Lecture Notes in Computer Science 11364

Commenced Publication in 1973
Founding and Former Series Editors:
Gerhard Goos, Juris Hartmanis, and Jan van Leeuwen

More information about this series at http://www.springer.com/series/7412

C. V. Jawahar · Hongdong Li ·
Greg Mori · Konrad Schindler (Eds.)

Computer Vision – ACCV 2018

14th Asian Conference on Computer Vision
Perth, Australia, December 2–6, 2018
Revised Selected Papers, Part IV

Editors
C. V. Jawahar
IIIT Hyderabad
Hyderabad, India

Hongdong Li
ANU
Canberra, ACT, Australia

Greg Mori
Simon Fraser University
Burnaby, BC, Canada

Konrad Schindler
ETH Zurich
Zurich, Zürich, Switzerland

ISSN 0302-9743 ISSN 1611-3349 (electronic)
Lecture Notes in Computer Science
ISBN 978-3-030-20869-1 ISBN 978-3-030-20870-7 (eBook)
https://doi.org/10.1007/978-3-030-20870-7

LNCS Sublibrary: SL6 – Image Processing, Computer Vision, Pattern Recognition, and Graphics

This Springer imprint is published by the registered company Springer Nature Switzerland AG
The registered company address is: Gewerbestrasse 11, 6330 Cham, Switzerland

Preface

The Asian Conference on Computer Vision (ACCV) 2018 took place in Perth, Australia, during December 2–6, 2018. The conference featured novel research contributions from almost all sub-areas of computer vision.

This year we received a record number of conference submissions. After removing the desk rejects, 979 valid, complete manuscripts were submitted for review. A pool of 34 area chairs and 1,063 reviewers was recruited to conduct paper reviews. Like previous editions of ACCV, we adopted a double-blind review process to determine which of these papers to accept. Identities of authors were not visible to reviewers and area chairs; nor were the identities of the assigned reviewers and area chairs visible to authors. The program chairs did not submit papers to the conference.

Each paper was reviewed by at least three reviewers. Authors were permitted to respond to the initial reviews during a rebuttal period. After this, the area chairs led discussions among reviewers. Finally, a physical area chairs was held in Singapore, during which panels of three area chairs deliberated to decide on acceptance decisions for each paper. At the end of this process, 274 papers were accepted for publication in the ACCV 2018 conference proceedings, of which five were later withdrawn by their authors.

In addition to the main conference, ACCV 2018 featured 11 workshops and six tutorials.

We would like to thank all the organizers, sponsors, area chairs, reviewers, and authors. Special thanks go to Prof. Guosheng Lin from Nanyang Technological University, Singapore, for hosting the area chair meeting. We acknowledge the support of Microsoft's Conference Management Toolkit (CMT) team for providing the software used to manage the review process.

We greatly appreciate the efforts of all those who contributed to making the conference a success.

December 2018

C. V. Jawahar
Hongdong Li
Greg Mori
Konrad Schindler

Organization

General Chairs

Kyoung-mu Lee	Seoul National University, South Korea
Ajmal Mian	University of Western Australia, Australia
Ian Reid	University of Adelaide, Australia
Yoichi Sato	University of Tokyo, Japan

Program Chairs

C. V. Jawahar	IIIT Hyderabad, India
Hongdong Li	Australian National University, Australia
Greg Mori	Simon Fraser University and Borealis AI, Canada
Konrad Schindler	ETH Zurich, Switzerland

Advisor

Richard Hartley	Australian National University, Australia

Publication Chair

Hamid Rezatofighi	University of Adelaide, Australia

Local Arrangements Chairs

Guosheng Lin	Nanyang Technological University, Singapore
Ajmal Mian	University of Western Australia, Australia

Area Chairs

Lourdes Agapito	University College London, UK
Xiang Bai	Huazhong University of Science and Technology, China
Vineeth N. Balasubramanian	IIT Hyderabad, India
Gustavo Carneiro	University of Adelaide, Australia
Tat-Jun Chin	University of Adelaide, Australia
Minsu Cho	POSTECH, South Korea
Bohyung Han	Seoul National University, South Korea
Junwei Han	Northwestern Polytechnical University, China
Mehrtash Harandi	Monash University, Australia
Gang Hua	Microsoft Research, Asia

Rei Kawakami	University of Tokyo, Japan
Tae-Kyun Kim	Imperial College London, UK
Junseok Kwon	Chung-Ang University, South Korea
Florent Lafarge	Inria, France
Laura Leal-Taixé	TU Munich, Germany
Zhouchen Lin	Peking University, China
Yanxi Liu	Penn State University, USA
Oisin Mac Aodha	Caltech, USA
Anurag Mittal	IIT Madras, India
Vinay Namboodiri	IIT Kanpur, India
P. J. Narayanan	IIIT Hyderabad, India
Carl Olsson	Lund University, Sweden
Imari Sato	National Institute of Informatics
Shiguang Shan	Chinese Academy of Sciences, China
Chunhua Shen	University of Adelaide, Australia
Boxin Shi	Peking University, China
Terence Sim	National University of Singapore, Singapore
Yusuke Sugano	Osaka University, Japan
Min Sun	National Tsing Hua University, Taiwan
Robby Tan	Yale-NUS College, USA
Siyu Tang	MPI for Intelligent Systems
Radu Timofte	ETH Zurich, Switzerland
Jingyi Yu	University of Delaware, USA
Junsong Yuan	State University of New York at Buffalo, USA

Additional Reviewers

Ehsan Abbasnejad
Akash Abdu Jyothi
Abrar Abdulnabi
Nagesh Adluru
Antonio Agudo
Unaiza Ahsan
Hai-zhou Ai
Alexandre Alahi
Xavier Alameda-Pineda
Andrea Albarelli
Mohsen Ali
Saad Ali
Mitsuru Ambai
Cosmin Ancuti
Vijay Rengarajan Angarai Pichaikuppan
Michel Antunes
Djamila Aouada
Ognjen Arandjelovic
Anil Armagan
Chetan Arora
Mathieu Aubry
Hossein Azizpour
Seung-Hwan Baek
Aijun Bai
Peter Bajcsy
Amr Bakry
Vassileios Balntas
Yutong Ban
Arunava Banerjee
Monami Banerjee
Atsuhiko Banno
Aayush Bansal
Dániel Baráth
Lorenzo Baraldi
Adrian Barbu
Nick Barnes
Peter Barnum
Joe Bartels
Paul Beardsley
Sima Behpour
Vasileios Belagiannis
Boulbaba Ben Amor
Archith Bency
Ryad Benosman
Gedas Bertasius
Ross Beveridge
Binod Bhattarai
Arnav Bhavsar
Simone Bianco
Oliver Bimber
Tolga Birdal
Horst Bischof
Arijit Biswas

Soma Biswas
Henryk Blasinski
Vishnu Boddeti
Federica Bogo
Tolga Bolukbasi
Terrance Boult
Thierry Bouwmans
Abdesselam Bouzerdoum
Ernesto Brau
Mathieu Bredif
Stefan Breuers
Marcus Brubaker
Anders Buch
Shyamal Buch
Pradeep Buddharaju
Adrian Bulat
Darius Burschka
Andrei Bursuc
Zoya Bylinskii
Weidong Cai
Necati Cihan Camgoz
Shaun Canavan
Joao Carreira
Dan Casas
M. Emre Celebi
Hakan Cevikalp
François Chadebecq
Menglei Chai
Rudrasis Chakraborty
Tat-Jen Cham
Kwok-Ping Chan
Sharat Chandran
Chehan Chang
Hyun Sung Chang
Yi Chang
Wei-Lun Chao
Visesh Chari
Gaurav Chaurasia
Rama Chellappa
Chen Chen
Chu-Song Chen
Dongdong Chen
Guangyong Chen
Hsin-I Chen
Huaijin Chen
Hwann-Tzong Chen
Jiacheng Chen
Jianhui Chen
Jiansheng Chen
Jiaxin Chen
Jie Chen
Kan Chen
Longbin Chen
Ting Chen
Tseng-Hung Chen
Wei Chen
Xi'ai Chen
Xiaozhi Chen
Xilin Chen
Xinlei Chen
Yunjin Chen
Erkang Cheng
Hong Cheng
Hui Cheng
Jingchun Cheng
Ming-Ming Cheng
Wen-Huang Cheng
Yuan Cheng
Zhi-Qi Cheng
Loong Fah Cheong
Anoop Cherian
Liang-Tien Chia
Chao-Kai Chiang
Shao-Yi Chien
Han-Pang Chiu
Wei-Chen Chiu
Donghyeon Cho
Nam Ik Cho
Sunghyun Cho
Yeong-Jun Cho
Gyeongmin Choe
Chiho Choi
Jonghyun Choi
Jongmoo Choi
Jongwon Choi
Hisham Cholakkal
Biswarup Choudhury
Xiao Chu
Yung-Yu Chuang
Andrea Cohen
Toby Collins
Marco Cristani
James Crowley
Jinshi Cui
Zhaopeng Cui
Bo Dai
Hang Dai
Xiyang Dai
Yuchao Dai
Carlo Dal Mutto
Zachary Daniels
Mohamed Daoudi
Abir Das
Raoul De Charette
Teofilo Decampos
Koichiro Deguchi
Stefanie Demirci
Girum Demisse
Patrick Dendorfer
Zhiwei Deng
Joachim Denzler
Aditya Deshpande
Frédéric Devernay
Abhinav Dhall
Anthony Dick
Zhengming Ding
Cosimo Distante
Ajay Divakaran
Mandar Dixit
Thanh-Toan Do
Jose Dolz
Bo Dong
Chao Dong
Jingming Dong
Ming Dong
Weisheng Dong
Simon Donne
Gianfranco Doretto
Bruce Draper
Bertram Drost
Liang Du
Shichuan Du
Jean-Luc Dugelay
Enrique Dunn
Thibaut Durand
Zoran Duric
Ionut Cosmin Duta
Samyak Dutta

Pinar Duygulu
Ady Ecker
Hazim Ekenel
Sabu Emmanuel
Ian Endres
Ertunc Erdil
Hugo Jair Escalante
Sergio Escalera
Francisco Escolano Ruiz
Bin Fan
Shaojing Fan
Yi Fang
Aly Farag
Giovanni Farinella
Rafael Felix
Michele Fenzi
Bob Fisher
David Fofi
Gian Luca Foresti
Victor Fragoso
Bernd Freisleben
Jason Fritts
Cheng-Yang Fu
Chi-Wing Fu
Huazhu Fu
Jianlong Fu
Xueyang Fu
Ying Fu
Yun Fu
Olac Fuentes
Jan Funke
Ryo Furukawa
Yasutaka Furukawa
Manuel Günther
Raghudeep Gadde
Matheus Gadelha
Jürgen Gall
Silvano Galliani
Chuang Gan
Zhe Gan
Vineet Gandhi
Arvind Ganesh
Bin-Bin Gao
Jin Gao
Jiyang Gao
Junbin Gao
Ravi Garg
Jochen Gast
Utkarsh Gaur
Xin Geng
David Geronimno
Michael Gharbi
Amir Ghodrati
Behnam Gholami
Andrew Gilbert
Rohit Girdhar
Ioannis Gkioulekas
Guy Godin
Nuno Goncalves
Yu Gong
Stephen Gould
Venu Govindu
Oleg Grinchuk
Jiuxiang Gu
Shuhang Gu
Paul Guerrero
Anupam Guha
Guodong Guo
Yanwen Guo
Ankit Gupta
Mithun Gupta
Saurabh Gupta
Hossein Hajimirsadeghi
Maciej Halber
Xiaoguang Han
Yahong Han
Zhi Han
Kenji Hara
Tatsuya Harada
Ali Harakeh
Adam Harley
Ben Harwood
Mahmudul Hasan
Kenji Hata
Michal Havlena
Munawar Hayat
Zeeshan Hayder
Jiawei He
Kun He
Lei He
Lifang He
Pan He
Yang He
Zhenliang He
Zhihai He
Felix Heide
Samitha Herath
Luis Herranz
Anders Heyden
Je Hyeong Hong
Seunghoon Hong
Wei Hong
Le Hou
Chiou-Ting Hsu
Kuang-Jui Hsu
Di Hu
Hexiang Hu
Ping Hu
Xu Hu
Yinlin Hu
Zhiting Hu
De-An Huang
Gao Huang
Gary Huang
Haibin Huang
Haifei Huang
Haozhi Huang
Jia-Bin Huang
Shaoli Huang
Sheng Huang
Xinyu Huang
Xun Huang
Yan Huang
Yawen Huang
Yinghao Huang
Yizhen Huang
Wei-Chih Hung
Junhwa Hur
Mohamed Hussein
Jyh-Jing Hwang
Ichiro Ide
Satoshi Ikehata
Radu Tudor Ionescu
Go Irie
Ahmet Iscen
Vamsi Ithapu
Daisuke Iwai
Won-Dong Jang

Dinesh Jayaraman
Sadeep Jayasumana
Suren Jayasuriya
Hueihan Jhuang
Dinghuang Ji
Mengqi Ji
Hongjun Jia
Jiayan Jiang
Qing-Yuan Jiang
Tingting Jiang
Xiaoyi Jiang
Zhuolin Jiang
Zequn Jie
Xiaojie Jin
Younghyun Jo
Ole Johannsen
Hanbyul Joo
Jungseock Joo
Kyungdon Joo
Shantanu Joshi
Amin Jourabloo
Deunsol Jung
Anis Kacem
Ioannis Kakadiaris
Zdenek Kalal
Nima Kalantari
Mahdi Kalayeh
Sinan Kalkan
Vicky Kalogeiton
Joni-Kristian Kamarainen
Martin Kampel
Meina Kan
Kenichi Kanatani
Atsushi Kanehira
Takuhiro Kaneko
Zhuoliang Kang
Mohan Kankanhalli
Vadim Kantorov
Nikolaos Karianakis
Leonid Karlinsky
Zoltan Kato
Hiroshi Kawasaki
Wei Ke
Wadim Kehl
Sameh Khamis
Naeemullah Khan
Salman Khan
Rawal Khirodkar
Mehran Khodabandeh
Anna Khoreva
Parmeshwar Khurd
Hadi Kiapour
Joe Kileel
Edward Kim
Gunhee Kim
Hansung Kim
Hyunwoo Kim
Junsik Kim
Seon Joo Kim
Vladimir Kim
Akisato Kimura
Ravi Kiran
Roman Klokov
Takumi Kobayashi
Amir Kolaman
Naejin Kong
Piotr Koniusz
Hyung Il Koo
Dimitrios Kosmopoulos
Gregory Kramida
Praveen Krishnan
Ravi Krishnan
Hiroyuki Kubo
Hilde Kuehne
Jason Kuen
Arjan Kuijper
Kuldeep Kulkarni
Shiro Kumano
Avinash Kumar
Soumava Roy Kumar
Kaustav Kundu
Sebastian Kurtek
Yevhen Kuznietsov
Heeseung Kwon
Alexander Ladikos
Kevin Lai
Wei-Sheng Lai
Shang-Hong Lai
Michael Lam
Zhenzhong Lan
Dong Lao
Katrin Lasinger
Yasir Latif
Huu Le
Herve Le Borgne
Chun-Yi Lee
Gim Hee Lee
Seungyong Lee
Teng-Yok Lee
Seungkyu Lee
Andreas Lehrmann
Na Lei
Spyridon Leonardos
Marius Leordeanu
Matt Leotta
Gil Levi
Evgeny Levinkov
Jose Lezama
Ang Li
Chen Li
Chunyuan Li
Dangwei Li
Dingzeyu Li
Dong Li
Hai Li
Jianguo Li
Stan Li
Wanqing Li
Wei Li
Xi Li
Xirong Li
Xiu Li
Xuelong Li
Yanghao Li
Yin Li
Yingwei Li
Yongjie Li
Yu Li
Yuncheng Li
Zechao Li
Zhengqi Li
Zhengqin Li
Zhuwen Li
Zhouhui Lian
Jie Liang
Zicheng Liao
Jongwoo Lim
Ser-Nam Lim

Kaimo Lin
Shih-Yao Lin
Tsung-Yi Lin
Weiyao Lin
Yuewei Lin
Venice Liong
Giuseppe Lisanti
Roee Litman
Jim Little
Anan Liu
Chao Liu
Chen Liu
Eryun Liu
Fayao Liu
Huaping Liu
Jingen Liu
Lingqiao Liu
Miaomiao Liu
Qingshan Liu
Risheng Liu
Sifei Liu
Tyng-Luh Liu
Weiyang Liu
Xialei Liu
Xianglong Liu
Xiao Liu
Yebin Liu
Yi Liu
Yu Liu
Yun Liu
Ziwei Liu
Stephan Liwicki
Liliana Lo Presti
Fotios Logothetis
Javier Lorenzo
Manolis Lourakis
Brian Lovell
Chen Change Loy
Chaochao Lu
Feng Lu
Huchuan Lu
Jiajun Lu
Kaiyue Lu
Xin Lu
Yijuan Lu
Yongxi Lu
Fujun Luan
Jian-Hao Luo
Jiebo Luo
Weixin Luo
Khoa Luu
Chao Ma
Huimin Ma
Kede Ma
Lin Ma
Shugao Ma
Wei-Chiu Ma
Will Maddern
Ludovic Magerand
Luca Magri
Behrooz Mahasseni
Tahmida Mahmud
Robert Maier
Subhransu Maji
Yasushi Makihara
Clement Mallet
Abed Malti
Devraj Mandal
Fabian Manhardt
Gian Luca Marcialis
Julio Marco
Diego Marcos
Ricardo Martin
Tanya Marwah
Marc Masana
Jonathan Masci
Takeshi Masuda
Yusuke Matsui
Tetsu Matsukawa
Gellert Mattyus
Thomas Mauthner
Bruce Maxwell
Steve Maybank
Amir Mazaheri
Scott Mccloskey
Mason Mcgill
Nazanin Mehrasa
Ishit Mehta
Xue Mei
Heydi Mendez-Vazquez
Gaofeng Meng
Bjoern Menze
Domingo Mery
Pascal Mettes
Jan Hendrik Metzen
Gregor Miller
Cai Minjie
Ikuhisa Mitsugami
Daisuke Miyazaki
Davide Modolo
Pritish Mohapatra
Pascal Monasse
Sandino Morales
Pietro Morerio
Saeid Motiian
Arsalan Mousavian
Mikhail Mozerov
Yasuhiro Mukaigawa
Yusuke Mukuta
Mario Munich
Srikanth Muralidharan
Ana Murillo
Vittorio Murino
Armin Mustafa
Hajime Nagahara
Shruti Nagpal
Mahyar Najibi
Katsuyuki Nakamura
Seonghyeon Nam
Loris Nanni
Manjunath Narayana
Lakshmanan Nataraj
Neda Nategh
Lukáš Neumann
Shawn Newsam
Joe Yue-Hei Ng
Thuyen Ngo
David Nilsson
Ji-feng Ning
Mark Nixon
Shohei Nobuhara
Hyeonwoo Noh
Mehdi Noroozi
Erfan Noury
Eyal Ofek
Seong Joon Oh
Seoung Wug Oh
Katsunori Ohnishi

Iason Oikonomidis
Takeshi Oishi
Takahiro Okabe
Takayuki Okatani
Gustavo Olague
Kyle Olszewski
Mohamed Omran
Roy Or-El
Ivan Oseledets
Martin R. Oswald
Tomas Pajdla
Dipan Pal
Kalman Palagyi
Manohar Paluri
Gang Pan
Jinshan Pan
Yannis Panagakis
Rameswar Panda
Hsing-Kuo Pao
Dim Papadopoulos
Konstantinos Papoutsakis
Shaifali Parashar
Hyun Soo Park
Jinsun Park
Taesung Park
Wonpyo Park
Alvaro Parra Bustos
Geoffrey Pascoe
Ioannis Patras
Genevieve Patterson
Georgios Pavlakos
Ioannis Pavlidis
Nick Pears
Pieter Peers
Selen Pehlivan
Xi Peng
Xingchao Peng
Janez Perš
Talita Perciano
Adrian Peter
Lars Petersson
Stavros Petridis
Patrick Peursum
Trung Pham
Sang Phan
Marco Piccirilli
Sudeep Pillai
Wong Ya Ping
Lerrel Pinto
Fiora Pirri
Matteo Poggi
Georg Poier
Marius Popescu
Ronald Poppe
Dilip Prasad
Andrea Prati
Maria Priisalu
Véronique Prinet
Victor Prisacariu
Hugo Proenca
Jan Prokaj
Daniel Prusa
Yunchen Pu
Guo-Jun Qi
Xiaojuan Qi
Zhen Qian
Yu Qiao
Jie Qin
Lei Qin
Chao Qu
Faisal Qureshi
Petia Radeva
Venkatesh Babu Radhakrishnan
Ilija Radosavovic
Bogdan Raducanu
Hossein Rahmani
Swaminathan Rahul
Ajit Rajwade
Kandan Ramakrishnan
Visvanathan Ramesh
Yongming Rao
Sathya Ravi
Michael Reale
Adria Recasens
Konstantinos Rematas
Haibing Ren
Jimmy Ren
Wenqi Ren
Zhile Ren
Edel Garcia Reyes
Hamid Rezatofighi
Hamed Rezazadegan Tavakoli
Rafael Rezende
Helge Rhodin
Alexander Richard
Stephan Richter
Gernot Riegler
Christian Riess
Ergys Ristani
Tobias Ritschel
Mariano Rivera
Antonio Robles-Kelly
Emanuele Rodola
Andres Rodriguez
Mikel Rodriguez
Matteo Ruggero Ronchi
Xuejian Rong
Bodo Rosenhahn
Arun Ross
Peter Roth
Michel Roux
Ryusuke Sagawa
Hideo Saito
Shunsuke Saito
Parikshit Sakurikar
Albert Ali Salah
Jorge Sanchez
Conrad Sanderson
Aswin Sankaranarayanan
Swami Sankaranarayanan
Archana Sapkota
Michele Sasdelli
Jun Sato
Shin'ichi Satoh
Torsten Sattler
Manolis Savva
Tanner Schmidt
Dirk Schnieders
Samuel Schulter
Rajvi Shah
Shishir Shah
Sohil Shah
Moein Shakeri
Nataliya Shapovalova
Aidean Sharghi
Gaurav Sharma

Pramod Sharma
Li Shen
Shuhan Shen
Wei Shen
Xiaoyong Shen
Zhiqiang Shen
Lu Sheng
Baoguang Shi
Guangming Shi
Miaojing Shi
Zhiyuan Shi
Takashi Shibata
Huang-Chia Shih
Meng-Li Shih
Sheng-Wen Shih
Atsushi Shimada
Nobutaka Shimada
Daeyun Shin
Young Min Shin
Koichi Shinoda
Tianmin Shu
Zhixin Shu
Bing Shuai
Karan Sikka
Jack Sim
Marcel Simon
Tomas Simon
Vishwanath Sindagi
Gurkirt Singh
Maneet Singh
Praveer Singh
Ayan Sinha
Sudipta Sinha
Vladimir Smutny
Francesco Solera
Amir Arsalan Soltani
Eric Sommerlade
Andy Song
Shiyu Song
Yibing Song
Humberto Sossa
Concetto Spampinato
Filip Šroubek
Ioannis Stamos
Jan Stuehmer
Jingyong Su
Jong-Chyi Su
Shuochen Su
Yu-Chuan Su
Zhixun Su
Ramanathan Subramanian
Akihiro Sugimoto
Waqas Sultani
Jiande Sun
Jin Sun
Ju Sun
Lin Sun
Min Sun
Yao Sun
Zhaohui Sun
David Suter
Tanveer Syeda-Mahmood
Yuichi Taguchi
Jun Takamatsu
Takafumi Taketomi
Hugues Talbot
Youssef Tamaazousti
Toru Tamak
Robert Tamburo
Chaowei Tan
David Joseph Tan
Ping Tan
Xiaoyang Tan
Kenichiro Tanaka
Masayuki Tanaka
Jinhui Tang
Meng Tang
Peng Tang
Wei Tang
Yuxing Tang
Junli Tao
Xin Tao
Makarand Tapaswi
Jean-Philippe Tarel
Keisuke Tateno
Joao Tavares
Bugra Tekin
Mariano Tepper
Ali Thabet
Spiros Thermos
Shangxuan Tian
Yingli Tian
Kinh Tieu
Massimo Tistarelli
Henning Tjaden
Matthew Toews
Chetan Tonde
Akihiko Torii
Andrea Torsello
Toan Tran
Leonardo Trujillo
Tomasz Trzcinski
Sam Tsai
Yi-Hsuan Tsai
Ivor Tsang
Vagia Tsiminaki
Aggeliki Tsoli
Wei-Chih Tu
Shubham Tulsiani
Sergey Tulyakov
Tony Tung
Matt Turek
Seiichi Uchida
Oytun Ulutan
Martin Urschler
Mikhail Usvyatsov
Alexander Vakhitov
Julien Valentin
Ernest Valveny
Ian Van Der Linde
Kiran Varanasi
Gul Varol
Francisco Vasconcelos
Pascal Vasseur
Javier Vazquez-Corral
Ashok Veeraraghavan
Andreas Velten
Raviteja Vemulapalli
Jonathan Ventura
Subhashini Venugopalan
Yashaswi Verma
Matthias Vestner
Minh Vo
Jayakorn Vongkulbhisal
Toshikazu Wada
Chengde Wan
Jun Wan
Renjie Wan

Baoyuan Wang
Chaohui Wang
Chaoyang Wang
Chunyu Wang
De Wang
Dong Wang
Fang Wang
Faqiang Wang
Hongsong Wang
Hongxing Wang
Hua Wang
Jialei Wang
Jianyu Wang
Jinglu Wang
Jinqiao Wang
Keze Wang
Le Wang
Lei Wang
Lezi Wang
Lijun Wang
Limin Wang
Linwei Wang
Pichao Wang
Qi Wang
Qian Wang
Qilong Wang
Qing Wang
Ruiping Wang
Shangfei Wang
Shuhui Wang
Song Wang
Tao Wang
Tsun-Hsuang Wang
Weiyue Wang
Wenguan Wang
Xiaoyu Wang
Xinchao Wang
Xinggang Wang
Yang Wang
Yin Wang
Yu-Chiang Frank Wang
Yufei Wang
Yunhong Wang
Zhangyang Wang
Zilei Wang
Jan Dirk Wegner
Ping Wei
Shih-En Wei
Wei Wei
Xiu-Shen Wei
Zijun Wei
Bihan Wen
Longyin Wen
Xinshuo Weng
Tom Whelan
Patrick Wieschollek
Maggie Wigness
Jerome Williams
Kwan-Yee Wong
Chao-Yuan Wu
Chunpeng Wu
Dijia Wu
Jiajun Wu
Jianxin Wu
Xiao Wu
Xiaohe Wu
Xiaomeng Wu
Xinxiao Wu
Yi Wu
Ying Nian Wu
Yue Wu
Zheng Wu
Zhirong Wu
Jonas Wulff
Yin Xia
Yongqin Xian
Yu Xiang
Fanyi Xiao
Yang Xiao
Dan Xie
Jianwen Xie
Jin Xie
Fuyong Xing
Jun Xing
Junliang Xing
Xuehan Xiong
Yuanjun Xiong
Changsheng Xu
Chenliang Xu
Haotian Xu
Huazhe Xu
Huijuan Xu
Jun Xu
Ning Xu
Tao Xu
Weipeng Xu
Xiangmin Xu
Xiangyu Xu
Yong Xu
Yuanlu Xu
Jia Xue
Xiangyang Xue
Toshihiko Yamasaki
Junchi Yan
Luxin Yan
Wang Yan
Keiji Yanai
Bin Yang
Chih-Yuan Yang
Dong Yang
Herb Yang
Jianwei Yang
Jie Yang
Jin-feng Yang
Jufeng Yang
Meng Yang
Ming Yang
Ming-Hsuan Yang
Tien-Ju Yang
Wei Yang
Wenhan Yang
Yanchao Yang
Yingzhen Yang
Yongxin Yang
Zhenheng Yang
Angela Yao
Bangpeng Yao
Cong Yao
Jian Yao
Jiawen Yao
Yasushi Yagi
Mang Ye
Mao Ye
Qixiang Ye
Mei-Chen Yeh
Sai-Kit Yeung
Kwang Moo Yi
Alper Yilmaz

Xi Yin
Zhaozheng Yin
Xianghua Ying
Ryo Yonetani
Donghyun Yoo
Jae Shin Yoon
Ryota Yoshihashi
Gang Yu
Hongkai Yu
Ruichi Yu
Shiqi Yu
Xiang Yu
Yang Yu
Youngjae Yu
Chunfeng Yuan
Jing Yuan
Junsong Yuan
Shanxin Yuan
Zejian Yuan
Xenophon Zabulis
Mihai Zanfir
Pablo Zegers
Jiabei Zeng
Kuo-Hao Zeng
Baochang Zhang
Cha Zhang
Chao Zhang
Dingwen Zhang
Dong Zhang
Guofeng Zhang
Hanwang Zhang
He Zhang
Hong Zhang
Honggang Zhang
Hua Zhang
Jian Zhang
Jiawei Zhang
Jing Zhang
Kaipeng Zhang
Ke Zhang
Liang Zhang
Linguang Zhang
Liqing Zhang
Peng Zhang
Pingping Zhang
Quanshi Zhang
Runze Zhang
Shanghang Zhang
Shu Zhang
Tianzhu Zhang
Tong Zhang
Wen Zhang
Xiaofan Zhang
Xiaoqin Zhang
Xikang Zhang
Xu Zhang
Ya Zhang
Yinda Zhang
Yongqiang Zhang
Zhang Zhang
Zhen Zhang
Zhoutong Zhang
Ziyu Zhang
Bin Zhao
Bo Zhao
Chen Zhao
Hengshuang Zhao
Qijun Zhao
Rui Zhao
Heliang Zheng
Shuai Zheng
Stephan Zheng
Yinqiang Zheng
Yuanjie Zheng
Zhonglong Zheng
Guangyu Zhong
Huiyu Zhou
Jiahuan Zhou
Jun Zhou
Luping Zhou
Mo Zhou
Pan Zhou
Yang Zhou
Zihan Zhou
Fan Zhu
Guangming Zhu
Hao Zhu
Hongyuan Zhu
Lei Zhu
Menglong Zhu
Pengfei Zhu
Shizhan Zhu
Siyu Zhu
Xiangxin Zhu
Yi Zhu
Yizhe Zhu
Yuke Zhu
Zhigang Zhu
Bohan Zhuang
Liansheng Zhuang
Karel Zimmermann
Maria Zontak
Danping Zou
Qi Zou
Wangmeng Zuo
Xinxin Zuo

Contents – Part IV

Poster Session P2

Oral Session O4: Detection, Segmentation, and Action

Poster Session P2

Gaussian Process Deep Belief Networks: A Smooth Generative Model of Shape with Uncertainty Propagation

Alessandro Di Martino[1(✉)], Erik Bodin[2], Carl Henrik Ek[2], and Neill D. F. Campbell[1]

[1] Department of Computer Science, University of Bath, Bath, UK
a.di.martino@bath.ac.uk
[2] Department of Computer Science, University of Bristol, Bristol, UK

Abstract. The shape of an object is an important characteristic for many vision problems such as segmentation, detection and tracking. Being independent of appearance, it is possible to generalize to a large range of objects from only small amounts of data. However, shapes represented as silhouette images are challenging to model due to complicated likelihood functions leading to intractable posteriors. In this paper we present a generative model of shapes which provides a low dimensional latent encoding which importantly resides on a smooth manifold with respect to the silhouette images. The proposed model propagates uncertainty in a principled manner allowing it to learn from small amounts of data and providing predictions with associated uncertainty. We provide experiments that show how our proposed model provides favorable quantitative results compared with the state-of-the-art while simultaneously providing a representation that resides on a low-dimensional interpretable manifold.

Keywords: Shape models · Unsupervised learning · Gaussian processes · Deep belief networks

1 Introduction

The space of silhouette images is challenging to work with as it is not smooth in terms of a representation as pixels. A transformation that we would consider semantically smooth might correspond to a drastic change in pixel values. Our goal is to learn a smooth low dimensional representation of silhouette images such that images can be generated in a natural manner. Further, as data is at a premium, we want to learn a fully probabilistic model that allows us to propagate uncertainty throughout the generative process. This will allow us to

Electronic supplementary material The online version of this chapter (https://doi.org/10.1007/978-3-030-20870-7_1) contains supplementary material, which is available to authorized users.

C. V. Jawahar et al. (Eds.): ACCV 2018, LNCS 11364, pp. 3–20, 2019.
https://doi.org/10.1007/978-3-030-20870-7_1

learn from *smaller amounts of data* and also associate a quantified uncertainty to its predictions. This uncertainty allows the model to be used as a building block in larger models.

The results of our model challenge the current trend in unsupervised learning towards maximum likelihood training of increasingly large parametric models with increasingly large datasets. We demonstrate that by propagating uncertainty throughout the model, our approach outperforms two standard generative deep learning models, a Variational Auto-Encoder (VAE [15]) and a Generative Adversarial Network (InfoGAN [5]) with comparable architectures and can achieve similar performance with far smaller training datasets.

In our work we revisit a few classic machine learning models with complementary properties. On the one hand, parametric models such as Restricted Boltzmann Machines (RBMs) [25] are particularly interesting as they are stochastic, generative and can be stacked easily into *deeper* models such as deep belief networks (DBNs); these can be trained in a greedy fashion, layer by layer [13]. RBMs can approximate a probability distribution on visible units. DBNs, in addition, learn deep representations by composing features learned by the lower layers, yielding progressively more abstract and flexible representations at higher layers and often leading to more expressive and efficient models compared to shallow ones [2].

However, DBNs suffer from a number of limitations. Firstly, they do not guarantee a smooth representation in the learned latent space. Secondly, the classic contrastive divergence algorithm used for greedy training is slow and can place limitations on architectures. Finally, a DBN does not provide any explicit generative process from a manifold, as the standard way to sample from a DBN is to start from a training example and perform iterations of Gibbs sampling.

The Gaussian Process Latent Variable Model (GPLVM) [17] combines a Gaussian process (GP) prior with a likelihood function in order to learn a representation. By specifying a prior that encourages smooth functions a smooth latent representation can be recovered. However, to make inference tractable the likelihood is also chosen to be Gaussian which does not reflect the statistics of natural images. Further, even though the mapping from the latent space is non-linear the posterior is linear in the observed space. This makes the GPLVM unsuitable for modelling images. To circumvent this one can compose hierarchies of GPs [6], however, these models are inherently difficult to train.

The characteristics of the DBN and GPLVM can be considered complementary, where the DBN excels the GPLVM fails and vice versa. Unfortunately, combining the two models into a single one by simply stacking a GPLVM on top of a DBN would not preserve uncertainty propagation. Furthermore, this would pose a challenge to training (while the GPLVM is a non-parametric model trained by optimizing an objective function, a DBN is a parametric model, with non-differentiable Bernoulli units, and is trained with contrastive divergence). Another important challenge is learning from very little data. The ability to learn from a small dataset expands the applicability of a model to domains where there is a lack of available data or where collection of data is costly or time-consuming.

Table 1. Summary of properties of related models.

	Non-Gaussian likelihood	Explicit smooth low-dim manifold	Fully generative	Propagates uncertainty
GPLVM [17]		✓	✓	✓
GPLVMDT [22]		✓	✓	✓
DBN [13]	✓			✓
SBM [10]	✓			✓
VAE [15]	✓	∼	✓	
InfoGAN [5]	✓	∼	✓	
ShapeOdds [8]	✓		✓	✓
This work	✓	✓	✓	✓

In this paper we address these challenges and present the following contributions:

1. A model (which we call GPDBN) that combines the properties of a smooth, interpretable manifold for synthesis with a data specific likelihood function (a deep structure) capable of decomposing images into an efficient representation while propagating uncertainty throughout the model in a principled manner.
2. We train the model end to end using back propagation with the same complexity as a standard feed-forward neural network by minimising a single objective function.
3. We also show that the model is able to learn from very little data, outperforming current generative deep learning models, as well as scaling linearly to larger datasets by the use of mini-batching.

2 Related Work

Modelling of shape is important for many computer vision tasks. It is beyond the scope of this paper to make a complete review of the topic, we refer the reader to the comprehensive work of Taylor *et al.* [7]. In our work we focus on recent unsupervised statistical models that operate directly on the pixel domain. Interest in these models was revived by the Shape Boltzmann Machine (SBM) work of Eslami et al. [10] and they have been shown to be useful for a variety of vision applications [9,16,28]. These deep models can also be readily extended into the 3D domain, *e.g.*, by recent work on 3D ShapeNets [31]. Detailed analysis of the DBN, GPLVM and SBM is provided in Sect. 3.

Desirable Properties. Table 1 highlights the desirable properties of the most closely related previous works. We have identified four advantageous properties: (i) It is well known that pixel silhouettes are not well modelled by a Gaussian likelihood. (ii) The utility of an unsupervised shape model is well described by the properties of its latent representation. Ensuring a smooth manifold opens up a number of applications to data in the pixel domain that previously required custom representations, *e.g.,* interactive drawing [29]. (iii) A fully generative model ensures that there is a well defined space that can be sampled as well as interpreted; *e.g.,* dynamics models can be defined in such a space to perform tracking [20,22]. (iv) Correctly propagating uncertainty is vital to perform data efficient learning, for example when data is scarce or expensive to obtain.

Auto-Encoders. The VAE model by Kingma and Welling [15] performs a variational approximation of a generative model with a non-Gaussian likelihood through a feed-forward or Multi-Layer Perceptron (MLP) network. In addition, it uses MLP networks to encode the variational parameters (in a similar manner to [18]). While this model provides a generative mapping, the feed-forward (decoder) network fails to propagate uncertainty from the latent space. Furthermore, the independent prior on the latent space does not promote a smooth manifold; any smoothness arises as a by-product of the MLP encoding network. This characteristic depends on the MLP architecture and is not directly parametrised. The key limitation of the VAE for our purposes is the lack of uncertainty propagation that results in poor results with limited training data.

The guided, non-parametric autoencoder model of Snoek et al. [26] appears similar, however, there are a number of important differences. They use label information (supervision) to guide a latent space learning process for an autoencoder; this is not a pure unsupervised learning task and we do not have label information available to us. Furthermore, as with the VAE, uncertainty is not propagated from the latent manifold to the output space due to the use of the feed-forward network to the output.

InfoGAN. Another prominent generative model in unsupervised learning is the Generative Adversarial Network (GAN) [11]. The model learns an implicit generator distribution using a minimax game between a deep generator network, which transforms a noise variable to a sample, and a deep discriminator network, which is used to classify between samples from the generator distribution and the true data distribution. One issue common with GAN models is that they do not provide a smooth latent manifold for synthesis nor uncertainty in their estimates (like the VAE). From the plethora of different variations of GANs models available in the literature we have chosen to include in our comparisons the InfoGAN model [5], since it also considers the goal of interpretable latent representations (by maximising the mutual information between a subset of GAN's noise variables and observations).

ShapeOdds. The recent ShapeOdds work of Elhabian and Whitaker [8] confers state-of-the-art performance and captures many of the desired properties including a generative probabilistic model that propagates uncertainty. The approach taken is quite different to ours as they specify a detailed probabilistic model including a Gaussian Markov Random Field (MRF) with individual Bernoulli random variables for the pixel lattice. In contrast, our model is more flexible, we allow the network to learn the structure from the data directly but ensure that we still maintain uncertainty quantification throughout. We would also argue that the specific form of the low dimensional manifold we generate is desirable with its guaranteed smoothness that makes the latent space readily interpretable. This provides the tradeoff between the two models. We expect the ShapeOdds model to perform very well at generalisation due to the inclusion of the MRF prior. In contrast, our model will be more data dependent in this respect (weaker prior assumptions on the nature of images), however, it provides a generative space that is highly interpretable and easy to work with. We identify that a topic for further work would be to combine our smooth priors with the likelihood model of ShapeOdds.

GPLVM Representations. A possible workaround to the problem of non-Gaussian likelihoods is to perform a deterministic transformation to a domain where the data is approximately Gaussian. This has been successful for domains where, for example, the shape can be represented in a new geometric representation away from pixels, *e.g.*, parametric curves [3,23]. However, this is application dependent and not suitable for arbitrary pixel based silhouettes considered here. A common approach that retains the pixel grid is to transform it into a level-set problem via the distance transform, *e.g.*, [22]. This can improve results in some settings, however, the uncertainty is not correctly preserved and therefore not correctly captured in predictions. We denote this model GPLVMDT in our comparisons.

3 Background

3.1 Deep Belief Networks

RBM. The restricted Boltzmann machine (RBM), or Harmonium, [25] is a generative stochastic neural network that learns a probability distribution over a vector of random variables. The RBM is when stacked the basic the basic component of a deep belief network. The graphical model of the RBM is an undirected bipartite graph, consisting of a set of visible random variables (or units): $\boldsymbol{v}$, and a set of hidden units $\boldsymbol{h}$ (Fig. 1(a)). Typically, all variables are binary (Bernoulli), taking on values from $\{0, 1\}$.

The RBM model specifies a probability distribution over both the visible and hidden variables jointly as

$$P(\boldsymbol{v}, \boldsymbol{h}) = \frac{1}{Z} \exp\left(-E(\boldsymbol{v}, \boldsymbol{h})\right) \tag{1}$$

which defines a Gibbs distribution with energy function

$$E(\boldsymbol{v}, \boldsymbol{h}) = -\boldsymbol{v}^\top \boldsymbol{W} \boldsymbol{h} - \boldsymbol{b}^\top \boldsymbol{v} - \boldsymbol{c}^\top \boldsymbol{h}, \tag{2}$$

where $\boldsymbol{W}$, $\boldsymbol{b}$, $\boldsymbol{c}$ are the parameters of the model: $\boldsymbol{W}$ as a linear weight matrix and $(\boldsymbol{b}, \boldsymbol{c})$ are bias vectors for the visible and hidden units respectively. The normalising constant Z is the, computationally intractable, sum over all possible random vectors $\boldsymbol{v}$ and $\boldsymbol{h}$.

The bipartite structure of the model (*i.e.*, the graph has no visible-visible or hidden-hidden connections, as shown in Fig. 1(a)), affords efficient Gibbs sampling from the visible units given the hidden variables (or vice versa). The conditional distribution of the hidden units given the visible ones, and vice versa, factorize as each set of variables are conditionally independent given the other:

$$P(\boldsymbol{h} \,|\, \boldsymbol{v}) = \prod_{j=1}^{H} P(h_j \,|\, \boldsymbol{v}), \;\; P(\boldsymbol{v} \,|\, \boldsymbol{h}) = \prod_{i=1}^{V} P(v_i \,|\, \boldsymbol{h}). \tag{3}$$

Replacing binary units with Gaussian units can be performed by modifying the energy function [12]. Unfortunately, parameter learning is difficult since direct calculation of the gradients of the log likelihood w.r.t. the parameters requires the intractable computation of the normalising constant Z. In *current* practice, the approximate maximum-likelihood contrastive divergence algorithm is used [4].

DBN. When multiple layers of RBMs are stacked on top of each other they form a deep belief network (Fig. 1(b)). Hinton *et al.* [13] demonstrated that a DBN can be trained in a greedy fashion, layer by layer. Essentially, the samples (activations) from the hidden units of a trained layer are used as the data to train the next layer in the stack.

Sampling. Sampling from an RBM proceeds by conditioning on some input data and performing a Gibbs sample for the hidden units. Subsequently, a Gibbs sample can be drawn for the visible units by conditioning the hidden units on this sample. This process is then repeated for a number of cycles. Since a DBN is a stack of RBMs, this process has to be repeated for all layers; the output of one layer becomes the input to condition on for the next layer. In this way, an input data point can be propagated up and down the network.

Limitations. Although a DBN is good at learning low-dimensional stochastic representations of high-dimensional data, it has three key drawbacks that we will address by combining the strengths of the DBN with a flexible non-parametric model in Sect. 4:

1. It lacks a directed generative sampling process from a well defined latent representation. In order to generate a sample one must condition on some input data and propagate it through the network back and forth until a sample from the lowest layer is obtained.
2. There is no explicit representation of the uncertainty, instead this only arises implicitly through the propagation of point estimates (samples) at each layer.
3. A side effect of the conditional independence assumption of (3) is that the correlations between the hidden units of the top layer of a DBN are not captured because each latent dimension is independent. Most importantly, a DBN does not, therefore, give any guarantee about learning a smooth latent space.

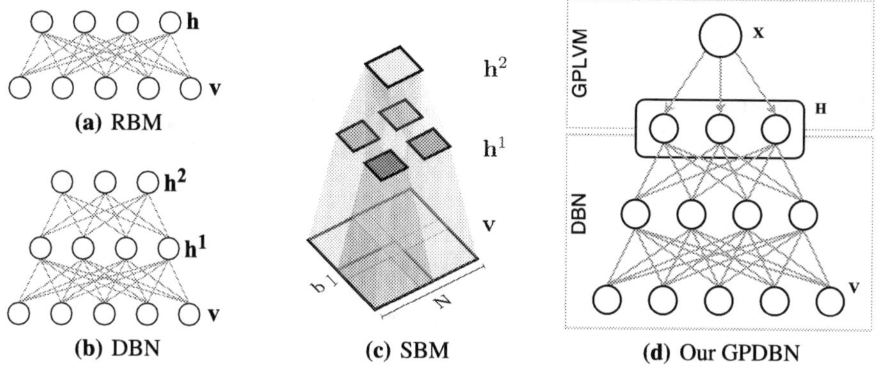

Fig. 1. Graphical representations of the (a) RBM, (b) DBN and (d) SBM. (d) A graphical representation of our proposed GPDBN model where $\boldsymbol{X}$ represents the latent variables, $\boldsymbol{H}$ the Gaussian activations (10), and $\boldsymbol{V}$ the observed (data) space. (The SBM figure is taken from [10]).

3.2 GPLVM

The Gaussian Process Latent Variable Model (GPLVM) [17] learns a generative representation by placing a Gaussian process (GP) prior over the mapping from the latent to the observed data. This approach has the benefit that it is very easy to ensure a smooth mapping from the latent representations to the observed data. Further, due to the principled uncertainty propagation of the GP, all predictions will have an associated uncertainty.

In specific, each observed datapoint $\boldsymbol{y}_n$, $n \in [1, N]$, is assumed to be generated by a latent location $\boldsymbol{x}_n$ through a mapping f. Due to the marginalising property of a Gaussian, the predictive posterior over function values $\boldsymbol{f}^*$ at a test location $\boldsymbol{x}^*$ can be reached in closed form as,

$$p(\boldsymbol{f}^* \mid \boldsymbol{Y}, \boldsymbol{x}^*, \boldsymbol{X}) = \mathcal{N}(\boldsymbol{m}_{\mathrm{GP}}, \sigma^2_{\mathrm{GP}}) \tag{4}$$

$$\boldsymbol{m}_{\mathrm{GP}} = k(\boldsymbol{x}^*, \boldsymbol{X})[k(\boldsymbol{X}, \boldsymbol{X})]^{-1}\boldsymbol{Y} \tag{5}$$

$$\sigma^2_{\mathrm{GP}} = k(\boldsymbol{x}^*, \boldsymbol{x}^*) - k(\boldsymbol{x}^*, \boldsymbol{X})[k(\boldsymbol{X}, \boldsymbol{X})]^{-1}k(\boldsymbol{X}, \boldsymbol{x}^*), \tag{6}$$

where $k(\cdot, \cdot)$ is the covariance function specifying the Gaussian process and $\boldsymbol{X} = [\boldsymbol{x}_1, \ldots, \boldsymbol{x}_N]^\top$. We used the common *squared exponential* kernel

$$k(\boldsymbol{x}, \boldsymbol{x}') = \alpha^2 \exp\left(-\frac{1}{2\ell^2}\left\|\boldsymbol{x} - \boldsymbol{x}'\right\|^2\right), \tag{7}$$

with hyperparameters α^2 (signal variance) and ℓ (lengthscale), to ensure a smooth manifold. Importantly, even though the function f can be non-linear, the relationship between the predicted mean (5) and the training data $\boldsymbol{Y}$ is linear. Due to this linearity, a GPLVM is inherently not suitable for modeling image data.

3.3 Shape Boltzmann Machine

The Shape Boltzmann Machine (SBM) [10] is a specific architecture of the Boltzmann machine. It consists of three layers: a rectangular layer of $N \times M$ visible units $\boldsymbol{v}$, and two layers of latent variables: $\boldsymbol{h}^1$ and $\boldsymbol{h}^2$. Each hidden unit in $\boldsymbol{h}^1$ is connected only to one of the four subsets of visible units of $\boldsymbol{v}$ (Fig. 1(c)). Each subset forms a rectangular patch and the weights of each patch (except the biases) are shared so that a patch effectively behaves as a local receptive field. To avoid boundary inconsistencies, the patches are slightly overlapped (in Fig. 1(c), the overlap has size b). Layer $\boldsymbol{h}^2$ is fully connected to $\boldsymbol{h}^1$.

While the SBM offers improved generalization over a DBN with the same number of parameters, the SBM has a fixed structure which is not easily extended to more layers or patches. In contrast, a DBN, as a stack of simple RBMs, has a more generic and flexible structure which can be adapted easily and combined with other models. Furthermore, like the DBN, the SBM lacks of a proper generative process.

4 The GPDBN Model

In our model, we connect a DBN and GPLVM so that the data space of the GPLVM corresponds the latent space of the DBN (Fig. 1(d)) to obtain a model that can be optimized by minimizing a single objective function.

New Concrete Layers. The uppermost hidden layer of the DBN has Gaussian units to interface with the Gaussian likelihood of the GPLVM. In the lower layers, we replace the standard binary units with a *Concrete distribution* [21]. This is a continuous relaxation to discrete random variables, in our case, to the Bernoulli distribution. This allows us to draw low bias samples, in an analogous manner to the reparameterization trick [15], using a function that is differentiable with respect to the model parameters,

$$\text{Concrete}\,(p, u) = \text{Sigmoid}\big(\tfrac{1}{\lambda}\big(\log p - \log(1-p) + \log u - \log(1-u)\big)\big)\,, \tag{8}$$

where p is the parameter of a Bernoulli distribution, λ is a scaling factor, which we fix to 0.1, and u is a uniform sample from $[0, 1]$.

Learning. Given a dataset $\mathcal{D} = \{\boldsymbol{t}_n\}_{n=1}^N$, we train the model end-to-end by minimizing the following objective function jointly with respect to all the parameters and the matrix of latent points $\boldsymbol{X}$ (omitted from the notation to avoid clutter):

$$L = \sum_{n=1}^{N} \underbrace{(\boldsymbol{t}_n \log(\boldsymbol{s}_n) + (1-\boldsymbol{t}_n)\log(1-\boldsymbol{s}_n))}_{\text{data term}} + \tfrac{1}{2}\underbrace{\mathrm{Tr}\big[\boldsymbol{K}^{-1}\boldsymbol{H}\boldsymbol{H}^\top\big]}_{\text{joint term}} + \tfrac{D}{2}\underbrace{\log|\boldsymbol{K}|}_{\substack{\text{complexity}\\ \text{term}}} + \underbrace{||\boldsymbol{X}||^2}_{\substack{\text{prior}\\ \text{term}}}. \tag{9}$$

Here, $\boldsymbol{t}_n$ is a training datapoint, $\boldsymbol{s}_n$ is a sample from the model, $\boldsymbol{K} = k(\boldsymbol{X}, \boldsymbol{X}) + \sigma^2 \boldsymbol{I}_N$ is the covariance matrix of the latent points and D is the number of Gaussian units in the uppermost DBN layer (equal to the dimension of the

GPLVM output space). We use a standard Gaussian as the prior on $\boldsymbol{X}$. The variance of the noise parameter is σ^2 and $\boldsymbol{I}_N$ is an $N \times N$ identity matrix.

To join the two models, the $N \times D$ matrix of activations $\boldsymbol{H}$, from the Gaussian units, is defined as:

$$\boldsymbol{H} = \boldsymbol{A} + \boldsymbol{\sigma}^{\text{GP}} \otimes \boldsymbol{\sigma}^{\text{DBN}} \odot \boldsymbol{\mathcal{E}}, \tag{10}$$

where $\boldsymbol{A} = [\boldsymbol{m}_1^{\text{GP}}, \ldots, \boldsymbol{m}_N^{\text{GP}}]^\top$ is a matrix in which each row is the mean output of the Gaussian units corresponding to each input training datapoint. This is combined with $\boldsymbol{\sigma}^{\text{GP}}$, the $N \times 1$ vector of predictive standard deviations from the GPLVM, and $\boldsymbol{\sigma}^{\text{DBN}}$, the $1 \times D$ vector of standard deviation parameters of the Gaussian units. Note that $\otimes$ is an outer product, and $\odot$ is an element-wise product.

The $\boldsymbol{H}$ matrix represents the observed data for the GPLVM and is updated at each training iteration by sampling $\boldsymbol{\mathcal{E}}$ a different $N \times D$ matrix of independent Gaussian noise, $\mathcal{E}_{n,d} \sim \mathcal{N}(0, 1)$. This is a second application of the reparameterization trick. At each iteration, $\boldsymbol{H}$ is always normalized, to match our zero mean GP assumption, by subtracting its column-wise mean and dividing by $\boldsymbol{\sigma}^{\text{DBN}}$.

Minibatches. The objective (9) can be evaluated on an uniformly drawn subset of data $\{\boldsymbol{t}_b\}_{b=1}^{B}$ yielding an estimator for the full objective,

$$\begin{aligned} L_{\text{batched}} \simeq \tfrac{N}{B} \textstyle\sum_{b=1}^{B} \left(\boldsymbol{t}_b \log(\boldsymbol{s}_b) + (1 - \boldsymbol{t}_b) \log(1 - \boldsymbol{s}_b)\right) + \tfrac{N}{2B} \operatorname{Tr}\left[\boldsymbol{K}_B^{-1} \boldsymbol{H}_B \boldsymbol{H}_B^\top\right] \\ + \tfrac{ND}{2B} \log|\boldsymbol{K}_B| + \tfrac{N}{B} ||\boldsymbol{X}_B||^2, \end{aligned} \tag{11}$$

where $\boldsymbol{H}_B$ and $\boldsymbol{K}_B$ corresponds to $\boldsymbol{H}$ and $\boldsymbol{K}$ evaluated on the subset $\boldsymbol{X}_B$ of $\boldsymbol{X}$. Using this estimator the model can be optimised using mini-batching to scale linearly to larger datasets. We note that the matrix inversion does introduce bias into the estimator; empirical results suggest this is small and removing it is a topic for future work.

Scaling via Convolutional Architecture. When defining the likelihood directly over the pixels, the fully-connected conditional independence of the RBM layers limits scalability in terms of image size. This can be circumvented by adding convolution and deconvolution steps to replace the dense matrix product in (2) in the lower layers.

Sampling. A sample $\boldsymbol{s}_n$ from the model is drawn by first generating a hidden sample $\boldsymbol{h}_n$ from latent point $\boldsymbol{x}_n$:

$$\boldsymbol{h}_n(\boldsymbol{x}) = (\boldsymbol{m}_n^{\text{GP}} + \sigma_n^{\text{GP}} \times \epsilon_n) \odot \boldsymbol{\sigma}^{\text{DBN}} + \boldsymbol{h}_\mu, \tag{12}$$

using $\boldsymbol{m}_n^{\text{GP}}$ and σ_n^{GP} as the predictive mean and standard deviation of the GPLVM given latent point $\boldsymbol{x}_n$. This is combined with a sample ϵ_n, a $1 \times D$ vector of spherical Gaussian noise. The term $\boldsymbol{h}_\mu$ is the mean vector that is subtracted from $\boldsymbol{H}$ in the normalization step. The sample $\boldsymbol{h}_n$ is then propagated down through the DBN, sampling layer-by-layer, to give an output sample $\boldsymbol{s}_n$.

Prediction and Projection. Since we have a simple sampling process, we can propagate uncertainty for our predictions by taking the empirical mean of a set of J samples from the model as $\boldsymbol{s}_* = \frac{1}{J}\sum_j^J \boldsymbol{s}_j(\boldsymbol{h}_j(\boldsymbol{x}_*))$ for the latent location $\boldsymbol{x}^*$. Since we can efficiently take gradients through the sampling process, we can project new observations into the latent space by minimizing the reprojection error w.r.t. the latent locations for predictions from a set of random starting locations in the manifold.

Interpretation. We note that the objective (9) consists of terms in contrast with each other. The first encodes a *data* term that ensures the observed data is well represented by the model. The third provides a *complexity* term that encourages a simple (low complexity) latent space $\boldsymbol{X}$ through the covariance matrix $\boldsymbol{K}$ to prevent overfitting.

The second term "glues" the two models together by ensuring that the covariance matrix $\boldsymbol{K}$ is a good model of the covariance of the Gaussian units at the top of the DBN. This in turn, ensures that the DBN learns an appropriate network to give sensible Gaussian activations rather than the unconstrained binary activations from a normal DBN. The last term encodes a *prior* which encourages the latent points to stay close to the origin.

The applications of the reparamerization trick ensures that efficient, low variance samples can be taken during training with gradients propagated throughout all parts of the network. The use of sampling and stochastic networks allows uncertainty to be propagated down through the entire model as well to ensure uncertainty is well quantified both at training and test time.

5 Experiments

In keeping with previous work, we evaluated our models in terms of four experiments: (i) *Synthesis*, that is, generating samples that are plausible. (ii) *Representation and Generalisation*, demonstrating the ability to capture the variability of the silhouettes away from the training data. (iii) *Smoothness*, evaluating the quality of the learned latent space through interpolation; smooth trajectories in the latent space should produce smooth variations in the silhouette space. (iv) *Scaling*, evaluating how the model performs with respect to the size of the training dataset.

Our Models. In the comparisons, our main model (which we will refer to as GPDBN) consists of a three-layer DBN plus a GPLVM layer connected as described in Sect. 4. From the bottom (observed) to the top (hidden) layer the architecture consists of 200 (Concrete units), 100 (Concrete) and 50 (Gaussian). The connected GPLVM layer has only 2 latent dimensions for easy visualisation. The model is optimized jointly as described in Sect. 4. Our second model, GPSBM, is similar to the GPDBN where the three-layer DBN has been replaced with an SBM architecture of [10] with hidden Concrete units in the bottom layer and hidden Gaussian units at the top. We implemented all our models in the TensorFlow [1] framework and trained using the Adam optimizer [14].

Baselines. For comparison, we compared our models to size baselines: (i) A vanilla GPLVM with 2 latent dimensions. (ii) GPLVMDT, a GPLVM operating on a signed distance function representation in a similar manner to [22]; samples are obtained by thresholding through the hyperbolic tangent function. (iii) The state-of-the-art ShapeOdds model [8]. (iv) A DBN with binary units and the same architecture as our GPDBN. (v) The SBM [10] model with binary units (trained layer by layer with contrastive divergence like the DBN) with the same architecture as our GPSBM. (vi) The VAE [15] model with the same architecture as our GPDBN (mirrored for the decoder) and 2 latent dimensions. (vii) An InfoGAN [5] with same architecture as the VAE and GPDBN (mirrored for the discriminator) and 2 latent dimensions of structured noise.

Datasets. In keeping with previous work, we trained the models on the Weizmann horse dataset [24], which consists of 328 binary silhouettes of horses facing left. The limited number of training samples and the high variability in the position of heads, tails, and legs make this dataset difficult. We also trained the models on 300 binary images from the Caltech101 dataset of motorbikes facing right [19]. All images in both datasets have been cropped and normalized to 32×32 pixels. The test datasets consisted of the challenging held-out data from [10]; an additional 14 horses and 9 motorbikes not contained in the training datasets.

Synthesis. Figure 2(a), shows the manifold learned by the GPDBN on the Weizmann horse dataset. Each blue point on the manifold represents the latent location corresponding to a training datapoint. The heat map is given by the log predictive variance (6) that encodes uncertainty in the latent space. The model is more likely to generate valid shapes from any location in the bright regions (*i.e.*,, low variance regions).

Unlike GP based models, a standard DBN (or the SBM) does not learn such a generative manifold. This implies, first of all, that a DBN does not allow us to sample "from the top" in a direct manner. Instead we must provide a test image to the visible units and condition on it before propagating it up and down the network for a few iterations to obtain a sample. Secondly, like the VAE and InfoGAN, a DBN does not provide information about how plausible a generated sample is.

A smooth generative manifold, such the one learned by our model in Fig. 2(a) is informative as it gives us an indication about where to sample from to get plausible silhouettes. Figure 2(b) compares silhouettes generated by the models that allow sampling from the manifold.[1] We note that the GPLVM and GPLVMDT produce blurry images since the shapes present interpolation artifacts from the Gaussian likelihood. In contrast, the results from both the GPDBN and GPSBM are sharper.

[1] When we show generated silhouettes from any model, we actually show grayscale images denoting pixel-wise probabilities of turning white rather than binary samples.

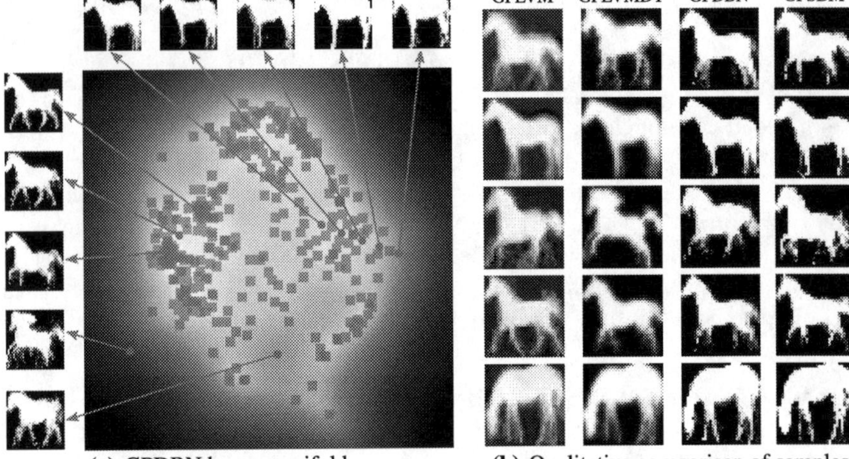

(a) GPDBN horse manifold. **(b)** Qualitative comparison of samples.

Fig. 2. (a) Manifold learned by the GPDBN model on the Weizmann horse dataset. Moving over the manifold changes the pose of the horse with smooth paths in the manifold producing smooth transitions in silhouette pose. The heat map encodes the predictive variance of the model with darker regions indicating higher uncertainty and lower confidence in the silhouette estimates. (b) Qualitative comparison of silhouettes generated from low variance manifold areas by each of the models (images manually ordered by visual similarity). (Color figure online)

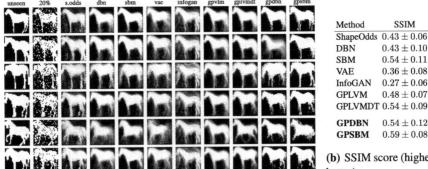

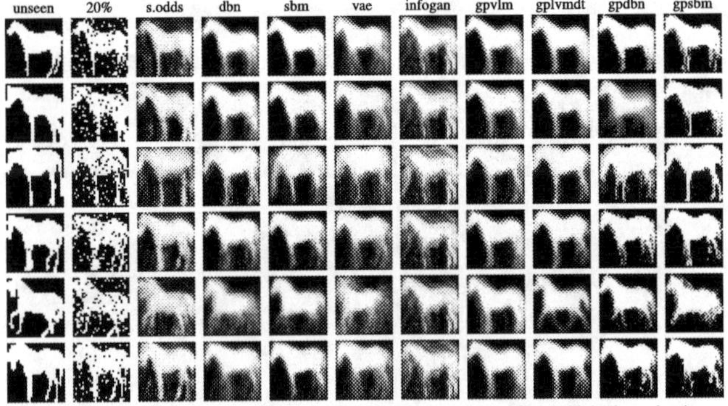

(a) Example results for projection onto manifold (20% noise).

Method	SSIM
ShapeOdds	0.43 ± 0.06
DBN	0.43 ± 0.10
SBM	0.54 ± 0.11
VAE	0.36 ± 0.08
InfoGAN	0.27 ± 0.06
GPLVM	0.48 ± 0.07
GPLVMDT	0.54 ± 0.09
GPDBN	0.54 ± 0.12
GPSBM	0.59 ± 0.08

(b) SSIM score (higher is better).

Fig. 3. Manifold projection from corrupted observations. (a) Test silhouettes (first column) are corrupted with 20% salt and pepper noise (second column). The remaining columns show estimated silhouettes from each model. (b) Mean and standard deviation of the SSIM score between silhouettes from each model against the original test data without noise.

Representation and Generalisation. In the recent literature on shape modelling, quantitative results are reported in terms of the distance between the test data not seen by the model and the most likely prediction under the model.

For the models that can be sampled from, this amounts to finding the location on the manifold that most closely represents the test input (discussed for our model in Sect. 4). For the models that learn an explicit manifold we find the closest silhouette to a test silhouette $\boldsymbol{t}^*$ by minimising the following objective with respect to a latent location $\boldsymbol{x}^*$ on the manifold:

$$L_{\text{proj}}(\boldsymbol{x}^*) = \frac{1}{P}\sum_{i=1}^{V} (\boldsymbol{t}^* \log(\boldsymbol{s}_i) + (1 - \boldsymbol{t}^*)\log(1 - \boldsymbol{s}_i)) + \gamma \times \log(\sigma^2(\boldsymbol{x}^*)), \quad (13)$$

where we use V samples to evaluate the cross entropy to the test silhouette. The second term is the log predictive variance of the latent location $\boldsymbol{x}^*$ (as defined in Eq. (6)), this encourages the model to generate plausible silhouettes from the manifold. The scaling factor γ ensures that the two term have approximatively the same scale.

Samples for a DBN (or SBM) are usually generated by conditioning on an observed sample and propagating it through the network for several cycles, as described in Sect. 3.1, with Gibbs samples taken after a burn in period. In our experiments, we fixed the conditioning on the test datapoint and averaged the results of a number of propagated samples through the model to prevent the sample chain from drifting away from the test data.

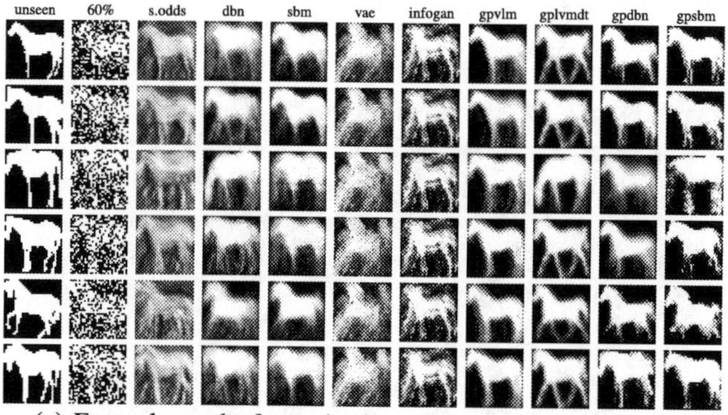

(a) Example results for projection onto manifold (60% noise).

Method	SSIM
ShapeOdds	0.25 ± 0.04
DBN	0.27 ± 0.05
SBM	0.35 ± 0.05
VAE	0.11 ± 0.02
InfoGAN	0.18 ± 0.03
GPLVM	0.44 ± 0.07
GPLVMDT	0.37 ± 0.03
GPDBN	0.42 ± 0.10
GPSBM	0.51 ± 0.09

(b) SSIM score (higher is better).

Fig. 4. Manifold projection from corrupted observations. (a) Test silhouettes (first column) are corrupted with 60% salt and pepper noise (second column). The remaining columns show estimated silhouettes from each model. (b) Mean and standard deviation of the SSIM score between silhouettes from each model against the original test data without noise.

Projection Under Noise. To provide a challenging evaluation, we take unseen test data, corrupt it with noise and ask each models to find their most likely silhouette. Simply asking to reconstruct the test data would not be a sufficient evaluation since an identity mapping would be able to perform this task. Instead, we need the model to demonstrate that it can reject data that should not be in the trained model (the noise). In Fig. 3(b), we report the results for our proposed model and the baseline methods. We use the Structured Similarity (SSIM) [30] metric (range [0, 1] with high values better) with a small window size of 3 to perform quantitative evaluations since it is known to outperform both cross-entropy and MSE as a perceptual metric. A random sample of corresponding silhouettes for the horse dataset are provided in Fig. 3(a). We also test our model in a more challenging environment, Fig. 4, where test data has been corrupted by significant noise. The quantitative comparisons shown that our GPDBN and GPSBM models have captured a high quality probabilistic estimate of the data manifold while still preserving interpretability.

Interpolation Test. We trained a GPDBN, VAE and InfoGAN models on a 30 image dataset (which we call *stars* dataset) generated from a *known* 1-dimensional manifold using a simple script. The full dataset is displayed in the top row of Fig. 5. The deterministically generated dataset allows us to determine quantitatively whether interpolations in the latent space are representative of the true data distribution. The middle rows of Fig. 5 show the model outputs for the interpolation between two latent points corresponding to a four-pointed *star* (leftmost sample) and a *square* (rightmost sample). The uncertainty information of the GPDBN allows us to go from one point to the other passing through low-variance regions by following a geodesic [27]. We can see that the GPDBN produces smoothly varying shapes of high quality that reflect the true manifold. In contrast, the VAE and InfoGAN results do not smoothly follow the true manifold and contain some erroneous interpolants that are not part of the true distribution; this is supported by the quantitative results that measure the quality of the samples to the true data using SSIM. The ability to exploit variance information in the GPDBN is clearly an advantage over the VAE and InfoGAN where the absence of direct access to the latent predictive posterior distribution prevents easy access to geodesics. Further demonstrations of the smoothness are available in supplementary material.

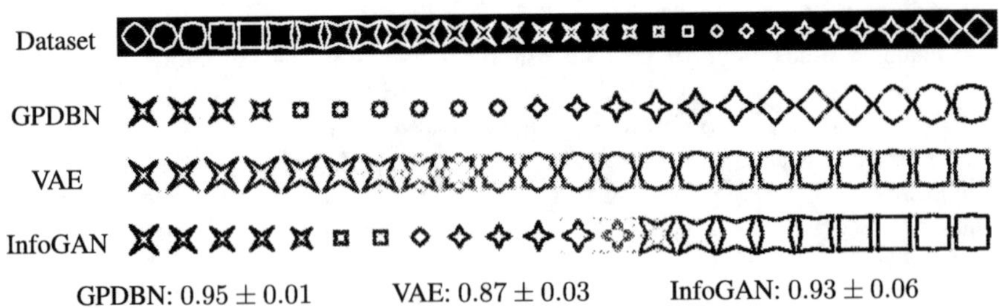

Fig. 5. Example results of the interpolation test between two training points from the stars dataset. The top row shows the geodesic interpolation generated by the GPDBN. The middle and the last rows are the linear interpolation generated by the VAE and InfoGAN respectively. The bottom row provides the mean and standard deviation of the SSIM score over 10 interpolation experiments. (In this picture black and white are inverted respect to the training dataset).

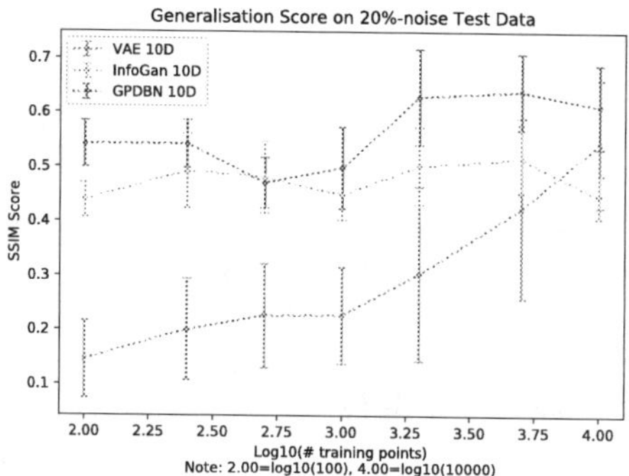

Fig. 6. Graph showing the SSIM score of the output of the GPDBN, InfoGAN and VAE models against the test data without noise as the training dataset size increases from 100 to 10000 points. A higher score is better.

Scaling Experiments. In Fig. 6 we compare the performance of the GPDBN, InfoGAN and VAE models as the size of the training dataset increases; here we use the standard MNIST digit dataset. We used a 10-dimensional latent space for all of the three models to account for the larger quantity of data. Similarly to the experiments in Figs. 3 and 4, we took 30 random images from the MNIST test data, add 20% salt-and-pepper noise, and calculated the SSIM score between the output of the models and the test data without noise. We plotted the score against dataset size (in log scale). We can see that the GPDBN model is able to capture a high quality model of the data manifold even from small datasets; for example, it achieves the same quality as a VAE trained on 10,000 images using only 100. We argue that the propagation of uncertainty throughout the model provides the advantage over both the VAE and InfoGAN which are both trained with only maximum likelihood approaches.

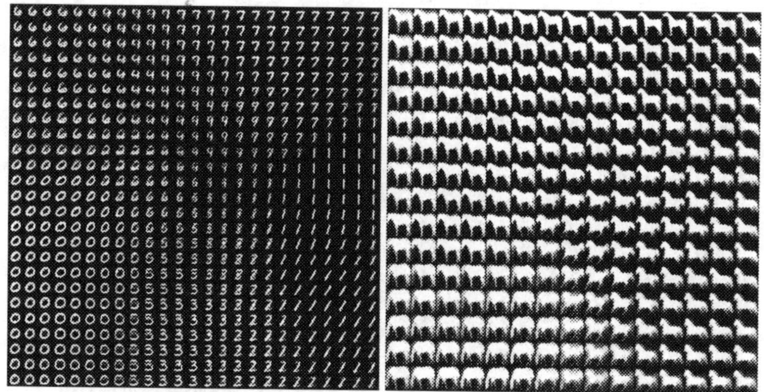

Fig. 7. The model can be made to scale to a large number of datapoints by optimizing the objective using mini-batching (11). Furthermore, scalability in the size of images can be obtained by adding upscaling and convolutions in the lowermost layer. Left: GPDBN trained on MNIST comprised of 60,000 28×28 images. Right: GPDBN trained on Weizmann Horses comprised of 328 300×300 images.

In Fig. 7 we provide results that demonstrate that our approach also overcomes scaling issues normally present in GP models and DBNs. Firstly, we show training on the 60,000 MNIST images via our proposed mini-batching approach. In addition, we also show the manifold for higher resolution images from the horse dataset (300×300). By using convolutional architectures, we can scale the number of parameters in an identical manner to convolutional feed-forward networks and our concrete layers allow us to train from random weight initialisation using back propagation without the need to use slow contrastive divergence. With both these approaches we still maintain our full uncertainty model so the same model can perform well with small and large datasets.

6 Conclusion

We have presented the GPDBN, a model that combines the properties of a smooth, interpretable low-dimensional latent representation with a data specific non-Gaussian likelihood function (for silhouette images). The model fully propagates and captures uncertainty in its estimates, it is trained end to end with the same complexity as a standard feed-forward neural network by minimising a single objective function, and is able to learn from very little data as well as scaling to larger datasets linearly by using mini-batching. We have shown both quantitatively and qualitatively that our model performs on par with the best shape models while at the same time introducing a smooth and low-dimensional latent representation with associated uncertainty that facilitates easy synthesis of data.

Acknowledgements. This work was supported by the EPSRC CAMERA (EP/M023281/1) grant and the Royal Society.

References

1. Abadi, M., et al.: TensorFlow: Large-Scale Machine Learning on Heterogeneous Systems (2015). Software available from tensorflow.org
2. Bengio, Y., LeCun, Y., et al.: Scaling learning algorithms towards AI. Large-Scale Kernel Mach. **34**(5), 1–41 (2007)
3. Campbell, N.D.F., Kautz, J.: Learning a manifold of fonts. ACM Trans. Graph. (SIGGRAPH) **33**(4), 91 (2014)
4. Carreira-Perpiñán, M.Á., Hinton, G.E.: On contrastive divergence learning. In: Cowell, R.G., Ghahramani, Z. (eds.) Proceedings of the Tenth International Workshop on Artificial Intelligence and Statistics, AISTATS 2005, Bridgetown, Barbados, 6–8 January 2005. Society for Artificial Intelligence and Statistics (2005)
5. Chen, X., Duan, Y., Houthooft, R., Schulman, J., Sutskever, I., Abbeel, P.: InfoGAN: interpretable representation learning by information maximizing generative adversarial nets. In: Lee, D.D., Sugiyama, M., von Luxburg, U., Guyon, I., Garnett, R. (eds.) Advances in Neural Information Processing Systems 29: Annual Conference on Neural Information Processing Systems 2016, Barcelona, Spain, 5–10 December 2016, pp. 2172–2180 (2016)

6. Damianou, A.C., Lawrence, N.D.: Deep Gaussian processes. In: Proceedings of the Sixteenth International Conference on Artificial Intelligence and Statistics, AISTATS 2013, Scottsdale, AZ, USA, 29 April–1 May 2013. JMLR Workshop and Conference Proceedings, vol. 31, pp. 207–215. JMLR.org (2013)
7. Davies, R., Twining, C., Taylor, C.: Statistical Models of Shape: Optimisation and Evaluation. Springer, Heidelberg (2008). https://doi.org/10.1007/978-1-84800-138-1
8. Elhabian, S.Y., Whitaker, R.T.: ShapeOdds: variational Bayesian learning of generative shape models. In: 2017 IEEE Conference on Computer Vision and Pattern Recognition, CVPR 2017, Honolulu, HI, USA, 21–26 July 2017, pp. 2185–2196. IEEE Computer Society (2017)
9. Eslami, S.M.A., Williams, C.K.I.: A generative model for parts-based object segmentation. In: Bartlett, P.L., Pereira, F.C.N., Burges, C.J.C., Bottou, L., Weinberger, K.Q. (eds.) Advances in Neural Information Processing Systems 25: 26th Annual Conference on Neural Information Processing Systems 2012. Proceedings of a Meeting Held Lake Tahoe, Nevada, USA, 3–6 December 2012, pp. 100–107 (2012)
10. Eslami, S.A., Heess, N., Williams, C.K., Winn, J.: The shape Boltzmann machine: a strong model of object shape. Int. J. Comput. Vis. **107**(2), 155–176 (2014)
11. Goodfellow, I.J., et al.: Generative adversarial nets. In: Ghahramani, Z., Welling, M., Cortes, C., Lawrence, N.D., Weinberger, K.Q. (eds.) Advances in Neural Information Processing Systems 27: Annual Conference on Neural Information Processing Systems 2014, Montreal, Quebec, Canada, 8–13 December 2014, pp. 2672–2680 (2014)
12. Hinton, G.E.: A practical guide to training restricted Boltzmann machines. In: Montavon, G., Orr, G.B., Müller, K.-R. (eds.) Neural Networks: Tricks of the Trade. LNCS, vol. 7700, pp. 599–619. Springer, Heidelberg (2012). https://doi.org/10.1007/978-3-642-35289-8_32
13. Hinton, G.E., Salakhutdinov, R.R.: Reducing the dimensionality of data with neural networks. Science **313**(5786), 504–507 (2006)
14. Kingma, D.P., Ba, J.: Adam: a method for stochastic optimization. In: International Conference on Learning Representations (ICLR) (2014)
15. Kingma, D.P., Welling, M.: Auto-encoding variational bayes. In: International Conference on Learning Representations (ICLR) (2013)
16. Kirillov, A., Gavrikov, M., Lobacheva, E., Osokin, A., Vetrov, D.P.: Deep part-based generative shape model with latent variables. In: Wilson, R.C., Hancock, E.R., Smith, W.A.P. (eds.) Proceedings of the British Machine Vision Conference 2016, BMVC 2016, York, UK, 19–22 September 2016. BMVA Press (2016)
17. Lawrence, N.D.: Probabilistic non-linear principal component analysis with Gaussian process latent variable models. J. Mach. Learn. Res. **6**, 1783–1816 (2005)
18. Lawrence, N.D., Candela, J.Q.: Local distance preservation in the GP-LVM through back constraints. In: Cohen, W.W., Moore, A. (eds.) Machine Learning, Proceedings of the Twenty-Third International Conference (ICML 2006), Pittsburgh, Pennsylvania, USA, 25–29 June 2006. ACM International Conference Proceeding Series, vol. 148, pp. 513–520. ACM (2006)
19. Li, F., Fergus, R., Perona, P.: Learning generative visual models from few training examples: an incremental Bayesian approach tested on 101 object categories. In: IEEE Conference on Computer Vision and Pattern Recognition Workshops, CVPR Workshops 2004, Washington, DC, USA, 27 June–2 July 2004, p. 178. IEEE Computer Society (2004)

20. Li, W., Viola, F., Starck, J., Brostow, G.J., Campbell, N.D.F.: Roto++: accelerating professional rotoscoping using shape manifolds. ACM Trans. Graph. (SIGGRAPH) **35**(4), 62 (2016)
21. Maddison, C.J., Mnih, A., Teh, Y.W.: The concrete distribution: a continuous relaxation of discrete random variables. abs/1611.00712 (2016)
22. Prisacariu, V.A., Reid, I.D.: PWP3D: real-time segmentation and tracking of 3D objects. Int. J. Comput. Vis. **98**(3), 335–354 (2012)
23. Prisacariu, V.A., Reid, I.D.: Nonlinear shape manifolds as shape priors in level set segmentation and tracking. In: The 24th IEEE Conference on Computer Vision and Pattern Recognition, CVPR 2011, Colorado Springs, CO, USA, 20–25 June 2011, pp. 2185–2192. IEEE Computer Society (2011)
24. Roy, A., Todorovic, S.: Combining bottom-up, top-down, and smoothness cues for weakly supervised image segmentation. In: 2017 IEEE Conference on Computer Vision and Pattern Recognition, CVPR 2017, Honolulu, HI, USA, 21–26 July 2017, pp. 7282–7291. IEEE Computer Society (2017)
25. Smolensky, P.: Information processing in dynamical systems: foundations of harmony theory. In: Parallel Distributed Processing: Explorations in the Microstructure of Cognition, vol. 1. pp. 194–281 (1986)
26. Snoek, J., Adams, R.P., Larochelle, H.: Nonparametric guidance of autoencoder representations using label information. J. Mach. Learn. Res. **13**, 2567–2588 (2012)
27. Tosi, A., Hauberg, S., Vellido, A., Lawrence, N.D.: Metrics for probabilistic geometries. In: Zhang, N.L., Tian, J. (eds.) Proceedings of the Thirtieth Conference on Uncertainty in Artificial Intelligence, UAI 2014, Quebec City, Quebec, Canada, 23–27 July 2014, pp. 800–808. AUAI Press (2014)
28. Tsogkas, S., Kokkinos, I., Papandreou, G., Vedaldi, A.: Semantic part segmentation with deep learning. arXiv preprint arXiv:1505.02438 (2015)
29. Turmukhambetov, D., Campbell, N.D.F., Goldman, D.B., Kautz, J.: Interactive sketch-driven image synthesis. Comput. Graph. Forum **34**(8), 130–142 (2015)
30. Wang, Z., Bovik, A.C., Sheikh, H.R., Simoncelli, E.P.: Image quality assessment: from error visibility to structural similarity. IEEE Trans. Image Process. **13**(4), 600–612 (2004)
31. Wu, Z., et al.: 3D ShapeNets: a deep representation for volumetric shapes. In: IEEE Conference on Computer Vision and Pattern Recognition, CVPR 2015, Boston, MA, USA, 7–12 June 2015, pp. 1912–1920. IEEE Computer Society (2015)

Gated Hierarchical Attention for Image Captioning

Qingzhong Wang and Antoni B. Chan(✉)

Department of Computer Science, City University of Hong Kong, Kowloon, Hong Kong
qingzwang2-c@my.cityu.edu.hk, abchan@cityu.edu.hk

Abstract. Attention modules connecting encoder and decoders have been widely applied in the field of object recognition, image captioning, visual question answering and neural machine translation, and significantly improves the performance. In this paper, we propose a bottom-up gated hierarchical attention (GHA) mechanism for image captioning. Our proposed model employs a CNN as the decoder which is able to learn different concepts at different layers, and apparently, different concepts correspond to different areas of an image. Therefore, we develop the GHA in which low-level concepts are merged into high-level concepts and simultaneously low-level attended features pass to the top to make predictions. Our GHA significantly improves the performance of the model that only applies one level attention, *e.g.*, the CIDEr score increases from 0.923 to 0.999, which is comparable to the state-of-the-art models that employ attributes boosting and reinforcement learning (RL). We also conduct extensive experiments to analyze the CNN decoder and our proposed GHA, and we find that deeper decoders cannot obtain better performance, and when the convolutional decoder becomes deeper the model is likely to collapse during training.

Keywords: Hierarchical attention · Image captioning · Convolutional decoder

1 Introduction

Image captioning aims to automatically generate sentences that are able to describe images. To achieve this goal, an image captioning model should contain at least three parts: (1) a vision module, which extracts features from images, (2) a language module, which is used to model the sentences, (3) a connection module, which is applied to fuse the vision and language context information.

Recently, CNNs are the most popular vision module, such as VGG nets [33], Google nets [35] and residual nets [14] (in this paper, we call them Image-CNNs). It is believed that introducing more information benefits the performance, and hence some models employ object detection or transfer image features into attributes to obtain more details or semantic information of an image [2,9,11,42,45,46]. However, applying object detection or attributes boosting methods requires more annotations, such as the bounding boxes of the

C. V. Jawahar et al. (Eds.): ACCV 2018, LNCS 11364, pp. 21–37, 2019.
https://doi.org/10.1007/978-3-030-20870-7_2

objects and their attributes, categories and actions, which is difficult to obtain. For the language module, LSTMs dominate the field of sentence generation [19,36,39,43]. Almost all previous image captioning models employ LSTMs or their variants. LSTMs apply gates and a memory cell to fuse the information of a sequence of words. In contrast, treating the sequence of word embeddings as a matrix, CNNs stack multiple convolution layers to merge words together [7] into higher-level concepts (in this paper, we call these Word-CNNs). While it is difficult to implement LSTMs in a parallel way, because there is a recurrent path during the computation, Word-CNNs only stack several layers and each layer is computed in parallel, increasing the speed. For example, to obtain the representation of 12 words, an LSTM needs 12 steps, while a Word-CNN with kernel size 3 only needs 6 layers. In terms of the connection module, a naive approach is to directly concatenate the image features and language context [25]. However different words correspond to different areas of an image, which limits the accuracy of the naive approach. The NIC model [39] first transfers the image features into another space at the first LSTM step and it outperforms m-RNN model [25]. However, [25,39] are not able to learn the correspondence between words and image areas. To address this issue, [43] introduces an attention mechanism to the LSTM-based captioning models, which is able to learn the relationship between words and image areas, and the performance improves.

The connection module plays a crucial role in image captioning models and the attention mechanism leads to both better performance and also better interpretation. For example, when a captioning model generates the word "person", the model will pay more attention to the area of the person – moreover it can also learn to find the appropriate image areas corresponding to the words that do not refer to objects. Word-CNNs are able to merge words to form high-level concepts, which mimics the tree structure of the sentence. Here we assume that each concept should correspond to an area of an image (e.g., as noted by image-text retrieval models [24,27]), and that multi-level attention is able to provide more accurate and detailed information [10,15,26,28].

Inspired by [24,27], we propose a gated hierarchical attention mechanism (GHA) for image captioning. The difference between our proposed GHA and other popular attention mechanisms is that GHA allows multi-level interaction between image encoder and language decoder, and the gating mechanism is applied to select low-level attention features and pass them to the high-level ones. Applying the proposed GHA, we obtain an increase of CIDEr score by 8.2% and SPICE by 8.6% on MSCOCO dataset, and obtain comparable results to the state-of-the-art models. Another contribution of this paper is that we conduct extensive experiments to analyze the proposed GHA and Word-CNNs.

2 Related Work

2.1 Image Captioning with Attention Mechanisms

Much work has shown that attention is able to significantly improve the captioning results [30,43,46]. In a captioning model, attention plays the role of connecting the image encoder and language decoder. The attention module normally takes the image feature map and context as input, and outputs a feature vector. In [43], an MLP is applied to learn the correspondence between words and image areas. When generating the current word, the attention module first computes an image representation by using the previous hidden state of the LSTM, and then the image representation and current hidden state are used to make predictions. After training, the attention module is able to show interpretable results. However, this attention mechanism computes attention feature for each word which is unreasonable because some words in the captions do not correspond to any object in an image. For example, the words "a" and "of" do not refer to any object, and therefore they are more likely to depend on the context instead of the image. To solve this problem, [23] introduces a visual sentinel to the attention module, which is a gate that decides whether the context or the attention feature is used to predict the current word. Other attention variants apply semantic, attribute and object detection results to introduce more information [2,30,46]. Generally, using more information results in better performance. In [31], multiple convolutional maps are employed to improve video captioning, which is similar to our GHA model. The decoder in [31] is an LSTM and to compute the attention maps at each time step, the same LSTM hidden state is applied. In contrast, our GHA model employs convolutional decoders, and therefore different concept representations are applied to compute attention maps, which reveals more about the relationships between concepts and image regions.

Moreover, our GHA model is able to obtain more visual information and hierarchically pass it from the bottom to the top level, while other models only employ attention at one layer. Although some models use gates, such as [23], the goals are different. The gates in our GHA filter out low-level information that cannot benefit prediction of the current word. In contrast, in [23], the gates decide whether the current word should depend on the image feature or the previous words. Moreover, in [23], all channels share the same gate, whereas, in our proposed GHA, a separate gate is used for each channel.

2.2 Word-CNNs for NLP

Word-CNNs have been widely applied in the field of NLP (e.g., text classification [5,17], language modeling [7], and machine translation [12]) due to several advantages: (1) convolution is faster than LSTMs, because convolution can be easily computed in parallel; (2) CNNs imitate a tree structure of the sentence, which is able to benefit solving NLP tasks.

In [13], a language CNN is applied to improve the long-term memory of LSTMs, however it also employs an LSTM to generate captions. [3,41] drop LSTMs and only apply CNNs to generate captions, which shows faster training. Although [3,41] both compute attention features at each convolutional layer, they use simple attention mechanisms, which just concatenates or adds low-level attended visual features to the high-level concept features. One disadvantage of this simple approach is that when the model becomes deeper, the influence of

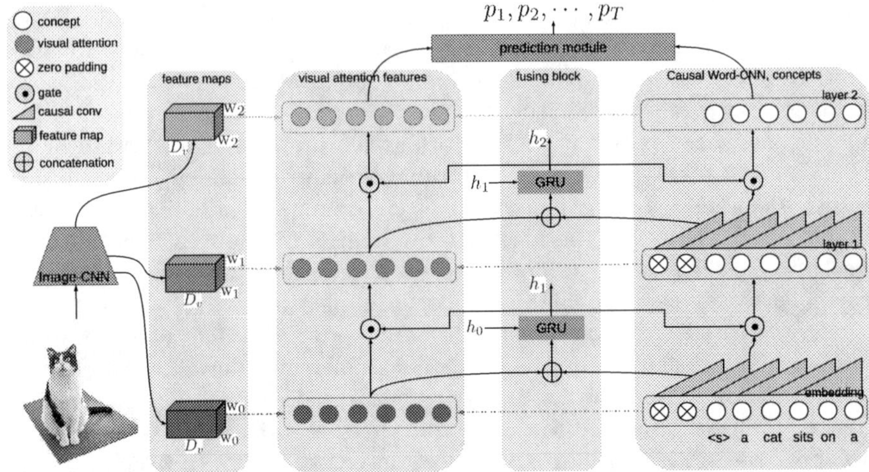

Fig. 1. An overview of our GHA. Here we show our captioning model with 2 causal convolutional layers. The dash arrows represent calculating the visual attention features using Eq. 2. The GHA can use different convolutional feature maps, which are represented by different colors. The fusing block selects the relevant visual and concept information to pass to the higher layer. (Color figure online)

low-level features could vanish. Another disadvantage is that sometimes the predictions only depend on high-level features, and introducing low-level features could result in unexpected predictions. In contrast, our GHA employs a gated recurrent unit (GRU) to learn to memorize or forget low-level features. Our proposed GHA first fuses the low-level concept features and the corresponding visual attention features, and then uses joint representations to calculate gates which decide which low-level concept and visual feature can pass to higher levels. By applying the fuse-select procedure, our proposed model with GHA outperforms other image captioning models that employ CNNs.

3 Gated Hierarchical Attention

In this section, we present our captioning model with gated-hierarchical attention (GHA). There are four parts in our proposed GHA model: (1) image encoder, (2) visual attention, (3) causal convolutional decoder, and (4) fusing block. An overview of the proposed GHA model is shown in Fig. 1. The image encoder and word decoder drive the visual attention to extract relevant features from the image feature maps. At each level, the fusing block plays the role of information fusion and selection, which allows interactions between Image-CNNs and Word-CNNs. There are gates between layer $l-1$ and layer l, which controls the bottom-up flow of visual and language information. The gates depend on both low-level visual and language features, and more details are in the following sections.

Image Encoder. The goal of the image encoder is to obtain a feature representation of an image. In this paper, we adopt an Image-CNN to extract visual features, which is similar to other image captioning models [3,13,39,43]. The main difference is that our GHA is able to use convolutional feature maps at different levels, which is shown in Fig. 1. Different convolutional feature maps have different receptive fields, and a feature map at lower layer can "see" smaller objects and more details of an image, while high-layer feature maps "see" parts of large objects or even the entire object. Therefore, applying multiple feature maps is able to benefit object recognition and word prediction [15]. The image feature maps at different levels are projected to the same channel-dimension using a learnable linear transformation. Thus, an image is represented by a set of feature maps $\mathbf{v} = \{v_{ij}^l | i = 1, \ldots, w; j = 1, \ldots, h; l = 0, \ldots, L\}$, where $v_{ij}^l \in \mathbb{R}^{D_v}$ is the image feature vector at image position (i, j) for layer l.

Causal Word-CNNs. The goal of Word-CNNs is to merge words to obtain a high-level representation of the sentence. Since we do not know the future words during inference time, we employ causal convolution, which only considers the previous words. In this paper, the Word-CNNs stack multiple causal convolutional layers (see Fig. 1, which shows a decoder with kernel size 3). The Word-CNN produces a set of concept representations at different levels, $\mathbf{c} = \{c_t^l | t = 1, \ldots, T; l = 0, \ldots, L\}$, where $c_i^l \in \mathbb{R}^{D_c}$ is the concept vector for level l and position i. L is the number of the convolutional layers in our decoder CNN, and $l = 0$ is the word embedding layer. T is the length of a caption.

For the activation function, gated linear units (GLU) show more advantages than ReLU in NLP [7], and other convolutional image captioning models also employ GLU [3,41]. In a standard GLU, both the gates and linear activations are computed using the hidden states of the previous layer of the decoder. For our GHA, we use a variant of GLU where the previous decoder layer is used to drive the linear unit and the fusing block is used to drive the gate,

$$c_{1:T}^l = \underbrace{(\mathbf{W}_a * c_{1:T}^{l-1})}_{\text{linear unit}} \odot \underbrace{\mathbf{sigmoid}\left(\mathbf{W}_b * h_{1:T}^l\right)}_{\text{gate}}, \tag{1}$$

where $c_{1:T}^l$ is the concepts at the l-th layer of the decoder, and $h_{1:T}^l$ is the hidden state of the fusing block (described later). $*$ denotes convolution, $\odot$ is element-wise multiplication, and $\{\mathbf{W}_a, \mathbf{W}_b\}$ are trainable weights. The advantage of using $h_{1:T}^l$ instead of $c_{1:T}^{l-1}$ for the gate is that the visual attention feature $\hat{v}_t^l$ are able to decide which concept features can pass to higher levels, resulting in more significant interaction between concepts and visual features.

Visual Attention. The visual attention module aims to learn the correspondence between concepts and image areas. In our GHA, the visual attention feature $\hat{v}_t^l$ at l-th level is composed of two parts[1]: (1) the current level visual attention feature $\tilde{v}_t^l$, (2) the previous level attention feature $\hat{v}_t^{l-1}$. The current-level

[1] For the word embedding layer $l = 0$, only the first part is used.

attention feature $\tilde{v}_t^l$ is calculated using the concepts c_t^l at the same level:

$$s_{ij}^{lt} = \frac{1}{\sqrt{D_c}}(v_{ij}^l)^{\mathrm{T}}\mathbf{W}c_t^l, \quad a_{ij}^{lt} = \frac{e^{s_{ij}^{lt}}}{\sum_{i=1}^{w}\sum_{j=1}^{h} e^{s_{ij}^{lt}}}, \quad \tilde{v}_t^l = \sum_{i=1}^{w}\sum_{j=1}^{h} a_{ij}^{lt} \cdot v_{ij}^l, \tag{2}$$

where $\mathbf{W} \in \mathbb{R}^{D_v \times D_c}$ is a parameter matrix. Note that, similar to [37], we apply a scaling factor $\frac{1}{\sqrt{D_c}}$ to s_{ij}^{lt} since it might take large values.

The final visual attention feature $\hat{v}_t^l$ is computed as follows:

$$\hat{v}_t^l = \tilde{v}_t^l + \mathbf{sigmoid}\left(\mathbf{W}_v h_t^l\right) \odot \hat{v}_t^{l-1}, \tag{3}$$

where $h_t^l \in \mathbb{R}^{D_h}$ is the hidden state of the fusing block, and $\mathbf{W}_v \in \mathbb{R}^{D_v \times D_h}$ are the trainable parameters. By using gates, GHA is able to select lower-level visual attention features ($\hat{v}_t^{l-1}$) and fuse them with current (higher) level features ($\tilde{v}_t^l$).

Fusing Block. The motivation of our GHA is to generate different level visual attention features for different concepts and pass low-level features to higher levels. To achieve the goal, we use a GRU to fuse the low-level concepts and the corresponding visual attention features. Concatenating the visual attention features and concepts $x_t^l = [\hat{v}_t^{l-1}, c_t^{l-1}]$, the hidden state of the fusing block h_t^l is computed as follows:

$$\begin{aligned} r_t^l &= \mathbf{sigmoid}\left(\mathbf{W}_r[h_t^{l-1}, x_t^l]\right), \quad \tilde{h}_t^l = \mathbf{tanh}\left(\mathbf{W}_{\tilde{h}} \cdot [r_t^l \odot h_t^{l-1}, x_t^l]\right), \\ z_t^l &= \mathbf{sigmoid}\left(\mathbf{W}_z[h_t^{l-1}, x_t^l]\right), \quad h_t^l = (1 - z_t^l) \odot h_t^{l-1} + z_t^l \odot \tilde{h}_t^{l-1}, \end{aligned} \tag{4}$$

where the initial hidden state is $h_t^0 = \mathbf{0}$. Note that we apply GRUs in a different way. Normally, GRUs are employed to modeling sequences, and thus the recurrent path is along with the time axis. In contrast, in our fusing block the recurrent path is along the hierarchical levels, from bottom to top.

Prediction and Loss Function. We employ a 3-layer MLP to predict the next word at sentence position t. Dropout layers are also applied to mitigate overfitting. At the t-th position, the prediction MLP takes $\hat{v}_t^L$ and c_t^L as input, and outputs the probability distribution p_t of the next word. The loss function is the cross-entropy loss between p_t and the ground-truth words in the sentence.

4 Experiments

4.1 Dataset and Preprocessing

In this paper, we conduct experiments on MSCOCO dataset [21], which contains 82,783 training and 40,504 validation images, where each image has at least 5 captions. We use the same train/validation/test split as [16] (denoted as "Karpathy split"), which uses 5,000 images for validation, 5,000 images for testing and the remaining images for training.

We drop the words that occur less than 6 times and obtain a vocabulary with 9,489 words, including 3 special tokens: starting token <start>, ending token <end> and unknown token <unk>. During training time, the images are resized to 256 × 256 and then we randomly crop a patch with the size of 224 × 224. Data is augmented using random horizontal flipping. During testing time, we resize all testing images to 224 × 224 and directly feed them into our trained model with the starting token. For the model that we submit to the testing server, we use our train+val split to train it.

4.2 Implementation Details

Baseline Model. To compare the effect of using GHA, we test baseline models where GHA is removed, and only visual attention at the top level is used, similar to [41]. The decoder in our baseline model has $L = 6$ convolutional layers, and the kernel size of each convolutional layer is 3 (this baseline is denoted as "Base-6-3"). Therefore each unit at the top layer can "see" 13 words, which is larger than the average length (11.6) of the captions in MSCOCO. The image encoder is Resnet101 without fully connected layers, therefore, $w = h = 7$ and $D_v = 2048$. The prediction module has 3 fully connected layers, and each hidden layer has 4096 units with ELU activation function [4]. After each hidden layer we employ a dropout [34] layer with the keep probability of 0.5. We use $D_c = 300$.

GHA Model. For the models with GHA, the number of hidden units of the GRU is 512, and we apply the same feature map—the output of conv5_x in Resnet101 to all levels. The same number of layers and kernel size is used for the decoder, and our GHA model is denoted as "GHA-6-3". For multi-scale GHA (MS-GHA), we use 3 different feature maps computed by Resnet101: the outputs of conv3_x, conv4_x and conv5_x, which have sizes of 28 × 28 × 512, 14 × 14 × 1024 and 7 × 7 × 2048. For easy implementation and reduce the computation complexity, we first transfer $\mathbb{R}^{512}$ and $\mathbb{R}^{1024}$ into $\mathbb{R}^{2048}$ and apply average pooling with $k = 2$ to the 28 × 28 feature map. After this, the feature maps become 14 × 14 × 2048, 14 × 14 × 2048 and 7 × 7 × 2048. Our MS-GHA models also have $L = 6$ convolutional layers plus an word embedding layer. For the word embedding layer and the first decoder level we use the conv3_x feature map to compute the attention features. For the subsequent 3 decoder levels, the conv4_x feature map are used for attention, and the last 2 decoder levels use the conv5_x feature map. The models with GHA employ the same prediction module as the baseline model.

Training and Inference. We apply the Adam optimizer [18] to train all models and use the pre-trained Resnet101 on the ImageNet dataset. The learning rate is fixed during training to 1×10^{-5} for the Resnet101 parameters, and 3×10^{-4} for the other parameters. We train all models for 50 epochs and report the performance of the best model during training. During inference, we apply beam search [3] with a beam width of 3. The maximum length of the generated sentences is 20 for all models.

Table 1. Performance on MSCOCO Karpathy test split. ⋆ denotes applying attributes or semantics, † denotes using reinforcement learning and ‡ means ensembling multiple trained models. B, M, R, C, S respectively represent BLEU [29], METEOR [8], ROUGE [20], CIDEr [38] and SPICE [1] metrics.

Method		B-1	B-2	B-3	B-4	M	R	C	S
LSTM	Hard-Att [43]	0.718	0.504	0.357	0.250	0.230	-	-	-
	ATT-FCN⋆‡ [46]	0.709	0.537	0.402	0.304	0.243	-	-	-
	SCN⋆‡ [11]	0.741	0.578	0.444	0.341	0.261	-	1.041	-
	Adaptive‡ [23]	0.742	0.580	0.439	0.332	0.266	-	1.085	-
	SCST:Att2in [32]	-	-	-	0.313	0.260	0.543	1.013	-
	SCST:Att2in† [32]	-	-	-	0.333	0.263	0.553	1.114	-
	MSM⋆‡ [45]	0.734	0.567	0.430	0.326	0.254	0.540	1.002	0.186
	PG-BCMR† [22]	0.754	0.591	0.445	0.332	0.257	0.550	1.013	-
	AG-CVAE [40]	0.732	0.559	0.417	0.311	0.245	0.528	1.001	0.179
CNN	CNN+RHN [13]	0.723	0.553	0.413	0.306	0.252	-	0.989	0.183
	CNN+Att [3]	0.722	0.553	0.418	0.316	0.250	0.531	0.952	0.179
	CNN+CNN [41]	0.685	0.511	0.369	0.267	0.234	0.510	0.844	-
Ours	Base-6-3	0.702	0.531	0.396	0.295	0.246	0.520	0.923	0.174
	GHA-6-3	0.733	0.564	0.426	0.321	0.255	0.538	0.999	**0.189**

4.3 Results on Karpathy Test Split

To compare with other methods, we first categorize the methods into 2 categories: (1) LSTM-based methods, and (2) CNN-based methods. Our proposed model is CNN-based. Results on the Karpathy test split are shown in Table 1.

Our GHA significantly improve the performance over the baseline model – BLEU-1,2,3,4 (B-1, etc.) scores increase by around 0.03 (relative improvement of 4.4%, 6.2%, 7.6%, and 8.8%), the CIDEr score increases from 0.923 to 0.999 (increase of 8.2%), and the SPICE score increases by 0.015 (increase of 8.6%), which are all significant improvements. Our GHA model outperforms other CNN-based models (CNN+RHN, CNN+Att and CNN+CNN) on all metrics, which suggests that the usefulness of our proposed GHA. Note that the goals of our convolutional decoder and the language CNNs in [13] are different. In [13], language CNNs are employed to make the LSTMs "see" more words, while our convolutional decoder is used to mimic the hierarchical structures of sentences (and therefore does not use LSTMs). Although CNN+Att and CNN+CNN apply attention at each decoder level, their simple approach without gates cannot filter out useless information, leading to worse performance.

Compared with Hard-Att [43], which applies an MLP to compute the attention weights, our baseline model obtains better results except for the B-1 score. By introducing our proposed GHA, the model obtains comparable performance on all metrics with LSTM-based models MSM [45] and AG-CVAE [40], which employ attributes or semantics. Note that applying attributes or semantics

Table 2. Performance on MSCOCO test dataset. The performance of other methods is from the latest version of their papers and the human performance is from the leaderboard (http://mscoco.org/dataset/#captions-leaderboard). The metrics are the same as Table 1. **c5** denotes that one image has 5 reference captions and **c40** represents one image corresponds to 40 reference captions. Note that the test dataset contains 40,775 images which is different from the Karpathy test split (5,000 images).

Method	c5							c40						
	B-1	B-2	B-3	B-4	M	R	C	B-1	B-2	B-3	B-4	M	R	C
Human	0.663	0.469	0.321	0.217	0.252	0.484	0.854	0.880	0.744	0.603	0.471	0.335	0.626	0.910
ATT-FCN [46]	0.731	0.565	0.424	0.316	0.250	0.535	0.943	0.900	0.815	0.709	0.599	0.335	0.682	0.958
Review Net [44]	-	-	-	-	-	-	-	-	-	-	0.597	0.347	0.686	0.969
MSM [45]	0.787	0.627	0.476	0.356	0.270	0.564	1.16	0.937	0.867	0.765	0.652	0.354	0.705	1.18
SCN [11]	0.740	0.575	0.436	0.331	0.257	0.543	1.003	0.917	0.839	0.739	0.631	0.348	0.696	1.013
SCST:Att2in [32]	-	-	-	0.344	0.268	0.559	1.112	-	-	-	-	-	-	-
CNN+Att [3]	0.715	0.545	0.408	0.304	0.246	0.525	0.910	0.896	0.805	0.694	0.582	0.333	0.673	0.914
GHA-6-3 (ours)	0.729	0.560	0.419	0.313	0.252	0.533	0.954	0.937	0.818	0.708	0.598	0.341	0.683	0.963

requires an extra branch to first predict the attributes or semantics, and the generated captions are highly related to the predicted semantics. If the semantics are incorrect or noisy, the captions could contain errors. SPICE correlates well with human judgements [6], and our GHA obtains higher SPICE than other methods.

Our GHA performs a little worse than SCST [32] and PG-BCMR [22], which use reinforcement learning (RL) to directly maximize the evaluation metrics. The GHA scores are lower by 0.01–0.02 than the models that apply RL. However, note that most of this improvement is from the RL method, because it is employed to fine-tune a model trained with cross-entropy loss. RL is able to suppress the words that cannot improve the evaluation metrics, and encourage the words that increase the metric scores, thus yielding better performance on these metrics. However, applying RL requires sampling during training, which is time-consuming.

4.4 Results on Online Test Set

Table 2 shows the comparison of the captioning methods on the online test dataset. Looking at CIDEr scores, our GHA model outperforms CNN+Att [3] and ATT-FCN [46], but obtain lower scores than MSM [45], SCN [11] and SCST:Att2in [32]. The results are mostly consistent with the Karpathy test split, although the CNN-based models perform slightly worse on the testing server. This is possibly due to overfitting since the CNN-based models have more trainable parameters compared to LSTM-based methods. For example, CNN+Att [3] has 20M parameters, while DeepVS [16] only has 13M parameters. Therefore to some extent, CNN-based models are more likely to overfit the dataset.

The BLEU, METEOR, ROUGE, and CIDEr (BMRC) metrics often do not correlate to human judgments, because they just consider the words or n-grams in the reference captions [6]. Under these metrics, the human captions actually have worse performance than most models. However, looking at the generated

1. a young boy swinging a baseball bat at a baseball
2. a young boy holding a baseball bat on a field
3. a young boy holding a baseball bat on a field
4. a boy in a baseball uniform holding a bat
5. a boy holding a baseball bat on a field
6. a young boy holding a baseball bat on a field
7. a young boy holding a baseball bat on a field
8. a young boy holding a baseball bat on a field
9. a young boy in a baseball uniform holding a bat
10.a little boy holding a baseball bat on a field
11.A boy in a green and yellow jersey holding a baseball bat
12.a close up of a baseball player holding a bat
13.A young boy ready to bat in a little league uniform.
14.A boy in a helmet and uniform holding a bat.
15.a boy holding a baseball bat next to fence and wearing a baseball helmet.

1. a kitchen filled with pots and pans and appliances
2. a kitchen filled with lots of clutter and clutter
3. a kitchen with a stove top oven next to a sink
4. a kitchen with a stove and pots on the counter
5. a bunch of pots are stacked up in a room
6. a kitchen with a lot of pots and pans
7. a room filled with lots of cooking utensils
8. a cluttered kitchen counter with many pots and pans
9. a kitchen with a bunch of cooking supplies and utensils
10.a kitchen with a lot of appliances and appliances
11.A concrete wall that has various types of tools hanging from it.
12.A room filled with lots of tools and other things.
13.a work bench and many tools hanging on a rack
14.A tool bench has a large assortment of tools above it.
15.A tool area with variety of tools hanging on nails on a board on a wall, with a table below with canisters, newspaper, and a box with small clear front drawers.

1. a wine glass and wine glass on a table
2. wine glasses and wine glasses are on a table
3. glasses of wine are set up on a table
4. three glasses of wine on a table with wine glasses
5. a group of wine glasses on a table
6. three wine glasses are sitting on a table
7. three glasses of red wine on a table
8. four wine glasses are sitting on a table
9. three glasses of red wine on a table
10.three glasses of wine sitting on a table
11.Three glasses of wine sitting on a wooden table.
12.Three glasses of wine on a wine tasting mat on a table.
13.Three wines sit on a wine tasting information card.
14.there are three glasses of wine for tasting
15.at a wine tasting they are given three different ones to try

1. a group of people sitting around a table eating food
2. a group of people sitting around a table
3. a group of people sitting at a table
4. a group of people sitting around a table eating
5. a group of people sitting around a wooden table
6. a group of people sitting on a couch
7. a group of people sitting on a bench
8. a couple of men sitting on a wooden bench
9. three people sitting at a table with plates and cups
10.a group of people sitting around a table
11.Man and two boys sitting in a corner booth of a restaurant.
12.The people sit at a restaurant with food and drinks.
13.Two boys and a man sit at a restaurant table
14.A father and two sons sitting down at a table eating a meal.
15.A man sits with two young boys at a table in a restaurant.

Fig. 2. Examples of the generated captions by our GHA model and base model. The baseline models are: (1) Base-6-3, (2) Base-6-5, (3) Base-6-7, (4) Base-10-3, and (5) Base-6B-3. The GHA models are: (6) GHA-6-3, (7) GHA-6-5, (8) GHA-6-7, (9) GHA-10-3, and (10) GHA-6B-3. The human (ground-truth) annotations are: (11)–(15).

captions reveals that most models just memorize the common words and phrases to describe images, and thus some similar images will have the same caption. In contrast, human annotations tend to have varying captions, since the background knowledge of each person varies, leading to lower BMRC metrics. SPICE [1] has been shown to be better correlated with human judgement [6]. Unfortunately, the SPICE metric is currently not available from the online test server.

4.5 Ablation Study and Analysis

To explore the impact of the depth and kernel size on our proposed models, we run an ablation study using model variants with different layers and kernel sizes, as listed in Table 3. For the model with 6 bottlenecks, which has an 18-layer decoder with 6 shortcut connections, we only use kernel size 3, because the best performances of the GHA and baseline models are obtained by using kernel size 3. The performance of all models is shown in Table 4.

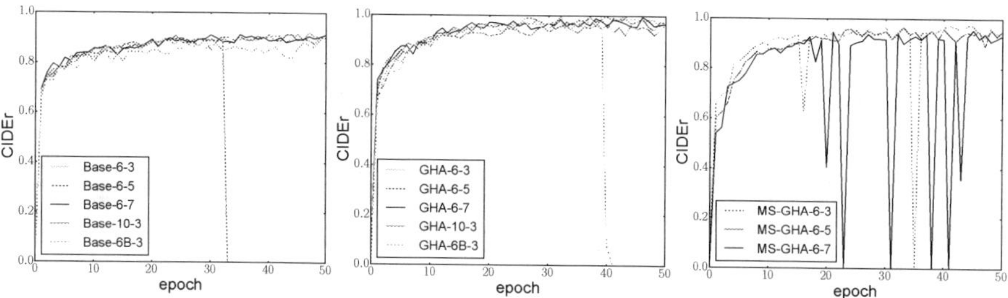

Fig. 3. CIDEr performance during training. Left: baseline models (without the proposed GHA). Middle: models with GHA. Right: models with multi-scale GHA.

Table 3. Model variants used in the ablation study. "M-l-k" represents a captioning model M, where l represents the number of convolutional layers of the decoder and k is the kernel size of each layer. B represents a model that applies bottleneck connections. "Base" represents a model without GHA, which only computes visual attention features at the top layer. GHA means using our proposed GHA and MS-GHA denotes multi-scale GHA, which applies different convolutional feature maps of the image encoder. In the table, $[k, D_c]$ represents the structure of the filter in the decoder, where D_c is the dimension of the concept space.

Base-6-3	Base-6-5	Base-6-7	Base-10-3	Base-6B-3	GHA-6-3	GHA-6-5
$[3, 300] \times 6$	$[5, 300] \times 6$	$[7, 300] \times 6$	$[3, 300] \times 10$	$\begin{bmatrix}1, 300\\3, 300\\1, 300\end{bmatrix} \times 6$	$[3, 300] \times 6$	$[5, 300] \times 6$
GHA-6-7	**GHA-10-3**	**GHA-6B-3**	**MS-GHA-6-3**	**MS-GHA-6-5**	**MS-GHA-6-7**	**-**
$[7, 300] \times 6$	$[3, 300] \times 10$	$\begin{bmatrix}1, 300\\3, 300\\1, 300\end{bmatrix} \times 6$	$[3, 300] \times 6$	$[5, 300] \times 6$	$[7, 300] \times 6$	-

Effectiveness of GHA. The models employing our GHA performs much better than the baseline models that do not use GHA. Applying GHA increases the BLEU scores by around 0.03 (a relative improvement of 4.4%, 6.2%, 7.6%, and 8.8%), and the CIDEr score by more than 0.07 (increase of 8.2%), and the SPICE score by 0.015 (increase of 8.6%), which are all significant improvements. However, the MS-GHA models performs worse than single-scale GHA models. One possible reason is that our image encoder is Resnet101, which contains shortcut connections that allow the top convolutional feature map to be fused with the low-level features. Therefore, the shortcut connections in residual nets work in the same manner to our MS-GHA model. Thus, it is unnecessary to employ multi-scale attention. Another possible reason is that MS-GHA introduces low-level visual features, such as edges and corners, which do not contain any semantic information. Table 5 shows the results of applying different feature maps of Resnet101. Applying low-level features could result in worse performance. In particular using conv3_x, the BMRC scores decrease drastically.

Some examples of generated captions are shown in Fig. 2. For the simple scenario with a few objects, all the models are able to recognize the objects, their

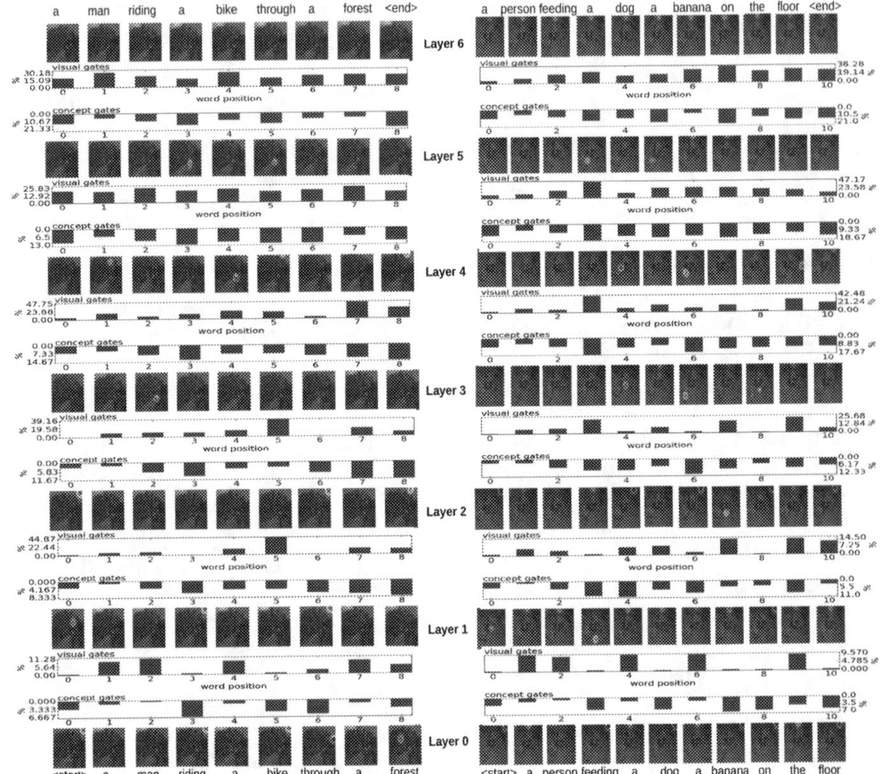

Fig. 4. Visualizing the attention weights and gate states of our GHA. The attention weights are visualized as a heat map on the image. The bar charts show the percentage of visual and concept gates that are "on", allowing lower-level information through. The bottom text are the input words and the top text are the predicted words.

relationships and the actions. However, if there are many different objects in an image, the models sometimes provide incorrect descriptions. Moreover, object counting can be difficult for the models. Introducing more visual information could benefit counting objects. For example, the models with GHA are able to recognize "three glasses" and "three people", while the baseline models without GHA are likely to ignore the numbers, even though the training data provide the numbers in the captions.

Is Deeper Better? In many cases, in particular object recognition, deeper neural networks perform better than shallow ones. Our experiments show that for image captioning, deeper convolutional decoders are not necessary. When the decoder becomes deeper, the performance becomes slightly worse. The goal of stacking more convolutional layers in the decoder is to increase the receptive field to "see" more words, however the average length of captions in MSCOCO is

Table 4. Performance of models with different kernel sizes and number of layers on Karpathy test split. The metrics are the same as Table 1.

Method		B-1	B-2	B-3	B-4	M	R	C	S
Baseline	Base-6-3	0.702	0.531	0.396	0.295	0.246	0.520	0.923	0.174
	Base-6-5	0.703	0.532	0.395	0.294	0.243	0.518	0.914	0.172
	Base-6-7	0.708	0.536	0.397	0.293	0.241	0.518	0.913	0.172
	Base-10-3	0.703	0.534	0.397	0.296	0.241	0.517	0.908	0.171
	Base-6B-3	0.701	0.530	0.392	0.288	0.239	0.515	0.894	0.172
GHA	GHA-6-3	0.733	0.564	0.426	0.321	0.255	0.538	0.999	0.189
	GHA-6-5	0.732	0.561	0.422	0.316	0.254	0.534	0.992	0.189
	GHA-6-7	0.726	0.559	0.421	0.318	0.255	0.535	0.996	0.185
	GHA-10-3	0.720	0.550	0.412	0.308	0.252	0.530	0.968	0.184
	GHA-6B-3	0.725	0.559	0.423	0.320	0.255	0.535	0.991	0.185
MS-GHA	MS-GHA-6-3	0.717	0.549	0.413	0.310	0.252	0.529	0.974	0.185
	MS-GHA-6-5	0.724	0.552	0.412	0.309	0.250	0.529	0.965	0.182
	MS-GHA-6-7	0.718	0.547	0.407	0.303	0.250	0.527	0.955	0.186

Table 5. The performance of GHA with different feature maps of Resnet101 on Karpathy test split.

Method	Convolutional map	B1	B2	B3	B4	M	R	C
GHA-6-3	conv3_x	0.600	0.416	0.291	0.208	0.191	0.446	0.597
	conv4_x	0.709	0.537	0.399	0.298	0.245	0.512	0.921
	conv5_x	0.733	0.564	0.426	0.321	0.255	0.538	0.999

11.6 words and our 6-layer decoder with kernel size 3 is able to "see" 13 words, which is enough to model the captions. Interestingly, if we fix the number of layers and increase the kernel size (e.g., Base-6-3 to Base-6-5 to Base-6-7), the performance marginally decreases (CIDEr drops from 0.923 to 0.914 and 0.913).

Another drawback of deeper decoders is that they are not stable during training. We found that the models with deeper decoders could collapse during training. In some epochs, the model predictions are all the same even though the input images are different, causing the CIDEr score to drop drastically (e.g., Fig. 3). The models that employ MS-GHA have the same problem, but finally they will stabilize and generate satisfying captions. One possible reason for this problem is that it is difficult to train deeper models. Moreover, deeper convolutional decoders require more training and testing time.

Attention and Gate Visualization. We visualize the attention maps and gates at each decoder layer (see Fig. 4). To visualize the 7×7 attention map, we first upsample it to 224×224, and then overlay it on the original image. We also show the percentage of the visual and concept gates that are "on", allowing information to flow from lower levels to higher levels (see the bar charts in Fig. 4). The gate values range from 0 (completely off) to 1 (completely on). The gate is considered on if its value is above 0.65 and 0.25 for the visual and concept gates, respectively. Note that there are 2,048 visual gates and 300 concept gates at each decoder level (one for each channel) and some gates could be on while others could be off at the same time.

From the attention maps, we can find that higher decoder levels are more likely to "see" the entire image and more gates are on at higher decoder levels. The gates are able to filter out the visual information when the model pays attention to the non-object areas, such as corners of an image. *E.g.*, in Fig. 4 (left), the first, fourth and sixth attention maps at layer 0 pay attention to the non-object areas, and the corresponding visual gates are off to filter out the information. Interestingly, if the attention weights are flat, the visual gates are likely to be on – thus the global representation of an image is able to benefit word prediction. For the correct object areas, some visual gates are on, which is reasonable. In Fig. 4 (left), the second and fifth attention maps at layer 4 pay attention to the person and the bike in the image, respectively, and the visual gates turn on, resulting in predicting the words "man" and "bike". This also occurs Fig. 4 (right) – in the fifth and seventh attention maps, dog and banana are attended when some visual gates are on.

Looking at the trends of the bar charts, our GHA exhibits a similar behavior as [23]: if more visual gates are off, then more concept gates will be on, in particular at lower decoder layers. Moreover, to predict a word that corresponds to an object in the image, such as "man" and "bike", more visual gates are open. In contrast, to predict the words "a", "through" and the ending token "<end>", more concept gates are on, which indicates that those words are more likely to depend on context instead of image features. Note that [23] switches between concept and visual features only at the highest feature-level, whereas our GHA performs the switching hierarchically, throughout the bottom-up flow of information.

5 Conclusion and Future Work

In this paper, we have presented gated hierarchal attention (GHA), which significantly improves the performance of the convolutional captioning models. Applying GHA, we obtained comparable performance with the state-of-the-art models, such as reinforcement learning methods, attributes boosting models, and LSTMs. We also analyzed the impact of hyper-parameters, such as depth and kernel size, and our experiments suggest that it is not necessary to use a deeper convolutional decoder.

Although we have conducted extensive experiments to show the abilities of GHA and convolutional decoders for image captioning, some issues should be solved in the future. One is that current attention mechanisms have limited ability to reveal the relationship between objects, therefore the image captioning models could generate strange descriptions. Hence, one direction of the future work could be learning better relationship representations to improve the quality of the generated captions. Another issue is that current captioning models could generate the same description for different images by using common words, which lacks distinctiveness. Therefore, another direction of the future work could be generating distinctive descriptions.

References

1. Anderson, P., Fernando, B., Johnson, M., Gould, S.: SPICE: semantic propositional image caption evaluation. In: Leibe, B., Matas, J., Sebe, N., Welling, M. (eds.) ECCV 2016. LNCS, vol. 9909, pp. 382–398. Springer, Cham (2016). https://doi.org/10.1007/978-3-319-46454-1_24
2. Anderson, P., et al.: Bottom-up and top-down attention for image captioning and VQA. arXiv preprint arXiv:1707.07998 (2017)
3. Aneja, J., Deshpande, A., Schwing, A.: Convolutional image captioning. In: CVPR (2018)
4. Clevert, D.A., Unterthiner, T., Hochreiter, S.: Fast and accurate deep network learning by exponential linear units (ELUs). arXiv preprint arXiv:1511.07289 (2015)
5. Conneau, A., Schwenk, H., Barrault, L., Lecun, Y.: Very deep convolutional networks for text classification. In: EACL (2017)
6. Cui, Y., Yang, G., Veit, A., Huang, X., Belongie, S.: Learning to evaluate image captioning. In: CVPR (2018)
7. Dauphin, Y.N., Fan, A., Auli, M., Grangier, D.: Language modeling with gated convolutional networks. In: ICML (2017)
8. Denkowski, M., Lavie, A.: METEOR universal: language specific translation evaluation for any target language. In: EACL Workshop on Statistical Machine Translation (2014)
9. Fang, H., et al.: From captions to visual concepts and back. In: CVPR (2015)
10. Fu, J., Zheng, H., Mei, T.: Look closer to see better: recurrent attention convolutional neural network for fine-grained image recognition. In: CVPR (2017)
11. Gan, Z., et al.: Semantic compositional networks for visual captioning. In: CVPR (2017)
12. Gehring, J., Auli, M., Grangier, D., Yarats, D., Dauphin, Y.N.: Convolutional sequence to sequence learning. In: ICML (2017)
13. Gu, J., Wang, G., Cai, J., Chen, T.: An empirical study of language CNN for image captioning. In: ICCV (2017)
14. He, K., Zhang, X., Ren, S., Sun, J.: Deep residual learning for image recognition. In: CVPR (2016)
15. Jetley, S., Lord, N., Lee, N., Torr, P.: Learn to pay attention. In: ICLR (2018)
16. Karpathy, A., Fei-Fei, L.: Deep visual-semantic alignments for generating image descriptions. In: CVPR (2015)
17. Kim, Y.: Convolutional neural networks for sentence classification. In: EMNLP (2014)
18. Kingma, D.P., Ba, J.L.: Adam: a method for stochastic optimization. In: ICLR (2015)
19. Krause, J., Johnson, J., Krishna, R., Fei-Fei, L.: A hierarchical approach for generating descriptive image paragraphs. In: CVPR (2017)

20. Lin, C.Y.: ROUGE: a package for automatic evaluation of summaries. In: ACL Workshop (2004)
21. Lin, T.Y., et al.: Microsoft COCO: common objects in context. In: Fleet, D., Pajdla, T., Schiele, B., Tuytelaars, T. (eds.) ECCV 2014. LNCS, vol. 8693, pp. 740–755. Springer, Cham (2014). https://doi.org/10.1007/978-3-319-10602-1_48
22. Liu, S., Zhu, Z., Ye, N., Guadarrama, S., Murphy, K.: Improved image captioning via policy gradient optimization of spider. In: ICCV (2017)
23. Lu, J., Xiong, C., Parikh, D., Socher, R.: Knowing when to look: adaptive attention via a visual sentinel for image captioning. In: CVPR (2017)
24. Ma, L., Lu, Z., Shang, L., Li, H.: Multimodal convolutional neural networks for matching image and sentence. In: ICCV (2015)
25. Mao, J., Xu, W., Yang, Y., Wang, J., Huang, Z., Yuille, A.: Deep captioning with multimodal recurrent neural networks (m-RNN). arXiv preprint arXiv:1412.6632 (2014)
26. Nam, H., Ha, J.W., Kim, J.: Dual attention networks for multimodal reasoning and matching. In: CVPR (2017)
27. Niu, Z., Zhou, M., Wang, L., Gao, X., Hua, G.: Hierarchical multimodal LSTM for dense visual-semantic embedding. In: ICCV (2017)
28. Osman, A., Samek, W.: Dual recurrent attention units for visual question answering. arXiv preprint arXiv:1802.00209 (2018)
29. Papineni, K., Roukos, S., Ward, T., Zhu, W.J.: BLEU: a method for automatic evaluation of machine translation. In: ACL (2002)
30. Pedersoli, M., Lucas, T., Schmid, C., Verbeek, J.: Areas of attention for image captioning. In: ICCV (2017)
31. Pu, Y., Min, M.R., Gan, Z., Carin, L.: Adaptive feature abstraction for translating video to text. In: AAAI (2018)
32. Rennie, S.J., Marcheret, E., Mroueh, Y., Ross, J., Goel, V.: Self-critical sequence training for image captioning. In: CVPR (2017)
33. Simonyan, K., Zisserman, A.: Very deep convolutional networks for large-scale image recognition. arXiv preprint arXiv:1409.1556 (2014)
34. Srivastava, N., Hinton, G., Krizhevsky, A., Sutskever, I., Salakhutdinov, R.: Dropout: a simple way to prevent neural networks from overfitting. JMLR **15**(1), 1929–1958 (2014)
35. Szegedy, C., Vanhoucke, V., Ioffe, S., Shlens, J., Wojna, Z.: Rethinking the inception architecture for computer vision. In: CVPR (2016)
36. Tan, Y.H., Chan, C.S.: phi-LSTM: a phrase-based hierarchical LSTM model for image captioning. In: Lai, S.-H., Lepetit, V., Nishino, K., Sato, Y. (eds.) ACCV 2016. LNCS, vol. 10115, pp. 101–117. Springer, Cham (2017). https://doi.org/10.1007/978-3-319-54193-8_7
37. Vaswani, A., et al.: Attention is all you need. In: NIPS (2017)
38. Vedantam, R., Zitnick, C.L., Parikh, D.: CIDEr: consensus-based image description evaluation. In: CVPR (2015)
39. Vinyals, O., Toshev, A., Bengio, S., Erhan, D.: Show and tell: a neural image caption generator. In: CVPR (2015)
40. Wang, L., Schwing, A., Lazebnik, S.: Diverse and accurate image description using a variational auto-encoder with an additive Gaussian encoding space. In: NIPS (2017)
41. Wang, Q., Chan, A.B.: CNN+CNN: convolutional decoders for image captioning. arXiv preprint arXiv:1805.09019 (2018)
42. Wu, Q., Shen, C., Liu, L., Dick, A., van den Hengel, A.: What value do explicit high level concepts have in vision to language problems? In: CVPR (2016)

43. Xu, K., et al.: Show, attend and tell: neural image caption generation with visual attention. In: ICML (2015)
44. Yang, Z., Yuan, Y., Wu, Y., Cohen, W.W., Salakhutdinov, R.R.: Review networks for caption generation. In: NIPS (2016)
45. Yao, T., Pan, Y., Li, Y., Qiu, Z., Mei, T.: Boosting image captioning with attributes. In: ICCV (2017)
46. You, Q., Jin, H., Wang, Z., Fang, C., Luo, J.: Image captioning with semantic attention. In: CVPR (2016)

Dealing with Ambiguity in Robotic Grasping via Multiple Predictions

Ghazal Ghazaei[1,2(✉)], Iro Laina[2], Christian Rupprecht[2], Federico Tombari[2], Nassir Navab[2], and Kianoush Nazarpour[1,3]

[1] School of Engineering, Newcastle University, Newcastle, UK
g.ghazaei1@newcastle.ac.uk
[2] Technische Universität München, Munich, Germany
[3] Institute of Neuroscience, Newcastle University, Newcastle, UK

Abstract. Humans excel in grasping and manipulating objects because of their life-long experience and knowledge about the 3D shape and weight distribution of objects. However, the lack of such intuition in robots makes robotic grasping an exceptionally challenging task. There are often several equally viable options of grasping an object. However, this ambiguity is not modeled in conventional systems that estimate a single, optimal grasp position. We propose to tackle this problem by simultaneously estimating multiple grasp poses from a single RGB image of the target object. Further, we reformulate the problem of robotic grasping by replacing conventional grasp rectangles with grasp belief maps, which hold more precise location information than a rectangle and account for the uncertainty inherent to the task. We augment a fully convolutional neural network with a multiple hypothesis prediction model that predicts a set of grasp hypotheses in under 60 ms, which is critical for real-time robotic applications. The grasp detection accuracy reaches over 90% for unseen objects, outperforming the current state of the art on this task.

Keywords: Robotic grasping · Deep learning · Multiple hypotheses

1 Introduction

Grasping is a necessary skill for an autonomous agent to interact with the environment. The ability to grasp and manipulate objects is imperative for many applications in the field of personal robotics and advanced industrial manufacturing. However, even under simplified working conditions, robots cannot yet match human performance in grasping. While humans can reliably grasp and manipulate a variety of objects with complex shapes, in robotics this is still an unsolved problem. This is especially true when trying to grasp objects in different positions, orientations or objects that have not been encountered before. Robotic grasping is a highly challenging task and consists of several components that need to take place in real time: perception, planning and control.

C. V. Jawahar et al. (Eds.): ACCV 2018, LNCS 11364, pp. 38–55, 2019.
https://doi.org/10.1007/978-3-030-20870-7_3

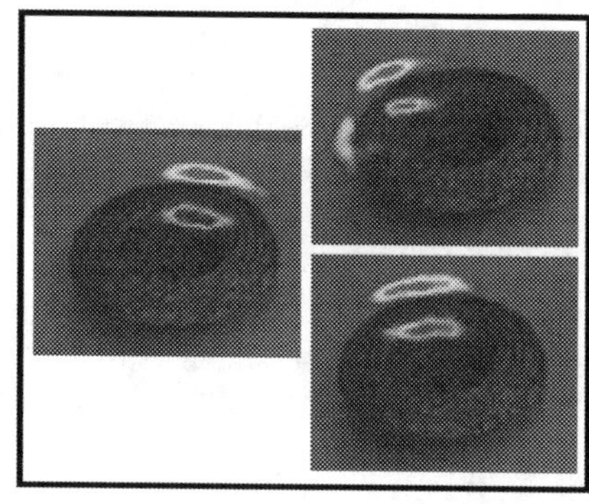

Fig. 1. We propose a model for regressing multiple grasp hypotheses as 2D belief maps, which tackles the ambiguity of grasp detection more effectively than a single grasp detection, in particular for completely unseen shapes, as the one depicted here.

In the field of robotic perception, a commonly studied problem is the detection of viable grasping locations. Visual recognition from sensors—such as RGB-D cameras—is required to perceive the environment and transfer candidate grasp points from the image domain to coordinates in the real world. The localization of reliable and effective grasping points on the object surface is a necessary first step for successful manipulation through an end effector, such as a robotic hand or a gripper. The detected target position is then used such that an optimal trajectory can be planned and executed. This visual recognition task has gained great attention in recent years [1,9,12,13,15,20,21,27,29,34,35,37,38,40] and led to the emergence of benchmark datasets, such as the Cornell grasp detection dataset [20], to evaluate the performance of approaches designed for this specific task.

Early approaches rely on explicitly estimating object geometry to localize grasping points [27,40]. This tends to slow down the overall run-time and fails in presence of complicated or unseen object shapes. Following the success of deep learning in a wide spectrum of computer vision applications, several recent approaches [9,15,20,24,29,37,38] employed Convolutional Neural Networks (CNNs) [14,18] to successfully detect grasping points from visual data, typically parametrized by 5-dimensional (5D) grasping representations [12,20]. It is worth noting that most of these methods rely on depth data, often paired with color information. All these approaches have contributed significantly to improving robotic grasp detection, however they have not exhaustively studied generalization to novel, complex shapes. In particular, although some prior work explicitly aims at grasp estimation for unseen objects from RGB-D/depth data, this aspect is still regarded as an open issue [40]. In this work we propose a novel grasp detection approach from RGB data only. Our method incorporates two measures to explicitly model ambiguity related to the task of robotic grasping. First, we redefine the task of grasp detection as dense belief estimation problem. Thus, instead of the conventional grasp representation based on bounding boxes [12] we model the grasp space with 2D belief maps to be predicted from an input image. This allows the model to predict a grasp distribution with spatial uncertainty that accounts for small-scale ambiguities and exploits the full potential of CNNs in learning spatial representations.

The reformulation of this problem further highlights the inherent ambiguity in grasp detection. Most objects can be gripped in different ways and, although some may be preferable, there is not necessarily a "best" grip. This is also reflected in that current benchmarks provide multiple grasp rectangles as ground truth for each object. However, aiming for a single output in an ambiguous problem can harm performance as the network typically learns the conditional average of all possible outcomes. To better model larger scale ambiguities, we employ a *multi-grasp prediction* framework and estimate multiple meaningful grasping positions for each input image. This approach allows to better model the output distribution and results in more precise and robust predictions especially in the case of unseen objects. The outcome of our method in comparison to a conventional single-prediction model is depicted in Fig. 1. Finally, for the selection of a single grasping position, we propose an additional ranking stage based on Gaussian Mixture Models (GMMs) [25]. This is particularly useful for practical applications of our approach and for fair comparisons with the state of the art. We demonstrate the effectiveness of our approach by evaluating on a common benchmark [20].

2 Related Work

Robotic Grasp Detection. Before the immense success of deep learning in computer vision applications, grasp estimation solutions were mostly based on analytic methods [3]. Some of these approaches, such as Graspit! [27], are dependent on the presence of a full 3D model to fit a grasp to it, not feasible for real-time applications. With the improvement of depth sensors, there are also recent methods that leverage geometrical information to find a stable grasp point using single-view point clouds [40].

In addition, the combination of both learning techniques and 3D shape information has led to interesting results. Varley *et al.* [35], use a deep learning based approach to estimate a 3D model of the target object from a single-view point cloud and suggest a grasp using 3D planning methods such as Graspit!. Mahler *et al.* [24] develop a quality measure to predict successful grasp probabilities from depth data using a CNN. Asif *et al.* [1] extract distinctive features from RGB-D point cloud data using hierarchical cascade forests for recognition and grasp detection.

The most recent robotic grasp estimation research is focused solely on deep learning techniques. Lenz *et al.* [20] pioneered the transfer of such techniques to robotic grasping using a two-step cascade system operating on RGB-D input images. A shallow network first predicts high-ranked candidate grasp rectangles, followed by a deeper network that chooses the optimal grasp points. Wang *et al.* [38] followed a similar approach using a multi-modal CNN. Another method [15] uses RGB-D data to first extract features from a scene using a ResNet-50 architecture [11] and then a successive shallower convolutional network applied to the merged features to estimate the optimal point of grasping.

Recent work in robotic grasp detection has also built on object detection methods [30,31] to directly predict candidate grasp bounding boxes. Redmon *et al.* [29] employ YOLO [30] for multiple grasp detection from RGB-D images. This model produces an output grid for candidate predictions including the confidence of grasp being correct in each grid cell. This MutiGrasp approach improved the state-of-the-art accuracy of grasp detection up to ∼10%. However, the results are only reported for the best ranked rectangle and the performance of other suggested grasps is not known. Guo *et al.* [9] instead propose a hybrid deep network combining both visual and tactile sensing. The multi-modal data is fed into a visual object detection network [31] and a tactile network during training and the features of both networks are concatenated as an intermediate layer to be employed in deep visual network during test.

Landmark Localization. In our method we define the grasping problem differently. Instead of approaching the task as object detection, *i.e.* detecting grasping rectangles as for example in [9,29], we express the rectangles as 2D belief maps around the grasping positions. This formulation is inspired by the latest methods in landmark localization, for example in human pose estimation [2,4,6,28,39], facial keypoint detection [5,26] and articulated instrument localization [8,16]. The use of heat maps to represent 2D joint locations has significantly advanced the state of the art in the localization problem. These models are trained so that the output matches the ground truth heat maps, for example through $\mathcal{L}_2$ regression, and the precise landmark locations can be then computed as the maxima of the estimated heat maps.

Multiple Hypothesis Learning. To better model the grasp distribution of varying objects as well as grasp uncertainty, we augment the belief maps along the lines of multiple hypothesis learning [19,33]. These methods model ambiguous prediction problems by producing multiple possible outcomes for the same input. However, they do not explore the possibility to select the best hypothesis out of the predicted set. The problem of selecting good hypotheses for multi-output methods has been typically addressed by training selection networks [10,22]. Here, we solve this problem in a task-specific fashion, by scoring the predictions based on their alignment with a parametric Gaussian distribution which was used in training.

3 Methods

In the following, we describe our approach in detail. First, we redefine the problem of robotic grasp detection as prediction of 2D grasp point belief maps

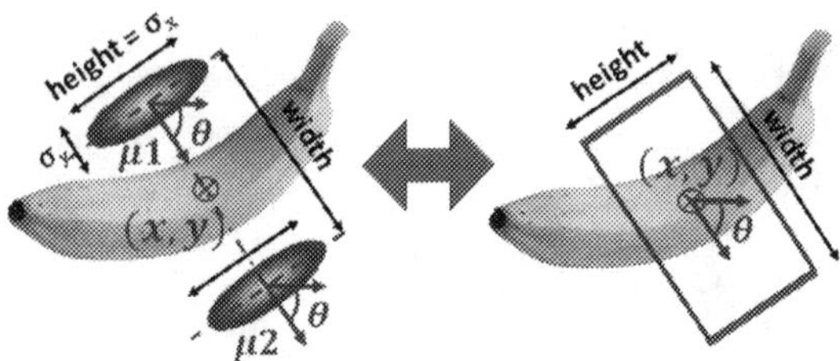

Fig. 2. An illustration of the adaptation of grasp rectangles to their associated grasp belief maps. The belief maps are constructed using the centers of the gripper plates as means for the normal distributions. The variance σ_x is proportional to the gripper height, while σ_y is a chosen constant.

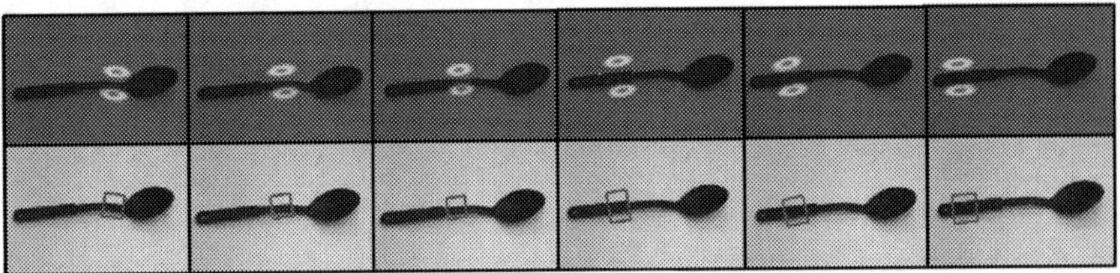

Fig. 3. Samples of rectangle grasps and grasp belief maps shown for the same item.

(Sect. 3.1). Specifically, we learn a mapping from a monocular RGB image to grasping confidence maps via CNN regression (Sect. 3.2). We then introduce our multi-grasp framework to tackle the inherent ambiguity of this problem by predicting multiple grasping possibilities simultaneously (Sect. 3.3). Finally, we rank all predicted grasps according to GMM likelihood in order to select the top ranked prediction (Sect. 3.4).

3.1 Grasp Belief Maps

The problem of robotic grasp detection can be formulated as that of predicting the size and pose of a rectangle, which, as suggested by [12], includes adequate information for performing the grasp; that is a 5-dimensional grasp configuration denoted by (x, y, θ, h, w), where (x, y) is the center of the rectangle and θ is its orientation relative to the horizontal axis. We denote width and height of the bounding box with w and h respectively. These correspond to the length of a grip and the aperture size of the gripper. This representation has been frequently used in prior work [1,9,15,20,29,38] as guidance for robotic grippers.

In this work, we propose an alternative approach to model the detection of a robotic grasp using 2D belief maps. For an N-finger robotic gripper, these belief maps can be represented as a mixture model of N bivariate normal distributions fitted around the finger locations.

For a parallel gripper, the previously used grasping rectangle representation can be encoded in belief maps as follows. The means $\boldsymbol{\mu}^{(n)} = (\mu_x^{(n)}, \mu_y^{(n)})^T$, with

$n \in \{1, 2\}$, around which the Gaussian distributions are centered correspond to the 2D centers (in Cartesian coordinates) of the gripper plates. The distance of the means $\|\boldsymbol{\mu}^{(1)} - \boldsymbol{\mu}^{(2)}\|_2 = w$ represents the width of the grasp. The Gaussian distributions are elliptical with $\Sigma = \mathrm{diag}(\sigma_x^{(n)}, \sigma_y^{(n)})^2$. The primary axis of the ellipse represents the grasp height h. The orientation of the Gaussian kernels is adjusted by the rotation matrix $R(\theta)$ to make up for the correct grasping pose with respect to the object. The mixture model can be then defined as

$$G(\mathbf{p}) = \sum_{n=1}^{N} \frac{\exp\Big(-\frac{1}{2}(\mathbf{p} - \boldsymbol{\mu}^{(n)})^T R(\theta)\, \Sigma^{-1}\, R(\theta)^T (\mathbf{p} - \boldsymbol{\mu}^{(n)})\Big)}{2\pi N\, \sigma_x^{(n)} \sigma_y^{(n)}}, \tag{1}$$

where $\mathbf{p}$ denotes a pixel's location inside the belief map. An illustration of our adapted grasp belief maps is shown in Fig. 2.

Grasp belief maps enclose the same information as the grasp rectangles, while expressing an encoding of the inherent spatial uncertainty around a grasp location. The proposed representation encourages the encoding of image structures, so that a rich image-dependent spatial model of grasp choices can be learned. Moreover, the amplitude as well as variance of the predicted belief maps can act as a measure of confidence for the exact location and orientation of the grasp. In Fig. 3, we show all possible grasp configurations for an item using both the traditional bounding box representation and our adapted continuous approach based on belief maps.

A model equipped with grasp belief maps can express its uncertainty spatially in the map, while direct regression of rectangles makes it harder to model spatial uncertainty. Further, such mixture models can be seamlessly extended to model grasp representations of other, more complex types of grippers, such as hand prostheses.

In practice, we create heat maps by constructing Gaussian kernels according to Eq. 1, parametrized by the centers and dimensions of the gripper fingers. The centers of the gripper plates specify the means of the Gaussian kernels, σ_x is proportional to the gripper height and σ_y is a chosen constant value.

3.2 CNN Regression

For the regression of confidence maps, a common design choice among deep learning methods have been fully convolutional networks (FCNs) [23]. For our purpose, we use the fully convolutional residual architecture proposed in [17], which has shown competitive performance for dense prediction tasks, in particular depth estimation, in real time. The encoder is based on ResNet-50 [11], which embeds the input into a low dimensional latent representation. The decoder is built from custom residual up-convolutional blocks, which increase the spatial resolution up to half of the input resolution. The architecture is shown in Fig. 4.

Given our problem definition, the network is trained to perform a mapping from a monocular RGB input to a single-channel heatmap comprised of the Gaussian mixture which represents the grasp belief. Since there are typically more than one viable grasp per object, choosing a single ground truth grasp

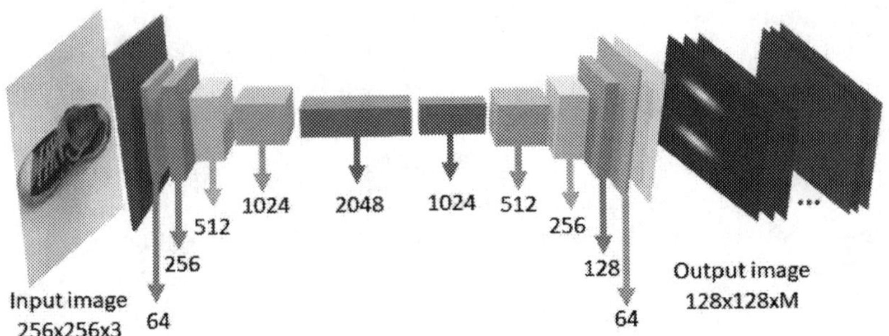

Fig. 4. The architecture of the fully convolutional residual network used in this paper. M refers to the number of grasp map predictions.

becomes an ambiguous problem. When training in the single-grasp setup, we choose the most stable available grasp as ground truth, that is the one with the maximum grasping area. To this end, the objective function to be minimized is the Euclidean norm between the predicted belief map $\tilde{G}$ and the chosen ground truth map:

$$\mathcal{L}(\tilde{G}, G) = \|\tilde{G} - G\|_2^2 \tag{2}$$

3.3 Multiple Grasp Predictions

Training the model with a single viable grasp is not optimal and could harm generalization, because the model gets penalized for predicting grasps which are potentially valid, but do not exactly match the ground truth. In other words, the samples that the model learns from do not cover the entire grasp distribution. Thus, in the case of known objects, the model would overfit to the single grasp possibility it has seen, while in the case of previously unseen objects the uncertainty which arises would prevent the model from producing a sharp and reliable belief map (Fig. 1).

To overcome this limitation we propose a multi-grasp estimation setup, Instead of forcing the model to produce exactly one grasp, we allow the same model to produce multiple simultaneous outputs $\tilde{G} = \{\tilde{G}^{(m)}\}_m$, $m \in \{1, 2, ..., M\}$. In practice, we replicate the last layer M times. Our goal is to then train the model such that it approximates the entire distribution of viable grasps. This problem can be formulated as an oracle meta-loss $\mathcal{M}$ that acts on top of the problem-specific objective function $\mathcal{L}$. By denoting the cost value of each grasp output as

$$\mathcal{L}_m = \mathcal{L}(\tilde{G}^{(m)}, G) \tag{3}$$

we can then define the meta-loss through the following minimum formulation:

$$\mathcal{M}(\tilde{G}, G) = (1 - \epsilon) \min_{m=1,\ldots,M} \mathcal{L}_m + \frac{\epsilon}{M-1} \sum_{m' \neq \arg\min_m \mathcal{L}_m} \mathcal{L}_{m'} \tag{4}$$

The proposed algorithm works as follows. At each training step, a grasp belief map is chosen randomly as the ground truth label among all available ground truth possibilities for the given input sample. In this way, the entire grasp distribution for each sample will be seen during training. Since the model cannot know which ground truth belief map will be chosen for a specific image, it will learn to disentangle the possibilities into the M grasping hypotheses. This is achieved by the loss $\mathcal{M}$ in Eq. 4. This objective is based on the hindsight loss, which only considers the output $\tilde{G}^{(m)}$ which is closest to the given ground truth G. Here we formulate it in a more intuitive way by using a soft approximation in which the oracle selects the best grasp with weight $1 - \epsilon$ and $\frac{\epsilon}{M-1}$ for all the other predictions, where $\epsilon = 0.05$. This enables the output branches to be trained equally well, especially if they were not initially selected.

3.4 Grasp Option Ranking

Our previously described model predicts M grasp hypotheses. For this system to be used in practice, we need a method to assess the hypotheses quality and find which one should be selected. Therefore, it is desirable to find a way to rank all candidate grasps and pick one with a high probability of successful grasping. As we train the model to produce two multivariate normal distributions, one way to rank the predicted belief maps is by fitting a two-component Gaussian mixture model (GMM) to each output map using finite mixture model estimation [25].

The main parameters of a Gaussian mixture model are the mixture component weights ϕ_k and the component means μ_k and variances/covariances σ_k with K being the number of components. The mathematical description of a GMM distribution over all the components is

$$p(\boldsymbol{x}) = \sum_{k=1}^{K} \phi_k \mathcal{N}(\boldsymbol{x} \mid \boldsymbol{\mu}_k, \sigma_k), \quad \sum_{k=1}^{K} \phi_k = 1 \tag{5}$$

where $\mathcal{N}(\boldsymbol{x} \mid \boldsymbol{\mu}, \sigma)$ represents a normal distribution with mean μ and variance σ. Mixture models can be estimated via the expectation maximization (EM) algorithm [7], as finding the maximum likelihood analytically is intractable. EM iteratively finds a numerical solution to the maximum likelihood estimation of the GMM. The EM algorithm follows two main steps: (E) computes an expectation of component assignments for each given data point given the current parameters and (M) computes a maximum likelihood estimation and subsequently updates the model parameters. The model iterates over E and M steps until the error is less than a desired threshold.

We fit the same parametric model that was used to create the ground truth belief maps (Eq. 1) and use the likelihood of the fit for each of the M predictions for ranking and choose the best fitted prediction as the system's final output.

4 Experiments and Results

In this section, we evaluate our method experimentally on a public benchmark dataset and compare to the state of the art. Further, we investigate the influence of the number of grasp hypotheses M on the performance of the method.

4.1 Dataset

Cornell Dataset. We evaluate our approach on the Cornell grasp detection dataset [20], which consists of 885 RGB-D images from 240 graspable objects with a resolution of 640×480 pixels. The annotated ground truth includes several grasping possibilities per object represented by rectangles. The dataset is mainly suited for 2D grippers with parallel plates, but as the grasp size and location are included in the representation, it has the potential to be used also for other types of grippers as it is used in [9] for a 3-finger gripper. There are 2 to 25 grasp options per object of different scales, orientations and locations, however, these annotated labels are not exhaustive and do not contain every possible grasp. Figure 5 shows some cropped samples of the dataset as used in this work. Here we only use the RGB images and disregard the depth maps.

Data Splits. We follow a cross-validation setup as in previous work [1,9,15,20, 29,38], using image-wise and object-wise data splits. The former split involves training with all objects, while some views remain unseen to evaluate the intra-object generalization capability of the methods. However, even an over-fitted model could perform well on this split. The object-wise split involves training on all available views of the same object and testing on new objects and thus is suitable for evaluating inter-object performance. However, the unseen objects are rather similar to ones used in training.

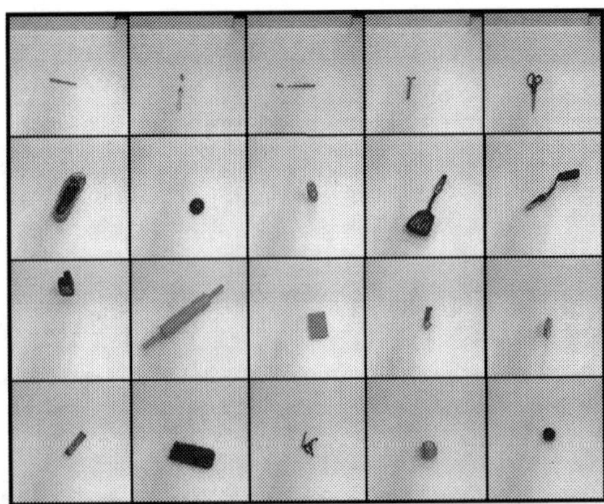

Fig. 5. A representation of a subset of the objects of the Cornell grasp detection dataset [20].

It is worth noting that none of the previous methods studied the potential of generalizing to truly novel *shapes*, as the dataset includes a variety of similar objects. For example, there are several objects with different colors but of the same shape. Therefore, the object-wise split may not be a good measure for generalization to novel shapes. To investigate our framework's performance on unseen shapes, we have created an additional *shape-wise* split, to encourage larger variation in objects between the train and test sets. We pick the train and test folds such that all the objects of similar shapes, *e.g.* various kinds of hats, are included in one of the test/train folds only and therefore novel when testing. Both image-wise and object-wise splits are validated in five folds. We perform two-fold cross validation for the shape-wise split, where we use the first 20% of objects for testing and the remainder for training. The second fold uses the same split but with reversed order of objects.

4.2 Implementation Details

In all our experiments we pre-process the images and annotations as detailed in the following. As the images contain a large margin of background around the objects, we crop them and their corresponding grasp maps to 350×350 pixels and then bilinearly down-sample the image to 256×256 and the grasp map to 128×128. Prior to cropping we apply data augmentation techniques. We sample a random rotation in $[-60°, 60°]$, center crops with a translation offset of $[-20, 20]$ pixels and scaling between 0.9 and 1.1. Each image is augmented six times. Thus, the final dataset contains 5310 images after augmentations. All the images and labels are normalized to a range of $[0, 255]$.

To train the single grasp prediction model, we choose the largest ground truth grasp rectangle as label since area is a good indicator for probability and stability of the grasp. This selection may be trivial, but training a single grasp model is not feasible without pre-selection of a fixed ground truth among the available grasps.

On the other hand, our multiple grasp prediction model can deal with a *variable* number of ground truth grasp maps per image. At each training step, we randomly sample one of the available ground truth annotations. We also add hypothesis dropout with rate 0.05 as regularization [33]. We investigate and report the performance of our framework for different numbers M of grasp hypotheses. To rank multiple predicted grasps, we performed EM steps for up to 1000 iterations and calculated the negative log-likelihood for the parameters σ_k and μ_k.

Training was performed on an NVIDIA Titan Xp GPU using MatConvNet [36]. The learning rate was set to 0.0005 in all experiments. For regularization we set weight decay to 0.0005 and add a dropout layer with rate equal to 0.5. The models were trained using stochastic gradient descent with momentum of 0.9 for 50 epochs and a batch size of 5 and 20 for training multiple and single prediction models respectively.

4.3 Grasp Detection Metric

We report quantitative performance using the rectangle metric suggested by [12] for a fair comparison. A grasp is counted as a valid one only when it fulfills two conditions:

- The intersection over union (IoU) score between the ground truth bounding box (B) and the predicted bounding box (B^*) is above 25%, where

$$\mathrm{IoU} = \frac{B \cap B^*}{B \cup B^*} \tag{6}$$

- The grasp orientation of the predicted grasp rectangle is within 30° of that of the ground truth rectangle.

This metric requires a grasp rectangle representation, while our network predicts grasp belief maps. We therefore calculate the modes μ_1 and μ_2 as the centers of each elliptical Gaussian for every predicted belief map. The Euclidean distance between these modes should be equal to the grasp rectangle's width w (Fig. 2). We compute the height h of the grasp rectangle as the major axis of the ellipse (after binarization of the belief map with a threshold of 0.2). We determine the gripper's orientation θ by calculating the angle of the major axis as $\arctan \frac{d_1}{d_2}$; where d_1 and d_2 are the vertical and horizontal distance between the centers of elliptical Gaussian maps respectively. We can then convert the belief maps to a grasping rectangle representation. Under high uncertainty, *i.e.* when a grasp map is considerably noisy, we discard the hypothesis as a rectangle cannot be extracted. We note that a valid grasp meets the aforementioned conditions with respect to *any* of the ground truth rectangles and compute the percentage of valid grasps as the *Grasp Estimation Accuracy*.

4.4 Evaluation and Comparisons

In the following, we compare our multiple grasp prediction method with the single-grasp baseline and state-of-the-art methods. As there are several ground truth annotations per object, we compare the selected prediction to all the ground truth grasp rectangles to find the closest match. Among the predictions there can be some which are not viable, while others are perfect matches. The selected prediction for each image is one with the maximum GMM likelihood.

Quantitative Results. We report the results in Table 1, where M indicates the number of hypotheses and consequently $M = 1$ refers to the regression of single belief map and can be seen as a baseline in the following experiments. The proposed model with $M = 5$ predicted grasps shows significant improvement in performance over the single-grasp model (the average number of grasps per object in the dataset is also approximately five). This performance boost reveals the potential of modeling ambiguity in robotic grasp detection. To study the effect of the number of grasping options, we also evaluated our approach with $M = 10$.

Table 1. Comparison of the proposed method with the state of the art. *multiple* refers to our multiple prediction models, while *multiple/reg* are the models trained with diversity regularization.

Method	Input	Grasp estimation accuracy (%)		
		Image-wise	Object-wise	Shape-wise
Lenz et al. [20]	RGB-D	73.9	75.6	-
Wang et al. [38]	RGB-D	85.3	-	-
Redmon et al. [29]	RGB-D	88.0	87.1	-
Asif et al. [1]	RGB-D	88.2	87.5	-
Kumra et al. [15]	RGB-D	89.2	89.0	-
Guo et al. [9]	RGB-D, tactile	**93.2**	89.1	-
Kumra et al. [15]	RGB	88.8	87.7	-
single $M = 1$	RGB	83.3	81.0	73.7
multiple $M = 5$	RGB	91.1	**90.6**	85.3
multiple/reg $M = 5$	RGB	89.1	89.2	82.5
multiple $M = 10$	RGB	**91.5**	90.1	**86.2**

While it only relies on RGB data as input, our multiple grasp approach outperforms all state-of-the-art methods that use additional depth information, except for Guo *et al.* [9] who also leverage tactile data. Moreover, both single and multiple grasp models have a faster grasp prediction run-time than the state of the art at 56 ms. GMM maximum likelihood estimation for hypothesis selection increases the run-time to 95 ms. Increasing the number of outputs M does not have a negative effect on speed.

It is worth noting that the comparable performance of the models in the image- and object-wise splits (also in prior work) suggests that task difficulty does not change much between the two scenarios. With the more challenging shape-wise scenario that we have proposed, we can better evaluate performance on novel objects. In this case, the accuracy of the single grasp baseline drops significantly. On the contrary, the multiple grasp model is still able to handle the increased difficulty with a large performance boost over the baseline. It can be observed that with an increasing number of grasp hypotheses the performance gap of the multiple-grasp over the single-grasp model is the highest for the shape-wise split, with over 12% increase in accuracy for unseen shapes/objects.

Diversity of Predictions. We also examine the diversity of the predicted hypotheses for each image. We have performed experiments adding a repelling regularizer [32] (weighted by a factor of 0.1) to the hindsight loss to further encourage diverse predictions. The accuracy of this model with $M = 5$ (Table 1) is slightly worse than our multiple prediction model without the regularizer. As a measure of hypothesis similarity, we calculate the average cosine distance among all predictions given an input. The average similarity for the object-wise

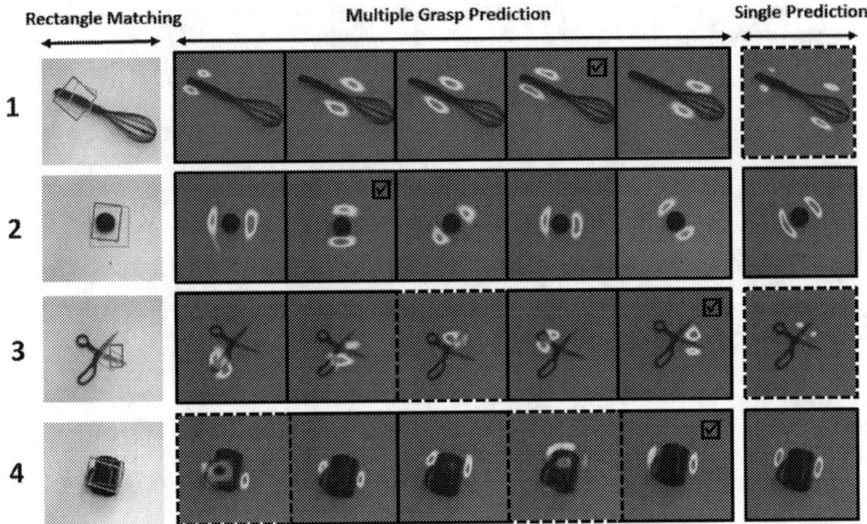

Fig. 6. Five and single grasp map predictions of sample objects in the dataset. A solid frame around an image is an indicator of grasp detection success, while a dashed line shows an incorrect detection. The predictions marked with ✓ are the top-ranked ones according to the GMM likelihood estimation. These predictions are converted back to grasp rectangles (magenta) and compared with the closest ground truth grasp (green). (Color figure online)

Fig. 7. Examples of diversity within predicted grasp maps (converted to rectangles).

split decreases only marginally from 0.435 (without regularizer) to 0.427 (with regularizer), suggesting that the multiple prediction framework does not really benefit by explicitly optimizing diversity. Our framework can naturally produce diverse predictions, which we intuitively attribute to the hypothesis dropout regularization used during training.

Qualitative Results. In Fig. 6 we show qualitative examples from our multi-grasp framework (with $M = 5$) and a comparison to the single grasp ($M = 1$) model's predictions, noting the advantage of multiple grasp predictions both in terms of accuracy and variability. We observe that for objects that have several distinct grasping options, our multiple prediction framework models the output distribution sufficiently. Object 3 (scissors) is undoubtedly a challenging object with many different grasping poses, which are successfully estimated

Table 2. Average grasp estimation accuracy of all hypotheses (lower limit) and average grasp success (upper limit).

Method	Image-wise	Object-wise	Shape-wise
Lower limit ($M = 5$)	80.0	77.4	75.0
Lower limit ($M = 10$)	76.5	73.3	72.1
Upper limit ($M = 5$)	98.0	98.5	96.3
Upper limit ($M = 10$)	99.2	98.4	99.1

via multiple predictions. In Fig. 7 we further emphasize the diversity among the grasp hypotheses, by showing multiple extracted rectangles for various objects.

4.5 Evaluation over Multiple Grasps

In Table 2 we report the lower and upper detection accuracy limits of the multi-grasp models. Instead of evaluating only the top-ranked grasp hypothesis, we first evaluate *all* predictions provided by our model. This evaluation gives the lower limit of the model's performance, as it computes the success rate of all hypotheses, including even those with a low probability of being chosen. This result suggests that the estimated belief maps correspond, in most cases, to valid grasps (75% overall accuracy compared to 85.3% for one chosen grasp in shape-wise split, when $M = 5$). This lower bound decreases as M increases, *i.e.* it is more likely to have a (noisy) prediction that does not match any of ground truth grasp rectangles with higher M. However, thresholding the "good" matches based on GMM likelihood can counteract this drop in performance while leaving multiple grasping choices to the robot.

Another observation is that the top-ranked prediction is not necessarily the best one in terms of grasping performance. This can be seen in the upper limit evaluation, in which if there exists at least one matching grasp detection among all hypotheses, it counts overall as successful. For $M = 10$ the upper limit exceeds 98% accuracy for the object-wise split. This implies that there is in almost all cases at least one valid prediction returned by our model, although GMM fitting might not always result in correct ranking. Still, the top-ranked prediction performance in Table 1 is closer to the upper rather than the lower limit.

4.6 Generalization

Finally, to evaluate the performance of the proposed model in a real-world scenario, we test it on several common household objects, such as cutlery, keys and dolls, in an own setup—and not test images from the same dataset. The differences to the Cornell dataset are not only in the type of objects used, but also in the camera views and illumination conditions. Through this setup we evaluate the generalization ability of the model under different conditions and challenging novel shapes and textures. Figure 8 illustrates the evaluated objects and the estimated grasp that is chosen as the maximum GMM likelihood. Our model is robust against these variations and results in viable and confident grasping options for all tested objects.

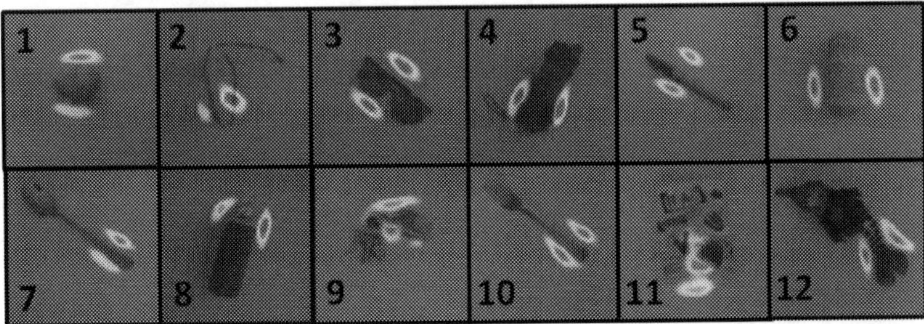

Fig. 8. The top ranked grasp map selected by the GMM likelihood estimation module for a $M = 5$ model evaluated on common household objects in real-time. Objects 1–5 have similar shapes to the objects in the Cornell grasp dataset. Objects 6–12, however, represent novel shapes and textures compared to the dataset used for training. Despite variations from the training distribution, our method produces reasonable grasp maps for all tested objects.

5 Conclusion

We have developed an efficient framework for robotic grasp detection. The representation of a grasp is redefined from an oriented rectangle to a 2D Gaussian mixture belief map that can be interpreted as the confidence of a potential grasp position. This allows us to handle the ambiguity stemming from the many possible ways to grasp an object. We employ a fully convolutional network for belief map regression and estimate a variety of viable grasp options per object. This approach embraces the ambiguous nature of the grasping task and provides a better approximation of the grasp distribution. This property manifests itself in the majority of the predicted grasps being viable solutions and the improvement over the single-grasp baseline becoming larger when tackling scenarios with increased difficulty, such as novel objects, shapes and textures. Our ranking approach selects the grasp positions with the highest likelihood, which result in real-time, state-of-the-art performance. Considering the fact that our belief map formulation also contains a measure of size, an interesting future direction could be the application of this method to prosthetic hands.

Acknowledgments. This work is supported by UK Engineering and Physical Sciences Research Council (EP/R004242/1). We also gratefully acknowledge the support of NVIDIA Corporation with the donation of a Titan Xp GPU used for the experiments.

References

1. Asif, U., Bennamoun, M., Sohel, F.A.: RGB-D object recognition and grasp detection using hierarchical cascaded forests. IEEE Trans. Rob. **33**(3), 547–564 (2017)
2. Belagiannis, V., Zisserman, A.: Recurrent human pose estimation. In: International Conference on Automatic Face & Gesture Recognition (FG 2017) (2017)
3. Bicchi, A., Kumar, V.: Robotic grasping and contact: a review. In: Proceedings of 2000 IEEE International Conference on Robotics and Automation (ICRA), vol. 1, pp. 348–353. IEEE (2000)
4. Bulat, A., Tzimiropoulos, G.: Human pose estimation via convolutional part heatmap regression. In: Leibe, B., Matas, J., Sebe, N., Welling, M. (eds.) ECCV 2016. LNCS, vol. 9911, pp. 717–732. Springer, Cham (2016). https://doi.org/10.1007/978-3-319-46478-7_44
5. Bulat, A., Tzimiropoulos, G.: Super-fan: integrated facial landmark localization and super-resolution of real-world low resolution faces in arbitrary poses with GANs. In: The IEEE Conference on Computer Vision and Pattern Recognition (CVPR), June 2018
6. Cao, Z., Simon, T., Wei, S.E., Sheikh, Y.: Realtime multi-person 2D pose estimation using part affinity fields. In: Proceedings of the IEEE Conference on Computer Vision and Pattern Recognition (CVPR) (2017)
7. Dempster, A.P., Laird, N.M., Rubin, D.B.: Maximum likelihood from incomplete data via the EM algorithm. J. R. Stat. Soc. Ser. B (Methodol.) (1977)
8. Du, X., et al.: Articulated multi-instrument 2D pose estimation using fully convolutional networks. IEEE Trans. Med. Imaging (2018)
9. Guo, D., Sun, F., Liu, H., Kong, T., Fang, B., Xi, N.: A hybrid deep architecture for robotic grasp detection. In: 2017 IEEE International Conference on Robotics and Automation (ICRA). IEEE (2017)
10. Guzman-Rivera, A., et al.: Multi-output learning for camera relocalization. In: Conference on Computer Vision and Pattern Recognition (2014)
11. He, K., Zhang, X., Ren, S., Sun, J.: Deep residual learning for image recognition. In: Proceedings of the IEEE Conference on Computer Vision and Pattern Recognition (CVPR) (2016)
12. Jiang, Y., Moseson, S., Saxena, A.: Efficient grasping from RGB-D images: learning using a new rectangle representation. In: International Conference on Robotics and Automation (ICRA). IEEE (2011)
13. Kehoe, B., Patil, S., Abbeel, P., Goldberg, K.: A survey of research on cloud robotics and automation
14. Krizhevsky, A., Sutskever, I., Hinton, G.E.: ImageNet classification with deep convolutional neural networks. In: Advances in Neural Information Processing Systems (2012)
15. Kumra, S., Kanan, C.: Robotic grasp detection using deep convolutional neural networks. arXiv preprint arXiv:1611.08036 (2016)
16. Laina, I., et al.: Concurrent segmentation and localization for tracking of surgical instruments. In: Descoteaux, M., Maier-Hein, L., Franz, A., Jannin, P., Collins, D.L., Duchesne, S. (eds.) MICCAI 2017. LNCS, vol. 10434, pp. 664–672. Springer, Cham (2017). https://doi.org/10.1007/978-3-319-66185-8_75
17. Laina, I., Rupprecht, C., Belagiannis, V., Tombari, F., Navab, N.: Deeper depth prediction with fully convolutional residual networks. In: 2016 Fourth International Conference on 3D Vision (3DV). IEEE (2016)

18. LeCun, Y., Bottou, L., Bengio, Y., Haffner, P.: Gradient-based learning applied to document recognition. In: Proceedings of the IEEE (1998)
19. Lee, S., Prakash, S.P.S., Cogswell, M., Ranjan, V., Crandall, D., Batra, D.: Stochastic multiple choice learning for training diverse deep ensembles. In: Advances in Neural Information Processing Systems (2016)
20. Lenz, I., Lee, H., Saxena, A.: Deep learning for detecting robotic grasps. Int. J. Rob. Res. (2015)
21. Levine, S., Pastor, P., Krizhevsky, A., Quillen, D.: Learning hand-eye coordination for robotic grasping with deep learning and large-scale data collection. arXiv preprint arXiv:1603.02199 (2016)
22. Li, Z., Chen, Q., Koltun, V.: Interactive image segmentation with latent diversity. In: Conference on Computer Vision and Pattern Recognition (CVPR) (2018)
23. Long, J., Shelhamer, E., Darrell, T.: Fully convolutional networks for semantic segmentation. In: Proceedings of the IEEE Conference on Computer Vision and Pattern Recognition (CVPR) (2015)
24. Mahler, J., et al.: Dex-net 2.0: deep learning to plan robust grasps with synthetic point clouds and analytic grasp metrics. arXiv preprint arXiv:1703.09312 (2017)
25. McLachlan, G., Peel, D.: Finite Mixture Models. Wiley, Hoboken (2004)
26. Merget, D., Rock, M., Rigoll, G.: Robust facial landmark detection via a fully-convolutional local-global context network. In: The IEEE Conference on Computer Vision and Pattern Recognition (CVPR), June 2018
27. Miller, A.T., Allen, P.K.: Graspit! a versatile simulator for robotic grasping. IEEE Rob. Autom. Mag. (2004)
28. Papandreou, G., et al.: Towards accurate multi-person pose estimation in the wild. In: Conference on Computer Vision and Pattern Recognition (CVPR) (2017)
29. Redmon, J., Angelova, A.: Real-time grasp detection using convolutional neural networks. In: 2015 IEEE International Conference on Robotics and Automation (ICRA). IEEE (2015)
30. Redmon, J., Divvala, S., Girshick, R., Farhadi, A.: You only look once: unified, real-time object detection. In: Conference on Computer Vision and Pattern Recognition (CVPR) (2016)
31. Ren, S., He, K., Girshick, R., Sun, J.: Faster R-CNN: towards real-time object detection with region proposal networks. In: Advances in Neural Information Processing Systems (2015)
32. Rochan, M., Ye, L., Wang, Y.: Video summarization using fully convolutional sequence networks. arXiv preprint arXiv:1805.10538 (2018)
33. Rupprecht, C., et al.: Learning in an uncertain world: representing ambiguity through multiple hypotheses. In: International Conference on Computer Vision (ICCV) (2017)
34. Saxena, A., Driemeyer, J., Ng, A.Y.: Robotic grasping of novel objects using vision. Int. J. Rob. Res. (2008)
35. Varley, J., DeChant, C., Richardson, A., Nair, A., Ruales, J., Allen, P.: Shape completion enabled robotic grasping. arXiv preprint arXiv:1609.08546 (2016)
36. Vedaldi, A., Lenc, K.: MatConvNet - convolutional neural networks for MATLAB. In: Proceeding of the ACM International Conference on Multimedia (2015)
37. Viereck, U., Pas, A., Saenko, K., Platt, R.: Learning a visuomotor controller for real world robotic grasping using simulated depth images. In: Conference on Robot Learning (2017)
38. Wang, Z., Li, Z., Wang, B., Liu, H.: Robot grasp detection using multimodal deep convolutional neural networks. Adv. Mech. Eng. (2016)

39. Wei, S.E., Ramakrishna, V., Kanade, T., Sheikh, Y.: Convolutional pose machines. In: Conference on Computer Vision and Pattern Recognition (CVPR) (2016)
40. Zapata-Impata, B.S.: Using geometry to detect grasping points on 3D unknown point cloud. In: International Conference on Informatics in Control, Automation and Robotics (2017)

Adaptive Visual-Depth Fusion Transfer

Ziyun Cai[1(✉)], Yang Long[2], Xiao-Yuan Jing[1], and Ling Shao[3]

[1] College of Automation, Nanjing University of Posts and Telecommunications, Nanjing, China
Ziyun.Cai@ieee.org

[2] Open Lab, School of Computing, University of Newcastle, Newcastle upon Tyne NE4 5TG, UK

[3] Inception Institute of Artificial Intelligence, Abu Dhabi, United Arab Emirates

Abstract. While RGB-D classification task has been actively researched in recent years, most existing methods focus on the RGB-D source to target transfer task. The application of such methods cannot address the real-world scenario where the paired depth images are not hold. This paper focuses on a more flexible task that recognizes RGB test images by transferring them into the depth domain. Such a scenario retains high performance due to gaining auxiliary information but reduces the cost of pairing RGB with depth sensors at test time. Existing methods suffer from two challenges: the utilization of the additional depth features, and the domain shifting problem due to the different mechanisms between conventional RGB cameras and depth sensors. As a step towards bridging the gap, we propose a novel method called adaptive Visual-Depth Fusion Transfer (aVDFT) which can take advantage of the depth information and handle the domain distribution mismatch simultaneously. Our key novelties are: (1) a global visual-depth metric construction algorithm that can effectively align RGB and depth data structure; (2) adaptive transformed component extraction for target domain that conditioned on invariant transfer on location, scale and depth measurement. To demonstrate the effectiveness of aVDFT, we conduct comprehensive experiments on six pairs of RGB-D datasets for object recognition, scene classification and gender recognition and demonstrate state-of-the-art performance.

Keywords: RGB-D data · Domain adaptation · Visual categorization

1 Introduction

Recent developments in low-cost RGB-D sensors, *e.g.*, the Microsoft Kinect, make the utilization of auxilliary depth information for RGB image classification and recognition more widely applicable, and thus aroused increasing interest throughout the computer vision community [3,5]. It becomes easier to acquire a large number of high quality pairwise RGB-D data for training. However, since the depth sensors are not widely used in our daily life, RGB test scenarios

C. V. Jawahar et al. (Eds.): ACCV 2018, LNCS 11364, pp. 56–73, 2019.
https://doi.org/10.1007/978-3-030-20870-7_4

still outnumber the pairwise RGB-D ones. Therefore, some recent approaches consider a more flexible task of recognizing RGB images while leveraging a set of labeled RGB-D [6,31].

In this paper, we address the above task by considering it as an Unsupervised Domain Adaptation (UDA) problem, which aims to take advantage of additional depth information in the source domain and reduce the data distribution mismatch between the source and target domains simultaneously. The training data in UDA consists of labeled RGB-D source data and the testing data are unlabeled RGB samples. In this assumption, the source and target domains follow different distributions, when images are acquired from different cameras, or in various conditions. It is noticeable that such a problem is different from conventional UDA, transfer learning and multi-view fusion problem. Rather than having all views during training and test, the depth information in our task is available during training only. The fact that the depth view is missing makes this problem challenging, since we cannot combine both of them like other multi-view learning techniques. In this work, there are two challenges to be addressed. First, traditional visual classification methods assume that training data and test data are drawn from the same distribution. Such an assumption can be violated since the training and test data are from different devices, *i.e.* conventional surveillance cameras and depth sensors. Therefore, how to address the domain mismatch problem between these two domains is the first challenge. Secondly, traditional UDA methods [7,22] only consider a single RGB modality and do not explore the depth information boost the performance further. On the other hand, many methods using the additional depth information have been proposed for classification tasks as well [19,34]. However, these methods take the unrealistic assumption that training and testing data are from same domain.

In this work, we aim to solve above two challenges simultaneously by our novel RGB-D method, referred to as **a**daptive **V**isual-**D**epth **F**usion **T**ransfer (aVDFT). The motivation behind our aVDFT is as follows: additional depth knowledge contain substantial discriminative information that might be used when constructing classifier, at the same time, in real-world problems, the source data and target data have different distributions, and the goal is to achieve reliable recognition performance on the test RGB domain. The pipeline of our idea is described in Fig. 1.

In the visual-depth metric fusion step, we construct the global metric in the source RGB domain, based on distance relations revealed by the depth information. This step can emphasize the exact values of the distances and incorporate the auxiliary depth information in the source domain resulting a transformed source domain. In the adaptive transfer step, our aim is to discover the components whose distribution is invariant across domains and estimate the target domain label distribution from the RGB-D and target domains. We can also explore the transfer components whose conditional distribution is invariant after location, scale and depth transformations.

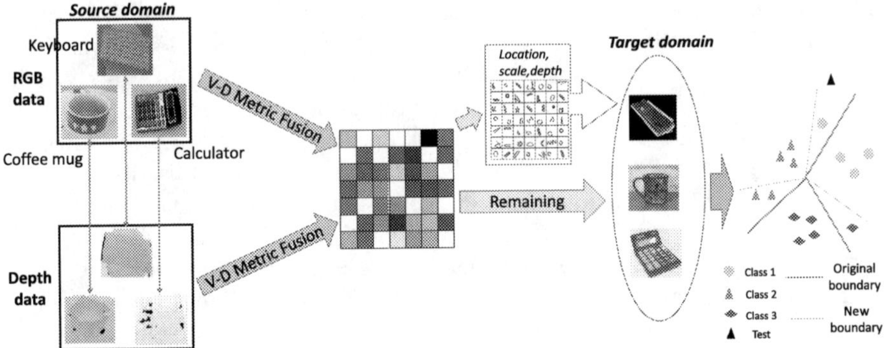

Fig. 1. The outline of the proposed method. We have RGB and depth features in the source domain, and RGB features in the target domain.

To summarize, our main contributions are:

- aVDFT can incorporate the auxiliary depth information in the source domain resulting a transformed source domain and simultaneously discover the components whose distribution is invariant across domains and estimate the target domain label distribution from the RGB-D and target domains.
- We propose a novel UDA method which can effectively leverage depth information to recognize new RGB images in target domain that does not contain the additional depth information.

2 Related Work

Recognizing RGB images from RGB-D data received limited attention. Our algorithm is mostly related to the methods in [4,6,28,31]. [6] attempts to seek an optimal projection matrix to map samples from two different domains into a common feature space such that the domain distribution mismatch can be reduced. Then [28] extends the work in [6] by defining various forms of regularizers in their framework. [28] provides different strategies which can be readily incorporated to learn robust SVM classifiers for classifying the target samples. [31] jointly accounts for the auxiliary view during training and for the domain shift by extending the information bottleneck method, and by combining it with risk minimization.

Our method is also related to UDA methods. Sampling Geodesic Flow (SGF) [17] creates intermediate representations of data between two domains through viewing the generative subspaces created from these domains as points on the Grassmann manifold, and then obtains subspaces which can provide a description of the underlying domain shift. Transfer Component Analysis (TCA) [32] tries to learn some transfer components across domains in a Reproducing Kernel Hilbert Space (RKHS) through Maximum Mean Discrepancy (MMD), which only takes advantage of feature matching but ignores the advantages of instance reweighting. Landmark (LMK) [15] exploits a subset of source domain that is most similar to the target domain. Besides, there still exist some approaches that use NMF to achieve domain adaptation. Unsupervised Nonnegative Embedding (UNE) [33] generates a non-negative embedding for the source and target tasks as a shared feature space of two aligned sets of their corresponding non-negative basis vectors for a prototype matrix. [16] models domain shift by integrating an infinite number of subspaces that characterize changes in geometric and statistical properties from source to target domain, which is computationally advantageous, automatically inferring important algorithmic parameters without requiring extensive cross validation or labeled data from either domain. However, these methods do not perform well on RGB-D scenarios. We provide the extensive comparison to these methods in our experiments, from which we demonstrate the advantages of our method.

3 Adaptive Visual-Depth Fusion Transfer

3.1 Notations

In this paper, we denote a vector by a lowercase letter in bold. The transpose of a vector or a matrix is denoted by the superscript T. We also define $\mathbf{I}$ as an identity matrix. In addition, Table 1 shows the list of frequently used notations.

Table 1. Notations and descriptions.

Notation	Description	Notation	Description
$\mathcal{D}_s$, $\mathcal{D}_t$	Source/target domain	$\mathbf{\Gamma}$	Invariant components
$\mathbf{A}$, $\mathbf{B}$	RGB/depth modality	ξ	Regularization parameter
$\mathbf{Y}_s$	Source label	$\mathbf{K}^{\mathbf{\Delta}}$, $\mathbf{K}^{\mathbf{\Gamma}}$	Kernel matrix
$\mathcal{T}^A$, $\mathcal{T}^B$	Metric tensor	$\mathbf{K}^{\mathbf{\Delta},\mathbf{\Gamma}}$	Kernel matrix
$\mathbf{M}$	Positive-definite matrix	$\mathbf{Z}$	Positive-definite matrix
$\mathbf{V}$	Full-rank matrix	$\mu(y_s)$	Density ratio
$\widetilde{\mathbf{A}}$	Transformed source	D_A, D_B	Sum of pairwise squared distances
$\mathbf{\Delta}$	Transfer components	λ	Scaling factor

Problem (Adaptive Visual-Depth Fusion Transfer). Given two pairwise modalities $\mathbf{A}$ and $\mathbf{B}$ in the source domain $\mathcal{D}_s$ with label space $\mathbf{Y}_s = [y_1, \cdots, y_{N_s}]$ and an target domain $\mathcal{D}_t$, the task is to find the transformed source domain $\widetilde{\mathbf{A}}$ through visual-depth metric fusion. Then given the target domain $\mathcal{D}_t$ is under a different marginal probability distribution and conditional probability distribution, $P_{\mathbf{Y}_s} \neq P_{\mathbf{Y}_t}$ and $P_{\mathbf{A}|\mathbf{Y}_s} \neq P_{\mathbf{B}|\mathbf{Y}_s} \neq P_{\mathbf{D}_t|\mathbf{Y}_t} \neq P_{\widetilde{\mathbf{A}}|\mathbf{Y}_s}$, we aim to obtain transfer components $\mathbf{\Delta}$ which holds $P_{\widetilde{\mathbf{A}}}(\mathbf{\Delta} \mid \mathbf{Y}_s) = P_{\mathcal{D}_t}(\mathbf{\Gamma} \mid \mathbf{Y}_t)$ after visual-depth transformations, and simultaneously discover how the changes occur on $P_{\mathbf{Y}_s}$ and $P_{\mathbf{Y}_t}$ between $\mathcal{D}_s$ and $\mathcal{D}_t$.

3.2 Visual-Depth Metric Fusion

We use $\mathbf{A}$ and $\mathbf{B}$ to define the two modalities in the source domain $\mathcal{D}_s$ with dimensions and sample sizes $M \times N_s$ and $M \times N_s$ respectively: $\mathbf{A} = [\mathbf{a}_1, \cdots, \mathbf{a}_{N_s}] \in \mathbb{R}^{M \times N_s}$ and $\mathbf{B} = [\mathbf{b}_1, \cdots, \mathbf{b}_{N_s}] \in \mathbb{R}^{M \times N_s}$. The target domain is defined as $\mathcal{D}_t = [\hat{\mathbf{a}}_1, \cdots, \hat{\mathbf{a}}_{N_t}] \in \mathbb{R}^{M \times N_t}$. $\mathbf{A}$ is represented as the main data view, that $\mathbf{B}$ is represented as the auxiliary depth information view, and that $\mathcal{D}_t$ is considered as the target data view. The marginal distribution and the conditional distribution change independently from each other across the domains: $P_{\mathbf{Y}_s} \neq P_{\mathbf{Y}_t}$ and $P_{\mathbf{A}|\mathbf{Y}_s} \neq P_{\mathbf{B}|\mathbf{Y}_s} \neq P_{\mathcal{D}_t|\mathbf{Y}_t}$, where $\mathbf{Y}_s = [\mathbf{Y}_s, \cdots, \mathbf{y}_{sN_s}]$ is given and $\mathbf{Y}_t = [\mathbf{y}_{t_1}, \cdots, \mathbf{y}_{tN_t}]$ is to be predicted.

We firstly incorporate the distance structure in the depth information view $\mathbf{B}$ into the metric in the main data view $\mathbf{A}$. Two positive definite global metric tensors $\mathcal{T}^A$ and $\mathcal{T}^B$ are considered on $\mathbf{A}$ and $\mathbf{B}$ respectively which parameterize the Mahalanobis distance:

$$d_{\mathcal{T}^A}(\mathbf{a}_i - \mathbf{a}_j) = (\mathbf{a}_i - \mathbf{a}_j)^T \mathcal{T}^A (\mathbf{a}_i - \mathbf{a}_j), (\mathbf{a}_i, \mathbf{a}_j) \in \mathbf{A}, \tag{1}$$

$$d_{\mathcal{T}^B}(\mathbf{b}_i - \mathbf{b}_j) = (\mathbf{b}_i - \mathbf{b}_j)^T \mathcal{T}^B (\mathbf{b}_i - \mathbf{b}_j), (\mathbf{b}_i, \mathbf{b}_j) \in \mathbf{B}. \tag{2}$$

The sum of pairwise squared distances in $\mathbf{A}$ and $\mathbf{B}$ are then expressed as:

$$D_A = \sum_{i<j}^{N_s} d_{\mathcal{T}^A}(\mathbf{a}_i - \mathbf{a}_j) \quad \text{and} \quad D_B = \sum_{i<j}^{N_s} d_{\mathcal{T}^B}(\mathbf{b}_i - \mathbf{b}_j). \tag{3}$$

λ is a scaling factor to rescale the distances in $\mathbf{B}$ for a direct distance comparison in $\mathbf{A}$ and $\mathbf{B}$ which levels out the difference in scales of D_A and D_B:

$$\lambda = \arg\min_{\lambda > 0} [D_A - \lambda D_B]^2, \quad \text{leading to} \quad \lambda = \frac{D_A}{D_B}. \tag{4}$$

To obtain a full-rank matrix $\mathbf{V} \in \mathbb{R}^{M \times M}$, parameterizing a positive-definite matrix $\mathbf{M} = \mathbf{V}^T\mathbf{V}$, we minimize the following cost function:

$$\begin{aligned} I(\mathbf{M}) = & \frac{2(1-\beta)}{N_s(N_s-1)} \sum_{i<j}^{N_s} (d_{\mathbf{M}}(\mathbf{a}_i - \mathbf{a}_j) - d_{\mathcal{T}^A}(\mathbf{a}_i - \mathbf{a}_j))^2 \\ & + \frac{2\beta}{N_s(N_s-1)} \sum_{i<j}^{N_s} (d_{\mathbf{M}}(\mathbf{a}_i - \mathbf{a}_j) - \lambda d_{\mathcal{T}^B}(\mathbf{b}_i - \mathbf{b}_j))^2, \end{aligned} \tag{5}$$

where $\beta \in [0, 1]$ is given to balance the importance of the two modalities. In our paper, since RGB information and depth data are assumed equally important, for simplicity, we set $\beta = 1/2$. Above expression prevents $d_{\mathbf{M}}$ from deviating too far from the distance $d_{\mathcal{T}^A}$ in the RGB data view $\mathbf{A}$. Meanwhile, the metric $d_{\mathbf{M}}$ is pulled in the direction of the metric $d_{\mathcal{T}^B}$ in the depth information view space $\mathbf{B}$. To find $\mathbf{M}$, we first differentiate:

$$\frac{\partial I}{\partial \mathbf{M}} = \frac{2}{N_s(N_s-1)}\left\{\sum_{i<j}^{N_s}\left[(\mathbf{a}_i-\mathbf{a}_j)^T\mathbf{M}(\mathbf{a}_i-\mathbf{a}_j)-(\mathbf{a}_i-\mathbf{a}_j)^T\mathbf{A}(\mathbf{a}_i-\mathbf{a}_j)\right]\right.$$
$$\cdot(\mathbf{a}_i-\mathbf{a}_j)(\mathbf{a}_i-\mathbf{a}_j)^T+\sum_{i<j}^{N_s}\left[(\mathbf{a}_i-\mathbf{a}_j)^T\mathbf{M}(\mathbf{a}_i-\mathbf{a}_j)-\lambda(\mathbf{b}_i-\mathbf{b}_j)^T\mathbf{B}(\mathbf{b}_i-\mathbf{b}_j)\right]$$
$$\left.\cdot(\mathbf{a}_i-\mathbf{a}_j)(\mathbf{a}_i-\mathbf{a}_j)^T\right\}. \tag{6}$$

Denoting the rank-1 matrix $(\mathbf{a}_i-\mathbf{a}_j)(\mathbf{a}_i-\mathbf{a}_j)^T$ by $\mathbf{U}^{ij}$, the optimal $\mathbf{M}$ is the solution of:

$$\frac{4}{N_s(N_s-1)}\sum_{i<j}^{N_s}(\mathbf{a}_i-\mathbf{a}_j)^T\mathbf{M}(\mathbf{a}_i-\mathbf{a}_j)\mathbf{U}^{ij} = \frac{2}{N_s(N_s-1)}\sum_{i<j}^{N_s}(\mathbf{a}_i-\mathbf{a}_j)^T\mathbf{A}(\mathbf{a}_i-\mathbf{a}_j)\mathbf{U}^{ij}$$
$$+\frac{2}{N_s(N_s-1)}\sum_{i<j}^{N_s}\lambda(\mathbf{b}_i-\mathbf{b}_j)^T\mathbf{B}(\mathbf{b}_i-\mathbf{b}_j)\mathbf{U}^{ij}. \tag{7}$$

Note that

$$(\mathbf{a}_i-\mathbf{a}_j)^T\mathbf{M}(\mathbf{a}_i-\mathbf{a}_j)\mathbf{U}^{ij} = \mathbf{U}^{ij}\mathbf{M}\mathbf{U}^{ij}. \tag{8}$$

The unconstrained solution $\mathbf{M}$ is typically already close to being symmetric positive-definite. The L_2 projection of $\mathbf{M}$ onto the space of matrices parameterized by $\mathbf{V}^T\mathbf{V}$ can be found by minimizing:

$$\mathbf{V}_0 = \arg\min_{\mathbf{V}} \|\mathbf{V}^T\mathbf{V}-\mathbf{M}\|_2, \tag{9}$$

which can be achieved through first find the 2-norm positive approximation $\mathbf{Z}$ of $\mathbf{M}$. Then the positive-definite matrix $\mathbf{Z} \succ \mathbf{0}$ is decomposed into the produced $\mathbf{V}_0^T\mathbf{V}_0$ through Cholesky decomposition.

The projection $\mathbf{V}_0$ then initializes a gradient descent algorithm:

$$\mathbf{V}_{t+1} = \mathbf{V}_t - \phi\frac{\partial I(\mathbf{V}_t^T\mathbf{V}_t)}{\partial \mathbf{V}_t}, \tag{10}$$

where $0 \le \phi \le 1$ is a positive step-size parameter and

$$\frac{\partial I(\mathbf{V}^T\mathbf{V})}{\partial \mathbf{V}} = \frac{4}{N_s(N_s-1)}\left\{\sum_{i<j}^{N_s}\left[(\mathbf{a}_i-\mathbf{a}_j)^T\mathbf{V}^T\mathbf{V}(\mathbf{a}_i-\mathbf{a}_j)-(\mathbf{a}_i-\mathbf{a}_j)^T\mathbf{A}(\mathbf{a}_i-\mathbf{a}_j)\right]\right.$$
$$\cdot\mathbf{V}(\mathbf{a}_i-\mathbf{a}_j)(\mathbf{a}_i-\mathbf{a}_j)^T+\sum_{i<j}^{N_s}\left[(\mathbf{a}_i-\mathbf{a}_j)^T\mathbf{V}^T\mathbf{V}(\mathbf{a}_i-\mathbf{a}_j)-\lambda(\mathbf{b}_i-\mathbf{b}_j)^T\mathbf{B}(\mathbf{b}_i-\mathbf{b}_j)\right]$$
$$\left.\cdot\mathbf{V}(\mathbf{a}_i-\mathbf{a}_j)(\mathbf{a}_i-\mathbf{a}_j)^T\right\}. \tag{11}$$

Unconstrained obtained minimizer $\mathbf{M}$ of Eq. (5) is projected onto a manifold $\mathcal{M}$ of symmetric positive-definite matrices with respect to the $L2$-norm. The projection $\mathbf{V}_0^T\mathbf{V}_0$ is not necessarily the constrained minimizer of I (constrained to the manifold $\mathcal{M}$). We therefore run a gradient descent on I constrained to $\mathcal{M}$ to find the minimizer of I parameterized as $\mathbf{V}^T\mathbf{V}$.

After the $d_\mathbf{M}$ is obtained from the parameterized form $\mathbf{M} = \mathbf{V}^T\mathbf{V}$, for any $\mathbf{a} \in \mathbf{A}$, we have

$$\|\mathbf{a}\|_\mathbf{M}^2 = \mathbf{a}^T\mathbf{V}^T\mathbf{V}\mathbf{a} = \widetilde{\mathbf{a}}^T\widetilde{\mathbf{a}} = \|\widetilde{\mathbf{a}}\|_2^2, \tag{12}$$

where $\widetilde{\mathbf{a}} = \mathbf{V}\mathbf{a}$ is the tansformed space which contains both of the $\mathbf{A}$ and $\mathbf{B}$ information. Meanwhile, $\widetilde{\mathbf{a}}$ reflects the similarity and dissimilarity information from $\mathbf{B}$. Therefore, data points with similar depth data representation will now in general be closer than in the original RGB data layout and vice versa.

3.3 Adaptive Transfer

Although above visual-depth metric fusion can incorporate the auxiliary depth information in the source domain under the basis transformation, the domain shifting problem between source domain and target domain remains unsolved. Recent transfer methods proposed to find invariant components which have similar distribution on different domains through minimizing a distribution mismatch measure. However, the conditional distribution of the invariant components in different domains is not similar when the conditional distribution of the different domain changes. In addition, transferable components are not limited to be invariant. We define the transformed source domain as $\widetilde{\mathbf{A}} = [\widetilde{\mathbf{a}}_1, \cdots, \widetilde{\mathbf{a}}_{N_s}] \in \mathbb{R}^{M\times N_s}$. The target domain which is mentioned above can be defined as $\mathcal{D}_t = [\hat{\mathbf{a}}_1, \cdots, \hat{\mathbf{a}}_{N_t}] \in \mathbb{R}^{M\times N_t}$. In the following, we focus on the case: $P_{\mathbf{Y}_s} \neq P_{\mathbf{Y}_t}$ and $P_{\widetilde{\mathbf{A}}|\mathbf{Y}_s} \neq P_{\mathbf{D}_t|\mathbf{Y}_t}$. For UDA problem, what types of information change, what types of information are invariant and how they change across the transformed source domain and target domain are interesting. Our aim is to extract the transferable components whose conditional distribution is invariant after the transformations. The changes in the components which are identifiable from the empirical joint distribution on the source domain and the empirical marginal distribution on the target domain can be used for UDA.

We define $\mathbf{\Gamma}$ as the d-dimensional invariant components which have the condition: $P_{\mathbf{\Gamma}|\mathbf{Y}_s} = P_{\mathbf{\Gamma}|\mathbf{Y}_t}$. If $\hat{\mathbf{\Gamma}}$ is considered as the rest of the components of $\mathcal{D}_t$, it may be dependent on $\mathbf{Y}_t$. Aim to discover more useful conditional transferable components, we make assumption that the transferable components can be estimated through location, scale and depth transformations across domains.

Since in most cases transformations occur in the conditional distribution of the labeled features, $\mathbf{\Delta}$ is defined as the d-dimensional components satisfying the condition: $P_{\mathbf{\Delta}|\mathbf{Y}_s} \neq P_{\mathbf{\Delta}|\mathbf{Y}_t}$ only in the location, scale and depth across domains for each value of $\mathbf{Y}_s$ and $\mathbf{Y}_t$. $\mathbf{\Gamma}$ and $\mathbf{\Delta}$ can be expressed as:

$$\mathbf{\Gamma} = \mathbf{G}^T\mathcal{D}_t \quad \text{and} \quad \mathbf{\Delta} = \mathbf{S} \circ (\mathbf{G}^T\widetilde{\mathbf{A}}) + \mathbf{D}, \tag{13}$$

where $\mathbf{G} \in \mathbb{R}^{M\times d}$, the i-th columns in $\mathbf{S} \in \mathbb{R}^{d\times N_s}$ and $\mathbf{D} \in \mathbb{R}^{d\times N_s}$ can be expressed as $\mathbf{a}(y_i)$ and $\mathbf{b}(y_i)$. $\circ$ denotes the Hadamard product. We have the constraint $\mathbf{G}^T\mathbf{G} = \mathbf{I}_d$ which can make sure no redundant information across dimensions of $\mathbf{\Gamma}$ and $\mathbf{\Delta}$. In UDA problem, we have no labels about the target domain. Therefore, only the empirical marginal distribution of $\mathcal{D}_t$ is available in the target domain. Matching the conditional distributions $P_{\widetilde{\mathbf{A}}}(\mathbf{\Delta} \mid \mathbf{Y}_s) = P_{\mathcal{D}_t}(\mathbf{\Gamma} \mid \mathbf{Y}_t)$ can be achieved by matching the marginal distribution under mild conditions:

$$P_*(\mathbf{\Delta}) = \int P_{\widetilde{\mathbf{A}}}(\mathbf{\Delta} \mid y_s) P_*(y_s) dy_s, \tag{14}$$

$$P_{\mathcal{D}_t}(\mathbf{\Gamma}) = \int P_{\mathcal{D}_t}(\mathbf{\Gamma} \mid y_t) P_{\mathcal{D}_t}(y_t) dy_t. \tag{15}$$

Our aim is to find the distribution $P^*_{\mathbf{Y}_s}$ and $\mathbf{\Delta}$ through enforcing $P^*(\mathbf{\Delta})$ as constructed in Eq. (14), which should be identical to $P_{\widetilde{\mathbf{A}}}(\mathbf{\Delta})$. Under mild conditions, if $P^*(\mathbf{\Delta}) = P_{\mathcal{D}_t}(\mathbf{\Gamma})$, $P_{\widetilde{\mathbf{A}}}(\mathbf{\Delta} \mid \mathbf{y}_s) = P_{\mathcal{D}_t}(\mathbf{\Gamma} \mid \mathbf{Y}_t)$ holds, the distribution of $\mathbf{Y}_t$ can also be recovered.

Our aim is to enforce the condition: $P^*(\mathbf{\Delta}) = P_{\mathcal{D}_t}(\mathbf{\Gamma})$. Since $P_*(\mathbf{Y}_s)$ is continuous, $P_*(\mathbf{Y}_s = y_s)$ is expressed as $P_*(y_s) = \mu(y_s) P_{\widetilde{\mathbf{A}}}(y_s)$. Here, $\mu(y_s) \geq 0$ is the density ratio. $\int \mu(y_s) P_{\widetilde{\mathbf{A}}} y_s dy = 1$. Minimize the squared maximum mean discrepancy to achieve $P^*(\mathbf{\Delta}) = P_{\mathcal{D}_t}(\mathbf{\Gamma})$:

$$\|\mathbb{E}_{\mathbf{\Delta} \sim P^*(\mathbf{\Delta})}[\psi(\mathbf{\Delta})] - \mathbb{E}_{\mathbf{\Gamma} \sim P_{\mathcal{D}_t}(\mathbf{\Gamma})}[\psi(\mathbf{\Gamma})]\|^2. \tag{16}$$

From Eq. (14), we have:

$$\|\mathbb{E}_{\mathbf{\Delta} \sim P^*(\mathbf{\Delta})}[\psi(\mathbf{\Delta})] = \mathbb{E}_{(\mathbf{Y}_s, \mathbf{\Delta}) \sim P^{\tilde{\mathbf{A}}}(\mathbf{Y}_s, \mathbf{\Delta})}[\mu(\mathbf{Y}_s)\psi(\mathbf{\Delta})]. \tag{17}$$

Equation (16) reduces to:

$$\|\mathbb{E}_{(\mathbf{Y}_s, \mathbf{\Delta}) \sim P^{\tilde{\mathbf{A}}}}[\mu(\mathbf{Y}_s)\mathbf{\Delta}] - \mathbb{E}_{\mathbf{\Gamma} \sim P_{\mathcal{D}_t}}[\psi(\mathbf{G}^{\mathbf{T}}\mathcal{D}_{\mathbf{t}})]\|^2. \tag{18}$$

In practice, we minimize the empirical version:

$$C = \|\frac{1}{N_s}\psi(\mathbf{\Delta})\boldsymbol{\mu} - \frac{1}{N_t}\psi(\mathbf{G}^T\mathcal{D}_t)\mathbf{1}\|^2 = \frac{1}{N_s^2}\boldsymbol{\mu}^T\mathbf{K}^{\mathbf{\Delta}}\boldsymbol{\mu} - \frac{2}{N_s N_t}\mathbf{1}^T\mathbf{K}^{\mathbf{\Delta},\mathbf{\Gamma}}\boldsymbol{\mu} + \frac{1}{N_t^2}\mathbf{1}^T\mathbf{K}^{\mathbf{\Gamma}}\mathbf{1}, \tag{19}$$

where $\boldsymbol{\mu} = [\mu_1, \cdots, \mu_{N_s}]^T$ which has the constraints $\mu_i \geq 0$ and $\sum_{i=1}^{N_s} \mu_i = N_s$. $\mathbf{K}^{\mathbf{\Delta}}$ denotes the kernel matrix on $\mathbf{\Delta}$. $\mathbf{K}^{\mathbf{\Delta},\mathbf{\Gamma}}$ is the cross kernel matrix between $\mathbf{\Delta}$ and $\mathbf{\Gamma}$. $\mathbf{K}^{\mathbf{\Gamma}}$ expresses the kernel matrix on $\mathbf{\Gamma}$. $\mathbf{1}$ is the $N_t \times 1$ vector of ones.

In addition, the changes in the distribution of $\mathbf{\Delta}$ given $\mathbf{Y}_s$ should be small. Therefore, we adopt a regularization term on $\mathbf{S}$ and $\mathbf{D}$:

$$R = \frac{\xi}{N_s}\|\mathbf{S} - \mathbf{1}\|^2_{\mathcal{F}} + \frac{\xi}{N_s}\|\mathbf{D}\|^2_{\mathcal{F}}, \tag{20}$$

where $\mathbf{1}$ is a $d \times N_s$ matrix of ones.

3.4 Reparametrization and Optimization

Our aim is to estimate the parameters $\boldsymbol{\mu}$, $\mathbf{G}$, $\mathbf{S}$ and $\mathbf{D}$ through minimizing the combination of empirical version of Eq. (18) and the regularization term Eq. (20):

$$\frac{1}{N_s^2}\boldsymbol{\mu}^T\mathbf{K}^{\mathbf{\Delta}}\boldsymbol{\mu} - \frac{2}{N_s N_t}\mathbf{1}^T\mathbf{K}^{\mathbf{\Delta},\mathbf{\Gamma}}\boldsymbol{\mu} + \frac{1}{N_t^2}\mathbf{1}^T\mathbf{K}^{\mathbf{\Gamma}}\mathbf{1} + \frac{\xi}{N_s}\|\mathbf{S} - \mathbf{1}\|^2_{\mathcal{F}} + \frac{\xi}{N_s}\|\mathbf{D}\|^2_{\mathcal{F}}, \tag{21}$$

under the constraints $\mathbf{G}^T\mathbf{G} = \mathbf{I}_d$, $\mu_i \geq 0$ and $\sum_{i=1}^{N_s} \mu_i = N_s$. Since we cannot directly minimize Eq. (21) with respect to $\boldsymbol{\mu}$, $\mathbf{S}$ and $\mathbf{D}$, we use new parameters to reparametrize them. H is the cardinality of $\mathbf{Y}_s$ and denote by the possible values $\kappa_1, \cdots, \kappa_C$. N_H is the number of samples with $\mathbf{Y}_s = \kappa_C$. A matrix is defined as $\boldsymbol{\Phi} \in \mathbb{R}^{N_s \times H}$, where $\boldsymbol{\Phi}_i = N_s/N_H$ if $y_i = v_i$, is 0 when else. Therefore, $\boldsymbol{\mu}$ can be expressed as $\boldsymbol{\Phi}\boldsymbol{\nu}$, where $\boldsymbol{\nu} \in \mathbb{R}^{H \times 1}$. $\mathbf{S}$ can be defined as $\boldsymbol{\Phi}\mathbf{O}$, where $\mathbf{O} \in \mathbb{R}^{H \times d}$. $\mathbf{D}$ is expressed as $\boldsymbol{\Phi}\mathbf{Q}$, where $\mathbf{Q} \in \mathbb{R}^{H \times d}$. The constraint $\mu_i \geq 0$ and $\sum_{i=1}^{N_s} \mu_i = N_s$ on $\boldsymbol{\mu}$ changes to the constraint on $\boldsymbol{\nu}$:

$$[\boldsymbol{\Phi}\boldsymbol{\nu}]_i \geq 0 \quad \text{and} \quad \mathbf{1}^T\boldsymbol{\nu} = 1. \tag{22}$$

We iteratively alternate between minimizing $\boldsymbol{\nu}$, $\mathbf{G}$ and $[\mathbf{Q}, \mathbf{O}]$. Moreover, quadratic programming (QP) is used to minimize Eq. (21) w.r.t. $\boldsymbol{\nu}$ under the constraint Eq. (22). For $\mathbf{G}$, we make sure that $\mathbf{G}$ is on the Grassmann manifold with $\mathbf{G}^T\mathbf{G} = 1$. $\mathbf{G}$ can be found through the conjugate gradient algorithm on the Grassmann manifold [10]. $[\mathbf{Q}, \mathbf{O}]$ can be obtained through standard conjugate gradient optimization procedure.

4 Experiments and Results

In this section, we evaluate the effectiveness of our aVDFT for object recognition, scene classification and gender recognition on six pairs of datasets. Since the images in source and target domains are from different types of cameras under various conditions, the domain difference between source and target is significant. The details of the datasets, experimental settings, relevant experimental results, important parameter analysis and algorithm analysis are shown in the rest of this section.

4.1 Datasets

Object Recognition. 1. Object→Caltech-256: Object dataset [27] and Caltech-256 dataset [18] share ten common categories: "ball", "calculator", "cereal box", "coffee mug", "flashlight", "keyboard", "light bulb", "mushroom", "soda can" and "tomato".

2. Object→ImageNet: RGB-D Object dataset and ImageNet dataset [8] share ten common categories: "apple", "banana", "coffee mug", "keyboard", "soda can", "water bottle", "plate", "calculator", "cereal box" and "light bulb".

3. B3DO→Caltech-256: B3DO [24] and Caltech-256 datasets share eight categories: "bottle", "can", "cup", "keyboard", "monitor", "mouse", "phone" and "spoon".

4. B3DO→ImageNet: The B3DO and ImageNet datasets share eight common categories: "bottle", "cup", "keyboard", "monitor", "mouse", "phone", "plate", "spoon".

Scene Classification. We select NYU Depth v1 dataset [36] as the source domain and Scene-15 dataset [12] as the target domain. We use the same four categories of NYU Depth v1 and Scene-15 datasets, "bedroom", "kitchen", "living room" and "office".

Gender Recognition. The RGB-D face dataset EURECOM [30] is chosen as the source domain. The RGB dataset Labeled Faces in the Wild-a (LFW-a) [38] is considered as the target domain. The EURECOM dataset includes 728 pairs of RGB-D images from 196 females and 532 males. The LFW-a contains color images with 13144 images from 2960 females and 10184 males which are captured in uncontrolled conditions.

4.2 Benchmarks and Settings

In our experiment, for a comprehensive and fair comparison, we compared our approach (aVDFT) with five categories baselines as following: (1) Naive Approach Single-view Classifiers: SVM_A and 1-Nearest Neighbor which are trained by the RGB features in the source domain without considering the domain adaptation and the depth information compensation for binary or multi-class SVM classifiers; (2) Multi-view (MV) Learning: Kernelisation of Canonical Correlation Analysis (KCCA) [21] and SVM2K [11] which use the two-view data in the source domain for training; (3) Learning Using Privileged Information (LUPI): SVM+ [37] and Rank Transfer (RT) [35] which use the additional depth features in the source domain as privileged information; (4) Unsupervised Domain Adaptation: Kernel Mean Matching (KMM) [22], Domain Adaptation Machine (DAM) [9], Sampling Geodesic Flow (SGF) [17], TJM [29], TCA [32], Landmark (LMK) [15], Subspace Alignment (SA) [13], Geodesic Flow Kernel (GFK) [16], UNE [33] and Domain Invariant Projection (DIP) [1] which use the visual features from both domains for training the classifiers, and then predict target data based on the visual features. (5) Using Privileged Information and Unsupervised Domain Adaptation (UPIUDA): Domain Adaptation from Multi-view to Single-view (DA-M2S), domain adaptation from multi-view to single-view_C (DAM2S_C) [28] and large-margin information bottleneck domain adaptation with privileged information (LMIBDAPI) [31] which use the additional depth features in the source domain as privileged information and reduces the data distribution mismatch between the source and target domains.

We also consider the performance gap between shallow and deep features, and thus choose both of them to evaluate aVDFT respectively. For shallow features, we extract Gradient kernel descriptors (KDES) features and LBP KDES features [2] which perform well on RGB-D object dataset from each pair of RGB/depth images. The vocabulary size is set as 1000. Three level of pyramids (1×1, 2×2, 3×3) are used. For deep features, we choose ImageNet-CNN features [26] which are learned from the pre-trained Caffe model [25] on image classification dataset (*i.e.* ImageNet) for object classification, and the Places-CNN [39] scene features which are learned from the pre-trained Caffe model on scene classification dataset (*i.e.* Places dataset) for scene classification. Both of these two kinds of models obtain great success for object and scene classification respectively. In addition, according to Object→ImageNet and B3DO→ImageNet, since the features are obtained by fine-tuning on ImageNet and the study includes experiments on the imageNet dataset, the experimental results on these two pairs of datasets will perform a little higher. We add some experiments based on CNN features which are not fine-tuned. In this case, we extract features directly on the fully connected layer (fc7) in the ImageNet trained network, which follows the strategy in [14]. More specifically, the CNN model is considered as a feature extractor in the added experiments. The feature dimension after CNN is 4096. Note that the depth image is encoded as HHA image as in [20] before extracting the features. Different from object and scene classification, we use the Gradient-LBP features [23] in gender recognition to represent the RGB and depth images for both of the source and target domains. In addition, 196 male images from EURECOM dataset are randomly sampled to balance the training and test samples, since male images are much more than female images. 3000 samples are randomly selected from the target samples for the baseline. The face images in the source and target domains are resized into 120×105 pixels. Then, each face image is uniformly divided into 8×7 non-overlapping subregions of 15×15 pixels. We concatenate the Gradient-LBP features from all 56 subregions into a single final feature vector.

In aVDFV, the standard deviation parameter δ used in MMD is calculated by the median distance among all source examples. In the adaptive transfer step, the sensitivity of regularization parameter ξ which is chosen for location, scale and depth transfer in Eq. (20) is explored by searching $\xi \in \{1, 10^{-1}, 10^{-2}, 10^{-3}, 10^{-4}, 10^{-5}\}$. $\boldsymbol{\mu}$-weighted SVM is considered for classification. The parameters H of SVM are decided by 5-fold cross validation on a grid. Besides, the dimension d is also related. We analyze the behavior of aVDFT by searching $d \in \{20, 40, 60, 80, 100, 120\}$.

5 Experimental Results

The experimental results of aVDFV compared with the 19 baseline methods discussed before on the two pairs of source and target domains are reported in Table 2. The first column is the number corresponding to the category of the selected benchmarks, the second column indicates method names, the third, forth, fifth, sixth, seventh, eighth, ninth and tenth columns present the recognition results when the RGB-D object dataset or B3DO dataset is used as the source domain and the Caltech-256 dataset or ImageNet dataset is used as the target domain, and the eleventh and twelfth columns give recognition rate when the NYU Depth v1 is used as the source domain and the Scene-15 dataset is used as the target domain, and the thirteenth and fourteenth columns show gender recognition rate. Further more, we illustrate some examples with highest recognition accuracies from selected datasets in Fig. 2. Five samples which are successfully classified by aVDFT but incorrectly classified by TCA are also showed. It may be because these samples have complex background or dark illumination, which results in an error classification by TCA. It demonstrates the effectiveness of our approach which explores the depth information boost the performance further.

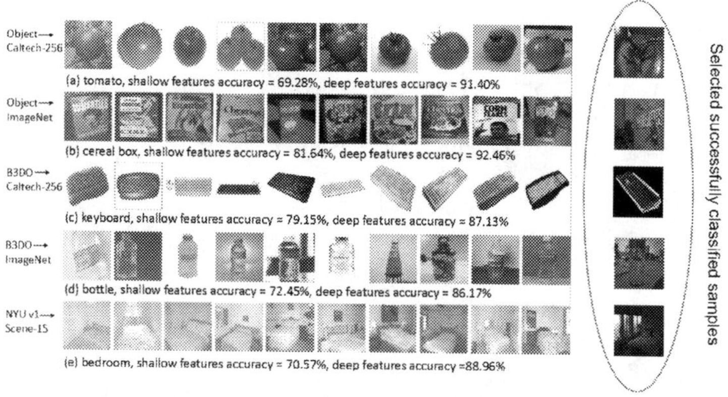

Fig. 2. Example images with highest accuracy results. 5 samples which are successfully classified by aVDFT but incorrectly classified by TCA are in the orange circle. (Color figure online)

Table 2. Accuracies (%) for object recognition, scene classification and gender recognition with shallow and deep features (bold numbers indicate the best results).

	Methods	Object→ Caltech-256		Object→ ImageNet		B3DO→ Caltech-256		B3DO→ ImageNet		NYU v1→ Scene-15		EURECOM→ Wild-a (LFW-a)
		KDES	ImageNet -CNN	KDES	ImageNet -CNN	KDES	ImageNet -CNN	KDES	ImageNet -CNN	KDES	Places -CNN	Gradient-LBP
1	SVM_A	18.21	47.21	26.65	51.76	24.61	47.81	21.80	46.13	17.42	49.46	64.22 ± 1.60
	1-NN	18.30	48.36	27.27	55.79	27.58	50.00	22.31	49.18	19.78	50.75	64.53 ± 1.82
2	KCCA	18.39	49.60	34.61	52.69	28.22	51.29	21.63	49.56	19.68	53.33	63.60± 1.34
	SVM2K	20.79	51.72	33.57	54.34	27.84	51.68	23.70	51.33	21.61	53.23	67.33± 1.92
3	SVM+	18.57	48.63	29.86	60.23	25.52	58.63	26.87	47.28	19.46	51.94	-
	RT	17.15	46.51	23.66	49.79	20.23	46.78	19.65	44.49	16.77	49.03	-
4	KMM	18.13	47.21	25.21	58.78	23.71	54.51	20.28	48.16	17.53	49.57	64.25± 1.43
	DAM	18.21	49.60	25.41	57.85	24.87	55.28	23.70	49.30	17.10	49.25	63.91± 1.57
	SGF	19.27	50.04	37.81	64.88	27.32	61.63	29.28	49.94	19.25	55.27	67.22± 1.38
	TJM	22.81	53.76	38.12	65.81	28.61	60.95	29.02	54.25	21.18	60.11	66.83± 0.97
	TCA	25.11	56.23	33.47	68.08	28.98	64.69	26.87	55.26	22.04	59.03	65.24± 0.88
	LMK	19.45	52.34	35.23	69.32	33.76	63.79	30.04	51.71	25.81	54.73	65.02± 1.55
	SA	21.13	54.64	36.57	70.35	34.54	54.77	25.48	56.27	27.42	62.69	67.38± 1.39
	GFK	18.48	51.02	41.63	68.70	41.24	61.21	30.16	50.57	24.19	53.23	66.78± 1.73
	UNE	24.76	56.23	42.25	71.90	40.72	64.56	29.78	53.23	26.34	59.68	67.83± 1.24
	DIP	25.46	57.38	41.63	69.21	40.21	60.57	29.91	57.67	25.48	58.60	64.84±4.80
5	DA-M2S	30.06	61.54	43.49	75.31	46.26	68.81	32.70	64.26	31.08	64.52	68.44± 1.44
	DAM2S_C	34.22	63.84	**44.32**	77.17	48.32	70.23	33.84	66.79	32.58	66.88	71.57± 1.16
	LMIBDAPI	34.22	62.78	42.77	76.55	49.74	70.75	34.60	67.30	31.72	65.91	72.43±1.34
	aVDFT	**35.81**	**70.20**	**44.32**	**78.72**	**50.13**	**72.68**	**35.74**	**68.19**	**32.15**	**68.71**	**74.87±1.69**

From Table 2, we observe that our aVDFT almost outperforms all other baseline methods, sometimes by a large margin. It demonstrates the effectiveness of our method by exploring additional depth information in the source domain and reducing the domain distribution mismatch between the source and target domains.

Generally, the domain difference in scene classification is larger than the domain difference between source and target in object recognition and gender recognition. From the results of selected datasets, we can see that not only the accuracy in object recognition has a significant improvement, but also the accuracy in scene classification increases dramatically. Meanwhile, we can obtain the similar observation in gender recognition. It demonstrates the effectiveness of our aVDFT in the condition of a larger domain difference. To view as a whole, since the MV based methods and the LUPI methods all suffer from the lack of adaptation, we observe that they perform worse than the UPIUDA methods. The UDA methods can perform better overall, which demonstrates that addressing the domain mismatch problem is more significant than taking advantage of the auxiliary information. Detailedly, RT performs the worst possibly because it is based on Rank SVM which is designed for ranking task rather than classification task. SVM_A and 1-NN which do not consider the depth information and domain discrepancy perform poorly. KCCA, SVM2K and SVM+ obtain better performance generally when compared with SVM_A and 1-NN by utilizing the additional depth features. However, these three methods do not reduce the distribution mismatch between the source and target domains. The domain adaptation methods as KMM and DAM perform in a general way or even worse than SVM_A and 1-NN, which maybe because both approaches are unsuitable in this application. SGF, TCA, LMK, TJM, SA, GFK, UNE and DIP perform better than other nonadaptation methods, which keeps consistent with our observation. Our proposed aVDFT outperforms the UPIUDA methods such as DA-M2S, DAM2S_C and LMIBDAPI as well, which is possible because aVDFT successfully discovers the transfer components and simultaneously can better identify how the changes occur between $P_{\mathbf{Y}_s}$ in the source domain and $P_{\mathbf{Y}_t}$ in the target domain.

The comparison of shallow and deep features shows that all deep features based performances outperform shallow features based performances. For example, the accuracy of our aVDFT method on Object→Caltech-256 classification task increases from 35.81% to 70.20%, which indicates that the deep features can effectively remove the domain bias. Besides the superiority of the deep learning models, it is possible because deep learning models (*i.e.* ImageNet model and Places model) are pre-trained by abundant images which are from different datasets and webs, which has achieved a preliminary domain adaptation. Note that the proposed method still outperforms other methods with deep features. The results comparison among the selected methods shows a similar rule with the shallow features and fine-tuned CNN features generally.

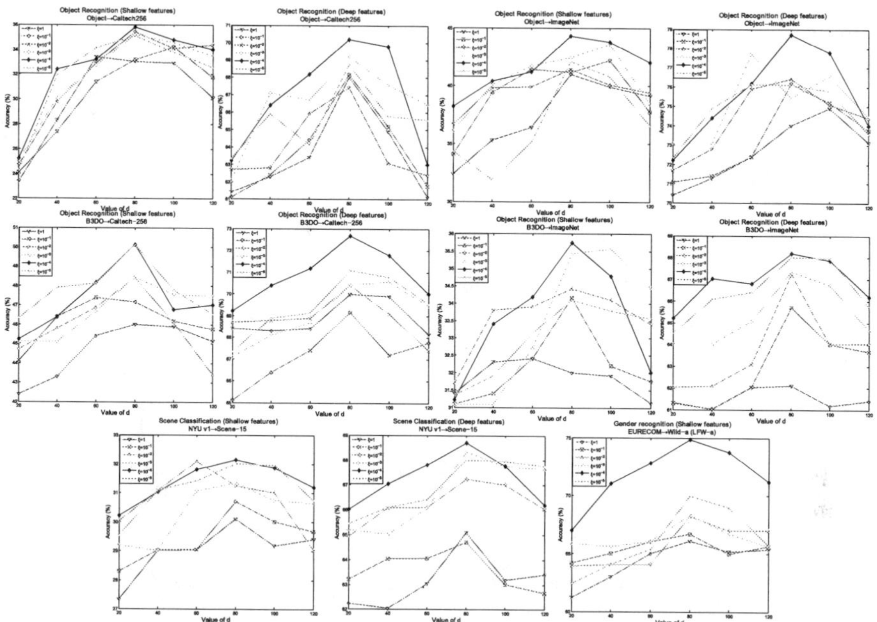

Fig. 3. Parameter sensitivity analysis on the datasets with shallow and deep features.

5.1 Parameter Sensitivity Analysis

Our aVDFT has two parameters d and ξ involved for model tuning. We demonstrate the accuracies with different values of d from $\{20, 40, 60, 80, 100, 120\}$ and different values of ξ from $\{1, 10^{-1}, 10^{-2}, 10^{-3}, 10^{-4}, 10^{-5}\}$ on six pairs of datasets with the shallow and deep features in Fig. 3. From Fig. 3, we can discover how the performances vary with the changes of dimensionality d of the learned components and ξ. It shows that with the increase of the dimensionality d, the performance of aVDFT (with $d \in \{20, 40, 60, 80, 100, 120\}$) becomes better and better until around 80 in general. Only few of them achieve the highest points when $\xi \neq 10^{-4}$ and $d \neq 80$, and other cases reach the best points when $\xi = 10^{-4}$ and $d = 80$. Therefore, we choose $\xi = 10^{-4}$ to guarantee the transfer of the location, scale and depth components can achieve an appropriate size.

5.2 Special Cases Analysis

Two special cases are explored for aVDFT which can provide a better understanding.

Case1: Depth information is not considered, which is denoted as aVT (adaptive Visual Transfer). We directly use the modality $\mathbf{A}$ in $\mathcal{D}_s$ to replace the transformed source domain $\widetilde{\mathbf{A}}$ which results in $\widetilde{\mathbf{\Delta}} = \mathbf{S} \circ (\mathbf{G}^T\mathbf{A}) + \mathbf{D}$ as the new d-dimensional components and minimize the squared maximum mean discrepancy:

$$\|\mathbb{E}_{\widetilde{\mathbf{\Delta}} \sim P^*(\widetilde{\mathbf{\Delta}})}[\psi(\widetilde{\mathbf{\Delta}})] - \mathbb{E}_{\mathbf{\Gamma} \sim P_{\mathcal{D}_t}(\mathbf{\Gamma})}[\psi(\mathbf{\Gamma})]\|^2. \tag{23}$$

Case2: The domain adaptation is not considered, which is denoted as VDF. The transformed source domain $\widetilde{\mathbf{A}}$ which is acquired from Eq. (12) to build a SVM classifier. Then the coming RGB target domain data $\mathcal{D}_t$ can be predicted.

Table 3. Comparison of accuracies (%) between aVDFT and the two special cases.

	Object→ Caltech-256		Object→ ImageNet		B3DO→ Caltech-256		B3DO→ ImageNet		NYUv1→ Scene-15		EURECOM→ Wild-a(LFW-a)
	KDES	**ImageNet -CNN**	**KDES**	**ImageNet -CNN**	**KDES**	**ImageNet -CNN**	**KDES**	**ImageNet -CNN**	**KDES**	**Places -CNN**	**Gradient-LBP**
aVT	26.70	57.12	41.84	68.60	40.98	64.82	30.67	56.78	26.45	61.94	67.80±1.46
VDF	25.46	58.71	36.78	64.77	39.18	61.73	28.39	56.15	25.81	59.89	65.43±1.91
aVDFT	**35.81**	**70.20**	**44.32**	**78.72**	**50.13**	**72.68**	**35.74**	**68.19**	**32.15**	**68.71**	**74.87±1.69**

From Table 3, we can find that aVDFT can perform better than the special cases, which shows it is beneficial to exploit the additional depth features and domain adaptation simultaneously for learning an adaptive classifier. Moreover, in Case 1, since depth features in the source domain contain additional information about shapes and depth, this advantage can help the correction of the noise and make the target domain take advantage of the shape and depth information from the source domain. In Case 1, it shows that the performance decreases by around 3% to 10%.

In addition, aVDFT outperforms the results in Case 2. aVT shows better performance than VDF in general, which verifies our observation that addressing domain mismatch problem is more significant than taking advantage of auxiliary information.

5.3 Conclusion

We proposed a new adaptive Visual-Depth Fusion Transfer (aVDFT) method for UDA problem under the setting of RGB and depth modalities with labeled instances and the RGB target domain with unlabeled instances. This approach improved visual recognition when auxiliary depth information was available at the training step. The auxiliary depth information was firstly incorporated into the model operating on the original space through metric learning. We then extracted the transfer location, scale and depth components whose conditional distribution is invariant given the target. At last, we estimated the target distribution about the target domain. On six real-world image datasets, aVDFT outperformed existing state-of-the-art methods, which demonstrated the effectiveness of the proposed approach. Our future work is to extend this approach to video and speech based applications which are often affected by distribution mismatch.

Acknowledgements. This work was sponsored by NUPTSF (Grant No. NY218120), and MRC Innovation Fellowship with ref MR/S003916/1.

References

1. Baktashmotlagh, M., Harandi, M.T., Lovell, B.C., Salzmann, M.: Unsupervised domain adaptation by domain invariant projection. In: IEEE International Conference on Computer Vision, pp. 769–776 (2013)
2. Bo, L., Ren, X., Fox, D.: Depth kernel descriptors for object recognition. In: IEEE International Conference on Intelligent Robots and Systems, pp. 821–826 (2011)
3. Cai, Z., Han, J., Liu, L., Shao, L.: RGB-D datasets using microsoft kinect or similar sensors: a survey. Multimed. Tools Appl. **76**(3), 4313–4355 (2017)
4. Cai, Z., Long, Y., Shao, L.: Adaptive RGB image recognition by visual-depth embedding. IEEE Trans. Image Process. **27**(5), 2471–2483 (2018)
5. Cai, Z., Shao, L.: RGB-D scene classification via multi-modal feature learning. Cogn. Comput. **10**, 1–16 (2018)
6. Chen, L., Li, W., Xu, D.: Recognizing RGB images by learning from RGB-D data. In: IEEE Conference on Computer Vision and Pattern Recognition, pp. 1418–1425 (2014)
7. Cui, Z., Li, W., Xu, D., Shan, S., Chen, X., Li, X.: Flowing on Riemannian manifold: domain adaptation by shifting covariance. IEEE Trans. Cybern. **44**(12), 2264–2273 (2014)
8. Deng, J., Dong, W., Socher, R., Li, L.J., Li, K., Fei-Fei, L.: ImageNet: a large-scale hierarchical image database. In: IEEE Conference on Computer Vision and Pattern Recognition, pp. 248–255 (2009)
9. Duan, L., Tsang, I.W., Xu, D.: Domain transfer multiple kernel learning. IEEE Trans. Pattern Anal. Mach. Intell. **34**(3), 465–479 (2012)
10. Edelman, A., Arias, T.A., Smith, S.T.: The geometry of algorithms with orthogonality constraints. SIAM J. Matrix Anal. Appl. **20**(2), 303–353 (1998)
11. Farquhar, J., Hardoon, D., Meng, H., Shawe-taylor, J.S., Szedmak, S.: Two view learning: SVM-2K, theory and practice. In: Advances in Neural Information Processing Systems, pp. 355–362 (2005)
12. Fei-Fei, L., Perona, P.: A Bayesian hierarchical model for learning natural scene categories. In: IEEE Conference on Computer Vision and Pattern Recognition, vol. 2, pp. 524–531 (2005)
13. Fernando, B., Habrard, A., Sebban, M., Tuytelaars, T.: Unsupervised visual domain adaptation using subspace alignment. In: IEEE International Conference on Computer Vision, pp. 2960–2967 (2013)
14. Girshick, R., Donahue, J., Darrell, T., Malik, J.: Rich feature hierarchies for accurate object detection and semantic segmentation. In: IEEE Conference on Computer Vision and Pattern Recognition, pp. 580–587 (2014)
15. Gong, B., Grauman, K., Sha, F.: Connecting the dots with landmarks: discriminatively learning domain-invariant features for unsupervised domain adaptation. In: International Conference on Machine Learning, pp. 222–230 (2013)
16. Gong, B., Shi, Y., Sha, F., Grauman, K.: Geodesic flow kernel for unsupervised domain adaptation. In: IEEE Conference on Computer Vision and Pattern Recognition, pp. 2066–2073 (2012)
17. Gopalan, R., Li, R., Chellappa, R.: Domain adaptation for object recognition: an unsupervised approach. In: International Conference on Computer Vision, pp. 999–1006 (2011)
18. Griffin, G., Holub, A., Perona, P.: Caltech-256 object category dataset (2007)
19. Gupta, S., Arbeláez, P., Girshick, R., Malik, J.: Indoor scene understanding with RGB-D images: bottom-up segmentation, object detection and semantic segmentation. Int. J. Comput. Vis. **112**(2), 133–149 (2015)

20. Gupta, S., Girshick, R., Arbeláez, P., Malik, J.: Learning rich features from RGB-D images for object detection and segmentation. In: Fleet, D., Pajdla, T., Schiele, B., Tuytelaars, T. (eds.) ECCV 2014. LNCS, vol. 8695, pp. 345–360. Springer, Cham (2014). https://doi.org/10.1007/978-3-319-10584-0_23
21. Hardoon, D.R., Szedmak, S., Shawe-Taylor, J.: Canonical correlation analysis: an overview with application to learning methods. Neural Comput. **16**(12), 2639–2664 (2004)
22. Huang, J., Gretton, A., Borgwardt, K.M., Schölkopf, B., Smola, A.J.: Correcting sample selection bias by unlabeled data. In: Advances in Neural Information Processing Systems, pp. 601–608 (2006)
23. Huynh, T., Min, R., Dugelay, J.-L.: An efficient LBP-based descriptor for facial depth images applied to gender recognition using RGB-D face data. In: Park, J.-I., Kim, J. (eds.) ACCV 2012. LNCS, vol. 7728, pp. 133–145. Springer, Heidelberg (2013). https://doi.org/10.1007/978-3-642-37410-4_12
24. Janoch, A., et al.: A category-level 3D object dataset: putting the kinect to work. In: Fossati, A., Gall, J., Grabner, H., Ren, X., Konolige, K. (eds.) Consumer Depth Cameras for Computer Vision. ACVPR, pp. 141–165. Springer, London (2013). https://doi.org/10.1007/978-1-4471-4640-7_8
25. Jia, Y., et al.: Caffe: convolutional architecture for fast feature embedding. In: ACM International Conference on Multimedia, pp. 675–678 (2014)
26. Krizhevsky, A., Sutskever, I., Hinton, G.E.: ImageNet classification with deep convolutional neural networks. In: Advances in Neural Information Processing Systems, pp. 1097–1105 (2012)
27. Lai, K., Bo, L., Ren, X., Fox, D.: A large-scale hierarchical multi-view RGB-D object dataset. In: IEEE International Conference on Robotics and Automation, pp. 1817–1824 (2011)
28. Li, W., Chen, L., Xu, D., Van Gool, L.: Visual recognition in RGB images and videos by learning from RGB-D data. IEEE Trans. Pattern Anal. Mach. Intell. **1**, 1 (2017)
29. Long, M., Wang, J., Ding, G., Sun, J., Yu, P.S.: Transfer joint matching for unsupervised domain adaptation. In: IEEE Conference on Computer Vision and Pattern Recognition, pp. 1410–1417 (2014)
30. Min, R., Kose, N., Dugelay, J.L.: KinectFaceDB: a kinect database for face recognition. IEEE Trans. Syst. Man Cybern.: Syst. **44**(11), 1534–1548 (2014)
31. Motiian, S., Doretto, G.: Information bottleneck domain adaptation with privileged information for visual recognition. In: Leibe, B., Matas, J., Sebe, N., Welling, M. (eds.) ECCV 2016. LNCS, vol. 9911, pp. 630–647. Springer, Cham (2016). https://doi.org/10.1007/978-3-319-46478-7_39
32. Pan, S.J., Tsang, I.W., Kwok, J.T., Yang, Q.: Domain adaptation via transfer component analysis. IEEE Trans. Neural Netw. **22**(2), 199–210 (2011)
33. Redko, I., Bennani, Y.: Non-negative embedding for fully unsupervised domain adaptation. Pattern Recogn. Lett. **77**, 35–41 (2016)
34. Shao, L., Cai, Z., Liu, L., Lu, K.: Performance evaluation of deep feature learning for RGB-D image/video classification. Inf. Sci. **385**, 266–283 (2017)
35. Sharmanska, V., Quadrianto, N., Lampert, C.H.: Learning to rank using privileged information. In: IEEE International Conference on Computer Vision, pp. 825–832 (2013)
36. Silberman, N., Fergus, R.: Indoor scene segmentation using a structured light sensor. In: IEEE International Conference on Computer Vision Workshops, pp. 601–608 (2011)

37. Vapnik, V., Vashist, A.: A new learning paradigm: learning using privileged information. Neural Netw. **22**(5), 544–557 (2009)
38. Wolf, L., Hassner, T., Taigman, Y.: Effective unconstrained face recognition by combining multiple descriptors and learned background statistics. IEEE Trans. Pattern Anal. Mach. Intell. **33**(10), 1978–1990 (2011)
39. Zhou, B., Lapedriza, A., Xiao, J., Torralba, A., Oliva, A.: Learning deep features for scene recognition using places database. In: Advances in Neural Information Processing Systems, pp. 487–495 (2014)

Solving Minimum Cost Lifted Multicut Problems by Node Agglomeration

Amirhossein Kardoost(✉) and Margret Keuper

Data and Web Science Group, University of Mannheim, Mannheim, Germany
kardoost@informatik.uni-mannheim.de, keuper@uni-mannheim.de

Abstract. Despite its complexity, the minimum cost lifted multicut problem has found a wide range of applications in recent years, such as image and mesh decomposition or multiple object tracking. Its solutions are decompositions of a graph into an optimal number of segments which are optimized w.r.t. a cost function defined on a superset of the edge set. While the currently available solvers for this problem provide high quality solutions in terms of the task to be solved, they can have long computation times for more difficult problem instances. Here, we propose two variants of a heuristic solver (primal feasible heuristic), which greedily generate solutions within a bounded amount of time. Evaluations on image and mesh segmentation benchmarks show the high quality of these solutions.

1 Introduction

This paper tackles the fast, heuristic optimization of a graph decomposition problem, the minimum cost *lifted* multicut problem. The minimum cost lifted multicut problem has first been proposed in [1], where its promise for the decomposition of pixel grid graphs as well as 3D shape meshes has been shown. It has been successfully applied in fields like multiple object tracking [2] and motion segmentation [3] and became known to produce state-of-the-art results on the segmentation of electron microscopy stacks of neuronal structures [4,5]. It is a generalization of the better-known minimum cost multicut problem [6,7] (also referred to as correlation clustering problem). For example, formulations of the image segmentation problem [8] as minimum cost multicut problem have been considered in [9–23]. This formulation is attractive because the feasible solutions of the multicut problem relate one-to-one to the decompositions of a graph, and the multicut problem does not favor balanced solutions a priori [24]. Furthermore, multicut algorithms are easy to use: They take as input a graph and, for every edge, a real-valued cost of the incident vertices being in distinct components, and output a 01-labeling of the edges which induce a decomposition of the graph. Assigned real-valued cost of the incident vertices ideally reflects the logit of the probability of the edge being cut, i.e. $\log \frac{1-p_e}{p_e} + \log \frac{1-p^*}{p^*}$, for a cut probability p_e at edge e, and a prior probability $p^* \in (0,1)$ of cuts. Cut probability p_e is generated based on the estimated boundary [8] at edge e.

C. V. Jawahar et al. (Eds.): ACCV 2018, LNCS 11364, pp. 74–89, 2019.
https://doi.org/10.1007/978-3-030-20870-7_5

Generalizations of the minimum cost multicut problem in terms of higher-order edges have been considered in [3,17,20]. In contrast to explicit higher-order terms, the generalization to minimum cost *lifted* multicuts allows introduction of additive edge costs, which alter the cost of a specific solution without modifying the set of feasible solutions. In practice, this property turned out to be useful for example in image segmentation, where it is easy to decide for a pair of distant points whether they are in distinct components, yet potentially hard for a pair of neighboring points. The minimum cost lifted multicut problem enables to encode this long range information directly in edge costs.

While this formulation is extremely useful, it turned out to be truely harder than the (NP-hard) minimum cost multicut problem [25]. In practice, it can be solved using heuristic solvers such as KLj [1] or Fusion Moves [4]. For large problem instances such as the pixel-wise image segmentation instances from [1], such solvers can take several minutes to converge or might require greedy pre-clustering.

In this paper, we propose a modification of a very simple primal feasible heuristic, the greedy additive edge contraction (GAEC) algorithm from [1]. The proposed algorithm produces results that are close to the ones generated by KLj [1] with a computation time similar to the one from GAEC [1] and a guaranteed worst case complexity. We evaluate the proposed heuristic on instances of (1) image segmentation problems on the BSDS-500 dataset [8], (2) mesh segmentation problems on the Princeton Mesh Segmentation benchmark [26], and (3), the challenging 3D segmentation instance from the ISBI 2012 challenge on segmentation of neuronal structures from electron microscopy images used in [4,5]. In all scenarios, the proposed algorithm can generate high quality results at a significantly reduced computation time.

2 Related Work

A canonical approach to solving instances of the minimum cost multicut problem is to solve the linear programming relaxation of the multicut polytope [6] as for example proposed in [27]. This procedure, with a subsequent thresholding to produce feasible solutions, has found wide application, e.g. in [16,19,20]. Yet, despite its NP-hardness, the minimum cost multicut problem has been solved to optimality for some practically relevant instances for example in [11,28]. Yet, for larger problem instances, heuristic solvers such as Cut, Glue & Cut (CGC) [15], KL [29,30] and its variant KLj [1], or the Fusion Moves approach [14] need to be employed. They have shown to generate good solutions in practice although no theoretical guarantee can be provided.

The latter two solvers, KLj [1] and Fusion Moves [4], can also be applied to the minimum cost *lifted* multicut problem which is of interest in this paper. Both have proven to provide good solutions in practice, generating results on par with the state-of-the-art in image segmentation in terms of the BSDS-500 benchmark [8], the mesh decomposition problem posed by the Princeton benchmark [26] and the ISBI2012 challenge on segmentation of neuronal structures in image stacks [31,32]. For problem instances for example on the image segmentation task, these heuristics still need several minutes to converge, while Fusion Moves [4] has an edge on KLj in terms of computation time, at the price of a greedy data pre-clustering.

The proposed approach is built on the fully greedy approach GAEC which has been proposed as an initialization procedure for KLj in [1]. As GAEC, KLj and Fusion Moves, it can not provide any bounds for the proposed solution. However, in contrast to KLj and Fusion Moves, it can provide a guaranteed worst case complexity. In practice, it generates results with a computation time slightly higher than GAEC while the resulting objective values can be close to the ones from KLj.

3 Optimization Problem

In this paper, we propose a heuristic solver for the minimum cost *lifted* multicut problem [1]. This problem is of interest, because its feasible solutions relate one-to-one to decompositions of a graph and because it provides a principled way to define a more general cost function decompositions than the minimum cost multicut problem. A decomposition of the graph $G = (V, E)$ is any partition Π of the vertices V such that every component $V' \in \Pi$ induces a connected subgraph of G. In the following, we define the minimum cost multicut problem [6,7] and the minimum cost *lifted* multicut problem [1,33].

3.1 Minimum Cost Multicut Problem

Given any graph $G = (V, E)$, a cost function $c : E \to \mathbb{R}$ and *edge* labels $y : E \to \{0, 1\}$, the optimization problem stated in Eq. (1) is an instance of the minimum cost multicut problem with respect to the graph G and costs c.

$$\min_{y \in \{0,1\}^E} \sum_{e \in E} c_e y_e \tag{1}$$

$$s.t. \quad \forall C \in cycles(G) \quad \forall e \in C : y_e \leq \sum_{e' \in C \setminus \{e\}} y_{e'}.$$

The inequality constraints stated over all cycles of G ensure that the edge labeling y induces a decomposition of G. It has been shown to be sufficient to ensure these constraints on the subset of all chordless cycles in [6]. The minimum cost multicut problem allows to assign a cost or reward (c_e) for every edge $e \in E$ to be cut.

3.2 Minimum Cost Lifted Multicut Problem

The minimum cost *lifted* multicut problem is defined w.r.t. a graph $G = (V, E)$ and a graph $G' = (V, E')$ with $E \subseteq E'$ and a cost function $c' : E' \to \mathbb{R}$ which allows to assign, for every edge in E' a cost or reward for being cut. Its feasible solutions relate one-to-one to decompositions of the graph G. Rigorously, for any undirected graph $G = (V, E)$, any $F = \binom{V}{2} \setminus E$ and any $c' : E \cup F \to \mathbb{R}$, the linear program written in Eqs. (2)–(5) is an instance of the minimum cost lifted multicut problem w.r.t. G, F and c'.

$$\min_{y \in \{0,1\}^{E'}} \sum_{e \in E'} c'_e y_e \tag{2}$$

$$s.t. \quad \forall C \in cycles(G) \quad \forall e \in C : y_e \leq \sum_{e' \in C \setminus \{e\}} y_{e'} \tag{3}$$

$$\forall vw \in F \quad \forall P \in vw\text{-paths}(G) : y_{vw} \leq \sum_{e \in P} y_e \tag{4}$$

$$\forall vw \in F \quad \forall C \in vw\text{-cuts}(G) : 1 - y_{vw} \leq \sum_{e \in C} (1 - y_e) \tag{5}$$

The linear inequalities in Eqs. (3)–(5) constrain y such that $\{e \in E | y_e == 1\}$ is a multicut of G. They ensure further that, for any edge $uv \in F, y_{uv} = 0$ iff there exists a path (uv-path) in the original graph G along which all edges are connected, i.e. labeled 0.

The set F of lifted edges is introduced to facilitate the modification of the cost function of the multicut problem without modifying the set of feasible solutions [1]. This is most intuitive in image segmentation. There, the connectivity should be defined on the image grid: two pixels in the same cluster should be connected in the image domain. However, for pairs of directly neighboring pixels, it is hard to decide whether they belong to the same segment or to different segments (due to blurred edges/textures). For pixels at a certain distance, it is easier to recognize boundaries separating one from the other. The lifted edge set F allows to introduce such information between distant pixels without modifying the connectivity [1].

4 Objectives

To generate fast solutions to minimum cost lifted multicut problems, we investigate the GAEC solver proposed in [1]. While other heuristic solvers such as [4] generate better solutions in terms of the resulting energy, GAEC is one of the fastest solvers currently available, although it operates directly on the nodes of the original graph without any local pre-clustering. GAEC provides deterministic solutions created in a greedy procedure of edge contractions and thus

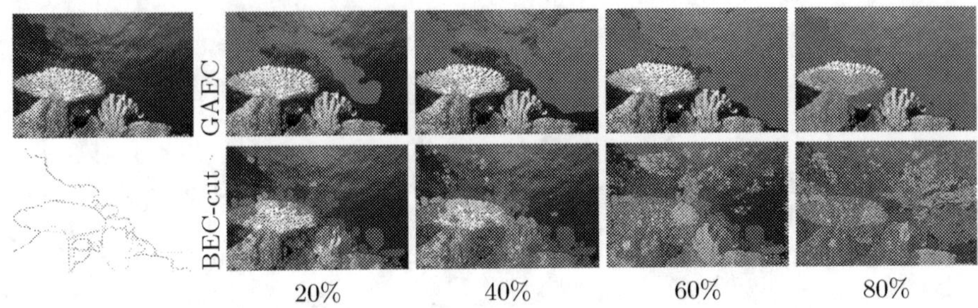

Fig. 1. For the BSDS-500 [8] image on the left (average ground-truth annotations depicted below), we show intermediate states during the execution of the GAEC solver [1] (top) and the proposed BEC-cut solver (bottom) after 20%, 40%, 60% and 80% of the total merges have been executed. GAEC tends to generate large segments that merge points across object boundaries. These merges can not be "repaired". In contrast, BEC-cut generates and grows many segments simultaneously. It starts generating these segments in vicinity to the object boundaries.

provides low computation times even for large and difficult problem instances [1]. While GAEC provides relatively low energy solutions on minimum cost multicut problems, it has major difficulties finding acceptable solutions to minimum cost *lifted* multicut problems. Where does this discrepancy come from? To analyze this effect, we visualize intermediate GAEC solutions in Fig. 1. We observe that large clusters are built pretty quickly. They tend to grow by adding small clusters or isolated nodes. In this scenario, long range repulsive edges are not in the scope of the greedy optimization until almost all nodes have been merged. Thus, the "difficult parts" of the problem, i.e. those parts possibly causing conflicts w.r.t. the objective, are only considered when most of the nodes have already been irreversibly merged.

We conclude that the GAEC algorithm would benefit from two aspects: (1) avoid creating very unbalanced clusters early on, such that repulsive edges are in the scope of intermediate regions early on, and (2) use information about repulsive edges directly as a criterion for merges.

5 Proposed Approach

We want to base our heuristic on the fast GAEC solver from [1] and follow a similar, greedy merging scheme such that running times remain affordable for large and difficult problem instances. In order to tackle aspects (1), avoid creating very unbalanced clusters early on, and (2), use information about repulsive edges in the merge criterion, we define an improved ranking scheme for the next best edge to be contracted. In the basic version of our proposed heuristic, we only tackle aspect (1) by proposing a greedy "Balanced Edge Contraction" scheme.

Algorithm 1. GAEC [1]

1 $\mathcal{E} := E$, $\mathcal{E}' := E'$
2 $\mathcal{V} := V$
3 **foreach** $ab \in \mathcal{E}'$ **do**
4     $\chi_{ab} := c_{ab}$
5 **while** $\mathcal{E} \neq \emptyset$ **do**
6     $ab := \underset{a'b' \in \mathcal{E}}{\text{argmax}}\ \chi_{a'b'}$
7   **if** $\chi_{ab} < 0$ **then**
8   **break**
9   **contract** ab in $\mathcal{G}$ and $\mathcal{G}'$
10   **foreach** $ab \neq ab' \in \mathcal{E}'$ **do**
11         $\chi_{ab'} := \chi_{ab'} + \chi_{bb'}$

Algorithm 2. BEC

1 $\mathcal{E} := E$, $\mathcal{E}' := E'$
2 $\mathcal{V} := V$
3 **foreach** $ab \in \mathcal{E}'$ **do**
4     $\chi_{ab} := c_{ab}$
5 **while** $\mathcal{E} \neq \emptyset$ **do**
6     $ab := \underset{a'b' \in \mathcal{E}}{\text{argmax}}\ \frac{\chi_{a'b'}}{|a'|+|b'|}$
7   **if** $\chi_{ab} < 0$ **then**
8   **break**
9   **contract** ab in $\mathcal{G}$ and $\mathcal{G}'$
10   **foreach** $ab \neq ab' \in \mathcal{E}'$ **do**
11         $\chi_{ab'} := \chi_{ab'} + \chi_{bb'}$

Instead of using the plain edge potentials as a merge criterion as in GAEC (see Algorithm 1, line 6), we propose to normalize these potentials by the size of the components to be merged (Algorithm 2, line 6). Note that this normalization only affects the order in which attractive edges are merged and not the actual edge potentials nor the cut objective.

In order to tackle aspect (2), we formulate a secondary merge criterion. Ultimately, we want to find a cut which minimizes the total energy of the cut (not maximize the energy of the joined components). We are motivated to encourage the solver to pursue this objective during the greedy optimization: We want to make join decisions that minimize the outgoing potentials of resulting components, i.e. minimize the intermediate cut.

To formalize this, lets look at the graph $G_d = (V, E_d)$ defined on G' (Sect. 3.2), and assign to every vertex v in V a unary potential $d_v = \sum_{\{b|e_{vb} \in E'\}} c_{vb}$, i.e. the degree of v. The outgoing potentials of a component in G resulting from joining two vertices u and v can be computed as $d_u + d_v - 2c_{u,v}$. Then, we define for edges $uv \in E_d$, edge weights $c^d_{u,v} = d_u + d_v - 2c_{u,v}$. Minimizing these "dual" edge weights is used as a secondary join criterion in Algorithm 3.

This modification of the order in which segments are agglomerated affects the intermediate stages of the solution during the optimization. Figure 1(bottom) shows such intermediate optimization stages after 20%, 40%, 60% and 80% of the total merges have been computed by the proposed algorithm. Unlike GAEC, it generates many small node agglomerations along both sides of the boundaries. Thus, repulsive terms on the boundary are in scope early on.

5.1 Algorithms

Algorithms 2 and 3 are adaptations of greedy agglomeration, more specifically, greedy additive edge contraction (Algorithm 1). Both take as input an instance of the lifted multicut problem (LMP) defined by $G = (V, E)$, F and $c : E \cup F \to \mathbb{R}$

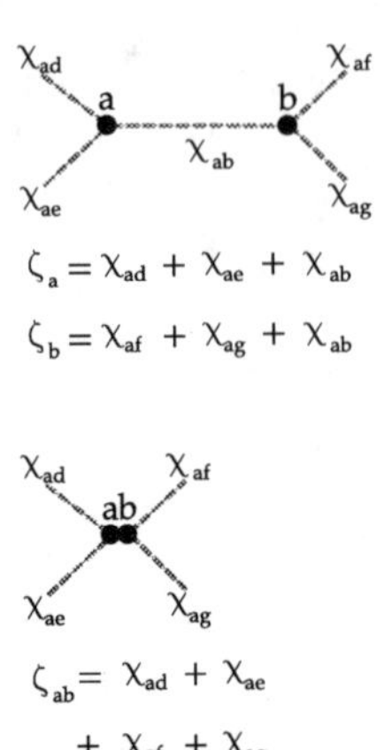

Fig. 2. Exemplary computation of ζ from χ before (top) and after (bottom) contraction of components a and b. χ encodes the sum of outgoing costs of a component.

Algorithm 3. BEC-cut

$\mathcal{E} := E$, $\mathcal{E}' := E'$
$\mathcal{V} := V$
foreach $ab \in \mathcal{E}$ **do**
  $\chi_{ab} := c_{ab}$
foreach $a \in \mathcal{V}$ **do**
  $\zeta_a := \sum_{\{b \mid e_{ab} \in E'\}} c_{ab}$
while $\mathcal{E} \neq \emptyset$ **do**
  $\mathcal{S} := \underset{a'b' \in \mathcal{E}}{\text{argmax}} \frac{\chi_{a'b'}}{|a'|+|b'|}$
  $ab := \underset{a'b' \in \mathcal{S}}{\text{argmin}} \frac{\zeta_{a'}+\zeta_{b'}-2\chi_{a'b'}}{|a'|+|b'|}$
  if $\chi_{ab} < 0$ **then**
    break
  contract $ab =: \bar{a}$ in $\mathcal{G}$ and $\mathcal{G}'$
  $\zeta_{\bar{a}} = \zeta_a + \zeta_b - 2\chi_{ab}$
  foreach $ab \neq ab' \in \mathcal{E}'$ **do**
    $\chi_{ab'} := \chi_{ab'} + \chi_{bb'}$

(Eqs. (2)–(5)) and construct as output a decomposition of the graph G. Both algorithms maintain a decomposition of G, represented by graph $\mathcal{G} = (\mathcal{V}, \mathcal{E})$ whose nodes $a \in \mathcal{V}$ are components of G and whose edges $ab \in \mathcal{E}$ connect any components a and b of G which are neighbors in G and $\chi : \mathcal{E} \to \mathbb{R}$ is an ordered sequence of costs for feasible joins. Objective values are computed w.r.t. the larger graph $G' = (V, E \cup F)$ and $c : E \cup F \to \mathbb{R}$.

Balanced Edge Contraction (BEC). Starting from the decomposition into single nodes, in every iteration, a pair of neighboring components is joined for which the join decreases the objective value. While for the basic GAEC algorithm, an edge is picked such that the objective value decreases maximally, we propose to weight the prospective gain by the size of the components. This weighting encourages components of similar size to merge earlier than components of different size if both merges are advantageous. Intuitively, this should lead to several balanced clusters (as opposed to one large cluster and many single nodes) at intermediate optimization states. If no join strictly decreases the objective value, the algorithm terminates.

BEC-cut. Starting from the decomposition into single nodes, at every iteration, a pair of neighboring components is joined for which the join decreases the objective value. If a unique pair of neighboring components exists whose join strictly decreases the *size-weighted* objective value maximally, this join is executed. From the set of all possible joins that decrease the weighted objective

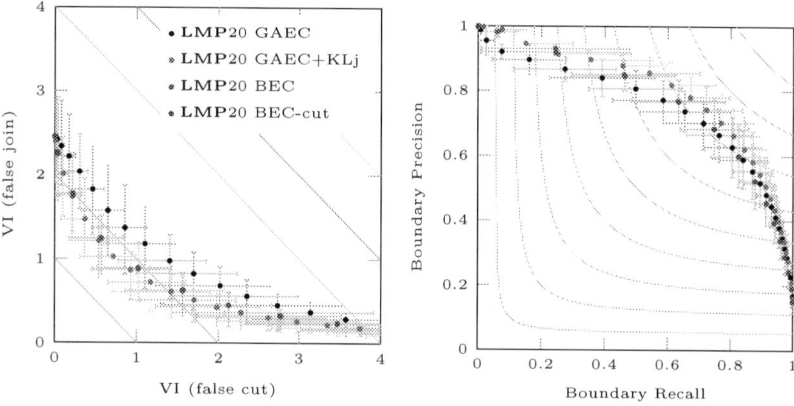

Fig. 3. Depicted above is an evaluation of the heuristics GAEC, (Algorithm 1), KLj [1] and the proposed BEC (Algorithm 2) and BEC-cut (Algorithm 3) on the large and difficult lifted multicut problem instances from [1] with lifting radius 20 (LMP20). These instances address the image decomposition problem posed by the BSDS-500 benchmark [8]. On the **left**, the variation of information (VI), split additively into a distance due to false cuts and a distance due to false joins is depicted (lower is better), on the **right**, the accuracy of boundary detection, split into recall and precision is shown (higher is better). Error bars depict the 0.25 and 0.75-quantile. Result of the proposed heuristics figure in between those of the solver GAEC and KLj in both metrics. In the region metric VI, results of the proposed solvers BEC and BEC-cut are very close to results of the KLj.

value maximally, the join is executed which minimizes the sum of outgoing costs, i.e. the prospective value ζ of the resulting component. Compare Fig. 2 for an illustration of the computation of ζ. If no join strictly decreases the objective value, the algorithm terminates.

It is important to notice that the balancing criteria in our heuristic methods never affects the original objective function, which is defined in Sect. 3.2.

Implementation. Our implementation is built upon GAEC [1]. As GAEC, it uses ordered adjacency lists for the graph $\mathcal{G}$ and for a graph $\mathcal{G}' = (\mathcal{V}, \mathcal{E}')$ whose edges $ab \in \mathcal{E}'$ connect any components a and b of G for which there is an edge $vw \in E \cup F$ with $v \in a$ and $w \in b$. It uses a *disjoint set data structure* for the partition of V and a *priority queue* for an ordered sequence of costs $\chi : \mathcal{E} \rightarrow \mathbb{R}$ of feasible joins, with a secondary sorting criterion $\bar{\chi} : \mathcal{E} \rightarrow \mathbb{R}$, $\bar{\chi}_{ab} = \frac{\zeta_a + \zeta_b - 2\chi_{ab}}{|a|+|b|}$ defined on ζ for Algorithm 3 (comp. line 9). As GAEC, its worst-case time complexity $O(|V|^2 \log |V|)$ is due to a sequence of at most $|V|$ contractions, in each of which at most $\deg \mathcal{G}' \leq |V|$ edges are removed, each in time $O(\log \deg \mathcal{G}') \in O(\log |V|)$.

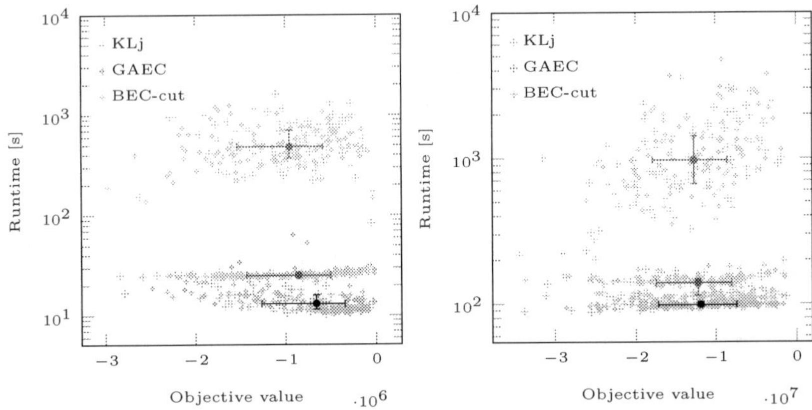

Fig. 4. Depicted above is a comparison of Algorithm 3 (BEC-cut) with GAEC and KLj [1]. Every point corresponds to one instance of the lifted multicut problem [1] defined w.r.t. one test image in the BSDS-500 benchmark [8] with lifting radius 10 (**left**) and 20 (**right**). The computation times of the proposed algorithm BEC-cut are close to the ones from GAEC while the resulting energy is improved.

6 Experiments

We evaluate the proposed heuristics on types of problem instances and w.r.t. three different tasks: lifted pixel-grid graphs [1] defined on the image segmentation problems of the BSDS-500 [8] benchmark, lifted graphs on 3D shape meshes [1] defined on the Princeton Mesh Segmentation benchmark [26] and the lifted superpixel adjacency graph [5] defined on the ISBI 2012 challenge data, a volumetric electron microscopy recording of neuronal structures [31,32].

6.1 Image Decomposition

On the image segmentation task posed by the BSDS-500 benchmark [8], we apply the proposed solvers BEC Algorithm 2 and BEC-cut 3 to the minimum cost lifted multicut instances proposed in [1]. These problem instances represent pixel grid graphs. Lifted "long range" edges are inserted to connect all pixels within a pre-defined pixel radius to provide more "global" information to the optimization problem. Lifting radii of 20 pixels showed best performance in [1].

Figure 3 shows the results of the proposed solvers in comparison to GAEC and KLj initialized with GAEC in terms of the variation of information (VI) [34] (Fig. 3 left, lower is better) and the boundary precision and recall (Fig. 3 right, higher is better). For the evaluation on these metrics results at different levels of granularity need to be generated. This can be done by modifying the prior probability of a cut in the lifted multicut problem instances. Every point in the plots of Fig. 3 shows, for one cut prior and algorithm, the average over all test images in the BSDS-500 benchmark.

Fig. 5. Qualitative segmentation results of the proposed BEC-cut solver on instances from the BSDS-500 benchmark. The lifted multicut problems are computed with lifted edges between all points at distance less than 10.

While BEC and BEC-cut show almost equivalent performance, the improvement over GAEC [1] especially on the region metric VI is evident.

Figure 4 shows scatter plots of the computation times and resulting objective values for the algorithms GAEC and KLj [1] and the proposed BEC-cut. With respect to the objective value, BEC-cut yields a clear improvement over GAEC while it is significantly faster than KLj.

Some of the qualitative results are shown in Fig. 5 for the proposed BEC-cut solver and lifting radius 10. Although its greedy merging procedure, it can produce nicely closed contours on these problem instances.

6.2 Mesh Segmentation

In this section, we evaluate the proposed methods on the Princeton Mesh Segmentation benchmark [26] which provides 380 meshes consisting 19 object categories with human-generated ground-truths [26].

On this dataset, the instance of the minimum cost lifted multicut problem for each mesh is generated based on Keuper et al. [1]. More specifically, the local edge costs for $e \in E$ are computed using curvatures and dihedral angle features which are computed based on the mesh data. The lifted edges are then inserted up to a fixed node distance of 70 (defined on the graph) and for cut prior 0.55 as proposed in [1] using their code[1]. Consequently, the created problem instances are solved by the proposed solvers. Some of the qualitative results for success and failure cases for the mesh segmentations are depicted in Figs. 8 and 7, respectively.

Table 1 shows a comparison of the resulting objective functions and the consumed optimization time of the different approaches. On this dataset, the optimization based on KLj when it is initialized with either GAEC or BEC converges

[1] https://www.mpi-inf.mpg.de/fileadmin/inf/d2/levinkov/iccv-2015/code.tar.gz.

Table 1. Average computation time and objective value of the different solvers on the Princeton Mesh Segmentation Benchmark.

	GAEC [1]	KLj-GAEC [1]	BEC	BEC-cut	KLj-BEC-cut	KLj-BEC
Avg. Comp. time [s]	576	755	589	574	797	755
Avg. Objective Value (lower is better)	−17840450	−18988930	−18484140	−18057480	−18991920	−18989332

Table 2. Resulting RI and VI score for the 3D mesh segmentation instances of the Princeton Mesh Segmentation Benchmark [26]. We evaluate the proposed solvers BEC and BEC-cut and compare to GAEC [1] and KLj [1] initialized by GAEC. We also evaluate KLj initialized with our results from BEC. "KLj-GAEC$_{opt}$" represents the results from Keuper et al. [1] when the lifting radius and cut prior were optimized per instance.

	GAEC [1]		BEC		BEC-cut		KLj-GAEC [1]		KLj-BEC		KLj-GAEC$_{opt}$ [1]	
	RI	VI	RI	VI	RI	VI	RI	VI	RI	VI	RI	VI
Human	0.77	1.90	0.84	1.77	0.85	1.74	0.86	1.63	0.86	1.60	0.87	1.79
Cup	0.83	0.53	0.88	0.44	0.86	0.45	0.88	0.40	0.89	0.37	0.90	0.39
Glasses	0.61	1.38	0.82	0.85	0.78	1.04	0.84	0.78	0.84	0.77	0.90	0.68
Airplane	0.89	0.93	0.91	0.92	0.91	0.86	0.91	0.84	0.91	0.85	0.92	0.83
Ant	0.93	0.70	0.97	0.48	0.96	0.52	0.97	0.43	0.97	0.44	0.98	0.42
Chair	0.85	0.85	0.92	0.67	0.89	0.84	0.92	0.58	0.92	0.58	0.93	0.55
Octopus	0.96	0.41	0.97	0.41	0.97	0.44	0.97	0.37	0.97	0.37	0.98	0.33
Table	0.87	0.48	0.91	0.40	0.83	0.63	0.93	0.29	0.93	0.29	0.94	0.29
Teddy	0.92	0.76	0.93	0.76	0.92	0.78	0.95	0.55	0.95	0.55	0.96	0.50
Hand	0.67	1.75	0.80	1.47	0.76	1.72	0.84	1.23	0.84	1.23	0.85	1.32
Plier	0.72	1.38	0.84	1.12	0.81	1.19	0.88	0.93	0.91	0.85	0.93	0.84
Fish	0.73	1.20	0.75	1.26	0.76	1.30	0.80	1.12	0.80	1.11	0.80	1.09
Bird	0.90	1.01	0.92	0.98	0.91	1.01	0.92	0.91	0.92	0.91	0.93	0.99
Armadillo	0.88	1.88	0.91	1.75	0.90	1.87	0.91	1.63	0.91	1.62	0.92	1.48
Bust	0.57	2.12	0.66	2.32	0.63	2.46	0.68	2.29	0.68	2.29	0.69	2.25
Mech	0.80	0.66	0.81	0.72	0.80	0.66	0.84	0.60	0.84	0.59	0.84	0.59
Bearing	0.79	0.76	0.82	0.75	0.83	0.70	0.84	0.69	0.84	0.69	0.84	0.69
Vase	0.77	1.02	0.80	1.06	0.77	1.13	0.84	0.87	0.84	0.87	0.84	0.87
FourLeg	0.81	1.94	0.82	1.98	0.81	2.04	0.83	1.87	0.83	1.89	0.84	1.72
Average	0.81	1.14	0.86	1.06	0.84	1.13	0.88	0.95	0.88	0.94	0.89	0.93

surprisingly fast. This might be an indication for a meaningful initial segmentation in these cases. Among the greedy heuristics BEC yields the lowest objective values. Initializing KLj with the proposed BEC yields a better objective value than KLj initialized with GAEC [1].

Table 2 provides a comparison between different solvers in terms of Rand's Index (RI) (higher is better) and Variation of Information (VI) (lower is better). In addition to report the plain results of our proposed solvers, we evaluate the quality of solutions from KLj initialized with BEC, i.e. KLj-BEC. The iterative, local move making heuristic KLj [1] is known to benefit from good initializations.

The evaluation shows that both proposed heuristics outperform GAEC. Specifically, BEC yields an improvement of 0.05 on the RI and a decrease of 0.08 in the VI. On this dataset, BEC performs better than BEC-cut. In fact, it yields a RI value close to the one from KLj-GAEC with the same lifting parameters. KLj, initialized with BEC yields slightly better results than KLj initialized with GAEC in terms of the VI. The column "KLj-GAEC$_{opt}$" in Table 2 corresponds to the results from Keuper et al. [1], which are obtained by KLj-GAEC when the lifting radius and cut prior were optimized per instance. KLj, initialized by BEC almost meets these results.

6.3 ISBI 2012 Challenge

In the ISBI 2012 challenge, a stack of electron microscopy images of neuronal structures [31,32] is provided for segmentation. The images are recorded by a

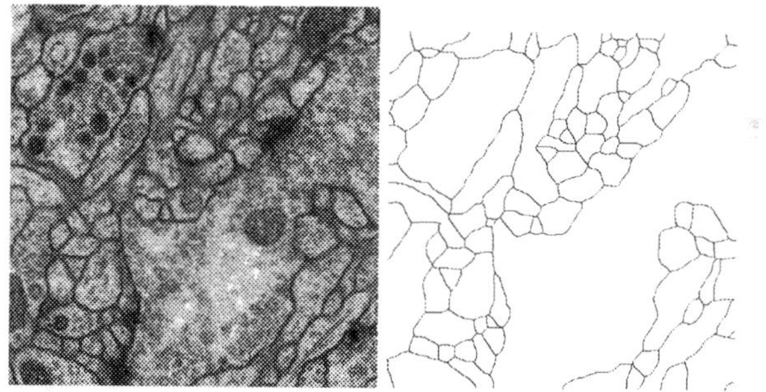

Fig. 6. First frame of the stack in the test data of ISBI 2012 with the corresponding segmentation boundaries are shown. The results for this dataset are acquired with BEC-cut solver.

Table 3. Comparison of the objective value and run time of our proposed solvers, BEC and BEC-cut with Fusion Move algorithm with the Randomized proposal generator (FM-R) [4] are provided. The results are generated based on the defined minimum cost lifted multicut problem for ISBI 2012 Challenge [31,32]. Leader board: http://brainiac2.mit.edu/isbi_challenge/leaders-board-new

Algorithm	Comp. time [s]	Objective Value (lower is better)	V^{Rand}	V^{Info}
FM-R [4]	10.43	−1.948524	0.9822	0.9884
BEC	2.53	−1.944767	–	–
BEC-cut	2.59	−1.944964	0.9811	0.9883

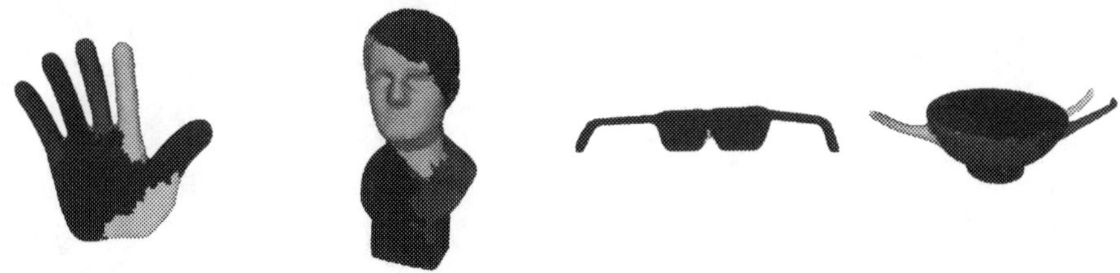

Fig. 7. Some of the failure cases for mesh decomposition are shown, where the instance of the lifted multicut problem is solved with BEC-cut. For success cases refer to the Fig. 8.

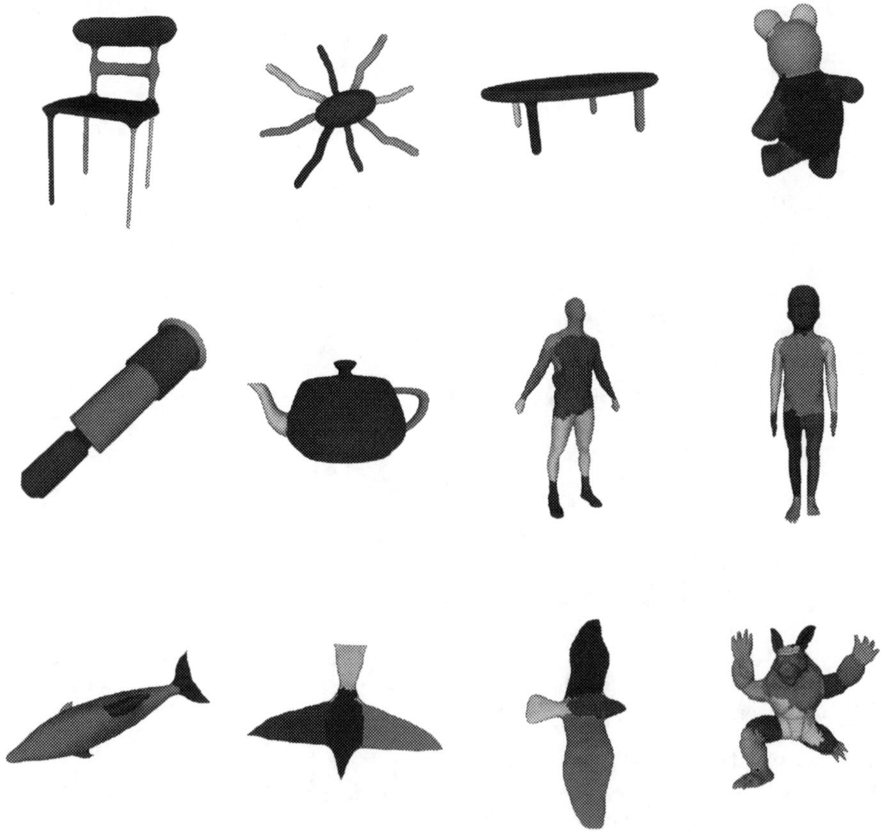

Fig. 8. Depicted above is a sample of success cases for mesh decompositions generated by solving an instance of the lifted multicut problem with BEC-cut.

serial section transmission electron microscope from the Drosophila larva ventral nerve cord.

We applied the proposed BEC and BEC-cut solvers to the instance of the minimum cost lifted multicut problem defined in [5]. The instance is based on a superpixel adjacency graph, i.e. every node corresponds to a superpixel and is connected to its direct neighbors. An additional *lifted* edge set encodes long range information. All edge weights are learned from training data using two random forest classifiers, one of them is trained to predict whether two adjacent superpixels should be assigned to the same cluster, the other one learns this prediction for non-adjacent superpixels. The trained classifiers are used to assign weights to the local and lifted edges, respectively. Table 3 shows results we achieve on this data with our heuristic solvers BEC and BEC-cut. At a significantly reduced computation time, we can get results close to the state-of-the-art in terms of objective value as well as segmentation quality. Figure 6 represents the first frame in the stack of the test data from ISBI 2012 with the corresponding segmentation boundaries which are resulted from the proposed BEC-cut solver.

7 Conclusion

In this paper, we propose two heuristic solvers BEC and BEC-cut. Both are modifications of the greedy agglomerative heuristic GAEC and provide a bounded worst case complexity. We evaluate our solvers on three application scenarios: image decomposition, 3D mesh segmentation and segmentation of neuronal structures from volumetric electron microscopic data. In all scenarios, the proposed solvers yield results close to the ones from more elaborate solvers KLj [1] or Fusion Moves [4], while the computation time is significantly lower.

Acknowledgements. We acknowledge funding by the DFG project KE 2264/1-1. We also acknowledge the NVIDIA Corporation for the donation of a Titan Xp GPU.

References

1. Keuper, M., Levinkov, E., Bonneel, N., Lavoué, G., Brox, T., Andres, B.: Efficient decomposition of image and mesh graphs by lifted multicuts. In: 2015 IEEE International Conference on Computer Vision (ICCV). pp. 1751–1759 (2015)
2. Tang, S., Andriluka, M., Andres, B., Schiele, B.: Multi people tracking with lifted multicut and person re-identification. In: IEEE Conference on Computer Vision and Pattern Recognition (CVPR) (2017)
3. Keuper, M.: Higher-order minimum cost lifted multicuts for motion segmentation. In: The IEEE International Conference on Computer Vision (ICCV) (2017)
4. Beier, T., Andres, B., Köthe, U., Hamprecht, F.A.: An efficient fusion move algorithm for the minimum cost lifted multicut problem. In: Leibe, B., Matas, J., Sebe, N., Welling, M. (eds.) ECCV 2016. LNCS, vol. 9906, pp. 715–730. Springer, Cham (2016). https://doi.org/10.1007/978-3-319-46475-6_44
5. Beier, T., et al.: Multicut brings automated neurite segmentation closer to human performance. Nat. Methods **14**, 101 (2017)
6. Chopra, S., Rao, M.: The partition problem. Math. Programm. **59**, 87–115 (1993)
7. Deza, M.M., Laurent, M.: Geometry of Cuts and Metrics. AC, vol. 15. Springer, Heidelberg (1997). https://doi.org/10.1007/978-3-642-04295-9
8. Arbelaez, P., Maire, M., Fowlkes, C., Malik, J.: Contour detection and hierarchical image segmentation. IEEE TPAMI **33**(5), 898–916 (2011)

9. Alush, A., Goldberger, J.: Ensemble segmentation using efficient integer linear programming. TPAMI **34**, 1966–1977 (2012)
10. Andres, B., Kappes, J.H., Beier, T., Köthe, U., Hamprecht, F.A.: Probabilistic image segmentation with closedness constraints. In: ICCV (2011)
11. Andres, B., et al.: Globally Optimal Closed-Surface Segmentation for Connectomics. In: Fitzgibbon, A., Lazebnik, S., Perona, P., Sato, Y., Schmid, C. (eds.) ECCV 2012. LNCS, vol. 7574, pp. 778–791. Springer, Heidelberg (2012). https://doi.org/10.1007/978-3-642-33712-3_56
12. Andres, B., et al.: Segmenting planar superpixel adjacency graphs w.r.t. non-planar superpixel affinity graphs. In: Heyden, A., Kahl, F., Olsson, C., Oskarsson, M., Tai, X.-C. (eds.) EMMCVPR 2013. LNCS, vol. 8081, pp. 266–279. Springer, Heidelberg (2013). https://doi.org/10.1007/978-3-642-40395-8_20
13. Bagon, S., Galun, M.: Large scale correlation clustering optimization. CoRR abs/1112.2903 (2011)
14. Beier, T., Hamprecht, F.A., Kappes, J.H.: Fusion moves for correlation clustering. In: CVPR (2015)
15. Beier, T., Kroeger, T., Kappes, J., Köthe, U., Hamprecht, F.: Cut, glue, & cut: a fast, approximate solver for multicut partitioning. In: CVPR (2014)
16. Kappes, J.H., Speth, M., Andres, B., Reinelt, G., Schnörr, C.: Globally optimal image partitioning by multicuts. In: Boykov, Y., Kahl, F., Lempitsky, V., Schmidt, F.R. (eds.) EMMCVPR 2011. LNCS, vol. 6819, pp. 31–44. Springer, Heidelberg (2011). https://doi.org/10.1007/978-3-642-23094-3_3
17. Kappes, J.H., Speth, M., Reinelt, G., Schnörr, C.: Higher-order segmentation via multicuts. CoRR abs/1305.6387 (2013)
18. Kappes, J.H., Swoboda, P., Savchynskyy, B., Hazan, T., Schnörr, C.: Probabilistic correlation clustering and image partitioning using perturbed multicuts. In: Aujol, J.-F., Nikolova, M., Papadakis, N. (eds.) SSVM 2015. LNCS, vol. 9087, pp. 231–242. Springer, Cham (2015). https://doi.org/10.1007/978-3-319-18461-6_19
19. Kim, S., Nowozin, S., Kohli, P., Yoo, C.D.: Higher-order correlation clustering for image segmentation. In: NIPS (2011)
20. Kim, S., Yoo, C.D., Nowozin, S.: Image segmentation using higher-order correlation clustering. IEEE TPAMI **36**, 1761–1774 (2014)
21. Nowozin, S., Jegelka, S.: Solution stability in linear programming relaxations: graph partitioning and unsupervised learning. In: ICML (2009)
22. Yarkony, J., Ihler, A., Fowlkes, C.C.: Fast planar correlation clustering for image segmentation. In: Fitzgibbon, A., Lazebnik, S., Perona, P., Sato, Y., Schmid, C. (eds.) ECCV 2012. LNCS, vol. 7577, pp. 568–581. Springer, Heidelberg (2012). https://doi.org/10.1007/978-3-642-33783-3_41
23. Yarkony, J., Zhang, C., Fowlkes, C.C.: Hierarchical planar correlation clustering for cell segmentation. In: Tai, X.-C., Bae, E., Chan, T.F., Lysaker, M. (eds.) EMMCVPR 2015. LNCS, vol. 8932, pp. 492–504. Springer, Cham (2015). https://doi.org/10.1007/978-3-319-14612-6_36
24. Shi, J., Malik, J.: Normalized cuts and image segmentation. TPAMI **22**, 888–905 (2000)
25. Horňáková, A., Lange, J.H., Andres, B.: Analysis and optimization of graph decompositions by lifted multicuts. In: ICML (2017)
26. Chen, X., Golovinskiy, A., Funkhouser, T.: A benchmark for 3D mesh segmentation. ACM Trans. Graph. (Proc. SIGGRAPH) **28**, 73 (2009)
27. Demaine, E.D., Emanuel, D., Fiat, A., Immorlica, N.: Correlation clustering in general weighted graphs. Theor. Comput. Sci. **361**, 172–187 (2006)

28. Kappes, J.H., et al.: A comparative study of modern inference techniques for structured discrete energy minimization problems. In: IJCV (2015)
29. Kernighan, B.W., Lin, S.: An efficient heuristic procedure for partitioning graphs. Bell Syst. Tech. J. **49**, 291–307 (1970)
30. Kappes, J., et al.: A comparative study of modern inference techniques for structured discrete energy minimization problems. Int. J. Comput. Vis. **115**, 155–184 (2015)
31. Cardona, A., et al.: An integrated micro- and macroarchitectural analysis of the drosophila brain by computer-assisted serial section electron microscopy. PLOS Biol. **8**, 1–17 (2010)
32. Carreras, I., et al.: Crowdsourcing the creation of image segmentation algorithms for connectomics. Frontiers Neuroanat. **9**, 1–13 (2015)
33. Andres, B.: Lifting of multicuts. CoRR abs/1503.03791 (2015)
34. Meilă, M.: Comparing clusterings-an information based distance. J. Multivar. Anal. **98**, 873–895 (2007)

Robust Deep Multi-modal Learning Based on Gated Information Fusion Network

Jaekyum Kim[1], Junho Koh[1], Yecheol Kim[1], Jaehyung Choi[2], Youngbae Hwang[3], and Jun Won Choi[1(✉)]

[1] Hanyang University, Seoul, Korea
{jkkim,jhkoh,yckim}@spa.hanyang.ac.kr, junwchoi@hanyang.ac.kr
[2] Phantom AI Inc., Burlingame, CA, USA
jaehyung@phantom.ai
[3] Korea Electronics Technology Institute (KETI), Seongnam-si, Korea
ybhwang@keti.re.kr

Abstract. The goal of multi-modal learning is to use complementary information on the relevant task provided by the multiple modalities to achieve reliable and robust performance. Recently, deep learning has led significant improvement in multi-modal learning by allowing for fusing high level features obtained at intermediate layers of the deep neural network. This paper addresses a problem of designing robust deep multi-modal learning architecture in the presence of the modalities degraded in quality. We introduce deep fusion architecture for object detection which processes each modality using the separate convolutional neural network (CNN) and constructs the joint feature maps by combining the intermediate features obtained by the CNNs. In order to facilitate the robustness to the degraded modalities, we employ the gated information fusion (GIF) network which weights the contribution from each modality according to the input feature maps to be fused. The combining weights are determined by applying the convolutional layers followed by the sigmoid function to the concatenated intermediate feature maps. The whole network including the CNN backbone and GIF is trained in an end-to-end fashion. Our experiments show that the proposed GIF network offers the additional architectural flexibility to achieve the robust performance in handling some degraded modalities.

Keywords: Object detection · Multi-modal fusion · Sensor fusion · Gated information fusion

This work was supported by Institute for Information & communications Technology Promotion (IITP) grant funded by the Korea government(MSIT) (2016-0-00564, Development of Intelligent Interaction Technology Based on Context Awareness and Human Intention Understanding).

Electronic supplementary material The online version of this chapter (https://doi.org/10.1007/978-3-030-20870-7_6) contains supplementary material, which is available to authorized users.

C. V. Jawahar et al. (Eds.): ACCV 2018, LNCS 11364, pp. 90–106, 2019.
https://doi.org/10.1007/978-3-030-20870-7_6

1 Introduction

Multi-modal learning refers to a machine learning problem aiming to improve learning performance using the experience acquired from the different types of data sources. Basically, such multi-modal data delivers rich and diverse information on the phenomenon relevant to the given task. Human is naturally born to be a good multi-modal learner in that it effectively learns from various modalities including audio, video, smell, touch, and so on. On the contrary, multi-modal fusion has been one of the most challenging problems in machine learning field due to the difficulty of combining the high level semantic information delivered by the different sources. Basically, multi-modal fusion concerns in which data processing stage the information fusion is conducted, which leads to the categorization into *early fusion* and *late fusion* [19]. While the early fusion aims to extract the joint representation directly from the raw or preprocessed data, the late fusion aggregates the decisions separately made by the machine learning models for each modality. The late fusion is considered to be easy to implement but its performance is limited in that the correlation structure underlying in multi-modal sources is not fully utilized. Early fusion is also difficult to find a good joint representation due to significantly different data structures between modalities. Recent emergence of deep neural network (DNN) technique (called deep learning) [18] has enabled the extraction of the hierarchical semantic features from the raw data and consequently led to better and flexible use of feature-level data fusion. The common practice for such feature-level fusion is to construct the shared representation by merging the intermediate features obtained by separate machine learning models. In this sense, this fusion approach is referred to as *intermediate fusion*. Leveraging the high level representation found by DNN, the *deep multi-modal learning* (DML) technique was shown to achieve remarkable performance for a variety of multi-modal learning problems including audio-visual speech recognition [21,23], multi-modal activity and emotion recognition [16,24,25], image analysis from RGBD data [7,10,11], and camera and Lidar sensor fusion [6,35].

The ultimate goal of the multi-modal learning is to achieve the highest level of reliability and robustness in performing the given task using the redundant information provided by multi-modal data. This implies that when the information provided by a single modality is not sufficiently good enough, the multi-modal learning uses the complementary information delivered by the different modalities and compensates for the performance degradation. The robustness against the degraded data quality can also be readily offered by the conventional late fusion approaches which aggregate the decisions in proportion to their credibility. On the contrary, it is not obvious how the intermediate fusion for DML can enjoy such selective information combining since it is difficult for the machine learning models to judge the reliability of the intermediate features. One conceivable approach is to train the fusion network with the data set containing various types of degradation, hoping that the architecture learns to use only reliable features from the multi-modal sources. However, our empirical evaluation reveals that the existing fusion architectures are not flexible enough to adapt their fusion strategy to the variation in data quality. This quests the new DML architecture which can take the information as needed from each modality to achieve the robust performance.

This paper proposes the DML architecture that can offer robust performance for missing or degraded modalities. Towards this end, we introduce a feature-level gated information fusion (GIF) network which combines the features obtained for each modality in a way that only information relevant to the task is aggregated. The GIF network controls the amount of information flow incoming from each modality through *gating mechanism*. Specifically, the GIF network selectively gates the contribution of the features by weighting each element of features by the factor between 0 and 1. These weights are independently calculated through the separate network called weight generation (WG) network. The WG network takes all concatenated features for all modalities as an input and produces the weights by applying the convolution layers followed by the sigmoid function. In fact, this operation resembles the gating operations used in long short term memory (LSTM) [13] in that it controls the operation of information gating in a data-dependent manner. We build the deep 2D object detection architecture based on the proposed multi-modal fusion method. The proposed method first applies the multiple convolutional neural network (CNN) networks (e.g. VGG [31], ResNet [12], etc.) to generate the intermediate feature maps for the different modalities. Then, we combine these feature maps across the modalities through the proposed GIF network. The rest of the procedure to perform the object detection based on the joint feature maps found by the GIF network follows that of the single shot detector (SSD) [20].

The prior work most closely related to our work is [1], in which the similar gated fusion was used to extract the joint features from the text and image data. While the work in [1] focuses on the role of gating function for modality selection, we aim to highlight the different aspect of the gated fusion for improving the robustness of deep multi-modal fusion in the context of object detection. The key contributions of our work are highlighted below.

- We demonstrate that our gated fusion network can effectively improve the robustness of multi-modal learning. Note that developing a robust perception system using redundant sensors is a crucial problem in various safety-critical applications such as autonomous driving and mobile robot.
- We present the robust 2D object detector built upon the proposed multi-modal fusion scheme. The idea of our weighted information fusion is not limited to the object detection and can readily extended to other learning models utilizing multi-modal data.
- In order to promote the robustness of our scheme, we train our model using the special data augmentation strategy. We generate the additional examples by corrupting some of modalities in various ways (e.g. blanking, noise addition, occlusion, severe change in illumination) and guide our model to learn the way to fuse the different modalities with the proper weights.
- The experiments conducted with the SUN-RGBD dataset [32] and KITTI camera and Lidar dataset [8] show that the proposed architecture achieves

better detection accuracy than the baseline object detectors even when the subset of modalities are severely corrupted.

The rest of the paper is organized as follows. In Sect. 2, we review the previous literature on the DML. In Sect. 3, we present the details on the proposed GIF network and the robust 2D object detector based on multi-modal fusion. The experimental results are provided in Sect. 4 and the paper is concluded in Sect. 5.

2 Related Works

In this section, we briefly review the existing works on the DML methods.

2.1 Deep Multi-modal Learning

The earliest research on DML goes back to the works in [22] and [33] first showing that the effective joint data representation can be found using deep models such as deep autoencoder and deep Boltzman machine (DBM). Since then, the DML has been shown to work for a variety of learning tasks including representation learning, data fusion, translation, and alignment. (See [2] and [26] for comprehensive review on DML.) Among them, we specifically review the multi-modal data fusion due to the relevance to our work. The multi-modal fusion aims to extract as much relevant information on the task as possible from the data having heterogeneous characteristics. Since the emerging DNN is good at finding high-level semantic features through the hierarchical pipelined data processing, the intermediate fusion, which combines the features found at the middle layers of the DNN, has given rise to an effective means for multi-modal fusion.

Thus far, various DML techniques have been proposed for different types of modalities. In [22], the speech recognition was enhanced by using the joint data representation learned from the voice record and the video of lip movement. In [16], the audio feature from CNN and the visual features from the deep belief network were aggregated into single video descriptor for emotion recognition. In [21] and [24], the feature-level multi-modal fusion was shown to achieve good performance in the application to speech recognition and sentiment analysis, respectively. The DML architecture was also designed to generate the effective features for RGB-D (RGB-depth) and multi-view images. In [7], the feature vectors obtained from the fully connected (FC) layer of two separate CNNs were combined to generate the joint features for RGB-D images. In [10], the performance of the RGB-D fusion was improved by finding the effective encoding scheme for depth image. In [19], multi-level fusion architecture was proposed to learn multi-modal features for semantic segmentation.

2.2 Object Detection Using Multi-modal Data

Recently, the CNN led to remarkable performance improvement for the recognition of 2D image. Thus far, various CNN-based object detectors have been proposed. Basically, these object detectors calculate the score for the bounding box candidate and the object class based on the feature map produced by the CNN. The state-of-the-art object detectors include the faster R-CNN [29], SSD [20], YOLO [27], and YOLOv2 [28]. The object detection can be extended for the multi-modal setup. In [36], object detection based on RGB-D data was performed using the cross-modality feature found by three CNN architectures. In [14], the deep fusion scheme based on RGB-D image was proposed using the *hallucination network* which learns a new RGB image representation by mimicking the depth network. In [6], the multi-view images are constructed from raw Lidar measurement data and used to perform 3D object detection along with RGB image in the context of automated driving. In [35], the authors proposed the *point-fusion network* which predicts the corner location of the 3D bounding box based on the Lidar 3D point data.

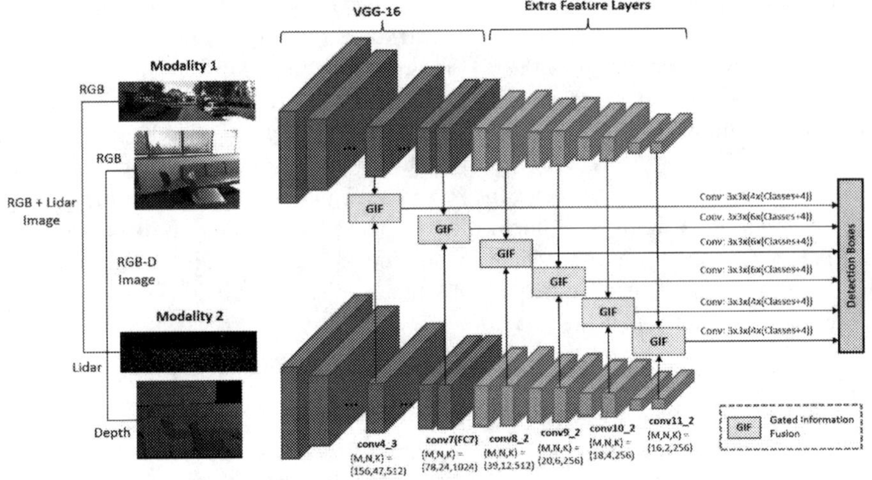

Fig. 1. Overall structure of the proposed R-DML. The R-DML takes the intermediate feature maps from both modality 1 and modality 2 using separate CNNs and combines them through the proposed GIF network. The joint feature maps produced by the GIF network are used to compute the score for object detection following the procedure of SSD.

3 Robust Deep Multi-modal Learning (R-DML)

In this section, we present our robust deep multi-modal learning (R-DML) architecture in details.

3.1 R-DML Architecture

Overall Architecture. The structure of the proposed R-DML is described in Fig. 1. Though our idea can be applied to the case of more than two modalities, we consider the example of two modalities. First, two separate CNN pipelines are used to extract the intermediate features to be fused. Each CNN consists of the CNN backbone network (e.g. VGG-16) followed by 8 extra convolutional layers. This configuration is similar to that of SSD. We combine the feature maps at the layers of conv4_3, conv7 (FC7), conv8_2, conv9_2, conv10_2, and conv11_2 layers.[1] These joint feature maps are used to perform object detection in different scales. As shown in Fig. 1, the GIF network is employed for feature-level information fusion. The GIF adjusts the contribution of the feature maps from each modality adaptively, whose detailed operation will be described next. In order to validate the benefit of the GIF, we compare our method with the baseline object detector referred to as the baseline DML (B-DML), which has the same structure as R-DML except that the combining weights in the GIF network are fixed to one.

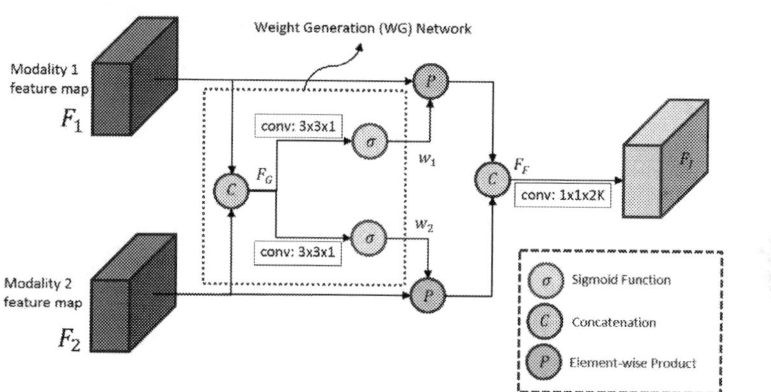

Fig. 2. The structure of the proposed GIF network. The GIF network produces the weight maps $\mathbf{w}_1$ and $\mathbf{w}_2$ by applying the convolutional layer and sigmoid function to the input features. Then, $\mathbf{w}_1$ and $\mathbf{w}_2$ are multiplied to the feature maps $\mathbf{F}_1$ and $\mathbf{F}_2$ for weighted information fusion.

Gated Information Fusion (GIF) Network. Figure 2 depicts the structure of the GIF network. The GIF network takes the intermediate feature maps from each CNN as an input and combines them with the weights calculated by the WG network. Let $\mathbf{F}_1$ and $\mathbf{F}_2$ be the $M \times N \times K$ feature maps obtained by two CNNs corresponding to two input modalities. The actual values of M, N and K for each layer are provided in Fig. 2. The GIF network consists of two parts: (1)

[1] We follow the notations of the SSD in [20].

the information fusion network and (2) the WG network. The information fusion network multiplies the $M \times N$ weight maps $\mathbf{w}_1$ and $\mathbf{w}_2$ to the feature maps $\mathbf{F}_1$ and $\mathbf{F}_2$, respectively. Such multiplication is done in element-wise for each feature map. Then, the weighted feature maps are concatenated across all modalities and $1 \times 1 \times 2K$ convolution is applied to fuse the feature maps. These operations result in the joint feature maps $\mathbf{F}_J$. Meanwhile, the WG network calculates the weights based on the input features as shown in Fig. 2. After concatenating the feature maps over all modalities, two separate $3 \times 3 \times 1$ CNN kernels $\mathbf{C}_1$ and $\mathbf{C}_2$ are applied in parallel to increase the depth in generate the high level features, which are used to calculate the combining weights[2]. Then, the sigmoid function is applied to produce the weight maps $\mathbf{w}_1$ and $\mathbf{w}_2$. We summarize the operation of the GIF network in the following equations.

$$\mathbf{F}_G = \mathbf{F}_1 \boxplus \mathbf{F}_2 \tag{1}$$

$$\mathbf{w}_1 = \sigma(\mathbf{C}_1 * \mathbf{F}_G + \mathbf{b}_1) \tag{2}$$

$$\mathbf{w}_2 = \sigma(\mathbf{C}_2 * \mathbf{F}_G + \mathbf{b}_2) \tag{3}$$

$$\mathbf{F}_F(i) = (\mathbf{F}_1(i) \odot \mathbf{w}_1) \boxplus (\mathbf{F}_2(i) \odot \mathbf{w}_2), \quad i = 1, ..., K, \tag{4}$$

$$\mathbf{F}_J = \mathit{ReLU}(\mathbf{C}_J * \mathbf{F}_F + \mathbf{b}_F) \tag{5}$$

where

- $\sigma(x) \triangleq \frac{1}{1+e^{-x}}$: sigmoid function(element-wise)
- $x * y$: convolutional layer
- $x \odot y$: element-wise product
- $x \boxplus y$: concatenation
- $\mathbf{F}(i)$: ith feature map of $\mathbf{F}$
- $\mathbf{b}_F, \mathbf{b}_1, \mathbf{b}_2$: biases of the convolution layers.

3.2 Training

Data Augmentation. In order to guide our network to learn to fuse the features appropriately in adverse environments, we design the data augmentation method. We generate the new training examples by applying various types of degradation to the subset of modalities. With such diverse training examples, our model would learn the robust multi-modal fusion. In our work, various type of modifications can be applied for data augmentation, including

- Blank Data (Type 1): we feed all pixel value to zero.
- Random occlusion (Type 2): we occlude the object using the black box whose size and location are randomly chosen.
- Severe illumination change (Type 3): we brighten the image in the rounded local region where the center and radius of the region and the brightness are randomly chosen.

[2] Our extensive experiments show that additional depth over single convolutional layer does not help improving the effectiveness of the gating operation.

- Additive random noise (Type 4): we add the random Gaussian noise where noise variance is randomly chosen within the certain range.
- No action.

The type of modification and which modalily will be degraded are chosen randomly with equal probability. Note that this data augmentation strategy is critical for our method to achieve the robust performance for the scenarios where some of modalities are corrupted.

Training Setup. Except for our data augmentation strategy, we use the same training setup used in SSD (e.g., matching strategy, hard negative mining, and multi-task loss function). We use VGG-16 pretrained model on ImageNet in two parallel CNN pipelines. The stochastic gradient descent (SGD) are used with the mini-batch size of 2 and the momentum parameter of 0.9. We set the initial learning rate to 0.0005. We set the weight decay parameter applied to L2 regularization term to 0.0005.

4 Experimental Results

In this section, we evaluate the performance of the proposed R-DML scheme using two public datasets: KITTI dataset [8] and SUN-RGBD dataset [32]. We first investigate the behavior of the gating operation to verify the effectiveness of the GIF network. Then, we compare the performance of our scheme with that of other multi-modal fusion schemes. Note that for fair comparison, we re-trained other algorithms using the same augmentation method as that used to train the R-DML. A total of 130 epochs and 200 epochs are executed with the KITTI dataset and SUN-RGBD dataset, respectively.

4.1 Datasets

KITTI Dataset. The KITTI dataset is collected by driving the car equipped with Pointgrey cameras and a Velodyne HDL-64E Lidar in various driving scenarios. The training set and test set contain 7,481 images and 7,518 images, respectively. Since the labels of the test images are not publicly available, we split the labeled training dataset into the training set and validation set by half as done in [5]. We evaluate the 2D detection performance with three object categories, i.e., car, pedestrian, and cyclist and three difficult levels, i.e., easy, moderate, hard as proposed in the KITTI Benchmark.

We consider the multi-modal fusion task which performs object detection using both RGB image and 3D lidar data. In order to preprocess the data for our object detector, we convert the 3D point cloud data into the 2D image in camera plane. The 3D point data in KITTI dataset contains the 3D coordinate (X, Y, Z) and the reflectivity R measured for each reflected laser pulse. Specifically, we map the 3D coordinate (X, Y, Z) of Lidar data into the 2D coordinate (x, y) on camera plane using

$$\begin{bmatrix} x \\ y \end{bmatrix} = calib\_matrix \cdot \begin{bmatrix} X \\ Y \\ Z \end{bmatrix}. \tag{6}$$

where $calib\_matrix$ is the matrix for coordinate transformation. Note that we quantize (x, y) to the nearest integer and limit the maximum range of (x, y) by that of camera plane. For the given 2D coordinate (x, y), we create three channel image by encoding the values of X, Z, and R to the pixel values. This creates the image with the depth, height, and intensity (DHI) channels. The pixel values for the DHI channels are obtained by

$$val_d = 255 \cdot (1 - \min[X/max\_X, 1]) \tag{7}$$
$$val_h = 255 \cdot (1 - \min[Z/max\_Z, 1]) \tag{8}$$
$$val_i = 255 \cdot (1 - \min[R/max\_R, 1]). \tag{9}$$

Note that $X \in [0, max\_X]$, $Z \in [0, max\_Z]$, and $R \in [0, max\_R]$ are mapped to the pixel values between $[0, 255]$ in a linear scale. For example, we set max_X, max_Z, and max_R to 80 m, 6 m, and 0.7. Note that the DHI Lidar image and the RGB camera image of the size 1242×375 are used as the multi-modal inputs for the proposed object detector. We apply data augmentation to these images. Since it is hard to introduce noise and illumination change to the Lidar image, we apply them only for RGB image.

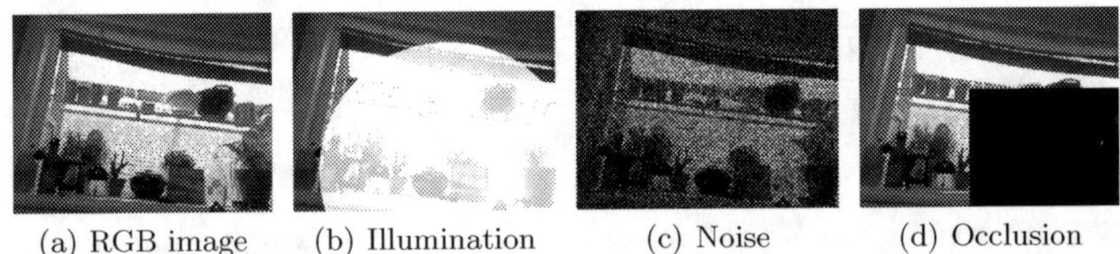

(a) RGB image (b) Illumination (c) Noise (d) Occlusion

Fig. 3. Examples of modifications applied to the camera image on SUN-RGBD dataset.

SUN-RGBD Dataset. The SUN-RGBD dataset is a large-scale RGB-D dataset collected in indoor environments. It contains 10,335 RGB image and depth image pairs including NYUDv2 depth [30], Berkeley B3DO [15], and SUN3D [34]. The dataset consists of 5,285 training set and 5,250 testing set. We evaluate the detection performance with 19 object categories as in [32]. Note that we apply the same data augmentation strategy used for the KITTI dataset and we set the size of the input image to 530×400. The examples of the modifications applied to the RGB camera image in SUN-RGBD dataset are illustrated in Fig. 3.

Extended Test Dataset. To evaluate the robustness of the proposed R-DML, we randomly generate the test dataset using the same types of data modification applied for the data augmentation. Both KITTI and SUN-RGBD datasets contain the RGB camera image while the modality 2 corresponds to the Lidar image and depth image, respectively. In our experiments, we come up with the following test cases:

- Total: Test with all normal and degraded examples together.
- RGB+modality2: Test with the normal test examples without any degradation.
- RGB (blank)+modality2: Test with the test examples with RGB image blanked.
- RGB+modality2 (blank): Test with the test examples with modality 2 blanked.
- RGB (occlusion)+modality2: Test with the test examples with RGB image occluded.
- RGB+modality2 (occlusion): Test with the test examples with modality 2 occluded.
- RGB (noise)+modality2: Test with the test examples with the noise of the RGB image changed.
- RGB (illumination)+modality2: Test with the test examples with the illumination of the RGB image changed.

Note that the performance evaluation is performed with the same number of test examples for each case.

4.2 Experimental Results on KITTI Dataset

First, we evaluate the performance of the proposed method when tested on KITTI dataset. As a baseline algorithm, the following multi-modal fusion methods are considered:

- B-DML: It has the same structure with R-DML except that both gating weights applied to two modalities are fixed to one.
- Early fusion: We concatenate two modality inputs and feed them into a single SSD.
- SSD-based fusion: We take the late fusion approach, which combines the detection boxes generated by two SSDs. Both SSDs are trained with the camera and Lidar images, separately. We combine the detection boxes found by two SSDs using non-maximum suppression.
- AVOD [17]: This is the state-of-the-art multi-modal object detection algorithm using both camera and Lidar data. Though the AVOD is capable of 3D object detection, we transform the 3D box information into the front view to compare it with our method.

Table 1 provides the average precision (AP) achieved by the algorithms of interest for *Car* category. The proposed data augmentation strategy is used for

Table 1. Detection performance (AP) for car category on the extended KITTI test dataset

Test input	Our R-DML			B-DML			Early fusion			SSD-based fusion [20]			AVOD [17]		
	Easy	Mod.	Hard	Easy	Mod.	Hard	Easy	Mod.	Hard	Easy	Mod.	Hard	Easy	Mod.	Hard
Total	**93.95**	**86.70**	**78.05**	89.86	82.21	72.21	91.10	85.65	75.83	89.69	82.03	72.96	-	-	-
RGB + Lidar	**98.69**	**90.31**	**82.16**	93.61	87.01	77.52	95.84	89.94	79.67	91.72	87.93	78.46	89.85	87.99	80.27
RGB (blank) + Lidar	88.86	78.12	69.68	86.56	74.30	64.71	**89.94**	**78.99**	69.56	87.92	77.83	69.11	86.42	69.82	**69.77**
RGB + Lidar (blank)	**97.39**	**90.29**	**81.84**	91.88	88.10	78.68	90.48	88.56	77.92	93.31	89.27	80.03	-	-	-
RGB (occl.) + Lidar	89.88	88.12	**79.03**	88.12	78.52	68.85	90.22	84.15	73.93	**91.78**	**88.22**	78.80	87.94	78.75	78.53
RGB + Lidar (occl.)	**97.72**	**90.23**	**81.94**	92.75	87.10	77.67	90.53	88.91	79.07	84.80	74.88	66.33	-	-	-
RGB (noise) Lidar	89.33	80.15	71.12	86.75	75.13	65.71	**90.18**	**81.29**	72.04	88.67	76.12	67.18	88.88	79.79	**79.46**
RGB (illum.) + Lidar	**95.82**	**89.71**	**80.58**	89.37	85.31	75.87	90.48	88.42	78.60	89.69	79.96	70.82	88.60	79.33	79.00

Table 2. Detection performance (AP) for car category on the extended KITTI test dataset with unseen types of modification

Test input	Our R-DML			B-DML		
	Easy	Mod.	Hard	Easy	Mod.	Hard
RGB + Lidar (Type1. blank)	-	-	-	-	-	-
RGB + Lidar (Type2. occl.)	**83.31**	**82.23**	**74.41**	80.50	77.37	68.89
RGB + Lidar (Type3. illum.)	**90.62**	**89.06**	**80.04**	89.70	87.22	78.59
RGB + Lidar (Type4. noise)	**83.10**	**73.34**	**65.67**	78.15	66.52	58.25

training all methods considered. The AP is evaluated using 3,740 test examples for each scenario. We observe that the proposed R-DML shows better detection accuracy than other algorithms in almost all cases. In particular, the R-DML significantly outperforms the B-DML, which shows the benefit of the proposed gated fusion method. We see that the performance gain of the R-DML over B-DML can go up to 5% of AP for some test scenarios (e.g. occlusion case). Interestingly, the proposed scheme outperforms the B-DML even when the normal KITTI data is used without any data corruption for test. Since this KITTI dataset might contain some natural but somewhat benign level of real world perturbation (e.g. camera noise and adverse illumination change), this could be a part of evidence showing that the R-DML is robust to real world perturbation as well as synthetic one. In essence, all these results show that the proposed GIF

Table 3. Detection performance (AP) on KITTI validation set. (*: trained by us, red text: ranked first, blue text: ranked second, green text: ranked third)

Method	Data	Easy	Moderate	Hard
SSD* [20]	Mono	93.31	89.27	80.03
3DOP [5]	Stereo	94.49	89.65	80.97
Mono3D [4]	Mono	95.75	90.01	80.66
Deep Manta [3]	Mono	97.58	90.89	82.72
MV3D [6]	Lidar+Mono	95.01	87.59	79.90
SSD-based fusion*	Lidar+Mono	91.72	87.93	78.46
B-DML*	Lidar+Mono	93.61	87.01	77.52
Our R-DML*	Lidar+Mono	98.69	90.31	82.16

network provides better model flexibility to improve the performance of multi-modal fusion. We evaluate the detection performance on *Pedestrian* and *Cyclist* categories as well. We obtain 70.59 (R-DML) versus 68.37 (B-DML) for moderate level for the pedestrian category and 70.11 (R-DML) versus 68.90 (B-DML) for the cyclist category. The whole results are provided in the supplemental material.

In Table 1, we have tested the models using the same type of modification used for training. However, the real world perturbation is hard to predict so that it is impossible to synthesize it in the training phase. Thus, the additional experiments are designed to evaluate how well the proposed method generalizes to the unseen types of modification. We train the models using the data augmented with the type 1 to $(i-1)$ modification and then test with the type i modification. For example, the models trained with the dataset augmented by the type 1 (blanking) and type 2 (occlusion) modification are tested with the type 3 (illumination change) modification. Table 2 shows that the R-DML achieves the performance gain over the B-DML when tested with each degradation type. This shows that the proposed method exhibits the robust behavior when encountered with unseen types of degradation.

Next, we look into the behavior of the gating operation in details. Figure 4 shows the histogram of the GIF weights (averaged over the whole weight map at the conv4_3 layer) for the case that the RGB image is completely blanked. Note that the weights multiplied to the RGB features are close to zero in order to reduce the contribution from the blanked data. On the contrary, we see that the weights for the normal Lidar image are close to one. In Fig. 5, we visualize the GIF weight maps learned by the GIF for the case where the RGB image is locally occluded by the black box. We find that the GIF weights in the camera side are small only within the locally occluded region while they are high for the rest of area. Note that the GIF weights for the Lidar image are relatively high for the whole region. This shows our gating mechanism controls the amount of information combined depending on the quality of the features for each interested region.

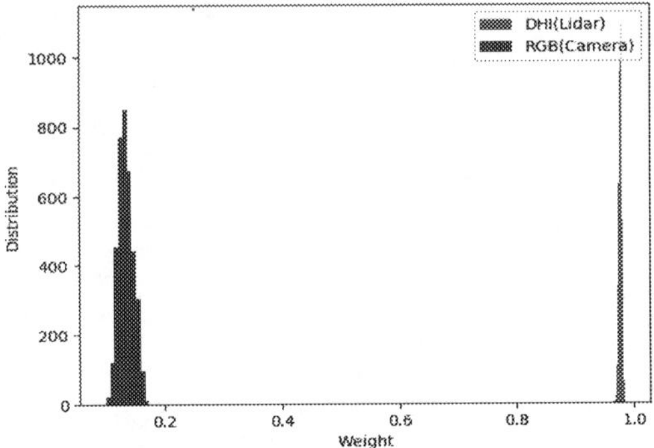

Fig. 4. The histogram of the averaged GIF weights at conv4_3 layer. The weights for the blanked data are close to zero. This demonstrates the operation for reducing the contribution from unreliable data.

(a) The locally occluded RGB image for test

(b) The weight map applied to RGB feature maps at conv4_3 layer

(c) The weight map applied to the Lidar feature maps at conv4_3 layer

Fig. 5. The visualization of the GIF weight maps at conv4_3 layer. Note that the weights for the RGB features are reduced significantly for the occluded region. This shows that the gating operation conducts locally controlled information fusion.

In Table 3, we compare the performance of the proposed method with other state of the art 2D object detectors when tested with the original KITTI dataset. The candidate detectors include SSD [20], 3DOP [5], Mono3D [4], Deep Manta [3], and MV3D [6]. For fair comparison, we use the same train/validation split method used in [3–6]. Note that SSD-based fusion, B-DML and the proposed R-DML are trained with the proposed data augmentation schemes. We observe that the performance of the proposed object detector is better or on par with the other algorithms for all difficulty levels. This shows that the proposed fusion method exhibits competitive performance for the normal environment while promising the robust performance in the adverse environment. Note that even though the proposed R-DML is built upon the baseline SSD, significant performance gain is achieved over the baseline SSD through the multi-modal fusion strategy proposed in our work. It is interesting that the B-DML does not perform better than the

SSD. This issue appears to be due to different data augmentation strategies used for training the B-DML and SSD. Due to the limitation of the SSD taking only single input modality, we could not train the SSD with our data augmentation strategy. On the other hand, the B-DML is trained with the data augmentation. We see that the B-DML does not achieve better performance than the SSD with the normal KITTI data. On the contrary when both methods are trained without data augmentation, the B-DML outperforms the SSD. Note that our R-DML significantly outperforms the B-DML and the SSD for both normal and extended KITTI datasets.

4.3 Experimental Results on SUN-RGBD Dataset

Table 4 provides the mean average precision (mAP) of the proposed object detection algorithm. Since there are not many recent 2D object detection algorithms using SUN-RGBD dataset, we compare our method with only the B-DML and supervision transfer (ST) methods [11]. The ST method is the fast-RCNN [9] based object detector which combines the detection boxes obtained by two separate object detectors. For fair comparison, we trained the B-DML and ST with the same augmentation method as that used for our R-DML. For each test case, we use the 5,250 test examples. We see in Table 4 that the proposed R-DML achieves better detection accuracy than the B-DML, which reveals the effectiveness of our gated fusion algorithm for the task of the RGB and depth image fusion as well. Note that the R-DML maintains the performance gain over the B-DML even when the normal SUN-RGBD dataset are used for test without any modification. The AP results per category are provided in the supplemental material.

Table 4. Results for detection performance (mAP) on extended SUN-RGBD test dataset

Test Input	Our R-DML	B-DML	Supervision transfer [11]
Total	**34.72**	29.13	21.35
RGB + depth	**40.43**	36.31	26.68
RGB (blank) + depth	**30.76**	28.37	15.81
RGB + depth (blank)	**32.69**	12.03	22.25
RGB (occlusion) + depth	**35.65**	29.39	22.95
RGB + depth (occlusion)	**35.04**	33.12	22.75
RGB (noise) + depth	**32.76**	31.50	16.65
RGB (illumination) + depth	**35.67**	33.19	22.40

5 Conclusions

In this paper, we proposed the robust multi-modal learning technique which fuses the intermediate features produced by the CNN with appropriate contributions. Inspired by the gating mechanism used in LSTM, we devised the gated information fusion network, which combines the features from each modality with the weights computed based on the input features to be fused. Such GIF network was used to perform 2D object detection using multi-modal inputs and the whole system is trained end-to-end. We used the special data augmentation strategy for promoting the robustness of our system, which corrupts some of modalities using various artificial operations. The experiments performed over KITTI dataset and SUR-RGBD dataset shows the superiority of the proposed method for the scenarios of missing or degraded modalities.

References

1. Arevalo, J., Solorio, T., Montes-y Gómez, M., González, F.A.: Gated multimodal units for information fusion. arXiv preprint arXiv:1702.01992 (2017)
2. Baltrušaitis, T., Ahuja, C., Morency, L.P.: Multimodal machine learning: a survey and taxonomy. IEEE Trans. Pattern Anal. Mach. Intell. **41**, 423–443 (2018)
3. Chabot, F., Chaouch, M., Rabarisoa, J., Teulière, C., Chateau, T.: Deep manta: a coarse-to-fine many-task network for joint 2D and 3D vehicle analysis from monocular image. In: Proceedings of IEEE Conference on Computer Vision Pattern Recog (CVPR) (2017)
4. Chen, X., Kundu, K., Zhang, Z., Ma, H., Fidler, S., Urtasun, R.: Monocular 3D object detection for autonomous driving. In: Proceedings of IEEE Conference on Computer Vision and Pattern Recognition (CVPR) (2016)
5. Chen, X., et al.: 3D object proposals for accurate object class detection. In: Advance in Neural Information Processing Systems (2015)
6. Chen, X., Ma, H., Wan, J., Li, B., Xia, T.: Multi-view 3D object detection network for autonomous driving. In: Proceedings of IEEE Conference on Computer Vision and Pattern Recognition (CVPR) (2017)
7. Eitel, A., Springenberg, J.T., Spinello, L., Riedmiller, M.A., Burgard, W.: Multimodal deep learning for robust RGB-D object recognition. In: Proceedings of IEEE/RSJ Interernational Conference on Intelligent Robots and Systems (IROS) (2015)
8. Geiger, A., Lenz, P., Urtasun, R.: Are we ready for autonomous driving? The kitti vision benchmark suite. In: Proceedings of IEEE Confernce on Computer Vision and Pattern Recognition (CVPR) (2012)
9. Girshick, R.: Fast R-CNN. In: Proceedings IEEE International Conference on Computer Vision (ICCV) (2015)
10. Gupta, S., Girshick, R., Arbeláez, P., Malik, J.: Learning rich features from RGB-D images for object detection and segmentation. In: Fleet, D., Pajdla, T., Schiele, B., Tuytelaars, T. (eds.) ECCV 2014. LNCS, vol. 8695, pp. 345–360. Springer, Cham (2014). https://doi.org/10.1007/978-3-319-10584-0_23
11. Gupta, S., Hoffman, J., Malik, J.: Cross modal distillation for supervision transfer. In: Proceedings of IEEE Conference on Computer Vision and Pattern Recognition (CVPR) (2016)

12. He, K., Zhang, X., Ren, S., Sun, J.: Deep residual learning for image recognition. In: Proceedings of IEEE Conference on Computer Vision and Pattern Recognition (CVPR) (2016)
13. Hochreiter, S., Schmidhuber, J.: Long short-term memory. Neural Comput. **9**(8), 1735–1780 (1997)
14. Hoffman, J., Gupta, S., Darrell, T.: Learning with side information through modality hallucination. In: Proceedings of IEEE Conference on Computer Vision and Pattern Recognition (CVPR) (2016)
15. Janoch, A., et al.: A category-level 3D object dataset: putting the kinect to work. In: Fossati, A., Gall, J., Grabner, H., Konolige, K., Ren, X. (eds.) Consumer Depth Cameras for Computer Vision. ACVPR, pp. 141–165. Springer, London (2013). https://doi.org/10.1007/978-1-4471-4640-7_8
16. Kahou, S.E., et al.: Emonets: multimodal deep learning approaches for emotion recognition in video. J. Multimodal User Interfaces **10**, 99–111 (2015)
17. Ku, J., Mozifian, M., Lee, J., Harakeh, A., Waslander, S.: Joint 3D proposal generation and object detection from view aggregation. arXiv preprint arXiv:1712.02294 (2017)
18. Lecun, Y., Bengio, Y., Hinton, G.: Deep learning. Nature **521**, 436–444 (2015)
19. Li, Y., Zhang, J., Cheng, Y., Huang, K., Tan, T.: Semantics-guided multi-level RGB-D feature fusion for indoor semantic segmentation. In: 2017 IEEE International Conference on Image Processing (ICIP) (2017)
20. Liu, W., et al.: SSD: single shot multibox detector. In: Leibe, B., Matas, J., Sebe, N., Welling, M. (eds.) ECCV 2016. LNCS, vol. 9905, pp. 21–37. Springer, Cham (2016). https://doi.org/10.1007/978-3-319-46448-0_2
21. Mroueh, Y., Marcheret, E., Goel, V.: Deep multimodal learning for audio-visual speech recognition. In: Proceedings of IEEE International Conference on Acoustics Speech and Signal Processing (ICASSP) (2015)
22. Ngiam, J., Khosla, A., Kim, M., Nam, J., Lee, H., Ng, A.Y.: Multimodal deep learning. In: Proceedings of International Conference on Machine Learning (ICML) (2011)
23. Noda, K., Yamaguchi, Y., Nakadai, K., Okuno, H.G., Ogata, T.: Audio-visual speech recognition using deep learning. Appl. Intell. **42**(4), 722–737 (2015)
24. Poria, S., Cambria, E., Gelbukh, A.: Deep convolutional neural network textual features and multiple kernel learning for utterance-level multimodal sentiment analysis. In: Proceedings of Conference Empirical Methods in Natural Language Processing, pp. 2539–3544 (2015)
25. Radu, V., Lane, N.D., Bhattacharya, S., Mascolo, C., Marina, M.K., Kawsar, F.: Towards multimodal deep learning for activity recognition on mobile devices. In: Proceedings of 2016 ACM Interernational Joint Confernce on Pervasive and Ubiquitous Computing, pp. 185–188 (2016)
26. Ramachandram, D., Taylor, G.W.: Deep multimodal learning. IEEE Signal Process. Mag. **34**(6), 96–108 (2017)
27. Redmon, J., Divvala, S., Girshick, R., Farhadi, A.: You only look once: unified, real-time object detection. In: Proceedings of IEEE Confernce on Computer Vision and Pattern Recognition (CVPR) (2016)
28. Redmon, J., Farhadi, A.: Yolo9000: better, faster, stronger. In: Proceedings of IEEE Conference on Computer Vision and Pattern Recognition (CVPR) (2017)
29. Ren, S., He, K., Girshick, R., Sun, J.: Faster R-CNN: Towards real-time object detection with region proposal networks. In: Advances in Neural Information Processing Systems (2015)

30. Silberman, N., Hoiem, D., Kohli, P., Fergus, R.: Indoor segmentation and support inference from RGBD images. In: Fitzgibbon, A., Lazebnik, S., Perona, P., Sato, Y., Schmid, C. (eds.) ECCV 2012. LNCS, vol. 7576, pp. 746–760. Springer, Heidelberg (2012). https://doi.org/10.1007/978-3-642-33715-4_54
31. Simonyan, K., Zisserman, A.: Very deep convolutional networks for large-scale image recognition. arXiv preprint arXiv:1409.1556 (2014)
32. Song, S., Lichtenberg, S.P., Xiao, J.: Sun RGB-D: a RGB-D scene understanding benchmark suite. In: Proceedings of IEEE Conference on Computer Vision and Pattern Recognition (CVPR) (2015)
33. Srivastava, N., Salakhutdinov, R.: Multimodal learning with deep boltzmann machines. J. Mach. Learn. Res. **15**, 2949–2980 (2014)
34. Xiao, J., Owens, A., Torralba, A.: Sun3D: a database of big spaces reconstructed using SFM and object labels. In: Proceedings of IEEE International Conference on Computer Vision (ICCV) (2013)
35. Xu, D., Anguelov, D., Jain, A.: Pointfusion: deep sensor fusion for 3D bounding box estimation. In: Proceedings of IEEE Conference on Computer Vision and Pattern Recognition (CVPR) (2017)
36. Xu, X., Li, Y., Wu, G., Luo, J.: Multi-modal deep feature learning for RGB-D object detection. Pattern Recogn. **72**, 300–313 (2017)

Hardware-Aware Softmax Approximation for Deep Neural Networks

Xue Geng[1(✉)], Jie Lin[1], Bin Zhao[2], Anmin Kong[2], Mohamed M. Sabry Aly[3], and Vijay Chandrasekhar[1]

[1] I²R, A*STAR, Singapore, Singapore
geng_xue@i2r.a-star.edu.sg
[2] IME, A*STAR, Singapore, Singapore
[3] School of CSE, NTU, Singapore, Singapore

Abstract. There has been a rapid development of custom hardware for accelerating the inference speed of deep neural networks (DNNs), by explicitly incorporating hardware metrics (*e.g.*, area and energy) as additional constraints, in addition to application accuracy. Recent efforts mainly focused on linear functions (matrix multiplication) in convolutional (Conv) or fully connected (FC) layers, while there is no publicly available study on optimizing the inference of non-linear functions in DNNs, with hardware constraints.

In this paper, we address the problem of cost-efficient inference for *Softmax*, a popular non-linear function in DNNs. We introduce a **hardware-aware linear approximation** framework by algorithm and hardware co-optimization, with the goal of minimizing the cost in terms of area and energy, without incurring significant loss in application accuracy. This is achieved by simultaneously reducing the operand bit-width and approximating cost-intensive operations in Softmax (*e.g.* exponential and division) with cost-effective operations (*e.g.* addition and bit shifts). We designed and synthesized a hardware unit for our approximation approach, to estimate the area and energy consumption. In addition, we introduce a training method to further save area and energy cost, by reduced precision. Our approach reduces area cost by 13× and energy consumption by 2× with 11-bit operand width, compared to baseline at 19-bit for VOC2007 dataset in Faster R-CNN.

Keywords: Softmax · Nonlinear operation · Power · Area

1 Introduction

Modern deep neural networks (DNNs) have achieved remarkable success in a broad of computer vision applications including image classification, object detection and instance segmentation, at the cost of huge amount of weights and activations. For instance, AlexNet-7 [19] has about 60M parameters, VGG-16 [27]

X. Geng and J. Lin—Both authors contributed equally to this work.

C. V. Jawahar et al. (Eds.): ACCV 2018, LNCS 11364, pp. 107–122, 2019.
https://doi.org/10.1007/978-3-030-20870-7_7

138M and ResNet-101 [14] 45M. There has been a rapid development of custom hardware for accelerating inference of DNNs at scale, such as Application-Specific Integrated Circuits (ASICs) - EIE [11], Eyeriss [5] and Google Tensor Processing Unit (TPU) [18]. On the other hand, plenty of work has been proposed to save hardware resources in terms of chip area and power, by reducing precision of operands (*e.g.*, DoReFa-Net [30], BinaryNet [6], XNOR-Net [25] and ternary quantization [31]), or reducing number of matrix multiplication operations (*e.g.*, compact networks like SqueezeNet [17] and MobileNet [16], or network pruning [12,15]). This in turn enables higher inference throughput, given limited hardware resources. For example, TPU [18] performs 8-bit integer multiplication for Conv and FC layers, enabling order of magnitude reduction in energy consumption. EIE [11] supports higher inference rate by pruning weights in FC layers, with lower energy and area cost.

However, these work mainly focused on linear matrix operations in Conv and FC layers which account for over 99% of total operations in modern DNNs [29]. To the best of our knowledge, no public study is available on optimizing the inference of non-linear blocks (*e.g.*, Softmax and Sigmoid) in DNNs with hardware constraints. Compared to linear operations in Conv and FC, nonlinear blocks pose unique challenges for hardware implementation. First, a Conv operation using a multiplier and an adder, is much cheaper than nonlinear functions like exponential, which usually requires either a complex hardware unit or an iterative routine in programmable hardware. Second, in current hardware accelerators, the compute ratio per unit area for nonlinear blocks is order of magnitude lower than that for Conv and FC layers, resulting in inefficient use of the chip area (*e.g.*, 20% of the total area allocated for compute operations is used by nonlinear unit, which only account for less than 1% of total operations in DNNs).

In this paper, we aim to address the problem of cost-efficient inference for *Softmax*, a popular non-linear function in a wide range of network architectures. We make the following contributions.

- We propose a framework of **hardware-aware linear approximation** for Softmax, with the goal of minimizing the design cost in terms of area and energy consumption, without incurring significant loss in application accuracy. The framework simultaneously reduces the operand bit-width and approximates cost-intensive operations in Softmax (*e.g.* exponential and division) with cost-effective operations (*e.g.*, addition and bit shifts).
- We develop a training approach to further save the chip area and energy cost with aggressively reduced bit-width of Softmax operands, by clipping Softmax input in a small range.
- We design and synthesize a hardware unit for our approximation approach to estimate area and energy costs. We present a comprehensive analysis of the impact of operand bit-width and operations on performance accuracy and hardware metrics. With comparable object detection and instance segmentation accuracy, our approach reduces area cost by 13× and energy cost by 2× with 11-bit operand width, compared to baseline at 19-bit.

We argue that our approach is not explicit to Softmax function. Many other nonlinear blocks in DNNs such as *Tanh*, *Sigmoid* can leverage our linear approximation approach. For instance, several of these nonlinear functions include exponential operation, rendering our approach a natural fit for approximating them at lower hardware cost.

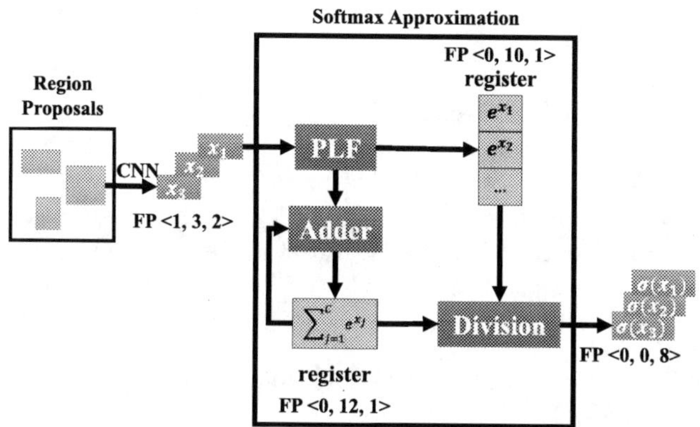

Fig. 1. The overall architecture for hardware-aware Softmax approximation. PLF - Piecewise Linear Function. FP - Fixed-point. Numbers in point bracket represent sign bit, integer bits and fractional bits respectively.

The paper is organized as follows. Section 2 describes background, motivation and overview of our approach. In Sect. 3, we explore the search space of operand bit-widths. Section 4 introduces several cost-effective operations for approximating Softmax. Section 5 presents a training approach for further reduction of hardware cost. We evaluate the performance in Sect. 6. Sections 7 and 8 are related work, conclusions and future work.

2 Background and Motivation

Softmax is a common building block for many DNN-based computer vision applications [8,13,26],

$$\sigma(x_c) = \frac{e^{x_c}}{\sum_{j=1}^{C} e^{x_j}}, \tag{1}$$

where C represents the number of classes and x is a C-dimensional input vector with arbitrary real-values. For image classification task, Softmax normalizes the C-dimensional input vector, so that all the entries add up to 1. For region-based object detection (*e.g.*, Faster R-CNN [26] and R-FCN [8]) and instance segmentation (*e.g.*, MNC [7] and Mask R-CNN [13]), Softmax generates a C-dimensional normalized confidence scores for each region proposal independently. Subsequently, for each class, the proposals are sorted by their scores, followed by non-maximum suppression (NMS) to filter overlapped ones.

Different from linear operations (*e.g.* matrix-matrix (matrix-vector) multiplication in Conv and FC layers), it is costly to implement nonlinear Softmax function in hardware. A single Conv operation is actually cheaper than Softmax or exponential. Conv uses a multiplier and an adder, while exponential requires either a complex hardware unit or an iterative routine in programmable hardware. As a result, more multipliers and adders can be placed in the same area to sustain the required CONV operations, compared to units that perform Softmax. Integrating numerous nonlinear operations, which may be required to improve the application runtime, consumes considerable hardware resources.

Take Google TPU [18] as an example, 20% of the total area allocated for computing resources is for non-linear functions – the remaining 80% is for CONV and FC operations. On the other hand, Conv (FC) layers account for over 99% of total operations in modern DNNs, versus less than 1% for nonlinear operations. One can see that the Compute Ratio Per Unit Area for nonlinear unit is 25× smaller than matrix multiply for CONV (FC). Thus, reducing the area of nonlinear unit by 10× leads to more efficient use of chip area, *e.g.*,

- faster nonlinear operation by integrating many such modules (*i.e.*, fostering parallel execution); or
- higher convolution rate by reclaiming the saved area to add more CONV hardware resources.

This motivates us to develop cost-efficient approximation method for Softmax in DNNs, from both algorithm and hardware perspectives. Towards lower area and energy cost, the key is to approximate Softmax with simple yet efficient linear operations - (1) approximate cost-intensive arithmetic operations (*e.g.*, exponential, division in Eq. 1.) with cost-effective operations (*e.g.* addition, logical operations) and (2) minimize the bit-width of operands in the operations. Figure 1 shows the overall flow for computing Softmax in simplified hardware architecture. This architecture contains several modules including the piecewise function (PLF), accumulation (Adder) and division (Division) with respective memory registers for storing intermediate operands.

It is worthy noting that we do not consider the complex polynomial approximation methods such as Taylor series [24] for exponential function, which would introduce many multiplication operations in order to preserve high accuracy. As compared to simple arithmetic operations like addition, multiplication leads to much higher energy and area cost, especially when the operand bit-width is large. For instance, 32-bit fixed-point addition can be 30× less energy and 25× less area than 32-bit fixed-point multiplication [9].

3 Exploring the Search Space of Operand Bit-Width

Representing operands in fixed-point precision with short bit-width would reduce energy consumption and area cost ref. Figure 1. Figure 2(b) shows an example of fixed-point representations for Softmax input x_c, output $\sigma(x_c)$ and intermediate values (*i.e.* the numerator e^{x_c} and the denominator $\sum_{j=1}^{C} e^{x_j}$). Once the number

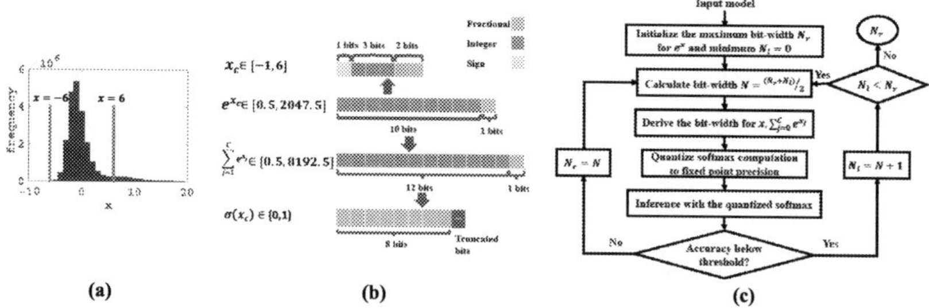

Fig. 2. (a) Distribution of Softmax input x. (b) Example of fixed-point representations for Softmax input x_c, output $\sigma(x_c)$ and intermediate values (*i.e.* the numerator e^{x_c} and the denominator $\sum_{j=1}^{C} e^{x_j}$). (c) Flow of binary search for the minimal operand bit-width that does not cause loss in application accuracy.

of integer bits of operand e^{x_i} is fixed as N, the integer bits for input $\mathbf{x}$ can be derived as follows.

$$N_{\mathbf{x}}^{I} = \lceil \log_2(\ln 2^N) \rceil \tag{2}$$

As we know, the negative part of x_i will decide the fractional part of e^{x_i}[1]. It is an asymmetric boundary. It is noteworthy that theoretically the bit-width for denominator is decided by the number of additions and bit-width of e^{x_i}. To shorten its bit-width, a data-driven manner is deployed to explore the minimum value. The range of $\sigma(x_c)$ is in $(0, 1)$, thus it only requires a small number of fractional bits truncated from the number computed by the division operation.

There is a trade-off between operand bit-width and application accuracy. We introduce an accuracy-aware approach to explore the minimal operand bit-width in Softmax. Figure 2(c) shows the flow of the minimal operand bit-width searching. It starts from an initialized integer bit N for e^{x_i}. With an input network model, each loop consists of reducing the integer bits for e^{x_i}, x_c and $\sum_{j=1}^{C} e^{x_j}$, quantizing Softmax with derived precision, followed by inference with the quantized Softmax.

4 Approximating Softmax Operation

The computation of Softmax can be roughly decomposed into 3 steps: the exponential function, the accumulation in the denominator and division. In this section, we introduce various cost-efficient strategies to approximate the exponential function and division respectively (see Fig. 3(a)). Finally, we integrate different operations for approximating Softmax.

Lookup Table of e^x (LUT-EXP). To approximate e^{x_i}, a straight-forward approach is to create a lookup table (LUT) which stores the fixed-point number of e^{x_i} over a discrete subset of x_i (see Fig. 3(b)). As analyzed in Sect. 3, once

[1] The fractional bits of e^{x_i} and x are fixed at small numbers (less than 2) as they contribute less to the precision, as compared to the integer bits.

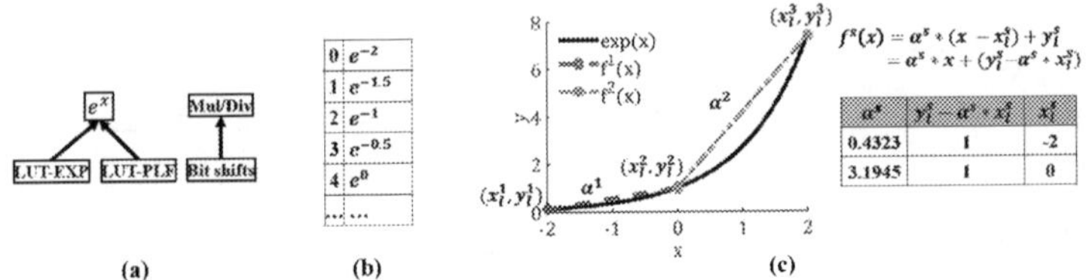

Fig. 3. (a) Approximate the exponential function and the division operation in Softmax function, respectively. (b) Lookup Table of e^x (LUT-EXP). (c) Piecewise Linear Function (LUT-PLF) for approximating e^{x_i}. Note that the entries in LUT are stored with fixed-point representations.

the integer bits of fixed-point operand e^{x_i} is fixed, we can derive the number of integer bits for the fixed-point input x_i as well as its range $x \in [x_l, x_r]$ that precise to a quantum of 1 (Fig. 2(a)–(b)). This would also determine the size of LUT-EXP, *i.e.* 2^{N_x} entries computed by e^{x_i}, where x_i is uniformly sampled in $[x_l, x_r]$ with a fixed step size.

Piecewise Linear Function (LUT-PLF). One drawback of LUT-EXP is the number of entries in the table increases exponentially with the bit-width of fixed-point input x. The larger the table size, the higher energy cost for memory access and bigger area cost for storage. To alleviate this issue, an alternate approach is Piecewise Linear Function (PLF), which typically approximates nonlinear function with a small number of line pieces [1,23]. In geometry, PLF approximates e^x with S continuous pieces uniformly defined over a finite range of $x \in [x_l^1, x_r^S]$, each of those pieces is an affine function with slope α^s

$$
\begin{aligned}
f^s(x) = \alpha^s * (x - x_l^s) + y_l^s = \alpha^s * x + (y_l^s - \alpha^s * x_l^s) \\
x \in [x_l^s, x_r^s], \quad y_l^s = e^{x_l^s}, \quad s \in [1, S]
\end{aligned}
\tag{3}
$$

A LUT of affine functions is built to store the value of x_l^s, α^s and the pre-computed $y_l^s - \alpha^s * x_l^s$ (see Fig. 3(c)). The number of bits for x_l^s and α^s is the same as input x, while $y_l^s - \alpha^s * x_l^s$ is the same as e^{x_i}. Given x, the entry nearest to x is chosen for computing the approximate value $f^s(x)$ in Eq. 3. The cost of computing $f^s(x)$ contains 1 multiply ($\alpha^s * x$) and 1 addition. At last, the minimal number of pieces S is determined in a similar way to the data-driven binary search of minimal operand bit-width introduced in Sect. 3.

Implement Multiplication and Division by Bit Shifts. The multiply term $\alpha^s * x$ in Eq. 3 can be simply implemented by bit shifts, via approximating α^s with the closet 2^b where b is an integer constant. Similarly, bit shifts is able to approximate the division operation in Eq. 1 by replacing the denominator with 2^b. Bit shifts can largely reduce energy/ares cost induced by multiplication and division, especially when the operand bit-width is large.

Approximate Softmax as a Whole. By assembling the 3 steps together, there are 6 possible combinations for Softmax approximation in total show in Table 1.

Table 1. Method naming and definitions.

Method names	Definition
Approx_A	Exponential function is implemented by the look-up table
Approx_B	Exponential function is implemented by the look-up table, while Division operation is implemented by bit shifting
Approx_C	Exponential function is implemented by piecewise linear function
Approx_D	Exponential function is implemented by piecewise linear function, in which the coefficients are power of two
Approx_E	Exponential function is implemented by piecewise linear function, while Division operation is implemented by bit shifting
Approx_F	Exponential function is implemented by piecewise linear function, in which the coefficients are power of two; While Division operation is implemented by bit shifting

And all method names appeared in text would refer to this table. In Sect. 6, we evaluate the performance (accuracy, energy/area cost) of Softmax approximation variants with varied operand bit-widths, on a wide range of network architectures as well as benchmarks. We observe that method Approx_D achieves the optimal tradeoff between accuracy and energy/area cost, especially at low operand bit-width.

5 Training with Softmax Approximation

The integration of LUT-PLF operation with the minimal operand bit-width trades off energy/area cost against application accuracy. If further reducing the operand bit-width, the energy/area cost is even lower, but there is a significant drop in accuracy. In this section, we propose a hybrid training method to simulate Softmax approximation error in the forward pass during training, which is able to adapt the network to the approximation method and retain accuracy even aggressively reducing operand bit-width.

Clipped Input for Aggressive Bit-Width Reduction. One can see from Eq. 3 that the range of y_l^s depends on the range of x_l^s. For instance, to avoid the loss of range and precision when comparing with floating point number representations, the minimal number of integer bits for $e^{y_l^s}$ is 18-bit for $x_l^s \in [-12, 12]$. This number dramatically drops to 10-bit when $x_l^s \in [-6, 6]$. To reduce bit-width for lower energy/area cost, a clipping operation is operated on input x, which is bounded in an asymmetric range $[-\hat{\gamma}, \gamma]$

$$h(x) = min(max(x, -\hat{\gamma}), \gamma), \tag{4}$$

where $\hat{\gamma}$ and γ are pre-defined positive thresholds. Note that $\hat{\gamma}$ is usually smaller than γ due to the asymmetric distribution of input x (see Fig. 2(a)).

Algorithm 1. Training with Softmax Approximation through STE

Initialization: DNN model weights M, input range $(-\hat{\gamma}, \gamma)$ and number of pieces S.
foreach s *in* S *pieces* **do**
  Derive x_l^s,x_r^s,
  $y_l^s = e^{x_l^s}$, $y_r^s = e^{x_r^s}$,
  $\alpha^s = \frac{y_r^s - y_l^s}{x_r^s - x_l^s}$.
end
foreach *batch* **do**
  foreach x_i *in input vector* $\boldsymbol{x}$ **do**
    Find relevant piece in LUT-PLF $s^* = \underset{s}{\text{argmin}}(x_i - x_l^s)$. $s.t., x_i > x_l^s$.
    $e^{x_i} \leftarrow y^{s^*}(x_i) = \alpha^{s^*} * (x_j - x_l^{s^*}) + y_l^{s^*}$
  end
  Calculate Softmax $\sigma(x_i) = \frac{y^{s^*}(x_i)}{\sum_j y^{s^*}(x_j)}$.
  Compute gradients of Softmax layer using STE.
  Update parameters M.
end
return M

Hybrid Training. One approach to compensate the loss in accuracy induced by Softmax approximation is to train the network by taking the approximation error into account. This can be accomplished by simulating the Softmax approximation in the forward pass, while the backward pass remains as usual. More specifically, the forward pass computes Softmax using the approximation method Approx_D with the clipped x as input. The hybrid training is described in Algorithm 1. As Eqs. 4 and 3 are non-differentiable functions, we use Straight Through Estimator (STE) [2] to enable the back-propagation. Note that the hybrid training method can be used to study the effect of aggressively reducing the minimal number of pieces S in LUT-PLF.

6 Experiments

We evaluate the performance on two challenging tasks: object detection and instance segmentation. First, we study the impact of operand bit-width on application performance, without approximating Softmax operation. Second, we evaluate the 6 Softmax approximation variants with floating point precision. Third, we perform the ASIC RTL simulation to measure the energy/area cost, as a function of operand bit-width and approximation operations. Finally, we perform extensive experiments on various benchmarks to verify the advantages of the training with aggressive bit-width reduction via clipped input x using Caffe on a NVIDIA Tesla V100 GPU.

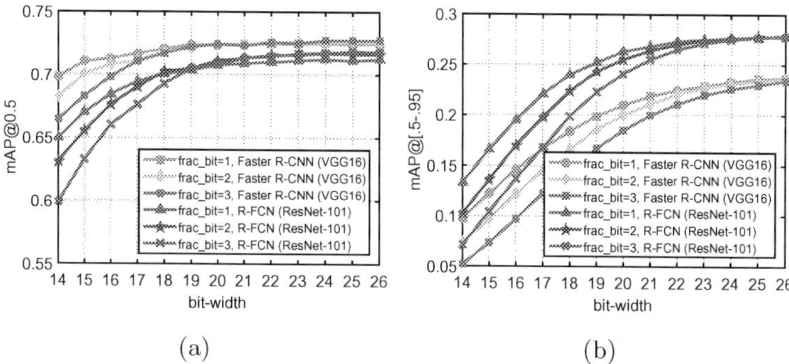

Fig. 4. (a) Object detection accuracy for Faster R-CNN (VGG16) and R-FCN (ResNet-50) on VOC2007, with varied bitwidths for operand e^{x_i}, including sign bit, integer bits and fractional bits. (b) Object detection accuracy for Faster R-CNN (VGG16) and R-FCN (ResNet-101) on COCO2014, with varied bit-widths for operand e^{x_i}. The number of fractional bits of e^{x_i} is varied from [1,2,3].

Datasets. For object detection, we evaluate our method on 2 standard benchmark datasets - PASCAL VOC2007 [10] and MS COCO2014 [20]. The VOC2007 dataset consists of about 5k train-val images and 5k test images over 20 object categories, while the MS COCO2014 dataset contains 80 foreground object classes and one background class. The training set has about 80 K images, and 5 K images for mini validation set. For instance segmentation, the models are trained on the PASCAL VOC 2012 training set, and evaluated on validation set.

Models and Metrics. For object detection, we integrate the Softmax approximation into Faster R-CNN [26] and R-FCN [8]. Following the standard protocol, we report results on VOC2007 test set using mean Average Precision (mAP) with IoU thresholds at 0.5 (denoted as mAP@0.5) and MS COCO2014 minival set using mAP averaged for IoU $\in$ [0.5 : 0.05 : 0.95] (denoted as mAP@[.5, .95]). For instance segmentation, the model MNC [7] is selection. The results are reported on VOC 2012 validation set using mAP with thresholds at 0.5 and 0.7 (denoted as mAP@0.5 and mAP@0.7).

6.1 Impact of Operand Bit-Width

Figures 4a and b evaluate the impact of operand bit-width (for e^{x_i}) on object detection, in terms of mAP@0.5 and mAP@[.5, .95] for VOC2007 and COCO2014 respectively. Besides, we also study the effect of the fractional bits for the fixed point of e^{x_i}. For clarity, we do not approximate Softmax operation when evaluating operand bit-width. We make the following observations - (1) the detection accuracy increases with the number of operand bit-width. (2) when the bit-width is at low range (*e.g.*, 15), the model with less fractional bits performs better. (3) when the bit-width is at large range (*e.g.*, 23), the model with more fractional bits performs slightly better. (4) for Faster-RCNN (VGG16), the bit-widths with comparable accuracy on VOC2007 and COCO2014 are different (the latter is larger). The possible reason is when the dataset becomes more challenging (*e.g.*, the number of targeted classes increases), the model would require more bits to preserve the application accuracy. (5) to maintain the detection accuracy, Faster-RCNN (VGG16) requires 19 bits (18 bits for integer part and 1 bit for fractional part), while R-FCN (ResNet-50) 22 bits, due to the fact that the distribution of input x from ResNet-50 is wider than that from VGG16.

Table 2. Object detection accuracy on VOC2007 and COCO2014 and instance segmentation accuracy on VOC 2012, with the 6 Softmax approximation variants.

Methods		Min. table size	VOC2007 mAP@0.5		COCO2014 mAP@[.5-.95]		VOC2012 mAP@0.5
e^{x_i}	$\sum e^x$		Faster R-CNN	R-FCN (ResNet50)	Faster R-CNN	R-FCN (ResNet101)	MNC (VGG16)
LUT-PLF	2^n	32	69.84	70.31	21.30	26.50	63.75
	/	32	72.30	71.69	24.10	28.10	64.65
LUT-PLF-B	2^n	32	68.12	68.86	20.80	25.10	64.27
	/	32	72.06	71.37	23.70	27.90	62.96
LUT-EXP	2^n	128	69.95	69.82	20.20	25.50	62.52
	/	128	72.68	71.64	24.10	27.40	64.40
e^{x_i}	/	-	72.52	71.76	24.20	28.20	63.50

6.2 Evaluations on Softmax Approximation Variants

Table 2 reports object detection accuracy on VOC2007 and COCO2014, and instance segmentation accuracy on VOC 2012, with the 6 Softmax approximation variants. At inference stage, we replace the exponential function in Softmax layer with either LUT-PLF or LUT-EXP, and the Division operation with bit shifts. The minimal LUT size for each Softmax approximation is derived by using the binary search algorithm described in Sect. 3. All experiments are performed in floating point precision.

We observe that (a) all LUT based approaches perform comparable to Softmax (the last row) in terms of accuracy, across different datasets and tasks; (b) bit shifts for approximating the division operation introduces considerable loss in accuracy, while it works well for approximating the multiplication in LUT-PLF (*i.e.* LUT-PLF-B). This might be because the bit shifts for division brings in higher approximation error, and (c) the table size of 4 times smaller than LUT-EXP, while with comparable accuracy.

6.3 Tradeoff Between Energy/Area Cost and Accuracy

Hardware Evaluation Methodology. We design ASIC RTL to simulate the Softmax approximation algorithms and measure the energy and area cost. All approaches are written in Verilog and is kept consistent with the algorithm model. We adopted logic gates to store LUT, because using memory to store lookup table is not efficient for the silicon area if table size is less than $1k$ entries. Registers are deployed for temporary storage of exponential value. The Cadence RTL compiler is deployed for synthesis with UMC 65 nm standard cell library. The power and area consumption are estimated with synthesis result under the condition of 500 MHz clock Synthesizers.

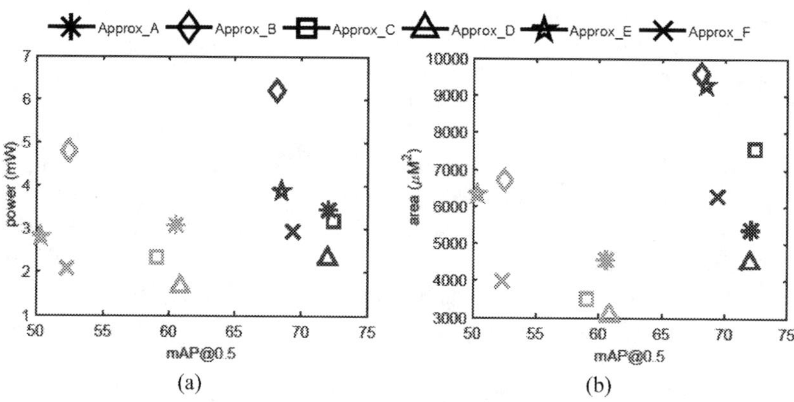

Fig. 5. Comparisons of 6 Softmax approximation variants with 2 operand bit-widths for Faster-RCNN (VGG16) model. (a) Trade-off between accuracy and power; and (b) Trade-off between accuracy and area. Green color represents 11-bit width for operand e^{x_i}, **Blue** 19-bit. (Color figure online)

Energy and Area Cost. Figure 5 reports energy and area cost with 2 operand bit-widths (11-bit and 19-bit) for e^{x_i}, for Faster-RCNN (VGG16) on VOC2007. We evaluate all the Softmax approximation variants. One can observe that (a) the energy/area cost is reduced as bit-width increases, (b) in most cases, the performance trend of area cost is consistent with energy cost, (c) among the 6 Softmax approximation variants, Approx_D achieves the optimal tradeoff between accuracy and energy/area cost, compared to the rest, (d) Approx_E and Approx_B performs the worst in terms of energy and area cost, as the search of n that 2^n is closet to the summation value in denominator costs considerable power.

Energy Breakdown. Figure 6 further studies the energy breakdown into cost-intensive operations including memory access, division and LUT-PLF (or LUT-EXP), for the 6 Softmax approximation variants. We observe that (a) memory

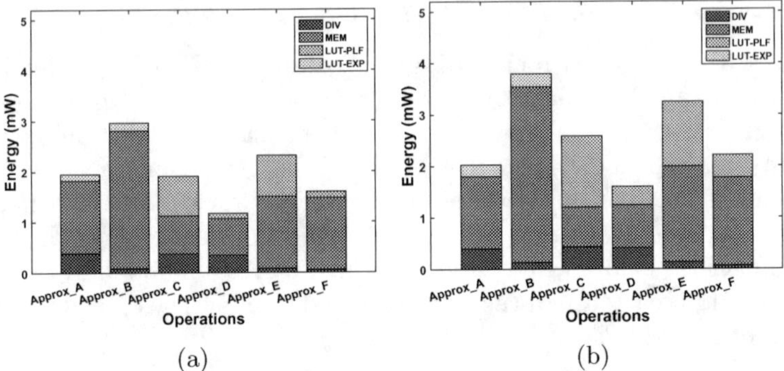

Fig. 6. Energy breakdown into cost-intensive operations on operand e^{x_i}. (a) 11-bit width; and (b) 19-bit width. There are 4 operations being evaluated, including division (DIV), memory access (MEM), LUT-PLF and LUT-EXP.

access, LUT-PLF and division consume most of energy during inference; (b) the energy consumption of all operations increases with bit-width, and memory access is the one with the most significant increase; (c) the shift operation in LUT-PLF-B saves some energy cost, compared to LUT-PLF and (d) DIV-B costs more power as compared to original DIV. It is because that memory access increases when it dynamically computes the closest value to the denominator.

Table 3. Performance of aggressive bit-width reduction with or without training, in terms of accuracy and energy/area cost, for Faster R-CNN (VGG16) on VOC2007. $*$ denotes measurements of area/energy are performed on e^{x_i} only.

Methods	mAP @0.5	Min. table size	Bit-width				Area* (μm²)	Power* (mW)
			x_i	e^{x_i}	$\sum_{j=1}^{C} e^{x_j}$	$\sigma(x_i)$		
Clip ($\gamma = 12$)	71.98	6	(1,4,2)	(0,18,1)	(0,20,1)	(0,0,8)	262	0.116
Clip ($\gamma = 6$)	54.18	2	(1,3,2)	(0,10,1)	(0,12,1)	(0,0,8)	19	0.067
Clip + Train ($\gamma = 6$)	70.58	2	(1,3,2)	(0,10,1)	(0,12,1)	(0,0,8)	19	0.067

6.4 Evaluations on Clipped Training

We evaluate the aggressive bit-width reduction with or without training using the clipped input x (*i.e.* Bounded Approx_D), and compare to the best Softmax approximation (*i.e.* Approx_D). Results are reported on 3 benchmarks for both object detection and instance segmentation, with the minimal number of LUT size as usual. The numbers in brackets represent the number of sign bit, integer bits and fractional bits for fixed-point number representations, respectively. It is worthy noting that the measurements of area and energy are performed on the approximation of e^{x_i} only, in order to fairly evaluate the advantages of aggressive bit-width reduction with clipped input (Clip) in Approx_D.

Table 3 reports the detection accuracy and energy/area on VOC2007. We observe that the Clip with training requires 2-3 times fewer LUT size to achieve comparable accuracy with the best baseline. The benefits of training on clipped input x is two-fold: (a) it leads to less area and energy ($2\times - 70\times$), and (b) the accuracy is dramatically improved compared to the aggressive bit-width reduction without training. These conclusions are consistent with the observations from Tables 4 and 5. The number of minimal LUT size is varied for different benchmarks. For instance, VOC2007 requires 6 entries to preserve accuracy while COCO2014 demands more. One may note that Clip + Train dropped about 5% in mAP on COCO2014, suggesting that the distribution of exponential value tends to be diverse with challenging datasets and complex tasks. Finally, results from all 3 tables show that the Softmax approximation approach generalize well in the wide range of tasks, datasets and models.

Table 4. Performance of aggressive bit-width reduction with or without training, in terms of energy and area cost, for R-FCN (ResNet-101) on COCO2014. $*$ denotes measurements of area/energy are performed on e^{x_i} only.

Methods	mAP @[.5-.95]	Min. table size	Bit-width				Area* (µm^2)	Power* (mW)
			x_i	e^{x_i}	$\sum_{j=1}^{C} e^{x_j}$	$\sigma(x_i)$		
Clip ($\gamma = 16$)	27.50	8	(1,5,2)	(0,24,1)	(0,28,1)	(0,0,8)	1020	0.598
Clip ($\gamma = 6$)	4.90	4	(1,3,2)	(0,10,1)	(0,14,1)	(0,0,8)	38	0.086
Clip + Train ($\gamma = 6$)	22.60	4	(1,3,2)	(0,10,1)	(0,14,1)	(0,0,8)	38	0.086

Table 5. Performance of aggressive bit-width reduction with or without training, in terms of accuracy and energy and area cost, for MNC (VGG16) on VOC 2012.

Methods	mAP @0.5	mAP @0.7	Min. table size	Bit-width				Area* (µm^2)	Power* (mW)
				x_i	e^{x_i}	$\sum_{j=1}^{C} e^{x_j}$	$\sigma(x_i)$		
Clip ($\gamma = 34$)	63.51	43.93	8	(1,5,2)	(0,23,1)	(0,26,1)	(0,0,8)	1049	0.641
Clip ($\gamma = 6$)	50.37	34.52	4	(1,3,2)	(0,10,1)	(0,13,1)	(0,0,8)	43	0.102
Clip + Train ($\gamma = 6$)	62.96	42.18	4	(1,3,2)	(0,10,1)	(0,13,1)	(0,0,8)	43	0.102

6.5 Discussion

In our experiments, we did not use the original softmax as a baseline as it would cost more energy. To demonstrate this, we conduct a software-based experiment. We measured the power consumption of softmax operation using a C-based implementation on CPUs using the Intel performance counter monitor toolset [28]. We find that such software-based softmax implementation consumes more than $10^3\times$ higher power (12.80 W on CPU vs. 3.78 mW with 19-bit Approx_A approximation in Table 1) than the baseline we consider in our work.

7 Related Work

Rectified Linear Unit (ReLU). A noteworthy example of function approximation in modern DNNs is ReLU, which uses piecewise linear function to replace saturated activation functions (*e.g. sigmoid* and *tanh*) [22]. ReLU is composed of 2 discontinuous pieces, the first assigns 0 to negative part of input features and the second retains the positive part. ReLU is to alleviate the vanishing gradient problem and accelerate the convergence speed during training, while our objective in this work is to design hardware-aware Softmax approximation that minimizes energy/area cost required during inference.

Softmax Approximation. In natural language modeling (*e.g.* word embedding), many Softmax approximation approaches [4] have been proposed to reduce the high complexity of computing Softmax, as the number of Softmax computation is proportional to the vocabulary size with typically more than million words. One group of work is to shortlist a subset of frequent words, thus avoid computing the normalization term over all words in the denominator of Softmax function (see Eq. 1). Examples include hierarchical tree structured Softmax [21] and differentiated Softmax [4]. Another group is to skip the expensive computation of normalization term by directly approximating it with sampling techniques like Monte-Carlo method [3].

Our work differs from these work in three-fold. (1) Objective - Most of these Softmax approximations are designed to accelerate neural network training only. Our approach is able to approximate Softmax for both inference and training. (2) Methodology - These Softmax approximation methods still compute the nonlinear Softmax function, while our method directly approximate the nonlinear function with cost-efficient linear operations in fixed-point precision, from a hardware perspective. (3) Task - Instead of language modeling, we target computer vision applications. Therefore, the design of approximation method requires different domain knowledge, for instance, hierarchical Softmax [21] builds tree structure based on word frequency in text, while our method is driven by the input and output distribution from images.

8 Conclusions and Future Work

In this work, we explored hardware-software co-optimization mechanism to approximate Softmax function in DNNs and performed extensive algorithmic and hardware synthesis experiments to demonstrate the trade-off between area/energy costs and application accuracy.

Future work includes benchmarking the Softmax approximation approach against other accelerators, extending the algorithm hardware co-optimization to other nonlinear functions such as Sigmoid and Tanh, and evaluating the hardware-aware approximation method in other application domains like language modeling. We believe that having a light-weight area-and-energy-efficient implementation of nonlinear operations is an innovative key to boost the inference rate of different DNNs – for image classification, language modeling and translation, etc. – particularly for resource constraints embedded devices.

Acknowledgement. This research is supported by the Agency for Science, Technology and Research (A*STAR) under its Hardware-Software Co-optimization for Deep Learning (Project No. A1892b0026).

References

1. Amin, H., Curtis, K.M., Hayes-Gill, B.R.: Piecewise linear approximation applied to nonlinear function of a neural network. In: IEE Proceedings-Circuits, Devices and Systems (1997)
2. Bengio, Y., Léonard, N., Courville, A.C.: Estimating or propagating gradients through stochastic neurons for conditional computation. CoRR (2013)
3. Bengio, Y., Senecal, J.S.: Adaptive importance sampling to accelerate training of a neural probabilistic language model. IEEE Trans. Neural Netw. **19**, 713–722 (2008)
4. Chen, W., Grangier, D., Auli, M.: Strategies for training large vocabulary neural language models. In: ACL (2016)
5. Chen, Y.H., Krishna, T., Emer, J.S., Sze, V.: Eyeriss: an energy-efficient reconfigurable accelerator for deep convolutional neural networks. IEEE J. Solid-State Circuits **52**, 127–138 (2017)
6. Courbariaux, M., Bengio, Y.: Binarynet: training deep neural networks with weights and activations constrained to +1 or −1. In: NIPS (2016)
7. Dai, J., He, K., Sun, J.: Instance-aware semantic segmentation via multi-task network cascades. In: CVPR (2016)
8. Dai, J., Li, Y., He, K., Sun, J.: R-FCN: object detection via region-based fully convolutional networks. In: NIPS (2016)
9. Dally, W.: High-performance hardware for machine learning. In: Cadence ENN Summit (2016)
10. Everingham, M., Van Gool, L., Williams, C.K., Winn, J., Zisserman, A.: The pascal visual object classes (voc) challenge. Int. J. Comput. Vis. **88**, 303–338 (2010)
11. Han, S., et al.: Eie: efficient inference engine on compressed deep neural network. In: ISCA (2016)
12. Han, S., Mao, H., Dally, W.J.: Deep compression: Compressing deep neural network with pruning, trained quantization and huffman coding. In: ICLR (2016)
13. He, K., Gkioxari, G., Dollár, P., Girshick, R.: Mask R-CNN. In: ICCV (2017)
14. He, K., Zhang, X., Ren, S., Sun, J.: Deep residual learning for image recognition. In: CVPR (2016)
15. He, Y., Zhang, X., Sun, J.: Channel pruning for accelerating very deep neural networks. In: ICCV (2017)
16. Howard, A.G., et al.: Mobilenets: Efficient convolutional neural networks for mobile vision applications. arXiv preprint arXiv:1704.04861 (2017)
17. Iandola, F.N., Han, S., Moskewicz, M.W., Ashraf, K., Dally, W.J., Keutzer, K.: Squeezenet: Alexnet-level accuracy with 50x fewer parameters and $<$ 0.5 MB model size. arXiv preprint arXiv:1602.07360 (2016)
18. Jouppi, N.P., et al.: In-datacenter performance analysis of a tensor processing unit. In: ISCA (2017)

19. Krizhevsky, A., Sutskever, I., Hinton, G.E.: Imagenet classification with deep convolutional neural networks. In: NIPs (2012)
20. Lin, T.-Y., et al.: Microsoft COCO: common objects in context. In: Fleet, D., Pajdla, T., Schiele, B., Tuytelaars, T. (eds.) ECCV 2014. LNCS, vol. 8693, pp. 740–755. Springer, Cham (2014). https://doi.org/10.1007/978-3-319-10602-1_48
21. Morin, F., Bengio, Y.: Hierarchical probabilistic neural network language model. In: Proceedings of the Tenth International Workshop on Artificial Intelligence and Statistics (2005)
22. Nair, V., Hinton, G.E.: Rectified linear units improve restricted boltzmann machines. In: ICML (2010)
23. Namin, A.H., Leboeuf, K., Muscedere, R., Wu, H., Ahmadi, M.: Efficient hardware implementation of the hyperbolic tangent sigmoid function. In: ISCAS (2009)
24. Nilsson, P., Shaik, A.U.R., Gangarajaiah, R., Hertz, E.: Hardware implementation of the exponential function using taylor series. In: NORCHIP, 2014 (2014)
25. Rastegari, M., Ordonez, V., Redmon, J., Farhadi, A.: XNOR-Net: ImageNet classification using binary convolutional neural networks. In: Leibe, B., Matas, J., Sebe, N., Welling, M. (eds.) ECCV 2016. LNCS, vol. 9908, pp. 525–542. Springer, Cham (2016). https://doi.org/10.1007/978-3-319-46493-0_32
26. Ren, S., He, K., Girshick, R., Sun, J.: Faster R-CNN: towards real-time object detection with region proposal networks. In: NIPS (2015)
27. Simonyan, K., Zisserman, A.: Very deep convolutional networks for large-scale image recognition. arXiv preprint arXiv:1409.1556 (2014)
28. Willhalm, T., Dementiev, R., Fay, P.: Intel performance counter monitor (2017)
29. Yang, T.J., Chen, Y.H., Sze, V.: Designing energy-efficient convolutional neural networks using energy-aware pruning. In: CVPR (2017)
30. Zhou, S., Wu, Y., Ni, Z., Zhou, X., Wen, H., Zou, Y.: DoReFa-net: training low bitwidth convolutional neural networks with low bitwidth gradients. CoRR (2016)
31. Zhu, C., Han, S., Mao, H., Dally, W.J.: Trained ternary quantization. In: ICLR (2017)

Video Object Segmentation with Language Referring Expressions

Anna Khoreva[1,2](✉), Anna Rohrbach[3], and Bernt Schiele[1]

[1] Max Planck Institute for Informatics, Saarbrücken, Germany
khoreva@mpi-inf.mpg.de
[2] Bosch Center for Artificial Intelligence, Renningen, Germany
[3] University of California, Berkeley, Berkeley, USA

Abstract. Most state-of-the-art semi-supervised video object segmentation methods rely on a pixel-accurate mask of a target object provided for the first frame of a video. However, obtaining a detailed segmentation mask is expensive and time-consuming. In this work we explore an alternative way of identifying a target object, namely by employing language referring expressions. Besides being a more practical and natural way of pointing out a target object, using language specifications can help to avoid drift as well as make the system more robust to complex dynamics and appearance variations. Leveraging recent advances of language grounding models designed for images, we propose an approach to extend them to video data, ensuring temporally coherent predictions. To evaluate our approach we augment the popular video object segmentation benchmarks, $DAVIS_{16}$ and $DAVIS_{17}$ with language descriptions of target objects. We show that our language-supervised approach performs on par with the methods which have access to a pixel-level mask of the target object on $DAVIS_{16}$ and is competitive to methods using scribbles on the challenging $DAVIS_{17}$ dataset.

Query: "A man in a red sweatshirt performing breakdance"

Fig. 1. Examples of the proposed approach. Classical semi-supervised video object segmentation relies on an expensive pixel-level mask annotation of a target object in the first frame of a video. We explore a more natural and more practical way of pointing out a target object by providing a language referring expression.

Electronic supplementary material The online version of this chapter (https://doi.org/10.1007/978-3-030-20870-7_8) contains supplementary material, which is available to authorized users.

C. V. Jawahar et al. (Eds.): ACCV 2018, LNCS 11364, pp. 123–141, 2019.
https://doi.org/10.1007/978-3-030-20870-7_8

1 Introduction

Video object segmentation has recently witnessed growing interest [3,6,15,37]. Segmenting objects at pixel level provides a finer understanding of video and is relevant for many applications, e.g. augmented reality, video editing, and rotoscoping.

Ideally, one would like to obtain a pixel-accurate segmentation of objects in video with no human input during test time. However, the current state-of-the-art unsupervised video object segmentation methods [17,40,47] have troubles segmenting the target objects in videos containing multiple objects and cluttered backgrounds without any guidance from the user. Hence, many recent works [3,15,43] employ a semi-supervised approach, where a pixel-level mask of the target object is manually annotated in the first frame and the task is to accurately segment the object in successive frames. Although this setting has proven to be successful, it can be prohibitive for many applications. It is tedious and time-consuming for the user to provide a pixel-accurate segmentation and usually takes more than a minute to annotate a single instance ([24] reports 79s for polygon annotations, precisely delineating an object would take even more). To make video object segmentation more applicable in practice, instead of costly pixel-level masks [2,29,37] propose to employ point clicks or scribbles to specify the target object in the first frame. This is much faster and takes an annotator on average 7.5s to label an object with point clicks [29] and 10s with scribbles [23]. However, on small touchscreen devices, such as tablets or phones, providing precise clicks or drawing scribbles using fingers could be cumbersome and inconvenient for the user.

To overcome these limitations we propose a new task - segmenting objects in video using language referring expressions - which is a more natural way of human-computer interaction. It is much easier for a user to say: "Segment the man in a red sweatshirt performing breakdance" (see Fig. 1), than to provide a tedious pixel-level segmentation mask or struggle with drawing a scribble which does not straddle the object boundary. Moreover, employing language specifications can make the system more robust to background clutter, help to avoid drift and better adapt to the complex dynamics inherent to videos, while not over-fitting to a particular view in the first frame (see Table 4).

We aim to investigate the capabilities and limitations of existing techniques on the proposed task and explore how far one can go while leveraging the advances in image-level language grounding and pixel-level segmentation in videos. We start by analyzing the performance of the state-of-the-art language grounding models [49,51] for localization of objects in videos via bounding boxes. We discover that they suffer from a number of issues, predicting temporally inconsistent and jittery boxes, and show a way to enhance their predictions by enforcing temporal coherency (see Fig. 3). Next we propose a convnet-based framework that utilizes referring expressions for video object segmentation task, where the output of the grounding model (bounding box) is used as a guidance for pixel-wise segmentation of the object. We also show that video object segmentation using the mask annotation on the first frame can be further improved by using language supervision, highlighting the complementarity of both modalities.

To evaluate the proposed approach we extend the popular benchmarks for segmenting single and multiple objects in videos, DAVIS_{16} [34] and DAVIS_{17} [38], with language descriptions of the target objects. We collect the annotations using two different settings, asking the annotators to provide a description of the target object based on the first frame only as well as on the full video. Future work may choose which setting they prefer to use. On average each video has been annotated with 7.5 referring expressions and it takes the annotator around 5s to provide a referring expression for a target object.

Our language-supervised approach performs on par with semi-supervised methods which have access to the pixel-accurate object mask on DAVIS_{16} and shows comparable results to the techniques that employ scribbles on the challenging DAVIS_{17} dataset.

In summary, our contributions are the following. We present a new task of segmenting objects in video using natural language referring expressions for which we augment two well-known video segmentation benchmarks with textual descriptions of target objects. We conduct an extensive analysis of the performance of the state-of-the-art language grounding models on video data and propose a way to improve their temporal coherency. To the best of our knowledge we are the first to perform an analysis of transferability of image-based grounding models to video. We show that high quality video object segmentation results can be obtained by employing language referring expressions, allowing a more natural and practical human-computer interaction. Moreover, we show that language descriptions are complementary to visual forms of supervision, such as masks, and can be exploited as an additional source of guidance for object segmentation. Thus, while proposing the new task and accompanying dataset, our work contributes the necessary benchmark analysis, a very competitive baseline and valuable insights for future work. We hope our findings would further promote the research in the field of video object segmentation via language expressions and help to discover better techniques that can be used in realistic scenarios.

2 Related Work

2.1 Grounding Natural Language Expressions

There has been an increasing interest in the task of grounding natural language expressions over the last few years [21,25,50]. We group the existing works by the type of visual domain: images and video.

Image Domain. Grounding natural language expressions is a task of localizing a given expression in an image with a bounding box [31,51] or a segmentation mask [21,25]. Referring expression comprehension is a closely related task, where the goal is to localize the non-ambiguous referring expression. Most existing approaches rely on external bounding box proposals which are scored to determine the top scoring box as the correct region [28,49]. A few recent works explore methods of inferring object regions by proposal generation network [4] or efficient subwindow search [48]. Multiple existing approaches model relationships between objects present in the scene [14,32]. In this work we choose two state-of-the-art grounding models for experimentation and analysis [49,51]. DBNet [51] frames grounding as a classification task, where an expression and an image region serve as input and a binary classification decision is an output. A key component of this approach is utilization of negative expressions and image regions to ensure discriminative training. DBNet currently leads on Visual Genome [20]. MattNet [49] is a modular network which "softly" decomposes referring expressions in three parts: subject, location, and relationship, each of which is processed by a different visual module. This allows MattNet to process referring expressions of general forms, as each module can be "enabled" or "disabled" depending on the expression. MattNet achieves top performance on RefCOCO(g/+) [31,50] both in terms of bounding box localization and pixel-wise segmentation accuracy.

Video Domain. The progress made in image-level natural language grounding leads to an increasing interest in application to video. The recent work of [22] studies object tracking in video using language expressions. They introduce a dynamic convolutional layer, where a language query is used to predict visual convolutional filters. [1] addresses object tracking in video with the language descriptions and human gaze as input. Our work falls in the same line of research, as we are exploring natural language as input for video object segmentation. To the best of our knowledge, this is the first work to apply natural language to this task. A concurrent work by [10] has addressed a task of actor/action segmentation in video based on sentence input. Their work focuses on seven classes of actors (adult, baby, etc.) and mostly action-oriented descriptions. In contrast, we consider arbitrary objects and unconstrained referring expressions.

2.2 Video Object Segmentation

Video object segmentation has witnessed considerable progress [3,19,33,40,41, 43]. In the following, we group the related work into unsupervised and semi-supervised.

Unsupervised Methods. Unsupervised methods assume no human input on the video during test time. They aim to group pixels consistent in both appearance and motion and extract the most salient spatio-temporal object tube. Several techniques exploit object proposals [19,47], saliency [9] and optical flow [33]. Convnet-based approaches [6,17,40] cast video object segmentation as a foreground/background classification problem and feed to the network both appearance and motion cues. Because these methods do not have any knowledge of the target object, they have difficulties in videos with multiple moving and dominant objects and cluttered backgrounds.

Semi-supervised Methods. Semi-supervised methods assume human input for the first frame, either by providing a pixel-accurate mask [3,41], clicks [29]

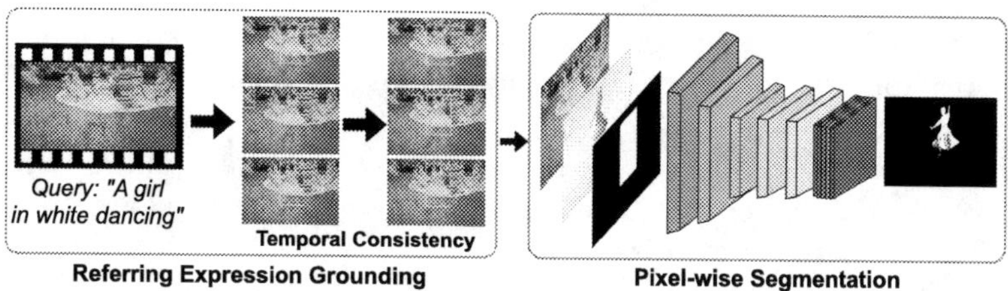

Fig. 2. System overview. We first localize the target object via grounding model using the given referring expression and enforce temporal consistency of bounding boxes across frames. Next we apply a segmentation convnet to recover detailed object masks.

or scribbles [37], and then propagate the information to the successive frames. Existing approaches focus on leveraging superpixels [46], constructing graphical models [41], utilizing object proposals [36] or employing optical flow and long-term trajectories [45]. Lately, convnets have been considered for the task [3,35,43]. These methods usually build the architecture upon the semantic segmentation networks [27] and process each frame of the video individually. [3] proposes to fine-tune a pre-trained generic object segmentation network on the first frame mask of the test video to make it sensitive to the target object. [35] employs a similar strategy, but also provides a temporal context by feeding the previous frame mask to the network. Several methods extend the work of [3] by incorporating the semantic information [30] or by integrating online adaptation [43]. [15] proposes to employ a recurrent network to exploit the long-term temporal information.

The above methods employ a pixel-level mask on the first frame. However, for many applications, particularly on small touchscreen devices, it can be prohibitive to provide a pixel-accurate segmentation. Hence, there has been a growing interest to integrate cheaper forms of supervision, such as point clicks [2,29] or scribbles [37], into convnet-based techniques. In spirit with these approaches, we aim to reduce the annotation effort on the first frame by using language referring expressions to specify the object. Our approach also builds upon convnets and exploits both linguistic and visual modalities.

3 Method

In this section we provide an overview of the proposed approach. Given a video $V = \{f_1, \ldots, f_N\}$ with N frames and a textual query of the target object Q, our aim is to obtain a pixel-level segmentation mask of the target object in every frame that it appears.

We leverage recent advances in grounding referring expressions in images [49,51] and pixel-level segmentation in videos [17,35]. Our method consists of two main steps (see Fig. 2). Using as input the textual query Q provided by the user, we first generate target object bounding box proposals for every frame of the video by exploiting referring expression grounding models, designed for images only. Applying these models off-the-shelf results in temporally inconsistent and jittery box predictions (see Fig. 3). Therefore, to mitigate this issue and make them more applicable for video data, we next employ temporal consistency, which enforces bounding boxes to be coherent across frames. As a second step, using as guidance the obtained box predictions of the target object on every frame of the video we apply a convnet-based pixel-wise segmentation model to recover detailed object masks in each frame.

3.1 Grounding Objects in Video by Referring Expressions

As discussed in Sect. 2, the task of natural language grounding is to automatically localize a region described by a given language expression. It is typically formulated as measuring the compatibility between a set of object proposals $O = \{o_i\}_{i=1}^{M}$ and a given textual query Q. The grounding model provides as output a set of matching scores $S = \{s_i\}_{i=1}^{M}$ between a box proposal and a textual query Q. The box proposal with the highest matching score is selected as the predicted region.

We employ two state-of-the-art referring expression grounding models – DBNet [51] and MattNet [49], to localize the object in each frame. Mask R-CNN [12] bounding box proposals are exploited as an initial set of proposals for both models, although originally DBNet has been designed to utilize EdgeBox proposals [8]. However, using the grounding models designed for images and picking the highest scoring proposal for each video frame lead to temporally incoherent results. Even with simple textual queries for adjacent frames that from a human perspective look very much alike, the referring model often outputs inconsistent predictions (see Fig. 3). This indicates the inherent instability of the grounding models trained on the image domain. To resolve this problem we propose to re-rank the object proposals by exploiting temporal structure along with the original matching scores given by a grounding model.

Temporal Consistency. The goal of the temporal smoothing step is to improve temporal consistency and to reduce id-switches for target object predictions across frames. Since objects tend to move smoothly through space and in time, there should be little changes from frame to frame and the box proposals should have high overlap between neighboring frames. By finding temporally coherent tracks of an object that are spread-out in time, we can focus on the predictions that consistently appear throughout the video and give less emphasis to objects that appear for only a short period of time.

The grounding model provides the likeliness of each box proposal to be the target object by outputting a matching score s_i. Then each box proposal is re-ranked based on its overlap with the proposals in other frames, the original objectness score given by [12] and its matching score from the grounding model. Specifically, for each proposal we compute a new score: $\hat{s}_i = s_i * (\sum_{j=1, j \neq i}^{M} r_{ij} * d_j * s_j / t_{ij})$, where r_{ij} measures an intersection-over-union ratio between box proposals i and j, t_{ij} denotes the temporal distance between two proposals ($t_{ij} = |f_i - f_j|$) and d_j is the original objectness score. Then, in each frame we select the proposals with the highest new score. The new scoring rewards temporally coherent predictions which likely belong to the target object and form a spatio-temporal tube. This step allows to improve temporal coherence boosting grounding and video segmentation performance (see Table 1 in Sect. 5 and Table 5 in Sect. 6) while being computational efficient (takes only a fraction of second).

3.2 Pixel-Level Video Object Segmentation

We next show how to output pixel-level object masks, exploiting the bounding boxes from grounding as a guidance for the segmentation network. The boxes are used as the input to the network to guide the network towards the target object, providing its rough location and extent. The task of the network is to obtain a pixel-level foreground/background segmentation mask using appearance and motion cues.

Approach. We model pixel-level segmentation as a box refinement task. The bounding box is transformed into a binary image (255 for the interior of the box, 0 for the background) and concatenated with the RGB channels of the input image and optical flow magnitude, forming a 5-channel input for the network. Thus we ask the network to learn to refine the provided boxes into accurate masks. Fusing appearance and motion cues allows to better exploit video data and handle better both static and moving objects.

We make one single pass over the video, applying the model per-frame. The network does not keep a notion of the specific appearance of the object in contrast to [3,35], where the model is fine-tuned during the test time to learn the appearance of the target object. Neither do we do an online adaptation as in [43], where the model is updated on its previous predictions while processing video frames. This makes the system more efficient during the inference time, which is more suitable for real-world applications.

Similar to [35], we train the network on static images, employing the saliency segmentation dataset [7] which contains a diverse set of objects. The bounding box is obtained from the ground truth masks. To make the system robust during test time to sloppy boxes from the grounding model, we augment the ground truth box by randomly jittering its coordinates (uniformly, $\pm 20\%$ of the original box width and height). We synthesize optical flow from static images by applying affine transformations for both background and foreground object to simulate the camera and object motion in the neighboring frames, as in [18]. This simple strategy allows us to train on diverse set of static images, while exploiting motion information during test time. We train the network on many triplets of RGB images, synthesized flow magnitude images and loose boxes in order for the model generalize well to different localization quality of boxes given by the grounding model and different dynamics of the object.

During inference we use the state-of-the-art optical flow estimation method Flow-Net2.0 [16]. We compute the optical flow magnitude by subtracting the median motion for each frame and averaging the magnitude of the forward and backward flow. The obtained image is further scaled to [0; 255] to maintain the same range as RGB channels.

Fig. 3. Qualitative results of language grounding with and w/o temporal consistency on DAVIS_{17}. The results are obtained using MattNet [49] trained on RefCOCO [50].

Network. As our network architecture we use ResNet-101 [13]. We adapt the network to the segmentation task following the procedure of [27] and employing atrous convolutions [5] with hybrid rates [44] within the last two blocks of ResNet to enlarge the receptive field as well as to alleviate the "gridding" issue. After the last block, we apply spatial pyramid pooling [5], which aggregates features at multiple scales by applying atrous convolutions with different rates, and augment it with the image-level features [26] to exploit better global context. The network is trained using a standard cross-entropy loss (all pixels are equally weighted). The final logits are upsampled to the ground truth resolution to preserve finer details for back-propagation.

For network initialization we use a model pre-trained on ImageNet [13]. The new layers are initialized using the "Xavier" strategy [11]. The network is trained on MSRA [7] for segmentation. To avoid the domain shift we fine-tune the model on the training sets of DAVIS_{16} [34] and DAVIS_{17} [38] respectively. We employ SGD with a polynomial learning policy with initial learning rate of 0.001, crop size of 513×513, random scale data augmentation (from 0.5 to 2.0) and left-right flipping during training. The network is trained for $20k$ iterations on MSRA and $20k$ iterations on the training set of $\text{DAVIS}_{16}/\text{DAVIS}_{17}$. During inference we employ test time augmentation as in [5].

Other Sources of Supervision. Additionally we consider variants of the proposed model using different sources of supervision. Our approach is flexible and can take advantage of the first frame mask annotation as well as language. We describe how language can be used on top of the mask supervision, improving the robustness of the system against occlusions and dynamic backgrounds (see Sect. 6 for results).

Mask. Here we discuss a variant that uses only the first frame mask supervision during test time. The network is initialized with the bounding box obtained from the object mask in the 1st frame and for successive frames uses the prediction from the preceding frame warped with the optical flow (as in [35]) to get the input box for the next frame. Following [3,35] we fine-tune the model for $1k$ iterations on an augmented set obtained from the first frame image and mask, to learn the specific properties of the object.

ID 1: "A man in a grey t-shirt and yellow trousers"
ID 2: "A woman in a black shirt"
ID 3: "A white truck on the road"
First frame annotation
ID 1: "A man in a grey shirt walking through the crossing"
ID 2: "A woman walking through the crossing"
ID 3: "A white truck moving from the left to right"
Full video annotation

Fig. 4. Example of annotations provided for the 1st frame vs. the full video. Full video annotations include descriptions of activities and overall are more complex.

Mask + Language. We show that using language supervision is complementary to the first frame mask. Instead of relying on the preceding frame prediction as in the previous paragraph, we use the bounding boxes obtained from the grounding model after the temporal consistency step. We initialize with the ground truth box in the first frame and fine-tune the network on the 1st frame.

4 Collecting Referring Expressions for Video

Our task is to localize and provide a pixel-level mask of an object on all video frames given a language referring expression obtained either by looking at the first frame only or the full video. To validate our approach we employ two popular video object segmentation datasets, DAVIS_{16} [34] and DAVIS_{17} [38]. These two datasets introduce various challenges, containing videos with single or multiple salient objects, crowded scenes, similar looking instances, occlusions, camera view changes, fast motion, etc.

DAVIS_{16} [34] consists of 30 training and 20 test videos of diverse object categories with all frames annotated with pixel-level accuracy. Note that in this dataset only a single object is annotated per video. For the multiple object video segmentation task we consider DAVIS_{17}. Compared to DAVIS_{16}, this is a more challenging dataset, with multiple objects annotated per video and more complex scenes with more distractors, occlusions, smaller objects, and fine structures. Overall, DAVIS_{17} consists of a training set with 60 videos, and a validation/test-dev/test-challenge set with 30 sequences each.

As our goal is to segment objects in videos using language specifications, we augment all objects annotated with mask labels in DAVIS_{16} and DAVIS_{17} with non-ambigu-ous referring expressions. We follow the work of [31] and ask the annotator to provide a language description of the object, which has a mask annotation, by looking only at the first frame of the video. Then another annotator is given the first frame and the corresponding description, and asked to identify the referred object. If the annotator is unable to correctly identify the object, the description is corrected to remove ambiguity and to specify the object uniquely. We have collected two referring expressions per target object annotated by non-computer vision experts (Annotator 1, 2).

However, by looking only at the 1st frame, the obtained referring expressions may potentially be invalid for an entire video. (We actually quantified that

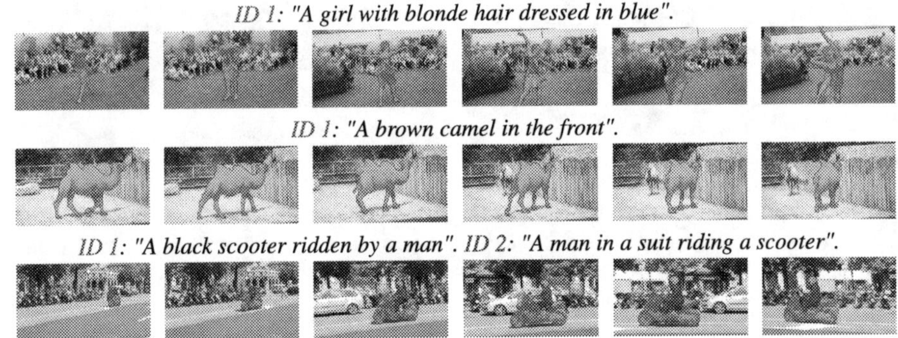

Fig. 5. Video object segmentation qualitative results using only referring expressions as supervision on DAVIS_{16} and DAVIS_{17}, val sets. Frames sampled along the video.

only ∼15% of the collected descriptions become invalid over time and it does not affect strongly segmentation results as temporal consistency step helps to disambiguate some of such cases, see the supp. material for details.) Besides, in many applications, such as video editing or video-based advertisement, the user has access to a full video. Providing a language query which is valid for all frames might decrease the editing time and result in more coherent predictions. Thus, on DAVIS_{17} we asked the workers to provide a description of the object by looking at the full video. We have collected one expression of the full video type per target object. Future work may choose to use either setting.

The average length for the first frame/full video expressions is 5.5/6.3 words. For DAVIS_{17} first frame annotations we notice that descriptions given by Annotator 1 are longer than the ones by Annotator 2 (6.4 vs. 4.6 words). We evaluate the effect of description length on the grounding performance in Sect. 5. Besides, the expressions relevant to a full video mention verbs more often than the first frame descriptions (44% vs. 25%). This is intuitive, as referring to an object which changes its appearance and position over time may require mentioning its actions. Adjectives are present in over 50% for all annotations. Most of them refer to colors (over 70%), shapes and sizes (7%) and spatial/ordering words (6% first frame vs. 13% full video expressions). The full video expressions also have a higher number of adverbs and prepositions, and overall are more complex than the ones provided for the first frame, see Fig. 4 for examples.

Overall augmented $\text{DAVIS}_{16/17}$ contains ∼1.2k referring expressions for more than 400 objects on 150 videos with ∼10k frames. We believe the collected data will be of interest to segmentation as well as vision and language communities, providing an opportunity to explore language as alternative input for video object segmentation.

5 Evaluation of Natural Language Grounding in Video

In this section we discuss the performance of natural language grounding models on video data. We experiment with DBNet [51] and MattNet [50]. DBNet is

Table 1. Comparison of the DBNet [51] and MattNet [49] models on $DAVIS_{16}$ training set and $DAVIS_{17}$ val set. Δ(A1,A2) denotes the difference between Annotator 1 and 2.

Method	Object proposals	Train. data	Temp. cons.	$DAVIS_{16}$		$DAVIS_{17}$		
				1st frame		1st frame		Full video
				mIoU	Δ(A1,A2)	mIoU	Δ(A1,A2)	mIoU
DBNet	EdgeBox	Vis.Gen.	-	54.1	1.0	-	-	-
	Mask R-CNN		-	64.9	2.1	48.4	1.3	49.6
MattNet	Mask R-CNN	RefCOCO	-	67.1	2.2	51.6	1.6	50.3
		RefCOCO+	-	69.1	3.2	50.8	1.2	50.1
DBNet	Mask R-CNN	Vis.Gen	✓	68.8	0.6	49.6	1.6	50.2
MattNet	Mask R-CNN	RefCOCO	✓	71.4	0.2	52.8	0.5	51.3
		RefCOCO+	✓	72.5	0.3	52.3	0.0	51.2

trained on Visual Genome [20] which contains images from MS COCO [24] and YFCC100M [39], and spans thousands of object categories. MattNet is trained on referring expressions for MS COCO images [24], specifically RefCOCO and RefCOCO+ [50]. Unlike RefCOCO which has no restrictions on the expressions, RefCOCO+ contains no spatial words and rather focuses on object appearance. Both aforementioned models rely on external bounding box proposals, such as EdgeBox [8] or Mask R-CNN [12].

We carry out most of our evaluation on $DAVIS_{16}$ and $DAVIS_{17}$ with the referring expressions introduced in Sect. 4. To evaluate the localization quality we employ the intersection-over-union overlap (IoU) of the top scored box proposal with the ground truth bounding box, averaged across all queries.

5.1 $DAVIS_{16}$/$DAVIS_{17}$ Referring Expression Grounding

Table 1 reports performance of the grounding models on $DAVIS_{16}$ and $DAVIS_{17}$ referring expressions. In the following we summarize our key observations.

(1) We see the effect of replacing EdgeBox with Mask R-CNN object proposals for DBNet model (54.1 to 64.9). Employing better proposals significantly improves the quality of this grounding method, thus we rely on Mask R-CNN proposals in all the following experiments. (2) We note the stability of grounding performance across two annotations (see Δ(A1,A2)), showing that the grounding methods are quite robust to variations in language expressions. (3) The grounding models trained on images are not stable across frames, even when small changes in appearance occur (e.g. see Fig. 3). We see that our proposed temporal consistency technique benefits both methods (e.g. DBNet: 64.9 vs. 68.8 on $DAVIS_{16}$, MattNet 51.6 vs. 52.8 on $DAVIS_{17}$). (4) On both datasets MattNet performs better than DBNet. The gap is particularly large on $DAVIS_{16}$ (72.5 vs. 68.8), as $DAVIS_{16}$ contains videos of a single foreground moving object, while DBNet is trained on a densely labeled Visual Genome dataset with many

foreground and background objects. (5) On DAVIS_{16} MattNet trained on RefCOCO+ outperforms MattNet trained on RefCOCO (72.5 vs. 71.4), while both perform similar on DAVIS_{17}. As RefCOCO+ contains no spatial words, MattNet trained on this dataset is more accurate in localizing queries mentioning object appearance. (6) Compared to DAVIS_{16}, DAVIS_{17} is significantly more challenging, as it contains cluttered scenes with multiple moving objects (e.g. for MattNet 71.4 vs. 52.8). (7) When comparing results on expressions provided for the first frame versus expressions provided for the full video, we observe diverging trends. While DBNet is able to improve its performance (48.4 vs. 49.6), MattNet performance decreases (52.8 vs. 51.3). We attribute this to the fact that DBNet is trained on the more diverse Visual Genome descriptions.

Attribute-Based Analysis. Next we perform a more detailed analysis of the grounding models on DAVIS_{17}. We split the textual queries/videos into subsets where a certain attribute is present and report the averaged results for the subsets. Table 2 presents attribute-based grounding performance on first-frame based expressions averaged across annotators. To estimate the upper bound performance and the impact of imperfect bounding box proposals we add an Oracle comparison, where performance is reported on the ground-truth object boxes. We summarize our findings in the following.

(1) As MattNet is trained on MS COCO images and both models rely on MS COCO-based Mask R-CNN proposals, we compare performance for expressions which include COCO versus non-COCO objects. Both models drop in performance on non-COCO expressions, showing the impact of the domain shift to DAVIS_{17} (e.g. for MattNet 59.6 vs. 36.9). Even DBNet which is trained on a larger training corpus suffers from the same effect (55.5 vs. 37.3). (2) We label the DAVIS_{17} expressions as “spatial” if they include some of the spatial words (e.g. left, right). Such queries are significantly harder for all models (e.g. for MattNet 33.8 vs. 58.5). (3) Verbs are important as they allow to disambiguate an object in a video based on its actions. Presence of verbs in expressions is a challenging factor for DBNet trained on Visual Genome, while MattNet does significantly better (37.4 vs. 55.8). (4) Expression length is also an important factor. We quantize our expressions into Short ($<$4 words), Medium (4–6 words) and Long ($>$6 words). All models demonstrate similar drop in performance as expression length increases (e.g. for MattNet 63.9 $\rightarrow$ 50.2 $\rightarrow$ 49.1). (5) Videos with more objects are more difficult, as these objects also tend to be very similar, such as e.g. fish in a tank (e.g. for MattNet 86.1 $\rightarrow$ 51.2 $\rightarrow$ 16.1). (6) From the Oracle performance on COCO versus non-COCO expressions, we see that all models are able to significantly improve their performance even for non-COCO objects (e.g. for DBNet 37.3 to 59.0). DBNet benefits more than MattNet from Oracle boxes, showing its higher potential to generalize to a new domain given better proposals.

Table 2. Grounding performance breakdown for different attributes on $DAVIS_{17}$, val set. Results obtained after the temporal consistency, using average between two annotators (1st frame based). Attributes: COCO/non-COCO, Spatial/non-Spatial, Verbs/no Verbs, Expression length (Short, Medium, Long) and Number of objects.

Method	Train. data	Obj. prop.	mIoU											
			CO.	~CO.	Sp.	~Sp.	Ve.	~Ve.	Expr. length			Num. obj.		
									S	M	L	1	2–3	>3
DBNet	Vis.Gen.	Mask	55.5	37.3	**36.5**	55.7	37.4	**52.0**	61.8	49.2	33.6	79.5	49.3	**22.6**
MattNet	RefCOCO	R-CNN	**59.6**	36.9	33.8	**58.5**	**55.8**	51.7	**63.9**	**50.2**	**49.1**	**86.1**	**51.2**	16.1
DBNet	Vis.Gen.	Oracle	**79.3**	**59.0**	**47.7**	**81.7**	70.3	**77.6**	**84.8**	**69.9**	**67.9**	100	**73.8**	**37.2**
MattNet	RefCOCO		73.2	46.6	42.2	72.5	**74.7**	62.9	79.0	61.1	59.0	100	64.5	23.2

6 Video Object Segmentation Results

In this section we present single and multiple video object segmentation results using natural language referring expressions on two datasets: $DAVIS_{16}$ [34] and $DAVIS_{17}$ [38]. In addition, we experiment with fusing two complementary sources of information, employing both the pixel-level mask and language supervision on the first frame. All results here are obtained using the bounding boxes given by the MattNet model [49] trained on RefCOCO [50] after the temporal consistency step (see Sect. 3.1).

For evaluation we use the IoU measure (also called Jaccard index - J) between the ground truth and the predicted segmentation, averaged across all video sequences and all frames. For $DAVIS_{17}$ we also employ the $J\&F$ measure proposed in [38].

6.1 $DAVIS_{16}$ Single Object Segmentation

Table 3 compares our results to previous work on $DAVIS_{16}$ [34]. As we employ MattNet [49], which exploits Mask R-CNN [12] box proposals, we also would like to compare to its segments. We report the oracle Mask R-CNN results, where on each frame the segment with the highest ground truth overlap was chosen. Even with the oracle assignment of segments, [12] under-performs compared to our segmentation model (71.5 vs. 83.1). This shows that for very detailed mask annotations (as in $DAVIS_{16/17}$) a more complex segmentation module than the Mask R-CNN segmentation head is required (which itself is a shallow FCN with reduced output resolution, resulting in coarse masks).

Our method, while only exploiting language, shows competitive performance, on par with techniques which use a pixel-level mask on the first frame (82.8 vs. 81.7 for OnAVOS [43]). This shows that high quality results can be obtained via a more natural way of human-computer interaction – referring to an object via language, making video segmentation techniques more applicable in practice. Compared to mask supervision employing language results in a runtime speed up: it is ~15 times faster to specify the object with language (79s [24] vs. 5s) plus online tuning is not needed for good performance ([30] reports 10min for

Table 4. Attribute-based results with different forms of supervision on $DAVIS_{16}$, val set. AC: appearance change, LR: low resolution, SV: scale variation, SC: shape complexity, CS: camera shake, DB: dynamic background, BC: background clutter, FM: fast motion, MB: motion blur, DEF: deformation, OCC: occlusions. See Sect. 6.1 for more details.

Supervision	AC	LR	SV	SC	CS	DB	BC	FM	MB	DEF	OCC
Language	80.1	**79.0**	74.4	77.6	85.7	66.4	**85.0**	77.7	78.1	84.3	80.1
Mask	**81.2**	78.1	75.9	79.0	85.6	68.0	82.8	79.0	79.9	85.6	80.5
Mask + Lang.	81.0	**79.0**	**76.8**	**80.4**	**86.8**	**72.2**	84.4	**79.5**	**80.4**	**85.9**	**82.3**

online tuning with 80.2 vs. our 82.8). Note that [30,43] show superior results to our approach (~86 mIoU). However, they employ additional cues by incorporating semantic information [30] or doing online adaptation [43]. Potentially, these techniques can also be applied to our method, though it is out of scope of this paper.

Compared to the approaches which use point click supervision [2,29], our method shows superior performance (82.8 vs. 80.6 and 80.9). This indicates that language can be successfully utilized as an alternative and cheaper form of supervision for video object segmentation, on par with clicks and scribbles.

Table 3. Comparison of video object segmentation results on $DAVIS_{16}$, val set.

Supervision		Method	mIoU
Oracle		Mask R-CNN [12]	71.5
Unsupervised		FusionSeg [17]	70.7
		LVO [40]	75.9
		ARP [19]	76.2
Semi-supervised	1st frame mask	SegFlow [6]	76.1
		MaskTrack [35]	79.7
		OSVOS[a] [30]	80.2
		MaskRNN [15]	80.4
		OnAVOS[b] [43]	81.7
		Our	83.1
	Clicks	iVOS [2]	80.6
		DEXTR [29]	80.9
	Language	Our	82.8
	Mask + Lang.	Our	**84.5**

[a] $OSVOS^S$ reports 86.0 mIoU by employing semantic segmentation as additional supervision.
[b] OnAVOS reports 64.5 mIoU by performing online adaptation on successive frames.

Maks and Language. In Table 3 we also report the results for variants using only mask supervision on the first frame or combining both mask and language (see Sect. 3.2 for details). Notice that employing either mask or language results in comparable performance (82.8 vs. 83.1), while fusing both modalities leads to a further improvement (82.8 vs. 84.5). This shows that referring expressions are complementary to visual forms of supervision and can be exploited as an additional source of guidance for segmentation, on top of not only pixel-level masks, but potentially scribbles and point clicks.

Table 4 presents a more detailed evaluation using video attributes. We report the averaged results on a subset of sequences where a certain challenging attribute is present. Note that using language alone leads to more robust performance for videos with low resolution, camera shake and background clutter without the need for an expensive pixel-level mask. When utilizing both mask and language we observe that the system becomes consistently more robust to various video challenges (e.g. fast motion, occlusions, motion blur, etc.) and compares favorably to mask only on all attributes, except appearance change. Overall, employing language can help the model to better handle occlusions, avoid drift and better adapt to complex dynamics inherent to video.

Ablation Study. We validate the contributions of the components in our method (see Sect. 3) by presenting an ablation study in Table 5 on DAVIS_{16}, training set. Augmenting the ground truth boxes by random jittering makes the system more robust to sloppy boxes at test time (82.5 vs. 80.6), while employing motion cues allows to better handle moving objects (80.6 vs. 75.9). Temporal consistency step helps to provide more temporally coherent boxes (4.3 mIoU point boost for grounding, see Table 1) and hence improve the final segmentation quality (75.9 vs. 72.5). Exploiting the proposed network architecture versus using the network proposed in [35] results in 3.7 point boost (75.9 vs. 72.2), providing more detailed object masks. Overall, all components introduced in our approach lead to the state-of-the-art results on DAVIS_{16}.

Table 5. Ablation study on DAVIS_{16}.

Variant	mIoU	Δ
Full system	82.5	-
No box jittering	80.6	−1.9
No optical flow magnitude	75.9	−4.7
No temporal consistency	72.5	−3.4
Backbone architecture of [35]	72.2	−3.7

6.2 DAVIS_{17} Multiple Object Segmentation

Table 6 presents results on DAVIS_{17} [38]. The lower numbers in comparison with Table 3 indicate that DAVIS_{17} is significantly more difficult than DAVIS_{16}. Even when employing mask supervision on the first frame the dataset presents a challenging task and there is much room for improvement. The semi-supervised methods perform well on foreground-background segmentation, but have problems separating multiple foreground objects, handling small objects and preserving the correct object identities [38].

Compared to mask supervision using language descriptions significantly under-performs. We believe that one of the main problems is a relatively unstable behavior of the underlying grounding model. There are a lot of identity switches, that are heavily penalized by the evaluation metric as every pixel should be assigned to one instance. We conducted an oracle experiment assigning Mask R-CNN box proposals to the correct object ids and then performing segmentation (denoted "Oracle - Grounding"). We observe a significant increase in performance (37.3 to 54.9), making the results competitive to mask supervision. If we utilize Mask R-CNN segment proposals for oracle case, the result is 2.1 points lower than using our segmentation model on top. The underlying choice of proposals for the grounding model could also have its effect. If the object is not detected by Mask R-CNN, the grounding model has no chances to recover the correct instance. To evaluate the influence of proposals we conduct an oracle experiment where the ground truth boxes are exploited in the grounding model (denoted "Oracle - Box proposals"). With oracle boxes we observe an increase in performance (37.3 to 42.1), however, recovering the correct identities still poses a problem for grounding.

Another factor influencing the results is the domain shift between the training and test data. Both Mask R-CNN and MattNet are trained on MS COCO [24], and have troubles recovering instances not belonging to 80 COCO categories. We split the DAVIS_{17} validation set into COCO and non-COCO objects/language queries (43 vs. 18) and evaluate separately on two subsets. As in Sect. 5, we observe much higher results for COCO queries (45 to 27.5), indicating the problem of generalization from training to test data.

The method which exploits scribble supervision [37] performs on par with our approach. Note that even for scribble supervision the task remains difficult.

Mask and Language. In Table 6 we also report the results for variants of our approach using only mask supervision or combining mask and language. Employing language on top of mask leads to an increase in performance over using mask only (58 to 59), again showing complementarity of both sources of supervision.

Figure 5 provides qualitative results of our method using only language as supervision. We observe successful handling of similar looking objects, fast motion, deformations and partial occlusions.

Table 6. Comparison of semi-supervised video object segmentation methods on DAVIS_{17}, val set. Numbers in italic are reported on subsets of DAVIS_{17} containing/non-containing COCO objects.

Supervision	Method	mIoU	$J\&F$
Oracle	Mask R-CNN [12]	52.8	53.3
	Grounding	54.9	57.4
	Box proposals	42.1	45.3
1st frame mask	OSVOS [3]	52.1	57.0
	OnAVOS[a] [42]	57.0	59.4
	MaskRNN [15]	60.5	-
	Our	58.0	60.8
Scribbles	CNN lin. class. [37]	-	39.3
	Scribble-OSVOS [37]	-	39.9
Language	Our	37.3	39.3
	Our, COCO	*45.0*	*47.5*
	Our, non-C.	*27.5*	*29.4*
Mask+Lang	Our	59.0	62.2

[a]OnAVOS reports 64.5 mIoU by performing online adaptation on successive frames.

Discussion. Our results indicate that language alone can be successfully used as an alternative and a more natural form of supervision. Particularly, high quality results can be achieved for videos with the salient target object. Videos with multiple similar looking objects pose a challenge for grounding models, as they have problems preserving object identities across frames. Experimentally we show that better proposals, grounding and proximity of training and test data can further boost the performance for videos with multiple objects. Language is complementary to mask supervision and can be exploited as an additional source of guidance for segmentation.

7 Conclusion

In this work we propose the task of video object segmentation using language referring expressions. We propose an approach to address this new task as well as extend two well-known video object segmentation benchmarks with textual descriptions of target objects. Our experiments indicate that language alone can be successfully exploited to obtain high quality segmentations of objects in videos. While allowing a more natural human-computer interaction, using guidance from language descriptions can also make video segmentation more robust to occlusions, complex dynamics and cluttered backgrounds. We show that classical semi-supervised video object segmentation which uses the mask annotation on the first frame can be further improved by the use of language descriptions. We believe there is a lot of potential in fusing lingual (referring expressions) and visual (clicks, scribbles or masks) forms of supervision for object segmentation in video. We hope that our results encourage more research on video object segmentation with referring expressions and foster discovery of new techniques applicable in realistic settings, which discard tedious pixel-level annotations.

References

1. Balajee Vasudevan, A., Dai, D., Van Gool, L.: Object referring in videos with language and human gaze. In: CVPR (2018)
2. Benard, A., Gygli, M.: Interactive video object segmentation in the wild. arXiv:1801.00269 (2017)
3. Caelles, S., Maninis, K.K., Pont-Tuset, J., Leal-Taixe, L., Cremers, D., Gool, L.V.: One-shot video object segmentation. In: CVPR (2017)
4. Chen, K., Kovvuri, R., Nevatia, R.: Query-guided regression network with context policy for phrase grounding. In: ICCV (2017)
5. Chen, L.C., Papandreou, G., Kokkinos, I., Murphy, K., Yuille, A.L.: DeepLab: semantic image segmentation with deep convolutional nets, atrous convolution, and fully connected CRFs. arXiv:1606.00915 (2016)
6. Cheng, J., Tsai, Y.H., Wang, S., Yang, M.H.: SegFlow: joint learning for video object segmentation and optical flow. In: ICCV (2017)
7. Cheng, M.M., Mitra, N.J., Huang, X., Torr, P.H.S., Hu, S.M.: Global contrast based salient region detection. PAMI **37**, 569–582 (2015)
8. Dollár, P., Zitnick, C.L.: Fast edge detection using structured forests. PAMI. **37**, 1558–1570 (2015)
9. Faktor, A., Irani, M.: Video segmentation by non-local consensus voting. In: BMVC (2014)
10. Gavrilyuk, K., Ghodrati, A., Li, Z., Snoek, C.G.: Actor and action video segmentation from a sentence. In: CVPR (2018)
11. Glorot, X., Bengio, Y.: Understanding the difficulty of training deep feedforward neural networks. In: AISTATS (2010)
12. He, K., Gkioxari, G., Dollár, P., Girshick, R.B.: Mask R-CNN. In: ICCV (2017)
13. He, K., Zhang, X., Ren, S., Sun, J.: Deep residual learning for image recognition. In: CVPR (2016)
14. Hu, R., Rohrbach, M., Andreas, J., Darrell, T., Saenko, K.: Modeling relationships in referential expressions with compositional modular networks. In: CVPR (2017)
15. Hu, Y.T., Huang, J., Schwing, A.G.: MaskRNN: instance level video object segmentation. In: NIPS (2017)
16. Ilg, E., Mayer, N., Saikia, T., Keuper, M., Dosovitskiy, A., Brox, T.: FlowNet 2.0: evolution of optical flow estimation with deep networks. In: CVPR (2017)

17. Jain, S.D., Xiong, B., Grauman, K.: FusionSeg: learning to combine motion and appearance for fully automatic segmentation of generic objects in videos. In: CVPR (2017)
18. Khoreva, A., Benenson, R., Ilg, E., Brox, T., Schiele, B.: Lucid data dreaming for multiple object tracking. arXiv:1703.09554 (2017)
19. Koh, Y., Kim, C.: Primary object segmentation in videos based on region augmentation and reduction. In: CVPR (2017)
20. Krishna, R., et al.: Visual genome: connecting language and vision using crowdsourced dense image annotations. arXiv:1602.07332 (2016)
21. Li, R., et al.: Referring image segmentation via recurrent refinement networks. In: CVPR (2018)
22. Li, Z., Tao, R., Gavves, E., Snoek, C.G.M., Smeulders, A.W.M.: Tracking by natural language specification. In: CVPR (2017)
23. Lin, D., Dai, J., Jia, J., He, K., Sun, J.: ScribbleSup: scribble-supervised convolutional networks for semantic segmentation. In: CVPR (2016)
24. Lin, T.Y., et al.: Microsoft COCO: common objects in context. In: Fleet, D., Pajdla, T., Schiele, B., Tuytelaars, T. (eds.) ECCV 2014. LNCS, vol. 8693, pp. 740–755. Springer, Cham (2014). https://doi.org/10.1007/978-3-319-10602-1_48
25. Liu, C., Lin, Z., Shen, X., Yang, J., Lu, X., Yuille, A.: Recurrent multimodal interaction for referring image segmentation. In: ICCV (2017)
26. Liu, W., Rabinovich, A., Berg, A.C.: ParseNet: looking wider to see better. arxiv:1506.04579 (2015)
27. Long, J., Shelhamer, E., Darrell, T.: Fully convolutional networks for semantic segmentation. In: CVPR (2015)
28. Luo, R., Shakhnarovich, G.: Comprehension-guided referring expressions. In: CVPR (2017)
29. Maninis, K., Caelles, S., Pont-Tuset, J., Gool, L.V.: Deep extreme cut: from extreme points to object segmentation. In: CVPR (2018)
30. Maninis, K., et al.: Video object segmentation without temporal information. arxiv:1709.06031 (2017)
31. Mao, J., Jonathan, H., Toshev, A., Camburu, O., Yuille, A., Murphy, K.: Generation and comprehension of unambiguous object descriptions. In: CVPR (2016)
32. Nagaraja, V.K., Morariu, V.I., Davis, L.S.: Modeling context between objects for referring expression understanding. In: Leibe, B., Matas, J., Sebe, N., Welling, M. (eds.) ECCV 2016. LNCS, vol. 9908, pp. 792–807. Springer, Cham (2016). https://doi.org/10.1007/978-3-319-46493-0_48
33. Papazoglou, A., Ferrari, V.: Fast object segmentation in unconstrained video. In: ICCV (2013)
34. Perazzi, F., Pont-Tuset, J., McWilliams, B., Gool, L.V., Gross, M., Sorkine-Hornung, A.: A benchmark dataset and evaluation methodology for video object segmentation. In: CVPR (2016)
35. Perazzi, F., Khoreva, A., Benenson, R., Schiele, B., Sorkine-Hornung, A.: Learning video object segmentation from static images. In: CVPR (2017)
36. Perazzi, F., Wang, O., Gross, M., Sorkine-Hornung, A.: Fully connected object proposals for video segmentation. In: ICCV (2015)
37. Pont-Tuset, J., et al.: The 2018 DAVIS challenge on video object segmentation. arXiv:1803.00557 (2018)
38. Pont-Tuset, J., Perazzi, F., Caelles, S., Arbeláez, P., Sorkine-Hornung, A., Van Gool, L.: The 2017 DAVIS challenge on video object segmentation. arXiv:1704.00675 (2017)

39. Thomee, B., et al.: YFCC100M: the new data in multimedia research. Commun. ACM (2016)
40. Tokmakov, P., Alahari, K., Schmid, C.: Learning video object segmentation with visual memory. In: ICCV (2017)
41. Tsai, Y.H., Yang, M.H., Black, M.J.: Video segmentation via object flow. In: CVPR (2016)
42. Voigtlaender, P., Leibe, B.: Online adaptation of convolutional neural networks for the 2017 DAVIS challenge on video object segmentation. In: DAVIS Challenge - CVPR Workshops (2017)
43. Voigtlaender, P., Leibe, B.: Online adaptation of convolutional neural networks for video object segmentation. In: BMVC (2017)
44. Wang, P., et al.: Understanding convolution for semantic segmentation. arXiv:1702.08502 (2017)
45. Wang, W., Shen, J.: Super-trajectory for video segmentation. arXiv:1702.08634 (2017)
46. Wen, L., Du, D., Lei, Z., Li, S.Z., Yang, M.H.: JOTS: joint online tracking and segmentation. In: CVPR (2015)
47. Xiao, F., Lee, Y.J.: Track and segment: an iterative unsupervised approach for video object proposals. In: CVPR (2016)
48. Yeh, R., Xiong, J., Hwu, W.M., Do, M., Schwing, A.: Interpretable and globally optimal prediction for textual grounding using image concepts. In: NIPS (2017)
49. Yu, L., et al.: MAttNet: modular attention network for referring expression comprehension. In: CVPR (2018)
50. Yu, L., Poirson, P., Yang, S., Berg, A.C., Berg, T.L.: Modeling context in referring expressions. In: Leibe, B., Matas, J., Sebe, N., Welling, M. (eds.) ECCV 2016. LNCS, vol. 9906, pp. 69–85. Springer, Cham (2016). https://doi.org/10.1007/978-3-319-46475-6_5
51. Zhang, Y., Yuan, L., Guo, Y., He, Z., Huang, I.A., Lee, H.: Discriminative bimodal networks for visual localization and detection with natural language queries. In: CVPR (2017)

Nonlinear Subspace Feature Enhancement for Image Set Classification

Mohammed E. Fathy(✉), Azadeh Alavi, and Rama Chellappa

Center for Automation Research, University of Maryland,
College Park, MD 20742, USA
{mefathy,azadeh,rama}@umiacs.umd.edu

Abstract. While several methods have been proposed for modeling and recognizing image sets, the success of these methods relies heavily on how well the image data follows the assumptions of the underlying models. Among the models that have been utilized by many image set classification methods, the physically inspired subspace model assumes that the images of an object lie on a union of low-dimensional subspaces. Despite their successful performance in controlled environments, the performance of such subspace-based classifiers suffers in practical unconstrained settings, where the data may not strictly follow the assumptions necessary for the subspace model to hold. In this paper, we propose Nonlinear Subspace Feature Enhancement (NSFE), an approach for nonlinearly embedding image sets into a space where they adhere to a more discriminative subspace structure. In turn, this improves the performance of subspace-based classifiers such as sparse representation-based classification. We describe how the structured loss function of NSFE can be optimized in a batch-by-batch fashion by a two-step alternating algorithm. The algorithm makes very few assumptions about the form of the embedding to be learned and is compatible with stochastic gradient descent and back-propagation. This makes NSFE usable with deep, feed-forward embeddings and trainable in an end-to-end fashion. We experiment with two different types of features and nonlinear embeddings over three image set datasets and we show that our method compares favorably to state-of-the-art image set classification methods.

1 Introduction

Image set classification aims to compute a single label for a set of images that are assumed to belong to the same class. The interest in the use of image sets for visual recognition tasks, such as face recognition, has grown in line with the increasing prevalence of video-capable consumer devices and surveillance cameras [1–19]. A video is typically believed to have richer information (i.e. more frames) than in a still image and so can lead to improved classification performance. However, the improvement in performance is sometimes limited in practice due to the challenges videos share with still images (*e.g.* variations in pose, illumination, motion-induced artifacts and occlusion) in addition to the

C. V. Jawahar et al. (Eds.): ACCV 2018, LNCS 11364, pp. 142–158, 2019.
https://doi.org/10.1007/978-3-030-20870-7_9

low resolution at which videos are sometimes captured to reduce bandwidth and storage requirements.

As reviewed in Sect. 2, several methods for modeling and classifying image sets have been proposed. Many of these have utilized the *subspace assumption* which (informally) states that the instances from a particular class lie on (or close to) a union of low-dimensional linear subspaces (the property is illustrated in Fig. 1). The assumption is theoretically founded on the work of [20] which shows that the images of a static convex Lambertian object, taken under varying Lambertian illumination from a fixed viewpoint, approximately lie on a low-dimensional subspace [20].

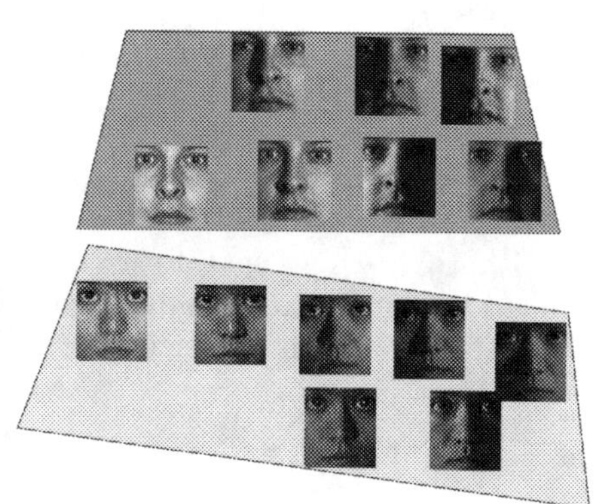
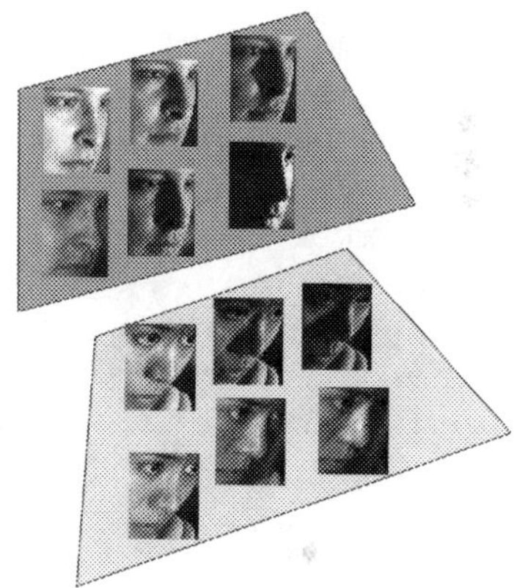

Fig. 1. An illustration of the discriminative subspace structure that is naturally exhibited by the *controlled* images of a visual object (*e.g.* a person's face) [20, 21]. The example illustrates the property for the face images of two different subjects, taken under two different poses and varying illumination. The images in which the visual object (i.e. face) has the same pose and identity lead to raw intensity vectors that lie close to a low-dimensional subspace regardless of the variations in Lambertian illumination. Our goal is to learn a nonlinear embedding that improves the discriminative subspace layout of image sets and consequently enhance the performance of subspace-based image set classifiers.

Despite the theoretical foundations of the subspace model, the success of the associated algorithms relies on how well these assumptions are satisfied in practice (i.e. the convexity of the imaged object, the fixing of viewpoint, the Lambertian illumination, and the use of raw intensities to represent images). In practical unconstrained settings, these requirements may not be met and so the data may not strictly follow the subspace model in such scenarios (*e.g.* varying pose and/or use of image features nonlinearly derived from intensities).

To mitigate this, we propose an algorithm to learn a nonlinear embedding that enhances the low-dimensional discriminative subspace structure of the image sets. Under such an embedding, an instance from one class is more likely to be closer to the subspace spanned by the samples of the same class than to the subspaces spanned by the samples from other classes. This can enhance the performance of subspace-based classifiers, such as Sparse-Representation-based Classification (SRC) [21], which essentially finds a low-dimensional subspace that is closest to the test sample and uses the labels in that subspace to decide a label for the particular test sample. Given a batch of samples, we formulate a novel structured loss function that encourages the distance between each sample and the subspace spanned by the same-class samples (within the batch) to be lower than the distances between the sample and the subspaces spanned by other classes (present in the batch). We then present a two-step alternating optimization algorithm to minimize the loss function in a way that is compatible with back-propagation. This allows the function to be minimized with Stochastic Gradient Descent (SGD)-based algorithms that are typically used to train deep networks [22,23]. At the end of training, the learned embedding is used to project the image sets and the Mean-Sequence SRC (MS-SRC) [10] is used to classify the test image sets.

The rest of this paper is organized as follows. A brief review of related work is presented in Sect. 2. We then describe in Sect. 3 the structured loss function and the optimization procedure of the NSFE algorithm. We experimentally evaluate NSFE in Sect. 4 where the results show the superiority of NSFE compared to several existing image set classification methods. We conclude the paper in Sect. 5.

2 Related Work

The image set classification problem has been formulated in various ways. One popular formulation is to compute the distance, either over a vector space or a manifold, between the probe set and each gallery set and then associate the probe with the class of its nearest gallery set. These include discriminative [2,5,8,16,18,19,24,25] and non-discriminative methods [1,3,4,7,11,12]. There are also other formulations that do not rely on nearest neighbor-based classification such as the binary SVM reverse-training approach of [15], the neural network-based methods [14,17], linear representation/coding methods [10,26] and clustering methods [6,13]. In what follows, we give a brief description of these methods.

Vector Space Methods: Several methods treat the whole image set as a subspace and measure the distance between subspaces by finding the pair of closest points inside them. Such methods include Affine (or Convex) Hull Image Set Distance (AHISD/CHISD) [3], Sparse-Approximated Nearest Points (SANP) [4], and Dual Linear Regression-based Classification (DLRC) [12]. The Sparse-Approximated Nearest Subspaces (SANS) [11] applies sparse coding to subspace-cluster each gallery image set and measures the distance from the gallery set to the probe set by finding the average distance of each cluster in the gallery set to its nearest subspace approximation from the probe set. Dictionary-based Face Recognition from Videos (DFRV) [7] learns a dictionary consisting of K sub-dictionaries for each gallery image set after clustering its images by appearance into K groups. The probe set is associated with the class whose gallery dictionaries result in the lowest reconstruction error for the majority of the images in the probe set. Simultaneous Feature and Dictionary Learning (SFDL) [16] discriminatively learns dictionaries for the different classes in addition to learning a linear projection $\mathbf{W}$ to improve the separation between the instances of the different classes. The classification algorithm is identical to DFRV except that the probe images are first transformed using $\mathbf{W}$. Hierarchical subspace clustering of the combined set of faces of the gallery and the probe has been proposed using either sparse codes [6] or Grassmann manifolds [13]. The probe set is associated with the class with the most similar distribution of elements over the clusters to the distribution of the probe elements.

Manifold Methods: Another approach is to represent the image sets as manifolds (or points on a manifold) and use the distance $d(\mathcal{P}, \mathcal{G})$ between the probe $\mathcal{P}$ and each gallery set $\mathcal{G}$ to label $\mathcal{P}$. Methods based on this general idea differ on how they represent an image set as/on a manifold and the way the distance between the sets is measured. Examples of methods that represent each image set as a separate manifold include the Manifold-Manifold Distance (MMD) method [1] and the Manifold Discriminant Analysis (MDA) method [2]. Other manifold methods have represented the subspace approximately spanning an image set as a point on a Grassmann manifold (as opposed to representing each set as a separate manifold). Kernels for Grassmann manifolds are then utilized to perform Discriminant Analysis (DA) [24] or graph-based DA [5] and the distances in the embedded space are used for classification. Kernel dictionary learning and sparse coding on Grassmann manifold have also been considered for image set classification [9]. Instead of using kernels, Projection Metric Learning (PML) [25] discriminatively learns a mapping into another, lower dimensional Grassmann manifold where the projection distance between a pair of points is used for nearest neighbor classification. Covariance Discriminant Learning (CDL) [8] treats the covariance of the image set as a point on a Riemannian manifold that is mapped to a Euclidean space via the logarithmic map. Partial Least Squares (PLS) is then used to learn the mapping from the gallery points to their labels and the resulting mapping is used to classify the probe point. Another related method learns a discriminative, geometry-preserving Mahalanobis metric over the logarithm of the mean-modified covariance matrices and is shown to outperform CDL in [18]. Discriminant Analysis on the Riemannian manifold of Gaussian distributions (DARG) models each image set as a Mixture of Gaussians (MoG) and then runs kernel discriminant analysis based on a combined kernel for Gaussians [19]. Kernel Density Estimation (KDE) has also been used to model image sets as probability density functions in [27] where kernel Fisher discriminant analysis is subsequently applied on the statistical manifold.

Neural Network Methods: With recent successes of deep networks in many vision tasks, different neural network architectures have been recently proposed for image set classification. Two such examples are the generative, per-class five-layer model proposed in [28] and the discriminative, per-class two-layer model

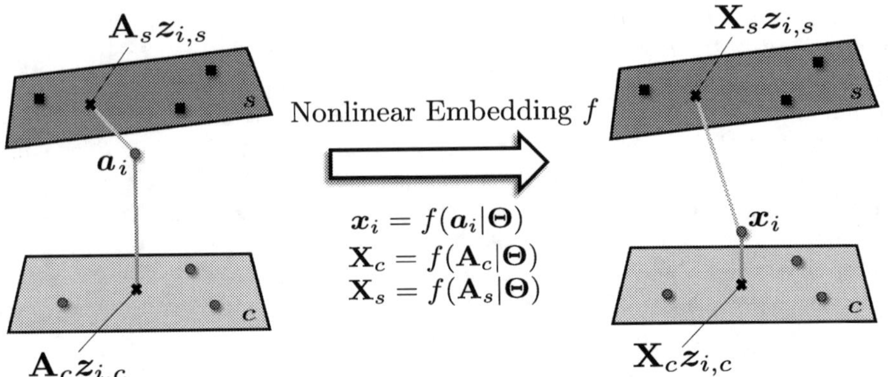

Fig. 2. An illustration of images and class-specific subspaces before and after the embedding. NSFE aims to improve the discriminative subspace arrangement of the data such that the images of a particular class c lie closer to the subspace $\mathbf{X}_c = f(\mathbf{A}_c)$ spanned by that class than any subspace $\mathbf{X}_s = f(\mathbf{A}_s)$ spanned by any other class s.

proposed in [17]. As we describe in Sects. 3.3 and 4, the two example embeddings we train with NSFE in this work are also based on neural networks.

Linear Representation (Coding) Methods: An effective approach, proposed in [21], for utilizing the subspace assumption for recognizing a given feature vector is to first compute its linear representation with respect to the gallery samples (i.e. project it on the gallery) then associate it with the class contributing the most to the representation. SRC [21], proposed for recognition of still face images, adopts this idea and casts the recognition problem as that of solving a convex Lasso optimization for the representation of the probe instance with respect to the gallery. It was then shown that replacing the l_1 regularization term with an l_2 term can yield similar performance with less processing time [29], resulting in the CRC method. Methods utilizing SRC and CRC for image set classification such as the Mean Sequence SRC (MS-SRC) [10] and Image Set CRC (ISCRC) [30] have also been developed.

Our goal in this paper is to learn nonlinear (or deep) features that can improve the performance of subspace-based classifiers like SRC. While some methods have been proposed previously with similar goals [16,31–33], they have been restricted to learning linear embeddings. In contrast, the proposed learning algorithm can be used with any embedding $\boldsymbol{x} = f(\boldsymbol{a}|\boldsymbol{\Theta})$, including deep ones, as long as the parameter subgradients $\partial f/\partial \boldsymbol{\Theta}$ are defined.

3 Nonlinear Subspace Feature Enhancement (NSFE)

We assume that there is a mapping $f : \mathcal{A} \rightarrow \mathbb{R}^m$ that maps every input image $\boldsymbol{a}$ from the vector space $\mathcal{A}$ (i.e. the space of raw intensity images) to $\boldsymbol{x} = f(\boldsymbol{a})$ in some feature space $\mathbb{R}^m$. We further assume that the mapping f is parameterized by a real tensor $\boldsymbol{\Theta}$ and that the parameter subgradients of f : $\partial f / \partial \boldsymbol{\Theta}$ are defined. For example, the mapping f could be a neural network and $\boldsymbol{\Theta}$ could be the network weights. Assuming that during training labeled samples arrive in batches, our goal is to learn a value of the parameter tensor $\boldsymbol{\Theta}$ that would make an embedded sample $\boldsymbol{x}$ from a particular class c closer to the subspace spanned by batch samples from c than to any subspaces spanned by batch samples from any other class $s \neq c$.

Definitions and Notations: In the following discussion, we use $\mathbf{B}$ to denote the current batch of samples and $|\mathbf{B}|$ to denote the number of samples in the batch. Furthermore, we use n_c to denote the number of samples from class c present in batch $\mathbf{B}$ while $\mathbf{X}_c = \left[\boldsymbol{x}_1, \ldots, \boldsymbol{x}_{n_c}\right] \in \mathbb{R}^{m \times n_c}$ is the matrix (dictionary) containing these samples along its columns. We use $C(\mathbf{B})$ to denote the set of class indices present in $\mathbf{B}$. In all our experiments, we sample each batch to contain nearly the same number of samples n_c from each class (the maximum difference between n_c and n_s is 1 for $c, s \in C(\mathbf{B})$). The sampling procedure ignores the boundaries between sets belonging to the same class and thus the subset drawn from a given class can contain samples from different sets within that class. In subsequent derivations, we assume $n_c > 1$ for all $c \in C(\mathbf{B})$ although in our experiments we have $6 \leq n_c \leq 20$. We also assume that the ith coordinate of a vector $\boldsymbol{z}$ is given by $\boldsymbol{z}^{(i)}$, the (i,j)th entry of a matrix $\mathbf{J}$ is given by $\mathbf{J}^{(i,j)}$, and the ith column is given by $\mathrm{col}_i(\mathbf{J})$.

3.1 Structured Loss Function

Before describing the loss function to be minimized, we need to formulate some measures of distance between a sample and different subspaces. Assuming the ith sample $\boldsymbol{x}_i$ is associated with class c (i.e. $c(i) = c$), we let $\boldsymbol{z}_{i,c}$ denote the linear representation of $\boldsymbol{x}_i$ with respect to the dictionary $\mathbf{X}_c$ (which is formed by the batch samples of class c present in $\mathbf{B}$). The representation $\boldsymbol{z}_{i,c}$ is obtained by solving the optimization problem

$$\boldsymbol{z}_{i,c} = \underset{\boldsymbol{z} \in \mathbb{R}^{n_c}}{\operatorname{argmin}} \left\|\boldsymbol{x}_i - \mathbf{X}_c \boldsymbol{z}\right\|_2^2 + \lambda \left\|\boldsymbol{z}\right\|_2^2, \text{s.t. } z^{(i)} = 0 \tag{1}$$

where we use l_2-norm instead of the sparsity inducing l_1-norm for efficiency purposes and also because n_c is typically small. It can be shown that

$$\boldsymbol{z}_{i,c} = \boldsymbol{u}_{i,c} - w_i \mathrm{col}_i(\mathbf{J}_c^{-1}) \tag{2}$$

where $\mathbf{J}_c = \mathbf{X}_c^T \mathbf{X}_c + \lambda \mathbf{I}$, $\boldsymbol{u}_{i,c} = \mathbf{J}_c^{-1} \mathbf{X}_c^T \boldsymbol{z}_{i,c}$, and $w_i = \boldsymbol{u}_{i,c}^{(i)} / \mathbf{J}_c^{-1(i,i)}$. Similarly, we define the linear representation $\boldsymbol{z}_{i,s}$ of the sample $\boldsymbol{x}_i$ with respect to the dictionary $\mathbf{X}_s$ formed by the batch samples of a different class $s \neq c = c(i)$ as a solution to the following optimization problem

$$\boldsymbol{z}_{i,s} = \underset{\boldsymbol{z} \in \mathbb{R}^{n_s}}{\operatorname{argmin}} \left\|\boldsymbol{x}_i - \mathbf{X}_s \boldsymbol{z}\right\|_2^2 + \lambda \left\|\boldsymbol{z}\right\|_2^2 \tag{3}$$

which has the closed form

$$\boldsymbol{z}_{i,s} = \mathbf{J}_s^{-1}\mathbf{X}_s^T\boldsymbol{x}_i \tag{4}$$

Our goal is to learn the embedding f such that we have

$$\|\boldsymbol{x}_i - \mathbf{X}_c\boldsymbol{z}_{i,c}\|_2^2 < \|\boldsymbol{x}_i - \mathbf{X}_s\boldsymbol{z}_{i,s}\|_2^2 \tag{5}$$

for all valid choices i, c, and s (Fig. 2). If such a discriminative subspace property is achieved for all choices of $c, s, \mathbf{X}_c$, and $\mathbf{X}_s$, a test sample $f(\boldsymbol{q})$ can be reconstructed using the samples of the true class more accurately compared to the samples of other classes. Applying a subspace classifier (like SRC) is thus more likely to associate $f(\boldsymbol{q})$ with its true class.

The proposed structured loss function, which we call Large-Margin Subspace Loss (LMSL), considers for every valid sample-to-subspaces-based triplet within the batch how well (5) is met. More specifically, LMSL is defined as

$$L = \frac{1}{T}\sum_{c\in C(\mathbf{B})}\sum_{\substack{i=1,\\ c(i)=c}}^{|\mathbf{B}|}\sum_{\substack{s\in C(\mathbf{B}),\\ s\neq c}}\Big[\|\boldsymbol{x}_i - \mathbf{X}_c\boldsymbol{z}_{i,c}\|_2^2 + m - \|\boldsymbol{x}_i - \mathbf{X}_s\boldsymbol{z}_{i,s}\|_2^2\Big]_+ \tag{6}$$

where m is the margin and the above sum is normalized by the number of terms/triplets T included the sum, which is $T = |\mathbf{B}|\,(|C(\mathbf{B})| - 1)$. It should be noted that the actual objective function being minimized is the sum of L and any other parameter regularization on $\boldsymbol{\Theta}$. LMSL can be thought of a kind of sample-to-subspace triplet loss [34,35]. The loss function treats as an anchor every sample $\boldsymbol{x}_i$ in the batch $\mathbf{B}$. For each anchor $\boldsymbol{x}_i$, LMSL considers as its corresponding positive point the class projection $\mathbf{X}_c\boldsymbol{z}_{i,c}$ and as a negative point its projection on one of the other-class subspaces $\mathbf{X}_s\boldsymbol{z}_{i,s}$. Thus, we have a total of $|C(B)| - 1$ triplets that have the sample $\boldsymbol{x}_i$ as the anchor.

3.2 Learning Algorithm

The LMSL function L can be difficult to optimize jointly with respect to both the sparse codes and $\boldsymbol{\Theta}$. Accordingly, we follow an alternating optimization approach. In this approach, we evaluate the sparse codes of all batch anchors using Eqs. (2, 4). Then, we treat the sparse codes as constants and use the chain rule and back-propagation to compute the parameter gradients of the loss function $\frac{\partial L}{\partial \theta_k}$, which are necessary for updating $\boldsymbol{\Theta}$ (see Fig. 3):

$$\frac{\partial L}{\partial \theta_k} = \sum_{b=1}^{|\mathbf{B}|}\Big(\frac{\partial L}{\partial \boldsymbol{x}_b}\Big)^T\frac{\partial \boldsymbol{x}_b}{\partial \theta_k} \tag{7}$$

If we assume $\boldsymbol{x}_b$ is associated with class s, b is its index within the batch, and r is its column index within $\mathbf{X}_s$, the left factor $\frac{\partial L}{\partial \boldsymbol{x}_b}$ in the above inner product is given by:

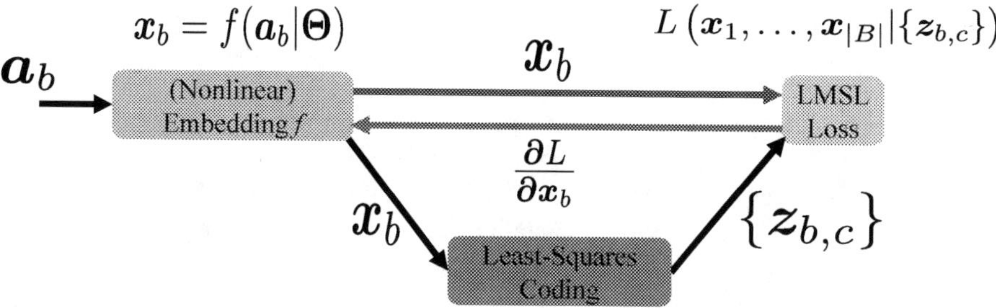

Fig. 3. An illustration of the alternating learning algorithm. After embedding the samples in the forward pass, the sparse codes $z_{b,c}$ are computed $\forall(b,c)$ and substituted into the loss function. The sparse codes are held constant, the loss function is evaluated, and the derivatives of loss function with respect to $x_b, \forall b$ are back-propagated. The chain rule (7) is then applied to evaluate the parameter subgradients $\partial L/\partial \theta_k$ of the loss function, which can then be used to update the parameters by an SGD-like algorithm.

$$
\begin{aligned}
\frac{\partial L}{\partial x_b} = \frac{2}{T} \sum_{c \in C(\mathbf{B}), c \neq s} & \Big\{ \Delta_{b,c} \left(x_b - \mathbf{X}_s z_{b,s} \right) \\
& - \Delta_{j,c} \sum_{j=1, c(j)=s, j \neq b}^{|\mathbf{B}|} z_{j,s}^{(r)} \left(x_j - \mathbf{X}_s z_{j,s} \right) \Big\} \\
& + \frac{2}{T} \sum_{i=1, c(i) \neq s}^{|\mathbf{B}|} \Delta_{i,s} z_{i,s}^{(r)} \left(x_i - \mathbf{X}_s z_{i,s} \right)
\end{aligned}
\tag{8}
$$

where $\Delta_{i,s}$ is a binary variable that is 1 iff the loss term corresponding to anchor sample i and negative class s is non-zero. The loss gradient in (8) is computed for each sample x_b in the batch and back-propagated for computing parameter updates. A summary of the learning algorithm of NSFE is given in Algorithm 1.

Input: A batch of samples $[a_1, \ldots, a_{|\mathbf{B}|}]$ and their labels.

1 Group batch samples by class.

2 Embed and l_2-normalize each sample in the batch: $x_b = f(a_b|\Theta_t)$.

3 For each class $c \in C(\mathbf{B})$, use Cholesky-Factorization to invert $\mathbf{J}_c = \mathbf{X}_c^T \mathbf{X}_c + \lambda \mathbf{I}$.

4 For each class $c \in C(\mathbf{B})$, use Eq. (2) to compute the code vector of its batch samples with respect to $\mathbf{X}_c$.

5 For each class $c \in C(\mathbf{B})$, use Eq. (4) to compute the code vector of other-class samples in the batch with respect to $\mathbf{X}_c$.

6 Compute the LMSL loss L using Eq. (6). Compute and back-propagate the LMSL gradient $\frac{\partial L}{\partial x_b}$, for $b = 1, \ldots, |\mathbf{B}|$.

7 Use the chain rule and Eq. (7) to compute the loss gradients $\frac{\partial L}{\partial \theta_k}$ of the parameters which can then be used to update these parameters.

Algorithm 1. NSFE Learning Algorithm Summary

3.3 Concrete Embeddings

Our method can work with any vector-space inputs and can easily utilize any nonlinear embeddings for which the parameter subgradients of f : $\partial f/\partial \mathbf{\Theta}$ are defined, including feed-forward neural networks. We test the proposed method with two types of vector-space inputs: raw intensity images and the hand-crafted Log-Euclidean Grid of Region Covariance Matrices (LE-GRCM) features proposed in [33]. With intensity images as inputs, we use the 32-layer deep fully convolutional residual network proposed in [36] for the CIFAR-10 dataset. The network has the following configuration:

(a) An initial $3 \times 3 \times 16$ convolutional layer. The notation specifies 16 filters, each has a weight kernel of dimensions 3×3. The stride is always 1 in both directions.
(b) A first block of ten $3 \times 3 \times 16$ convolutional layers, with residual connections made every two layers. The last layer is followed by a 2×2 average pooling with a stride of 2 in both directions.
(c) A second block of ten $3 \times 3 \times 32$ convolutional layers. Residual connections and a final average pooling are defined for this block.
(d) A third block of ten $3 \times 3 \times 64$ convolutional layers. It uses residual connections in a similar fashion but does not have a subsequent pooling layer.
(e) A final $1 \times 1 \times 10$ convolutional layer that is not followed by any nonlinearities or batch normalization [37]. The output of that layer is reshaped as a vector and l_2-normalized to produce the final embedded feature vector.

The final layer replaces the global average pooling operation used in [36] in an attempt to retain spatial information in the computed features. Unless otherwise stated, we add batch normalization and ReLU nonlinearities according to the architecture in [36]. The total number of parameters in this architecture is 463,856, which is less than 0.5 million.

Since an LE-GRCM vector input is not a 2D image, we cannot use a conventional CNN for the embedding to process such hand-crafted features. Instead, we use a very basic, fully-connected 2-layer network with the following architecture: FC-3600 $\rightarrow$ ReLU $\rightarrow$ FC-406 $\rightarrow$ l_2-normalization, where FC-k is a linear fully-connected layer with k units.

3.4 Classification

After training, the learned embedding f is used to map the training data then we use the Online Dictionary Learning (ODL) algorithm described in [38] to compute a dictionary $\mathbf{D}_c$ for each class c. Given a test set, we use the learned embedding f to map it and we follow the MS-SRC approach [10] by computing the mean vector $\bar{\boldsymbol{y}}$ of the embedded test set and then using SRC to find a label for $\bar{\boldsymbol{y}}$. The details of ODL and MS-SRC algorithms can be found in [38] and [10], respectively.

It is worth noting that ODL is an unsupervised algorithm and enhanced performance can be further achieved by using any of the discriminative dictionary learning algorithms instead of ODL. However, we only use ODL in the next section to objectively and more precisely evaluate the effect of NSFE on accuracy.

4 Experiments

We experimentally compare the performance of NSFE against several existing algorithms for image-set classification. The compared methods include Affine Hull-based Image Set Distance (AHISD) [3], its convex variant (CHISD) [3], Sparse-Approximated Nearest Points (SANP) [4], Dictionary-based Face Recognition from Videos (DFRV) [7], Mean Sequence Sparse Representation-based Classification (MS-SRC) [10], Set to Set Distance Metric Learning (SSDML) [26], Deep Reconstruction Models (DRM) [14], Covariance Discriminative Learning (CDL) [8], Log-Euclidean Metric Learning (LEML) [18], and the shallow subspace Feature Learning+SRC (FL+SRC) approach of [33] both with intensity images as inputs (FL+SRC) as well as LE-GRCM features (LE-FL+SRC). We show the results of our method with both intensity features as inputs (NSFE) and LE-GRCM features (LE-NSFE). For comparability, the results of other Log-Euclidean methods (i.e. CDL and LEML) are obtained using LE-GRCM features.

In all experiments, each method is given a set of labeled image sets for training and is required to classify (or more specifically identify) a number of test image sets. For performance comparison, we use the classification accuracy (i.e. recognition rate) as a metric by measuring the percentage of test image sets that are correctly classified.

For existing methods, we have used the source code provided by the original authors and set the parameters according to the recommendations made in their respective papers.

NSFE Parameter Settings: In all experiments, we use SGD with momentum to update the weights of the embedding network in each iteration for a total of 50 K iterations. The momentum is set to 0.9 and we use a learning rate schedule of 0.1 for the first 20 K iterations then we divide it by 10 for each subsequent 10 K iterations. For the 2-layer fully-connected network, we train for 20 K iterations with a learning rate of 0.01 that we decrease to 0.001 after 10 K iterations. We use a batch of size 128. We also set the representation regularization parameter λ of NSFE to 0.01, the margin $m = 0.5$, and the desired number of atoms in each class-specific dictionary computed by ODL to 50.

To guarantee a fair comparison with other methods and to accurately measure the ability of our method to learn effective features, we do not perform any pre-training on any external data and we initialize the weights of our embeddings randomly.

Fig. 4. Sample face pairs from YTC, YTF and MobFaces. Each pair of faces in each column belong to the same subject. YTC and YTF photos reveal large intra-class appearance variations and low resolution. MobFaces photos are relatively frontal but they reveal some challenges such as blur and intra-class variations in illumination and context due to the change in sessions.

The datasets used in our experiments are described below. Figure 4 shows examples from each dataset.

4.1 YouTube Celebrities (YTC)

The YTC dataset contains 1,910 YouTube-downloaded videos of 47 subjects [39]. For a given subject, the videos are short segments clipped from three longer, parent videos downloaded from YouTube. YTC has been built to be very challenging for face tracking and recognition by choosing very low resolution videos with wild variations in pose, scale, hair style, make-up, illumination, motion and number of people per frame.

We perform ten-fold cross-validation experiment. Each fold contains nine distinct videos for each subject: three for training and six for testing, randomly drawn in the same manner of previous works [28,33]. The $9 \times 47 = 423$ videos in each fold are randomly selected from the complete dataset while minimizing the overlap between different folds as much as possible.

Feature Extraction: We use the Viola-Jones (VJ) detector [40] as in prior works [18,33] to locate the faces in each video. Then we use the eye locations detected using the method of [41] to align the subject's face to a standard, 30×36 pixel frame. The intensities of each frame are histogram equalized and we use the faces detected in each video to define the corresponding image set. To test the robustness of the compared methods to outliers, we have not cleaned any of the bad detections or misaligned faces.

4.2 YouTube Faces (YTF)

The YTF dataset contains 3,425 videos of 1,595 subjects with diverse ethnicities [42]. Similar to YTC, YTF videos are downloaded from YouTube and are very challenging for face recognition. Since our method is used for identification rather verification, we adopt the experimental protocol of [33] which is more suitable for testing identification: We use those subjects with four or more videos available. This results in 226 subjects. After randomly dropping one subject, we randomly split the remaining 225 subjects into five mutually exclusive groups, with 45 subjects each. We run the experiment on each group where we use the first three videos of each subject as gallery sets and the remaining videos for testing. Since the dataset provides aligned face images, we extract intensity features from each image by cropping the central 100×100 box, resizing it to 30×36, and histogram-equalizing it.

4.3 Mobile Faces (MobFaces)

The MobFaces dataset has 750 videos of 50 subjects recorded by a smartphone's front camera during usage [43]. Each subject provides 3 sessions $\times$ 5 videos/session (one enrollment + four tasks) where each session is taken under a different illumination and/or in a different place. The dataset includes some mobile camera-specific such as wild variations in illumination and context due to the mobility of the device. We compute the features as for the YTC dataset. We adopt the two evaluation protocols suggested by [43] by dividing the task videos into ten-second long clips and treating each clip as a separate query set. In the first protocol (MobFaces-I), training is done using only the 50 enrollment videos from one session and testing is performed on the ten-second long task video clips from the two other sessions. In the second protocol (MobFaces-II), training is done on the 100 enrollment videos of two sessions and testing is done on the task video clips of the remaining session. Results are reported for each of the six scenarios possible with these protocols. The clipping of the 600 task videos results in 1065 ten-second clips for the first session, 587 the second, and 666 for the third. Note that training sets under these protocols contain relatively very few images with limited appearance (*e.g.* some classes have a single image set with nine almost-identical images only available for training) which makes it challenging.

Table 1. The mean recognition rates obtained with the compared methods on YTC and YTF.

Methods	YTC	YTF
AHISD	57.27	17.18
CHISD	64.79	32.99
SANP	66.99	31.62
DFRV	66.70	36.77
SSDML	69.22	34.02
DRM	70.35	43.99
MS-SRC	74.68	45.02
FL+SRC	75.71	45.36
NSFE (ours)	***78.23**	**54.91**
Methods with LE-GRM input		
CDL	67.62	41.92
LEML	73.26	48.45
LE-FL+SRC	76.28	53.26
LE-NSFE (ours)	**76.42**	***56.66**

4.4 Results

Table 1 shows the mean recognition rate of the compared methods for the YTC and YTF datasets where we group the methods by the type of input features (raw images vs LE-GRCM). For each group, we highlight in **bold** the highest performance under each setting and we place an asterisk $*$ next to the single highest overall performance for that setting. For both datasets and types of input features, the proposed method, NSFE/LE-NSFE, achieves the highest mean recognition rate. Table 2 shows the recognition rates for the six different splits for the MobFaces dataset where we use the same grouping and highlighting adopted by Table 1. The training image sets of this dataset contain very limited visual variations (namely once short video per subject for each setting in MobFaces-I and two such videos in MobFaces-II) while the test image sets are captured under ambient conditions different from those of training. Meanwhile, our method (NSFE/LE-NSFE) ranks among the top two best performing methods under each individual setting and it is the best performing on average for each of the two protocols, with a significant margin on MobFaces-II due to the availability of more images and visual variations during training in that protocol. This shows that our method achieves relatively higher gain in performance as more deta and variations become available for training.

Table 2. The recognition rates obtained on the MobFaces dataset under the different protocols. The setting ($1 \rightarrow \{2,3\}$) involves training on session 1 (i.e. the lit session) and testing on sessions 2 and 3 (i.e. the unlit and day-lit sessions). The other five settings are defined in a similar manner. Each 'avg' column contains the average of the rates obtained under the three settings to its left. Since each session has a different number of test video clips, the average column weighs the rate of each setting by its number of test sets.

Methods	MobFaces-I			
	$1 \rightarrow \{2,3\}$	$2 \rightarrow \{1,3\}$	$3 \rightarrow \{1,2\}$	Avg
AHISD	15.00	31.14	29.30	26.12
CHISD	10.61	26.57	25.73	21.96
SANP	9.34	27.09	26.15	21.96
DFRV	19.39	32.29	30.87	28.30
SSDML	10.53	28.89	26.15	22.95
DRM	33.28	38.94	37.95	37.06
MS-SRC	32.40	46.56	42.49	41.29
FL+SRC	32.88	**46.97**	42.25	41.48
NSFE (ours)	**47.01**	46.27	**46.49**	**46.55**
Methods with LE-GRM input				
CDL	41.66	36.78	42.68	40.21
LEML	42.70	45.93	44.07	44.39
LE-FL+SRC	48.20	***56.21**	54.90	53.58
LE-NSFE (ours)	***49.08**	49.68	***61.38**	***53.69**
Methods	MobFaces-II			
	$\{2,3\} \rightarrow 1$	$\{1,3\} \rightarrow 2$	$\{1,2\} \rightarrow 3$	Avg
AHISD	24.41	51.28	52.85	39.39
CHISD	23.29	44.97	47.60	35.76
SANP	20.38	48.89	45.95	34.94
DFRV	32.11	50.60	52.40	42.62
SSDML	21.31	50.09	54.95	38.27
DRM	**53.62**	70.53	69.37	62.42
MS-SRC	43.29	71.89	75.53	59.79
FL+SRC	44.98	72.40	76.58	61.00
NSFE (ours)	52.11	***81.43**	**83.63**	**68.59**
Methods with LE-GRM input				
CDL	63.57	67.12	65.32	64.97
LEML	49.39	66.95	74.62	61.09
LE-FL+SRC	62.72	75.64	86.19	72.74
LE-NSFE (ours)	***68.92**	**76.15**	***87.84**	***76.19**

5 Conclusion

We presented NSFE, an approach for discriminatively learning a nonlinear embedding that can improve the subspace structured representation of image sets, and thus improve the performance of subspace-based classifiers such as MS-SRC. Since the proposed structured loss function LMSL is minimized in an online fashion, the proposed approach can be used to train existing feed-forward architectures via back-propagation. The minimization algorithm can also utilize the capabilities of modern GPUs, which provide APIs for solving batches of small linear systems of equations. In fact, all the linear systems solved in our batch processing algorithm are small, ranging from 6×6 to 22×22 systems of equations, depending on the number of samples from a certain class available in the batch. Consequently, we were able to train and test many copies of our model for the different experiments described above without facing any unusual delays.

Acknowledgment. This research is based upon work supported by the Office of the Director of National Intelligence (ODNI), Intelligence Advanced Research Projects Activity (IARPA), via IARPA R&D Contract No. 2014-14071600012. The views and conclusions contained herein are those of the authors and should not be interpreted as necessarily representing the official policies or endorsements, either expressed or implied, of the ODNI, IARPA, or the U.S. Government. The U.S. Government is authorized to reproduce and distribute reprints for Governmental purposes notwithstanding any copyright annotation thereon.

References

1. Wang, R., Shan, S., Chen, X., Gao, W.: Manifold-manifold distance with application to face recognition based on image set. In: CVPR, pp. 1–8 (2008)
2. Wang, R., Chen, X.: Manifold discriminant analysis. In: CVPR, pp. 429–436 (2009)
3. Cevikalp, H., Triggs, B.: Face recognition based on image sets. In: CVPR, pp. 2567–2573 (2010)
4. Hu, Y., Mian, A.S., Owens, R.: Sparse approximated nearest points for image set classification. In: CVPR, pp. 121–128 (2011)
5. Harandi, M.T., Sanderson, C., Shirazi, S., Lovell, B.C.: Graph embedding discriminant analysis on Grassmannian manifolds for improved image set matching. In: CVPR, pp. 2705–2712 (2011)
6. Mahmood, A., Mian, A.: Hierarchical sparse spectral clustering for image set classification. In: BMVC, pp. 1–11 (2012)
7. Chen, Y.-C., Patel, V.M., Phillips, P.J., Chellappa, R.: Dictionary-based face recognition from video. In: Fitzgibbon, A., Lazebnik, S., Perona, P., Sato, Y., Schmid, C. (eds.) ECCV 2012. LNCS, vol. 7577, pp. 766–779. Springer, Heidelberg (2012). https://doi.org/10.1007/978-3-642-33783-3_55
8. Wang, R., Guo, H., Davis, L.S., Dai, Q.: Covariance discriminative learning: a natural and efficient approach to image set classification. In: CVPR, pp. 2496–2503 (2012)
9. Harandi, M., Sanderson, C., Shen, C., Lovell, B.C.: Dictionary learning and sparse coding on Grassmann manifolds: an extrinsic solution. In: ICCV, pp. 3120–3127 (2013)

10. Ortiz, E.G., Wright, A., Shah, M.: Face recognition in movie trailers via mean sequence sparse representation-based classification. In: CVPR, pp. 3531–3538 (2013)
11. Chen, S., Sanderson, C., Harandi, M.T., Lovell, B.C.: Improved image set classification via joint sparse approximated nearest subspaces. In: CVPR, pp. 452–459 (2013)
12. Chen, L.: Dual linear regression based classification for face cluster recognition. In: CVPR, pp. 2673–2680 (2014)
13. Mahmood, A., Mian, A., Owens, R.: Semi-supervised spectral clustering for image set classification. In: CVPR, pp. 121–128 (2014)
14. Hayat, M., Bennamoun, M., An, S.: Learning non-linear reconstruction models for image set classification. In: CVPR, pp. 1915–1922 (2014)
15. Hayat, M., Bennamoun, M., An, S.: Reverse training: an efficient approach for image set classification. In: Fleet, D., Pajdla, T., Schiele, B., Tuytelaars, T. (eds.) ECCV 2014. LNCS, vol. 8694, pp. 784–799. Springer, Cham (2014). https://doi.org/10.1007/978-3-319-10599-4_50
16. Lu, J., Wang, G., Deng, W., Moulin, P.: Simultaneous feature and dictionary learning for image set based face recognition. In: Fleet, D., Pajdla, T., Schiele, B., Tuytelaars, T. (eds.) ECCV 2014. LNCS, vol. 8689, pp. 265–280. Springer, Cham (2014). https://doi.org/10.1007/978-3-319-10590-1_18
17. Lu, J., Wang, G., Deng, W., Moulin, P., Zhou, J.: Multi-manifold deep metric learning for image set classification. In: CVPR (2015) 1137–1145
18. Huang, Z., Wang, R., Shan, S., Li, X., Chen, X.: Log-Euclidean metric learning on symmetric positive definite manifold with application to image set classification. In: ICML, pp. 720–729 (2015)
19. Wang, W., Wang, R., Huang, Z., Shan, S., Chen, X.: Discriminant analysis on Riemannian manifold of Gaussian distributions for face recognition with image sets. In: CVPR, pp. 2048–2057 (2015)
20. Basri, R., Jacobs, D.W.: Lambertian reflectance and linear subspaces. PAMI **25**, 218–233 (2003)
21. Wright, J., Yang, A.Y., Ganesh, A., Sastry, S.S., Ma, Y.: Robust face recognition via sparse representation. PAMI **31**, 210–227 (2009)
22. Duchi, J., Hazan, E., Singer, Y.: Adaptive subgradient methods for online learning and stochastic optimization. JMLR **12**, 2121–2159 (2011)
23. Sutskever, I., Martens, J., Dahl, G.E., Hinton, G.E.: On the importance of initialization and momentum in deep learning. In: ICML, pp. 1139–1147 (2013)
24. Hamm, J., Lee, D.D.: Grassmann discriminant analysis: a unifying view on subspace-based learning. In: ICML, pp. 376–383 (2008)
25. Huang, Z., Wang, R., Shan, S., Chen, X.: Projection metric learning on Grassmann manifold with application to video based face recognition. In: CVPR, pp. 140–149 (2015)
26. Zhu, P., Zhang, L., Zuo, W., Zhang, D.: From point to set: extend the learning of distance metrics. In: ICCV, pp. 2664–2671 (2013)
27. Harandi, M., Salzmann, M., Baktashmotlagh, M.: Beyond Gauss: image-set matching on the Riemannian manifold of PDFs. In: ICCV, pp. 4112–4120 (2015)
28. Hayat, M., Bennamoun, M., An, S.: Deep reconstruction models for image set classification. PAMI **37**, 713–727 (2015)
29. Zhang, L., Yang, M., Feng, X.: Sparse representation or collaborative representation: which helps face recognition? In: ICCV, pp. 471–478 (2011)

30. Zhu, P., Zuo, W., Zhang, L., Shiu, S.C.K., Zhang, D.: Image set-based collaborative representation for face recognition. IEEE Trans. Inf. Forens. Secur. **9**, 1120–1132 (2014)
31. Zhang, H., Zhang, Y., Huang, T.S.: Simultaneous discriminative projection and dictionary learning for sparse representation based classification. Pattern Recogn. **46**, 346–354 (2013)
32. Qiu, Q., Sapiro, G.: Learning transformations for clustering and classification. JMLR **16**, 187–225 (2015)
33. Fathy, M.E., Alavi, A., Chellappa, R.: Discriminative Log-Euclidean feature learning for sparse representation-based recognition of faces from videos, pp. 3359–3367 (2016)
34. Weinberger, K.Q., Blitzer, J., Saul, L.K.: Distance metric learning for large margin nearest neighbor classification. In: NIPS, pp. 1473–1480 (2005)
35. Schroff, F., Kalenichenko, D., Philbin, J.: FaceNet: a unified embedding for face recognition and clustering. In: CVPR, pp. 815–823 (2015)
36. He, K., Zhang, X., Ren, S., Sun, J.: Deep residual learning for image recognition. In: CVPR, pp. 770–778 (2016)
37. Ioffe, S., Szegedy, C.: Batch normalization: accelerating deep network training by reducing internal covariate shift. In: ICML, pp. 448–456 (2015)
38. Mairal, J., Bach, F., Ponce, J., Sapiro, G.: Online dictionary learning for sparse coding. In: ICML, pp. 689–696 (2009)
39. Kim, M., Kumar, S., Pavlovic, V., Rowley, H.: Face tracking and recognition with visual constraints in real-world videos. In: CVPR, pp. 1–8 (2008)
40. Viola, P., Jones, M.J.: Robust real-time face detection. IJCV **57**, 137–154 (2004)
41. Asthana, A., Zafeiriou, S., Cheng, S., Pantic, M.: Robust discriminative response map fitting with constrained local models. In: CVPR, pp. 3444–3451 (2013)
42. Wolf, L., Hassner, T., Maoz, I.: Face recognition in unconstrained videos with matched background similarity. In: CVPR, pp. 529–534 (2011)
43. Fathy, M.E., Patel, V.M., Chellappa, R.: Face-based active authentication on mobile devices. In: ICASSP, pp. 1687–1691 (2015)

Continual Occlusion and Optical Flow Estimation

Michal Neoral(✉), Jan Šochman, and Jiří Matas

Center for Machine Perception, Faculty of Electrical Engineering,
Czech Technical University in Prague, Prague, Czech Republic
{neoramic,jan.sochman,matas}@fel.cvut.cz

Abstract. Two optical flow estimation problems are addressed: (i) occlusion estimation and handling, and (ii) estimation from image sequences longer than two frames. The proposed ContinualFlow method estimates occlusions before flow, avoiding the use of flow corrupted by occlusions for their estimation. We show that providing occlusion masks as an additional input to flow estimation improves the standard performance metric by more than 25% on both KITTI and Sintel. As a second contribution, a novel method for incorporating information from past frames into flow estimation is introduced. The previous frame flow serves as an input to occlusion estimation and as a prior in occluded regions, i.e. those without visual correspondences. By continually using the previous frame flow, ContinualFlow performance improves further by 18% on KITTI and 7% on Sintel, achieving top performance on KITTI and Sintel.

1 Introduction

Optical flow is a two-dimensional displacement field describing the projection of scene motion between two images. Occlusions caused by scene motion contribute to the ill-posedness of optical flow estimation – at occluded pixels no visual correspondences exist. Classical non-CNN methods address this problem by using regularisation which extrapolates the flow from the surrounding non-occluded area. Current state-of-the-art CNN algorithms for optical flow use the correlation cost volume [9,16,18,26,31,35] to estimate the most likely correspondences. Their regularisation is only implicit and the network has to learn when to rely on the cost volume and when to extrapolate. In both cases, the occluded areas are processed the same way as non-occluded ones which leads to errors in the occluded areas as well as in the nearby non-occluded regions.

Approaches dealing with occlusions [1,26] usually first estimate initial forward and backward optical flows. Occlusions are found by a forward-backward consistency check and occlusion maps are then used for estimating of the final optical flow. The problem here is that occlusions affect the initial flow and thus the final output.

As our first contribution, we extend a current state-of-the-art CNN optical flow method [35] by estimating the occluded areas first, *without estimating the*

C. V. Jawahar et al. (Eds.): ACCV 2018, LNCS 11364, pp. 159–174, 2019.
https://doi.org/10.1007/978-3-030-20870-7_10

flow, and then passing the occlusion maps to the optical flow estimation network. The correlation cost volume for flow estimation is re-used for occlusion estimation. Intuitively, the cost will be low in non-occluded areas with good correspondences and high in occluded regions. While preserving end-to-end trainability, we accurately estimate occlusions and significantly improve the estimated flow.

Optical flow estimation over more than two frames is a problem whose difficulty stems from the need for the pixels to be mapped to a reference coordinate system before loss evaluation. The mapping is defined by the unknown optical flow itself. Hence, it is difficult to apply temporal regularisation before the flow is known. A typical solution over three frames is to use the middle one as the reference defining the coordinate system and to compute the forward flow to the future frame and the backward flow to the past frame and to apply regularisation to these two flows. Published multi-frame approaches assume various motion constraints: constant rigid motion for three images [41], adaptive trajectory regularisation over five images [38], multi-frame subspace constrains [19] and other complex motion models [12] over the whole sequence.

We avoid modelling the motion regularity explicitly and let a CNN model learn the relations of the current and previous optical flows. The CNN is fed pairs of consecutive images together with the flow computed between the penultimate and last images. We solve the coordinate system mapping by bilinear warp [20]. The proposed method is not limited to a fixed temporal horizon, the network uses previously estimated flows and thus, by recursion, all prior frames.

The two above-mentioned problems – occlusion estimation and the use of multiple frames – are related. Since there are no correspondences in occluded areas, optical flow cannot be estimated from the cost volume and the CNN is forced to use regularisation. Knowing the occlusions and given the previous flow, the network has prior information about the motion to be used when no correspondences are available. So, the last estimated flow is also fed into the occlusions estimation as it is a source of information about possible occlusions.

Finally, we add a specialised refinement network [18,29] to the proposed architecture. It has been shown to improve fine detail accuracy of the flow, which is confirmed by our experiments. We integrate this network with both occlusion estimation and temporal processing.

Contributions. We introduce integrated occlusion estimation, i.e. the algorithm does not operate on an occlusion-ignorant flow estimate, to the state-of-the-art PWC-net [35]. Second, we propose a novel method that implicitly uses all previous frames for optical flow estimation. Finally, we add refinement blocks with additional feature map inputs leading to improved spatial resolution of the final flow. ContinualFlow is state-of-the-art on several public benchmarks[1]: 1st place in Sintel [6][2] and 1st place in the KITTI'15 [27] optical flow benchmark among Robust Vision Challenge (ROB) participants and 3rd over all optical

[1] As of the submission date, July 7, 2018.

[2] The "Final pass" category.

flow methods[3] with a large margin in precision in occluded areas. Continual flow ranked 3rd in ROB [32] for the optical flow category.

2 Related Work

Occlusion Estimation and Occlusion Handling. Most optical flow methods detect occlusions as outliers of the correspondence field [1,2,13] or by a consistency check on the estimated forward and backward optical flows [8,36]. The optical flow is then extrapolated into the occluded areas. The shortcoming of such approaches is that the initial flow is already adversely affected by the occlusions. Other methods incorporate occlusion estimation directly into the energy minimisation [34,37,42] by truncating the data term, avoiding the problematic post-processing of already affected optical flow. The current best performing non-CNN method [17] formulates optical flow estimation symmetrically - estimating the forward and backward flows, occlusions and dis-occlusions in a single joint optimisation.

Most of the current state-of-the-art CNN networks [9,18,31,35] do not explicitly deal with occlusions. The network in [26] estimates the forward and backward flows independently and uses the forward-backward consistency check to estimate the occlusions. The estimated occlusions are then used for network training only. In LiteFlowNet [16] an occlusion probability map is a function of brightness inconsistency between the reference frame and warped target frame. The occlusion probability map is used in a flow regularisation module.

To our best knowledge, no published CNN method estimates occlusions prior to optical flow estimation to improve the flow in the test phase.

Using Multiple Frames. Most methods that process more than two frames impose some kind of regularisation on the flow. Murray and Buxton [28] introduced an approach that uses spatio-temporal smoothness term which regularises optical flow trajectory over multiple frames. However, the algorithm does not work well for large displacements. Black et al. [5] extrapolate the flow from the previous frame as a starting point for the optimisation in the current frame. In Garg et al. [11], the motion regularisation was relaxed from several rigid motions into multi-frame subspace constraints allowing non-rigid motions. Multi-frame subspace constraints were used in [19] over long trajectories. Its extension [12] allows more complex motions using soft constraints between frames. An adaptive trajectory regularisation over five consecutive frames was used in [38], where optical flow was parametrised w.r.t. the central reference frame. Wulff *et al.* [41] use super-pixel segmentation and a rigid motion assumption over triplets of images. ProFlow [23] uses three consecutive frames, a CNN regularises non-CNN-estimated forward ($I_t \rightarrow I_{t+1}$) and backward ($I_{t-1} \rightarrow I_t$) optical flows.

While many non-CNN algorithms use more than two frames in some form, to our best knowledge, no CNN-based method using more frames has been published. Unlike the above-mentioned approaches, the proposed method trains the regularisation from data and does not need any hand-crafted approximations.

[3] Excluding scene flow methods.

The Refinement Network. The last important component added to the proposed architecture is a specialised refinement network [18,29]. We confirm it improves accuracy of fine details of the flow. We integrate the network with both occlusion estimation and temporal processing.

The refinement network was introduced in [18] for optical flow estimation as a part of an architecture specialised on optical flow fine detail refinement. The inputs to the network are the optical flow estimated by previous blocks, the brightness error of the warped image and the input images themselves. In [18,29], it was shown that training the first flow estimation block and the refinement network sequentially leads to improvements in estimated optical flow.

3 ContinualFlow

The proposed ContinualFlow method builds on the state-of-the-art PWC-Net architecture [35]. We extend the architecture by adding (i) occlusion estimation blocks and use the estimated occlusions for flow estimation, (ii) an refinement network to improve fine detail accuracy, and (iii) temporal connections for utilising the previous flow for estimation of both the flow and the occlusions. Figure 1 shows a schematic of the PWC-Net with both the occlusions estimation blocks and temporal connections. Another diagram containing also the refinement network is shown in Fig. 2.

The original PWC-Net [35] is composed of two networks: a *feature pyramid extractor* and a coarse-to-fine *optical flow decoder*. The feature pyramid extractor takes as input two images I_t and I_{t+1} and encodes them into a pyramid of feature vectors $\mathcal{F}_t^s$ and $\mathcal{F}_{t+1}^s$ with gradually decreasing spatial resolution (indexed by s) and with increasing channel dimension. The decoder, in a coarse-to-fine manner, takes features from the corresponding resolution s, warps features $\mathcal{F}_{t+1}^s$ using the up-sampled flow F_{t+1}^{s-1} estimated at a coarser iteration $s-1$ (if not at the coarsest resolution) and builds a correlation cost volume - a volume of feature correlations over a limited displacement range. The cost volume is then fed to the optical flow estimator, which produces the current scale optical flow F^s and the process is repeated for higher resolution. We refer the reader to the original paper for further details. We are using the version with DenseNet [15] and a context network as described in the original paper.

3.1 Occlusion Estimation

PWC-Net and many other state-of-the-art approaches rely on the correlation cost volume for estimation of the optical flow [9,18,26,31,35]. Apart from being useful for the flow estimation, it is also indicative of possible occlusions. Intuitively, when the cost for all displacements for some pixel is high, the pixel is likely occluded in the next frame. In order to utilise this information, we propose to connect the occlusions estimator directly after the cost volume computation, even before any flow is estimated as shown in Fig. 1. The output of the occlusions estimator is then sent to the optical flow estimator together with the cost

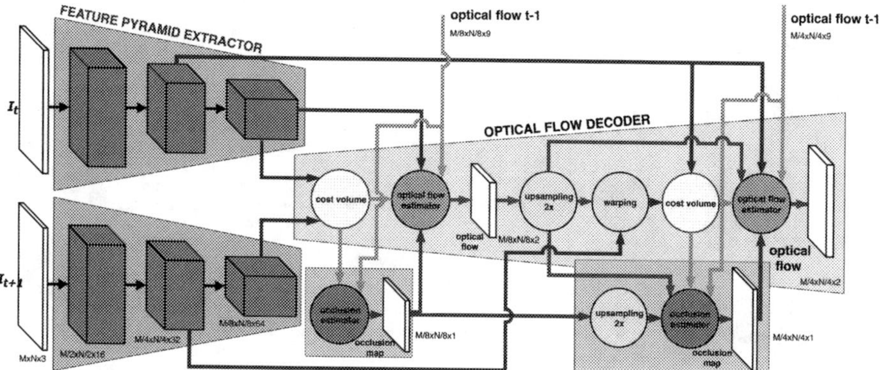

Fig. 1. ContinualFlow - optical flow and occlusion decoder, which extends the PWC-Net [35] flow decoder for occlusion estimation. The feature pyramid extractor (in blue) is a convolutional network which produces a feature pyramid given an input image. A correlation cost volume is computed on each scale from warped features from the second frame using up-sampled flow estimated at a coarser level of decoder. The cost volume is used to estimate occlusions in occlusion estimator (in magenta). The cost volume and the occlusion map are inputs to the optical flow estimator. For clarity, the diagram shows only three of the six levels of the ContinualFlow pyramid extractor. The output resolution is quarter of the input reference frame. Please, refer to the text for additional network details and inputs explanation. (Color figure online)

volume itself. This way the occlusion estimation does not rely on the imprecise flow estimation and the flow estimator benefits from the additional input. Same as the flow estimator, the occlusions estimator works in a coarse-to-fine manner with higher resolution estimators receiving also up-sampled flow estimate from the lower resolution.

In experiments, we use an occlusion estimator with five convolutional layers with D, $\lfloor \frac{D}{2} \rfloor$, $\lfloor \frac{D}{4} \rfloor$, $\lfloor \frac{D}{8} \rfloor$ and two output channels (occluded/not occluded maps), where $D = 89$ in our case (the number of correlation cost volume layers + 8). All layers use ReLU activation except for the last one, which uses soft-max.

3.2 Refinement Network

It was shown that a specialised refinement network which processes the output of the initial network boosts the precision of the flow estimate, especially the fine details recovery [18, 29]. The refinement network takes several extra inputs, like the current estimate of the optical flow, image I_{t+1} warped back to time step t and brightness error between I_t and the warped I_{t+1}, and produces a refined optical flow [18].

The refinement network used in ContinualFlow has the same architecture as the optical flow decoder, but without the DenseNet connections. The main difference is in the network inputs. Instead of using the input images and their warps as in [18], we use the features from the feature pyramid on the corresponding

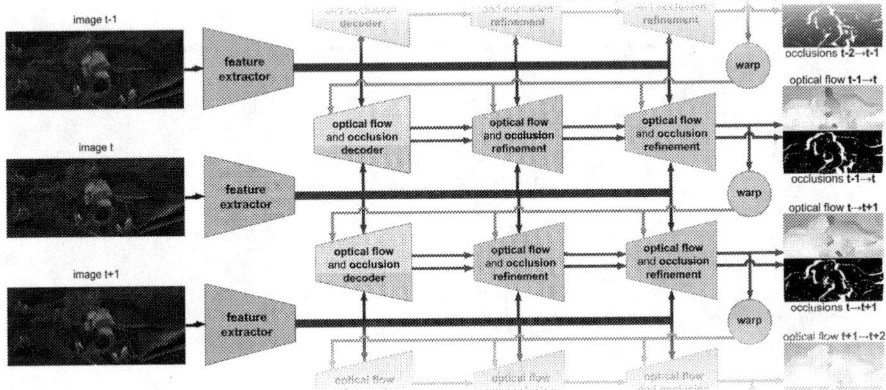

Fig. 2. Block diagram of ContinualFlow. Feature extractors with shared weights compute a feature pyramid from the input images. Features are input to the optical flow and occlusion decoder and the refinement blocks. The decoder estimates the optical flow and the occlusion map from the input features and from the temporal connection – the warped optical flow from the previous time step. Optical flow and occlusion maps are finalised by the refinement blocks.

scale and their warps as a richer input representation. The input error channel for these features is computed as a sum of the L_1 distance and structure similarity (SSIM) [39]. We applied the refinement two times, additional refinements did not improve the accuracy in our experiments.

3.3 ContinualFlow Estimation over Image Sequence

We use temporal connections, which give the optical flow decoder, the occlusions decoder and the refinement network an additional input: the flow estimated in the previous time step (see the orange arrows in Figs. 1 and 2). When processing sequences longer than two frames these connections allow the network to learn typical relations between the previous and current flows and use them in the current frame flow estimation.

However, as discussed in Sect. 1, the coordinate systems in which the two flows are expressed differ and need to be transformed onto each other in order to apply the previous flow to the correct pixels in the current time step. Here we describe two such transformations, forward and backward warping, and we test them independently as well as in combination (concatenation of both) in Sect. 4.

Forward Warping Transformation. Forward warping transforms the coordinate system from time step $t-1$ using the optical flow F_{t-1} itself. The warped flow $\hat{F}_{t-1}$ is computed as

$$\hat{F}_{t-1}(\mathbf{x} + \mathrm{round}(F_{t-1}(\mathbf{x}))) = F_{t-1}(\mathbf{x}), \tag{1}$$

for all pixel positions $\mathbf{x}$. For positions to which the flow F_{t-1} maps more than once we preserve the larger of the mapped flows. This prioritises larger motions, thus faster moving objects. Although the experiments show usefulness of this warping, the main disadvantage of this approach is that the transformation is not differentiable. Thus, the training cannot propagate gradients through this step and relies on the shared weights only.

Backward Warping Transformation. Alternatively, the coordinate system could be transformed using the backward flow B_t from frame t to frame $t-1$. This requires an extra evaluation of the network, but then the warping is a direct application of the differentiable spatial transformer [20]. Thus, in this case the gradients are propagated through the temporal connections during training. A disadvantage of this approach is the computationally expensive computation of the backward flow.

Combining Forward and Backward Warping. It is possible to use both warpings at the same time. In ContinualFlow we combine forward warped previous flow, backward warped previous flow and backward flow by simply concatenating their outputs. The only difference becomes that the previous flow input has nine channels: three times two for the flow warps and a validity masks for each warp (set to zero if the measurement is not available, e.g. at the beginning of the sequence).

Multi-frame Sequence Initialisation. The network is fed a pair of input images and the previously estimated flow. For the first frame in the sequence, no previous flow estimation is available. We estimate the initial optical flow between the first and second frame twice. First, we mask out the temporal connection and, in the second estimation, we use the first estimate as a temporal input.

3.4 Training Loss

The network is trained end-to-end with a weighted multi-task loss over the flow and occlusions estimators at all scales,

$$\mathcal{L} = \sum_{s=1}^{S} \alpha^s \mathcal{L}_F^s + \alpha_O \sum_{s=1}^{S} \alpha^s \mathcal{L}_O^s, \tag{2}$$

where α^s is the weight of individual scale s losses and α_O is the occlusion estimation weight. The sums are over all S spatial resolutions. The flow estimator loss $\mathcal{L}_F$ is the same as in PWC-Net, i.e. the end-point error

$$\mathcal{L}_F^s = \sum_{\mathbf{x}} \gamma(\mathbf{x}) ||F^s(\mathbf{x}) - F_{gt}^s(\mathbf{x})||_2, \tag{3}$$

where F^s is the estimated optical flow at scale s, F_{gt}^s the corresponding ground-truth optical flow and γ is the valid ground-truth flow mask (one for valid flow and zero otherwise). The sum is over all pixel positions. As in [7,43] we adopted the weighted pixel-wise cross-entropy loss for occlusion map estimation

$$\begin{aligned} \mathcal{L}_O^s = &- w_{noc} \sum_{\mathbf{x}:\, O_{gt}(\mathbf{x})=1} \rho(\mathbf{x}) \log \Pr(O(\mathbf{x}) = 1|X) \\ &- w_{occ} \sum_{\mathbf{x}:\, O_{gt}(\mathbf{x})=0} \rho(\mathbf{x}) \log \Pr(O(\mathbf{x}) = 0|X), \end{aligned} \tag{4}$$

where $\Pr(O(\mathbf{x}) = 1|X)$ is computed using soft-max $\sigma(\cdot)$ function on the occlusion estimator output O, O_{gt} is the ground truth occlusion map, ρ the valid ground-truth occlusion mask used for masking out images without ground-truth occlusions, and w_{occ} and w_{noc} are the fractions of occluded and non-occluded ground truth pixels respectively.

As suggested by [35], we modify this loss for the final fine-tuning on the most complex evaluation benchmark datasets. Here we change the $\mathcal{L}_F^s$ loss to the generalised Charbonnier loss (with $q = 0.4$, $\epsilon = 0.01$ as in [35]):

$$\mathcal{L}_F^s = \sum_{\mathbf{x}} \gamma(\mathbf{x}) \left(|\hat{F}^s(\mathbf{x}) - F_{\mathbf{gt}}^s(\mathbf{x})| + \epsilon \right)^q . \tag{5}$$

4 Experiments

Training Details. The ContinualFlow network is trained using a curriculum learning approach [4] starting from a dataset with less complex motions and increasing gradually the task complexity [18,35]. First, we train on FlyingChairs dataset [9] using the training parameters introduced in [35] and following the learning rate schedule from [18]. We do not use rotation, scaling and translation augmentations. Since the FlyingChairs dataset contains only two frames sequences and no occlusion ground truth, we cannot train the full ContinualFlow model with temporal connections and the occlusion map estimation. Instead, we use it for pre-training the PWC-Net part of the ContinualFlow network. The network is trained for 1200k iteration and the learning rate 1e−4 is divided by 2 each 200k iteration, starting from 400k. Images in a batch of size eight are randomly cropped to 448×384 px.

Next, the all parts of the ContinualFlow network are trained on the FlyingThings dataset [25]. Since occlusion maps were not available for this dataset, we computed them using the available backward and forward ground truth flows and the object segmentation masks. The mask $O_t(\mathbf{x})$ is set to "occluded" for pixel x when the object labels $L_t(\mathbf{x})$ and $L_{t+1}(F_{gt}(\mathbf{x}))$ differ or the bi-directional consistency between backward and forward flows differs by more than one pixel. The network is trained for 500k iteration and the learning rate, set to 1e−4 for the first 200k iterations, is divided by 2 at that point and after 100k iterations. First, we train the network without the refinement. Then, only the refinement is trained while all other weights are fixed. Images in the batch of size four are

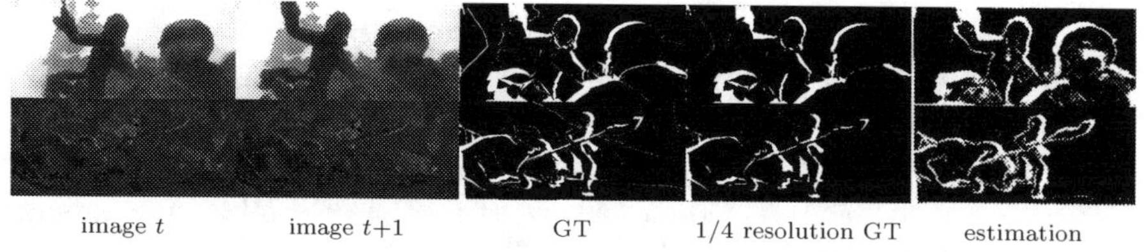

Fig. 3. Example estimated occlusion maps on the Sintel (final) dataset, our validation split. ContinualFlow estimates occlusions up to quarter resolution.

randomly cropped to 768 × 384 px. After cropping, optical flow pointing out of the frame is labelled as occluded.

Finally, the ContinualFlow is trained on data from six datasets: Driving [25], KITTI'15 [27], VirtualKITTI [10], Sintel [6], HD1K [22] and the FlyingChairs small motions dataset [18]. These datasets, except for FlyingChairs, contain sequences longer than two frames and are suitable for the training of temporal connections. We used the first image twice for the FlyingChairs dataset to obtain the same batch size for all input data, the loss on the estimate of the (zero) flow $F^{0,1}$ is not used. Dense occlusion maps are available only for the Sintel and Driving datasets. We set occlusion estimation loss to zero on the rest. The network is fine-tuned for 500k iteration and the learning rate, set to 1e−5 for the first 200k interactions, is divided by 2 at that point and after 100k iterations. Images in batches of size four are randomly cropped to 768 × 320 px. We sample images from all datasets uniformly.

We set weights for individual scales as in [35]. Maximal displacement in the cost volume is set to four. The same scale weights are set to train the refinement network and for the occlusion map estimation. The occlusion estimation weight α_O is set to 0.1. All experiments are trained with the ADAM optimiser [21] and 0.0004 weight decay. All parts of the network are implemented in TensorFlow.

The ContinualFlow training has the same three phases as training of PWC-Net. Only when training the refinement network separately, there is an additional phase which updates only the refinement parameters as mentioned above. ContinualFlow without the refinement network has 9.6M parameters, 0.8M more than the PWC-Net. The refinement network adds 5.0M parameters, it is based on the PWC-Net-small architecture. ContinualFlow runs at 8 FPS on KITTI-resolution of 1240 × 375 px.

In the following, we focus on the Robust Vision Challenge [32], where one trained model with the same parameters has to be evaluated on four individual benchmarks [3,6,22,27] instead of fine-tuning for each particular dataset independently.

4.1 Ablation Study

In this section, we experimentally evaluate the individual contributions and design choices for the ContinualFlow network trained on FlyingChairs [9] and fine-tuned on FlyingThings [25] as described above. Below, the term *baseline* refers to our TensorFlow implementation of PWC-Net. Unlike the PWC-Net settings [35], we trained the network without rotation, scaling and translation augmentation of input frames.

Occlusion Map Learning. Table 1 shows the results of optical flow estimation with and without occlusion learning. Temporal connections are not used. Application of the occlusion map estimator improves performance on all tested datasets not only in occluded regions but also in all non-occluded regions. Figure 3 shows example estimated occlusion maps.

The Specialised Refinement Block. improves results of the estimated optical flow as is shown in [18]. Table 1 compares the optical flow estimation with and without the refinement block. No temporal connections are used. The refinement block improves the estimated optical flow, especially in occluded areas.

Influence of the Coordinate Warping Methods. We evaluated the three approaches for warping the previous flow estimate introduced in Sect. 3.3. Results for individual datasets are shown in Table 1. Forward warping W_f is beneficial for the KITTI dataset [27] and the Sintel Clean dataset [6], while backward warping W_b is more suitable for the complex Sintel Final sequences. The combination of both, W_{bf}, is the most accurate on FlyingThings sequences [25]. All evaluated variants use the occlusion estimator in the decoder and no refinement.

Temporal Connection Placement. We experimented with passing the warped optical flow from previous frame to different network components, thus creating different temporal connections. In one variant, only the refinement network received the previous frame flow estimates. In another variant, all temporal connections as depicted in Fig. 2 were used. Table 1 shows how feeding these connections with different warpings influences the estimated flow. The best results were obtained with temporal connections leading into both the decoder and refinement networks and the combination of forward and backward warpings.

Number of Refinement Blocks. Table 1 shows results for 1, 2, 3 and 5 stacked refinement networks. Stacking more than two refinement networks is not beneficial. Thus the final network architecture contains only two refinements. All evaluated variants use the occlusion estimator and warps the previously estimated optical flow using both warping methods in the first part of the network and the refinement.

Multi-frame Sequences Initialisation. For the first frame in the sequence, no previous frame flow estimate is available to be passed to the temporal connections. Unsurprisingly, the estimation on the first frame is usually slightly worse than at the consecutive frames. We tested two initialisations of the first frame flow estimation: (i) no flow (zero displacements) instead of the previously estimated optical flow and, (ii) a two-pass initial estimation of the currently estimated optical flow as described in Sect. 3.3. We evaluated both approaches for an increased length of the sequence on different datasets. As shown in Table 1,

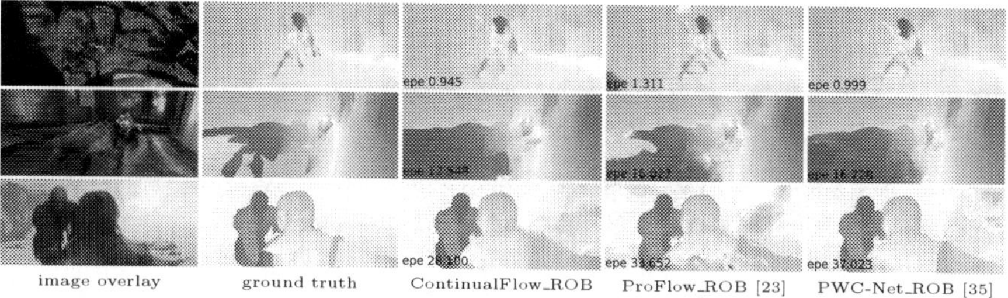

Fig. 4. Example results on Sintel final-pass for ContinualFlow closest competitors in the Robust Vision Challenge. End-point-error for each method is shown for particular scenes.

the two-pass initialisation leads to quicker convergence and is most beneficial for the first optical flow estimation in the sequence.

4.2 Comparison with State of the Art

We start by noting that a single model was used for all benchmarks without further fine-tuning to individual datasets. We were not able to evaluate occlusions on public benchmarks since there is no benchmark available for occlusion map estimation. ContinualFlow achieves recall 0.87 and F1-score 0.83 for the validation split of FlyingThings [25] and recall 0.72 and F1-score 0.48 for Sintel [6]. Examples of estimated occlusion maps are shown in Fig. 3.

KITTI'15. optical flow benchmark [27] results are reported in Table 2. Fl refers to the KITTI evaluation metric – the percentage of pixels with end-point-error greater than 3 px. Our method ranked first among methods participating in the Robust Vision Challenge (ROB) and third for all optical flow estimation methods with score 10.03% on all evaluated pixels. We are interested in ROB Challenge since methods outside ROB fine-tune on each particular dataset, resulting in over-fitting, which we wanted to avoid.

Sintel. Figure 4 shows visual comparison with the closest competitors. Results of ROB participants on the Sintel dataset are reported in Table 3. ContinualFlow ranked first on Sintel Final for the all pixels end-point-error evaluation. As we are focused on occlusion estimation and handling, we point out that ContinualFlow achieves best results for estimation in occluded areas with significant margin.

Robust Vision Challenge. A snapshot of the leaderboard[4] of optical flow Robust Vision Challenge [32] is shown in Table 4. ContinualFlow is built on our implementation of PWC-Net [35]. While ContinualFlow did not achieve a better results in the ROB than the original PWC-Net, the experiments show that our contributions outperform the results of our baseline.

[4] As of July 7, 2018.

Table 1. Ablation study of ContinualFlow. The leftmost column codes the experiment configurations: occlusion estimator (+OC); refinement network (+R); temporal connection with forward warping (W_f), backward warping (W_b) and both warping methods (W_{bf}); previous flow input in the refinement (RW_x); and two pass (2pass) initialisation of the first frame of the sequence N frames long. Performance measure are the KITTI 3-pixel error metric (column Fl) and the end-point error (in pixels, all other columns) for background (bg), foreground (fg), occluded (occ), non-occluded (noc) and all (all) pixels. The best performance in bold. All models trained on FlyingChairs and fine-tuned on FlyingThings. See Sect. 3 for details.

	FlyingThings					KITTI'15 noc		KITTI'15 occ		Sintel Clean			Sintel Final		
	all	occ-bg	occ-fg	noc-bg	noc-fg	Fl-all	all	Fl-all	all	all	occ	noc	all	occ	noc
common: baseline	**Occlusion map learning**														
	22.79	25.31	53.88	10.64	26.78	37.73	7.82	43.56	14.16	3.45	9.29	2.38	5.36	12.03	4.17
+OC	**18.01**	**18.27**	**47.53**	**7.10**	**20.13**	**23.98**	**5.22**	**31.12**	**10.60**	**2.45**	**7.46**	**1.53**	**4.02**	**9.99**	**2.91**
common: baseline+OC	**The specialised refinement block**														
	18.01	18.27	47.53	**7.10**	**20.13**	23.98	5.22	31.12	10.60	2.45	7.46	1.53	4.02	9.99	2.91
+R	**17.80**	**17.49**	**45.90**	7.31	21.46	**21.14**	**4.78**	**28.61**	**9.83**	**2.30**	**7.11**	**1.42**	**3.87**	**9.68**	**2.76**
common: baseline+OC	**Influence of coordinate warping methods**														
	18.01	18.27	47.53	7.10	20.13	23.98	5.22	31.12	10.60	2.45	7.46	1.53	4.02	9.99	2.91
$+W_f$	14.90	14.89	38.75	6.55	**16.69**	**20.78**	**4.13**	**27.85**	**8.28**	**2.18**	**6.67**	**1.37**	4.04	9.48	3.03
$+W_b$	16.33	17.10	39.68	6.49	20.72	26.52	4.56	33.80	10.64	2.58	7.49	1.70	**3.79**	9.27	**2.80**
$+W_{bf}$	**14.64**	**14.84**	**36.05**	**6.10**	17.65	23.64	4.56	30.92	9.46	2.36	6.79	1.59	3.81	**8.97**	2.87
common: baseline+OC	**Temporal connection placement**														
$+RW_f$	16.10	15.87	38.71	6.76	19.01	23.11	4.88	30.35	9.82	2.27	6.89	**1.45**	3.92	9.34	2.90
$+RW_{bf}$	14.90	15.35	37.55	**5.78**	17.69	24.54	4.84	32.18	10.12	2.35	6.93	1.54	**3.55**	**8.62**	**2.65**
$+W_{bf}$	14.64	14.84	36.05	6.10	17.65	23.64	4.56	30.92	9.46	2.36	6.79	1.59	3.81	8.97	2.87
$+W_{bf}+RW_{bf}$	**14.28**	**14.24**	**35.58**	5.82	**17.56**	**21.72**	**4.41**	**29.48**	**9.33**	**2.26**	**6.66**	1.49	3.70	8.81	2.76
common: baseline+OC+W_{bf}	**Number of refinement blocks**														
$+1xRW_{bf}$	14.28	14.24	35.58	5.82	**17.56**	**21.72**	**4.41**	**29.48**	**9.33**	**2.26**	**6.71**	**1.47**	**3.76**	**8.93**	2.80
$+2xRW_{bf}$	**14.26**	**14.13**	**35.60**	5.78	17.62	21.77	4.45	29.62	9.35	**2.26**	6.72	**1.47**	**3.76**	8.96	**2.79**
$+3xRW_{bf}$	14.30	**14.13**	35.71	**5.75**	17.77	21.98	4.50	29.86	9.40	**2.26**	6.74	**1.47**	3.77	8.99	2.80
$+5xRW_{bf}$	14.43	14.24	36.16	**5.75**	17.93	22.48	4.58	30.35	9.49	2.28	6.80	1.48	3.80	9.03	2.83
common: baseline+OC+W_{bf}+RW_{bf}	**Multi-frame sequence initialisation**														
2 frames	-	-	-	-	-	25.08	5.50	32.59	11.56	2.48	7.72	1.48	3.84	9.64	2.75
2 frames+2pass	-	-	-	-	-	**23.06**	**5.03**	**30.92**	**11.00**	**2.41**	**7.60**	**1.41**	**3.74**	**9.48**	**2.66**
3 frames	-	-	-	-	-	21.72	4.41	29.48	9.33	2.26	6.71	**1.47**	3.76	8.93	2.80
3 frames+2pass	-	-	-	-	-	**21.65**	**4.36**	**29.42**	**9.23**	**2.26**	**6.71**	1.48	**3.73**	**8.92**	**2.76**
4 frames	-	-	-	-	-	**21.53**	4.30	**29.32**	9.05	**2.23**	6.59	1.46	3.75	8.83	2.82
4 frames+2pass	-	-	-	-	-	21.54	**4.30**	29.33	**9.02**	2.24	**6.59**	**1.46**	**3.73**	**8.80**	**2.80**
5 frames	-	-	-	-	-	**21.48**	**4.25**	**29.27**	**8.92**	**2.21**	**6.51**	**1.45**	3.80	8.85	2.87
5 frames+2pass	-	-	-	-	-	**21.48**	**4.25**	29.28	**8.92**	**2.21**	6.52	1.46	**3.79**	**8.83**	**2.86**
10 frames	-	-	-	-	-	21.49	**4.24**	29.28	8.90	-	-	-	-	-	-
10 frames+2pass	-	-	-	-	-	**21.48**	**4.24**	**29.27**	**8.89**	-	-	-	-	-	-

The source code for PWC-Net was released by the authors just days before the ACCV submission deadline, so a direct comparison was possible only through ROB vision challenge submissions, which are limited in number by the challenge rules. We did our best to follow the paper regarding the architecture, parameters and training. Later, when analysing the results, we found two main differences: (i) Due to implementation issues, we omitted rotation and scaling data augmentations, which in retrospect could harm the performance significantly as suggested in [24]. (ii) Our implementation is in Tensorflow whereas the original implementation is in Caffe, so some of the suggested training parameter values

Table 2. KITTI'15 optical flow benchmark results of Robust Vision Challenge participants as of June 7, 2018. Performance measured by the KITTI 3-pixel error metric (column Fl) and the end-point error (in pixels, all other columns) for background (bg), foreground (fg), occluded (occ), non-occluded (noc) and all (all) pixels. The best results in bold. Anonymous entries in time of paper submission are marked [anon]. Methods are sorted according to Fl-all, the default ranking for KITTI.

Fl (%)	KITTI'15 occ (%)			KITTI'15 noc (%)		
	bg	fg	all	bg	fg	all
ContinualFlow_ROB	**8.54**	17.48	**10.03**	**5.90**	14.99	7.55
LFNet_ROB [anon]	11.18	10.20	11.01	6.14	6.87	**6.27**
PWC-Net_ROB [35]	11.22	13.69	11.63	7.12	10.29	7.69
ProFlow_ROB [23]	14.15	21.82	15.42	8.44	17.90	10.15
FF++_ROB [33]	15.32	19.27	15.97	7.82	15.33	9.18
ResPWCR_ROB [anon]	16.63	16.18	16.55	10.10	12.23	10.49
AugFNG_ROB [anon]	19.77	**9.95**	18.14	13.75	**6.71**	12.47
DMF_ROB [40]	30.74	30.07	30.63	19.32	25.60	20.46

Table 3. Sintel benchmark results for Robust Vision Challenge participants. Performance measured the end-point error (EPE, in pixels) for matched (noc), unmatched (occ) and all (all) pixels. The best results in bold. Anonymous entries marked [anon]. Methods are sorted by EPE all, the default ranking for Sintel.

	Sintel final			Sintel clean		
	all	noc	occ	all	noc	occ
ContinualFlow_ROB	**4.528**	2.723	**19.248**	3.341	1.752	**16.292**
PWC-Net_ROB [35]	4.903	**2.454**	24.878	3.897	1.726	21.637
ProFlow_ROB [23]	5.015	2.659	24.192	**2.709**	**1.013**	16.549
AugFNG_ROB [anon]	5.500	2.978	26.052	3.606	1.603	19.939
LFNet_ROB [anon]	5.966	3.278	27.893	4.815	2.333	25.065
FF++_ROB [33]	6.496	2.990	35.057	3.953	1.148	26.836
ResPWCR_ROB [anon]	6.530	3.849	28.371	5.674	3.138	26.380
DMF_ROB [40]	7.475	3.575	39.245	5.368	1.742	34.899

may need to be fine-tuned for this framework. Still, the ablation study clearly shows the impact and significance of the novelties (occlusion estimation, feeding the previous estimate of optical flow as input).

Table 4. Robust Vision Challenge. Performance measured by ranking of all metrics in individual datasets. The best results in bold. Anonymous entries marked [anon]. Methods are sorted by the Robust Vision Challenge rank.

	Middlebury	KITTI	MPI Sintel	HD1K
PWC-Net_ROB [35]	2	4	2	1
ProFlow_ROB [23]	1	6	1	4
ContinualFlow_ROB	5	2	3	3
LFNet_ROB [anon]	7	1	6	5
AugFNG_ROB [anon]	9	3	4	2
FF++_ROB [33]	3	5	5	6
DMF_ROB [40]	4	8	7	8
ResPWCR_ROB [anon]	6	7	8	7
WOLF_ROB [anon]	8	9	9	9
TVL1_ROB [30]	10	10	10	10
H+S_ROB [14]	11	11	11	11

5 Conclusion

The ContinualFlow network for optical flow estimation was introduced, with two novelties - occlusion estimation integrated in the optic flow computation and the use of the optic flow from the previous time instant, and, through recursion, of all prior flows. We showed that the two contributions improve performance, especially in occluded areas or areas close to motion discontinuities. In evaluation on standard dataset ContinualFlow is top ranked in Sintel and 3rd in KITTI.

Acknowledgements. The research was supported by Toyota Motor Europe, CTU student grant SGS17/185/OHK3/3T/13 and the OP VVV MEYS project CZ.02.1.01/0.0/0.0/16_019/0000765 Research Center for Informatics.

References

1. Bailer, C., Taetz, B., Stricker, D.: Flow fields: dense correspondence fields for highly accurate large displacement optical flow estimation. In: ICCV (2015)
2. Bailer, C., Varanasi, K., Stricker, D.: CNN-based patch matching for optical flow with thresholded hinge embedding loss. In: CVPR, pp. 3250–3259 (2017)
3. Baker, S., Scharstein, D., Lewis, J.P., Roth, S., Black, M.J., Szeliski, R.: A database and evaluation methodology for optical flow. IJCV (2011). https://doi.org/10.1007/s11263-010-0390-2
4. Bengio, Y., Louradour, J., Collobert, R., Weston, J.: Curriculum learning. In: International Conference on Machine Learning, pp. 41–48. ACM (2009)
5. Black, M.J., Anandan, P.: Robust dynamic motion estimation over time. In: CVPR (1991)

6. Butler, D.J., Wulff, J., Stanley, G.B., Black, M.J.: A naturalistic open source movie for optical flow evaluation. In: Fitzgibbon, A., Lazebnik, S., Perona, P., Sato, Y., Schmid, C. (eds.) ECCV 2012. LNCS, vol. 7577, pp. 611–625. Springer, Heidelberg (2012). https://doi.org/10.1007/978-3-642-33783-3_44
7. Caelles, S., Maninis, K.K., Pont-Tuset, J., Leal-Taixé, L., Cremers, D., Van Gool, L.: One-shot video object segmentation. In: CVPR 2017. IEEE (2017)
8. Chen, Q., Koltun, V.: Full flow: optical flow estimation by global optimization over regular grids. In: CVPR (2016)
9. Dosovitskiy, A., et al.: FlowNet: learning optical flow with convolutional networks. In: ICCV, pp. 2758–2766, December 2015
10. Gaidon, A., Wang, Q., Cabon, Y., Vig, E.: Virtual worlds as proxy for multi-object tracking analysis. In: CVPR (2016)
11. Garg, R., Pizarro, L., Rueckert, D., Agapito, L.: Dense multi-frame optic flow for non-rigid objects using subspace constraints. In: Kimmel, R., Klette, R., Sugimoto, A. (eds.) ACCV 2010. LNCS, vol. 6495, pp. 460–473. Springer, Heidelberg (2011). https://doi.org/10.1007/978-3-642-19282-1_37
12. Garg, R., Roussos, A., Agapito, L.: A variational approach to video registration with subspace constraints. IJCV **104**(3), 286–314 (2013)
13. Güney, F., Geiger, A.: Deep discrete flow. In: Lai, S.-H., Lepetit, V., Nishino, K., Sato, Y. (eds.) ACCV 2016. LNCS, vol. 10114, pp. 207–224. Springer, Cham (2017). https://doi.org/10.1007/978-3-319-54190-7_13
14. Horn, B.K., Schunck, B.G.: Determining optical flow. Artif. Intell. **17**(1–3), 185–203 (1981)
15. Huang, G., Liu, Z., Weinberger, K.Q., van der Maaten, L.: Densely connected convolutional networks. In: CVPR (2017)
16. Hui, T.W., Tang, X., Loy, C.C.: LiteFlowNet: a lightweight convolutional neural network for optical flow estimation. In: CVPR, June 2018
17. Hur, J., Roth, S.: MirrorFlow: exploiting symmetries in joint optical flow and occlusion estimation. ICCV (2017)
18. Ilg, E., Mayer, N., Saikia, T., Keuper, M., Dosovitskiy, A., Brox, T.: FlowNet 2.0: evolution of optical flow estimation with deep networks. In: CVPR (2017)
19. Irani, M.: Multi-frame correspondence estimation using subspace constraints. IJCV **48**(3), 173–194 (2002)
20. Jaderberg, M., Simonyan, K., Zisserman, A., et al.: Spatial transformer networks. In: ANIPS (2015)
21. Kingma, D.P., Ba, J.: Adam: a method for stochastic optimization. In: ICLR (2015)
22. Kondermann, D., et al.: The HCI benchmark suite: stereo and flow ground truth with uncertainties for urban autonomous driving. In: CVPR (2016)
23. Maurer, D., Bruhn, A.: ProFlow: learning to predict optical flow. In: BMVC (2018)
24. Mayer, N., et al.: What makes good synthetic training data for learning disparity and optical flow estimation? IJCV **126**(9), 942–960 (2018)
25. Mayer, N., et al.: A large dataset to train convolutional networks for disparity, optical flow, and scene flow estimation. In: CVPR (2016)
26. Meister, S., Hur, J., Roth, S.: UnFlow: unsupervised learning of optical flow with a bidirectional census loss. In: AAAI (2018)
27. Menze, M., Geiger, A.: Object scene flow for autonomous vehicles. In: CVPR (2015)
28. Murray, D.W., Buxton, B.F.: Scene segmentation from visual motion using global optimization. PAMI **9**, 220–228 (1987)
29. Pang, J., Sun, W., Ren, J.S., Yang, C., Yan, Q.: Cascade residual learning: a two-stage convolutional neural network for stereo matching. In: CVPR (2017)

30. Pérez, J.S., Meinhardt-Llopis, E., Facciolo, G.: TV-L1 optical flow estimation. Image Process. Line **3**, 137–150 (2013)
31. Ranjan, A., Black, M.J.: Optical flow estimation using a spatial pyramid network. In: CVPR (2018)
32. Robust vision challenge team: robust vision challenge (2018). http://www.robustvision.net. Accessed 8 July 2018
33. Schuster, R., Bailer, C., Wasenmüller, O., Stricker, D.: FlowFields++: accurate optical flow correspondences meet robust interpolation. In: ICIP (2018)
34. Sun, D., Liu, C., Pfister, H.: Local layering for joint motion estimation and occlusion detection. In: CVPR, pp. 1098–1105 (2014)
35. Sun, D., Yang, X., Liu, M.Y., Kautz, J.: PWC-Net: CNNs for optical flow using pyramid, warping, and cost volume. In: CVPR (2018)
36. Sundaram, N., Brox, T., Keutzer, K.: Dense point trajectories by GPU-accelerated large displacement optical flow. In: Daniilidis, K., Maragos, P., Paragios, N. (eds.) ECCV 2010. LNCS, vol. 6311, pp. 438–451. Springer, Heidelberg (2010). https://doi.org/10.1007/978-3-642-15549-9_32
37. Unger, M., Werlberger, M., Pock, T., Bischof, H.: Joint motion estimation and segmentation of complex scenes with label costs and occlusion modeling. In: CVPR, pp. 1878–1885. IEEE (2012)
38. Volz, S., Bruhn, A., Valgaerts, L., Zimmer, H.: Modeling temporal coherence for optical flow. In: ICCV (2011)
39. Wang, Z., Bovik, A.C., Sheikh, H.R., Simoncelli, E.P.: Image quality assessment: from error visibility to structural similarity. IEEE Trans. Image Process. **13**(4), 600–612 (2004)
40. Weinzaepfel, P., Revaud, J., Harchaoui, Z., Schmid, C.: DeepFlow: large displacement optical flow with deep matching. In: ICCV (2013)
41. Wulff, J., Sevilla-Lara, L., Black, M.J.: Optical flow in mostly rigid scenes. In: CVPR (2017)
42. Xiao, J., Cheng, H., Sawhney, H., Rao, C., Isnardi, M.: Bilateral filtering-based optical flow estimation with occlusion detection. In: Leonardis, A., Bischof, H., Pinz, A. (eds.) ECCV 2006. LNCS, vol. 3951, pp. 211–224. Springer, Heidelberg (2006). https://doi.org/10.1007/11744023_17
43. Xie, S., Tu, Z.: Holistically-nested edge detection. In: ICCV, pp. 1395–1403 (2015)

Adversarial Learning for Visual Storytelling with Sense Group Partition

Lingbo Mo[1(✉)], Chunhong Zhang[2], Yang Ji[2], and Zheng Hu[1]

[1] State Key Laboratory of Networking and Switching Technology, Beijing University of Posts and Telecommunications, Beijing 100876, China
molingbochn@gmail.com, huzheng@bupt.edu.cn

[2] Key Laboratory of Universal Wireless Communications, Ministry of Education, Beijing, China
{zhangch,jiyang}@bupt.edu.cn

Abstract. Visual storytelling aims to investigate the generation of a paragraph to describe the content of a photo stream. Despite the substantial progress in vision and language research, the techniques for sequential vision-to-language are still far away from being perfect. Due to the limitation of maximum likelihood estimation on training, the majority of existing models encourage high resemblance to texts in the training database, which makes the description overly rigid and lack in diverse expressions. Therefore, We cast the task as a reinforcement learning problem and propose an Adversarial All-in-one Learning (AAL) framework to learn a reward model, which simultaneously incorporates the information of all images in the photo stream and all texts in the paragraph, and optimize a generative model with the estimated reward. Specifically, in light of the linguistic reading theory with sense group as the unit, we propose to do the paragraph generation at sense group level instead of sentence level. Experiments on the widely-used dataset show that our approach generates higher-quality descriptions than previous baselines.

Keywords: Vision and language · Sense group · Adversarial learning

1 Introduction

Generating a natural story for an ordered image sequence, known as visual storytelling, is a challenging task in the field of both computer vision and natural language processing. Compared with image caption generation, it requires not only to understand each image fully in the sequence, as well as relations among different images, but also to generate a human-like paragraph to describe the content of images. Before dealing with this task, a fundamental question needs to be answered: what are crucial aspects that define an ideal story for an image stream? According to the common sense, we expect to produce a story that possesses three properties: (1) **Correctness:** the generated descriptions should be able to reflect the visual content. (2) **Expressiveness:** imagine that, if you tell

C. V. Jawahar et al. (Eds.): ACCV 2018, LNCS 11364, pp. 175–190, 2019.
https://doi.org/10.1007/978-3-030-20870-7_11

someone a story I told you today, it probably won't be word for word exactly as I said it. Still, it will be basically the same story, but is more likely to produce notably different expressions. (3) **Coherence:** when presented with a few images, stories should be coherent and take into account the temporal context. Figure 1 shows an example of visual storytelling with these three properties.

Story #1 : Many people were on the street. Two women sat on the tractor. There were a lot of balloons. A few people wore colored hats. The woman was very happy.

Story #2 : The family was excited to participate in a parade. My aunts sat waiting for the parade to start. They had their balloons of all shapes and colors. There were hats and balloons for everyone. We made pom-poms to celebrate.

Fig. 1. An example of visual storytelling. We present two stories that match the same image sequence. The first story is a poor one, and the second is an ideal story. The colored words demonstrate the coherence of the story, and the underlined words shows the expressiveness. (Color figure online)

From the perspective of how paragraphs are generated, previous visual storytelling works can be basically classified into two types. The first type is to view visual storytelling as a retrieval task, which is an information search task that requires a ranked list of existed sentences related to input images. This type of method creates the final paragraph for narrating the image stream by concatenating individual sentences retrieved from training database. In this case, there is one obvious problem that the generated paragraph is lack of **expressiveness**. It is widely known that given a sequence of images, different people could produce descriptions in different ways. Thus, expressive languages are essential to the goal of generating human-like paragraphs. However, every sentence in the present paragraph is totally the same as a certain sentence existed in the training data, which makes it impossible to generate something new.

The second type is to firstly generate sentences word by word according the input images in parallel, and then concatenate all the generated sentences as a full paragraph. Nevertheless, it is because these methods do the paragraph at the sentence level that the generated paragraph tends to have a poor performance on **coherence**. Due to the simple concatenation of relatively independent sentences, the paragraph would hardly maintain the coherence that captures text relatedness, especially at the level of sentence-to-sentence transitions. Moreover, these methods are mainly trained by a learning principle that is to maximize the likelihood of training samples. This principle encourages high resemblance to the ground-truth descriptions with limited **expressiveness**.

In order to resolve the problems mentioned above and produce more human-like stories, we propose an Adversarial All-in-one Learning (AAL) framework for visual storytelling. In terms of the **expressiveness**, we all know that different people would describe images in different ways. A story without high resemblance to the 'standard' answer, but correctly describes the input images, is still a good one. Such a goal suggests a training objective similar to the idea of the Turing test [10]. Therefore, we cast the visual storytelling task as a reinforcement learning (RL) problem and propose the AAL system to learn a comprehensive reward. Inspired by the progress in generative adversarial networks (GANs [4]), which can be viewed as actor-critic methods of RL in an environment where the actor cannot affect the reward [16], we thus design two models. Specifically, a generative model (G) defines the probability of generating a paragraph for description. A reward model (R) learns a value function to predict reward that evaluates the generated paragraph. Then the estimated reward could be used back to optimize the generative model. Additionally, in order to improve the **correctness** of descriptions, we define the value function that simultaneously incorporates the information of both images and texts.

For the problem of **coherence**, we view visual storytelling as a generation task. Instead of producing paragraphs by concatenating several sentences, we propose a finer-grained way to do the paragraph generation at the level of ***sense group***. Sense group is a concept in speaking. When we speak, we want the listener to understand what we say. Often we speak without visual aid, such as the form of a written script. Unless we speak clearly, the message can not be shared with the listener fully. Therefore, the speaker will facilitate the listener to share the message completely by giving brief units of meaning each at a time, in order to reach the total meaning of the utterance without confusion. Each brief unit, discretely spoken, is called a sense group. We believe that a coherent paragraph is semantically constituted by several sense groups.

Overall, the contributions of the paper can be summarized as follow: (1) We propose an adversarial all-in-one learning framework to improve the performance of visual story generation. (2) Especially, we propose to do the paragraph generation at the level of sense group to improve the coherence of descriptions. (3) We evaluate our approach on the Visual Storytelling dataset (VIST) and take advantage of different linguistic information as a new indicator to measure the quality of the generated paragraphs.

2 Related Work

With the prospective growth of research interest in vision-to-language translation, a large number of related works have been carried out. According to both input and output dimension, these works can be approximately divided into three categories: (1) image caption (single-image to single-sentence), such as [7,11,19]. (2) video caption (multi-image to single-sentence), such as [3,15,20]. (3) visual storytelling (multi-image to multi-sentence). In this paper, we concentrate on the third category, visual storytelling.

Visual storytelling is a task of generating a human-like paragraph to describe an ordered image sequence. Park and Kim [14] have done some pioneering work on storytelling. They develop coherence recurrent convolutional network (CRCN), and use an entity-based local coherence model to focus on sentence-level transition. Liu et al. [9] design a bidirectional attention-based recurrent neural network (BARNN), which additionally uses a coherence matrix to enforce the sentence-to-sentence coherence. Although these works adopt different methods to improve the coherence, the basic scheme of them is generally to retrieve the candidate sentences from a pre-provided corpus. As a result, the generated paragraph is formed by sentences that have already appeared, which could barely maintain **expressiveness** of stories.

Then, some more sophisticated works have been proposed to explore the generation of more human-like stories. Huang et al. [5] have released a standard dataset for visual storytelling (VIST), and use a sequence-to-sequence recurrent neural net approach to train the story generation model. Yu et al. [24] propose a multi-task model, which is composed of three hierarchically-attentive recurrent neural nets, for both album summarization and story generation. These methods mainly follow the Encoder-and-Decoder paradigm proposed in [12], and adopt the *maximum likelihood* principle for learning. Such a framework usually works as follows. Given a sequence of images $I = \{i_1, i_2, \ldots, i_N\}$, it first extracts the visual representation $f(I_i)$, and then generates the words $w_1, \ldots, w_T$ sequentially to form a sentence for each image. The model parameters are learned via maximum likelihood estimation (MLE [21]), maximizing the conditional log-likelihood of the training samples like:

$$\sum_{(I_i,S_i)} \sum_{t=0}^{T_i} \log p\left(w_i^t \mid f(I_i), w_i^{t-1}, \ldots, w_i^{t-n}\right) \tag{1}$$

where I_i and S_i are the image and the corresponding sentence of the i-th sample in the story sequence. The distribution of the current word depends on n preceding words. Despite the evolution of the models, MLE remains the predominant learning principle. To best match with the ground truth texts, these methods encourage producing the n-gram patterns that have appeared frequently in the training samples. As illustrated in Fig. 2, models following the principle of MLE tend to generate sentences that contain the frequent n-grams from the training set.

Meanwhile, various evaluation metrics have been proposed to assess the quality of generated paragraph. Traditional metrics like BLEU in [13] and ROUGE in [8], respectively concentrates on the precision and recall of n-grams. METEOR in [2] makes a combination of both precision and recall of n-grams. CIDEr in [18] computes weighted statistics based on n-grams. However, these metrics also mainly focus on matching n-grams with ground truth. Consequently, the generated paragraph tends to achieve high scores on these traditional metrics, but become rigid with limited **expressiveness** in language.

Reference annotations:
• There are plenty of people gathering to celebrate.
• There is a local parade on the street.
• People are gathering for the parade.
Description 1: =>
• People are gathering on the street.
Description 2: =>
• The parade is so colorful and funny, people always have a great time.

Fig. 2. We illustrate the sentence generation following the principle of MLE or not. Description 1 encourages producing the frequent n-gram patterns from the training set, but is apparently less human-like than Description 2. Best viewed in color. (Color figure online)

Recently, generative adversarial network (GAN) has achieved great success in image generation. GAN simultaneously trains two models, a generative model G and a discriminative model D, to play a minimax two-player game:

$$\min_{D} \max_{G} E_{x \sim p_{data}} [\log D(x)] + E_{z \sim p_z} [\log D(G(z))] \tag{2}$$

As reported in previous works, GAN can generate new images that can be hardly distinguished from real ones. However, this idea has not achieved comparable success in natural language processing (NLP). This is because data in NLP is discrete, which makes it hard to back propagate the error outputted from the discriminator to the generator. Some recent works have begun to deal with this issue. To the best of our knowledge, there are basically two strategies. The first one is to provide the discriminator with the intermediate hidden representations of the generator instead of its output samples [6]. The other one is SeqGAN [23] that uses policy gradient in reinforcement learning to back propagate the error from the discriminator. Considering about the limitation of traditional metrics on evaluating story quality, Wang at el. [22] adopt the second strategy and apply the idea of adversarial training to storytelling. They propose an adversarial reward learning (AREL) framework, learning a reward function, to boost visual story generation. Despite the advantage of generating more expressive descriptions, the basic scheme of this framework is to firstly generate sentences word by word in parallel, and form the paragraph by simply concatenating all the generated sentences. Due to the concatenation of relatively independent sentences, the final paragraph would have the problem of **coherence**, especially at the level of sentence-to-sentence transitions.

Our work is distantly related to recent work that formalizes storytelling as an action-taking problem in reinforcement learning (RL). We construct an adversarial All-in-one Learning architecture named AAL consisting of a generative model G and a reward model R. The basic idea is to consider the production of each token in the generative model G as an *actor*, for which the *reward* comes from the reward model R. One the one hand, we give up MLE method and use the reward as the learning principle, which could contribute to the **expressiveness** of descriptions. One the other hand, our reward model considers not only the content of paragraph but also the input images, which is beneficial to the alignment of vision and language, to improve **correctness**. Especially, we propose to do the paragraph generation in a finer-grained way to improve the **coherence**. Specifically, we produce the paragraph at the level of sense group, which mentioned above, instead of sentences. We view the paragraph as a sequence, and the element of the sequence is sense group.

3 Model of Adversarial Storytelling

In this section, details will be described about the components of the proposed AAL architecture, as is shown in Fig. 3. We formulate visual storytelling as an action-taking process in reinforcement learning. In action-taking, there is an *agent* A_1 that interacts with the *environment*, and executes a series of *actions*. There is another *agent* A_2 that produces the reward to optimize a *goal*. In the task of visual storytelling, the goal is, given a sequence of ordered images $I = \{i_1, i_2, ..., i_N\}$, to generate a paragraph $Y = \{y_1, y_2, ..., y_T\}$, which correctly describes the content of images, where N is the length of image sequence, y_t is a token in paragraph Y and T is the length of paragraph. In our architecture, the generative model G is the agent A_1 and the reward model R is the agent A_2; the environment is the given image sequence I and the tokens predicted so far $\{y_1, y_2, ..., y_t\}$; and the action is to predict the next token y_{t+1}. After each action, a state is observed. In our problem, the state at time step t consists of the image sequence I and the tokens predicted until t.

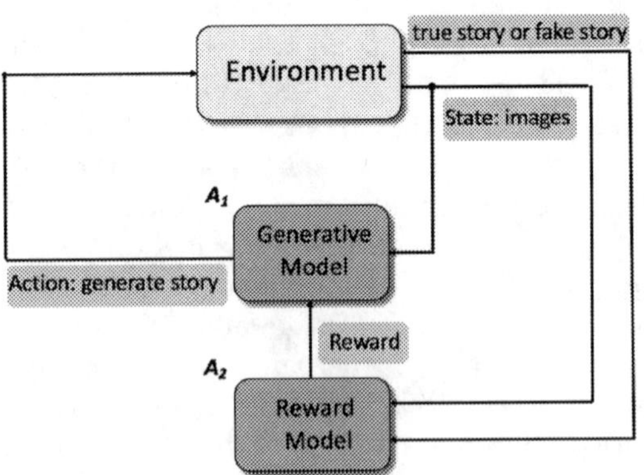

Fig. 3. Our AAL architecture for visual storytelling.

3.1 Sense Group

With regard to visual storytelling, we could take it as a text generation task from the perspective of its output. Text generation is a process of producing a series of basic units, such as words, sentences or other kinds of units. The final generated text should be made up of these units. However, facing the storytelling task now, if we choose sentence as the basic unit, the generated-paragraph would come across the problem of coherence as we mentioned above. Or if we do the paragraph generation based on individual words, it is not appropriate to train long sequences, which has the length of a whole paragraph.

Considering this situation, we introduce an alternative unit, sense group. Sense group is a group or sequence of words that are structurally and semantically related to each other. Combining a group of concepts together according to certain association, sense group represents the intended meaning through a cluster of such interrelated units of words. Two examples in Fig. 4 illustrate the sense group partition of paragraphs. Vertical lines in red color between sense groups are used to delineate the borders between adjacent sense groups. As is shown in Fig. 4, a paragraph can be constituted by these sense groups. We find that sense group can capture some words that are often used together, such as "best wishes" marked in orange in the Fig. 4. Also, between the adjacent sense groups, this kind of partition can capture some grammar information. For example, the combination of verb and preposition such as "wants to" marked in green in Fig. 4, and the combination of noun and preposition such as "goal of" marked in purple. We believe that these regular collocations could contribute to the **coherence** of a paragraph.

- Example 1:
- *There is a great deal difference | between the eager man | who wants | to read a book, | and the tired man | who wants a book | to read.*
- Example 2:
- *Diligence | is the key | of good fortune, | and idleness never brought a man | to the goal | of his best wishes.*

Fig. 4. Two examples of sense group partition. Vertical lines in red color are used to delineate the borders between adjacent sense group. Words marked in orange, green or purple are used to demonstrate the grammar information captured by sense group. (Color figure online)

However, there is no automatic tool to do sense group partition. In this paper, we separate the sense group units according to some grammatical cues. As we can see, the sense group units are basically introduced by grammatical words such as relative pronoun, conjunction and preposition. Therefore, we create an extra corpus consisting of these grammatical words. There are totally 66 words in this corpus, including grammatical words like "who", "since", "from" and so on. We use the words that appear in this corpus to partition each paragraph into sense groups. Admittedly, this method of partition may make some mistakes partly because of the incompleteness of the corpus, but experiments show that this is acceptable.

Therefore, in this paper, instead of choosing sentence or word, we introduce **sense group** as the basic unit to do the generation. In particular, sense group is the token y_t in each paragraph Y that we mentioned above.

3.2 Generative Model

Given the image sequence $I = \{i_1, \ldots i_N\}$, the generative model G provides the probability to take actions at each time step t. The current state is $\{I, y_1, \ldots y_t\}$ and the action is y_{t+1}. As is shown in Fig. 5, the generative model takes a form that is similar to Seq2Seq model [17] with an attention mechanism [1]. Firstly, we take the image sequence $I = \{i_1, i_2, \ldots, i_N\}$ as the input. To extract image features $X = \{x_1, x_2, \ldots, x_N\}$, we feed the images into a pre-trained Convolutional Neural Network (CNN). We then employ Gated Recurrent Units (GRU) as a image encoder to map the image features into hidden vectors $H = \{h_1, h_2, \ldots, h_N\}$. This is where we introduce the mechanism of attention. We compute the image-context vector c_t depending on the sequence of hidden image vectors. Each image-context vector c_t contains information about the whole input image sequence with a focus on the parts surrounding the n-th

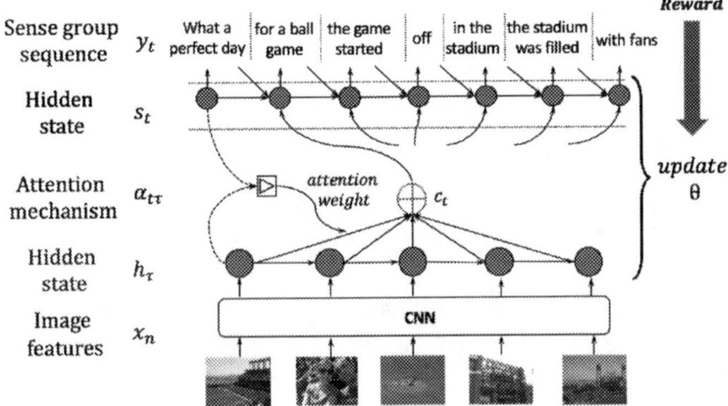

Fig. 5. An illustration of our generative model G. It consists of three parts: a CNN for image feature extraction, a RNN plus attention mechanism as an image encoder and another RNN as a text decoder. The generative model computes the probability of executing an action at a certain state. The reward from reward model R is used to optimize all the parameters θ of G.

image of the input sequence. The process of image encoder is governed by the following equations:

$$x_n = CNN(i_n) \tag{3}$$
$$h_n = GRU(h_{n-1}, x_n) \tag{4}$$
$$c_t = \sum_{\tau=1}^{N} \alpha_{t\tau} h_\tau \tag{5}$$
$$\alpha_{t\tau} = \frac{e^{\phi(s_{t-1}, h_\tau)}}{\sum_{\tau'} e^{\phi(s_{t-1}, h_{\tau'})}} \tag{6}$$

where s_t denotes the t-th hidden vector of the text decoder. In the decoder part, we feed each image-context vector c_t into a GRU. As the hidden state s_t of GRU evolves at time t, the generative model computes the probability of generating each output sense group y_t using a softmax output layer. The process of text decoder is demonstrated as the following equations:

$$s_t = GRU(y_{t-1}, s_{t-1}, c_t) \tag{7}$$
$$p_\theta(y_t \mid i_{i:N}, y_{1:t-1}) = softmax(W s_t + b) \tag{8}$$

where θ includes all the parameters of G model. The final paragraph Y for description is the concatenation of y_t.

3.3 Reward Model

The reward model R serves as an evaluation of the current state $\{I, y_1, \ldots y_t\}$, which consists of the image sequence I and the tokens predicted until t, and produces a reward to optimize the generative model G. However, for the storytelling task, we can't make the evaluation until the story is finished. That means R can only provide a reward for an entire sense group sequence. In order to evaluate the reward for each action step, we adopt Monte Carlo search with a roll-out policy to sample the last sense groups $y_{(t+1):T}$.

Meanwhile, to fuse both visual features $x_{1:N}$ and textual features $y_{1:T}$ into the reward, we adopt a hierarchical RNN architecture as the reward model that comprised of two RNN layers, as is shown in Fig. 6. In the first layer, one RNN is utilized as a image encoder to encode the visual information of I, another RNN is designed as a text encoder to encode the semantic information of the generated sense group sequence. The process of text encoder is illustrated by the following equations.

$$h_t^1 = LSTM(e_t^1, h_{t-1}^1) \tag{9}$$
$$e_s^2 = h_{end}^1 \tag{10}$$

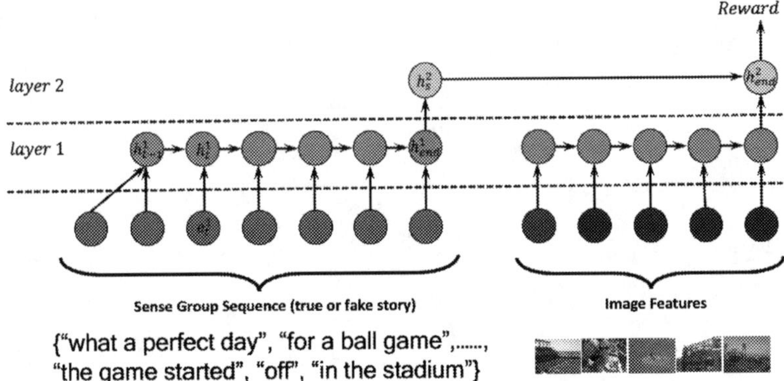

Fig. 6. An illustration of our reward model R. It is a hierarchical network with two layers of RNN. Given a state that contains the image sequence I and a partially generated paragraph until t, the reward model evaluates its value and produces the reward.

where h_t^1 denotes hidden vectors, the superscript means the layer number and the subscript means the current time step. e_t^1 denotes sense group embedding[1] at position t. The vector output h_{end}^1 at the ending time step is fed to the second layer as the input e_s^2. Similarly, the process of image encoder is also like this.

In the second layer, one RNN is used to fuse both visual and textual features:

$$h_s^2 = LSTM(e_s^2, h_{s-1}^2) \tag{11}$$

$$R(x, y) = softmax(h_{end}^2) \tag{12}$$

where h_s^2 denotes hidden vectors of the second RNN layer. Similarly, h_{end}^2 computed at the ending time step is used to represent the current state. Then the vector h_{end}^2 is fed to a 2-class softmax function, computing the probability of the input story being a fake story (denoted as $R_-(x, y)$) or a true story (denoted as $R_+(x, y)$). This probability is used as the reward for generative model G. Then the objective of G can be defined as:

$$J_\theta = \sum_x P(x) \sum_y R(x, y) G_\theta(y|x) \tag{13}$$

where θ includes all the parameters of G. $P(x)$ is the probability distribution of input image features, and the sum of $P(x)$ is 1. Then the gradient of the objective function with the generative model's parameters θ can be derived as:

$$\nabla J_\theta = E_{x \sim P(x), y \sim G_\theta(y|x)}[R(x, y) \nabla \log G_\theta(y \mid x)] \tag{14}$$

[1] We compute a sense group embedding by making the sum of embedding of each word in the sense group.

4 Experiments

4.1 Dataset

To evaluate our model on the visual storytelling task, we make use of the dataset VIST [5], which is the first dataset particularly created for sequential vision-to-language tasks. It contains 48K stories with 210K unique images. The image streams are extracted from Flickr and the text stories are written by AMT. Each story is composed of 5 images and 5 corresponding sentences. The dataset has been split into 38K stories as training set, 4K as test set and 4K as validation set.

4.2 Evaluation

Table 1 shows a summary of the methods we investigate, including: (1) Seq2Seq: standard Seq2Seq model that maps the source sequence to a vector representation using a recurrent net and then generates each token in the target; (2) SeqGAN [23]: a sequence generation method to train generative nets for structured sequences generation; (3) AAL: this is our adversarial all-in-one learning architecture; (4) G-mle: It shares the same architecture with our generative model, but it is trained via maximum likelihood estimation. Meanwhile, we combine these models respectively with word partition or sense group partition to do the paragraph generation.

Table 1. The summary of models in our experiment

	Word	Sense group
Seq2Seq	*	Seq2Seq-sg
SeqGAN	*	SeqGAN-sg
G-mle	G-mle-w	G-mle-sg
AAL	AAL-w	AAL-sg

Metrics. We evaluate the quality of generated-paragraphs based on three aspects: correctness, expressiveness and coherence. For quantitative measure, we compute several evaluation metrics, which can be categorized into three types: (1) Traditional metrics: BLEU, METEOR, ROUGE-L and CIDEr, they mainly focus on matching n-grams with ground truth; (2) linguistic metrics: the average numbers of noun, verb, adjective and pronoun in each paragraph, which are mainly related to part of speech; (3) Recurring-words: the average number of recurring words with the same root in each paragraph.

For Correctness. One important criterion of generated paragraphs' quality is to check whether these paragraphs can correctly describe the contents of images. To evaluate the correctness, we choose traditional metrics for evaluation because these metrics focus on similarity with ground truth. Table 2 lists the results

Table 2. Metrics for correctness

	BLEU-1	BLEU-3	METEOR	ROUGE_L	CIDEr
Seq2Seq-sg	23.5	16.0	16.1	28.1	0.806
SeqGAN-sg	35.0	25.6	19.5	32.8	0.853
AAL-sg	42.4	33.4	23.3	39.5	2.531
G-mle-sg	**43.1**	**35.5**	**25.2**	**44.9**	**3.265**

produced by four methods with sense group partition. For one thing, our method AAL-sg remarkably outperforms the first two methods. Take the result of BLEU-1 for example, our method is about 45% higher than Seq2Seq-sg method, 17% higher than SeqGAN-sg method. This suggests our AAL-sg method has a good performance of correctness.

Although the G-mle-sg method yields slightly higher scores, this actually makes sense. As we mentioned above, the adversarial method encourages producing diverse texts, but these automatic evaluation metrics overly focus on n-grams matching with ground truth. Consequently, paragraphs written with variant expressions tend to get lower scores. Therefore, these traditional metrics only partially reflect the quality of generated paragraphs.

For Expressiveness. In order to measure expressiveness, we propose to use linguistic metrics. Specifically, we compute the average number of nouns, verbs and adjectives in each paragraph. It is known that nouns, verbs and adjectives are content words in linguistics. They signify actual living things, family members, natural phenomena, common actions, characteristics and so on. Therefore, we believe that more content words could indicate more expressiveness. As is shown in Table 3, we divide those candidate methods into two groups: (1) AAL and G-mle methods with word partition; (2) AAL and G-mle methods with sense group partition. In the first group, compared with G-mle method, our AAL method achieves a better performance in terms of the average number of content words. For example, AAL has 1.49 nouns, 0.87 verb and 0.71 adjective more than G-mle. Similarly, in the second group, AAL has 1.77 nouns, 2.04 verb and 0.64 adjective more than G-mle. The results of both two groups show that our AAL architecture makes effect in improving expressiveness.

For Coherence. To the best knowledge of us, there is no general metric to measure the coherence in the field of text generation. In our experiment, we quantify the coherence by computing the average number of pronouns and recurring words in each paragraph. For one thing, think about that, in a coherent paragraph, the same entity is high likely to be mentioned more than once. Then it is natural to refer these entities by replacing with the corresponding pronouns after the first mention. For another, a coherent paragraph should be logically integrated, and semantically around one global topic. For example, when talking about the

Table 3. Linguistic metrics for expressiveness

	Noun	Verb	Adjective
G-mle-word	5.65	4.63	2.27
AAL-word	**7.14**	**5.50**	**2.98**
G-mle-sg	7.63	5.79	3.35
AAL-sg	**9.40**	**7.83**	**3.99**

Table 4. Linguistic metrics for coherence

	Pronoun	Recurring-words
G-mle-word	2.50	1.87
G-mle-sg	**3.49**	**3.72**
AAL-word	2.35	1.98
AAL-sg	**4.91**	**4.82**

sunset, you are likely to use words like 'beautiful', 'beauty', 'beauties' and so on. From this perspective, we believe that the number of recurring words with the same root in a paragraph could reflect the coherence.

As is shown in Table 4, we divide those candidate methods into two groups: (1) G-mle methods with word or sense group partition; (2) AAL methods with word or sense group partition. In the first group, compared to G-mle with word partition, G-mle with sense group partition achieves a better performance. For instance, G-mle-sg has about 1 pronoun and 1.85 recurring words more than G-mle-w. Similarly, in the second group, AAL with sense group partition has about 2.56 pronouns and 2.84 recurring words more than AAL with word partition. The results of both two groups show that sense group partition makes better effect than word partition in improving coherence.

User Study. We perform pairwise human evaluation to test the preference on the stories by ground truth, G-mle model and our AAL method. We randomly choose 100 image sequences from dataset VIST, each associated with three stories: story from ground truth, story generated by G-mle-sg method and story by our AAL-sg method. Please see Fig. 7 for example. Then, each story is assigned to 5 judges to eliminate human variance. The result is presented in Table 5. Consistently on all the comparisons, our models achieve better performance.

Table 5. Pairwise human comparisons

	AAL-sg *vs* G-mle-sg			AAL-w *vs* G-mle-w			G-mle-sg *vs* G-mle-w			AAL-sg *vs* AAL-w		
Choice (%)	AAL-sg	G-mle-sg	Tie	AAL-w	G-mle-w	Tie	G-mle-sg	G-mle-w	Tie	AAL-sg	AAL-w	Tie
Correctness	**58**	31	11	**49**	31	20	**40**	20	40	**49**	27	24
Expressiveness	**53**	32	15	**32**	21	47	**27**	24	49	**41**	21	38
Coherence	**45**	36	19	**40**	20	40	**21**	16	63	**38**	29	33

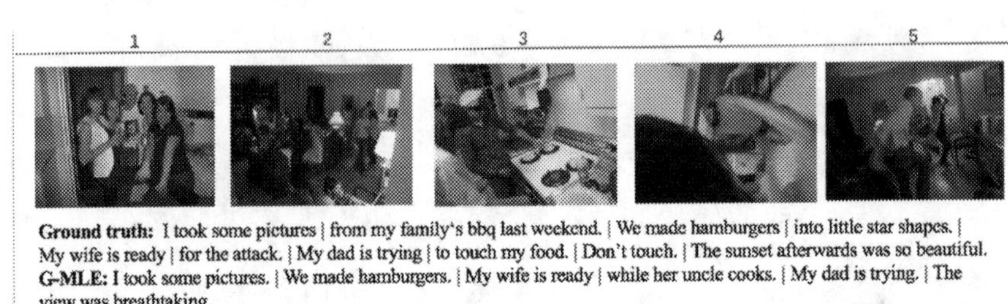

Ground truth: I took some pictures | from my family's bbq last weekend. | We made hamburgers | into little star shapes. | My wife is ready | for the attack. | My dad is trying | to touch my food. | Don't touch. | The sunset afterwards was so beautiful.
G-MLE: I took some pictures. | We made hamburgers. | My wife is ready | while her uncle cooks. | My dad is trying. | The view was breathtaking.
Our method: We gathered | to set | at dark. | Our friends trickled | by one. | We got all the food | to cook and ready | to eat. | The sunset was amazing that night.

Ground truth: We went | to the local parade this weekend. | There were funny clowns | on mini motorcycles. | Our veterans were also represented | by a few people. | The local fire department decked | out their truck | in flags. | We had a good time | everyone was happy | and all smiles.
G-MLE: We went | to the local parade this weekend. | on mini motorcycles. | The local fire department decked | out their truck | in flags. | everyone was happy | and all smiles.
Our method: The parade was going | through main street. | The local fire department decked | out their truck | The firefighters brought their fire truck | through the parade | and everyone had a good time.

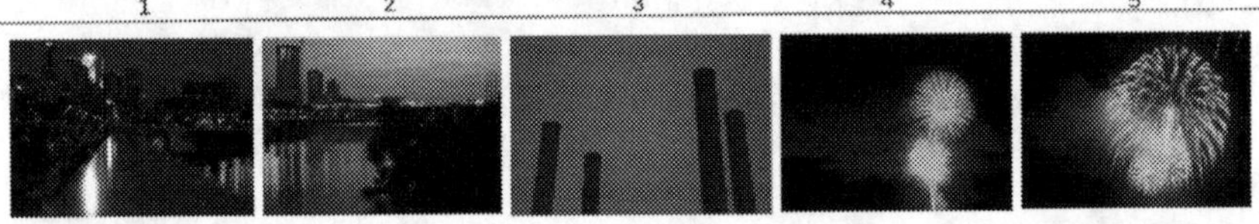

Ground truth: Today I marveled | at the beauty | of the sunrise. | I was amazed | at how man could build the Golden Gate Bridge. | I looked out | over the bay and counted my blessings. | The sun set | over the mountains was glorious. | Then I watched | as night crawled in.
G-MLE: It is going | to be a great day today | up bright and early. | We are taking a road trip | to cross the bridge. | We are headed | over.
Our method: It is going | to be a great day today | up bright and early. | When we first arrived | to cross the bridge. | the sunset

Ground truth: Today is a good day | to invite family over. | It is such a nice day today | and we finished cleaning | up the yard. | We should water all the grass | before people come over. | Some | of the guests made a campfire | to cook some | of the food. | Everyone is having a great time | the meal was great today.
G-MLE: It is going | to be a great day today | up bright and early. | We are taking a road trip | to cross the bridge. | We are headed | over.
Our method: It is going | to be a great day today | up bright and early. | When we first arrived | to cross the bridge. | the sunset was beautiful | from the plane. | I had a great time.

Fig. 7. Examples of visual storytelling results on VIST. Each image sequence is associated with three stories: (1) story from ground truth; (2) story generated by G-mle-sg method; (3) story generated by our AAL-sg method. Vertical lines in red color between sense groups are used to delineate the borders between adjacent sense groups. (Color figure online)

5 Conclusion

In this paper, we propose an alternative approach AAL architecture to deal with the task of visual storytelling. Compared to the existing methods, which mostly focus on retrieving sentences from corpus or doing the paragraph generation by concatenation of sentences, our approach is a generative method that aims at improving the overall quality including correctness, expressiveness and coherence. We cast this task into a reinforcement learning problem, and construct an adversarial system including a generative model and a reward model. Specially, we propose to use sense group as the basic language unit, and the generated story is semantically constituted by these sense group units. On the VIST dataset, the experiments quantitatively demonstrate the effectiveness and advantage of our method. In the future, we will continue to do the vision-to-language research, and explore the possibility of applying sense group partition into other text generation task or text classification.

Acknowledgement. This work is partially supported by Funds for Creative Research Groups of China (No. 61421061), and Natural Science Foundation of China (No. 61601046, No. 61602048).

References

1. Bahdanau, D., Cho, K., Bengio, Y.: Neural machine translation by jointly learning to align and translate. arXiv preprint arXiv:1409.0473 (2014)
2. Denkowski, M., Lavie, A.: Meteor universal: language specific translation evaluation for any target language. In: Proceedings of the Ninth Workshop on Statistical Machine Translation, pp. 376–380 (2014)
3. Donahue, J., et al.: Long-term recurrent convolutional networks for visual recognition and description. In: Proceedings of the IEEE Conference on Computer Vision and Pattern Recognition, pp. 2625–2634 (2015)
4. Goodfellow, I., et al.: Generative adversarial nets. In: Advances in Neural Information Processing Systems, pp. 2672–2680 (2014)
5. Huang, T.H.K., et al.: Visual storytelling. In: Proceedings of the 2016 Conference of the North American Chapter of the Association for Computational Linguistics: Human Language Technologies, pp. 1233–1239 (2016)
6. Lamb, A.M., Goyal, A.G.A.P., Zhang, Y., Zhang, S., Courville, A.C., Bengio, Y.: Professor forcing: a new algorithm for training recurrent networks. In: Advances In Neural Information Processing Systems, pp. 4601–4609 (2016)
7. Li, F.F., Karpathy, A., Johnson, J.: CS231n: Convolutional neural networks for visual recognition. University Lecture (2015)
8. Lin, C.Y.: ROUGE: a package for automatic evaluation of summaries. In: Text Summarization Branches Out (2004)
9. Liu, Y., Fu, J., Mei, T., Chen, C.W.: Storytelling of photo stream with bidirectional multi-thread recurrent neural network. arXiv preprint arXiv:1606.00625 (2016)
10. Machinery, C.: Computing machinery and intelligence-AM turing. Mind **59**(236), 433 (1950)
11. Mao, J., Xu, W., Yang, Y., Wang, J., Huang, Z., Yuille, A.: Deep captioning with multimodal recurrent neural networks (m-RNN). arXiv preprint arXiv:1412.6632 (2014)

12. Mishima, H., Itow, T.: Encoder and decoder, uS Patent 5,488,418, 30 January 1996
13. Papineni, K., Roukos, S., Ward, T., Zhu, W.J.: BLEU: a method for automatic evaluation of machine translation. In: Proceedings of the 40th Annual Meeting on Association for Computational Linguistics, pp. 311–318. Association for Computational Linguistics (2002)
14. Park, C.C., Kim, G.: Expressing an image stream with a sequence of natural sentences. In: Advances in Neural Information Processing Systems, pp. 73–81 (2015)
15. Peris, Á., Bolaños, M., Radeva, P., Casacuberta, F.: Video description using bidirectional recurrent neural networks. In: Villa, A.E.P., Masulli, P., Pons Rivero, A.J. (eds.) ICANN 2016. LNCS, vol. 9887, pp. 3–11. Springer, Cham (2016). https://doi.org/10.1007/978-3-319-44781-0_1
16. Pfau, D., Vinyals, O.: Connecting generative adversarial networks and actor-critic methods. arXiv preprint arXiv:1610.01945 (2016)
17. Sutskever, I., Vinyals, O., Le, Q.V.: Sequence to sequence learning with neural networks. In: Advances in Neural Information Processing Systems, pp. 3104–3112 (2014)
18. Vedantam, R., Lawrence Zitnick, C., Parikh, D.: CIDEr: consensus-based image description evaluation. In: Proceedings of the IEEE Conference on Computer Vision and Pattern Recognition, pp. 4566–4575 (2015)
19. Vendrov, I., Kiros, R., Fidler, S., Urtasun, R.: Order-embeddings of images and language. arXiv preprint arXiv:1511.06361 (2015)
20. Venugopalan, S., Rohrbach, M., Donahue, J., Mooney, R., Darrell, T., Saenko, K.: Sequence to sequence-video to text. In: Proceedings of the IEEE International Conference on Computer Vision, pp. 4534–4542 (2015)
21. Vinyals, O., Toshev, A., Bengio, S., Erhan, D.: Show and tell: a neural image caption generator. In: Proceedings of the IEEE Conference on Computer Vision and Pattern Recognition, pp. 3156–3164 (2015)
22. Wang, X., Chen, W., Wang, Y.F., Wang, W.Y.: No metrics are perfect: adversarial reward learning for visual storytelling. arXiv preprint arXiv:1804.09160 (2018)
23. Yu, L., Zhang, W., Wang, J., Yu, Y.: SeqGAN: sequence generative adversarial nets with policy gradient. In: AAAI, pp. 2852–2858 (2017)
24. Yu, L., Bansal, M., Berg, T.L.: Hierarchically-attentive RNN for album summarization and storytelling. arXiv preprint arXiv:1708.02977 (2017)

Laser Scar Detection in Fundus Images Using Convolutional Neural Networks

Qijie Wei[1,2,3], Xirong Li[1,2(✉)], Hao Wang[1,2], Dayong Ding[3], Weihong Yu[4], and Youxin Chen[4]

[1] Key Lab of DEKE, Renmin University of China, Beijing, China
xirong@ruc.edu.cn
[2] AI & Media Computing Lab, Renmin University of China, Beijing, China
[3] Vistel Inc., Beijing, China
[4] Peking Union Medical College Hospital, Beijing, China

Abstract. In diabetic eye screening programme, a special pathway is designed for those who have received laser photocoagulation treatment. The treatment leaves behind circular or irregular scars in the retina. Laser scar detection in fundus images is thus important for automated DR screening. Despite its importance, the problem is understudied in terms of both datasets and methods. This paper makes the first attempt to detect laser-scar images by deep learning. To that end, we contribute to the community *Fundus10K*, a large-scale expert-labeled dataset for training and evaluating laser scar detectors. We study in this new context major design choices of state-of-the-art Convolutional Neural Networks including Inception-v3, ResNet and DenseNet. For more effective training we exploit transfer learning that passes on trained weights of ImageNet models to their laser-scar counterparts. Experiments on the new dataset shows that our best model detects laser-scar images with sensitivity of 0.962, specificity of 0.999, precision of 0.974 and AP of 0.988 and AUC of 0.999. The same model is tested on the public LMD-BAPT test set, obtaining sensitivity of 0.765, specificity of 1, precision of 1, AP of 0.975 and AUC of 0.991, outperforming the state-of-the-art with a large margin. Data is available at https://github.com/li-xirong/fundus10k/.

Keywords: Laser scar detection · Fundus image · Convolutional Neural Network

1 Introduction

Diabetic retinopathy (DR) refers to damages occurring to retinal blood vessels caused by diabetes mellitus. Since the retina is a very vulnerable tissue, such damages could lead to vision loss or even blindness. DR typically progresses through four stages, *i.e.*, mild nonproliferative DR (NPDR), moderate NPDR, severe NPDR and proliferative DR (PDR) [20]. There are 425 million adults

C. V. Jawahar et al. (Eds.): ACCV 2018, LNCS 11364, pp. 191–206, 2019.
https://doi.org/10.1007/978-3-030-20870-7_12

on the planet that suffer from diabetes[1] and more than one-third of diabetic patients are likely to have DR [12]. To fully carry out eye screening programme, especially for countries of large population, automated screening is an inevitable trend.

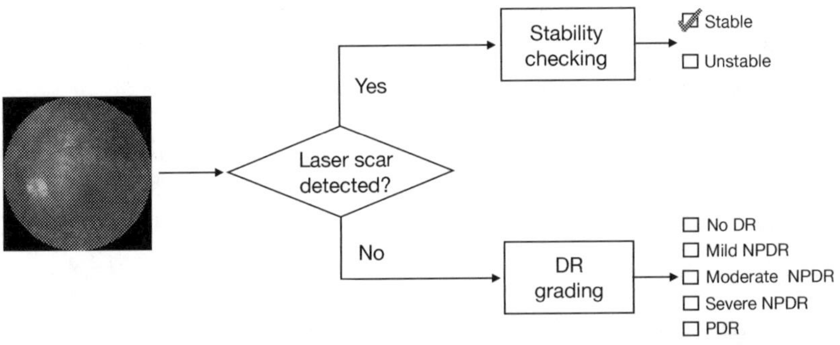

Fig. 1. Diagram of a standard DR screening process, according to the Diabetic Eye Screening Guidance of the NHS, UK [20]. Laser scar detection is an important module for automated DR screening in a real scenario.

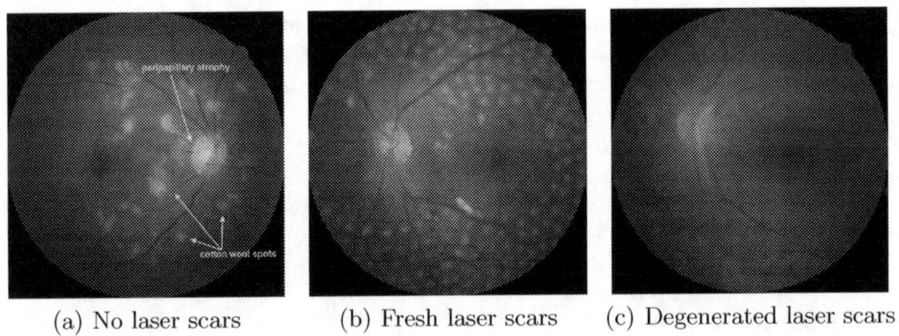

(a) No laser scars (b) Fresh laser scars (c) Degenerated laser scars

Fig. 2. Examples of fundus color images of posterior pole, with 45° field of view. Cotton wool spots in (a) resemble fresh laser scars to some extent, while peripapillary atrophy looks like degenerated scars. This paper aims for automated classification of fundus images with and without laser scars. (Color figure online)

Exciting progress is being made on automated DR screening [4,5,14], thanks to the groundbreaking deep learning algorithms for visual recognition [10] and the public availability of large-scale DR-graded data such as Kaggle DR [9]. However, there is an (implicit) condition for these systems to be applicable: *the*

[1] http://www.diabetesatlas.org.

person in consideration has not taken any laser photocoagulation. Laser photocoagulation is a common treatment for severe NPDR and PDR [1], preventing further vision loss by destroying abnormal blood vessels in the retina. According to the Diabetic Eye Screening Guidance of the NHS, UK [20], if there is evidence of previous photocoagulation, judgement should be made differently, see Fig. 1. Due to cauterization of the laser, laser treatment leaves behind circular or irregular scars in the retina, see Fig. 2(b) and (c). Therefore, detecting the presence of laser scars in fundus images is important for automated DR screening in a real scenario.

Despite its importance, the problem of laser scar detection is largely unexplored. Few methods have been developed [3,16,17,19], all relying on hand-crafted visual features. Although fresh laser scars are clearly visible with regular shapes, see Fig. 2(b), they degenerate over time, resulting in irregular boundaries and lower contrast against the background. Moreover, DR lesions such as cotton wool spots resemble fresh scars to some extent, while peripapillary atrophy looks like old scars, as exemplified in Fig. 2(a). All this makes hand-crafted features less effective.

Laser scars are local patterns. They might appear anywhere in a fundus image except for few specific areas including the optic disk, the macular, and main vessels. Meanwhile, they may scatter around a relatively large area. For these two properties we consider a deep Convolutional Neural Network (CNN) appealing for laser scar detection, as the network finds local patterns in its early layers and perform multi-scale analysis in its deeper layers. Probably due to the absence of large-scale labeled laser scar data, we see no effort in developing deep learning techniques for this problem.

In this paper we make the following three contributions.

- First, we present a large-scale dataset consisting of 10,861 fundus images, with expert labels indicating presence or absence of laser scars in each image. The previous largest dataset of this kind has 671 images only[2] [16].
- Second, to the best of our knowledge, this paper is the first deep learning entry for laser scar detection. To reveal what CNNs are the most suited, we systematically investigate major design choices of existing CNNs with good practices identified. In particular, simply and properly adjusting the last pooling layer allows the CNNs to accept input images of a higher resolution, without the need of increasing the number of network parameters.
- Lastly, the proposed deep learning based solution outperforms the best result previously reported on LMD-BAPT [16] (the only public test set). Even though the performance increase can be arguably expected due to the tremendous success of deep learning in varied applications, the optimal use of the technique is task-dependent. By proper adaption of the technique, we establish a new baseline for the task of laser scar detection, which is important for automated diabetic retinopathy screening.

The rest of the paper is organized as follows. We review related work in Sect. 2, followed by a description of the newly constructed dataset in Sect. 3. The

[2] 622 images for training plus 49 images for test [16].

proposed deep learning approach to laser scar detection is depicted in Sect. 4, with its effectiveness verified in Sect. 5. We conclude in Sect. 6.

2 Related Work

There is a paucity of literature on laser scar detection. Dias *et al.* make an initial attempt [3], building a binary classifier with a set of color, focus, contrast and illumination features. A 5-fold cross validation experiment is performed on a dataset composed of 40 fundus images with laser scars and 176 fundus images without laser scars. Syed *et al.* [17] and Tahir *et al.* [19] exploit color, shape and texture based features, with their experiments conducted on a locally gathered dataset consisting of 380 images, among which 51 images have laser scars. More recently, Sousa *et al.* propose to extract geometric, texture, spatial distribution and intensity based features [16], and train a decision tree and a random forest as their laser scar detectors. A common disadvantage of the above methods is their dependency on hand-crafted features which often do not generalize well. Extracting the hand-crafted features involves specifying a number of ad-hoc (and implicit) parameters, making replicability of previous methods extremely difficult, if not impossible. Moreover, previous studies were performed on private datasets, except for [16] where the authors have generously made a training set of 622 images (termed LMD-DRS) and a test set of 49 images (termed LMD-BAPT) publicly accessible. Nevertheless, a large-scale benchmark dataset is missing, making one difficult to understand the state of the art. Probably due to the lack of such a dataset, no effort has ever made to investigate deep learning techniques. We show in Sect. 5 that CNN models trained on the small LMD-DRS dataset do not generalize well.

For deep learning based medical image analysis, some efforts on transfer learning are made [13,15]. Orlando *et al.* adopt two CNNs pre-trained on ImageNet, *i.e.,* OverFeat and VggNet, as feature extractors [13] for glaucoma identification. The CNN weights keep unchanged. For organ localization, Ravishankar *et al.* adopt a CaffeNet pre-trained on ImageNet, reporting that adjusting weights for all layers is better than having weights of some layers fixed [15]. Note that both [13] and [15] use the network architecture of the pre-trained CNNs as is. By contrast, we propose to adjust the last pooling layer. This allows us to double the size of the input, but with the amount of the network parameters unchanged.

3 A Large-Scale Dataset for Laser Scar Detection

In order to construct a large-scale dataset for laser scar detection, we adopted fundus images used in the Kaggle Diabetic Retinopathy Detection task [9]. The Kaggle dataset contains 88,702 fundus color images of posterior pole (with 45° field of view) provided by EyePACS, a free platform for retinopathy screening [2]. To make the subsequent manual labeling manageable, the size of the

Kaggle dataset was reduced to around 11K by random down-sampling. In addition, we gathered from a local hospital 2K fundus color images of posterior pole (also with 45° field of view) of diabetic patients.

For ground-truth labeling, we employed a panel of 45 China licensed ophthalmologists. Each image was assigned to at least three distinct annotators. They were asked to provide a binary label indicting either presence or absence of laser scars in the given image. The number of expert-labeled images was 12,550 in total. As five annotators did not fully complete their assignments, each image has been labeled 2.5 times, approximately. Excluding 1,317 images that were labeled by only one annotator and 372 images receiving diverse labels, we obtained a set of 10,861 expert-labeled images. We term the dataset *Fundus10K*.

We split Fundus10K into three disjoint subsets as follows. We first constructed a hold-out test set by randomly sampling 20% of the images. The remaining data is split at random into a training set of 7,602 images and a validation set of 1,086 images. Table 1 shows data statistics.

Table 1. Laser-scar datasets used in this work. We have constructed a large-scale dataset of 10,861 fundus images with expert annotations. A hold-out test set is constructed by randomly sampling 20% of the images. We term the set Test-2k. In addition, we include LMD-BAPT [16], the only public test set, as our second test set.

	Our contribution (10,861 images)			LMD-BAPT from [16]
	Training (70%)	*Validation (10%)*	*Testing (20%)*	
No. images	7,602	1,086	2,173	49
No. images with laser scars	282	42	80	34

4 Our Approach

We aim to build a CNN that predicts if any laser scar is present in a given fundus image. For a formal description, let x be a specific image and $y \in \{0, 1\}$ as a binary label, where $y = 1$ indicates the image contains laser scars and 0 otherwise. We define $p(y = 1|x)$ as a probabilistic output of the classifier, larger values indicating higher chances of laser scar occurrence. Such a soft classification enables laser scar detection in multiple scenarios. By specifying a particular operating point on a precision-recall curve, one can aim for either high-recall (sensitivity) or high-precision detection. We simply use 0.5 as a decision threshold, *i.e.*, test images having $p(y = 1|x) > 0.5$ will be classified as having laser scars, unless stated otherwise. Also, one might employ $p(y = 1|x)$ as a ranking criterion to retrieve laser-scar images from a large unlabeled collection.

4.1 CNNs for Laser Scar Detection

We express a CNN implementation of $p(y|x)$ as

$$p(y|x) := softmax(\cdots CNN(x)), \tag{1}$$

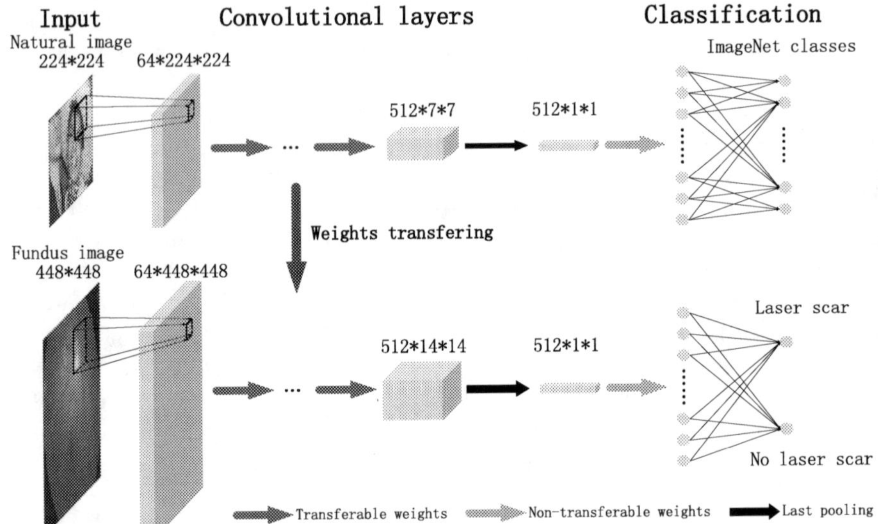

Fig. 3. Diagram of transferring weights from a trained ImageNet CNN model for laser scar detection. The convolutional layers of our laser scar detector are initialized by the corresponding weights from a pre-trained (ResNet-18) model. By adjusting the last pooling layer, we use a double-sized input (448×448), without increasing the number of trainable parameters. Best viewed in color.

where $\cdots CNN$ indicates stacked CNN layers that take a fix-sized RGB image as input and sequentially produce an array of feature maps that describe the visual content at multiple scales. The $softmax$ module employs fully connected layers to convert the last feature map (and optionally some preceding feature maps if skip connections are used) to final predictions.

Choices of CNNs. It remains open what CNN architectures are suited for laser scar detection. Hence, instead of inventing new architectures, we investigate existing options. We consider Inception-V3 [18], ResNet [7], and DenseNet [8], for their state-of-the-art performance on the ImageNet visual recognition task. To reveal the influence of the network depth on the performance, we exploit ResNet-18, ResNet-34, ResNet-50, DenseNet-121, DenseNet-169 and DenseNet-201. The three DenseNet networks have nearly the same architecture, with deeper network repeating a common convolutional block for more times. The case is similar in ResNet, except that ResNet-50 uses so-called BottleNeck convolutional blocks which are deeper but with less parameters.

4.2 Transfer Learning

Instead of training CNNs from scratch, we aim for a better starting point by transferring weights from their counterparts pre-trained on ImageNet. A straightforward strategy is to follow exactly the same configuration as the existing models, by enforcing the size of the input image to be the de facto 224×224. This strategy is unlikely to be optimal, because a fundus image has a much larger resolution than a consumer picture. Since laser scars are not so big, resolution may affect the ability of the CNN to distinguish them. However, a double-sized input means the feature maps will be four times as large as the original ones. Consequently, the amount of parameters in the first fully connected layer will increase substantially. We consider a simple yet effective trick: adjusting the last pooling layer to maintain the size of the last feature map. The adjustment varies over CNNs. As for ResNet, DenseNet and Inception-v3, they all use global average pooling as their last pooling layer. So we double the pooling size, from 7×7 to 14×14 for ResNet and DenseNet and from 12×12 to 24×24 for Inception-v3. We refer to Fig. 3 for a conceptual illustration.

5 Evaluation

5.1 Experimental Setup

Training Procedure. We use SGD with a mini-batch of 20, a weight decay factor of 1×10^{-4}, and a momentum of 0.95. The initial learning rate is set to be 1×10^{-3}. Validation is performed every 800 batches. An early stop occurs when the validation performance does not improve in 10 consecutive validation steps. For data augmentation we perform random rotation, crop, flip and changes in brightness, saturation and contrast. As the two classes are highly imbalanced, we over sample the laser-scar images to make each batch nearly balanced.

CNN Ensemble. As the SGD based training yields models of slightly different performance, for each CNN we repeat the training procedure three times and use model averaging to obtain its final prediction. Considering that CNNs with varied depth might be complementary to each other, we further investigate two ensembled CNNs, namely ResNet-Ensemble which equally combines ResNet-18, ResNet-34 and ResNet-50 and DenseNet-Ensemble which combines the three variants of DenseNet.

Performance Metrics. We report *Sensitivity*, *Specificity* and AUC as commonly used as performance metrics of a screening or diagnostic test. In particular, we consider laser-scar images as positive instances, and images without laser cars as negatives. As such, *Sensitivity* is defined as the number of correctly detected positives divided by the number of true positives. *Specificity* is defined as the number of correctly detected negatives divided by the number of true negatives. AUC is the area under a receiver operating characteristic (ROC) curve. Given an extremely imbalanced test set, like our Test-2k with only 3.68% positive examples, AUC and *Specificity* tend to be high and less discriminative. Under this circumstance, *Precision* and *Average Precision* (AP) are better metrics. *Precision* is defined as the number of correctly detected positives divided by the number of images detected as positives. AP is a rank-based measure [11]. Higher numbers of the five metrics indicate better performance.

5.2 Experiments

All models are evaluated on our test set of 2,173 images (which we term Test-2k for the ease of reference), unless otherwise stated.

Experiment 1. Choice of CNNs. Table 2 shows performance of different CNNs. Concerning the network architecture, DenseNet leads the performance in terms of AP, followed by ResNet and Inception-v3. Concerning the individual models, the best overall performance of DenseNet-121 suggests that this CNN strikes a proper balance between model capability and learnability for laser scar detection. Its performance can be further improved by model ensembling, as shown in Table 2 and Fig. 4.

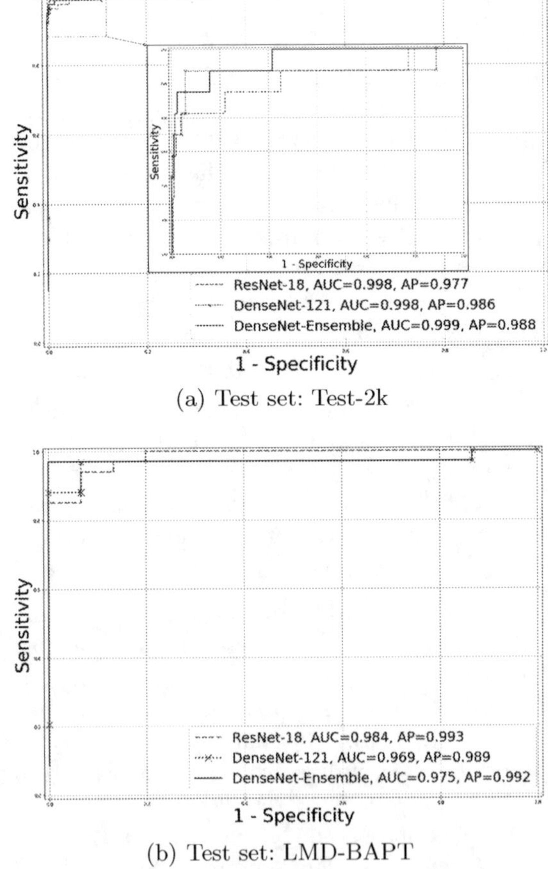

(a) Test set: Test-2k

(b) Test set: LMD-BAPT

Fig. 4. ROC curves of ResNet-18, DenseNet-121 and DenseNet-Ensemble on the two test sets. Best viewed in color.

Experiment 2. CNN Initialization Strategies. In order to justify the effectiveness of transfer learning described in Sect. 4.2, we compare CNNs trained with randomly initialized weights and the same models but with their initial weights transfered from their ImageNet counterparts. For random initialization, the weights are initialized using Gaussian distribution with zero-mean and variance calculated according to [6]. We found that when randomly initialized, CNNs with an input size of 448 × 448 did not converge. So this experiment uses a smaller input size of 224 × 224. To reduce redundancy, we show only the results of the ResNet series and Inception-v3 in Table 3. DenseNet has similar results. Transfer learning not only leads to better models but also reduces the training time by around 50%.

Table 2. Performance of different CNNs. The input size of each CNN is 448 × 448, with its initial weights transfered from the corresponding ImageNet model.

Model	Sensitivity	Specificity	Precision	AP	AUC
ResNet-18	0.938	0.998	0.949	0.977	0.998
ResNet-34	0.950	0.998	0.938	0.973	0.997
ResNet-50	0.950	0.996	0.905	0.976	0.996
ResNet-Ensemble	0.950	0.997	0.927	0.977	0.998
Inception-v3	0.938	**0.999**	0.962	0.968	0.996
DenseNet-121	0.938	**0.999**	**0.974**	0.986	0.998
DenseNet-169	0.950	0.997	0.916	0.979	0.998
DenseNet-201	**0.962**	**0.999**	0.962	0.987	**0.999**
DenseNet-Ensemble	0.950	**0.999**	**0.974**	**0.988**	**0.999**

Table 3. Performance of CNNs trained with and without transfer learning, respectively. Note that the input size of each CNN is 224 × 224. Weight transferring consistently improves the performance.

Model	Initialization	Sensitivity	Specificity	Precision	AP	AUC
ResNet-18	Random	0.812	0.991	0.774	0.882	0.980
	Transfer	**0.913**	**0.994**	**0.849**	**0.954**	**0.992**
ResNet-34	Random	**0.887**	0.990	0.780	0.905	0.988
	Transfer	**0.887**	**0.998**	**0.947**	**0.962**	**0.997**
ResNet-50	Random	0.850	0.991	0.791	0.888	0.989
	Transfer	**0.900**	**0.997**	**0.923**	**0.957**	**0.997**
Inception-v3	Random	0.762	0.998	0.938	0.894	0.977
	Transfer	**0.887**	**0.999**	**0.959**	**0.969**	**0.998**

Experiment 3. The Influence of CNN Input Size. Table 4 shows performance of CNNs trained with two input sizes, *i.e.*, 224×224 and 448×448, separately. Using the larger input is more beneficial for less deeper models. Compare ResNet-18 and ResNet-50 for instance. For ResNet-18, increasing the input size lifts its AP from 0.954 to 0.977, while the corresponding number of ResNet-50 increases from 0.959 to 0.976. Enlarging the input further, say up to 896×896, gives a marginal improvement at the cost of much increased GPU memory. Hence, we do not go further in this direction. Additionally, we observe that among the five performance metrics, Precision and AP are more discriminative than the other three.

Table 4. Performance of CNNs with two different input sizes. The initial weights of each CNN is passed from the corresponding ImageNet model. Given the same CNN architecture, the larger input tends to be more helpful for less deeper models.

Model	Input size	Sensitivity	Specificity	Precision	AP	AUC
ResNet-18	224 × 224	0.913	0.994	0.849	0.954	0.992
	448 × 448	**0.938**	**0.998**	**0.949**	**0.977**	**0.998**
ResNet-34	224 × 224	0.887	**0.998**	**0.947**	0.962	**0.997**
	448 × 448	**0.950**	**0.998**	0.938	**0.973**	**0.997**
ResNet-50	224 × 224	0.900	**0.997**	**0.923**	0.959	**0.997**
	448 × 448	**0.950**	0.996	0.905	**0.976**	0.996
ResNet-Ensemble	224 × 224	0.925	**0.998**	**0.937**	0.964	0.996
	448 × 448	**0.950**	0.997	0.927	**0.977**	**0.998**
Inception-v3	224 × 224	0.887	**0.999**	0.959	**0.969**	**0.998**
	448 × 448	**0.938**	**0.999**	**0.962**	0.968	0.996
DenseNet-121	224 × 224	0.913	0.998	0.948	0.963	0.993
	448 × 448	**0.938**	**0.999**	**0.974**	**0.986**	**0.998**
DenseNet-169	224 × 224	0.925	**0.999**	**0.961**	0.970	0.994
	448 × 448	**0.950**	0.997	0.916	**0.979**	**0.998**
DenseNet-201	224 × 224	0.913	0.996	0.901	0.973	0.997
	448 × 448	**0.962**	**0.999**	**0.962**	**0.987**	**0.999**
DenseNet-Ensemble	224 × 224	0.913	**0.999**	0.961	0.970	0.997
	448 × 448	**0.950**	**0.999**	**0.974**	**0.988**	**0.999**

Experiment 4. Comparison to the State-of-the-Art. For existing methods [3,17,19], their code and data are not publicly available. As they rely heavily on low-level image processing with implementation details not clearly documented, it is difficult to replicate the methods with the same preciseness as intended by their developers. So we do not include them for comparison. Alternatively, we

Table 5. Laser scar detection performance on LMD-BAPT. High AP indicates the sensitivity of our CNN models can be further optimized, see also ROC curves in Fig. 4.

Model	Sensitivity	Specificity	Precision	AP	AUC
Decision tree [16]	0.618	0.933	–	–	–
Random forest (500 trees) [16]	0.676	0.867	–	–	–
This paper					
Fine-tuned ResNet-18	0.765	0.933	0.963	0.955	0.878
ResNet-18	0.706	**1.0**	**1.0**	**0.993**	**0.984**
DenseNet-121	0.765	**1.0**	**1.0**	0.989	0.969
DenseNet-Ensemble	0.765	**1.0**	**1.0**	0.992	0.975
DenseNet-Ensemble (*decision threshold*: 0.216)	**0.971**	**1.0**	**1.0**	0.992	0.975

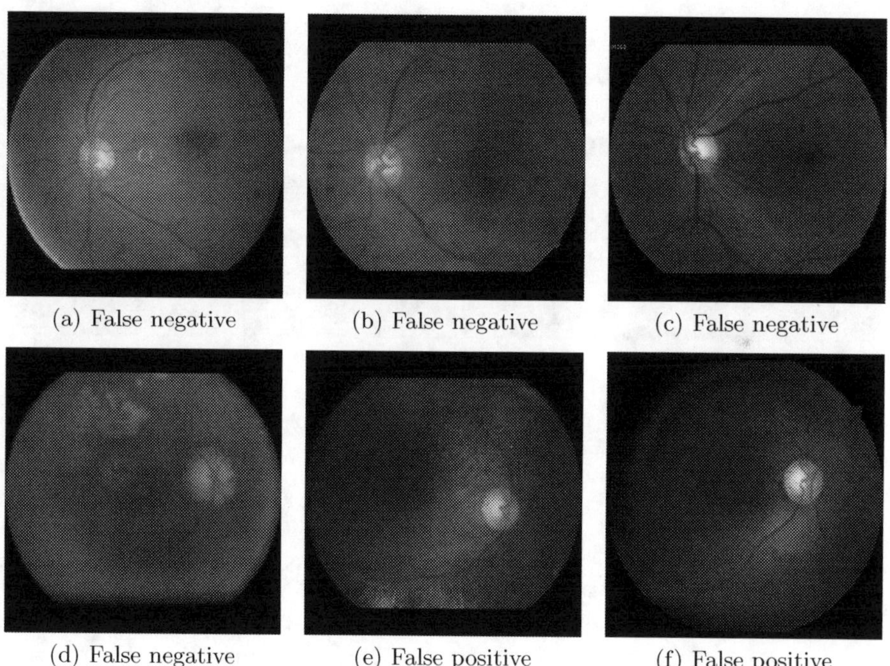

(a) False negative (b) False negative (c) False negative

(d) False negative (e) False positive (f) False positive

Fig. 5. Misclassification by DenseNet-Ensemble on the Test-2k test set. False negative images (a)–(d) are severely degenerated laser scars. False positive image (e) is peripapillary atrophy visually similar to laser scars, while False positive image (f) is affected by dirty marks from camera lens. Best viewed digitally in close-up.

add a fine-tuning baseline that uses pre-trained ResNet-18 as feature extractor, as used by [13] for glaucoma identification. To the best of our knowledge, LMD-DRS and LMD-BAPT from [16] are the only two laser-scar datasets that are publicly accessible, with LMD-BAPT as a test set. As Table 5 shows, our CNN models surpass the state-of-the-art. Recall that our decision threshold is 0.5.

As indicated by the ROC curve of DenseNet-Ensemble in Fig. 4, an adjusted threshold of 0.216 would yield sensitivity of 0.941 and specificity of 1.

For a more intuitive understanding, all misclassification by DenseNet-Ensemble are shown in Figs. 5 and 6. In particular, the number of misclassified images is six and eight on our test set and LMD-BAPT, respectively. Misclassification is largely due to severe degeneration of laser scars, making them either mostly invisible or visually similar to peripapillary atrophy.

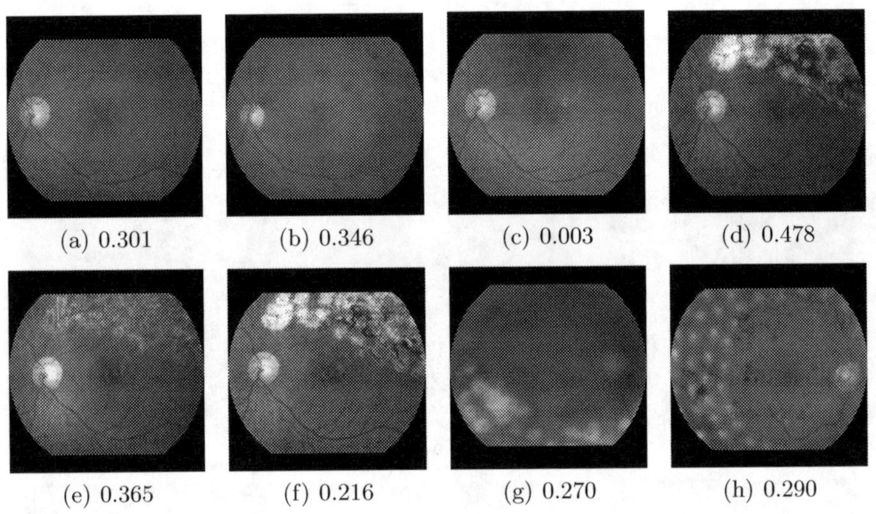

Fig. 6. Misclassification by DenseNet-Ensemble on the LMD-BAPT test set, all false negatives given 0.5 as decision threshold. Score below each image is $p(y = 1|x)$ by DenseNet-Ensemble. Image (a)–(c) are over degenerated, (d)–(f) have large laser scars visually similar to peripapillary atrophy, (g) is fresh laser scars, while (h) is out of focus and obscured.

To further justify the necessity of the newly constructed dataset, we have also trained models using LMD-DRS [16], the only training set that is publicly accessible. As ROC curves in Fig. 7 show, our training data results in better models on both test sets. Moreover, for the models trained on LMD-DRS, a clear drop of their AP scores indicate that they do not generalize well across datasets.

Discussion. As we have noted, given a highly imbalanced test set AUC is less informative. Despite the high AUC of 0.99, for key metrics such as Sensitivity, Precision and AP, there remains room for improvement. The number of positive

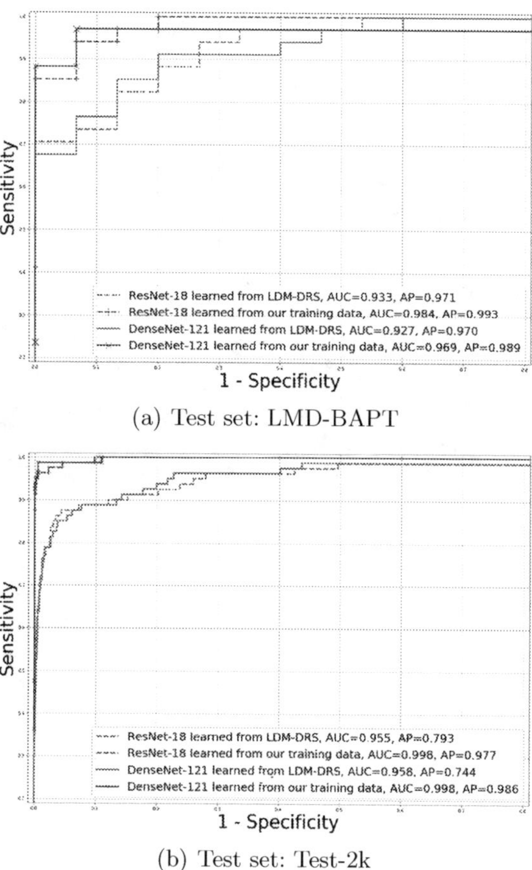

(a) Test set: LMD-BAPT

(b) Test set: Test-2k

Fig. 7. ROC curves of ResNet-18 and DenseNet-121 learned from our dataset and the LMD-DRS dataset, respectively. Best viewed in color.

images in Test-2k is only 80, meaning the differences shown between compared methods are only in few misclassified images. This might weaken our conclusion. To resolve the concern, with much efforts we collected 80 new positive images from our hospital partners, and added them to Test-2k. On the expanded test set, which we term Test-2k$^+$, we re-test the previously trained models. The new results are given in Table 6. Similar conclusions can be drawn as those in Experiment 1. That is, DenseNet performs better than ResNet and Inception-v3 in terms of the overall performance, which can be further improved by model ensembling. Miss detections of the newly added test images by DenseNet-Ensemble are shown in Fig. 8.

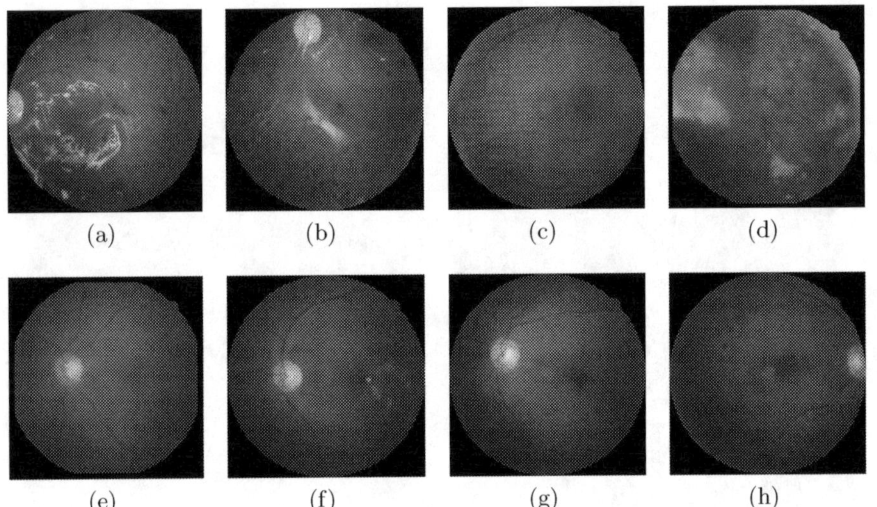

Fig. 8. All eight miss detections in the 80 newly added positive examples, made by DenseNet-Ensemble. Best viewed digitally in close-up.

Table 6. Performance of different CNNs on the expanded Test-2k$^+$ test set. The input size of each CNN is 448 × 448, with its initial weights transfered from the corresponding ImageNet model. The default decision threshold of 0.5 is used.

Model	Sensitivity	Specificity	Precision	AP	AUC
ResNet-18	0.925	0.997	0.974	0.981	**0.998**
ResNet-34	0.919	0.993	0.967	0.973	0.996
ResNet-50	0.919	0.996	0.948	0.974	0.995
ResNet-Ensemble	0.925	0.997	0.974	0.981	**0.998**
Inception-v3	0.919	**0.999**	0.980	0.968	0.994
DenseNet-121	0.919	**0.999**	**0.987**	0.982	0.998
DenseNet-169	0.931	0.997	0.955	0.977	0.996
DenseNet-201	**0.938**	**0.999**	0.980	**0.983**	**0.998**
DenseNet-Ensemble	0.925	**0.999**	**0.987**	**0.983**	**0.998**

6 Conclusions

We present the first deep learning approach to laser scar detection in fundus images. By performing transfer learning on the recent DenseNet models, a highly effective laser scar detector is developed. The detector obtains Precision of 1.0 and AP of 0.993 on the public LMD-BAPT test set, and Precision of 0.974 and AP of 0.988 on the newly built Test-2k test set. The success of our deep learning approach is largely attributed to the large expert-labeled laser-scar dataset proposed by this work.

Acknowledgments. This work was supported by the National Natural Science Foundation of China (No. 61672523), the Fundamental Research Funds for the Central Universities and the Research Funds of Renmin University of China (No. 18XNLG19). The authors thank anonymous reviewers for their feedbacks.

References

1. AAO: Diabetic retinopathy ppp - updated 2017 (2017). https://www.aao.org/preferred-practice-pattern/diabetic-retinopathy-ppp-updated-2017
2. Cuadros, J., Bresnick, G.: EyePACS: an adaptable telemedicine system for diabetic retinopathy screening. JDST **3**(3), 509–516 (2009)
3. Dias, J., Oliveira, C., da Silva Cruz, L.: Detection of laser marks in retinal images. In: CBMS (2013)
4. Gargeya, R., Leng, T.: Automated identification of diabetic retinopathy using deep learning. Ophthalmology **124**(7), 962–969 (2017)
5. Gulshan, V., et al.: Development and validation of a deep learning algorithm for detection of diabetic retinopathy in retinal fundus photographs. JAMA **316**(22), 2402–2410 (2016)
6. He, K., Zhang, X., Ren, S., Sun, J.: Delving deep into rectifiers: surpassing human-level performance on ImageNet classification. In: ICCV (2015)
7. He, K., Zhang, X., Ren, S., Sun, J.: Deep residual learning for image recognition. In: CVPR (2016)
8. Huang, G., Liu, Z., Weinberger, K., van der Maaten, L.: Densely connected convolutional networks. In: CVPR (2017)
9. Kaggle: Diabetic retinopathy detection (2015). https://www.kaggle.com/c/diabetic-retinopathy-detection
10. Krizhevsky, A., Sutskever, I., Hinton, G.: ImageNet classification with deep convolutional neural networks. In: NIPS (2012)
11. Li, X., Uricchio, T., Ballan, L., Bertini, M., Snoek, C., Del Bimbo, A.: Socializing the semantic gap: a comparative survey on image tag assignment, refinement and retrieval. ACM Comput. Surv. **49**(1), 14:1–14:39 (2016)
12. Liu, Y., et al.: Prevalence of diabetic retinopathy among 13473 patients with diabetesmellitus in China: a cross-sectional epidemiological survey in sixprovinces. BMJ Open **7**(1), e013199 (2017)
13. Orlando, J., Prokofyeva, E., del Fresno, M., Blaschko, M.: Convolutional neural network transfer for automated glaucoma identification. In: ISMIPA (2017)
14. Pratt, H., Coenen, F., Broadbent, D., Harding, S., Zheng, Y.: Convolutional neural networks for diabetic retinopathy. Procedia Comput. Sci. **90**, 200–205 (2016)
15. Ravishankar, H., et al.: Understanding the mechanisms of deep transfer learning for medical images. In: Carneiro, G., et al. (eds.) LABELS/DLMIA -2016. LNCS, vol. 10008, pp. 188–196. Springer, Cham (2016). https://doi.org/10.1007/978-3-319-46976-8_20
16. Sousa, J., Oliveira, C., Silva Cruz, L.: Automatic detection of laser marks in retinal digital fundus images. In: EUSIPCO (2016)
17. Syed, A., Akbar, M., Akram, M., Fatima, J.: Automated laser mark segmentation from colored retinal images. In: INMIC (2014)

18. Szegedy, C., Vanhoucke, V., Ioffe, S., Shlens, J., Wojna, Z.: Rethinking the inception architecture for computer vision. In: CVPR (2016)
19. Tahir, F., Akram, M., Abbass, M., Khan, A.: Laser marks detection from fundus images. In: HIS (2014)
20. Taylor, D.: Diabetic eye screening revised grading definitions (2012). http://bmec.swbh.nhs.uk/wp-content/uploads/2013/03/Diabetic-Screening-Service-Revised-Grading-Definitions-November-2012.pdf

Gradient-Guided DCNN for Inverse Halftoning and Image Expanding

Yi Xiao[1], Chao Pan[1], Yan Zheng[2(✉)], Xianyi Zhu[1], Zheng Qin[1], and Jin Yuan[1]

[1] College of Computer Science and Electronic Engineering, Hunan University, Changsha, Hunan Province, China

[2] College of Electrical and Information Engineering, Hunan University, Changsha, Hunan Province, China

yanzheng@hnu.edu.cn

Abstract. Inverse halftoning and image expanding refer to the ill-posed problems which restore higher-bit images from lower bit ones. Many scholars have studied these problems so far, but the restored images still suffer either quantization artifacts or fine detail losses. Although recent deep convolutional neural network (DCNN) based methods have shown its advantage in these two problems, it is hard to restore high quality images with fine details if no extra information is feeded to the network. To solve this problem, this paper proposes a gradient-guided DCNN model for inverse halftoning and image expanding. The DCNN model consists of two stages. In the first stage, two subnetworks are designed to explicitly predict the gradient maps of the input image, which account for the detail information of image. In the second stage, the gradient maps, concatenated with the input image, are feeded to another subnetwork to guide the reconstruction of the final results. Experimental results show that our method outperforms the state-of-arts in terms of both visual quality and numerical evaluation. In particular, our method better recovers the fine details of the images.

Keywords: Gradient-guided · Inverse halftoning · Image expanding

1 Introduction

Image quantization is widely used to save memory or bandwidth in storage and transmission, or to fit the accuracy level of display devices or printers. In this case, only a few bits per pixel are used to store the image information. An extreme example is halftone image, whose pixels are 1's and 0's (1 bit per pixel). Compared to the original digital images, these quantized images may suffer a

The work is supported by the National Key R&D Program of China (2018YFB0203904), NSFC from PRC (61872137, 61502158, 61502157, 61472131, 61772191), Hunan NSF (2017JJ3042), and Science and Technology Key Projects of Hunan Province (2015TP1004, 2015SK2087, 2015JC1001, 2016JC2012).

C. V. Jawahar et al. (Eds.): ACCV 2018, LNCS 11364, pp. 207–222, 2019.
https://doi.org/10.1007/978-3-030-20870-7_13

considerable amount of information loss, contouring artifacts and blocking artifacts. Also, typical image processing techniques such as scaling or enhancing may be hard to apply to them [13,33]. With the widespread applications of image quantization, how to restore high quality continuous tone images from quantized images is becoming a research focus. In this paper, we mainly focus on methods to recover continuous tone images from images which have only 1 bit per pixel (inverse halftoning) or a few bits per pixel (image expanding).

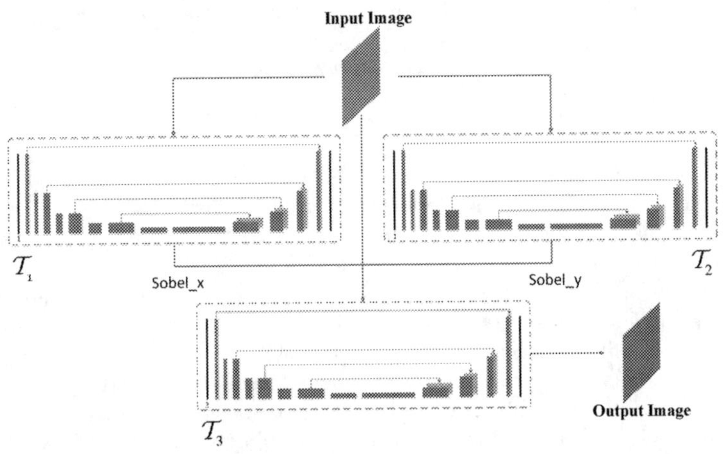

Fig. 1. The overall structure of our framework. Symbol $\mathcal{T}_x$ denotes subnetwork, Sobel_x and Sobel_y denotes gradient map of horizontal and vertical direction respectively. Each subnetwork in framework is an U-shaped encoder-decoder with skip connections between the encoder and decoder. Use gradient maps generated by $\mathcal{T}_1$ and $\mathcal{T}_2$ along with input image as inputs to $\mathcal{T}_3$. More details of subnetwork are shown in Fig. 2.

Inverse halftoning and image expanding are ill-posed problems without unique solutions. Even if the quantization and halftone methods are known in advance, there can exist arbitrary number of outputs for an input image. An general idea for these two problem is to infer the value of each pixel from the features contained in its neighbour region. Based on this idea, a large number methods have been proposed, include filtering [16,30], projection on convex sets (POCS) [3,7,32], maximum a-posteriori (MAP) estimation [27,28], wavelets [26,36], look-up table (LUT) [22,23,34] and neural networks [8–10,35]. However, most of the aforementioned methods tend to compromise between the reduction of the artifacts and recover of image details. Either the artifacts due to quantization cannot be fully removed or the details of the image can not be restored.

In recent years, convolution neural networks (CNN) has shown their superiority in the field of image processing. Hou et al. [8] suggested using a deep convolution neural network (DCNN) model can give a good solution to this two image processing problems. Xiao et al. [35] improved the DCNN model [8] and obtained better results for inverse halftoning. But there are still plenty of space to improve the detail textures of the restored images.

When analyzing the DCNN based methods [8,35], we find that it is difficult to restore high quality images with fine details if no extra information is feeded to the network. The possible reason is that convolution neural network is a kind of black-box approach, it could be too tough to control the direction of the optimization of network only with loss functions, such as mean square error (MSE). If extra information such as gradient maps can be feeded to the network, the network can be better guided to a better solution. Similar views also appeared in works of predecessors, such as [19,24], which proposed to direct the data generation process by conditioning the model to accept additional information. Based on this insight, we propose a gradient-guided DCNN model for inverse halftoning and image expanding. Our model consists of two stages (shown in Fig. 1.). In the first stage, we designs two subnetworks to explicitly predict the gradient maps in vertical and horizontal directions. In the second stage, the gradient maps, together with the input image, are then feeded to another subnetwork to guide the recover of the final results. Each subnetwork is a U-net structural [35], which is proven to perform well in many applications. Experimental results show that our method achieves state-of-art results both in numerical evaluation and visual effects when compared to previous methods. In particular, the fine details of the images are better restored in our method.

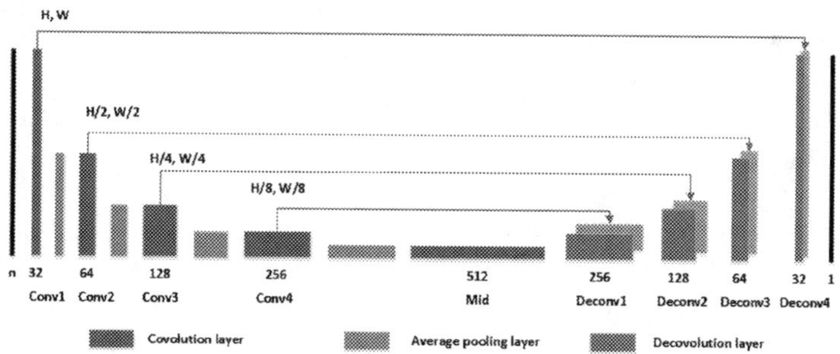

Fig. 2. The details of subnetwork. Every subnetwork has the same architecture. $n = 1$ in $\mathcal{T}_1$ and $\mathcal{T}_2$, $n = 3$ in $\mathcal{T}_3$.

2 Background and Related Work

2.1 Halftoning and Inverse Halftoning

Halftoning is a technology of transferring the continuous-tone images into binary images. It breaks up an image into a series of dots, varying either in size (Amplitude Modulated, AM) or in spatial frequency (Frequency Modulated, FM), and hence generates a gradient-like effect. This technology is widely used in image compression, output printing, LED display and other fields. Halftoning methods can be roughly divided into 3 categories according to the computational types involved: point processes [1,18,29], neighborhood processes [5,6,11], and iterative processes [12,14].

Despite the popularity of halftoning technology, inverse halftoning, which converts halftone images back to the continuous-tone images, also has a wide range of applications. There are many good outcomes about inverse halftoning in literatures so far. One of the most classic methods is a low-pass filter reduction method. The Gaussian filter is the optimal pre-smoothing filter for gradient estimation in continuous signals [4], but halftones introduce extra requirements on the pre-smoothing filter besides the conjoint minimization of spatial domain and frequency domain variances. Kite et al. [16] presented a single-pass method, which consists of multi-scale directional gradient estimation followed by adaptive low-pass filtering. Although this method eliminates the high frequency noise in the image, the details of the original image are removed, and the effect it achieves is very limited. The wavelet based methods offer a decomposition of the halftone image that allows us to selectively choose appropriate information from all frequency bands for good inverse halftoning performances [36]. Motivated by Kite et al.'s linear approximation model [16], Neelamani et al. [26] proposed a wavelet-based inverse halftoning via Deconvolution (WInHD) to perform inverse halftoning of error-diffused halftones. A method based on LUT is proposed by Mese et al. [22], the LUT is obtained from the histogram gathered from a few sample halftone-original image pairs. This approach is very fast because no filtering is required, but its performance greatly depends on the choice of template, which is hard to determine. In [9], Wen et al. proposed to search the optimal template using elitist genetic algorithm, but the quality of the restored image is still not satisfactory.

With the development of neural networks, some researchers applied the neural network to inverse halftoning. Huang et al. proposed an hybrid neural system [10] to handle halftoning and inverse halftoning simultaneously. Jimenez et al. proposed a multi-layer perceptron network based inverse halftoning method [25]. Before training, the halftone images are smoothed with a low-pass filter. Then each pixel and its 4×4 neighbors are used to train a two-layer prospector. In fact, this MLP [25] based method is equivalent to a two-layer convolution neural network. If more layers are used, the quality of restored images can be further improved. Hou et al. [8] and Xiao et al. [35] proposed using the DCNN model to tackle this problem and achieved much better results. But the fine details of the restored images still require further improvement.

2.2 Image Companding

Image companding [2,20,37] is the combination of two processes, namely compresssing and expanding. This technique squeezes higher-bit images to lower bit ones for tasks such as transmission, and restore the dynamic range after the task. Many literature on high dynamic range (HDR) compression has been conducted. The most straightforward techniques, sometimes called "global" tone-mapping methods, use compressive point nonlinearities [17,31]. Li et al. [20] proposed a multi-scale subband architecture to compress high dynamic range images to displayable low dynamic range (LDR) ones. They also stated that with the similar scheme as the previous compression, low dynamic range images can be expanded to approximate the original higher-bit ones with minimal degradation. Hou et al. [8] formulated the image companding and inverse halftoning as image transformation problems and employ the convolutional neural network (CNN) as non-linear functions to map input images to output images for different purposes.

3 Proposed Method

In this work, we propose a two-stage DCNN model to tackle the two image processing problems, i.e. inverse halftoning and expanding. In Sect. 3.1, we describe the overall structure of our model and the details of the subnetworks. In Sect. 3.2, we define the loss function of the network. We then describe the two stage of our system (i) the gradient map generating stage in Sect. 3.1, which takes halftoned images or low bit images as input and infers corresponding gradient maps, and (ii) the information integrating stage in Sect. 3.1, which combines the original input images and gradient maps and infers high qualified output images.

Because of the nature similarity of inverse halftoning and image expanding, we will only take inverse halftoning problem as an example for simplicity in Sect. 3.1.

(a) halftoned image

(b) horizontal-gradient map

(c) vertical-gradient map

Fig. 3. An example of guidance information generating stage.

3.1 Two-Stage DCNN

As aforementioned, it is hard to reconstruct high quality image with fine details in a single DCNN model [8,35], if no extra information is provided. To better train the network to form a good solution, we break the problem into two stages. In the first stage, we directly predict the gradient maps from the input image, and use them to guide the final image recovery in the second stage. With this arrangement, the network can be better trained to restore more fine details of the images. Similar ideas also appears in joint image super-resolution [19], and conditional generative adversarial networks [24].

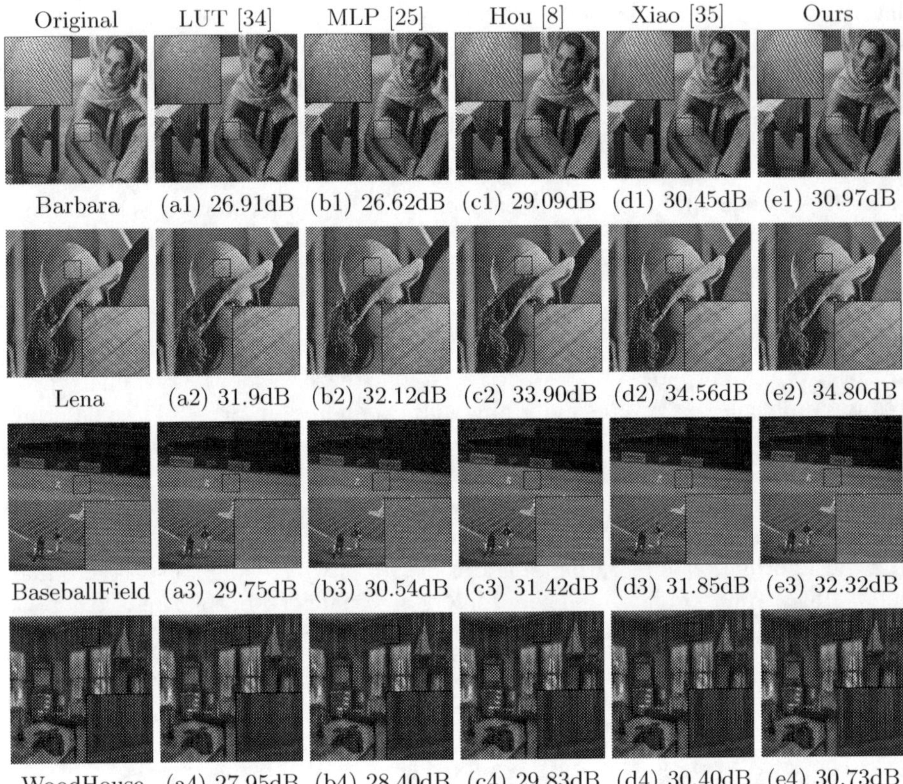

Fig. 4. Visual comparison of inverse halftoning methods (grayscale). Barbara and Lena are selected from classic image processing set. BaseballField and WoodHouse are selected from COCO testing set.

The overall structure of our framework is illustrated in Fig. 1. The framework is composed of 3 subnetworks, denoted as $\mathcal{T}_1, \mathcal{T}_2, \mathcal{T}_3$. In the first stage, we train $\mathcal{T}_1$ and $\mathcal{T}_2$ to generate the gradient map of horizontal direction and vertical direction. In the second stage, we take original input image along with predicted gradient maps of two directions as input and train the subnetwork $\mathcal{T}_3$ to restore high quality image. We directly use the model in [35] as our subnetwork, which is proven the superiority for tackling inverse halftoning problem.

The structure of subnetwork is shown in Fig. 2. It is an U-shaped encoder-decoder with skip connections between the encoder and decoder. Each convolution layer in the encoder follows an average pooling layer for down-sampling. Since each deconvolution layer will reduce the number of feature channels by a half, Xiao [35] added an extra 1×1 convolution layer to increase the feature maps to $\frac{H}{16} \times \frac{W}{16} \times 512$. The first deconvolution layer will generate a $\frac{H}{8} \times \frac{W}{8} \times 256$ tensor, which will concatenate the output of the fourth convolution layer "conv4", also a $\frac{H}{8} \times \frac{W}{8} \times 256$ tensor, to form a $\frac{H}{8} \times \frac{W}{8} \times 512$ tensor. An extra convolution layer with kernel size 1×1 is used to reduce the tensor to reduce tensor to $\frac{H}{8} \times \frac{W}{8} \times 256$. The steps are similar for the other deconvolution layers. Batch normalization layers is used in all convolution and deconvolution layers (except input and output layers).

Gradient Map Generating Stage. In [8] and [35], they take halftoned image as input directly, and get well restored results. But we found that when we add gradient map of ground truth image to the input and retrain the network, the peak signal to noise ratio (PSNR) results has increased nearly 10dB on average. This finding inspires us that getting gradient map from halftoned image helps improving the performance of the model.

In this stage, we use gradient maps obtained from ground truth images as label images, and MSE between input images and label images to train the subnetwork. Then, we train network $\mathcal{T}_1$ (as shown in Fig. 1) to reason the gradient map of horizontal direction, and network $\mathcal{T}_2$ to reason the gradient map of vertical direction respectively. Figure 3 shows an example of this procedure. Once $\mathcal{T}_1$ and $\mathcal{T}_2$ have been trained, we then feed the output of the two subnetwork to the last network $\mathcal{T}_3$ to synthesize fine detailed images.

Information Integrating Stage. In the second stage, we concatenate the original input image with the predicted gradient maps to form a 3-channel input. Then we use the loss function define in Eq. (5) to guide the training process of subnetwork $\mathcal{T}_3$. We will demonstrate the effectiveness of gradient maps by experiments in Sect. 4.

3.2 Loss Function and Training

We use I to denote the input halftoned image, Y to denote the ground truth image, and $\mathcal{T}_1(I), \mathcal{T}_2(I), \mathcal{T}_3(I, \mathcal{T}_1(I), \mathcal{T}_2(I))$ denotes the output of the three subnetwork. For the sake of simplicity, we use $\mathcal{T}_3(\cdot)$ to denote the output the the subnetwork $\mathcal{T}_3$. Since we will choose the mean squared error (MSE) of two images O_1 and O_2 as our basic loss function, we define it as

$$\mathcal{L}_{MSE}(O_1, O_2) = \frac{1}{H \times W} \sum_{i,j} (O_1(i,j) - O_2(i,j))^2, \tag{1}$$

where $O_1(i,j)$ is the pixel value of position (i,j), H and W is the height and width of the image, respectively.

We use the Sobel operator to calculate the gradient maps, given by

$$G_x = \begin{bmatrix} -1\,0\,1 \\ -2\,0\,2 \\ -1\,0\,1 \end{bmatrix}, G_y = \begin{bmatrix} 1 & 2 & 1 \\ 0 & 0 & 0 \\ -1 & -2 & -1 \end{bmatrix} \tag{2}$$

where G_x is for horizontal gradients, G_y is for vertical gradients. By using the Sobel operator, horizontal and vertical gradient maps of an image $\mathcal{G}_x(O), \mathcal{G}_y(O)$

can be obtained. Because the value range of gradient map obtained by Sobel operator isn't in the range [0, 1], we map them to this range by the Sigmoid function. Then, the gradient maps $\mathcal{G}_x(O), \mathcal{G}_y(O)$ are given by

$$\begin{aligned}\mathcal{G}_x(O) &= \sigma(O \otimes G_x) \\ \mathcal{G}_y(O) &= \sigma(O \otimes G_y)\end{aligned} \tag{3}$$

where $\sigma(\cdot)$ is the Sigmoid function, symbol $\otimes$ denotes the convolution operation.

The three subnetworks in our model are trained separately. For subnetwork $\mathcal{T}_1$, we train it using the MSE between the output image and the horizontal gradient map of the ground truth $\mathcal{L}_{MSE}(\mathcal{T}_1(I), \mathcal{G}_x(Y))$. Similarly, the loss function of the subnetwork $\mathcal{T}_2$ is $\mathcal{L}_{MSE}(\mathcal{T}_2(I), \mathcal{G}_y(Y))$.

The loss function of $\mathcal{T}_3$ is composed of two parts, the first part is the MSE between output image and the ground truth image $\mathcal{L}_{MSE}(\mathcal{T}_3(\cdot), Y)$. Different with the method in [35], we further introduce the MSE of the gradient of the output image and the ground truth in the loss function. The gradient loss term can help better restore the details of images. The gradient loss term is given by

$$\mathcal{L}_{GRAD} = \mathcal{L}_{MSE}(\mathcal{G}_x(\mathcal{T}_3(\cdot)), \mathcal{G}_x(Y)) + \mathcal{L}_{MSE}(\mathcal{G}_y(\mathcal{T}_3(\cdot)), \mathcal{G}_y(Y)) \tag{4}$$

Our final loss function of the subnetwork $\mathcal{T}_3$ is

$$Loss = \mathcal{L}_{MSE}(\mathcal{T}_3(\cdot), Y) + \lambda \cdot \mathcal{L}_{GRAD}, \tag{5}$$

where λ is a parameter that weights the relative importance of gradient loss. Setting $\lambda = 0$ would disable the gradient loss and only use the grayscale loss. We set $\lambda = 10$ in this paper by experience.

4 Experimental Results

We detail the qualitative and quantitative experiments of our gradient-guided DCNN model. In Sect. 4.1, we first introduce our experiment settings, including data set and detailed training parameters. Then we evaluate the inverse halftoning and image companding task in Sects. 4.2 and 4.3 respectively.

4.1 Experiment Settings

We choose Microsoft COCO data set [21] for experiment, which is a large-scale database containing more than 80,000 images for training, and more than 40,000 images for testing. In our experiments, we randomly select 2000 images from the testing images as our testing set, and resize the training and testing images to the size of 256. Furthermore, we add 6 classical 512 × 512 images frequently used in image processing to our testing set, including Baboon, Barbara, Boat, Goldhill, Lena and Peppers.

We implement our two-stage DCNN model using Google's Tensorflow framework, and train it on a GeForce GTX1080 Ti GPU. For each subnetwork, Adam

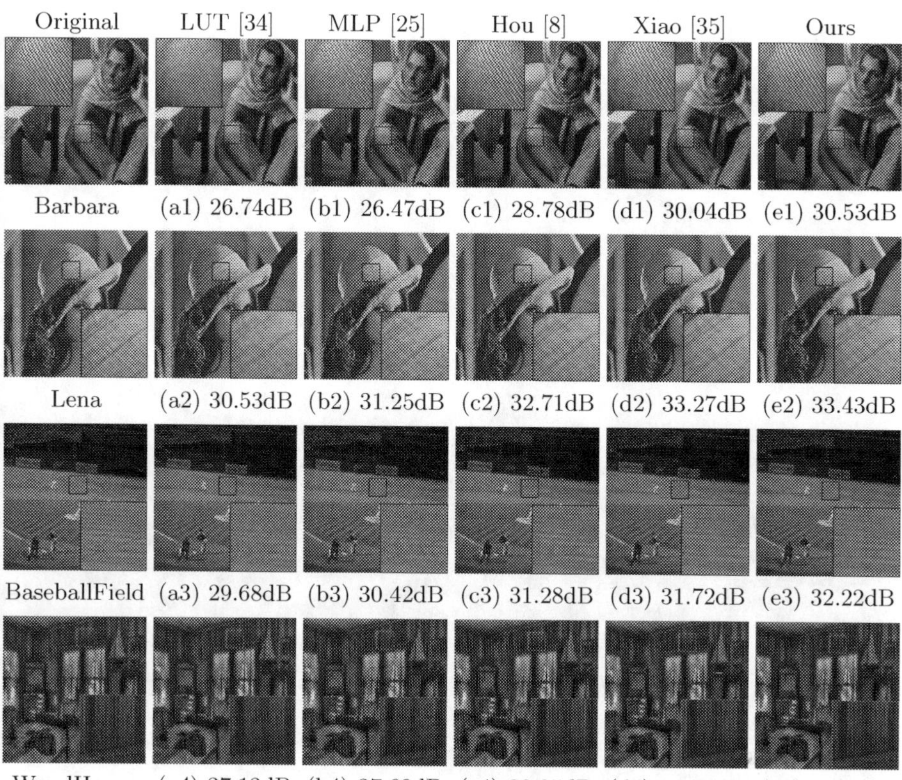

Fig. 5. Visual comparison of inverse halftoning methods (color). Barbara and Lena are selected from classic image processing set. BaseballField and WoodHouse are selected from COCO testing set.

algorithm [15] is chosen as the optimizer. We select the batch size of 32 and the number of iterations is 100,000 times by experiments. The initial value of the learning factor is set to 0.001, which is reduced to 0.7 times in every 10,000 steps. Diminishing learning rate is proven to improve training effectiveness of the model.

And we also compare our methods with several recent advanced approaches, including LUT [34], MLP [25], Hou's DCNN method [8] and Xiao's DCNN method [35]. We implement the LUT [34] method and MLP [25] method in Matlab, and Hou's method [8] and Xiao's method [35] in TensorFlow with Python. Each of these implementations achieves nearly identical precision compared with the original.

4.2 Inverse Halftoning

Inverse halftoning is a task to generate a continuous-tone image from a halftoned binary image. This is a ill-posed problem since there could exist multiple continuous-tone images corresponding to the halftoned ones. We use Floyd-Steinberg error diffusion (FS) [6] and its edge enhanced version (E-FS) [5] to preprocess the data set getting halftoned images for training and testing. We experiment with both grayscale and color images by using the same approach. In the case of processing a color image, we directly apply inverse halftoning methods to 3 color channels (RGB) separately and merge 3 channels to a color image.

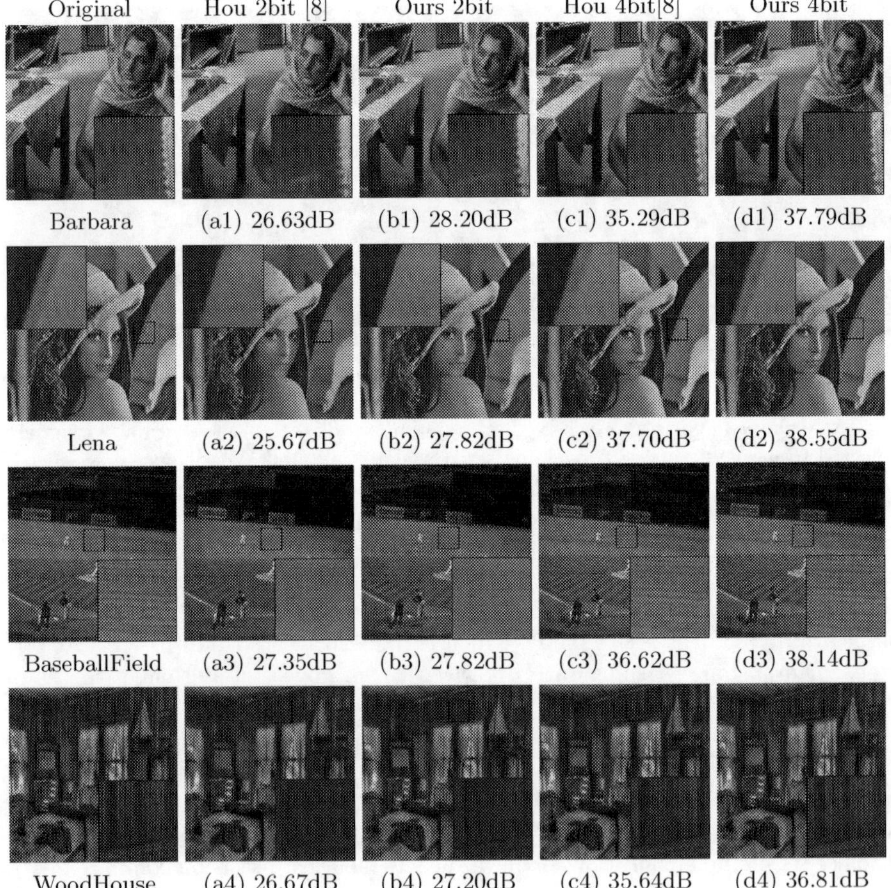

Fig. 6. Visual comparison of image expanding methods (grayscale). Barbara and Lena are selected from classic image processing set. BaseballField and WoodHouse are selected from COCO testing set.

We test our method on the 2 K testing set of size 256 and 512, as well as 6 classical image processing figures of size 512, and use peak signal to noise ratio (PSNR) as quality metrics to quantitatively evaluate our inverse halftoning results. As the quantitative results shown in Table 1, our method achieves the best numerical results for both color and grayscale images. And it is not difficult to find that images containing abundant regular textures have more significantly improvement. For example, the PSNR of Barbara (containing many black and white stripes) increases 0.52 dB over Xiao's method [35], while the PSNR of Peppers (lacking textures) only increases 0.08 dB. The visual results are shown in Figs. 4 and 5.

As we can see in Figs. 4 and 5, our method gives the best reconstruction of input halftoned image. For example, stripes in Fig. 4(e1) are more distinct than other methods. In the third row figures in Fig. 4, Hou's method [8] and Xiao's method [35] only restore the horizontal stripes from halftoned image while our method restores the crisscrossed stripes. We owes it to the introduction of gradient guidance information.

Table 1. Numerical comparison of inverse halftoning methods (PSNR). In second column, g and c denote gray image and color image respectively. Last two columns is the results of 2K test set with size of 256 and 512.

Images		Baboon	Barbara	Boat	Goldhill	Lena	Peppers	256×	512×
LUT FS [34]	g	24.44	26.91	30.33	29.93	31.29	30.95	28.11	-
	c	23.94	26.74	30.25	29.53	30.53	30.01	27.94	-
MLP FS [25]	g	24.18	26.62	31.23	30.48	32.12	31.56	28.61	-
	c	23.74	26.47	31.07	30.07	31.25	30.54	28.46	-
Hou [8] FS	g	25.28	29.09	32.80	31.57	33.90	33.21	29.97	31.04
	c	24.76	28.78	32.60	31.04	32.71	31.68	29.77	30.76
Xiao [35] FS	g	25.68	30.45	33.64	32.10	34.56	34.02	30.71	30.74
	c	25.16	30.04	33.36	31.54	33.27	32.22	30.51	31.47
Ours FS	g	**25.73**	**30.97**	**33.95**	**32.30**	**34.80**	**34.10**	**30.89**	**31.98**
	c	**25.21**	**30.53**	**33.62**	**31.70**	**33.43**	**32.29**	**30.67**	31.66
Hou [8] E-FS	g	26.10	30.18	33.90	32.90	35.27	33.14	29.91	31.20
	c	25.43	29.88	33.23	31.97	33.77	31.58	29.56	30.83
Xiao [35] E-FS	g	26.72	31.02	35.04	33.47	35.84	33.69	30.55	31.86
	c	26.05	30.61	34.39	32.55	34.30	31.91	30.18	31.45
Ours E-FS	g	**26.91**	**31.15**	**35.12**	**33.60**	**35.85**	**33.63**	**30.72**	32.07
	c	**26.69**	**30.97**	**34.67**	**32.83**	**34.34**	**31.83**	**30.34**	31.66

4.3 Image Expanding

The second image processing problem we concerned is image expanding. Expanding lower bit images to higher bit outputs is a classic problem of image companding. This technique has been investigated in the context of high dynamic

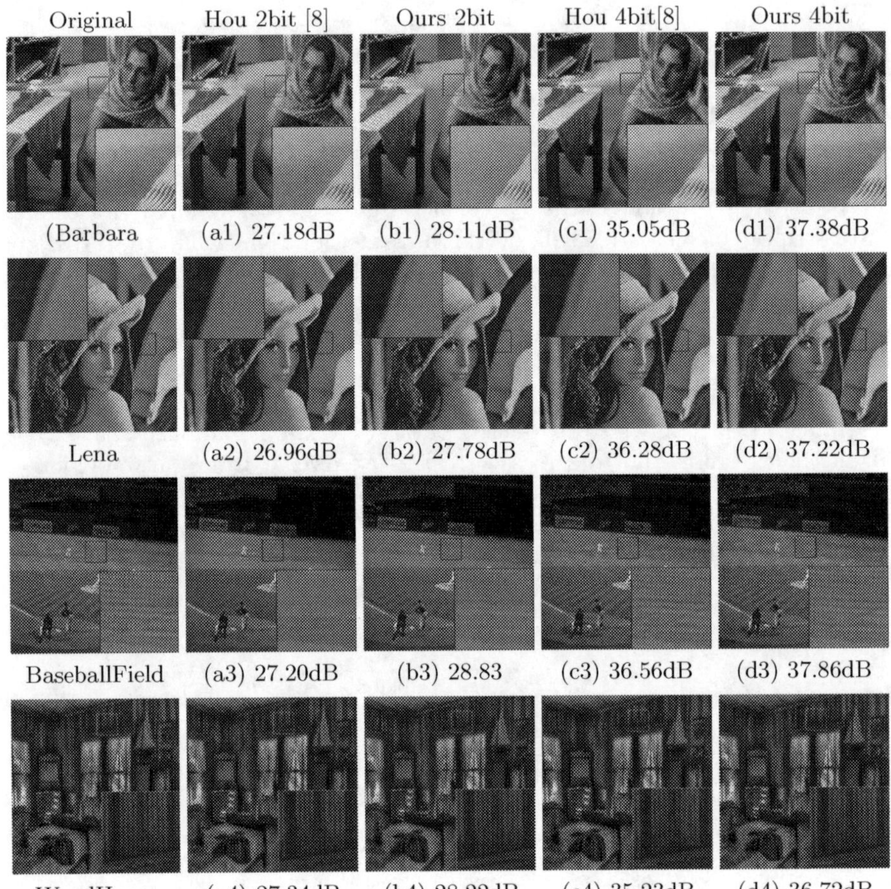

Fig. 7. Visual comparison of image expanding methods (color). Barbara and Lena are selected from classic image processing set. BaseballField and WoodHouse are selected from COCO testing set.

range (HDR) imaging [20], firstly compressing the range of an HDR image into an LDR image for less storage memory, and then retrieve it to higher bit depth image that close to original HDR image. Considering the most frequently images are 8 bits per pixel per channel, we use 8 bit (per channel) images as the highest bit depth images in our experiments. We first compress the 8 bit images to 2 bit and 4 bit depth images in a channel wise manner, then expand them back to 8 bits. A common method [20] for compressing high bit images is to quantize the color level from 256 to the corresponding low level, which will be then scaled up to fill the full range of the display. Mathematically we can use the formula below to easily convert high bit images to different lower bit outputs.

$$P_{low} = \lfloor \frac{P_{high}}{2^{h-l}} \rfloor 2^{h-l}. \tag{6}$$

where P_{low} and P_{high} denote the pixel intensity of converted lower and higher bit depth images respectively, l and h denote the bit depth for low bit depth and high bit depth images. We use 8 bit images as ground truth and lower bit images preprocessed by Eq. (6) as inputs to train the model. In this paper, we only take 2 bit and 4 bit depth images for experiments.

Table 2. Numerical comparison of image expanding methods (PSNR). In second column, g and c denote gray image and color image respectively. Last two columns is the results of 2K test set with size of 256 and 512.

Images		Baboon	Barbara	Boat	Goldhill	Lena	Peppers	256×	512×
Hou 2bit [8]	g	25.90	26.63	26.96	27.36	25.67	27.59	26.66	26.74
	c	26.01	27.18	26.57	27.57	26.96	28.02	27.05	27.15
Ours 2bit	g	**25.92**	**28.20**	**28.84**	**28.07**	**27.82**	**28.30**	**27.56**	**27.84**
	c	**26.41**	**28.11**	**28.48**	**27.96**	**27.78**	**28.37**	**27.70**	**27.98**
Hou 4bit [8]	g	33.41	35.29	36.84	36.65	37.70	36.70	35.94	36.10
	c	32.84	35.05	36.97	36.44	36.82	35.73	35.58	35.88
Ours 4bit	g	**35.68**	**37.79**	**38.41**	**37.17**	**38.55**	**37.42**	**37.32**	**37.65**
	c	**35.25**	**37.38**	**38.06**	**36.93**	**37.22**	**36.45**	**37.23**	**37.53**

As shown in Table 2, our method can improve the images by a large margin for both color and grayscale images. The comparisons of visual effects are shown in Figs. 6 and 7. Compared to the visual results of inverse halftoning, the enhancements in the details do have, but are not so obvious in some cases, e.g. Barbara and Lena. There are more improvements in pixel intensity uniformity. This is because when compressing HDR images to LDR images using Eq. (6), many of information in the picture has completely disappeared while the halftoning process distribute texture information into the neighbourhoods. Our framework cannot generate textures out of thin air, but existing gradient border could help limiting the color evenness of local patches. Compared to Hou's method [8], our method results in less blocking and contouring artifacts.

4.4 Model Analysis

As mentioned earlier, our two stage gradient-guided model leads to better image quality. In this section, we conduct ablative analysis on the model we have built. Table 3 shows the results of ablation study with having different ground truth image-gradient maps, removing gradient-guide structure and removing L_{Grad}, as well as naive baseline by using multi-task learning (Fig. 8).

Table 3. Ablation study (PSNR)

Images	Baboon	Barbara	Boat	Goldhill	Lena	Peppers	256×
w Canny maps	26.84	31.04	34.85	33.18	35.50	34.46	31.89
w Laplacian maps	31.08	36.22	39.47	38.01	40.16	37.95	36.21
w Sobel maps	35.49	42.58	46.17	44.52	45.11	41.41	41.51
Multi-task	25.68	30.38	33.67	32.12	34.59	33.97	30.74
w/o Grad-guide	25.67	30.43	33.68	32.12	34.59	34.02	30.71
w/o L_{Grad}	25.69	30.92	33.94	32.28	34.82	34.01	30.82
Full	**25.73**	**30.97**	**33.95**	**32.30**	**34.80**	**34.10**	**30.89**

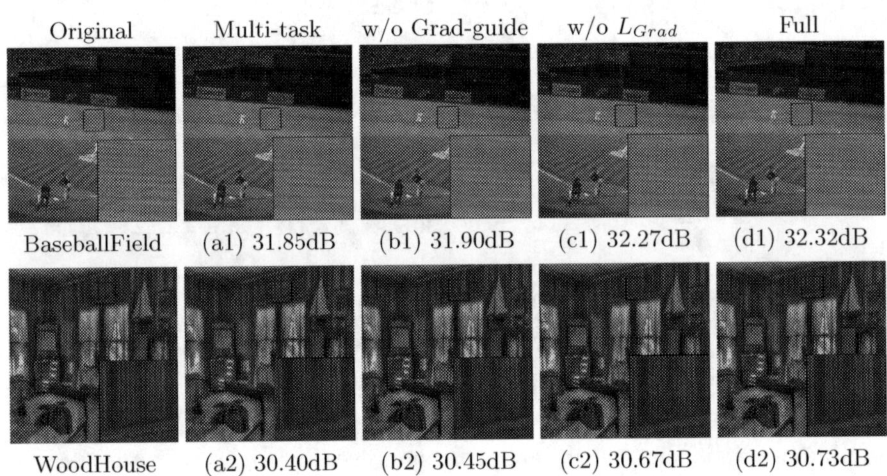

Fig. 8. Ablative analysis results on inverse halftoning.

5 Conclusions

In this paper, we propose a two-stage framework for inverse halftoning and image expanding. In the first stage, we generate the corresponding gradient maps of horizontal and vertical directions based on the input image. In the second stage, we concatenate original input images with the gradient maps as the input and get the high qualified results. Experimental results show that our model outperforms the state-of-arts in terms of both visual quality and numerical evaluation.

References

1. Bayer, B.E.: An optimal method for two-level rendition of continuous-tone pictures. In: International Conference on Communications (1973)
2. Bhooshan, S., Kumar, V.: 2D T-law: a novel approach for image companding (2010)

3. Bozkurt, G., Cetin, A.E.: Restoration of error-diffused images using POCS. In: 1999 IEEE International Conference on Acoustics, Speech, and Signal Processing, pp. 3225–3228 (1999)
4. Catté, F., Lions, P.L., Morel, J.M., Coll, T.: Image selective smoothing and edge detection by nonlinear diffusion. SIAM J. Numer. Anal. **29**(1), 182–193 (1992). https://doi.org/10.1137/0729012
5. Eschbach, R., Knox, K.T.: Error-diffusion algorithm with edge enhancement. J. Opt. Soc. Am. A **8**(12), 1844–1850 (1991)
6. Floyd, R.W.: An adaptive algorithm for spatial grayscale. In: Proceedings of Society Information Display, vol. 17, pp. 75–77 (1976)
7. Hein, S., Zakhor, A.: Halftone to continuous-tone conversion of error-diffusion coded images. IEEE Trans. Image Process. Publ. IEEE Signal Process. Soc. **4**(2), 208–16 (1995)
8. Hou, X., Qiu, G.: Image companding and inverse halftoning using deep convolutional neural networks. CoRR abs/1707.00116 (2017)
9. Huang, W.B., Chang, W.C., Lu, Y.W., Su, A.W.Y., Kuo, Y.H.: Halftone/contone conversion using neural networks. In: 2004 International Conference on Image Processing, ICIP 2004, vol. 5, pp. 3547–3550, October 2004. https://doi.org/10.1109/ICIP.2004.1421882
10. Huang, W.B., Su, A.W.Y., Kuo, Y.H.: Neural network based method for image halftoning and inverse halftoning. Expert Syst. Appl. **34**(4), 2491–2501 (2008)
11. Jarvis, J., Roberts, C.: A new technique for displaying continuous tone images on a bilevel display. IEEE Trans. Commun. **24**(8), 891–898 (1976). https://doi.org/10.1109/TCOM.1976.1093397
12. Mulligan, J.B., Ahumada, J.A.: Principled halftoning based on human vision models (1992). https://doi.org/10.1117/12.135960
13. Kang, H.R.: Digital Color Halftoning. Society of Photo-Optical Instrumentation Engineers. SPIE, Bellingham (1999)
14. Kim, S.H., Allebach, J.P.: Impact of HVS models on model-based halftoning. IEEE Trans. Image Process. Publ. IEEE Signal Process. Soc. **11**(3), 258–69 (2002)
15. Kingma, D.P., Ba, J.: Adam: a method for stochastic optimization. Computer Science (2014)
16. Kite, T.D., Damera-Venkata, N., Evans, B.L., Bovik, A.C.: A fast, high-quality inverse halftoning algorithm for error diffused halftones. IEEE Trans. Image Process. Publ. IEEE Signal Process. Soc. **9**(9), 1583–92 (2000)
17. Larson, G.W., Rushmeier, H., Piatko, C.: A visibility matching tone reproduction operator for high dynamic range scenes. IEEE Trans. Vis. **3**(4), 291–306 (1997)
18. Li, P., Allebach, J.P.: Look-up-table based halftoning algorithm. IEEE Trans. Image Process. **9**(9), 1593–1603 (2000)
19. Li, Y., Huang, J.-B., Ahuja, N., Yang, M.-H.: Deep joint image filtering. In: Leibe, B., Matas, J., Sebe, N., Welling, M. (eds.) ECCV 2016. LNCS, vol. 9908, pp. 154–169. Springer, Cham (2016). https://doi.org/10.1007/978-3-319-46493-0_10
20. Li, Y., Sharan, L., Adelson, E.H.: Compressing and companding high dynamic range images with subband architectures. ACM Trans. Graph. **24**(3), 836–844 (2005). https://doi.org/10.1145/1073204.1073271
21. Lin, T., et al.: Microsoft COCO: common objects in context. CoRR abs/1405.0312 (2014). http://arxiv.org/abs/1405.0312
22. Mese, M., Vaidyanathan, P.P.: Look-up table (LUT) method for inverse halftoning. IEEE Trans. Image Process. Publ. IEEE Signal Process. Soc. **10**(10), 1566–78 (2001)

23. Mese, M., Vaidyanathan, P.P.: Tree-structured method for LUT inverse halftoning and for image halftoning. IEEE Trans. on Image Process. **11**, 644–655 (2002)
24. Mirza, M., Osindero, S.: Conditional generative adversarial nets. CoRR abs/1411.1784 (2014). http://arxiv.org/abs/1411.1784
25. Pelcastre-Jimenez, F., Nakano-Miyatake, M., Toscano-Medina, K., Sanchez-Perez, G., Perez-Meana, H.: An inverse halftoning algorithm based on neural networks and UP(x) atomic function. In: International Conference on Telecommunications and Signal Processing, pp. 523–527 (2015)
26. Neelamani, R., Nowak, R.D., Baraniuk, R.G.: WInHD: wavelet-based inverse halftoning via deconvolution. IEEE Trans. Image Process. (2002)
27. Saika, Y., Inoue, J.I., Tanaka, H., Okada, M.: Bayes-optimal solution to inverse halftoning based on statistical mechanics of the Q-ising model. Central Eur. J. Phys. **7**(3), 444–456 (2009)
28. Stevenson, R.L.: Inverse halftoning via map estimation. IEEE Trans. Image Process. Publ. IEEE Signal Process. Soc. **6**(4), 574 (1997)
29. Sullivan, J.R., Ray, L.A., Miller, R.: Design of minimum visual modulation halftone patterns. IEEE Trans. Syst. Man Cybern. **21**(1), 33–38 (1991). https://doi.org/10.1109/21.101134
30. Thao, N.T.: Set theoretic inverse halftoning. In: Proceedings of International Conference on Image Processing, vol. 1, pp. 783–786 (1997)
31. Tumblin, J., Rushmeier, H.: Tone reproduction for realistic images. Comput. Graph. **13**(6), 42–48 (1993)
32. Unal, G.B., Cetin, A.E.: Restoration of error-diffused images using projection onto convex sets. IEEE Trans. Image Process. **10**, 1836–1841 (2001)
33. Wang, L., Hua, B.-S., Li, X.: Adaptive energy diffusion for blind inverse halftoning. In: Qiu, G., Lam, K.M., Kiya, H., Xue, X.-Y., Kuo, C.-C.J., Lew, M.S. (eds.) PCM 2010. LNCS, vol. 6297, pp. 470–480. Springer, Heidelberg (2010). https://doi.org/10.1007/978-3-642-15702-8_43
34. Wen, Z.Q., Lu, Y.L., Zeng, Z.G., Zhu, W.Q., Ai, J.H.: Optimizing template for lookup-table inverse halftoning using elitist genetic algorithm, January 2015
35. Xiao, Y., Pan, C., Xianyi Zhu, H.J., Zheng, Y.: Deep neural inverse halftoning. In: International Conference on Virtual Reality and Visualization (ICVRV 2017) (2017, to appear)
36. Xiong, Z., Orchard, M.T., Ramchandran, K.: Inverse halftoning using wavelets. IEEE Trans. Image Process. Publ. IEEE Signal Process. Soc. **8**(10), 1479–83 (1999)
37. Yang, B., Schmucker, M., Funk, W., Busch, C., Sun, S.: Integer DCT-based reversible watermarking for images using companding technique. In: Proceedings of SPIE - The International Society for Optical Engineering, vol. 5306, pp. 405–415 (2004)

Learning from PhotoShop Operation Videos: The PSOV Dataset

Jingchun Cheng[2], Han-Kai Hsu[1], Chen Fang[3], Hailin Jin[3], Shengjin Wang[2(✉)], and Ming-Hsuan Yang[1]

[1] University of California, Merced, Merced, USA
[2] Tsinghua University, Beijing, China
wgsgj@tsinghua.edu.cn
[3] Adobe Research, San Jose, USA

Abstract. In this paper, we present the PhotoShop Operation Video (PSOV) dataset, a large-scale, densely annotated video database designed for the development of software intelligence. The PSOV dataset consists of 564 densely-annotated videos for Photoshop operations, covering more than 500 commonly used commands in the Photoshop software. Videos in this dataset are obtained from YouTube, manually watched and annotated precisely to seconds by experts. There are more than 74 h of videos with 29,204 labeled commands. To the best of our knowledge, the PSOV dataset is the first large-scale software operation video database with high-resolution frames and dense annotations. We believe that this dataset can help advance the development of intelligent software, and has extensive application aspects. In this paper, we describe the dataset construction procedure, data attributes, proposed tasks and their corresponding evaluation metrics. To demonstrate that the PSOV dataset has sufficient data and labeling for data-driven methods, we develop a deep learning based algorithm for the command classification task. We also carry out experiments and analysis with the proposed method to encourage better understanding and usage of the PSOV dataset.

Keywords: Software intelligence · The PSOV dataset · Photoshop operation video

1 Introduction

Recent years have witnessed rapid development in software intelligence. With the performance leap made by deep learning, there is an explosion of works in automatic human-assisting techniques, e.g. advanced driver assistance system [4,5,22,28], machine translation [2,8], interactive robots [21,26,36], and

J. Cheng and H.-K. Hsu—Equal contribution.

Electronic supplementary material The online version of this chapter (https://doi.org/10.1007/978-3-030-20870-7_14) contains supplementary material, which is available to authorized users.

C. V. Jawahar et al. (Eds.): ACCV 2018, LNCS 11364, pp. 223–239, 2019.
https://doi.org/10.1007/978-3-030-20870-7_14

virtual player [14,15,30,40,41]. As many state-of-the-art algorithms are data-driven, well-designed datasets [1,11,29] contribute a lot to this prosperity. For example, [9,12,23] boost the development in image classification, [13,34] enable rapid progress in robotic vision; [19,27,33] assist researches in action recognition largely. In spite of the numerous existing datasets, there is still a lack of data for one particular use: computer software intelligence.

Fig. 1. Example frames of the PSOV dataset. Each row represents a video clip for one specific Photoshop operation.

Computer software plays an important role in everyday life. Due to the never-satiable appetite of computer users, there exist an rapidly-growing number of computer software, varying a lot in function, operation, and etc. Therefore, it is important for software to provide easy access for beginners. A common solution is to put all technical details in a user-guide. However, the long, boring, rich-text user-guide itself causes trouble for starters. We propose that software intelligence could be incorporated here to help solve this problem. Starters of a software can first refer to an intelligent agent, which briefly narrates shared Internet instructional videos, and advises users with instructional videos in correspondence with specific needs. With the help of these highly related, readily comprehensible instruction videos recommended by intelligent software agents, the software can be much easier to understand, operate and spread.

We consider software intelligence as a next research hotspot due to the predictable huge potentials. However, there are few published datasets designed to help algorithms understand software operations. The most closely related dataset, MiniWoB [29], aims to provide simulated environment and data helping software agents to learn interactive tasks on the web. But this dataset only uses synthetic video data, which has small window size (160×210 pixels), simple operations and primitive interfaces. Motivated by this observation, we propose to construct a computer software dataset that can further encourage research and development of intelligent software in real-world situations. For concreteness, we first focus on one widely-used software with hundreds of complex operations, Photoshop. We collect a large number of Photoshop operation videos (mostly instructional videos), annotate them and also propose some tasks for easy entry.

In this paper, we present a large-scale, densely-annotated PhotoShop Operation Video (PSOV) dataset (Fig. 1). The PSOV dataset contains videos and dense command annotations for real-world Photoshop Software. Each annotation includes command name, start and end time accurate to seconds. There are 74 h of videos and 29,204 labeled commands in the dataset. In addition, we define three tasks on the PSOV dataset: command classification, command tube prediction, and command recognition. The details of each task and evaluation metrics are described in Sect. 3. To have a better insight of the proposed dataset, we also construct a 3-D convolutional neural network based algorithm for the command classification task. By experimenting with the proposed network, we validate that the PSOV dataset is capable of supporting deep learning methods, and encourage further understanding of this database. The dataset, task definition, evaluation code as well as annotation tool are available at http://vllab1.ucmerced.edu/~hhsu22/PSOV/.

The main contributions of this work are: (1) a first-of-its-kind, large-scale, real-world PSOV dataset containing dense command annotations; (2) three well-designed tasks with evaluation metrics to help develop software intelligence; (3) a baseline algorithm for better usage and comprehension of the proposed dataset.

2 Dataset Construction Procedure

Raw videos for Photoshop operations are downloaded from YouTube[1]. The videos are collected using the Youtube Data API[2], which allows users to search for corresponding video information (such as video title, views, likes, and duration) using keywords We use keywords like *Photoshop*, *Photoshop Introduction*, *Photoshop Operation* and *Photoshop Tutorial* to search for potential Photoshop videos. The API does not return all the related videos on Youtube due to some restrictions. In order to look for as many videos related to the given keyword as possible, we set different time windows and make multiple searches for each keyword. We take the union of all the search results and remove duplicate videos programmatically. We also filter these videos with the requirement of a minimum 720p resolution. This procedure results in a collection of 184,626 videos. We observe that videos which are more related to Photoshop operations often have some creator input, i.e. caption data in the video metadata file. To guarantee high quality, we only keep the videos which have caption data, resulting in 3,734 remaining videos. Then, we go through captions of each video and sort out

[1] www.youtube.com.

[2] developers.google.com/youtube/v3/.

more than 2,000 low-quality or non-related ones. Finally, each video is watched and evaluated manually until we reach the final 564 high-quality Photoshop operation videos.

For labeling, we use a crowdsourcing platform due to the huge amount of this work. We annotate each and every command performed in the collected videos with the help of several workers, who has experience in using Photoshop. The workers are hired from Upwork[3], a global freelancing platform which enables remote communication and collaboration. Upwork provides the option to specify skill-level requirements for tasks, allowing us to hire workers with a certain level of Photoshop software knowledge. Other than their Photoshop skills, we also set a rating requirement for workers (each worker has an averaged rating from their previous jobs). Only the top-ranked workers in the platform are invited for our labeling project. Before labeling, we also conduct an interview and a training process to ensure the qualification of the workers.

Fig. 2. Labeling tool for Photoshop videos. This figure shows an example interface of our online labeling tool, by which workers can easily annotate a Photoshop operation video. Past annotations are listed on the left. See detailed descriptions in Sect. 2.

During the annotation process, we implement an online annotation tool to help facilitate remote working as well as simplify the labeling process (released with the dataset). Figure 2 shows an interface of the annotation tool, a web application based on the Express.js framework[4]. The tool shows a progress bar for each video, enabling workers to easily navigate through a video and precisely locate commands. In the bottom-right corner, there are two additional time bars designed for fine adjustment of the start and end time point, respectively. These progress bars each represents a 20-s interval with the selected time point in

[3] www.upwork.com.

[4] www.expressjs.com.

the center. They contribute a lot to time precision during annotation. Workers can select an approximate time on the full-length progress bar, and make small adjustments here to be accurate to seconds. Users can change the video playback speed (next to the full-length progress bar) in case that the candidate video is fast forwarded by its creator. We also consider other factors like interface color which differs due to software versions or themes, and video zoom-in selection when the software does not occupy the full screen (e.g. the bottom row in Fig. 6).

Before starting the labeling process, each worker is assigned an account name for user identification. Workers need to log in to their own account to start labeling. Videos are assigned randomly to workers one at a time, with the text input from video creator as a reference during labeling (see the text box in the bottom-left of Fig. 2). Workers are allowed to add, delete, and insert command labels. The labeling process also requires the user to select an interface color of the Software. In the labeling process, we set these two pre-defined colors for workers to choose from (dark gray and light gray). The most important and time-consuming part is for workers is to label the start and finish time, as well as the specific operation name of each command. Along with that, workers are required to judge whether the entire software interface is within the screen during each command, because videos may be post-edited by creators to zoom into a specific region in some cases, and video frames vary a lot after zooming in (see bottom row in Fig. 6 for an example). After labeling the candidate video, workers can either click *Finish Video* to receive the next assignment and upload the current one onto the server, or click *Save Progress* and return to where they left off afterwards. Finally, the labeled commands are double checked by ourselves to ensure the correctness.

We show the pipeline of our dataset construction procedure in Fig. 3, and describe details of the PSOV dataset in Sect. 3.

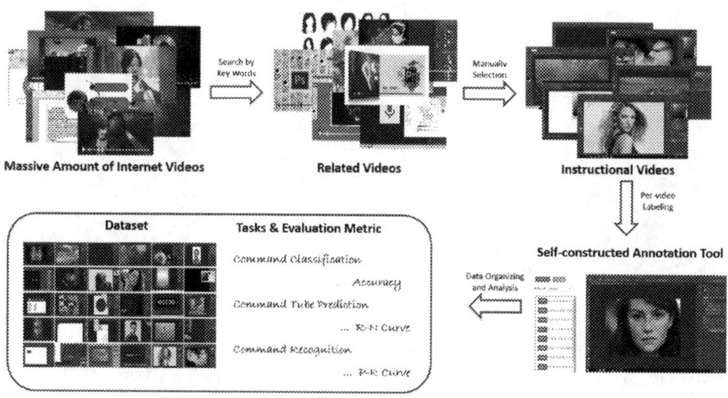

Fig. 3. Pipeline of dataset construction procedure.

3 Dataset Description

In this Section, we introduce the PSOV dataset, a large-scale, densely-annotated video dataset, specially designed for development of software intelligence. Example frames of some typical Photoshop commands are shown in Fig. 1; and the dataset structure is illustrated in Fig. 5.

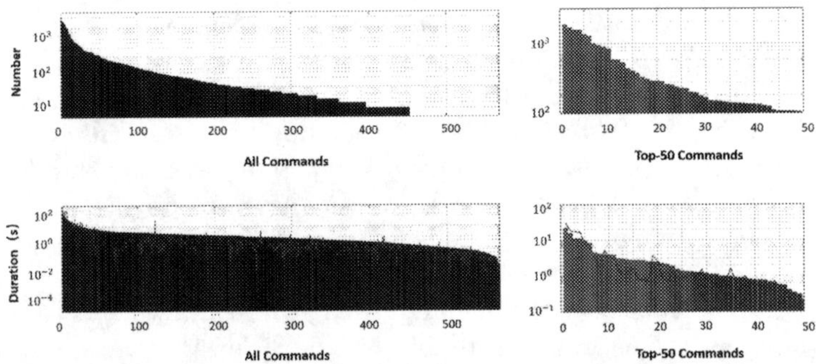

Fig. 4. Data distribution in the PSOV dataset. From left to right, we show data distribution of all labeled commands and the top-50. The first row shows the number of each command, and the second row shows the average duration (finish time minus start time) of the commands, all sorted by value. The blue lines in duration figures denote duration variance values of each bar. The top-left figure shows that about 150 commands only have 1 labeled sequence, and that the top-50 commands have the number of sequences more than 100. We provide labeling data for all command sequences in the dataset, but only evaluate tasks on the top-50 to guarantee enough training data. More details will be presented in the supplementary materials. (Color figure online)

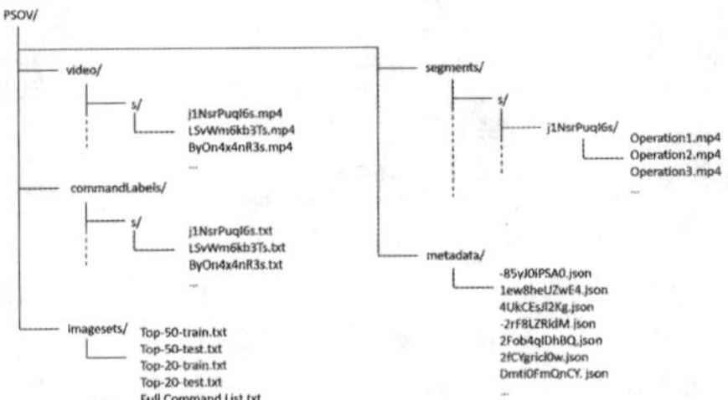

Fig. 5. Dataset structure. This figure illustrates the data storage path in the dataset, where folder *video*, *commandLabels*, *segments*, *metadata* contains whole videos, per-video annotation file, operation frames, and video caption information respectively.

Data Amount and Quality. The PSOV dataset consists of 564 densely-annotated Photoshop operation videos. There are 74 h of video with 29,204 labeled commands. Each video has the minimum resolution of 720p. Labels of command operations in Photoshop are predefined by ourselves by exploiting user guides, technique books, etc. The command definition is in a concise and effective manner, for instance, *Layer Panel > Select Layer*, *Image > Adjustments > Brightness/Contrast*, and *Apply on canvas: Brush Tool.* All 29,204 commands are labeled by the workers hired from Upwork (see details in Sect. 2). Note that besides a large portion of usual mouse click interactions, the labels also include keyboard short-cuts (e.g. Control-N, Control-C, Control-P) which are often used in Photoshop software. These keyboard short-cuts make the dataset more challenging and more realistic, since they are hard to recognize for beginners. The number of samples for each command is shown in Fig. 4. We select the top-50 commands (those with larger amount) for tasks on this dataset to ensure a sufficient volume of data for data-driven techniques like CNN-based video processing algorithms [18,19,24,31,42]. In Sect. 6, we demonstrate that the PSOV dataset has enough data quantity and diversity for training deep-learning based algorithms.

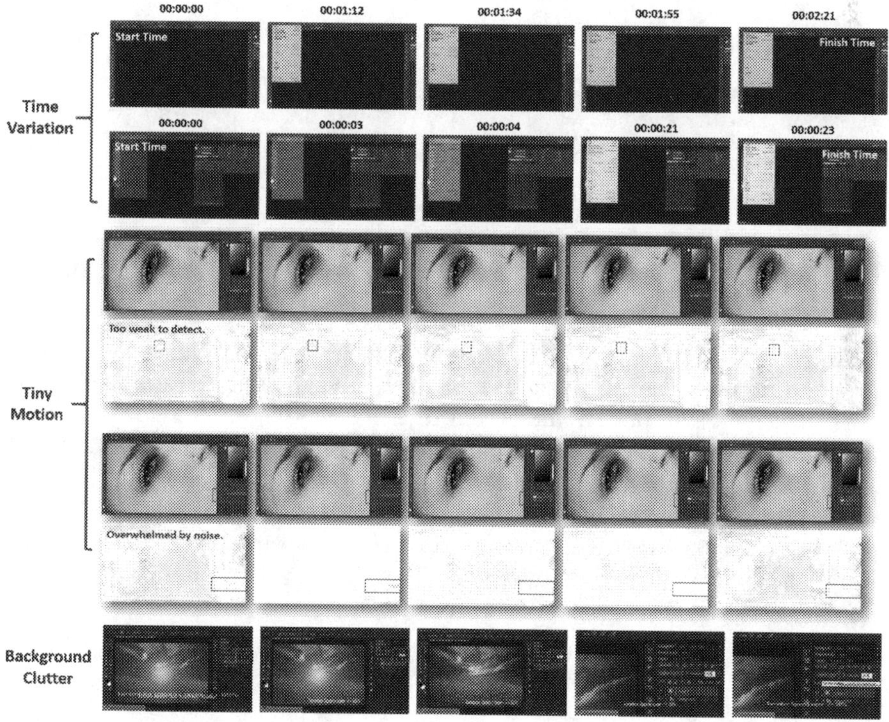

Fig. 6. Key difficulties in the PSOV dataset. This figure shows examples of three key difficulties in the PSOV dataset, i.e. duration variance, tiny motion and background clutter. (1) For time variance, each row shows a sequence of class *File > New*. This same operation has a two-second difference in the two sequences. (2) For tiny movement, optical flow [10] is used to illustrate what can be seen in motion space: the brush moving around lower eyelid in the first sequence is too weak to be detected; and the new layer appeared in the right panel has no stronger response than background noises. (3) For background clutter, we show an extreme example where the center region is zoomed in by the creator, largely changing the background of the operation. (Color figure online)

Challenges. The PSOV dataset is a challenging dataset, as the video data collected have fast but minor motion, with large variance in duration and background (see Fig. 6 for an example). In addition, data samples of different commands are imbalanced. Figure 4 presents an example of the duration difference between two command sequences with the same label *File* > *New*, showing a key difficulty of time variance in this dataset. The figure also gives examples of two other challenges: minor motion and background clutter. The PSOV dataset holds many sequences where motion happens in a tiny local area that can not be distinguished by current optical flow methods [10,17,25,35]. Furthermore, some operation sequence may contain severe background clutter (zooming-in, panel change, etc.), causing confusion for recognition. We analyze the influence of some challenging factors using the proposed method in Sect. 6, providing a better insight and understanding of the PSOV dataset.

4 Tasks and Evaluation

In this section, we describe three tasks as well as the corresponding evaluation metrics on the PSOV dataset. Tasks share common training and testing set, which contains 433 and 131 videos, respectively (training and testing sets are split in a manner that the command distributions are similar). To ensure a sufficient amount of labeling data for deep learning methods, we only conduct these tasks on the top-50 and top-20 popular commands. We also provide the evaluation functions in the development kit to release together with the dataset (see supplementary for details).

Command Classification. The command classification task aims to recognize the operation performed in a given video tube[5]. In this task, the start and finish time of commands in both training and testing sets are given. Algorithms need to learn a classifier from the 433 training set videos and predict the command label for the operation tubes in the test set. We use the simple and intuitive classification accuracy to evaluate the performance of different methods on this task. Using our development kit, the classification accuracy and per-class precision will be given once obtaining a 50-dimension probability vector from the algorithm.

Command Tube Prediction. This task aims to predict the begin and finish time of each command in Photoshop videos. With the available training set videos and corresponding command labels, methods need to predict the two time points (start time t_{start} and finish time t_{end}) for each operation in the test set videos. We propose to use a R&N Curve[6] as the evaluation metric, where a tube is considered 'hit' when a proposal has the IoU (intersection over union between ground truth time interval and the proposal) greater than 0.5. Note that commands not in the top-50 are not calculated in this task. The methods on this

[5] Video tube denotes a sequence of video frames which contains one specific command.

[6] R denotes recall, and N denotes the number of proposals averaged over the number of ground truth commands.

task predict proposals for command tubes ($[t_{start}, t_{end}]$); and are evaluated by R&N Curve where higher curves denote better performance.

Command Recognition. Command recognition is a comprehensive and the most complicated one among three tasks. This task is a further step from classification and tube prediction, it aims to recognize commands (predict start time, end time, command name of operations) from a raw video. Given a test video, the algorithm needs to decide which time period exists an operation and exactly which one it is. It is closest to reality, as the method understands when and what commands are performed in videos with no manually provided information. Algorithms for this task can be directly applied to Photoshop operation videos outside of the PSOV dataset. They can sketch instructional videos with step by step operation list, relieving users from browsing over tens of thousands of video searching results. They can also dig useful data from massive amount of videos uploaded to the Internet every day, and provide assistance to researchers and software developers. Furthermore, their output operations can also be transformed back into computer commands, so that the computer can reproduce automatically in real-world software. The command recognition task is evaluated by AUC (the Area Under precision-recall Curve). Note that the correct prediction here has an IoU with the ground truth over a certain threshold and a correct command label prediction. Both precision-recall curve and AUC value are provided by development kit in evaluation.

5 Methodology

We develop a command classification algorithm on the PSOV dataset to: (1) show an example usage of the proposed database; (2) validate that the PSOV dataset has sufficient data volume for developing data-driven algorithms; and (3) provide a baseline comparison for the command classification task. This section describes the details of our method construction.

Convolutional neural network (CNN) plays an important role in computer vision these years for the effectiveness and robustness of CNN features and classifiers. Many algorithms [3,6,16,42] use CNN for video recognition, which usually process each frame independently and use feature fusion to obtain video descriptions. However, such methods make little use of the motion information in time dimension since the feature of each frame is extracted separately. In this paper, we propose to use a 3-D CNN [18,37] for the challenging PSOV dataset. First, we design an attention-aware preprocessing method to draw attention to operation-critical regions. Then we regularize each video to a fixed length with reference to the attention information. Finally, a 3-D CNN structure is trained for the command classification task.

5.1 Attention-Aware Filtering

In video-related tasks, it is common to leverage temporal features [7,32]. Optical flow is one of the most commonly used descriptors for such information. However,

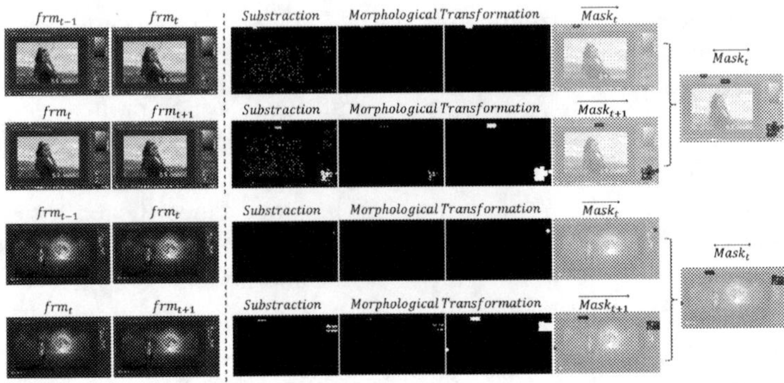

Fig. 7. Attention-aware filtering. We show the attention filtering results on example frames from two commands: *Layer Panel > Select Layer* and *Layer Panel > Duplicate Layer*. $\overrightarrow{Mask}$ denotes the attention computing in single direction ($frm_{t-1} \Rightarrow frm_t$, $frm_t \Rightarrow frm_{t+1}$); and $\overleftrightarrow{Mask}$ denotes the result considering bi-directional context ($frm_{t-1} \Rightarrow frm_t \Leftarrow frm_{t+1}$).

this traditional feature does not take effect in the PSOV dataset, for that key motions are usually weak or located in a tiny region in this dataset (Fig. 6). If we use the whole image frame as network input, information from key regions can easily be overwhelmed by surrounding background noises. Thus, we propose an Attention-aware Filtering algorithm that directly extracts features from the strongest motion part by filtering out useless area. Figure 7 shows an example of the process for our filtering method, which helps the network to focus more on the informative and effective region, boosting its recognition ability (see Sect. 6.1).

Difference Filtering. The purpose of our Attention-aware Filtering method is to focus on the informative motion region. As shown in Fig. 6, the motion that determines specific operation often takes place in a small fraction of area. An intuitive way to find this area is to use the difference map between two adjacent frames ($frm_t - frm_{t-1}$). However, due to video compression artifacts, the direct subtraction has a noisy result (column three in Fig. 6), making it difficult to locate true movement. To deal with this phenomenon, we propose to use morphological image processing methods: erosion and dilation. First, we apply erosion with a disk-shaped kernel (radius 1 pixel) on the subtraction result, removing noisy points here and there. As the erosion procedure comes with region shrinking, we then apply a dilation kernel (this time by a disk-shaped kernel with a radius of 20 pixels) to ensure that most information remains in the outcoming mask ($\overrightarrow{Mask_t}$). Figure 7, shows that Difference Filtering can effectively locate main movement region, relieving the difficulty caused by minor motion in the PSOV dataset.

Bi-direction Context. As movement happens between two frames, context information is needed for both before and after the action ($frm_{t-1} - frm_{t+1}$). While $\overrightarrow{Mask_t}$ is calculated between two frames, it only knows what happened before the action but has no idea about the temporal context afterward. This can cause serious information loss. For example, command *Layer Panel > Select Layer* and *Layer Panel > Duplicate Layer* share similar actions in the former part of the operation in Fig. 7. Simply using Difference Filtering leads to a confusion on $\overrightarrow{Mask}$ in the first and third row. Based on this observation, we propose to compute bi-directional context that preserves temporal context information both before and after the current frame. As shown in Fig. 7, $\overrightarrow{Mask_t}$ and $\overrightarrow{Mask_{t+1}}$ are obtained using Difference Filtering introduced above. These two masks are combined together to obtain a $\overleftrightarrow{Mask}$ which preserves bi-direction temporal information. We show the classification difference with and without bi-direction context in Fig. 10, where class 0 and 12 denotes class *Layer Panel > Select Layer* and *Layer Panel > Duplicate Layer* respectively. The left side figure shows that a large proportion of class 12 video clips are miss-categorized into class 0 due to information loss caused by Difference Filtering. The right-side figure demonstrates that adding bi-direction context can effectively relieve this problem.

As described above, our Attention-aware Filtering uses Difference Filtering with Bi-direction Context. It can find the main active region as well as examine the temporal context in both forward and backward direction. We demonstrate in Sect. 6.1 that this process is a significant step in the proposed algorithm.

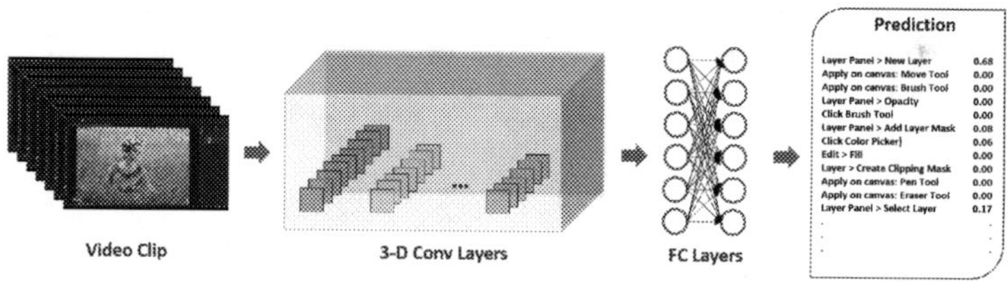

Fig. 8. Network structure.

5.2 Video Regularization

All the video sequences are processed to the same size (in both spatial and temporal dimension) for convenience during training and testing in the proposed framework. Unlike images which can easily be resized to a fixed size, videos vary a lot in temporal extent (the first row in Fig. 6), especially for the proposed PSOV dataset. To regularize the Photoshop command video clips, one significant point is to select frames which keep the most important information. We note that simple uniform sampling can miss such important information severely in the PSOV dataset, for that the key moments (frames that determines the command like clicking a button) distribute randomly in each video. Therefore, we take advantage of the attention area in Sect. 5.1. Redundant frames with no information left after attention filtering are removed from the video. During down-sampling, we start by taking away frames with less information; when it comes to up-sampling, we simply pad the video via random duplicating.

5.3 3-D CNN

Our network is modified from [38], with 5 convolution layers, two fully connected layers, and one classification output layer. Figure 8 shows the structure of our proposed network. Different from 2-D CNNs, 3-D network does convolution and pooling in 2-D surface and an additional time dimension, so sizes and strides in this network have three parameters: width, height and time. Our detailed parameter settings are as follow: (1) convolution layers all have $3 \times 3 \times 3$ kernels with $2 \times 2 \times 2$ strides; (2) pooling layers have $2 \times 2 \times 2$ kernels with strides of $2 \times 2 \times 2$ (except the first pooling layer which has a $2 \times 2 \times 1$ stride, with no operations in temporal channel); (3) the two fully connected layers both have 2,048 output channels and are followed by drop-out layers.

Table 1. Ablation study. This table shows the performance for different combinations of components in the proposed framework, where 3D-Conv, Diff-Filter, Bi-Context, DataAug denote 3-D convolution, Difference Filtering, Bi-direction context, data augmentation respectively (details in Sect. 6.1).

	3-D CNN	Diff-Filter	Bi-Context	DataAug	acc-50	acc-20
2-D CNN		✓			17.02	23.18
2-D CNN*		✓	✓		19.15	24.70
RGB input	✓				51.17	54.66
3-D CNN	✓	✓			63.15	69.14
3-D CNN*	✓	✓	✓		63.76	69.73
Ours	✓	✓	✓	✓	66.37	74.97

The training process is done with Pytorch on a 12G TitanX GPU. The proposed network is trained from scratch, using SGD optimizer with learning rate of 1e−5, and momentum of 0.9. Videos are regularized to 100×100 pixels in spatial domain and 50 frames in the temporal domain. It takes about 250 epochs to reach convergence with batch size of 10. Evaluation of the proposed network can be found in Sect. 6.

5.4 Data Augmentation

Data augmentation is widely used in various computer vision fields [10,20,39]. It can help introduce more diversity and make up for the data imbalance among different classes (Fig. 4). Although the PSOV is a large dataset, data augmentation is still helpful for network training. We use the following sets of data augmentation methods to augment training data: (1) image enhancement, where we adjust the brightness, saturation, contrast, and sharpness of each video frame to augment training data, (frames within one command period have the same augmentation setting); (2) noise, where we randomly add two kinds of noises to each frame during training: the Gaussian white noise and the salt and pepper noise; (3) translation, where we add a bit of movement to frames and use neighboring pixels to compensate for the corresponding blank area.

6 Experiments

We carry out extensive experiments and analysis on the PSOV dataset. First, we validate the effectiveness of each method component. Then we test the influence of command duration variance, filtered area, and analyze the confusion matrix. Through these experiments, we demonstrate that the PSOV dataset is sufficient to support deep learning, and hope to encourage better understanding and usage of this dataset.

6.1 Ablation Study

First, we validate the necessity and effectiveness of each component in the proposed algorithm via ablation study on the PSOV dataset. The proposed framework mainly have the following components:

- **3D-Conv**, 3-D Convolution, without which network does calculations in space domain only without temporal dimension;
- **Diff-Filter**, Difference Filtering, primary step in Attention-aware Filtering, without which network takes in original RGB images;
- **Bi-Context**, Bi-direction Context, without which network only uses Difference Filtering (in Sect. 5);
- **DataAug**, Data Augmentation, without which network does not use data augmentation during training.

We implement methods with different sets of components, and compare their performance for classifying top-20 and top-50 commands respectively. Note for top-20 command classification, networks are trained with top-20 classes on the training set; while for top-50 classification, networks are trained with top-50 classes.

Table 1 shows the statistical results, where components used in each method are denoted by check-marks. We observe that 3-D Convolution contributes largely (3-D CNN vs 2-D CNN), improving the accuracy by more than 40%. It demonstrates that temporal information is essential in recognizing Photoshop operations. The Difference Filtering (Diff-Filter) and Bi-direction Context (Bi-Context) also consistently improve performance by about 10% and 1%, illustrating the effectiveness of our Attention-aware Filtering step (Diff-Filter+Bi-Context). We also evaluate the data augmentation (DataAug) step, and find a 2%–5% improvement (3D CNN* vs Ours) in top-50 and top-20 respectively, proving that data augmentation helps on the PSOV dataset.

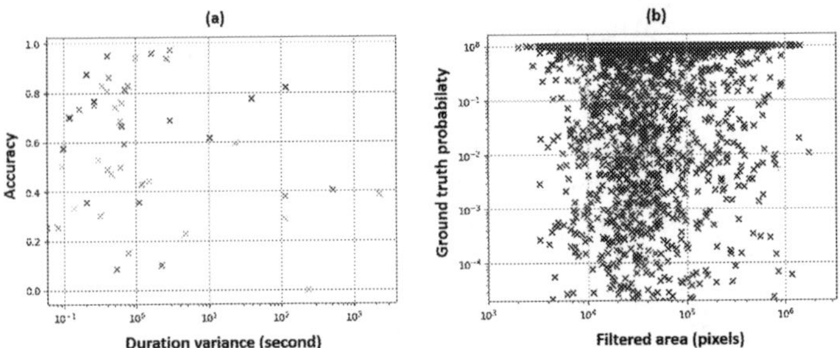

Fig. 9. Accuracy distribution. Image (a) shows the per-class accuracy distribution on training set class duration variance; image (b) shows the per-sequence prediction versus averaged attention filter area curve. See details in Sect. 6.2.

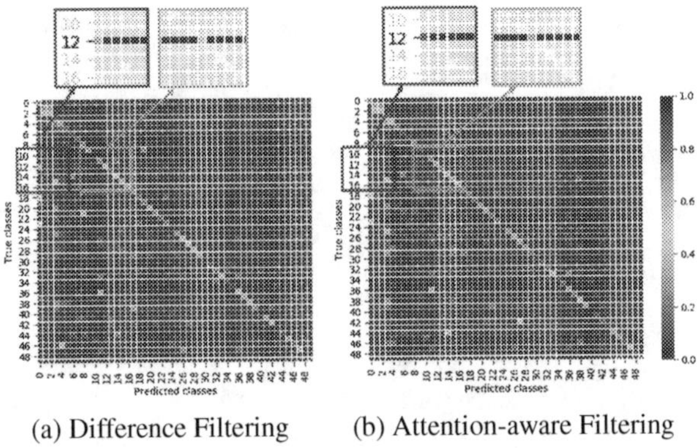

(a) Difference Filtering (b) Attention-aware Filtering

Fig. 10. Confusion matrix for Difference Filtering and Attention-aware Filtering. Index of each row and column denotes a top-50 class; color blue to red in each pixel indicates the proportion of its row-class classified into column-class; class 0 and 12 are *Layer Panel > Select Layer* and *Layer Panel > Duplicate Layer* respectively. (Color figure online)

6.2 Analysis on the Command Classification Task

We draw the figure of per-class accuracy versus class duration variance in training set (image (a) in Fig. 9). This figure shows that command sequences with extremely large duration variance (right side of the image) tend to be hard to classify (the five points in the bottom-right corner; while other videos with smaller duration variance (<1 s) do not have clear correspondence between accuracy and variance. It demonstrates that the proposed network can handle time variance in the PSOV dataset to a large extent.

We also draw the true class prediction probability of each sequence with the averaged pixel number of our Attention-aware Filtering to see whether the filtered motion area is related to classification difficulty. Image (b) in Fig. 9 shows the results of this distribution, illustrating that the proposed algorithm is robust to motion area.

Figure 10 shows two confusion matrix for with and without Bi-direction Context, respectively. Index of each row or column represents a top-50 class. Color blue to red in each pixel indicates the proportion of its row-class classified into column-class. Figure 10 shows an intuitive inter-class similarity (similar pairs like class 0 and 12, class 14 and 44), indicating that bi-direction context helps in correcting wrong predictions. For example, class 0 (*Layer Panel > Select Layer*) and class 12 (*Layer Panel > Duplicate Layer*) are largely misclassified with using only Difference Filtering, but the miss-classifications are corrected via adding bi-direction context (the Attention-aware Filtering). Detailed explanation of how this happens is in Sect. 5.1 and Fig. 7.

7 Conclusion

In this paper, we present the PSOV dataset, a novel, large-scale, densely-annotated, Photoshop Operation Video dataset. The PSOV dataset consists of 564 videos with 29,204 dense annotations. To the best of our knowledge, it is the first real-world software operation dataset with large amount of videos and detailed labeling. We believe that this database can fuel researches in software intelligence, e.g. instruction video mining, autonomous software component, etc. To have a better insight into the PSOV dataset, we also propose a baseline algorithm for the command classification task. By experimenting with the proposed framework, we (1) validate that the PSOV dataset has sufficient data quantity for deep learning, (2) evaluate the effectiveness of each algorithm component, and (3) encourage better understanding and usage of the database. In the future, we plan on extending our dataset to more popular software, and provide online challenges.

Acknowledgement. This work is supported in part by the NSF CAREER Grant #1149783, and gifts from Adobe.

References

1. Abbeel, P., Coates, A., Ng, A.Y.: Autonomous helicopter aerobatics through apprenticeship learning. IJRR **29**(13), 1608–1639 (2010)
2. Bahdanau, D., Cho, K., Bengio, Y.: Neural machine translation by jointly learning to align and translate. arXiv preprint arXiv:1409.0473 (2014)
3. Caelles, S., Maninis, K.K., Pont-Tuset, J., Leal-Taixé, L., Cremers, D., Van Gool, L.: One-shot video object segmentation. In: CVPR (2017)
4. Chen, C., Seff, A., Kornhauser, A., Xiao, J.: DeepDriving: learning affordance for direct perception in autonomous driving. In: ICCV (2015)
5. Chen, X., Ma, H., Wan, J., Li, B., Xia, T.: Multi-view 3D object detection network for autonomous driving. In: CVPR (2017)
6. Cheng, J., et al.: Learning to segment instances in videos with spatial propagation network. arXiv preprint arXiv:1709.04609 (2017)
7. Cheng, J., Tsai, Y.H., Wang, S., Yang, M.H.: SegFlow: joint learning for video object segmentation and optical flow. In: ICCV (2017)

8. Cho, K., et al.: Learning phrase representations using RNN encoder-decoder for statistical machine translation. arXiv preprint arXiv:1406.1078 (2014)
9. Deng, J., Dong, W., Socher, R., Li, L.J., Li, K., Fei-Fei, L.: ImageNet: a large-scale hierarchical image database. In: CVPR, pp. 248–255 (2009)
10. Dosovitskiy, A., et al.: FlowNet: learning optical flow with convolutional networks. In: ICCV (2015)
11. Dosovitskiy, A., Ros, G., Codevilla, F., Lopez, A., Koltun, V.: CARLA: an open urban driving simulator. In: CoRL (2017)
12. Everingham, M., Van Gool, L., Williams, C.K., Winn, J., Zisserman, A.: The Pascal visual object classes (VOC) challenge. IJCV **88**(2), 303–338 (2010)
13. Geiger, A., Lenz, P., Stiller, C., Urtasun, R.: Vision meets robotics: the KITTI dataset. IJRR **32**(11), 1231–1237 (2013)
14. Gelly, S., Silver, D.: Achieving master level play in 9 × 9 computer go. In: AAAI (2008)
15. Gelly, S., Silver, D.: Monte-Carlo tree search and rapid action value estimation in computer go. Artif. Intill. **175**(11), 1856–1875 (2011)
16. Girdhar, R., Ramanan, D., Gupta, A., Sivic, J., Russell, B.: ActionVLAD: learning spatio-temporal aggregation for action classification. In: CVPR (2017)
17. Ilg, E., Mayer, N., Saikia, T., Keuper, M., Dosovitskiy, A., Brox, T.: FlowNet 2.0: evolution of optical flow estimation with deep networks. In: CVPR (2017)
18. Ji, S., Xu, W., Yang, M., Yu, K.: 3D convolutional neural networks for human action recognition. PAMI **35**(1), 495–502 (2013)
19. Karpathy, A., Toderici, G., Shetty, S., Leung, T., Sukthankar, R., Fei-Fei, L.: Large-scale video classification with convolutional neural networks. In: CVPR (2014)
20. Khoreva, A., Benenson, R., Ilg, E., Brox, T., Schiele, B.: Lucid data dreaming for multiple object tracking. arXiv preprint arXiv:1703.09554 (2017)
21. Kim, M., Kim, S., Park, S., Choi, M.T., Kim, M., Gomaa, H.: Service robot for the elderly. RAM **16**(1), 34–45 (2009)
22. Lefèvre, S., Carvalho, A., Gao, Y., Tseng, H.E., Borrelli, F.: Driver models for personalised driving assistance. VSD **53**(12), 1705–1720 (2015)
23. Lin, T.-Y., et al.: Microsoft COCO: common objects in context. In: Fleet, D., Pajdla, T., Schiele, B., Tuytelaars, T. (eds.) ECCV 2014. LNCS, vol. 8693, pp. 740–755. Springer, Cham (2014). https://doi.org/10.1007/978-3-319-10602-1_48
24. Oh, J., Guo, X., Lee, H., Lewis, R.L., Singh, S.: Action-conditional video prediction using deep networks in atari games. In: NIPS (2015)
25. Revaud, J., Weinzaepfel, P., Harchaoui, Z., Schmid, C.: EpicFlow: edge-preserving interpolation of correspondences for optical flow. In: CVPR (2015)
26. Rhee, C., Chung, W., Kim, M., Shim, Y., Lee, H.: Door opening control using the multi-fingered robotic hand for the indoor service robot. In: ICRA (2004)
27. Rodriguez, M.D., Ahmed, J., Shah, M.: Action mach a spatio-temporal maximum average correlation height filter for action recognition. In: CVPR (2008)
28. Shashua, A., Gdalyahu, Y., Hayun, G.: Pedestrian detection for driving assistance systems: single-frame classification and system level performance. In: IEEE Intelligent Vehicles Symposium, 2004, pp. 1–6. IEEE, June 2004
29. Shi, T., Karpathy, A., Fan, L., Hernandez, J., Liang, P.: World of bits: an open-domain platform for web-based agents. In: ICML (2017)
30. Silver, D., et al.: Mastering the game of go without human knowledge. Nature **550**, 354–359 (2017)
31. Simonyan, K., Zisserman, A.: Two-stream convolutional networks for action recognition in videos. In: NIPS (2014)

32. Song, S., Lan, C., Xing, J., Zeng, W., Liu, J.: An end-to-end spatio-temporal attention model for human action recognition from skeleton data. In: AAAI (2017)
33. Soomro, K., Zamir, A.R., Shah, M.: UCF101: a dataset of 101 human actions classes from videos in the wild. CoRR (2012)
34. Sturm, J., Engelhard, N., Endres, F., Burgard, W., Cremers, D.: A benchmark for the evaluation of RGB-D SLAM systems. In: IROS (2012)
35. Sun, D., Yang, X., Liu, M.Y., Kautz, J.: PWC-Net: CNNs for optical flow using pyramid, warping, and cost volume. In: CVPR (2018)
36. Taggart, W., Turkle, S., Kidd, C.D.: An interactive robot in a nursing home: preliminary remarks. In: COGSCI Workshop (2005)
37. Tran, D., Bourdev, L., Fergus, R., Torresani, L., Paluri, M.: Learning spatiotemporal features with 3D convolutional networks. In: ICCV (2015)
38. Varol, G., Laptev, I., Schmid, C.: Long-term temporal convolutions for action recognition. PAMI **40**(6), 1510–1517 (2017)
39. Voigtlaender, P., Leibe, B.: Online adaptation of convolutional neural networks for video object segmentation. arXiv preprint arXiv:1706.09364 (2017)
40. Wang, J., Xiao, C., Zhu, T., Hsueh, C.H., Tseng, W.J., Wu, I.C.: Only-one-victor pattern learning in computer go. IEEE Trans. Comput. Intell. AI Games **9**(1), 88–102 (2017)
41. Yannakakis, G.N.: Game AI revisited. In: CF (2012)
42. Yue-Hei Ng, J., Hausknecht, M., Vijayanarasimhan, S., Vinyals, O., Monga, R., Toderici, G.: Beyond short snippets: deep networks for video classification. In: CVPR (2015)

A Joint Local and Global Deep Metric Learning Method for Caricature Recognition

Wenbin Li[1], Jing Huo[1], Yinghuan Shi[1], Yang Gao[1(✉)], Lei Wang[2], and Jiebo Luo[3]

[1] National Key Laboratory for Novel Software Technology, Nanjing University, Nanjing, China
liwenbin.nju@gmail.com, {huojing,syh,gaoy}@nju.edu.cn

[2] School of Computing and Information Technology, University of Wollongong, Wollongong, Australia
leiw@uow.edu.au

[3] Department of Computer Science, University of Rochester, Rochester, USA
jluo@cs.rochester.edu

Abstract. Caricature recognition is a novel, interesting, yet challenging problem. Due to the exaggeration and distortion, there is a large cross-modal gap between photographs and caricatures, making it nontrivial to match the features of photographs and caricatures. To address the problem, a joint local and global metric learning method (LGDML) is proposed. First, joint local and global feature representation is learnt with convolutional neural networks to find both discriminant features of local facial parts and global distinctive features of the whole face. Next, in order to fuse the local and global similarities of features, a unified feature representation and similarity measure learning framework is proposed. Various methods are evaluated on the caricature recognition task. We have verified that both local and global features are crucial for caricature recognition. Moreover, experimental results show that, compared with the state-of-the-art methods, LGDML can obtain superior performance in terms of Rank-1 and Rank-10.

Keywords: Caricature recognition · Deep metric learning

1 Introduction

Caricature is a popular artistic drawing style in social media. One caricature is a facial sketch beyond realism, attempting to portray a facial essence by exaggerating some prominent characteristics and oversimplifying the rest. Interestingly, it can be recognized lightly by human at a glance. Moreover, since caricature contains abundant non-verbal information, it is widely used in news and social media. The retrieval between photograph and caricature will be a high demand.

C. V. Jawahar et al. (Eds.): ACCV 2018, LNCS 11364, pp. 240–256, 2019.
https://doi.org/10.1007/978-3-030-20870-7_15

However, there are only a few studies on caricature recognition [1,19,29], which mainly focus on designing and learning mid-level facial attribute features. Moreover, these attributes usually need to be ad-hoc designed and laboriously labeled. Considering the prominent representation ability of deep convolutional neural networks (CNNs), we adopt CNN to learn the features automatically in this paper.

Fig. 1. Local and global similarities between photographs and caricatures.

It is observed, when human verify whether a pair of photograph and caricature belongs to the same person or not, we can first easily connect the special characteristic of photograph with the artistic exaggeration of caricature [26]. For example, the small eyes of Ban Ki moon (Fig. 1(a)), the wing nose of George W. Bush (Fig. 1(b)), the plump lips of Angelina Jolie (Fig. 1(d)), and the pointed chin of Bingbing Fan (Fig. 1(e)). Then, the overall appearance similarity between photograph and caricature from global perspective is taken into consideration [35]. For instance, the long face of Benedict Cumberbatch (Fig. 1(c)).

The above observations imply that the fusion of local and global similarities will benefit measuring the similarity between photograph and caricature. To obtain the fusion of local and global similarities, we present a novel deep metric learning to jointly train a global sub-network and four local part sub-networks. In this method, feature representation and similarity measure are learnt simultaneously, which is end-to-end. Specifically, the global sub-network is used to extract the global features from the whole face for global similarity measure, and the four local part sub-networks are employed to capture the local features from four local parts (*i.e.*, eye, nose, mouth and chin parts) for local similarity measure. By integrating the local and global similarities, we can obtain better similarity measure for photograph and caricature. Thus, the proposed method is termed as *Local and Global Deep Metric Learning (LGDML)*.

In summary, our major contributions include:

- **Joint local and global feature representation:** As a new strategy, joint local and global feature representation learning, is developed for the caricature recognition task. Based on this strategy, discriminative local and global features of photograph and caricature are learnt, leading to better recognition performance.

- **Unified feature representation and similarity measure learning:** To learn the local and global feature representation and similarity measure (or measure fusion) in a unified framework, we design a novel deep metric learning (DML) method and apply it to the caricature recognition task for the first time. The framework allows us to learn feature representation and similarity measure in a consistent fashion. Under the constraint of metric loss, five single siamese networks are trained, where four are for learning local features and one is for learning global features.
- **Promising results:** Through various experiments, the proposed DML method and the strategy of fusing local and global features prove the most effective for the caricature recognition task. Compared with various network structures, the five single siamese network structures prove the best.
- **Interesting insights:** We verify that an intermediate domain indeed can help reduce the huge semantic gap between two domains when performing a cross-modal recognition task. Moreover, learning feature and metrics simultaneously is more effective for deriving better feature and better metrics than the two-stage process in shallow metric learning.

2 Related Work

2.1 Caricature Recognition

Although many works are proposed for caricature generation [3–5,36,40], there are only few works about caricature recognition [1,19,29]. Klare *et al.* [19] proposed a semi-automatic caricature recognition method by utilizing crowdsourcing. Through crowdsourcing, they define and collect a set of qualitative facial attributes. However, these facial attributes need to be annotated manually, which is difficult and subjective in practical use. On the contrary, Ouyang *et al.* [29] employed attribute learning methodology to automatically estimate the facial attributes. Similar to the aforementioned two works, Abaci *et al.* [1] defined a set of slightly different facial attributes. They adopted a genetic algorithm to evaluate the importance of each attribute and matched the caricature and photograph. Recently, Huo *et al.* [16,17] collected a large caricature dataset and offered four evaluation protocols.

The above methods mainly focus on extracting mid-level facial attributes and conducting experiments on small-scale datasets (*i.e.*, the total number of pairs is less than 200). Our contribution is to design a novel DML-based method on a much larger dataset (*i.e.*, the total number of pairs is more than 1.5×10^5).

2.2 Deep Metric Learning

Compared with conventional shallow metric learning [8,24,32,39], which mainly focuses on learning linear metrics (*e.g.*, Mahalanobis distance based metrics),

DML can learn better non-linear metrics by using deep networks. Several DML methods have been proposed, which can be roughly classified into three categories: (1) CNN combined with metric loss [7,15,28,38,41]; (2) CNN combined with fully connected (FC) layers [11]; (3) Deep structure metric learning [9,13,14].

In the first kind of DML methods, the network structure usually contains two (three) sub-networks, trained by pairwise loss (triplet loss) which is usually used in metric learning. For example, Yi *et al.* [41] adopted a binomial deviance loss to train a siamese neural network for person re-identification task. Cui *et al.* [7] employed a triplet-based DML method to solve the fine-grained visual categorization problem. Huang *et al.* [15] introduced a position dependent deep metric unit, aiming to learn a similarity metric adaptive to local feature structure. In the second kind of DML methods, the FC layers are taken as the metric learning part, while the loss is still cross-entropy loss. A typical representative is MatchNet proposed by Han *et al.* [11]. In the third kind of DML methods, the structure of metric learning is modelled on deep structure (*i.e.*, multilayer perceptron (MLP)) to learn a set of hierarchical nonlinear transformations. However, the inputs of these methods are still hand-crafted features or pre-extracted deep features. Representative works are series of works of Hu and Lu *et al.* [9,13,14].

Our proposed LGDML method belongs to the first category, but the differences include (1) LGDML is a joint local and global multi-view metric method, (2) LGDML focuses on cross-modal verification based on single siamese network and much more sub-networks (*i.e.*, five single siamese networks) are learnt at the same time.

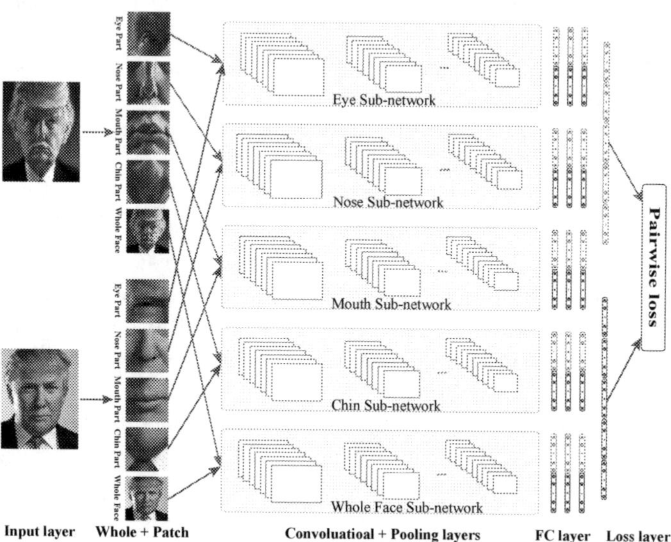

Fig. 2. The framework of the proposed LGDML, containing five single siamese sub-networks.

3 Joint Local and Global Deep Metric Learning

3.1 Network Structure

The framework of LGDML is illustrated in Fig. 2. For each input photograph (caricature), four key parts, *i.e.*, eye, nose, mouth and chin parts, which have abundant local information for recognition (see Fig. 1), are picked and cropped. Combined with the original whole face, these parts are fed into five single sub-networks. In the loss layer, all features of the last FC layers (*i.e.*, Fc8) in these five sub-networks are concatenated. Typically, pairwise loss is adopted to calculate the loss between photograph and caricature. When performing back propagation, the gradients are used for parameter updating of all the sub-networks.

In fact, there should be a total of ten separate sub-networks in this structure for there are ten inputs (*i.e.*, five parts of photograph and five parts of caricature), but it is too difficult and bloated to train this network (*e.g.*, memory limit issue). In order to train this network efficiently, we employ five single siamese sub-networks instead of ten separate sub-networks. Specifically, photograph and caricature share one single sub-network in the same part (*e.g.*, eye part). In other words, two inputs are entered into a single sub-network simultaneously instead of two separate sub-networks which share the same parameters. In addition, compared with traditional siamese network with two identical separate sub-networks or two-tower network with two different separate sub-networks, the single siamese network with only one sub-network can learn better modality invariant features, because data of two modalities are both used to update the same sub-network.

Hence, the advantages of the proposed network structure are that, on one hand, it can leverage the local and global similarities between photograph and caricature simultaneously; on the other hand it can learn good modality invariant features.

3.2 Pairwise Loss Function

For each pair of photograph and caricature, four local metrics and one global metric are learnt together, which can be seen as a multi-view metric. To learn a joint, overall metric, a uniform pairwise loss is used to train all the sub-networks. The goal is to make the fused distance metric between the same-class (*i.e.*, same-individual) pair small and the different-class pair large. From the perspective of different types of metric function, two typical loss functions: Binomial deviance loss [10,41] which focuses on similarity measure and Generalized logistic loss [13, 27] which focuses on distance measure are employed. We describe them in detail as follows:

Binomial deviance loss: Inspired by Yi *et al.* [41], we use cosine similarity to calculate the similarity between two samples, and then adopt binomial deviance to train the network. Given a pair of samples $\boldsymbol{x}_i, \boldsymbol{x}_j \in \mathbb{R}^d$, and the corresponding similarity label $l_{ij} \in \{1, -1\}$ (*i.e.*, $l_{ij} = 1$ if $\boldsymbol{x}_i$ and $\boldsymbol{x}_j$ belong to the same class, and $l_{ij} = -1$ otherwise), the formulation can be denoted as follow,

$$\mathcal{L}_{dev} = \ln\left[\exp\Big(-2\cos(\boldsymbol{x}_i, \boldsymbol{x}_j) l_{ij}\Big) + 1\right], \tag{1}$$

where $\cos(\boldsymbol{x}_i, \boldsymbol{x}_j)$ denotes the cosine similarity between two vectors $\boldsymbol{x}_i$ and $\boldsymbol{x}_j$. If $\boldsymbol{x}_i$ and $\boldsymbol{x}_j$ are from the same class, and the cosine similarity is small, then there will be a large loss of Eq. (1). Otherwise, there will be a small loss of Eq. (1). In this way, the similarity between same-class pair is increased, and the similarity between different-class pair is decreased.

Generalized logistic loss: In metric learning, the major goal is to learn a feature transformation to make the distance between $\boldsymbol{x}_i$ and $\boldsymbol{x}_j$ in the transformed space smaller than $\tau - 1$ when $\boldsymbol{x}_i$ and $\boldsymbol{x}_j$ belong to the same class (*i.e.*, $l_{ij} = 1$), and larger than $\tau + 1$ otherwise (*i.e.*, $l_{ij} = -1$). The constraints can be formulated as follow,

$$\begin{aligned} d^2(\boldsymbol{x}_i, \boldsymbol{x}_j) &\le \tau - 1, l_{ij} = 1 \\ d^2(\boldsymbol{x}_i, \boldsymbol{x}_j) &\ge \tau + 1, l_{ij} = -1, \end{aligned} \tag{2}$$

where $d^2(\boldsymbol{x}_i, \boldsymbol{x}_j) = \|\boldsymbol{x}_i - \boldsymbol{x}_j\|_2^2$, and $\tau > 1$. For simplicity, the constraints can be written as $l_{ij}\big(\tau - d^2(\boldsymbol{x}_i, \boldsymbol{x}_j)\big) \ge 1$. With the generalized logistic loss function, the loss function is given by

$$\mathcal{L}_{log} = g\bigg(1 - l_{ij}\Big(\tau - \|\boldsymbol{x}_i - \boldsymbol{x}_j\|_2^2\Big)\bigg), \tag{3}$$

where $g(z) = \frac{1}{\beta}\log\big(1 + \exp(\beta z)\big)$ is the generalized logistic loss function and β is the *sharpness* parameter.

3.3 Implementation

As AlexNet [21] is a popular and effective network, we take it as the base network in our LGDML. Another reason is that the number of caricature data is still too limited to train deeper networks well, such as VGG-VD [33], GoogLeNet [34] and ResNet [12] *etc.* Usually, the pre-trained AlexNet, which has been trained on the ImageNet dataset, shall be employed. Nevertheless, we observed that directly fine-tuning the pre-trained AlexNet does not produce desirable recognition performance. The reason is that there is a significant semantic gap between the source data (*i.e.*, natural image) and target data (*i.e.*, caricature). To this end, we first adopt other available face image dataset (*e.g.*, PubFig [22]) to fine-tune this pre-trained AlexNet. Afterwards, the fine-tuned AlexNet will be fine-tuned again by caricature data.

During training, we minimize the pairwise loss by performing mini-batch stochastic gradient descent (SGD) over a training set of n photograph-caricature pairs with a batch size of 256 (*i.e.*, 128 pairs). Specifically, we maintain a dropout layer after each FC layer except Fc8 layer, and set the values of momentum and weight decay to 0.9 and 5×10^{-4} respectively. The filter size of the last FC layer is set to $1 \times 1 \times 4096 \times 4096$, the weights are randomly initialized from a zero-mean Gaussian distribution with 10^{-2} standard deviation, and the biases are initialized to zero. We generate a set of $N = 40$ (*i.e.*, the number of epoches) logarithmically equally spaced points between $10^{-2.7}$ and 10^{-4} as the learning rates.

During forward propagation, a pair of photograph and caricature images are cropped into four pairs of local patches. Then the five pairs of patches (combined with the pair of original images) subtracted their corresponding mean RGB values respectively are fed into five single siamese networks. For each modality, one global feature and four local features can be extracted from the last FC layer. In the final loss layer, the global and local features of each modality are concatenated together to calculate the loss according to the designed cost function. Note that a ℓ_2 normalization layer is added before the loss layer. During back propagation, the parameters of the network are fine-tuned by freezing the first m layers. The reason is that the first several layers mainly learn generic features of images which are transferable between these two modalities [42].

4 Experiments

In this section, we implement various deep networks by changing the structure and loss function. Then, we compare the performance of these methods by conducting caricature recognition task on the WebCaricature dataset [17]. Our implementations are based on the publicly available MATLAB toolbox MatConvNet [37] on one NVIDIA K80 GPU.

4.1 Dataset

PubFig Dataset: To reduce the semantic gap between natural images and caricature images, we choose the PubFig [22] dataset to fine-tune the pre-trained AlexNet. PubFig dataset is a large, real-world face dataset, consisting of a development set and an evaluation set. In our setting, these two subsets are integrated together (36604 images of 200 individuals). After data augmentation, all images (*i.e.*, 512456 images) of the 200 individuals are used to fine-tune a 200-class classification network (*i.e.*, the pre-trained AlexNet). The fine-tuned AlexNet model is named as AlexNet-PubFig.

Caricature Dataset: Our experiments are mainly developed on the WebCaricature dataset, which contains 6042 caricatures and 5974 photographs of 252 individuals. In our experiments, the dataset is divided into two parts, one for training (*i.e.*, 126 individuals) and the other for testing (*i.e.*, the rest 126 individuals). These two parts are disjoint by individual, that is, no individual will appear in both the training and testing sets. Because there are 51 overlapped individuals between PubFig dataset and WebCaricature dataset, the overlapped individuals are only divided into the training set. Besides, in the training set, 30% images of each individual are randomly picked for validation and the rest is used for training.

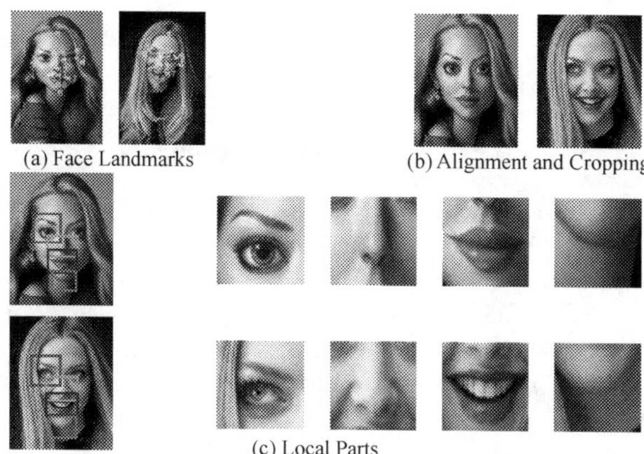

Fig. 3. Illustration of data preprocessing. (a) shows the 17 facial landmarks; (b) exhibits the cropped face images after alignment and rotating; (c) illustrates the cropped local parts.

4.2 Data Preprocessing

Preprocessing: As for each image, 17 landmarks have been provided (Fig. 3(a)) [17]. According to the landmarks, the following face alignment process are employed which includes three major steps: First, each image is aligned by image rotation to make two eyes in a horizontal line. Second, the image is resized to guarantee the distance between two eyes of 75 pixels. Third, the image is cropped by enlarging the bounding box encircled by the face landmarks {# 1, 2, 3, 4} with a scale of 1.2 in both width and height. Finally, the image is eventually resized to 256×320. All the processes are illustrated in Fig. 3.

Augmentation: To better fine-tune our LGDML, we augment the caricature dataset by image flipping in horizontal direction. In this way, we can construct a large-scale image pairs with a magnitude greater than 1.5×10^5. Before using the pre-trained AlexNet, we need to fine-tune this network by utilizing other natural face dataset. In this setting, we also need data augmentation. This time, besides image flipping we also perform random translation inspired by [2]. For each image, we crop a central region 227×227 and randomly sample another 5 images around the image center. Moreover, every image is also horizontally flipped. Thus, 14 images including the resized original image can be obtained after augmentation.

Cropping: To capture the local features of a face, we pick four key parts on the face, *i.e.*, eye part (just left eye), nose part, mouth part and chin part. For the left eye part, landmarks {# 5, 6, 9, 10} (see Fig. 3(a)) are considered, and a rectangle patch is cropped which covers the whole left eye and eyebrow. For the nose part, landmarks {# 9, 10, 11, 12, 13, 14} are taken into account. As for the mouth part, a rectangle patch is cropped according to landmarks {# 13, 14,

15, 16, 17}. So as to the chin part, landmarks {# 3, 15, 16, 17} are considered. Then, all the local patches are resized to 227 × 227 (see Fig. 3(c)).

4.3 Results of Different Deep Network Structures

We report the comparison with different deep methods, which have different network structures. All the methods are evaluated on the caricature recognition task, which is a cross-modal face identification task. Given a caricature (photograph), the goal is to search the corresponding photographs (caricatures) from a photograph (caricature) gallery. For the "Caricature to Photograph" setting, all the caricatures in the testing set (126 individuals) will be used as probes (*i.e.*, 2961 images) and photographs will be used as gallery. Specifically, only one photograph of each individual is selected to the gallery (*i.e.*, 126 images). The setting of "Photograph to Caricature" is similar to the one of "Caricature to Photograph". As these two settings are similar, we only focus on the setting of "Caricature to Photograph". Rank-1 and Rank-10 are chosen as the evaluation criteria.

Table 1. Rank-1 (%) and Rank-10 (%) of deep methods with different network structures. Columns 3–4 show the results of raw features. The last two columns exhibit the results after dimensionality reduction by t-SNE.

Structure	Loss	Rank-1	Rank-10	Rank-1 t-SNE	Rank-10 t-SNE
Single	Cross-entropy	24.28	60.79	26.56	54.58
Triplet	Triplet	24.42	61.63	28.57	54.91
Two-tower	Binomial	24.65	62.45	20.63	50.19
Two-tower	Logistic	24.89	62.41	20.42	51.08
Siamese	Binomial	26.21	65.21	30.23	61.06
Siamese	Logistic	27.09	66.60	34.04	62.51
LGDML	Binomial	28.40	**67.65**	36.14	**65.96**
LGDML	Logistic	**29.42**	67.00	**36.27**	64.37

According to the network structure, these deep methods can be divided into five categories as follows:

- **Single Network Methods:** These methods consisting of single network are usually used for classification task. The pre-trained AlexNet-PubFig will be taken as the baseline method without any postprocessing.
- **Siamese Network Methods:** These networks contain two parameter sharing sub-networks which are based on AlexNet-PubFig model. Here, we adopt the single siamese network structure like LGDML. Two loss functions, *i.e.*, binomial deviance loss and generalized logistic loss, would be employed to fine-tune these networks. The depth of back propagation is 11, *i.e.*, updating to conv5 layer.

- **Two-tower Network Methods:** Different from the siamese network, the two sub-networks of two-tower network don't share parameters completely. The binomial deviance loss or generalized logistic loss is used to fine-tune these networks by freezing first several layers (*i.e.*, top 12 layers) which keep the pre-trained parameters unchanged.
- **Triplet Network Methods:** There are three sub-networks with parameter sharing in these networks. Like above networks, these networks also take AlexNet-PubFig as the base network. Moreover, we design a new triplet loss by adding an extra pairwise loss to maximize the use of the provided triplet. Given a triplet $\langle \boldsymbol{x}_i, \boldsymbol{x}_j, \boldsymbol{x}_k \rangle$, the new triplet loss can be formalized as $\mathcal{L}_{triplet} = \mu\|\boldsymbol{x}_i - \boldsymbol{x}_j\|_2^2 + (1-\mu)(1 + \|\boldsymbol{x}_i - \boldsymbol{x}_j\|_2^2 - \|\boldsymbol{x}_i - \boldsymbol{x}_k\|_2^2)_+$, where $\boldsymbol{x}_i$ and $\boldsymbol{x}_j$ belong to the same class, while $\boldsymbol{x}_i$ and $\boldsymbol{x}_k$ belong to different classes. μ is the hyper-parameter and $(z)_+ = \max(0, z)$ indicates the hinge loss.
- **Our LGDML:** This is the proposed method, containing five single siamese networks. According to the different losses chosen, the proposed method can be named as LGDML-Binomial or LGDML-Logistic.

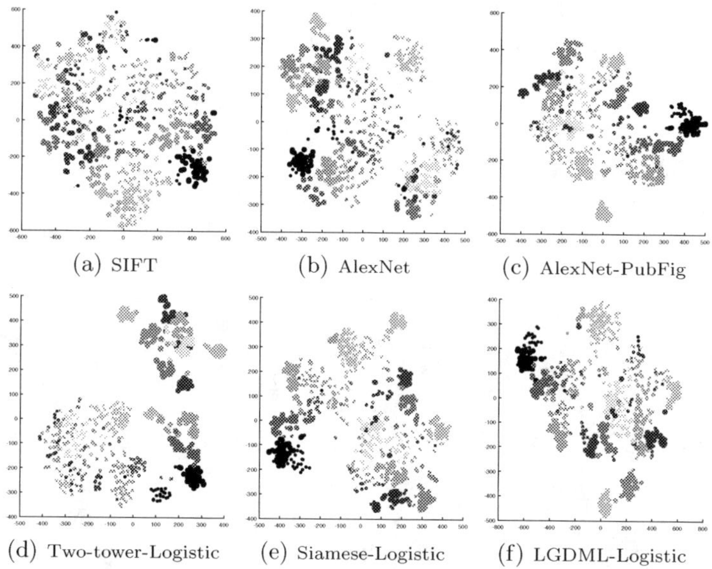

Fig. 4. Feature visualization of six representative methods using t-SNE. Different colors denote different individuals (*i.e.*, 11 individuals), big/small dot indicates the photograph/caricature modality, respectively. (Color figure online)

It is worth noting that although we do not explicitly compare the proposed LGDML with other existing cross-modal methods, the competitive network structures implicitly represent some existing methods. For example, in [30], a two-tower network combined with the contrastive loss was employed to solve the near-infrared heterogeneous face recognition problem. In addition, [31] adopted a triplet loss to train a face recognition network, which is equivalent to the triplet network in our experiments. All these deep methods aim to learn a good feature representation. Hence, for the first four deep methods, a 4096-dimensional feature is extracted from the first FC layer (*i.e.*, Fc6 layer), which is proved to be more expressive than Fc7 and Fc8 in feature representation. LGDML extracts a 20480-dimensional feature by integrating all the features of the four local parts and the whole image. A popular dimensionality reduction method t-SNE [25] is also employed to make all features into a same dimensionality (*i.e.*, 300). Table 1 reports the results of all the methods. LGDML achieves the best rank-1 and rank-10 performance with 29.42% and 67.65%. When performing dimensionality reduction, the results are 36.27% and 65.95%. From the results, we can observe that:

Influence of loss function: Binomial deviance loss (denoted as Binomial) performs similar with generalized logistic loss (denoted as Logistic). While the triplet loss (denoted as Triplet) does not achieve promising results, the reason may be that three separate sub-networks are employed in the triplet network, which cannot learn good modality invariant features.

Influence of network structure: Under the same loss function setting, two-tower structure performs worse than the single siamese structure. The reason is that single siamese structure is more tend to learn modality invariant feature (see Fig. 4(d), (e)). From Fig. 4(f), we can see that the features learnt from LGDML are blended together in the modality, but are distinguishable between different individuals. LGDML can learn both modality invariant and discriminant features, which makes LGDML achieve the state-of-the-art result.

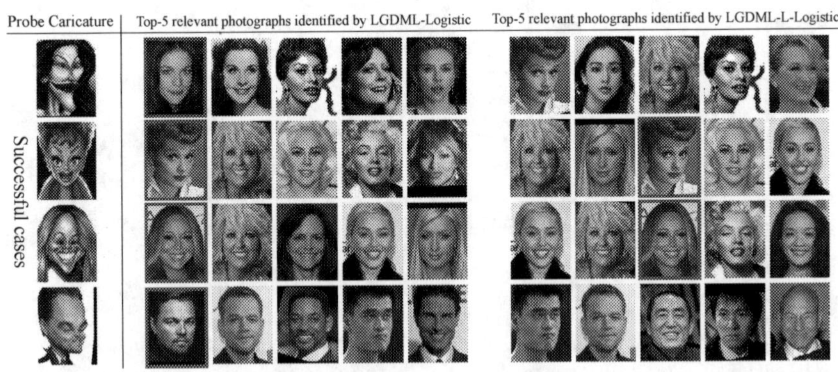

Fig. 5. Success cases of caricature recognition results by LGDML and LGDML-Local. For each probe caricature, top 5 relevant photographs are exhibited, where the photographs annotated with red rectangular boxes are the ground-truth. (Color figure online)

4.4 Local and Global Methods

LGDML can learn local and global features simultaneously. To illustrate the effectiveness of fusion of the local and global features, we reduce LGDML to a simpler variant by only learning local features namely LGDML-Local. It can be seen that if we only learn local features (see Table 2), the result becomes worse due to the lack of global information. We also reduce LGDML to another simpler variant by only learning global features namely LGDML-Global. In fact, LGDML-Global is same as AlexNet-PubFig-Siamese in Table 1. The results in Table 2 show that it is beneficial to integrate local and global features. A clear effect of this integration can also be seen in Fig. 5. We can see that LGDML is obviously superior to LGDML-Local.

Table 2. Local and global methods.

Method	Loss	Type	Rank-1 (%) t-SNE	Rank-10 (%) t-SNE
LGDML-Local	Binomial	Local	23.57	50.35
LGDML-Local	Logistic	Local	21.65	45.80
LGDML-Global	Binomial	Global	30.23	61.06
LGDML-Global	Logistic	Global	34.04	62.51
LGDML	Binomial	Local+Global	36.14	**65.96**
LGDML	Logistic	Local+Global	**36.27**	64.37

4.5 Indirect and Direct Fine-Tuning

From Table 3, we can see that if we directly perform fine-tuning on the AlexNet which is pre-trained on the ImageNet, the rank-1 performance can only reach 18.34% (*i.e.*, the result of AlexNet-Siamese-Logistic). However, if we perform fine-tuning on the AlexNet-PubFig, which is fine-tuned based on the pre-trained AlexNet, the rank-1 performance can reach 34.04% (AlexNet-PubFig-Siamese-Logistic). This inspires us that when we perform fine-tuning on two domains that have huge semantic gap (*i.e.*, natural image and caricature), we can resort to an intermediate domain (*i.e.*, natural face image) between these two domains first.

4.6 Deep and Hand-Crafted Features

In addition to deep features, we also compare deep methods with hand-crafted feature extraction methods. Three hand-crafted features will be extracted for each image respectively, that is, LBP, Gabor and SIFT [1,19,29]. For LBP feature, the original image (256×320) is partitioned into 4×5 patches of 64×64.

Table 3. Indirect and direct fine-tuning.

Base network	Architecture	Loss	Rank-1 t-SNE	Rank-10 t-SNE
AlexNet	Siamese	Binomial	17.76	39.28
AlexNet	Siamese	Logistic	18.34	40.19
AlexNet-Pubfig	Siamese	Binomial	30.23	61.06
AlexNet-Pubfig	Siamese	Logistic	**34.04**	**62.51**

Table 4. Deep and hand-crafted features.

Base network	Feature/loss	Rank-1 t-SNE	Rank-10 t-SNE
–	LBP	1.65	12.23
	Gabor	3.24	15.30
	SIFT	9.56	29.08
AlexNet	Cross-entropy	14.39	36.68
AlexNet-Pubfig	Cross-entropy	**26.56**	**54.58**

In each patch, a 30-dimensional uniform LBP feature is extracted. We can get a 600-dimensional LBP feature after combining the features of all patches. To extract Gabor feature, the original 256×320 image is resized to 256×256 and 40 filters are used. After filtering, the filtered image is down sampled to $\frac{1}{16}$ of its original size. Then, the vectorized images are concatenated to obtain a 10240-dimensional Gabor feature. For SIFT feature, the original image is divided into 10×13 patches of 64×64 with a stride of 20 pixels. In each 64×64 patch, a 32-dimensional SIFT feature is extracted. Then all the features are concatenated to get a 4160-dimensional SIFT feature.

Hand-crafted features perform poorly on this task (see Table 4), which reflects the difficulty of this task. Interestingly, the pre-trained AlexNet achieves better performance than the best hand-crafted feature (*i.e.*, SIFT), although the feature of AlexNet is just learnt from natural images. AlexNet-PubFig, which is just fine-tuned by natural face images, achieves significant performance improvement (more than 15% performance improvement in rank-1). This verifies again, through the caricature recognition task, that, compared with hand-crafted methods, deep learning indeed has stronger ability of feature representation.

4.7 Deep and Shallow Metric Learning

We compare our DML method with traditional shallow metric learning methods. Several state-of-the-art shallow metric learning methods are picked, including large margin nearest neighbor (LMNN) [39], information-theoretic metric learning (ITML) [8], KISSME [20], logdet exact gradient online (LEGO) [18], online algorithm for scalable image similarity (OASIS) [6] and OPML [23]. All these methods learn from the deep features extracted from the AlexNet-PubFig network. For fair comparison, all features are reduced to features with a suitable dimensions (*i.e.*, 300) by PCA. We summarized the results in Table 5. From the results, we can see that most shallow metric learning methods can hardly improve the performance. Among them, ITML achieves the best result (just about 2% performance improvement in rank-1). In contrast, DML methods can further improve the performance.

The above results can be explained as follows. Traditional shallow metric learning generally focuses on learning new feature representation based on the given input feature representation. It is a two-stage process, in which feature extraction and distance measure are usually separated. The given input feature representation has limited the upper bound of the optimization of metric learning algorithms, and their quality directly affects the performance improvement of metric learning. In other words, metric learning could make large performance improvement on weak feature representation (*e.g.*, hand-crafted features), but can only make a small improvement on powerful feature representation (*e.g.*, deep features). In contrast, DML integrates feature extraction and distance measure together. It can learn feature and metrics simultaneously, and makes them to work best with each other. In this way, DML can achieve better feature and better metrics. In addition, shallow metric learning methods usually learn a linear transformation, which cannot effectively capture the non-linear structure in the data. On the contrary, the non-linear features learnt from DML, *e.g.*, our proposed LGDML, are more capable in this regard.

Table 5. Deep and shallow metric learning.

Method	Rank-1 (%) PCA	Rank-10 (%) PCA
AlexNet-PugFig	23.74	60.15
KissMe	21.28	55.56
OASIS	21.61	64.00
OPML	23.98	61.03
LEGO	24.38	60.22
LMNN	25.60	62.60
ITML	26.02	63.07
Siamese-Logistic	26.98	66.26
LGDML-Binomial	28.06	**66.57**
LGDML-Logistic	**28.88**	66.30

5 Conclusions

Caricature recognition is a challenging and interesting problem, but has not been sufficiently studied. Furthermore, the existing methods mainly pay attention to mid-level facial attributes, which are expensive to annotate manually, and need ad-hoc settings. In this paper, taking advantage of the strong representation ability of deep learning and discriminative transformation of metric learning, we propose LGDML to solve the caricature recognition task. In LGDML, local and global features of caricature are jointly learnt. In addition, metric loss is chosen to optimize the entire network, allowing feature representation and distance metric to be learnt simultaneously. The experiments have been conducted extensively to evaluate all the comparable methods, and our proposed LGDML outperform all the other methods.

Acknowledgements. This work is supported by the National NSF of China (Nos. 61432008, 61673203, 61806092, U1435214), Primary R&D Plan of Jiangsu Province, China (Nos. BE2015213), Jiangsu Natural Science Foundation (Nos. BK20180326), CCF-Tencent RAGR (Nos. 20180114) and the Collaborative Innovation Center of Novel Software Technology and Industrialization.

References

1. Abaci, B., Akgul, T.: Matching caricatures to photographs. SIVP **9**(1), 295–303 (2015)
2. Ahmed, E., Jones, M., Marks, T.K.: An improved deep learning architecture for person re-identification. In: CVPR, pp. 3908–3916 (2015)
3. Akleman, E.: Making caricatures with morphing. In: SIGGRAPH, p. 145 (1997)
4. Akleman, E., Reisch, J.: Modeling expressive 3D caricatures. In: SIGGRAPH, p. 61 (2004)
5. Brennan, S.E.: Caricature generator: the dynamic exaggeration of faces by computer. Leonardo **40**(4), 392–400 (2007)
6. Chechik, G., Sharma, V., Shalit, U., Bengio, S.: Large scale online learning of image similarity through ranking. JMLR **11**, 1109–1135 (2010)
7. Cui, Y., Zhou, F., Lin, Y., Belongie, S.: Fine-grained categorization and dataset bootstrapping using deep metric learning with humans in the loop. In: CVPR, pp. 1153–1162 (2016)
8. Davis, J.V., Kulis, B., Jain, P., Sra, S., Dhillon, I.S.: Information-theoretic metric learning. In: ICML, pp. 209–216 (2007)
9. Duan, Y., Lu, J., Feng, J., Zhou, J.: Deep localized metric learning. TCSVT **28**, 2644–2656 (2017)
10. Friedman, J., Hastie, T., Tibshirani, R.: The Elements of Statistical Learning: Data Mining, Inference, and Prediction. Springer Series in Statistics. Springer, Heidelberg (2009). https://doi.org/10.1007/978-0-387-84858-7
11. Han, X., Leung, T., Jia, Y., Sukthankar, R., Berg, A.C.: MatchNet: unifying feature and metric learning for patch-based matching. In: CVPR, pp. 3279–3286 (2015)
12. He, K., Zhang, X., Ren, S., Sun, J.: Deep residual learning for image recognition. In: CVPR, pp. 770–778 (2016)
13. Hu, J., Lu, J., Tan, Y.P.: Discriminative deep metric learning for face verification in the wild. In: CVPR, pp. 1875–1882 (2014)
14. Hu, J., Lu, J., Tan, Y.P.: Deep metric learning for visual tracking. TCSVT **26**(11), 2056–2068 (2016)
15. Huang, C., Loy, C.C., Tang, X.: Local similarity-aware deep feature embedding. In: NIPS, pp. 1262–1270 (2016)

16. Huo, J., Gao, Y., Shi, Y., Yin, H.: Variation robust cross-modal metric learning for caricature recognition. In: ACMMM Workshop, pp. 340–348. ACM (2017)
17. Huo, J., Li, W., Shi, Y., Gao, Y., Yin, H.: WebCaricature: a benchmark for caricature face recognition. In: BMVC (2018)
18. Jain, P., Kulis, B., Dhillon, I.S., Grauman, K.: Online metric learning and fast similarity search. In: NIPS, pp. 761–768 (2009)
19. Klare, B.F., Bucak, S.S., Jain, A.K., Akgul, T.: Towards automated caricature recognition. In: ICB, pp. 139–146 (2012)
20. Koestinger, M., Hirzer, M., Wohlhart, P., Roth, P.M., Bischof, H.: Large scale metric learning from equivalence constraints. In: CVPR, pp. 2288–2295 (2012)
21. Krizhevsky, A., Sutskever, I., Hinton, G.E.: ImageNet classification with deep convolutional neural networks. In: NIPS, pp. 1097–1105 (2012)
22. Kumar, N., Berg, A.C., Belhumeur, P.N., Nayar, S.K.: Attribute and simile classifiers for face verification. In: ICCV, pp. 365–372 (2009)
23. Li, W., Gao, Y., Wang, L., Zhou, L., Huo, J., Shi, Y.: OPML: a one-pass closed-form solution for online metric learning. Pattern Recogn. **75**, 302–314 (2018)
24. Li, W., Huo, J., Shi, Y., Gao, Y., Wang, L., Luo, J.: Online deep metric learning. arXiv:1805.05510 (2018)
25. van der Maaten, L., Hinton, G.: Visualizing data using t-SNE. JMLR **9**(Nov), 2579–2605 (2008)
26. Mauro, R., Kubovy, M.: Caricature and face recognition. Mem. Cogn. **20**(4), 433–440 (1992)
27. Mignon, A., Jurie, F.: PCCA: a new approach for distance learning from sparse pairwise constraints. In: CVPR, pp. 2666–2672 (2012)
28. Oh Song, H., Xiang, Y., Jegelka, S., Savarese, S.: Deep metric learning via lifted structured feature embedding. In: CVPR, pp. 4004–4012 (2016)
29. Ouyang, S., Hospedales, T., Song, Y.-Z., Li, X.: Cross-modal face matching: beyond viewed sketches. In: Cremers, D., Reid, I., Saito, H., Yang, M.-H. (eds.) ACCV 2014. LNCS, vol. 9004, pp. 210–225. Springer, Cham (2015). https://doi.org/10.1007/978-3-319-16808-1_15
30. Reale, C., Nasrabadi, N.M., Kwon, H., Chellappa, R.: Seeing the forest from the trees: a holistic approach to near-infrared heterogeneous face recognition. In: CVPR Workshop, pp. 54–62 (2016)
31. Schroff, F., Kalenichenko, D., Philbin, J.: FaceNet: a unified embedding for face recognition and clustering. In: CVPR, pp. 815–823 (2015)
32. Shi, Y., Li, W., Gao, Y., Cao, L., Shen, D.: Beyond IID: learning to combine non-IID metrics for vision tasks. In: AAAI, pp. 1524–1531 (2017)
33. Simonyan, K., Zisserman, A.: Very deep convolutional networks for large-scale image recognition. arXiv:1409.1556 (2014)
34. Szegedy, C., et al.: Going deeper with convolutions. In: CVPR, pp. 1–9 (2015)
35. Tanaka, J.W., Farah, M.J.: Parts and wholes in face recognition. Q. J. Exp. Psychol. **46**(2), 225–245 (1993)
36. Tseng, C.C., Lien, J.J.J., Member, I.: Colored exaggerative caricature creation using inter-and intra-correlations of feature shapes and positions. IVC **30**(1), 15–25 (2012)
37. Vedaldi, A., Lenc, K.: MatConvNet: convolutional neural networks for MATLAB. In: ACMMM, pp. 689–692 (2015)
38. Wang, J., et al.: Learning fine-grained image similarity with deep ranking. In: CVPR, pp. 1386–1393 (2014)
39. Weinberger, K.Q., Blitzer, J., Saul, L.K.: Distance metric learning for large margin nearest neighbor classification. In: NIPS, pp. 1473–1480 (2005)

40. Yang, W., Toyoura, M., Xu, J., Ohnuma, F., Mao, X.: Example-based caricature generation with exaggeration control. TVC **32**(3), 383–392 (2016)
41. Yi, D., Lei, Z., Liao, S., Li, S.Z.: Deep metric learning for person re-identification. In: ICPR, pp. 34–39 (2014)
42. Yosinski, J., Clune, J., Bengio, Y., Lipson, H.: How transferable are features in deep neural networks? In: NIPS, pp. 3320–3328 (2014)

Fast Single Shot Instance Segmentation

Zuoxin Li[1], Fuqiang Zhou[1](✉), and Lu Yang[2]

[1] Beihang University, Beijing 100191, China
{lizuoxin,zfq}@buaa.edu.cn
[2] Beijing University of Posts and Telecommunication, Beijing 100876, China
soeaver@bupt.edu.cn

Abstract. In this work, we propose fast single shot instance segmentation framework (FSSI), which aims at jointly object detection, segmenting and distinguishing every individual instance (instance segmentation) in a flexible and fast way. In the pipeline of FSSI, the instance segmentation task is divided into three parallel sub-tasks: object detection, semantic segmentation, and direction prediction. The instance segmentation result is then generated from these three sub-tasks' results by the post-process in parallel. In order to accelerate the process, the SSD-like detection structure and two-path architecture which can generate more accurate segmentation prediction without heavy calculation burden are adopted. Our experiments on the PASCAL VOC and the MSCOCO datasets demonstrate the benefits of our approach, which accelerate the instance segmentation process with competitive result compared to MaskRCNN. Code is public available (https://github.com/lzx1413/FSSI).

Keywords: Instance segmentation · Multi-task learning · Convolutional Neural Networks

1 Introduction

Benefited from the Deep Convolutional Neural Networks (CNNs) [16], the field of category-level semantic segmentation and object detection has a rapid progress over a short period of time [3,23–25,29]. However, instance segmentation is more complex since it requires segmenting each instance in an image. To tackle this challenging task, several approaches have been proposed, such as MaskR-CNN [12] and FCIS [17]. Those methods can achieve state-of-the-art performance on the instance segmentation task but usually require a complicated pipeline and a huge amount of computations. Our goal in this work is to build a system which can split the instance segmentation task into several lightweight, parallel and computing sharing tasks. Hence they can run at a faster speed while retaining the competitive results with other methods.

There are mainly two kinds of methods to solve the instance segmentation problem. The first one is developing a system which focuses on bounding box detection first and then refining the prediction to obtain mask segmentation.

C. V. Jawahar et al. (Eds.): ACCV 2018, LNCS 11364, pp. 257–272, 2019.
https://doi.org/10.1007/978-3-030-20870-7_16

The state-of-the-art instance segmentation model MaskRCNN [12], generates the instance masks from the features cropped and resized by ROIAlign. The operator of ROIAlign is very heavy when there are numerous proposals. Besides, reducing the resolution of input images will decrease the performance markedly according to our experiments. Another type is to assign pixel predictions to instances in a bottom-up way. The prior work of [31] produces three predictions: semantic segmentation, instance direction (predicting the pixel's direction towards its corresponding instance center) and depth estimation. However, the complicate template matching which is used to decode the instance mask slows the speed of the pipeline.

In this work, we propose a fast single shot instance segmentation method (FSSI) which is a fast and flexible approach to tackle instance segmentation task. The instance segmentation task is decomposed into three parallel tasks: object detection, semantic segmentation, and direction prediction. In order to reduce the computational cost, the fusion feature generated from the base model is shared among the three tasks. We adopt the SSD-like head structure for object detection rather than crop-and-resize method introduced in [12,17]. Then the instance mask is produced by clustering the patch of masks from segmentation tasks according to the detected boxes, which is simpler and faster than template matching in the work [31]. As shown in Fig. 1, FSSI is designed in a multi-task way using one full convolutional network (FCN). Therefore, FSSI can be trained in an end-to-end way and the performance of instance segmentation can be further improved while better results can be produced by the three sub-tasks. Our main contributions can be summarized as follows:

(1) We decompose instance segmentation task into three sub-tasks: object detection, semantic segmentation, and direction prediction. We propose a novel and lightweight multi-task framework (FSSI) which shares the fusion feature and generates the outputs of the three sub-tasks.
(2) Our proposed FSSI adopts SSD-like object detection structure and two-path segmentation architecture to reduce the computational cost, which let FSSI perform about 4 times faster than MaskRCNN while having the competitive performance.
(3) We propose a simple and parallel post-process algorithm to generate instance segmentation masks from the three sub-task results.

2 Related Work

In this section, we summarize current instance segmentation algorithms based on deep neural networks and categorize them into two types, depending on the framework of the pipeline: Top-down or Bottom-up.

Top-Down Based Methods. Top-down based methods generate instance segmentation by producing the bounding box of objects firstly. Then the regions of features in the bounding boxes are cropped and resized to be used to either classify mask regions or refine boxes to obtain instance masks. There have been several methods proposed to tackle the instance segmentation task. MCG [1], SharpMask [28] and instance-sensitive FCNs [4] are proposed to generate mask proposals. MNC [5] decomposes the instance segmentation into three cascade problems including box localization, mask refinement, and instance classification. The former result is used as the input of the following tasks. Hayer*et al.* [9] suggest reducing the mask boundary error to improve MNC. Higher-order Conditional Random Fields (CRFs) are used in [2] to refine the instance mask. FCIS [17] is the first Fully Convolutional Network (FCN) for instance segmentation. It adopts position-sensitive score maps from InstanceFCN [4] and considers inside/outside score maps further to produce instance masks. Recently, Mask-RCNN [12], which is built on the top of FPN [20], adopts another small FCN branch to obtain refined mask results from box predictions.

Bottom-Up Based Methods. Bottom-up based methods generally adopt the following two stages, including segmentation and clustering. The segmentation module predicts the pixel-level labels, and the clustering process is used to group the per-pixel predictions together for each object instance. PFN [19] adopts spectral clustering to group the semantic segmentation results from DeepLab [3] depending on the prediction of object number and the bounding box every pixel belongs to. Zhang *et al.* [34] apply depth order to distinguish different instances. Uhrig *et al.* [31] train an FCN to predict the direction to the object center of each pixel, semantic mask, and depth information to generate instance segmentations. Liu *et al.* [22] segment objects from patches of images with multi-scales and aggregate them together. However, existing methods seldom pay attention to the efficiency of instance segmentation and they are hard to be deployed to platforms which have limited computational capability. For instance, MaskRCNN based on ResNet-50 [13] can only run at 5 FPS on the advanced GPUs. To tackle this problem, our proposed FSSI model combines the advantages from both top-down and bottom-up advantages and aims at supplying a fast and lightweight approach to generate instance masks. Our proposed method divides the instance segmentation task into three parallel sub-tasks: object detection, semantic segmentation, and direction segmentation. Different from FCIS or MaskRCNN, which are built on the two-stage object directors and refine the mask from the features w.r.t the detected boxes, our FSSI adopts SSD-like head for object detection and the results of instance segmentation initialized by the boxes are generated from the semantic segmentation and direction prediction directly. Benefited from the two-path architecture described in Sect. 3, the computational cost for segmentation tasks is reduced observably.

3 Fast Single Shot Instance Segmentation

In this section, we first introduce the sub-tasks designed to accomplish the final instance segmentation task. Then we demonstrate the global view of our FSSI pipeline and the architecture of each sub-task. Finally, we explain how to aggregate results from the sub-tasks to generate the instance segmentation result and the loss functions which are used to optimize our FSSI.

3.1 Multi-task Design for Instance Segmentation

In our FSSI framework, instance segmentation can be decomposed into three parallel tasks including object detection, semantic segmentation and auxiliary information for distinguishing individual instances which belong to the same category. The object detection result can supply the category label and bounding box information which can be regarded as the initial region of interest to generate a refined instance mask. Semantic segmentation logits are designed to predict the pixel-wise semantic logits, which have the ability to separate instances of different semantic labels. However, semantic labels are not sufficient to make a distinction between instance objects which belong to the same class and are connected to each other. Auxiliary information for distinguishing them is necessary at this time. There are several ways to tackle this task, such as direction, boundary, and depth prediction. In this work, we adopt the direction prediction proposed by [31] as the auxiliary information. The direction prediction logits can be used to predict each pixel's direction towards of the center of its corresponding instance. However, our direction target is different from [31], which will be discussed in Sect. 3.6. The instance segmentation results can be obtained by a simple post-processing method which will be described in Sect. 3.7 in details.

3.2 Global View of the Pipeline

As presented in Fig. 1, we design one fully convolutional network, which performs object detection, semantic segmentation, and direction prediction synchronously. Our motivation is as follows: Firstly, we consider generating a comprehensive representation of the input image. Then the general feature will be regarded as the input feature for three subnets which are corresponding to the three sub-tasks. Finally, outputs of the three sub-tasks will be aggregated together to generate the instance segmentation results with a post-process module.

3.3 Fusion Feature

Inspired by HyperNet [15] and FSSD [18], we produce the fusion feature by fusing the multi-level feature maps generated by the base model. Considering the trade-off between the performance and speed in image classification task, we choose ResNet-50 [13] as the base model. The fusion feature is the comprehensive representation of the input image. Following FSSD [18], we choose the feature maps with feature stride 8, 16, 32 to generate the fusion feature, whose feature stride is 8. In order to reduce the time consumed in the fusion feature extraction, we resize the input image to 300×300 before feeding it into the base model.

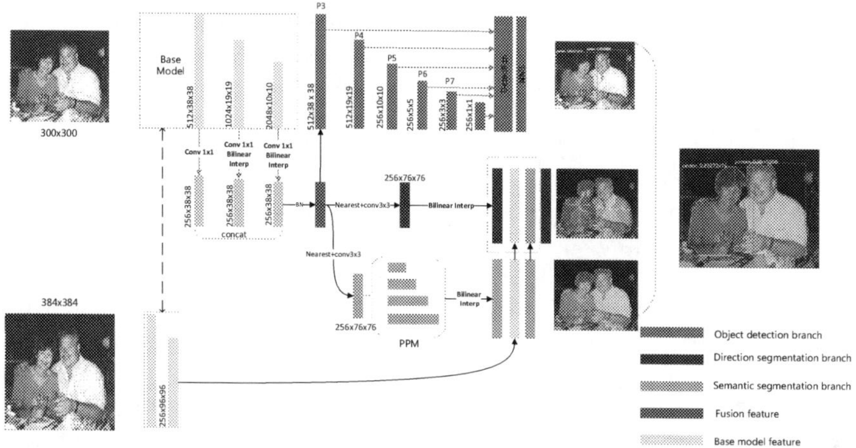

Fig. 1. The FSSI architecture. The size of the input image is 384×384. FSSI consists of three branches for **object detection**, **semantic segmentation,** and **direction prediction**. We adopt ResNet50 [13] as the **BaseModel** to extract the **fusion feature**(orange). The green part is the single shot object detection sub-net which takes the **fusion feature** as the input. As for the segmentation tasks, the original large input image is used to generate **low level feature** by a shallow FCN (shares weights with part of the base model). Then one pyramid pooling module (PPM) is appended after the fusion feature to generate high-level semantic feature map. Next, the low-level and high-level feature maps are concatenated together to generate the semantic segmentation results, which will be concatenated with the feature maps from the direction segmentation sub-net to produce the direction prediction outputs. Finally, the instance segmentation results can be generated by a post-process.

3.4 SSD Head for Object Detection

SSD [23] is an excellent object detector architecture which can achieve outstanding performance while running at a very fast speed. Inspired by FSSD [18], we generate new feature pyramid from the fusion feature with a cascade of convolutional layers whose stride is 2. Then the feature pyramid will be adopted to generate classification and coordinate correction for a set of default bounding boxes. At test time, non-maximum suppression (NMS) will be used to filter the final object detection results. Since we only use the image with 300×300 to process object detection, the object detection process is very efficient.

3.5 Segmentation Sub-networks

As shown in Fig. 1, we append two sub-nets after the fusion feature to generate prediction map for the semantic mask and direction mask. Since the spatial size of the fusion feature is 38×38, it is insufficient to generate the mask with high quality, especially for the direction map whose spatial size is much smaller than the semantic mask (semantic masks are divided into direction masks). Therefore, we adopt the two-path structure, which means that we also extract the low-level feature maps from the original input image (384×384) using a sequence of convolutional layers which share the weights with the first stage of ResNet-50 to refine the mask prediction results.

Semantic Segmentation Branch. As the feature stride of the fusion feature is 8, we firstly up-sample the feature map by the nearest interpolation layer with up-scale factor 2 followed by one convolutional layer. We also leverage the pyramid pooling module (PPM) which is proposed by PSPnet [35] to enhance the capacity of the semantic segmentation branch. The high-level feature maps generated from the fusion feature will be concatenated to the low-level feature maps to generate the ultimate semantic segmentation results. The output semantic prediction map will be up-sampled by bilinear interpolation to match the size of the input image.

Direction Segmentation Branch. The target of direction segmentation is described in Sec. 3.6. Compared with semantic segmentation target, the direction segmentation target has a smaller area. Therefore, we discard the PPM and only up-sample the fusion feature by a nearest up-sample layer with scale factor 2 and a convolutional layer. Since the direction segmentation only needs to be conducted on the region of objects, the output of the semantic segmentation is concatenated with the up-sampled fusion feature to serve as a reference for the objects' spatial distribution. However, the gradient of the direction segmentation branch does not be back-propagated to the semantic segmentation branch. Different from the FCIS [17], our proposed direction results are class-agnostic instead of having the logits for each category to yield more compact models. Hence the outputs of direction segmentation are only 9 channels (8 for 8 directions and 1 for the background.)

3.6 Direction Map of Objects

As shown in Fig. 2(b), semantic segmentation will only predict the category results of the pixels rather than instance results. In order to discriminate the different object instances which belong to the same category and are connected together in the image, we adopt the direction map (Fig. 2(c)) which is inspired by [31]. [31] splits the instance mask into 8 different directions with the angle interval of 45 degrees. Different from the [31], we use the diagonal and the lines between the midpoints on the sides of the bounding boxes to split the instance mask into 8 regions (We do not adopt 4 or 16 regions because they do not perfrom as well as 8 regions in our experiments.). We propose this method according to fact that the input image will be resized before being processed by the network. Our approach can preserve the constant direction label with image-ratio varieties. Besides, this strategy can also make the direction logits become easier to collaborate with the object detection results, which will be described in Sect. 3.7. Besides, since the area of each individual direction segmentation mask is smaller than the original category mask and only the regions where objects exist need to generate direction

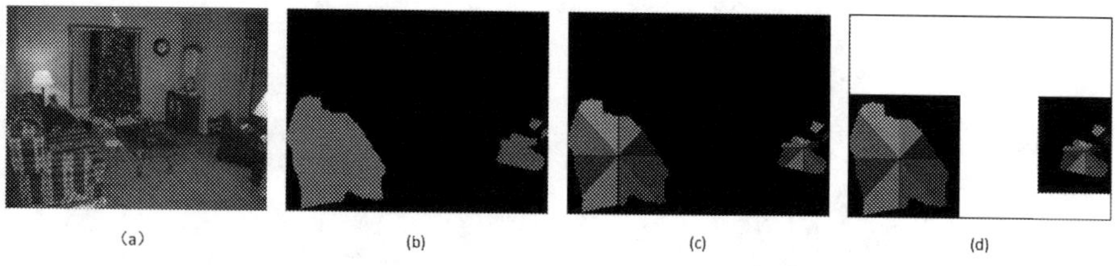

Fig. 2. Segmentation targets. (a) input image. (b) semantic segmentation target. (c) original direction segmentation target. (d) direction segmentation target after ignoring the background regions (in white color).

predictions, we ignore the region (Fig. 2(d)) which is outside of the expanded bounding boxes from the ground truths to reduce the jamming effect from the background.

3.7 Post-process for Generating Instance Mask

The multi-task network called FSSI can generate the object detection, semantic segmentation and direction segmentation of the input image. The post-process will take these three parts of information as the inputs and generate the instance segmentation results. For the objects in one image, we process them with groups which are clustered by their category labels from the object detection results. Different groups of objects can be processed in parallel to accelerate the process. For each group of objects, as shown in Fig. 3, there are two stages for post-process.

1. Find and match the bounding boxes (det-box) with the individual semantic masks, which means that the masks are not connected with other objects in the same group. First, connected components of the semantic masks are extracted and the bounding box of these connected components (mask-box) can be calculated. Then the intersection over union (IoU) between each det-box and mask-box can be obtained. One det-box and one mask-box are matched successfully if the IoU between them is higher than a threshold t_{bs} which is 0.7 in our experiments. Therefore, we can confirm one object with both it's bounding box and mask. In order to avoid the problem that the det-box is not large enough to surround the object (last row in Fig. 4), which leads to failure to produce the full mask of the object, we set the union set of mask-box and det-box to be the final object box in this stage.
2. Discriminate the instance masks which are connected together with the guide of direction predictions. First, given one predicted bounding box and category label, we crop the regions in the semantic segmentation map and direction map w.r.t the predicted bounding box. The semantic patch is transformed into a binary mask according to the category label and used to perform as the mask to filter the direction patches. Regions in the direction map which are not in the semantic mask will turn to be background. Then the direction

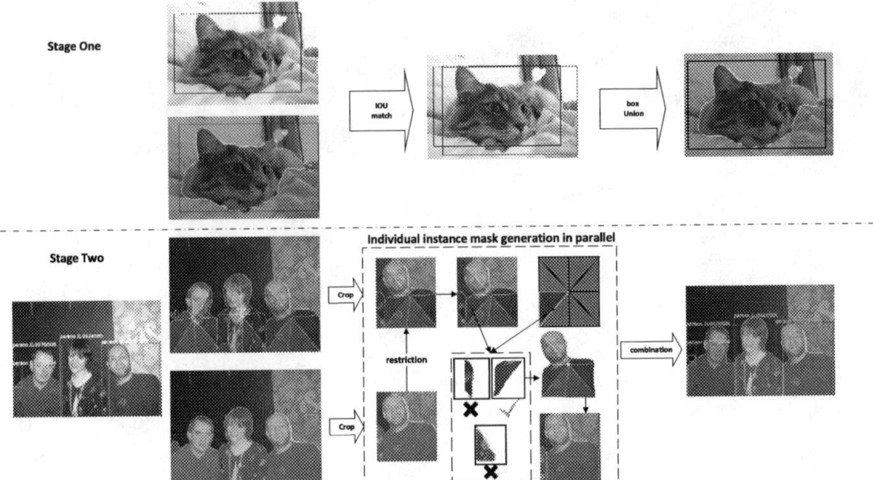

Fig. 3. Pipeline of the post-process for instance results. Details can be found in Sect. 3.7.

patch can be used to determine the mask of center objects according to their location distribution as follows: First, we define a direction template w.r.t the predicted box as shown in Fig. 3. The regions of 8 different directions are separated. The direction template is with the same size as the det-box. Then the mask patches of 8 directions are processed in parallel. For each direction, the mask patches which belong to this direction will be extracted by finding their connected components. For each mask patch, the occupancy rate (O_r) will be calculated to confirm whether this patch is in the corresponding direction to the center object. The occupancy rate is defined as follows:

$$O_r = \frac{Mask_d \cap Mask_t}{Mask_d} \tag{1}$$

where $Mask_d$ is the binary mask of the direction patch and $Mask_t$ is the mask of the corresponding direction in the direction template. If O_r is higher than a threshold O_t(0.2 in our experiments), the direction patch is regarded as part of the center object's mask. This method can tolerate det-box's error within limits. After the direction patches of 8 directions which belong to the center obje ct are collected, we can get a coarse mask of the object by piecing them together. In order to fill the small holes in the mask, we apply a close morphology operation on the coarse mask to refine the mask.

To illustrate the mechanism of how to use direction map to reject the mask patches which are not part of the center object more clearly, we supply an example. As shown in stage 2 of Fig. 3, the rightmost person's det-box contains the masks of both its center object and another person near him. Take the direction in red as an instance, two mask patches which are in the region of the direction are predicted as other directions. Therefore, it is apparent that those two mask patches are not from the center objects. The final instance mask does not contain these mask patches.

3.8 Training and Loss Functions

Given the dataset which is annotated with instance masks, the bounding box, semantic segmentation targets and direction segmentation targets can be extracted from the instance annotations. The loss function used to optimize the model is the sum of three sub-task loss functions including object detection (L_{det}), semantic segmentation (L_s), and direction segmentation (L_d). The loss is defined as follows:

$$L = L_{det} + \alpha L_s + \beta L_d \tag{2}$$

where α and β are the scale factors to reweight the three loss functions and in our experiments, the α and β are set to 100.

As for the object detection loss, we adopt the same loss proposed in SSD [23]. We adopt the same data augmentation and matching strategy suggested in the conventional SSD framework.

For both of the two segmentation tasks, the loss is the cross-entropy between the predicted and target class distribution for each pixel. To boost the segmentation performance on the hard cases in images, we adopt the bootstrapping cross-entropy proposed by Wu *et al.* [33]. Supposing C is the number of categories, and $y_1, ..., y_N \in \{1, ..., c\}$ are the target labels for the pixels $1, ..., N$, and $p_{i,j}$ is the posterior class probability for pixel i and class j, the bootstrapping cross-entropy loss can be defined as follows:

$$L_s = -\frac{1}{K}\sum_{1}^{K} log(p_k) \qquad log(p_k) \in TopK(log(p_{i,j})), y_i = j \tag{3}$$

The misclassified pixels or pixels where we predict the correct label with a small probability will be selected to be optimized in the first place depending on the number of pixels K (16384 in our experiments) that we consider.

4 Experiments

In this section, we show that our FSSI can achieve competitive performance in terms of object detection, semantic segmentation and instance segmentation with a fast speed. We implement FSSI with PyTorch[1] throughout all the experiments. We conduct experiments on PASCAL VOC [7] and MSCOCO [21] for which both bounding box annotations and segmentation maps or instance annotations are available.

[1] https://github.com/pytorch/pytorch.

4.1 Experiments on PASCAL VOC

PASCAL VOC includes 20 object categories for detection, semantic segmentation, and instance segmentation. All images in PASCAL VOC have bounding box annotations but there are only 1464 fully labeled images in the train set and another 1449 in the validation set for segmentation. We evaluate the semantic segmentation performance on the VOC2012 segmentation test set. We also augment the train set with extra annotations from the semantic boundaries dataset (SBD) [8]. Therefore, there are 10582 images in the train set (we call this set VOC12-sem-seg-aug-train). Besides, VOC07 trainval set (VOC07-trainval) has 5011 images, and VOC07 test set (VOC07-test) has 4952 images for object detection.

As for the instance segmentation task on PASCAL VOC dataset, we use the annotations in SBD [8] and follow the common protocols used in several recent works [10,17]. There are 5623 images in the train set (SBD-train) and 5732 images in the validation set (SBD-val) according to the PASCAL VOC 2012 splits. We train the models with the train set and evaluate them with the validation set as there is no annotation for the test set.

The performance of semantic segmentation and direction segmentation on PASCAL VOC dataset is mainly measured with mean intersection over union (mIoU). mAP@0.5 is used to measure the object detection quality. mAP@0.5 and mAP@0.7 are used to evaluate the performance of instance segmentation task.

While training models on the PASCAL VOC dataset, we train the FSSI on two Nvidia 1080Ti GPUs with batch size 32 for 60 epochs with initial learning rate 0.01. We decay the learning rate with cosine annealing which is proposed by [26] for each epoch.

Table 1. Ablation study results for FSSI. The performance is evaluated on the SBD-val set. **DP**: Initialize FSSI with detection model pre-trained on VOC07-trainval and VOC07-test. **BTL**: Replace the conventional cross-entropy loss with bootstrapping cross-entropy loss. **MR**: The outputs of semantic segmentation are used to generate the direction predictions. **TP**: Adopt two-path architecture to produce segmentation results. **MT**: Double the epoches in the training phase. **DET**: Object detection. **SEM**: Semantic segmentation. **DRT**: Direction segmentation. **INS**: Instance segmentation.

DP	BTL	MR	TP	MT	DET mAP@0.5	SEM mIoU	DRT mIoU	INS mAP@0.5	INS mAP@0.7
				✓	67.39	68.28	54.29	50.12	34.95
✓					74.00	69.02	55.82	53.99	37.77
✓	✓				73.50	70.60	56.63	55.44	40.79
✓	✓	✓			**74.85**	70.84	57.14	56.47	40.88
✓	✓	✓		✓	74.07	69.56	57.33	56.70	41.01
✓	✓	✓	✓		74.02	**71.30**	**58.23**	**58.40**	**41.95**

Ablation on PASCAL VOC. We run a lot of ablation studies to analyze FSSI on the structure design and training strategy. Results are shown in Table 1 and discussed as follows.

Extra Data for Detection from VOC07 Set: As illustrated in Fig. 1, our FSSI is designed for multitasks. Therefore we want to figure out whether more data of bounding box annotations is beneficial to the performance of FSSI. In Table 1, we note that training model with VOC07-trainval and VOC07-test set can improve the performance of FSSI effectively.

Bootstrapping Cross-Entropy vs. Cross-Entropy. As mentioned in [33], continuing to learn from the pixels which are easy to be classified can not improve the segmentation performance. The model should focus on the hard pixels (edge of objects or complex surfaces) during training. In order to enhance the ability of the model to discriminate the edge of the center object, we adopt the bootstrapping cross-entropy to mine the hard pixels during the training phase. We compare the effect of conventional cross-entropy and bootstrapping cross-entropy. As shown in Table 1, bootstrapping cross-entropy can improve the mIoU of both semantic segmentation and direction segmentation, which contributes to the progress of instance segmentation performance.

Direction Segmentation Takes Semantic Results as a Reference or Not: As shown in Fig. 1, the output of semantic segmentation is used as part of feature maps to generate the direction segmentation. In order to evaluate the effectiveness of this design, we remove this link and compare their performance. As shown in Table 1, approximate 1% improvement can be obtained while taking the output of semantic segmentation as the reference of the direction segmentation.

Adopt Two Path Architecture or Not for Segmentations: In order to illustrate the effectiveness of the two-path structure, we compare the one-path and two-path structure. As shown in Table 1, we can observe the improvement with a large margin while adopting the design of two-path architecture.

Effectiveness of the Three Sub-task Design. In this section, we evaluate gains from the three sub-tasks. We evaluate the instance segmentation performance in different ways as shown in Table 2. It is obvious that the direction segmentation task can improve the performance effectively. Besides, if we replace the predicted mask with the ground truth, the performance can be improved further, which means that future advances in semantic segmentation methods can further improve the performance of our approach.

Table 2. The effectiveness of the three sub-tasks for instance segmentation. **box**: The region of box is regarded as the instance mask. **sem-mask**: The semantic mask in the box is regarded as the instance mask. **direct-mask**: The direction mask joins the post-process. **gt-sem**: The semantic mask is replaced by the ground truth. **gt-direct**: The direction mask is replaced by the ground truth.

box	sem-mask	direct-mask	gt-sem	gt-direct	mAP@0.5	mAP@0.7
✓					33.51	7.93
✓	✓				53.20	36.25
✓	✓	✓			56.70	41.00
✓		✓	✓		65.77	54.11
✓	✓			✓	62.28	51.63

Table 3. Object detection and semantic segmentation evaluation on PASCAL VOC dataset.

method	*BaseModel*	*input size*	mAP_{50}
SSD300[23]	VGG16	300	77.2
RSSD300[14]	VGG16	300	78.5
DSSD300[30]	Res101	321	78.6
Blitz300[6]	Res50	300	79.1
FSSD300[18]	VGG16	300	78.8
FSSI(ours)	Res50	300	**79.6**

(a) Detection results of PASCAL VOC2007 test set. Blitz300 and FSSI are trained with mask annotations.

method	mAP_{50}
FCN[25]	62.2
DeepLab[3]	71.6
DeconvNet[27]	72.5
Blitz300[6]	72.8
GCRF[32]	73.2
DPN[24]	74.1
FSSI(ours)	**75.1**

(b) Semantic segmentation results of PASCAL VOC2012 segmentation test dataset.

Results on PASCAL VOC

Object Detection. We first evaluate our FSSI on the object detection task on PASCAL VOC 2007 test. Our FSSI is trained with VOC2007 trainval and VOC2012 trainval. Apart from the bounding box annotations, semantic segmentation labels of VOC2012 are also used to optimize the FSSI model. As shown in Table 3(a), our FSSI can achieve 79.6 mAP@0.5, and outperform the BlitzNet which is also trained with extra semantic mask annotations.

Semantic Segmentation. Since semantic segmentation is one task of our FSSI, we also evaluate the performance of FSSI with other semantic segmentation algorithms. As shown in Table 3, even though the input image of FSSI is only 384×384 pixels, FSSI still can produce competitive results with other methods (http://host.robots.ox.ac.uk:8080/anonymous/BHMCV1.html).

Fig. 4. Instance segmentation results. (a) Input image. (b) Semantic segmentation results. (c) Direction prediction results. (d) Instance segmentation results of our FSSI. (e) Instance segmentation results of MaskRCNN.

Instance Segmentation. We compare the results of our FSSI with the state-of-the-art approaches on PASCAL VOC 2012 dataset. As shown in Table 4, note that our approach can achieve better performance than MaskRCNN with the approximate same size of input images, even though our FSSI cannot catch up with other complex models such as MNC, FCIS, and BAIS which adopt input images with higher resolution. There are some sample results on the VOC2012 validation set as shown in Fig. 4. It is evident that our model produces competitive results with MaskRCNN[2]. Moreover, our FSSI can produce more refined masks than MaskRCNN.

[2] This result is produced by ourselves based on https://github.com/roytseng-tw/Detectron.pytorch.

Table 4. Evaluation of different methods on the PASCAL VOC2012 validation set.

Method	Input size	mAP@0.5	mAP@0.7	Time/img (ms)
SDS [10]	-	49.7	25.3	48000
PFN [19]	-	58.7	42.5	1000
InstanceFCN [4]	-	61.5	43.0	1500
MNC [5]	600˜	63.5	41.5	360
FCIS [17]	600˜	66.0	51.9	230
BAIS [11]	-	65.7	48.3	780
MaskRCNN [12]	300˜500	56.7	39.2	53
FSSI (ours)	384×384	58.4	42.0	17

4.2 Inference Time Comparison

As shown in Table 4, our FSSI only consumes 17 ms (network inference + post-process) for each input image averagely on the Nvidia 1080Ti GPU, which is about 4 times faster than Mask-RCNN with the approximate same size of input images.

4.3 Microsoft COCO Dataset

We further evaluate FSSI on the MSCOCO dataset. MSCOCO dataset includes 80 categories for detection and instance segmentation. There are no official semantic annotations for training and validation. In this work, we generate the semantic segmentation targets by combining instances of one category. As shown in Table 5(a), our FSSI can reach 53.8 mIoU with 384×384 input, which is better than BlitzNet whose input size is 512×512. As for the instance segmentation, our FSSI can achieve 17.5 mAP@[0.5:0.95], which is competitive with the MaskRCNN.

Table 5. Results of MSCOCO dataset. The *mmAP* denotes mAP@[0.5:0.95].

method	*Backend*	*input*	*mIoU*
Blitznet[6]	Res50	512	53.5
FSSI(ours)	Res50	384	53.8

(a) Semantic segmentation results on COCO validation set.

method	*Backend*	*input*	*val mmAP*	*test mmAP*
MaskRCNN[12]	Res50	300˜500	18.1	18.3
FSSI(ours)	Res50	384	17.5	17.8

(b) Instance segmentation results on COCO validation and test-dev set.

5 Conclusions

In this work, we propose fast single shot instance segmentation (FSSI), a lightweight and fast framework for instance segmentation. The paradigm represents the instance segmentation task by a combination of three sub-tasks: object detection, semantic segmentation and direction prediction. We have designed a new FCN architecture that utilizes this paradigm. The three sub-tasks share the fusion feature generated from the base model. Two path architecture is also adopted to supply feature maps with low-level information to produce more accurate masks. The proposed framework can run at 4 times faster than MaskRCNN while having the competitive performance on PASCAL VOC and MSCOCO.

Acknowledgements. This work was supported by the National Natural Science Foundation of China (No. 61471123).

References

1. Arbeláez, P., Pont-Tuset, J., Barron, J., Marques, F., Malik, J.: Multiscale combinatorial grouping. In: 2014 IEEE Conference on Computer Vision and Pattern Recognition, pp. 328–335 (2014)
2. Arnab, A., Jayasumana, S., Zheng, S., Torr, P.H.S.: Higher order conditional random fields in deep neural networks. In: Leibe, B., Matas, J., Sebe, N., Welling, M. (eds.) ECCV 2016. LNCS, vol. 9906, pp. 524–540. Springer, Cham (2016). https://doi.org/10.1007/978-3-319-46475-6_33
3. Chen, L., Papandreou, G., Kokkinos, I., Murphy, K., Yuille, A.L.: DeepLab: semantic image segmentation with deep convolutional nets, atrous convolution, and fully connected CRFs. IEEE Trans. Pattern Anal. Mach. Intell. **40**(4), 834–848 (2018)
4. Dai, J., He, K., Li, Y., Ren, S., Sun, J.: Instance-sensitive fully convolutional networks. In: Leibe, B., Matas, J., Sebe, N., Welling, M. (eds.) ECCV 2016. LNCS, vol. 9910, pp. 534–549. Springer, Cham (2016). https://doi.org/10.1007/978-3-319-46466-4_32
5. Dai, J., He, K., Sun, J.: Instance-aware semantic segmentation via multi-task network cascades. In: CVPR (2016)
6. Dvornik, N., Shmelkov, K., Mairal, J., Schmid, C.: BlitzNet: a real-time deep network for scene understanding. In: ICCV (2017)
7. Everingham, M., Van Gool, L., Williams, C.K.I., Winn, J., Zisserman, A.: The pascal visual object classes (VOC) challenge. Int. J. Comput. Vis. **88**(2), 303–338 (2010)
8. Hariharan, B., Arbeláez, P., Bourdev, L., Maji, S., Malik, J.: Semantic contours from inverse detectors. In: 2011 International Conference on Computer Vision, pp. 991–998 (2011)
9. Hariharan, B., Arbelaez, P., Girshick, R., Malik, J.: Hypercolumns for object segmentation and fine-grained localization. In: CVPR (2015)
10. Hariharan, B., Arbeláez, P., Girshick, R., Malik, J.: Simultaneous detection and segmentation. In: Fleet, D., Pajdla, T., Schiele, B., Tuytelaars, T. (eds.) ECCV 2014. LNCS, vol. 8695, pp. 297–312. Springer, Cham (2014). https://doi.org/10.1007/978-3-319-10584-0_20
11. Hayder, Z., He, X., Salzmann, M.: Boundary-aware instance segmentation. In: CVPR (2017)
12. He, K., Gkioxari, G., Dollar, P., Girshick, R.: Mask R-CNN. In: ICCV (2017)
13. He, K., Zhang, X., Ren, S., Sun, J.: Deep residual learning for image recognition. In: CVPR (2016)
14. Jeong, J., Park, H., Kwak, N.: Enhancement of SSD by concatenating feature maps for object detection. CoRR abs/1705.09587 (2017)

15. Kong, T., Yao, A., Chen, Y., Sun, F.: HyperNet: towards accurate region proposal generation and joint object detection. In: CVPR, pp. 845–853 (2016). 00026
16. Krizhevsky, A., Sutskever, I., Hinton, G.E.: ImageNet classification with deep convolutional neural networks. Commun. ACM **60**(6), 84–90 (2017)
17. Li, Y., Qi, H., Dai, J., Ji, X., Wei, Y.: Fully convolutional instance-aware semantic segmentation. In: CVPR (2017)
18. Li, Z., Zhou, F.: FSSD: feature fusion single shot multibox detector. CoRR abs/1712.00960 (2017)
19. Liang, X., Wei, Y., Shen, X., Yang, J., Lin, L., Yan, S.: Proposal-free network for instance-level object segmentation. CoRR abs/1509.02636 (2015)
20. Lin, T., Dollár, P., Girshick, R.B., He, K., Hariharan, B., Belongie, S.J.: Feature pyramid networks for object detection. CoRR abs/1612.03144 (2016)
21. Lin, T.-Y., et al.: Microsoft COCO: common objects in context. In: Fleet, D., Pajdla, T., Schiele, B., Tuytelaars, T. (eds.) ECCV 2014. LNCS, vol. 8693, pp. 740–755. Springer, Cham (2014). https://doi.org/10.1007/978-3-319-10602-1_48. 01470
22. Liu, S., Qi, X., Shi, J., Zhang, H., Jia, J.: Multi-scale patch aggregation (MPA) for simultaneous detection and segmentation. In: CVPR (2016)
23. Liu, W., et al.: SSD: single shot multibox detector. In: Leibe, B., Matas, J., Sebe, N., Welling, M. (eds.) ECCV 2016. LNCS, vol. 9905, pp. 21–37. Springer, Cham (2016). https://doi.org/10.1007/978-3-319-46448-0_2
24. Liu, Z., Li, X., Luo, P., Loy, C.C., Tang, X.: Semantic image segmentation via deep parsing network. In: ICCV (2015)
25. Long, J., Shelhamer, E., Darrell, T.: Fully convolutional networks for semantic segmentation. In: CVPR (2015)
26. Loshchilov, I., Hutter, F.: SGDR: stochastic gradient descent with restarts. CoRR abs/1608.03983 (2016)
27. Noh, H., Hong, S., Han, B.: Learning deconvolution network for semantic segmentation. In: ICCV (2015)
28. Pinheiro, P.O., Lin, T.-Y., Collobert, R., Dollár, P.: Learning to refine object segments. In: Leibe, B., Matas, J., Sebe, N., Welling, M. (eds.) ECCV 2016. LNCS, vol. 9905, pp. 75–91. Springer, Cham (2016). https://doi.org/10.1007/978-3-319-46448-0_5
29. Ren, S., He, K., Girshick, R., Sun, J.: Faster R-CNN: towards real-time object detection with region proposal networks. In: Cortes, C., Lawrence, N.D., Lee, D.D., Sugiyama, M., Garnett, R. (eds.) Advances in Neural Information Processing Systems, vol. 28, pp. 91–99. Curran Associates, Inc. (2015)
30. Shen, Z., Liu, Z., Li, J., Jiang, Y.G., Chen, Y., Xue, X.: DSOD: learning deeply supervised object detectors from scratch. In: ICCV (2017)
31. Uhrig, J., Cordts, M., Franke, U., Brox, T.: Pixel-level encoding and depth layering for instance-level semantic labeling. In: Rosenhahn, B., Andres, B. (eds.) GCPR 2016. LNCS, vol. 9796, pp. 14–25. Springer, Cham (2016). https://doi.org/10.1007/978-3-319-45886-1_2
32. Vemulapalli, R., Tuzel, O., Liu, M.Y., Chellapa, R.: Gaussian conditional random field network for semantic segmentation. In: CVPR (2016)
33. Wu, Z., Shen, C., van den Hengel, A.: Bridging category-level and instance-level semantic image segmentation. CoRR abs/1605.06885 (2016)
34. Zhang, Z., Fidler, S., Urtasun, R.: Instance-level segmentation for autonomous driving with deep densely connected MRFs. In: CVPR (2016)
35. Zhao, H., Shi, J., Qi, X., Wang, X., Jia, J.: Pyramid scene parsing network. In: CVPR (2017)

A Stable Algebraic Camera Pose Estimation for Minimal Configurations of 2D/3D Point and Line Correspondences

Lipu Zhou[1(✉)], Jiamin Ye[2], and Michael Kaess[1]

[1] Robotics Institute, Carnegie Mellon University, Pittsburgh, PA 15213, USA
{lipuz,kaess}@andrew.cmu.edu

[2] Institute of Engineering Thermophysics, Chinese Academy of Sciences, Beijing, China
yejiamin@iet.cn

Abstract. This paper proposes an algebraic solution for the problem of camera pose estimation using the minimal configurations of 2D/3D point and line correspondences, including three point correspondences, two point and one line correspondences, one point and two line correspondences, and three line correspondences. In contrast to the previous works that address these problems in specific geometric ways, this paper shows that the above four cases can be solved in a generic algebraic framework. Specifically, the orientation of the camera is computed from a polynomial equation system of four quadrics, then the translation can be solved from a linear equation system. To make our algorithm stable, the key is the polynomial solver. We significantly improve the numerical stability of the efficient three quadratic equation system solver, E3Q3 [17], with a slight computational cost. The simulation results show that the numerical stability of our algorithm is comparable to the state-of-the-art Perspective-3-Point (*P3P*) algorithm [14], and outperforms the state-of-the-art algorithms of the other three cases. The numerical stability of our algorithm can be further improved by a rough estimation of the rotation matrix, which is generally available in the Localization and Mapping (SLAM) or Visual Odometry (VO) system (such as the pose from the last frame). Besides, this algorithm is applicable to real-time applications.

Keywords: Minimal solution · Pose estimation · SLAM

1 Introduction

Estimating the pose of a camera from a set of 2D/3D point and correspondences has many applications in computer vision and robotics, such as robot autonomous navigation, Augmented Reality (AR) [35], SLAM [23,29,30] and VO [13,20]. Recent studies [25,26,34] show that jointly using point and line features for pose estimation give improved results. As there may exist false matchings in the real scenarios, RANSAC algorithm [5] is generally used to point out

C. V. Jawahar et al. (Eds.): ACCV 2018, LNCS 11364, pp. 273–288, 2019.
https://doi.org/10.1007/978-3-030-20870-7_17

these outliers. The solution of the minimal problem is an essential part of the RANSAC algorithm. This paper focuses on solving the minimal configurations of the 2D/3D point and line correspondences.

There are four minimal configurations for the 2D/3D point and line correspondences. Existing works generally focus on finding a specific solution for each of these minimal configurations. The similarity between the 2D/3D line correspondence and the 2D/3D point correspondence has been used in the literature. In [31], they apply such similarity to solve the least-squares problem of 2D/3D line and point correspondences. Kuang *et al.* [16] propose a minimal solution to estimate the pose of a camera with unknown focal length by points, directions and lines. Direct algebraic solution is generally adopted for pose estimation when the camera intrinsic parameters are unknown, because it is hard to get the 3D information of points and lines in the image plane without the intrinsic parameters. However, it is not clear whether the direct algebraic solution using the basic constraints is comparable to the methods based on well-designed geometric transformations when the intrinsic parameters are known. The specific geometric transformation can eliminate the unknown or even get lower order equation. Such simplification is thought to probably result in a more stable algorithm. This paper shows that directly solving the basic constraints can result in more stable or comparable results. We significantly improve the stability of the efficient three quadrics solver, E3Q3 [17], by selecting a proper unknown elimination order. This can benefit the vision tasks that resort to a three quadrics solver. We compare our algorithm with the previous algorithms by simulations. The results show that our algebraic algorithm is comparable to the state-of-the-art *P3P* algorithm [14], and is superior to the state-of-the-art algorithms of the other three cases in terms of stability. In addition, our algorithm is efficient and can be applied in real-time applications.

2 Related Work

The four minimal problems mentioned above have been solved case by case in the literature.

P3P Problem. Calculating the camera pose from three 2D/3D point correspondences is known as the *P3P* problem, which have been extensively studied in the literature. The first solution for the *P3P* problem dates back to 1841 presented by Grunert [7]. This algorithm applies the law of cosines to generate three quadratic equations about the lengths between the three 3D points and the camera origin. This is a specific quadratic polynomial system without first order monomials, which can result in a quartic equation with a closed-form solution. Several works [4, 18, 22] follow this formulation with difference in the specific variable elimination approach used to get the quartic equation. Haralick *et al.* [9] present a detailed comparison about these algorithms. More general approaches are also used to explore this specific quadric system. Quan *et al.* [27] apply the Sylvester resultant [19] to solve the quadric system. Gao *et al.* [6] employ

Wu-Ritt's zero decomposition algorithm [32] to systematically study this equation system, and provide a complete analytical solution. They also give criteria to determine the number of solutions and the number of real physical solutions. The drawback of this series of algorithms is that they need to solve a 3D/3D point alignment problem [1] to get the pose. This increases the computational time. Additionally, due to the finite representation of a digital number, the numerical error accumulated in the extra step may degrade the accuracy. Kneip *et al.* [15] and Masselli *et al.* [21] address this problem by introducing the intermediate coordinate frame to eliminate the variable. Most recently, Ke *et al.* [14] give an algebraic solution to directly compute the camera pose. Due to avoiding extra transformations, this algorithm is efficient and accurate. These approaches make use of the specific property of the *P3P* problem. Therefore, they can not be generalized to the other three minimal problems.

Two Point and One Line, and One Point and Two Line Correspondences. These two cases have not been studied thoroughly in the literature. Ramalingam *et al.* [28] give a solution to both problems. They apply the collinearity of the 2D/3D point correspondence, and the coplanarity of the 2D/3D line correspondence to construct constraints on the camera pose. They design two intermediate coordinate systems for each problems to eliminate the variables. Their transformations involve tangent function. This may cause numerical problem. Our algorithm also uses the collinearity and coplanarity constraints. But our algorithm does not require any transformation. This can avoid numerical error propagation, thus can increase accuracy. Besides, their algorithm needs to calculate the Singular-Value Decomposition (SVD) of a relative large matrix. This reduces the speed of the algorithm.

P3L Problem. Determining the camera pose by three line correspondences is known as the Perspective-3-Line (*P3L*) problem. Several solutions [2,3,33] have been proposed for this problem. Chen [2] analyzes the degenerate condition of the *P3L* problem. Xu *et al.* [33] study the number of potential solutions of the *P3L* problem. These methods adopt the similar methodology. They introduce intermediate coordinate systems to make one of the constraints on the rotation matrix automatically satisfied. Two transformations are required by [3], and one transformation is needed by [2,33]. The simplified problem then can be solved by using the elementary linear algebra and the trigonometric identity. Our algorithm does not need such transformation, thus reduces the numerical error accumulation.

3 Notation and Geometrical Constraints

In this paper, we use italic, boldfaced lowercase and boldfaced uppercase letters to represent scalars, vectors and matrices, respectively. The aim of this paper is to calculate the rotation $\mathbf{R}$ and translation $\mathbf{t}$ between a world frame $O^wX^wY^wZ^w$ and a camera frame $O^cX^cY^cZ^c$ from the minimal configurations of 2D/3D point and line correspondences, including three point correspondences, two point and

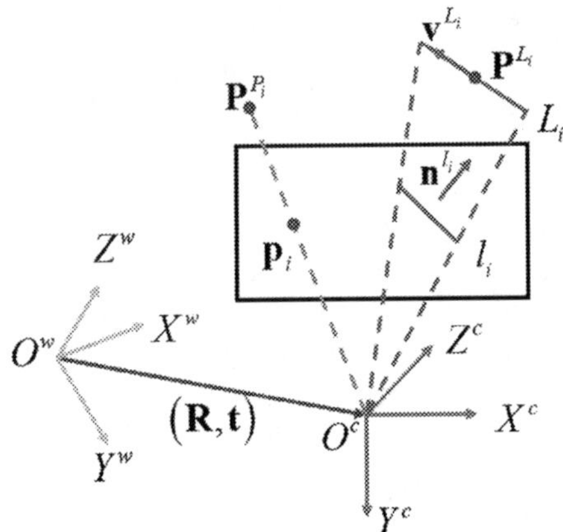

Fig. 1. Geometric constraints from one 2D/3D point correspondence and one 2D/3D line correspondence.

one line correspondences, one point and two line correspondences, and tree line correspondences. As mentioned above, determining the camera pose from three 2D/3D point correspondences and three 2D/3D line correspondences are known as the *P3P* and *P3L* problem, respectively. To simplify the notation, we call determining the camera pose from two point and one line correspondences as the Perspective-2-Point-and-1-Line (*P2P1L*) problem, and determining the pose from one point and two line correspondences as the Perspective-1-Point-and-2-Line (*P1P2L*) problem. This section describes the notation and geometrical constraints yielded by one 2D/3D point correspondence and one 2D/3D line correspondence, illustrated in Fig. 1.

3.1 2D/3D Point Correspondence

In this paper, we use a quaternion $\mathbf{q} = [w, x, y, z]^T$ [12] to represent the rotation matrix $\mathbf{R}$ as:

$$\mathbf{R} = \begin{bmatrix} w^2 + x^2 - y^2 - z^2 & 2xy - 2wz & 2wy + 2xz \\ 2wz + 2xy & w^2 - x^2 + y^2 - z^2 & 2yz - 2wx \\ 2xz - 2wy & 2wx + 2yz & w^2 - x^2 - y^2 + z^2 \end{bmatrix} \tag{1}$$

Let $\mathbf{P}^{P_i}$ denote a 3D point and $\mathbf{p}_i$ the back-projection ray of its image. To avoid extra transformation, we do not adopt the law of cosines widely used in the *P3P* problem [9]. As $\mathbf{p}_i$ is collinear with $\mathbf{P}^{P_i}$, we have:

$$\mathbf{p}_i \times \left(\mathbf{R}\mathbf{P}_i^P + \mathbf{t}\right) = \mathbf{0} \tag{2}$$

where $\times$ represents the cross product, which can be calculated as:

$$[\mathbf{p}_i]_\times \left(\mathbf{R}\mathbf{P}_i^P + \mathbf{t}\right) = \mathbf{0} \tag{3}$$

where $[\mathbf{p}_i]_\times$ is a skew-symmetric matrix having the form:

$$[\mathbf{p}_i]_\times = \begin{bmatrix} p_{i1} \\ p_{i2} \\ p_{i3} \end{bmatrix}_\times = \begin{bmatrix} 0 & -p_{i3} & p_{i2} \\ p_{i3} & 0 & -p_{i1} \\ -p_{i2} & p_{i1} & 0 \end{bmatrix} \tag{4}$$

Substituting (1) and (4) into (3), we have the following three quadric equations:

$$\begin{aligned} & c_{j,1}^{p_i} x^2 + c_{j,2}^{p_i} y^2 + c_{j,3}^{p_i} z^2 + c_{j,4}^{p_i} w^2 + c_{j,5}^{p_i} xy + c_{j,6}^{p_i} xz \\ & + c_{j,7}^{p_i} xw + c_{j,8}^{p_i} yz + c_{j,9}^{p_i} yw + c_{j,10}^{p_i} zw - p_{i3} t_2 + p_{i2} t_3 = 0, j = 1,2,3 \end{aligned} \tag{5}$$

where t_k $(k = 1, 2, 3)$ are the three components of $\mathbf{t}$. Define

$$\mathbf{r} = \left[x^2, y^2, z^2, w^2, xy, xz, xw, yz, yw, zw\right]^T \tag{6}$$

We can simplify the j-th equation of the i-th point correspondences in (5) as

$$\mathbf{c}_j^{p_i} \cdot \mathbf{r} + \mathbf{n}_j^{p_i} \cdot \mathbf{t} = 0, \quad j = 1, 2, 3 \tag{7}$$

where $\cdot$ represents the dot product, $\mathbf{c}_j^{p_i}$ is a 10×1 vector and $\mathbf{n}_j^{p_i}$ is a 3×1 vector. As $[\mathbf{p}_i]_\times$ is a rank-2 matrix, this equation system only provides 2 linear independent constraints.

3.2 2D/3D Line Correspondence

Let L_i and l_i represent a 3D line and its corresponding 2D line. Denote the direction of L_i as $\mathbf{v}^{L_i}$ and a 3D point on L_i as $\mathbf{P}^{L_i}$. The back-projection of l_i is a plane π_i that passes through the origin of the camera frame. Denote the normal of π_i as $\mathbf{n}^{l_i}$. Since L_i should be on π_i, we get the following constraints:

$$\begin{aligned} & \mathbf{n}^{l_i} \cdot \mathbf{R}\mathbf{v}^{L_i} = 0, \\ & \mathbf{n}^{l_i} \cdot \left(\mathbf{R}\mathbf{P}^{L_i} + \mathbf{t}\right) = 0 \end{aligned} \tag{8}$$

Substituting (1) into (8) and using the definition of (6), we obtain two quadrics:

$$\begin{aligned} & \mathbf{c}_1^{l_i} \cdot \mathbf{r} = 0, \\ & \mathbf{c}_2^{l_i} \cdot \mathbf{r} + \mathbf{n}^{l_i} \cdot \mathbf{t} = 0 \end{aligned} \tag{9}$$

4 Minimal Solution

4.1 P3P

We give a new approach for the *P3P* problem. As we seek to give a generic framework for all the minimal configurations of 2D/3D point and line correspondences, we avoid adopting the specific property of the *P3P* problem used by the previous works [9,14]. As mentioned above, each 2D/3D correspondence provides two constraints. Without loss of generality, we pick up the first two equations of (3) from the first two correspondences, and the first and the last equations from the third correspondence. According to (7), we have the following quadratic equation system:

$$\begin{aligned} \mathbf{c}_1^{p_1} \cdot \mathbf{r} + \mathbf{n}_1^{p_1} \cdot \mathbf{t} = \mathbf{c}_1^{p_2} \cdot \mathbf{r} + \mathbf{n}_1^{p_2} \cdot \mathbf{t} = \mathbf{c}_1^{p_3} \cdot \mathbf{r} + \mathbf{n}_1^{p_3} \cdot \mathbf{t} = 0 \\ \mathbf{c}_2^{p_1} \cdot \mathbf{r} + \mathbf{n}_2^{p_1} \cdot \mathbf{t} = \mathbf{c}_2^{p_2} \cdot \mathbf{r} + \mathbf{n}_2^{p_2} \cdot \mathbf{t} = \mathbf{c}_3^{p_3} \cdot \mathbf{r} + \mathbf{n}_3^{p_3} \cdot \mathbf{t} = 0 \end{aligned} \tag{10}$$

Divide this equation system into two parts, so that the first part contains the first 3 equations and the second part contains the remaining ones. Then we have:

$$\begin{aligned} &\mathbf{C}_1\mathbf{r} + \mathbf{N}_1\mathbf{t} = \mathbf{0}, \quad \mathbf{C}_2\mathbf{r} + \mathbf{N}_2\mathbf{t} = \mathbf{0} \\ &\mathbf{C}_1 = \left[\mathbf{c}_1^{p_1}, \mathbf{c}_1^{p_2}, \mathbf{c}_1^{p_3}\right]^T, \ \mathbf{N}_1 = \left[\mathbf{n}_1^{p_1}, \mathbf{n}_1^{p_2}, \mathbf{n}_1^{p_3}\right]^T \\ &\mathbf{C}_2 = \left[\mathbf{c}_2^{p_1}, \mathbf{c}_2^{p_2}, \mathbf{c}_3^{p_3}\right]^T, \ \mathbf{N}_2 = \left[\mathbf{n}_2^{p_1}, \mathbf{n}_2^{p_2}, \mathbf{n}_3^{p_3}\right]^T \end{aligned} \tag{11}$$

where $\mathbf{C}_1$ and $\mathbf{C}_2$ are 3×10 matrices, $\mathbf{N}_1$ and $\mathbf{N}_2$ are 3×3 matrices. Using $\mathbf{C}_2\mathbf{r} + \mathbf{N}_2\mathbf{t} = \mathbf{0}$ in (11), we get a closed-form solution for $\mathbf{t}$ as

$$\mathbf{t} = -(\mathbf{N}_2)^{-1}\mathbf{C}_2\mathbf{r} \tag{12}$$

Other choices are also valid, if the coefficient matrix of $\mathbf{t}$ is invertible. Replace $\mathbf{t}$ in $\mathbf{C}_1\mathbf{r} + \mathbf{N}_1\mathbf{t} = \mathbf{0}$ in (11). Together with the norm one constraint of $\mathbf{q}$, we get four quadratic equations for the four elements in $\mathbf{q}$ as:

$$\begin{aligned} &\mathbf{A}\mathbf{r} = 0 \\ &w^2 + x^2 + y^2 + z^2 = 1 \end{aligned} \tag{13}$$

where

$$\mathbf{A} = \mathbf{C}_1 - \mathbf{N}_1(\mathbf{N}_2)^{-1}\mathbf{C}_2 \tag{14}$$

We will show that the other three minimal cases also have the same quadric forms of $\mathbf{q}$. Therefore, we will give the solution to it at the end of this section.

4.2 P2P1L

For the two 2D/3D point correspondences, we chose the first two equations of (7). Together with constraints in (9) from the line correspondence, we can obtain the following equation system:

$$\begin{aligned} \mathbf{c}_1^{l_1} \cdot \mathbf{r} = \mathbf{c}_1^{p_1} \cdot \mathbf{r} + \mathbf{n}_1^{p_1} \cdot \mathbf{t} = \mathbf{c}_1^{p_2} \cdot \mathbf{r} + \mathbf{n}_1^{p_2} \cdot \mathbf{t} = 0 \\ \mathbf{c}_2^{l_1} \cdot \mathbf{r} + \mathbf{n}^{l_1} \cdot \mathbf{t} = \mathbf{c}_2^{p_1} \cdot \mathbf{r} + \mathbf{n}_2^{p_1} \cdot \mathbf{t} = \mathbf{c}_2^{p_2} \cdot \mathbf{r} + \mathbf{n}_2^{p_2} \cdot \mathbf{t} = 0 \end{aligned} \tag{15}$$

There are 5 equations in $\mathbf{t}$. Without loss of generality, we choose one equation involving $\mathbf{t}$ from each correspondence to solve $\mathbf{t}$. To simplify the notation, we use the same notation as (11). Rearranging (15), we have

$$\begin{aligned} &\mathbf{c}_1^{l_1} \cdot \mathbf{r} = 0, \quad \mathbf{C}_1\mathbf{r} + \mathbf{N}_1\mathbf{t} = 0, \quad \mathbf{C}_2\mathbf{r} + \mathbf{N}_2\mathbf{t} = 0 \\ &\mathbf{C}_1 = \left[\mathbf{c}_1^{p_1}, \mathbf{c}_1^{p_2}\right]^T, \ \mathbf{N}_1 = \left[\mathbf{n}_1^{p_1}, \mathbf{n}_1^{p_2}\right]^T \\ &\mathbf{C}_2 = \left[\mathbf{c}_2^{l_1}, \mathbf{c}_2^{p_1}, \mathbf{c}_2^{p_2}\right]^T, \ \mathbf{N}_2 = \left[\mathbf{n}^{l_1}, \mathbf{n}_2^{p_1}, \mathbf{n}_2^{p_2}\right]^T \end{aligned} \tag{16}$$

where $\mathbf{C}_1$ is a 2×10 matrix, and $\mathbf{N}_1$ is a 2×3 matrix. Using $\mathbf{C}_2\mathbf{r}+\mathbf{N}_2\mathbf{t}=\mathbf{0}$, we can obtain a closed-form solution for $\mathbf{t}$ as (12). Substituting the expression of $\mathbf{t}$ into $\mathbf{C}_1\mathbf{r}+\mathbf{N}_1\mathbf{t}=\mathbf{0}$, we get a quadric equation system as (13), with

$$\mathbf{A}=\left[\mathbf{c}_1^{l_1},\left(\mathbf{C}_1-\mathbf{N}_1(\mathbf{N}_2)^{-1}\mathbf{C}_2\right)^T\right]^T \tag{17}$$

4.3 P1P2L

Given one 2D/3D point and two 2D/3D line correspondences, according to (7) and (9), we can have the following equations:

$$\begin{aligned}&\mathbf{c}_1^{l_1}\cdot\mathbf{r}=\mathbf{c}_1^{l_2}\cdot\mathbf{r}=\mathbf{c}_1^{p_1}\cdot\mathbf{r}+\mathbf{n}_1^{p_1}\cdot\mathbf{t}=0\\&\mathbf{c}_2^{l_1}\cdot\mathbf{r}+\mathbf{n}^{l_1}\cdot\mathbf{t}=\mathbf{c}_2^{l_2}\cdot\mathbf{r}+\mathbf{n}^{l_2}\cdot\mathbf{t}=\mathbf{c}_2^{p_1}\cdot\mathbf{r}+\mathbf{n}_2^{p_1}\cdot\mathbf{t}=0\end{aligned} \tag{18}$$

Here we use the first two equations of (7). Other choices are also valid. Each line correspondence provides one constraint on $\mathbf{t}$. Together with another constraint from the point correspondence, we can obtain three linear equations with respect to $\mathbf{t}$. Rearranging the equations, we can have:

$$\begin{aligned}&\mathbf{c}_1^{l_1}\cdot\mathbf{r}=\mathbf{c}_1^{l_2}\cdot\mathbf{r}=\mathbf{c}_1^{p_1}\cdot\mathbf{r}+\mathbf{n}_1^{p_1}\cdot\mathbf{t}=0\\&\mathbf{C}_2\mathbf{r}+\mathbf{N}_2\mathbf{t}=0\\&\mathbf{C}_2=\left[\mathbf{c}_2^{l_1},\mathbf{c}_2^{l_2},\mathbf{c}_2^{p_1}\right]^T,\ \mathbf{N}_2=\left[\mathbf{n}^{l_1},\mathbf{n}^{l_2},\mathbf{n}_2^{p_1}\right]^T\end{aligned} \tag{19}$$

Using (12), we can get $\mathbf{t}$. Substituting (12) into $\mathbf{c}_1^{p_1}\cdot\mathbf{r}+\mathbf{n}_1^{p_1}\cdot\mathbf{t}=0$, we can get a quadratic equation system the same as (13) with

$$\mathbf{A}=\left[\mathbf{c}_1^{l_1},\mathbf{c}_1^{l_2},\mathbf{c}_1^{p_1}-\left((\mathbf{N}_2)^{-1}\mathbf{C}_2\right)^T\mathbf{n}_1^{p_1}\right]^T \tag{20}$$

4.4 P3L

Given three line correspondences, we can have the following quadratic equation system according to (9):

$$\begin{aligned}&\mathbf{c}_1^{l_1}\cdot\mathbf{r}=\mathbf{c}_1^{l_2}\cdot\mathbf{r}=\mathbf{c}_1^{l_3}\cdot\mathbf{r}=0\\&\mathbf{c}_2^{l_1}\cdot\mathbf{r}+\mathbf{n}^{l_1}\cdot\mathbf{t}=\mathbf{c}_2^{l_2}\cdot\mathbf{r}+\mathbf{n}^{l_2}\cdot\mathbf{t}=\mathbf{c}_2^{l_3}\cdot\mathbf{r}+\mathbf{n}^{l_3}\cdot\mathbf{t}=0\end{aligned} \tag{21}$$

It is clear that the first three quadrics only involving the quaternion $\mathbf{q}$. Combining with the norm one constraint of $\mathbf{q}$, we have a form the same as (13) with

$$\mathbf{A}=\left[\mathbf{c}_1^{l_1},\mathbf{c}_1^{l_2},\mathbf{c}_1^{l_3}\right]^T \tag{22}$$

Besides, $\mathbf{t}$ can be computed from the last three equations of (21) using (12) with

$$\mathbf{C}_2=\left[\mathbf{c}_2^{l_1},\mathbf{c}_2^{l_2},\mathbf{c}_2^{l_3}\right]^T,\ \mathbf{N}_2=\left[\mathbf{n}^{l_1},\mathbf{n}^{l_2},\mathbf{n}^{l_3}\right]^T \tag{23}$$

4.5 Solve the Rotation Matrix

As mentioned above, in all of the four minimal configurations, $\mathbf{R}$ can be obtained by solving a quadratic equation system with the form (13). It seems that there are 16 solutions according to the Bézout's Theorem [19]. However, as (1) only includes degree 2 monomials, signs of unknowns do not impact on the value of $\mathbf{R}$. Thus, there are at most 8 real solutions for $\mathbf{R}$. In this section, we show how to solve this quadratic equation system. Assume w is not 0. Let us define

$$x = aw, \quad y = bw, \quad z = cw \tag{24}$$

Divide both side of $\mathbf{Ar} = \mathbf{0}$ in (13) by w. We can have

$$\mathbf{a}_i \left[a^2, b^2, c^2, ab, ac, bc, a, b, c, 1\right]^T = 0, \quad i = 1, 2, 3 \tag{25}$$

where $\mathbf{a}_i$ is the i-th row of $\mathbf{A}$. It is easy to find that $[a, b, c]^T$ is the intersection of three quadrics. This can be solved by the E3Q3 algorithm [17].

For completeness, we briefly introduce the E3Q3 algorithm. By regarding a as a constant, we get three equations about b and c. Dividing the six monomials of b and c into two parts, *i.e.*, $\{b^2, c^2, bc\}$ and $\{b, c, 1\}$, we can obtain:

$$\mathbf{H} \begin{bmatrix} b^2 \\ c^2 \\ bc \end{bmatrix} = \begin{bmatrix} p_{11}(x), p_{12}(x), p_{13}(x) \\ p_{21}(x), p_{22}(x), p_{23}(x) \\ p_{31}(x), p_{32}(x), p_{33}(x) \end{bmatrix} \begin{bmatrix} b \\ c \\ 1 \end{bmatrix} \tag{26}$$

Assume $\mathbf{H}$ is invertible. Multiplying $\mathbf{H}^{-1}$ to both side of (26), we get the relationship between $\{b^2, c^2, bc\}$ and $\{b, c, 1\}$. Using this relationship and the identities $(b^2)c = (bc)b$, $(bc)c = (c^2)b$, and $(bc)(bc) = (b^2)(c^2)$, we can get a homogeneous linear system whose coefficients $\mathbf{M}(a)$ are polynomials in a. According to the linear algebra, the homogeneous linear system has a non-trivial solution, if and only if the determinant of $\mathbf{M}(a)$ is zero. This results in a degree 8 polynomial in a. Solve this for a, then back-substitute a into the linear system to get b and c.

Given a, b and c, w^2 can be obtained from the norm one constraint of the quaternion by $w^2 = 1/\left(a^2 + b^2 + c^2 + 1\right)$. Substituting (24) into (1) and using w^2, we can easily obtain $\mathbf{R}$. There are two assumptions for computing $\mathbf{R}$. The first is $\mathbf{H}$ is invertible, and the second is w is not zero. Therefore, singularity occurs when the assumptions do not satisfy. We address both singularities in the following two sections.

Robust E3Q3 (RE3Q3). Kukelova *et al.* [17] find that there are 8 degenerate configurations when $\mathbf{H}$ is rank deficient, and they give the solution for each of them. However, this method is hard to handle the situation when $\mathbf{H}$ approximates singularity, which will significantly degrade the performance of the algorithm as shown in Fig. 2a.

As we can treat any of a, b and c as a constant, and the other two as unknowns in (25), there actually exist three choices for $\mathbf{H}$. Let $\mathbf{H}_a$, $\mathbf{H}_b$ and $\mathbf{H}_c$ represent the coefficient matrices obtained by choosing a, b and c as a constant, respectively. If the coefficient matrix of the second order monomials in (25) is nondegenerate, it is probable that when $\mathbf{H}_a$ is ill-conditioned, but $\mathbf{H}_b$ or $\mathbf{H}_c$ is still in good condition. We try to find the one with the best condition. As the condition number of a matrix describes to what extent a matrix approaches singularity. The larger the condition number is, the closer the matrix approaches singularity. We calculate the condition number of $\mathbf{H}_a$, $\mathbf{H}_b$ and $\mathbf{H}_c$, and choose the one with the minimal condition number to replace $\mathbf{H}$ in (25). This just needs to interchange the coefficient of (25), and do not need to implement different algorithm for different choice. Thus, it is efficient. We call this approach Robust E3Q3 (RE3Q3). Figure 2a shows that RE3Q3 is much more stable than the original E3Q3 algorithm [17] in the degenerate configuration. Besides, in the general situation, RE3Q3 still improves the stability of E3Q3, as shown in Fig. 2b.

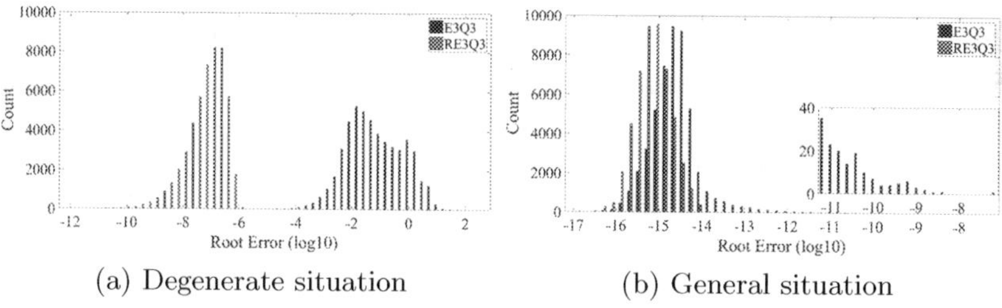

Fig. 2. Compare RE3Q3 with E3Q3 in degenerate situation (a) and in general situation (b). We randomly generate the coefficients of (25) except for the constants. Then we randomly generate a solution, and substitute it into (25) to calculate the constants. For the degenerate cases, we get $\mathbf{H}$ in (26) and randomly set the smallest singular value within $(0, 10^{-6})$. We run the algorithm 50,000 times.

Reference Rotation. When w in $\mathbf{q}$ is small, according to (24), a, b and c are probably greater than 1. Thus, they may amplify the estimation error of w when we compute x, y and z. This effect increases, when w gets smaller. The performance of our algorithm will degrade if w is a very tiny value, as shown in Fig. 3, where $w \in (0, 10^{-6})$. If we have a reference rotation represented as a quaternion $\mathbf{q}_{ref}$, which gives a rough estimation of the rotation, we can easily solve this problem. Given a $\mathbf{q}_{ref}$, we can exchange w with the element that has the maximum absolute value in $\mathbf{q}_{ref}$ to get $\mathbf{q}'$. This makes a, b and c all smaller than 1. Exchanging the element of $\mathbf{q}'$ equals to permute the coefficients in (25), and the computational cost is negligible. When $\mathbf{q}'$ is calculated, we can get the original $\mathbf{q}$ by applying the exchange again.

In the application, we can generally have a $\mathbf{q}_{ref}$. For example, in the SLAM system, camera pose is sequentially estimated. Therefore, the last rotation can be used as the reference rotation. In addition, the minimal solution is generally used in the RANSAC algorithm [5], the current optimal rotation estimation can be a reference rotation. One question is that whether our algorithm can generate a valid reference matrix in the degenerate configuration. To verify this,

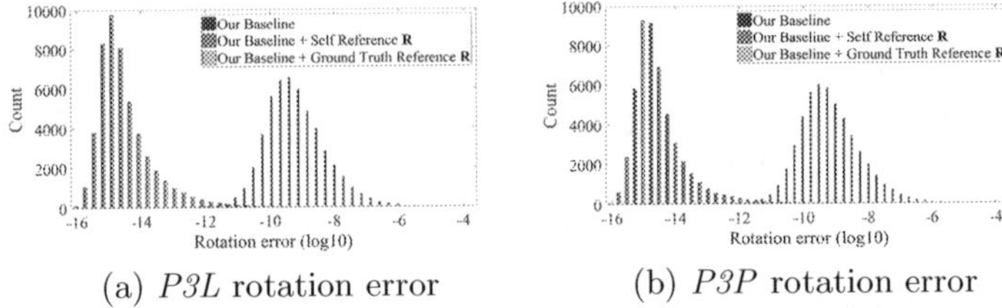

(a) *P3L* rotation error

(b) *P3P* rotation error

Fig. 3. Rotation error for *P3L* and *P3P* when $w \in (0, 10^{-6})$, which is degenerate for the baseline algorithm. We generate 3 extra points to find the most accurate rotation $\mathbf{R}_{self}$. Then we use $\mathbf{R}_{self}$ as a reference rotation to calculate the rotation again (labeled as Self Reference $\mathbf{R}$). We run the algorithm 50,000 times. This method gives almost the same result as using the ground truth as the reference matrix. It is clear that our algorithm can provide valid reference rotation even in the degenerate situation.

we run our *P3L* and *P3P* algorithm on 50,000 randomly generated degenerate configurations where $w \in (0, 10^{-6})$. Three additional points are generated to select the most accurate rotation, denoted as $\mathbf{R}_{self}$. $\mathbf{R}_{self}$ is then used as the reference rotation. We also use the ground truth rotation $\mathbf{R}_{gt}$ as the reference rotation. The experimental results in Fig. 3 show that $\mathbf{R}_{self}$ and $\mathbf{R}_{gt}$ gives almost the small results. As we only use the relative order of $\mathbf{q}_{ref}$, $\mathbf{q}_{ref}$ can be rather rough. This makes our algorithm stable even in the degenerate case.

4.6 Algorithm Summary

As mentioned above, the rotation matrix $\mathbf{R}$ of all the four minimal configurations can be obtained by solving a quadric equation system having the form of (13). Given $\mathbf{R}$, the translation $\mathbf{t}$ can be calculated from a linear system (12). One 2D/3D point correspondence gives three equations in (3). We use one of them for $\mathbf{R}$ estimation. Given $\mathbf{R}$, we use the remaining 2 equations for the estimation of $\mathbf{t}$. Our algorithm is summarized in Algorithm 1.

Algorithm 1. Solve the minimal problems of 2D/3D point and line correspondences

---

1. Calculate the coefficient matrix $\mathbf{A}$ of the quadric equations, *i.e.*, using (14) for *P3P*, (17) for *P2P1L*, (20) for *P1P2L*, (22) for *P3L*.
2. If $\mathbf{q}_{ref}$ is available, find the max absolute element in $\mathbf{q}_{ref}$. Exchange it with w, and rearrange the coefficients accordingly.
3. Solve (25) by the RE3Q3 algorithm. If $\mathbf{q}_{ref}$ is used, rearrange the solution accordingly.
4. Use the norm one constraint of the quaternion and the definition (1) to get $\mathbf{R}$.
5. Solve $\mathbf{t}$ from the linear system including all the remaining constraints on $\mathbf{t}$.

---

5 Simulation Results

As the previous works [2,3,6,9,14,15,28], we compare our algorithm with the state-of-the-art algorithms by simulations. We can evaluate the algorithms by a large number of configurations in the simulation. As the same input will generate the same result, the simulation results will unfold the performance of different algorithms in real applications.

Given the estimation $(\hat{\mathbf{R}}, \hat{\mathbf{t}})$ and the ground truth $(\mathbf{R}_{gt}, \mathbf{t}_{gt})$, the estimation error of $\hat{\mathbf{R}}$ is measured by the absolute angle of the axis-angle representation of $\hat{\mathbf{R}}\mathbf{R}_{gt}^{-1}$ as [17], and the estimation error of $\hat{\mathbf{t}}$ is measured by $\left\|\hat{\mathbf{t}} - \mathbf{t}_{gt}\right\|_2 / \left\|\mathbf{t}_{gt}\right\|_2$. We randomly generate the rotation matrix by Euler angle. The position of the camera is within a cube $[-5, 5]^3$. The camera has resolution 640×480 and focal length 800. A line is generated by two random points. The depth of the 3D point is within $[2, 8]$. We also study the behavior of our algorithm with or without a reference rotation. As shown in Fig. 3, the rotation matrix calculated by our algorithm is as valid as the ground truth. Thus, we use the ground truth rotation matrix as the reference. Our algorithm without a reference rotation is labeled as the baseline. The following results are obtained from 50,000 trials. Table 1 lists the mean, standard deviation, median, and maximal estimation errors. It shows that our baseline algorithm is comparable to the state-of-the-art *P3P* algorithm [14], and outperforms the previous algorithms of the other three problems. Besides, a reference rotation can further increase the performance.

5.1 Results of P3P Problem

We compare our algorithm with Ke's algorithm [14], Kneip's algorithm [15] and Gao's algorithm [6]. For fairness, we do not apply root polishing for Ke's algorithm. As all of these algorithms have publicly available c++ implementation, we also implement our algorithm in c++. We use Hartley's Sturm sequences [10] implementation to solve the eighth degree polynomial equation. The relative error is set to 10^{-14} as [17].

The histograms of rotation and translation errors are shown in Fig. 4. Table 1 lists the quantitative results of different algorithms. It is clear that the reference rotation can increase the stability of our algorithm. Ke's algorithm is better than our algorithm in rotation. Our algorithm gives better results in translation, as we use more equations for the translation estimation, and solve it in the least-squares manner. Our algorithm outperforms other *P3P* algorithms. This is because both Ke's algorithm and our algorithm avoid the unnecessary intermediate transformation, therefore reduce the numerical error accumulation.

5.2 Results of P2P1L and P1P2L Problem

We compare our algorithm with Ramalingam's algorithm [28] for the *P2P1L* and *P1P2L* problems. The error histograms are shown in Figs. 5 and 6. Table 1 gives the statistics of the estimation error. It is obvious that our algorithm

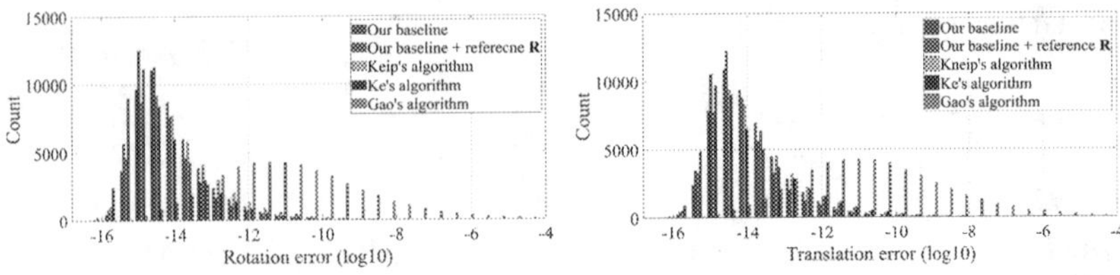

Fig. 4. Histograms of rotation **R** (left) and **t** (right) errors for *P3P* algorithms.

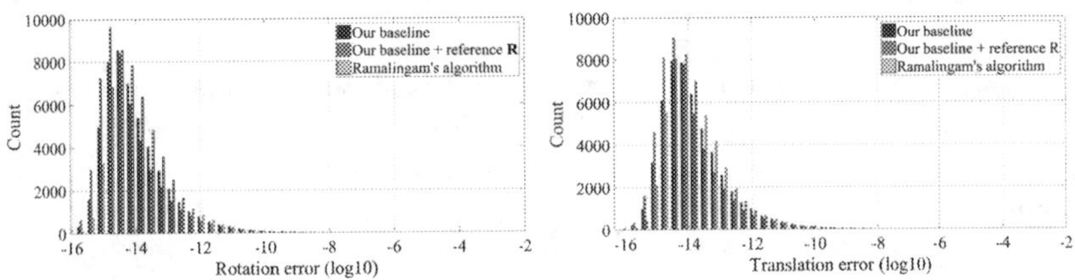

Fig. 5. Histograms of **R** (left) and **t** (right) errors for different *P2P1L* algorithms.

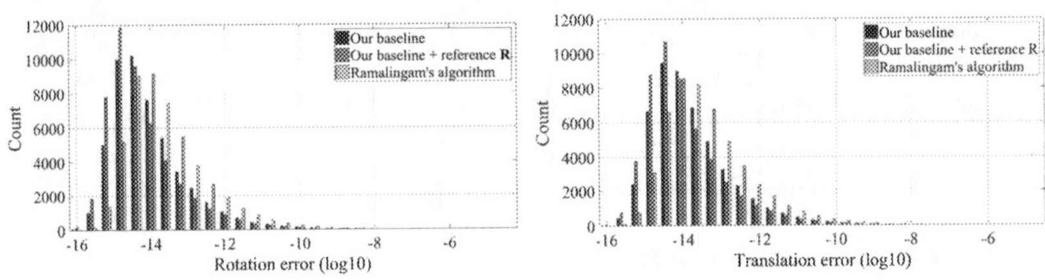

Fig. 6. Histograms of **R** (left) and **t** (right) errors for *P1P2L* algorithms.

outperforms Ramalingam's algorithm in terms of accuracy. Ramalingam's algorithm requires two intermediate transformations. Numerical errors accumulated in these transformations potentially decrease the accuracy. Besides, their transformations involve tangent function, which may case numerical issue.

5.3 Results of P3L Problem

As mentioned in the Sect. 2, The *P3L* algorithms [2,3,33] are similar. We compare our algorithm with the latest *P3L* algorithm [33]. Figure 7 shows the results of different algorithms. In the area of very small rotation error (the first two bins in Fig. 7a), Xu's algorithm has a higher probability than our algorithm. However, as shown by the sub-windows in Fig. 7, Xu's algorithm has a very long tail. Besides, the statistics listed in Table 1 also verify that our algorithm is more stable than Xu's algorithm. The maximal rotation and translation errors of Xu's algorithm approximate 0.1 rad and 0.8, respectively. Our maximal rotation and translation errors are much smaller than theirs.

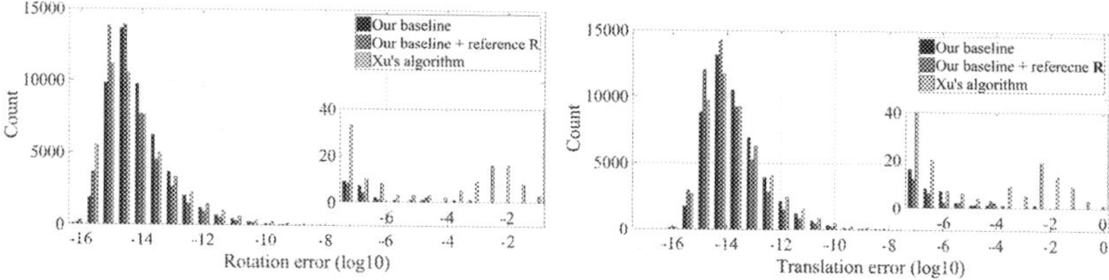

Fig. 7. Histograms of **R** (left) and **t** (right) errors for *P3L* algorithms.

Table 1. Mean, standard deviation (STD), median, and max of the pose errors. The best result is highlighted by the boldface.

	Algorithm	Rotation				Translation			
		Mean	STD	Median	Max	Mean	STD	Median	Max
P3P	Our baseline	1.2e−09	2.1e−07	5.4e−15	4.6e−05	1.2e−09	2.0e−07	7.4e−15	4.4e−05
	Baseline+ref. **R**	6.6e−10	6.9e−08	3.2e−15	1.3e−05	**1.2e−09**	**1.6e−07**	**4.5e−15**	**3.4e−05**
	Kneip	1.6e−08	3.2e−06	6.3e−15	7.1e−04	2.2e−08	4.3e−06	8.3e−15	9.5e−04
	Ke	**1.4e−10**	**2.0e−08**	**2.5e−15**	**4.4e−06**	7.9e−09	1.1e−06	5.5e−15	1.7e−04
	Gao	1.9e−04	1.8e−02	7.7e−12	2.7	4.1e−04	3.4e−02	1.5e−11	5.4
P2P1L	Our baseline	2.2e−08	4.3e−06	5.5e−15	9.5e−04	3.0e−08	6.0e−06	9.0e−15	1.3e−03
	Baseline+ref. **R**	**7.9e−09**	**1.2e−06**	**3.3e−15**	**2.6e−04**	**9.0e−09**	**1.4e−06**	**5.6e−15**	**3.1e−04**
	Ramalingam	1.6e−07	3.4e−05	7.8e−15	7.6e−03	8.7e−08	1.9e−05	1.1e−14	4.2e−03
P1P2L	Our baseline	9.1e−10	1.2e−07	5.6e−15	2.6e−05	1.2e−09	1.3e−07	1.0e−14	2.6e−05
	Baseline+ref. **R**	**3.0e−10**	**2.9e−08**	**3.3e−15**	**5.2e−06**	**4.3e−10**	**4.7e−08**	**6.1e−15**	**9.5e−06**
	Ramalingam	1.9e−09	1.9e−07	1.6e−14	3.6e−05	2.3e−09	2.1e−07	2.6e−14	3.1e−05
P3L	Our baseline	2.0e−08	3.6e−06	4.6e−15	8.0e−04	6.6e−08	1.4e−05	1.3e−14	3.1e−03
	Baseline+ref. **R**	**6.6e−10**	**7.8e−08**	**2.5e−15**	**1.2e−05**	**3.0e−09**	**3.5e−07**	**6.9e−15**	**5.1e−05**
	Xu	1.1e−05	6.6e−04	3.4e−15	9.1e−02	3.9e−05	3.8e−03	1.2e−14	8.0e−01

5.4 Computational Time

Our algorithm is implemented in C++ using Eigen linear algebra library [8] for the *P3P* problem. We use the OpenCV's [24] implementation of Ke's algorithm [14]. For the other minimal problems, we compare the time using the Matlab implementations. Here, we only list our running time with reference rotation, as the running of our baseline algorithm is very similar to our algorithm with reference rotation. As all the four minimal problems are solved in a uniform framework, the computational time of the other three cases in c++ should be similar to the time of the *P3P* problem. In the application, we can use the reference rotation to reduce the computational time of the translation. For fairness, we compute all the eight solutions of translation here. All the results are obtained by 50,000 trials on a laptop with a 2.9 GHZ intel core i7 CPU.

Table 2 gives the results. Compared to E3Q3, RE3Q3 slightly increases the running time. It is not surprising that our algorithm is slower that Ke's algorithm [14], as we need to solve an eighth degree equation for the rotation and eight linear equation systems for the translation, but they only need to solve a quartic equation for the rotation and four linear systems for the translation. For the *P3L* problem, Xu's algorithm [33] is slightly faster than ours. This is

Table 2. Computational time comparison. RE3Q3, E3Q3, and *P3P* algorithms are tested by c++. Others are tested by Matlab.

	Algorithm	Time (μs)
Solver	RE3Q3	11
	E3Q3	8.3
P3P	Our baseline + reference **R**	21
	Ke's algorithm	3.1
P2P1L	Our baseline + reference **R**	290
	Ramalingam's algorithm	429
P1P2L	Our baseline + reference **R**	279
	Ramalingam's algorithm	439
P3L	Our baseline + reference **R**	261
	Xu's algorithm	202

because they use a transformation to directly eliminate one of the rotation variable. Ramalingam's algorithm [28] is slower than our algorithm. This is because their algorithm needs to compute SVD of a 6×8 matrix for the *P2P1L* problem, and 6×9 matrix for the *P1P2L* problem. The SVD is time-consuming. Although our algorithm is slower than Ke's algorithm, it is still efficient for a real-time application. Minimal solution is generally used in the RANSAC algorithm [5]. Suppose the ratio of the outlier is 0.5. To ensure with a probability, such as 0.99, that at least one of the random minimal samples is without outliers, we need at least 35 trials [11]. This will be finished within 0.8 ms.

6 Conclusion

In this paper, we propose an algebraic algorithm for the four minimal configurations of 2D/3D point and line correspondences. This is useful for many robotics and computer vision applications. Our algorithm directly uses the collinearity and coplanarity constraints to construct the equation system, and does not need any intermediate transformation. This can avoid numerical error accumulation. We increase the stability of our algorithm by a reference matrix which is generally available in real applications. We present the RE3Q3 algorithm which significantly increases the stability of the E3Q3 algorithm [17]. The simulation results show that our baseline algorithm is comparable to the state-of-the-art *P3P* algorithm [14], and outperforms the stat-of-the-art algorithms of the other three minimal cases. A reference rotation matrix, which is generally available in the SLAM or VO system, can further increase the numerical stability of our algorithm. Additionally, our algorithm is efficient for real-time applications.

References

1. Arun, K.S., Huang, T.S., Blostein, S.D.: Least-squares fitting of two 3-D point sets. IEEE Trans. Pattern Anal. Mach. Intell. **5**, 698–700 (1987)
2. Chen, H.H.: Pose determination from line-to-plane correspondences: existence condition and closed-form solutions. IEEE Trans. Pattern Anal. Mach. Intell. **13**(6), 530–541 (1991). https://doi.org/10.1109/34.87340
3. Dhome, M., Richetin, M., Lapreste, J.T., Rives, G.: Determination of the attitude of 3D objects from a single perspective view. IEEE Trans. Pattern Anal. Mach. Intell. **11**(12), 1265–1278 (1989). https://doi.org/10.1109/34.41365
4. Finsterwalder, S., Scheufele, W.: Das rückwärtseinschneiden im raum. Verlag d. Bayer. Akad. d. Wiss. (1903)
5. Fischler, M.A., Bolles, R.C.: Random sample consensus: a paradigm for model fitting with applications to image analysis and automated cartography. Commun. ACM **24**(6), 381–395 (1981)
6. Gao, X.S., Hou, X.R., Tang, J., Cheng, H.F.: Complete solution classification for the perspective-three-point problem. IEEE Trans. Pattern Anal. Mach. Intell. **25**(8), 930–943 (2003)
7. Grunert, J.A.: Das pothenotische problem in erweiterter gestalt nebst über seine anwendungen in der geodäsie. Grunerts archiv für mathematik und physik **1**(238–248), 1 (1841)
8. Guennebaud, G., Jacob, B., et al.: Eigen v3 (2010). http://eigen.tuxfamily.org
9. Haralick, B.M., Lee, C.N., Ottenberg, K., Nölle, M.: Review and analysis of solutions of the three point perspective pose estimation problem. Int. J. Comput. Vis. **13**(3), 331–356 (1994)
10. Hartley, R., Li, H.: An efficient hidden variable approach to minimal-case camera motion estimation. IEEE Trans. Pattern Anal. Mach. Intell. **34**(12), 2303–2314 (2012)
11. Hartley, R., Zisserman, A.: Multiple View Geometry in Computer Vision. Cambridge University Press, Cambridge (2003)
12. Horn, B.K.: Closed-form solution of absolute orientation using unit quaternions. JOSA A **4**(4), 629–642 (1987)
13. Jose Tarrio, J., Pedre, S.: Realtime edge-based visual odometry for a monocular camera. In: Proceedings of the IEEE International Conference on Computer Vision, pp. 702–710 (2015)
14. Ke, T., Roumeliotis, S.I.: An efficient algebraic solution to the perspective-three-point problem. In: 2017 IEEE Conference on Computer Vision and Pattern Recognition (CVPR), pp. 4618–4626, July 2017. https://doi.org/10.1109/CVPR.2017.491
15. Kneip, L., Scaramuzza, D., Siegwart, R.: A novel parametrization of the perspective-three-point problem for a direct computation of absolute camera position and orientation. In: 2011 IEEE Conference on Computer Vision and Pattern Recognition (CVPR), pp. 2969–2976. IEEE (2011)
16. Kuang, Y., Åström, K.: Pose estimation with unknown focal length using points, directions and lines. In: ICCV, pp. 529–536 (2013)
17. Kukelova, Z., Heller, J., Fitzgibbon, A.: Efficient intersection of three quadrics and applications in computer vision. In: Proceedings of the IEEE Conference on Computer Vision and Pattern Recognition, pp. 1799–1808 (2016)
18. Linnainmaa, S., Harwood, D., Davis, L.S.: Pose determination of a three-dimensional object using triangle pairs. IEEE Trans. Pattern Anal. Mach. Intell. **10**(5), 634–647 (1988)

19. Little, J.B., O'Shea, D.: Ideals, Varieties, and Algorithms: An Introduction to Computational Algebraic Geometry and Commutative Algebra. Springer, New York (2007). https://doi.org/10.1007/978-0-387-35651-8
20. Lu, Y., Song, D.: Robust RGB-D odometry using point and line features. In: Proceedings of the IEEE International Conference on Computer Vision, pp. 3934–3942 (2015)
21. Masselli, A., Zell, A.: A new geometric approach for faster solving the perspective-three-point problem. In: 2014 22nd International Conference on Pattern Recognition (ICPR), pp. 2119–2124. IEEE (2014)
22. Merritt, E.: Explicit three-point resection in space. Photogram. Eng. **15**(4), 649–655 (1949)
23. Mur-Artal, R., Montiel, J.M.M., Tardos, J.D.: ORB-SLAM: a versatile and accurate monocular slam system. IEEE Trans. Robot. **31**(5), 1147–1163 (2015)
24. OpenCV: Open source computer vision library (2017). https://github.com/itseez/opencv
25. Proença, P.F., Gao, Y.: SPLODE: Semi-probabilistic point and line odometry with depth estimation from RGB-D camera motion. arXiv preprint arXiv:1708.02837 (2017)
26. Pumarola, A., Vakhitov, A., Agudo, A., Sanfeliu, A., Moreno-Noguer, F.: PL-SLAM: real-time monocular visual SLAM with points and lines. In: 2017 IEEE International Conference on Robotics and Automation (ICRA), pp. 4503–4508. IEEE (2017)
27. Quan, L., Lan, Z.: Linear N-point camera pose determination. IEEE Trans. Pattern Anal. Mach. Intell. **21**(8), 774–780 (1999)
28. Ramalingam, S., Bouaziz, S., Sturm, P.: Pose estimation using both points and lines for geo-localization. In: 2011 IEEE International Conference on Robotics and Automation (ICRA), pp. 4716–4723. IEEE (2011)
29. Sola, J., Vidal-Calleja, T., Civera, J., Montiel, J.M.M.: Impact of landmark parametrization on monocular EKF-SLAM with points and lines. Int. J. Comput. Vis. **97**(3), 339–368 (2012)
30. Taylor, C.J., Kriegman, D.J.: Structure and motion from line segments in multiple images. IEEE Trans. Pattern Anal. Mach. Intell. **17**(11), 1021–1032 (1995)
31. Vakhitov, A., Funke, J., Moreno-Noguer, F.: Accurate and linear time pose estimation from points and lines. In: Leibe, B., Matas, J., Sebe, N., Welling, M. (eds.) ECCV 2016. LNCS, vol. 9911, pp. 583–599. Springer, Cham (2016). https://doi.org/10.1007/978-3-319-46478-7_36
32. Wu, W.: Basic principles of mechanical theorem proving in elementary geometries. In: Selected Works Of Wen-Tsun Wu, pp. 195–223. World Scientific (2008)
33. Xu, C., Zhang, L., Cheng, L., Koch, R.: Pose estimation from line correspondences: a complete analysis and a series of solutions. IEEE Trans. Pattern Anal. Mach. Intell. **39**(6), 1209–1222 (2017)
34. Yang, S., Scherer, S.: Direct monocular odometry using points and lines. arXiv preprint arXiv:1703.06380 (2017)
35. Zhou, F., Duh, H.B.L., Billinghurst, M.: Trends in augmented reality tracking, interaction and display: a review of ten years of ISMAR. In: Proceedings of the 7th IEEE/ACM International Symposium on Mixed and Augmented Reality, pp. 193–202. IEEE Computer Society (2008)

Symmetry-Aware Face Completion with Generative Adversarial Networks

Jiawan Zhang[1], Rui Zhan[1], Di Sun[2(✉)], and Gang Pan[1]

[1] Tianjin University, Tianjin, China
[2] Tianjin University of Science and Technology, Tianjin, China
dsun@tju.edu.cn

Abstract. Face completion is a challenging task in computer vision. Unlike general images, face images usually have strong semantic correlation and symmetry. Without taking these characteristics into account, existing face completion techniques usually fail to produce a photo-realistic result, especially for the missing key components (e.g., eyes and mouths). In this paper, we propose a symmetry-aware face completion method based on facial structural features using a deep generative model. The model is trained with a combination of a reconstruction loss, a structure loss, two adversarial losses and a symmetry loss, which ensures pixel faithfulness, local-global contents integrity and symmetrical consistency. We conduct a dedicated symmetry detection technique for facial components and show that the symmetrical attention module significantly improves face completion results. Experiments show that our method is capable of synthesizing semantically valid and visually plausible contents for the missing facial key parts from random mask. In addition, our model outperforms other methods for detail completion of facial components.

Keywords: Face completion · GAN · Symmetry · Image inpainting

1 Introduction

Face completion, also known as face inpainting, is an important topic in computer vision and image processing. It refers to the task of filling missing pixels or removing unwanted parts from a face image. It is often used in conjunction with face recognition [31–33] and face editing [4,24].

The core challenge of face completion lies in synthesizing visually realistic and semantically plausible pixels for the missing areas that are coherent with the existing contents in a face image. However, the semantics of facial components are related to each other and do not exist independently. This makes the face completion task significantly more difficult than general image inpainting or completion.

This work was supported by Tianjin Philosophy and Social Science Planning Program under grant TJSR15-008.

The original version of this chapter was revised: the address of the author Di Sun was incorrect. The correction to this chapter is available at https://doi.org/10.1007/978-3-030-20870-7_46

C. V. Jawahar et al. (Eds.): ACCV 2018, LNCS 11364, pp. 289–304, 2019.
https://doi.org/10.1007/978-3-030-20870-7_18

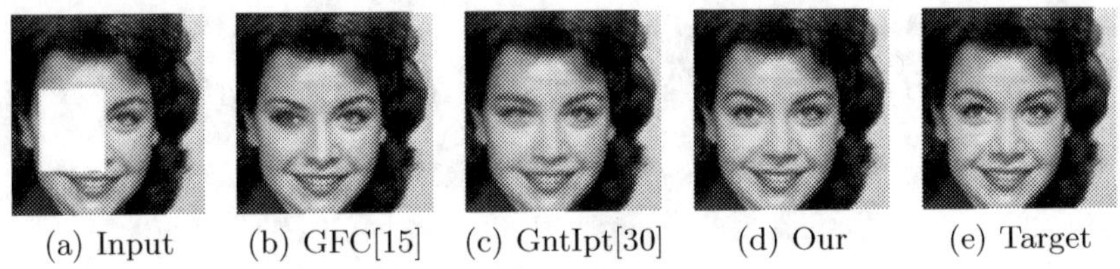

(a) Input (b) GFC[15] (c) GntIpt[30] (d) Our (e) Target

Fig. 1. From left to right: (a) input image with mask. (b) inpainted result of GFC [15]. (c) inpainted result of GntIpt [30]. (d) inpainted result of our method. (e) target image.

Early face completion methods [5,6,10,19,34] are mainly based on texture synthesis or patch matching. These approaches based on texture synthesis work well on images with small missing or meshed occlusion. But they are unsuitable for situations with large areas occlusion. Besides, the approaches based on patch matching often require a reference image or database to complete the repair, which makes it impossible to obtain better repair results when similar semantic patches are not found in the reference image or database. Recently, great progress has been made in deep learning, especially in generative adversarial networks (GANs) [9]. At the same time, learning-based face completion methods [7,11,15, 17,28,30] have also achieved remarkable results. These methods are suitable for images with small or large missing areas which may include individual semantic components.

However, the above methods mostly ignore the property of symmetry for the facial components. The symmetry does not only refer to the shape similarity between the symmetric components. It refers to the overall feature similarity which includes many factors, such as color, texture, shape, etc. Neglecting the symmetry of the face in face completion methods may cause great inconsistency in the completion result. For example, when half the face is occluded (see Fig. 1(a)), the symmetrical components, such as eyes, eyebrows and nose, are all missing a part. In this case, the existing generative face completion (GFC) method [15] can only maintain the shape feature of the semantic components but cannot guarantee the consistency of the texture and other details between symmetrical semantic components. As shown in Fig. 1(b), there is a great asymmetry between the completed left eye and the existing right eye. The generative image inpainting method with contextual attention (GntIpt) [30] can borrow or copy texture and color information from known background patches to generate the missing parts, but it cannot ensure the shape similarity of symmetrical components. In Fig. 1(c), it still causes a huge gap between eyes. Therefore, the consideration of the symmetry in face image is the key to achieve better face completion.

In this paper, we propose a symmetry-aware face completion method based on deep learning. We adopt a generative adversarial networks as our completion model. The input is a face image with a random mask. First, the encoder of the generator is utilized to extract the structural features of the input image, and then a decoder is employed to generate a completion result based on the structural features. To optimize the completion of the generator, we design three adversarial losses and a structure loss to regularize the training process. Among these, commonly used global adversarial loss and local adversarial loss [11] are adopted to constrain the global semantic integrity and local semantic consistency with surrounding pixels of the completion result. The symmetry adversarial loss is posed to constrain the symmetry of the completion result and the structure loss is used to guide the generation of completion image. By adopting the above mechanism, the proposed model can not only repair large missing area, but also can well maintain the symmetry of facial components, as shown in Fig. 1(d).

To summarize, our contributions are as follows: (1) We propose a deep generative face completion model. A U-Net network is utilized to generate the completion result and three additional networks are adopted to optimize the completion model. (2) Considering the symmetry characteristics of human face, we introduce a strategy for symmetrical components detection of face images. (3) We design a new loss function, of which a symmetry loss is added to constrain the symmetry and consistency between symmetrical facial components, and a structure loss is adopted to guide the structure generation of the completion result.

2 Related Work

A variety of different approaches have been proposed for the image completion task. Traditionally, image completion mainly uses diffusion-based or patch-based methods. Diffusion-based inpainting [3,8] uses smoothness priors via parametric models or partial differential equations (PDEs) to propagate the low-level features around the target holes to the interior of the hole. It can be naturally applied to small regions inpainting, but are not suitable for large missing areas cases. Patch-based methods [2,10,34] differ from the diffusion-based methods, they repair the missing regions by searching similar patches from the background or image database. Since the patch-based methods require external patch to fill in the unknown regions, it fails if similar patches do not exist in the surrounding region or database.

Recently, with the rapid development of deep learning, many learning-based approaches [14,16,22,26] have emerged and produced remarkable achievements. At first, learning-based methods can only work on small and thin damage. Later, Goodfellow et al. propose a new network architecture - GANs [9], which can be effectively applied to image completion. The completion methods based on GANs [11,17,20,27,28] achieve good completion results.

There are also some researchers who focus on face completion and have achieved remarkable research results [5–7,11,17,19,28,34]. Here we'd like to highlight two representative work. One is proposed by Li et al. [15] which adopts an encoding-decoding generator and two discriminators (global discriminator and local discriminator) to generate the completion result with truly global and local content. Motivated by this, we also adopt this similar network architecture in our work. In addition, in order to ensure the semantic structure similarity between completion result and ground-truth, it also utilizes a semantic parsing network. This method can effectively generate completion results with similar structure to the ground-truth, but it lacks the detailed constraints on semantic components. Hence, there is still a great inconsistency of color or texture for symmetrical facial components.

Later, Yu et al. [30] pose a generative image inpainting method with contextual attention (GntIpt). This method integrates the advantages of the traditional patch-based methods and the current learning-based methods. It can solve the inconsistency of color and texture between the completed patches and the background pixels, but it lacks structure and shape constraints for facial components. Therefore, there is also a great asymmetry when completing symmetrical facial components.

To sum up, the above methods can achieve good performance for face completion, but they do not fully consider the symmetry of the face, so there are some distortions or inconsistencies when processing face images. Hence, in our work we need to take symmetrical facial components into account and specialize in face completion technique.

3 Proposed Method

Given a masked image, our goal is to synthesize the missing contents that are both semantically consistent with the whole object and visually realistic. Our method is based on generative adversarial networks trained for the face completion task. A generator is used for the image completion. Three additional networks, the global, local and symmetry discriminator networks, are used in order to train this network to realistically complete images. An overview of our method can be seen in Fig. 2.

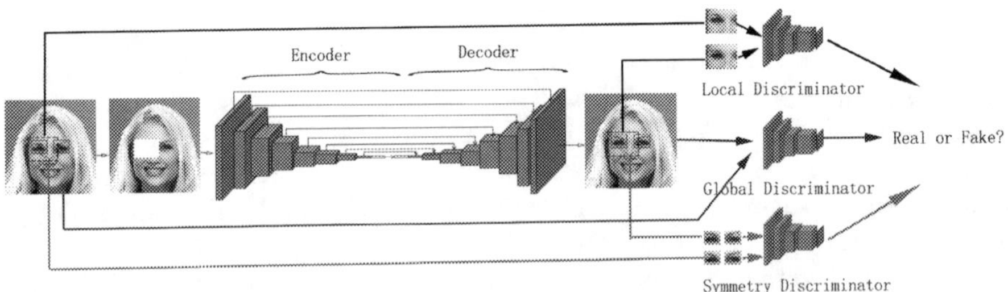

Fig. 2. Network architecture. It consists of one generator and three discriminators. The global discriminator and local discriminator are learned to distinguish the whole generated image and synthesize contents in the mask as real and fake. The symmetry discriminator is to further ensure the newly generated contents symmetric and encourage consistency between new and old pixels. (Color figure online)

3.1 Generator

Our approach is motivated by Generative Adversarial Networks (GANs) [9]. It trains two networks, a generator G, and a discriminator D. G is designed as an autoencoder to construct new contents given input images with missing regions, while D plays an adversarial role, discriminating between the image generated from G and the real image.

In this work, we adopt a "U-Net" network [23] as the generator which follows an encoder-decoder structure similar to the one used in [12]. The input of the generator is an RGB image with a binary mask (1 for a pixel to be completed), and the output is an RGB completed image. The encoder employs a down sampling process to extract the structural features of the masked input image, and then the decoder utilizes an up sampling process to gradually fill the contents of the missing area according to the structural features extracted by the encoder. It is worth mentioning that the skip connection of the U-Net network can keep more information for the generation of unmasked part. This eliminates the need to replace the unmasked area with original image in subsequent processing. In order to get more spatial support to generate the masked area, we add two dilated convolution layer [29] between the encoder and decoder which are represented by the yellow rectangle in Fig. 2.

3.2 Discriminator

The generator can be trained to fill the masked area with small reconstruction and structure losses. However, it does not ensure that the filled area is visually realistic and natural. As shown in Fig. 4(c), the generated pixels are quite fuzzy and only capture the coarse shape of missing face components. To encourage more photorealistic results, we design three discriminators, that is, global discriminator, local discriminator and symmetry discriminator. These three discriminators' structure is similar to [12] which uses batch normalization layer and LeakyReLU layer after each convolution layer.

The global discriminator is designed to determine the faithfulness of an entire image, so the inputs of it are the whole completion result and the ground-truth. The local discriminator follows the same pattern, except for the purpose of checking whether the generated contents of the missing area are real or not. It takes the 8-pixels dilation of the masked areas from the completion result and the ground-truth as inputs. The inputs of 8-pixels dilation around the masked area can make our model fully exploit the spatial correlation between adjacent pixels. With the global and local discriminators' further optimization, the completion result can be more realistic with less fuzzy artifacts.

In order to maintain the symmetry of the completion result, we further utilize the symmetry discriminator to optimize the generation of symmetrical face components. The inputs of the symmetry discriminator are the symmetrical components detection results taken from the completion image and the corresponding ground-truth as inputs. With the unmasked part of the symmetrical components as a condition [18], the completion of corresponding components can be further optimized. Here the key of this issue is twofold: one is what these so-called symmetrical components should be, and the other is how to detect these symmetrical components for face images. We will introduce them in next subsection.

3.3 Symmetry Detection for Face Components

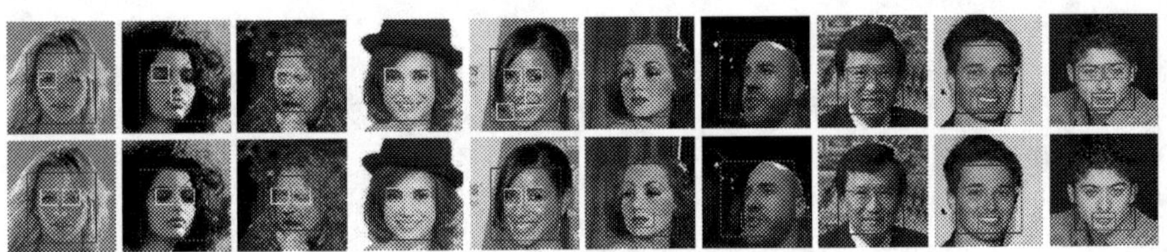

Fig. 3. Results of symmetrical components detection. The first row are the eye and mouth detection results by using the Haar cascade method [25] directly. The second row are the corresponding detection results after optimization using our detection strategy.

The face contains five components, eyes, eyebrows, nose, mouth and ears. The geometrical position of these components is relatively fixed and each can be seen as symmetrical, for example, the eyes are in pairs, and the nose itself is also bilaterally symmetrical. In this paper, we collectively refer to them as symmetrical components. Since the ears are always unpaired in most of the face images, we ignore the ears during the actual detection and symmetric optimization process. In addition, we also treat the eyebrows as parts of the eyes. To sum up, during the detection and optimization process, the symmetrical components involve only the eyes (eyebrows), nose and mouth.

As symmetrical components are important feature description of the human face, we need to detect them at first. We use the Haar feature cascade classifiers proposed in [25] as our detection method. Although the Haar cascade method can improve its detection accuracy by adjusting the "minNeighbors" parameters, there are still some false detections, see the first row in Fig. 3. Therefore, we adopt an optimization method to improve the detection accuracy. Firstly, we recognize the face and detect the symmetrical components to be optimized within the facial region, this can improve the detection rate efficiently. Next, we exclude the wrong detections based on the detection number and the relative position of the symmetrical components in the face image. Finally, we set a default value by averaging the past accurate detections for the wrong detection.

As the wrong detections exclusion is the most important part, we give more details about this filtering strategy. For each individual symmetrical component (mouth, nose), the correct detection number is one. For paired symmetrical components (eyes, eyebrows, ears), the correct detection number is two. We set four position parameters [x1, x2, y1, y1] to define the position of each symmetry component. x1, x2 represent the minimum and maximum horizontal positions, and y1, y2 represent the minimum and maximum vertical positions. Based on the detection number and position range of components, we can exclude three types of errors. The first one is that the detection number is less than the correct detection number. (See in the first and sixth columns of Fig. 3). The second one is that the detection number is equal to the correct detection number, but the component is not within the correct position range. (See in the second and seventh columns of Fig. 3). For both cases, we use the default value to replace the detection value. The third one is that the detection number is greater than the correct detection number (See in the fourth, fifth and ninth and tenth columns of Fig. 3). In this case, we exclude the detections that the components are not within the correct position range and randomly select the one that the components are within the correct position range as the final detection result. In this detection process, the position parameters need to be manually set by experience and the others are all automatic.

With our optimization method, the detection accuracy can be significantly improved. The second row of Fig. 3 show the detection results after optimization.

3.4 Loss Functions

We first introduce a per-pixel reconstruction loss $\mathcal{L}_r$ to the generator, which is the $L1$ distance between the network output and the ground-truth image. The reason we use $L1$ loss is that $L2$ loss penalizes outliers heavily and tends to generate blurry contents. The $\mathcal{L}_r$ loss is defined as below:

$$\mathcal{L}_r(x, M) = \|G(x, M) - x\|_1 \tag{1}$$

where x is the ground-truth, M is the mask image, G represents the generator.

In order to make the generated image have a high structural similarity with the ground-truth, we then adopt a structure loss $\mathcal{L}_s$. The structure loss is similar to the perceptual loss used in [16]. Instead of using an additional VGG-16 network, we directly use the generator to obtain the structure loss. We take both the masked image and the ground truth as input. Note that the feature maps of the masked image at each layer of the decoder should be consistent with the corresponding feature maps of the ground-truth. The structure loss $\mathcal{L}_s$ is defined as

$$\mathcal{L}_s(x, M) = \sum_{k=1}^{N} \alpha_k \|\Psi_k(x, M) - \Psi_k(x)\|_1 + \beta \|G(x) - x\|_1 \tag{2}$$

Here, the former item computes the $L1$ distances between the feature maps of the raw output image and the ground truth image. It can improve the structural similarity between the output and the ground truth. Ψ_k is the activation map of the kth selected layer, α_k is the corresponding weight. The latter item is a constraint to guarantee the output of the ground-truth is consistent with itself. β is the weight of the constraint.

We further employ the global and local adversarial loss. They both adopt the sigmoid cross-entropy loss but have different inputs. The inputs for the global discriminator are the overall completion result and the ground-truth, and for the local discriminator, the inputs are a patch with 8-pixel dilation around the completed region and the corresponding ground truth. The global adversarial loss $\mathcal{L}_g$ and local adversarial loss $\mathcal{L}_l$ are defined by:

$$\mathcal{L}_g(x, M) = \min_G \max_D \mathbb{E}\left[\log D(x) + \log(1 - D(G(x, M))\right] \tag{3}$$

$$\mathcal{L}_l(x, M) = \min_G \max_D \mathbb{E}\left[\log D(x, M) + \log(1 - D(G(x, M), M)\right] \tag{4}$$

The symmetry discriminator network also works as a kind of loss, called the symmetry loss. The symmetry loss is used to optimize the completion of symmetrical components, which includes symmetry adversarial loss and symmetry pixel loss. The symmetry adversarial loss adopt the sigmoid cross-entropy adversarial loss, but it takes the symmetrical components of the ground-truth and the completion result as inputs. The symmetry pixel loss is the L1 distance between the symmetrical components of the ground-truth and completion result. If the symmetrical components are in pairs, such as eyes, eyebrows and ears, we use P_l to represent the left part of the symmetrical components and P_r to represent the right part. When P_l is masked and P_r is unmasked, the symmetry loss function is defined as:

$$\mathcal{L}_{sym}(x, M) = \gamma \mathcal{L}_{sym_a}(x, M) + \mathcal{L}_{sym_b}(x, M) \tag{5}$$

$$\mathcal{L}_{sym_a}(x, M) = \min_G \max_D \mathbb{E}\left[\log D(P_l, P_r) + \log(1 - D(\bar{P}_l, P_r)\right] \tag{6}$$

$$\mathcal{L}_{sym_b}(x, M) = \left\|\bar{P}_l - P_l\right\|_1 \tag{7}$$

Here, we set $\gamma = 0.1$ in our experiments. $\bar{P}_l$ is the left part of the generated symmetrical components in completion result. If P_r is unmasked while P_l is masked, the loss function needs to replace $\overline{P_l}$ with $\overline{P_r}$. If the missing component is a single symmetrical component, such as nose or mouth, we simply input the single component as a whole and have no need to divide it into two parts. The simplified formulation is changed as below:

$$\mathcal{L}_{sym_a}(x, M) = \min_G \max_D \mathbb{E}\left[\log D(P) + \log(1 - D(\bar{P})\right] \tag{8}$$

$$\mathcal{L}_{sym_b}(x, M) = \left\|\bar{P} - P\right\|_1 \tag{9}$$

P and $\bar{P}$ represent the single symmetrical component of the ground truth and the completion result, respectively. By using the symmetry loss, we can use the known part of the symmetrical components as a constraint to generate the unknown part, this will make the completion result have better symmetry and consistency.

The overall loss function is defined by:

$$\mathcal{L} = \omega_1 \mathcal{L}_r + \omega_2 \mathcal{L}_s + \omega_3 \mathcal{L}_g + \omega_4 \mathcal{L}_l + \omega_5 \mathcal{L}_{sym} \tag{10}$$

where ω_i is the weight to balance the effects of different losses. We set $\omega_1 = 100$, $\omega_2 = 5$, $\omega_3 = 1$, $\omega_4 = 1$, $\omega_5 = 1$ in our experiments.

3.5 Training

The training process can be scheduled in three stages. Firstly, we train the network using the reconstruction loss and structure loss to get the initial result. Secondly, we utilize the global adversarial loss and local adversarial loss to fine-tune the network so as to obtain the completion results with less fuzzy. Finally, the symmetry loss is incorporated to optimize the completion of symmetrical components. For the third stage, we need to optimize all the symmetrical components in turn.

(a) Input (b) L1 (c) Stage1 (d) Stage2 (e) Stage3

Fig. 4. Comparison results of different training stages. (a) is the input, (c) shows the first stage with both reconstruction loss and structure loss, (d) displays the second stage with additional global and local adversarial loss, (e) indicates the last stage with additional symmetry loss, (b) are the results obtained by only using reconstruction loss.

Figure 4 shows the experimental results of different stages. Figure (a) are inputs, Figure (c–e) are respectively the outputs of each progressive stage with different optimization. Each stage is an optimization of its previous stage. As shown in Fig. 4, the first stage produces a fuzzy initial result with a white border. While the second stage, after the optimization of the global discriminator and the local discriminator, the blurring is reduced and the white border is eliminated, but the paired symmetrical components such as eyes and eyebrows are still asymmetrical. In the third stage, the completion results look more symmetrical and natural by using the symmetry loss. Figures (b) shows the results obtained by only using reconstruction loss with the same training number as the first phase. The comparison of the (b) and (c) reveals that the structure loss can guide the generator to produce completion results with similar structure to the ground-truth. In order to improve the stability of training, we adopt the training procedure proposed by [21] and use Adam [13] to optimize. The initial learning rate is 0.00005.

4 Experimental Results

4.1 Datasets

We use the CelebA dataset to train and test our model. The CelebA dataset contains 202,599 face images and each image is cropped and rescaled to $256 \times 256 \times 3$ pixels for data normalization. We randomly select 2599 images for testing and 200,000 images for training. To ensure our network can complete missing contents with different sizes and positions, we generate a random mask for the input image with the mask size between $[30 \times 30,\ 130 \times 130]$ during training. Besides, the position of the mask is also randomly selected.

4.2 Qualitative Results

Figure 5 shows some results on the test dataset. In each test image, the mask covers at least one key facial components. The first row shows the examples with large square-like mask from which more than two facial components are occluded. In these examples, any of the facial components covered by the mask are relatively complete. For example, both eyes or the entire nose is blocked. For this case, the model can generate pleasing results even without the symmetrical components optimization.

In the second and third row, only one part of the paired symmetrical components is missing, then the symmetry optimization is required so as to obtain

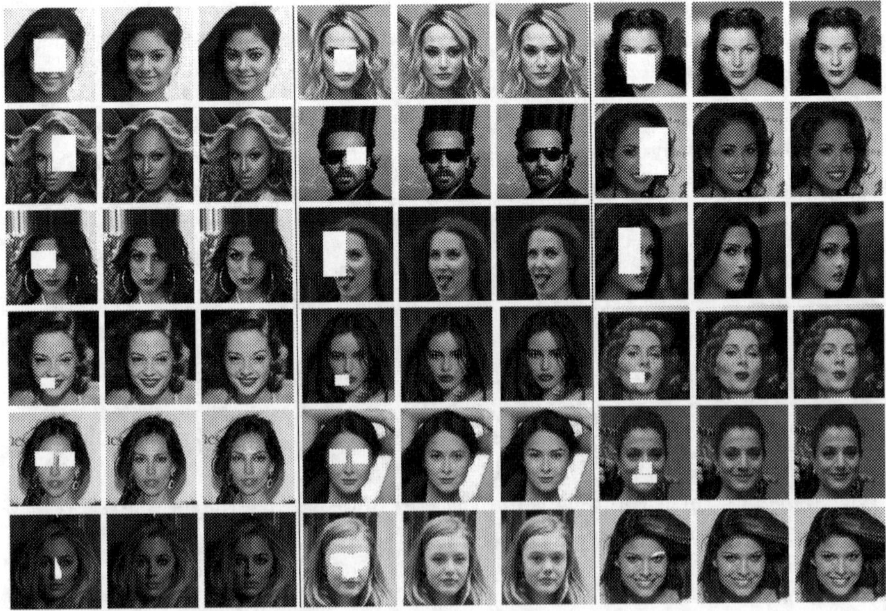

Fig. 5. Face completion results on the CelebA test dataset. In each panel from left to right: masked inputs, our completion results, ground truth images.

symmetrical and natural completion results. It is worth noting that the symmetry optimization not only has a better optimization effect on the geometrically symmetric facial components, but also has a better optimization effect on the facial components with a certain view angle. The fourth row displays some results for individual symmetrical component. Taking lips as examples, our method is capable of maintaining both the shape symmetry and the texture consistency. Note that the color of the lips is well recovered. The fifth row shows the completion results with multiple masks, and the sixth row exhibits the results with irregular masks. For both cases, Our method can get photo-realistic and pleasing results.

Fig. 6. Face completion results with irregular masks. In each panel from left to right: masked inputs, our completion results, ground truth images.

Figure 6 shows more results with irregular masks. In a real-world scenario, our method can perform face completion by replacing irregular masks with multiple rectangular masks, and also can give completion results that are consistent with their contextual semantics.

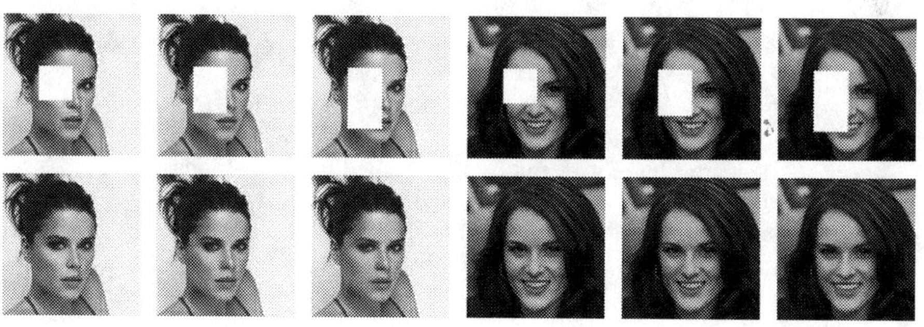

Fig. 7. Completion results with different mask sizes: 64×64, 84×64, and 120×64.

We also give some completion examples with different mask sizes in Fig. 7. In these examples, each image is processed by three different masks whose sizes are respectively 64×64, 84×64, and 120×64. As can be seen from the results, the completion effect does not change significantly as the mask increases.

Overall, our completion algorithm is competent for images with missing symmetrical facial components or large missing area, or partially/completely corrupted by the masks with different shapes and sizes.

Fig. 8. Qualitative comparison with different methods.

4.3 Comparison with the State of the Art

We compare our model with some current learning-based methods [11,15,30] in Fig. 8.

As can be seen from the results, the GL [11] method can identify the contents to be completed, but the completion results have large semantic distortion. The GFC [15] method can maintain the shape similarity of semantic components to some extent, but there are still inconsistencies in colors and textures for symmetrical components. The GntIpt [30] method can effectively alleviate the inconsistency of color and texture between symmetrical components, but it cannot guarantee the shape symmetry. Note that our method can make up for the above deficiencies and obtain natural and consistent results.

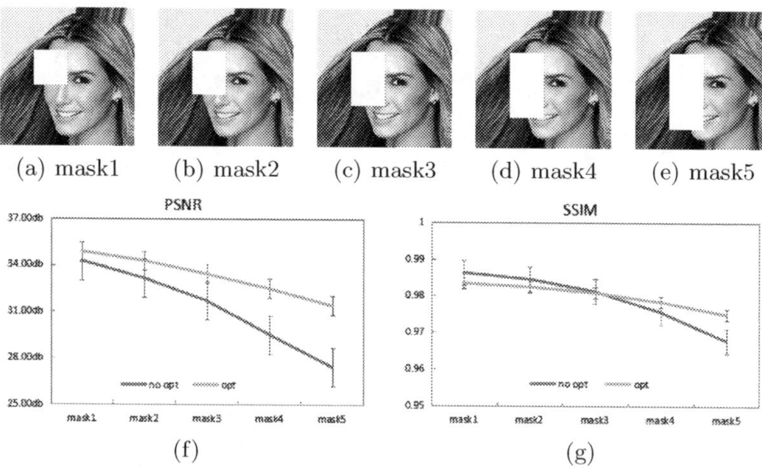

Fig. 9. Quantitative comparison. (a–e) represent five masks which size are 64×64, 64×80, 64×100, 64×120, 64×140. (f) is the result of the PSNR evaluation. (g) is the result of the SSIM evaluation. In (f) and (g), the blue line represents the evaluation curve obtained without symmetry optimization, the orange line represents the evaluation curve obtained using symmetry optimization. (Color figure online)

4.4 Quantitative Comparison

A quantitative comparison experiment is adopted to evaluate the effectiveness of the symmetry optimization. In this quantitative comparison experiment, two metrics, PSNR and SSIM are used for evaluation. In this experiment, we only focus on the completion of the symmetry components, so we use five masks as shown in Fig. 9(a–e) to occlude the symmetric area. The evaluation results of PSNR and SSIM are shown in Fig. 9(f–g). It can be seen that the completion results with symmetry optimization have higher PSNR values, and the PSNR curve decreases relatively slowly when the mask size increases. As for the SSIM evaluation, the results without optimization have a higher structural similarity when the mask size is small. But as the mask size increases, the value drops faster. When the input images have a large mask size, the symmetry optimization can make the completion results have higher structural similarity. Through the quantitative comparison, we can conclude that symmetry optimization has a better improvement effect on face completion.

4.5 Limitations and Discussion

Though our model performs well at completing various images, it has some limitations. The mask size used in this paper is between $[30 \times 30, 130 \times 130]$. When it is close to or less than the floor, the generated patch will be inconsistent with the surrounding pixels in color (see in Fig. 10(b)). To handle this problem, we use a modified Poisson blending method (MPB) proposed in [1] for post-processing. However, post-processing can only alleviate this problem but can

(a) Input (b) Output (c) MPB Result (d) Input (e) Output (f) target

Fig. 10. Model limitation. (a) is the input with small mask. (b) is the directly result of the proposed method. (c) is the MPB [1] optimization of (b). (d) is the input with large mask. (e) is completion result after optimization. (f) is the target image.

not eliminate it completely, as shown in Fig. 10(c). In addition, when the mask size larger than 130×130, the completion result will become more and more blurred (see in Fig. 10(e)). If the mask is too large to provide enough context information, it will be impossible to generate pleasant completion results. If we want to completely solve those problem, the lower and upper limits of the mask size should be set to $[0 \times 0, 256 \times 256]$, but meanwhile it will result in an increase in training time.

5 Conclusions

In this paper, we have proposed a deep generative network for face completion. The network is based on a GAN, with an structure-constraint autoencoder as the generator, two adversarial loss functions (local and global) and a symmetry correction as the discriminators. Our method automatically detects symmetrical facial components and completes them without any user interaction. We show that the symmetrical attention module significantly improves face completion results for the missing facial key parts from random mask. We provide in-depth comparisons with existing approaches and show semantically valid and visually plausible completion results.

References

1. Afifi, M., Hussain, K.F.: MPB: a modified poisson blending technique. Comput. Vis. Media **1**(4), 331–341 (2015)
2. Barnes, C., Shechtman, E., Finkelstein, A., Goldman, D.B.: PatchMatch: a randomized correspondence algorithm for structural image editing. ACM Trans. Graph. (ToG) **28**(3), 24 (2009)
3. Bertalmio, M., Sapiro, G., Caselles, V., Ballester, C.: Image inpainting. In: Proceedings of the 27th Annual Conference on Computer Graphics and Interactive Techniques, pp. 417–424. ACM Press/Addison-Wesley Publishing Co. (2000)
4. Bitouk, D., Kumar, N., Dhillon, S., Belhumeur, P., Nayar, S.K.: Face swapping: automatically replacing faces in photographs. ACM Trans. Graph. (TOG) **27**, 39 (2008)

5. Deng, Y., Dai, Q., Zhang, Z.: Graph Laplace for occluded face completion and recognition. IEEE Trans. Image Process. **20**(8), 2329–2338 (2011)
6. Deng, Y., Li, D., Xie, X., Lam, K.M., Dai, Q.: Partially occluded face completion and recognition. In: 2009 16th IEEE International Conference on Image Processing (ICIP), pp. 4145–4148. IEEE (2009)
7. Dolhansky, B., Ferrer, C.C.: Eye in-painting with exemplar generative adversarial networks. In: Proceedings of the IEEE Conference on Computer Vision and Pattern Recognition, pp. 7902–7911 (2018)
8. Elad, M., Starck, J.L., Querre, P., Donoho, D.L.: Simultaneous cartoon and texture image inpainting using morphological component analysis (MCA). Appl. Comput. Harmonic Anal. **19**(3), 340–358 (2005)
9. Goodfellow, I., et al.: Generative adversarial nets. In: Advances in Neural Information Processing Systems, pp. 2672–2680 (2014)
10. Hays, J., Efros, A.A.: Scene completion using millions of photographs. ACM Trans. Graph. (TOG) **26**, 4 (2007)
11. Iizuka, S., Simo-Serra, E., Ishikawa, H.: Globally and locally consistent image completion. ACM Trans. Graph. (TOG) **36**(4), 107 (2017)
12. Isola, P., Zhu, J.Y., Zhou, T., Efros, A.A.: Image-to-image translation with conditional adversarial networks. arXiv preprint (2017)
13. Kingma, D.P., Ba, J.: Adam: a method for stochastic optimization. arXiv preprint arXiv:1412.6980 (2014)
14. Köhler, R., Schuler, C., Schölkopf, B., Harmeling, S.: Mask-specific inpainting with deep neural networks. In: Jiang, X., Hornegger, J., Koch, R. (eds.) GCPR 2014. LNCS, vol. 8753, pp. 523–534. Springer, Cham (2014). https://doi.org/10.1007/978-3-319-11752-2_43
15. Li, Y., Liu, S., Yang, J., Yang, M.H.: Generative face completion. In: The IEEE Conference on Computer Vision and Pattern Recognition (CVPR), vol. 1, p. 3 (2017)
16. Liu, G., Reda, F.A., Shih, K.J., Wang, T.C., Tao, A., Catanzaro, B.: Image inpainting for irregular holes using partial convolutions. arXiv preprint arXiv:1804.07723 (2018)
17. Liu, P., Qi, X., He, P., Li, Y., Lyu, M.R., King, I.: Semantically consistent image completion with fine-grained details. arXiv preprint arXiv:1711.09345 (2017)
18. Mirza, M., Osindero, S.: Conditional generative adversarial nets. arXiv preprint arXiv:1411.1784 (2014)
19. Mo, Z., Lewis, J.P., Neumann, U.: Face inpainting with local linear representations. In: BMVC, vol. 1, p. 2 (2004)
20. Pathak, D., Krahenbuhl, P., Donahue, J., Darrell, T., Efros, A.A.: Context encoders: feature learning by inpainting. In: Proceedings of the IEEE Conference on Computer Vision and Pattern Recognition, pp. 2536–2544 (2016)
21. Radford, A., Metz, L., Chintala, S.: Unsupervised representation learning with deep convolutional generative adversarial networks. arXiv preprint arXiv:1511.06434 (2015)
22. Ren, J.S., Xu, L., Yan, Q., Sun, W.: Shepard convolutional neural networks. In: Advances in Neural Information Processing Systems, pp. 901–909 (2015)
23. Ronneberger, O., Fischer, P., Brox, T.: U-Net: convolutional networks for biomedical image segmentation. In: Navab, N., Hornegger, J., Wells, W.M., Frangi, A.F. (eds.) MICCAI 2015. LNCS, vol. 9351, pp. 234–241. Springer, Cham (2015). https://doi.org/10.1007/978-3-319-24574-4_28

24. Saito, Y., Kenmochi, Y., Kotani, K.: Estimation of eyeglassless facial images using principal component analysis. In: Proceedings of the 1999 International Conference on Image Processing, ICIP 1999, vol. 4, pp. 197–201. IEEE (1999)
25. Viola, P., Jones, M.: Rapid object detection using a boosted cascade of simple features. In: Proceedings of the 2001 IEEE Computer Society Conference on Computer Vision and Pattern Recognition, CVPR 2001, vol. 1, p. I. IEEE (2001)
26. Xie, J., Xu, L., Chen, E.: Image denoising and inpainting with deep neural networks. In: Advances in Neural Information Processing Systems, pp. 341–349 (2012)
27. Yang, C., Lu, X., Lin, Z., Shechtman, E., Wang, O., Li, H.: High-resolution image inpainting using multi-scale neural patch synthesis. In: The IEEE Conference on Computer Vision and Pattern Recognition (CVPR), vol. 1, p. 3 (2017)
28. Yeh, R.A., Chen, C., Lim, T.Y., Schwing, A.G., Hasegawa-Johnson, M., Do, M.N.: Semantic image inpainting with deep generative models. In: CVPR, vol. 2, p. 4 (2017)
29. Yu, F., Koltun, V.: Multi-scale context aggregation by dilated convolutions. arXiv preprint arXiv:1511.07122 (2015)
30. Yu, J., Lin, Z., Yang, J., Shen, X., Lu, X., Huang, T.S.: Generative image inpainting with contextual attention. arXiv preprint (2018)
31. Zhang, S., He, R., Sun, Z., Tan, T.: Multi-task convnet for blind face inpainting with application to face verification. In: 2016 International Conference on Biometrics (ICB), pp. 1–8. IEEE (2016)
32. Zhang, S., He, R., Sun, Z., Tan, T.: DeMeshNet: blind face inpainting for deep MeshFace verification. IEEE Trans. Inf. Forensics Secur. **13**(3), 637–647 (2018)
33. Zhang, W., Shan, S., Chen, X., Gao, W.: Local Gabor binary patterns based on Kullback–Leibler divergence for partially occluded face recognition. IEEE Signal Process. Lett. **14**(11), 875–878 (2007)
34. Zhuang, Y.T., Wang, Y.S., Shih, T.K., Tang, N.C.: Patch-guided facial image inpainting by shape propagation. J. Zhejiang Univ.-SCIENCE A **10**(2), 232–238 (2009)

GrowBit: Incremental Hashing for Cross-Modal Retrieval

Devraj Mandal[1(✉)], Yashas Annadani[2], and Soma Biswas[1]

[1] Indian Institute of Science, Bangalore, India
{devrajm,somabiswas}@iisc.ac.in
[2] ETH, Zurich, Switzerland
ayashas@student.ethz.ch

Abstract. Cross-modal retrieval using hashing techniques is gaining increasing importance due to its efficient storage, scalability and fast query processing speeds. In this work, we address a related and relatively unexplored problem: given a set of cross-modal data with their already learned hash codes, can we increase the number of bits to better represent the data without relearning everything? This scenario is especially important when the number of tags describing the data increases, necessitating longer hash codes for better representation. To tackle this problem, we propose a novel approach called *GrowBit*, which incrementally learns the bits in the hash code and thus utilizes all the bits learned so far. We develop a two-stage approach for learning the hash codes and hash functions separately, utilizing a recent formulation which decouples over the bits so that it can incorporate the incremental approach. Experiments on MirFlickr, IAPR-TC-12 and NUS-WIDE datasets show the usefulness of the proposed approach.

Keywords: Cross-modal retrieval · Hashing · Incremental learning

1 Introduction

Due to the availability of large amounts of multimedia data, cross-modal retrieval has become an active area of research [5,8,15]. For example, given an image query, it is often required to retrieve relevant textual documents from the database. Hashing techniques designed to generate good binary encodings for capturing the semantic relations between the data have gained popularity because of their impressive retrieval results, low-storage costs and efficient retrieval. Hashing techniques for both unsupervised [5,23,35,36] and supervised settings [1,13,31,36] have been proposed.

Multimedia data is often described using multiple tags (or labels or attributes) which gives a richer description of the data. Some illustrative examples of cross-modal multimedia data are shown in Fig. 1. Since for training, the data is usually manually annotated or requires manual supervision, getting all the tags for the data at once might not be feasible due to limited human

C. V. Jawahar et al. (Eds.): ACCV 2018, LNCS 11364, pp. 305–321, 2019.
https://doi.org/10.1007/978-3-030-20870-7_19

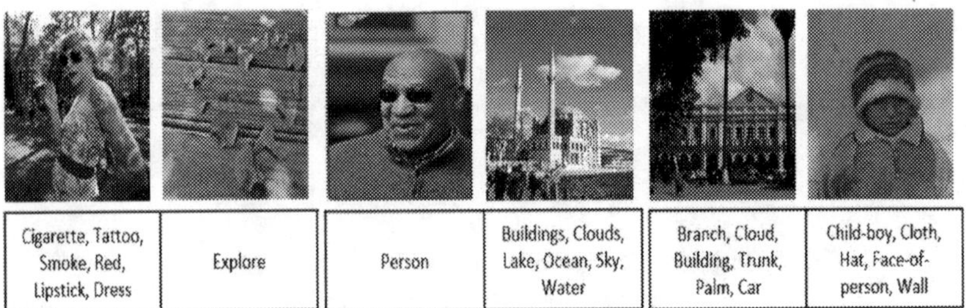

Fig. 1. Some illustrative image-text data pairs from the three datasets - MirFlickr [10] (left), NUS-WIDE [3] (middle) and IAPR TC-12 [6] (right).

resources. Let us consider that the training data $\{X_{tr}, Y_{tr}\}$ has been annotated with L_{tr} tags, using which we learn a hash bit representation of k_1 bits. Gradually, with more human resources, more annotations of the data become available. Let us assume that now a total of $\hat{L}_{tr}$ tags become available. Consider an example, where, an existing dress catalogue which has been stored based on their category (like shirt, top) may now be annotated with finer details like sleeve length, etc., which requires a better representation using more bits so that it can be correctly retrieved using a textual description. Most of the current algorithms require relearning the entire set of hash codes and hash functions. In this work, we propose a novel incremental hashing approach termed *GrowBit*, which can efficiently utilize the already learned hash codes, and incrementally learn the additional bits, without compromising on the retrieval performance.

Inspired by the success of the two-stage hashing approaches [14,15,20,27], we design our *GrowBit* as a two-stage approach, in which the additional hash bits are learned in the first stage and the new hash functions are learned in the second stage based on these additional hash bits. More specifically, we build upon the formulation of a recent state-of-the-art technique [20] which decouples over the bit representation and allows us to learn the bits in an incremental manner. In the first stage, in order to utilize the already learned hash codes, we compute the additional bits such that they learn the semantic information not captured by the initially learned bits. We utilize a deep neural network to learn the respective hash functions in the second stage. To learn the hash functions for the newly learned additional bits, we efficiently re-utilize parts of the network which was previously trained and modify it accordingly. This has an added advantage of significantly reducing the training time as compared to completely retraining the model. In addition, we propose a novel unification scheme to generate common hash codes using complementary information from multiple modalities. We perform an exhaustive evaluation on three standard cross-modal datasets, namely MirFlickr [10], IAPR-TC-12 [6] and NUS-WIDE [3] and show that the proposed algorithm can efficiently learn the hash codes under different scenarios. The contributions of this work are as follows:

1. We propose a novel incremental hashing approach *GrowBit*, which can seamlessly integrate the increasing tags in an incremental fashion, while utilizing the already learned hash code representations. To the best of our knowledge, this is the first work on incremental hashing in a cross-modal setting.
2. We also propose a unification strategy to generate common hash codes for representation.
3. The proposed approach results in a significant decrease in the number of new parameters to be trained in the second stage without compromising much on the retrieval performance.

2 Related Work

For cross-modal retrieval, algorithms to learn binary embeddings have been developed using both unsupervised and supervised techniques. Unsupervised approaches like [5,23,35,36] uses the criterion of inter and intra affinity preservation for design of the binary latent embedding space. The work in CMFH [5] uses matrix factorization to learn a unified hash code. A recent method, inspired from dictionary learning, called quantization, has been proposed in [18,26,34] and shows good promise in retrieval performance.

Supervised approaches use label information to learn effective and more discriminative binary embedding like CMSSH [1] and CVH [13]. Incorporating label information in a matrix factorization based approach is proposed in [19]. In addition, the work in [19] is capable of handling large amounts of data seamlessly. SePH [15] converts the label information into probability distribution and uses the criterion of low Kullback-Leibler divergence to learn the bits. It also uses a unification stage which further boosts the retrieval performance. A generalized method to handle both paired and unpaired data in cross-modal settings with unification has been proposed in [20]. In [17], in the learning phase, each bit of the code can be sequentially learned with a discrete optimization scheme that jointly minimizes the empirical loss based on a boosting strategy. In a bitwise manner, hash functions are then learned for each modality, mapping the corresponding representations into unified hash codes [17]. The discriminative capability of the labels has been used to learn the hash code and hash function in [29]. Furthermore, care has been taken to suitably design constraints for the objective function to reduce the quantization error. Deep learning techniques for cross-modal hashing has been developed in [11]. The deep learning models [11] have shown major improvements whenever end-to-end training network with non-linear hash functions have been used. The semantic structure of the multi-modal data has been effectively captured by a deep generative framework in [32].

The problem of online hashing [7,28] studies models which can deal with new incoming data while retaining important information learned from all previous data. This work considers the problem of adapting an already learned model to incorporate the ever-expanding set of tags (or attributes or descriptions) of data samples whereas, in an online setting, the incoming data is usually spread

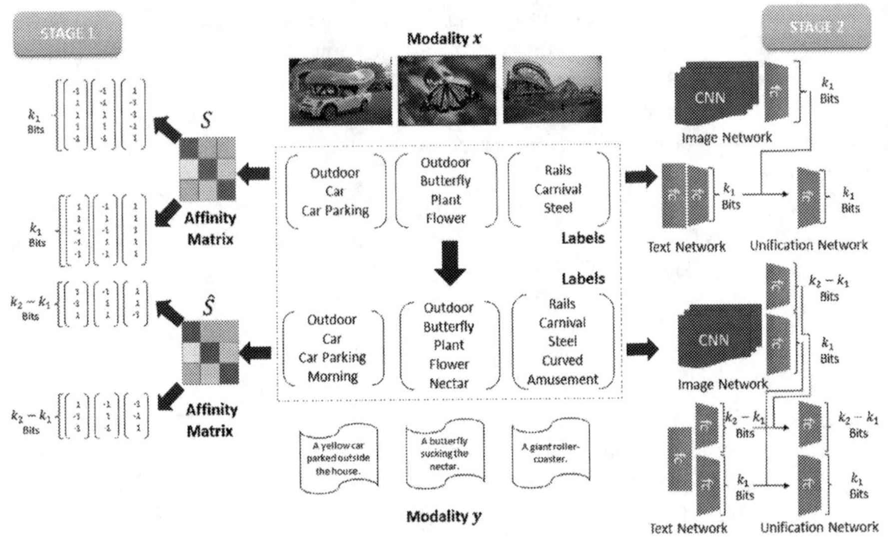

Fig. 2. An illustration of the proposed approach. (Color figure online)

across the same set of categories as the previously available examples. Sequential learning of hash codes have been proposed in the works of [25,31] where hash functions are learned incrementally to correct the errors made by the previous bits sequentially. However, those methods [25,31] uses linear transformations to learn hash functions which usually gives poor retrieval performance as compared to non-linear based methods.

In this work, for developing an incremental hashing approach, we draw inspiration from the recent two-stage approaches [14,15,27]. Instead of learning the optimal hash codes and mapping functions in a joint optimization framework, the two-stage approaches first learn the hash codes followed by learning the hash functions, which often lead to simpler formulations. A schematic of the proposed algorithm is shown in Fig. 2. Here, the affinity information (S) encoded in the labels is decomposed to generate the hash codes and a deep neural network (DNN) is used to learn the hash functions. A change in the affinities ($\hat{S}$, provided by the new tags highlighted in red) can be captured by learning the extended hash codes. The corresponding hash functions can then be learned by reusing parts of the previous DNN resulting in significant savings in computation and time without adversely affecting the retrieval performance. The work in [2] came to our notice recently and we believe that both the works help to advance the state-of-the-art in hashing. The main differences with GrowBit (vs [2]) are - (1) usage of standard hamming distance (weighted hamming metric) (2) ability to learn extendable hash bits (3) a novel unification scheme for cross-modal retrieval and (4) use of mean square loss (hinge loss) to learn the hash functions.

3 Proposed Approach

Problem Definition and Notation: Let the training data for the two modalities be denoted as $X_{tr} \in \mathbb{R}^{N \times d_x}$ and $Y_{tr} \in \mathbb{R}^{N \times d_y}$, where N is the number of training examples and d_x, d_y are the dimensionality of the data (in general $d_x \neq d_y$). Suppose, the initial set of tags available is denoted as $L_{tr} \in [0,1]^{N \times a}$, where a is the total number of tags and (0/1) denotes the (absence/presence) of the individual tag. The already learned hash code representations for X_{tr} and Y_{tr} are denoted as $H^x \in [-1,1]^{N \times k_1}$ and $H^y \in [-1,1]^{N \times k_1}$, where k_1 is the number of bits in the hash codes. Let $\hat{L}_{tr} \in [0,1]^{N \times \hat{a}}$ denote the new set of tags, where $\hat{a}$ denotes the increased set of tags. As a result of more number of tags, the data has richer representation. We would like to represent this data with a richer representation using hash codes with more number of bits (say k_2), which should result in better cross-modal retrieval. Even if the number of tags remain the same, we may want to increase the number of bits to better represent the data for improved retrieval performance. One option is to learn all the k_2 bits from scratch. In this work, we explore whether we can utilize the already learned k_1 bits, and only learn the additional $(k_2 - k_1)$ bits, such that they capture the semantic relation between the data not captured by the initial bits. Since we are not relearning everything, there is significant savings in computation. In the second stage, we utilize deep learning architectures in a block-wise fashion to learn the hash functions for the additional hash bits.

In this work, X represents a matrix, x_{i*}, x_{*j} represents its ith row, j^{th} column and x_{ij} represents its $(i,j)^{th}$ element. $\|\cdot\|_F$ denotes the Frobenius norm: $\|X\|_F^2 = \mathrm{Tr}(X^T X)$. The operation $x^*_{ij} = \mathrm{Proj}_{[-1,1]} x_{ij}$ can be defined as $x^*_{ij} = \{-1, x_{ij}, 1\}$; if, $\{x_{ij} < -1, x_{ij} \in [-1,1], x_{ij} > 1\}$ respectively. The sign operation is defined as $\mathrm{sign}(x_{ij}) = 1$ if $x_{ij} \geq 0$, and $= -1$ otherwise. Proj and sign applied to vector and matrix respectively are done point-wise.

Motivation and Background: One way to design an incremental hash code learning framework is to utilize a formulation which decouples over the variables (bits) to be learned. In literature, such formulation can be found in [4,20,33,38], which relate the similarity measure such that it can easily decouple over the bits. Here, the similarity between the ith and j^{th} samples of the two modalities are measured using inner product of the k_1 bits i.e., $s_{ij} = {h^x_{i*}}^T h^y_{j*}$, which is equivalent to $s_{ij} = \sum_{k=1}^{k_1} h^x_{ik} h^y_{jk}$, i.e. the objective remains decoupled over the bit dimension. Similarly, the new similarity $\hat{s}_{ij}$ can be expressed in terms of the expanded set of k_2 bits and can also be written in terms of the previously computed bits as

$$\hat{s}_{ij} = \sum_{k=1}^{k_1} h^x_{ik} h^y_{jk} + \sum_{k=k_1+1}^{k_2} \overline{h^x_{ik}}\,\overline{h^y_{jk}} \tag{1}$$

where the new hash bits $\overline{h^x_{ik}}, \overline{h^y_{jk}}$ of $(k_2 - k_1)$ length captures the difference in similarity between $\hat{s}_{ij}$ and s_{ij} that has not already been captured by the k_1

length hash bits h^x_{ik}, h^y_{jk}. [20] utilizes a similar formulation to learn the hash codes, but does not use any incremental updates.

Another such formulation can be found in [4,33,38] which deals with the triplet ranking loss whose general form is

$$\mathcal{L}\left(h^x_{i*}, h^y_{j*}, h^y_{k*}\right) = \max\left(0, 1 - \left(\|h^x_{i*} - h^y_{k*}\|_2^2 - \|h^x_{i*} - h^y_{j*}\|_2^2\right)\right) \tag{2}$$

where, $\{h^x_{i*}, h^y_{j*}, h^y_{k*}\}$ are the bit representations of three data samples. The squared norm is the sum of the square of the elements [9] ($\|x\|_2^2 = \sum_i x_i^2$) and hence the above objective can be expressed as a summation over the individual bits. The work in [38] utilizes this fact to design fast and efficient hash learning protocols for the single modal applications.

In this work, we build upon the first kind of formulation and show how it can be modified for incremental hashing. The second formulation is also suitable for a similar approach. The formulations in [25,31] can also be used to learn the hash functions sequentially. However, as the two stages are coupled together, the form of the hash function is limited to a linear transformation. Our two stage method removes this restriction and enables us to efficiently use DNN to learn better functions for hash bit representations. Also using DNN to learn Stage 2 allows us to re-use parts of the network to learn hash functions incrementally with considerable savings in time and computation.

3.1 Stage 1: Learning the Hash Code

We will first briefly describe the formulation in [20] and then extend it for our problem. During training, the binary representations of the ith data of x modality and j^{th} data of y modality are computed in such a way that its similarity (${h^x_{i*}}^T h^y_{j*}$) is consistent with the semantic affinity given by their associated labels ($s_{ij} =< L^i_{tr}, L^j_{tr} >$). $< ., . >$ denotes the normalized inner product operation [15,20]. The two hash codes H^x and H^y (of k_1 dimension) are computed using the affinity matrix S by solving the following least square formulation [20], [27] which encodes all possible relations between the data using the initial labels L_{tr}

$$\begin{aligned} \min_{H^x, H^y} \quad & \|k_1 S - H^x {H^y}^T\|_F^2 \\ \text{s.t.} \quad & H^x \in \{-1, 1\}^{N \times k_1}, \quad H^y \in \{-1, 1\}^{N \times k_1}. \end{aligned} \tag{3}$$

The above objective deals with discrete variables and is difficult to solve. Thus the discrete constraint is relaxed and it is then solved using an alternating minimization technique [16,20,27]. For each variable update of H^x and H^y, we use the projected gradient descent approach [22]. Denoting the above objective as a function f with respect to a single variable, say U, where $U = \{H^x \text{ or } H^y\}$, with the other variable fixed, we need to solve the following

$$\begin{aligned} \min_{U} \quad & f(U) \\ \text{s.t.} \quad & U \in [-1, 1]^{N \times k_1}. \end{aligned} \tag{4}$$

Following [22], we compute $\frac{\partial f(U)}{\partial U}$ and then update U as $\text{Proj}_{[-1,1]}\left(U - \eta\frac{\partial f(U)}{\partial U}\right)$, where η is the step size. These steps are repeated for both H^x, H^y until convergence.

Computing the Additional Hash Bits: Assume that we have already learned the hash bit representation of the training data as H^x, H^y of k_1 bit length. Now, in addition to the original tags $L_{tr} \in \mathcal{R}^{N\times a}$, we have access to an additional set of tags, and let the increased set be denoted as $\hat{L}_{tr} \in \mathcal{R}^{N\times \hat{a}}$ ($a \subset \hat{a}$). One can always reconstruct the new affinity as $\hat{s}_{ij} =< \hat{L}^i_{tr}, \hat{L}^j_{tr} >$ and relearn the hash bit representation $\hat{H^x}, \hat{H^y}$ from scratch. Instead, we propose to reuse the already learned hash bits H^x, H^y of k_1 bits and extend it to $\hat{H^x}, \hat{H^y}$ of k_2 bits to incorporate the additional semantic information. This way, we can utilize the already learned bits. The additional bits are computed as:

$$\begin{aligned}
&\min_{\hat{H^x},\hat{H^y}} \quad \|k_2\hat{S} - \hat{H^x}\hat{H^y}^T\|_F^2 \\
&= \min_{\overline{H^x},\overline{H^y}} \quad \|k_2\hat{S} - (H^x {H^y}^T + \overline{H^x}\overline{H^y}^T)\|_F^2 \\
&= \min_{\overline{H^x},\overline{H^y}} \quad \|D - \overline{H^x}\overline{H^y}^T\|_F^2
\end{aligned} \tag{5}$$

Here, $\overline{H^x}$ and $\overline{H^y}$ are the additional hash bits of length $(k_2 - k_1)$ to be learnt for the x and y modalities. Since $D = k_2\hat{S} - H^x {H^y}^T$, we see that the additional hash bits are trying to learn the semantic information not captured by the original bit representation. The above objective (5) can be solved using a similar strategy as in (3).

A sub-problem of the one addressed above is when we want to increase the hash bit length to better capture the relationship between the data for better retrieval, even though the tags remain unchanged. This scenario is relevant since the retrieval performance of standard state-of-the-art hashing techniques [11,20] increases with the increase in hash bits. We can use the same formulation as above to learn the additional bits and reuse the already learned k_1 bits. For this, we use (5) by replacing $\hat{S}$ with S since the tags remain the same.

3.2 Stage 2: Learning the Hash Functions

We first describe how to learn two hash functions $\mathcal{F}_x : x \rightarrow H^x$ and $\mathcal{F}_y : y \rightarrow H^y$ to generate the hash codes for the x and y modalities. Next, we will discuss how to learn the hash functions for the extended bits. Here, we consider the two modalities as image and text, but the proposed approach is equally applicable for other modalities.

Owing to the success of deep learning approaches for learning data representations, we formulate a multilayer neural network based approach to learn the hash functions. The proposed setup (Fig. 3) consists of two networks, corresponding to image and text. For the image modality, we use the AlexNet [12] architecture which has convolutional (conv) layers followed by fully connected

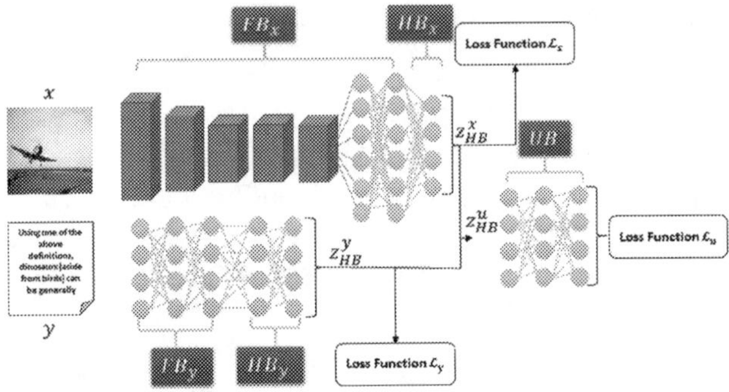

Fig. 3. The basic network architecture to learn the hash function.

(fc) layers and replace the last fc layer with a new one of k_1 dimensions. For the text modality, the text data represented using bag-of-words is passed through a series of fc layers to learn the hash function, with the final layer being of k_1 dimensions. Additionally, we define a unification network which takes as input the concatenated output of the image and text networks and generates a unified hash code. The output of each of these three networks is passed through a tanh activation to bring the values between -1 and 1 which are finally quantized using bit-wise sign operation to get the final hash codes.

We consider each part of the network as independent modules or blocks with a specific function. For the image network, the initial part of the network up to the penultimate fc layer is defined as the Feature Block (FB_x) which generates feature vector specific to the input image. This feature vector is used by the last fc layer termed as Hashing Block (HB_x) to learn semantically rich hash codes. We define the blocks in the above manner so that more hashing blocks can be added after the feature block to increase the number of hash bits, which enables us to train only a part of the network while obtaining better hash representations. The text domain network can be considered to have similar modules with the initial fc layers before the last two fc layers constituting the Feature Block (FB_y) and the last two fc layers making up the Hashing Block (HB_y).

We designate the functions approximated by FB and HB for the two modalities as $\{f^t_{FB}, f^t_{HB}\}$, with $t = \{x, y\}$. The functions are defined as $f^t_{FB} : t \rightarrow z^t_{FB}$ and $f^t_{HB} : z^t_{FB} \rightarrow z^t_{HB}$. Hence, $\mathcal{F}_t$ can be written as $\mathcal{F}_t = f^t_{HB}(f^t_{FB}(.))$. We concatenate the output (before the tanh layer) from the two networks f^x_{HB}, f^y_{HB} to form the concatenated vector z^u_{HB} which is then passed through the Unification Block (UB) to get the unified hash bits. We employ mean squared error (MSE) loss at the output of the two networks to learn the hash bits H^x and H^y. MSE is also used to get the unified hash code (choosing either H^x or H^y was found to be equally good). The overall loss function is $\mathcal{L} = \mathcal{L}_x + \mathcal{L}_y + \mathcal{L}_u$ with each loss $\mathcal{L}_t, (t \in \{x, y, u\})$ defined as

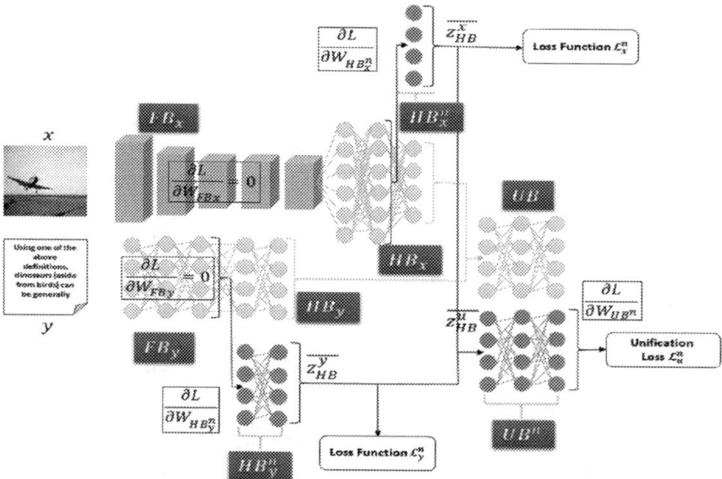

Fig. 4. The network architecture to learn the extended hash functions using the new network blocks (marked in green). The previously reused network blocks (marked in blue and yellow) are not trained again. (Color figure online)

$$\mathcal{L}_t = \sum_{i=1}^{N}\sum_{j=1}^{k_1}\left(z_{HB,ij}^t - h_{ij}^t\right)^2 + \lambda\sum_{i=1}^{N}\sum_{j=1}^{k_1}\left(\log\cosh(\left|z_{HB,ij}^t\right| - 1)\right) \quad (6)$$

The second term helps to reduce the quantization loss [37], with λ as the weight parameter. The quantization loss is essential because the variable h_{ij}^t (hash bits from the first stage) is discrete, whereas $z_{HB,ij}^t$ is the output after passing through the tanh layer.

Learning the Additional Hash Functions: Now, given the extended hash codes of length $k_2 (k_2 > k_1)$ bits, we show how the network described above can be seamlessly adapted to the new set of bits. In Stage 1, we keep the initially learned hash codes H^x, H^y of length k_1 fixed, and only learn the additional bits $\overline{H^x}, \overline{H^y}$ of length $(k_2 - k_1)$. Thus in Stage 2, we only introduce new hashing blocks and unification block $\{HB_x^n, HB_y^n, UB^n\}$ corresponding to the new $(k_2 - k_1)$ bits, which have the same architecture as $\{HB_x, HB_y, UB\}$ respectively. The original FB, HB and UB blocks for the initial k_1 bits need not be retrained. This is illustrated in Fig. 4. The new loss is $L^n = \mathcal{L}_x^n + \mathcal{L}_y^n + \mathcal{L}_u^n$ with each loss $\mathcal{L}_t^n, (t \in \{x, y, u\})$ defined as

$$\mathcal{L}_t^n = \sum_{i=1}^{N}\sum_{j=k_1+1}^{k_2}\left(\overline{z_{HB^n,ij}^t} - \overline{h_{ij}^t}\right)^2 + \lambda\sum_{i=1}^{N}\sum_{j=k_1+1}^{k_2}\left(\log\cosh(\left|\overline{z_{HB^n,ij}^t}\right| - 1)\right) \quad (7)$$

Since we do not retrain the original blocks FB_x, FB_y, we fix $\{\frac{\partial L^n}{\partial W_{FBx}} = 0, \frac{\partial L^n}{\partial W_{FBy}} = 0\}$ (W denotes the weights and biases of the network blocks) so as not to update their network parameters, which helps to significantly reduce the training time.

There are two fc layers in the HB_y block for the text network as it is not pre-trained. The unification block needs to be repeated as the function to learn the additional bits have to be trained from scratch.

For a test query, hash codes are generated by passing it through the network and using sign() for quantization. For a paired data sample, the unified hash representation is generated by passing it further through the unification block with subsequent quantization.

This work has differences from the recent state-of-the-art technique in [20] - (1) here, we are integrating a deep based architecture to learn the hash functions which performs better than the non-deep based ones, (2) the unification scheme outperforms the unification scheme in [20] and (3) this algorithm can learn the bits in an incremental fashion. This incremental method can also be applied for unimodal hashing purpose though here we have specifically focussed on cross-modal applications.

4 Experiments

4.1 Datasets and Evaluation Protocol

The three datasets we have used for our evaluation are MIRFLICKR-25K [10], IAPR TC-12 [6] and NUS-WIDE [3]. We follow the standard experimental protocol as in [11]. MIRFLICKR-25K [10] has 25,000 images accumulated from Flickr website with each described by textual tags, of which only those pairs with at-least 20 tags are considered. We use Convolutional Neural Network (CNN) features for images and 1386-dimensional bag-of-words (BOW) feature vectors [11] for the text. Each pair has multiple annotations out of 24 possible unique labels. The IAPR TC-12 dataset [6] has 20,000 image-text pairs with annotation spread over 255 labels. Following the same protocol as in [11], we use the entire dataset in IAPR TC-12 for our experiments. CNN features and 2912-dimensional BOW features are used for image and text data respectively [11]. NUS-WIDE [3] has 260,648 images designated with multiple labels across 81 categories. As in [11], we consider only those pairs that belong to the 21 most frequent concepts to form a reduced dataset of 195,834 image-text pairs for our experiments. For textual data, we use a 1000-dimensional BOW representation, while for images we use CNN features. All the features are taken from the work in [11].

The retrieval performance is measured using Mean Average Precision (MAP). It is computed as the mean of the Average Precision (AP) of all the queries where $AP(q) = \frac{\sum_{r=1}^{R} P_q(r)\delta(r)}{\sum_{r=1}^{R} \delta(r)}$. R is the number of retrieved items and $P_q(r)$ is the precision at position r for query q. $\delta(r)$ is defined to be 1 if the rth retrieved item shares at least one label with the label of the query q, else it is set to 0.

4.2 Baseline and Implementation Details

We compare the proposed approach with the state-of-the-art cross-modal supervised hashing methods like SePH [15], STMH [24], SCM [31], GSPH [20], DCMH [11], PRDH [30] and some unsupervised methods like CMFH [5] and CCA [8]. We report the results of the above baseline algorithms from the work in [11] whenever available. We report the results of GSPH and SePH using the unification strategy for fair comparison. We use the open source deep learning toolbox PyTorch [21] on a NVIDIA Titan X GPU card to perform our evaluations. For the text based network, the FB and HB consist of one and two fc layers respectively and the UB consists of three fc layers. The hidden layer is taken to be 500-dimensional except for the NUS-WIDE dataset, where it is chosen as 1500. The learning rate for training the network initially and re-training it for the extended bits is set to be $lr = 1e^{-3}$ and $lr = 1e^{-4}$. It took around 10–30 iterations for our network to converge. Now, we describe the results obtained by our algorithm.

4.3 Results

Results for Protocol I (P-I). P-I is the standard cross-modal evaluation protocol as in [11]. We randomly sample 2000 examples to form the query set and the remaining form the retrieval set for MIRFLICKR-25K [10] and IAPR TC-12 [6] datasets. For NUS-WIDE [3], randomly chosen 2100 examples form the query set and the remaining examples form the retrieval set. The training data is formed by sampling from the retrieval set itself as in [11]. We use $\{10000, 10000, 10500\}$ examples as the training set for MIRFLICKR-25K, IAPR TC-12, and NUS-WIDE datasets respectively. As in [11,15,20], a retrieval is considered correct if it shares at least one common label with the query. The MAP results for *GrowBit* and comparison with the state-of-the-art on the three datasets is given in Table 1. $I \rightarrow T$ denotes that image query is used to retrieve text data and vice-versa. We report the comparisons with PRDH [30] in Table 1 by following the same protocol as in [30] (results marked with *). We observe that *GrowBit* outperforms the other approaches for all the three datasets. The performance of our approach increases monotonically with an increase in the number of bits. Interestingly, it also outperforms DCMH [11] and PRDH [30] though ours is not an end-to-end deep learning approach. Figure 5 shows some text-image retrieval (top-5) results for the MirFlickr [10] dataset.

Results for Protocol II (P-II). In P-II, we want to increase the length of hash bits to get better retrieval performance without changing the number of tags/labels. The results for P-II for the three datasets are given in Table 2. Here $16 \rightarrow 64$ denotes that the initial hash code length is 16 and it is increased to 64 using *GrowBit*. Comparing the results with that in Table 1, we observe that the improved performance obtained by increasing the number of bits eg. $16 \rightarrow 64$ and $32 \rightarrow 64$ does not significantly deviate from the expected result if we would have learned all the 64 hash bits from scratch. This is observed across both the

Table 1. MAP for MIRFLICKR-25K, IAPR TC-12 and NUS-WIDE datasets for P-I.

Task	Method	MIRFLICKR-25K			IAPR TC-12			NUS-WIDE		
		16 bits	32 bits	64 bits	16 bits	32 bits	64 bits	16 bits	32 bits	64 bits
$I \rightarrow T$	CCA	0.5719	0.5693	0.5672	0.3422	0.3361	0.3300	0.3604	0.3485	0.3390
	CMFH	0.6377	0.6418	0.6451	0.4189	0.4234	0.4251	0.4900	0.5053	0.5097
	SCM	0.6851	0.6921	0.7003	0.3692	0.3666	0.3802	0.5409	0.5485	0.5553
	STMH	0.6132	0.6219	0.6274	0.3775	0.4002	0.4130	0.4710	0.4864	0.4942
	SePH	0.7123	0.7194	0.7232	0.4442	0.4563	0.4639	0.6037	0.6136	0.6211
	DCMH	0.7410	0.7465	0.7485	0.4526	0.4732	0.4844	0.5903	0.6031	0.6093
	GSPH	0.7706	0.7866	0.7984	0.4799	0.5128	0.5372	0.7074	0.7258	0.7381
	GrowBit	**0.7951**	**0.8053**	**0.8232**	**0.4987**	**0.5371**	**0.5621**	**0.7069**	**0.7283**	**0.7408**
	PRDH*	0.7126	0.7128	0.7201	-	-	-	0.6348	0.6529	0.6506
	GrowBit*	**0.7675**	**0.7898**	**0.8008**	-	-	-	**0.7275**	**0.7491**	**0.7584**
$T \rightarrow I$	CCA	0.5742	0.5713	0.5691	0.3493	0.3438	0.3378	0.3614	0.3494	0.3395
	CMFH	0.6365	0.6399	0.6429	0.4168	0.4212	0.4277	0.5031	0.5187	0.5225
	SCM	0.6939	0.7012	0.7060	0.3453	0.3410	0.3470	0.5344	0.5412	0.5484
	STMH	0.6074	0.6153	0.6217	0.3687	0.3897	0.4044	0.4471	0.4677	0.4780
	SePH	0.7216	0.7261	0.7319	0.4423	0.4562	0.4648	0.5983	0.6025	0.6109
	DCMH	0.7827	0.7900	0.7932	0.5185	0.5378	0.5468	0.6389	0.6511	0.6571
	GSPH	0.7388	0.7522	0.7653	0.4881	0.5260	0.5523	0.6561	0.6716	0.6860
	GrowBit	**0.7778**	**0.7919**	**0.7994**	**0.5205**	**0.5614**	**0.5828**	**0.6595**	**0.6864**	**0.6945**
	PRDH*	0.7467	0.7540	0.7505	-	-	-	0.6808	0.6961	0.6943
	GrowBit*	**0.7496**	**0.7728**	**0.7793**	-	-	-	**0.6893**	**0.7060**	**0.7082**

Fig. 5. Few text-image retrieval (top-5) results for the MirFlickr dataset [10] under P-I protocol.

scenarios $I \rightarrow T$ and $T \rightarrow I$ and across all the datasets. Figure 6 shows some $T \rightarrow I$ retrieval (top-5) results for the MirFlickr [10] dataset. We observe that using extended hash bits ($16 \rightarrow 64$), there is a noticeable improvement in the images that are retrieved corresponding to the text query.

Results for Protocol III (P-III). In this third and most challenging protocol, the number of tags increases which needs to be accounted for by the new bits. Here, we initially learn the hash codes using 50% of the tags and use the extended hash bits to learn the full semantic relations using all the tags. The 50% split is generated randomly and we repeat our experiments three times and report the average. The results for the three datasets for P-III are shown in Table 2. We observe that (1) the performance of the incremented hash bits as compared to

Table 2. MAP for the three datasets for P-II and P-III.

Protocol	Dataset	$I \rightarrow T$			$T \rightarrow I$		
		$16 \rightarrow 32$	$16 \rightarrow 64$	$32 \rightarrow 64$	$16 \rightarrow 32$	$16 \rightarrow 64$	$32 \rightarrow 64$
P-II	MIRFLICKR-25K	0.8108	0.8180	0.8253	0.7970	0.7983	0.8085
	IAPR TC-12	0.5325	0.5449	0.5599	0.5550	0.5610	0.5820
	NUS-WIDE	0.7248	0.7394	0.7413	0.6860	0.6884	0.7001
P-III	MIRFLICKR-25K	0.7907	0.8094	0.8010	0.7700	0.7777	0.7733
	IAPR TC-12	0.5143	0.5574	0.5525	0.5310	0.5647	0.5635
	NUS-WIDE	0.6933	0.7188	0.7143	0.6426	0.6540	0.6629

Fig. 6. Few text-image retrieval (top-5) results for the MirFlickr [10] dataset under P-II protocol. We observe that the extended hash bits ($16 \rightarrow 64$) helps to better capture the semantic relation and shows a noticeable improvement in the retrieved items.

Table 1 is slightly lower, and (2) the performance drop in $I \rightarrow T$ is smaller as compared to that in $T \rightarrow I$.

4.4 Analysis of the Proposed Approach.

Effect of Unification: Figure 7 shows the retrieval performance (MAP) on the three datasets with and without unification for hash bit length of 16, 32 and 64 for Protocol I. We observe that the unified bits gives a significant boost in the performance. Thus the complementary information from both the modalities results in significant improvement in the retrieval performance for both $I \rightarrow T$ and $T \rightarrow I$ scenarios.

Effect of Number of Hash Bits: We observe from Fig. 8 (left) that the retrieval performance (MAP) improves monotonically with increase in the number of bits (from 16 to 128) for both the datasets MIRFLICKR-25K and IAPR TC-12.

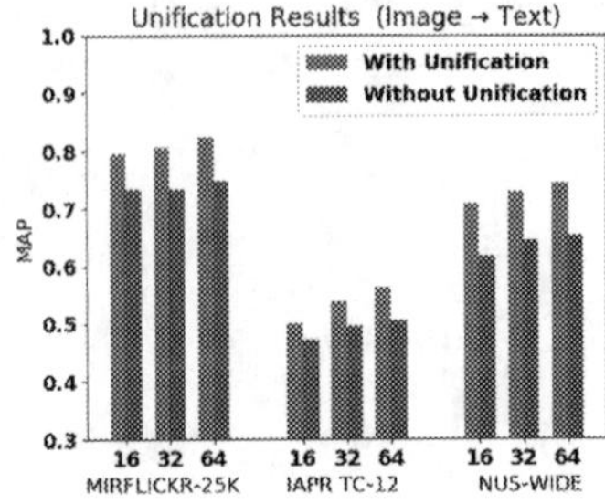

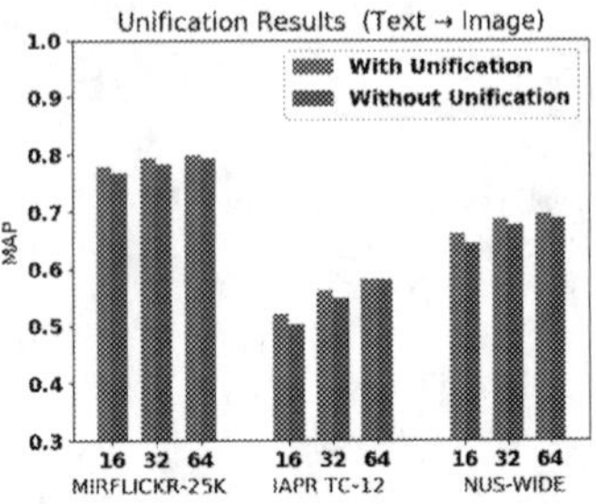

Fig. 7. MAP (y-axis) for the three datasets with and without unification for P-I.

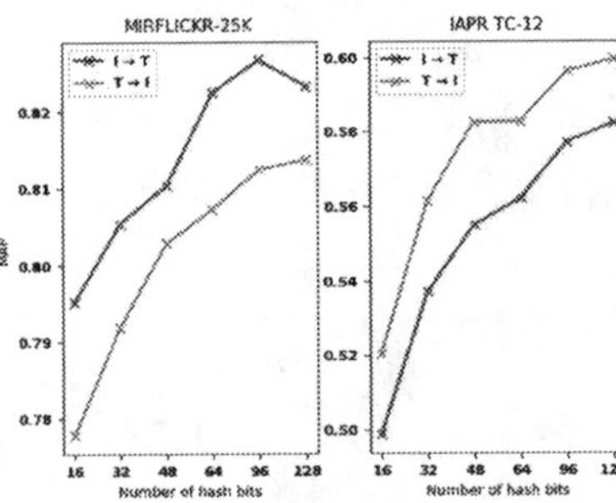

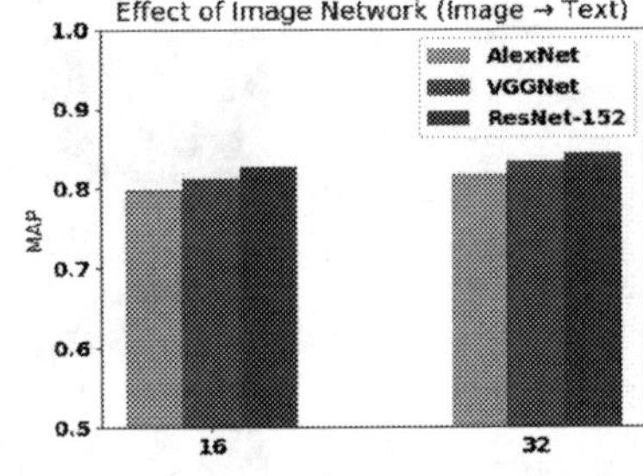

Fig. 8. (Left) MAP with increasing number of bits for both $I \rightarrow T$ and $T \rightarrow I$ scenarios under P-I protocol. (Right) MAP performance on MIRFLICKR-25K using different networks.

Effect of Better Network Architecture: Here we study the effects of using networks with better representation capabilities on the retrieval performance. The $I \rightarrow T$ results for the MIRFLICKR-25K dataset with different architectures [21] for the image domain is shown in Fig. 8 (right). We observe that better networks improve the retrieval performance for both 16 and 32 bits. Since the network for the text data remains unchanged, the $T \rightarrow I$ results do not improve much, which can potentially be improved with a better network for the text modality.

Savings in Computation: Now we show the computation savings in both Stage 1 and Stage 2 of our algorithm when we learn extended hash codes. Table 3 shows the computation required for the MIRFLICKR-25K dataset when we extend the hash bits from $k_1 = 16$ to $k_2 = \{32, 64\}$ for a training data size of $N = 10,000$. We observe that most of the savings is obtained when the number of fc layers in the HB block is reduced. The relative number of parameters saved using GrowBit is also provided. Considerable savings will also be there during testing as k_1 bits for the test data can be reused.

Table 3. Comparison of MAP obtained for P-I and P-II. The relative gain in performance (%) obtained ($k_1 \rightarrow k_2$ vs k_1) is shown. The parameters (in millions for both Stages s_1, s_2) required for training $10K$ data of MIRFLICKR-25K is also noted with relative savings $\left(1 - \frac{\#(k_1 \rightarrow k_2)}{\#k_2}\right)$ given in %.

	$I \rightarrow T$ ($T \rightarrow I$)		
	16 bits	32 bits	64 bits
P-I	0.7951 (0.778)	0.805 (0.792)	0.823 (0.799)
P-II	-	0.8108 (0.797) $_{16 \rightarrow 32}$	0.818 (0.7983) $_{16 \rightarrow 64}$
Gain	-	1.975% (2.469%)	2.880% (2.636%)
$\#k_1$	$0.32^{s_1} + 59.50^{s_2}$	$0.64^{s_1} + 59.65^{s_2}$	$1.28^{s_1} + 59.80^{s_2}$
$\#(k_1 \rightarrow k_2)$	-	$(0.32^{s_1} + 0.59^{s_2})_{16 \rightarrow 32}$	$(0.96^{s_1} + 0.76^{s_2})_{16 \rightarrow 64}$
Parameters saved (in %)	-	$50.0\%^{s_1} + 98.9\%^{s_2}$	$25.0\%^{s_1} + 98.7\%^{s_2}$

5 Summary

In this work, we have proposed a novel incremental hashing approach *GrowBit* for cross-modal retrieval which can incrementally learn the hash codes for better representation of the data, especially when the number of tags increases. The novel hash code unification block gives significant performance boost by using the complementary information of the two modalities effectively. To the best of our knowledge, this is the first work which addresses this problem. Extensive evaluation on three cross-modal datasets under different protocols justifies the usefulness of the proposed approach.

References

1. Bronstein, M.M., Bronstein, A.M., Michel, F., Paragios, N.: Data fusion through cross-modality metric learning using similarity-sensitive hashing. In: 2010 IEEE Conference on Computer Vision and Pattern Recognition (CVPR), pp. 3594–3601 (2010)
2. Cakir, F., He, K., Sclaroff, S.: Hashing with binary matrix pursuit. arXiv preprint arXiv:1808.01990 (2018)
3. Chua, T.S., Tang, J., Hong, R., Li, H., Luo, Z., Zheng, Y.: NUS-WIDE: a real-world web image database from National University of Singapore. In: 2009 ACM International Conference on Image and Video Retrieval (ACM-CIVR), pp. 48–56 (2009)
4. Dai, Q., Li, J., Wang, J., Jiang, Y.G.: Binary optimized hashing. In: 2016 ACM on Multimedia Conference (ACM-MM), pp. 1247–1256 (2016)
5. Ding, G., Guo, Y., Zhou, J.: Collective matrix factorization hashing for multimodal data. In: 2014 IEEE Conference on Computer Vision and Pattern Recognition (CVPR), pp. 2075–2082 (2014)
6. Escalante, H.J., et al.: The segmented and annotated IAPR TC-12 benchmark. Comput. Vis. Image Underst. **114**, 419–428 (2010)
7. Fatih, C., He, K., Bargal, S.A., Sclaroff, S.: MIHash: online hashing with mutual information. In: 2017 IEEE International Conference on Computer Vision (ICCV), pp. 437–445 (2017)

8. Hardoon, D.R., Szedmak, S., Shawe-Taylor, J.: Canonical correlation analysis: an overview with application to learning methods. Neural Comput. **16**, 2639–2664 (2004)
9. Horn, R.A., Johnson, C.R.: Matrix Analysis. Cambridge University Press, Cambridge (1990)
10. Huiskes, M.J., Lew, M.S.: The MIR Flickr retrieval evaluation. In: 2008 ACM International Conference on Multimedia Information Retrieval (ACM-MIR), pp. 39–43 (2008)
11. Jiang, Q.Y., Li, W.J.: Deep cross-modal hashing. In: 2017 IEEE Conference on Computer Vision and Pattern Recognition (CVPR), pp. 3232–3240 (2017)
12. Krizhevsky, A., Sutskever, I., Hinton, G.E.: ImageNet classification with deep convolutional neural networks. In: 2012 Advances in Neural Information Processing Systems (NIPS), pp. 1097–1105 (2012)
13. Kumar, S., Udupa, R.: Learning hash functions for cross-view similarity search. In: 2011 International Joint Conference on Artificial Intelligence (IJCAI), pp. 1360–1365 (2011)
14. Lin, G., Shen, C., Suter, D., van den Hengel, A.: A general two-step approach to learning-based hashing. In: 2013 IEEE International Conference on Computer Vision (ICCV), pp. 2552–2559 (2013)
15. Lin, Z., Ding, G., Han, J., Wang, J.: Cross-view retrieval via probability-based semantics-preserving hashing. IEEE Trans. Cybern. **47**, 4342–4355 (2017)
16. Lin, Z., Ding, G., Hu, M., Wang, J.: Semantics-preserving hashing for cross-view retrieval. In: 2015 IEEE Conference on Computer Vision and Pattern Recognition (CVPR), pp. 3864–3872 (2015)
17. Liu, L., Lin, Z., Shao, L., Shen, F., Ding, G., Han, J.: Sequential discrete hashing for scalable cross-modality similarity retrieval. IEEE Trans. Image Process. **26**, 107–118 (2017)
18. Long, M., Cao, Y., Wang, J., Yu, P.S.: Compositional correlation quantization for large-scale multimodal search. In: 2016 International ACM SIGIR Conference on Research & Development in Information Retrieval (SIGIR), pp. 579–588 (2016)
19. Mandal, D., Biswas, S.: Label consistent matrix factorization based hashing for cross-modal retrieval. In: 2017 IEEE International Conference on Image Processing (ICIP), pp. 2901–2905 (2017)
20. Mandal, D., Chaudhury, K.N., Biswas, S.: Generalized semantic preserving hashing for n-label cross-modal retrieval. In: 2017 IEEE Conference on Computer Vision and Pattern Recognition (CVPR), pp. 2633–2641 (2017)
21. Paszke, A., et al.: Automatic differentiation in PyTorch. In: 2017 Advances in Neural Information Processing Systems Workshop (NIPS-W) (2017)
22. Shen, F., Zhou, X., Yang, Y., Song, J., Shen, H.T., Tao, D.: A fast optimization method for general binary code learning. IEEE Trans. Image Process. **25**, 5610–5621 (2017)
23. Song, J., Yang, Y., Yang, Y., Huang, Z., Shen, H.T.: Inter-media hashing for large-scale retrieval from heterogeneous data sources. In: 2013 ACM SIGMOD International Conference on Management of Data (SIGMOD), pp. 785–796 (2013)
24. Wang, D., Gao, X., Wang, X., He, L.: Semantic topic multimodal hashing for cross-media retrieval. In: 2015 International Joint Conference on Artificial Intelligence (IJCAI), pp. 3890–3896 (2015)
25. Wang, J., Kumar, S., Chang, S.F.: Sequential projection learning for hashing with compact codes. In: 2010 International Conference on Machine Learning (ICML), pp. 1127–1134 (2010)

26. Wu, B., Yang, Q., Zheng, W.S., Wang, Y., Wang, J.: Quantized correlation hashing for fast cross-modal search. In: 2015 International Joint Conference on Artificial Intelligence (IJCAI), pp. 3946–3952 (2015)
27. Xia, R., Pan, Y., Lai, H., Liu, C., Yan, S.: Supervised hashing for image retrieval via image representation learning. In: 2014 AAAI Conference on Artificial Intelligence (AAAI), pp. 2156–2162 (2014)
28. Xie, L., Shen, J., Han, J., Zhu, L., Shao, L.: Dynamic multi-view hashing for online image retrieval. In: 2017 International Joint Conference on Artificial Intelligence (IJCAI), pp. 3133–3139 (2017)
29. Xu, X., Shen, F., Yang, Y., Shen, H.T., Li, X.: Learning discriminative binary codes for large-scale cross-modal retrieval. IEEE Trans. Image Process. **26**, 2494–2507 (2017)
30. Yang, E., Deng, C., Liu, W., Liu, X., Tao, D., Gao, X.: Pairwise relationship guided deep hashing for cross-modal retrieval. In: 2017 AAAI Conference on Artificial Intelligence (AAAI), pp. 1618–1625 (2017)
31. Zhang, D., Li, W.J.: Large-scale supervised multimodal hashing with semantic correlation maximization. In: 2014 AAAI Conference on Artificial Intelligence (AAAI), pp. 2177–2183 (2014)
32. Zhang, J., Peng, Y., Yuan, M.: Unsupervised generative adversarial cross-modal hashing. In: 2018 AAAI Conference on Artificial Intelligence (AAAI), pp. 539–546 (2018)
33. Zhang, R., Lin, L., Zhang, R., Zuo, W., Zhang, L.: Bit-scalable deep hashing with regularized similarity learning for image retrieval and person re-identification. IEEE Trans. Image Process. **24**, 4766–4779 (2015)
34. Zhang, T., Wang, J.: Collaborative quantization for cross-modal similarity search. In: 2016 IEEE Conference on Computer Vision and Pattern Recognition (CVPR), pp. 2036–2045 (2016)
35. Zhou, J., Ding, G., Guo, Y.: Latent semantic sparse hashing for cross-modal similarity search. In: 2014 International ACM SIGIR Conference on Research & Development in Information Retrieval (SIGIR), pp. 415–424 (2014)
36. Zhou, J., Ding, G., Guo, Y., Liu, Q., Dong, X.: Kernel-based supervised hashing for cross-view similarity search. In: 2014 IEEE International Conference on Multimedia and Expo (ICME), pp. 1–6 (2014)
37. Zhu, H., Long, M., Wang, J., Cao, Y.: Deep hashing network for efficient similarity retrieval. In: 2016 AAAI Conference on Artificial Intelligence (AAAI), pp. 2415–2421 (2016)
38. Zhuang, B., Lin, G., Shen, C., Reid, I.: Fast training of triplet-based deep binary embedding networks. In: 2016 IEEE Conference on Computer Vision and Pattern Recognition (CVPR), pp. 5955–5964 (2016)

Region-Semantics Preserving Image Synthesis

Kang-Jun Liu, Tsu-Jui Fu, and Shan-Hung Wu(✉)

National Tsing Hua University, Hsinchu, Taiwan, R.O.C.
{kjliu,zrfu}@datalab.cs.nthu.edu.tw, shwu@cs.nthu.edu.tw

Abstract. We study the problem of *region-semantics preserving* (RSP) image synthesis. Given a reference image and a region specification R, our goal is to train a model that is able to generate realistic and diverse images, each preserving the same semantics as that of the reference image within the region R. This problem is challenging because the model needs to (1) understand and preserve the *marginal semantics* of the reference region; i.e., the semantics excluding that of any subregion; and (2) maintain the compatibility of any synthesized region with the marginal semantics of the reference region. In this paper, we propose a novel model, called the *fast region-semantics preserver* (Fast-RSPer), for the RSP image synthesis problem. The Fast-RSPer uses a pre-trained GAN generator and a pre-trained deep feature extractor to generate images without undergoing a dedicated training phase. This makes it particularly useful for the interactive applications. We conduct extensive experiments using the real-world datasets and the results show that Fast-PSPer can synthesize realistic, diverse RSP images efficiently.

1 Introduction

Image synthesis is a long-standing goal in computer vision, graphics, and machine learning. Recent advances in image modeling with neural networks [7,8,14,18,24,26] have made it feasible to generate photorealistic and diverse/creative images. While such unconditional models are fascinating, many practical applications of image synthesis require a model to be conditioned on prior information, motivating further studies on *controlling* the synthesis.

One common way to control the model is to use a *reference image*; that is, given an image as the input, the model is expected to generate images that resemble the input image. This strategy advances the state-of-the-art in density estimation [2], compression [30], in-painting [12,23], super-resolution [17] and image-to-image translation [13,35]. However, the reference image may be a too stringent control that limits the *diversity* of synthesized images. In many other applications, such as interactive photo editing [1] and stimuli generation in psycho-physical experiments [6], diversity is a key to success. There is a need for a new form of control that guides the model in a *soft* manner.

In this paper, we study the problem of *region-semantics preserving* (RSP) image synthesis, as shown in Fig. 1(a). Specifically, given one or more reference

C. V. Jawahar et al. (Eds.): ACCV 2018, LNCS 11364, pp. 322–337, 2019.
https://doi.org/10.1007/978-3-030-20870-7_20

(a) Input/output (b) Interactive editor

Fig. 1. Region semantic preserving (RSP) image synthesis problem. (a) A user provides reference regions R, which can be copied from different sources, then get synthesized, complete images preserving the semantics behind the reference regions. (b) An interactive editor based on real-time RSP image synthesis.

images and the region specification R, our goal is to train a model that is able to generate realistic and diverse images, each showing the same semantics as that of the reference image within the region R. We call the pixels enclosed by R in the reference image and synthesized image the *reference region* and *synthesized region*, respectively. Depending on the application, R could be specified in either a coarse grain (coordinates of a bounding box) or fine grain (pixel identifiers) manner. For example, one can ask the model to synthesis images with the semantic "happy mouth plus female eyes" by giving the reference regions shown in Fig. 1(b). Note that the mouth or eyes in a synthesized region need *not* be identical to that in the reference region since only the *semantics* is preserved. One can also obtain many bedroom images with the same partial layout by giving some reference bedroom regions, as shown in Fig. 1(a). Note that in an image, the semantics of a region R may be closely related to that of other regions residing either inside or outside R. So, to preserve the semantics of the reference region, the model will generate images that are compatible with the semantics everywhere. In other words, although being regional, the reference region is able to guide *all* pixels in a synthesized image, and we can expect "bedroom-only" decorators to appear in Fig. 1(a) and "female faces" in Fig. 1(b).

The RSP image synthesis is a challenging problem because when generating an image, the model needs to (1) understand and preserve the *marginal semantics* of the reference region. By "marginal" we mean that the semantics excludes the meaning of any other region (residing in or out R). For example, in Fig. 1(a), the marginal semantics of R is "a bedroom with partial layout" despite that any subregion of R could have its own meaning (e.g., a bed, scene outside the window, etc.); (2) maintain the compatibility of any generated region with the marginal semantics of the reference region. To the best of our knowledge, the Ladder-VAEs [22,29] are the only off-the-shelf models that can be used to synthesize RSP images. Another solution could be a modified generative adversarial network [7] (GAN). However, in practice, these approaches usually produce images with sub-optimal quality and/or are very slow to train and run.

Here, we propose a novel model, called the *fast region-semantics preserver* (Fast-RSPer), that can produce high-quality RSP images and are fast to run.

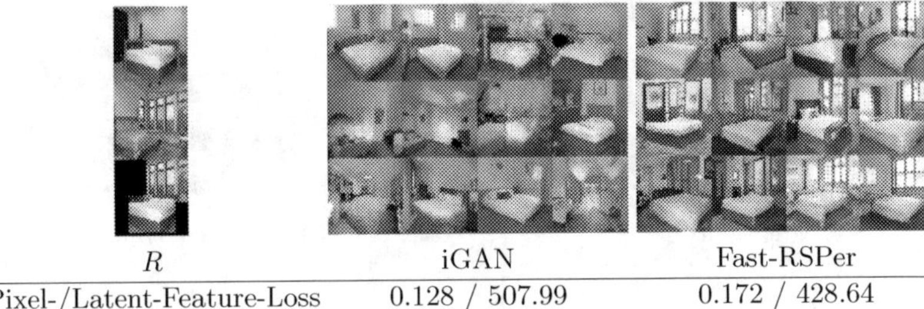

	R	iGAN	Fast-RSPer
Pixel-/Latent-Feature-Loss		0.128 / 507.99	0.172 / 428.64

Fig. 2. Pixel- vs. semantics-preserving. iGAN [34], whose goal is to align pixels of synthesized images with those in R, gives lower pixels-losses but higher feature losses at a deep CNN layer. As the pixels in R become more diverse, the semantics is harder to preserve by aligning pixels. (Color figure online)

The Fast-RSPer is based on GANs but unlike most GANs where a generator and a discriminator are trained jointly, it uses a pre-trained generator and feeds the output (images) into a pre-trained deep feature extractor. Given a reference image and R, the Fast-RSPer synthesis an image by finding (using the gradient descent) an input variable $\boldsymbol{z}$ for the generator such that, at a deep layer where neurons capture the semantics of the reference R, the feature extractor maps the synthesized region to features similar to those of the reference region. Since both the generator and feature extractor are pre-trained, the Fast-RSPer has no dedicated training phase and can generate images efficiently. Furthermore, it has been shown [20] that a properly trained generator can map $\boldsymbol{z}$ to a high quality image at a high resolution.

However, in practice there are still many technical problems to solve to synthesize a high-quality RSP image. The first problem is how to align the semantics of R with that of the synthesized region while maintaining its compatibility with other regions. Fast-RSPer uses both the *macro-* and *micro-*alignment techniques to achieve these goals. Second, the gradient descent algorithm may find $\boldsymbol{z}$'s (for different images) close to each other, resulting in the lack of diversity among multiple synthesized images. Fast-RSPer adds *gradient noises* to create visual diversity. Furthermore, a pre-trained generator may fail to generate satisfactory images in some cases. We investigate the cause and discuss pitfalls to avoid when using a pre-train generator. Following summarizes our contributions:

- We propose the problem of region-semantics preserving (RSP) image synthesis that allows a user to easily guide the synthesis using a reference image in a soft manner.
- We present the Fast-RSPer model that generates realistic, diverse RSP images in near realtime.
- We discuss practical tricks to use and pitfalls to avoid to synthesize high-quality RSP images.
- We conduct experiments using the real-word datasets and the results show that the Fast-PSPer can synthesize photorealistic, diverse RSP images efficiently, enabling new interactive applications.

2 Related Work

Studies have explored different ways other than using a reference image to control the image synthesis. Mirza et al. [19] train a GAN by feeding the class labels and show that the generator can learn to produce images conditioned on a given label. Reed et al. [25] extend the GAN architecture to synthesis images from text. Güçlütürk et al. [9] use deep neural networks for inverting face sketches to synthesize face images. Studies [4,31,33] propose models that synthesize images based on domain-specific attributes such as the orientation with respect to the camera. The goals of the above studies are orthogonal to ours–to present an easy-to-use, powerful, soft control over the reference image.

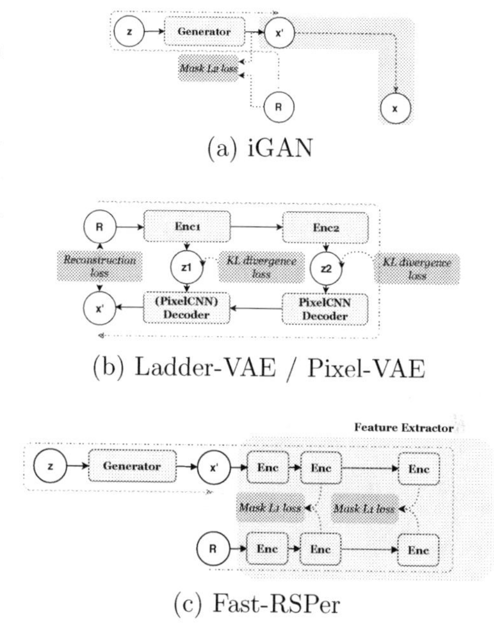

(a) iGAN

(b) Ladder-VAE / Pixel-VAE

(c) Fast-RSPer

Fig. 3. Model architecture of (a) Ladder-VAE and Pixel-VAE; (b) iGAN; (c) Fast-RSPer. The $\boldsymbol{x}$ is a reference image, R is the reference region, $\boldsymbol{x}'$ is a synthesized image, and $\boldsymbol{z}$ is a latent variable. Red dashed lines denote the computation flows for generating an image while the blue line denotes post-processing.

The style transfer [5,15] and image analogies [11] can be seen as ways to synthesize images using a soft control. The former expects a *style image* to come along with the reference image (serving as the content image); while the latter takes *a pair of images* as additional input and synthesis images following the example analogy between the images in the pair. These soft controls (i.e., the style image and the image pair) are very different from the reference region R proposed in this paper, and their applications normally don't emphasize on diversity of the synthesize results.

iGAN. This idea of using a pre-trained generator to speed up image synthesis is not new and has appeared in iGAN [34], whose model architecture is shown in Fig. 3(a). However, the work studied a different problem, where there are two types of input: one the "base image" and another the "changes" to the base image, and the goal is to synthesis images that preserve the semantics of the base image while having the changes applied. The optimization procedure in [34] finds a $\boldsymbol{z}$ so that the generated image $G(\boldsymbol{z})$ satisfies two constraints: (1) the semantics of the base image is preserved and (2) the changes are applied to $G(\boldsymbol{z})$. For the constraint (2), the changes are applied *at the pixel level* (see the data term in Eqs. (4) and (5) in [34]), which is different from our region-semantic-preserving image synthesis problem where only the latent marginal semantic should be preserved. In iGAN, the $\boldsymbol{z}$ can only output images that helps an *auxiliary algorithm* measure and apply the same amount of geometric and color changes to the original base image to produce the final result. The images synthesized by iGAN and Fast-RSPer has different characteristics, as shown in Fig. 2. When pixels in R (e.g., window scene) are diverse, images synthesized by iGAN may end up preserving the *average* of pixels in R, destroying the semantics.

Ladder-VAEs/Pixel-VAE. To overcome the challenges of the RSP image synthesis discussed in Sect. 1, an image model needs to be able to extract and manipulate the semantics of *any* region in an image. One way to achieve this is to use the Ladder-VAE [29], whose architecture is shown in Fig. 3(b). Assuming that the encoding and decoding of an image follow two multi-layer distributions recursively parametrized by a series of shared latent variables $\boldsymbol{z}^{(i)}$'s, the Ladder-VAE learns the $\boldsymbol{z}^{(i)}$'s from a training dataset and synthesizes images following the multi-layer decoding distribution parametrized by the learned $\boldsymbol{z}^{(i)}$'s. To preserve the marginal semantics of the reference region, one can encode the reference image using the Ladder-VAE encoder, identify the dimensions of $\boldsymbol{z}^{(i)}$ parameterizing the reference region at a deep layer i, and then *fix* the decoding distribution along those dimensions in the Ladder-VAE decoder when synthesizing images. To create diversity while maintaining the compatibility of any region in a synthesized image with the reference region, one can add *sampling variances* to decoding distributions parametrized the rest dimensions of $\boldsymbol{z}^{(i)}$ and all dimensions of $\boldsymbol{z}^{(j)}$, $j \neq i$. However, the VAE variants are known to produce blurry images [14]. To solve this problem, one can use the Pixel-VAE [22] that replaces the decoder of Ladder-VAE with an autoregressive decoder based on the Pixel-CNN [23]. But this creates another problem that the decoder needs to generate pixels one-by-one (due to the autoregressive nature) and becomes very slow. Furthermore, the autoregressive decoder may occasionally generate "bad" pixels (due to the sampling for diversity) that degrades the quality of following pixels and creates local artifacts in the synthesized images.

3 Fast RSP Image Synthesis

In this section, we present a fast, end-to-end algorithm [7] for synthesizing RSP images based on GANs. As compared to (non-autoregressive) VAEs, GANs are able to produce sharp images. In a GAN model, the generator maps a random noise vector $\boldsymbol{z}$ to an image $\boldsymbol{x}'$ and tries to trick the discriminator into believing that $\boldsymbol{x}'$ is a real image coming from the training dataset. To synthesize RSP images, a GAN-based generator needs to be capable of extracting and manipulating the semantics of any region in an image (see the challenges discussed in Sect. 1).

One naive way to do so is to extend the VAE-GAN [16], by replacing the generator with a Ladder-VAE. This allows us to control the multi-layer decoding distributions using the sampling techniques discussed in Sect. 2. So, the extended VAE-GAN model is able to output crisp RSP images without resorting to the autoregressive alternatives, which are slow at generating images. However, the model suffers from a practical drawback that it requires a dedicated training phase *for each* given reference image and R. The training cost prevents the model from being useful in interactive scenarios, such as the interactive photo editing [1].

Here, we propose a novel model, called the *fast region-semantics preserver* (Fast-RSPer), that uses a pre-trained GAN generator G and a pre-trained deep feature extractor $\Phi = \{\Phi^{(1)}, \Phi^{(2)}, \cdots, \Phi^{(L)}\}$ (e.g., a deep CNN), where $\Phi^{(L)}$ is the deepest layer, to synthesize RSP images. We feed the output of the generator to the feature extractor, as shown in Fig. 3(d). Given a reference image $\boldsymbol{x}$ and a region specification R, the Fast-RSPer synthesizes an image by solving the input $\boldsymbol{z}^*$ for G first, where

$$\boldsymbol{z}^* = \arg\min_{\boldsymbol{z}} \Sigma_{i=l}^{L} \|\Phi^{(i)}(G(\boldsymbol{z})) - \Phi^{(i)}(\boldsymbol{x})\|_{mask}^{(i)}, \tag{1}$$

l is a sufficiently deep layer in Φ, and $\|\cdot\|_{mask}^{(i)}$ is a masked one-norm taking into account only the dimensions/features/activations of neurons whose receptive fields overlaps with R at layer i. The model then feeds $\boldsymbol{z}^*$ into G to synthesize an RSP image $G(\boldsymbol{z}^*)$. Intuitively, the Fast-RSPer generates an image by finding an input variable $\boldsymbol{z}^*$ for the generator G such that, at deep layers where neurons are able to capture the semantics of the reference region, the feature extractor Φ maps the synthesized region to features similar to those of the reference region. Note that the marginal semantics of the reference region is preserved in $G(\boldsymbol{z}^*)$ by explicitly solving Eq. (1). On the other hand, the compatibility of other regions in $G(\boldsymbol{z}^*)$ with the semantics of the reference region is maintained *implicitly* by the GAN generator–if the generator produced incompatible regions, it wouldn't have fooled the discriminator during the GAN training process.

Merits. The Fast-RSPer is an unsupervised model and does not requires human labels to train. As compared with native GAN extensions discussed above, the Fast-RSPer has an advantage that there is no dedicated training phase since both the generator G and feature extractor Φ are pre-trained. As compared with iGAN, our model preserves the semantics of R and is *end-to-end*–no auxiliary algorithm is needed to output the final results. Furthermore, the Fast-RSPer can generate an RSP image more efficiently than the autoregressive Pixel-VAE because Eq. (1) can be solved efficiently using the gradient descent and G generates all pixels at once.

3.1 Technical Contributions

Next, we discuss some engineering "tricks" we used to deliver good results. We also discuss some pitfalls to avoid when using a pre-trained generator.

Semantics Alignment. We align the semantics of synthesized images with R at both the macro- and micro-scales. *Macro-alignment*: Given a reference image and R, one needs to decide the value of l in Eq. (1) and make sure that the features extracted by $\|\cdot\|_{mask}^{(i)}$, $i \geq l$, capture the marginal semantics of the reference region. There are several ways to choose an appropriate l. For example, we can use the visualization techniques [32] to understand what each neuron "sees" in Φ and then pick the layer l that can capture sufficiently complex concepts. We can also choose different l's for different R's based on the visualization techniques. However, these approaches require human intervention and may not be acceptable to the interactive applications. Instead, we use a simple strategy that selects l based on the *size of receptive fields*–the layer l is the shallowest layer in Φ where the receptive field of a neuron is larger than the minimal bounding box of R. The size of receptive fields can be calculated automatically, and it turns out that this strategy works well in our experiments. *Micro-alignment*: When finding $\boldsymbol{z}$, one can follow the style transfer [5,15] to align the convolution output (before it is applied to an activation function) of $G(\boldsymbol{z})$ and R at a deep layer. However, we find that aligning the *RELU output* of $G(\boldsymbol{z})$ and R instead can significantly improve the quality of the synthesized images. This observation may be valuable to future studies on semantic preserving.

Diversity. The vanilla Fast-RSPer has a problem that different synthesized images based on the same R may lack diversity, because the gradient descent algorithm may find the same $\boldsymbol{z}^*$ (or multiple $\boldsymbol{z}^*$'s close to each other) for different synthesized images. One way to solve this problem is to transform Eq. (1) to an energy-based model [21] and sample iteratively from such a model using a sampling algorithm (e.g., an approximate Metropolis-adjusted Langevin sampling). Here, we propose a simple alternative by taking advantage of the fact that *only the semantics* of the reference region needs to be preserved. During the gradient descent, the Fast-RSPer adds random noises to the gradients at different iterations. This leads to diverse $\boldsymbol{z}^*$'s and in turn diverse synthesized images $G(\boldsymbol{z}^*)$'s having different features at layers shallower than l. Since the layer l in Eq. (1) is a deep layer, the synthesized images $G(\boldsymbol{z}^*)$'s can have different features at shallow layers, which encode textures or colors or shapes, and can look very different from each other.

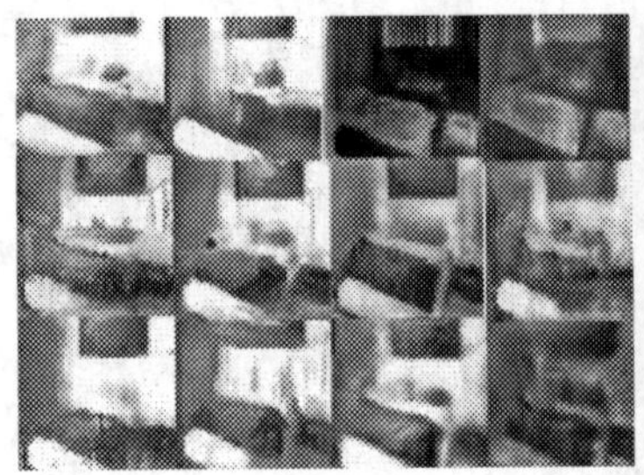

Fig. 4. Images synthesized by batch-normalized generator may have degraded quality due to the bias of moments in the current input batch. (Color figure online)

Generator Selection. We have tried pairing up Fast-RAPer with many types of pre-trained generators but found that some generators failed to deliver good results. After investigation, we find that the root cause is due to the batch-normalization. Most existing GANs employ the batch-normalization *without* learning moving moments. They only normalize the latent outputs based on the moments of individual training batches rather than the moments of entire training data. If this is the case, we suggest that one should turn *off* the batch-normalization in G, because it introduces dependency between batch inputs during training and seriously degrades the quality of images generated by G, as shown in Fig. 4. To ensure the best quality, we use pre-trained generators *without* batch normalization layers in our experiments.

4 Experiments

In this section, we evaluate the performance of Fast-RSPer by comparing it with existing models. We use the CelebA[1] and LSUN Bedroom[2] datasets for training the models and choosing the reference images/regions for problems of RSP image synthesis. We implement the models using Tensorflow.[3] Following summarizes the models we implemented:

Pixel-VAE. To the best of our knowledge, the only off-the-shelf models that can be used for RSP image synthesis is the Ladder-VAE [29] and its variant Pixel-VAE [22]. We implement both the models but find that the Ladder-VAE consistently yields blurry images that are *not* comparable to other approaches in terms of image quality. Therefore, we omit its results in order to save space. The Pixel-VAE model consists of a Ladder-VAE and a Pixel-CNN [23]. When generating an image, the Ladder-VAE part ensures the global coherence of the image while the Pixel-CNN part enhances the details at the pixel level. We implement Pixel-VAE by following the architecture described in the original paper [22]. Note that in this architecture, the encoder and decoder of the Ladder-VAE part have two layers parametrized by the latent variables $\boldsymbol{z}^{(1)}$ and $\boldsymbol{z}^{(2)}$ respectively (see Fig. 3(a)), and its is sufficient for $\boldsymbol{z}^{(2)}$ to control the semantics of *any* region in an image since the second-layer encoder and decoder are fully-connected layers. The number of weights to learn is about 67M.

Extended VAE-GAN. We also implement the naive extension of VAE-GAN [16] discussed in Sect. 3. We follow the architecture used in [16] and replace the VAE part with the Ladder-VAE described above. Unfortunately, despite applying many GAN-training techniques [27] and careful engineering, we are not able to train the VAE-GAN extension successfully. It turns out this is due to the limitation of VAE-GAN–it can be trained to generate face images but not bedrooms. We believe this is because that a face have relatively simpler parametrization than a bedroom. And the distribution assumption of the VAE-GAN (in the VAE part) limits the model complexity and stops the model from learning a complex parametrization. We therefore omit the results of this model.

Fast-RSPer. We use a pre-trained VGG-19 [28] as the feature extractor. Note that in VGG-19, the convolution, pooling, and activation layers are grouped into *blocks*. We set l at the *start* of a block instead of in the middle because this leads to better results empirically. For the CelebA and LSUN Bedroom datasets, we pre-train two generators following the BEGAN [3] and WGAN-GP

[1] http://mmlab.ie.cuhk.edu.hk/projects/CelebA.html.
[2] http://lsun.cs.princeton.edu/.
[3] https://www.tensorflow.org/.

[10], respectively. As discussed in Sect. 3, we do *not* employ normalization layers in both generators. The numbers of model weights to learn are about 23M for CelebA dataset and 29M for Bedroom dataset, respectively.

iGAN. Although the iGAN [34] was not proposed to solve the RSP image synthesis problem, we implement it as a baseline to study the difference between pixel- and semantics-preserving. Like Fast-RSPer, iGAN needs a pre-trained generator. So, for fairness, we let it use the same generators as in Fast-RSPer (i.e., BEGAN on CelebA dataset and WGAN-GP on LSUN Bedroom dataset). Following the settings reported in the iGAN paper [34], we use L2 pixel loss for alignment and update the $\boldsymbol{z}$ variable without gradient noise. And we use the same optimizer and maximum step as in Fast-RSPer during training. The numbers of model weights for different datasets are also roughly the same as Fast-RSPer.

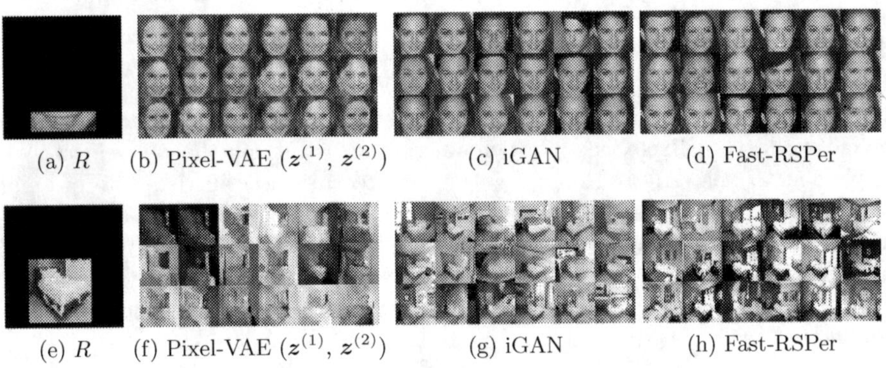

(a) R (b) Pixel-VAE ($\boldsymbol{z}^{(1)}$, $\boldsymbol{z}^{(2)}$) (c) iGAN (d) Fast-RSPer

(e) R (f) Pixel-VAE ($\boldsymbol{z}^{(1)}$, $\boldsymbol{z}^{(2)}$) (g) iGAN (h) Fast-RSPer

Fig. 5. Synthesized images given simple reference regions containing only a single object. (a) A laughing mouth as a reference region. (b–d) Images synthesized by Pixel-VAE, iGAN, and Fast-RSPer trained on the CelebA dataset. (e) A bed as a reference region. (f–h) Images synthesized by Pixel-VAE, iGAN, and Fast-RSPer trained on the LSUN Bedroom dataset.

4.1 Results Given Single-Object Regions

We first study the images synthesized by different models given a simple reference region consisting of one object. We choose a "laughing mouth" as the reference region for models trained on CelebA and a "bed" as the reference region for models trained on LSUN Bedroom, as sown in Figs. 5(a)(e). In Pixel-VAE, we fix the decoding distributions parametrized by both $\boldsymbol{z}^{(1)}$ and $\boldsymbol{z}^{(2)}$ along the dimensions whose receptive field covers R in order to make it preserve the semantics of the reference region. The synthesized images are shown in Figs. 5(b)(c)(e)(f).

As we can see, the iGAN and Fast-RSPer give relatively better results than Pixel-VAE. The iGAN performs well because the pixels in the reference region are simple thus aligning pixels amounts to aligning the semantics. On the other hand, the images synthesized by Pixel-VAE are less satisfactory. First, they contains local artifacts. This is because the images are synthesized by the Pixel-CNN part, which is an autoregressive model. A "bad" pixel sampled by Pixel-CNN creates a negative impact on the following pixels and finally leads to a local artifact. The iGAN and Fast-RSPer avoid this problem by generating all pixels of an image at once.[4] Moreover, the images produced by Pixel-VAE have less diversity–most images share the same global tone. Since $\boldsymbol{z}^{(2)}$ is the output of fully connected layer, its receptive field covers the entire face region. So when $\boldsymbol{z}^{(2)}$ was fixed, the output would have low diversity, even $\boldsymbol{z}^{(1)}$ can be sampled. Fast-RSPer avoids this problem by using a GAN without feature parametrization. We can also see that, on LSUN Bedroom, Pixel-VAE is less capable of preserving the semantics of the reference region than Fast-RSPer (Figs. 5(e)(f)). A bedroom scene is usually more complex than a face, implying a wider feature space to learn at each layer. Images in the LSUN Bedroom dataset usually look very different from each other, and it is hard to learn a shared parametrization of such complex feature spaces for the encoder and decoder.

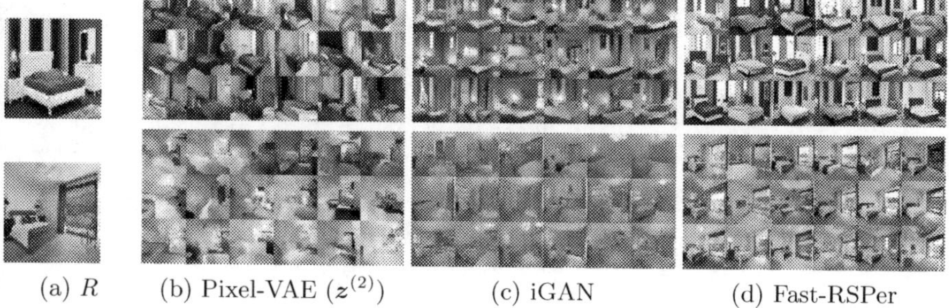

Fig. 6. Synthesized images given a complex reference region containing many objects. (a) A bedroom scene as a reference region. (b–d) Images synthesized by PixelVAE, iGAN, and Fast-RSPer respectively.

4.2 Results Given Complex Regions

Here, we investigate the images synthesized by different models given a complex reference region representing the entire bedroom scene, as shown in Fig. 6(a). In a complex region, subregions may have their own semantics. For example, a bedroom image may contain beds, desks, lamps, or pictures on the wall. The goal of RSP image synthesis is to preserve the *marginal* semantics of the reference region; that is, the semantics excluding that of any subregion. In this case, the marginal semantics should be the layout of a bedroom. The synthesized

[4] One may notice that the images synthesized by iGAN and Fast-RSPer contains some small "holes" on the CelebA dataset. This is due to the pre-trained generator BEGAN, not the synthesis models themselves, as evidenced by Fig. 8(a).

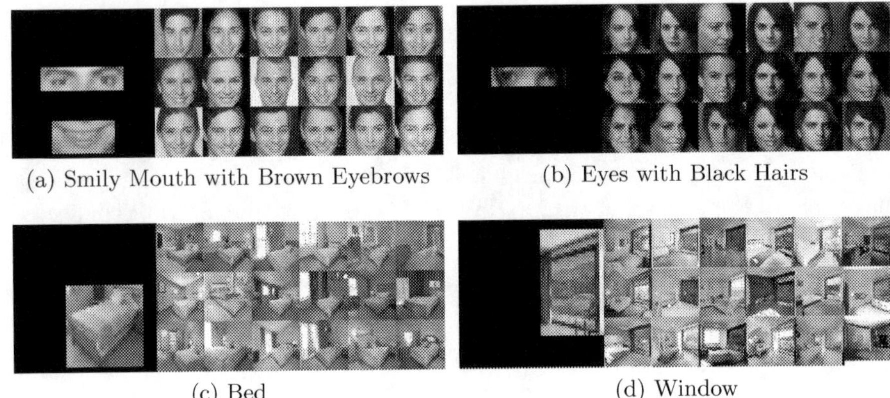

Fig. 7. Images synthesized by Fast-RSPer given different reference regions. In each image block, the left (large) image shows R in which the marginal semantics needs to be preserved.

images are shown in Figs. 6(b)(c)(d). As we can see, only Fast-RSPer generates satisfactory images this time.

The iGAN, which is based on pixel-alignment, cannot well preserve the semantics of R because the pixels in R are diverse. Aligning pixels of synthesized images with those in R results in a group of images whose average resembles R but lack semantics individually.

In Pixel-VAE, we fix only the decoding distribution parametrized by $\boldsymbol{z}^{(2)}$ (not the one by $\boldsymbol{z}^{(1)}$) along the dimensions whose receptive field covers R in order to make it preserve the marginal semantics of the reference region. As we can see from Fig. 6(b), the layout is less preserved by the images generated by Pixel-VAE than by Fast-RSPer. This is because the shared parametrization is harder to train on a complex dataset, as discussed in the previous subsection.

4.3 Semantics Preserving Vs. Mode Collapse

Next, we look into the capability of semantics preserving of Fast-RSPer. We can see from Figs. 7(a–d) that Fast-RSPer can successfully synthesize images given various reference regions with different facial/bedroom semantics.

Note that, in some cases, the images synthesized by Fast-RSPer render less variety as compared to those that could have been generated by a well-trained, unconstrained GAN generator. One may conjecture that a poor-trained GAN generator with significant mode collapse is used. However, this is not the case. Figure 8 shows the images synthesized by our pre-trained generator, which include a variety of modes. The reason behind the reduced variety is because of the constraints imposed by the *semantics* of the reference region. When comparing Fast-RSPer with Pixel-VAE (which is also conditioned) in Figs. 5 and 6, our method clearly gives more diversity.

(a) CelebA (b) LSUN Bedroom

Fig. 8. Images synthesized by our pre-trained generators do not have the problem of mode collapse, showing that the reduced variety among synthesized images is due to the semantics constraints. Note that the CelebA images have small "holes" because BEGAN [3] clips color ranges of pixels. The WGAN-GP [10], which generates bedroom images, does not have the same problem. (Color figure online)

4.4 Quantitative Comparison

To quantitatively compare the level of semantics preserving, quality and diversity of images synthesized by Pixel-VAE, iGAN and Fast-RSPer, we conduct human evaluations. We invite 103 external users from the Internet. Each user is asked to decide the winners in terms of quality, diversity and level of semantics preserving for 13 experiments. In each experiment, we display 36 images synthesized by Pixel-VAE, iGAN and Fast-RSPer respectively given the same reference region. The number of wins of each model is shown in Table 1. It is clear that people think Fast-RSPer (1) gives better-quality images on both the CelebA and LSUN Bedroom datasets; and (2) preserves more semantics on the LSUN Bedroom dataset while (3) giving more diversity. Table 1 also includes the average time required to generate an image. The time applies to both the datasets since they contain images of the same size (64×64 pixels). Both the iGAN and Fast-RSPer can synthesize images in near realtime. The average generating time of iGAN is 0.1 second faster since it doesn't need to feed forward the VGG. In summary, Fast-RSPer is able to efficiently generate RSP images of higher quality and diversity. This is important when one wants to synthesize a large amount of images for, e.g., data augmentation.

Table 1. Quantitative comparison results. Average image synthesis time is reported on a machine with an Intel Core-i7 6900K CPU, 128 GB RAM, and an Nvidia GeForce GTX 1070 GPU.

	CelebA			LSUN Bedroom			Avg. time
	Semantics	Quality	Diversity	Semantics	Quality	Diversity	
Pixel-VAE	328 wins	416 wins	310 wins	201 wins	525 wins	291 wins	43 secs
iGAN	451 wins	347 wins	482 wins	508 wins	227 wins	408 wins	**0.3** sec
Fast-RSPer	**560** wins	**576**wins	**547** wins	**630** wins	**587** wins	**640** wins	0.4 sec

We have also used two standard metrics, the Inception Score (IS) and structural similarity (SSIM), to evaluate the quality and diversity of synthesized images. The higher the IS (and the lower the SSIM) the better. We conduct experiments where there are 25 reference images and we generate 64 images for each reference image using PixelVAE, iGAN, and our Fast-RSPer. We average the IS and SSIM scores of the synthesized images and give the results in Table 2.

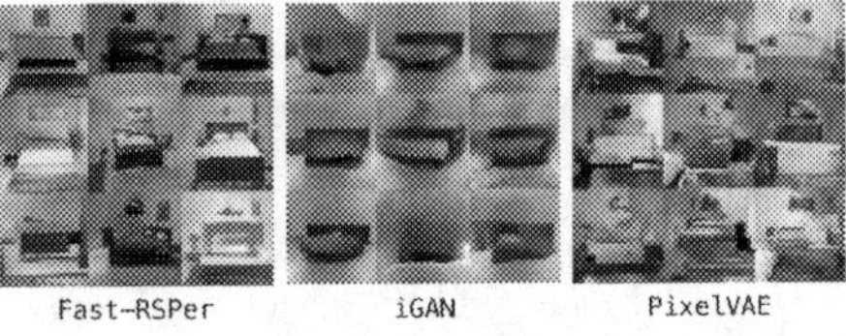

Fig. 9. Synthesized images

We also show some randomly sampled synthesized images in Fig. 9 As we can see, neither IS nor SSIM can truly indicate the quality and diversity in our problem. Although giving the highest quality through human eyes, Fast-RSPer does not top the Inception Scores because it can generate some objects that are out of the classes which the Inception model was trained for. Also, the low SSIM values given by PixelVAE are not from diversity but from distortion and artifacts. This is why we employ human evaluation instead.

Table 2. Inception Scores and SSIM.

	Inception		SSIM	
	CelebA	Bedroom	CelebA	Bedroom
PixelVAE	1.39	2.17	0.92	**0.20**
iGAN	**1.56**	**2.61**	1.01	0.66
Ours	1.51	2.23	**0.89**	0.28

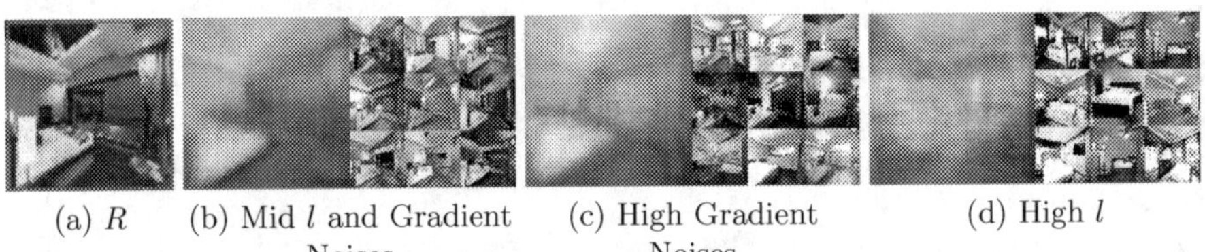

(a) R (b) Mid l and Gradient Noises (c) High Gradient Noises (d) High l

Fig. 10. Images synthesized by Fast-RSPer given different l's and levels of gradient noises. In each image block, the large image at left is the average of synthesized images.

4.5 Effect of l and Gradient Noises

We study the impact of l in Eq. (1) and the noises added to the gradients at each iteration when solving $\boldsymbol{z}^*$ using the gradient descent. The layer l controls the minimal receptive fields of neurons in the feature extractor used to capture the semantics of the reference regions. The larger the l, the higher-level concepts are captured and preserved by Fast-RSPer. On the other hand, the level of gradient noises controls how diverse the features in the shallow layers of the feature extractor when generating an image. The larger the gradient noises, the more visual diversity we can expect *given the same preserved semantics.* To see how l and the level of gradient noises affect a synthesized image, we show images synthesized by Fast-RSPer given enlarged l and noise level in Fig. 10. In Fig. 10, we use Fig. 10(b) as the baseline and change *one hyperparameter at a time* in Fig. 10(c) and (d). Figure 10(c) and (d) show the impact of increasing gradient noises and l, respectively. As we can see, with a high noise level (Fig. 10(c)), the diversity of synthesized images increases, but in average the image does not change too much. The diversity is added over the same semantics. A larger l (Fig. 10(d)) also leads to more diversity. But such diversity comes from less preserved semantics. In this case, the only preserved semantics is the layout of the roof, excluding the layout of furnitures in the room which was preserved in Fig. 10(b). In practice, these two parameters offer a flexible way for users to fine-control the diversity and what semantics to preserve (Fig. 11).

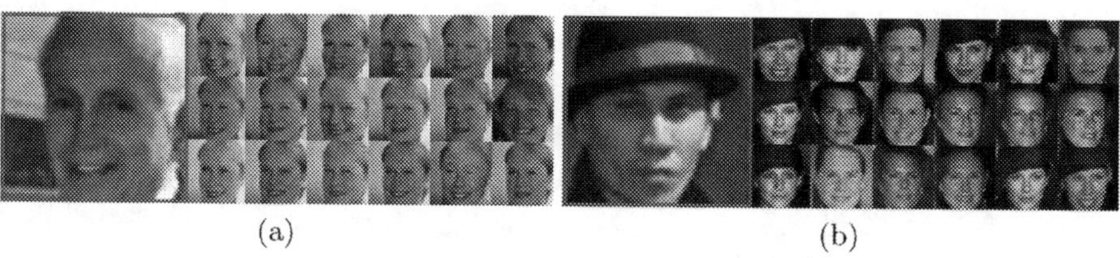

Fig. 11. Cross-domain RSP image synthesis, where the source domain is "male," the target domain is "female," and the region semantics is "face." Given a source domain A, a target domain B, and the reference region R in the source domain, the goal is to synthesize an image $\boldsymbol{y}'$ *in the target domain* that keeps the high-level semantics of R. In Fast-RSPer, we replace the single-domain feature extractor with a cross-domain feature extractor and use an ordinary GAN generator for domain B. This way, an image generated by the generator ($\boldsymbol{x}'$ in Fig. 3(c)) can lie in domain B while preserving the high-level semantics of $\boldsymbol{x}$ in domain A. Note that the cross-domain feature extractor can be trained in an unsupervised manner using an autoencoder that takes both example images from domains A and B as the input.

5 Conclusion

We study the problem of region-semantics preserving (RSP) image synthesis that allows a user to easily guide the synthesis using a reference image in a soft manner. We then propose the Fast-RSPer model based on a pre-trained GAN generator and a pre-trained deep feature extractor. The Fast-RSPer is able to generate images without undergoing a dedicated training phase, making it particularly useful for the interactive applications. We conduct extensive experiments using the real-world datasets and the results show that Fast-PSPer can synthesize realistic, diverse RSP images efficiently.

References

1. Agarwala, A., et al.: Interactive digital photomontage. In: ACM Transactions on Graphics (TOG), vol. 23, pp. 294–302. ACM (2004)
2. Ballé, J., Laparra, V., Simoncelli, E.P.: Density modeling of images using a generalized normalization transformation. arXiv preprint arXiv:1511.06281 (2015)
3. Berthelot, D., Schumm, T., Metz, L.: Began: boundary equilibrium generative adversarial networks. arXiv preprint arXiv:1703.10717 (2017)
4. Dosovitskiy, A., Tobias Springenberg, J., Brox, T.: Learning to generate chairs with convolutional neural networks. In: Proceedings of the IEEE Conference on Computer Vision and Pattern Recognition (CVPR), pp. 1538–1546 (2015)
5. Gatys, L.A., Ecker, A.S., Bethge, M.: A neural algorithm of artistic style. arXiv preprint arXiv:1508.06576 (2015)
6. Gatys, L.A., Ecker, A.S., Bethge, M.: Texture synthesis and the controlled generation of natural stimuli using convolutional neural networks. arXiv preprint arXiv:1505.07376 12 (2015)
7. Goodfellow, I., et al.: Generative adversarial Nets. In: Advances in Neural Information Processing systems, pp. 2672–2680 (2014)
8. Gregor, K., Danihelka, I., Graves, A., Rezende, D., Wierstra, D.: Draw: a recurrent neural network for image generation. In: International Conference on Machine Learning, pp. 1462–1471 (2015)
9. Güçlütürk, Y., Güçlü, U., van Lier, R., van Gerven, M.A.J.: Convolutional sketch inversion. In: Hua, G., Jégou, H. (eds.) ECCV 2016. LNCS, vol. 9913, pp. 810–824. Springer, Cham (2016). https://doi.org/10.1007/978-3-319-46604-0_56
10. Gulrajani, I., Ahmed, F., Arjovsky, M., Dumoulin, V., Courville, A.: Improved training of Wasserstein GANs. arXiv preprint arXiv:1704.00028 (2017)
11. Hertzmann, A., Jacobs, C.E., Oliver, N., Curless, B., Salesin, D.H.: Image analogies. In: Proceedings of the 28th Annual Conference on Computer Graphics and Interactive Techniques, pp. 327–340. ACM (2001)
12. Iizuka, S., Simo-Serra, E., Ishikawa, H.: Globally and locally consistent image completion. ACM Trans. Graph. (TOG) **36**(4), 107 (2017)
13. Isola, P., Zhu, J.Y., Zhou, T., Efros, A.A.: Image-to-image translation with conditional adversarial networks. arXiv preprint arXiv:1611.07004 (2016)
14. Kingma, D.P., Welling, M.: Auto-encoding variational Bayes. arXiv preprint arXiv:1312.6114 (2013)
15. Kyprianidis, J.E., Collomosse, J., Wang, T., Isenberg, T.: State of the "art": a taxonomy of artistic stylization techniques for images and video. IEEE Trans. Vis. Comput. Graph. **19**(5), 866–885 (2013)
16. Larsen, A.B.L., Sønderby, S.K., Larochelle, H., Winther, O.: Autoencoding beyond pixels using a learned similarity metric. In: International Conference on Machine Learning, pp. 1558–1566 (2016)
17. Ledig, C., et al.: Photo-realistic single image super-resolution using a generative adversarial network. arXiv preprint arXiv:1609.04802 (2016)
18. Lee, H., Grosse, R., Ranganath, R., Ng, A.Y.: Convolutional deep belief networks for scalable unsupervised learning of hierarchical representations. In: Proceedings of the 26th Annual International Conference on Machine Learning, pp. 609–616. ACM (2009)
19. Mirza, M., Osindero, S.: Conditional generative adversarial Nets. arXiv preprint arXiv:1411.1784 (2014)

20. Nguyen, A., Dosovitskiy, A., Yosinski, J., Brox, T., Clune, J.: Synthesizing the preferred inputs for neurons in neural networks via deep generator networks. In: Advances in Neural Information Processing Systems, pp. 3387–3395 (2016)
21. Nguyen, A., Yosinski, J., Bengio, Y., Dosovitskiy, A., Clune, J.: Plug & play generative networks: Conditional iterative generation of images in latent space. arXiv preprint arXiv:1612.00005 (2016)
22. van den Oord, A., Kalchbrenner, N., Espeholt, L., Vinyals, O., Graves, A., et al.: Conditional image generation with PixelCNN decoders. In: Advances in Neural Information Processing Systems, pp. 4790–4798 (2016)
23. van den Oord, A., Kalchbrenner, N., Kavukcuoglu, K.: Pixel recurrent neural networks. In: International Conference on Machine Learning, pp. 1747–1756 (2016)
24. Radford, A., Metz, L., Chintala, S.: Unsupervised representation learning with deep convolutional generative adversarial networks. arXiv preprint arXiv:1511.06434 (2015)
25. Reed, S., Akata, Z., Yan, X., Logeswaran, L., Schiele, B., Lee, H.: Generative adversarial text to image synthesis. In: International Conference on Machine Learning, pp. 1060–1069 (2016)
26. Salakhutdinov, R., Hinton, G.: Deep Boltzmann machines. In: Artificial Intelligence and Statistics, pp. 448–455 (2009)
27. Salimans, T., Goodfellow, I., Zaremba, W., Cheung, V., Radford, A., Chen, X.: Improved techniques for training GANs. In: Advances in Neural Information Processing Systems, pp. 2234–2242 (2016)
28. Simonyan, K., Zisserman, A.: Very deep convolutional networks for large-scale image recognition. arXiv preprint arXiv:1409.1556 (2014)
29. Sønderby, C.K., Raiko, T., Maaløe, L., Sønderby, S.K., Winther, O.: Ladder variational autoencoders. In: Advances in Neural Information Processing Systems, pp. 3738–3746 (2016)
30. Toderici, G., et al.: Full resolution image compression with recurrent neural networks. arXiv preprint arXiv:1608.05148 (2016)
31. Yan, X., Yang, J., Sohn, K., Lee, H.: Attribute2Image: conditional image generation from visual attributes. In: Leibe, B., Matas, J., Sebe, N., Welling, M. (eds.) ECCV 2016. LNCS, vol. 9908, pp. 776–791. Springer, Cham (2016). https://doi.org/10.1007/978-3-319-46493-0_47
32. Zeiler, M.D., Fergus, R.: Visualizing and understanding convolutional networks. In: Fleet, D., Pajdla, T., Schiele, B., Tuytelaars, T. (eds.) ECCV 2014. LNCS, vol. 8689, pp. 818–833. Springer, Cham (2014). https://doi.org/10.1007/978-3-319-10590-1_53
33. Zhou, T., Tulsiani, S., Sun, W., Malik, J., Efros, A.A.: View synthesis by appearance flow. In: Leibe, B., Matas, J., Sebe, N., Welling, M. (eds.) ECCV 2016. LNCS, vol. 9908, pp. 286–301. Springer, Cham (2016). https://doi.org/10.1007/978-3-319-46493-0_18
34. Zhu, J.-Y., Krähenbühl, P., Shechtman, E., Efros, A.A.: Generative visual manipulation on the natural image manifold. In: Leibe, B., Matas, J., Sebe, N., Welling, M. (eds.) ECCV 2016. LNCS, vol. 9909, pp. 597–613. Springer, Cham (2016). https://doi.org/10.1007/978-3-319-46454-1_36
35. Zhu, J.Y., Park, T., Isola, P., Efros, A.A.: Unpaired image-to-image translation using cycle-consistent adversarial networks. arXiv preprint arXiv:1703.10593 (2017)

SemiStarGAN: Semi-supervised Generative Adversarial Networks for Multi-domain Image-to-Image Translation

Shu-Yu Hsu[1], Chih-Yuan Yang[1], Chi-Chia Huang[2], and Jane Yung-jen Hsu[1,2](✉)

[1] Computer Science and Information Engineering, National Taiwan University, Taipei, Taiwan
{r05922059,yangchihyuan,yjhsu}@ntu.edu.tw

[2] Graduate Institute of Networking and Multimedia, National Taiwan University, Taipei, Taiwan
d01944003@ntu.edu.tw

Abstract. Recent studies have shown significant advance for multi-domain image-to-image translation, and generative adversarial networks (GANs) are widely used to address this problem. However, to train an effective image generator, existing methods all require a large number of domain-labeled images, which may take time and effort to collect for real-world problems. In this paper, we propose SemiStarGAN, a semi-supervised GAN network to tackle this issue. The proposed method utilizes unlabeled images by incorporating a novel discriminator/classifier network architecture—Y model, and two existing semi-supervised learning techniques—pseudo labeling and self-ensembling. Experimental results on the CelebA dataset using domains of facial attributes show that the proposed method achieves comparable performance with state-of-the-art methods using considerably less labeled training images.

Keywords: Image-to-image translation · Generative adversarial network · Semi-supervised learning

1 Introduction

Image-to-image translation is the study of converting an image's representation, e.g., its colors and tone, painting style, or objects' attributes such as an identity's

This research was supported in part by the Ministry of Science and Technology of Taiwan (MOST 107-2633-E-002-001, 106-2218-E-002-043, 107-2811-E-002-018), National Taiwan University (NTU-107L104039), Intel Corporation, and Delta Electronics.

Electronic supplementary material The online version of this chapter (https://doi.org/10.1007/978-3-030-20870-7_21) contains supplementary material, which is available to authorized users.

C. V. Jawahar et al. (Eds.): ACCV 2018, LNCS 11364, pp. 338–353, 2019.
https://doi.org/10.1007/978-3-030-20870-7_21

gender. Numerous GAN-based methods have been proposed in the literature to address this problem [1,6,7,14,15,23,25,29] because GANs can generate realistic images and achieve effective translation.

Existing GAN-based image translation methods are designed with various principles such as keeping consistency between source and target images [7,25, 29] or sharing same semantic space [14]. But most of them take only a source and target domain into consideration except StarGAN [1], which is the first method designed for directly translating images from a source domain to multiple target domains. The success of StarGAN relies on a prerequisite that a large number of domain-labeled training images are available. Although it is a common assumption for many existing GAN-based methods, it may require a high level of cost and effort to generate labels for real-world problems. Therefore, there will be a great merit to develop a method which requires less labeled data but achieves comparable performance.

Such a motivation has been widely adopted by many semi-supervised methods, from which we integrate two existing techniques—pseudo labeling and self-ensembling [9]—into our method to address the multi-domain image-to-image translation problem.

Furthermore, we propose a novel architecture of the discriminator/classifier component in a GAN framework. We name it Y model due to its shape—a few sharing base layers plus two separated branches of layers: one for the discriminator and the other for the classifier. Such a design is motivated by an observation that a discriminator and a classifier serve for different purposes, so that they can be better optimized if they have individual branches of layers. However, because low-level image features such as edges, corners and spots extracted by CNNs are highly similar, we retain a few common low-level layers to reduce the total number of weights and increase the stability of the training process.

We evaluate the proposed method using the CelebA dataset [16] for facial attributes synthesis and measure its performance by three metrics: Inception accuracy, human perceptual study, and classification accuracy of the auxiliary classifier. Our experimental results show that SemiStarGAN uses less labeled training images and generates comparable translated images with a state-of-the-art method, StarGAN.

In short, our contributions are threefold:

- We propose a novel method, which first utilizes semi-supervised learning to exploit unlabeled data for multi-domain image-to-image translation.
- We introduce a novel partially-splitting discriminator/classifier model, designed to improve the auxiliary classifier's accuracy and reduce the uncertainty caused by unlabeled images.
- We conduct experiments on hair color translation and validate the effectiveness of the proposed method, which generates higher Inception and classification accuracy by using merely one-third labeled images of a compared supervised method.

2 Related Work

Generative Adversarial Network. Generative adversarial networks (GANs) [4] are capable of generating various high-quality images so that they are widely used to tackle assorted computer vision problems including text to image synthesis [19,27], image-to-image translation [1,6,23,29], image editing [28], and image super-resolution [10]. There are two fundamental parts contained in GANs: a generator and a discriminator. During the loops of training, the former improves its ability to generate realistic images difficult to distinguish, and the latter also improves its expertise to make better judgments. As a result at the end of the training process, an effective generator is trained to work for a specific task.

GAN-based Image-to-Image Translation. Due to the effectiveness of handling complicated translation functions as a generator under a GAN framework, many GAN-based image-to-image translation methods have been proposed to generate promising results. Pix2pix [6] regulates a conditional GAN (cGAN) by a pixel-wise L1 loss to reduce the difference between a translated image and a target image. However, the method requires many highly matched pairs of images from both source and target domains to train its network, and it is a challenging preparation. To free this constraint of paired training images, two different approaches have been proposed. One of them introduces a cycle consistency loss to enable direct image translation [7,25,29], and the other trains two image encoders for projecting images from both source and target domain into the shared semantic space; then trains another two decoders for reconstructing images from semantic features [14,15,23]. As the foregoing methods deal with bi-domain translation, StartGAN is the first method designed for multi-domain translation. StartGAN uses an auxiliary classifier to guide its generator so that it can sidestep the trouble of using multiple bi-domain translation. However, all of these GAN-based methods require a large amount of domain-labeled data, which take cost and effort to collect. Unlike those approaches mentioned above, our framework can reduce the need of labeled data and achieve comparable performance.

We would like to point out the detailed difference of the terms *unsupervised* used by two existing methods [14,29] and *semi-supervised* used by the proposed method. The authors call their method unsupervised because they no longer need to use paired training images, which means that their training data are unsupervised on the pixel level. In contrast, the proposed method utilizes both labeled and unlabeled images so that its learning process is semi-supervised on the domain level.

Semi-supervised Learning. Compared with fully supervised learning methods, semi-supervised learning (SSL) methods take advantage of unlabeled data and show promising results in many real-world problems because it is more feasible to collect a large number of unlabeled data than labeled ones. There are several regularization-based and GAN-based SSL methods in the literature highly related to the proposed method. The two methods temporal ensembling and self-ensembling [9] are proposed to develop a robust classifier which can work reliably against various perturbations. To validate this idea, their authors introduce stochastic augmentations and dropouts to enhance their classifier so that the classifier can make consistent predictions under highly altered source data. Similarly, virtual adversarial training [17] regularizes a classifier with images added with virtual adversarial perturbations.

In order to cope with unlabeled data, many GAN-based methods have been proposed by changing their objectives of output images or adversarial losses. CatGAN [21] extends a binary discriminator to a multi-class classifier and replaces a conventional GAN objective with entropy minimization of unlabeled data. SGAN [18], ImprovedGAN [20] and BadGAN [2] add an auxiliary classifier aside the discriminator and enhance the classifier with generated data. Although the classifier of these GAN- based methods can achieve favorable classification accuracy, their generated images are blurred and incomprehensible. To address this issue, TripleGAN [12] proposes two independent parts—a discriminator and classifier—to prevent their conflict of learning optimized CNN weights, which also prevents the generator from generating incomprehensible output images. In short, we adopt the techniques used by self-ensembling into the proposed method, and inspired by SGAN and TripleGAN, we design a novel Y model of the discriminator/classifier architecture, which owns a few shared layers of the discriminator and auxiliary classifier but two separated branches to reach a balance between classification accuracy and training stability.

3 Proposed Method

The proposed method, SemiStarGAN, is motivated by an existing method StarGAN [1] and takes advantage of unlabeled training images to address the issue of lacking labeled images. The success of StarGAN relies on a prerequisite that abundant domain-labeled training images are available to train its classifier to generate correct labels to give its generator the information whether the generated images contain expected attributes. However, it may take time and effort to collect a large number of labeled data for real-world tasks, and two problems will come up if only limited labeled data are available. First, its generator may create unexpected output images such as broken or over-blurred due to incorrect data models learned from insufficient training examples. Second, there may be an over-fitting problem of the auxiliary classifier because of the limited number of training examples. As a result, the generator will wrongly translate an image to an unexpected target domain. To address this problem, we propose a method which utilizes unlabeled images and considerably less labeled training images to achieve comparable performance. We will first introduce the notations widely used in GAN-based image-to-image translation methods, and then explain the details of each component contained in the proposed SemiStarGAN.

3.1 Formulation

We define the problem of multi-domain image-to-image translation as the following. Let X be a partially labeled image set, C be the label set of X on multiple domains, and X_L be the subset of X in which every image is well labeled, x be an image in X, and c be the label of x if available. Given the training set X and C, the problem is about developing an image translation function which generates a new image y from a given x in the training set X with a parameter of a target domain label c' and the new image y will be classified as being of the domain label c'. Multi-domain GAN-based image-to-image translation methods contains three major components: an image generator G to generate translated images, an image discriminator D_{src} to tell the difference between real/fake images, and an auxiliary classifier D_{cls} to indicate domain labels. To use both labeled and unlabeled images to train an effective image generator for multi-domian image translation, we propose a training process as illustrated in Fig. 1 and its architecture is shown in the supplementary material.

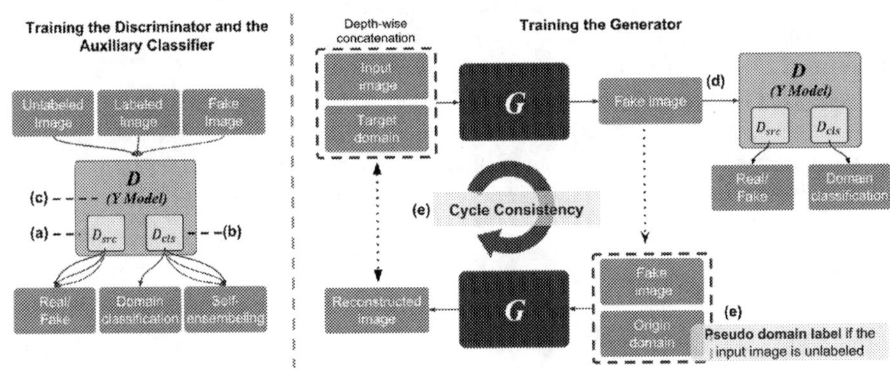

Fig. 1. Training of SemiStarGAN. (a) The discriminator D_{src} learns to distinguish between real and fake images. (b) The auxiliary classifier D_{cls} learns to correctly classify a labeled image. We enhance the classifier's robustness by applying self-ensembling which uses unlabeled data. (c) We propose Y model, a novel parameter-sharing structure between D_{src} and D_{cls} for stabilizing the training process. (d) Given an image and a target domain label, the generator G learns to generate a fake image that can fool D_{src} and still be correctly classified by D_{cls}. (e) G remains the cycle consistency by translating a fake image back to the image's original domain. A pseudo domain label is used if the input image is unlabeled.

3.2 GAN Objectice

To make generated images realistic, we adopt the GAN objective

$$\mathcal{L}_{GAN} = \mathbb{E}_x[D_{src}(x)] - \mathbb{E}_{x,c'}[D_{src}(G(x,c'))] - \lambda_{gp}\mathbb{E}_{\hat{x}}[(\|\nabla_{\hat{x}} D_{src}(\hat{x})\|_2 - 1)^2], \quad (1)$$

where c' is a given target domain label to generate a fake image $G(x, c')$, λ_{gp} is a weighting parameter to balance a gradient penalty term $\mathbb{E}_{\hat{x}}[(\|\nabla_{\hat{x}} D_{src}(\hat{x})\|_2 - 1)^2]$ which increases the stability of a GAN's training process [5]. The symbol $\hat{x}$ stands for any image linearly mixed by x and $G(x, c')$ in their image space. The generator G aims to minimize this objective while the discriminator D_{src} tries to maximize it.

3.3 Domain Classification Loss and Self-Ensembling

The auxiliary classifier D_{cls} is designed to let G know whether generated images $G(x, c')$ own expected attributes so that they can be correctly recognized. That is, D_{cls} is utilized to optimize G. Hence, it is essential to improve the classification accuracy of D_{cls}. We design a labeled images' classification loss

$$\mathcal{L}^r_{cls} = \mathbb{E}_{x,c}[-\log D_{cls}(c|x)], \tag{2}$$

which penalizes D_{cls} if it wrongly predicts x's domain label.

But for a training set containing many unlabeled images, we propose to integrate established learning techniques to improve the classifier's robustness. To do it, we adopt self-ensembling [9], a method generates robust prediction results by using two stochastic augmentations to alter its input stimulus and adding a few dropouts to enhance its classifier. The choices of the two stochastic augmentations are made upon the input data, and we select Gaussian noise and random horizontal flipping for our experiments conducted on facial attribute domains, which remain consistent after either augmentation. Figure 2 shows the proposed auxiliary classifier and its self-ensembling components, and we define a domain classification loss for unlabeled images

$$\begin{aligned} \mathcal{L}^u_{cls} &= \mathbb{E}_x[\|D_{cls}(\phi(x, \epsilon)) - D_{cls}(\phi(x, \epsilon'))\|_2^2 \\ &\quad + \mathbb{E}_{x,c'}[\|D_{cls}(\phi(G(x, c'), \epsilon)) - D_{cls}(\phi(G(x, c'), \epsilon'))\|_2^2], \end{aligned} \tag{3}$$

where ϕ is the stochastic augmentation function, and ϵ and ϵ' are two different parameter settings of ϕ for generating different augmentation. Self-ensembling not only is applied to the unlabeled images but also to the fake images $G(x, c')$ and labeled images. To make G translate images to target domains correctly, we adopt domain classification loss for fake images

$$\mathcal{L}^f_{cls} = \mathbb{E}_{x,c'}[-\log D_{cls}(c'|G(x, c'))], \tag{4}$$

which punishes G if its fake image $G(x, c')$ is not classified as the domain c'.

3.4 Cycle Consistency and Pseudo Cycle Consistency Loss

We aim to develop a network which can not only generate realistic images containing correct domain attributes, but also prevent random permutation often

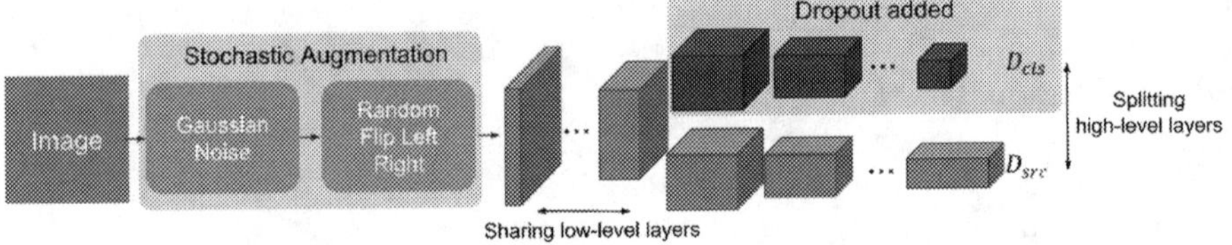

Fig. 2. The proposed Y model architecture and self-ensembling components of the classifier. The discriminator D_{src} and the auxiliary classifier D_{cls} share a few early-stage layers for extracting common low-level features and then split into two branches for learning their individual high-level features. For the two stochastic augmentations required by self-ensembling, we propose to use the Gaussian noise and random horizontal flipping. We only apply the dropouts used by self-ensembling to D_{cls}.

occurring in large networks. Thus we adopt an approach of remaining cycle consistency [29] and define a consistency loss

$$\mathcal{L}^{l}_{rec} = \mathbb{E}_{x,c,c'}[\|x - G(G(x, c'), c)\|_1], \tag{5}$$

which regulates the generator G by translating a generated image $G(x, c')$ back to its origin domain c and encouraging the image $G(G(x, c'), c)$ to be similar with the original image x. To apply cycle consistency for unlabeled images which do not have domain labels, we define a loss of pseudo cycle consistency

$$\mathcal{L}^{u}_{rec} = \mathbb{E}_{x,c'}[\|x - G(G(x, c'), D_{cls}(x))\|_1], \tag{6}$$

where we utilize the auxiliary classifier D_{cls} to predict unlabeled data's labels, which are required to brought into a loss of cycle consistency. Our use of pseudo labels is inspired by an existing method, pseudo labeling [11], but we do not follow its approach of joining genuine and pseudo labeled images to train a classifier. We only use pseudo labels to enable cycle consistency for unlabeled data.

3.5 Y Model: Splitting Classifier and Discriminator

Many existing methods design their classifiers and discriminators in a convenient way that both classifier and discriminator share most neural network layers except the last one. Such a type of straightforward architecture is based on a hypothesis that a common set of image features from low- to high-level is sufficient for both classifier and discriminator; nevertheless, it remains an open question under which situation the hypothesis works.

Based on an observation that a discriminator and auxiliary classifier serve for different purposes, i.e. telling real/fake images and predicting domain labels, and another observation that adopting self-ensembling must create a new sort of network architecture, we propose a partially splitting model of the classifier and discriminator, named Y model due to its shape similar to the letter Y, as shown in Fig. 2.

The architecture of Y model is inspired from TripleGAN [12], which totally splits its discriminator and classifier. However, since most convolutional neural networks extract similar low-level image features such as edges, corners, and spots [26], we propose to share a few common layers in the early stage used by both discriminator and auxiliary classifier. Beyond those common layers, either the discriminator or the auxiliary classifier owns its individual convolutional layers for learning specific high-level features. To the best of our knowledge, no similar architecture has been proposed in the literature to address the problem of image translation.

3.6 Full Objective

Finally, we make the overall objective for the generator G as

$$\mathcal{L}_G = \mathcal{L}_{GAN} + \lambda_{cls}\mathcal{L}_{cls}^{f} + \lambda_{rec}\mathcal{L}_{rec}^{l} + \lambda_{rec}\mathcal{L}_{rec}^{u} \tag{7}$$

and for the discriminator D_{scr} and the auxiliary classifier D_{cls} as

$$\mathcal{L}_D = -\mathcal{L}_{GAN} + \lambda_{cls}\mathcal{L}_{cls}^{r} + \lambda_{cls}^{u}\mathcal{L}_{cls}^{u} \tag{8}$$

where λ_{cls}, λ_{rec}, and λ_{cls}^{u} are weight parameters make losses balanced.

4 Experimental Validation

We conduct two experiments to validate the proposed method, and report its performance by two sets of numerical evaluation and one human perceptual study. The code is publicly available at GitHub[1].

CelebA_HAG Image Set. The CelebA dataset [16] is a widely used face image dataset, which contains 202,599 face images collected from 10,177 identities with large pose variations and background clutter. Each image in the CelebA dataset is labeled with 40 binary attributes, among which three attributes—*black hair*, *blond hair* and *brown hair* indicate hair colors, but a few images are annotated as positive in more than one of the three attributes because the hair colors of those images are between the three given colors. To create an unambiguous image set in which hair colors become mutually exclusive, we extract all images from the CelebA dataset labeled as positive for only one of the three hair color attributes, i.e., images with multiple positive hair color attributes are excluded. We name the image set CelebA_HAG, which contains 115309 images. The letters H, A, and G stand for hair color, age, and gender because we take two more attributes—young and male—into account, and the statistics of the CelebA_HAG image set is shown in Table 1. Those attributes, three hair colors, two age states (young, not young), and two genders (male, not male) are all mutually exclusive and make up 12 domains. For a fair comparison with a state-of-the-art method StarGAN,

[1] https://github.com/KevinYuimin/SemiStarGAN.

Table 1. Statistics of the CelebA_HAG image sets used for the experimental validation of the proposed method.

	Male +		Male −		
Hair color	Young +	Young −	Young +	Young −	Total
Black	19722	4939	21104	1568	47333
Blond	1026	565	22691	4478	28760
Brown	9475	2664	24091	2986	39216
Total	30223	8168	67886	9032	115309

we generate images for experiments using its release code, which crops a central region of 178×178 pixels from the original CelebA images of 178×218 pixels, and then downsamples cropped images using bilinear interpolation into a smaller size of 128×128 pixels.

4.1 Evaluation Metrics

We evaluate the performance of the proposed method using three metrics: Inception accuracy, classification accuracy, and human perceptual rating.

Inception Accuracy. In order to fairly access the effectiveness of a generator by its translated images, we utilize a strong classifier to objectively evaluate the saliency of the translated images [20]. We choose Inception-v3 [22] as the classifier due to its state-of-the-art performance for object recognition. We use its publicly released model pretrained on the ImageNet dataset [3], and refine it using our CelebA_HAG dataset. Each test image is translated to another domain and classified by the strong classifier. The inception accuracy Acc_{incept} is defined as the fraction of translated test images which are correctly classified by the refined Inception-v3 network. Note that though a high Acc_{incept} value means good translation saliency, it reveals little information about the quality of the translated images, so that we need human perceptual studies to measure their visual quality.

Human Perceptual Study. We carry out our human perceptual studies through Amazon Mechanical Turk (AMT). We present each translated image to 5 different turkers and ask two multiple-choice questions. First, which domain does the subject on the translated image belongs to? That is, turkers work in the same manner as Inception-v3 to classify translated images. Second, how is the quality of the translated image compared with its original image? and we offer three choices: similar, slightly worse, and worse. Because the image quality of the CelebA dataset varies significantly, when we ask the second question, we present not only a translated image but also its original one. To increase the reliability of this perceptual study, we set up a criterion to hire turkers whose approve rate and submission history exceed 90% and 30 times, and accept the result of a HIT (human intelligence task) only if at least 3 of 5 turkers select the same choice for both questions.

Classification Accuracy of the Auxiliary Classifier. In the proposed method, the auxiliary classifier takes an important role to guide the generator to translate images with eligible saliency. To evaluate the effectiveness of the proposed auxiliary classifier, we compute the classifier's accuracy Acc_{aux}, which is defined as the fraction of the number of correctly classified test images divided by the total number.

4.2 Implementation and Training

Implementation. Our generator use the same CNN architecture as [1], which is composed of three convolutional downsampling layers, six residual blocks and three transposed convolutional layers for upsampling. Each convolutional layer except the last one is followed by a step of instance normalization [24]. Our discriminator and auxiliary classifier share the first two convolution layers and then split into two branches. Our discriminator branch, similar to StarGAN's discriminator, contains four convolutional layers and PatchGANs [1,6,13,29], which divides an image into several patches and discriminates between real and fake patches. Our auxiliary classifier branch contains six convolutional layers, three dropout layers, and one 1×1 convolutional layer. More details of our network architecture is shown in the supplementary material.

Training Detail. We initialize SemiStarGAN using random numbers and train it using batches of eight labeled samples and eight unlabeled samples in 250K iterations (20 epochs including unlabeled data). We use the Adam optimizer [8] to train SemiStarGAN and set the optimizer's two exponential decay rates for the moment estimates β_1 and β_2 as 0.5 and 0.999 respectively.

We set the initial learning rate as 0.0001 and keep it unchanged for the first half of iterations, and linearly reduce it to 0 for the second half. Regarding the parameters of the proposed method, we set the classification weight λ_{cls} as 1, gradient penalty weight λ_{gp} as 10, and reconstruction weight λ_{rec} as 10. We use Gaussian ramp up weighting function proposed by self-ensembling to set the classification weight for unlabeled images λ_{cls}^{u} as 2 for the first one-third training iterations, and reduce it to 0 for the last one-third training images.

4.3 Experimental Results

Experiment on Three Domains of Hair Colors. In this experimental setting, we only create three domains using the hair color attributes of our CelebA_HAG image set in order to assure large numbers of samples available in all domains to investigate the performance of the proposed method affected by the numbers of labeled training images. We randomly split the CelebA_HAG

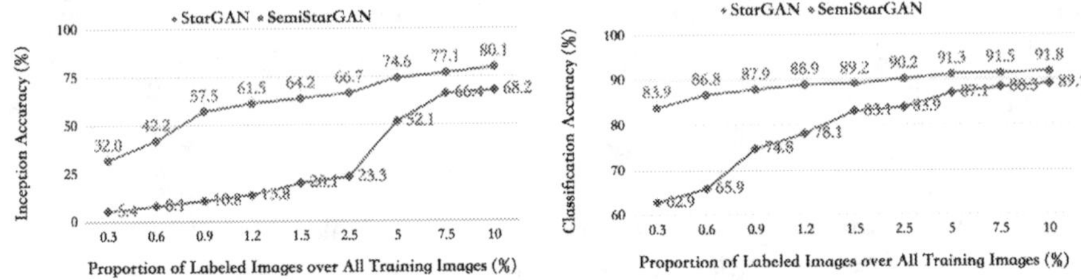

Fig. 3. Learning curves of StarGAN and SemiStarGAN generated from the experiment of the three hair color domains in terms of the Inception and classification accuracy shown in the left and right subfigures respectively. SemiStarGAN successfully exploits unlabeled images to generate translated images with higher accuracy over StarGAN for a wide range of numbers of labeled training images.

Fig. 4. Qualitative comparison between the proposed method (Semi) and a state-of-the-art method StarGAN (Star) over three hair color domains. (Top-left) A source image belonging to the domain of blond hair. (Top) Proportions of labeled images over all training images of the unit of percentage. (Left) The method and the target domain. StarGAN needs 5% labeled images while SemiStarGAN only needs 1.2% to achieve desirable translation saliency and quality.

Table 2. Human perceptual study results of the experiment using three hair colors as domains. The #HITs indicates the number of HITs in which at least 3 of 5 turkers reach a consensus. When using only 1/3 amount (2.5% v.s. 7.5%) of labeled training images used by StarGAN, the proposed SemiStarGAN method generates higher accuracy and better image quality evaluated by AMT turkers. Note a smaller percentage of the two worse options means better quality.

Method	Prop.	Question 1		Question 2			
		Accuracy	#HITs	Similar	Slightly worse	Worse	#HITs
SemiStarGAN	2.5%	**64.29%**	196	**66.22%**	**21.62%**	**12.16%**	148
StarGAN	7.5%	59.90%	197	57.82%	24.49%	17.69%	147

image set into training and test sets where the test set contains 5001 images (1667 images per domain), and the training set contains the remaining 110308 images. We use all images in the training set with their hair color labels to train the Inception-v3-based strong classifier and reach an accuracy rate of 92.4%. We randomly select 11031 images (3677 images per domain, 10% of all training images) to make up a labeled training set, and use the remaining 99277 (90%) images as the unlabeled training set. From the maximal proportion as 10%, we gradually reduce the number but keep the three domains balanced to do a series of experiments. In order to reduce the uncertainty caused by random selection, we repeat the experiments 3 times using 3 different seed numbers (0, 1, 2) and report their averaged Inception and classification accuracy in Fig. 3, and a set of translated images in Fig. 4. For a fair comparison with a state-of-the-art method StarGAN, we use its publicly released code and original setting to train its network on our CelebA_HAG dataset. Using the same labeled training images, the proposed SemiStarGAN generates higher accuracy rates over StarGAN because the SemiStarGAN takes advantage of a large number of unlabeled training images. Even only a small portion of labeled training images are used (0.3% of the total), due to the capability of exploiting a large portion of unlabeled images (90% of the total), the proposed method generated images with better quality than StarGAN. The results of our human perception study as shown in Table 2 also indicate that the proposed method generate better image quality.

Experiment on 12 Domains of Hair Colors, Age, and Gender. We take gender and age into account to evaluate the proposed method under a large domain number 12. We randomly select 2400 images, 200 per domain, to make up a test image set. In order to generate multi-domain classification labels composed by 3 fields (hair color, gender, and age), we replace the two softmax layers used in Inception-v3 (one at the end of the main branch, and another at the end of its auxiliary branch, more details are reported in the supplementary material) with two sigmoid layers. We use the remaining 112909 images to train the strong classifier and reach a classification accuracy rate of 87.7%. Since the numbers of images belonging to the 12 domains are uneven as shown in Table 1, we randomly select 3600 images, 300 per domain, from the training image set as the labeled training image set, and treat the remaining 109509 images as the unlabeled images. We repeat the experiments 3 times using 3 different seed numbers (0, 1, 2) and show their averaged performance in Fig. 6 and qualitative comparisons in Fig. 5. The proposed method generates both higher Inception and classification accuracy rates then StarGAN.

The Effectiveness of the Y Model. To investigate the effectiveness of the Y model, we take two other models into consideration: the mixed model similar to the architecture used in StarGAN, and a model whose discriminator and classifier branches are totally separated. We name the former D/C model due to its combined architecture and the latter II model due to its shape of two inde-

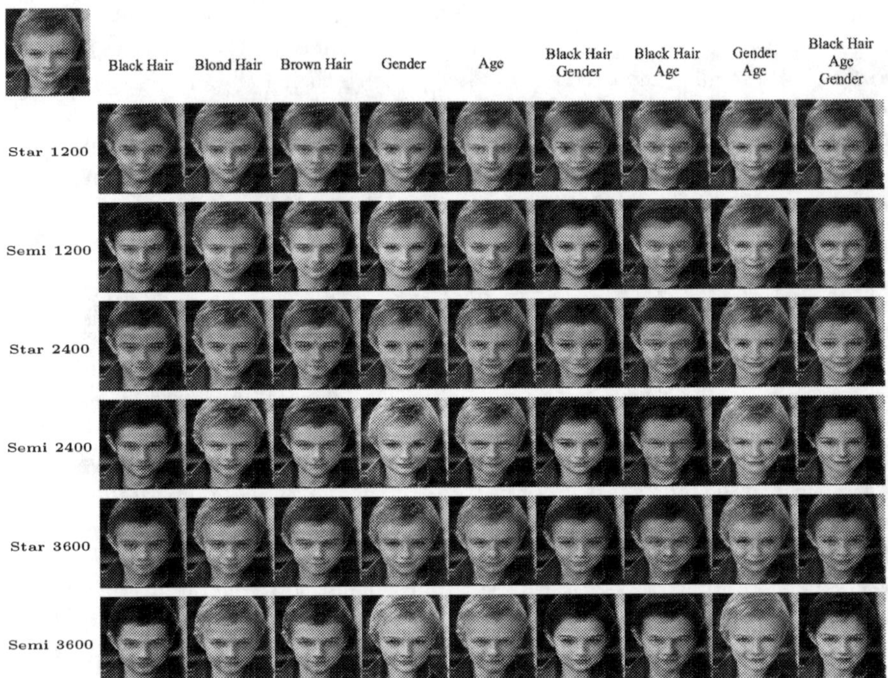

Fig. 5. Qualitative comparison between the proposed method (Semi) and a state-of-the-art method StarGAN (Star) over the 12-domain problem. (Top-left) A source image belonging to the domain of blond young male. (Top) The changed facial attributes. (Left) Methods and the numbers of used labeled training images. Compared with StarGAN, SemiStarGAN generates images with better saliency in terms of expected target domains. For example of the target domain of black hair using the same 1200 labeled training images (the two images at the first column and first two rows), SemiStarGAN generates obvious black hair, but StarGAN does not. For another example of the target domain of black hair, and different gender and age using the same 3600 labeled training images (the two image at the last column and last two rows), SemiStarGAN generates blacker hair, clearer eyes and smoother skin than StarGAN.

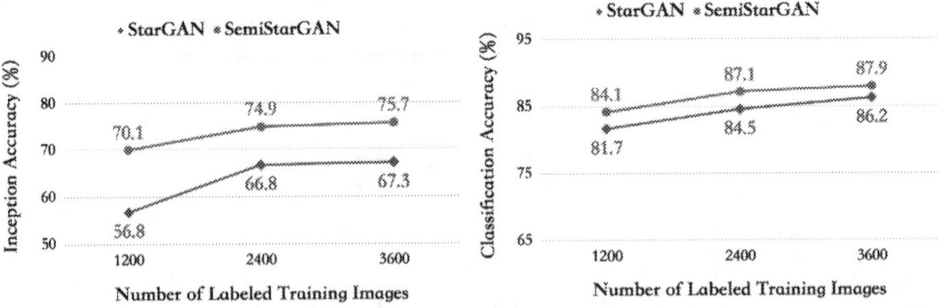

Fig. 6. Learning curves of StarGAN and SemiStarGAN of the facial attribute synthesis experiments using 12 domains. Images of both test and labeled training sets are evenly sampled from the 12 domains.

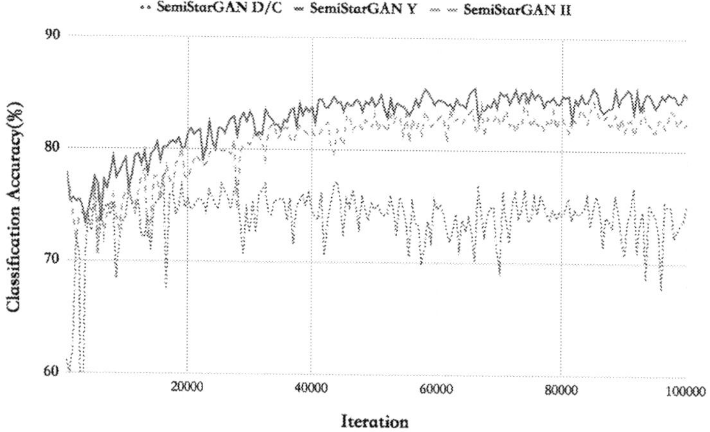

Fig. 7. Performance comparison of three different architecture models applicable to the discriminator and auxiliary classifier. D/C stands for the mixed model similar to the architecture used in StarGAN, and II stands for a model whose discriminator and classifier branches are totally separated.

pendent branches. For a fair comparison, the three types of architecture use the same stochastic augmentations and dropouts, and their classification accuracy of the three hair color domains test images is shown in Fig. 7 for every interval of 500 training iterations using 0.3% labeled training data. All of the three models reach their accuracy plateaus before 6000 iterations, and the proposed Y model not only generates higher accuracy but also performs more stably than the D/C model, which shows that the partially split structure can learn better high-level features and achieve better performance. We ascribe the superiority of the Y model over the II model to our used GAN objective. As mentioned in several papers presenting semi-supervised GAN methods [2,18,20], generated samples and an adversarial loss provided by the discriminator can regularize the classifier and improve the robustness. To sum up, the Y model lets the discriminator and classifier not only learn their own suitable high-level features in the same manner of TripleGAN but also gain benefits from GAN objectives proved effective by other semi-supervised GANs.

5 Conclusion

In this paper, we present a novel method SemiStarGAN, which utilizes unlabeled data for the problem of multi-domain image-to-image translation. Experimental results show the method's effectiveness for facial attribute transferring. For hair color transferring, SemiStarGAN only needs one third of the labeled data used by StarGAN to achieve the same Inception accuracy rate.

References

1. Choi, Y., Choi, M., Kim, M., Ha, J.W., Kim, S., Choo, J.: StarGAN: unified generative adversarial networks for multi-domain image-to-image translation. In: CVPR (2018)
2. Dai, Z., Yang, Z., Yang, F., Cohen, W.W., Salakhutdinov, R.: Good semi-supervised learning that requires a bad GAN. In: NIPS (2017)
3. Deng, J., Dong, W., Socher, R., Li, L.J., Li, K., Fei-Fei, L.: ImageNet: a large-scale hierarchical image database. In: CVPR (2009)
4. Goodfellow, I., et al.: Generative adversarial nets. In: NIPS (2014)
5. Gulrajani, I., Ahmed, F., Arjovsky, M., Dumoulin, V., Courville, A.: Improved training of wasserstein GANs. In: NIPS (2017)
6. Isola, P., Zhu, J.Y., Zhou, T., Efros, A.A.: Image-to-image translation with conditional adversarial networks. In: CVPR (2017)
7. Kim, T., Cha, M., Kim, H., Lee, J.K., Kim, J.: Learning to discover cross-domain relations with generative adversarial networks. In: ICML (2017)
8. Kingma, D.P., Ba, J.L.: Adam: a method for stochastic optimization. In: ICML (2015)
9. Laine, S., Aila, T.: Temporal ensembling for semi-supervised learning. In: ICLR (2017)
10. Ledig, C., et al.: Photo-realistic single image super-resolution using a generative adversarial network. In: CVPR (2017)
11. Lee, D.H.: Pseudo-label: the simple and efficient semi-supervised learning method for deep neural networks. In: Workshop on Challenges in Representation Learning, ICML (2013)
12. Li, C., Xu, K., Zhu, J., Zhang, B.: Triple generative adversarial nets. In: NIPS (2017)
13. Li, C., Wand, M.: Precomputed real-time texture synthesis with Markovian generative adversarial networks. In: Leibe, B., Matas, J., Sebe, N., Welling, M. (eds.) ECCV 2016. LNCS, vol. 9907, pp. 702–716. Springer, Cham (2016). https://doi.org/10.1007/978-3-319-46487-9_43
14. Liu, M.Y., Breuel, T., Kautz, J.: Unsupervised image-to-image translation networks. In: NIPS (2017)
15. Liu, M.Y., Tuzel, O.: Coupled generative adversarial networks. In: NIPS (2016)
16. Liu, Z., Luo, P., Wang, X., Tang, X.: Deep learning face attributes in the wild. In: ICCV (2015)
17. Miyato, T., Maeda, S., Koyama, M., Ishii, S.: Virtual adversarial training: a regularization method for supervised and semi-supervised learning. ArXiv e-prints, April 2017
18. Odena, A.: Semi-supervised learning with generative adversarial networks. In: Workshop at ICML (2016)
19. Reed, S., Akata, Z., Yan, X., Logeswaran, L., Schiele, B., Lee, H.: Generative adversarial text to image synthesis. In: ICML (2016)
20. Salimans, T., Goodfellow, I., Zaremba, W., Cheung, V., Radford, A., Chen, X.: Improved techniques for training GANs. In: NIPS (2016)
21. Springenberg, J.T.: Unsupervised and semi-supervised learning with categorical generative adversarial networks. In: ICLR (2016)
22. Szegedy, C., Vanhoucke, V., Ioffe, S., Shlens, J., Wojna, Z.: Rethinking the inception architecture for computer vision. In: CVPR (2016)

23. Taigman, Y., Polyak, A., Wolf, L.: Unsupervised cross-domain image generation. In: ICLR (2017)
24. Ulyanov, D., Vedaldi, A., Lempitsky, V.: Instance normalization: the missing ingredient for fast stylization. ArXiv e-prints (Jul 2016)
25. Yi, Z., Zhang, H., Tan, P., Gong, M.: DualGAN: unsupervised dual learning for image-to-image translation. In: ICCV (2017)
26. Zeiler, M.D., Fergus, R.: Visualizing and understanding convolutional networks. In: Fleet, D., Pajdla, T., Schiele, B., Tuytelaars, T. (eds.) ECCV 2014. LNCS, vol. 8689, pp. 818–833. Springer, Cham (2014). https://doi.org/10.1007/978-3-319-10590-1_53
27. Zhang, H., et al.: StackGAN: text to photo-realistic image synthesis with stacked generative adversarial networks. In: ICCV (2017)
28. Zhu, J.-Y., Krähenbühl, P., Shechtman, E., Efros, A.A.: Generative visual manipulation on the natural image manifold. In: Leibe, B., Matas, J., Sebe, N., Welling, M. (eds.) ECCV 2016. LNCS, vol. 9909, pp. 597–613. Springer, Cham (2016). https://doi.org/10.1007/978-3-319-46454-1_36
29. Zhu, J.Y., Park, T., Isola, P., Efros, A.A.: Unpaired image-to-image translation using cycle-consistent adversarial networkss. In: ICCV (2017)

Gated Transfer Network for Transfer Learning

Yi Zhu[1(✉)], Jia Xue[2], and Shawn Newsam[1]

[1] University of California at Merced, Merced, CA 95343, USA
{yzhu25,snewsam}@ucmerced.edu
[2] Rutgers University, New Brunswick, NJ 08901, USA
jia.xue@rutgers.edu

Abstract. Deep neural networks have led to a series of breakthroughs in computer vision given sufficient annotated training datasets. For novel tasks with limited labeled data, the prevalent approach is to transfer the knowledge learned in the pre-trained models to the new tasks by fine-tuning. Classic model fine-tuning utilizes the fact that well trained neural networks appear to learn cross domain features. These features are treated equally during transfer learning. In this paper, we explore the impact of feature selection in model fine-tuning by introducing a transfer module, which assigns weights to features extracted from pre-trained models. The proposed transfer module proves the importance of feature selection for transferring models from source to target domains. It is shown to significantly improve upon fine-tuning results with only marginal extra computational cost. We also incorporate an auxiliary classifier as an extra regularizer to avoid over-fitting. Finally, we build a Gated Transfer Network (GTN) based on our transfer module and achieve state-of-the-art results on six different tasks.

Keywords: Transfer learning · Feature selection · Sparse coding

1 Introduction

Deep convolutional neural networks (CNNs) are good at accurately mapping inputs to outputs from large amounts of labeled data. For example, deep residual learning [10] already achieves superhuman performance at recognizing objects on the ImageNet challenge [7]. However, these successful models rely on large amounts of annotated data to achieve such performances. For tasks and domains that do not have sufficient training data, deep models may have inferior performance to traditional classification algorithms that utilize hand crafted features. Transfer learning is helpful to deal with these novel scenarios that go beyond tasks where labeled data is abundant. The essence is to transfer the knowledge learned in the pre-trained models to new domains.

The first two authors contributed equally.

C. V. Jawahar et al. (Eds.): ACCV 2018, LNCS 11364, pp. 354–369, 2019.
https://doi.org/10.1007/978-3-030-20870-7_22

Transfer learning is a broad research topic, and is studied in several forms such as domain adaptation, multi-task learning and model fine-tuning. In this work, we focus on model fine-tuning and try to answer the question of how to best adapt a pre-trained CNN model to new tasks. We start with the observations of existing model fine-tuning approaches for classification: The common approach is to pre-train a CNN architecture on a source domain with sufficient training data (e.g., ImageNet, which contains 1.2 million images in 1000 categories), and then employ the pre-trained CNN as a feature extraction module, combined with a classification module for the task domain. When the task domain contains limited training data (e.g., CUB-200 [26], which contains 11 thousand images in 200 categories), two types of prevalent classifier models are employed in transfer learning. The first one is to remove the classification layer from the pre-trained CNN, treat the remaining CNN as a fixed feature extractor, and train a linear classifier for classification. The second type is to replace the pre-trained classification layer with a new classification layer (e.g., a new 200-way classification layer for CUB-200 classification), fine-tuning all (or a portion of) the layers of the network by continuing the back-propagation with a relatively small learning rate. For both scenarios, the underlying thesis is that the well trained CNNs appear to learn cross domain features.

However, both scenarios have their own drawbacks. When we regard a pre-trained CNN as a fixed feature extractor, the features are not tailored for the target domain, which limits their performance. When we fine-tune the pre-trained CNN to learn task specific features in an end-to-end manner, we will encounter the over-fitting problem quite often. How can we best leverage the information from both the source and target domains?

A recent study [6] shows that there exists a similarity ratio between the source and target domains, termed domain similarity. Inspired by this, we argue that features extracted from pre-trained CNNs also have a similarity ratio: some features share more similarity between the source and target domains than other features. The features with a higher similarity ratio should get more attention. Hence, a feature selection mechanism is expected to be helpful during model fine-tuning. In this paper, we consider some novel questions. *Should the features extracted from the pre-trained CNN be treated equally? Are some features more important and thus be weighted more than others in the novel target domain? Will a feature selection mechanism be helpful for better knowledge transfer?* We aim to answer these questions by introducing a gating architecture, acting like a weight assignment, to the extracted features before classification. We refer to it as a *transfer module* and illustrate the details in later sections. Specifically, our contributions include the following:

- First, we prove that a feature selection mechanism is helpful during model fine-tuning and introduce the transfer module as a gating mechanism to decide feature importance when transferring from pre-trained CNNs to target domains.
- Second, we incorporate an auxiliary classifier to stabilize the training and avoid over-fitting.

– Finally, our proposed gated transfer network achieves state-of-the-art results on six different domains, which demonstrates its superior transferability.

2 Related Work

There is a large body of literature on transfer learning; here we review only the most related work. Starting from [9], off-the-shelf CNN features have shown promising performance in various computer vision domains. Later, Yosinski et al. [29] raised the question of "How transferable are features in deep neural networks", and experimentally quantified the generality versus specificity of neurons in each layer of a deep CNN. However, features from the pre-trained models are not tailored for the target domain, which limits their performance. The common practice now is to not only replace and retrain the classifier on top of the CNN on the new dataset, but also fine-tune the weights of the pre-trained network by continuing the back-propagation, which is known as model fine-tuning [17]. Depending on the size of the new dataset, we could either train all the layers or only part of the network. Hence, task-specific features could be learned in an end-to-end manner.

Recently, there have been several attempts to explore more information between the source and target domains for better knowledge transfer [14,15]. [27] tries to grow a CNN with additional units, either by widening existing layers or deepening the overall network, and achieves moderate success over traditional fine-tuning. [8] proposes a source-target selective joint fine-tuning scheme based on the observation that low-level characteristics (shallow network features) are similar between the source and target domains. Their method obtains state-of-the-art results on several benchmarks. However, the joint fine-tuning pipeline consists of multiple stages and is not end-to-end optimized. [6] introduces a measure to estimate domain similarity via the Earth Mover's Distance and demonstrates that transfer learning benefits from pre-training on a source domain that is similar to the target domain by such a measure.

Our work lies in the recent direction that explores the source-target domain relationship, and is most similar to [27] in terms of increasing model capacity for more natural model adaptation through fine-tuning. However, we differ in several aspects. First, [27] makes an analogy to developmental learning while our work is inspired by sparse learning. Our transfer module acts like a gating mechanism without learning new features. We are interested in how to make existing features more distinctive for various target domains. Thus, we can better handle over-fitting in the insufficient training data scenario. Second, [27] proposes to make the fully connected layers deeper or wider to increase model capacity. This technique does not scale well to recent deeper networks like ResNet [10] or DenseNet [12] because they do not have fully connected layers. In contrast, our proposed transfer module is generally applicable. Third, we design our transfer module based on a "Squeeze-and-Excitation" block [11]. Squeeze aims at embedding global information while excitation learns to use the global information to selectively emphasize informative features and suppress less useful ones.

We show that our transfer module outperforms [27] on several widely adopted benchmarks for transfer learning.

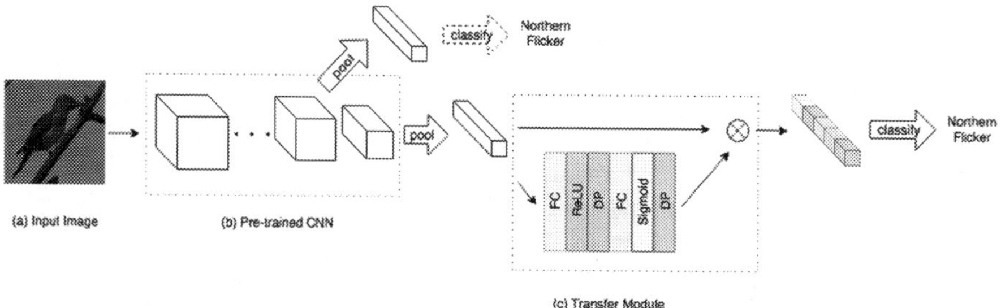

Fig. 1. Overview of our proposed gated transfer network. Our idea is that feature selection makes more sense than learning new features when we fine-tune a pre-trained CNN. The transfer module functions as a gating mechanism to assign weights to features from the pre-trained CNN. $\otimes$ denotes the point-wise multiplication. An auxiliary classifier is only used during the training phase.

3 Gated Transfer Network

In this section, we first introduce our transfer module as a feature attention mechanism and interpret its relation to other approaches. Then we incorporate the auxiliary classifier to stabilize the model fine-tuning and avoid over-fitting to domains with insufficient training data. Finally, we describe the details of our proposed gated transfer network.

3.1 Transfer Module

A weight assigning mechanism, which transforms features from the source domain to target domain, is very important for transfer learning. Intuitively, knowledge transfer will be easier if the source and target domains are similar: models trained on more images will likely to learn features in an unbiased manner, and lead to better transfer learning performance. However, as studied in [16,22], transfer learning performance is logarithmically related with the scale of training data. This indicates that the performance gained from using more training data would be insignificant when we already have a large-scale dataset (e.g., ImageNet [7] or Places [32]). Hence, feature selection makes more sense than learning new features when we fine-tune a pre-trained CNN.

The ground rule of our approach is that there should be common features (knowledge) between the source and target domains in order to do transfer learning. We should give more attention to the common features and ignore the dissimilar ones. In addition, during back propagation, the common features should be focused on and finely adjusted, instead of treating all features from a pre-trained model equally.

Let x denote the extracted features from the aforementioned feature extractor module, with y denoting the target features. Our transfer module is defined as:

$$y = F(x) \otimes x \tag{1}$$

where the function $F(x)$ is the gating function and represents the feature map weights to be learned. $\otimes$ is the channel-wise multiplication between the feature maps x and the feature weights $F(x)$. When $F(x)$ contains all 1s, it passes all the learned features through without gating, which is basically a classic fine-tuning approach. We will provide more interpretations on our proposed transfer module in the next section.

In addition, over-fitting is a non-trivial problem in transfer learning, especially when the training images are limited. To prevent over-fitting, we adopt the dropout [21] function in our transfer module. As shown in Fig. 1, our transfer module is designed as:

$$F(x) = \rho\delta(W_2\rho\sigma(W_1x)) \tag{2}$$

in which σ denotes the ReLU function, ρ refers to the dropout function, and δ is the sigmoid function. W_1 and W_2 are two fully-connected layers.

3.2 Interpretation

We introduce the transfer module as a feature selection mechanism into CNN fine-tuning approaches with minimal extra computational cost. Here, we interpret why it works by relating it to classic fine-tuning and sparse coding.

Classic Fine-Tuning. Classic fine-tuning replaces the pre-trained classification layer with a new classification layer for the target domain. All (or a portion of) the layers of the network continue back-propagation until the new model converges. It does not consider feature importance during the knowledge transfer process. If our transfer module learns the extracted features as being equally important for the target domain, our network will assign same weights to the features. In the end, our transfer module will simply become the classic fine-tuning approach.

Sparse Coding. Sparse coding assumes that a task's parameters are well approximated by sparse linear combinations of the atoms of a dictionary on a high or infinite dimensional space. The sparsity acts as regularization and works well for transfer learning tasks. When considering sparse coding in CNNs, most literature utilizes it for model compression and reduced computational cost. The overall idea is that some sparse representations embedded in the pre-trained model are vital for visual recognition. If our transfer module learns that only a few features are important for the target domain, our network will assign high weights to these important features and low weights to the other features. In the end, our transfer module will function like sparse coding.

3.3 Auxiliary Classifier

[10,19,23] demonstrate that deeper networks generally lead to better performance in images classification. However, a very deep network may be unstable during training, due to vanishing gradients and information forgetting [10]. In the transfer learning regime, the problems are even more severe because of the additional optimization difficulty brought by the limited training set.

Motivated by the observation in [23], we believe that features produced by the intermediate layers of the network should be very discriminative. Instead of only using the output layer, we can provide additional feedback signals to the network by adding auxiliary classifiers after the intermediate representations. In this manner, we expect to learn more distinctive features for the target domain in the lower layers of the network. Furthermore, the extra gradient signal will provide additional regularization, and alleviate the common problem of vanishing gradients.

Hence, we introduce an auxiliary classifier as shown in Fig. 1. The total loss of the network is the sum of original loss from the output layer and the new loss from the auxiliary classifier. We aim to let the auxiliary classifier and transfer module separately do their own jobs. The auxiliary classier learns realizable features for the target domain, and the transfer module selects the features based on the attention weights. We only employ the auxiliary classifier during the training phase, and in later sections, we will show that the auxiliary classifier provides performance improvement even when there are already multiple dropout layers and batch normalization. Thus, we have the same observation as in [24] that the auxiliary classifier acts as regularizer.

3.4 Network Architecture

With the proposed transfer module and auxiliary classifier, we build our gated transfer network as illustrated in Fig. 1. Given an input image, we use a pre-trained CNN while removing the last fully connected layer to extract the feature maps. The pre-trained CNN could be of any architecture, e.g., AlexNet, VGGNet, ResNet, DenseNet, etc. This is followed by the transfer module to assign attention weights to the features. The auxiliary classifier is on another branch to provide feedback for more regularization. In our experiments, we branch it out before the last convolutional group. Finally, the network makes a prediction based on the gated features with a new classification layer for the target domain.

To improve model efficiency and aid generalization, inspired by [10,11], we reduce the feature map channels between the fully connected layers in the transfer module with a manually defined reduction ratio r. If the channel for input features is C, then the dimension of the weights for the first fully connected layer is $W_1 \in \mathbb{R}^{\frac{C}{r} \times C}$ and the dimension of the weights for the second fully connected layer is $W_2 \in \mathbb{R}^{C \times \frac{C}{r}}$. In our experiments, we set the reduction ratio to 16 for a good trade-off between accuracy and efficiency.

4 Experiments

4.1 Datasets

We choose six different datasets for evaluating of our proposed transfer module: MIT67, CUB200, MINC, DTD, UCF101 and FashionAI. MIT67 and CUB200 are widely adopted benchmarks for evaluating CNN transferability. We also report performance on four other large-scale datasets, MINC for material recognition, DTD for texture classification, UCF101 for video human action recognition and FashionAI for attribute recognition of apparel. These tasks are quite challenging for existing transfer learning techniques because they are conceptually different from what the pre-trained CNN was designed to do (e.g., object recognition). We follow the standard experimental setup (e.g., the train/test splits) for these datasets, and demonstrate the effectiveness of our approach in later sections.

In brief, MIT Indoor 67 (MIT67) [18] is an indoor scene categorization dataset with 67 categories. A standard subset of 80 images per-category for training and 20 for testing is used. Caltech-UCSD Birds 200-2011 (CUB200) [26] is a fine grained recognition dataset containing 200 categories of birds. There are 5994 training images and 5794 test images. For MIT67 and CUB200, we report the mean class accuracy on the test set. Materials in Context Database (MINC) [2] is a large scale material dataset. In this work, a publicly available subset MINC-2500 is evaluated, containing 23 material categories and 2,500 images per-category. Describable Textures Dataset (DTD) [4] is a collection of textural images in the wild. This texture database consists of 5640 images and is organized according to a list of 47 categories. UCF101 [20] is composed of realistic action videos from YouTube. It contains 13320 video clips distributed among 101 action classes. Each video clip lasts for an average of 7 seconds. For MINC, DTD and UCF101, we report the average recognition accuracy. FashionAI [1] is a global challenge aiming to make AI insights on fashion. There are two tasks in the challenge, and we focus on the attribute recognition of apparel task. The training dataset has 79573 images from 8 attributes. Each attribute has multiple attribute values. We submit our results on the held out test set to the evaluation server, and report the mean average precision.

4.2 Implementation Details

We use stochastic gradient descent (SGD) with a mini-batch size of 64 for our deep model training and evaluation. For data augmentation, the input images are first resized to 256 along the short edge, and normalized by pixel mean subtraction and standard deviation division. The images are then randomly cropped to size 224, keeping the aspect ratio between 3/4 and 4/3. We also flip the images horizontally with a 50% chance. For fine-tuning, the learning rate starts at 0.01 and is divided by 10 when the validation error plateaus. During fine-tuning, we first freeze the pre-trained CNN for the first several epochs to get a good initialization of our transfer module, and then we make them learn at the same pace. We use a weight decay of 0.0001 and a momentum of 0.9. In testing, we adopt the standard center crop evaluation strategy.

4.3 Ablation Study

In this section, we will perform a series of ablation studies on MIT67, MINC and CUB200, to both justify our network design and demonstrate the effectiveness of our proposed transfer module. To be specific, we first show how significant dropout can help the fine-tuning process to avoid over-fitting. Second, we show the impact of the auxiliary classifier through a grid search of loss weights. Third, we compare with a strong baseline method [27] to indicate the superiority of our gating mechanism. Fourth, we compare our transfer module with widely adopted residual block [10] to confirm our design choice. For all the experiments, we use ResNet50 as the backbone CNN architecture.

Table 1. Impact of dropout. TM: transfer module. AUX: auxiliary objective. Numbers in parentheses are mean accuracies with dropout.

Method	MIT67	CUB200	MINC
Baseline fine-tuning	76.95	77.64	77.88
Pre-trained + TM	77.17 (77.29)	77.85 (79.72)	79.83 (80.41)
Pre-trained + TM + AUX	77.54 (**77.77**)	77.96 (**79.95**)	**81.05** (80.80)

Dropout as Good Practice: For transfer learning to a target domain with little annotated data, over-fitting is usually the most challenging problem to deal with. This is true for classic fine-tuning as well as more recent domain adaption approaches, and our approach is no exception.

As shown in Table 1, our transfer module brings significant improvement over baseline fine-tuning on all three benchmarks. Here, baseline indicates directly fine-tuning on the target domain using a ResNet50 model pre-trained on ImageNet. Similarly, due to the extra regularization, our model with both the transfer module and auxiliary objective performs the best. However, we observe that for CUB200, the improvement is rather limited (77.64 $\Rightarrow$ 77.96). On the other hand, our proposed method achieves much higher accuracy (77.88 $\Rightarrow$ 81.05) than the baseline on the MINC dataset. We believe that we are experiencing over-fitting since CUB200 has too little training data (e.g., 20 images per class), while MINC has many more images (e.g., 2500 images per class).

Hence, we incorporate dropout [21] as a good practice in our transfer module. As shown in Fig. 1, we add two dropout layers after each fully connected layer, with dropout rates of 0.5 and 0.7, respectively. The dropout rates are empirically determined based on cross-validation. The numbers inside the parentheses in Table 1 are the recognition accuracy after adding dropout layers. We observe a clear performance boost on CUB200 (77.64 $\Rightarrow$ 79.95), and moderate improvement on MIT67 and MINC. This confirms that our initial model without dropout layers suffers from serious over-fitting on CUB200. There is one interesting observation that adding dropout does not improve MINC (81.05 $\Rightarrow$ 80.80) when the auxiliary classifier is also present. This is because the auxiliary loss can regularize the training given sufficient data, and thus there is no need for extra dropout layers. Next, we will investigate the impact of the auxiliary loss.

Impact of Auxiliary Classifier: Intermediate features are also capable of discriminating different classes because they are extracted from earlier layers in which the gradients carry information. Hence, the auxiliary classifier is introduced to regularize the network fine-tuning especially when the training data is small. Here, we perform an ablation study to justify its impact.

As show in Table 2, we assign different weights to the auxiliary loss during CNN optimization. A loss weight of 0 indicates we do not use the auxiliary loss. We can see that the auxiliary loss does bring improvement on all three datasets. The optimal weight of the auxiliary loss dependa on the dataset. We choose 0.2 as a trade-off, and use it for all our experiments hereafter. Although the improvements seem marginal, they are actually significant considering we already use state-of-the-art techniques such as batch normalization and dropout to regularize model training. In addition, our model converges about 10% faster due to the strong supervision signals flowing to earlier layers in the network.

Table 2. The impact of the weight of the auxiliary loss on classification performance. We find that the auxiliary loss performs best with a weight of 0.2 and use this value for the remaining experiments.

Loss weights	MIT67	CUB200	MINC
0	77.29	79.72	80.41
0.1	77.09	78.93	80.56
0.2	**77.77**	**79.95**	80.80
0.4	77.07	79.81	80.47
0.8	76.27	79.24	**80.87**

Transfer Module vs Grow a Brain [27]**:** We mentioned in Sect. 2 that [27] is the most related work. [27] proposed several structures, such as depth-augmented (DA)-CNN, width-augmented (WA)-CNN, etc., but the basic idea is to deepen or widen the fully connected layers in the CNN model. Here, we compare our GTN to this strong baseline [27].

Because [27] reported its performance using VGG16, for fair comparison, we report our numbers using both VGG16 and ResNet50. As we can see in Table 3, our recognition accuracies outperform [27] by a large margin on MIT67 and CUB200 using VGG16. We also re-implement [27] using ResNet50. Since ResNets do not have fully connected layers, we could not width-augment the network. Thus, to depth-augment the network as in [27], we add one fully connected layer and one batch normalization layer before the classifier. As shown in in Table 3, our GTN with ResNet50 still obtains better performance than [27] with

ResNet50 on all three benchmarks. Note that, for MIT67, the depth-augmented ResNet50 performs even worse than the baseline model fine-tuning (as shown in Table 1, 75.38 < 76.95). This indicates that [27] may not generalize well to deeper architectures like ResNet and DenseNet.

Table 3. Comparison with DA-CNN [27] using both VGG16 and ResNet50 models. GTN outperforms DA-CNN on all three datasets.

Method	MIT67	CUB200	MINC
[27] with VGG16	66.3	69.0	–
GTN with VGG16	71.19	72.14	–
[27] with ResNet50	75.38	76.28	78.56
GTN with ResNet50	**77.77**	**79.95**	**80.80**

Table 4. Performance comparisons of classification accuracy (%) on the target datasets between the transfer module (multiplication) and a residual block (summation) based on ResNet50.

Method	MIT67	CUB200	MINC
Summation	76.47	78.39	80.23
Multiplication	**77.29**	**79.72**	**80.41**

Transfer Module vs Residual Block: Continuing the discussion from the last paragraph, it is straightforward to grow network capacity by deepening or widening fully connected layers in AlexNet and VGG16. However, for recent widely-adopted deeper networks like ResNet and DenseNet, it is more natural to add residual blocks to grow the network capacity. A residual block [10] aims to utilize additional shortcut connections to pass the input directly to the output and ease the model optimization procedure. But it still needs to learn the corresponding residuals. In this work, we argue that features from models pre-trained on ImageNet are already good enough. We only need to select those features instead of learning new ones.

Simply, if we design our transfer module by replacing the last multiplication with a summation operation in Fig. 1, we will transform it to a standard residual block. In this way, we expect the network to learn residuals to make the feature set more distinctive. The comparison results are shown in Table 4. We observe that multiplication obtains better results than summation, especially on CUB200 (78.39 $\Rightarrow$ 79.72). This indicates that our transfer module with multiplication is more easily optimized when dealing with insufficient data. The reason is because we only need to learn how to select the original features instead of learning something new.

4.4 Visualizing Transfer Module

To demonstrate what the transfer module is learning, we visualize its weight distribution. Since the last layer of the transfer module is a sigmoid activation function, the output will be in the range [0, 1]. The dimension of the output is the same as the original features from the pre-trained model (e.g., 2048 in our case). This represents a one-to-one gating score. A value closer to 1 indicates the feature is important for target domain classification, while a value closer to 0 means it is irrelevant.

Here, we show three histograms to visualize the selection weight distribution. For each dataset, we randomly select a batch of 100 images as input. For the x-axis, we divide 0~1 into 10 bins, and group the values of neurons in each group. As we can see in Fig. 2 top, the selection score distributions are different for different datasets. Such distributions could be used to describe the domain similarity between source and target domains. MINC is a material recognition dataset, which is quite different from ImageNet. It requires low-level information instead of the high-level object features. Hence, most of the weights are small (below 0.5), which means the original features are not important for the target domain. MIT67 is a scene classification dataset and, although different from the object recognition task, most of the scenes contain objects. There are some common features (knowledge) that can be transferred, thus most of the features have a gating score of 0.7. CUB200 is a fine-grained dataset for bird species recognition. It is also an object recognition task like ImageNet. In addition, some of the images are from ImageNet. Hence, the source domain and target domain are very similar. As expected, most weights are large (above 0.7), which means most of the original features (knowledge) are useful for the target domain. The observation demonstrates that our transfer module indeed functions as a gating mechanism. We select useful features based on the domain similarity between the source and target domains.

In addition, we plot the mean and standard deviation of the weights for each feature in the gating module and the weights in the classification layer in Fig. 2 bottom. We have the same observation as demonstrated by the histograms. The higher the domain similarity (CUB200 > MIT67 > MINC) between the source and target domains, the more features we select for the target application.

To gain insight into the effect of the transfer module in feature space, we also visualize the features extracted from the MIT67 and MINC validation datasets using the t-SNE algorithm [25]. As shown in Fig. 3, based on ResNet50, we embed the 4096 dimension features before the classification layer of the pre-trained networks, DA-CNN and GTN, into a 2 dimensional space and plot them as points colored based on their semantic categories. From the t-SNE manifold, our GTN consistently shows better semantic separation, which is compatible with its improved classification performance.

4.5 Learning Without Forgetting

A must-have property of transfer learning is that new tasks can be learned without suffering from catastrophic forgetting. In particular, for a CNN model,

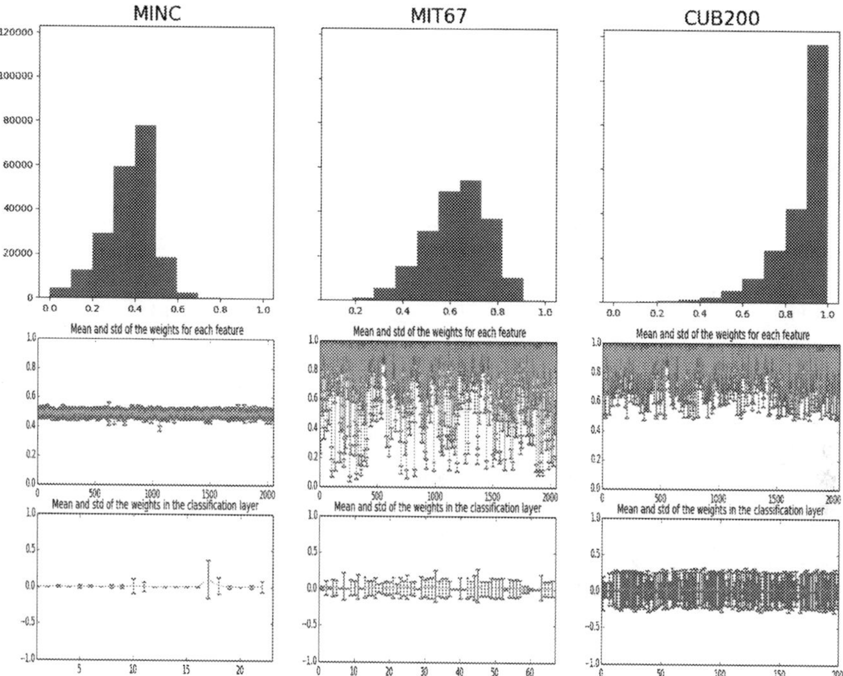

Fig. 2. Top: Histogram of the attention weights from the transfer module. It visualizes how our transfer module selects useful features for the target domain. Values on the Y axis indicate the number of neurons. Our transfer module indeed functions as a gating mechanism based on the domain similarity. Bottom: Mean (blue) and standard deviation (gray) of the weights for each feature in our gating module and in the classification layer. Same observation holds. (Color figure online)

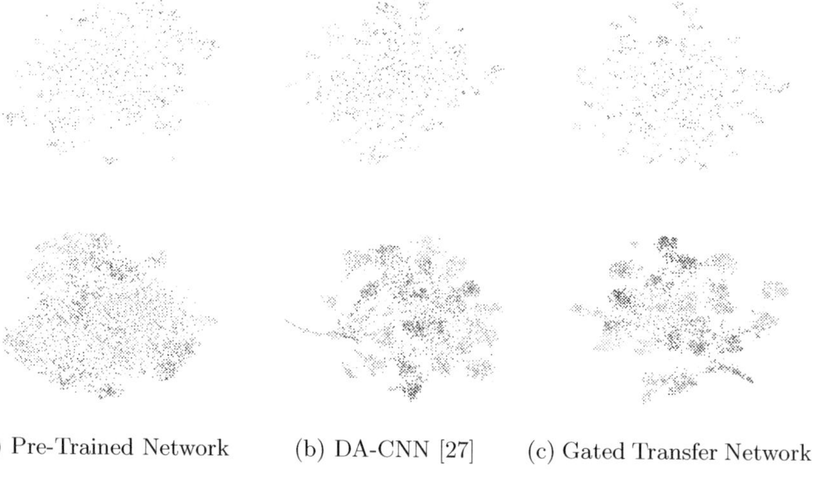

(a) Pre-Trained Network (b) DA-CNN [27] (c) Gated Transfer Network

Fig. 3. t-SNE visualization of the features from top layers on the MIT67 (top) and MINC (below) validation set. Our GTN shows better semantic separations.

we would like to use the same or similar sets of parameters to adapt to new target domains without sacrificing accuracy on the source domain.

Initial attempts include feature extraction and model fine-tuning for which we have already noted the drawbacks in Sect. 1. In order to avoid domain shift, a joint training scheme is proposed. Simply put, all the model parameters are jointly optimized by interleaving samples from all tasks. This method's performance may be considered as an upper bound of a model's robustness. However, joint training becomes increasingly cumbersome as more tasks are learned and is not possible if the training data for the previously learned tasks is unavailable. There are quite a few works making progress in this direction [14,27]. Here, we compare to two recent state-of-the-art works that focus on learning without forgetting, [14] and [27].

We take our fine-tuned model and re-fine-tune it on the source domain, which is the ImageNet training set [7]. We fix the convolutional layers and only fine tune the transfer module and the new 1000-way classifier. For fair comparison, we report accuracy using an AlexNet architecture. As shown in Table 5, our proposed GTN consistently outperforms previous methods, regardless of which target domain it is fine-tuned on. Even when the target domain is video action recognition (quite different from image object classification), our re-trained model can achieve higher accuracy than LwF [14] and DA-CNN [27]. Oracle indicates the original AlexNet trained on ImageNet. Note that we almost achieve the upper bound set by joint training. We believe such robustness of our approach is because our gating mechanism aims to select features instead of learning new ones, thus we are not designed to "forget". In addition, other existing approaches [14] can be naturally incorporated into our approach to further improve the performance on both source and target tasks.

Table 5. Learning without forgetting on the ImageNet [7] validation set. Experiments based on an AlexNet architecture. The dataset in brackets indicates the target domain on which the model is fine-tuned. Our proposed GTN consistently outperforms previous approaches, regardless of which target domain it is fine-tuned on.

Method	Acc (%)
Oracle	56.9
LwF [14]	55.9
Joint [14]	56.4
DA-CNN [27]	55.3
WA-CNN [27]	51.5
GTN (CUB200)	56.3
GTN (UCF101)	56.2

4.6 Comparison to State-of-the-art

We evaluate our proposed transfer module on six benchmarks: MIT67 for scene classification, CUB200 for fine-grained recognition, MINC for material recognition, DTD for texture classification, UCF101 for video action recognition and FashionAI for apparel attribute recognition. Here, we use ResNet152 as the backbone CNN architecture. CUB200 and MIT67 are widely adopted benchmarks to evaluate CNN transferability, thus we compare to previous transfer learning literature. For the other four datasets, we compare to transfer learning approaches as well as to the popular baselines for each dataset.

As shown in Table 6, our proposed GTN consistently outperforms previous state-of-the-art results on all benchmarks. Most importantly, our transfer module can be combined with other transfer learning techniques [8] or deeper networks [12] for further improvement. Note that [8] reported a better result on MIT67 than us. However, they used a better CNN backbone (identity mapping based ResNet152) and extra training data (Places dataset [32]) for the source domain. We believe this is not a fair comparison. Since MIT67 is a scene classification dataset, it has higher domain similarity with Places rather than ImageNet. For equal comparison, we re-implement [8] using vanilla ResNet152 without the extra training data from Places, and our GTN outperforms it by 0.9%.

Table 6. Performance comparisons of classification accuracy (%) with previous work on scene classification, fine-grained recognition, material recognition and action recognition. * indicates our reimplementation result. Our approach achieves state-of-the-art performance on these challenging benchmark datasets.

MIT67		CUB200		MINC		DTD		UCF101		FashionAI	
	Acc		Acc		Acc		Acc		Acc		Acc
[14]	64.5	[14]	56.6	[5]	63.1	[5]	72.3	[35]	63.3	[10]	84.2
[27]	66.3	[27]	57.7	[27]	80.4*	[27]	71.7*	[33]	82.4	[27]	86.5*
[8]	78.1	[31]	73.9	[30]	80.4	[30]	69.6	[13]	79.5	[19]	81.2
[15]	72.5	[3]	75.7	[28]	81.2	[28]	73.2	[34]	82.3	[23]	85.6
GTN	**79.0**	GTN	**83.4**	GTN	**81.3**	GTN	**74.3**	GTN	**85.6**	GTN	**92.0**

5 Conclusion

In this work, we propose gated transfer network for transfer learning. By analyzing domain similarity, we argue that weighting features from pre-trained CNN models for target domains is a more effective approach. Hence, we introduce a transfer module as a feature selection mechanism with minimal extra computational cost. The novel transfer module can be interpreted as classic fine-tuning or sparse coding depending on the learned gating scores. In addition, the transfer module can be easily incorporated with other transfer learning techniques for further improvement. We evaluate our proposed GTN on six different domains and prove its effectiveness by achieving state-of-the-art results on all benchmarks.

Acknowledgement. We gratefully acknowledge the support of NVIDIA Corporation through the donation of the Titan Xp GPUs used in this work.

References

1. FashionAI Global Challenge: Make AI Insight to Fashion. fashionai.alibaba.com/ (2018)
2. Bell, S., Upchurch, P., Snavely, N., Bala, K.: Material recognition in the wild with the materials in context database. In: The IEEE Conference on Computer Vision and Pattern Recognition (CVPR) (2015)
3. Branson, S., Horn, G.V., Belongie, S., Perona, P.: Bird species categorization using pose normalized deep convolutional nets. In: British Machine Vision Conference (BMVC) (2014)
4. Cimpoi, M., Maji, S., Kokkinos, I., Mohamed, S., Vedaldi, A.: Describing textures in the wild. In: The IEEE Conference on Computer Vision and Pattern Recognition (CVPR) (2014)
5. Cimpoi, M., Maji, S., Vedaldi, A.: Deep filter banks for texture recognition and segmentation. In: The IEEE Conference on Computer Vision and Pattern Recognition (CVPR) (2015)
6. Cui, Y., Song, Y., Sun, C., Howard, A., Belongie, S.: Large scale fine-grained categorization and domain-specific transfer learning. In: The IEEE Conference on Computer Vision and Pattern Recognition (CVPR) (2018)
7. Deng, J., Dong, W., Socher, R., Li, L.J., Li, K., Fei-Fei, L.: ImageNet: a large-scale hierarchical image database. In: The IEEE Conference on Computer Vision and Pattern Recognition (CVPR) (2009)
8. Ge, W., Yu, Y.: Borrowing treasures from the wealthy: deep transfer learning through selective joint fine-tuning. In: The IEEE Conference on Computer Vision and Pattern Recognition (CVPR) (2017)
9. Gong, Y., Wang, L., Guo, R., Lazebnik, S.: Multi-scale orderless pooling of deep convolutional activation features. In: Fleet, D., Pajdla, T., Schiele, B., Tuytelaars, T. (eds.) ECCV 2014. LNCS, vol. 8695, pp. 392–407. Springer, Cham (2014). https://doi.org/10.1007/978-3-319-10584-0_26
10. He, K., Zhang, X., Ren, S., Sun, J.: Deep residual learning for image recognition. In: The IEEE Conference on Computer Vision and Pattern Recognition (CVPR) (2016)
11. Hu, J., Shen, L., Sun, G.: Squeeze-and-excitation networks. In: The IEEE Conference on Computer Vision and Pattern Recognition (CVPR) (2018)
12. Huang, G., Liu, Z., van der Maaten, L., Weinberger, K.Q.: Densely connected convolutional networks. In: The IEEE Conference on Computer Vision and Pattern Recognition (CVPR) (2017)
13. Lan, Z., Zhu, Y., Hauptmann, A.G., Newsam, S.: Deep local video feature for action recognition. In: The IEEE Conference on Computer Vision and Pattern Recognition (CVPR) (2017)
14. Li, Z., Hoiem, D.: Learning without forgetting. In: Leibe, B., Matas, J., Sebe, N., Welling, M. (eds.) ECCV 2016. LNCS, vol. 9908, pp. 614–629. Springer, Cham (2016). https://doi.org/10.1007/978-3-319-46493-0_37
15. Liu, J., Wang, Y., Qiao, Y.: Sparse deep transfer learning for convolutional neural network. In: Association for the Advancement of Artificial Intelligence (AAAI) (2017)
16. Miao, X., Zhen, X., Liu, X., Deng, C., Athitsos, V., Huang, H.: Direct shape regression networks for end-to-end face alignment. In: The IEEE Conference on Computer Vision and Pattern Recognition (CVPR) (2018)

17. Oquab, M., Bottou, L., Laptev, I., Sivic, J.: Learning and transferring mid-level image representations using convolutional neural networks. In: The IEEE Conference on Computer Vision and Pattern Recognition (CVPR) (2014)
18. Quattoni, A., Torralba, A.: Recognizing indoor scenes. In: The IEEE Conference on Computer Vision and Pattern Recognition (CVPR) (2009)
19. Simonyan, K., Zisserman, A.: Very deep convolutional networks for large-scale image recognition. In: International Conference on Learning Representations (ICLR) (2015)
20. Soomro, K., Zamir, A.R., Shah, M.: UCF101: a dataset of 101 human action classes from videos in the wild. In: CRCV-TR-12-01 (2012)
21. Srivastava, N., Hinton, G., Krizhevsky, A., Sutskever, I., Salakhutdinov, R.: Dropout: a simple way to prevent neural networks from overfitting. J. Mach. Learn. Res. (JMLR) **15**, 1929–1958 (2014)
22. Sun, C., Shrivastava, A., Singh, S., Gupta, A.: Revisiting unreasonable effectiveness of data in deep learning era. In: International Conference on Computer Vision (ICCV) (2017)
23. Szegedy, C., et al.: Going deeper with convolutions. In: The IEEE Conference on Computer Vision and Pattern Recognition (CVPR) (2015)
24. Szegedy, C., Vanhoucke, V., Ioffe, S., Shlens, J., Wojna, Z.: Rethinking the inception architecture for computer vision. In: The IEEE Conference on Computer Vision and Pattern Recognition (CVPR) (2016)
25. Van Der Maaten, L.: Accelerating T-SNE using tree-based algorithms. J. Mach. Learn. Res. (JMLR) **15**(1), 3221–3245 (2014)
26. Wah, C., Branson, S., Welinder, P., Perona, P., Belongie, S.: The Caltech-UCSD Birds-200-2011 Dataset (2011)
27. Wang, Y.X., Ramanan, D., Hebert, M.: Growing a brain: fine-tuning by increasing model capacity. In: The IEEE Conference on Computer Vision and Pattern Recognition (CVPR) (2017)
28. Xue, J., Zhang, H., Dana, K.: Deep texture manifold for ground terrain recognition. The IEEE Conference on Computer Vision and Pattern Recognition (CVPR) (2018)
29. Yosinski, J., Clune, J., Bengio, Y., Lipson, H.: How transferable are features in deep neural networks? In: Neural Information Processing Systems (NIPS) (2014)
30. Zhang, H., Xue, J., Dana, K.: Deep TEN: texture encoding network. In: The IEEE Conference on Computer Vision and Pattern Recognition (CVPR) (2017)
31. Zhang, N., Donahue, J., Girshick, R., Darrell, T.: Part-based R-CNNs for fine-grained category detection. In: Fleet, D., Pajdla, T., Schiele, B., Tuytelaars, T. (eds.) ECCV 2014. LNCS, vol. 8689, pp. 834–849. Springer, Cham (2014). https://doi.org/10.1007/978-3-319-10590-1_54
32. Zhou, B., Lapedriza, A., Xiao, J., Torralba, A., Oliva, A.: Learning deep features for scene recognition using places database. In: Neural Information Processing Systems (NIPS) (2014)
33. Zhu, Y., Lan, Z., Newsam, S., Hauptmann, A.G.: Hidden two-stream convolutional networks for action recognition. In: Asian Conference on Computer Vision (ACCV) (2018)
34. Zhu, Y., Long, Y., Guan, Y., Newsam, S., Shao, L.: Towards universal representation for unseen action recognition. In: The IEEE Conference on Computer Vision and Pattern Recognition (CVPR) (2018)
35. Zhu, Y., Newsam, S.: Depth2Action: exploring embedded depth for large-scale action recognition. In: Hua, G., Jégou, H. (eds.) ECCV 2016. LNCS, vol. 9913, pp. 668–684. Springer, Cham (2016). https://doi.org/10.1007/978-3-319-46604-0_47

Detecting Anomalous Trajectories via Recurrent Neural Networks

Cong Ma[1(✉)], Zhenjiang Miao[1], Min Li[1], Shaoyue Song[1], and Ming-Hsuan Yang[2]

[1] Beijing Jiaotong University, Beijing, China
{13112063,zjmiao,16112066,14112060}@bjtu.edu.cn
[2] University of California, Merced, USA
mhyang@ucmerced.edu

Abstract. Detecting anomalies from trajectory data is an important task in video surveillance. However, it is difficult to give a precise definition of this term since trajectory data obtained from different camera views may vary in shape, direction, and spatial distribution. In this paper, we propose trajectory distance metrics based on a recurrent neural network to measure similarities and detect anomalies from trajectory data. First, we use an autoencoder to capture the dynamic features of a trajectory. The distance between two trajectories is defined by the reconstruction errors based on the learned models. We then detect anomalies based on the nearest neighbors using the proposed metric. As such, we can deal with various kinds of anomalies in different scenes and detect anomalous trajectories in either a supervised or unsupervised manner. Experiments show that the proposed algorithm performs favorably against the state-of-the-art anomaly detections on the benchmark datasets.

1 Introduction

Anomaly detection is important in numerous vision tasks including traffic monitoring, motion analysis, and public safety. Trajectories of moving targets are good representations of object behaviors in video data and useful in detecting unusual events. On one hand, compared with appearance and low-level motion features, trajectories can provide object-level long-term information of target behaviors and motion patterns. On the other hand, compared with raw image data, trajectories are more compact and require less computational resources for motion analysis. In addition, thanks to the recent rapid development of object detection and tracking algorithms, fairly accurate trajectories can be extracted and analyzed for event analysis. Anomalies are usually defined as irregular patterns

This work is supported in part by NSFC (No. 61672089, 61273274, and 61572064), National Key Technology R&D Program of China 2012BAH01F03, the Fundamental Research Funds for the Central Universities 2017YJS043, the NSF CAREER Grant (No. 1149783), and gifts from Adobe and Nvidia. Cong Ma and Shaoyue Song are supported by a scholarship from China Scholarship Council.

C. V. Jawahar et al. (Eds.): ACCV 2018, LNCS 11364, pp. 370–382, 2019.
https://doi.org/10.1007/978-3-030-20870-7_23

that are different from the mainstream. However, in real-world video surveillance scenarios, due to the difference of camera positions, sampling rates, and scene structures, the obtained trajectories usually vary in temporal and spatial characteristics. Therefore, it is challenging to properly define and analyze trajectory properties and detect anomalous patterns. Furthermore, in some cases, we can obtain a video segment that contains only normal patterns for building regular models, and yet in other cases, we only have a test video to detect anomalies without any prior knowledge of normal patterns. A flexible method that facilitates anomaly detection in both cases is of great interest for numerous applications. Existing trajectory anomaly detection methods [13,14,19] usually construct statistical path models based on clustering to learn normal patterns and determine deviated samples as irregular ones. However, when the number of samples in the dataset is small, it is difficult to construct reliable statistical models. Other approaches [17,18,22] learn regular models based on the normal distributions and detect outliers. These algorithms usually rely on labeled data to estimate the distributions. Constructing reliable statistical models usually require a fair amount of data. In contrast, non-parametric models offer more flexibility when only scarce and rare samples are at our disposal. If we treat each normal sample as a single regular model, we can avoid this problem and detect the anomalies with a k-nearest neighbor based method, as shown in [16] and [9]. For unlabeled datasets, we can also measure the anomaly level of a trajectory by computing the distance to its nearest neighbor. A similar strategy is developed in [28]. However, the trajectory distances used in these methods are less sensitive to some anomalous patterns and thus limit performance and application scenarios.

In this paper, we use the simple but effective nearest neighbor method to deal with the trajectory anomaly detection problem in different settings. In order to obtain robust detection results in challenging scenes, we propose a new trajectory similarity measure based on an autoencoder constructed from recurrent neural networks (RNNs) to compute the distances between trajectories and facilitate the distance-based anomaly detector. Our contributions can be summarized as follows:

- We propose an RNN autoencoder based similarity measure for two, three or higher dimensional trajectory data.
- We demonstrate that the proposed similarity measure is effective for distinguishing various types of trajectory anomalies.
- We show that the proposed anomaly detection method performs favorably against the state-of-the-art algorithms in both supervised and unsupervised settings.

2 Related Work

2.1 Trajectory Anomaly Detection

In order to detect anomalous trajectories, numerous methods aim to learn a regular model first. Clustering based methods [13–15,19] learn path models for normal patterns via grouping trajectory data in an unsupervised manner. Hu et al. [13] cluster trajectories based on spatial and temporal information using Gaussian distributions. For a trajectory sample, if the probabilities under known patterns are lower than a threshold, it is detected as an anomaly. Jiang et al. [14] represent trajectories with hidden Markov models (HMMs) and propose a dynamic hierarchical clustering method to learn normal patterns. HMMs are also used in [19] to model activity paths and evaluate the likelihoods of trajectory samples. However, it is difficult for these methods to handle the ambiguities that are clustered near the boundaries of normal and anomalous patterns. A few methods learn regular models when some labeled normal samples are available. Trajectories that deviate from the learned model are considered as anomalies. Li et al. [17] use the sparse reconstruction analysis and construct a dictionary based on normal samples. For a test trajectory, when the reconstruction error on the normal dictionary is lower than a threshold, it is identified as an anomaly. In [20] Piciarelli et al. learn the regular model with a one-class SVM and use the novelty detection method to find anomalies. Additionally, they propose an approach to tune the SVM parameters without labeled data. A recent method developed in [18] is based on the concept of tube and droplets. For anomaly detection, it first constructs thermal transfer fields based on the training set and then evaluates test samples by the derived droplet vectors. Nearest neighbor based methods are simple but usually effective for anomaly detection. Such approaches require few parameters and can be applied to both supervised and unsupervised settings. Yankov et al. [28] propose an efficient method based on the Euclidean distance to discover unusual samples in huge unlabeled datasets. This method performs favorably against the SVM-based scheme by Piciarelli et al. [20]. For online and sequential anomaly detection, Laxhammar [16] propose a detector based on the Hausdorff distance, nearest neighbor principle, and non-conformity measure. The detector can be used with or without supervisory signals. More recently, Ergezer and Leblebicioğlu [9] apply sparse representations to the nearest neighbor method based on the covariance trajectory descriptors and achieve favorable results. In these methods, it is critical to compute sample distances accurately. Therefore, trajectory similarity measures with better sensitivity to anomalies are likely to improve the detection performance and studied in this work.

2.2 Trajectory Similarity Measures

Numerous trajectory distances or similarity measures have been proposed in the literature. On one hand, warping based distance metrics take the temporal dimension into consideration. The simplest one is the Euclidean distance that averages the differences between each pair of corresponding points [21,30]. In this case, lengths of the two trajectories are required to be the same. In addition, the DTW [2] and LCSS [25] methods have been used for time sequences to measure similarities. When these metrics are applied to trajectory data, the distances between each time steps are computed based on the Euclidean distance. Furthermore, Chen et al. design ERP [4] and EDR [5] distance metrics for time series to support local time shifts and deal with data noises. On the other hand, shape-based distance metrics such as the Hausdorff [11] and Fréchet [1] measures have been applied to measure the similarities between spatial trajectory sequences. A more recent shape-based distance metric is the SSPD introduced in [3] for trajectory clustering. Different from these methods, a set of HMM-based distances are proposed in [21]. The distance between two trajectories is defined with the probabilities of each sample to be generated by the models learned on each other. Experiments in [21] show that such a model-based distance is able to handle more unrestricted trajectories and has strong discriminative abilities. However, distances based on more powerful trajectory models remain unexplored.

2.3 RNN-Based Autoencoder

An autoencoder can be seen as a special encoder-decoder architecture where the target is the same as the input. The autoencoders based on RNNs are introduced in [6] and [24] to address the machine translation problem. The RNN autoencoders have also been used to construct representations for videos, such as in [23] and [27]. Hasan et al. [10] use convolutional autoencoders to learn regularity models in videos and detect anomalies. In addition, the spatio-temporal autoencoders have been developed for anomaly detection in [7]. These two approaches use autoencoders as a one-class learning approach and detect frame-level anomalies based on raw image data, rather than trajectories. In addition, Yao et al. [29] learn fixed-size representations of geographical trajectories with sequence-to-sequence autoencoders for clustering. However, to the best of our knowledge, autoencoders based on RNNs have not been applied to measure trajectory distances for anomaly detection.

3 Proposed Method

3.1 RNN Autoencoder Based Trajectory Distance

Consider a trajectory T formed by a moving object in an image sequence, at each time step t the state of T is represented by the spatial coordinates (x, y). Thus we have the sequence notation $T = \{(x_1, y_1), (x_2, y_2), \ldots, (x_N, y_N)\}$, where N is the time duration. In order to measure the similarity between two trajectories, we propose a model-based method.

We first train an RNN autoencoder model for each trajectory sample in a sequence-to-sequence manner. The autoencoder consists of an encoder and a decoder while the network input and the decoding target are identical. In the encoder part, we use a GRU-based RNN [8] to capture the dynamic characteristics of the input trajectory sequence. In practice, the state of the input sequence at each time step can be multi-dimensional. To emphasize the sequential information, we explicitly embed a time axis starting from 0 to the input sequence during training. Thus at each time step k, the state of a sequence is denoted as (x_k, y_k, t_k). The final hidden states of the encoder are fed to the decoder network as initial hidden states. In the decoder part, we use a GRU layer and a linear layer to reconstruct the input sequence along the time dimension. The two parts of the autoencoder model are trained together by minimizing the reconstruction error. Since the output sequence and the target are in the same dimensions, we use mean squared error (MSE) as the loss function. The training stage ends when the loss is small enough (we use a threshold of 10^{-5}). In addition, we normalize the data values of the input sequence to $[0, 1]$ for a better convergence performance. We define the distance between two trajectories based on the trained models. For a pair of trajectory sequences T_a and T_b, we denote the autoencoder models learned from each trajectory as M_a and M_b. When we take trajectory T_b as the input of model M_a, we compute the reconstruction error $e(T_b, M_a)$. Therefore, the one-way distance from T_a to T_b can be computed by:

$$d(T_a, T_b) = |e(T_b, M_a) - e(M_a)|, \tag{1}$$

where $e(M_a)$ denotes the final loss of model M_a during training. Conversely, the one-way distance $d(T_b, T_a)$ from T_b to T_a can be computed by $|e(T_a, M_b) - e(M_b)|$.

From the definition above we know that $d(T_a, T_b) > 0$ and $d(T_a, T_a) = 0$. However, due to the randomness and noise during model training, we cannot obtain $d(T_a, T_b) = d(T_b, T_a)$. To have a symmetric distance measure, we define the bidirectional dissimilarity between trajectory pair T_a and T_b as:

$$D(T_a, T_b) = |e(T_b, M_a) + e(T_a, M_b) - e(M_a) - e(M_b)|. \tag{2}$$

Since RNN models can process sequences with variable time steps, trajectories T_a and T_b need not be of the same lengths.

Furthermore, considering that the autoencoder model can be trained with a batch of samples at the same time, we can expand the application of this model to computing the distance from a cluster of trajectories C_T to a query trajectory T_q. Similarly, this one-way distance can be defined as:

$$D_C(C_T, T_q) = |e(T_q, M_C) - e(M_C)|, \tag{3}$$

where M_C denotes the model learned from the cluster of trajectories.

The set of distances defined above can be naturally applied to the nearest neighbor based anomaly detection depending on different data settings.

3.2 Distance Based Anomaly Detection

In trajectories obtained from surveillance videos, anomalies tend to show irregular motion patterns. However, it is difficult to differentiate between anomalies and samples with noise. When there is a training set indicating the normal patterns as a limited supervision, it is easier to define and detect the anomalies. Instead of the statistical methods that may require a lot of training samples, we use a nearest neighbor detector based on the proposed one-way autoencoder distance (Eq. 1). Considering each training sample as an individual normal model, the anomaly score can be defined by the directional distance of a test sample from its nearest training sample.

However, labeled data are not always available. In unsupervised scenes, researchers usually use novelty detection methods to find anomalies. A nearest neighbor based detector can still perform by measuring the deviation of a trajectory sample to its neighbors. We use the bidirectional distance definition (Eq. 2) in this case to obtain a symmetric distance matrix. Since the proposed trajectory similarity measure is sufficiently robust, we use the one-nearest neighbor distance as the anomaly score for a test trajectory.

4 Experimental Results

4.1 Comparison of Distances on Different Trajectory Patterns

In order to evaluate the sensitivity of a trajectory distance to different kinds of anomalies, we measure the similarities of several trajectory pattern pairs inspired by [21]. In a surveillance video scene, an anomalous object trajectory may be different from the normal ones in several aspects including position, orientation, and speed. Therefore, we list six pattern pairs including: *Translation*, *Deviation*, *Opposite*, *Loop*, *Wait*, and *Speed*, as shown in Fig. 1.

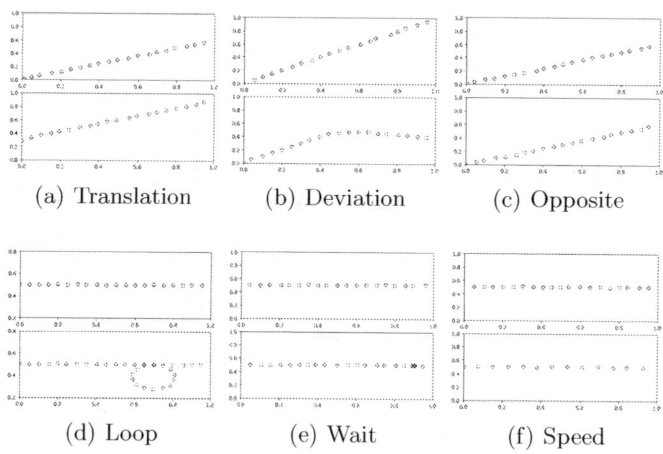

(a) Translation (b) Deviation (c) Opposite

(d) Loop (e) Wait (f) Speed

Fig. 1. Different pattern pairs illustrating various types of anomalies

For each pair of trajectories T_a and T_b, considering T_a as a normal sample and T_b as an anomaly, we compute the distance $D(a,b)$ between them. We then construct another pair of trajectories T_a and T_c, where T_c is built by adding T_a with a Gaussian noise. The distance $D(a,c)$ between this pair is computed as a baseline. Therefore, we can evaluate the distance sensitivity $S_{pattern}$ to a certain pattern by computing the ratio between $D(a,b)$ and $D(a,c)$ as:

$$S_{pattern} = D(a,b)/(D(a,c)+\epsilon), \tag{4}$$

where ϵ is the machine epsilon for avoiding division by zero. A ratio close to 1.0 indicates that it is difficult for the distance to distinguish a pattern from noises. On the other hand, a higher ratio value indicates that the similarity measure is more sensitive to this pattern.

We generate a synthetic dataset consisting of 100 pair examples for each pattern. The length of each normal trajectory sample is set to 50. Due to the pattern definition, in the last three cases *Loop*, *Wait*, and *Speed*, the lengths of anomalous samples are different from those of the normal ones. This inequality also contributes to the data variety. In addition, a Gaussian white noise is added to each sample for a better simulation of real situations.

We use nine trajectory distances to compare with the proposed method. They are: Euclidean, DTW [2], LCSS [25], ERP [4], EDR [5], Hausdorff [11], Fréchet [1], SSPD [3], and the HMM-based distance [21]. Experimental results are shown in Table 1.

From the table we can know that most of the distances cannot identify the temporal anomalies *Wait* and *Speed*, while non-directional distances SSPD and Hausdorff (undirected) are not sensitive to the *Opposite* case. Among these, the ERP metric performs well over all the patterns. Compared to other distances, our method is sensitive to all the six anomalous pattern cases.

Table 1. Sensitivity scores of different trajectory distances on the six anomaly patterns.

Distances	Translation	Deviation	Opposite	Loop	Wait	Speed
Euclidean	42.47	54.73	82.42	15.10	5.34	1.10
DTW	40.88	54.73	82.42	6.86	1.51	1.38
SSPD	62.35	75.06	1.01	3.52	0.98	0.99
LCSS	10.12	8.00	9.12	1.00	0.94	1.04
EDR	10.04	8.00	9.04	1.78	2.57	3.63
ERP	42.47	54.73	56.06	30.29	47.99	35.73
Frechet	22.25	72.68	83.97	8.50	1.01	1.05
Hausdorff	22.08	69.36	1.00	10.71	1.01	1.05
HMM	750.64	2919.38	1249.74	98.86	2.43	1.34
Ours (One-way)	4679.26	10544.19	14865.79	1050.85	746.84	584.86
Ours (Bidirectional)	198125.56	693815.05	641080.44	44645.88	27131.89	20250.79

4.2 Anomaly Detection Performances

Based on the proposed trajectory distance, we implement the anomaly detection task with the nearest neighbor detector as described in Sect. 3.2. In order to show the wide applicability of our method, we conduct experiments on four datasets that are under quite different configurations, as summarized in Table 2. Since the anomaly detection results vary with different threshold values, we use the Receiver Operating Characteristic (ROC) curve and the Area Under Curve (AUC) to evaluate the overall performance of the detector.

Table 2. Dataset properties: a brief view.

Datasets	Supervision	Dataset size	Scene number	Data source
CROSS [19]	Yes	Big	1	Synthetic
TRAFFIC [18]	Yes	Small	1	Realistic
VMT [12]	No	Big	1	Realistic
DETRAC [26]	No	Medium	31	Realistic

CROSS Dataset. This is a widely used dataset for motion pattern learning and anomaly detection under a cross-traffic scene, introduced in [19]. The training set contains 1900 traffic trajectory samples divided to 19 classes. The test set has 9700 samples while 200 of them are labeled as anomalous. In order to make a fair comparison and reduce noise effects, trajectory data in this and the following experiments are normalized to the same length of 12 points using least-squares cubic spline curves approximation [17,22].

First, we compare the performances of several different trajectory distances using the same nearest neighbor anomaly detector. Since there exists a training set, we use the one-way distance as defined in Eq. 1. In order to make use of the class labels, we construct 19 normal models with the average trajectory of each class. The anomaly score is defined with the distance of a test sample from the nearest normal model. With the scores obtained, we can vary the threshold and draw ROC curves as shown in Fig. 2. The AUC scores are summarized in Table 3. The distances compared are the same as those in Sect. 4.1. We can see that the proposed distance metric performs favorably against the others when applied to anomaly detection.

Table 3. AUCs of anomaly detectors based on different trajectory distances on the CROSS dataset. The best result is in bold and the second best results are underlined.

Methods	Euclidean	DTW	SSPD	LCSS	EDR	ERP	Fréchet	Hausdorff	HMM	Ours
AUCs	<u>0.9985</u>	0.9976	0.9520	0.9916	0.9920	<u>0.9985</u>	0.9923	0.9961	0.8600	**0.9996**

Then, the comparison with several state-of-the-art methods is shown in Table 4. Since the available results in the literature are evaluated by the detection rates (DR) and abnormality false positive rates (FPR) [18,19], we report our results under the same metrics. The results are obtained directly from [18]. From Table 4 we can know that our method achieves a significantly low false alarm rate while keeping a high detection rate. It is worth mentioning that the listed methods [12,18,19] are not specially designed for anomaly detection, so their results may not seem competitive.

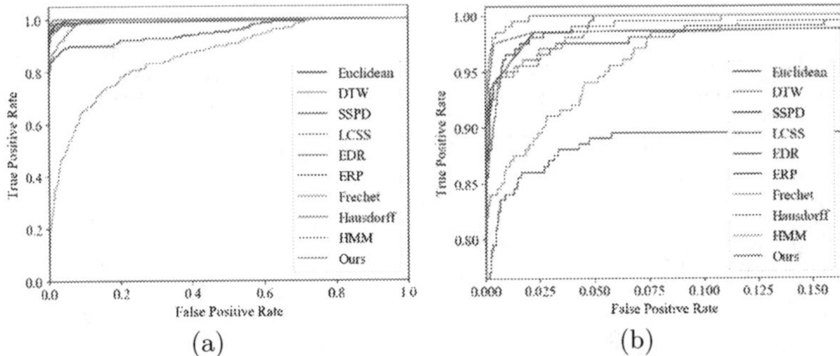

Fig. 2. ROC curves of anomaly detection based on different trajectory distances on the CROSS dataset. Sub-figure (b) is the zoomed out version of the left top part of (a)

Table 4. Comparison of anomaly detection results on the CROSS dataset.

Methods	DR (%)	FPR (%)
tDPMM [12]	91.0	23.3
3SHL [19]	85.5	23.5
3D Tube [18]	91.3	23.5
Ours	**96.0**	**9.9**

TRAFFIC Dataset. This dataset is introduced in a recent work [18]. It contains 300 trajectories collected from a real-world cross-traffic scene. As shown in [18], the small sample number, large data variations, and oblique camera view all make the TRAFFIC dataset challenging, especially for learning reliable normal models. We also use the nearest neighbor detector based on our RNN autoencoder distance measure to handle this situation. We keep the same experimental settings with [18], namely: equally dividing the dataset into training/test sets and running the random division for four times to obtain an average score. For each test trajectory, we compute the nearest one-way distance from the training samples as the anomaly score. Since the results are averaged, we do not present ROC curves. The average AUCs computed from different distances are shown in Table 5. From the experimental results, we can know the best performing distance metrics are Hausdorff, Fréchet and ours. This indicates that the anomalies in the TRAFFIC dataset are best distinguished by shape features.

Table 5. AUCs of anomaly detectors based on different trajectory distances on the TRAFFIC dataset.

Methods	Euclidean	DTW	SSPD	LCSS	EDR	ERP	Fréchet	Hausdorff	HMM	Ours
AUCs	0.9987	0.9987	0.9977	0.9937	0.9909	0.9987	**1.0000**	<u>0.9999</u>	0.9922	**1.0000**

VMT Dataset. In order to evaluate our method on more real-world data, we employ the Vehicle Motion Trajectory (VMT) dataset [12] that contains 1500 trajectory samples. Since the dataset is not labeled with anomalies, we manually label 24 anomalous trajectories that deviate from the others in spatial or shape features. Some examples of labeled anomalies are shown in Fig. 3. We do not label normal data and directly run our method in an unsupervised manner.

As discussed in Sect. 3.2, we use the symmetric version of the proposed distance metric (Eq. 2) in this experiment. The ROC curves of different trajectory distances are shown in Fig. 4 and AUCs are summarized in Table 6. Due to the fact that the anomalies in this dataset are more difficult to distinguish, we can see that the overall results are not so good, but the detector based on our distance metric still performs the best.

Fig. 3. Illustration of some anomalous trajectory samples in the VMT dataset

DETRAC Dataset. This is a video dataset originally introduced as a large-scale real-world benchmark for object detection and multi-object tracking [26]. We generate trajectories based on the tracking ground-truth of the training set. We divide the behaviors of vehicle trajectories to several types including *Driving through*, *Changing lane*, *Turn*, *Wait* and some ambiguities. In order to define a proper amount of anomalous samples, we label the trajectories with *Turn* and *Wait* behaviors as anomalies. Finally, there are 31 scenes labeled with anomalies out of the 60 training videos. The number of trajectory samples in each scene ranges from 8 to 89 and there are 3 anomalies out of 43 trajectories in each scene on average. Therefore, the labeled trajectory dataset is challenging due to the sparse data, different vehicle behaviors and various scenes. For this dataset, we use the nearest neighbor based anomaly detector without the supervision of normal data. The AUCs of the nearest neighbor detector based on different distances are listed in Table 7. The results are averaged over the 31 scenes of the dataset. Overall, the HMM-based distance metric performs the best on this dataset. The Euclidean distance and our method also achieve comparable results. The experimental results above show that our method is suitable for both supervised and unsupervised anomaly detection and sufficiently flexible to obtain satisfactory results on datasets with various properties. The results indicate the robustness and wide applicability of our RNN autoencoder based trajectory distance. All the source code and datasets will be made available to the public.

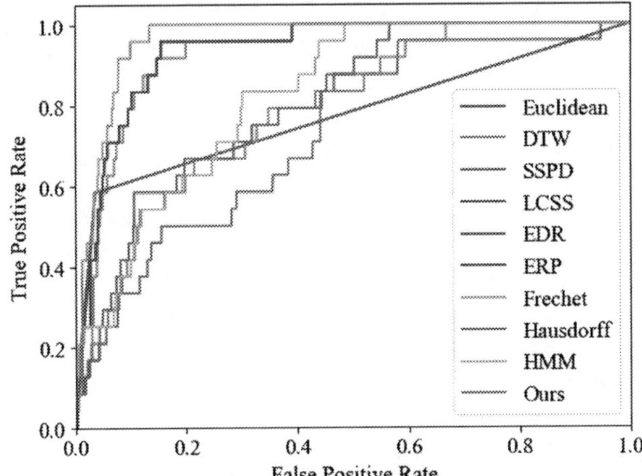

Fig. 4. ROC curves of anomaly detectors based on different trajectory distances on the VMT dataset.

Table 6. AUCs of anomaly detectors based on different trajectory distances on the VMT dataset.

Methods	Euclidean	DTW	SSPD	LCSS	EDR	ERP	Fréchet	Hausdorff	HMM	Ours
AUCs	0.9339	0.9261	0.7300	0.7734	0.7744	0.9339	0.7871	0.8049	0.8246	**0.9608**

Table 7. AUCs of anomaly detectors based on different trajectory distances on the DETRAC dataset.

Methods	Euclidean	DTW	SSPD	LCSS	EDR	ERP	Fréchet	Hausdorff	HMM	Ours
AUCs	0.8956	0.9044	0.8981	0.8976	0.8979	0.8956	0.8557	0.8572	**0.9071**	0.9022

5 Conclusion

In this paper, we present trajectory distance metrics based on an RNN-based autoencoder to measure the similarity between trajectories and apply them to anomaly detection. Experimental results show that the proposed metrics are sensitive to anomalies and perform favorably in the trajectory anomaly detection task when incorporated in a nearest neighbor based detector. We also demonstrate an anomaly detector based on our metrics is flexible and effective under various dataset configurations. In practice, the proposed distance metrics can also be applied to other distance-based detectors. We will address these issues in our future work.

References

1. Alt, H., Godau, M.: Computing the fréchet distance between two polygonal curves. Int. J. Comput. Geom. Appl. **5**, 75–91 (1995)
2. Berndt, D.J., Clifford, J.: Using dynamic time warping to find patterns in time series. In: Workshop on Knowledge Discovery in Databases (1994)
3. Besse, P., Guillouet, B., Loubes, J.M., François, R.: Review and perspective for distance based trajectory clustering. arXiv preprint arXiv:1508.04904 (2015)
4. Chen, L., Ng, R.: On the marriage of LP-norms and edit distance. In: International Conference on Very Large Data Bases (2004)
5. Chen, L., Ozsu, M.T., Oria, V.: Robust and fast similarity search for moving object trajectories. In: ACM SIGMOD International Conference on Management of Data (2005)
6. Cho, K., et al.: Learning phrase representations using RNN encoder-decoder for statistical machine translation. arXiv preprint arXiv:1406.1078 (2014)
7. Chong, Y.S., Tay, Y.H.: Abnormal event detection in videos using spatiotemporal autoencoder. arXiv preprint arXiv:1701.01546 (2017)
8. Chung, J., Gulcehre, C., Cho, K., Bengio, Y.: Empirical evaluation of gated recurrent neural networks on sequence modeling. arXiv preprint arXiv:1412.3555 (2014)
9. Ergezer, H., Leblebicioğlu, K.: Anomaly detection and activity perception using covariance descriptor for trajectories. In: Hua, G., Jégou, H. (eds.) ECCV 2016. LNCS, vol. 9914, pp. 728–742. Springer, Cham (2016). https://doi.org/10.1007/978-3-319-48881-3_51
10. Hasan, M., Choi, J., Neumann, J., Roy-Chowdhury, A.K., Davis, L.S.: Learning temporal regularity in video sequences. In: IEEE Conference on Computer Vision and Pattern Recognition (2016)
11. Hausdorff, F.: Grundz uge der mengenlehre (1914)
12. Hu, W., Li, X., Tian, G., Maybank, S., Zhang, Z.: An incremental DPMM-based method for trajectory clustering, modeling, and retrieval. IEEE Trans. Pattern Mach. Intell. **35**(5), 1051–1065 (2013)
13. Hu, W., Xiao, X., Fu, Z., Xie, D., Tan, T., Maybank, S.: A system for learning statistical motion patterns. IEEE Trans. Pattern Mach. Intell. **28**(9), 1450–1464 (2006)
14. Jiang, F., Wu, Y., Katsaggelos, A.K.: A dynamic hierarchical clustering method for trajectory-based unusual video event detection. IEEE Trans. Image Process. **18**(4), 907–913 (2009)
15. Kumar, D., Bezdek, J.C., Rajasegarar, S., Leckie, C., Palaniswami, M.: A visual-numeric approach to clustering and anomaly detection for trajectory data. Vis. Comput. **33**(3), 265–281 (2017)
16. Laxhammar, R., Falkman, G.: Online learning and sequential anomaly detection in trajectories. IEEE Trans. Pattern Mach. Intell. **36**(6), 1158–1173 (2014)
17. Li, C., Han, Z., Ye, Q., Jiao, J.: Visual abnormal behavior detection based on trajectory sparse reconstruction analysis. Neurocomputing **119**, 94–100 (2013)
18. Lin, W., et al.: A tube-and-droplet-based approach for representing and analyzing motion trajectories. IEEE Trans. Pattern Mach. Intell. **39**(8), 1489–1503 (2017)
19. Morris, B.T., Trivedi, M.M.: Trajectory learning for activity understanding: Unsupervised, multilevel, and long-term adaptive approach. IEEE Trans. Pattern Mach. Intell. **33**(11), 2287–2301 (2011)
20. Piciarelli, C., Micheloni, C., Foresti, G.L.: Trajectory-based anomalous event detection. IEEE Trans. Circ. Syst. Video Technol. **18**(11), 1544–1554 (2008)

21. Porikli, F.: Trajectory distance metric using hidden Markov model based representation. In: ECCV 2004, PETS Workshop (2004)
22. Sillito, R.R., Fisher, R.B.: Semi-supervised learning for anomalous trajectory detection. In: British Machine Vision Conference (2008)
23. Srivastava, N., Mansimov, E., Salakhudinov, R.: Unsupervised learning of video representations using LSTMs. In: International Conference on Machine Learning (2015)
24. Sutskever, I., Vinyals, O., Le, Q.V.: Sequence to sequence learning with neural networks. In: Neural Information Processing Systems (2014)
25. Vlachos, M., Kollios, G., Gunopulos, D.: Discovering similar multidimensional trajectories. In: IEEE International Conference on Data Engineering (2002)
26. Wen, L., et al.: UA-DETRAC: a new benchmark and protocol for multi-object detection and tracking. arXiv preprint arXiv:1511.04136 (2015)
27. Yang, H., Wang, B., Lin, S., Wipf, D., Guo, M., Guo, B.: Unsupervised extraction of video highlights via robust recurrent auto-encoders. In: IEEE International Conference on Computer Vision (2015)
28. Yankov, D., Keogh, E., Rebbapragada, U.: Disk aware discord discovery: finding unusual time series in terabyte sized datasets. In: IEEE International Conference on Data Mining, pp. 381–390 (2007)
29. Yao, D., Zhang, C., Zhu, Z., Huang, J., Bi, J.: Trajectory clustering via deep representation learning. In: International Joint Conference on Neural Networks (2017)
30. Zhang, Z., Huang, K., Tan, T.: Comparison of similarity measures for trajectory clustering in outdoor surveillance scenes. In: International Conference on Pattern Recognition (2006)

A Binary Optimization Approach for Constrained K-Means Clustering

Huu M. Le[1(✉)], Anders Eriksson[1], Thanh-Toan Do[2], and Michael Milford[1]

[1] Queensland University of Technology, Brisbane, Australia
{huu.le,anders.eriksson,michael.milford}@qut.edu.au
[2] University of Liverpool, Liverpool, England
thanh-toan.do@liverpool.ac.uk

Abstract. K-Means clustering still plays an important role in many computer vision problems. While the conventional Lloyd method, which alternates between centroid update and cluster assignment, is primarily used in practice, it may converge to solutions with empty clusters. Furthermore, some applications may require the clusters to satisfy a specific set of constraints, e.g., cluster sizes, must-link/cannot-link. Several methods have been introduced to solve constrained K-Means clustering. Due to the non-convex nature of K-Means, however, existing approaches may result in sub-optimal solutions that poorly approximate the true clusters. In this work, we provide a new perspective to tackle this problem by considering constrained K-Means as a special instance of Binary Optimization. We then propose a novel optimization scheme to search for feasible solutions in the binary domain. This approach allows us to solve constrained K-Means clustering in such a way that multiple types of constraints can be simultaneously enforced. Experimental results on synthetic and real datasets show that our method provides better clustering accuracy with faster run time compared to several existing techniques.

1 Introduction

Since the early days of computer vision and machine learning research, K-Means [17] has been shown to be an outstanding algorithm for a wide range of applications involving data clustering, such as image retrieval, segmentation, object recognition, etc. Despite a long history of research and developments, K-Means is still being employed as an underlying sub-problem for many state-of-the-art algorithms. Take vector quantization (VQ) [8], a well-known algorithm for approximate nearest neighbor (ANN) search, as an example. In order to learn a code-book containing k code-words from the given dataset, VQ uses K-Means to partition the training data into k non-overlapping clusters (the value of k depends on the applications and storage requirements). The k centroids provided by K-Means are then used as k code-words. During the training process,

This work was supported by an Asian Office of Aerospace Research and Development Grant FA2386-16-1-4027 and an ARC Future Fellowship FT140101229 to MM. Eriksson was supported by FT170100072.

C. V. Jawahar et al. (Eds.): ACCV 2018, LNCS 11364, pp. 383–398, 2019.
https://doi.org/10.1007/978-3-030-20870-7_24

each data point is then encoded by associating it with the nearest centroid and is stored by the index of the corresponding codeword using $\log_2 k$ bits. The success of VQ in nearest neighbor search and image retrieval has inspired many of its variants [6,9,11,13]. Among such methods, the task of data clustering is still primarily handled by K-Means, thus the effectiveness of K-Means clustering contributes substantially to the overall performance of quantization techniques.

Although being considered as a prime method underpinning many applications, K-Means is in fact NP-Hard, even for instances in the plane [18]. Therefore, the task of searching for its globally optimal solution is almost computationally intractable for datasets containing large number of clusters. As a result, one can only expect to obtain sub-optimal solutions to this problem, given that good initializations of the clusters' centroids are available. Lloyd's algorithm [17] is the commonly used algorithm for K-Means. Starting from the initial centroids and cluster assignments, which can be obtained from random guesses or by employing different initialization strategies [12,21], it solves K-Means by alternating between updating centroids and assigning data points into updated clusters. This iterative process is repeated until convergence (no more improvements can be made to the clusters). Lloyd's approach has the advantage of being simple and can be easily implemented.

One of the main drawbacks of Lloyd's algorithm, however, lies in its inability to enforce constraints, which may become a disadvantage in certain applications. For example, several photo query systems [1] require the number of data points distributed into the clusters to be approximately equal. It's also worth mentioning that due to the dependence on initializations of the conventional Lloyd's approach, this algorithm poses a risk of converging to solutions in which one or many clusters contain zero or very few data points (which are more likely to be outliers). In practice, it has also been empirically shown that by enforcing the constraints on the cluster sizes, one gets a better clustering performance [3,26]. Furthermore, in order to take advantage of a-priori contextual information, it can be beneficial for some applications to enforce must-link/cannot-link constraints (i.e., some particular points must/must not be in the same cluster). Recently, there have been much interests in developing deep learning approaches that require the use of K-Means [4,25]. Such deep networks can also be benefited from a K-Means algorithms with some specific requirements on the clusters. Henceforth, a K-Means clustering algorithm that strictly enforces constraints during its iterations is highly desirable for many practical applications.

There have been several works that address K-Means clustering with constraints [3,15,16,19,26]. A large number of works focus on the special case of balanced clusters [1,16,19]. Among them, several methods propose different heuristic schemes to distribute data points into clusters such that the constraints are satisfied [23,26]. On the other hand, [3] solves the assignment step by optimizing the linear assignment problem. The authors in [19] proposed to use max-flow to address constrained K-Means. However, their algorithm can only work for problem instances containing a small number of clusters, as it is rather computationally expensive to optimize the min-cut algorithm for a large number of nodes. Balanced K-Means has recently been considered in [16] where the balance constraint is enforced by solved by minimizing a least squares problem. This approximation scheme requires an annealing parameter, which needs to be separately tuned for each problem instance. Also, [16] can only handle balance constraints, which makese it inflexible for problems that require different cardinality constraints for different clusters, not to mention the fact that must-link and cannot-link constraints are unable to be enforced in [16].

Contributions. In this paper, we revisit the constrained K-Means clustering problem and propose a novel approach to address it in such a way that different types of constraints can be simultaneously enforced. Particularly, we look at the problem at the perspective of a binary optimization problem and devise an algorithm to optimize it so that all the constraints are strictly enforced at each iteration. Unlike other relaxation schemes, our algorithm aims to find feasible solutions in the binary domain, i.e., the cluster assignments are represented by a binary matrix that satisfies the given constraints. One notable feature of our technique is that different types of constraints can be easily integrated into the proposed framework. The experiment results on multiple synthetic and real datasets show that our technique provides much better clustering quality while the run time is comparable to (or even faster than) other approaches.

2 Related Work

Among other works on constrained clustering [3,15,16,19,26], our method is closely related to the methods proposed in [3] and [23]. In particular, [3] concerns the problem of K-Means clustering in which the number of points in cluster l must be greater than τ_l, $l = 1, \ldots, k$, with the main goal is to prevent K-Means from providing clusters containing zero or very few points. Similar to the conventional K-Means, the algorithm proposed in [3] comprises two steps: centroid update and cluster assignment. To address the constraints on the cluster sizes, the cluster assignment step in [3] is formulated as a linear programming (LP) problem, in which the requirements for the cluster sizes are expressed as linear constraints on the assignment matrix. In fact, the task of solving for the assignment matrix is a Mixed Integer Program (MIP). However, with the special case in [3], it can be proven that the solutions of LP are guaranteed to be binary, i.e., each element of the assignment matrix returned from LP is guaranteed to be either 0 or 1. Therefore, the task of solving a MIP boils down to solving an LP as the integrality of the solutions can always be assured. Due to the relationship between the task of distributing points into the clusters and the linear assignment problem, the constrained clustering with cluster size constraints can also be consider as finding a minimum flow on a network. A balanced K-Means algorithm based on this approach is proposed in [19].

Another type of constraint that finds its use in many clustering problems is the must-link (or cannot-link) constraints [23]. These constraints require a subset of data points must (or must not) be assigned to the same clusters.

They are usually incorporated into the clustering process when prior application domain information is available, with the aim to boost the overall accuracy. Note that the must-link and cannot-link constraints can also be formulated as linear constraints (as will be explained in the later sections). However, the solutions of LP is no longer guaranteed to be binary. A heuristic scheme is proposed by [23] to tackle the constrained clustering problem, where the points are distributed into the cluster in such a way that the constraint violations are minimized.

Besides [3] and [23], there are also many other works that address clustering with constraints, with a majority of them focusing on the cluster-size constraints. Our work can be considered as a generalized version of [3], in which the must-link and cannot-link constraints discussed in [23] can also be integrated into a binary optimization framework. Due to the introduction of additional constraints, the solutions of the LP proposed in [3] are no longer guaranteed to be binary. Our method addresses this by proposing an alternating optimization scheme which aims to find the feasible solutions in the binary domain.

3 Problem Formulation

3.1 K-Means Clustering

Given a set $\mathcal{X}$ containing N data points $\mathcal{X} = \{\mathbf{x}_j\}_{j=1}^N$, where $\mathbf{x}_j \in \mathbb{R}^d$, the goal of K-Means is to partition $\mathcal{X}$ into k non-overlapping clusters. Specifically, K-Means finds a set $\mathcal{C}$ containing k centroids $\mathcal{C} = \{\mathbf{c}_i\}_{i=1}^k$, and an assignment that distributes the points into k distinct groups $\mathcal{S}_1, \dots, \mathcal{S}_k$, where $\mathcal{S}_1 \cup \dots \cup \mathcal{S}_k = \mathcal{X}$ and $\mathcal{S}_i \cap \mathcal{S}_j = \emptyset\ \forall i \neq j$, that minimizes the *within cluster sum of squares* (WCSS) distortion. Mathematically speaking, K-Means clustering can be formulated as the following optimization problem

$$\min_{\mathcal{C}, \mathcal{S}_1, \dots, \mathcal{S}_k} \sum_{i=1}^{k} \sum_{\mathbf{x}_j \in \mathcal{S}_i} ||\mathbf{x}_j - \mathbf{c}_i||_2^2. \tag{1}$$

3.2 Constrained K-Means

In several applications, it is sometimes desirable to impose some particular restrictions on the clustering. For the ease of representation, we focus on the cluster size constraints [3,16], and must-link/cannot-link constraints [23], while other types of constraints (assuming that they can be converted into linear constraints), depending on the applications, can also be integrated into our proposed framework in a similar manner. Assume that we are given as a priori m subsets $\mathcal{M}_1, \dots, \mathcal{M}_m$, where $\mathcal{M}_i \subset \mathcal{X}$ and points belonging to a particular set $\mathcal{M}_i$ *must* be grouped into the same cluster. Likewise, assume that h subsets $\mathcal{D}_1, \dots, \mathcal{D}_h$ are given, where $\mathcal{D} \subset \mathcal{X}$ and each set $\mathcal{D}_i$ contains points that *must not* be in the same cluster. Let f represent the cluster assignment operation, i.e., $f(\mathbf{x})$ is the cluster that $\mathbf{x}$ is assigned to. Similar to (1), constrained K-Means also seeks to find the set of k cluster centroids $\mathcal{C}$ and the subsets $\mathcal{S}_i$ that minimize the WCSS distortion with additional constraints on the clusters, which can be mathematically expressed as

$$\min_{\mathcal{C},f,\mathcal{S}_1,\ldots,\mathcal{S}_k} \quad \sum_{i=1}^{k} \sum_{\mathbf{x}_j \in \mathcal{S}_i} ||\mathbf{x}_j - \mathbf{c}_i||_2^2, \tag{2a}$$

$$\text{subject to} \quad l_i \leq |\mathcal{S}_i| \leq u_i, \quad \forall i = 1 \ldots k, \tag{2b}$$

$$f(\mathbf{p}^t) = f(\mathbf{q}^t) \;\; \forall (\mathbf{p}^t, \mathbf{q}^t) \in \mathcal{M}_t, \; t = 1 \ldots m, \tag{2c}$$

$$f(\mathbf{p}^t) \neq f(\mathbf{q}^t) \;\; \forall (\mathbf{p}^t, \mathbf{q}^t) \in \mathcal{D}_t, \; \mathbf{p}^t \neq \mathbf{q}^t \;\; t = 1 \ldots h, \tag{2d}$$

where the notation $|\,.\,|$ denotes the cardinality of a set, and the pairs $\{(l_i, u_i)\}_{i=1}^{k}$ represent the lower and upper bound on the sizes of the corresponding clusters. The constraints (2b) limit the sizes of the clusters, while the must-link and cannot-link constraints are reflected by (2c) and (2d), i.e., f must assign all points in $\mathcal{M}_t$ to the same cluster and, similarly, points reside in the same $\mathcal{D}_t$ must be distributed into different clusters.

4 Constrained K-Means as Binary Optimization

Before introducing our approach to tackle constrained K-Means, let us first re-formulate (2a–2d) as a binary optimization problem. Let $\mathbf{X} \in \mathbb{R}^{d \times N}$ be the matrix containing the set of N data points, where each point $\mathbf{x}_i \in \mathbb{R}^d$ corresponds to the i-th column of $\mathbf{X}$), and $\mathbf{C} \in \mathbb{R}^{d \times k}$ be the matrix that stores the set of k centroids (each centroid lies in one column of $\mathbf{C}$). Additionally, let the cluster assignments be represented by a matrix $\mathbf{S} \in \mathbb{R}^{k \times N}$, where $\mathbf{S}_{ij}$ has the value of 1 if the data point $\mathbf{x}_j$ is assigned to the i-th cluster and 0 otherwise. The problem (2a–2d) can now be written as follows

$$\min_{\mathbf{C},\mathbf{S}} \quad ||\mathbf{X} - \mathbf{C}\mathbf{S}||_F^2, \tag{3a}$$

$$\text{subject to} \quad \mathbf{S}_{ij} \in \{0, 1\} \;\; \forall i, j, \tag{3b}$$

$$\sum_{i=1}^{k} \mathbf{S}_{ij} = 1 \;\; \forall j = 1 \ldots N, \tag{3c}$$

$$l_i \leq \sum_{j=1}^{N} \mathbf{S}_{ij} \leq u_i \;\; \forall i = 1 \ldots k, \tag{3d}$$

$$\mathbf{S}_{ip} = \mathbf{S}_{iq}, \;\; i = 1 \ldots k \;\; \forall (\mathbf{x}_p, \mathbf{x}_q) \in \mathcal{M}_t, \; t = 1 \ldots m, \tag{3e}$$

$$\mathbf{S}_{ip} + \mathbf{S}_{iq} \leq 1, \;\; i = 1 \ldots k \;\; \forall (\mathbf{x}_p, \mathbf{x}_q) \in \mathcal{D}_t, \; t = 1 \ldots m. \tag{3f}$$

With the re-arrangements of variables into the matrices $\mathbf{X}$, $\mathbf{C}$ and $\mathbf{S}$, the objective function (2a) translates to (3a) where $||.||_F$ denotes the Frobenius norm of a matrix. The constraint (3b) restricts $\mathbf{S}$ to be a binary assignment matrix, while the second constraint (3c) allows each point to be assigned to only one cluster. The set cardinality requirements in (2b) are reflected by the third constraint (3d), as the sum of all elements on the i-th row of $\mathbf{S}$ is the number of points being assigned to the i-th cluster. Finally, (3e) and (3f) enforce the must-link and cannot-link constraints. The intuition behind (3e) is that if two data points $\mathbf{x}_p$ and $\mathbf{x}_q$ have the same cluster assignment, the p-th column and q-th column of $\mathbf{S}$ must be identical. Consequently, if two data points $\mathbf{x}_p$ and $\mathbf{x}_q$ belong to the same cluster, the element-wise sum of the p-th column and q-th column of $\mathbf{S}$ must contain a value of 2. Therefore, by restricting the element-wise sum to be less than 2 as (3f), the cannot-link constraint can be enforced.

Henceforth, for the sake of brevity, we define $\boldsymbol{\Omega}$ as the convex domain in which the linear constraints (3c), (3d), (3e), (3f) are satisfied, i.e.,

$$\boldsymbol{\Omega} = \{\mathbf{S} \in \mathbb{R}^{k \times N} |\ (3c),\ (3d),\ (3e),\ (3f)\}. \tag{4}$$

With the re-formulation (3a–3f) of the constrained K-Means problem, besides the introduced constraints, other restrictions on point assignments can be explicitly enforced by introducing additional constraints for the matrix $\mathbf{S}$. Therefore, our proposed method for addressing constrained K-Means by solving (3a–3f) can be generalized to incorporate different types of constraints.

5 Optimization Strategy

In this section, we introduce our optimization technique to tackle the constrained K-Means problem with the binary formulation (3a–3f). Clearly, (3a–3f) is a non-convex quadratic programming problem with binary constraints, thus solving it optimally is a computationally challenging task. This section introduces a novel alternating optimization approach to solve (3a–3f). In contrast to other relaxation schemes, we introduce an optimization technique aiming at finding feasible solutions for (3a–3f), i.e., $\mathbf{S} \in \{0,1\}^{k \times N}$ and $\mathbf{S} \in \boldsymbol{\Omega}$. This allows us to devise a better approximation approach compared to other heuristic or relaxation methods, which will be empirically demonstrated in our experiments.

First, observe that the optimization problem (3a–3f) consists of two sets of variables, namely, $\mathbf{C}$ and $\mathbf{S}$, where the constraints are only enforced on the matrix $\mathbf{S}$. This allows us, similar to the conventional K-Means approach, to set up an optimization strategy that involves alternatively updating $\mathbf{C}$ and $\mathbf{S}$ until convergence. Particularly, the update step for $\mathbf{C}$ with a fixed matrix $\mathbf{S}$ can be written as

$$\min_{\mathbf{C}} \quad \|\mathbf{X} - \mathbf{C}\mathbf{S}\|_F^2, \tag{5}$$

while with $\mathbf{C}$ fixed, updating $\mathbf{S}$ can be written as

$$\begin{aligned} \min_{\mathbf{S}} \quad & \|\mathbf{X} - \mathbf{C}\mathbf{S}\|_F^2, \\ \text{subject to} \quad & \mathbf{S} \in \{0,1\}^{k \times N}, \\ & \mathbf{S} \in \boldsymbol{\Omega}. \end{aligned} \tag{6}$$

In the following, we provide more details on the updating steps.

5.1 Updating the Centroids

To solve (5), notice that it is a convex quadratic problem in which solutions can be derived in closed-form. However, to avoid numerical issues of the solutions for large-scale problems, we update $\mathbf{C}$ by solving the regularized least square problem [22]:

$$\min_{\mathbf{C}} \quad \|\mathbf{X} - \mathbf{C}\mathbf{S}\|_F^2 \;+\; \lambda\|\mathbf{C}\|_F^2, \tag{7}$$

where λ is the regularize parameter. The problem (7) also admits a closed-form solution

$$\mathbf{C} = \mathbf{X}\mathbf{S}^T(\mathbf{S}\mathbf{S}^T + \lambda\mathbf{I})^{-1}. \tag{8}$$

The advantage of (8) is that $(\mathbf{S}\mathbf{S}^T + \lambda\mathbf{I})$ is guaranteed to be full-rank, allowing the inversion to be computed efficiently by several matrix factorization techniques. We choose λ to be 10^{-4} in all the experiments to prevent λ from affecting the solution of $\mathbf{C}$.

5.2 Updating the Assignment Matrix

Due to the special structure of $\mathbf{S}$, the problem of finding the cluster assignments (6) can be written as an optimization problem with linear objective function [3]. Let $\mathbf{Y} \in \mathbb{R}^{k\times N}$ be a matrix where each element $\mathbf{Y}_{i,j}$ is defined as $\mathbf{Y}_{i,j} = \|\mathbf{c}_i - \mathbf{x}_j\|_2^2$ ($\mathbf{x}_j$ is the j-th column of $\mathbf{X}$ and $\mathbf{c}_i$ is the i-th column of $\mathbf{C}$). The problem (6) is equivalent to

$$\min_{\mathbf{S}} \qquad \langle \mathbf{Y}, \mathbf{S} \rangle, \tag{9a}$$

$$\text{subject to} \qquad \mathbf{S} \in \boldsymbol{\Omega}, \;\; \mathbf{S} \in \{0,1\}^{k\times N} \tag{9b}$$

If the binary constraints in (9b) are ignored, (9a–9b) becomes a convex linear programming (LP) problem. Based on that observation, a straightforward relaxation technique to tackle (9a–9b) is to allow $\mathbf{S}_{ij}$ to be in the continuous domain, i.e., $0 \le \mathbf{S}_{i,j} \le 1 \;\; \forall i,j$. Then, $\mathbf{S}$ can be updated efficiently by solving the relaxed version (9a–9b), which can be done by taking advantage of several state-of-the-art LP solvers. However, the solutions returned by LP may not be feasible w.r.t. (9a–9b), i.e., $\exists (i,j), \mathbf{S}_{i,j} \notin \{0,1\}$. In order to project the LP solutions back to the binary domain of (9a–9b), a thresholding step needs to be executed, which may lead to loose approximation if the threshold is not chosen properly.

To overcome such drawbacks, we introduce an alternating optimization approach to find the feasible solutions for (9a–9b) in an optimal way. Our approach is inspired by several algorithms on feasibility pump [2,5,7], which aim to find feasible solutions for mixed integer programming (MIP) problems. Our formulation allows the problem to be tackled using alternating optimization. As will be shown in the experiments, our algorithm provides a better solution for the constrained K-Means problem compared to other approximation techniques.

Let us first introduce the auxiliary variable $\mathbf{V} \in \mathbb{R}^{k\times N}$ that has the same size as $\mathbf{S}$. Furthermore, with the constraint that $\mathbf{V} \in \{0,1\}^{k\times N}$, the problem (9a–9b) can now be written equivalently as

$$\begin{aligned} \min_{\mathbf{S},\mathbf{V}} \quad & \langle \mathbf{Y}, \mathbf{S} \rangle, \\ \text{subject to} \quad & 0 \le \mathbf{S}_{i,j} \le 1 \ \forall i,j, \ \ \mathbf{S} \in \boldsymbol{\Omega}, \\ & \mathbf{V} \in \{0,1\}^{k\times N}, \ \ \mathbf{S} = \mathbf{V}. \end{aligned} \tag{10}$$

Note that by introducing the auxiliary matrix $\mathbf{V}$, the task of optimizing (10) w.r.t. $\mathbf{S}$ can be done within the continuous domain. However, due to the binary restrictions on $\mathbf{V}$, solving (10) is still a challenging problem.

In this work, we propose to tackle (10) by using the ℓ_1 penalty method [24]. Specifically, by incorporating the coupling constraint $\mathbf{S} = \mathbf{V}$ into the cost function of (10), in the context of ℓ_1 penalty method, the penalty problem can be written as follows

$$\begin{aligned} \min_{\mathbf{S},\mathbf{V}} \quad & \langle \mathbf{Y}, \mathbf{S} \rangle + \rho \|\mathbf{S} - \mathbf{V}\|_1, \\ \text{subject to} \quad & 0 \le \mathbf{S}_{i,j} \le 1 \ \forall i,j, \\ & \mathbf{S} \in \boldsymbol{\Omega}, \ \ \mathbf{V} \in \{0,1\}^{k\times N}, \end{aligned} \tag{11}$$

where the notation $\|.\|_1$ of a matrix $\mathbf{X}$ is defined as $\|\mathbf{X}\|_1 = \sum_{i,j} |\mathbf{X}_{i,j}|$ and $\rho > 0$ is the penalty parameter. Intuitively, by minimizing the sum of $\sum_{i,j} |\mathbf{S}_{i,j} - \mathbf{V}_{i,j}|$ with a penalty parameter ρ, the element-wise differences between the two matrices $\mathbf{S}$ and $\mathbf{V}$ are penalized during the optimization process, where the penalization strength is controlled by ρ.

Furthermore, observe that the equality constraint $\mathbf{S}_{i,j} = \mathbf{V}_{i,j}$ can also be represented by two inequality constraints, i.e., $\mathbf{S}_{i,j} \ge \mathbf{V}_{i,j}$ and $\mathbf{V}_{i,j} \ge \mathbf{S}_{i,j}$. This allows us to write the second term containing the ℓ_1 norm in (11) as the sum of two separate terms. Specifically, let $[x]^- = \max\{0, -x\}$, and introduce two non-negative matrices $\boldsymbol{\rho}^+ \in \mathbb{R}^{k\times N}$ and $\boldsymbol{\rho}^- \in \mathbb{R}^{k\times N}$ that store the penalty parameters, the penalty problem (11) becomes

$$\begin{aligned} \min_{\mathbf{S},\mathbf{V}} \quad & \langle \mathbf{Y}, \mathbf{S} \rangle + \sum_{i,j} \boldsymbol{\rho}^+_{i,j} [\mathbf{S}_{i,j} - \mathbf{V}_{i,j}]^- + \sum_{i,j} \boldsymbol{\rho}^-_{i,j} [\mathbf{V}_{i,j} - \mathbf{S}_{i,j}]^-, \\ \text{subject to} \quad & 0 \le \mathbf{S}_{i,j} \le 1 \ \forall i,j, \\ & \mathbf{S} \in \boldsymbol{\Omega}, \ \ \mathbf{V} \in \{0,1\}^{k\times N}. \end{aligned} \tag{12}$$

Note that instead of using one penalty parameter ρ as in (11), we associate each matrix index (i,j) with two penalty parameters $\boldsymbol{\rho}^+_{i,j} > 0$ and $\boldsymbol{\rho}^-_{i,j} > 0$ that correspond to the constraints $\mathbf{S}_{i,j} \ge \mathbf{V}_{i,j}$ and $\mathbf{V}_{i,j} \ge \mathbf{S}_{i,j}$, respectively.

We are now ready to introduce the alternating optimization scheme to solve the problem (12). The algorithm consists of iteratively updating $\mathbf{S}$ and $\mathbf{V}$ until convergence. Particularly, let t denote the iteration, the update steps for $\mathbf{S}$ and $\mathbf{V}$ can be formulated as follows

S Update Step. With $\mathbf{V}$ fixed to the value at iteration t, updating $\mathbf{S}$ at iteration $t+1$ amounts to solving a linear programming (LP) problem. Specifically, by introducing two non-negative matrices $\boldsymbol{\gamma}^+ \in \mathbb{R}^{k\times N}$ and $\boldsymbol{\gamma}^- \in \mathbb{R}^{k\times N}$, the LP problem to update $\mathbf{S}$ can be written as follows

$$\mathbf{S}^{(t+1)} = \arg\min_{\mathbf{S},\gamma} \quad \langle \mathbf{Y}, \mathbf{S}\rangle + \sum_{i,j} \boldsymbol{\rho}^+_{i,j}\gamma^+_{i,j} + \sum_{i,j} \boldsymbol{\rho}^-_{i,j}\gamma^-_{i,j}, \tag{13a}$$

$$\text{subject to} \quad \mathbf{V}^{(t)}_{i,j} - \mathbf{S}_{i,j} \le \gamma^+_{i,j} \ \forall i,j, \tag{13b}$$

$$\mathbf{S}_{i,j} - \mathbf{V}^{(t)}_{i,j} \le \gamma^-_{i,j} \ \ \forall i,j, \tag{13c}$$

$$\gamma^+_{i,j}, \gamma^-_{i,j} \ge 0 \ \ \forall i,j, \tag{13d}$$

$$0 \le \mathbf{S}_{i,j} \le 1 \ \ \forall i,j, \quad \mathbf{S} \in \boldsymbol{\Omega}. \tag{13e}$$

Note that the purpose of introducing $\boldsymbol{\gamma}^+$ and $\boldsymbol{\gamma}^-$ is to eliminate the $[.]^-$ operator in the objective function of (12) – based on the observation that $[x]^- \ge 0 \ \forall x$. Therefore, the problem (12) and (13a–13e) with fixed $\mathbf{V}$ are equivalent. As (13a–13e) is a convex LP problem, it can be solved efficiently using any off-the-shelf solver.

V Update Step. After $\mathbf{S}$ is updated by solving the LP problem (13a–13e), starting from (12), the task of updating $\mathbf{V}$ with fixed $\mathbf{S}$ can be written as

$$\mathbf{V}^{(t+1)} = \arg\min_{\mathbf{V}} \quad \sum_{i,j} \boldsymbol{\rho}^+_{i,j}[\mathbf{S}^{(t+1)}_{i,j} - \mathbf{V}_{i,j}]^- + \sum_{i,j} \boldsymbol{\rho}^-_{i,j}[\mathbf{V}_{i,j} - \mathbf{S}^{(t+1)}_{i,j}]^-,$$
$$\text{subject to} \quad \mathbf{V} \in \{0,1\}^{k\times N}. \tag{14}$$

Due to the fact that the objective function of (14) consists of non-negative terms, solving for $\mathbf{V}$ can be done element-wise. Moreover, as each element $\mathbf{V}_{i,j} \in \{0,1\}$, it can be updated by choosing the value that results in the smaller objective value

$$\mathbf{V}^{(t+1)}_{i,j} = \begin{cases} 0, & \text{if } \boldsymbol{\rho}^-_{i,j}\mathbf{S}^{(t+1)}_{i,j} \le \boldsymbol{\rho}^+_{i,j}\left(1 - \mathbf{S}^{(t+1)}_{i,j}\right), \\ 1, & \text{otherwise.} \end{cases} \tag{15}$$

Updating Penalty Parameters. From (15), it can be seen that for a fixed value of $\mathbf{S}^{(t+1)}_{i,j}$, the penalty parameters $\boldsymbol{\rho}^+_{i,j}$ and $\boldsymbol{\rho}^-_{i,j}$ control the weights for updating $\mathbf{V}^{(t+1)}_{i,j}$. Particularly, if $\boldsymbol{\rho}^+_{i,j}$ is much larger than $\boldsymbol{\rho}^-_{i,j}$, the value of 0 is more favorable for $\mathbf{V}^{(t+1)}_{i,j}$ (since $\boldsymbol{\rho}^+_{i,j}(1 - \mathbf{S}^{(t+1)}_{i,j}) \gg \boldsymbol{\rho}^-_{i,j}\mathbf{S}^{(t+1)}_{i,j}$), and vice versa. Thus, in other to prevent early convergence to a bad local minima, if $\mathbf{V}^{(t+1)}_{i,j} = 0$ at iteration $t+1$, we increase $\boldsymbol{\rho}^-_{i,j}$ to give $\mathbf{V}_{i,j}$ chances to be assigned with the value of 1 in the later iterations. Similar argument can be applied for the case of $\mathbf{V}^{(t+1)}_{i,j} = 1$. The penalty parameters, therefore, are updated as follows

$$\boldsymbol{\rho}^{-(t+1)}_{i,j} = \begin{cases} \kappa \boldsymbol{\rho}^{-(t)}_{i,j}, & \text{if } \mathbf{V}^{(t+1)}_{i,j} = 0, \\ \boldsymbol{\rho}^{-(t)}_{i,j}, & \text{otherwise,} \end{cases} \quad \text{and} \quad \boldsymbol{\rho}^{+(t+1)}_{i,j} = \begin{cases} \kappa \boldsymbol{\rho}^{+(t)}_{i,j}, & \text{if } \mathbf{V}^{(t+1)}_{i,j} = 1, \\ \boldsymbol{\rho}^{+(t)}_{i,j}, & \text{otherwise,} \end{cases} \tag{16}$$

where κ is a positive number that controls the increase rate. Note that besides controlling the updating of $\mathbf{V}$ in (15), the $\boldsymbol{\rho}^+$ and $\boldsymbol{\rho}^-$ parameters also affect the solution of (13a–13e). Specifically, by gradually increasing $\boldsymbol{\rho}^+$ and $\boldsymbol{\rho}^-$ as in (16), the weights for the second and third terms in the objective function (13a) become higher in the later iterations, forcing (13a–13e) to drive $\mathbf{S}$ to integrality.

6 Main Algorithm

Based on the discussions in the previous sections, Algorithm 1 summarizes our main approach for solving the constrained K-Means problem (2a–2d). The algorithm alternates between updating the centroids (Line 3, Algorithm 1) and

Algorithm 1. Binary Optimization Based Constrained K-Means (BCKM)

Require: Input data $\mathbf{X}$, number of clusters `n_clusters`, convergence threshold ϵ_c, `max_iter`, initial assignment $\mathbf{S}^{(0)}$, initial centroids $\mathbf{C}^{(0)}$

1: $t \leftarrow 1$;
2: **while** $t <$ `max_iter` **do**
3: $\quad \mathbf{C}^{(t)} \leftarrow \arg\min_{\mathbf{C}} \|\mathbf{X} - \mathbf{C}\mathbf{S}^{(t-1)}\|_F^2$
4: $\quad \mathbf{S}^{(t)} \leftarrow$ UpdateClusterAssignment($\mathbf{X}, \mathbf{C}^{(t)}, \mathbf{S}^{(t-1)}$) /*Alg.2 */
5: $\quad$ **if** $\|\mathbf{C}^{(t)} - \mathbf{C}^{(t-1)}\|_F^2 \le \epsilon$ **then**
6: $\qquad$ break
7: $\quad$ **end if**
8: $\quad t \leftarrow t + 1$
9: **end while**
10: **return** Cluster centroids $\mathbf{C}$, cluster assignment matrix $\mathbf{S}$

Algorithm 2. Update Cluster Assignment

Require: Data matrix $\mathbf{X}$, set of centroids $\mathbf{C}$, $\mathbf{S}^{(0)}$, initial penalty parameter ρ_0, penalty increase rate κ, convergence threshold ϵ_s, `max_iter`

$t \leftarrow 1$; $\quad \mathbf{Y}_{i,j} \leftarrow \|\mathbf{c}_i - \mathbf{x}_j\|_2^2$
$\boldsymbol{\rho}^+ \leftarrow \rho_0 \mathbf{1}^{k \times N}$; $\boldsymbol{\rho}^- \leftarrow \rho_0 \mathbf{1}^{k \times N}$
$\mathbf{V}^{(0)} \leftarrow \lceil \mathbf{S}^{(0)} \rfloor$ /*$\lceil . \rfloor$ denotes rounding to nearest integer*/
while $t <$ `max_iter` **do**
$\quad$ Update $\mathbf{S}^{(t)}$ using (13) with $\mathbf{V}$ fixed to $\mathbf{V}^{(t-1)}$
$\quad$ Update $\mathbf{V}^{(t)}$ using (15) with $\mathbf{S}$ fixed to $\mathbf{S}^{(t)}$
$\quad$ Update $\boldsymbol{\rho}^{+(t)}$ and $\boldsymbol{\rho}^{-(t)}$ using (16)
$\quad$ **if** $\|\mathbf{S}^{(t)} - \mathbf{S}^{(t-1)}\|_F^2 + \|\mathbf{V}^{(t)} - \mathbf{V}^{(t-1)}\|_F^2 \le \epsilon_s$ **then**
$\qquad$ break
$\quad$ **end if**
end while
return $\mathbf{S}$

updating the cluster assignments (Algorithm 2). Note that in Line 4 of Algorithm 1, the current value of $\mathbf{S}$ is supplied to Algorithm 2 for initialization. In Algorithm 1, ϵ_c is the convergence threshold of the clusters, i.e., we stop the algorithm if the Frobenius norm of two consecutive centroid matrices is less than ϵ_c. Similarly, the parameter ϵ_s in Algorithm 2 determines the stopping condition for two consecutive set of variables $(\mathbf{S}, \mathbf{V})$. In Algorithm 2, each elements of the penalty parameter matrices $\boldsymbol{\rho}^+$ and $\boldsymbol{\rho}^-$ are initialized to the same value ρ_0 (note that $\mathbf{1}^{k \times N}$ denotes a matrix of size $k \times N$ with all elements equal to 1).

7 Experiments

In this section, we evaluate the performance of our proposed algorithm (BCKM – Binary Optimization based Constrained K-Means) on synthetic and real datasets and compare BCKM with several popular approaches. Among a large body of works on constrained K-Means, we only select some commonly used and state-of-the-art representatives to benchmark our algorithm against, including: The conventional K-Means clustering algorithm (KM) [17]; Hierarchical K-Means (HKM) [10]; Constrained K-Means with Background Knowledge (COP-KM) [23]; Balanced K-Means (BKM) [19]; Constrained K-Means (CKM) [3]; Constrained K-Means with Spectral Clustering (CKSC) [15]; Balanced Clustering with Least Square Regression (BCLR) [16].

All experiments are executed on a standard Ubuntu desktop machine with 4.2 GHz CPU and 32 GB of RAM. We implement our proposed method in Python. All the runs are initialized with standard K-Means. The ρ_0 parameter is set to the starting value of 0.5 and is increased by a rate of $\kappa = 1.1$ for all experiments. For KM and HKM, we employ the implementation provided by the Scikit-learn library [20] with 10 random initializations and the maximum number of iterations is set to 100. For BCLR, we use the MATLAB code and parameters provided by the authors [16], with maximum number of iterations set to 2000. We use our own Python implementation of Constrained K-Means [3] and Balanced K-Means [19]. To measure the performance of the algorithms, we report the Normalized Mutual Information (NMI), which is a commonly used metric for clustering problems. Additionally, in order to evaluate the efficiency of our method compared to other approaches, we also report the run time (in seconds) for all the experiments.

7.1 Balanced Clustering on Synthetic Data

In this experiment, we test the performance of the methods on the task of balanced clustering with must-link and cannot-link constraints on high dimensional data. Note that our algorithm, based on the formulation (3a–3f), is capable of handling different bounds on cluster sizes. However, we conduct experiments on balanced clustering to provide a fair comparison for algorithms that can only handle balance constraints [16]. We randomly generate k clusters, where each cluster contains n data points. We choose $N = kn \approx 500$ data points, and each data point $\mathbf{x}_i$ belongs the space of $\mathbb{R}^d$ (with $d = 512$). To generate the set containing k cluster centers $\{\mu_i\}_{i=1}^k$, we uniformly sample k points in the hyperbox $[-1, 1]^d$. For each i-th cluster, its members are generated by randomly drawing n points from a Gaussian distribution with mean μ_i and covariance matrix of $\sigma\mathbf{I}$ ($\mathbf{I}$ is the identity matrix). To achieve balanced clustering, we set the lower bounds on the cluster sizes for all clusters to be n. Besides, within each cluster, 20% of the points are randomly sampled to generate must-link and cannot-link constraints.

Figure 1 shows experiment results for $\sigma = 0.1$ (top row), $\sigma = 0.5$ (second row) and $\sigma = 0.7$ (bottom row), respectively. On each row of Fig. 1, we plot the NMI (left) and run time (right) for all the methods. As can be observed from this figure, with small values of k, all methods provide relatively good clustering results. As k increases, however, the performances of all methods also degrade (with lower NMI). Among them, our proposed method provides the best NMI result due to its ability to strictly enforce the constraints. Note that although the linking constraints are also added to the LP formulation in [3], our method is able to achieve much higher NMI due to its ability to find good binary solutions, while our runtime is only slightly higher compared to that of [3]. Observe that as the value of σ increases, the performance of the methods also degrade, but ours is able to achieve the best NMI compared to others as the constraints are properly enforced.

To demonstrate the ability to provide balanced clusters, we plot in Fig. 2 the number of points distributed into each cluster by K-Means and our method for three different values of k (we use K-Means to initialize our method). Observe that as k increases, the clusters provided by K-Means becomes highly unbalanced. With such unbalanced initializations, however, our method is able to refine the initial solutions and return balanced clusters, while the must-link and cannot-link constraints are also enforced to provide better NMI compared to other approaches.

7.2 Clustering on Real Datasets

Besides testing with synthetic data, we also conduct experiments on some real datasets that are often employed to benchmark clustering algorithms, including MNIST [14], ORL Face Dataset[1], UMIST Face Datset[2], Yale Dataset[3] and YaleB Dataset[4]. For each dataset, we randomly sample data points from 10 to 15 clusters, and each cluster contains the same number of instances (for the task of balanced clustering). Within each cluster, we randomly select 20% of the points to enforce the must-link and cannot-link constraints. For large datasets, we repeat the experiment with different random subsets of data (the subset indexes are shown by the number in the parentheses). The NMI and the run

[1] http://www.cl.cam.ac.uk/research/dtg/attarchive/facedatabase.html.
[2] https://www.sheffield.ac.uk/eee/research/iel/research/face.
[3] http://vision.ucsd.edu/content/yale-face-database.
[4] http://vision.ucsd.edu/content/extended-yale-face-database-b-b.

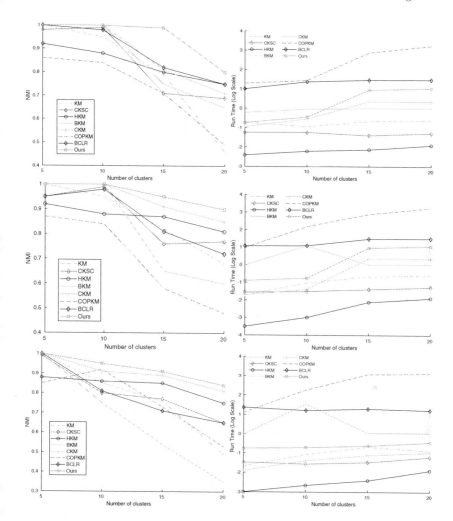

Fig. 1. NMI (left column) and run time (right) for different values of clusters with $N = 500$ points and $d = 512$. First row: NMI and run time for $\sigma = 0.1$. Second row: NMI and run time for $\sigma = 0.5$. Last row: NMI and run time for $\sigma = 0.7$.

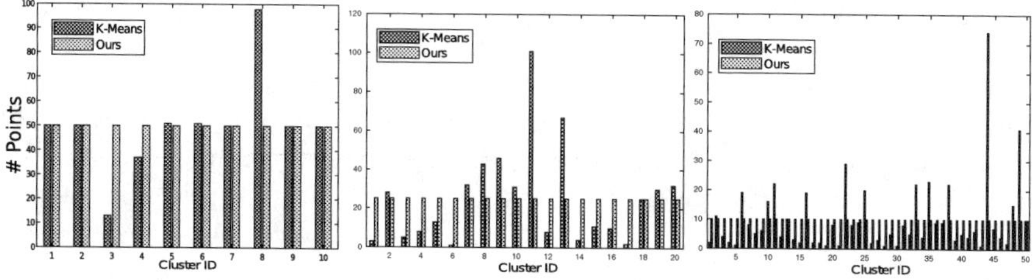

Fig. 2. Cluster distribution of K-Means and our method for 3 different values of $k = 10, 20, 50$ (from left to right).

time of the methods are shown in Table 1. Similar to the case of synthetic data, throughout most of the experiments, our method provides better NMI compared to other approaches due to its ability to provide assignments that satisfy the constraints. Note that in some cases, the NMI results provided by BCLS and COP are very close to ours, while our run time is much faster. We also apply the must-link and cannot-link constraints to the LP formulation of CKM [3], yet we are able to achieve better NMI. This demonstrates that our binary optimization technique provides better solutions compared to the LP relaxation approach.

Table 1. Experiment results on real datasets. For each dataset, different subsets (indexed by the number in the parentheses) are sampled to run the experiments. Run time is in seconds.

Datasets		KM [17]	CKSC [15]	HKC [10]	BKM [19]	CKM [3]	BCLS [16]	COP [23]	Ours
MNIST (1)	NMI	0.49	0.62	0.57	0.51	0.68	0.62	0.68	**0.69**
	Time	0.63	0.15	0.11	0.52	0.40	2.52	5.54	0.49
MNIST (2)	NMI	0.52	0.55	0.54	0.52	0.58	0.50	0.48	**0.60**
	Time	0.77	0.12	0.14	0.47	0.33	3.36	4.07	0.40
MNIST (3)	NMI	0.53	0.59	0.57	0.50	0.59	0.55	0.56	**0.61**
	Time	0.77	0.12	0.14	0.47	0.45	2.19	4.52	0.54
Yale (1)	NMI	0.51	0.54	0.59	0.51	0.67	0.55	0.61	**0.73**
	Time	0.34	0.09	0.15	0.23	0.24	4.13	2.13	0.30
Yale (2)	NMI	0.54	0.52	0.51	0.50	0.64	0.68	0.56	**0.72**
	Time	0.34	0.17	0.13	0.27	0.33	3.21	3.11	0.39
YaleB (1)	NMI	0.55	0.62	0.59	0.48	0.68	0.60	0.64	**0.71**
	Time	0.34	0.11	0.21	0.31	0.19	1.95	2.48	0.22
YaleB (2)	NMI	0.52	0.53	0.54	0.50	0.61	0.55	0.54	**0.66**
	Time	0.34	0.09	0.08	0.43	0.20	2.39	2.40	0.25
YaleB (3)	NMI	0.51	0.61	0.60	0.48	0.67	**0.72**	0.69	**0.72**
	Time	0.34	0.21	0.15	0.20	0.35	4.12	2.65	0.37
ORL (1)	NMI	0.67	0.70	0.75	0.64	0.79	0.75	**0.85**	0.81
	Time	0.38	0.15	0.17	0.29	0.41	2.35	3.51	0.54
ORL (2)	NMI	0.61	0.71	0.69	0.61	0.68	0.75	0.75	**0.83**
	Time	0.38	0.14	0.17	0.26	0.37	2.35	3.50	0.45
UMIST	NMI	0.76	**0.81**	0.67	0.75	0.72	0.75	0.78	**0.81**
	Time	0.25	0.09	0.15	0.52	0.30	2.15	6.45	0.39

8 Conclusion

In this work, we propose a binary optimization approach for the constrained K-Means clustering problem, in which different types of constraints can be simultaneously enforced. We then introduce a novel optimization technique to search for the solutions of the problem in the binary domain, resulting in better solutions for the cluster assignment problem. Empirical results show that our method outperforms other heuristic or relaxation techniques while the increase in run time is negligible. The method proposed in this paper can be considered as a generic framework for constrained K-Means which can be embedded into different problems that require the use constrained clustering.

References

1. Althoff, T., Ulges, A., Dengel, A.: Balanced clustering for content-based image browsing. Series of the Gesellschaft fur Informatik, pp. 27–30 (2011)
2. Bertacco, L., Fischetti, M., Lodi, A.: A feasibility pump heuristic for general mixed-integer problems. Discret. Optim. **4**(1), 63–76 (2007)
3. Bradley, P., Bennett, K., Demiriz, A.: Constrained K-Means Clustering, pp. 1–8. Microsoft Research, Redmond (2000)
4. Fard, M.M., Thonet, T., Gaussier, E.: Deep k-means: jointly clustering with k-means and learning representations. arXiv preprint arXiv:1806.10069 (2018)
5. Fischetti, M., Glover, F., Lodi, A.: The feasibility pump. Math. Program. **104**(1), 91–104 (2005)
6. Ge, T., He, K., Ke, Q., Sun, J.: Optimized product quantization for approximate nearest neighbor search. In: 2013 IEEE Conference on Computer Vision and Pattern Recognition (CVPR), pp. 2946–2953. IEEE (2013)
7. Geißler, B., Morsi, A., Schewe, L., Schmidt, M.: Penalty alternating direction methods for mixed-integer optimization: a new view on feasibility pumps. SIAM J. Optim. **27**(3), 1611–1636 (2017)
8. Gersho, A., Gray, R.M.: Vector Quantization and Signal Compression, vol. 159. Springer, Heidelberg (2012). https://doi.org/10.1007/978-1-4615-3626-0
9. Jegou, H., Douze, M., Schmid, C.: Product quantization for nearest neighbor search. IEEE Trans. Pattern Anal. Mach. Intell. **33**(1), 117–128 (2011)
10. Johnson, S.C.: Hierarchical clustering schemes. Psychometrika **32**(3), 241–254 (1967)
11. Kalantidis, Y., Avrithis, Y.: Locally optimized product quantization for approximate nearest neighbor search. In: Proceedings of the IEEE Conference on Computer Vision and Pattern Recognition, pp. 2321–2328 (2014)
12. Khan, S.S., Ahmad, A.: Cluster center initialization algorithm for k-means clustering. Pattern Recogn. Lett. **25**(11), 1293–1302 (2004)
13. Le Tan, D.K., Le, H., Hoang, T., Do, T.T., Cheung, N.M.: DeepVQ: a deep network architecture for vector quantization. In: Proceedings of the IEEE Conference on Computer Vision and Pattern Recognition Workshops, pp. 2579–2582 (2018)
14. LeCun, Y., Bottou, L., Bengio, Y., Haffner, P.: Gradient-based learning applied to document recognition. Proc. IEEE **86**(11), 2278–2324 (1998)
15. Li, Z., Liu, J.: Constrained clustering by spectral kernel learning. In: 2009 IEEE 12th International Conference on Computer Vision, pp. 421–427. IEEE (2009)
16. Liu, H., Han, J., Nie, F., Li, X.: Balanced clustering with least square regression (2017)
17. MacQueen, J., et al.: Some methods for classification and analysis of multivariate observations. In: Proceedings of the Fifth Berkeley Symposium on Mathematical Statistics and Probability, Oakland, CA, USA, vol. 1, pp. 281–297 (1967)
18. Mahajan, M., Nimbhorkar, P., Varadarajan, K.: The planar k-means problem is NP-hard. Theor. Comput. Sci. **442**, 13–21 (2012)
19. Malinen, M.I., Fränti, P.: Balanced K-means for clustering. In: Fränti, P., Brown, G., Loog, M., Escolano, F., Pelillo, M. (eds.) S+SSPR 2014. LNCS, vol. 8621, pp. 32–41. Springer, Heidelberg (2014). https://doi.org/10.1007/978-3-662-44415-3_4
20. Pedregosa, F., et al.: Scikit-learn: machine learning in python. J. Mach. Learn. Res. **12**(Oct), 2825–2830 (2011)
21. Pena, J.M., Lozano, J.A., Larranaga, P.: An empirical comparison of four initialization methods for the k-means algorithm. Pattern Recogn. Lett. **20**(10), 1027–1040 (1999)

22. Rifkin, R.M., Lippert, R.A.: Notes on regularized least squares (2007)
23. Wagstaff, K., Cardie, C., Rogers, S., Schroedl, S.: Constrained k-means clustering with background knowledge. In: Proceedings of the Eighteenth International Conference on Machine Learning, pp. 577–584. Citeseer (2001)
24. Wright, S., Nocedal, J.: Numerical optimization. Springer Sci. **35**(67–68), 7 (1999)
25. Yang, B., Fu, X., Sidiropoulos, N.D., Hong, M.: Towards k-means-friendly spaces: simultaneous deep learning and clustering. arXiv preprint arXiv:1610.04794 (2016)
26. Zhu, S., Wang, D., Li, T.: Data clustering with size constraints. Knowl.-Based Syst. **23**(8), 883–889 (2010)

LS3D: Single-View Gestalt 3D Surface Reconstruction from Manhattan Line Segments

Yiming Qian[1], Srikumar Ramalingam[2], and James H. Elder[1](✉)

[1] York University, Toronto, Canada
{yimingq,jelder}@yorku.ca
[2] University of Utah, Salt Lake City, USA
srikumar@cs.utah.edu

Abstract. Recent deep learning algorithms for single-view 3D reconstruction recover rough 3D layout but fail to capture the crisp linear structures that grace our urban landscape. Here we show that for the particular problem of 3D Manhattan building reconstruction, the explicit application of linear perspective and Manhattan constraints within a classical constructive perceptual organization framework allows accurate and meaningful reconstructions to be computed. The proposed Line-Segment-to-3D (LS3D) algorithm computes a hierarchical representation through repeated application of the Gestalt principle of proximity. Edges are first organized into line segments, and the subset that conforms to a Manhattan frame is extracted. Optimal bipartite grouping of orthogonal line segments by proximity minimizes the total gap and generates a set of Manhattan spanning trees, each of which is then lifted to 3D. For each 3D Manhattan tree we identify the complete set of 3D 3-junctions and 3-paths, and show that each defines a unique minimal spanning cuboid. The cuboids generated by each Manhattan tree together define a solid model and the visible surface for that tree. The relative depths of these solid models are determined by an L1 minimization that is again rooted in a principle of proximity in both depth and image dimensions. The method has relatively fewer parameters and requires no training. For quantitative evaluation, we introduce a new 3D Manhattan building dataset (3DBM). We find that the proposed LS3D method generates 3D reconstructions that are both qualitatively and quantitatively superior to reconstructions produced by state-of-the-art deep learning approaches.

1 Introduction

Most 3D computer vision research focuses on multi-view algorithms or direct ranging methods (e.g., LiDAR, structured light). However, the human ability to appreciate the 3D layout of a scene from a photograph shows that our brains also make use of single-view cues, which complement multi-view analysis by providing instantaneous estimates, even for distant surfaces, where stereoscopic disparity signals are weak.

C. V. Jawahar et al. (Eds.): ACCV 2018, LNCS 11364, pp. 399–416, 2019.
https://doi.org/10.1007/978-3-030-20870-7_25

Recent work on single-view 3D reconstruction has focused on supervised deep learning to directly estimate depth from pixels. Here we take a different approach, focusing instead on identifying a small set of principles that together lead to a simple, unsupervised method for estimating 3D surface geometry for buildings that conform to a Manhattan constraint [1].

This approach has three advantages. First, it provides an interpretable scientific theory with a clear set of assumptions and domain of validity. Second, it leads to a well-specified hierarchical solid model 3D representation that may be more useful for downstream applications than a range map. Finally, as we will show, it generates results that are qualitatively and quantitatively superior to state-of-the-art deep learning methods for the domain of 3D Manhattan building reconstruction.

Single-view 3D reconstruction is ill-posed and thus solvable only for scenes that satisfy strong regularity conditions. Linear perspective - the assumption that features of the 3D scene are arranged over systems of parallel lines - is perhaps the most powerful of these constraints; its discovery is often cited as a defining achievement of the Early Renaissance. Linear perspective is a particularly valuable cue for urban environments, which abound with piecewise planar and often parallel surfaces that generate families of parallel 3D line segments in the scene.

A stronger constraint than linear perspective is the so-called Manhattan constraint [1], which demands that there be three dominant and mutually orthogonal families of parallel line segments. Application of this additional regularity allows line segments to be labelled with their 3D orientation, but does not directly provide an estimate of the 3D surfaces or solid shapes in the scene.

To bridge this gap, we appeal to a long history of research in Gestalt psychology that identifies a principle of proximity and related cues of connectedness and common region as dominant factors in the perceptual organization of visual information [2–5]. We use this principle of proximity repeatedly to construct successively more global and three-dimensional representations of the visual scene.

The proposed approach is anchored on a sparse line segment representation - Fig. 1 provides an overview of our Line-Segment-to-3D (LS3D) algorithm. Principles of proximity and good continuation are used to group local image edges into line segments, which are then labelled according to their Manhattan directions (Fig. 1(a)). A principle of proximity is then again employed to optimally group neighbouring orthogonal segments, forming local 2D minimal spanning Manhattan trees (MTs, Figs. 1(b–c)). Each of these local trees is then lifted to 3D using the Manhattan constraints. Note, however, that the relative depth of each 3D MT remains undetermined (Fig. 1(d)).

One of our main contributions is to show that each of these 3D Manhattan trees can be decomposed into a maximal set of non-subsuming 3D 3-junctions, 3-paths and L-junctions. Each of the 3-junctions and 3-paths defines a unique minimal covering cuboid, and each L-junction defines a unique minimal covering rectangle. The union of these cuboids and rectangles defines the 3D surface model for the tree (Fig. 1(e)).

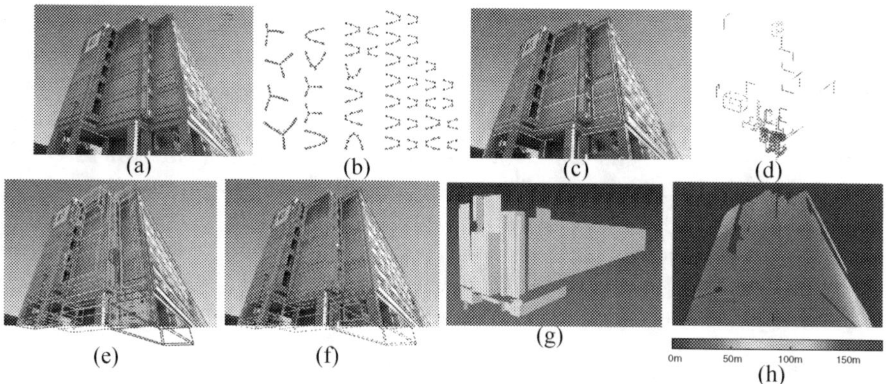

Fig. 1. LS3D processing stages. (a) Detected Manhattan line segments. (b) Graphical structure of identified Manhattan spanning trees (MTs). Each vertex represents a line segment endpoint, and each edge represents either a real line segment or a junction between orthogonal segments. (c) MTs localized in the image (d) MTs lifted to 3D. Note that the relative depth of each MT remains unknown. (e) Minimal spanning cuboid/rectangle models. (f) Compound 3D models of connected structures. (g) Final model of visible surfaces. (h) Range map.

The definition of these surfaces now allows the relative depth of these local 3D models to be resolved through a two-stage constrained optimization procedure. We first apply a principal of common region [5], minimizing the L_1 distance between parallel planes from different models that overlap in the image, forming sets of compound 3D models corresponding to connected regions in the image (Fig. 1(f)). Finally, we apply a principle of proximity to resolve the relative depth of these disjoint compound 3D models, minimizing the L_1 distance between parallel planes from distinct models, weighted by their inverse separation in the image. For both stages, occlusion constraints [6] play a crucial role in preventing physically unrealizable solutions. The resulting 3D scale model (Fig. 1(g)) can be used to generate a range map (Fig. 1(h)) for comparison with competing approaches.

Unlike deep learning methods, LS3D is not designed to recover an estimate of absolute depth for every pixel in the image, but rather an estimate of the Euclidean 3D layout of the Manhattan structures in the scene, up to a single unknown scaling factor. We therefore introduce a new 3D ground-truth dataset of solid massing building models and evaluation framework suitable for the evaluation of such algorithms.

To summarize, our contributions are three: (1) We introduce a novel, explainable single-view 3D reconstruction algorithm called LS3D that infers the 3D Euclidean surface layout of Manhattan buildings, up to an unknown scaling factor, (2) We introduce a new 3DBM ground truth dataset of 3D Manhattan building models and a novel evaluation framework that allows single-view methods for 3D Manhattan building reconstruction to be evaluated and compared, and

(3) Using this dataset and framework, we find that the LS3D method outperforms state-of-the-art deep-learning algorithms, both qualitatively and quantitatively. The goal of this work is not to reconstruct general scenes. This is consistent with the computer vision tradition of focusing on important sub-problems, and making use of domain constraints. As we argue here, Manhattan structures are extremely common in our built environment and many non-Manhattan scenes can be modelled as a mixture of Manhattan frames. Thus it makes sense to have a specialized module for their reconstruction. Any system that does not take explicit advantage of Manhattan regularity will, we expect, fail to reconstruct crisp orthogonal structure (See DNN output in Fig. 4).

2 Prior Work

Single-view 3D reconstruction is a classical computer vision problem that goes back to Roberts' PhD thesis [7–11]. More recent work has attempted to reconstruct piecewise planar 3D models of real scenes but under somewhat stronger assumptions. In their Photo Pop-up work, Hoiem *et al.* [12] modeled scenes as comprising three types of surfaces: ground, vertical and sky. Boosted decision tree classifiers were used to label superpixels from the image into one of these three semantic classes using a feature descriptor that includes appearance and geometric cues. The set of polylines defining the ground/vertical boundary was identified to estimate the 3D orientations of the vertical surfaces in the scene. Subsequent work globally optimizes the ground/vertical boundary [13] and generalizes to a larger range of camera poses and more fine-grained surface estimation [14].

While Hoiem *et al.* allowed vertical surfaces of arbitrary orientation, Coughlan and Yuille [15] observed that in the built environment, 3D scenes are often dominated by three mutually orthogonal directions (vertical + 2 horizontal) and developed a probabilistic approach to recover the rotation of this so-called Manhattan frame relative to the camera. Subsequent work [16,17] refined this model to deliver more accurate Manhattan frames and to label the lines in the image according to their Manhattan direction.

The Manhattan constraint has been productively exploited by numerous subsequent 3D reconstruction algorithms. Delage *et al.*[18] developed a Bayes net model to identify the floor/wall boundary in indoor scenes and thus to recover the Euclidean floor/wall geometry. Hedau et al. [19] employed an even stronger constraint for indoor 3D room reconstruction, assuming that the room could be modeled as a single cuboid with intervening clutter. Subsequent improvements to indoor reconstruction based on this cuboid constraint has relied on novel features [20–22], physics-based constraints [6], Bayesian modeling [23], better inference machinery [24,25], larger field-of-view [26], and supervised deep learning [27].

While these indoor room scenes are highly constrained, a more recent approach returns to the problem of reconstructing more general Manhattan scenes, indoor and outdoor [28]. Line segments are first detected and labelled with their

Manhattan directions, and then a large set of potential 3D connectivities are identified between segment pairs. While many of these potential connectivities are false, an L1 minimization framework can identify the 3D solution that respects the maximal number of connection hypotheses, allowing the detected 3D line segments to be backprojected into 3D space.

As an alternative to the ground/vertical and Manhattan constraints one can assume that surfaces are linear 3D sweeps of lines or planar contours detected in the image. This constraint had led to interesting interactive systems, although fully automatic reconstruction is challenging [29].

The main competing fully automatic approach to constrained piecewise planar models attempts to recover an unconstrained range map, using supervised machine learning techniques. An early example is Make3D [30], which models range as a conditional random field (CRF) with naïve Bayes unary potentials over local edge, texture, and colour features and a data-dependent binary smoothness term.

More recent range map approaches tend to use deep neural networks [31–39]. For example, Eigen *et al.* train and evaluate a multi-scale CNN on their own NYU RGBD dataset of indoor scenes and the KITTI LiDAR dataset of road scenes [31,40], while Laina *et al.* train and evaluate a single-scale but deeper ResNet concatenated with up-sampling layers [33] on Make3D [30] and NYU2 [31] datasets. Joint estimation of depth with surface orientation and/or semantic category has been found to improve the accuracy of depth estimates [31,37,38].

One criticism of deep network approaches is the requirement for large amounts of labelled training data, but recent work demonstrates that deep networks for single-view range map estimation can be trained from calibrated stereo pairs [39,41] or even uncalibrated video sequences [42] using reprojection error as the supervisory signal.

Recent research has also been exploring fusion of deep networks with more traditional computer vision approaches. The IM2CAD system [43], for example, focuses on the modeling of room interiors, optimizing configurations of 3D CAD models of furnishings and wall features by projection error, using metrics trained by CNNs.

While deep networks have become the dominant approach to single-view 3D reconstruction, this approach has limitations. First, DNN models have millions of free parameters and are thus not easily interpretable. Second, while deep networks can provide an estimate of rough scene layout, they typically fail to deliver the crisp and accurate geometry that is typical of urban environments. Third, most deep network approaches deliver a range map, which may be appropriate for some applications (e.g., navigation), but for applications such as construction, interior design and architecture a succinct CAD model is more useful.

We thus return in this paper to the classical geometry-driven approach. In particular, we ask, for the particular problem of single-view 3D Manhattan building reconstruction, how much can be achieved by a method that uses geometry alone, without relying upon any form of machine learning or appearance features.

While the geometric approach has been criticized as unreliable [20], we show here that by integrating several key novel ideas with state-of-the-art line segment detection [44], reliable single-view 3D reconstruction of Manhattan objects can be achieved. By keeping the model simple we keep it interpretable, and by focusing on geometry, we deliver the crisp surfaces we experience in built environments, in a highly compact 3D CAD model form.

The focus on geometry and application of the Manhattan constraint links the proposed LS3D approach most directly to the line lifting algorithm of Ramalingam and Brand [28]. However, in this prior work there was no explicit grouping of line segments into larger structures, no inference of surfaces or solid models, and no quantitative evaluation of 3D geometric accuracy. LS3D thus goes far beyond this prior work in delivering quantitatively-evaluated 3D surface models. This is achieved through **three key contributions:**

1. While prior approaches [20, 45] use a 'line sweeping' heuristic to go from line segments to independent Manhattan rectangles, here we introduce a novel, principled approach to identify more complex 3D Manhattan trees, solving a series of three optimal bipartite matching problems to deliver spanning tree configurations of orthogonal Manhattan line segments that together maximize proximity between grouped endpoints.
2. We introduce a novel method for converting these 3D Manhattan trees to surface models. The idea is based on decomposing each Manhattan tree into a maximal set of non-subsuming 3D 3-junctions, 3-paths and L-junctions. Each of the 3-junctions and 3-paths defines a unique minimal spanning cuboid, and each L-junction defines a unique minimal spanning rectangle. The union of these cuboids and rectangles defines the 3D surface model for the tree.
3. These 3D surface models contain multiple planes, providing stronger cues for estimating the relative depth of disconnected structures. We introduce a novel two-stage L_1 minimization approach that gives precedence to the Gestalt principle of common region [5] to first form compound 3D models of structures connected in the image, and later resolving distances between these disjoint structures.

3 The LS3D Algorithm

The LS3D algorithm is summarized in Fig. 1 and detailed below. Line segments are first detected and labelled according to Manhattan direction (Fig. 1(a), Sect. 3.1). From these, Manhattan spanning trees (MTs) are recovered (Fig. 1(b–c), Sect. 3.2) and then lifted to 3D (Fig. 1(d), Sect. 3.3). A maximal set of minimal cuboids and rectangles that span each 3D MT is then identified (Fig. 1(e), Sect. 3.4) and their surfaces aligned in depth through a constrained L_1 optimization first for overlapping MTs (Fig. 1(f)) and finally for disjoint MTs (Sect. 3.5). The resulting 3D CAD model Fig. 1(g)) can be rendered as a range map (Fig. 1(h)) to compare with algorithms that only compute range maps.

3.1 Manhattan Line Segment Detection

We employ the method of Tal and Elder [17] to estimate Manhattan lines, based upon probabilistic Houghing and optimization on the Gauss sphere, and then the MCMLSD line segment detection algorithm [44], which employs an efficient dynamic programming algorithm to estimate segment endpoints. MCMLSD produces line segment results that are quantitatively superior to prior approaches - Fig. 1(a) shows an example.

The MCMLSD algorithm identifies line segments that are co-linear: LS3D groups nearby co-linear segments into a single 'super-segment', but retains a record of the intermediate endpoints to support later surface creation (see below). We retain only segments over a threshold length.[1]

3.2 Manhattan Tree Construction

Prior line-based single-view 3D algorithms [20,45] attempt to leap directly from line segments to 3D with no intermediate stages of perceptual organization. One of our main hypotheses is that the Gestalt principle of proximity coupled with sparsity constraints can yield a much stronger intermediate Manhattan tree representation that will subsequently facilitate global 3D model alignment.

First, a dense graph is formed by treating each segment as a vertex, and defining edges between pairs of vertices representing orthogonal segments with endpoints separated by less than a threshold distance.[2] (Note that an endpoint can lie on the interior of a super-segment.) To sparsify the graph we apply the constraint that each endpoint connects to at most one other endpoint in each of the two orthogonal Manhattan directions. This is achieved through a series of three optimal bipartite matchings, using a proximity-based objective function. Specifically, we seek the bipartite matching of all X segment endpoints to all Y segment endpoints that minimizes the total image distance between matched endpoints, and repeat for X and Z segments as well as Y and Z segments. These optimal bipartite matches are found in cubic time using the Hungarian algorithm [46]. We further sparsify the graph by computing the minimum spanning tree (MST) for each connected subgraph, generating what we will call local Manhattan trees (MTs, Fig. 1(b–c)).

3.3 Lifting 2D MTs to 3D

Each of the MTs can be back-projected from 2D to 3D space using Manhattan direction constraints, up to an unknown distance/scaling constant λ. Assume a camera-centered world coordinate frame (X, Y, Z) in which the X and Y axes are aligned with the x and y axes of the image. Then any endpoint $\mathbf{x}_i = (x_i, y_i)^\top$

[1] We use a minimum segment length of 100 pixels, and maximum gap between co-linear segments of 300 pixels. Sensitivity to these threshold is studied in Sect. 5.

[2] We use a threshold distance of 100 pixels - sensitivity to this threshold is studied in Sect. 5.

in the image back-projects to a 3D point $\mathbf{X}_i = \lambda(x_i, y_i, f)^\top$ in the scene, where f is the focal length of the camera. Note that while λ is unknown it must be the same for all endpoints in the MT.

Due to noise, Manhattan line segments will never be perfectly aligned with the Manhattan directions. Lifting an MT thus entails rectifying each segment to the exact Manhattan direction. We employ a sequential least-squares process. One of the endpoints $\mathbf{X}_0$ of the MT is first randomly selected as the 3D anchor of the tree: the 3D tree is assumed to pass exactly through $\mathbf{X}_0$. Then a depth-first search from $\mathbf{X}_0$ is executed, during which the Manhattan 3D location $\mathbf{X}'_j$ of each endpoint $\mathbf{X}_j$ is determined from the Manhattan location $\mathbf{X}'_i$ of its parent on the depth-first path by $\mathbf{X}'_j = \mathbf{X}'_i + \alpha\lambda\mathbf{V}_{ij}$, where $\mathbf{V}_{ij}$ is the 3D vanishing point direction for segment (i, j) and α is determined by minimizing $||\mathbf{X}'_i + \alpha\lambda\mathbf{V}_{ij} - \mathbf{X}_j||_2$. (Note that λ factors out of this minimization.) Figures 1(c–d) show the MTs for an example image, each lifted to 3D up to a random scaling constant λ.

3.4 From Line Segments to Surfaces

A key contribution of our work is a novel method for inferring surface structure from 3D MTs. We define a Manhattan three-junction as a triplet of orthogonal line segments that meet at a vertex of the MT, and a Manhattan three-path as a sequence of three orthogonal segments meeting end-to-end (Fig. 2). Since each segment can radiate from a junction in two ways, there are eight types of three-junctions, four that may be observed below the horizon and four that may be observed above (Fig. 2 Columns 2–3). Each three-path must begin at one of two endpoints of one of three segment types, and then continue to one of two endpoints of one of the remaining two segment types, and finally one of two endpoints of the remaining segment type. This leads to $2 \times 3 \times 2 \times 2 \times 2 = 48$ three-paths, however each of these has a metamer path that has been traversed in the opposite direction, so there are only 24 distinct three-paths, 12 that can be observed above the horizon and 12 that can be observed below (Fig. 2 Columns 4–9). Our main insight is that this collection of 32 three-junctions and three-paths can be viewed as the outcome of a generative process involving just four generic cuboid poses, two lying above the horizon and two below (Fig. 2 Columns 1).

This observation leads to a simple algorithm for bridging line segments to surfaces. We first decompose an MT into an exhaustive set of Manhattan three-junctions and three-paths. If any segments remain these are used to form two-paths with neighbouring orthogonal segments. This collection of three-junctions, three-paths and

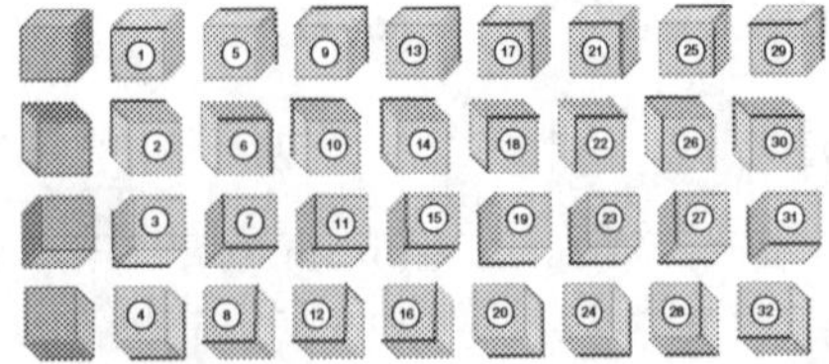

Fig. 2. The 32 unique classes of Manhattan three-junctions and three-paths shown on the four classes of generic Manhattan cuboid poses.

two-paths spans the MT. Three-junctions and three-paths are then used to spawn minimal spanning Manhattan cuboids as per Fig. 2, and two-paths, if they exist, span minimum spanning Manhattan rectangles. (Note that at an intermediate endpoint of a super-segment, the entire super-segment is considered to support the generated cuboid or rectangle - this serves to complete occluded surfaces.) Together, these cuboids and rectangles form a surface model for the MT.

It is important to distinguish our approach to inferring 3D surface models from prior work on recovering indoor scenes that 'sweeps' segments in orthogonal Manhattan directions [20,45]. This sweeping approach estimates the 3D orientation of Manhattan rectangles, but not their relative depth, which must be resolved using strong constraints on the structure of the room (single floor and single ceiling connected by 'accordion' Manhattan walls).

By first connecting proximal orthogonal line segments into minimal Manhattan spanning trees, we provide the connectivity constraints necessary for producing more complex locally-connected 3D surface models, which generate much stronger constraints for resolving relative depth (next section). This approach can be considered a quantitative expression of the 3D reasoning philosophy advocated by Gupta *et al.* [6], who argued for the use of simple solid models to make qualitative inferences about 3D scenes. While their goal was to compute qualitative spatial relationships between independent cuboids, we show that it is possible to recover *quantitative* 3D scene structure involving much more complex compound objects composed of many cuboids and rectangular surfaces.

3.5 Constrained L1-Minimization for Manhattan Building Reconstruction

A typical building generates many MTs and their relative distance/scaling must be determined. Our surface models allow us now to formulate a constrained L_1 optimization that identifies the scaling parameters minimizing separation between parallel planes while respecting occlusion constraints [6]. We partition the process into two stages based upon Gestalt principles of common region and proximity [5].

Stage 1 (Common Region): Let M represent the number of MTs in the model and let $\{\lambda_1, \ldots \lambda_M\}$ represent the unknown scaling parameters for these MTs. Visible rectangular facets from all MTs are projected to the image. The overlap in these projections defines an undirected common region graph $\mathcal{G}_{cr} = (\mathcal{V}_{cr}, \mathcal{E}_{cr})$ in which each vertex $i \in \mathcal{V}_{cr}$ represents a facet and each edge $(i, j) \in \mathcal{E}_{cr}$ represents overlap between parallel facets from different MTs. Figure 1(f) shows the MTs within each connected component of this graph.

For each connected component $c \in [1, \ldots, C]$ of the graph we identify the MT m_c with the largest image projection and clamp its scaling parameter to $\lambda_{m_c} = 1$. Our goal is now to use linear programming (LP) to determine the remaining scaling parameters $\Lambda = \{\lambda_1, \ldots, \lambda_M\} \setminus \{\lambda_{m_1}, \ldots, \lambda_{m_C}\}$ that minimize the weighted distance between overlapping parallel planes from different MTs.

This minimization must, however, respect depth ordering constraints induced by the visibility of line segments. To code these constraints, for each MT i we identify all line segment endpoints $p_{ijk} \in P_{ij}$ that lie within a rectangular facet from another MT j. Letting d^-_{ijk} represent the depth of endpoint p_{ijk} when $\lambda_i = 1$ and d^+_{ijk} represent the distance to the overlapping facet from MT j along the ray from the camera centre to endpoint p_{ijk} when $\lambda_j = 1$, we have the depth ordering constraint $\lambda_i d^-_{ijk} \leq \lambda_j d^+_{ijk}$.

The resulting constrained optimization is thus:

$$\begin{aligned} \min_{\Lambda} \quad & \sum_{(i,j)\in\mathcal{E}_{cr}} |A_i \cap A_j| \cdot |\lambda_i d_i - \lambda_j d_j| \\ \text{s.t.} \quad & \lambda_i d^-_{ijk} \leq \lambda_j d^+_{ijk}, p_{ijk} \in P_{ij} \end{aligned} \tag{1}$$

Here $|\lambda_i d_i - \lambda_j d_j|$ is the distance between two parallel planes. We weight this distance by the area of overlap $|A_i \cap A_j|$ of the two planar facets in the image.

Stage 2: (Proximity): Even after the scaling parameters of MTs within each connected component of the common region graph have been optimized to merge parallel planes in 3D, the relative scaling of each connected component will remain unknown.

To resolve these remaining degrees of freedom, we first identify a disjoint region graph $\mathcal{G}_{dr} = (\mathcal{V}_{dr}, \mathcal{E}_{dr})$ in which each vertex $i \in \mathcal{V}_{dr}$ represents a facet and each edge $(i, j) \in \mathcal{E}_{dr}$ represents two parallel facets from different MTs and different components that do *not* overlap in the image.

We then identify the connected component c with the largest image area and clamp its scaling parameter to $\lambda_{m_c} = 1$. We will now again use LP to determine the remaining scaling parameters $\Lambda_C = \{\lambda_{m_1}, \ldots, \lambda_{m_C}\} \setminus \lambda_{m_c}$ that minimize the weighted distance between non-overlapping parallel planes from different MTs and different components. We weight this minimization by the sum of the areas $|A_i \cup A_j|$, and inversely by the minimum separation l_{ij} of the two planar facets in the image.

Note that although the pairs of planar facets entered into the minimization do not overlap, there may still be overlap between one or more visible line segments from one component and one or more facets from the other, and these must again be encoded as ordering constraints. The resulting constrained minimization is thus:

$$\begin{aligned} \min_{\Lambda_C} \quad & \sum_{(i,j)\in\mathcal{E}_{dr}} \frac{1}{l_{ij}} |A_i \cup A_j| \cdot |\lambda_i d_i - \lambda_j d_j| \\ \text{s.t} \quad & \lambda_i d^-_{ijk} \leq \lambda_j d^+_{ijk}, p_{ijk} \in P_{ij} \end{aligned} \tag{2}$$

Figure 1(g) shows the 3D surface model that results from this two-stage constrained minimization for an example image.

4 Evaluation Dataset

To evaluate the LS3D algorithm and compare against state-of-the-art, we have created a new 3D ground truth dataset of 57 urban buildings that largely conform to the Manhattan constraint. The 3D building massing models (3DBMs) were obtained through the City of Toronto Open Data project from www.toronto.ca/city-government/data-research-maps/open-data and were simplified in MeshLab [47] to speed processing. Figure 3 shows some examples.

The number of images taken of each building depended upon access and the complexity of the architecture - 118 images were taken in total. We used a Sony NEX-6 camera with 4912 × 3264 pixel resolution. The camera was calibrated using the MATLAB Camera Calibration Toolbox to determine focal length (15.7 mm) and principal point. The NEX-6 corrects for barrel distortion - our calibration procedure confirmed that it is negligible.

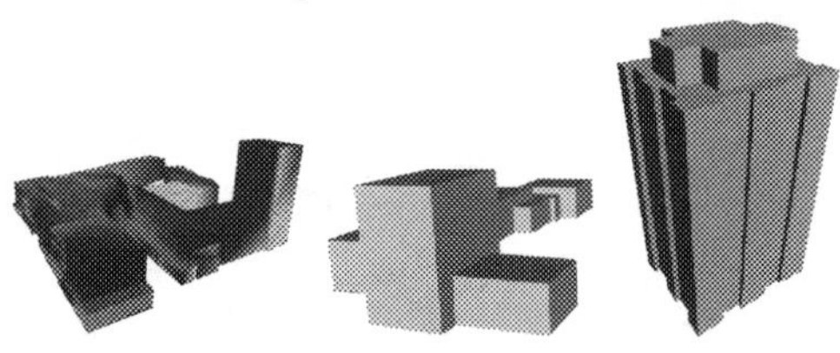

Fig. 3. Some examples of 3DBM models in our dataset.

The camera was held roughly horizontally, but no attempt was made to precisely control height, roll or tilt. We attempted to take generic views of the buildings, but the exact viewing distance and vantage depended upon access and foreground obstructions. This dataset will be made available at elderlab.yorku.ca/resources.

To use the 3DBM dataset to evaluate single-view 3D reconstruction algorithms, we need to determine the rotation $\boldsymbol{\Omega}$ and translation τ of the camera relative to each of the 3DBMs. To this end, we manually identified between 5–20 point correspondences $(\mathbf{w_i}, \mathbf{x_i})$ in the 3DBM model and the 2D image, and then used a standard nonlinear optimization method (MATLAB fmincon) to minimize projection error.

5 Evaluation

We compare LS3D against the CRF-based Make3D algorithm [30] and four state-of-the-art deep learning approaches: the multi-scale deep network of Eigen *et al.* [48], the fully convolutional residual network (FCRN) of Laina *et al.* [33], the deep ordinal regression network(DORN) of Fu *et al.* [36] and the very recent PlaneNet algorithm of Liu *et al.*[49].

The LS3D method estimates range only up to an unknown scaling factor α. Although the FCRN and DORN algorithm are trained to estimate absolute range, the Eigen algorithm is trained to minimize a partially scale-invariant loss function, and therefore should not be expected to deliver accurate absolute range estimates. Moreover, global scaling error has been reported as a significant contributor to overall error for such methods [48]. For these reasons we estimate a global scaling factor α for each algorithm and image independently by fitting the range estimates to the 3DBM ground truth. In particular, we estimate the value of α that minimizes the RMS deviation of estimated range $\hat{d}$ from ground truth range d, over all pixels that project from the 3DBM model.

The LS3D algorithm is not guaranteed to return a range estimate for every pixel that projects from the 3DBM, particularly when foliage and other objects intervene. To account for this, we employ two different methods to compare error between the LS3D and competing methods. In the *intersection* method, we measure the RMS error for all algorithms only for the intersection of the pixel set that projects from the 3DBM and the pixel set for which LS3D returns a range estimate. In the *diffusion* method, we interpolate estimates of range at 3DBM pixels for which LS3D does not return an estimate by solving Laplace's equation, with boundary conditions given by the LS3D range estimates at pixels where estimates exist and reflection boundary conditions at the frame of the image. This allows us to compare RMS error for all algorithms over all pixels projecting from the 3DBMs. The input and output resolution of each algorithm varies - our 4912×3264 pixels images were resized to meet the input requirements of each algorithm.

Qualitative results are shown in Fig. 4. Make3D and the deep networks deliver range estimates that are sometimes correlated with ground truth, but these estimates are noisy and highly regularized. They generally fail to capture the dynamic range of depths over the 3DBM surfaâce (deep red to dark blue). Moreover in some cases the estimates seem wildly inaccurate. In Column 1, for example, both versions of FCRN completely fail. In Column 2, all competing algorithms except perhaps DORN estimate the left face of the building as farther away than the right. In Column 3, all networks seem to fail. In Column 4 all networks fail to capture the receding depth of the left wall of the building.

The LS3D results are qualitatively different. The crisp architectural structure of each building is captured, along with the full dynamic range of depths. As expected, where good connectivity is achieved errors are minimal (Columns 2, 4). In Column 1 and 3, however, some limitations can be seen, stemming from the failure to extract parts of the building occluded by vegetation.

We find that on average the LS3D method returns a range estimate for 83.3% of pixels projecting from the 3DBM model. For quantitative evaluation, we first average error over all images of a particular building, and then report the mean and standard error over the 57 buildings in the dataset. Table 1 shows quantitative results based on the intersection measure of error. Of the prior algorithms, we find that PlaneNet [49] performs best, achieving a mean error of 9.35 m (23.4%). However, LS3D beats this by a substantial margin (24.6%), achieving a mean error of 7.05 m (17.7%). Matched-sample t-tests confirm that this improvement is statistically significant (Table 1). A comparison of LS3D performance with and without occlusion constraints shows that these constraints yield a substantial improvement in performance. Mean errors are somewhat higher for all methods when using the diffusion method to evaluate over all pixels projecting from the 3DBM model (Table 2). PlaneNet is again the best of the deep networks, achieving a mean error of 10.6 m (26.1%). However, LS3D beats this by 22.9%, achieving a mean error of 8.17 m (19.4%). Matched-sample t-tests again confirm that this improvement is statistically significant (Table 2).

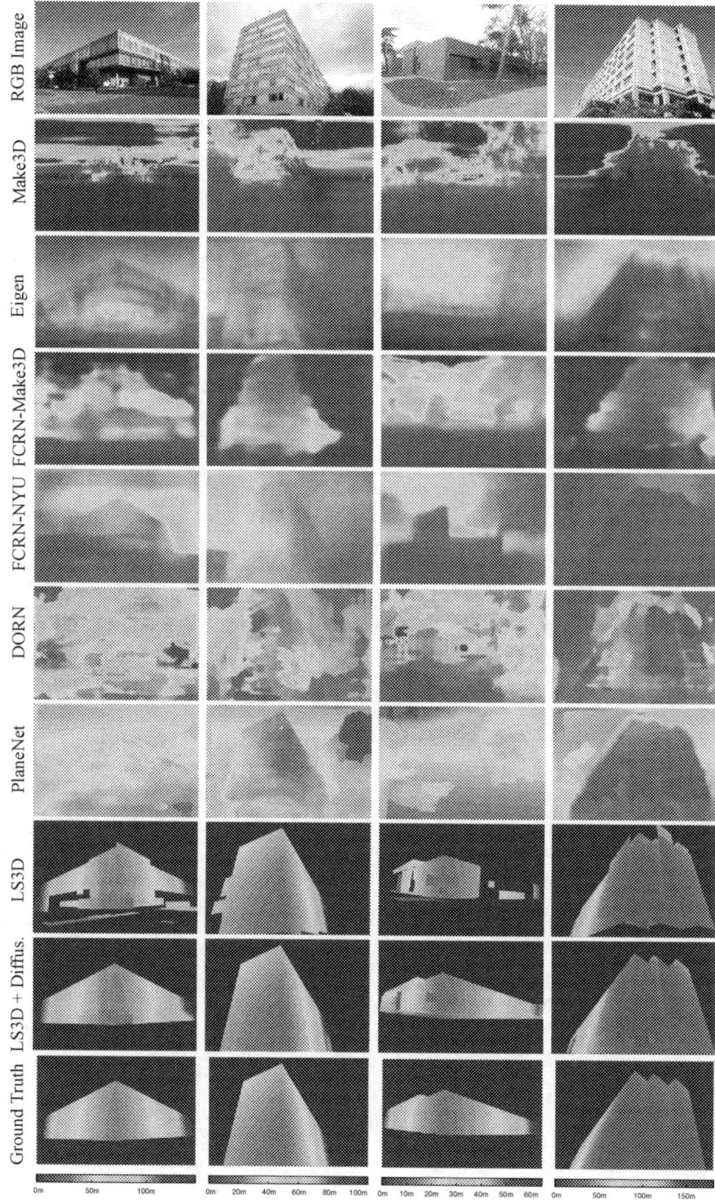

Fig. 4. Example results for Make3D [30], Eigen [48], FCRN [33], DORN [36], PlaneNet [49], and the proposed LS3D method, with and without diffusion. (Color figure online)

Our method is not intended to reconstruct an entire image or to operate on non-Manhattan structure. Nevertheless, we have evaluated its performance on the indoor $NYU2$ dataset. We achieve a mean error of 1.08 m on the subset

Table 1. Quantitative results using the intersection method of evaluation. Errors are computed only for pixels where the LS3D method returns a range estimate. p-values for matched-sample t-tests of the LS3D method (with occlusion constraint) against competing deep network algorithms are reported.

Methods	Error rate		p-value	
	RMSE (m)	RMSPE (%)	RMSE	RMSPE
Make3D [30]	25.3	63.3	7.11E−18	4.36E−30
Eigen [48]	11.9	31.4	2.59E−07	2.74E−10
FCRN(Make3D) [33]	14.1	34.9	1.40E−10	1.32E−13
FCRN(NYU) [33]	11.0	28.1	3.91E−08	1.42E−09
DORN [36]	11.5	29.0	1.23E−08	1.05E−10
planeNet [49]	9.33	24.0	8.1E−03	1.2E−03
LS3D (no occlusion constraint)	8.02	20.2	5.60E−03	3.21E−02
LS3D (with occlusion constraint)	**7.03**	**18.0**	N/A	N/A

Table 2. Quantitative results using the diffusion method of evaluation. Errors are computed for all pixels projecting from the 3DBM model. p-values for matched-sample t-tests of the LS3D method (with occlusion constraint) against competing deep network algorithms are reported.

Methods	Error rate		p-value	
	RMSE (m)	RMSPE (%)	RMSE	RMSPE
Make3D [30]	27.1	65.9%	1.72E−19	7.52E−33
Eigen [48]	13.2	34.2	2.88E−08	4.21E−12
FCRN(Make3D) [33]	15.8	38.1	1.60E−12	5.76E−16
FCRN(NYU) [33]	12.3	30.7	2.01E−09	1.64E−12
DORN [36]	13.0	31.8	5.42E−12	3.60E−13
PlaneNet [49]	10.6	26.5	1.98E−05	1.49E−04
LS3D (with occlusion constraint)	**8.11**	**19.7**	N/A	N/A

of pixels for which a range estimate is returned. This is not competitive with deep networks trained on NYU, for which mean error is on the order of 0.5–0.64 m over the entire image, but is better than Make3D (1.21 m). We believe the higher performance of deep networks on NYU2 is due to deviation from Manhattan constraints and the fact that DNNs overfit to the constant camera pose and similarity of environments in the dataset.

Figure 5(a) shows best, median and worst case performance of our LS3D algorithm on our dataset. The worst case does not actually look that bad qualitatively, but the algorithm incorrectly underestimates the depth of a small part of the building in the lower right corner of the image, and this leads to a large quantitative error.

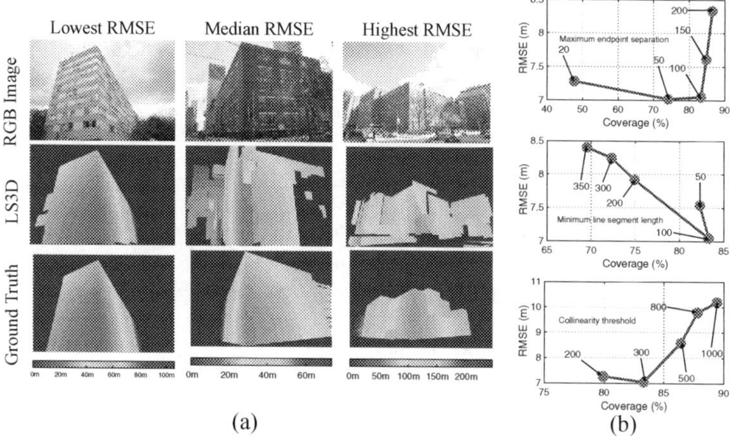

Fig. 5. (a) Best, median and worst case LS3D performance on the 3DBM dataset. (b) LS3D parameter sensitivity analysis.

LS3D has three main free parameters: (1) the minimum length of a line segment, (2) the maximum endpoint separation of connected orthogonal segments, and (3) the maximum threshold of connected collinear line segments. Both (1) and (2) are currently set to 100 pixels, and (3) is set to 300 pixels. The dependence of performance on the exact value of these parameters is shown in Fig. 5(b). This analysis shows that these threshold values are reasonable, and that variation of up to $\pm 50\%$ in threshold values leads to at most a 10% reduction in coverage and a 7% increase in error.

Our current Matlab implementation of LS3D takes about 21 s to produce a 3D model from a 640×480 image. It could be made much faster by optimizing in C++.

6 Conclusion and Future Work

We have developed a novel algorithm called LS3D for single-view 3D Manhattan reconstruction. This geometry-driven method uses no appearance cues or machine learning yet outperforms state-of-the-art deep learning methods on the problem of 3D Manhattan building reconstruction. While this algorithm is not designed to reconstruct general 3D environments, we believe it will be useful for architectural applications. Future work will explore a mixture-of-experts approach which fuses the LS3D approach to reconstructing Manhattan portions of the environment with deep learning approaches for estimating the 3D layout of non-Manhattan structure.

Acknowledgements. This research was supported by the NSERC Discovery program and the NSERC CREATE Training Program in Data Analytics & Visualization, the Ontario Research Fund, and the York University VISTA and Research Chair programs.

References

1. Coughlan, J.M., Yuille, A.L.: Manhattan world: orientation and outlier detection by Bayesian inference. Neural Comput. **15**, 1063–1088 (2003)
2. Kubovy, M., Wagemans, J.: Grouping by proximity and multistability in dot lattices: a quantitative Gestalt theory. Psychol. Sci. **6**, 225–234 (1995)
3. Kubovy, M., Holcombe, A.O., Wagemans, J.: On the lawfulness of grouping by proximity. Cogn. Psychol. **35**, 71–98 (1998)
4. Elder, J.H., Goldberg, R.M.: Ecological statistics of Gestalt laws for the perceptual organization of contours. J. Vis. **2**, 324–353 (2002)
5. Wagemans, J., et al.: A century of Gestalt psychology in visual perception: I. Perceptual grouping and figure-ground organization. Psychol. Bull. **138**, 1172 (2012)
6. Gupta, A., Efros, A.A., Hebert, M.: Blocks world revisited: image understanding using qualitative geometry and mechanics. In: Daniilidis, K., Maragos, P., Paragios, N. (eds.) ECCV 2010. LNCS, vol. 6314, pp. 482–496. Springer, Heidelberg (2010). https://doi.org/10.1007/978-3-642-15561-1_35
7. Roberts, L.G.: Machine perception of three-dimensional solids. Ph.D. thesis, Massachusetts Institute of Technology (1963)
8. Guzman, A.: Computer recognition of three-dimensional objects in a visual scene. Ph.D. thesis, MIT (1968)
9. Waltz, D.L.: Generating semantic descriptions from drawings of scenes with shadows. Technical Report AITR-271, MIT (1972)
10. Kanade, T.: A theory of Origami world. Artif. Intell. **13**, 279–311 (1980)
11. Sugihara, K.: Machine Interpretation of Line Drawings, vol. 1. MIT Press, Cambridge (1986)
12. Hoiem, D., Efros, A.A., Hebert, M.: Recovering surface layout from an image. Int. J. Comput. Vis. **75**, 151–172 (2007)
13. Barinova, O., Konushin, V., Yakubenko, A., Lee, K.C., Lim, H., Konushin, A.: Fast automatic single-view 3-D reconstruction of urban scenes. In: Forsyth, D., Torr, P., Zisserman, A. (eds.) ECCV 2008. LNCS, vol. 5303, pp. 100–113. Springer, Heidelberg (2008). https://doi.org/10.1007/978-3-540-88688-4_8
14. Haines, O., Calway, A.: Recognising planes in a single image. IEEE TPAMI **37**, 1849–1861 (2015)
15. Coughlan, J.M., Yuille, A.L.: Manhattan world: compass direction from a single image by Bayesian inference. In: CVPR, vol. 2, pp. 941–947 (1999)
16. Denis, P., Elder, J.H., Estrada, F.J.: Efficient edge-based methods for estimating Manhattan frames in urban imagery. In: Forsyth, D., Torr, P., Zisserman, A. (eds.) ECCV 2008. LNCS, vol. 5303, pp. 197–210. Springer, Heidelberg (2008). https://doi.org/10.1007/978-3-540-88688-4_15
17. Tal, R., Elder, J.H.: An accurate method for line detection and Manhattan frame estimation. In: Park, J.-I., Kim, J. (eds.) ACCV 2012. LNCS, vol. 7729, pp. 580–593. Springer, Heidelberg (2013). https://doi.org/10.1007/978-3-642-37484-5_47
18. Delage, E., Lee, H., Ng, A.Y.: Automatic single-image 3D reconstructions of indoor Manhattan world scenes. In: Thrun, S., Brooks, R., Durrant-Whyte, H. (eds.) Robotics Research. STAR, vol. 28, pp. 305–321. Springer, Heidelberg (2007). https://doi.org/10.1007/978-3-540-48113-3_28

19. Hedau, V., Hoiem, D., Forsyth, D.: Recovering the spatial layout of cluttered rooms. In: ICCV, pp. 1849–1856 (2009)
20. Gupta, A., Hebert, M., Kanade, T., Blei, D.M.: Estimating spatial layout of rooms using volumetric reasoning about objects and surfaces. In: Lafferty, J.D., Williams, C.K.I., Shawe-Taylor, J., Zemel, R.S., Culotta, A. (eds.) NIPS. Curran Associates, Inc. (2010)
21. Ramalingam, S., Pillai, J.K., Jain, A., Taguchi, Y.: Manhattan junction catalogue for spatial reasoning of indoor scenes. In: CVPR 2013, pp. 3065–3072 (2013)
22. Mallya, A., Lazebnik, S.: Learning informative edge maps for indoor scene layout prediction. In: ICCV, pp. 936–944 (2015)
23. Pero, L.D., Bowdish, J., Fried, D., Kermgard, B., Hartley, E., Barnard, K.: Bayesian geometric modeling of indoor scenes. In: CVPR, pp. 2719–2726 (2012)
24. Felzenszwalb, P.F., Veksler, O.: Tiered scene labeling with dynamic programming. In: CVPR, pp. 3097–3104 (2010)
25. Schwing, A.G., Urtasun, R.: Efficient exact inference for 3D indoor scene understanding. In: Fitzgibbon, A., Lazebnik, S., Perona, P., Sato, Y., Schmid, C. (eds.) ECCV 2012. LNCS, vol. 7577, pp. 299–313. Springer, Heidelberg (2012). https://doi.org/10.1007/978-3-642-33783-3_22
26. Yang, H., Zhang, H.: Efficient 3D room shape recovery from a single panorama. In: CVPR, pp. 5422–5430 (2016)
27. Dasgupta, S., Fang, K., Chen, K., Savarese, S.: Delay: robust spatial layout estimation for cluttered indoor scenes. In: CVPR, pp. 616–624 (2016)
28. Ramalingam, S., Brand, M.: Lifting 3D Manhattan lines from a single image. In: ICCV, pp. 497–504 (2013)
29. Kushal, A., Seitz, S.M.: Single view reconstruction of piecewise swept surfaces. In: 3DV, pp. 239–246 (2013)
30. Saxena, A., Sun, M., Ng, A.Y.: Make3D: learning 3D scene structure from a single still image. IEEE TPAMI **31**, 824–840 (2009)
31. Eigen, D., Fergus, R.: Predicting depth, surface normals and semantic labels with a common multi-scale convolutional architecture. In: CVPR, pp. 2650–2658 (2015)
32. Liu, F., Shen, C., Lin, G., Reid, I.: Learning depth from single monocular images using deep convolutional neural fields. IEEE TPAMI **38**, 2024–2039 (2016)
33. Laina, I., Rupprecht, C., Belagiannis, V., Tombari, F., Navab, N.: Deeper depth prediction with fully convolutional residual networks. In: 3DV, pp. 239–248 (2016)
34. Liu, F., Shen, C., Lin, G.: Deep convolutional neural fields for depth estimation from a single image. In: CVPR, pp. 5162–5170 (2015)
35. Zhuo, W., Salzmann, M., He, X., Liu, M.: 3D box proposals from a single monocular image of an indoor scene. In: AAAI (2018)
36. Fu, H., Gong, M., Wang, C., Batmanghelich, K., Tao, D.: Deep ordinal regression network for monocular depth estimation. In: CVPR (2018)
37. Xu, D., Ouyang, W., Wang, X., Sebe, N.: PAD-Net: multi-tasks guided prediction-and-distillation network for simultaneous depth estimation and scene parsing. In: CVPR (2018)
38. Qi, X., Liao, R., Liu, Z., Urtasun, R., Jia, J.: GeoNet: geometric neural network for joint depth and surface normal estimation. In: CVPR (2018)
39. Li, Z., Snavely, N.: MegaDepth: learning single-view depth prediction from internet photos. In: CVPR (2018)
40. Geiger, A., Lenz, P., Stiller, C., Urtasun, R.: Vision meets robotics: the KITTI dataset. Int. J. Rob. Res. **32**, 1231–1237 (2013)

41. Garg, R., B.G., V.K., Carneiro, G., Reid, I.: Unsupervised CNN for single view depth estimation: geometry to the rescue. In: Leibe, B., Matas, J., Sebe, N., Welling, M. (eds.) ECCV 2016. LNCS, vol. 9912, pp. 740–756. Springer, Cham (2016). https://doi.org/10.1007/978-3-319-46484-8_45
42. Zhou, T., Brown, M., Snavely, N., Lowe, D.G.: Unsupervised learning of depth and ego-motion from video. In: CVPR (2017)
43. Izadinia, H., Shan, Q., Seitz, S.M.: IM2CAD. In: CVPR, pp. 2422–2431. IEEE (2017)
44. Almazan, E.J., Tal, R., Qian, Y., Elder, J.H.: MCMLSD: a dynamic programming approach to line segment detection. In: CVPR (2017)
45. Lee, D., Hebert, M., Kanade, T.: Geometric reasoning for single image structure recovery. In: CVPR, pp. 2136–2143. IEEE (2009)
46. Munkres, J.: Algorithms for the assignment and transportation problems. J. Soc. Ind. Appl. Math. **5**, 32–38 (1957)
47. Cignoni, P., Callieri, M., Corsini, M., Dellepiane, M., Ganovelli, F., Ranzuglia, G.: MeshLab: an open-source mesh processing tool. In: Eurographics Italian Chapter Conference (2008)
48. Eigen, D., Puhrsch, C., Fergus, R.: Depth map prediction from a single image using a multi-scale deep network. In: NIPS, pp. 2366–2374 (2014)
49. Liu, C., Yang, J., Ceylan, D., Yumer, E., Furukawa, Y.: PlaneNet: piece-wise planar reconstruction from a single RGB image. In: CVPR, pp. 2579–2588 (2018)

Deep Supervised Hashing with Spherical Embedding

Stanislav Pidhorskyi[1(✉)], Quinn Jones[1], Saeid Motiian[2], Donald Adjeroh[1], and Gianfranco Doretto[1]

[1] Lane Department of Computer Science and Electrical Engineering, West Virginia University, Morgantown, WV 26508, USA
{stpidhorskyi,qjones1,daadjeroh,gidoretto}@mix.wvu.edu
[2] Adobe Applied Research, San Francisco, CA 94103, USA
motiian@adobe.com

Abstract. Deep hashing approaches are widely applied to approximate nearest neighbor search for large-scale image retrieval. We propose Spherical Deep Supervised Hashing (SDSH), a new supervised deep hashing approach to learn compact binary codes. The goal of SDSH is to go beyond learning similarity preserving codes, by encouraging them to also be balanced and to maximize the mean average precision. This is enabled by advocating the use of a different relaxation method, allowing the learning of a spherical embedding, which overcomes the challenge of maintaining the learning problem well-posed without the need to add extra binarizing priors. This allows the formulation of a general triplet loss framework, with the introduction of the spring loss for learning balanced codes, and of the ability to learn an embedding quantization that maximizes the mean average precision. Extensive experiments demonstrate that the approach compares favorably with the state-of-the-art while providing significant performance increase at more compact code sizes.

1 Introduction

Indexing and searching large-scale image databases leverage heavily hashing based approximate nearest neighbor search technology. The goal of hashing is to map high dimensional data, such as images, into compact codes in a way that visually, or semantically similar images are mapped into similar codes, according to the Hamming distance. Given a query image, hierarchically structured based methods can then be used for the rapid retrieval of the neighbors within a certain distance from the query [1].

Recent data-dependent methods for hashing images (as opposed to data-independent methods [12]) leverage deep neural networks due to their ability

Electronic supplementary material The online version of this chapter (https://doi.org/10.1007/978-3-030-20870-7_26) contains supplementary material, which is available to authorized users.

C. V. Jawahar et al. (Eds.): ACCV 2018, LNCS 11364, pp. 417–434, 2019.
https://doi.org/10.1007/978-3-030-20870-7_26

to integrate the image feature representation learning with the objective of the hashing task [3,9,21,42,45], leading to a superior efficiency and compactness of the codes. However, so far the focus of these approaches has been on designing architectures only with the similarity preserving goal of mapping similar images to similar codes. On the other hand, hashing methods based on hand-crafted image features [28], have improved performance also by requiring codes to have certain properties, for example, to be balanced, uncorrelated, or to be obtained with a small quantization error [13,25,26,30,36,39,44].

Balanced codes are such that bits partition data in equal portions [39,44]. It is a desirable property because it increases the variance of bits since they approach 50% chance of being one or zero. Also code bits that are uncorrelated, or even better independent, increase their information content. In addition, learning hash functions generally require solving intractable optimization problems that are made tractable with the continuous relaxation of the codomain of the function. This means that quantization is required to discretize the continuous embedding into codes, and controlling the quantization error has been shown to improve performance [13].

In this work, we propose a deep supervised hashing approach that goes beyond similarity preserving, and that aims at learning hashing functions that map onto codes with good quality, by encouraging them to be *balanced*, and to *maximize the mean average precision.* We do so by advocating the use of a different continuous relaxation strategy that has several advantages, into overcome the challenge of maintaining the learning problem well-posed, without the addition of costly priors that typically encourage a binary output, and that have led deep hashing approaches to focus, so far, only on similarity preserving codes. This approach allows learning a hashing function composed of a *spherical embedding* followed by an optimal *quantization.* Specifically, the embedding is based on a convolutional neural network, learned with a triplet loss framework [34], that has the advantage of being more general, because it allows the use of different triplet losses, and it allows introducing a new *triplet spring loss* that aims at learning balanced codes. Moreover, the loss framework is rotation invariant in the embedded space, which allows optimizing the quantization for a rotation that provides the highest mean average precision. We call the resulting model *Spherical Deep Supervised Hashing (SDSH)*, and provides state-of-the-art performance on standard benchmarks, including a significantly greater performance at more compact code dimensions.

2 Related Work

The existing variety of data-dependent, learning based hashing methods can be categorized into unsupervised and supervised methods [40].

Unsupervised methods [11,13,15,16,19,20,27,44] use unlabeled data to learn a hashing function that preserves some metric distance between data points. This work instead falls into the supervised category, which tries to improve the quality of hashing by leveraging label information to learn compact codes. Supervised

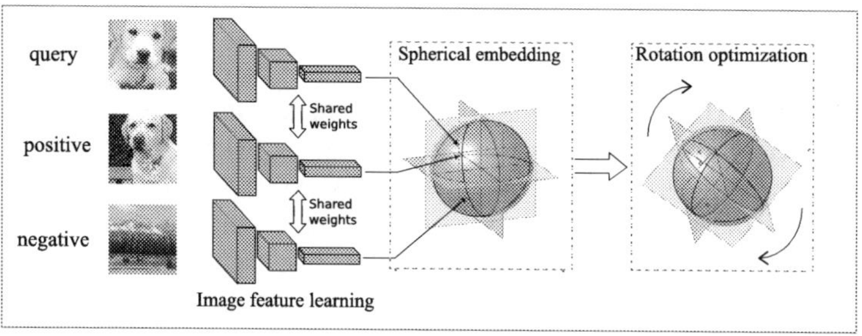

Fig. 1. Overview. Overview of the approach, highlighting the stages of the hash embedding learning, and the optimal quantization.

methods can be divided into those which use off-the-shelf visual features versus those that leverage deep networks. Representative examples of non-deep methods include Minimal Loss Hashing (MLH) [31], Supervised Hashing with Kernels (KSH) [26] and Latent Factor Hashing (LFH) [46].

The initial attempts to utilize deep learning [18,37,38,41] for hashing included CNNH [45] and DNNH [21]. Deep Hashing Network (DHN) [50] and Deep Supervised Hashing (DSH) [24] extend DNNH by performing a continuous relaxation of the intractable discrete optimization by introducing a quantization error prior which is controlled by a quantization loss. DHN uses a cross entropy loss to link the pairwise Hamming distances with the pairwise similarity labels, while DSH uses max-margin loss. Deep Cauchy Hashing (DCH) [2] improves DHN by utilizing Cauchy distribution. Deep Pairwise-Supervised Hashing (DPSH) [23] uses pairwise similarity labels and a loss-function similar to LFH, which maximizes the log-likelihood of the pairwise similarities. The log-likelihood is modeled as a function of the Hamming distance between the corresponding data points. Deep Triplet-Supervised Hashing (DTSH) [42] extends DPSH by using triplet label information.

The learning problem of deep hashing methods (DHN, DSH, DPSH, DTSH, etc.) turns out to be NP-complete, due to the discrete nature of the codomain of the hash function being sought, which is the Hamming space. The workaround is to relax the native space into the continuous Euclidean counterpart. This makes the original learning problem ill-posed, and a regularizing prior becomes necessary, which is often chosen to encourage the sought mapping to produce a nearly binary output. While needed, such prior complicates the training and might lead to performance reduction. Discrepancy Minimizing Deep Hashing (DMDH) [7] suggests an alternating optimization approach with a series expansion of the objective. Our work instead, leverages a different relaxation, which has the advantage of maintaining a well-posed learning problem, without the need for extra priors. Besides the obvious computational advantage, the framework allows to identify a class of triplet losses, and to define new ones, tailored to seeking good hash functions.

Another line of work, like Deep Quantization Network (DQN) [4], avoid the use of relaxation by incorporating quantization methods into the approach [10,43,48]. DQN performs a joint learning of image representations and a product quantization for generating compact binary codes. Deep Visual-Semantic Quantization (DVSQ) [3] extends DQN by adding semantic knowledge extracted from the label space. In this way, hash codes are directly optimized. While being an interesting direction, it significantly increases the complexity of the learning process. Indeed, that might be one of the contributing factors that make our approach comparing favorably against those.

Finally, our approach also considers the quantization problem. Indeed, the proposed relaxation suggests learning a spherical embedding, which is an equivalence class of solutions, because the loss turns out to be rotation invariant with respect to the embedded spherical space. This allows picking, as a solution, a representative of the class that will affect the quantization of the spherical embedding in such a way that it directly maximizes the mean average precision. This is different from previous approaches, and it is different also from approaches like Iterative Quantization (ITQ) [13], which is unsupervised, and it aims at minimizing the quantization error. Our comparison with ITQ shows that linking the quantization directly to the retrieval metric leads to better solutions.

3 Problem Overview

Given a training set of N images $\mathcal{I} = \{I_1, \cdots, I_N\}$, with labels $\mathcal{Y} = \{y_1, \cdots, y_N\}$, we are interested in learning a *hash function* h that maps an image I onto a compact binary code $\mathbf{b} = h(I) \in \{+1, -1\}^B$ of length B. The typical approach based on deep learning assumes that given three images I_i, I_j, I_k, with labels y_i, y_j, y_k, such that $y_i = y_j$, and $y_i \neq y_k$, then the hash function should be such that the corresponding binary codes $\mathbf{b}_i$ and $\mathbf{b}_j$ should be close, while $\mathbf{b}_i$ and $\mathbf{b}_k$ should be far away in the Hamming space. If $d_H(\cdot, \cdot)$ indicates the Hamming distance, this means that $d_H(\mathbf{b}_i, \mathbf{b}_j)$ should be as small as possible, while $d_H(\mathbf{b}_i, \mathbf{b}_k)$ should be as large as possible.

In addition to that, ideally, we would want to encourage hash codes to be maximally informative, where bits are independent and balanced, and to ultimately maximize the mean average precision (mAP). These aspects have been of secondary importance thus far, because deep learning approaches have to use binarizing priors to regularize loss functions that are already computationally intensive to optimize.

We overcome the major hurdle of the binarizing prior by advocating the use of a different relaxation method, which does not require additional priors, and learns a *spherical embedding*. This modeling choice has ripple effects. Besides simplifying the learning by eliminating the binarizing prior, it enables a unified formulation of a class of triplet losses [34] that are *rotation invariant*, and it allows to introduce one, which we name *spring loss*, that encourages balanced hash codes. In addition, the rotation invariance allows us to look for a rotation of

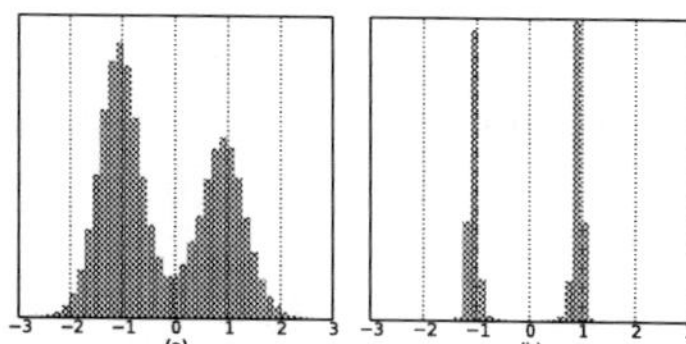

Fig. 2. Embedding distribution. Bimodal distribution of the hash embedding components (a) early on during training, and (b) at advanced training stage, when modes are separated.

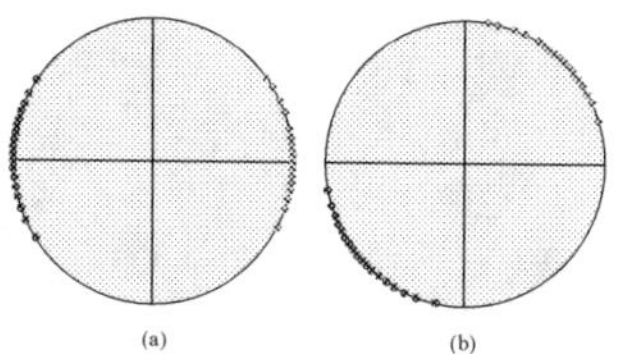

Fig. 3. Quantization. (a) Distribution of hash embeddings on the unit circle for two classes. The sign quantization assigns different hash codes to samples in the same class. (b) Rotated distribution of hash embeddings. The sign quantization assigns same hash codes to samples in the same class, thus increasing the mAP.

the embedding hypersphere that leads to its optimal *quantization* for producing hash codes that directly maximize the retrieval mAP. This two-stage approach is depicted in Fig. 1.

4 Hash Function Learning

The desired hash function should ensure that the code $\mathbf{b}_i$ of image I_i would be closer to all other codes $\mathbf{b}_j$ of I_j because $y_i = y_j$, than it would be to any code $\mathbf{b}_k$ of I_k since $y_i \neq y_k$. Therefore, if $\mathcal{T} = \{(i,j,k)|y_i = y_j \neq y_k\}$ is the set of the allowed triplet labels, then we certainly desire this condition to be verified

$$d_H(\mathbf{b}_i, \mathbf{b}_j) < d_H(\mathbf{b}_i, \mathbf{b}_k) \quad \forall (i,j,k) \in \mathcal{T}. \tag{1}$$

A loss function that aims at achieving condition (1) could simply be written as

$$L(h) = \sum_{(i,j,k)\in\mathcal{T}} \ell(d_H(\mathbf{b}_i, \mathbf{b}_j) - d_H(\mathbf{b}_i, \mathbf{b}_k)) \tag{2}$$

where $\ell(\cdot) : \mathbb{R} \to [0, +\infty)$ is the cost for a triplet that does not satisfy (1). Equation (2) is a more general version of the well known triplet loss [34].

As pointed out in [42], it is easy to realize that

$$d_H(\mathbf{b}_i, \mathbf{b}_j) - d_H(\mathbf{b}_i, \mathbf{b}_k) = \frac{1}{2}\mathbf{b}_i^\top \mathbf{b}_k - \frac{1}{2}\mathbf{b}_i^\top \mathbf{b}_j. \tag{3}$$

In particular, the Hamming space where codes are defined, and through which depends the estimation of the hash function h, makes the optimization of (2) intractable [23]. Therefore, the typical approach is to relax the domain of $\mathbf{b}$ from the Hamming space to the continuous space $\mathbb{R}^B$ [23, 42]. However, this method has severe drawbacks. The first and most important one is that optimizing (2) becomes an ill-posed problem, with trivial solutions corresponding to pulling infinitely apart relaxed codes with label mismatch. This forces the introduction of a regularizing prior to the loss, which typically is designed to encourage the relaxed code $\tilde{\mathbf{b}}$ to be also "as binary as possible", or in other words, to stay close to one of the vertices of the Hamming space.

Computationally, adding a prior is a major setback because it increases the number of hyperparameters at best, with all the consequences. In addition, if we look at the distribution of the values of the components of $\tilde{\mathbf{b}}$, we have observed experimentally that as the two main modes around $+1$ and -1 become separated, the corresponding hash codes, obtained simply by taking $\mathbf{b} = \text{sgn}(\tilde{\mathbf{b}})$, stop changing during the training procedure. See Fig. 2. This "locking" behavior might prevent from learning a hash function that could potentially be more efficient if it still had room to adjust the outputs. Finally, we note that (3) does not hold in the relaxed space, meaning that

$$\left\| \frac{\tilde{\mathbf{b}}_i - \tilde{\mathbf{b}}_j}{2} \right\|^2 - \left\| \frac{\tilde{\mathbf{b}}_i - \tilde{\mathbf{b}}_k}{2} \right\|^2 \neq \frac{1}{2}\tilde{\mathbf{b}}_i^\top \tilde{\mathbf{b}}_k - \frac{1}{2}\tilde{\mathbf{b}}_i^\top \tilde{\mathbf{b}}_j . \tag{4}$$

even though there are approaches that rely on the left-hand-side of (4) being approximately equal to the right-hand-side [42].

The following section addresses the drawbacks outlined above by advocating the use of a different relaxation for hash function learning.

5 Spherical Embedding

The hash function learning problem can be summarized as learning a function $\tilde{h}$ such that $h(I) = \text{sgn}[\tilde{h}(I)]$, where $\tilde{h}$ optimizes a relaxed version of (2). Differently from previous hashing work, we propose to use a relaxation where $\tilde{h}$ is a *spherical embedding*, meaning that we constrain the output $\mathbf{s} = \tilde{h}(I)$ to be defined on the $(B-1)$-dimensional unit sphere. This means that, using the previous notation, $\mathbf{s} \doteq \tilde{\mathbf{b}}/\|\tilde{\mathbf{b}}\|$, and the meaning of Eqs. (1), (2), and (3) remain valid by simply substituting $\mathbf{b}$ with $\mathbf{s}$, and $d_H(\mathbf{b_i}, \mathbf{b_j})$ with $\|(\mathbf{s}_i - \mathbf{s}_j)/2\|^2$. Therefore, we advocate the end-to-end learning of a function $\tilde{h}$, given by minimizing the loss

$$L(\tilde{h}) = \sum_{(i,j,k) \in \mathcal{T}} \ell(\mathbf{s}_i^\top \mathbf{s}_k - \mathbf{s}_i^\top \mathbf{s}_j). \tag{5}$$

This approach, also used in [34] to regularize the spreading of the embedding, is leveraged here to address the limitations of the continuous relaxation described in Sect. 4. Indeed, a spherical embedding makes the optimization of the relaxed version of (2) (which is (5)) a well-posed problem, and this was the main reason why previous works required a regularizing prior. In addition, previous priors encouraged the embedding space to be "as binary as possible" by moving $\tilde{\mathbf{b}}$ closer to a vertex of the Hamming cube, without direct evidence that this was producing better hash codes. On the other hand, we observed this practice to encourage a "locking" behavior, which we do not have with the spherical embedding because there are no forces pushing towards the Hamming cube, and $\mathbf{s}$ is free to move on the unit sphere. Moreover, if $\tilde{h}$ is an optimal spherical embedding, so is $R\tilde{h}$, where R is a rotation matrix, since it still minimizes (5). Therefore, since (5) is *rotation invariant*, $\tilde{h}$ is found modulo a rotation, which can be estimated at a later stage to optimize other hash code properties (Sect. 6).

In Sect. 7 we design different triplet loss functions $\ell(\cdot)$, leading to different spherical embeddings. In practice, the spherical embedding comprises a convolutional neural network with a number of layers aiming at learning visual features from images, followed by fully connected layers with an output dimension equal to the number of bits B of the hash code. We adopt the VGG-F architecture [5], and replace the last fully connected layer, but other architectures can also be used [14,18].

6 Quantization

Given an image I, its hash code is computed with a *sign quantization* as $\mathbf{b} = \text{sgn}(\tilde{h}(I))$. Since $\tilde{h}$ minimizes (5), we observed that also a rotated version $R\tilde{h}$ does, so it is important to analyze the difference between the two solutions. Figure 3(a) shows a case where the spherical embeddings of two classes along the unit circle are such that the sign quantization assigns different hash codes to samples of the same class. Therefore, a rotation R could be applied to the embeddings as in Fig. 3(b), where the sign quantization would now produce the expected results.

We propose to use the extra degrees of freedom due to the *rotation invariance* of (5) for learning a rotation matrix R that finds the quantization that produces the best hash function. We do so by estimating the rotation R that maximizes the mean average precision (mAP), which is the metric that we value the most for retrieval

$$\hat{R} = \arg\max_{R} \text{mAP}(R). \tag{6}$$

Since mAP$(\cdot)$ is not a smooth function, and has zero gradient almost everywhere, (6) is not easy to optimize, even with derivative-free methods. On the other hand, we found that a standard random search optimization with a linear annealing schedule allows to achieve good results quickly. At the i-th iteration we apply a random perturbation $Q^{(i)}$ to the current rotation matrix $R^{(i)}$ to obtain the update $R^{(i+1)} = Q^{(i)}R^{(i)}$, which we retain if it improves the mAP. Since the perturbation should be random, uniform, and with a controllable magnitude, we generate it by setting $Q^{(i)} = P^{(i)}E(\theta){P^{(i)}}^{\top}$, where $P^{(i)}$ is a random unitary matrix, generated with a simplified approach based on the SVD decomposition of a matrix with normally sampled elements [29,32]. $E(\theta)$ instead represents a rotation by θ on the plane identified by the first two basis vectors. The angle θ defines the perturbation magnitude and varies linearly with the iteration number, starting with $\theta_0 = 1.0$ down to 0 when the maximum number of iterations is reached, which was 800 in our experiments. Algorithm 1 summarizes the steps. We compute the mAP with a C++ implementation, where we take 1000 samples from the training set as queries and 16000 samples as database, or a smaller

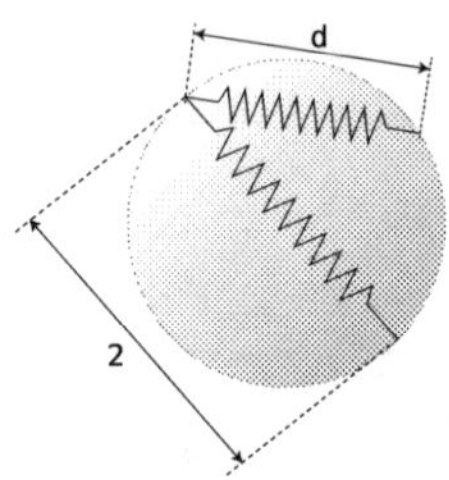

Fig. 4. Spring loss. Unit sphere where two points with different class labels are pulled apart by an elastic force proportional to the displacement $2 - d$, while constrained to remain on the sphere.

number if the training set is smaller. With a PC workstation with CPU Core i7 5820K 3.30 GHz the running time for one iteration update is around 0.4 s, keeping the time for the random search optimization very small, if compared with the time for training the deep network of the spherical embedding.

We now note that if R is an optimal solution, by swapping two columns of R we obtain a new solution, corresponding to swapping two bits in all hash codes. Since there are $B!$ of these kind of changes, it means that the order of growth of the solution space is $O(B!)$. Therefore, as B increases, estimating R according to (6) becomes less important because the likelihood that a random R is not far from an optimal solution has increased accordingly. The experimental section supports this observation.

7 Triplet Spherical Loss

In this section we give three examples of *rotation invariant* triplet loss ℓ that can be used in (5), namely the *margin loss*, the *label likelihood loss*, and the new *spring loss*. To shorten the notation, we define the quantity $d_{i,j,k} \doteq \mathbf{s}_i^\top \mathbf{s}_k - \mathbf{s}_i^\top \mathbf{s}_j$.

7.1 Margin Loss

The first loss that we consider is well known, and stems from requiring condition (1) to be verified with a certain margin α, in combination with using the standard hinge loss. This translates into the following *margin loss*

$$\ell(d_{i,j,k}) = \max\{0, d_{i,j,k} + \alpha\}. \tag{7}$$

7.2 Label Likelihood Loss

The second loss has been originally proposed in [42], where it was used with the Hamming space relaxed into the continuous space $\mathbb{R}^B$ for learning a hashing function. Here we extend it for learning a spherical embedding. The loss is derived

```
Result: Returns the optimal matrix R according to a random search
R^(0) = I;
i = 0 ;
while i < number of iterations do
    // f(i) is a linear annealing schedule to update the rotation
       magnitude
    θ^(i) ← f(i); E^(i) ← E(θ^(i)); P^(i) ← random unitary matrix ;
    Q^(i) ← P^(i) E^(i) P^(i)^⊤ ; R' ← Q^(i) R^(i);
    if mAP(R') > mAP(R^(i)) then
        R^(i+1) ← R';
    else
        R^(i+1) ← R^(i);
    end
    i ← i + 1;
end
return R^i
```

Algorithm 1. Random search for the optimal rotation R.

from a probabilistic formulation of the likelihood of the triplet labels $\mathcal{T}$, where triplets that verify condition (1) by bigger margins have a bigger likelihood, and where the margin parameter α can affect the speed of the training process. This *label likelihood loss*, adapted to our framework becomes

$$\ell(d_{i,j,k}) = d_{i,j,k} + \alpha + \log(1 + e^{-d_{i,j,k} - \alpha}). \tag{8}$$

7.3 Spring Loss

While both the margin loss and the label likelihood loss produce remarkable results, none of them make explicit efforts towards clustering samples in the spherical embedding space, according to their classes, and in a way that classes cover the sphere in a spatially uniform manner. This last property is very important because if we assume an equal number of samples per class, for each bit b, balanced codes satisfy the property

$$\sum_{i=1}^{N} h_b(I_i) = 0, \quad b = 1, \cdots, B. \tag{9}$$

Therefore, we note that condition (9) is satisfied whenever the spherical embedding distributes the classes uniformly on the unit sphere, thus producing balanced codes, where code bits have higher variance and are more informative. This has motivated the design of the loss that we introduce.

Let us consider two points $\mathbf{s}_i$ and $\mathbf{s}_k$ on the $(B-1)$-dimensional sphere of unit radius, and let us assume that a spring is connecting them. The Euclidean distance $d = \|\mathbf{s}_i - \mathbf{s}_k\| \doteq \sqrt{d_{i,k}}$, between the points varies in the range $[0, 2]$. At distance 2, we consider the spring unstretched, while at distance $d < 2$,

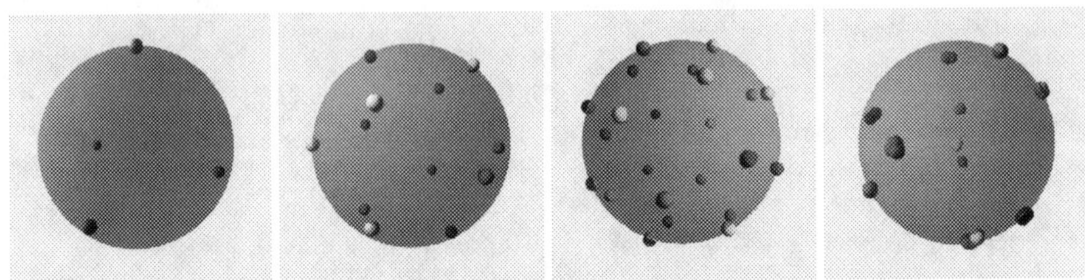

Fig. 5. Regular polyhedrons. Three left-most images: Three unit spheres with $5 \times n$ points at minimum elastic potential, where n is the number of classes. From left to right n is equal to 4, 12, 24. The 5 points per class coincide with the class centroid at equilibrium. Right-most image: For $n = 12$, the points at minimum margin loss do not reach a uniform distribution on the sphere.

the spring will have accumulated an elastic potential energy proportional to $(2-d)^2$. See Fig. 4. This suggests that we could train the hash embedding by minimizing (5), with $\ell(d_{i,k}) = (2 - \sqrt{d_{i,k}})^2$, where we would limit the summation to the pairs $(i,k) \in \mathcal{Q} = \{(i,j) | y_i \neq y_j\}$. In this way, the training would aim at minimizing the total elastic potential energy of the system of springs. The effect is that samples from different classes would be mapped on the sphere, but as far apart as possible. We note that minimizing this loss is equivalent to solving a first order linear approximation to the Thomson's Problem [35], which concerns the determination of the minimum electrostatic potential energy configuration of N electrons, constrained to the surface of a unit sphere. The solution has been rigorously identified in only a handful of cases, which mostly correspond to spatial configurations forming regular polyhedrons, which we have observed also in our simulations using the spring loss described before, as it can be seen in Fig. 5. If we were to perform a Voronoi tessellation on the sphere based on the class centroids, we clearly would obtain a pretty uniform partition of the sphere, which is our main goal. For comparison, the right-most image in Fig. 5 is obtained with the margin loss, which stops pulling apart query and negative samples once they are more far apart than the margin. This leads to a less uniform distribution of the classes.

We have experimented with the loss described above and indeed, it provides fairly good results. However, we argue that it can be improved because it does not explicitly pull closer samples that belong to the same class, besides pulling apart samples with different labels. We address that issue with the *triplet spring loss*, which we define as follows

$$\ell(d_{i,j,k}) = (2 - \sqrt{2 - d_{i,j,k}})^2. \tag{10}$$

Note that $d_{i,j,k}$ varies in the range $[-2,2]$, thus the square root varies in the range $[0,2]$, and the loss varies in the range $[0,4]$. The loss is minimized when $d_{i,j,k}$ approaches -2. Since $d_{i,j,k}$ is proportional to $\|\mathbf{s}_i - \mathbf{s}_j\|^2 - \|\mathbf{s}_i - \mathbf{s}_k\|^2$, convergence is approached by maximally pulling closer $\mathbf{s}_i$ and $\mathbf{s}_j$, while maximally pushing apart $\mathbf{s}_i$ and $\mathbf{s}_k$. Note that, differently than before, now even when $\mathbf{s}_i$ and $\mathbf{s}_k$ have reached a distance of 2, the loss still works to pull $\mathbf{s}_i$ and $\mathbf{s}_j$ closer.

8 Experiments

We tested our approach on the most relevant datasets for deep hashing applications, namely *CIFAR-10* [17], *NUS_WIDE* [8], and we also tested on *MNIST* [22] to compare with some older methods. For each experimental setting, we report the average mAP score over 5 runs for comparison against the previous works for hashes of size as low as 4 and up to 48 bits.

8.1 Experimental Setup

Similar to other deep hashing methods we use raw image pixels as input. Following [23,42,49], for the spherical embedding we adopt VGG-F [6] pre-trained on ImageNet. We replace the last layer with our own, initialized with normal distribution. The output layer doesn't have activation function and the number of outputs matches the needed number of bits - B. The input layer of VGG-F is 224×224, so we crop and resize images of the *NUS_WIDE* dataset and upsample images of the *CIFAR-10* dataset to match the input size.

CIFAR-10: CIFAR-10 [17] is a publicly available dataset of small images of size 32×32 which have each been labeled to one of ten classes. Each class is represented by 6,000 images for a total of 60,000 available samples. In terms of evaluation in the CIFAR domain, two images are counted as relevant to each other if their labels match. In order for our experiments to be comparable to as many works as possible, including [42] and [3], we use two different experimental settings, which are labeled "Full" and "Reduced".

"Full" Setting: For this setting, 1,000 images are first selected randomly from each class of the dataset to make up the test images. Which, by extension, results in 10,000 query images. The remaining 50,000 images are used as the database images and as the images used in training.

"Reduced" Setting: For this setting, 100 images are selected randomly from each class for use as 1,000 total test images. From the remaining 59,000 samples we randomly sample 500 images per category to form the reduced training set with only 5,000 images. The database is composed of all 59,000 samples which were not selected for testing.

The mAP for CIFAR-10, full and reduced setting, is computed based on all samples from the database set. We have used for training purposes a system with only one NVIDIA Titan X GPU, in this configuration training takes about four hours for the Cifar Full setting.

NUS_WIDE: NUS_WIDE [8] is another publicly available dataset, but unlike CIFAR-10 each sample image is multi-labeled from a set of 81 possible labels across all 269,643. This is reduced slightly, as [42] and [3] have also done in their

Table 1. Mean average precision (MAP) results for different number of bits of CIFAR-10: In the case of DTSH and DVSQ we have filled some additional results which were not presented by the original papers by using the authors' respective released source code to replicate their experiments such that we may compare with them across more hash sizes.

	CIFAR-10 Full setting: Number of Bits							CIFAR-10 Reduced setting: Number of Bits						
Method	4	8	12	16	24	32	48	4	8	12	16	24	32	48
DQN[4]	-	-	-	-	-	-	-	-	-	0.554	-	0.558	0.564	0.580
DSH[24]	-	-	0.616	-	0.651	0.661	0.676	-	-	-	-	-	-	-
DPSH[23]	-	-	0.763	-	0.781	0.795	0.807	-	-	0.763	-	0.727	0.744	0.757
DMDH [7]	-	-	-	-	-	-	-	-	-	-	0.704	-	0.719	0.732
DTSH[42]	-	0.814	0.859	0.915	0.923	0.925	0.926	-	0.641	0.710	0.723	0.750	0.765	0.774
DVSQ[3]	-	0.839	-	0.839	0.843	0.840	0.842	-	**0.715**	-	0.727	0.730	0.733	0.764
BL[33]	0.870							-						
SDSH-ML	-	0.839	0.882	0.886	0.939	0.880	0.878	-	0.657	0.712	0.756	0.747	0.765	0.764
SDSH-LL	0.481	0.763	0.854	**0.942**	**0.945**	**0.944**	**0.947**	0.407	0.673	**0.757**	0.782	0.799	**0.815**	**0.822**
SDSH-S	**0.755**	**0.911**	**0.939**	0.938	0.939	0.939	0.934	**0.569**	0.697	0.723	**0.783**	**0.801**	0.810	0.813

experiments, by first removing every image which does not have any of the 21 most common labels associated with it. This is done as many of the less common labels have very few samples associated with them, but prepared in this way each of the 21 labels are represented by at least 5,000 samples. In terms of evaluation in the NUS_WIDE domain two images are counted as relevant to each other if any of their labels match. Note, that despite the usage of samples associated with the 21 most frequent labels, all 81 labels are used for determining similarity between samples. To compare with previous work we use three different settings, labeled "Full", "Reduced A", and "Reduced B".

"Full" Setting: For this setting, 100 samples from each of the 21 most frequent labels are reserved for the test set. And the remaining images are used both as the database and as the training set. The mAP is computed based on the top 50000 returned neighbors.

"Reduced A" Setting: For this setting, the 2100 test samples are selected as in the Full setting. From the remaining samples, 500 were sampled from the 21 most frequent labels to compose the training set. The remaining were used for the database. The mAP is computed based on top 5000 returned neighbors.

"Reduced B" Setting: For this setting, the training set was chosen by sampling the available images uniformly 5,000 times. From the remaining samples the training set was uniformly sampled 10,000 times. All of the remaining samples from these two operations were used as the database. The mAP is computed based on top 5000 returned neighbors.

8.2 Results

Our method is abbreviated as SDSH, and the combination with the margin loss, label likelihood loss, and spring loss are indicated as SDSH-ML, SDSH-LL, and SDSH-S respectively. All reported results are from our publicly available

Table 2. Mean average precision (MAP) results for different number of bits on NUS_WIDE

Method	Number of Bits 16	24	32	48
DTSH[42]	0.756	0.776	0.785	0.799
DPSH[23]	0.715	0.722	0.736	0.741
SDSH-ML	0.794	0.800	0.797	0.805
SDSH-LL	0.452	0.808	0.810	0.812
SDSH-S	**0.812**	**0.817**	**0.821**	**0.821**

(a) Full settings

Method	Number of Bits 8	12	16	24	32	48
DTSH[42]	-	0.773	-	**0.808**	**0.812**	**0.824**
SDSH-ML	0.758	0.770	0.784	0.798	0.802	0.810
SDSH-LL	0.751	0.780	0.792	0.805	0.810	0.817
SDSH-S	**0.774**	**0.789**	**0.796**	0.807	**0.812**	0.820

(b) Reduced A settings

Method	Number of Bits 8	16	24	32
DVSQ[3]	**0.780**	**0.790**	**0.792**	**0.797**
DMDH [7]	-	0.751	-	0.781
SDSH-ML	0.739	0.771	0.785	0.791
SDSH-LL	0.750	0.771	0.782	0.789
SDSH-S	0.755	0.783	0.786	0.790

(c) Reduced B settings

Table 3. Mean average precision (MAP) results for different number of bits of MNIST

Method	Number of Bits 16	24	32	48
CNNH[45]	0.957	0.963	0.956	0.960
CNNH+[45]	0.969	0.975	0.971	0.975
DSCH[47]	0.965	0.966	0.972	0.975
DRSCH[47]	0.969	0.974	0.979	0.979
SDSH-ML	0.993	**0.995**	0.994	0.995
SDSH-LL	**0.994**	0.994	**0.995**	**0.996**
SDSH-S	**0.994**	**0.995**	**0.995**	0.995

implementation[1]. The average mAP scores for all methods on CIFAR-10 are listed in Table 1, which includes also the baseline (BL) classification accuracy. As pointed out in [33], the BL value can be interpreted as mAP attainable by a supervised system retrieving samples, one class at a time, with classes ranked according to the class probability of the query. Therefore, a retrieval approach should surpass the BL threshold to be effective. Table 1 shows that the proposed SDSH-S is above BL starting from 8-bits, and it always outperforms the state-of-the-art methods. In full setting and $B = 8$, and 12, SDSH-S shows large improvements, and outperforms DVSQ by 7.2% and 5.7%. SDSH-LL performs slightly better than SDSH-S for $B > 12$, but has worse performance for lower number of bits. For reduced setting, SDSH-S and SDSH-LL perform about the same, and always outperforms the state-of-the-art methods with an exception for the 8-bit case. Figure 6 presents the data of Table 1 in the form of plots.

Figure 7 shows the comparison of the precision-recall curves of SDSH-S with those produced by two state-of-the-art approaches, namely DTSH [42] and DVSQ [3], highlighting the promising performance of the proposed approach.

Tables 2a, b, and c show average mAP scores on NUS_WIDE for Full, Reduced A, and Reduced B settings respectively. Unfortunately, the protocol of this experiment does not allow to compare against the BL value. Although [33] describes two additional protocols, since they are suitable for tasks other than supervised hashing, for comparison with the state-of-the-art, here we follow protocols that have been in use by the widest majority of the literature. In particular, SDSH-S, SDSH-LL, and SDSH-ML always outperform the state-of-the-art methods on Full setting except for SDSH-LL at 8-bit case, where it converged

[1] https://github.com/podgorskiy/SDSH.

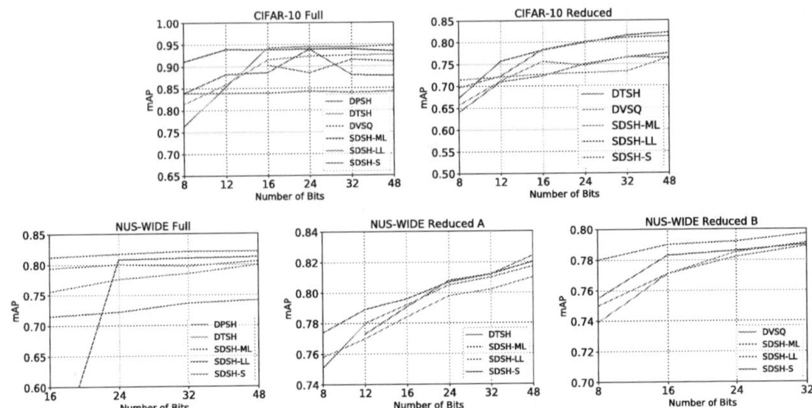

Fig. 6. Average mAP scores. Comparison of mAP values w.r.t. bit number for our method (SDSH-ML, SDSH-LL, SDSH-S) with DPSH [23], DTSH [42] and DVSQ [3].

poorly. On full setting, SDSH-S outperforms other type of losses for all bit numbers. On Reduced A setting, SDSH-S outperforms the state-of-the-art methods for $B < 24$ and for higher B it stays about the same as DTSH and slightly below for $B = 48$. On Reduced B setting our method is outperformed by DVSQ. It is important to note that NUS_WIDE has 81 labels but only 500 samples from the 21 most frequent labels are used for training. Therefore, even though the training set for NUS-WIDE's reduced setting is still about twice as large as the training set for CIFAR-10's reduced setting, the ratio of samples per label for CIFAR is 500, while the ratio for this NUS_WIDE setting is on average 129.6 per label. Therefore, for NUS_WIDE reduced setting, the network is more prone to overfitting. As for CIFAR-10, the bottom row of Fig. 6 presents the data of Tables 2a, b, and c in the form of plots.

In Table 3 we show a comparison between CNNH, CNNH+ [45], and DSCH, DRSCH [47] on the MNIST [22] dataset, noticing that all the three losses provide a performance increase.

8.3 Ablation Study

The proposed approach requires two steps for learning a hash function. The first step learns a spherical embedding that identifies an equivalence class of solutions because of the rotation invariance of the loss, and then a rotation needs to be identified to pick a representative of the equivalence class. Here we analyze what happens if use the identity as rotation, versus using the proposed method, versus using an off-the-shelve method like ITQ [13]. The summary of the results is shown in Fig. 9, where the three approaches have been applied to SDSH-S, which has been tested on CIFAR-10, and NUS_WIDE. The first observation is that estimating the optimal rotation becomes more important at lower number of bits. As we suggested in Sect. 6, when B grows, the solution space

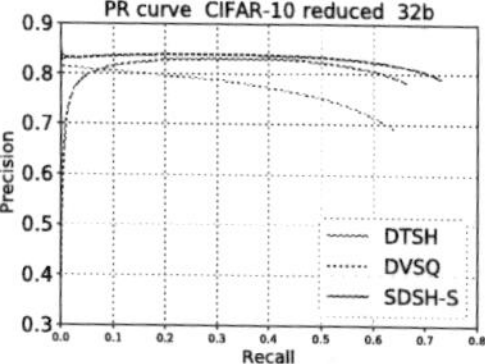

Fig. 7. Precision-recall curves. Comparison of P-R curves from our method, DVSQ [3] and DTSH [42] on CIFAR-10 reduced, top 5000 samples @ 32 bits.

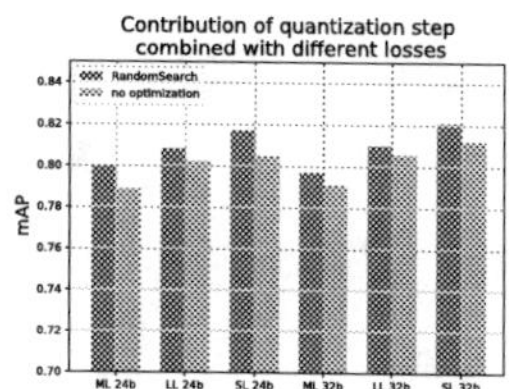

Fig. 8. Effect of quantization step. Contribution of quantization step for different losses on NUS-WIDE Full @ 24 bits, 32 bits.

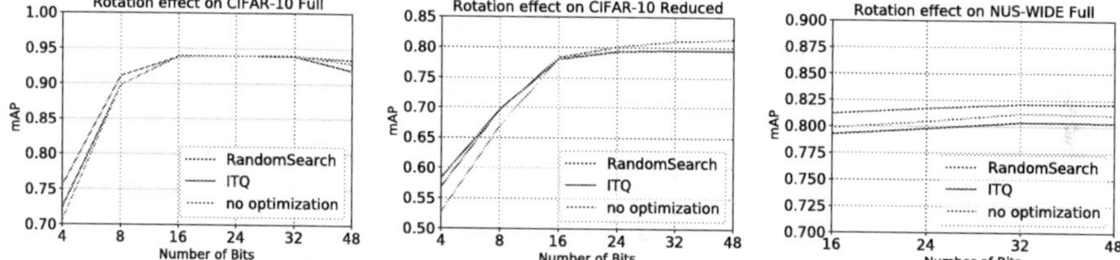

Fig. 9. Effect of learning rotation. Comparison of mAP values for a range of bit number for three scenarios: ITQ [13] and random search optimization and no rotation optimization.

grows significantly, so a random solution is more likely to do well. In addition, we note that ITQ tends to underperform our approach, and often decreases the performance of the identity solution. We note that ITQ differs from the proposed approach at least in two important aspects. First, ITQ is an unsupervised method, whereas our random search leverages the label information. In addition, ITQ aims at minimizing the quantization error, whereas the proposed method looks for the best quantization that maximizes the mAP. Finally, Fig. 8 shows the performance improvement that adds rotation optimisation for different loss types, highlighting, as expected, that each of them can benefit from that step.

9 Conclusions

We have introduced SDSH, a novel deep hashing method that moves beyond the sole goal of similarity preserving, and explicitly learns a hashing function that produces quality codes. This is achieved by leveraging a different relaxation method that eliminates the need for regularizing priors, and it enables the design of loss functions for learning balanced codes, and it allows to optimize the quantized hash function to maximize the mAP. Extensive experiments on three standard benchmark datasets demonstrated the strength of the approach. In particular, addressing the issue of quality in deep hashing approaches has revealed to be valuable, because the performance has increased particularly for more compact codes, which is very important for building efficient retrieval systems.

Acknowledgments. This material is based upon work supported in part by the Center for Identification Technology Research and the National Science Foundation under Grant No. 1650474.

References

1. Andoni, A., Indyk, P.: Near-optimal hashing algorithms for approximate nearest neighbor in high dimensions. In: IEEE FOCS, pp. 459–468 (2006)
2. Cao, Y., Long, M., Liu, B., Wang, J., KLiss, M.: Deep cauchy hashing for hamming space retrieval. In: CVPR, pp. 1229–1237 (2018)
3. Cao, Y., Long, M., Wang, J., Liu, S.: Deep visual-semantic quantization for efficient image retrieval. In: CVPR (2017)
4. Cao, Y., Long, M., Wang, J., Zhu, H., Wen, Q.: Deep quantization network for efficient image retrieval. In: AAAI, pp. 3457–3463 (2016)
5. Chatfield, K., Simonyan, K., Vedaldi, A., Zisserman, A.: Return of the devil in the details: delving deep into convolutional nets. In: BMVC (2014)
6. Chatfield, K., Simonyan, K., Vedaldi, A., Zisserman, A.: Return of the devil in the details: delving deep into convolutional nets. arXiv preprint arXiv:1405.3531 (2014)
7. Chen, Z., Yuan, X., Lu, J., Tian, Q., Zhou, J.: Deep hashing via discrepancy minimization. In: CVPR, pp. 6838–6847 (2018)
8. Chua, T.S., Tang, J., Hong, R., Li, H., Luo, Z., Zheng, Y.: NUS-WIDE: a real-world web image database from National University of Singapore. In: ACM CIVR, pp. 48:1–48:9 (2009)
9. Erin Liong, V., Lu, J., Wang, G., Moulin, P., Zhou, J.: Deep hashing for compact binary codes learning. In: CVPR, pp. 2475–2483 (2015)
10. Ge, T., He, K., Ke, Q., Sun, J.: Optimized product quantization. IEEE TPAMI **36**(4), 744–755 (2014)
11. Ghasedi Dizaji, K., Zheng, F., Sadoughi, N., Yang, Y., Deng, C., Huang, H.: Unsupervised deep generative adversarial hashing network. In: CVPR, pp. 3664–3673 (2018)
12. Gionis, A., Indyk, P., Motwani, R., et al.: Similarity search in high dimensions via hashing. In: VLDB, vol. 99, 518–529 (1999)
13. Gong, Y., Lazebnik, S., Gordo, A., Perronnin, F.: Iterative quantization: a procrustean approach to learning binary codes for large-scale image retrieval. IEEE TPAMI **35**(12), 2916–2929 (2013)
14. He, K., Zhang, X., Ren, S., Sun, J.: Deep residual learning for image recognition. In: CVPR, pp. 770–778 (2016)
15. He, K., Wen, F., Sun, J.: K-means hashing: an affinity-preserving quantization method for learning binary compact codes. In: CVPR, pp. 2938–2945 (2013)
16. Heo, J., Lee, Y., He, J., Chang, S., Yoon, S.: Spherical hashing: binary code embedding with hyperspheres. IEEE Trans. Pattern Anal. Mach. Intell. **37**(11), 2304–2316 (2015). https://doi.org/10.1109/TPAMI.2015.2408363
17. Krizhevsky, A.: Learning multiple layers of features from tiny images (2009)
18. Krizhevsky, A., Sutskever, I., Hinton, G.E.: ImageNet classification with deep convolutional neural networks. In: NIPS, pp. 1097–1105 (2012)

19. Kulis, B., Darrell, T.: Learning to hash with binary reconstructive embeddings. In: NIPS, pp. 1042–1050 (2009)
20. Kulis, B., Grauman, K.: Kernelized locality-sensitive hashing for scalable image search. In: ICCV, pp. 2130–2137. IEEE (2009)
21. Lai, H., Pan, Y., Liu, Y., Yan, S.: Simultaneous feature learning and hash coding with deep neural networks. In: CVPR, pp. 3270–3278 (2015)
22. LeCun, Y., Bottou, L., Bengio, Y., Haffner, P.: Gradient-based learning applied to document recognition. Proc. IEEE **86**(11), 2278–2324 (1998)
23. Li, W.J., Wang, S., Kang, W.C.: Feature learning based deep supervised hashing with pairwise labels. arXiv preprint arXiv:1511.03855 (2015)
24. Liu, H., Wang, R., Shan, S., Chen, X.: Deep supervised hashing for fast image retrieval. In: CVPR, pp. 2064–2072 (2016)
25. Liu, W., Mu, C., Kumar, S., Chang, S.F.: Discrete graph hashing. In: NIPS, pp. 3419–3427 (2014)
26. Liu, W., Wang, J., Ji, R., Jiang, Y.G., Chang, S.F.: Supervised hashing with kernels. In: CVPR, pp. 2074–2081. IEEE (2012)
27. Liu, W., Wang, J., Kumar, S., Chang, S.F.: Hashing with graphs. In: ICML, pp. 1–8 (2011)
28. Lowe, D.G.: Distinctive image features from scale-invariant keypoints. IJCV **60**(2), 91–110 (2004)
29. Mishkin, D., Matas, J.L.: All you need is a good init. CoRR abs/1511.06422 (2015)
30. Norouzi, M., Blei, D.M., Salakhutdinov, R.R.: Hamming distance metric learning. In: NIPS (2012)
31. Norouzi, M., Blei, D.M.: Minimal loss hashing for compact binary codes. In: ICML, pp. 353–360 (2011)
32. Ozols, M.: How to generate a random unitary matrix (2009)
33. Sablayrolles, A., Douze, M., Usunier, N., Jégou, H.: How should we evaluate supervised hashing? In: ICASSP, pp. 1732–1736 (2017)
34. Schroff, F., Kalenichenko, D., Philbin, J.: FaceNet: a unified embedding for face recognition and clustering. In: CVPR, pp. 815–823 (2015)
35. Schwartz, R.E.: The five-electron case of Thomson's problem. Exp. Math. **22**(2), 157–186 (2013)
36. Strecha, C., Bronstein, A., Bronstein, M., Fua, P.: LDAHash: improved matching with smaller descriptors. IEEE TPAMI **34**(1), 66–78 (2012)
37. Szegedy, C., Toshev, A., Erhan, D.: Deep neural networks for object detection. In: NIPS, pp. 2553–2561 (2013)
38. Taigman, Y., Yang, M., Ranzato, M., Wolf, L.: DeepFace: closing the gap to human-level performance in face verification. In: CVPR, pp. 1701–1708 (2014)
39. Wang, J., Kumar, S., Chang, S.F.: Semi-supervised hashing for scalable image retrieval. In: CVPR, pp. 3424–3431 (2010)
40. Wang, J., Zhang, T., Sebe, N., Shen, H.T., et al.: A survey on learning to hash. IEEE TPAMI **40**(4), 769–790 (2018)
41. Wang, N., Yeung, D.Y.: Learning a deep compact image representation for visual tracking. In: NIPS, pp. 809–817 (2013)
42. Wang, X., Shi, Y., Kitani, K.M.: Deep supervised hashing with triplet labels. In: Lai, S.-H., Lepetit, V., Nishino, K., Sato, Y. (eds.) ACCV 2016. LNCS, vol. 10111, pp. 70–84. Springer, Cham (2017). https://doi.org/10.1007/978-3-319-54181-5_5
43. Wang, X., Zhang, T., Qi, G.J., Tang, J., Wang, J.: Supervised quantization for similarity search. In: CVPR, pp. 2018–2026 (2016)
44. Weiss, Y., Torralba, A., Fergus, R.: Spectral hashing. In: NIPS, pp. 1753–1760 (2009)

45. Xia, R., Pan, Y., Lai, H., Liu, C., Yan, S.: Supervised hashing for image retrieval via image representation learning. In: AAAI, vol. 1, pp. 2156–2162 (2014)
46. Zhang, P., Zhang, W., Li, W.J., Guo, M.: Supervised hashing with latent factor models. In: ACM SIGIR, pp. 173–182 (2014)
47. Zhang, R., Lin, L., Zhang, R., Zuo, W., Zhang, L.: Bit-scalable deep hashing with regularized similarity learning for image retrieval and person re-identification. IEEE TIP **24**(12), 4766–4779 (2015)
48. Zhang, T., Du, C., Wang, J.: Composite quantization for approximate nearest neighbor search. In: ICML, no. 2, pp. 838–846 (2014)
49. Zhao, F., Huang, Y., Wang, L., Tan, T.: Deep semantic ranking based hashing for multi-label image retrieval. In: CVPR, pp. 1556–1564 (2015)
50. Zhu, H., Long, M., Wang, J., Cao, Y.: Deep hashing network for efficient similarity retrieval. In: AAAI, pp. 2415–2421 (2016)

Semantic Aware Attention Based Deep Object Co-segmentation

Hong Chen, Yifei Huang(✉), and Hideki Nakayama

The University of Tokyo, Tokyo, Japan
chen@nlab.ci.i.u-tokyo.ac.jp, hyf@iis.u-tokyo.ac.jp,
nakayama@ci.i.u-tokyo.ac.jp

Abstract. Object co-segmentation is the task of segmenting the same objects from multiple images. In this paper, we propose the Attention Based Object Co-Segmentation for object co-segmentation that utilize a novel attention mechanism in the bottleneck layer of the deep neural network for the selection of semantically related features. Furthermore, we take the benefit of attention learner and propose an algorithm to segment multi-input images in linear time complexity. Experiment results demonstrate that our model achieves state of the art performance on multiple datasets, with a significant reduction of computational time.

Keywords: Co-segmentation · Attention · Deep learning

1 Introduction

Image segmentation is one of a fundamental computer vision problem which aims to segment images into semantically different regions. Recently, remarkable success have been made based on the rapid development of deep learning [2,4,22,36,40]. First proposed by Rother et al. [30], *object co-segmentation* which aims at extracting similar objects from multiple inputs, utilizes joint information from two images and achieves higher accuracy compared to segmenting the objects independently. This can be used in various applications like image retrieval [30] and object discovery [26].

While considerable attention has been paid to object segmentation, there are limited previous works focusing on object co-segmentation [6,9,16–18,20,23,25,26,30,38]. Intuitively thinking, the advantage of co-segmentation against segmentation is to utilize information from both images to perform better segmentation jointly. In particular, this information includes (1) appearance similarity, (2) background similarity and (3) semantic similarity. There are previous works that leverage (1) and (2) [9,18], but these are not general since appearance or background is not always similar. Recently, a deep learning based method [20]

Electronic supplementary material The online version of this chapter (https://doi.org/10.1007/978-3-030-20870-7_27) contains supplementary material, which is available to authorized users.

C. V. Jawahar et al. (Eds.): ACCV 2018, LNCS 11364, pp. 435–450, 2019.
https://doi.org/10.1007/978-3-030-20870-7_27

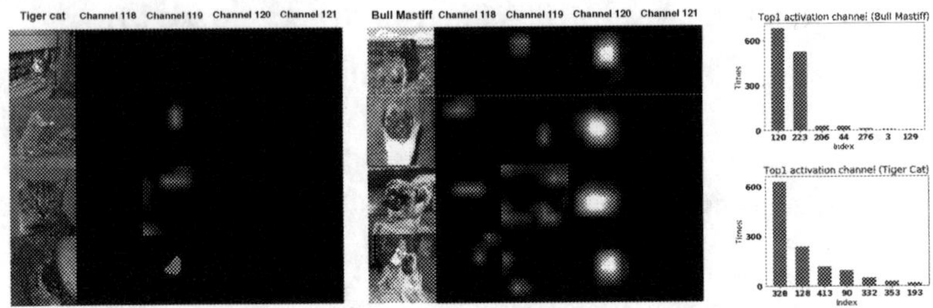

Fig. 1. Visualization activation of channels 118–121 (*conv5_3 layer of VGG16*) with Grad-Cam [27] for two different classes: (a) Bull Mastiff (b) Tiger Cat. Different classes correspond to different layer activations. We leverage this property and propose our semantic aware attention based object co-segmentation model, by using an attention learner to find relevant channels to enhance and irrelevant channel to suppress.

focused on semantic similarity; they can co-segment objects in the same semantic class even with different appearance and background, and outperformed other conventional methods by a large margin. They use a correlation layer [8] to compute localized correlations between semantic features of two input images, then predict the mask of common objects. However, since the correlation is computed in a pair-wise manner, their method is hard to extend to co-segmentation of more than two images. If the number of images in the group is large, the time complexity of co-segmentation with multiple (i.e., more than three) images will increase drastically when considering all different pairs in the group.

In this work, we aim to co-segment the objects of the same semantic class in multiple input images, even with different appearance and background. We also intend to enable instant group co-segmentation, without suffering extra time complexity by pair-wisely considering all possible image pairs.

In a deep neural network, higher abstract semantic information is encoded in deeper layers, and different channels correspond to different semantic meanings [34]. Figure 1 is a visualization of the channel activation of the *conv5_3* layer of VGG16 to different input images. We can see that strong activations are observed in channel 120 and 223 with respect to class *Bull Mastiff*, while the same channel only have very weak activations with respect to class *Tiger Cat*. Motivated by this observation, we argue that by applying attention in deep features (i.e., emphasizing channels whose activation is strong in both images' features and suppressing the other channels), semantic information can be selected and enhanced. Thus co-segmentation can be performed. According to this disentangled property, when dealing with multiple inputs, we can regard attention as semantic selectors which can be applied globally instead of taking care of intra semantic relationship pair-wisely. Also, attention learner can be effectively implemented as fully connected layers and average pooling layers, which makes it faster than correlation layer used in [20] in one forward operation.

In this paper, we propose a novel attention based co-segmentation model that leverages attention in bottleneck layers of the deep neural network. The proposed model is mainly composed of three modules: an encoder, a semantic attention learner, and a decoder. The encoder encodes the images into highly abstract features, in this work we take the convolutional layers of VGG16 as the encoder. The semantic attention learner takes the encoded feature and learns to pay attention to the co-existing objects. We propose three mechanisms for this attention learner and will describe them in detail in Sect. 3. The decoder then uses the attended deep features to output the final segmentation mask.

We summarize the main contributions of this work as follows:

- We propose a simple yet efficient deep learning architecture for object co-segmentation: Attention Based Deep Object Co-segmentation model. In our model, we use a semantic attention learner to spotlight feature channels that have high activation in all input images and suppress other irrelevant feature channels. To the best of our knowledge, this is the first work that leverages the attention mechanism for deep object co-segmentation.
- Compared with previous works that perform co-segmentation in quadratic time complexity, our proposed model can do co-segmentation of multiple images in linear time complexity.
- Our model achieves state of the art performance in multiple object co-segmentation datasets and is able to generalize to unseen objects absent from the training dataset.

2 Related Work

Object Co-segmentation. The term Object Co-segmentation that segment "object" instead of "stuff" was first proposed by Rother et al. [30] in 2011. Rubinstein et al. [26] captured the sparsity and visual variability of the common object over the entire database using dense correspondences between images to avoid noise while finding saliency. Utilizing the clustering method, Joulin et al. [18] pointed out that discriminative clustering is well adapted to the co-segmentation problem and they extended its formulation to fit the co-segmentation task.

With the assistance of deep learning, Mukherjee et al. [23] generated object proposals from two images and turned them into vectors by a Siamese network. During the training, they built an Annoy (Approximate Nearest Neighbor) Library to measure their Euclidean distance or Cosine distance between two vectors. Recently, DOCS [20] turned PASCAL VOC dataset into a co-segmentation dataset, producing more paired data. They applied a correlation layer [8] to find out similar features. They proposed group co-segmentation to test on several datasets and demonstrated that their result had achieved state-of-the-art. However, their pairwise scheme makes the testing cost a lot of computation time when performing group co-segmentation, so testing on the whole Internet dataset becomes computationally intractable. They only tested on the subset of it. In this paper, our method can run in linear time and the meantime, achieve state of the art performance. Our proposed model has a much simpler structure, yet can still get better performance.

Pixel Objectness. Pixel Objectness was first proposed in [15]. Their research revealed that the feature map from the model pretrained by Imagenet [7] could be used in the task called *object discovery*. Similar with our model, they extended a decoder after the last convolutional layer of VGG16 to produce the segmentation mask. Though they only trained the model on PASCAL VOC Dataset, their model can segment other objects even not existed in the training dataset.

Our model extended their work with a novel attention learner. By this means, we can not only perform image co-segmentation task but also enhance the model's ability for object discovery.

Attention. As far as we know, visual attention was first proposed in [31]. Since then many attention based models have been used in many computer vision tasks such as VQA [10,33,35,41] and image captioning [1,5,31,37]. Recently, attention models have been widely used in many other research domains [11–13, 21,32,39]. Attention can be considered as laying weights on channels of feature map to enhance some semantic information and, at the same time, remove other unwanted semantic information.

In our paper, we utilize the channel-wise attention model as semantic selectors, since specific channels contribute to the specific semantic class. In this object co-segmentation task, we generate channel-wise attention from one image to decide which semantic information should be removed in the other. To the best of our knowledge, this is the first work to use channel-wise attention model in the task of object co-segmentation.

3 Model

Figure 2 presents an overview of our model. For simplicity, we demonstrate our model using two inputs, which is the typical case of co-segmentation. We will show in Sect. 3.4 that our model can be extended to multiple inputs when testing. Our model is composed of an encoder, a semantic attention learner, and a decoder. The encoder is identical with the convolutional layers of VGG16. Thus the output from the encoder is a 512-channel feature map. The feature maps are forwarded into the semantic attention learner. Here we propose three different architectures for the semantic attention learner: channel-wise attention model (CA), fused-channel-wise attention model (FCA) and channel-spatial-wise attention model (CSA). Processed by semantic attention learner, we obtain the attended feature map and forward it to the decoder. We adopt the up-sampling method for the decoder and add a dropout layer after each layer to avoid overfitting. For the last layer, we use a convolution layer to output two channels, representing the foreground and the background respectively. To be emphasized, unlike [20], we do not concatenate the original feature with the processed feature since the innovative feature tends to segment every "object-like stuff" and ignore the semantic selector, which is contrary to the goal of this task.

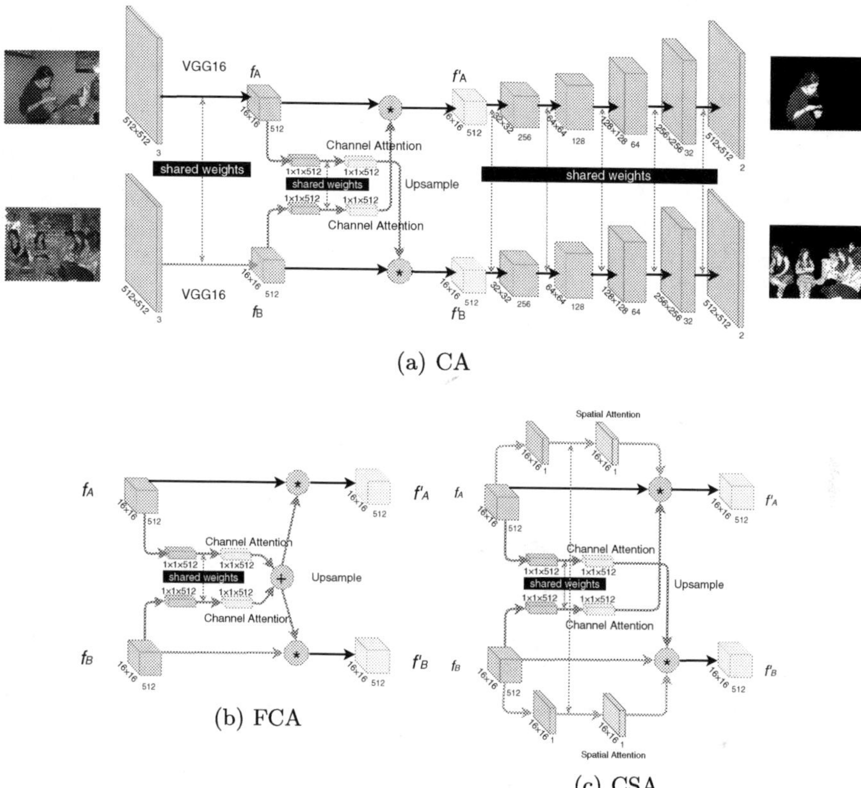

Fig. 2. Model overview. Our model contains three parts: Siamese encoder, attention learner and Siamese decoder. The encoder uses general VGG16, and the decoder uses the up-sampling method. In the middle part, we propose three different architectures of attention learner: CA, FCA, and CSA. (a) Channel-wise Attention (CA): Generating the channel-wise attention from each image separately and apply it on the other feature map. (b) Fused Channel-wise Attention (FCA): Combining both attention and generate new attention for both images. (c) Channel Spatial Attention (CSA): Generating spatial-wise attention as well as channel-wise attention.

3.1 Channel Wise Attention (CA)

It is known that each channel contains different semantic information with respect to different semantic classes [34] as mentioned in Fig. 1. We construct the Channel-wise attention (CA) to help us enhance the semantic information we need and suppress the remaining. To be specific, we first do global average pooling for the output of the encoder f_A and f_B and forward to a learnable fully connected (FC) layer to get two weight vectors $\boldsymbol{\alpha}_A, \boldsymbol{\alpha}_B \in R^{512}$. $\boldsymbol{\alpha}_A, \boldsymbol{\alpha}_B$ contain semantic information of two inputs: if the i-th index of $\boldsymbol{\alpha}_A$ is large, it indicates the i-th channel has high activation, and thus the image contains the semantic represented by channel i. By performing channel-wise multiplication with $\boldsymbol{\alpha}_A$ and f_A, $\boldsymbol{\alpha}_B$ and f_B, we can get the attended feature maps f'_A and f'_B. Here f_A receives the attention weights computed from f_B, so if f_A has high activation in channel i while f_B contains no such semantic ($\boldsymbol{\alpha}_{B,i}$ is small), this channel will be suppressed. On the other hand, if f_A does not have high activation in channel j while the j-th index of $\boldsymbol{\alpha}_B$ is large, channel j will not be activated since this channel activation is initially small. Same will happen to f_B. As a consequence, by applying this channel wise attention mechanism, only the channels with high activations in both inputs are preserved and enhanced relatively. Other channels which do not contain semantics in both inputs will be suppressed. We also show the property of the channel wise disentanglement in our supplementary material. We present details in Eqs. (1)–(4). In all of the equations below, * represents matrix multiplication, and $\odot$ represents element-wise multiplication with broadcasting.

$$\boldsymbol{\alpha}_A = \sigma(W^T * AvgPool_{channel}(f_A) + b) \tag{1}$$

$$\boldsymbol{\alpha}_B = \sigma(W^T * AvgPool_{channel}(f_B) + b) \tag{2}$$

$$f'_A = \boldsymbol{\alpha}_B \odot f_A \tag{3}$$

$$f'_B = \boldsymbol{\alpha}_A \odot f_B \tag{4}$$

Note that here we use a sigmoid function instead of the generally used softmax function because our approach is to use attention for retaining or removing semantic information. If two objects with different semantics both appear in both images, according to our assumption, the weights of related channels of the objects appear in the other image need to be close to 1 to maintain their information. However, if we use a softmax layer, both related and irrelevant channel weights may become less than 0.5, which will affect the performance of attention co-segmentation.

3.2 Fused Channel Wise Attention (FCA)

Since we aim to find the same semantic information in both inputs, the output attention weights from the semantic attention learner for both input images should be the same. Therefore, we propose another way of finding common semantic information from $\boldsymbol{\alpha}_A$ and $\boldsymbol{\alpha}_B$, by using one FC layer to fuse the two attention weights. Figure 2(b) shows the architecture of our fused channel-wise attention. We take the same procedure from CA to generate $\boldsymbol{\alpha}_A$ and $\boldsymbol{\alpha}_B$. $\mathcal{A}_C$ is the combined results of both attention:

$$\boldsymbol{\alpha}_C = \sigma(W^T * (\boldsymbol{\alpha}_A + \boldsymbol{\alpha}_B) + b) \tag{5}$$

$$f'_A = \boldsymbol{\alpha}_C \odot f_A \tag{6}$$

$$f'_B = \boldsymbol{\alpha}_C \odot f_B \tag{7}$$

3.3 Channel Spatial Attention (CSA)

While Global Average Pooling can extract global information from the feature map, spatial information will be lost due to this pooling operation. To further improve CA, inspired by [5], we propose to lay some spatial information for further improving its segmentation performance. We can find that our spatial attention produces reasonable heat map on objects in different pictures. We show visualizations of spatial wise attention in supplementary material.

For this channel spatial attention architecture, we first generate channel wise attention $\boldsymbol{\alpha}_A^c, \boldsymbol{\alpha}_B^c$ using the same fashion as CA. For generating the spatial-wise attention, we calculate mean value of each spatial location across all channels to generate spatial attention maps $\boldsymbol{\alpha}_A^s, \boldsymbol{\alpha}_B^s \in R^{W\times H}$:

$$\boldsymbol{\alpha}_A^c = \sigma(W^T * AvgPool_{channel}(f_A) + b) \quad (8)$$
$$\boldsymbol{\alpha}_B^c = \sigma(W^T * AvgPool_{channel}(f_B) + b) \quad (9)$$
$$\boldsymbol{\alpha}_A^s = \sigma(AvgPool_{spatial}(f_A)) \quad (10)$$
$$\boldsymbol{\alpha}_B^s = \sigma(AvgPool_{spatial}(f_B)) \quad (11)$$
$$f_A' = \boldsymbol{\alpha}_B^c \odot \boldsymbol{\alpha}_A^s \odot f_A \quad (12)$$
$$f_B' = \boldsymbol{\alpha}_A^c \odot \boldsymbol{\alpha}_B^s \odot f_B \quad (13)$$

3.4 Instant Group Co-segmentation

With group co-segmentation proposed in [20], we have to match all possible image pairs separately. Co-segmenting n images needs quadratic $\big(O(n^2)\big)$ computation time. Thus, it becomes computationally intractable to test on a large scale dataset. Moreover, because of their fixed structure, the existing deep learning models show weaknesses when co-segmenting more than two images at the same time. For example, we can hardly use [20] to discover and segment the most frequently appearing object among several (more than 2) images, since it is hard to measure frequency due to the lack of global semantical understanding in correlation modules.

To address this problem, thanks to our attention mechanism, we present an approach to accomplish co-segmentation in a single shot by controlling their generated attention. Without loss of generality, we use CA (the first proposed model) to demonstrate the procedure.

Algorithm 1. Instant Group Co-segmentation

Input N: Numbers of inputs. I: Images I_1,I_2,$I_3\dots I_N$.
Output S: Segment mask S_1,S_2,$S_3\dots S_N$.

Split the model into AttentionGeneration() and Segmentation().
for $i = 1, 2, 3 \ldots N$ **do**
  compute attention $\boldsymbol{\alpha}_i = AttentionGeneration(I_i)$;
end for
Calculate Group Average Attention from all $\boldsymbol{\alpha}_i$. $\boldsymbol{\alpha}_{avg} = mean(\boldsymbol{\alpha})$
for $i = 1, 2, 3 \ldots N$ **do**
  S_i = Segmentation(I_i,$\boldsymbol{\alpha}_{avg}$)
end for

Although our model is trained end to end by pairs of input images, when testing, our model can be seen as a composition of two parts: an attention-generating module and a segmentation module. When forwarding images $\{I_1, \cdots, I_N\}$ into our model, each image I_k will generate an attention weight $\boldsymbol{\alpha}_k$. Each $\boldsymbol{\alpha}_k$ represents the disentangled semantic information of each I_k. To get the common semantic information for all the input images, we take the averaged attention weight $\overline{\boldsymbol{\alpha}} = \sum_{i=1}^{k} \boldsymbol{\alpha}_k$ and use $\overline{\boldsymbol{\alpha}}$ for attending on each image features. We name this procedure **Group Average Attention** and show in detail in Algorithm 1. Thus, we reduce time complexity into linear time $\big(O(n)\big)$. Based on specific task and dataset, the global average attention can also be changed to global minimum attention, by changing the averaging operation to minimum operation of all $\boldsymbol{\alpha}_k$ along all dimensions. By this means we can strictly co-segment objects that appear in all input images.

3.5 Training and Implementation Details

We use PyTorch [24] library to implement our model. For the training, we rescale every image into spatial size $512 * 512$. As for the decoder we adopt the architecture: upsample → conv (512, 256) → upsample → conv (256, 128) → upsample → conv (128, 64) → upsample → conv (64, 32) → upsample → conv (32, 2), in which conv (a, b) indicates a convolution layer whose input channel is a and output channel is b. For all convolution layers we use kernel size 3 and stride 1, followed by a Rectified Linear Unit (ReLU) layer and Batch Normalize Layer [14]. We compute loss using cross entropy loss, and back propagate gradients to all layers. We use Adam [19] optimizer with learning rate 1e−5 for optimization.

4 Experiments

4.1 Datasets

For training, we use the same dataset as [20], where the image pairs are extracted from the PASCAL VOC 2012 training sets. The total pair number is over 160k.

For validation and testing our model, we randomly separate the PASCAL VOC2012 validation set into 724 validation images and 725 test images like [20], by pairing the images we get 46973 and 37700 pairs respectively.

We also test our model using other datasets commonly used in object co-segmentation. They include:

- MSRC [28,29] sub-dataset. In this dataset, there are 7 classes: bird, car, cat, cow, dog, plane, sheep. Each class contains 10 images.
- Internet [26] sub-dataset, each of the 3 classes: car, horse and airplane contains 100 images.
- Internet [26] dataset. The three classes car, horse and airplane contain 1306, 879 and 561 images correspondingly. Note that the MSRC dataset and two Internet dataset all contains classes within the training data. Here we refer to these object classes as *Seen Objects*.

- ICoseg [3] sub-dataset. This dataset contains 8 classes, each with a different number of images. Different from the previous datasets, the class in ICoseg dataset is different from the training dataset. We adopt this dataset to test the generalizability of our model. We refer to the objects in ICoseg dataset as *Unseen Objects*.

4.2 Baselines

For result comparison, we use the following baselines: [30] is a conventional method which first extracts the features from image pairs and then trains a Random Forest Regressor based on these features. [16,17,26] do co-segmentation based on saliency. [6,18] utilize clustering method to find the similarity of the image. [38] uses conditional random fields to find the relationship between pixels. [25] connects the superpixel nodes located in the image boundaries of the entire image group, then infers via the proposed GO-FMR algorithm. [9] first induces affinities between image pairs and then co-segments objects from co-occurring regions. They further improve their results with Consensus Scoring. Other than the pre deep learning conventional methods, [20,23] both utilized deep learning method for object co-segmentation. [23] found the objects with object proposals, encoded them into feature vectors with VGG16, then they compared the similarity of the feature vectors and decided which to segment. Recently, [20] proposed an end-to-end deep learning model with VGG16, a correlation layer and a decoder, which achieved state of the art in this area.

Pixel Objectness [15] is the state of the art method of object discovery, and it is capable of segmenting all the existing objects with a single input image. The network architecture of Pixel Objectness is a VGG16 encoder directly followed by a decoder. So in the view of network architecture, our model can be viewed as adding attention learner in the middle of Pixel Objectness. So since the task is different, it is unfair to compare their method with co-segmentation methods quantitatively. We, therefore, demonstrate qualitative results to show that our model can inherit (and even perform better than) the object discovery ability of Pixel Objectness.

4.3 Results and Visualization of Co-segmentation

We first show the performance comparisons of conventional pairwise co-segmentation. For PASCAL VOC Datasets, we test our models on 37700 images pairs. We gain the Jaccard accuracy 59.24%, 59.41% and 59.76% for CA, FCA, and CSA respectively. Tables 1 and 2 show quantitative results on different MSRC and Internet sub-dataset. We can see that our model can get state of the art performance when segmenting *Seen Objects*. Among the three proposed attention mechanisms, CSA is best at the co-segmentation of *Seen Objects*.

Table 1. Results on MSRC sub dataset with pairwise co-segmentation.

MSRC	[30]	[26]	[9]	[23]	[20]	CA (ours)	FCA (ours)	CSA (ours)
Precision	90.2	92.16	92.0	84	92.43	**96.6**	96.31	95.26
Jaccard	70.6	74.7	77	67	**79.89**	76.49	76.94	77.7

Table 2. Results comparison on Internet sub dataset with pairwise co-segmentation.

Internet (Jaccard)	Cars	Horse	Airplane	Average
[18]	37.1	30.1	15.3	27.5
[26]	64.4	51.6	55.8	57.3
[6]	64.9	33.4	40.3	46.2
[25]	66.8	58.1	56.3	60.4
[38]	72.0	65.0	66.0	67.7
[20]	**82.7**	64.6	63.5	70.3
CA (ours)	80.0	67.3	**71.4**	72.8
FCA (ours)	76.9	69.1	65.9	70.6
CSA (ours)	79.9	**71.4**	68.0	**73.1**

Table 3 shows quantitative result of *Unseen Objects* from the ICoseg sub-dataset. We can see that our model (especially FCA) outperforms all baseline methods. In particular, we get 1.8% performance gain compared with [20] which also uses deep learning based method.

Table 3. Results on ICoseg sub-dataset with pairwise co-segmentation.

iCoseg (Jaccard)	[26]	[16]	[9]	[17]	[20]	CA (ours)	FCA (ours)	CSA (ours)
bear2	65.3	70.1	72.0	67.5	88.3	90.2	88.3	**90.6**
brownbear	73.6	66.2	92.0	72.5	92.0	92.9	91.5	**93.0**
cheetah	69.7	**75.4**	67.0	78.0	68.8	65.7	71.3	51.4
elephant	68.8	73.5	67.0	79.9	84.6	82.5	84.4	**85.1**
helicopter	80.3	76.6	**82.0**	80.0	79.0	74.2	76.5	77.1
hotballoon	65.7	76.3	88.0	80.2	91.7	92.9	**94.0**	93.7
panda1	75.9	80.6	70.0	72.2	82.6	**92.2**	91.8	92.5
panda2	62.5	71.8	55.0	61.4	86.7	**91.1**	90.3	89.1
Average	70.2	73.8	78.2	70.4	84.2	85.2	**86.0**	84.0

In Fig. 3, we visualize some co-segmentation results from three models. These demonstration images are selected from all of the three datasets containing *Seen Objects*: MSRC, Internet, PASCAL VOC, and MSCOCO dataset. We can see

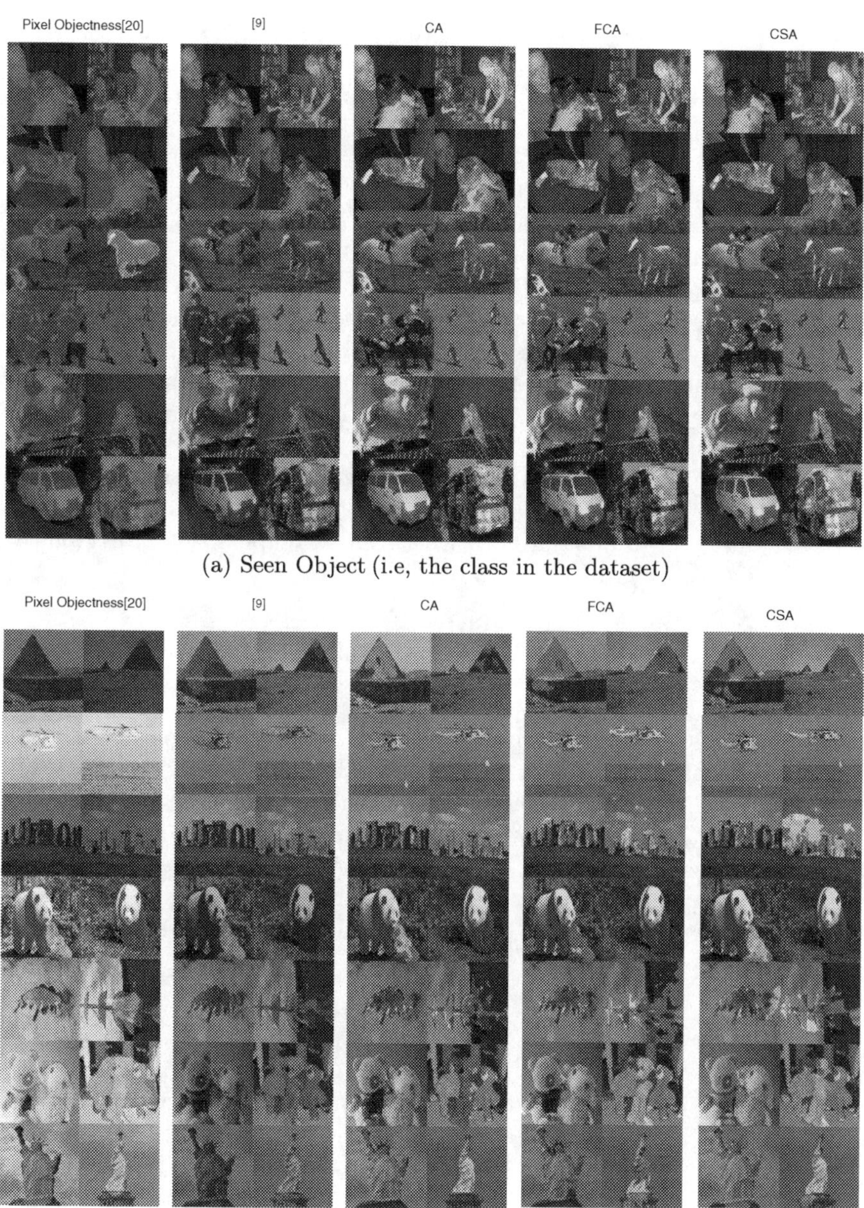

(a) Seen Object (i.e, the class in the dataset)

(b) Unseen Object (i.e, the class beyond the dataset)

Fig. 3. Qualitative co-segmentation results. Each row indicate the input image pairs to different methods. Red masks are the output by [20], yellow by Pixel Objectness [15], and the output of our proposed methods are shown in green masks. (Color figure online)

that Pixel Objectness [15] tends to over segment since it outputs the segmentation of all possible objects. We can see that our method performs comparably well as the state of the art deep learning based method [20]. We will further demonstrate that our method has much less time complexity compared with [20] in Sect. 4.4.

In Fig. 3(b), the comparison between our method and Pixel Objectness [15] demonstrates that our approach has a stronger ability in object discovery, thanks to the attention learner that can help to reduce semantic noise and enhance some semantic information in the feature map. For example, from the first row in Fig. 3(b), with Pixel Objectness, no object could be detected but assisted with reference attention from another image, our model can detect and segment the pyramid precisely. Also, we can see that our method achieves better performance in co-segmentation task compared with [15] and [20]. FCA is the best architecture for co-segmentation of *Unseen Objects*. According to the architecture, CSA remains most information from the original images because of spatial attention. However, it is unclear that spatial attention also has the disentangle properties which may lead to miss-segment in the unseen objects. On the other hand, FCA aims at finding the common attention between two inputs, so noises from two generated attention will be suppressed.

4.4 Instant Group Co-segmentation Results

Algorithm 1 shows each step in instant group co-segmentation. With this method, we reduce the time complexity of group co-segmentation to linear time complexity. All of the previous work has quadratic time complexity which made it computationally intractable testing on the whole Internet dataset. In Table 4, we show the results using instant group co-segmentation in the whole Internet dataset which contains 1306 car, 879 horse, and 561 airplane images labeled. We reach state-of-the-art performance without doing co-segmentation pair-wisely. Figure 4 shows some qualitative results of our instant group co-segmentation.

Table 4. Instant group co-segmentation results on whole Internet Dataset (time cost 590 s). We cannot compare the result with [20] since it's computational intractable.

Avg Jaccard	[26]	[6]	CA-instant
Car	63.4	64.7	**83.4**
Horse	53.9	57.6	**70.9**
Airplane	55.6	60.0	**60.6**
Average	57.6	60.7	**71.7**

To show that our instant group co-segmentation method does not sacrifice accuracy compared with previous methods based on pairwise co-segmentation, we carry out the same quantitative experiment in the same dataset as done

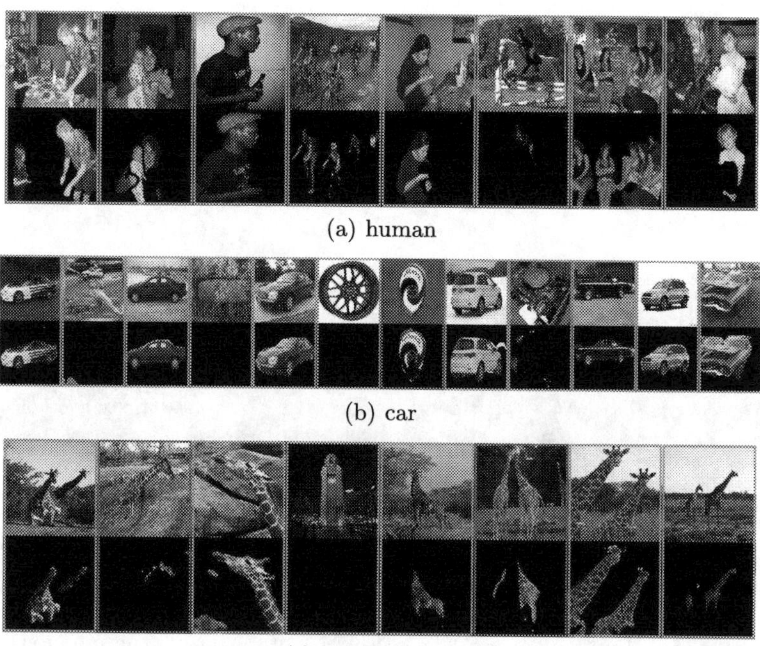

(a) human

(b) car

(c) giraffe (unseen)

Fig. 4. Results of instant group co-segmentation. The green bounding boxes present the correct answers and red bounding boxes show failures. (Color figure online)

in Sect. 4.3. From Table 5, we can see that the instant group co-segmentation achieves higher accuracy for *Unseen Objects* of iCoseg dataset, while performing comparably well in *Seen Objects* from other two datasets, compared with [20] and our CA model used pair-wisely. This demonstrates that the global average attention helps us filtering some semantic noises in the irrelevant channels.

There are three typical failure cases in co-segmentation task: loss of segmentation accuracy, over-segmentation, and under-segmentation. For example in Fig. 4(b), the 7th image is over-segmented and in Fig. 4(c), the 2nd image is under-segmented.

Table 5. Instant group co-segmentation results on different datasets, compared with results using pairwise co-segmentation.

Avg Jaccard (test time)	[20]	CA	CA-instant
MSRC (seen)	**79.9** (203)	76.5 (51)	73.9 (17)
Internet (seen)	70.3 (9531)	**72.8** (2179)	70.9 (63)
ICoseg (unseen)	84.2 (1077)	85.2 (268)	**87.1** (43)

According to [15], the pretrained model is well capable of segmenting unseen objects. Our models find the balance between attention learners and the pre-trained model during training. If the pretrained model dominates, it tends to segment all objects in the image, resulting in over-segment. On the other hand, if the attention learner overfits, unseen objects would be ignored, leading to under-segment.

Fig. 5. Compare segmentation results with two processions. The 2nd row shows the results using the **Global Average Attention**: 8/9 of the images contain human class, so humans will be segmented in this case. The 3rd row demonstrates the results using the **Global Minimum Attention**. In the 4th image, there is no human, so nothing will be segmented in all images with this method.

Group Average Attention is not the only meaningful procession in our model. For other tasks, such as segmenting the common objects existed in all images, we can choose the minimum weight for each channel from the generated attention and obtain **Global Minimum Attention**. Figure 5 shows an example of comparing global average attention and global minimum attention. **Group Average Attention** can segment the most common object in multiple images, while **Group Minimum Attention** strictly finds the objects appear in all images.

5 Conclusion

In this paper, we propose three different architectures of attention learner as semantic selectors. With proposed instant group co-segmentation, we can co-segment multiple images in the linear time. We present that our results have achieved state-of-the-art in the object co-segmentation task and outperformed [15] in object discovering ability. We also visualize the channel-wise attention and the spatial-wise attention to show the correctness of our proposed models.

However, using our proposed model, if the inputs do not contain the same object, our model will output the wrong results since there's no common semantic class. Together with applying zero-shot learning to improve segmentation of unseen objects, we leave this for our future work.

Acknowledgements. This work was supported by JSPS KAKENHI Grant Number 16H05872.

References

1. Anderson, P., et al.: Bottom-up and top-down attention for image captioning and visual question answering. In: CVPR (2018)
2. Badrinarayanan, V., Kendall, A., Cipolla, R.: SegNet: a deep convolutional encoder-decoder architecture for image segmentation. IEEE Trans. Pattern Anal. Mach. Intell. **39**(12), 2481–2495 (2017)
3. Batra, D., Kowdle, A., Parikh, D., Luo, J., Chen, T.: iCoseg: interactive co-segmentation with intelligent scribble guidance. In: CVPR (2010)
4. Chen, L.C., Papandreou, G., Kokkinos, I., Murphy, K., Yuille, A.L.: DeepLab: semantic image segmentation with deep convolutional nets, atrous convolution, and fully connected CRFs. IEEE Trans. Pattern Anal. Mach. Intell. **40**(4), 834–848 (2018)
5. Chen, L., et al.: SCA-CNN: spatial and channel-wise attention in convolutional networks for image captioning. arXiv preprint arXiv:1611.05594 (2016)
6. Chen, X., Shrivastava, A., Gupta, A.: Enriching visual knowledge bases via object discovery and segmentation. In: CVPR (2014)
7. Deng, J., Dong, W., Socher, R., Li, L.J., Li, K., Fei-Fei, L.: ImageNet: a large-scale hierarchical image database. In: CVPR (2009)
8. Dosovitskiy, A., et al.: FlowNet: learning optical flow with convolutional networks. In: CVPR (2015)
9. Faktor, A., Irani, M.: Co-segmentation by composition. In: ICCV (2013)
10. Gan, C., Li, Y., Li, H., Sun, C., Gong, B.: VQS: linking segmentations to questions and answers for supervised attention in VQA and question-focused semantic segmentation. In: ICCV (2017)
11. Hu, J., Shen, L., Sun, G.: Squeeze-and-excitation networks. arXiv preprint arXiv:1709.01507 (2017)
12. Huang, Y., Cai, M., Kera, H., Yonetani, R., Higuchi, K., Sato, Y.: Temporal localization and spatial segmentation of joint attention in multiple first-person videos. In: ICCVW (2017)
13. Huang, Y., Cai, M., Li, Z., Sato, Y.: Predicting gaze in egocentric video by learning task-dependent attention transition. arXiv preprint arXiv:1803.09125 (2018)
14. Ioffe, S., Szegedy, C.: Batch normalization: accelerating deep network training by reducing internal covariate shift. arXiv preprint arXiv:1502.03167 (2015)
15. Jain, S.D., Xiong, B., Grauman, K.: Pixel objectness. arXiv preprint arXiv:1701.05349 (2017)
16. Jerripothula, K.R., Cai, J., Meng, F., Yuan, J.: Automatic image co-segmentation using geometric mean saliency. In: ICIP (2014)
17. Jerripothula, K.R., Cai, J., Yuan, J.: Image co-segmentation via saliency co-fusion. IEEE Trans. Multimedia **18**(9), 1896–1909 (2016)
18. Joulin, A., Bach, F., Ponce, J.: Discriminative clustering for image co-segmentation. In: CVPR (2010)
19. Kingma, D.P., Ba, J.: Adam: a method for stochastic optimization. arXiv preprint arXiv:1412.6980 (2014)
20. Li, W., Jafari, O.H., Rother, C.: Deep object co-segmentation. arXiv preprint arXiv:1804.06423 (2018)

21. Li, Z., Tao, R., Gavves, E., Snoek, C.G., Smeulders, A., et al.: Tracking by natural language specification. In: CVPR (2017)
22. Long, J., Shelhamer, E., Darrell, T.: Fully convolutional networks for semantic segmentation. In: CVPR (2015)
23. Mukherjee, P., Lall, B., Lattupally, S.: Object cosegmentation using deep Siamese network. arXiv preprint arXiv:1803.02555 (2018)
24. Paszke, A., et al.: Automatic differentiation in PyTorch (2017)
25. Quan, R., Han, J., Zhang, D., Nie, F.: Object co-segmentation via graph optimized-flexible manifold ranking. In: CVPR (2016)
26. Rubinstein, M., Joulin, A., Kopf, J., Liu, C.: Unsupervised joint object discovery and segmentation in internet images. In: CVPR (2013)
27. Selvaraju, R.R., Cogswell, M., Das, A., Vedantam, R., Parikh, D., Batra, D.: Grad-CAM: visual explanations from deep networks via gradient-based localization. In: ICCV (2017)
28. Shotton, J., Winn, J., Rother, C., Criminisi, A.: *TextonBoost*: joint appearance, shape and context modeling for multi-class object recognition and segmentation. In: Leonardis, A., Bischof, H., Pinz, A. (eds.) ECCV 2006. LNCS, vol. 3951, pp. 1–15. Springer, Heidelberg (2006). https://doi.org/10.1007/11744023_1
29. Vicente, S., Kolmogorov, V., Rother, C.: Cosegmentation revisited: models and optimization. In: Daniilidis, K., Maragos, P., Paragios, N. (eds.) ECCV 2010. LNCS, vol. 6312, pp. 465–479. Springer, Heidelberg (2010). https://doi.org/10.1007/978-3-642-15552-9_34
30. Vicente, S., Rother, C., Kolmogorov, V.: Object cosegmentation. In: CVPR (2011)
31. Xu, K., et al.: Show, attend and tell: neural image caption generation with visual attention. In: ICML (2015)
32. Yang, C., Kim, T., Wang, R., Peng, H., Kuo, C.C.J.: Show, attend and translate: unsupervised image translation with self-regularization and attention. arXiv preprint arXiv:1806.06195 (2018)
33. Yang, Z., He, X., Gao, J., Deng, L., Smola, A.: Stacked attention networks for image question answering. In: CVPR (2016)
34. Yosinski, J., Clune, J., Nguyen, A., Fuchs, T., Lipson, H.: Understanding neural networks through deep visualization. arXiv preprint arXiv:1506.06579 (2015)
35. Yu, D., Fu, J., Mei, T., Rui, Y.: Multi-level attention networks for visual question answering. In: CVPR (2017)
36. Yu, F., Koltun, V.: Multi-scale context aggregation by dilated convolutions. arXiv preprint arXiv:1511.07122 (2015)
37. Yu, Y., Choi, J., Kim, Y., Yoo, K., Lee, S.H., Kim, G.: Supervising neural attention models for video captioning by human gaze data. In: CVPR (2017)
38. Yuan, Z., Lu, T., Wu, Y.: Deep-dense conditional random fields for object co-segmentation. In: IJCAI (2017)
39. Zhang, H., Goodfellow, I., Metaxas, D., Odena, A.: Self-attention generative adversarial networks. arXiv preprint arXiv:1805.08318 (2018)
40. Zhao, H., Shi, J., Qi, X., Wang, X., Jia, J.: Pyramid scene parsing network. In: CVPR (2017)
41. Zhu, C., Zhao, Y., Huang, S., Tu, K., Ma, Y.: Structured attentions for visual question answering. In: ICCV (2017)

PIRC Net: Using Proposal Indexing, Relationships and Context for Phrase Grounding

Rama Kovvuri(✉) and Ram Nevatia(✉)

University of Southern California, Los Angeles, CA 90007, USA
{nkovvuri,nevatia}@usc.edu

Abstract. Phrase Grounding aims to detect and localize objects in images that are referred to and are queried by natural language phrases. Phrase grounding finds applications in tasks such as Visual Dialog, Visual Search and Image-text co-reference resolution. In this paper, we present a framework that leverages information such as phrase category, relationships among neighboring phrases in a sentence and context to improve the performance of phrase grounding systems. We propose three modules: Proposal Indexing Network (PIN); Inter-phrase Regression Network (IRN) and Proposal Ranking Network (PRN) each of which analyze the region proposals of an image at increasing levels of detail by incorporating the above information. Also, in the absence of ground-truth spatial locations of the phrases (weakly-supervised), we propose knowledge transfer mechanisms that leverages the framework of PIN module. We demonstrate the effectiveness of our approach on the Flickr 30k Entities and ReferItGame datasets, for which we achieve improvements over state-of-the-art approaches in both supervised and weakly-supervised variants.

Keywords: Phrase grounding · Phrase localization · Object proposals

1 Introduction

Our goal is to detect and localize objects in images that are referred to, are queried by, natural language phrases. This objective is also commonly referred to as "phrase grounding". The key difference with conventional object detection approaches is that the categories of objects is not pre-specified; furthermore the queries may contain attributes (such as a"red car") and relations between objects ("baby holding a pacifier"). Phrase grounding finds applications in tasks such as Visual Dialog [32], Visual Search [9] and Image-text co-reference resolution [28].

Grounding faces several challenges beyond those present for learning detectors for pre-specified categories. These include generalizing the models from limited data, resolving semantic ambiguities from an open-ended vocabulary and localizing small, hard-to-detect visual entities. Current approaches ([4,12,23,27]) adopt a two stage process for phrase grounding. In the first stage, a region proposal module [31,36] generates proposals to identify regions likely to contain

C. V. Jawahar et al. (Eds.): ACCV 2018, LNCS 11364, pp. 451–467, 2019.
https://doi.org/10.1007/978-3-030-20870-7_28

objects or groups of objects in an image. In the second stage, the grounding system employs a multimodal subspace [1] that projects queries (textual modality) and their corresponding proposals (visual modality) to have high correlation score.

Various approaches are suggested to learn this subspace such as knowledge transfer from image captioning [12]; Canonical Correlation Analysis [17,23] and query-specific attention for region proposals [4,27]. To provide visual context, [21] augments the proposals' visual features using bounding box features while [35] employs neighboring proposal features. Query phrases are often generated from image descriptions and neighboring phrases from a description can provide useful context like relative locations and relationships between them to reduce semantic ambiguity. Using this context, [3,22] ground multiple queries for the same image together to resolve ambiguity and reduce conflicting predictions.

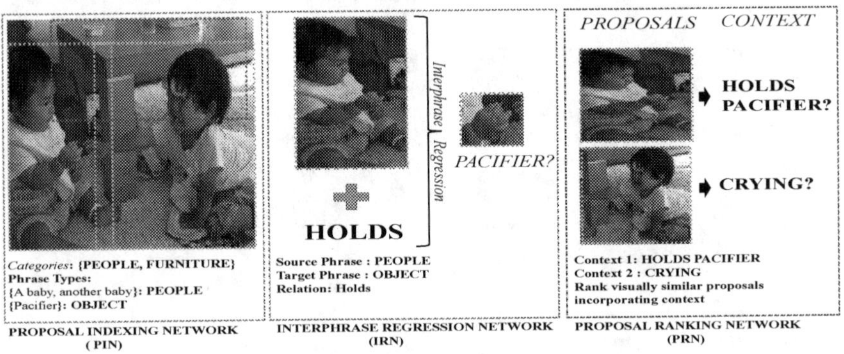

Fig. 1. Overview of the PIRC Net framework

Given a query phrase, above approaches consider all the proposals extracted from the image for grounding. This can result in inter-class errors especially for object classes with few corresponding query phrases in the training dataset. The existing approaches are also upperbound by the accuracy of proposal generator, since a query phrase is only able to choose from pre-generated proposals. Further, the existing approaches provide bounding box location and/or image visual representation as context for a proposal. However, many of the queries are defined by attributes and the suitability of an attribute to a proposal is relative. For example, for a query phrase "short boy" we need to compare each boy with all other boys in the image to figure out which one is the "short boy".

To address the above challenges, we present a framework that uses Proposal Indexing, Relationship and Context for Grounding ("PIRC Net"), whose overview is presented in Fig. 1. We propose an architecture with three modules; each succeeding module analyzes the region proposals for a query phrase at increasing levels of detail. The first module, Proposal Indexing Network (PIN) is a two stage network that is trained to reduce the generalization errors and volume of proposals required per query. The second module, Inter-phrase Regression Network (IRN) functions as an enhancement module by generating positive proposals for the cases where PIN does not generate a positive proposal. The third and final module, Proposal Ranking Network (PRN) scores the proposals generated by PIN and IRN by incorporating query specific context. A brief description of each of the modules is provided below.

In the first stage, PIN module classifies the region proposals into higher-level phrase categories. The phrase categories are generated by grouping semantically similar query phrases together using clustering. Intuitively, if the training data has no query phrases from object class "bus", queries such as "red bus" should consider the proposals that have similar appearance to other queries from same phrase category like "sports car" and "yellow truck". Skip-thought vectors [15] are used to encode the phrases since they latently identify the important nouns in a phrase to map semantically similar phrases. In the next stage, PIN learns to attend the proposals most relevant to query phrase to further reduce the volume of region proposals. IRN module employs a novel method estimate the location of one neighbor phrase from another given the relationship between them. For example, for a phrase tuple 'small baby', 'holds', 'a pacifier' while it is difficult to detect 'a pacifier' alone, the relationship 'holds' can help localize 'a pacifier' from the location of its neighboring phrase 'small baby'. PRN module trains a bimodal network which uses learned embeddings to score the region proposals (visual modality) given a query phrase (textual modality). To encode the visual context given a query phrase, we compare a region proposal to other proposals from the same phrase category by encoding their relative appearance.

During training, IRN and PRN learn to predict the proposals with high overlap to ground truth bounding box. However, the ground truth annotation is costly and most vision and language datasets do not provide this information. While it is difficult to train IRN and PRN without this information, we provide methodologies to train PIN with ground truth (supervised) and without ground truth (weakly-supervised) annotations. For supervised setting, PIN is trained using a RPN to predict the proposals close to the groundtruth bounding boxes for a phrase category. For the weakly supervised setting, we propose to use knowledge transfer learning from an object detection system for training PIN and retrieving region proposals that may belong to query phrase category.

We evaluate our framework on two common phrase grounding datasets: Flickr 30K entities [23] and Refer-it Game [13]. For supervised setting, experiments show that our framework outperforms existing state-of-the-art [4], achieving 6%/8% and 10%/15% improvements using VGG/ResNet architectures on Flickr30K and Referit datasets respectively. For weakly-supervised setting, our framework achieves 5% and 4% improvements over state-of-the-art [27] for both datasets.

Our contributions are: (a) Designed a query-guided Proposal Indexing Network that reduces generalization errors for grounding; (b) Introduced novel Inter-phrase Regression and Proposal Ranking Networks that leverage the context provided by multiple phrases in a caption; (c) Proposed knowledge transfer mechanisms that employ object detection systems to index proposals in weakly supervised setting.

2 Related Work

Phrase Grounding. Improving hugely on early phrase grounding attempts that used limited vocabulary [14,16], Karpathy et al. [2] employ bidirectional RNN to align the sentence fragments and image regions in common embedding space. Hu et al. [12] proposed to rank proposals using knowledge transfer from image captioning. Rohrbach et al. [27] employ attention to rank proposals in a latent subspace. Chen et al. [3] extended this approach to account for regression based on query semantics. Plummer et al. [23] suggest using Canonical Correlation Analysis (CCA) and Wang et al. [17] suggest Deep CCA to learn similarity among visual and language modalities. Wang et al. [33] employ structured matching and boost performance using partial matching of phrase pairs. Plummer et al. [22] further augment CCA model to take advantage of extensive linguistic cues in the phrases. All these approaches are upperbound by the performance of the proposal generation systems.

Recently, Chen et al. [4] proposed QRC that overcomes some limitations of region proposal generators by regressing proposals based on query and employs reinforcement learning techniques to punish conflicting predictions.

Visual and Semantic Context. Context provides broader information that can be leveraged to resolve semantic ambiguities and rank proposals. Hu et al. [12] used global image context and bounding box encoding as context to augment visual features. Yu et al. [35] further encode the size information and jointly predict all query regions to boost performance in a referring task. Plummer et al. [22] jointly optimize neighboring phrases by encoding their relations for better grounding performance. Chen et al. [3,4] employ semantic context to jointly ground multiple phrases to filter conflicting predictions among neighboring phrases. The existing approaches for grounding do not take full advantage of the rich context provided by visual context, semantic context and inter-phrase relationships.

Knowledge Transfer. Knowledge transfer involves solving a target task by learning from a different but related source task. Li et al. [18] employ knowledge transfer, Rohrbach et al. [29] use linguistic knowledge bases to automatically transfer information from source to target classes. Deselaers et al. [5] and Rochan et al. [26] employ knowledge transfer in weakly-supervised object detection and localization respectively using skip vectors [20] as a knowledge base. In this work, we propose to use knowledge transfer from object detection task to index region proposals for weakly supervised phrase grounding.

3 Our Network

In this section, we present the architecture of our PIRC network (Fig. 2). First, we provide an overview of the entire framework followed by detailed descriptions of each of the three subnetworks: Phrase Indexing Network (PIN), Inter-phrase Regression Network (IRN) and Proposal Ranking Network (PRN).

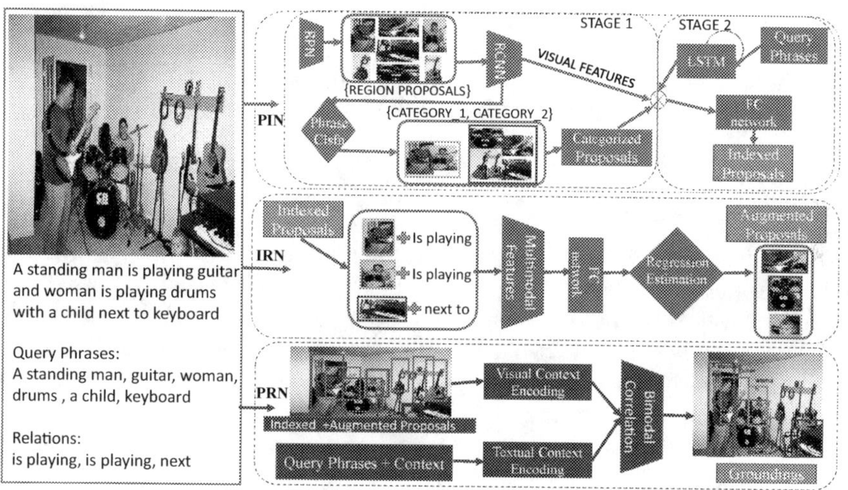

Fig. 2. Architecture of PIRC Net

3.1 Framework Overview

Given an image $\mathbb{I}$ and query phrases $p_i \in \{\mathbb{C}\}$, the goal of our system is to predict the location of visual entities specified by the queries. PIN takes each query phrase and image as input and in two stages, retrieves a set of "indexed region proposals". IRN generates the region proposals for each query phrase by predicting its location using its relationship with neighboring query phrases of the same image (Note: This information is only available if multiple query phrases are generated from the same image description). The union of proposals generated by PIN and IRN is referred to as "candidate proposals". Finally, PRN uses context-incorporated features to rank the candidate proposals and choose the one that is most relevant to the query phrase.

3.2 Proposal Indexing Network (PIN)

PIN retrieves a subset of region proposals that are likely correlated to a given query phrase in two stages. Classification is used by PIN to categorize the region proposals in the Stage 1. In Stage 2, PIN ranks the proposals and chooses a subset for which complex analysis is performed in later stages by IRN and PRN subnetworks.

Stage 1. Architecture of stage 1 of PIN is analogous to Faster RCNN [25] and has two subnetworks: A proposal generator (RPN) and a proposal classifier (RCNN). For proposal generation, we finetune a pretrained object detection network to generate region proposals like [4] instead of object proposals. For classification (RCNN), since each query phrase is distinct from another, we propose to group them into fixed number of higher level phrase categories. To achieve this, we encode phrases as skip-thought vectors [15] and cluster them into a set number of phrase categories $C_j, j \in [1, N]$. Skip-thought vectors [15] employ a data-driven encoder-decoder framework to embed semantically similar sentences into similar vector representations. Given a query phrase p_i, it is embedded into a skip-thought vector ep_i and then categorized as follows:

$$p_i \in C_j : ep_i \cdot \mu_j > ep_i \cdot \mu_J, \forall_{J \neq j} J \in [1, N] \tag{1}$$

where μ_j is center of cluster j.

Stage 2. In stage 1, classification chooses the region proposals that likely belong to the query phrase category (Eq. 1). In stage 2, these proposals are ranked based on their relevance to the query phrase.

For stage 2, we employ visual attention on each region proposal from stage 1 to rank their similarity to query phrase. For each region proposal, its visual feature is concatenated to the query phrase embedding and these multimodal features are projected through a FC layer network to get a 5 dimensional prediction vector s_p^i. The first element of the vector indicates the similarity score between proposal and query embedding and the next four elements indicate the regression parameters of the proposals. Visual features of proposals are obtained from the penultimate layer of the classification network in Stage 1. An LSTM is used to encode a query phrase as an embedding vector. For a region proposal with visual feature vf_j and query feature g_{p_i} generated for a query phrase p_i, the loss function is calculated as a combination of ranking $\mathcal{L}_{rnk}$ and regression loss $\mathcal{L}_{reg}$ mentioned below:

$$\mathcal{L}_{rnk}(\{vf_j\}, g_{p_i}) = -log(s_p^i[0]) \tag{2}$$

$$\mathcal{L}_{reg}(\{vf_j\}, g_{p_i}) = \frac{1}{4}\sum_{k=1}^{4} f(\|s_p^i[k] - s_{g_i}^j[k]\|) \tag{3}$$

where s_{g_i} are regression parameters for proposals relative to ground-truth and f is a smooth-L1 loss function. The region proposals $\{V_S^i\}$ with highest similarity to query phrase are chosen as indexed region proposals for further inspection.

While the proposals chosen in PIN have fairly high accuracy, they still do not consider any relative attributes and relationships while ranking the proposals. The next modules, IRN and PRN incorporate inter-phrase relations and context knowledge to improve ranking among these indexed region proposals.

3.3 Inter-phrase Regeression Network (IRN)

Inter-phrase Regression Network uses a novel architecture to take advantage of the relationship among two neighboring query phrases (from an image description) to estimate the relative location of a target phrase from a source phrase. Given a phrase tuple of source phrase, relationship, target phrase; IRN estimates the regression parameters to predict the location of target phrase given the location of source phrase and vice-versa. To model the visual features for regression, the representation of source phrase must encode not only its visual appearance fv but also its spatial configuration and its interdependence with the target phrase. For example, the interdependence of 'person-in-clothes' is different to that of 'person-in-vehicle' and is dependent on where the 'person' is. To encode the spatial configuration lv, we employ a 5D vector that is encoded as $\left[\frac{x_{min}}{W}, \frac{y_{min}}{H}, \frac{x_{max}}{W}, \frac{y_{max}}{H}, \frac{\Delta x \cdot \Delta y}{W \cdot H}\right]$ where (W, H) are width and height of the image respectively. To encode the interdependence of the phrases, we suggest to use the phrase categories (from PIN) of source and target phrases embedded as a one-hot-vector rv. The relation between the two phrases is encoded using an LSTM (Er); concatenated with visual feature and is projected using a Fully Connected Layer to obtain regression parameters for target phrase location. For a query phrase p_i and its neighboring phrases Np_i, the regression Rp_i is estimated as follows:

$$Rp_i = \phi(\mathbf{W}_{rl}(fv_k || lv_k || rv_k || Er_i) + \mathbf{b}_{rl}); v_k \in \{V_S^{Np_i}\} \tag{4}$$

where '$||$' denotes the concatenation operator, p_i is the query phrase whose regression parameters are predicted and $\{V_S^{Np_i}\}$ is the set of region proposals chosen by PIN for neighboring phrases Np_i of query phrase p_i. $\mathbf{W}_{rl}$ and $\mathbf{b}_{rl}$ are projection parameters and ϕ is the non-linear activation function.

During training, the regression loss $\mathcal{L}_{rlReg}$ for predicted regression parameters Rp_i is calculated as follows:

$$\mathcal{L}_{rlReg}(Rp_i, g_{p_i}) = \sum_{k=1}^{4} f(||rp_i[k] - g_{p_i}[k]||) \tag{5}$$

given the ground truth regression parameters g_{p_i} calculated from ground truth location g of target phrase p_i.

The proposals $\{rV_S^i\}$ estimated from both the neighboring phrases (subject and object) are added to the proposals generated by PIN

$$\{V_{S_a}^i\} \equiv \{V_S^i\} \bigcup \{rV_S^i\} \tag{6}$$

IRN enhances the proposal set and is especially useful for smaller objects which are often missed by proposal generators (Fig. 4, query 3). The candidate proposal set$\{V_{S_a}^i\}$ is next passed to the Proposal Ranking Network.

3.4 Proposal Ranking Network (PRN)

Proposal Ranking Network (PRN) is designed to incorporate visual and semantic context while ranking the region proposals. PRN employs a bimodal network to generate a confidence score for each region proposal using a discriminative correlation metric. For the visual modality, we employ contrastive visual features to differentiate among the region proposals from the same phrase category.

Each proposal is encoded by aggregating its relative appearance with respect to other candidate proposals (Eq. 6). This relative appearance between a given proposal and any other candidate proposal is computed by L2 normalization of the difference in visual features of the two proposals. To compute the feature representation, this relative appearance is aggregated using average pooling for a given proposal as follows:

$$cfv_k = \sum_{l \neq k} \frac{fv_k - fv_l}{\|fv_k - fv_l\|}; v_k \in \{V^i_{S_a}\}$$

For location and size feature representation, we encode relative position and size of a given proposal with respect to all the other candidate proposals. This representation helps in capturing the attributes of a proposal compared with other candidate proposals and is especially helpful in relative references. This feature representation is encoded as a 5 D vector: $\left[\frac{[x_{c_k} - x_{c_{Nk}}]}{w_k}, \frac{[y_{c_k} - y_{c_{Nk}}]}{h_k}, \frac{[w_k - w_{Nk}]}{w_k}, \frac{[h_k - h_{Nk}]}{h_k}, \frac{[w_{Nk} * h_{Nk}]}{[w_k * h_k]}\right]$ using the relative distance between centers, relative width, relative height and relative size of the given proposal and any other candidate proposal respectively. The final visual representation is the concatenation of all the above representations (Eq. 7).

To encode the text modality (Eq. 8), we concatenate the query embedding, g_{p_i} with embedding, g_{fc} of the entire image description $\mathbb{C}$.

$$Rv_k = \phi(\mathbf{W}_V(fv_k||cfv_k||lv_k) + \mathbf{b}_V) \tag{7}$$

$$Rp_i = \phi(\mathbf{W}_T(g_{p_i}||g_{fc}) + \mathbf{b}_T) \tag{8}$$

To compute the cross modal similarity, first the textual representation is projected into the same dimensionality as the visual representation. Then, the discriminative confidence score $\zeta(v_k, p_i)$ is computed by accounting for the bias between the two modalities as follows:

$$Vp_i = \phi(\mathbf{W}_P(Rp_i)), bp_i = \phi(\mathbf{b}_P(Rp_i)) \tag{9}$$

$$\zeta(v_k, p_i) = Vp_i.Rv_k + \mathbf{b}_{p_i} \tag{10}$$

To learn the projection weights and bias for both modalities during training, we employ the max-margin ranking loss $\mathcal{L}_{rnk}$ that assigns higher scores to positive proposals. To account for multiple positive proposals in the candidate set, we experiment with both maximum and average pooling to get the representative positive score from the proposals. In our experiments, maximum pooling operator performed better. The ranking loss is formulated below:

$$\mathcal{L}_{rnk} = \sum_{N_k} max[0, \lambda + \zeta(v_{N_k}, p_i) - max(\zeta(v_{P_k}, p_i))] \tag{11}$$

The loss implies that the score of the highest scoring positive proposal, $v_{P_k} \in \{V^i_{S_a}\}$ should be greater than each of the negative proposal $v_{N_k} \in \{V^i_{S_a}\}$ by a margin λ.

3.5 Supervised Training and Inference

The proposal generator for PIN is pre-trained using RPN [25] architecture on PASCAL VOC [7] dataset. The fully-connected network of PIN is alternatively optimized with RPN to index the proposals. Stage 2 of PIN is trained independently for 30 epochs with a learning rate of 1e−3. IRN and PRN for are trained for 30 epochs with starting learning rate of 1e−3 that is reduced by a factor of 10 every 10 epochs. During testing, the region proposal with the highest score from PRN is chosen as the prediction for a query phrase.

4 Weakly Supervised Training

We present our framework for weakly-supervised training in this section.

4.1 Weak Proposal Indexing Network (WPIN)

For weakly-supervised grounding, to overcome the lack of ground truth information, we employ knowledge transfer learning from object detection systems for indexing relevant proposals for a query phrase. The knowledge transfer is two-fold: data-driven knowledge transfer and appearance based knowledge transfer. We describe both methodologies below.

Data-Driven Knowledge Transfer. For Data-driven Knowledge Transfer, our training objective is to learn the representations of phrase categories from a pre-trained object detection network. The pre-trained network's relevant object classes provide a strong initialization for generating proposals of phrase categories (defined similarly as Sect. 3.2). For a region proposal $v_k \in \{V_T\}$, the network trains to predict probability $\{pc_j\}$ for a phrase category $C_j, j \in [1, N]$. Final scoring layer of pre-trained network is replaced to predict the probabilities of N phrase categories. Each region proposal v_k is represented as the distribution of the phrase category probabilities $[pc_1^k..pc_J^k]$. For training the network, the representations of K region proposals for an image $\mathbb{I}$ are added and loss function $\mathcal{L}_{dkt}$ is calculated as a multi-label sigmoid classification loss as follows:

$$\mathcal{L}_{dkt} = \frac{1}{N}\sum_{j=1}^{N} y_j * log(PC_j) + (1 - y_j) * log(1 - PC_j) \tag{12}$$

where $PC_j = \sigma(\frac{1}{K}\sum_{k=1}^{K} pc_j^k)$. σ denotes the sigmoid function. $y_i = 1$ if the image contains phrase category and 0 otherwise. During test time, the region proposals with highest scores $\{pc_j^{max}\}$ for a query phrase $p \in C_j$, are chosen as the indexed query proposals $\{V_I\}$.

Appearance-Based Knowledge Transfer. Appearance-based knowledge Transfer is based on the expectation that semantically related object classes have visually similar appearances. While this may not hold true universally and could mislead the system in few cases, it provides a strong generalization among classes that do. Given probability scores $\{pc_o\}$ of a set of source classes $\{sc_o\}$ for a region proposal $v_k \in \{V_T\}$, the goal of the knowledge transfer is to learn the correlation score S^j_{pk} for a query phrase p for that region proposal v_k. To measure the correlation among different classes, we employ skip vectors [20] that embed semantically related words in similar vector representations. For a query phrase p, we employ its constituent nouns NP extracted using Stanford POS tagger along with phrase category $\{C_j\}, j \in [1, N]$ for its semantic representation. For a set of K proposals $\{v_k\}$ given by an object detection system with source class probability scores $\{pc^k_o\}$; we measure their correlation S^j_{pk} to target phrase class C_j and phrase's constituent nouns NP as follows:

$$S^j_{pk} = \frac{\sum_{o=1}^{O} pc_o * Vsc_o}{||\sum_{o=1}^{O} pc_o * Vsc_o||} \cdot \frac{V(C_j) + V(NP)}{||V(C_j) + V(NP)||} \quad (13)$$

An average of appearance-based correlation S^j_{pk} and data-driven probability pc^k_j is employed as the final score for correlation of proposal v_k with query phrase p.

4.2 Training and Inference

Faster RCNN system [25] pretrained on MSCOCO [19] dataset using VGG [30] architecture is employed for knowledge transfer. For training the weakly supervised grounding system, the encoder-decoder network with attention is used to compute reconstruction loss similar to [27]. The learning rate of the network is set to 1e−4.

5 Experiments and Results

We evaluate our framework on Flickr30K Entities [24] and Referit Game [13] datasets for phrase grounding task.

5.1 Datasets

Flickr30k Entities. We use a standard split of 30,783 training and 1000 testing images. Each image has 5 captions, 360K query phrases are extracted from these captions and refer to 276K manually annotated bounding boxes. Each phrase is assigned one of eight pre-defined phrase categories. We treat the connecting words between two phrases in the caption as a 'relation' and use relations occurring > 5 times for training IRN.

ReferIt Game. We use a standard split of 9,977 training and 9974 testing images. A total of 130K query phrases are annotated to refer to 96K distinct objects. Unlike Flick30K, the query phrases are not extracted from a caption and do not come with an associated phrase category. Hence, we skip training IRN for ReferIT.

5.2 Experimental Setup

Phrase Indexing Network (PIN). A Faster RCNN pre-trained on PASCAL VOC 2007 [7] is finetuned on the respective datasets for proposal generation. Flickr30k [24] and ReferIt Game [13] employ 10 and 20 cluster centers obtained from clustering training query phrases as target classes respectively. Vectors from the last fc layers are used as visual representation for each proposal. For Stage 2, hidden size and dimension of bi-LSTM are set to 1024.

InterPhrase Regression Network (IRN). Since query phrases of ReferIt game are annotated individually, IRN is only applicable to Flickr30k dataset. The visual features from PIN are concatenated with 5D spatial representation (for regression) and 8*8 one-hot embedded vector for source and target phrase categories; for generating representation vector. Both left and right neighboring phrases, if available, are used for regression prediction.

Proposal Ranking Network (PRN). For visual stream, the visual features from PIN are augmented with contrastive visual features and 5D relative location features; generating an augmented feature vector. For text stream, lstm features are generated for both query phrase and corresponding caption. Each stream has 2 fully connected layers followed by a ReLU non-linearity and Dropout layers with probability $\bar{0}.5$ The intermediate and output dimensions of visual and text streams are [8192, 4096].

Network Parameters. All convolutional and fully connected layers are initialized using MSRA and Xavier respectively. All the features are l2 normalized and batch normalization is employed before similarity computation. Training batch size is set to 40 and learning rate is 1e$-$3 for both flickr30k and referit. VGG architecture [30] is used for PIN to be comparable to existing approaches. Further, ResNet [11] architecture is used to establish the new state-of-the-art with improved visual representation. In the experiments, we use VGG net for comparison with other methods and ResNet for performance analysis. We set L as 10 and 20 for VGG net and ResNet respectively.

Evaluation Metrics. Accuracy is adopted as the evaluation metric and a predicted proposal is considered positive, if it has an overlap of $>$0.5 with the ground-truth location. For evaluating the efficiency of indexing network, Top 3 and Top 5 accuracy are also presented.

5.3 Results on Flickr30k Entities

Performance. We compare performance of PIRC Net to other existing approaches for Flickr30k dataset. As shown in Table 1, PIN alone achieves 1.13% improvement while using a fraction of proposals compared to existing approaches. Adding IRN with ranking objective, we achieve 5.05% increase in accuracy. Adding PRN along with PIN, we achieve 5.83% improvement. Our overall framework achieves 6.02% improvement over QRC which is the existing

Table 1. Relative performance of our approach on Flickr30k dataset. Different combinations of our modules are evaluated.

Approach	Accuracy (%)
Compared approaches	
SCRC [12]	27.80
Structured Matching [33]	42.08
GroundeR [27]	47.81
MCB [8]	48.69
CCA embedding [23]	50.89
SPPC [22]	55.85
MSRC [3]	57.53
QRC [4]	65.14
Our approaches	
PIN (VGG Net)	66.27
PIN + IRC (VGG Net)	70.17
PIN + PRN (VGG Net)	70.97
PIRC Net (VGG Net)	**71.16**
PIN (Res Net)	69.37
PIN + IRC (Res Net)	71.42
PIN + PRN (Res Net)	72.27
PIRC Net (Res Net)	**72.83**

Table 2. Relative performance of our approach for Weakly supervised Grounding on Flickr30k dataset.

Approach	Accuracy (%)
Compared approaches	
Deep Fragments [14]	21.78
GroundeR [27]	28.94
Our approach	
PIRC Net	**34.28**

Table 3. Performance evaluation of efficiency of supervised PIN on Flickr30k Entities

Retrieval rate	Top 1	Top 3	Top 5
QRC (see footnote 1) [4]	65.14	73.70	78.47
PIRC Net	**66.27**	**79.80**	**83.46**
Proposal limit (no regression)			83.12

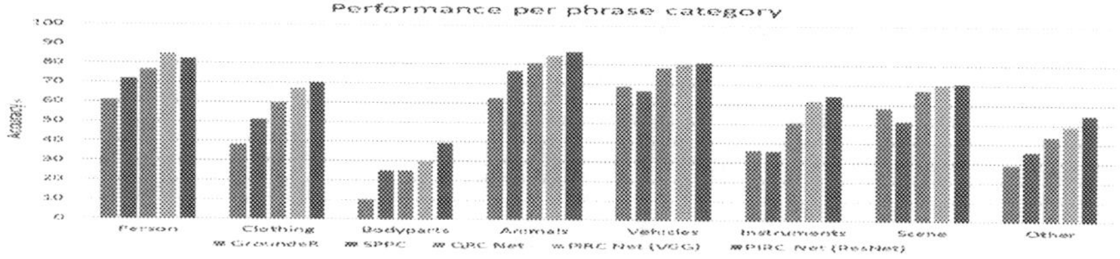

Fig. 3. Grounding performance per phrase category for different methods on Flickr30K Entities

Table 4. Relative performance of our approach on Referit Game dataset.

Approach	Accuracy (%)
Compared approaches	
SCRC [12]	17.93
GroundeR [27]	26.93
MSRC [3]	32.21
Context-aware RL [34]	36.18
QRC [4]	44.07
Our approaches	
PIN (VGG Net)	51.67
PIRC Net (PIN+PRN) (VGG Net)	**54.32**
PIN (Res Net)	56.67
PIRC Net (PIN+PRN) (Res Net)	**59.13**

state-of-the-art approach. Further, employing Resnet architecture for PIN gives an additional 1.67% improvement.

Weakly-Supervised Grounding Performance. We compare performance of PIRC Net to two other existing approaches for Weakly-supervised Grounding. As shown in Table 2, we achieve 5.34% improvement over existing state-of-the art.

PIN Indexing Performance. The effectiveness of PIN is measured by its ability to index proposals for query phrase. For this, we measure the accuracy of proposals at Top 1, Top 3 and Top 5 ranks. We compare the results to QRC, which is the current state of the art in Table 3. The upperbound i.e., the maximum accuracy possible with RPN is mentioned in the last row. PIN consistently outperforms QRC [4][1] in Top 3 and Top 5 retrieval showcasing its effectiveness in indexing the proposals. Our method employs regression to move proposals to positive locations improving over upperbound.

Per Category Performance. For the predefined phrase categories of Flickr30K Entities, PIRC Net consistently performs better across all categories 3.

[1] Results provided by authors.

Table 5. Relative performance of our approach for Weakly supervised Grounding on Referit dataset.

Approach	Accuracy (%)
Compared approaches	
LRCN [6](reported in [12])	8.59
CAFFE-7K [10](reported in [12])	10.38
GroundeR [27]	10.69
Our approach	
PIRC Net	**14.39**

5.4 Results on ReferIt Game

Performance. Table 4 shows the performance of PIRC Net compared to existing approaches. PIN network gives a 7.6% improvement over state-of-the-art approaches. The high gains could be attributed to richer diversity of objects in ReferIt Game than Flickr30k Entities dataset. Employing PRN in addition to PIN, gives a 10.25% improvement over QRC. Using ResNet architecture gives an additional 4.81% improvement; leading to 15.06% improvement over the state-of-the-art.

Weakly-Supervised Grounding Performance. We compare performance of PIRC Net to two other existing approaches for Weakly-supervised Grounding on Referit. As shown in Table 5, we achieve 3.70% improvement over existing state-of-the art.

PIN Indexing Performance. Similar to Flickr30k, we do performance analysis to judge the effectiveness of PIN. The results are presented in Table 6. PIN consistently performs better for Top 3 and Top 5 retrieval.

Table 6. Performance evaluation of efficiency of supervised PIN on Referit Game

Retrieval rate	Top 1	Top 3	Top 5
QRC (see footnote 1) [4]	44.07	54.96	59.45
PIRC Net	**51.67**	**68.49**	**73.69**
Proposal limit			77.79

5.5 Qualitative Results

We present qualitative results for few samples on Flickr30K Entities and ReferItGame datasets (Fig. 4). For Flickr30K (top row), we show an image with its caption and five associated query phrases. We can see the importance of context in localizing the queries. For ReferIt (middle row), we show the query phrase and the associated results. Bottom row shows the failure cases.

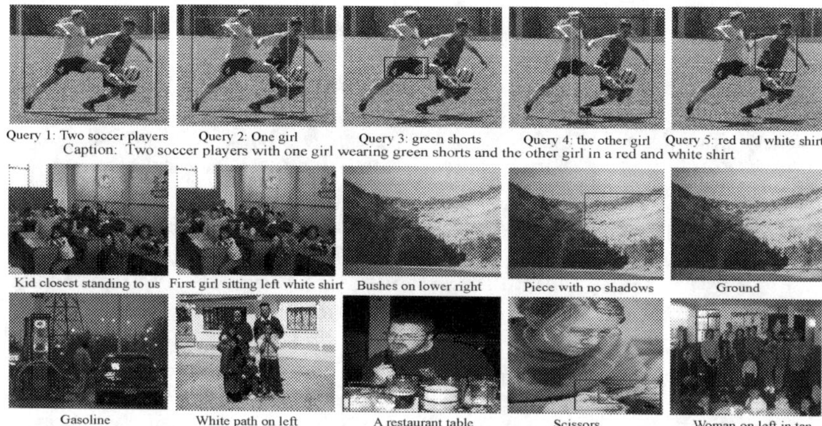

Fig. 4. Qualitative results on the test sets of Flickr30K Entities (top row) and ReferIT Game (middle row). Last row shows failure cases from both the datasets. Green: Correct Prediction, Red: Wrong Prediction, Blue: Groundtruth (Color figure online)

6 Conclusions

In this paper, we addressed the problem of phrase grounding using PIRC Net, a framework that incorporates semantic and contextual cues to rank visual proposals. By incorporating these cues, our framework outperforms other baselines for phrase grounding. Further, we demonstrate the benefit of knowledge transfer from object detection systems for weakly-supervised grounding.

Acknowledgements. This paper is based, in part, on research sponsored by the Air Force Research Laboratory and the Defense Advanced Research Projects Agency under agreement number FA8750-16-2-0204. The U.S. Government is authorized to reproduce and distribute reprints for Governmental purposes notwithstanding any copyright notation thereon. The views and conclusions contained herein are those of the authors and should not be interpreted as necessarily representing the official policies or endorsements, either expressed or implied, of the Air Force Research Laboratory and the Defense Advanced Research Projects Agency or the U.S. Government.

References

1. Agharwal, A., Kovvuri, R., Nevatia, R., Snoek, C.G.M.: Tag-based video retrieval by embedding semantic content in a continuous word space. In: Applications of Computer Vision (WACV) (2016)
2. Karpathy, A., Li, F.F.: Deep visual-semantic alignments for generating image descriptions. In: CVPR (2015)
3. Chen, K., Kovvuri, R., J., G., Nevatia, R.: MSRC: multimodal spatial regression with semantic context for phrase grounding. In: ICMR (2017)
4. Chen, K., Kovvuri, R., Nevatia, R.: Query-guided regression network with context policy for phrase grounding. In: ICCV (2017)

5. Deselaers, T., Alexe, B., Ferrari, V.: Weakly supervised localization and learning with generic knowledge. IJCV **100**, 275–293 (2012)
6. Donahue, J., et al.: Long-term recurrent convolutional networks for visual recognition and description. In: CVPR (2015)
7. Everingham, M., Van Gool, L., Williams, C.K.I., Winn, J., Zisserman, A.: The PASCAL visual object classes challenge. IJCV **88**, 303–338 (2010)
8. Fukui, A., Park, D.H., Yang, D., Rohrbach, A., Darrell, T., Rohrbach, M.: Multimodal compact bilinear pooling for visual question answering and visual grounding. In: EMNLP (2016)
9. Gordo, A., Almazán, J., Revaud, J., Larlus, D.: Deep image retrieval: learning global representations for image search. In: Leibe, B., Matas, J., Sebe, N., Welling, M. (eds.) ECCV 2016. LNCS, vol. 9910, pp. 241–257. Springer, Cham (2016). https://doi.org/10.1007/978-3-319-46466-4_15
10. Guadarrama, S., Rodner, E., Saenko, K., Darrell, T.: Understanding object descriptions in robotics by open-vocabulary object retrieval and detection. IJRR **35**, 265–280 (2016)
11. He, K., Zhang, X., Ren, S., Sun, J.: Deep residual learning for image recognition (2016)
12. Hu, R., Xu, H., Rohrbach, M., Feng, J., Saenko, K., Darrell, T.: Natural language object retrieval. In: CVPR (2016)
13. Kazemzadeh, S., Ordonez, V., Matten, M., Berg, T.L.: ReferItGame: referring to objects in photographs of natural scenes. In: EMNLP (2014)
14. Karpathy, A., Joulin, A., Li, F.F.: Deep fragment embeddings for bidirectional image sentence mapping. In: NIPS (2014)
15. Kiros, R., et al.: Skip-thought vectors. In: NIPS (2015)
16. Kong, C., Lin, D., Bansal, M., Urtasun, R., Fidler, S.: What are you talking about? text-to-image coreference. In: CVPR (2014)
17. Wang, L., Li, Y., Lazebnik, S.: Learning deep structure-preserving image-text embeddings. In: CVPR (2016)
18. Li, F.F.: Knowledge transfer in learning to recognize visual objects classes. In: ICDL (2006)
19. Lin, T.Y., et al.: Microsoft COCO: common objects in context. In: Fleet, D., Pajdla, T., Schiele, B., Tuytelaars, T. (eds.) ECCV 2014. LNCS, vol. 8693, pp. 740–755. Springer, Cham (2014). https://doi.org/10.1007/978-3-319-10602-1_48
20. Mikolov, T., Sutskever, I., Chen, K., Corrado, G., Dean, J.: Distributed representations of words and phrases and their compositionality. In: NIPS (2013)
21. Nagaraja, V.K., Morariu, V.I., Davis, L.S.: Modeling context between objects for referring expression understanding. In: Leibe, B., Matas, J., Sebe, N., Welling, M. (eds.) ECCV 2016. LNCS, vol. 9908, pp. 792–807. Springer, Cham (2016). https://doi.org/10.1007/978-3-319-46493-0_48
22. Plummer, B.A., Mallya, A., Christopher, M.C., Hockenmaier, J., Lazebnik, S.: Phrase localization and visual relationship detection with comprehensive image-language cues. In: ICCV (2017)
23. Plummer, B.A., Wang, L., Cervantes, C.M., Caicedo, J.C., Hockenmaier, J., Lazebnik, S.: Flickr30k entities: collecting region-to-phrase correspondences for richer image-to-sentence models. In: IJCV (2016)
24. Plummer, B.A., Wang, L., Cervantes, C.M., Caicedo, J.C., Hockenmaier, J., Lazebnik, S.: Flickr30k entities: collecting region-to-phrase correspondences for richer image-to-sentence models. In: ICCV (2015)
25. Ren, S., He, K., Girshick, R., Sun, J.: Faster R-CNN: towards real-time object detection with region proposal networks. In: NIPS (2015)

26. Rochan, M., Wang, Y.: Weakly supervised localization of novel objects using appearance transfer. In: CVPR (2015)
27. Rohrbach, A., Rohrbach, M., Hu, R., Darrell, T., Schiele, B.: Grounding of textual phrases in images by reconstruction. In: Leibe, B., Matas, J., Sebe, N., Welling, M. (eds.) ECCV 2016. LNCS, vol. 9905, pp. 817–834. Springer, Cham (2016). https://doi.org/10.1007/978-3-319-46448-0_49
28. Rohrbach, A., Rohrbach, M., Tang, S., Oh, S.J., Schiele, B.: Generating descriptions with grounded and co-referenced people. In: CVPR (2017)
29. Rohrbach, M., Stark, M., Schiele, B.: Evaluating knowledge transfer and zero-shot learning in a large-scale setting. In: CVPR (2011)
30. Simonyan, K., Zisserman, A.: Very deep convolutional networks for large-scale image recognition. CoRR (2014)
31. Uijlings, J.R., Van De Sande, K.E., Gevers, T., Smeulders, A.W.: Selective search for object recognition. IJCV **104**, 154–171 (2013)
32. de Vries, H., Strub, F., Chandar, S., Pietquin, O., Larochelle, H., Courville, A.: Guesswhat?! visual object discovery through multi-modal dialogue. In: CVPR (2017)
33. Wang, M., Azab, M., Kojima, N., Mihalcea, R., Deng, J.: Structured matching for phrase localization. In: Leibe, B., Matas, J., Sebe, N., Welling, M. (eds.) ECCV 2016. LNCS, vol. 9912, pp. 696–711. Springer, Cham (2016). https://doi.org/10.1007/978-3-319-46484-8_42
34. Wu, F., Xu, Z., Yang, Y.: An end-to-end approach to natural language object retrieval via context-aware deep reinforcement learning. arxiv (2017)
35. Yu, L., Poirson, P., Yang, S., Berg, A.C., Berg, T.L.: Modeling context in referring expressions. In: Leibe, B., Matas, J., Sebe, N., Welling, M. (eds.) ECCV 2016. LNCS, vol. 9906, pp. 69–85. Springer, Cham (2016). https://doi.org/10.1007/978-3-319-46475-6_5
36. Zitnick, C.L., Dollár, P.: Edge boxes: locating object proposals from edges. In: Fleet, D., Pajdla, T., Schiele, B., Tuytelaars, T. (eds.) ECCV 2014. LNCS, vol. 8693, pp. 391–405. Springer, Cham (2014). https://doi.org/10.1007/978-3-319-10602-1_26

Paired-D GAN for Semantic Image Synthesis

Duc Minh Vo[1(✉)] and Akihiro Sugimoto[2]

[1] Department of Informatics,
The Graduate University for Advanced Studies (SOKENDAI), Tokyo, Japan
[2] National Institute of Informatics, Tokyo, Japan
{vmduc,sugimoto}@nii.ac.jp

Abstract. Semantic image synthesis is to render foreground (object) given as a text description into a given source image. This has a wide range of applications such as intelligent image manipulation, and is helpful to those who are not good at painting. We propose a generative adversarial network having a pair of discriminators with different architectures, called *Paired-D GAN*, for semantic image synthesis where the two discriminators make different judgments: one for foreground synthesis and the other for background synthesis. The generator of paired-D GAN has the encoder-decoder architecture with skip-connections and synthesizes an image matching the given text description while preserving other parts of the source image. The two discriminators judge foreground and background of the synthesized image separately to meet an input text description and a source image. The paired-D GAN is trained using the effective adversarial learning process in a simultaneous three-player minimax game. Experimental results on the Caltech-200 bird dataset and the Oxford-102 flower dataset show that Paired-GAN is capable of semantically synthesizing images to match an input text description while retaining the background in a source image against the state-of-the-art methods.

1 Introduction

Very recently proposed semantic image synthesis [1] is to manipulate a given source image semantically with given text descriptions, while still maintain features that are irrelevant to what text descriptions. Text descriptions are usually on foreground (objects), and thus the task is to render foreground given as a text description into a given source image. Since text descriptions [2] is easier and more natural for us than image descriptions such as attributes [3], textures [4] or styles [5], semantic image synthesis is promising to widen the range of applications of image synthesis.

Generative Adversarial Network (GAN) [6] is capable of synthesizing images, and work has been proposed that conditions GAN on either text descriptions [2, 7] or images [8–10] to synthesize images for various tasks. Almost all work on image synthesis [1,2,7,11] follows the original GAN architecture where a single

C. V. Jawahar et al. (Eds.): ACCV 2018, LNCS 11364, pp. 468–484, 2019.
https://doi.org/10.1007/978-3-030-20870-7_29

discriminator judges whether a synthesized image is realistic. Despite obtaining remarkable results, synthesizing realistic images directly from text descriptions is still difficult. This is due to the gap between the semantic levels of images and text descriptions.

Semantic image synthesis requires to disentangle the semantics contained in image and text information and then combine the disentangled semantics to synthesize realistic images. This suggests to separately deal with text descriptions and images with different semantic levels. We thus design a GAN with a pair of discriminators, called *Paired-D GAN*, to separately condition text descriptions and images. Indeed, dual discriminator GAN [12] showed that having two discriminators is more effective than GANs with one discriminator for image synthesis. Different from dual discriminator GAN, we design different architectures for two discriminators to deal with different levels of semantics of text descriptions and images. The two discriminators separately judge foreground and background of the synthesized image to meet an input text description and a source image. Furthermore, we employ the skip-connection in the generator to more precisely retain background information in the source image. We also introduce a training process for adversarial learning in the three-player minimax game of the generator and two discriminators. In this way, Paired-D GAN improves the quality of synthesized images. Experiments on the Caltech-200 bird dataset [13] and the Oxford-102 flower dataset [14] demonstrate outperformances of Paired-D GAN against [1,15]. Figure 1 shows an example of our results.

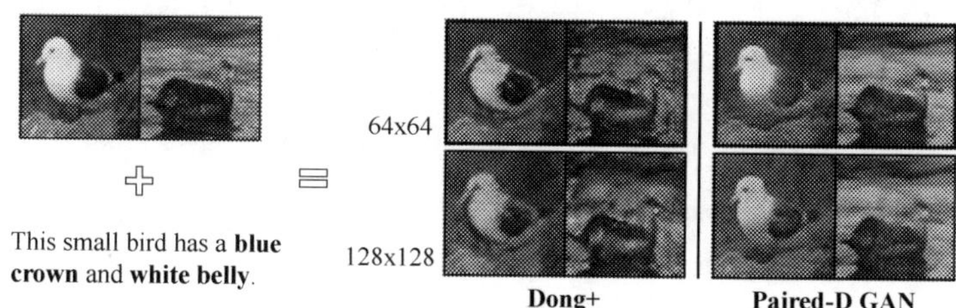

Fig. 1. Examples of synthesized images. Our results match the text description more precisely than [1] while successfully retaining background of the source image. The performance of our method does not change for different sizes of images (64×64 and 128×128 images).

2 Related Work

With the rapid development of deep learning, many models for image synthesis have been proposed to achieve highly realistic images. They include variational auto-encoder [16,17], auto-regressive models [18,19], and GAN [1,2,6,15]. Among them, GAN and its variants show remarkably realistic results.

GAN [6] consists of a generator and a discriminator. The generator maps the latent variable into the data space while the discriminator judges whether the output of the generator is real or fake. The generator and the discriminator are simultaneously trained in a minimax game. Interestingly, GAN can be constrained on various conditions not only to generate plausible images but also to meet the conditions. Some work conditions GANs on the attribute label [3,20] or images [10,21–24] for domain transfer [21,22], photo editing [23], image super-resolution [10], and style transfer [24].

Among various conditions on GAN, text descriptions make image synthesis easier and more friendly to us. Reed et al. [2] proposed an end-to-end GAN using the text condition. They employed a pre-trained text encoder [25] to extract text features from an input text, and then combined text features with a vector representing random noise to produce the input of the generator. They also employed the combination of text features and image features in the discriminator to discriminate real images and generated images. Their proposed model [2] became the baseline of the GAN framework for generating images from text descriptions.

As an extension, a model conditioned on texts and location information was proposed [26]. Models with two stages of GAN, Stack-GAN [7] (and Stack-GAN++ [11]), were also proposed, showing successfully generated higher resolution images (256×256), compared to [2] (64×64). These models [2,7,11,15] condition on GAN only texts or a pair of texts and location information [26].

Addressing the background problem in image synthesis, Yang et al. [15] proposed to decompose the image synthesis into two phases using foreground and background generators. They fed random noise vectors to a long short-term memory (LSTM) network to obtain hidden states for the foreground generator and used the first hidden state to generate background. They then combined foreground and background by a compositor operator. However, decomposing foreground and background may cause less realistic images.

The model proposed by Dong et al. [1] is most related with ours. It also conditions text and source image on GAN. The architecture of the model is, however, similar to [2] and has a single discriminator: the noise vector in [2] is replaced by image features from the image encoder. Though it generates images that match the semantic meaning of the input text description while maintaining other parts of a source image, it does not preserve background precisely because the discriminator is used only for foreground; synthesized images are less realistic images.

Different from the above mentioned models, we fully take into account each role of foreground and background in synthesized images. More precisely, our proposed Paired-D GAN is conditioned on both text descriptions and images, has skip-connections in its generator to preserve background information as much as possible, and has two discriminators with different architectures for synthesizing realistic images. Paired-D GAN generates simultaneously foreground and background.

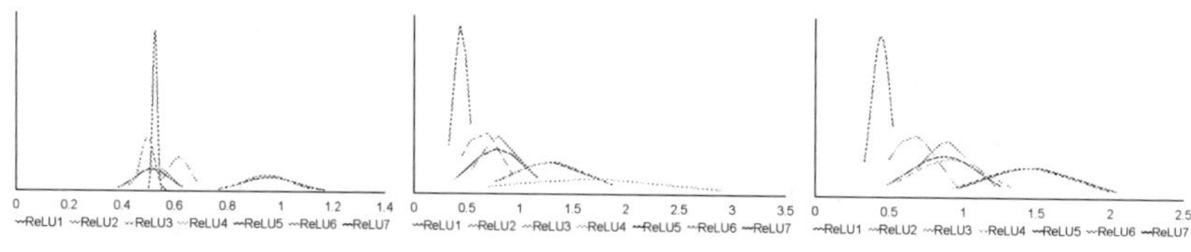

(a) Same background (with different foregrounds). (b) Different backgrounds (with one foreground). (c) Different backgrounds (with another foreground).

Fig. 2. Distribution of the mean values of the first 7 ReLU layers in VGG-16.

3 Semantic Levels of Image Features for Foreground/Background

Convolution Neural Network (CNN) has proved the effectiveness in many tasks. Along with the depth, CNN extracts different semantic levels of image features in layers. Gatys et al. [5] pointed out that features in early layers reflect color or texture of images while features in latter layers convey foreground information. The work [27] also found that features in early layers address background while foreground is obtained in latter layers. As [28] learned the statistic of image features, we experimentally exploit semantic levels of image features in VGG-16 [29].

We randomly prepare 10 foreground images and 8 background ones. We then generated 100 images for each pair of foreground-background images with randomly localizing foreground (we have 8000 images in total). We feed these generated images into the VGG-16 [29] pre-trained on ImageNet dataset [30] without any fine-tuning to compute the mean activation at each Rectified Linear Unit (ReLU) layer [31].

The distribution of the mean activations in all 13 ReLU layers shows that the first 7 ReLU layers are more sensitive to background and foreground than the other ReLU layers. In the case where background is the same (Fig. 2a), the distribution of the mean values is small at the 1st – 3rd ReLU layers and becomes larger from the 4th ReLU layer. This suggests that VGG-16 recognizes the similarity of images at the 1st – 3rd ReLU layers and starts to learn differences of images from the 4th ReLU layer (though not strictly clear at the 4th layer).

On the other hand, in the case where backgrounds are different (Fig. 2b, c), the values at the 1st – 3rd ReLU layers are larger and similar with each other even if foregrounds are different (compared to the same background case). This observation is in good harmony with the same background case. If we change foreground (Fig. 2b, c), the distribution of mean values is completely different from the layer 4th to the 7th layer (at each layer respectively).

Combining insights given by [5,27], we may thus conclude that VGG-16 weights background in early layers and foreground at latter layers. More precisely, from the 1st to the 3rd ReLU layers capture background while from the 5th to the 7th ReLU layers do foreground, and the 4th ReLU layer seems to be in-between as a transition.

Using appropriate semantic levels of image features for discriminators is crucial. We use above observation for employing appropriate semantic levels of image features for foreground and background. Namely, we use features from the 1st to the 3rd ReLU layers for background and those from the 5th to the 7th ReLU layers for foreground. We remark that more deeply exploring background-foreground relation is preferable.

4 Proposed Method

4.1 Network Design

Our network follows the GAN architecture [6] for image synthesis [1,2,7,11]. Like [1], we condition GAN on both text descriptions and a source image. As seen in Sect. 3, we use different semantic levels of features depending on foreground and background. Namely, we design the network in which a text description on foreground matches features in latter layers while features of a source image in early layers are preserved as much background information as possible. This appropriate-level selection allows our model to synthesize realistic images that meet both a text description and a source image.

Nguyen et al. [12] argued that dual discriminators in GAN generate better images in quality than a single discriminator, though the two discriminators has the same architecture. To deal with foreground and background separately and more precisely, we employ a pair of discriminators where each of them independently judges foreground/background of synthesized images. For different semantic levels of foreground and background, we design our discriminators with different architectures and make each play a different role. Namely, we design one discriminator to evaluate matching foreground between a text description and a synthesized image following [1,2,7] and the other discriminator to evaluate whether background of a source image is retained in the synthesized image. We also introduce an effective training strategy for adversarial learning in a three-player minimax game.

4.2 Network Architecture

We build our network, called Paired-D GAN, upon the GAN architecture with one generator G and a pair of discriminators, foreground discriminator D_{FG} and background discriminator D_{BG} (Fig. 3). We employ the end-to-end encoder-decoder architecture for our generator G following [1]. The generator G receives a source image and a text description where the source image is with the size of $n \times n \times 3$ (n can be 64, 128 or 256; 3 are for RGB channels) and the text description is with maximum of 50 words. G synthesizes an image of $n \times n \times 3$ that adaptively changes foreground to match the text description while retaining background of the source image.

Two discriminators D_{FG}, D_{BG} evaluate whether the synthesized image is real or generated. D_{FG} receives the generated image and the ground-truth foreground image with the text feature extracted from the text description to focus

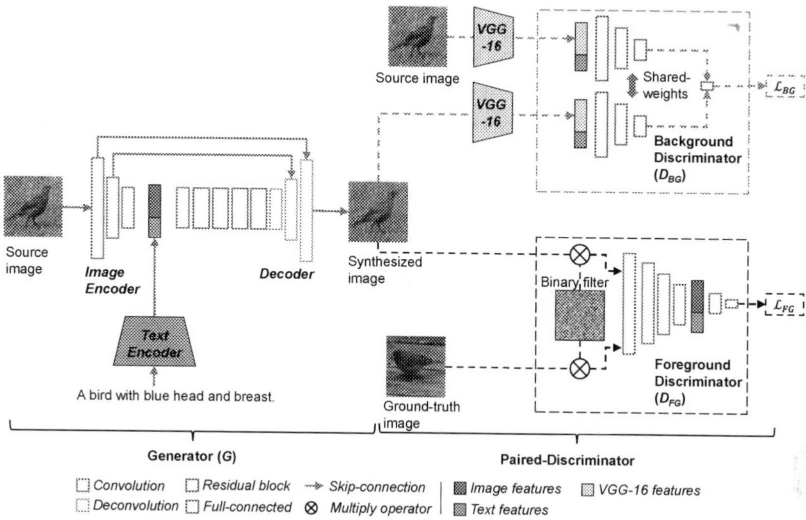

Fig. 3. Framework of our proposed Paired-D GAN.

on foreground evaluation. D_{BG}, on the other hand, receives the image feature extracted from the source image and the text feature extracted from the text description to focus on background evaluation. We use the pre-trained VGG-16 to extract image features from input images for D_{BG} as mentioned in Sect. 3. We remark that the two discriminators do not share their parameters.

We train G, D_{FG}, and D_{BG} simultaneously in a three-player minimax game using adaptive loss functions. This adversarial learning process enables our generator G to generate plausible images that mach text descriptions while preserving background information of the source image.

4.2.1 Generator

Our generator G consists of an image encoder, a text encoder, and a decoder.

The image encoder is a stack of three convolution layers that receives the source image size of $n \times n \times 3$ to produce an image feature with the size of $m \times m \times 512$ (m can be 16, 32 or 64 depending on n) at the top. We adopt the pre-trained text encoder [25] for our text encoder and use the text embedding augmentation [7] to produce a text feature with the size of 1×128. The channel of the text feature is duplicated to the size of $m \times m \times 128$ to be consistent with that of the image feature.

The image feature and the text feature are then concatenated to produce an image-text feature as the input of the decoder.

The decoder in our generator consists of one convolution layer, four residual blocks [32], and two deconvolution layers. The convolution layer reduces the channel of the image-text feature, and the four residual blocks enrich feature maps. The two deconvolution layers, on the other hand, upscale the feature maps.

We remark that each of the convolution and deconvolution layers in the image encoder and the decoder is followed by a batch normalization (BN) layer [33] and a ReLU layer. The only exception is the last deconvolution layer in the decoder where it uses the tanh activation to guarantee that the range of the output can be normalized to be $[0, 255]$ (in the test step). We remark that we use images with the range $[-1, 1]$ in the training step.

To reflect the features at early layers weighting background information into a synthesized image, we employ the skip-connection from the image encoder to the decoder. More precisely, the first layer in the image encoder is connected to the last layer in the decoder while the second layer in the image encoder is paired with the second last layer in the decoder.

4.2.2 Foreground Discriminator

The foreground discriminator should be able to discriminate foreground of real images and that of generated images. We employ the foreground-text matching in the foreground discriminator. Following previous work [1,2,7,11], we design our foreground discriminator D_{FG} as a classification task that rewards high probability scores to real images and low ones to generated images in the adversarial learning phase.

Our D_{FG} is a stack of six convolution layers.

Each of the first four convolution layers uses the filter size of 4×4, the reflection-padding size of 1×1, and the stride size of 2×2, producing 64, 128, 256, 512 output channels, respectively. These convolution layers encode an input to produce the high-level semantic image features containing mostly foreground information (cf. Sect. 3). These image features are then concatenated with the text feature obtained from the input text description using the text encoder to produce a image-text feature.

Next, the image-text feature is fed into the last two convolution layers, each of which is with the filter size of 1×1, and 4×4, respectively, no padding, the stride size of 1×1, outputting 512, 4 channels respectively. The output of the last convolution layer indicates how realistic the image input to D_{FG} is using the similarity probability.

We remark that each of the all convolution layers except for the last one is followed by a BN layer and a ReLU layer. We follow Reed et al. [2] to train D_{FG} (Eq. 1).

D_{FG} need not access all image information but focuses on foreground image information. To enhance the performance of D_{FG}, we introduce a processing before feeding an input image to D_{FG}. Namely, we create a binary filter where 0 at each pixel is generated with the probability of p. We then apply the binary filter to the image input to D_{FG}, and feed the filtered image to D_{FG}. This processing brings two benefits: (1) D_{FG} has more chance to focus on only foreground information, helping to extract semantic image features of foreground, and (2) this operation prevents quick convergence [34].

4.2.3 Background Discriminator

The background discriminator evaluates how real and generated images are different in background. We therefore design the background discriminator as a verification task with the limited number of samples in each category. This is because each image in a dataset has different background in general, and the number of samples with the same (very similar) background is limited. To this end, we follow the idea of the Siamese network [35] because it shows the effectiveness for the verification task.

Our D_{BG} consists of four fully-connected layers in which the first three layers are two shared-parameter layers and the last one is the joint layer, producing 512, 100, 10, 1 outputs, respectively. D_{BG} receives two input features (one from the source image with the text description and the other from the generated image with the text description) and passes them to the two shared-parameter layers separately before being jointly trained at the last layer.

In order to create the input of D_{BG}, we feed the input image into the pre-trained VGG-16 to compute the mean and variance at the first four ReLU layers (cf. Sect. 3), and then concatenate them with the text feature extracted from the input text description using the pre-trained text encoder [25] (without using the text embedding augmentation [7]). The text feature is useful to disentangle background and foreground information (e.g. images with the same background and different foreground information can be positive samples for the background verification task). We remark that the size of the input is 1×1068 where the image feature is with the size of 1×768 and the text feature is with the size of 1×300.

We propose a new training strategy for D_{BG}, which is based on the contrastive loss function [35] that fully uses a source image and a text description.

4.3 Adversarial Learning for Paired-GAN

Training the generator G, and a pair of discriminators D_{FG} and D_{BG} becomes a three-player minimax game conditioned on images and text descriptions. Using positive/negative training samples, we first update the parameters of D_{FG} with fixing the parameters of D_{BG} and G, and then update the parameters of D_{BG} with fixing the parameters of D_{FG} and G, and finally update the parameters of G with fixing the parameters of the two discriminators. We iterate this adversarial training to minimize each loss function separately.

For the adversarial training for Paired-D GAN, we use positive and negative samples whose definitions depend on D_{FG} and D_{BG}. A positive sample of D_{FG} is a sample in which foreground is the ground-truth and its text description is matching. A sample is negative if (1) foreground is the ground-truth but its text description is mismatching or (2) foreground is generated even if its text description is matching. A positive sample of D_{BG}, on the other hand, is the one where the background of the source image used in training the generator and discriminators for each iteration is the same regardless of whether text descriptions are matching or mismatching. A sample is negative if background is generated even if the text descriptions match foreground.

Table 1. Types of input pairs used in the adversarial leaning process.

	D_{FG}	D_{BG}
Positive	$\{g, \varphi(t)\}$	$\{(s,t), (s,\bar{t})\}$
Negative	$\{g, \varphi(\bar{t})\}$, $\{G(s,\varphi(t)), \varphi(t)\}$	$\{(G(s,\varphi(t)),t), (G(\bar{s},\varphi(t)),t)\}$

Let s be an image in a dataset and t be a text description. Then, we let g be an image in the dataset whose foreground is the ground-truth to t (t is thus a matching text description to g). We denote by $\bar{s}$ a randomly selected image (from the dataset) having different background from s, and by $\bar{t}$ a different text description from t (a mismatching text description to g). We also denote by $\varphi(\cdot)$ the text embedding augmentation [7]. Then, positive/negative samples of D_{FG} and D_{BG} can be classified as in Table 1.

Let $D(\cdot)$ denote the discriminators (D_{FG} and D_{BG}). At each iteration in training $D(\cdot)$, we randomly select all the types of samples in Table 1 from the training dataset, and feed them one by one to $D(\cdot)$ to obtain the probability whether the sample is positive or negative. We train the two discriminators to reward a high score to a positive sample and a low score to a negative sample. Through the training, we maximize the ability of $D(\cdot)$ to assign relevant scores to the samples. The loss functions for $D(\cdot)$ are defined as follows:

$$\mathcal{L}_{\mathrm{FG}} = \mathbb{E}_{(g,t)\sim p_{\mathrm{data}}}[\log D_{\mathrm{FG}}(g,\varphi(t))] + \frac{1}{2}\mathbb{E}_{(g,\bar{t})\sim p_{\mathrm{data}}}[\log(1 - D_{\mathrm{FG}}(g,\varphi(\bar{t})))] + \frac{1}{2}\mathbb{E}_{(s,t)\sim p_{\mathrm{data}}}[\log(1 - D_{\mathrm{FG}}(G(s,\varphi(t)),\varphi(t)))]. \tag{1}$$

$$\mathcal{L}_{\mathrm{BG}} = \mathbb{E}_{(s,t,s,\bar{t})\sim p_{\mathrm{data}}}[\log D_{\mathrm{BG}}((s,t),(s,\bar{t}))] + \mathbb{E}_{(s,t,\bar{s},t)\sim p_{\mathrm{data}}}[\log(1 - D_{\mathrm{BG}}((G(s,\varphi(t)),t),(G(\bar{s},\varphi(t)),t)))], \tag{2}$$

where p_{data} denotes the all the training data and $\mathbb{E}_{(\cdot)\sim p_{\mathrm{data}}}$ means the expectation over p_{data}. Each term in Eqs. 1 and 2 corresponds to the type of samples: $\log(D(\cdot))$ for positive samples and $\log(1 - D(\cdot))$ for negative samples. Note that Eq. 1 follows [2].

Since our adversarial learning process is a three-player minimax game, we also train the generator G in which we minimize the terms of $\log(1 - D(\cdot))$ in Eqs. 1 and 2. In practice, however, maximizing $\log(D(\cdot))$ is known to be better than minimizing $\log(1 - D(\cdot))$ in training G [6]. We also introduce the reconstruction loss to keep the structure of the input source image. Now the loss function for G is:

$$\mathcal{L}_{\mathrm{G}} = \mathbb{E}_{(s,t)\sim p_{\mathrm{data}}}[\log(D_{\mathrm{FG}}(G(s,\varphi(t)),\varphi(t))] + \mathbb{E}_{(s,t,s,\bar{t})\sim p_{\mathrm{data}}}[\log(D_{\mathrm{BG}}((G(s,\varphi(t)),t)),(G(s,\varphi(\bar{t})),\bar{t})))] + \lambda\mathbb{E}_{(s,t)\sim p_{\mathrm{data}}}\|s - G(s,\varphi(t))\|_2, \tag{3}$$

where λ is the hyperparameter, and $\|.\|_2$ is the Euclidean distance. To train G, we randomly select an image s, and two text descriptions t and $\bar{t}$ to generate the synthesized images. We then feed them to the D_{FG} and D_{BG} to receive feedback signals for updating parameters of G. We remark that since our aim is not to reconstruct the source image, λ can be small (we set $\lambda = 0.0001$ in our experiments).

As discussed in [2], training D_{FG} with match and mismatching text descriptions enables D_{FG} to feedback stronger image-text matching signals, allowing G to generate plausible images that match text descriptions. Our usage of a pair of image and a text description in training D_{BG}, on the other hand, enables D_{BG} to generate stronger signals as well, leading to the capability of G of retaining background information (though at the beginning, D_{BG} spends more time to verify background, D_{BG} gradually need not concern foreground thanks to text descriptions, and has ability of easily judging whether the image is real or generated). Accordingly, the above adversarial learning brings to Paired-D GAN the capability of generating realistic images that match text descriptions in foreground and precisely retain background of source images.

5 Experiments

5.1 Dataset and Compared Methods

Dataset. We used the Caltech-200 bird dataset [13] and the Oxford-102 flower dataset [14]. The Caltech-200 bird dataset contains 11,788 images belonging to one of 200 different bird classes. The Oxford-102 flower dataset has 8,189 images with 102 classes of the flower. Each image in the datasets has 10 captions collected by Reed et al. [25]. Following previous work [1,2], we split the Caltech-200 dataset into 150 training classes and 50 testing classes, and the Oxford-102 dataset into 82 training classes and 20 testing classes. We remark that we resized the images used in our experiments to ones with 64×64.

Compared Methods. We employed the model proposed by Dong+ [1] as the baseline. We also compared our method with Yang+ [15] that generates image foreground and background separately and recursively from input text descriptions (we chose this though the task is different because it generates realistic images). For Dong+ [1], we used the re-implementation by Seonghyeon [36] (as recommended by the authors of Dong+ [1]). For Yang+ [15], we used the publicly available source codes with the parameters recommended by the authors [37]. We remark that we used the combination of a noise vector and a text feature [2] as an input for Yang+ [15].

5.2 Implementation and Training Details

We implemented our model in PyTorch. We adopted the pre-trained text encoder [25] without any fine-tuning. To extract image features for the background discriminator input, we employed the VGG-16 [29] pre-trained on ImageNet dataset [30] without any fine-tuning. Like [1], we also used the image augmentation technique (e.g., flipping, rotating, zooming and cropping). We conducted all the experiments using a PC with CPU 6-cores Xeon 3.7 GHz, 64 GB of RAM, and GTX1080 Titan GPU (11 GB of VRAM).

We optimized the adaptive loss functions (Sect. 4.3) using Adam optimizer [38] with the learning rate of 2×10^{-3}, the learning rate decay of 0.5 performed every 100 epochs, the momentum $\beta_1 = 0.9$ and $\beta_2 = 0.999$, and the division from zero parameter $\epsilon = 10^{-8}$. We did not use the weight decay. We trained our model with the batch size of 48 for 600 epochs.

5.3 Evaluation Metrics

We use the inception score (IS) [39] to evaluate the overall quality of synthesized images. We also use two metrics, foreground score (FGS) and background score (BGS) for evaluating foreground and background of synthesized images separately.

IS is widely used for the generative model evaluation through the output of the Inception-v3 network [40]: $IS(G) \approx \exp(\frac{1}{N}\sum_{i=1}^{N} D_{\mathrm{KL}}(p(y|\hat{x}^{(i)}||\hat{p}(y))))$, where $\hat{x}$ is a synthesized image by the generator G, N is the number of generated images, D_{KL} is the Kullback–Leibler divergence, y indicates an instance of all classes given in the dataset, $p(y|\hat{x})$ is the conditional class distribution, and $\hat{p}(y) = \frac{1}{N}\sum_{i=1}^{N} p(y|\hat{x}^{(i)})$ is the empirical marginal-class distribution.

We employ the visual-text shared-space [25] and compute the matching between text descriptions and foreground for the foreground evaluation: $FGS = \|f_{\mathrm{img}} - f_{\mathrm{text}}\|_2$ where f_{img} and f_{text} are the features from the image encoder and the text encoder.

For background evaluation, we use $BGS = \|\hat{x} \odot \overline{x_{\mathrm{seg}}} - x \odot \overline{x_{\mathrm{seg}}}\|_2$ where x is the source image, and $\odot$ is the element-wise multiplication. $\overline{x_{\mathrm{seg}}}$ is the inverse map of x_{seg} where x_{seg} is the binary segmentation map of x provided from the dataset. We use $\overline{x_{\mathrm{seg}}}$ to mask foreground for x and $\hat{x}$.

5.4 Qualitative Evaluation

Figures 4 and 5 illustrate some examples of the results obtained by our method (with $p = 0.8$) and Dong+ [1]. They show that the synthesized images by our method match the text descriptions more precisely than Dong+ [1] while successfully retaining background of the source images.

On the Caltech-200 dataset, we see that the results by our method are clearer in foreground and background with less noise than Dong+ [1] (Fig. 4). Though foreground of the results by Dong+ [1] also matches the text descriptions (not always though), we observe that background is not preserved well.

On the Oxford-102 dataset, on the other hand, we see that our method and Dong+ [1] both have some failures in synthesizing images (red rectangles in Fig. 5). This is because images in the dataset are too complex; for example, the detail of flowers such as a stamen is too small. Nevertheless, we still observe that our method outperforms Dong+ [1]. We note that Dong+ [1] generated different flowers from the source images (blue rectangles in Fig. 5).

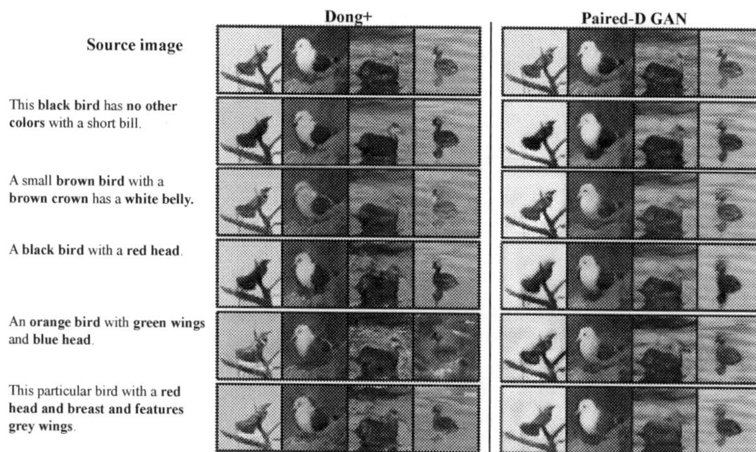

Fig. 4. Visual comparison of our method against Dong+ [1] on the Caltech-200 bird dataset [13]. First row: source images, most left column: text descriptions. Each image is generated using a source image and a text description.

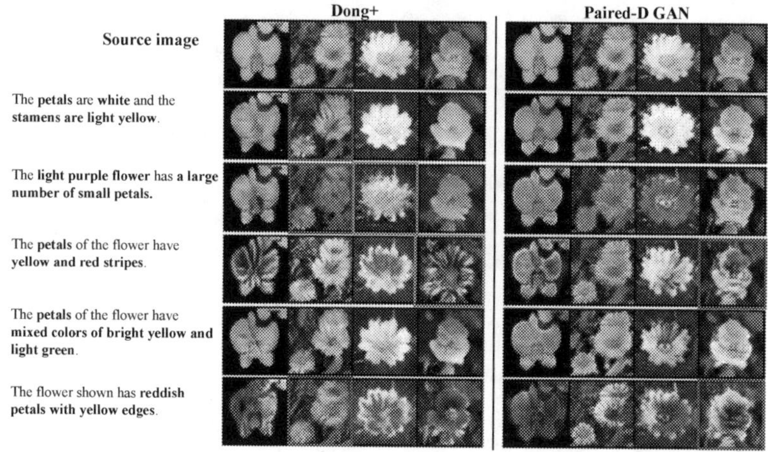

Fig. 5. Visual comparison of our method against Dong+ [1] on Oxford-102 flower dataset [14]. First row: source image, most left column: text descriptions. Each image is generated using its source image and text. The red rectangles indicate the failure synthesized images in both Dong+ [1] and ours. The blue rectangles indicate the generated images different from their source images. (Color figure online)

5.5 Quantitative Evaluation

For the quantitative evaluation, we computed IS, FGS, and BGS of the synthesized images, which are shown in Table 2. To compute IS, we iterated 10 times the experiment that we synthesize 8000 images, and computed the average and the standard deviation of the resulting scores, as recommended in [39]. For FGS

Table 2. Quantitative comparison using IS (larger is better), FGS, and BGS (smaller is better). The best results are given in blue.

Dataset	Caltech-200 [13]			Oxford-102 [14]		
Metric	$IS \Uparrow$	$FGS \Downarrow$	$BGS \Downarrow$	$IS \Uparrow$	$FGS \Downarrow$	$BGS \Downarrow$
Paired-D GAN	6.39 ± 0.18	17.26 ± 0.21	9.03 ± 0.06	4.41 ± 0.08	8.81 ± 0.08	8.87 ± 0.04
Dong+ [1]	5.56 ± 0.14	18.60 ± 0.09	11.83 ± 0.06	4.03 ± 0.11	9.71 ± 0.11	9.47 ± 0.14
Yang+ [15]	5.92 ± 1.04	18.34 ± 0.14	–	3.49 ± 0.04	10.32 ± 0.09	–

and BGS, we iterated 5 times the experiment that we synthesize 600 images, and computed the average and the standard deviation of the resulting scores. Note that we cannot compute BGS for Yang+ [15] because no ground-truths of background images exit for Yang+ [15]. We also remark that we used the visual-text shared-space model [25] pre-trained on the Caltech-200 (or Oxford-102) dataset to compute features for FGS.

Table 2 shows that our method achieves the best performances in all the metrics, meaning that the images synthesized by our method are superior not only in the overall quality (IS) but also in foreground-text matching (FGS) and in background preservation (BGS). The outperformance of our method against Dong+ [1] in all the metrics confirms that evaluating foreground and background separately in the training phase is effective. Compared to Yang+ [15], we see that our method and Dong+ [1] generate more realistic image, suggesting that for semantic image synthesis, generating foreground and background at the same time is better than separately and recursively generating foreground and background.

5.6 Detailed Analysis

First of all, we evaluated the effectiveness of employing D_{BG} through comparing our complete model with models using D_{FG} only or D_{BG} only. As shown in Table 3, the method using D_{FG} only achieves FGS best, and the method using D_{BG} only achieves BGS best. This means that the method using D_{FG} is correctly tuned to the foreground while the method using D_{BG} is correctly tuned to the background, and that D_{FG} and D_{BG} properly work for foreground and background each. Our completed method, on the other hand, balances foreground and background well as it achieves IS best.

Table 3. Evaluation on the effectiveness of employing D_{BG}.

Dataset	Caltech-200			Oxford-102		
Metric	$IS \Uparrow$	$FGS \Downarrow$	$BGS \Downarrow$	$IS \Uparrow$	$FGS \Downarrow$	$BGS \Downarrow$
Complete model ($D_{FG} + D_{BG}$)	6.39 ± 0.18	17.26 ± 0.21	9.03 ± 0.06	4.41 ± 0.08	8.81 ± 0.08	8.87 ± 0.04
Model with D_{FG} only	5.83 ± 0.19	16.74 ± 0.12	11.89 ± 0.08	4.21 ± 0.07	8.52 ± 0.13	10.02 ± 0.08
Model with D_{BG} only	6.02 ± 0.15	20.33 ± 0.11	7.63 ± 0.08	4.24 ± 0.10	10.68 ± 0.14	8.32 ± 0.15

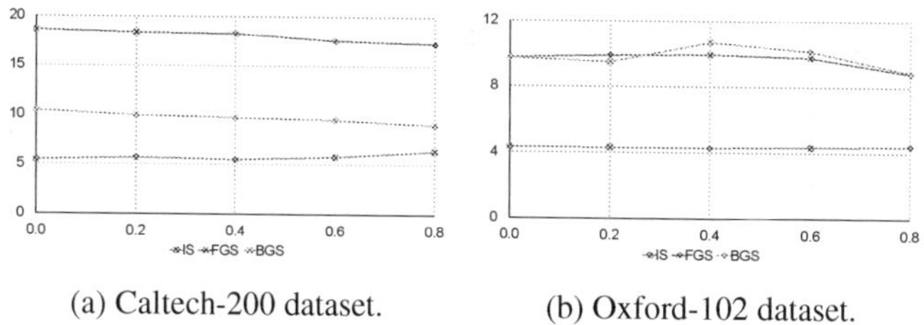
20
15
10
5
0
0.0 0.2 0.4 0.6 0.8
IS FGS BGS
12
8
4
0
0.0 0.2 0.4 0.6 0.8
IS FGS BGS

(a) Caltech-200 dataset. (b) Oxford-102 dataset.

Fig. 6. Quantitative comparison by changing p by 0.2 from 0.0 to 0.8.

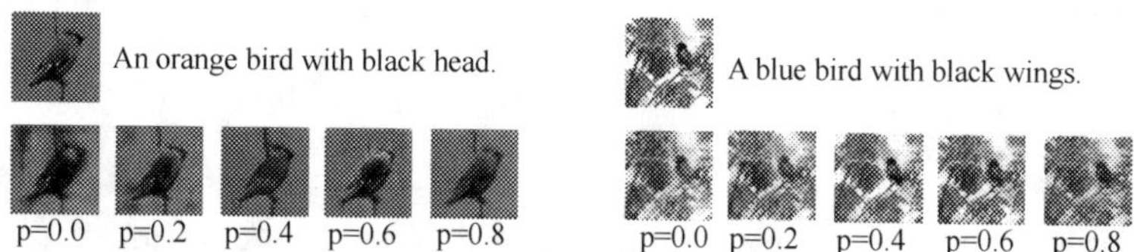
An orange bird with black head.
p=0.0 p=0.2 p=0.4 p=0.6 p=0.8
A blue bird with black wings.
p=0.0 p=0.2 p=0.4 p=0.6 p=0.8

Fig. 7. Zero-shot results by changing p by 0.2 from 0.0 to 0.8. The source image has simple background (right) or complex background (left).

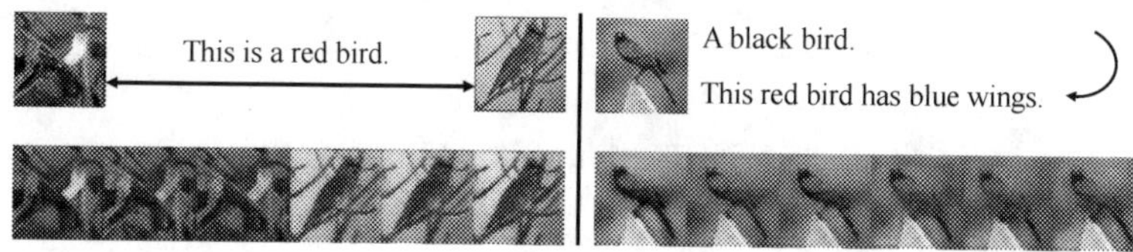
This is a red bird.
A black bird.
This red bird has blue wings.

Fig. 8. Zero-shot results of interpolation. Left: interpolation between two source images with the same target text description. Right: interpolation between two target text descriptions for the same source image.

The petals of this flower are **white** with a large stigma.
A **yellow** bird with a **black** on wings.
The **red** flower has no visible stamens.
This bird is **completely white**.

Fig. 9. Zero-shot results from a source image and text descriptions that are not related to each other, showing the effectiveness of foreground and background discriminators.

The bird is blue and red in color with a black beak.
This bird is completely red with black swing.

Fig. 10. Zero-shot results from the same source image and text descriptions, showing variety of foregrounds.

Then, we evaluated the impact on the results by different p's (the probability of generating zero at each pixel) used in creating the binary filter for the foreground discriminator D_{FG}. We changed p by 0.2 from 0.0 (no mask) to 0.8 and computed IS, BGS, FGS at each p (Fig. 6). Visual comparison with different p's are illustrated in Fig. 7 (two examples with simple/complex background). Figure 6 indicates that all the metrics become better at $p = 0.8$ (80% in probability of a source image are masked to focus on foreground). The explanation for this can be as follows, which is also supported by Fig. 7. When $p = 0.0$ (no mask), D_{FG} accesses the whole source image in the training phase, affecting background of generated images. By increasing p, D_{FG} is likely to focus on only foreground, leading to improving the quality of generated images. We note that background discriminator D_{BG} also succeeds in maintaining background of the source image (we can see that the background is kept well in most cases).

We next demonstrated the smooth interpolation between the source image and the target image. Figure 8 show synthesized images obtained by the linear interpolation between the source and the target images. In Fig. 8 (left), we interpolated two source images with a fixed text description. In contrast, we keep the source image fixed while changing text descriptions in Fig. 8 (right). These results indicate that our method is capable of independently interpolating between source images and text descriptions. We remark that our method preserve background well regardless of interpolation.

Figure 9 shows the generated images obtained using source images from the Caltech-200 [13] dataset with text descriptions from the Oxford-102 [14] dataset (not used in training phase), and vice verse. Figure 9 shows that our model retains background of source images and changes only foreground to match text descriptions (e.g. color) even if they are not used in the training (regardless of untrained text descriptions). This illustrates the flexible capability of our model to disentangle foreground and background.

We also show in Fig. 10 the effectiveness of text embedding augmentation [7] in our method to synthesize various images using the same source image and text descriptions.

6 Conclusion

We proposed Paired-D GAN conditioned on both text descriptions and images for semantic image synthesis. Paired-D GAN consists of one generator and two discriminators with different architectures where one discriminator is used for judging foreground and the other is for judging background. Our method is able to synthesize a realistic image where an input text description matches its corresponding part (foreground) of the image while preserving background of a given source image. Experimental results on the Caltech-200 and the Oxford-102 datasets demonstrate the effectiveness of our method.

References

1. Dong, H., Yu, S., Wu, C., Guo, Y.: Semantic image synthesis via adversarial learning. In: ICCV (2017)
2. Reed, S., Akata, Z., Yan, X., Logeswaran, L., Schiele, B., Lee, H.: Generative adversarial text-to-image synthesis. In: ICML (2016)
3. Yan, X., Yang, J., Sohn, K., Lee, H.: Attribute2Image: conditional image generation from visual attributes. In: Leibe, B., Matas, J., Sebe, N., Welling, M. (eds.) ECCV 2016. LNCS, vol. 9908, pp. 776–791. Springer, Cham (2016). https://doi.org/10.1007/978-3-319-46493-0_47
4. Efros, A.A., Freeman, W.T.: Image quilting for texture synthesis and transfer. In: SIGGRAPH (2001)
5. Gatys, L.A., Ecker, A.S., Bethge, M.: Image style transfer using convolutional neural networks. In: CVPR (2016)
6. Goodfellow, I., et al.: Generative adversarial nets. In: NIPS (2014)
7. Zhang, H., Xu, T., Li, H., Zhang, S., Wang, X., Huang, X., Metaxas, D.: StackGAN: text to photo-realistic image synthesis with stacked generative adversarial networks. In: ICCV (2017)
8. Isola, P., Zhu, J.Y., Zhou, T., Efros, A.A.: Image-to-image translation with conditional adversarial networks. In: CVPR (2017)
9. Wang, X., Gupta, A.: Generative image modeling using style and structure adversarial networks. In: Leibe, B., Matas, J., Sebe, N., Welling, M. (eds.) ECCV 2016. LNCS, vol. 9908, pp. 318–335. Springer, Cham (2016). https://doi.org/10.1007/978-3-319-46493-0_20
10. Ledig, C., et al.: Photo-realistic single image super-resolution using a generative adversarial network. In: CVPR (2017)
11. Zhang, H., et al.: StackGAN++: realistic image synthesis with stacked generative adversarial networks. arXiv: 1710.10916 (2017). (IEEE TPAMI, to appear)
12. Nguyen, T., Le, T., Vu, H., Phung, D.: Dual discriminator generative adversarial nets. In: NIPS (2017)
13. Wah, C., Branson, S., Welinder, P., Perona, P., Belongie, S.: The Caltech-UCSD Birds-200-2011 Dataset. California Institute of Technology, Technical report CNS-TR-2011-001 (2011)
14. Nilsback, M.-E., Zisserman, A.: Automated flower classification over a large number of classes. In: Proceedings of the Indian Conference on Computer Vision, Graphics and Image Processing (2008)
15. Yang, J., Kannan, A., Batra, D., Parikh, D.: LR-GAN: layered recursive generative adversarial networks for image generation. In: ICLR (2017)
16. Kingma, D.P., Welling, M.: Auto-encoding variational bayes. In: ICLR (2014)
17. Rezende, D.J., Mohamed, S., Wierstra, D.: Stochastic backpropagation and approximate inference in deep generative models. In: ICML (2014)
18. Van Den Oord, A., Kalchbrenner, N., Kavukcuoglu, K.: Pixel recurrent neural networks. In: ICML (2016)
19. Van den Oord, A., Kalchbrenner, N., Vinyals, O., Espeholt, L., Graves, A., Kavukcuoglu, K.: Conditional image generation with pixelcnn decoders. In: NIPS (2016)
20. Chen, X., Duan, Y., Houthooft, R., Schulman, J., Sutskever, I., Abbeel, P.: InfoGAN: interpretable representation learning by information maximizing generative adversarial nets. In: NIPS (2016)

21. Taigman, Y., Polyak, A., Wolf, L.: Unsupervised cross-domain image generation. In: ICLR (2017)
22. Zhu, J.-Y., et al.: Toward multimodal image-to-image translation. In: NIPS (2017)
23. Perarnau, G., van de Weijer, J., Raducanu, B., Álvarez, J.M.: Invertible conditional GANs for image editing. In: NIPS Workshop on Adversarial Training (2016)
24. Li, C., Wand, M.: Precomputed real-time texture synthesis with Markovian generative adversarial networks. In: Leibe, B., Matas, J., Sebe, N., Welling, M. (eds.) ECCV 2016. LNCS, vol. 9907, pp. 702–716. Springer, Cham (2016). https://doi.org/10.1007/978-3-319-46487-9_43
25. Reed, S., Akata, Z., Lee, H., Schiele, B.: Learning deep representations of fine-grained visual descriptions. In: CVPR (2016)
26. Reed, S., Akata, Z., Mohan, S., Tenka, S., Schiele, B., Lee, H.: Learning what and where to draw. In: NIPS (2016)
27. Ha, M.L., Franchi, G., Moller, M., Kolb, A., Blanz, V.: Segmentation and shape extraction from convolutional neural networks. In: WACV (2018)
28. Wu, R., Li, X., Yang, B.: Identifying computer generated graphics via histogram features. In: ICIP (2011)
29. Simonyan, K., Zisserman, A.: Very deep convolutional networks for large-scale image recognition. In: ICLR (2015)
30. Russakovsky, O., et al.: ImageNet large scale visual recognition challenge. Int. J. Comput. Vis. **115**, 211–252 (2015)
31. Nair, V., Hinton, G.E.: Rectified linear units improve restricted Boltzmann machines. In: ICML (2010)
32. He, K., Zhang, X., Ren, S., Sun, J.: Deep residual learning for image recognition. In: CVPR (2016)
33. Ioffe, S., Szegedy, C.: Batch normalization: accelerating deep network training by reducing internal covariate shift. In: ICML (2015)
34. Ashish Bora, A.D., Price, E.: AmbientGAN: generative models from lossy measurements. In: ICLR (2018)
35. Chopra, S., Hadsell, R., LeCun, Y.: Learning a similarity metric discriminatively, with application to face verification. In: CVPR (2005)
36. https://github.com/woozzu/dong_iccv_2017. Accessed 01 June 2018
37. https://github.com/jwyang/lr-gan.pytorch. Accessed 01 June 2018
38. Kingma, D.P., Ba, J.: Adam: a method for stochastic optimization. In: ICLR (2015)
39. Salimans, T., et al.: Improved techniques for training GANs. In: NIPS (2016)
40. Szegedy, C., Vanhoucke, V., Ioffe, S., Shlens, J., Wojna, Z.: Rethinking the inception architecture for computer vision. In: CVPR (2016)

Skeleton Transformer Networks: 3D Human Pose and Skinned Mesh from Single RGB Image

Yusuke Yoshiyasu[1,2(✉)], Ryusuke Sagawa[1,2], Ko Ayusawa[1,2], and Akihiko Murai[1]

[1] National Institute of Advanced Industrial Science and Technology (AIST), Tokyo, Japan
{yusuke-yoshiyasu,ryusuke.sagawa,k.ayusawa,a.murai}@aist.go.jp
[2] CNRS-AIST JRL (Joint Robotics Laboratory), UMI3218/RL, Tsukuba, Japan

Abstract. In this paper, we present Skeleton Transformer Networks (SkeletonNet), an end-to-end framework that can predict not only 3D joint positions but also 3D angular pose (bone rotations) of a human skeleton from a single color image. This in turn allows us to generate skinned mesh animations. Here, we propose a two-step regression approach. The first step regresses bone rotations in order to obtain an initial solution by considering skeleton structure. The second step performs refinement based on heatmap regressor using a 3D pose representation called cross heatmap which stacks heatmaps of xy and zy coordinates. By training the network using the proposed 3D human pose dataset that is comprised of images annotated with 3D skeletal angular poses, we showed that SkeletonNet can predict a full 3D human pose (joint positions and bone rotations) from a single image in-the-wild.

Keywords: Convolutional neural networks · 3D human pose · Skeleton

1 Introduction

Estimating 3D human pose from a single image is an important yet very challenging problem in computer vision, where applications range from surveillance to robotics. Recent work has shown that convolutional neural networks (ConvNets) can detect 2D joint positions accurately. The key to achieving accurate predictions is to represent 2D joint locations as heatmaps and iteratively refines them gradually by incorporating context information [3,16]–early approaches [25] on the other hand directly perform regression of the 2D joint coordinates using ConvNets, which is a difficult problem that needs to model a highly-nonlinear

Electronic supplementary material The online version of this chapter (https://doi.org/10.1007/978-3-030-20870-7_30) contains supplementary material, which is available to authorized users.

C. V. Jawahar et al. (Eds.): ACCV 2018, LNCS 11364, pp. 485–500, 2019.
https://doi.org/10.1007/978-3-030-20870-7_30

mapping from an input image to real values. Recent techniques, such as OpenPose [5], can robustly detect 2D joints of multiple people in an image.

In contrast to its 2D counterpart, the progress of 3D human pose detection has been relatively slow. The main challenges regarding to 3D human pose estimation is as follows:

3D Pose Representation. To predict 3D joint locations using ConvNets, 3D pose representation used is critical, which affects prediction accuracy. Previous approaches have shown that regression of a 3D pose using heatmaps (e.g., volumetric [18] and 2D heatmaps + depth [27]) leads to accurate 3D joint predictions. On the other hand, regression of joint angles using ConvNets [10,28] has not been successful so far in contributing to accurate 3D joint localizations, because they are difficult to learn with ConvNets due to their high non-linearity. From the application point of view, such as computer animation and biomechanics, it is desirable to predict not only 3D joint locations but also angular pose of skeleton, e.g., joint angles or segment rotations.

Data Scarcity. Compare to 2D human pose dataset, 3D human pose dataset is smaller in size. This is because obtaining a 3D human pose dataset where the images paired with 3D joint annotations requires time and effort to construct. In particular, annotations of 3D angular skeletal poses are difficult to obtain. One common way to achieve this is to use a motion capture (MoCap) system and RGB video cameras at the same time. However, such dataset are usually limited to a small variety of subjects—for example, Human 3.6M dataset [9], which is the most common dataset for 3D human pose, is limited to around 10 subjects. Consequently, it is difficult to learn sufficient visual features from 3D pose dataset solely to localize 2D/3D joints accurately.

Skeletal structure has been incorporated into 3D human pose estimation as a form of constraints or subspace. In biomechanics and robotics, forward and inverse kinematics have been well-studied and are used to generate human pose from MoCap by controlling joint angles of a skeleton. Previous approaches in the computer vision field estimated 3D human pose from 2D key points using a statistical model and enforcing constraints such as segment length [21], joint limit [1] and symmetry. In computer graphics, human skeletal pose is often represented using linear or affine transformation matrices, as can be seen for example in linear blend skinning for character animation.

In this paper, we propose skeleton transformer networks (SkeletonNet) for 3D human pose detection which respects skeletal structure while attaining 3D joint prediction accuracy. SkeletonNet combines and benefits from the two paradigms, skeleton and heatmap representations. SkeletonNet first regresses bone rotations to an input image in order to have an initial solution which is not precisely accurate but considers skeletal structure. Starting from this initial solution, the second step refines it using ConvNet heamap regressor. This strategy allows us to recover reasonably accurate predictions of full 3D human poses (joint positions and bone rotations) from a single in-the-wild image. To contribute to solving the data scarcity problem, we also construct a dataset where 3D angular skeletal poses are annotated on in-the-wild images, based on a human-validation approach. By fusing the proposed dataset and Mocap dataset captured under a controlled environment (Human3.6M), SkeletonNet can predict a full 3D pose (joint positions and bone rotation) from a single image in-the-wild. In addition, experimental results showed that SkeletonNet outperforms previous approaches based on joint angles [10,28] in terms of MPJPE joint position accuracy.

The contributions of this work is summarized as follows:

- We propose an end-to-end ConvNet framework for predicting a full 3D human pose (joint positions and bone rotations).
- We propose a bone rotation regressor which predicts 3D human pose using 3×3 transformation matrices. To make arbitrarily linear transformations into rotations, we propose a Gram Schmidt orthogonalization layer. This combination is the key to learning angular pose accurately using ConvNets.
- We propose a 3D human pose representation called cross heatmap for accurate 3D joint detection. This representation combines two heat maps, one for representing 2D joints in image space (xy space) and the other for zy space. The benefit of this representation is that it is more efficient than the volumetric heatmaps [18], while accurately predicting 3D joint positions when trained using Mocap-video dataset (Human 3.6M) and in-the wild dataset (MPII with 3D pose annotations).
- We built a 3D human pose dataset in-the-wild which includes annotations of 3D bone rotations.

2 Related Work

Estimating 2D Joint Positions Using ConvNets. Recent work has shown that the detection of 2D joint positions can be done very accurately using convolutional neural networks (ConvNets). Toshev et al. [25] first proposed a method based on ConvNets for detecting human pose i.e., 2D key points representing joint locations from a single image. Tompson et al. instead represented joint locations in images using 2D heat maps so that it can avoid complicated a non-linear mapping that goes from an image to xy pixel coordinates. The recent techniques, such as the stacked hourglass network [16] and its variants [6,7], accurately predict 2D joint positions by iteratively refining 2D heatmaps.

Predicting 3D Joint Positions. The early approaches predicts 3D joint positions from key points [20]. These approaches assume that the almost perfect 2D key points are already extracted from an image. Li et al. [13] first used ConvNets to directly regress 3D human joints with an image. There are two main reasons for the improvements on accuracy of 3D human pose detection. First, the recent approach combines multiple data sources to increase the 3D pose dataset [15,27]. Second, the recent techniques make use of more natural 3D joint representation. For example, Pavlakos et al. [18] uses a volumetric heatmap representation, which can avoid regressing the real values in a highly nonlinear manner. Other methods first predicts 2D joints with heatmaps and then regress 3D joint positions or depths from them. Tome et al. [24] have tried to iteratively update 3D joints represented as a weighted combination of PCA basis that is constructed from 3D MoCap dataset.

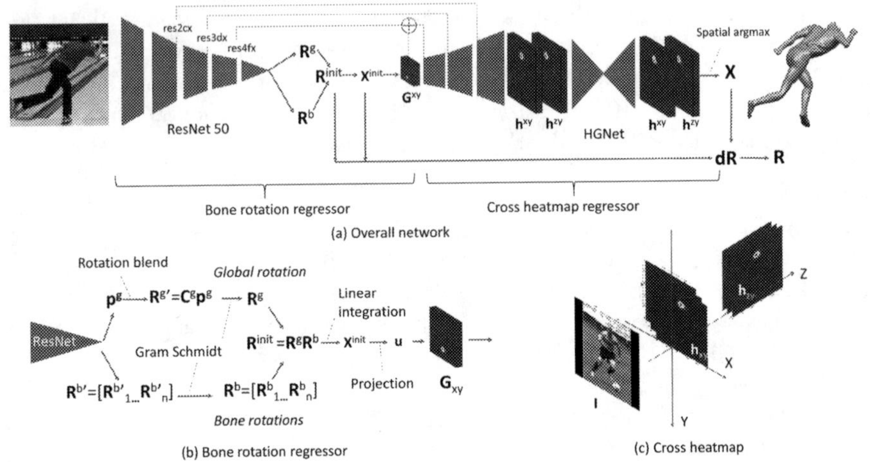

Fig. 1. Network architecture of SkeletonNet. (a) SkeletonNet is a two-step regressor. (b) The first part performs regression of bone rotations. (c) The second part detects heatmaps of xy and zy spaces.

Exploiting Skeletal Structure and Predicting Angular Pose. In biomechanics, robotics and computer animation fields, inverse kinematics has been well-studied and used to generate human pose from MoCap by controlling joint angles. Previous approaches [4,20] estimated 3D human pose from 2D key points by combining a statistical model and constraints such as joint limit [1], segment length [20] and symmetry. Some methods perform regression of joint angles or axis angles [10,28] to estimate angular skeletal pose using ConvNets but the high nonlinearity prevents them from accurate prediction of joint locations.

Weakly Supervision and Predictions from in-the-wild Images. Recent works tackle the data scarcity problem by using both 3D human pose dataset captured in the experimental room and 2D human pose dataset captured in a wide range of environment [15,23,27]. Sun et al. [23] used compositional loss function that is defined by integrating 2D positions and depths by properly normalizing the regression target values. Zhou et al. [27] took a weak supervised approach and used bone length constraint when 3D information (depths) is not available. The use of this approach not only enables 3D joint predictions from in-the wild images but also performance boost in joint prediction accuracy. We go further by building a 3D human pose dataset in-the-wild which includes annotations of 3D bone rotations.

3 Skeleton Transformer Networks

Skeleton Transformer Networks (SkeletonNet) is based on deep ConvNets, which predicts not only 3D joint positions but also rotations of body segments. Our approach is based on an end-to-end two-step regression approach. The network architecture of SkeletonNet is depicted in Fig. 1(a). The first step is called *bone rotation regressor* that performs regression of angular skeletal pose using 3×3 rotation matrices to provide an initial solution. The resulting pose is not precisely accurate but it respects skeletal structure, without having to produce large errors such as left and right confusions. The second step, *cross heatmap regressor*, starts from this initial solution and refine the joint predictions using heatmap regression. We benefit from the two different paradigms, i.e., skeleton and ConvNets, to achieve accuracy and preservation of structure.

3.1 Bone Rotation Regressor

Bone rotation regressor predicts bone rotations of a human skeleton. We achieve this by solving two simpler problems separately: predicting (1) a global rotation and (2) transformations of bone segments relative to the root. The idea behind this strategy is that the global orientation of the body has some discrete patterns e.g., sit, stand and lie, which can be effectively solved as a classification problem. On the other hand, bone rotations have more continuous distributions within some range, which can be effectively modeled as a regression problem.

To predict a global rotation, we convert the rotation estimation problem into a classification problem. Specifically, we first cluster the training dataset into 200 clusters based on its global rotations with k-means clustering. The samples within the same cluster is put in the same class. ConvNets is trained to output rotation class probabilities $\mathbf{p}^{\mathrm{g}}$ using Softmax. We use a classification loss (cross entropy) for supervision:

$$\mathcal{L}_{\mathrm{RotG}} = L_{cls}(\mathbf{p}^{\mathrm{g}}, \bar{\mathbf{p}}^{\mathrm{g}})$$

where L_{cls} is the log loss and $\bar{\mathbf{p}}^{\mathrm{g}}$ is the one-hot class label of global rotation. From the output probabilities $\mathbf{p}^{\mathrm{g}}$, we obtain a 3×3 global transformation matrix by blending cluster centers $\mathbf{C}^{\mathrm{g}}$, $\mathbf{R}^{\mathrm{g}'} = \mathbf{C}^{\mathrm{g}}\mathbf{p}^{\mathrm{g}}$. We tried linear blending of axis angles but found that blending matrices works better.

Since bone rotations relative to the root have more continuous distributions than global rotation, regression is more suitable in this case than classification. Bone rotations $\mathbf{R}^{\mathrm{b}'} = [\mathbf{R}_1^{\mathrm{b}'} \dots \mathbf{R}_n^{\mathrm{b}'}]$, where n is the number of bones, are thus predicted directly using a 3×3 rotation matrix (9 parameters). The loss for bone rotations is defined using the mean squared error (MSE) loss as:

$$\mathcal{L}_{\mathrm{RotB}} = \sum_{i}^{n} ||\mathrm{vec}(\mathbf{R}_i^{\mathrm{b}'}) - \mathrm{vec}(\bar{\mathbf{R}}_i^{\mathrm{b}})||_2^2$$

where $\mathrm{vec}(\cdot)$ makes a matrix to a vector and $\bar{\mathbf{R}}^{\mathrm{b}}$ is the ground truth bone rotations. Note that regression of rotation matrices demands more memory spaces because they need more parameters than other rotation representation, such as Euler angles, quaternions and axis angles. However, for 3D human pose detection, we have under 20 joints to predict, which means that the additional costs are almost negligible. The down side of Euler angles and quaternions are their nonlinearities and ambiguities (sign flips for quaternions and periodical angle jumps for Euler angles), which is difficult to use as the regression targets—we could not train a network properly using Euler angles as supervisions as reported in [28].

Gram Schmidt Orthogonalization Layer. The problem of the above strategy is that it does not guarantee to produce orthonormal matrices. This means the resulting skeleton is deformed in an undesirable way with scales and shears. To solve this issue, we propose the Gram Schmidt (GS) orthogonalization layer which performs GS to make transformations into rotations. GS requires elemental functions only, such as dot product, subtraction and division, which is differentiable and can be relatively easily incorporated into ConvNets. We input global transformation $\mathbf{R}^{\mathrm{g}'}$ and bone transformations $\mathbf{R}^{\mathrm{b}'}$ into the GS layer to make transformations to rotations, obtaining $\mathbf{R}^{\mathrm{g}}$ and $\mathbf{R}^{\mathrm{b}}$.

Once transformations are orthonormalized, we multiply a global rotation $\mathbf{R}^{\mathrm{g}}$ and bone rotations $\mathbf{R}^{\mathrm{b}}$ in order to obtain the absolute bone rotations. Finally, 3D joint positions are computed by applying these absolute rotations to the original bone vectors in the rest pose and performing linear integration to add up bone vectors from the root (Fig. 1(b)).

3.2 Cross Heatmap Regressor

We propose cross heatmap regressor which is used for refining the 3D joints obtained using bone rotation regressor. In the current design, cross heatmap regressor stacks xy and zy heatmaps (Fig. 1(c)) because they sufficiently cover xyz coordinates and the variance of human joint locations in zy coordinates are usually larger than that of zx space.

To integrate bone rotation regressor and cross heatmap regressor, we project 3D joint positions obtained in Sect. 3.1 into the image plane (xy plane). Here, we did not estimate a camera pose and scale explicitly. Instead we scale the xy coordinates to 90% of the width of the first upsampling layer, which is 16 pixels. From the projected 2D joints, 2D Gaussian maps [18] are obtained and, after convolutions, they are summed up with the feature maps from bone rotation regressor to serve as approximate positions of 2D joints for cross heatmap regressor. Note that all of these process are differentiable, which can be optimized using back propagation.

Once the feature maps are up-sampled three times to the size of 64 × 64, a single stack of hourglass module [16] is used to compute cross heatmaps. The cross heatmap representation concatenates two heatmaps, one for representing 2D joints in image space (xy space) $\mathbf{h}^{\mathrm{xy}}$ and the other for the zy space, $\mathbf{h}^{\mathrm{zy}}$. For training we use the MSE loss as:

$$\mathcal{L}_{\mathrm{hm}} = \sum_{i}^{m}\sum_{j,k} ||\mathbf{h}^{\mathrm{xy}}_{(j,k)} - \bar{\mathbf{h}}^{\mathrm{xy}}_{(j,k)}||_2^2 + \sum_{i}^{m}\sum_{j,k} ||\mathbf{h}^{\mathrm{zy}}_{(j,k)} - \bar{\mathbf{h}}^{\mathrm{zy}}_{(j,k)}||_2^2$$

where $\bar{\mathbf{h}}^{\mathrm{xy}}$ and $\bar{\mathbf{h}}^{\mathrm{zy}}$ are the ground truth heatmaps for xy and zy spaces. In addition, m is the number of joints. The benefit of this representation is that it is more compact and efficient than the volumetric heatmaps, while maintaining accuracy. To extract xyz coordinates from cross heatmaps in an end-to-end manner, we use spatial argmax layers similar to those proposed in [12,14]. Finally, we compute rotations $\mathbf{dR}$ that align bone vectors obtained using bone rotation regressor with that of the final predicted positions. They are multiplied with the predicted absolute bone rotations $\mathbf{R}^{\text{init}}$ to make them consistent with the final joint positions $\mathbf{x}$. This way, we can exploit accurate heatmaps to refine rotations, avoiding a difficult regression problem of nonlinear angle parameters. Now that the loss for the final positions $\mathbf{x}$ and rotations $\mathbf{R}$ are defined as:

$$\mathcal{L}_{\text{pos}} = \sum_{i}^{m} ||\mathbf{x}_i - \bar{\mathbf{x}}_i||_2^2, \ \mathcal{L}_{\text{Rot}} = \sum_{i}^{n} ||\text{vec}(\mathbf{R}_i) - \text{vec}(\bar{\mathbf{R}}_i)||_2^2$$

where and $\bar{\mathbf{x}}_i$ and $\bar{\mathbf{R}}_i$ are the ground truth labels of positions and rotations.

With the final positions $\mathbf{x}$ and rotations $\mathbf{R}$, linear blend skinning can be done to produce a 3D mesh. Note that we perform skinning outside the network but this process can also be done within the network in an end-to-end manner, as this is a linear matrix multiplication.

3.3 Loss Function

For supervision, a standard cross entropy loss and MSE loss is used for comparing the predictions and ground truth labels of the global rotation class probability, bone rotations and cross heatmaps. In total, we minimize the loss function of the form:

$$\mathcal{L}_{\text{total}} = \mathcal{L}_{\text{RotG}} + \alpha\mathcal{L}_{\text{RotB}} + \beta\mathcal{L}_{\text{Rot}} + \gamma\mathcal{L}_{\text{pos}} + \lambda\mathcal{L}_{\text{hm}}$$

where $\mathcal{L}_{\text{RotG}}$, $\mathcal{L}_{\text{RotB}}$, $\mathcal{L}_{\text{Rot}}$, $\mathcal{L}_{\text{pos}}$ and $\mathcal{L}_{\text{hm}}$ are a cross entropy loss for global rotation and MSE loss for bone rotations $\mathbf{R}^{\text{b}}$, final rotations $\mathbf{R}$, final positions $\mathbf{x}$ and cross heatmaps ($\mathbf{h}^{\text{xy}}$ and $\mathbf{h}^{\text{zy}}$), respectively. In addition, α, β, γ and λ are the respective weights.

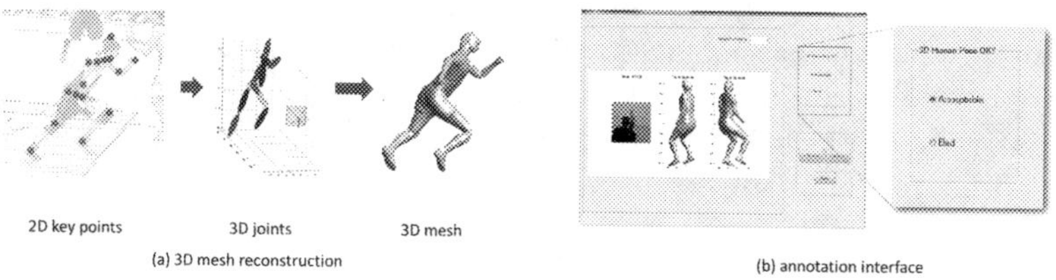

Fig. 2. 3D pose annotation system. (a) Given 2D key points as inputs, we compute 3D joints using the projected matching pursuit (PMP) technique. Next, skeleton rotations are obtained using a skeleton transformation optimization method. 3D mesh is obtained from rotations and positions. (b) With the annotation tool, the annotator is just needed to judge whether the 3D pose is acceptable or not by comparing the real image and the rendered image created from the mesh.

4 In-the-wild 3D Human Pose Dataset

To build 3D human pose dataset that have variations in clothes and background, we annotate 3D positions and bone rotations on MPII human pose dataset as shown in Fig. 2. To this end, we followed the human verification approach [17]. Here a 3D human pose is obtained from 2D key points using a previous technique, which will then be sorted by human annotators whether each result is acceptable or not. This is in spirit similar to the concurrent work of [11]. The aim for constructing our dataset is not to provide accurate 3D pose annotations but to obtain reasonable ones on in-the-wild images, including joint positions and rotations, such that they can be used for training our bone rotation regressor. In fact, the annotators are instructed to judge whether the pose is 'acceptable' or 'bad', e.g., if the global rotation of the resulting pose looks deviating from the true pose more than 30°, the pose is 'bad'. As a consequence, our dataset have more 3D pose annotations than [11], possibly at the cost of accuracy.

To obtain 3D joint positions from 2D key points, we use the projected matching pursuit (PMP) approach [20]. This method calculates a camera pose, scale and 3D joint positions as a combination of PCA basis that is constructed from Mocap database. From the resulting 3D joint positions, rotations of bones are obtained based on a method which is conceptually similar non-rigid surface deformation techniques [22]. Specifically, the skeleton in the rest shape is fitted to the PMP result by balancing the rigidity of bones, the smoothness between bone rotations and the position constraints to attract the skeleton to them. The initial rotations are obtained from local coordinate frames, which are defined in a similar manner using [1]. Reconstructing one model from 2D key points takes approx. 1 min.

We also designed a simple annotation tool Fig. 2(b) to simplify the process of 3D pose annotations. With this tool, human annotators are just required to decide a 3D pose is acceptable or not. In addition, we obtained skin meshes from the 3D pose using linear blend skinning and showed rendered images. By visualizing a skin mesh, it makes the annotators' decisions significantly easier and quicker. From among the images in MPII dataset, we extracted those with all 16 joints are inside the image region, which was approximately 20000 poses. After annotations, we were able to collect 10291 images with 3D pose annotations. Note that we remove 'bad' poses and do not use them in the training. It took about 2–3 hrs for an annotator to process 1000 images.

5 Experiments

5.1 Dataset and Evaluation Protocols

MPII [2]. This dataset contains in-the-wild images for 2D human pose estimation, which includes 25k training images and 3k validation images. Those images are annotated with 2D joint locations and bounding boxes. In Sect. 4, we constructed a 3D pose dataset on top of MPII dataset by annotating 3D joints to images. This dataset is used in training.

Human3.6M. Human 3.6M dataset [9] is used in training and testing. Human 3.6M dataset is a large scale dataset for 3D human pose detection. This dataset contains 3.6 million images of 15 everyday activities, such as walking, sitting and making a phone call, which is performed by 7 professional actors. 3D positions of joint locations captured by motion capture (Mocap) systems are also available in the dataset. In addition, 2D projections of those 3D joint locations into images are available. The images are taken from four different views. As with previous researches, we down-sampled the video from 50 fps to 10 fps in order to reduce redundancy in video frames. We followed the same evaluation protocol used in previous approaches [18,27] for evaluation, where we use 5 subjects (S1, S5, S6, S7, S8) for training and the rest 2 subjects (S9, S11) for testing. We used the 3D model of an actor provided in Human3.6 to generate mesh animations but this could be replaced with any 3D models.

The error metric used is called mean per joint position error (MPJPE) in mm. In the evaluation protocol, the position of the root joints is aligned with the ground truth but the global orientation is kept as is. Following [27] the output joint positions from ConvNets is scaled so that the sum of all 3D bone lengths is equal to that of a canonical average skeleton. This is done by:

$$\mathbf{P}_j = (\mathbf{P}_j^{\text{pred}} - \mathbf{P}_0^{\text{pred}}) \cdot l^{\text{ave}} / l^{\text{pred}} \tag{1}$$

where $\mathbf{P}_j^{\text{pred}}$ is the predicted position, $\mathbf{P}_0$ is the root position, l^{pred} is the sum of skeleton length of the predicted skeleton and l^{ave} is the average of sum of skeleton length for all the training subjects in Human 3.6M dataset.

We also evaluated the method with the error measure called the reconstruction error, where, before calculating the error, the result is aligned to the ground truth with a similarity transformation.

5.2 Baselines

Four baseline methods are implemented to conduct ablation studies. We trained the first three networks using Human3.6M dataset only and the fourth one with both Human3.6M and MPII dataset.

Rotation Regress (Rot Reg) Only. This only uses bone rotation regressor. The position is computed from linear integration of bone rotations.

Heatmap (HM) Only. This on the other hand only uses cross heatmap regressor.

Rot Reg + HM. This method is our proposed method which combines bone rotation regressor and cross heatmap regressor.

All. This is our proposed method trained using Human 3.6M and MPII dataset with 3D annotations obtained using the method presented in Sect. 4.

5.3 Implementation and Training Detail

Our method is implemented using MatConvNet toolbox [26]. For the bone rotation regressor, we use ResNet50 [8] as the base network, which is pre-trained on the ImageNet dataset. A single up-sampling layer and a single hourglass module is followed by the base network to predict heatmaps. We also use skip connections to connect skeleton regression layers and up-sampling layers. We used a skeleton with 16 joints and 15 segments each of them have 9 rotational parameters. The definition of joints is same as that of MPII dataset. Training a whole model takes about 1 day using three NVIDIA Quadro P6000 graphics cards with 24 GB memory. The batch size is 30 for each GPU. As for augmentation, we used left/right flip only—no scaling and rotation augmentation is used. We trained a model with SGD for 70 epochs, starting from the learning late of 0.001 and decreasing it to 0.00001. During test time, a single forward pass of our network is approx. 0.12 s, which means the performance of our method is approx. 8–9 fps.

We set the parameters in the loss function as $\alpha = \beta = \gamma = 0.1$ and $\lambda = 0.001$. When training with both Human 3.6M and MPII datasets, we randomly selected the images from both dataset such that half of the batch is filled with Human 3.6M and the other half by MPII dataset, following [27]. Since the 3D annotations of MPII are not accurate, we use them for supervising bone rotation regressor only. Thus, when training images are from MPII, we do not back propagate gradients from the losses that include the final 3D pose, $\mathbf{h}^{zy}$, $\mathbf{x}$ and $\mathbf{R}$, (i.e., L_{pos}, L_{Rot} and the right term of L_{hm}) to the network. On the other hand, when the training sample is from Human3.6M dataset, which has accurate 3D annotations, we minimize all the losses.

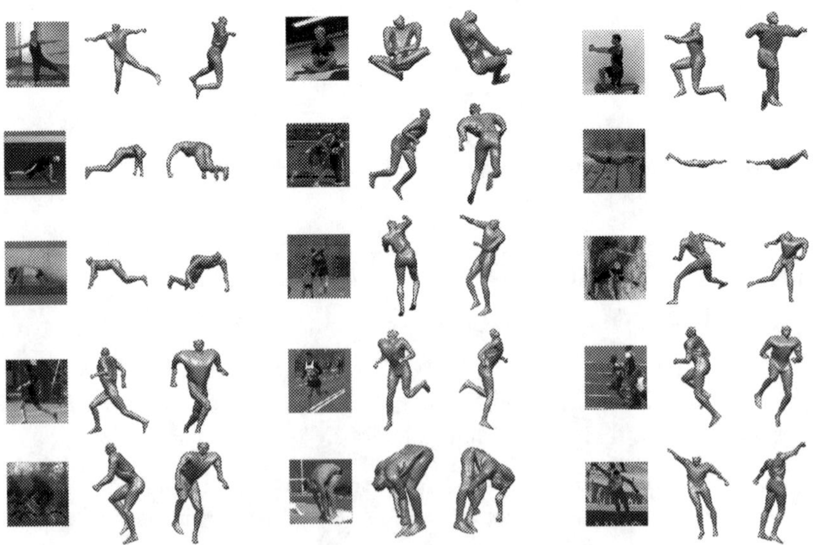

Fig. 3. Some results on in-the-wild images.

5.4 Results

Qualitative Results. In Figs. 3 and 6, we show the result of our 3D pose prediction method. Our method is able to predict 3D joint positions and bone orientations reasonably accurately even on in-the wild-images. Because our method can predict bone rotations of human body skeletons, we can produce mesh animations from 3D joint positions and rotations using linear blend skinning. Note that the rotations of hands and feet are not supervised.

Comparisons to Other State-of-the-art. We have compared our techniques against other state-of-the-art in Table 1. Our technique is comparable with other state-of-the-art in terms of MPJPE. Volumetric heatamaps [18] can achieve MPJPE approx. 71 mm. However, it got worse results when including MPII (MPJPE 78 mm) with their decoupled structure, whereas we are around MPJPE 70 mm. Also, compared with [18] with two stacks of hourglass networks, cross heatmap is more compact, which requires 1/32 of memory spaces to store.

Compared with the previous techniques that predict angular poses [10,28], SkeletonNet is more accurate. In fact, MPJPE of our result is 69.9 mm, whereas that of Kanazawa et al. [10] is 87.97 mm. In Table 2, we also compared the reconstruction error with previous approaches. Our technique outperforms previous techniques that iteratively optimizes joint angles [4] and perform regression of joint angles [19]. The benefit of SkeletonNet is, in addition to estimating 3D joint positions relatively accurately, we can predict 3D bone rotations, which is useful in animating a human body mesh or possibly predicting dynamics such as joint torques.

Table 1. Comparisons to other state-of-the-art. MPJPE [mm] is used for error metric.

	Directions	Discussion	Eating	Greeting	Phoning	Photo	Posing	Purchases
Zhou et al. [28]	91.8	102.4	97.0	98.8	113.4	90.0	93.8	132.2
Tome et al. [24]	64.98	73.47	76.82	86.43	86.28	110.67	68.93	74.79
Mehta et al. [15]	59.69	69.74	60.55	68.77	76.36	85.42	59.05	75.04
Pavlakos et al. [18]	67.38	71.95	66.70	69.07	71.95	76.97	65.03	68.30
Ours (All)	63.33	71.59	61.39	70.40	69.90	83.17	62.98	68.77
	Sitting	**SittingDown**	**Smoking**	**Waiting**	**WalkDog**	**Walking**	**WalkPair**	**Average**
Zhou et al. [28]	159.0	106.9	125.2	94.4	79.0	126.0	99.0	107.3
Tome et al. [24]	110.19	172.91	84.95	85.78	86.26	71.36	73.14	88.39
Mehta et al. [15]	96.19	122.92	70.82	68.45	54.41	82.03	59.79	74.14
Pavlakos et al. [18]	83.66	96.51	71.74	65.83	74.89	59.11	63.24	71.90
Ours (All)	76.81	98.90	68.24	67.45	73.74	57.72	57.13	69.95

Table 2. Comparison of reconstruction errors on Human 3.6M dataset.

Zhou et al. [29]	Bogo et al. [4]	Lassener et al. [11]	Pavlakos et al. [19]	Ours
106.7	82.3	80.7	75.9	61.4

Table 3. Comparisons between baselines. MPJPE [mm] is used for error metric.

Rot reg only	Heatmap only	Rot reg + HM	All
112.43	128.55	87.05	69.95

Comparisons Between Baselines. In Table 3 and Fig. 4, we show comparisons between the baselines. As can be seen from Fig. 4a, the result of bone rotation regressor preserves skeletal structure, but the joint positions are not accurate enough. With only heatmaps, however, skeletal structure is sometimes destructed e.g., by the left and right flips. By combining our bone rotation and cross heatmap regressor, a more accurate result is produced, while preserving skeletal structure. Note that in previous work this kind of confusions are remedied by incorporating recurrence [3] or using many stacks of a hourglass module [16]. By training with both Human 3.6M and MPII, we get the best result (Table 3). In addition, we found that annotating 3D rotations is important for reconstructing human poses from in-the-wild images (Fig. 4b). Thus, the key to our improvements in MPJPE is the use of cross heatmap and the use of MPII dataset in training. Even when MPII dataset is not provided for training, SkeletonNet can predict reasonably accurately 3D human pose by exploiting the combination of skeletal structure and heatmaps.

Comparisons Between Rotation Representation. We have also compared the results of bone rotation regressor by changing its rotation representation. Specifically, we tested the network that (1) regressess axis angles but indirectly supervised with rotation matrices (AA), (2) regressess axis angles but supervised with relative joint rotation matrices and converts them back to the absolute space using forward kinematics, which is equivalent as SMPL [4] (FKAA), (3) regresses absolute rotations (AbsRotReg), (4) regresses rotations without the GS layer (w/o GS), (5) regresses a global rotation (GlobalReg), (6) classifies a global rotation (GlobalClass) and (7) is same as GlobalClass but aligns rotations with heatmaps (All), respectively. The networks are trained with Human 3.6M, except for All that was trained with both MPII and Human 3.6M. To compare the rotation prediction accuracy, we compute relative rotations between the ground truth and predicted bone rotations, convert them to axis angles and take the norms in degrees, which reflects all three DoFs of rotations.

In Table 4, Global Rot. Err. indicates the error of global rotations. Bone Rot. Err. indicates the average error of bone rotations relative to the root. As shown in Table 4, the proposed method based on the GS layer, which classifies a global rotation, is the best in terms of MPJPE accuracy. AbsRotReg is also high in accuracy but it produces bone rotations with its determinant of -1, which collapse skeletal structure. The method based on axis angle tends to produce large errors probably because of their high non-linearity, requiring an iterative process [10] or a more informative geometric loss, e.g., the one using differences between silhouettes [19]. In summary, our method can benefit from the use of 3×3 rotation matrices, which can probably be modeled as simpler functions than other angle representations, which is more friendly to ConvNets to learn with. As reported in [28], we could not train a network properly using Euler angles as supervisions, where training and validation losses remained high. In contrast, SkeletonNet can model subtle pose appearances due to e.g., medial and lateral rotations around segment axes by providing supervisions on both rotations and positions. With joint position supervisions only and no rotational supervisions, it is possible to get reasonable results in joint position predictions [28] but is difficult to obtain good results for bone orientations.

Table 4. Comparison of rotation representation.

	AA	FKAA	AbsRotReg	w/o GS	GlobalReg	GlobalClass	All
MPJPE	175.06	197.44	114.70	124.06	119.18	112.42	69.95
Global Rot. Err	30.46	35.81	18.83	21.28	21.64	20.81	12.93
Bone Rot. Err	37.34	44.77	—	28.72	29.08	29.46	21.94

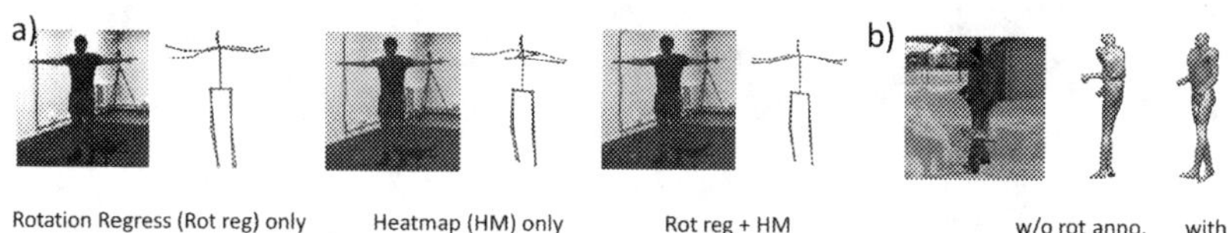

Fig. 4. Comparisons of baselines. (a) Bone rotation regressor preserves skeletal structure but the joint positions are not accurate enough. With only heatmaps, skeletal structure is sometimes destructed e.g., with the left and right flips. By combining both, it produces more accurate result while preserving structure. (b) The rotation annotation is important for reconstructing a pose from in the wild images.

Failure Cases and Limitations. In Fig. 5, we show failure cases. Our technique fails when there are large self-occlusions and occlusions by objects or other humans. In addition, our network is currently designed for the single-person detection and thus fails when multiple humans exist in the image. Since we scale a skeleton, we are not be able to model absolute bone lengths. Cross heatmap regressor possesses the ability to alter relative bone lengths but our method have generalization issues when the body type is extremely different from the original skeleton, e.g., prediction of small children's poses. Also our network does not take into account hand and foot orientations.

Fig. 5. Failure cases.

Fig. 6. More results.

6 Conclusion

We have presented SkeletonNet, a novel end-to-end 3D human pose detection technique from a single image. The first step regresses bone segment rotations to obtain an initial solution without large errors by considering skeleton structure. The second step performs refinement based on heatmap regressor that is based on the representation called cross heatmap which stacks heatmaps of xy and zy coordinates. This combination allows us to predict bone orientations and joint positions accurately, which may provide useful information to applications like animation and biomechanics. We also presented a 3D human pose dataset constructed by adding 3D rotational annotations to publicly-available 2D human pose dataset.

In future work, we would like to address monocular detections of other human body properties, such as body shape, body weight, contact forces and joint forces/torques. We are also interested in generative adversarial networks (GAN) to improve pose prediction results using an unsupervised manner based on the image dataset that does not have 3D annotations.

Acknowledgment. I would like to thank Rie Nishihama and CNRS-AIST JRL members for supporting us constructing 3D human pose dataset. This work was partly supported by JSPS Kakenhi No. 17K18420 and No. 18H03315.

References

1. Akhter, I., Black, M.J.: Pose-conditioned joint angle limits for 3D human pose reconstruction. In: CVPR, pp. 1446–1455 (2015)
2. Andriluka, M., Pishchulin, L., Gehler, P., Bernt, S.: 2D human pose estimation: new benchmark and state of the art analysis. In: CVPR, June 2014
3. Belagiannis, V., Zisserman, A.: Recurrent human pose estimation. arXiv preprint arXiv:1605.02914 (2016)
4. Bogo, F., Kanazawa, A., Lassner, C., Gehler, P., Romero, J., Black, M.J.: Keep it SMPL: automatic estimation of 3D human pose and shape from a single image. In: Leibe, B., Matas, J., Sebe, N., Welling, M. (eds.) ECCV 2016. LNCS, vol. 9909, pp. 561–578. Springer, Cham (2016). https://doi.org/10.1007/978-3-319-46454-1_34
5. Cao, Z., Simon, T., Wei, S.-E., Sheikh, Y.: Realtime multi-person 2D pose estimation using part affinity fields. In: CVPR (2017)
6. Chen, Y., Shen, C., Wei, X., Liu, L., Yang, J.: Adversarial poseNet: a structure-aware convolutional network for human pose estimation. CoRR, abs/1705.00389 (2017)
7. Chu, X., Yang, W., Ouyang, W., Ma, C., Yuille, A.L., Wang, X.: Multi-context attention for human pose estimation. CoRR, abs/1702.07432 (2017)
8. He, K., Zhang, X., Ren, S., Sun, J.: Deep residual learning for image recognition. CoRR, abs/1512.03385 (2015)
9. Ionescu, C., Papava, D., Olaru, V., Sminchisescu, C.: Human3. 6m: large scale datasets and predictive methods for 3D human sensing in natural environments. IEEE Trans. Pattern Anal. Mach. Intell. **36**(7), 1325–1339 (2014)
10. Kanazawa, A., Black, M.J., Jacobs, D.W., Malik, J.: End-to-end recovery of human shape and pose. In: Computer Vision and Pattern Regognition (CVPR) (2018)
11. Lassner, C., Romero, J., Kiefel, M., Bogo, F., Black, M.J., Gehler, P.V.: Unite the people: Closing the loop between 3D and 2D human representations. In: CVPR, July 2017
12. Levine, S., Finn, C., Darrell, T., Abbeel, P.: End-to-end training of deep visuomotor policies. CoRR, abs/1504.00702 (2015)

13. Li, S., Chan, A.B.: 3D human pose estimation from monocular images with deep convolutional neural network. In: Cremers, D., Reid, I., Saito, H., Yang, M.-H. (eds.) ACCV 2014. LNCS, vol. 9004, pp. 332–347. Springer, Cham (2015). https://doi.org/10.1007/978-3-319-16808-1_23
14. Luvizon, D.C., Tabia, H., Picard, D.: Human pose regression by combining indirect part detection and contextual information. CoRR, abs/1710.02322 (2017)
15. Mehta, D., Rhodin, H., Casas, D., Sotnychenko, O., Xu, W., Theobalt, C.: Monocular 3D human pose estimation using transfer learning and improved CNN supervision. arXiv preprint arXiv:1611.09813 (2016)
16. Newell, A., Yang, K., Deng, J.: Stacked hourglass networks for human pose estimation. In: Leibe, B., Matas, J., Sebe, N., Welling, M. (eds.) ECCV 2016. LNCS, vol. 9912, pp. 483–499. Springer, Cham (2016). https://doi.org/10.1007/978-3-319-46484-8_29
17. Papadopoulos, D.P., Uijlings, J.R.R., Keller, F., Ferrari, V.: We don't need no bounding-boxes: training object class detectors using only human verification. CoRR, abs/1602.08405 (2016)
18. Pavlakos, G., Zhou, X., Derpanis, K.G., Daniilidis, K.: Coarse-to-fine volumetric prediction for single-image 3D human pose. CoRR, abs/1611.07828 (2016)
19. Pavlakos, G., Zhu, L., Zhou, X., Daniilidis, K.: Learning to estimate 3D human pose and shape from a single color image. In: CVPR (2018)
20. Ramakrishna, V., Kanade, T., Sheikh, Y.: Reconstructing 3D human pose from 2D image landmarks. In: Fitzgibbon, A., Lazebnik, S., Perona, P., Sato, Y., Schmid, C. (eds.) ECCV 2012. LNCS, vol. 7575, pp. 573–586. Springer, Heidelberg (2012). https://doi.org/10.1007/978-3-642-33765-9_41
21. Simo-Serra, E., Ramisa, A., Alenyà, G., Torras, C., Moreno-Noguer, F.: Single image 3D human pose estimation from noisy observations. In: CVPR, po. 2673–2680. IEEE (2012)
22. Sorkine, O., Alexa, M.: As-rigid-as-possible surface modeling. In: Proceedings of the Fifth Eurographics Symposium on Geometry Processing, SGP 2007, Aire-la-Ville, Switzerland, Switzerland, pp. 109–116. Eurographics Association (2007)
23. Sun, X., Shang, J., Liang, S., Wei, Y.: Compositional human pose regression. arXiv preprint arXiv:1704.00159 (2017)
24. Tome, D., Russell, C., Agapito, L.: Lifting from the deep: Convolutional 3D pose estimation from a single image. arXiv preprint arXiv:1701.00295 (2017)
25. Toshev, A., Szegedy, C.: DeepPose: human pose estimation via deep neural networks. In: CVPR, pp. 1653–1660 (2014)
26. Vedaldi, A., Lenc, K.: Matconvnet - convolutional neural networks for MATLAB. In: Proceeding of the ACM International Conference on Multimedia (2015)
27. Zhou, X., Huang, Q., Sun, X., Xue, X., Wei, Y.: Weakly-supervised transfer for 3D human pose estimation in the wild. arXiv preprint arXiv:1704.02447 (2017)
28. Zhou, X., Sun, X., Zhang, W., Liang, S., Wei, Y.: Deep kinematic pose regression. In: Hua, G., Jégou, H. (eds.) ECCV 2016. LNCS, vol. 9915, pp. 186–201. Springer, Cham (2016). https://doi.org/10.1007/978-3-319-49409-8_17
29. Zhou, X., Zhu, M., Leonardos, S., Derpanis, K.G., Daniilidis, K.: Sparseness meets deepness: 3D human pose estimation from monocular video. In: CVPR, pp. 4966–4975 (2016)

Detecting Text in the Wild with Deep Character Embedding Network

Jiaming Li(✉), Chengquan Zhang, Yipeng Sun, Junyu Han, and Errui Ding

Baidu Inc., Beijing, China
{liujiaming03,zhangchengquan,yipengsun,hanjunyu,dingerrui}@baidu.com

Abstract. Most text detection methods hypothesize texts are horizontal or multi-oriented and thus define quadrangles as the basic detection unit. However, text in the wild is usually perspectively distorted or curved, which can not be easily tackled by existing approaches. In this paper, we propose a deep character embedding network (CENet) which simultaneously predicts the bounding boxes of characters and their embedding vectors, thus making text detection a simple clustering task in the character embedding space. The proposed method does not require strong assumptions of forming a straight line on general text detection, which provides flexibility on arbitrarily curved or perspectively distorted text. For character detection task, a dense prediction subnetwork is designed to obtain the confidence score and bounding boxes of characters. For character embedding task, a subnet is trained with contrastive loss to project detected characters into embedding space. The two tasks share a backbone CNN from which the multi-scale feature maps are extracted. The final text regions can be easily achieved by a thresholding process on character confidence and embedding distance of character pairs. We evaluated our method on ICDAR13, ICDAR15, MSRA-TD500, and Total Text. The proposed method achieves state-of-the-art or comparable performance on all of the datasets, and shows a substantial improvement in the irregular-text datasets, i.e. Total-Text.

Keywords: Text detection · Character detection · Embedding learning

1 Introduction

Optical Character Recognition (OCR) is a long-standing problem that attracts the interest of many researchers with its recent focus on scene text. It enables computers to extract text from images, which facilitates various applications, such as scene text translation, scanned document reading, etc.

J. Liu and C. Zhang—These authors contribute equally in this work.

C. V. Jawahar et al. (Eds.): ACCV 2018, LNCS 11364, pp. 501–517, 2019.
https://doi.org/10.1007/978-3-030-20870-7_31

As the first step of OCR, the flexibility and robustness of text detection significantly affect the overall performance of OCR system. The goal for text detection algorithms is to generate bounding boundaries of text units as tight as possible.

When dealing with different kinds of text, different text unit should be defined in advance. When detecting text in Latin, the text unit is usually "word"; while if in Asian language, it is "text line" instead. Words or lines have a strong prior by their nature. The characters in them tend to usually cluster as straight lines. Therefore, it is natural to define rectangles or quadrangles that wrap text as the objective of detection. This prior has been widely used in many text detection works and achieved promising results [5,12,17,18,24,25,31,32,41].

However, when text appears in the wild, it often suffers from severe deformation and distortion. Even worse, some text are curved as designed. In such scenario, this strong prior does not hold. Figure 1 shows curved text with quadrangle bounding boxes and curved tight bounding boundaries. It can be easily observed the quadrangle bounding box inevitably contains extra background, making it more ambiguous than curved polygon boundaries.

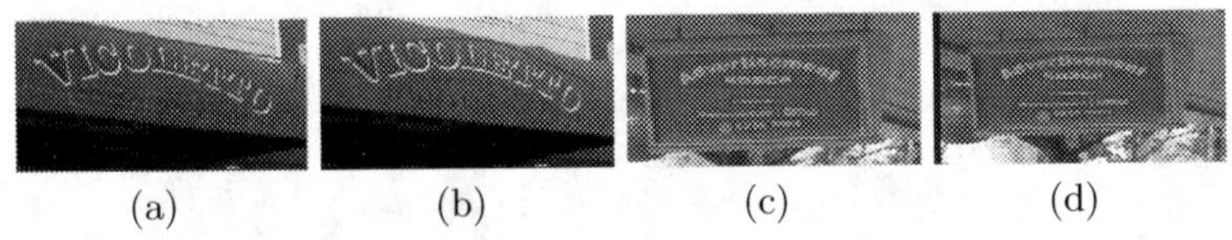

(a) (b) (c) (d)

Fig. 1. Examples of curved text from Total-Text and ICDAR15. Detected texts are labeled with quadrangle bounding box in (a) and (c), and with polygon by our proposed method in (b) and (d). Note that the image is cropped for better presentation. The dark blue lines represent the detected text boundaries.

We realized that if characters can be detected and a flexible way to group them into text can be found, tight bounding boundaries will be easily generated with the boundary of characters. Characters are also fundamental elements of text, this idea can be naturally extended to irregular text. In early attempts [31,36,37], scholars turned to use a heuristic clustering method with hand-crafted features to link detected character parts into text lines. The non data-driven heuristic clustering methods are fragile, requiring a thorough check on corner cases manually. Also, the hand-crafted features ignore large parts of visual context information of text, making it less discriminative to determine the closeness between characters.

Thereby, we propose a Character Embedding Network (CENet) in a fully data-driven way. The model detects characters as the first step. After characters being detected, they are projected into an embedding space by the same model where characters belonging to the same text unit are close to each other, and characters belonging to different text units are far from each other. During the training stage, the network is jointly trained with a character detection loss and a character embedding loss. During the inference stage, a single forward pass could produce character candidates as well as their representation in the embedding space. A simple distance thresholding is then applied to determine connected character pairs. Connected character pairs further form text groups by chaining the characters together. After the connection relationships are properly learned, the text units could be detected regardless of text length or distortion the text suffers.

To the best of our knowledge, the proposed CENet is the first to model text grouping problem as a character embedding learning problem. It does not rely on strong priors, making it capable of detecting arbitrarily curved or distorted text. Moreover, since both character detection and character grouping tasks are based on local patch of images, our model could be directly expand from "word" detection to"line" detection without modifying the backbone model for larger receptive field. Our model also avoids complicated heuristic grouping rules or hand-crafted features. At last, our single model performs two tasks with a single forward pass, only adding minimal overhead over character detection network.

The contributions of this paper are three-fold:

- We propose a multi-task network to detect arbitrarily curved text in the wild. The character detection subnet is trained to detect character proposals, and the character embedding subnet learns a way to project characters into embedding space. Complicated post-processing steps, e.g. character grouping and word partition, are then be simplified as a simple distance thresholding step in the embedding space.
- We adopt a weakly supervised method to train character detector with only word-level polygon annotations, without the strong hypothesis that text should appear in a straight line.
- We conduct extensive experiments on several benchmarks to detect horizontal words, multi-oriented words, multi-oriented lines and curved words, demonstrating the superior performance of our method over the existing methods.

2 Related Works

Scene Text Detection. Based on the basic elements produced in the pipeline of text detection, we roughly classify the scene text detection methods into three categories:

Text Component Based Methods. MSER [25] and SWT [5] are classical text component extraction methods. In the era of deep learning, CTPN [32] extracts horizontal text components with fixed-size width using a modified Faster R-CNN framework. Horizontal text lines are easily generated, since CTPN adjusted the Faster R-CNN [26] framework to output dense text components. SegLink [28] proposed a kind of oriented text component (i.e. segment) and a component-pair connection structure (i.e. link). A link indicates which two segments should be connected. Naturally, SegLink dealt better with multi-oriented texts than CTPN. PixelLink [4] provided an instance segmentation based solution that detects text pixels and their linkage with neighbor pixels. Positive pixels with positive links are grouped as the collection of connected components. Besides, Markov Clustering Network [22] regarded detected text pixels as nodes and associated them with computed attractors by a designed markov clustering networks. The above mentioned methods provided inspiring ideas on text detection. However, the regions between characters are sometimes in-discriminative with background in some cases, especially in text lines where distances between characters are large.

Character Based Methods. The character is the fundamental semantic element of text, regardless of whatever the language is. Additionally, characters have a precise definition. Compared with components, the position, scale and orientation information of characters could be provided in a well-defined way. Therefore, the character seems to be a more natural choice to set up a general text detection engine. Previously, some character based methods [9,14,31,42] have achieved good performances on some public benchmarks that have character-level annotations (such as ICDAR13 [16]). However, as it is not convenient and economic to acquire character-level annotations, more and more public benchmarks (such as ICDAR15 [15] and MSRA-TD500 [35]) provide only word-level annotations. Hence, these methods can not get sufficient fine-tuning on those datasets. In order to deal with this problem, Tian et al. [30] (WeText) and Hu et al. [12] (WordSup) proposed two different solutions for character detection from word annotations.

Unfortunately, both methods can not deal with the datasets (such as Total-Text [2]) with polygon annotations for curved text lines, because they are based on the strong hypothesis that text should appear in a straight line. Our method is also a character-based method with weak supervision, but a more general mechanism of updating character supervision is proposed, which makes our method capable of learning from arbitrary annotation formats including rectangle, quadrangle and polygon.

Word Based Methods. Recently, quite a few works [6,8,10,18,21,23,40,41] have put emphasis on adjusting some popular object detection frameworks including Faster R-CNN [26], SSD [20] and Densebox [13] to detect word boundary. In contrast to general objects, texts appearing in the real-world have larger varieties of aspect ratios and orientations. Liao et al. [18] and Zhong et al. [40] directly added more anchor boxes of large aspect ratio to cover texts of wider range. Gupta et al. [6] and Liu et al. [21] added the angle property to the bounding box to deal with the problem of multiple orientations, while EAST [41] and He et al. [10] provided a looser representation namely quadrangle. These methods seem to easily achieve high performance on benchmarks with word-level annotations, but not on non-Latin scripts or curved text with polygon-level annotations.

Deep Metric Learning. The goal of metric learning or embedding methods [3,27,33] is to learn a function that measures how similar two samples are. There are many successful applications of metric learning [3,11,27,33], such as ranking, image retrieval, face verification, speaker verification and so on. By far, applications of metric learning on document analysis or text reading were limited to the problem of word spotting and verification [1,26,34]. In this work, we verify the effectiveness of deep metric learning in text detection task. Based on character candidates, we provide an end-to-end trainable network that can output the character bounding boxes and their embedding vectors simultaneously. Text regions could be easily detected by grouping characters which embedding distances are small.

3 Method

There are two tasks that our model is supposed to solve. One is to detect characters and the other is to project characters into an embedding space where characters belonging to the same group are close, and characters belonging to different groups are far from each other. Sharing a backbone CNN, the two tasks are implemented by separate subnets, i.e., a character detection subnet and a character embedding subnet. To put it another way, our framework is a single backbone network with two output heads. With the calculated character candidates and their corresponding embedding vectors, the post processing removes false positive and groups characters in an efficient and effective manner.

3.1 Network Design

We use ResNet-50 [7] as the backbone network of our model. Following recent network design practices [12,19,31], we concatenate semantic features from three different layers of the backbone ResNet-50 network. After deconvolutional operations, the features are concatenated as shared feature maps which are 1/4 of the original image in size. A character detection subnet and a character embedding subnet are stacked on top of the shared feature maps.

The character detection subnet is a convolutional network that produces 5 channels as the final output. The channels are offsets Δx_{tl}, Δy_{tl}, Δx_{br}, Δy_{br} and confidence score, where *tl* means top left and *br* means bottom right. The top left and bottom right bounding box coordinates of detected character candidates could be calculated by $(x - \Delta x_{tl}, y - \Delta y_{tl})$ and $(x + \Delta x_{br}, y + \Delta y_{br})$, where x and y are coordinates of pixel whose confidence score greater than a threshold s. The bounding boxes further serve as RoIs of characters.

The character embedding subnet takes the residual convolution unit (RCU) as the basic blocks which is simplified residual block without batch normalization. The design was inspired by [31] where the authors showed that the scores and bounding box sizes of character proposals offer strong clues on whether they belong to the same group, and the feature maps extracted by the backbone network contains such information. Therefore, residual units were chosen to preserve score and bounding box information from feature maps, directly passing them to top layers by skip connection. On top of the RCU blocks, we employ a 1×1 convolution layer with linear activation function to output a 128-channel final embedding map. RoI pooing with 1×1 kernel is applied on the embedding maps extracting embedding vectors for each character.

During inference, we extract confidence map, offset maps and embedding maps from the two heads of the model. After thresholding on the score map and performing NMS on character proposals, the embedding vectors are extracted by 1×1 RoI pooling on embedding map. In the end, we output character candidates with the format of {score, coordinates(x, y) of character center, width, height, 128D embedding vector}. Characters are finally clustered into text blocks as the last post-processing step. The overall structure of the model and pipeline are shown in Fig. 2.

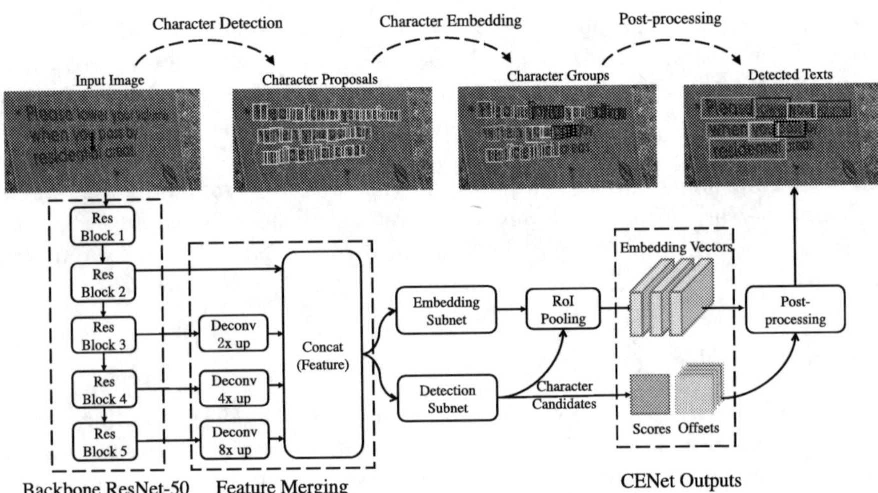

Fig. 2. Overall process of the model. Blue bounding boxes in "character proposals" are character candidates with high confidence scores."Character Clusters" is the character clusters in embedding space, where candidates in the same cluster use the same color. The final detected words represented in quadrangles are shown in "Detected text". Better view in color.

3.2 Training Character Detector

Loss Definition. The character detector consists of two tasks that include text/non-text classification and box regression. The loss can be formulated as

$$L_{char} = L_{cls} + \lambda_1 L_{reg}, \tag{1}$$

where L_{cls} denotes the binary classification loss, L_{reg} represents the box regression loss, and λ_1 is a factor to balance the two losses. In this paper, we use pixel-wise hinge-loss as classification cost. Some measures for class balance or boosting (e.g., OHEM [29]) are adopted in our experiments. Usually, we set the sampling ratio of 1:3 to balance the positive and negative samples, where 30% of negative samples selected from the top hardest in a training batch. Here, IoU-loss [38] is adopted as the regression cost which handles the problem of bounding box accuracy bias between large and small objects instead of L2-loss.

Learning Character Detector from Coarse Annotation. Since it is labor-intensive to annotate character-level boxes, most of public benchmarks like ICDAR15 [15] and Total-Text [2] provide only quadrangle or polygon annotations for words, and MSRA-TD500 provides annotations for sentences. Those annotations are all coarse annotations. Inspired by WordSup [12], which recursively rectifies character-level supervisions and updates the model parameters with the rectified character-level supervision, a new rectification rule is designed for producing character-level supervision. This rule is capable of training character detector from bounding boundary annotations with polygon format, while WordSup may fail.

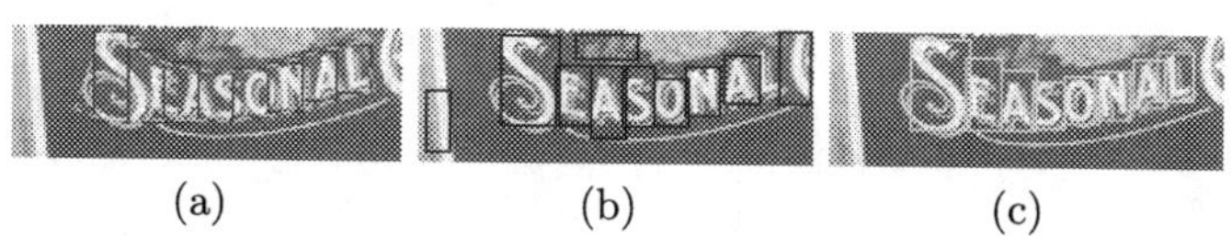

Fig. 3. Learning character detector from word-level annotation. (a) are some coarse-char boxes (blue) with the polygon annotation (red), (b) are some pred-char boxes, and (c) are the fine-char boxes whose height is the same as (a). (Color figure online)

Our design follows the general observation that the short side of a nearly horizontal (or vertical) text is approximately equal to the heights (or width) of characters in it. The short side could be used to rectify the imprecise predicted characters with the following pipeline. Firstly, each annotated quadrangle or polygon is uniformly divided into N bounding boxes along the center line, where N denotes the character number of the text transcript. We call the preliminary bounding box segmentations as coarse-char boxes. After one forward pass, some candidate character boxes (namely pred-char boxes) with high confidence are collected. Finer character boxes (namely fine-char boxes) are produced from coarse-char boxes and their corresponding matched pred-char boxes. If no matched pred-char is founded, the coarse-char box is used as a fine-char box directly. Otherwise, if the annotated text is more horizontal, the width of the fine-char box is set to be the width of pred-char box, and the height is set to the height of the coarse-char box; if more vertical, the width is the width of coarse-char box, and the height is the height of pred-char box. The obtained fine-char boxes are used as "ground truth" in Eq. 1 to update model.

The matched pred-char box p of a coarse-char box c should meet the following constraints:

$$\begin{cases} S(p) > t_1 \\ IoU(p,c) > t_2, \end{cases} \tag{2}$$

where $S(p)$ denotes the confidence score of pred-char box p, $IoU(p,c)$ means Intersection over Union between the pred-char box and coarse-char box. t_1 and t_2 are predefined to 0.2 and 0.5 in our experiments. The visualization of the rectification procedure is shown in Fig. 3.

3.3 Learning Character Embedding

The character embedding subnet is another crucial part in our model. In an ideal case, we hope the subnet projects the characters into an embedding space. Distances between characters among the same text unit are small in the learned space, and that between those belong to different units to be large. Therefore we can group characters into text blocks by performing clustering in the embedding space. This case resembles the objective of metric learning, which aims to learn a distance function to measure similarities between samples.

Inspired by previous works in metric learning, we select the most straightforward contrastive loss to train our model. Contrastive loss takes *pairs* of characters into calculation. Let i and j denote the index of character candidates in a pair, v_i and v_j denote their embedding vectors that are extracted by the embedding subnet, and $l_{i,j}$ denotes whether they belong to the same text unit. If they do, we name pair (i, j) to be positive pair and $l_{i,j} = 1$. Otherwise, pair (i, j) is defined as negative pair and $l_{i,j} = 0$. The Contrastive Loss is defined as

$$J(i,j) = l_{i,j}[D(v_i, v_j)]^2 + (1 - l_{i,j})\max(0, 1 - D(v_i, v_j))^2, \tag{3}$$

where D denotes the distance measure. In training, v_i and v_j are pulled close to each other if $l_{i,j} = 1$. If $l_{i,j} = 0$, v_j and v_i are pushed away from each other until $D(v_i, v_j) > 1$.

Constructing Local Character Pairs. It is worth-noting that in every definition of text, characters in the same text unit are naturally close in the image. Two small characters are unlikely from the same text unit if they are too far from each other in the image. However, if they are on the endpoints of a line of characters, the probability of their belonging to same text line are significantly increased. The key difference is whether there are closely scattered characters, namely *local character pairs*, that connect individual characters in one text unit.

In addition, it is unnecessary to train models with all possible character pairs. Instead, when all the local character pairs are correctly labeled, all of the text units would be correctly detected. Working with local character pairs also reduces the requirement of large receptive field when detecting long text.

In this work, we employ k nearest neighbor with radius (r-KNN) to incorporate such information. When producing possible pairs, each character was selected as *anchor* in turn. With an *anchor* selected, at most k characters which are closest to *anchor* in the image were taken form *pairs*. Another useful heuristic rule is that a character is more likely to be connected with characters with similar box size. Therefore, only characters within radius were kept. To formalize this empirical pair sampling method, we define c_i, w_i, and h_i as the center coordinates, width, and height of character i in image respectively; and KNN(i) be a function that generates the set of k nearest neighbors of character i in the image. Then $j \in$ r-KNN$(i, \beta r(i))$ represents j is in KNN(i) and the spatial distance $D(c_i, c_j) < \beta\sqrt{w_i^2 + h_i^2}$. Both k and β were set to 5 in our experiments.

When $j \in$ r-KNN(i), we call i and j produces a locally connected pair. Here we define the set of all locally connected pairs as $LCP = \{(i, j), i \in$

$M, j \in$ r-KNN$(i)\}$, where M is the total number of character candidates in one image. With r-KNN preprocessing, there are only $O(kM)$ locally connected pairs remaining, reducing the size of character pairs to a reasonable level.

We noticed that the positive pairs are redundant. The minimum requisite for error-less positive pairs is that at least one chain connects all characters in a text unit. Positive pairs with large embedding distances do not contribute any text level error as long as the minimum requisite is satisfied. However, a negative pair with small embedding distance will certainly mis-connect two text units and generate text level error. Meanwhile, we found there are about 3/4 of local character pairs are positive. According to the above analysis, we assume the negative pairs should be weighted more than the positive pairs in training.

Therefore, we sample R pairs from LCP of batch images so that there are α pairs are negative in a batch. Let's denote the sampled pairs set as SP, the final re-weighted loss for learning embedding is defined as Eq. 4. We found $R = 1024$ and $\alpha = 60\%$ work well in our experiments.

$$L_{emb} = \frac{\sum_{i,j \in SP} J(i,j)}{R}. \tag{4}$$

The loss function to train the whole network then becomes

$$L = L_{cls} + \lambda_1 L_{reg} + \lambda_2 L_{emb}, \tag{5}$$

where λ_1 and λ_2 control the balance among the losses. We set both λ_1 and λ_2 to 1 in our experiments.

3.4 Post-processing

In testing, we employ two threshold values (s and d) to filter false character candidates and group characters into text units. After a forward pass, the proposed model would provide a set of character candidates and their corresponding embedding vectors. Then, the character candidates with confidence scores greater than s are kept. Next, r-KNN is performed on each character, outputting the local character pairs in whole image. To address the character grouping problem, we simply cut down the connected pairs whose embedding distances are over d.

Following the steps above, we can quickly find characters from the same groups. The final step is to represent the character groups in a suitable way. In this paper, we adopted the piecewise linear method that used in WordSup [12] to format the boundary of character groups. This method provides various configurable boundary formats, which meet the requirements of different benchmarks. On ICDAR15, a filtering strategy that removes short words with less than two detected characters are applied. This strategy aims to further remove false alarm from the detection results.

4 Experiments

We conduct experiments on ICDAR13, ICDAR15, MSRA-TD500, and Total-Text datasets, to explore how the proposed approach performs in different scenarios. The four chosen datasets focus on horizontal-oriented text, multi-oriented text, sentence-level long text, as well as curved-oriented text respectively. Experiments on synthetic data are also conducted for structural search and pretraining. We also list recent state-of-art methods for comparison.

4.1 Datasets and Evaluation

Five datasets are used in the experiments:

- VGG 50k. The VGG SynthText dataset [6] consists of 800,000 images, where the synthesized text are rendered in various background images. The dataset provides detailed character-level, word-level and line-level annotations. For the experimental efficiency, we randomly select 50,000 images for training and 500 images for validation. This subset is referred as VGG 50k.
- ICDAR13. The ICDAR13 dataset [16] is from ICDAR 2013 Robust Reading Competition. The texts are well focused and horizontal oriented. Annotations on character-level and word-level bounding boxes are both provided. There are 229 training images and 233 testing images.
- ICDAR15. The ICDAR15 dataset [15] is from ICDAR 2015 Robust Reading Competition. The images are captured in an incidental way with Google Glass. Only word-level quadrangles annotations are provided in ICDAR15. There are 1000 natural images for training and 500 for testing. Experiments under this dataset shows our method's performance in word-level Latin text detection task.
- MSRA-TD500. The MSRA-TD500 dataset [35] is a dataset comprises of 300 training images and 200 test images. Text regions are arbitrarily orientated and annotated at sentence level. Different from the other datasets, it contains both English and Chinese text. We test our method on this dataset to show it is scalability across different languages and different detection level (line level in this dataset).
- Total-Text. The Total-Text dataset [2] is recently released in ICDAR2017. Unlike the ICDAR datasets, there are plenty of curved-oriented text as well as horizontal and multi-oriented text in Total-Text. There are 1255 images in training set, and 300 images in test set. Two kinds of annotations are provided: one is word level polygon bounding regions that bind ground-truth words tightly, and word level rectangular bounding boxes as other datasets provided. Since many of the words in this datasets are curved or distorted, it is adopted to validate the generalization ability of our method on irregular text detection tasks.

4.2 Implementation Details

Since the training samples are not abundant in these available datasets, we use VGG 50k data to pretrain a base model, and then finetune the base model on other benchmark datasets accordingly. Two models are trained with the word-level annotation and line-level annotation of VGG 50k data respectively. The backbone ResNet-50 model was first pretrained on ImageNet dataset. Then the models are trained on VGG 50k dataset for character detection and further finetuned with both character detection and character embedding loss. The converged models are used as pretrained models for training other benchmarks.

We have not adopted any more data augmentation when training models with VGG 50k data. For the remaining benchmark datasets, we perform multi scale data augmentation by resizing the image to [0.65, 0.75, 1, 1.2] scales of the original image respectively, and cropped with a sliding window of size 512×512 with stride 256 to generate images for training. During training, we randomly rotate the cropped image to 90°, 180° or 270°, and distort brightness, contrast and color on all three benchmark datasets.

When training with data without character level annotation, the supervision for character detection comes from the weak supervision mechanism depicted above. Boxes used to train character embedding are the same coarse-char box used for character detection. We found a "mixing batch" trick helps. In practice, a half of the mixing batch are sampled from benchmark data, and the other half are from VGG 50k which provide character-level annotation. Character supervision for data from VGG 50k comes from their character annotation.

The optimizer is SGD with momentum in all the model training. We train the models 50k iteration at learning rate of 0.001, 30K iterations at 0.0001, and 20K iterations at 0.00001. The momentum was set to 0.9 in all the experiments. The two threshold for post-processing, i.e. s and g, are tuned by grid search on training set.

All the experiments are carried out on a shared server with a NVIDIA Tesla P40 GPU. Training a batch takes about 2 s. Inference was done on original images. The average inference time cost is 276 ms per image with size 768×1280, the forward pass, r-KNN search, NMS, and other operations cost 181 ms, 21 ms, 51 ms and 23 ms, respectively.

4.3 Ablation Study

As shown in Table 1, ablation experiments have been done on ICDAR15 dataset. Three key components in our pipeline are evaluated. Specifically, the mixing batch trick used in weak supervision, the positive-negative pair reweighting strategy, and short word removal strategy are added progressively to show their impact on overall performance.

Without bells and whistles, the model trained merely with weak character supervision and local character pairs converges successfully but gives mediocre results (73% in Recall). The character detection subnet was more likely overfitted on text components instead of characters.

With "mixing batch" trick, word recall is improved strikingly by about 4% with similar precision. The finding here may imply that this trick, as a regularization measure, prevents the weak character supervision from prevailing. In other words, weak character supervision tends to results in a certain amount of

Table 1. Text detection results using CENet evaluated on the ICDAR15 [15].

Mixing batch trick	Reweighting	Short word removal	Recall	Precision	F1
✗	✗	✗	73.8	80.5	77.0
✓	✗	✗	77.4	79.4	78.4
✓	✓	✗	79.2	82.3	80.9
✓	✓	✓	79.2	86.1	82.5

"soft" ground truths while the precise character supervision can pull the trained model to its correct position.

If we further add positive-negative pair reweighting trick in character embedding, performances in both precision and recall increase by 2%. In accordance to our previous analysis in Sect. 3.3, more balanced positive-negative pairs are behind the improvement. In addition, a detected word is error-prone if it is too short. Removal of the word less than 2 characters is adopted, which indicates 3.8% improvement in precision without hurting recall.

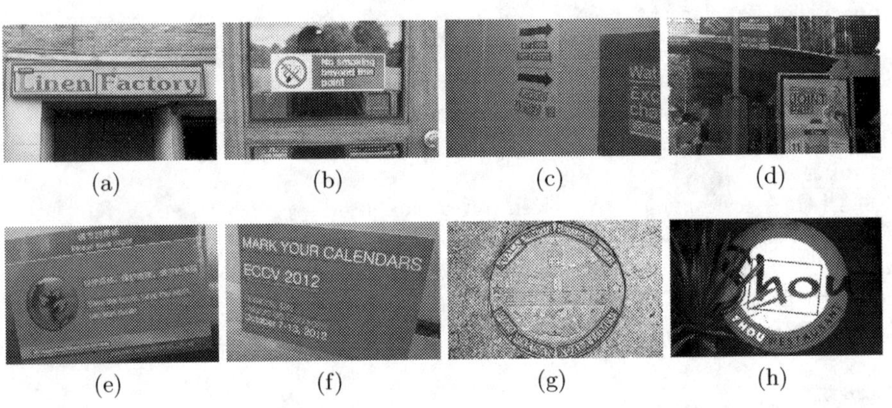

Fig. 4. Qualitative evaluation of the proposed CENet. Dark blue bounding boundaries show our text detection results on the datasets. (a, b) are from ICDAR13; fig. (c, d) are from ICDAR15; (e, f) are from MSRA-TD500; and (g,h) are from Total-Text dataset. Zoom in to see better. (Color figure online)

4.4 Experiments on Scene Text Benchmarks

Table 2 lists the results on ICDAR13 dataset of various state-of-art methods. Our model presents a competitive performance on this scenario. The demonstrated that the proposed CENet is capable of learning horizontal text line. Note that WordSup adopted the horizontal nature of text directly when grouping characters into text lines, and the data-driven CENet could achieve a similar performance without utilizing that strong prior. s, d are set to 0.4 and 0.45 in this dataset.

We conduct experiments on ICDAR15 dataset, comparing the results of the proposed CENet with other state-of-the-art methods. As shown in Table 3, our single scale CENet outperforms most of the existing approaches in terms of F-measure. This shows that character detection and character embedding together can handle most cases in regular text word detection. Our model learns both the character proposals and their relationship in terms of grouping, reducing wrongly-grouped and wrongly-split characters compared with word based methods [10,41]. s, d are set to 0.35 and 0.38 in this dataset.

Table 4 lists the results on MSRA-TD500 dataset. Our model achieve best result w.r.t F-measure on this dataset. The dataset is multilingual and is a good test-bed for generalization. For our model, it is basic unit is character which is dependent on local patch and character embedding connects neighboring units by propagation. Therefore it escapes from the large receptive field requirement of one stage methods. s, d are set to 0.4 and 0.3 in this dataset.

Table 2. Performances of ICDAR13, the evaluation criteria are from DetEval.

Method	Recall	Precision	F-measure
MCLAB-FCN [39]	79.65	88.40	83.80
Gupta et al. [6]	75.5	92.0	83.0
Zhu et al. [42]	81.64	93.40	87.69
CTPN [32]	81.64	93.40	87.69
WeText [30]	83.1	91.1	86.9
Wordsup [12]	87.53	93.34	**90.34**
EAST [41]	82.67	92.64	87.37
He et al. [10]	92	81	86
PixelLink [4]	88.6	87.5	88.1
CENet (VGG 50k+icdar13 finetune)	85.94	93.18	89.41

On the most challenging Total-text dataset, the proposed method presents an overwhelming advantage over other methods in comparison, as is shown in Table 5. The baseline comes from DeconveNet that predicts a score map of text followed by connected component analysis. VGG 50K dataset contains some curved text, therefore the model trained on VGG 50k solely works reasonably well. With finetuning on the provided training set, our final model significantly outperforms the baseline method. Besides, this result strongly exhibits the effectiveness of our weak supervision mechanism for training the character detector. s, d are set to 0.4 and 0.38 in this dataset.

We visualize detection results of our model on four benchmarks, illustrates in Fig. 4. Results show our model can tackle text detection in various scenarios, especially on curved texts.

Table 3. Performances of different methods on ICDAR15.

Method	Recall	Precision	F-measure
RRPN-2 [24]	72.65	68.53	70.53
seglink [28]	73.1	76.8	75.0
Wordsup [12]	77.03	79.33	78.16
EAST [41]	78.33	83.27	80.78
He et al. [10]	80	82	81
PixelLink [4]	82.0	85.5	**83.7**
CENet (VGG 50k+icdar15 finetune)	79.2	86.1	82.5

Table 4. Results of different methods on MSRA-TD500.

Method	Recall	Precision	F-measure
Zhang et al. [39]	67	83	74
EAST [41]	67.43	87.28	76.08
He et al. [10]	70	77	74
PixelLink [4]	83.0	73.2	77.8
CENet (VGG 50k+MSRA TD500 finetune)	75.26	85.88	**80.21**

4.5 Future Works

Our model predicts rich information including text level boundaries as well as character bounding boxes. With a view to these advantages, we hope to incorporate the acquired detection information into the follow-up text recognition. For instance, we may use the predicted character position to align the attention weight or boost CTC based recognition.

5 Conclusion

Observing the demerits of previous text detection methods, we present a novel scene text detection model. The model is more flexible to detect texts that captured unconstrained, the curved or severely distorted texts in particular. It is completely data-driven in an end-to-end way and thus makes little use of heuristic rules or handcrafted features. It is also trained with two correlated tasks,

Table 5. Performances on Total-Text dataset.

Method	Recall	Precision	F-measure
DeconvNet [2]	33	40	36
CENet (VGG 50k)	42.39	58.17	49.04
CENet (VGG 50k+Total Text finetune)	54.41	59.89	**57.02**

i.e., the character detection and character embedding, which is unprecedented. To train the network smoothly, we also propose several measures, i.e., weak supervision mechanism for training character detector and positive-negative pair reweighting, to facilitate training and boost the performance. Extensive experiments on benchmarks show that the proposed framework could achieve superior performances even though texts are displayed in multi-orientated, line-level or curved ways.

References

1. Almazán, J., Gordo, A., Fornés, A., Valveny, E.: Word spotting and recognition with embedded attributes. IEEE Trans. PAMI **36**(12), 2552–2566 (2014)
2. Chng, C.K., Chan, C.S.: Total-text: a comprehensive dataset for scene text detection and recognition. CoRR abs/1710.10400 (2017)
3. Chopra, S., Hadsell, R., LeCun, Y.: Learning a similarity metric discriminatively, with application to face verification. In: Proceedings of CVPR, vol. 1, pp. 539–546. IEEE (2005)
4. Deng, D., Liu, H., Li, X., Cai, D.: PixeLlink: detecting scene text via instance segmentation. arXiv preprint arXiv:1801.01315 (2018)
5. Epshtein, B., Ofek, E., Wexler, Y.: Detecting text in natural scenes with stroke width transform. In: Proceedings of CVPR, pp. 2963–2970 (2010)
6. Gupta, A., Vedaldi, A., Zisserman, A.: Synthetic data for text localisation in natural images. In: Proceedings of CVPR, pp. 2315–2324 (2016)
7. He, K., Zhang, X., Ren, S., Sun, J.: Deep residual learning for image recognition. In: Proceedings of the IEEE Conference on Computer Vision and Pattern Recognition, pp. 770–778 (2016)
8. He, P., Huang, W., He, T., Zhu, Q., Qiao, Y., Li, X.: Single shot text detector with regional attention. In: Proceedings of ICCV (2017)
9. He, T., Huang, W., Qiao, Y., Yao, J.: Text-attentional convolutional neural network for scene text detection. IEEE Trans. Image Process. **25**(6), 2529–2541 (2016)
10. He, W., Zhang, X.Y., Yin, F., Liu, C.L.: Deep direct regression for multi-oriented scene text detection. In: Proceedings of ICCV (2017)
11. Hoi, S.C., Liu, W., Lyu, M.R., Ma, W.Y.: Learning distance metrics with contextual constraints for image retrieval. In: Proceedings of CVPR, vol. 2, pp. 2072–2078. IEEE (2006)
12. Hu, H., Zhang, C., Luo, Y., Wang, Y., Han, J., Ding, E.: WordSup: exploiting word annotations for character based text detection. arXiv preprint arXiv:1708.06720 (2017)
13. Huang, L., Yang, Y., Deng, Y., Yu, Y.: DenseBox: unifying landmark localization with end to end object detection. arXiv preprint arXiv:1509.04874 (2015)
14. Jaderberg, M., Vedaldi, A., Zisserman, A.: Deep features for text spotting. In: Fleet, D., Pajdla, T., Schiele, B., Tuytelaars, T. (eds.) ECCV 2014. LNCS, vol. 8692, pp. 512–528. Springer, Cham (2014). https://doi.org/10.1007/978-3-319-10593-2_34
15. Karatzas, D., et al.: ICDAR 2015 competition on robust reading. In: Proceedings of ICDAR, pp. 1156–1160. IEEE (2015)
16. Karatzas, D., et al.: ICDAR 2013 robust reading competition. In: Proceedings of ICDAR, pp. 1484–1493. IEEE (2013)

17. Li, H., Wang, P., Shen, C.: Towards end-to-end text spotting with convolutional recurrent neural networks. arXiv preprint arXiv:1707.03985 (2017)
18. Liao, M., Shi, B., Bai, X., Wang, X., Liu, W.: TextBoxes: a fast text detector with a single deep neural network. In: Proceedings of AAAI, pp. 4161–4167 (2017)
19. Lin, T.Y., Dollár, P., Girshick, R., He, K., Hariharan, B., Belongie, S.: Feature pyramid networks for object detection. In: CVPR (2017)
20. Liu, W., et al.: SSD: single shot multibox detector. In: Leibe, B., Matas, J., Sebe, N., Welling, M. (eds.) ECCV 2016. LNCS, vol. 9905, pp. 21–37. Springer, Cham (2016). https://doi.org/10.1007/978-3-319-46448-0_2
21. Liu, Y., Jin, L.: Deep matching prior network: toward tighter multi-oriented text detection. In: Proceedings of CVPR (2017)
22. Liu, Z., Lin, G., Yang, S., Feng, J., Lin, W., Ling Goh, W.: Learning Markov clustering networks for scene text detection. In: Proceedings of the IEEE Conference on Computer Vision and Pattern Recognition, pp. 6936–6944 (2018)
23. Lyu, P., Yao, C., Wu, W., Yan, S., Bai, X.: Multi-oriented scene text detection via corner localization and region segmentation. In: Proceedings of the IEEE Conference on Computer Vision and Pattern Recognition, pp. 7553–7563 (2018)
24. Ma, J., et al.: Arbitrary-oriented scene text detection via rotation proposals. arXiv preprint arXiv:1703.01086 (2017)
25. Neumann, L., Matas, J.: Real-time scene text localization and recognition. In: Proceedings of CVPR, pp. 3538–3545 (2012)
26. Ren, S., He, K., Girshick, R.B., Sun, J.: Faster R-CNN: towards real-time object detection with region proposal networks. In: NIPS, pp. 91–99 (2015)
27. Schroff, F., Kalenichenko, D., Philbin, J.: FaceNet: a unified embedding for face recognition and clustering. In: Proceedings of CVPR, pp. 815–823 (2015)
28. Shi, B., Bai, X., Belongie, S.: Detecting oriented text in natural images by linking segments. arXiv preprint arXiv:1703.06520 (2017)
29. Shrivastava, A., Gupta, A., Girshick, R.: Training region-based object detectors with online hard example mining. In: CVPR (2016)
30. Tian, S., Lu, S., Li, C.: WeText: scene text detection under weak supervision. In: Proceedings of ICCV (2017)
31. Tian, S., Pan, Y., Huang, C., Lu, S., Yu, K., Lim Tan, C.: Text flow: A unified text detection system in natural scene images. In: Proceedings of ICCV, pp. 4651–4659 (2015)
32. Tian, Z., Huang, W., He, T., He, P., Qiao, Y.: Detecting text in natural image with connectionist text proposal network. In: Leibe, B., Matas, J., Sebe, N., Welling, M. (eds.) ECCV 2016. LNCS, vol. 9912, pp. 56–72. Springer, Cham (2016). https://doi.org/10.1007/978-3-319-46484-8_4
33. Wang, J., Zhou, F., Wen, S., Liu, X., Lin, Y.: Deep metric learning with angular loss. In: Proceedings of ICCV, October 2017
34. Wilkinson, T., Lindstrom, J., Brun, A.: Neural ctrl-F: segmentation-free query-by-string word spotting in handwritten manuscript collections. In: Proceedings of ICCV, October 2017
35. Yao, C., Bai, X., Liu, W., Ma, Y., Tu, Z.: Detecting texts of arbitrary orientations in natural images. In: 2012 IEEE Conference on Computer Vision and Pattern Recognition (CVPR), pp. 1083–1090. IEEE (2012)
36. Yin, F., Liu, C.L.: Handwritten chinese text line segmentation by clustering with distance metric learning. Pattern Recogn. **42**(12), 3146–3157 (2009)
37. Yin, X.C., Pei, W.Y., Zhang, J., Hao, H.W.: Multi-orientation scene text detection with adaptive clustering. IEEE Trans. PAMI **37**(9), 1930–1937 (2015)

38. Yu, J., Jiang, Y., Wang, Z., Cao, Z., Huang, T.: UnitBox: an advanced object detection network. In: Proceedings of ACMMM, pp. 516–520. ACM (2016)
39. Zhang, Z., Zhang, C., Shen, W., Yao, C., Liu, W., Bai, X.: Multi-oriented text detection with fully convolutional networks. In: Proceedings of CVPR (2016)
40. Zhong, Z., Jin, L., Huang, S.: DeepText: a new approach for text proposal generation and text detection in natural images. In: Proceedings of ICASSP, pp. 1208–1212 (2017)
41. Zhou, X., et al.: EAST: an efficient and accurate scene text detector. arXiv preprint arXiv:1704.03155 (2017)
42. Zhu, S., Zanibbi, R.: A text detection system for natural scenes with convolutional feature learning and cascaded classification. In: Proceedings of CVPR, pp. 625–632 (2016)

Design Pseudo Ground Truth with Motion Cue for Unsupervised Video Object Segmentation

Ye Wang[1(✉)], Jongmoo Choi[1], Yueru Chen[1], Qin Huang[1], Siyang Li[1], Ming-Sui Lee[2], and C.-C. Jay Kuo[1]

[1] University of Southern California, Los Angeles, CA 91754, USA
{wang316,jongmooc,yueruche,qinhuang,siyangl,cckuo}@usc.edu
[2] National Taiwan University, Taipei 10617, Taiwan
mslee@csie.ntu.edu.tw

Abstract. One major technique debt in video object segmentation is to label the object masks for training instances. As a result, we propose to prepare inexpensive, yet high quality pseudo ground truth corrected with motion cue for video object segmentation training. Our method conducts semantic segmentation using instance segmentation networks and, then, selects the segmented object of interest as the pseudo ground truth based on the motion information. Afterwards, the pseudo ground truth is exploited to finetune the pretrained objectness network to facilitate object segmentation in the remaining frames of the video. We show that the pseudo ground truth could effectively improve the segmentation performance. This straightforward unsupervised video object segmentation method is more efficient than existing methods. Experimental results on DAVIS and FBMS show that the proposed method outperforms state-of-the-art unsupervised segmentation methods on various benchmark datasets. And the category-agnostic pseudo ground truth has great potential to extend to multiple arbitrary object tracking.

Keywords: Pseudo ground truth · Unsupervised · Video object segmentation

1 Introduction

Video object segmentation (VOS) is the task to segment foreground objects from background across all frames in a video clip. The VOS methods can be classified into two categories: semi-supervised and unsupervised VOS methods. Semi-supervised VOS methods [2,23,28,34,35] require the ground truth segmentation mask in the first frame as the input and, then, segment the annotated object in the remaining frames. Unsupervised VOS methods [4,12,15,17,18,32] identify and segment the main object in the video automatically.

Recent image-based semantic and instance segmentation tasks [9–11] have achieved great success due to the emergence of deep neural networks such as

C. V. Jawahar et al. (Eds.): ACCV 2018, LNCS 11364, pp. 518–533, 2019.
https://doi.org/10.1007/978-3-030-20870-7_32

the fully convolutional network (FCN) [22]. The one-shot video object segmentation (OSVOS) method [2] uses large classification datasets in pretraining and applies the foreground/background segmentation information obtained from the first frame to object segmentation in the remaining frames of the video clip. It converts the image-based segmentation method to a semi-supervised video-based segmentation method by processing each frame independently without using the temporal information.

However, since manual annotation is expensive, it is desired to develop the more challenging unsupervised VOS solution. This is feasible due to the following observation. Inspired by vision studies [29], moving objects can attract infant and young animals' attention who can group things properly without knowing what kinds of objects they are. Furthermore, we tend to group moving objects and separate them from background and other static objects. In other words, semantic grouping is acquired after motion-based grouping in the VOS task.

In this paper, we propose to tag the main object in a video clip by combining the motion information and the instance segmentation result. We use optical flow to group segmented pixels to a single object as the pseudo ground truth and, then, take it as the first frame mask to perform the OSVOS. The pseudo ground truth is the estimated object mask for the first frame to replace the true ground truth in the semi-supervised VOS methods. The main idea is sketched below. We apply a powerful instance segmentation algorithm, called the Mask R-CNN [9], to the first frame of a video clip as shown in Fig. 1, where different objects have different labels. Then, we extract optical flow from the first two frames and select and group different instance segmentations to estimate the foreground object. Next, we finetune a pretrained CNN using the estimated foreground object from the first frame as the pseudo ground truth and propagate the foreground/background segmentation to the remaining frames of the video one frame at a time. Finally, we achieve state-of-the-art performance in the benchmark datasets by incorporating online adaptation [35]. Example results are shown in Fig. 2.

Our goal is to segment the primary video object without manual annotations. The proposed method does not use the temporal information of the whole video clip at once but one frame at a time. Errors from each consequent frames do not propagate along time. As a result, the proposed method has higher tolerance against occlusion and fast motion. We evaluate the proposed method extensively on the DAVIS dataset [27], the FBMS dataset [24]. Our method gives state-of-the-art performance in both datasets with the mean intersection-over-union (IoU) of 79.3% on DAVIS, and 77.9% on FBMS.

Main contributions in this work are summarized below. First, we introduce a novel unsupervised video object segmentation method by combining instance segmentation and motion information. Second, we transfer a recent semi-supervised network architecture to the unsupervised context. Finally, the proposed method outperforms state-of-the-art unsupervised methods on several benchmarks datasets.

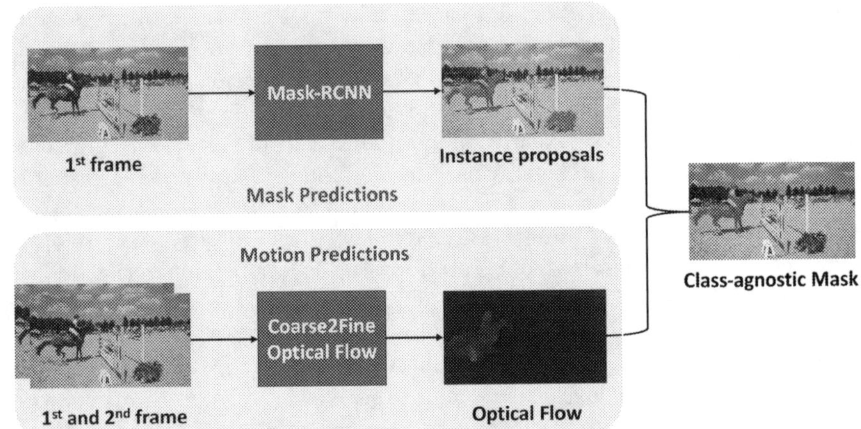

Fig. 1. Overview of tagging the main object. We use instance segmentation algorithm to segment objects in the static image. We then utilize optical flow to select and group the segments to one foreground object.

The rest of this paper is organized as follows. Related work is reviewed in Sect. 2. Our novel unsupervised video object segmentation method is proposed in Sect. 3. Experimental results are shown in Sect. 4. Finally, concluding remarks are given in Sect. 5.

Fig. 2. Example results of our method, where the pseudo ground truth of the first frame is in yellow, and the other seven images in green are sample segmentations of the rest of the video clip. Best viewed in color.

2 Related Work

Instance Segmentation. Many video object segmentation methods [2,12,28,35] are based on semantic segmentation networks [36] for static images. State-of-the-art semantic segmentation techniques are dominated by fully convolutional networks [3,22]. Semantic segmentation segments the same category of objects with one mask while instance segmentation [9] provides a segmentation mask independently for each instance. One key reason that these deep learning based methods for instance segmentation have developed very rapidly is that there are large datasets with instance mask annotations such as COCO [20]. It is difficult to annotate all categories of objects and apply a supervised training. It is more difficult to extend image instance segmentation to video instance segmentation due to the lack of large-scale manual labeled instance video object segmentation datasets. In contrast, we focus on generic object segmentation in the video and we do not care whether the object category is in the training dataset or not. We propose a method to transfer the image instance segmentation to enable finetuning the pretrained fully convolutional network.

Semi-supervised Video Object Segmentation. Semi-supervised VOS requires the manual labels for the first frame and then propagate it to the rest of the video. The annotation provides a good initialization for the object appearance model and the problem can be considered as a foreground/background segmentation guided by the first frame annotation. Deep learning approaches have achieved higher performance [35], most of the recent work are based on OSVOS [2] and MaskTrack [28]. OSVOS creates a new model for each new video initialized with the pretrained model and finetunes on the first frame without using any temporal information. OSVOS treats each frame independently while MaskTrack considers the relationship between consecutive frames when training the network. Lucid data dreaming [14] proposed a data augmentation technique by cutting-out foreground, in-painting the background, perturbing both the foreground and background and finally reconstructed the frames. VOS with re-identification [19] adds a re-identification step to recover the lost instances in the long term by feeding the cropped patch contained the object instead of forwarding the entire image to the network. OnAVOS [35] proposed a online finetuning approach to segment future frames based on the first frame annotation and the previous predicted segmented frames.

Unsupervised Video Object Segmentation. Unsupervised VOS algorithms [12,15] discover the primary object segmentation in a video and assume no manual annotations. Some approaches formulate segmentation as foreground and background labeling problem, such as Gaussian Mixture Models and Graph Cut [23,34]. ARP [15] proposed a unsupervised video object segmentation approach by iteratively refining the augmentation with missing parts or reducing them by excluding noisy parts. Recently more CNN-based approaches identify the primary object by using motion boundaries, saliency maps [12,32]. LMP [32] trains an encoder-decoder architecture using ground truth optical flow and motion segmentation and then refines by the objectness map. Both LVO [33] and FSEG [12] have two-stream fully convolutional neural networks that combine appearance features and motion features, LVO further improves the segmentation by forwarding the features to bidirectional convolutional GRU, while FSEG fuses these two models and put it as an end-to-end training. Unsupervised approach is more desired since it needs no human interactions and we focus on the unsupervised VOS in this paper.

3 Proposed Method

Our goal is to segment generic object in the video in an unsupervised approach. In the semi-supervised VOS, the first frame ground truth label is needed. Inspired by the semi-supervised approach, we propose a method to tag the "pseudo ground truth" and then take it as input for the pretrained network, and then output the segmentation masks for the rest of the video. To our best knowledge, this is the first attempt to transfer semi-supervised VOS approach to unsupervised VOS approach by utilizing "pseudo ground truth". Figure 3 shows the overview of the proposed method, which includes three key components, the criterion to tag the primary object, appearance model and online adaptation.

3.1 Learning to Tag the Foreground Object

Image Instance Segmentation. We apply an image-based instance segmentation algorithm to the first frame of the given video. Specifically, we choose Mask R-CNN [9] as our instance segmentation framework and generate instance masks. We further exploit the error analysis to demonstrate that better initial instance segmentations improve the performance in a large margin which suggests that our proposed method has the potential to improve further with more advanced instance segmentation methods.

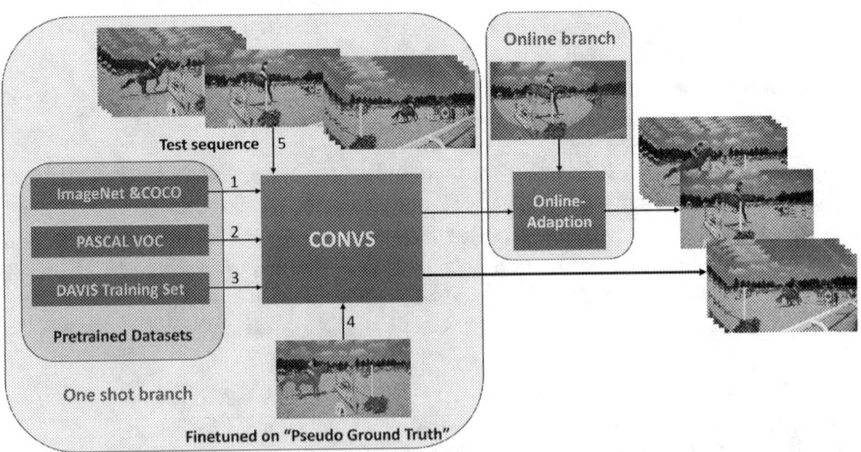

Fig. 3. Overview of the proposed method. We trained the appearance model on the DAVIS training set with a pre-trained wider-ResNet from ImageNet, COCO and PASCAL VOC. We then finetuned the model on the first frame "pseudo ground truth", and online adaptation is applied afterwards. The pixels in yellow and green are selected positive and negative examples respectively in the online branch. (Color figure online)

Mask R-CNN is a simple yet high performance instance segmentation model. Specifically, Mask R-CNN adds an additional FCN mask branch to the original Faster R-CNN [30] model. The mask branch and the bounding box branch are trained simultaneously in the training, while the instance masks are generated from the detection results at inference time. The box prediction branch generates bounding boxes based on the proposals followed by non-maximum suppression. The mask branch is then applied to predict segmentation masks from the 100 detection boxes with the highest scores. This step speeds up the inference time and improves accuracy, which is different from the training step with parallel computation. For each region of interests (ROIs), the mask can predict n times where n is the class number in the training set, and the only used k-th mask is from the predicted class by the classification branch.

We note that the mask branch generates class-specific instance segmentation masks for the given image whereas VOS focuses on class-agnostic object segmentation. Our experiments show that even though Mask R-CNN can only generate limited-class labels due to the labels of COCO [20] and PASCAL [6], we can still output instance segmentation masks with closest class label. Our algorithm needs to further force all the classes to one foreground class, and thus the mis-classification has little influence to the performance of VOS.

Optical Flow Thresholding. There are two important cues in video object segmentations: appearance and motion. To use the information from both spatial and temporal domain, we incorporate optical flow with instance segmentation to learn to segment the primary object. Instance segmentation can generate precise class-specific segmentation masks, however, the algorithm cannot determine the primary object in the video. While optical flow can separate moving objects from the background, however the optical flow estimation is still far from perfect. Motivated by the moving objects attract people's attention [26], so we use motion information to select and group the static image instance segmentation proposals, which takes advantage of the merits of optical flow and instance segmentation. We apply optical flow algorithm Coarse2Fine [21] to extract the optical flow between the first frame and the second frame of a given video clip. To combine with the instance segmentation proposals, we normalize the flow magnitude and then threshold and select the optical flow motivated by the faster motions are more likely to attract attentions.

We select instance segmentation proposals which have more than 80% overlap with optical flow mask. We further group the selected proposal masks with different class labels to one foreground class without any class labels. In image-based instance segmentation, the same object may be separated into different parts due to the differences of colors, textures and the influence of occlusions. We can efficiently group the different parts to one primary object without knowing the categories of the objects. We named this foreground object as "pseudo ground truth" and forward it to the pretrained appearance model. Sample "pseudo ground truths" are shown in Fig. 1.

3.2 Unsupervised Video Object Segmentation

Our proposed method is built on one-shot video object segmentation (OSVOS) [2] which finetunes the pretrained appearance model on the first annotated frame. We replace the first annotated frame with our estimated "pseudo ground truth" so that semi-supervised network architecture can be used in our proposed approach. Our goal is to train a ConvNet to segment a generic object in a video.

Network Overview. We adopt a more recent ResNet [36] architecture pretrained on ImageNet [5] and MS-COCO [20] to learn powerful features. In more detail, the network uses the model A of the wider ResNet with 38 hidden layers as the backbone. The data in DAVIS training datasets is very scarce and we further pretrain the network using PASCAL [6] by mapping all the 20-class labels to one foreground label and keep background unchanged. As demonstrated in OnAVOS [35], the two steps of finetuning on DAVIS and PASCAL are complementary. Hence, we finetune the network using DAVIS training datasets and obtain the final pretrained network. The above training steps are all offline training to construct a model to identify foreground object. At inference time, we finetune the network on the "pseudo ground truth" of the first frame to tell the network which object to be segmented. However, the first frame does not provide all the information through the whole video, and thus online adaptation is needed during the test time.

Online Adaptation. The major difficulty for video object segmentation is the appearance may change dramatically throughout the video. A model learned only from the first frame cannot address the severe appearance changes. Therefore online adaptation for the model is needed to exploit the information from the rest frames during inference time.

We adopt test data augmentation method from Lucid Data Dreaming augmentation [14] and online adaptation approach from OnAVOS [35] to perform our online finetuning. We generate augmentation of the first frame using Lucid Data Dreaming approach. As each frame is segmented, foreground pixels with high confidence predictions are taken as further positive training examples, while pixels far away from the last assumed object position are taken as negative examples. Then an additional round of fine-tuning is performed on the newly acquired data.

4 Experiments

To evaluate the effectiveness of our proposed method, we conduct experiments on three challenging video object segmentation datasets: DAVIS [27], Freiburg-Berkeley Motion Segmentation (FBMS) dataset [24], SegTrack-v2 [16]. We use region similarity, which is defined as the intersection-over-union (IoU) between the estimated segmentation and the ground truth mask, and F-score evaluation protocol proposed in [24] to estimate the accuracy.

Table 1. Comparison of the mIoU scores (%) of different unsupervised VOS approaches in the DAVIS 2016 validation dataset. Our method achieves the highest mIoU compared with state-of-the-art methods

	NLC [7]	FST [25]	LMP [32]	FSEG [12]	LVO [33]	ARP [15]	Ours
mIoU	55.1	55.8	70.0	70.7	75.9	76.2	**79.3**

4.1 Datasets

We provide a detailed introduction to evaluation benchmarks below.

DAVIS. The DAVIS dataset is composed of 50 high-definition video sequences, 30 in the training set and the remaining 20 in the validation set. There are totally 3, 455 densely annotated, pixel-accurate frames. The videos contain challenges such as occlusions, motion blur, and appearance changes. Only the primary moving objects are annotated in the ground truth.

FBMS. The Freiburg-Berkeley motion segmentation dataset is composed of 59 video sequences with 720 frames annotated. In contrast to DAVIS, it has multiple moving objects in several videos with instance-level annotations. We do not train on any of these sequences and evaluate using mIoU and F-score respectively. We also convert the instance-level annotations to binary ones by merging all foreground annotations, as in [32].

SegTrack-v2. The SegTrack-v2 dataset contains 14 videos with a total of 1, 066 frames with pixel-level annotations. For videos with multiple objects with individual ground-truth segmentations, each object can be segmented in turn, treating each as a problem of segmenting that object from the background.

4.2 Implementation Details

We jointly use optical flow and semantic instance segmentation to group foreground objects that move together into a single object. We use the optical flow from a re-implementation of Coarse2Fine optical flow [21]. We implemented the objectness network using Tensorflow [1] library and set wider ResNet [36] with 38 hidden layers as the backbone. The segmentation network is simple without using upsampling, skip connections or multi-scale structures. In some convolution layers, increasing the dilation rates and removing the down-sampling operations accordingly are applied to generate score maps at 1/8 resolution. Large field-of-view setting in Deeplabv2 [3] is used to replace the top linear classifier and global pooling layer which exist in the classification network. Besides, the batch normalization layers are freezed during finetuning.

We adopted the initial network weights provided by the repository which were pre-trained on the ImageNet and COCO dataset. We further finetune the

Fig. 4. Qualitative results on DAVIS validation set: the first column in yellow is the "pseudo ground truth" of the first frame of each video. The other four columns are the output segmentation masks of our proposed approach. Our algorithm performs well on videos with fast motion (first and forth row), gesture changes (second row), unseen category (third row) and complex background (fifth row). Best viewed in color.

objectness network based on the augmented PASCAL VOC ground truth from [8] with a total of 12, 051 training images. Note that we force all the foreground objects in a certain image to one single foreground object and keep background the same.

For the DAVIS dataset evaluation, we further train the network on DAVIS training set and then apply a one-shot finetuning on the first frame with "pseudo ground truth". The segmentation network is trained on the first frame image/"pseudo ground truth" pair, by Adam with learning rate 3×10^{-6}. We set the number of finetuning n_f on the first frame as 100, we found that a relative small n_f can improve the accuracy which is opposite with semi-supervised VOS. For the online part, we used the default parameters in OnAVOS [35] by setting the number of finetuning as 15, finetuning interval as 5 frames, and learning rate as 1×10^{-5} and adopted the CRF parameters from DeepLab [3]. For completeness, we also conduct experiments on FBMS and SegTrack-v2 datasets, we conduct the same procedures for FBMS as DAVIS. To check the effectiveness of the "pseudo ground truth" we only perform one-shot branch for SegTrack-v2 without online adaption.

Table 2. Comparison of the mIoU scores (%) per video of several methods for the DAVIS 2016 validation dataset. (1) blackswan, (2) bmx-trees, (3) breakdance, (4) camel, (5) car-roundabout, (6) car-shadow, (7) cows, (8) dance-twirl, (9) dog, (10) drift-chicane, (11) drift-straight, (12) goat, (13) horsejump-high, (14) kite-surf, (15) libby, (16) motocross-jump, (17) paragliding-launch, (18) parkour, (19) scooter-black, (20) soapbox

Method	No.1	No.2	No.3	No.4	No.5	No.6	No.7	No.8	No.9	No.10	No.11	No.12	No.13	No.14	No.15	No.16	No.17	No.18	No.19	No.20	meanIoU
FSEG [12]	81.2	43.3	51.2	83.6	90.7	89.6	86.9	70.4	88.9	59.6	81.1	83.0	65.2	39.2	58.4	77.5	57.1	76.0	68.8	62.4	70.7
ARP [15]	**88.1**	**49.9**	**76.2**	**90.3**	81.6	73.6	**90.8**	**79.8**	71.8	79.7	71.5	77.6	**83.8**	59.1	65.4	82.3	**60.1**	82.8	74.6	84.6	76.2
Ours-oneshot	83.3	39.8	50.3	76.1	82.9	91.9	87.5	77.3	**90.1**	**86.1**	85.4	85.1	74.1	60.1	75.5	75.5	57.3	**89.9**	72.7	74.9	75.8
Ours-online	82.0	46.0	60.7	75.5	**93.0**	**94.6**	87.6	78.9	89.3	82.9	**91.7**	**85.7**	76.8	**60.3**	**76.0**	**84.7**	56.9	**89.9**	**88.1**	**85.1**	**79.3**

4.3 Comparison with State-of-the-art Methods

DAVIS. We compare our proposed approach with state-of-the-art unsupervised techniques, NLC [7], LMP [32], FSEG [12], LVO [33], and ARP [15] in Table 1. We achieve the best performance for unsupervised video object segmentation: 3.1% higher than the second best ARP. Besides, we achieve mIoU of 71.2% on the DAVIS validation set by extracting the pseudo ground-truth on each frame of a given video. When we break down the performance on each DAVIS sequence, we outperform the majority of the videos shown in Table 2, and especially for drift-straight, libby and scooter-black, our results are more than 10% higher than the second best results. As shown in Fig. 4, our approach could segment unknown object classes which do not need to be in the PASCAL/COCO vocabulary. The goat in the third row is an unseen category in the training data, the closest semantic category horse is matched instead. Note that our algorithm only needs the foreground mask without knowing the specific category, and performs better than state-of-the-art methods. Our method performs even better when the object classes are in the MS COCO, the top two rows show a single instance segmentation with large appearance changes (first row) and viewing angle and gesture changes (second row). The bottom two rows show that our algorithm works well when merging multiple object masks to one single mask with viewing angle changes (forth row) and messy background (fifth row).

To verify where the improvements come from, we utilize similar backbone with previous method. We test OSVOS [2] by replacing the first frame annotations with pseudo ground truths. OSVOS uses the VGG architecture, and we set the number of first-frame fine-tuning to 500 without applying boundary snapping. The mIoUs of our approach and the original OSVOS are 72.3% and 75.7%, respectively. Our approach in the VGG architecture still outperforms FSEG (70.7%) without online adaptation, CRF, test time data augmentation.

We further analyze the finetuning times on the first frames for both semi-supervised and unsupervised approaches in Table 3. In the table, the second column shows that the performance improves with the increasing finetuning times for semi-supervised approach in terms of mIoU, which indicates more finetuning times with image/ground truth pairs can predict better results. The right two columns show the different relationships between the performance in mIoU and finetuning times on the first frames for unsupervised approach. They

Table 3. Comparison of mIoU scores (%) of different finetuning times on the first frames of the DAVIS validation set

Finetuning times	Semi-supervised oneshot	Unsupervised oneshot	Unsupervised online
50	80.4	73.1	77.6
100	80.7	**75.8**	**79.3**
500	81.4	74.4	77.7
2000	**82.1**	74.8	77.9

Table 4. Comparison of the F-score and mIoU scores (%) of different unsupervised VOS approaches on the FBMS test dataset. Our method achieves the highest compared with state-of-the-art methods

	NLC [7]	FST [25]	CVOS [31]	MP-Net-V [32]	LVO [33]	ARP [15]	Ours
mIoU	44.5	55.5	-	-	-	59.8	**77.9**
F-score	-	69.2	74.9	77.5	77.8	-	**85.1**

both achieve the highest performance by setting the number of finetuning as 100, which indicates the model learns better with an appropriate number of finetuning since the pseudo ground truth is not as accurate as the ground truth.

FBMS. We evaluate the proposed approach on the test set, with 30 sequences in total. The results are shown in Table 4. Our method is outperformed in both evaluation metrics, with an F-score of 85.1% which is 7.3% higher than the second best method LVO [33], and the mIoU of 77.9% which is 18.1% better than ARP [15], which performs the second best on DAVIS. Figure 5 shows qualitative results of our method, our algorithm performs well for most of the sequences. The last row shows the failure case for rabbits04 since there are severe occlusions in this video and the rabbit is also an unseen category in the MS COCO. To recover a better prediction mask, further motion information should be used to address this problem.

SegTrack-V2. Our method achieves mIoU of 58.7% on this dataset, which is higher than other methods that do well on DAVIS, CUT [13] (47.8%), FST [25] (54.3%), and LVO [33] (57.3%). Note that we did not apply online adaptation on this dataset which could further improve the performance. Our method performs worse than NLC [7] (67.2%) due to low resolution of SegTrack-v2 and the fact that NLC is designed and evaluated on this dataset. We outperform NLC on both FBMS and DAVIS datasets by a large margin. Figure 6 shows qualitative results of the proposed method on the SegTrack-v2. All these visual results demonstrate the effectiveness of our approach where the category of the object is not existed in MS COCO [20] or PASCAL VOC 2012 [6]. The accurate category is not needed in our approach, as long as the foreground object is consistent in the whole video. The objectness of the worm sequence in the third row cannot be

Fig. 5. Qualitative results on FBMS dataset: the first column in yellow is the "pseudo ground truth" of the first frame of each video. The other four columns are the output segmentation masks of our proposed approach. Best viewed in color.

detected using instance segmentation algorithm, in this case the thresholded flow magnitude is used as the pseudo ground truth mask instead.

4.4 Ablation Studies

Table 5 presents our ablation study on DAVIS 2016 validation set on the three major components: online adaptation, CRF [3] and test time data augmentation. The baseline ours-oneshot in Table 5 is the wider-ResNet trained on the PASCAL VOC 2012 dataset and the DAVIS 2016 training set. Online adaptation provides 1.4% improvement over the baseline in terms of mIoU. Additional CRF post processing brings further 1.1% boost in terms of mIoU. Combining with test time data augmentation (TTDA) gives the best performance of 79.3% in mIoU which is 3.5% higher than the baseline without any post processing.

Figure 7 shows qualitative comparisons for oneshot and online approaches on the video sequences camel and car-roundabout. Our online approach outperforms our oneshot approach for the sequence car-roundabout in the second row, which is due to the right bottom pixels are considered as negative training examples

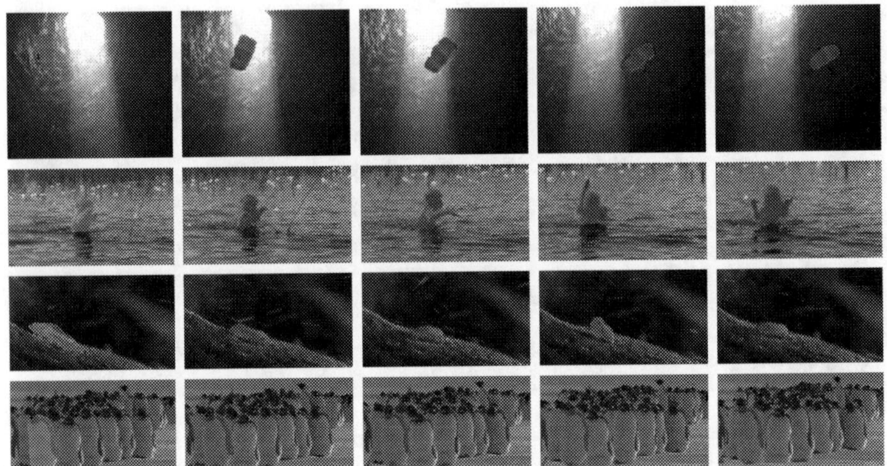

Fig. 6. Qualitative results on SegTrack-v2 dataset: the first column in yellow is the "pseudo ground truth" of the first frame of each video. The other four columns are the output segmentation masks of our proposed approach. Best viewed in color.

Table 5. Ablation study of our approach on DAVIS 2016 validation set.TTDA denotes the test time data augmentation and CRF denotes conditional random field

	Ours-oneshot	+Online	+Online +CRF	+Online +CRF +TTDA
mIoU(%)	75.8	77.2	78.3	79.3

from the previous frames. The additional round of fintuning is performed on the newly acquired data to remove the false positive masks. The first row shows the failure case for the two approaches, the two branches both wrongly predict the foreground mask when the moving camel is walking across the static camel. This example shows the weakness of the oneshot approaches by propagating thoughout the whole video without using motion information.

Error Analysis. To analyze the effect of the first frame tagging, we apply OSVOS to the entire DAVIS validation set using the pseudo ground truth and the ground truth of the first frame respectively, the mIoUs of the entire dataset and two difficult sequences are shown in Table 6. The mIoUs of the entire DAVIS validation set is 5.5% lower when using pseudo ground truth of the first frame. This demonstrates that more accurate mask prediction for the first frame can generate better segmentation masks for the remaining frames of the whole video, which shows the potential performance improvement when using more advanced tagging technique.

We also erode and dilate the pseudo ground truth by 5 pixels respectively and use the erosion and dilation masks as the new pseudo ground truths to

"pseudo ground truth" Ours-oneshot Ours-online

Fig. 7. Comparison of qualitative results on two sequences, camel and car-roundabout, on DAVIS validation set: the first column in yellow is the "pseudo ground truth" of the first frame of each video. The other two columns are the output segmentation masks of our oneshot and online approaches respectively. Best viewed in color.

Table 6. Error analysis for the entire DAVIS 2016 validation set and two difficult videos (bmx-trees and kite-surf)

Sequences	Erosion	Dilation	Pseudo ground truth	Ground truth
bmx-trees	33.9	42.4	46.0	52.5
kite-surf	51.0	56.4	60.3	66.6
mIoU	68.4	76.1	79.3	84.8

apply OSVOS approach to the videos. The performances have largely degraded from 3.2% to 10.9% compared with those of the original pseudo ground truth. This demonstrates accurate tagging is the key component for our tagging and segmenting approach.

5 Conclusion and Future Work

In this paper, we present a simple yet intuitive approach for unsupervised video object segmentation. Specifically, instead of manually annotating the first frame like existing semi-supervised methods, we proposed to automatically generate the approximate annotation, pseudo ground truth, by jointly employing instance segmentation and optical flow. Experimental results on the DAVIS, FBMS and SegTrack-v2 demonstrate that our approach enables effective transfer from semi-supervised VOS to unsupervised VOS and improves the mask prediction performance by a large margin. Our error analysis shows that using better instance segmentation has a dramatic performance boost which shows great potential for further improvement. Our approach is able to extend from single object tracking to multiple arbitrary object tracking based on the category-agnostic ground truths or pseudo ground truths.

References

1. Abadi, M., et al.: TensorFlow: a system for large-scale machine learning. In: OSDI, vol. 16, pp. 265–283 (2016)
2. Caelles, S., Maninis, K.K., Pont-Tuset, J., Leal-Taixé, L., Cremers, D., Van Gool, L.: One-shot video object segmentation. In: CVPR 2017. IEEE (2017)
3. Chen, L.C., Papandreou, G., Kokkinos, I., Murphy, K., Yuille, A.L.: DeepLab: semantic image segmentation with deep convolutional nets, atrous convolution, and fully connected CRFs. arXiv preprint arXiv:1606.00915 (2016)
4. Cheng, J., Tsai, Y.H., Wang, S., Yang, M.H.: SegFlow: joint learning for video object segmentation and optical flow. In: 2017 IEEE International Conference on Computer Vision (ICCV), pp. 686–695. IEEE (2017)
5. Deng, J., Dong, W., Socher, R., Li, L.J., Li, K., Fei-Fei, L.: ImageNet: a large-scale hierarchical image database. In: IEEE Conference on Computer Vision and Pattern Recognition, CVPR 2009, pp. 248–255. IEEE (2009)
6. Everingham, M., Van Gool, L., Williams, C.K., Winn, J., Zisserman, A.: The pascal visual object classes (VOC) challenge. Int. J. Comput. Vis. **88**(2), 303–338 (2010)
7. Faktor, A., Irani, M.: Video segmentation by non-local consensus voting. In: BMVC, vol. 2, p. 8 (2014)
8. Hariharan, B., Arbeláez, P., Girshick, R., Malik, J.: Simultaneous detection and segmentation. In: Fleet, D., Pajdla, T., Schiele, B., Tuytelaars, T. (eds.) ECCV 2014. LNCS, vol. 8695, pp. 297–312. Springer, Cham (2014). https://doi.org/10.1007/978-3-319-10584-0_20
9. He, K., Gkioxari, G., Dollár, P., Girshick, R.: Mask R-CNN. In: 2017 IEEE International Conference on Computer Vision (ICCV), pp. 2980–2988. IEEE (2017)
10. Huang, Q., Xia, C., Li, S., Wang, Y., Song, Y., Kuo, C.C.J.: Unsupervised clustering guided semantic segmentation. In: 2018 IEEE Winter Conference on Applications of Computer Vision (WACV), pp. 1489–1498. IEEE (2018)
11. Huang, Q., et al.: Semantic segmentation with reverse attention. arXiv preprint arXiv:1707.06426 (2017)
12. Jain, S.D., Xiong, B., Grauman, K.: FusionSeg: learning to combine motion and appearance for fully automatic segmention of generic objects in videos. arXiv preprint arXiv:1701.05384 **2**(3), 6 (2017)
13. Keuper, M., Andres, B., Brox, T.: Motion trajectory segmentation via minimum cost multicuts. In: 2015 IEEE International Conference on Computer Vision (ICCV), pp. 3271–3279. IEEE (2015)
14. Khoreva, A., Benenson, R., Ilg, E., Brox, T., Schiele, B.: Lucid data dreaming for object tracking. arXiv preprint arXiv:1703.09554 (2017)
15. Koh, Y.J., Kim, C.S.: Primary object segmentation in videos based on region augmentation and reduction. In: Proceedings of the IEEE Conference on Computer Vision and Pattern Recognition, vol. 1, p. 6 (2017)
16. Li, F., Kim, T., Humayun, A., Tsai, D., Rehg, J.M.: Video segmentation by tracking many figure-ground segments. In: 2013 IEEE International Conference on Computer Vision (ICCV), pp. 2192–2199. IEEE (2013)
17. Li, S., Seybold, B., Vorobyov, A., Fathi, A., Huang, Q., Kuo, C.C.J.: Instance embedding transfer to unsupervised video object segmentation. In: Proceedings of the IEEE Conference on Computer Vision and Pattern Recognition, pp. 6526–6535 (2018)

18. Li, S., Seybold, B., Vorobyov, A., Lei, X., Kuo, C.-C.J.: Unsupervised video object segmentation with motion-based bilateral networks. In: Ferrari, V., Hebert, M., Sminchisescu, C., Weiss, Y. (eds.) ECCV 2018. LNCS, vol. 11207, pp. 215–231. Springer, Cham (2018). https://doi.org/10.1007/978-3-030-01219-9_13
19. Li, X., et al.: Video object segmentation with re-identification. arXiv preprint arXiv:1708.00197 (2017)
20. Lin, T.-Y., et al.: Microsoft COCO: common objects in context. In: Fleet, David, Pajdla, Tomas, Schiele, Bernt, Tuytelaars, Tinne (eds.) ECCV 2014. LNCS, vol. 8693, pp. 740–755. Springer, Cham (2014). https://doi.org/10.1007/978-3-319-10602-1_48
21. Liu, C., et al.: Beyond pixels: exploring new representations and applications for motion analysis. Ph.D. thesis, Massachusetts Institute of Technology (2009)
22. Long, J., Shelhamer, E., Darrell, T.: Fully convolutional networks for semantic segmentation. In: Proceedings of the IEEE Conference on Computer Vision and Pattern Recognition, pp. 3431–3440 (2015)
23. Märki, N., Perazzi, F., Wang, O., Sorkine-Hornung, A.: Bilateral space video segmentation. In: Proceedings of the IEEE Conference on Computer Vision and Pattern Recognition, pp. 743–751 (2016)
24. Ochs, P., Malik, J., Brox, T.: Segmentation of moving objects by long term video analysis. IEEE Trans. Pattern Anal. Mach. Intell. **36**(6), 1187–1200 (2014)
25. Papazoglou, A., Ferrari, V.: Fast object segmentation in unconstrained video. In: 2013 IEEE International Conference on Computer Vision (ICCV), pp. 1777–1784. IEEE (2013)
26. Pathak, D., Girshick, R., Dollár, P., Darrell, T., Hariharan, B.: Learning features by watching objects move. In: Proceedings of the CVPR, vol. 2 (2017)
27. Perazzi, F., Pont-Tuset, J., McWilliams, B., Van Gool, L., Gross, M., Sorkine-Hornung, A.: A benchmark dataset and evaluation methodology for video object segmentation. In: Computer Vision and Pattern Recognition (2016)
28. Perazzi, F., Khoreva, A., Benenson, R., Schiele, B., Sorkine-Hornung, A.: Learning video object segmentation from static images. In: Computer Vision and Pattern Recognition (2017)
29. Port, R.F., Van Gelder, T.: Mind as Motion: Explorations in the Dynamics of Cognition. MIT press, Cambridge (1995)
30. Ren, S., He, K., Girshick, R., Sun, J.: Faster R-CNN: towards real-time object detection with region proposal networks. In: Advances in Neural Information Processing Systems, pp. 91–99 (2015)
31. Taylor, B., Karasev, V., Soatto, S.: Causal video object segmentation from persistence of occlusions. In: Proceedings of the IEEE Conference on Computer Vision and Pattern Recognition, pp. 4268–4276 (2015)
32. Tokmakov, P., Alahari, K., Schmid, C.: Learning motion patterns in videos. In: 2017 IEEE Conference on Computer Vision and Pattern Recognition (CVPR), pp. 531–539. IEEE (2017)
33. Tokmakov, P., Alahari, K., Schmid, C.: Learning video object segmentation with visual memory. arXiv preprint arXiv:1704.05737 (2017)
34. Tsai, Y.H., Yang, M.H., Black, M.J.: Video segmentation via object flow. In: Proceedings of the IEEE Conference on Computer Vision and Pattern Recognition, pp. 3899–3908 (2016)
35. Voigtlaender, P., Leibe, B.: Online adaptation of convolutional neural networks for video object segmentation. arXiv preprint arXiv:1706.09364 (2017)
36. Wu, Z., Shen, C., Hengel, A.v.d.: Wider or deeper: revisiting the resnet model for visual recognition. arXiv preprint arXiv:1611.10080 (2016)

Identity-Enhanced Network for Facial Expression Recognition

Yanwei Li[1,2], Xingang Wang[1(✉)], Shilei Zhang[3], Lingxi Xie[4], Wenqi Wu[1,2], Hongyuan Yu[1,2], and Zheng Zhu[1,2]

[1] Institute of Automation, Chinese Academy of Sciences, Beijing, China
{liyanwei2017,xingang.wang,wuwenqi2013, yuhongyuan2017,zhuzheng2014}@ia.ac.cn
[2] University of Chinese Academy of Sciences, Beijing, China
[3] IBM Research, Beijing, China
slzhang@cn.ibm.com
[4] The Johns Hopkins University, Baltimore, USA
198808xc@gmail.com

Abstract. Facial expression recognition is a challenging task, arguably because of large intra-class variations and high inter-class similarities. The core drawback of the existing approaches is the lack of ability to discriminate the changes in appearance caused by emotions and identities. In this paper, we present a novel identity-enhanced network (IDEnNet) to eliminate the negative impact of identity factor and focus on recognizing facial expressions. Spatial fusion combined with self-constrained multi-task learning are adopted to jointly learn the expression representations and identity-related information. We evaluate our approach on three popular datasets, namely Oulu-CASIA, CK+ and MMI. IDEnNet improves the baseline consistently, and achieves the best or comparable state-of-the-art on all three datasets.

1 Introduction

Facial expression recognition (FER) is a classic problem in the field of computer vision that attracts a lot of attentions for its wide range of applications in human-computer interaction (HCI) [3]. FER is challenging mainly due to the large intra-class variations and high inter-class similarities. Identity is a key issue, because the change in identities can bring even heavier variations than the change in expressions. Typical examples are shown in Fig. 1. Consequently, this may cause the same expression with different identities to be ranked lower than different expressions. From the perspective of machine learning, this requires projecting the features to another space in which the change in expressions is enhanced and the change in identities is depressed. Some loss functions were designed for this purpose [14,16], but they were more focused on data-level (reorganizing training data into groups and using metric learning to cancel out ID information) and cannot learn the identities well because of the limited amount of ID cases.

C. V. Jawahar et al. (Eds.): ACCV 2018, LNCS 11364, pp. 534–550, 2019.
https://doi.org/10.1007/978-3-030-20870-7_33

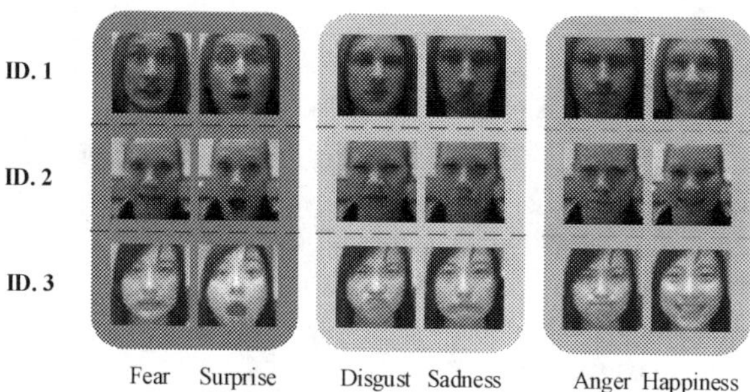

Fig. 1. Examples of six basic facial expressions, including fear, surprise, disgust, sadness, anger, and happiness. Each row includes examples of six facial expressions with the same identity, and each column includes examples of one specific facial expression with different identities. They are organized by similarities between two facial expressions. Here, we give examples of three people.

Identity information shares similar facial characteristics with expression features, and these characteristics are concentrated on different facial areas among people. As is presented in Fig. 1, the differences of the same expression among people mainly focus on several facial areas (e.g. mouth, nose, eye, and eyebrow), which also reveal their unique identities. However, the relationship between expression features and identity information has seldom been deeply studied in previous works.

For these reasons, we propose a novel identity-enhanced network (IDEnNet) to maximally discriminate identity information from expressions. This is done by jointly learning identity information with expression features and performing expression recognition and identity classification simultaneously. With the enhancement of identity information, the learned expression features are supervised to focus more on several representative facial regions among different expressions and adapt to the changes of identity at the same time. This can be easily learned from Figs. 4 and 5 in ablation study (Sect. 4.5).

The proposed network structure is illustrated in Fig. 2, in which feature extraction groups are adopted to extract identity information together with emotion features from input images and fusion dense block is designed for discriminative expression learning. In order to train this model efficiently, spatial fusion and self-constrained multi-task learning are adopted. Additional loss function whose value decays with the training process is designed to constrain sub-tasks, which facilitates continuous identity learning in the whole training stage.

We introduce multi-level identity information into FER tasks to extend the feature space and enhance ID. The enhancement of identity information also shows effectiveness in well known FER datasets. For example, the accuracy over the baseline is up to **6.77%** on the Oulu-CASIA database [27].

Overall, the key contributions of this work are summarized as follows:

- We propose a novel identity-enhanced network that can effectively discriminate the effect of facial expression changes from that of identity changes with the help of additional identity supervision.
- We introduce a loss function whose value decays with learning process to eliminate the over-training risk of auxiliary tasks without early-stopping it during multi-task learning stage.
- We present extensive experiments on the three well known FER datasets (namely Oulu-CASIA [27], CK+ [15], and MMI [18]), and our proposed method achieves better or comparable results of the state-of-the-art methods in all the three datasets.

2 Related Work

2.1 Facial Expression Recognition

Numerous approaches have been proposed to extract emotion features from frames and sequences, such as hand-crafted feature-based method and learned feature-based method [3,21]. Traditional hand-crafted features use predesigned appearance [9,11,27,28], or geometrical features such as Landmark distances [17] to describe relevant facial information. Learned features are usually trained through a joint feature and classification pipeline. Over the past years, deep learning architectures have been developed for end-to-end classification.

More recently, Jung et al. [7] proposed a joint fine-tuning method to fuse geometric features (facial landmarks) with appearance features (images) using deep temporal geometry network and deep temporal appearance network. In [29], PPDN was proposed to improve the performance of non-peak expressions under the supervision of peak expressions. In [4], a regularization function called FaceNet2ExpNet was designed to train expression classification net with the help of pre-trained face net. Related works also considered the impact of identity information in FER tasks. For example, in order to separate identity information from emotion features, Liu et al. [14] extended triplet loss to $(N{+}M)$-tuplet clusters loss function by incorporating N negative sets with the same identity and M examples with the same expression. The deep model with $(N{+}M)$-tuplet clusters loss function is subtle, but still hard to train. In contrast with the method mentioned on [14], our proposed IDEnNet introduces identity information into FER tasks rather than reducing it. Meng et al. [16] tried to alleviate the effect of IDs by adding another FC branch of identity. However, limited amount of ID cases in datasets cannot afford sufficient information for this method.

2.2 Multi-task Learning

Multi-task learning has proven its effectiveness in many computer vision problems [20,25]. On one hand, if there is no proper constrain, the performance of main task would be harmed by the over-trained auxiliary tasks. On the other hand, too-early stopping would "erase" the features learned by auxiliary tasks. Most of existing multi-task deep models [2] assume similar learning difficulties across all tasks, which are not suitable for our problem. In [20], many tasks were trained together and balanced by changeless weights in loss function through the whole training stage. In order to appropriately end the learning process of auxiliary tasks, Zhang et al. [26] proposed "Task-Wise Early Stopping", which terminated auxiliary tasks using highly complex judgements. Such "early-stopping" operations in our task may erase IDs as training process goes on. Different from previous methods, our proposed loss function (whose value decays with training process) keeps the auxiliary task through the whole training stage in a simple but effective way.

3 Identity-Enhanced Network

In this work, we introduce the identity-enhanced network for facial expression recognition. As is illustrated in Fig. 2, our designed framework introduces identity information to FER tasks in a fusion way and enhances it by self-constrained multi-task learning (Identity Enhancing Branch in Fig. 2). In detail, the proposed IDEnNet includes five pre-trained DenseNet [6] style blocks. Respectively, Identity Dense Block 1 and 2, Emotion Dense Block 1 and 2 are pre-trained with Identity Dense Block 3 and Emotion Dense Block 3 to extract identity features and facial expression features from the input image. And the other dense block (Fusion Dense Block, shares weights with Emotion Dense Block 3) is designed to deeply fuse facial expression representations with identity-related features by several convolution operations.

To clearly illustrate these processes, we start with a cropped image which contains the facial region. It is a 48×48 grayscale image, then expression feature map x_t^e and identity feature map x_t^i with exactly the same size $H \times W \times D$ are extracted by feature extraction groups after "Identity Dense Block 2" and "Emotion Dense Block 2". The following procedures can be decomposed into spatial fusion (Sect. 3.1) and self-constrained multi-task learning section (Sect. 3.2).

3.1 Spatial Fusion

Considering the limited number of sequences in FER datasets, we propose a fusion method ("Concatenate", "Conv", "Pooling" layers and Fusion Dense Block in Fig. 2) to combine facial expression features with identity information. Moreover, two feature streams are combined by convolution, and fusion dense block is designed for a further combination.

The feature map $\mathrm{y}^{\mathrm{cat}}$ after concatenation function can be represented as:

$$\mathrm{y}^{\mathrm{cat}} = f^{\mathrm{cat}}(\mathrm{x}_t^e, \mathrm{x}_t^i) \tag{1}$$

where $\mathrm{y}^{\mathrm{cat}} \in \mathbb{R}^{H \times W \times 2D}$.

The two feature maps x_t^e and x_t^i are stacked at the same spatial location across the feature channels after concatenation. To better fuse expression features with

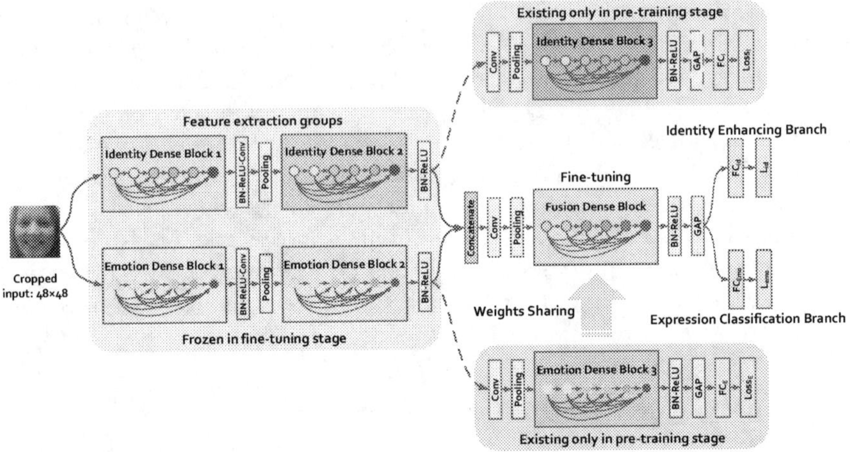

Fig. 2. The proposed network structure. Here, "BN" represents batch normalization and "GAP" means global average pooling. Feature extraction groups (pre-trained) are frozen in the fine-tuning stage to prevent the damage to extracted features during back propagation. Identity Dense Block 3 and Emotion Dense Block 3 are used to train feature extraction groups only in per-training stage. In the testing stage, only the feature extraction groups, fusion dense block (shares weights with pre-trained Emotion Dense Block 3) and expression classification branch are used to recognize a single image.

identity information, we adopt convolution filter $\mathbf{f}$ with size $1 \times 1 \times 2D \times D^{\mathrm{c}}$. Thus, the feature map $\mathrm{y}^{\mathrm{conv}}$ can be written as follows after convolution:

$$\mathrm{y}^{\mathrm{conv}} = \mathrm{y}^{\mathrm{cat}} * \mathbf{f} + b \tag{2}$$

where filter $\mathbf{f} \in \mathbb{R}^{1 \times 1 \times 2D \times D^{\mathrm{c}}}$, bias $b \in \mathbb{R}^{1 \times 1 \times 2D}$, D^{c} is the number of output channels. Here, the filter $\mathbf{f}$ is adopted to reduce the dimensionality and combine two feature maps $\mathrm{x}_t^e, \mathrm{x}_t^i$ at the same spatial location.

The advantage of convolutional fusion is that the filter $\mathbf{f}$ and bias b here can be optimized to combine expression features with identity information in a subtle way after back propagation. And the concatenated features are further learned by the following "Fusion Dense Block", which enhances several representative facial regions between similar expressions and encourages the network to be more adaptive to identity change. The effect of spatial fusion is evaluated and visualized in the ablation study (Sect. 4.5).

3.2 Self-constrained Multi-task Learning

The above method introduces identity information stream to the network in a fusion way, but it may not use up the capability of two streams. Consequently, we propose a self-constrained multi-task learning method (Identity Enhancing Branch in Fig. 2) to enhance the identity characteristics contained in expression features, which boosts the network performance in FER tasks.

Firstly, the proposed network architecture is reused, as shown in Fig. 2. Next, we add another linear fully connected layer (FC_{Id}) to the network for identity classification, which is located below the global average pooling function. Note that the identity classification is an auxiliary task utilized to enhance identity information. Thus, an additional function is needed to constrain the identity classification task before it is over-trained and harms the FER task.

Here we propose a novel method called self-constrained multi-task learning to constrain the auxiliary task. This method uses additional loss function (L_{id} in Fig. 2) whose value decays quickly with training process to prevent over-training of the auxiliary task. In the designed function, the loss of expression recognition, the main task, is cross-entropy loss, which can be written as:

$$L_{emo} = -\sum_{i=1}^{c} y_i \log(p_i) \tag{3}$$

where y_i is i-th value (0 or 1) of the ground truth label, and p_i is the i-th value of softmax activation function.

To constrain identity classification training process, we introduce the loss function of identity L_{id} by extending binary Focal loss [10] to multi-class style:

$$L_{id} = -\sum_{j=1}^{c} \alpha(1 - p_j)^{\gamma} y_j \log(p_j) \tag{4}$$

where y_j is j-th value (0 or 1) of the ground truth label, p_j is the j-th value of softmax activation function, α and γ are hyper parameters used to constrain training process, with α and $\gamma \geq 0$.

Obviously, the format of L_{id} is similar with L_{emo}, which just multiply a constrain parameter $\alpha(1 - p_j)^{\gamma}$. With the training process going deeper, the value of $\alpha(1 - p_j)^{\gamma}$ decays quickly due to the increase of p_j. Consequently, the training process of identity classification is constrained by this parameter. Thus, the joint loss function can be defined as:

$$L_{joint} = L_{emo} + L_{id} \tag{5}$$

Theoretically and experimentally we find that due to the use of parameter $\alpha(1 - p_j)^{\gamma}$, the auxiliary task (identity classification) is constrained in the whole training stage. In the designed loss, auxiliary tasks are considered as background roles, which means loss value of identity classification could be much smaller than the main task, but bigger than zero. With the use of designed loss function, auxiliary tasks can be utilized to supervise the training process as well as enhance robustness of the main task without stopping in the whole training stage. In practice, we find that the network performs best when $\gamma = 15$ and $\alpha = 0.1$. Furthermore, self-constrained multi-task learning can be extended to multiple auxiliary tasks learning by adding other loss functions in a similar form to L_{id}.

3.3 Network Architecture

Each dense block in the network contains six layers which consists of BN-ReLU-Conv(1×1)-BN-ReLU-Conv(3×3), and concatenates input with the output of each layer. Here, each convolution layer includes 12 filters. All of the pooling layers except global average pooling in the network are 2×2 average pooling with stride 2. The dimension of $\mathrm{FC_{Id}}$ and $\mathrm{FC_{Emo}}$ adjust to the number of identities and facial expressions respectively. Depending on whether to use spatial fusion and self-constrained multi-task learning, the proposed method can be divided into four sub-networks: Original Network (baseline without additional identity information, contains Emotion Dense Block 1 and 2, Fusion Dense Block, and Expression Classification Branch), $\mathrm{IDEnNet}_I$ (contains Original Network and additional Identity Enhancing Branch), $\mathrm{IDEnNet}_F$ (contains Feature extraction groups, Fusion Dense Block, and Expression Classification Branch), and $\mathrm{IDEnNet}_{IF}$ (contains all of the dense blocks and branches).

4 Experiments

We empirically demonstrate the effectiveness of proposed method on three public databases: Oulu-CASIA [27], CK+ [15], and MMI database [18]. The following shows details and results of these experiments as well as ablation study (Sect. 4.5).

4.1 Dataset Description

Oulu-CASIA. The Oulu-CASIA database [27] includes 480 sequences consist of 80 subjects and six basic expressions (anger, disgust, fear, happiness, sadness, and surprise) taken under dark, strong and weak illumination conditions. The same way as before [4], we use videos with strong condition captured by a VIS camera in this experiment. Each sequence of the database begins with neutral and ends with a peak expression. Thus, only the last three frames of each sequence are kept for training and testing. We adopt 10-fold cross validation protocol for training and validating.

CK+. CK+ [15] is a widely used database for FER tasks, which includes 118 subjects consist of seven emotions: anger, contempt, disgust, fear, happiness, sadness, and surprise. There are 327 image sequences in the database, which begin with neutral and end with a peak expression. Similar to the Oulu-CASIA database, we only use last three frames of each sequence and adopt 10-fold cross validation protocol for training and validating.

MMI. For further experiments, we use MMI database [18], which contains 312 image sequences from 30 individuals with six basic expressions (same expressions with Oulu-CASIA). Here, we select 205 sequences captured in a front view. Different from Oulu-CASIA and CK+, each sequence in MMI starts from a neutral face, reaches the peak in the middle and returns to neutral expression at the end. So we use three frames in the middle of each sequence following the protocol of 10-fold cross validation. Moreover, this database includes individuals who wear glasses or pose expression non-uniformly. Consequently, the facial expression recognition task is relatively challenging compared to other databases.

4.2 Preprocessing

To reduce the variation in face scale, we apply SeetaFace face detection [22] and alignment [24] modules for face detection and landmark detection. Then, the region of interest based on the coordinate of detected landmarks is cropped and resized to 60×60. Due to the limited images in FER datasets, several data augmentation procedures are employed to alleviate the over-fitting problem. Following [7], we horizontally flip the whole cropped images at first. Then, the region of interest in each image is rotated by each angle in $\{-15°, -10°, -5°, 5°, 10°, 15°\}$. Thus, we obtain a new dataset 14 times larger than the original one: original, flipped, rotated with six angles, and their flipped version.

4.3 Implementation Details

For network training, we firstly pre-trained two networks respectively with exactly the same architecture (as is illustrated in Fig. 2) in FER+ dataset [1] and CASIA-WebFace dataset [23] for facial expression and identity recognition (our accuracy is up to 81.22% on CASIA-WebFace with no bells and whistles). Both of them are trained with initial learning rate set to 0.1, which is divided by 10 at 50% and 75% of the total training epochs.

In the fine-tuning stage, we only fine-tune the layers below concatenation operation, and freeze the feature extraction groups. In this stage, we randomly crop images to 48×48 when training. A single center crop with size 48×48 is used for testing. We optimize the network using Stochastic Gradient Descent with a momentum of 0.9. The initial learning rate for fine-tuning is 0.01, and decreased by 0.1 at 50% and 75% of the total training epochs. The mini-batch size, weight decay parameter and drop out rate are set to 128, 0.0001 and 0.5.

As described in Sect. 3.3, there are original network and other three types of proposed IDEnNet. Here, we adopt original network as our baseline, and do comparative experiments based on it.

4.4 Results

Among all the compared databases, our proposed IDEnNet outperforms the state-of-the-art methods including handcraft-based methods (LBP-TOP [28], and HOG 3D [9]), video-based methods (MSR [19], AdaLBP [27], Atlases [5], STM-ExpLet [13], and DTAGN [7]), and CNN-based methods (3D-CNN [12], 3D-CNN-DAP [12], DTAGN [7], PPDN [29], GCNet [8], and FN2EN [4]).

Table 1. Average accuracy of Oulu-CASIA database.

Method	Average accuracy (%)
HOG 3D [9]	70.63
AdaLBP [27]	73.54
STM-ExpLet [13]	74.59
Atlases [5]	75.52
DTAGN [7]	81.46
PPDN [29]	84.59
GCNet [8]	86.39
FN2EN [4]	87.71
Original network (baseline)	87.18
Ours (IDEnNet$_I$)	**87.66**
Ours (IDEnNet$_F$)	**91.39**
Ours (IDEnNet$_{IF}$)	**93.95**

Table 2. Average accuracy of CK+ database, 7 expressions.

Method	Average accuracy (%)
3D-CNN [12]	85.9
LBP-TOP [28]	88.99
MSR [19]	91.4
HOG 3D [9]	91.44
3D-CNN-DAP [12]	92.4
STM-ExpLet [13]	94.19
IACNN [16]	95.37
(N+M) Softmax [14]	97.1
DTAGN [7]	97.25
GCNet [8]	97.93
Original network (baseline)	98.23
Ours (IDEnNet$_I$)	**98.46**
Ours (IDEnNet$_F$)	**98.42**
Ours (IDEnNet$_{IF}$)	**98.42**

Oulu-CASIA. Table 1 reports the average accuracy of 10-fold cross validation results. Compared with other state-of-the-art algorithms, our proposed algorithm achieves substantial improvement. As is shown, our method is superior to the previous best performance achieved by FN2EN [4], with a gain of 6.24%. Respectively, IDEnNet$_I$, IDEnNet$_F$, and IDEnNet$_{IF}$ have improved 0.48%, 4.21% and 6.77% over the baseline of 87.18%. We can find that IDEnNet$_I$ have slight improvement over the original one, while the network with spatial

Table 3. Average accuracy of MMI database.

Method	Average accuracy (%)
3D-CNN [12]	53.2
LBP-TOP [28]	59.51
HOG 3D [9]	60.89
3D-CNN-DAP [12]	63.4
DTAGN [7]	70.24
IACNN [16]	71.55
CSPL [30]	73.53
STM-ExpLet [13]	75.12
$(N+M)$ Softmax [14]	78.53
GCNet [8]	81.53
Original network (baseline)	73.62
Ours (IDEnNet$_I$)	**73.82**
Ours (IDEnNet$_F$)	**79.41**
Ours (IDEnNet$_{IF}$)	80.19

fusion improves a lot. What's more, the result shows that self-constrained multi-task learning after spatial fusion further learns difference between similar facial expressions. This is consistent with the analysis in ablation study (Sect. 4.5).

CK+. In Table 2, we compare our method with other state-of-the-art algorithms which use 7 expressions for training and validating. Our proposed method shows a better performance than all other compared algorithms including GCNet [8] which compares given images with generative faces to generate contrastive representation for classification. Due to the high accuracy of benchmark algorithm, the improvement of our proposed method in CK+ is less obvious than in Oulu-CASIA. As the number of individuals in CK+ is bigger, the contribution of multi-task learning (IDEnNet$_I$) is relatively greater than that in Oulu-CASIA when compared with spatial fusion method (IDEnNet$_F$), which could also be learned from Table 2. The slight drop (0.04%) of IDEnNet$_{IF}$ is mainly due to some random factors, *e.g.* network initialization. This can be verified by using weaker networks on the CK+ dataset, as is reported in Table 4.

MMI. Due to the small size of this database, it is difficult for deep networks to learn features. Thus, we adopt 16 layers instead of 40 layers as backbone network. As is presented in Table 3, the previous top accuracy was only 81.53%. In more detail, IDEnNet$_{IF}$ improves 6.57% over the baseline, while IDEnNet$_I$ and IDEnNet$_F$ increase by 0.20% and 5.79% respectively. Here, we strongly recommend using large database in practice. Totally, even under the limitation of this database, the proposed network still has a better ability for FER.

Table 4. Average accuracy of CK+ in different backbones.

Method	16 layers	22 layers	40 layers
Original	91.19%	95.16%	98.23%
IDEnNet$_I$	**92.13%**	**96.57%**	**98.46%**
IDEnNet$_F$	**92.87%**	**96.49%**	**98.42%**
IDEnNet$_{IF}$	**93.46%**	**96.63%**	**98.42%**

Table 5. Average accuracy of FER+ in different backbones.

Method	16 layers	22 layers	40 layers
Original	76.37%	79.93%	80.11%
IDEnNet$_F$	**78.42%**	**80.67%**	**82.96%**

4.5 Ablation Study

In this subsection, we will reveal the effect of backbone network as well as the amount of IDs in training data. Moreover, in order to better demonstrate the effectiveness of our proposed network, heatmaps after "Fusion Dense Block" of expressions with same identity and expressions with different identities in Oulu-CASIA database [27] are visualized.

Backbone Network. In order to prove our generalization performance on different backbone network and databases, we apply different backbones (16-, 22- and 40-layer DenseNets) on CK+ [15] and FER+ [1] dataset. For the lack of identity label of images in FER+ dataset, we only adopt IDEnNet$_F$ for experiments. As is elaborated in Tables 4 and 5, our proposed IDEnNet consistently boosts the performance on two datasets whatever the backbone network is. What's more, IDEnNet also improves 2.85% on FER+ without data augmentation.

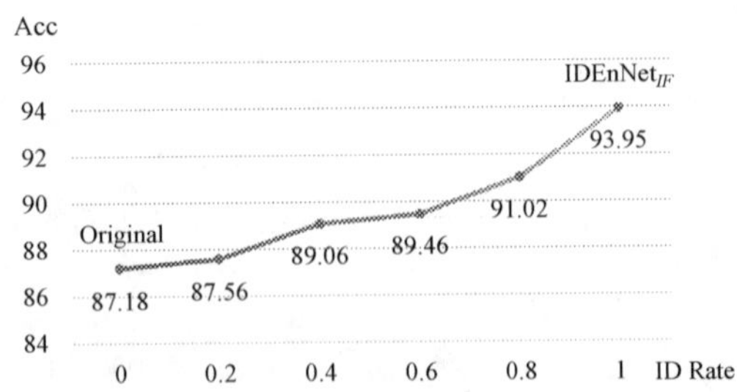

Fig. 3. Accuracy of IDEnNet on Oulu-CASIA with different ID rates.

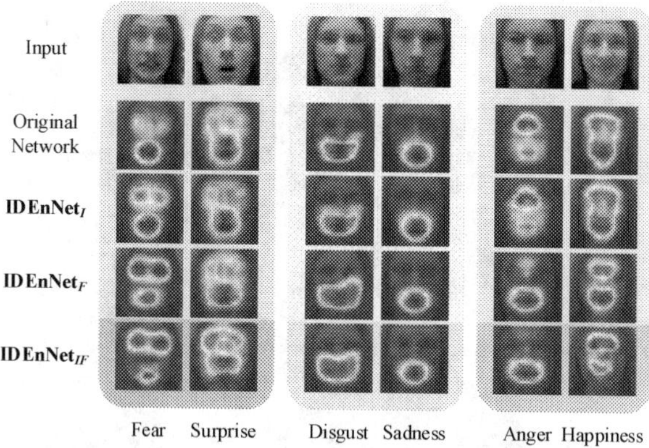

Fig. 4. Heatmaps of facial expressions with same identity in Oulu-CASIA database [27]. The images in the first row are used as input. The second to fifth rows are heatmaps under original network, IDEnNet$_I$, IDEnNet$_F$, and IDEnNet$_{IF}$ respectively. Blue and red in each heatmap represent the low and high response value. They are organized in pairs according to the similarity between two expressions as well as corresponding regions in the heatmaps under the original network. (Color figure online)

Identity Contribution. To evaluate the contribution of identity, We perform an ablation study on Oulu-CASIA by using all training images but only a subset of ID information. Unsurprisingly, more IDs are utilized, better results are obtained, as is presented in Fig. 3. The curve in Fig. 3 also proves the effectiveness of ID information when adopting IDEnNet.

Expressions with Same Identity. To further explore the effect of the proposed network for expressions in the same identity, we draw the heatmaps in each proposed method. As is presented in Fig. 4, heatmaps in the "Original Network" show different areas which are highly respond to the corresponding expressions. These heatmaps are drawn under the original network which means identity information in the network has not been enhanced. It can be seen that the areas with high response are mainly concentrated on the mouth, nose, eyes and eyebrows, which is consistent with our prior knowledge.

With the addition of identity information, the high response areas trend to be more focused and change their corresponding priorities according to different expressions, as is illustrated in Fig. 4. From two similar expressions (Fear and Surprise), we can find that our proposed IDEnNet$_I$, IDEnNet$_F$, and IDEnNet$_{IF}$ adjust their attention to eyes and mouth when recognizing fear, while concentrating more on nose wing and eyebrows when identifying surprise. And this also can be learned from other pairs of similar classes. Moreover, the addition of identity information encourages the network to use features which represent the specific identity. For different expressions, the identity characteristics tend to locate in different facial areas, which also encourages the network to use different facial regions. Thus, our proposed IDEnNet have the ability to focus more on

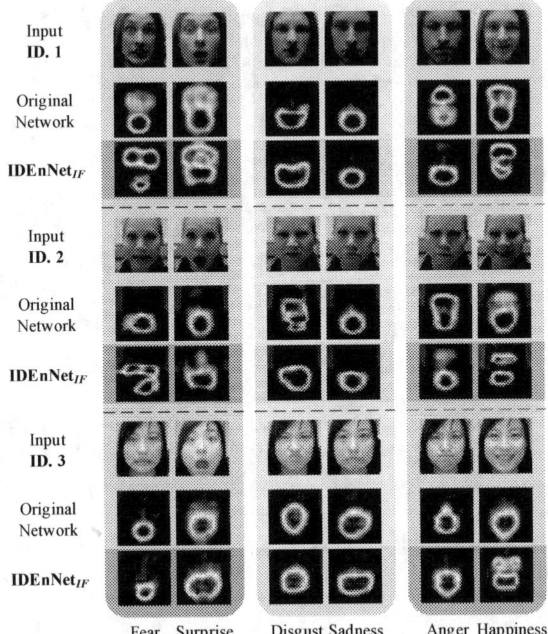

Fig. 5. Heatmaps of facial expressions with different identities in Oulu-CASIA database [27]. The images in the first, fourth, and seventh row are input images of three people. The following two rows after each input are heatmaps under original network and IDEnNet$_{IF}$ respectively. Blue and red in each heatmap represent the low and high response value. They are organized in pairs according to the similarities between two expressions as well as corresponding regions in the heatmaps under the original network. (Color figure online)

distinguishable facial regions when classifying similar expression classes. That is to say, IDEnNet enlarge the inter-class difference of facial expressions due to the enhancement of identity information.

Expressions with Different Identities. As well known, the performance of different people have great difference when doing the same facial expression. Here, we compare performance of the proposed IDEnNet for these people.

Concerning the same expression of three people, we can learn from Fig. 5 that IDEnNet$_{IF}$ trends to use similar facial regions of people for the same expression, adapting slightly to different identities at the same time. For example, original network mainly uses mouth, nose wing and eyebrows areas of the ID. 1 man to recognize his happiness, but mainly uses mouth and nose wing areas of both the ID. 2 and ID. 3 woman to represent the same expression. With the addition of identity information, our proposed IDEnNet$_{IF}$ mainly concentrate on both mouth and eyes areas of three people to recognize their happiness. The proposed IDEnNet$_{IF}$ also shows the same effect on other expressions. As for classes

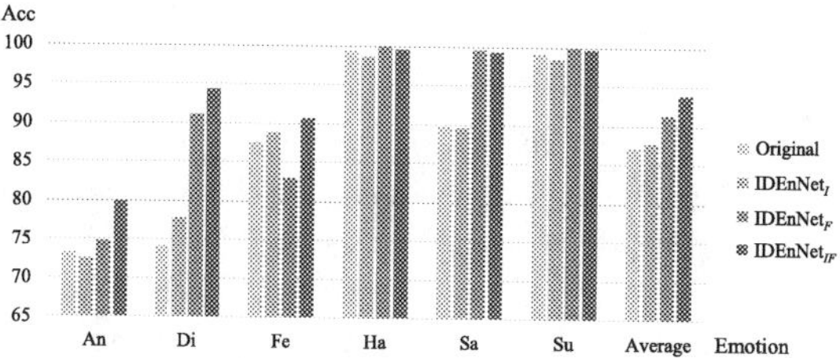

Fig. 6. Comparison of accuracy in the Oulu-CASIA database [27] according to each emotion among the proposed networks.

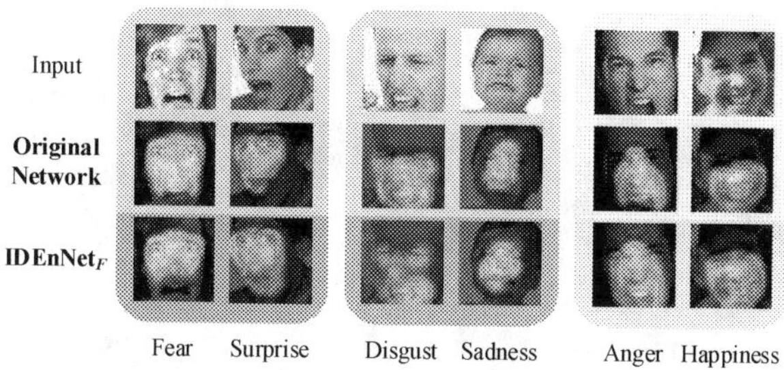

Fig. 7. Heatmaps of facial expressions with weakly-aligned faces in FER+ database [1].

of fear and surprise, IDEnNet$_{IF}$ inclines to focus on mouth areas for fear and nose wing areas for the other. Furthermore, the proposed network also uses the eyes areas for fear expression of ID. 1 man and ID. 2 woman, and uses the eyes with wider areas to recognize the surprise expression of the ID. 1 man, which can be attributed to adaptation of IDEnNet$_{IF}$ to different identities. With the enhancement of identity information, our proposed IDEnNet trends to learn the key representation which is helpful to the identity recognition, and the representative features are often located in similar regions for different people. This is also confirmed by Fig. 6, which shows that IDEnNet$_{IF}$ has a great improvement over the original network, especially in the cases of anger, disgust and sadness. Therefore, we can draw the conclusion that the proposed IDEnNet trends to focus more on several similar facial regions of different people for the same expression. Namely, it reduce the intra-class variations of the same expression among people.

We also visualize some profile face images from FER+. As shown in Fig. 7, IDEnNet works well in dealing with these weakly-aligned cases. In addition, the attention areas in Figs. 5 and 7 share the same trend, indicating that IDEnNet learns to focus on semantic regions even in profile faces rather than learns a face template.

5 Conclusions

In this paper, we propose a novel identity-enhanced network which explicitly learns from identity information so that the network can focus on representative facial regions between similar expressions as well as adapt to different identities. In the proposed IDEnNet, feature extraction groups are adopted to extract identity information together with expression features and fusion dense block is designed for identity-related expression learning. In order to train this network efficiently, spatial fusion and self-constrained multi-task learning are adopted, which also enables the identity cues to be combined in expression recognition. Extensive experiments on several datasets demonstrate the effectiveness of our proposed method.

Furthermore, the feature enhancement approach proposed in this work has potential application value for other fine-grained recognition tasks. The recognition performance could be much better if the pose information is utilized for supervision in a feature enhancement method when recognizing different kinds of birds or dogs.

Acknowledgement. This work has been supported by the National Key Research and Development Program of China No. 2018YFD0400902 and National Natural Science Foundation of China under Grant 61573349.

References

1. Barsoum, E., Zhang, C., Ferrer, C.C., Zhang, Z.: Training deep networks for facial expression recognition with crowd-sourced label distribution. In: ACM International Conference on Multimodal Interaction (2016)
2. Collobert, R., Weston, J.: A unified architecture for natural language processing: deep neural networks with multitask learning. In: International Conference on Machine Learning (2008)
3. Corneanu, C.A., Simon, M.O., Cohn, J.F., Guerrero, S.E.: Survey on RGB, 3D, thermal, and multimodal approaches for facial expression recognition: History, trends, and affect-related applications. IEEE Trans. Pattern Anal. Mach. Intell. **38**, 1548–1568 (2016)
4. Ding, H., Zhou, S.K., Chellappa, R.: FaceNet2ExpNet: regularizing a deep face recognition net for expression recognition. In: IEEE International Conference on Automatic Face and Gesture Recognition (2017)
5. Guo, Y., Zhao, G., Pietikäinen, M.: Dynamic facial expression recognition using longitudinal facial expression atlases. In: Fitzgibbon, A., Lazebnik, S., Perona, P., Sato, Y., Schmid, C. (eds.) ECCV 2012. LNCS, pp. 631–644. Springer, Heidelberg (2012). https://doi.org/10.1007/978-3-642-33709-3_45
6. Huang, G., Liu, Z., van der Maaten, L., Weinberger, K.Q.: Densely connected convolutional networks. In: IEEE Conference on Computer Vision and Pattern Recognition (2017)
7. Jung, H., Lee, S., Yim, J., Park, S., Kim, J.: Joint fine-tuning in deep neural networks for facial expression recognition. In: IEEE International Conference on Computer Vision (2015)

8. Kim, Y., Yoo, B., Kwak, Y., Choi, C., Kim, J.: Deep generative-contrastive networks for facial expression recognition. arXiv preprint arXiv:1703.07140 (2017)
9. Klaser, A., Marszałek, M., Schmid, C.: A spatio-temporal descriptor based on 3D-gradients. In: British Machine Vision Conference (2008)
10. Lin, T.Y., Goyal, P., Girshick, R., He, K., Dollar, P.: Focal loss for dense object detection. In: IEEE International Conference on Computer Vision (2017)
11. Littlewort, G., et al.: The computer expression recognition toolbox (CERT). In: IEEE International Conference on Automatic Face and Gesture Recognition Workshops (2011)
12. Liu, M., Li, S., Shan, S., Wang, R., Chen, X.: Deeply learning deformable facial action parts model for dynamic expression analysis. In: Cremers, D., Reid, I., Saito, H., Yang, M.-H. (eds.) ACCV 2014. LNCS, vol. 9006, pp. 143–157. Springer, Cham (2015). https://doi.org/10.1007/978-3-319-16817-3_10
13. Liu, M., Shan, S., Wang, R., Chen, X.: Learning expressionlets on spatio-temporal manifold for dynamic facial expression recognition. In: IEEE Conference on Computer Vision and Pattern Recognition (2014)
14. Liu, X., Kumar, B.V., You, J., Jia, P.: Adaptive deep metric learning for identity-aware facial expression recognition. In: IEEE Conference on Computer Vision and Pattern Recognition Workshops (2017)
15. Lucey, P., Cohn, J.F., Kanade, T., Saragih, J., Ambadar, Z., Matthews, I.: The extended Cohn-Kanade dataset (CK+): a complete dataset for action unit and emotion-specified expression. In: IEEE Conference on Computer Vision and Pattern Recognition Workshops (2010)
16. Meng, Z., Liu, P., Cai, J., Han, S., Tong, Y.: Identity-aware convolutional neural network for facial expression recognition. In: IEEE International Conference on Automatic Face and Gesture Recognition (2017)
17. Pantic, M., Patras, I.: Dynamics of facial expression: recognition of facial actions and their temporal segments from face profile image sequences. IEEE Trans. Syst. Man Cybern. Part B (Cybern.) **36**, 433–449 (2006)
18. Pantic, M., Valstar, M., Rademaker, R., Maat, L.: Web-based database for facial expression analysis. In: IEEE International Conference on Multimedia and Expo (2005)
19. Ptucha, R., Tsagkatakis, G., Savakis, A.: Manifold based sparse representation for robust expression recognition without neutral subtraction. In: IEEE International Conference on Computer Vision Workshops (2011)
20. Ranjan, R., Patel, V.M., Chellappa, R.: HyperFace: a deep multi-task learning framework for face detection, landmark localization, pose estimation, and gender recognition. IEEE Trans. Pattern Anal. Mach. Intell. **41**, 121–135 (2017)
21. Sariyanidi, E., Gunes, H., Cavallaro, A.: Automatic analysis of facial affect: a survey of registration, representation, and recognition. IEEE Trans. Pattern Anal. Mach. Intell. **37**, 1113–1133 (2015)
22. Wu, S., Kan, M., He, Z., Shan, S., Chen, X.: Funnel-structured cascade for multi-view face detection with alignment-awareness. Neurocomputing **221**, 138–145 (2017)
23. Yi, D., Lei, Z., Liao, S., Li, S.Z.: Learning face representation from scratch. arXiv preprint arXiv:1411.7923 (2014)
24. Zhang, J., Shan, S., Kan, M., Chen, X.: Coarse-to-fine auto-encoder networks (CFAN) for real-time face alignment. In: Fleet, D., Pajdla, T., Schiele, B., Tuytelaars, T. (eds.) ECCV 2014. LNCS, vol. 8690, pp. 1–16. Springer, Cham (2014). https://doi.org/10.1007/978-3-319-10605-2_1

25. Zhang, T., Ghanem, B., Liu, S., Ahuja, N.: Robust visual tracking via structured multi-task sparse learning. Int. J. Comput. Vis. **101**, 367–383 (2013)
26. Zhang, Z., Luo, P., Loy, C.C., Tang, X.: Facial landmark detection by deep multi-task learning. In: Fleet, D., Pajdla, T., Schiele, B., Tuytelaars, T. (eds.) ECCV 2014. LNCS, vol. 8694, pp. 94–108. Springer, Cham (2014). https://doi.org/10.1007/978-3-319-10599-4_7
27. Zhao, G., Huang, X., Taini, M., Li, S.Z., Pietikäinen, M.: Facial expression recognition from near-infrared videos. Image Vis. Comput. **29**, 607–619 (2011)
28. Zhao, G., Pietikainen, M.: Dynamic texture recognition using local binary patterns with an application to facial expressions. IEEE Trans. Pattern Anal. Mach. Intell. (2007)
29. Zhao, X., et al.: Peak-piloted deep network for facial expression recognition. In: Leibe, B., Matas, J., Sebe, N., Welling, M. (eds.) ECCV 2016. LNCS, vol. 9906, pp. 425–442. Springer, Cham (2016). https://doi.org/10.1007/978-3-319-46475-6_27
30. Zhong, L., Liu, Q., Yang, P., Liu, B., Huang, J., Metaxas, D.N.: Learning active facial patches for expression analysis. In: IEEE Conference on Computer Vision and Pattern Recognition (2012)

A Novel Multi-scale Invariant Descriptor Based on Contour and Texture for Shape Recognition

Jishan Guo[1], Yi Rong[1], Yongsheng Gao[2], Ying Liu[1], and Shengwu Xiong[1](✉)

[1] Wuhan University of Technology, Wuhan, China
{214166,yrong,liuynnly,xiongsw}@whut.edu.cn
[2] School of Engineering, Griffith University, Brisbane, QLD 4111, Australia
yongsheng.gao@griffith.edu.au

Abstract. This paper proposes a novel multi-scale descriptor for shape recognition. The contour of shape is represented by a sequence of sample points with uniform spacing. Straight lines connected between two moving contour points are used to cut the shape. The lengths of the contour segments between the two sampled contour points determine the levels of scales. Then the geometric features of the cut contour and the interior texture features around the straight lines are extracted at each scale. This method not only has the powerful discriminability to describe a shape from coarse to fine, but also is invariant to scale, rotation, translation and mirror transformations. Experiments conducted on five image datasets (COIL-20, Flavia, Swedish, Leaf100 and ETH-80) demonstrate that the proposed method significantly outperforms the state-of-the-art methods.

Keywords: Multi-scale · Shape recognition · Contour · Texture

1 Introduction

In human perception, shape is one of the basic features for object recognition. Shape recognition is a fundamental problem which has been attracting increasing attentions from the researchers in the field of computer vision, pattern recognition and machine learning. It has been widely employed in many practical applications, such as plant leaf species recognition [7,13,20,22], logo recognition [15], medical image retrieval [9] and animal species recognition [23]. For shape recognition task, how to effectively describe the shape of object plays a key role. A number of shape description techniques have been proposed which can be roughly divided into two major categories: contour-based methods and region-based methods [12,25].

Contour-based methods only rely on the shape boundary information, such as circularity, eccentricity, convexity and ratio of principle axis. Alajlan et al. [2] employed the areas of the triangles formed by the boundary points to measure the convexity/concavity of each point at different scales (or triangle side

C. V. Jawahar et al. (Eds.): ACCV 2018, LNCS 11364, pp. 551–564, 2019.
https://doi.org/10.1007/978-3-030-20870-7_34

lengths). This representation is effective in capturing both local and global characteristics of a shape. Wu et al. [24] utilized some basic geometric features (diameter, perimeter, physiological length and width et al.) and morphological features (rectangularity, perimeter ratio of diameter, aspect ratio et al.) to represent the shape. Ling [11] proposed the inner-distance shape context (IDSC) to describe shape, and used dynamic programming approaches for the shape matching. Wang [20] proposed a hierarchical string cuts (HSC) method, which uses strings to cut shape contour into two parts and extract the geometric and distribution properties about the cut profile. All above methods can achieve impressive shape recognition results, when there are large contour differences between different shapes. However, in some real-world applications, the contours of two different objects are similar, which will significantly reduce the recognition accuracies of these contour-based descriptors. For example, in Fig. 1(b), the contours of different species leaf A and leaf B are very similar. It is not enough to only rely on the contour for shape recognition.

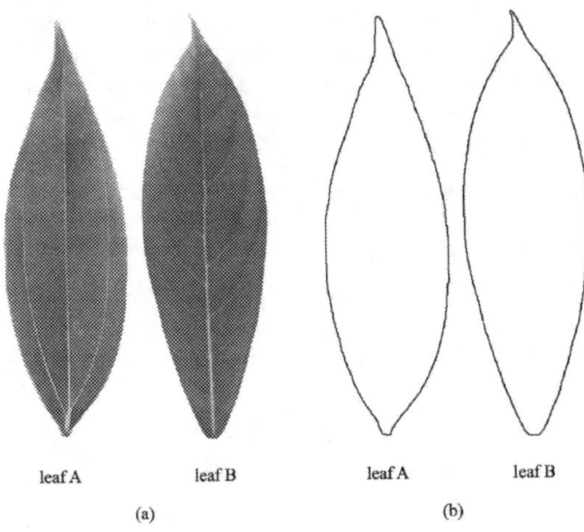

Fig. 1. (a) Two leaves of different species in Flavia dataset; (b) the shape contours of the two leaves in (a).

To overcome this limitation, region-based descriptors [4,8,21] attempt to make use of the interior information in shapes, rather than only consider the boundary information like contour-based methods. The well-known method Shape Contexts [4] is proposed to extract the internal features inside the shape. But this method only describes the internal contour, thus the detailed structure information and the texture information inside the shape are ignored. To this end, Structure Integral Transform (SIT) [21] utilizes two orthogonal integrals over a 2D K-cross dissecting structure to bisect shape regions in each integral along a varying orientation. In this way, the interior structure information can be effectively captured. However, SIT only describes the lengths of line segments fall in the shape region through a line integral transform, the interior texture information inside the shape is still not utilized for shape recognition. In Fig. 1(a), the interior texture information of the two leaf shapes with similar contours is very different from each other. Thus, in this case, we can make the best use of interior texture information to distinguish the two different species. All of these inspire us to propose an approach to capture both contour information and details of internal texture information.

In order to effectively utilize both contour and interior texture information of the shape, we propose a novel hierarchical coarse-to-fine descriptor for shape recognition. More specifically, the shape contour is represented by a sequence of sampled points. Then, straight lines between two moving contour sample points cut the shape into pieces. At each scale, features are extracted to reflect the geometric and distribution properties about the contour points and internal texture details of the shape.

The contribution of our work can be summarized as follows: (1) the interior texture informations insides shapes are captured by line-based LBP at multiple scales, which describe a shape from center to outline; (2) all the features are designed to be invariant with respect to group transformations including translation, mirror, scale and rotation.

The remainder of the paper is organized as follows: Sect. 2 first introduces the extracting process of our shape descriptor in details. Then, the invariance of the descriptor is discussed. After that, dissimilarity measure is defined for shape matching. In Sect. 3, we report the experimental results compared with the state-of-the-art methods, which demonstrate the effectiveness of the proposed method. Finally, the conclusions are presented in Sect. 4.

2 The Proposed Method

In this section, we present the proposed descriptor for shape recognition in details. Our descriptor attempts to extract the shape features from both external contour and inner texture. Moreover, a multi-scale framework is also introduced into the feature extraction process, thus, the proposed descriptor has a hierarchical coarse-to-fine representation characteristic. Then, the invariance of the proposed descriptor is discussed. Finally, the dissimilarity measure is presented for shape matching.

2.1 Feature Extraction

The contour of shape can be represented by a sequence of sample points with uniform spacing [1–3,6,11,20]. The benefits of this representation is that the approximate shape contour information can be reserved without extra time costs for seeking key-point such as points of maximum curvature. Therefore, a shape contour A can be represented as $A = \{p_i(x_i, y_i), i = 1, 2, \ldots, N\}$, where i is the index of the sample point in counter-clockwise direction, (x_i, y_i) is the coordinate of the sample point p_i, and N is the total number of the contour sample points (N is designed to be in the power of two in our experiments for segmentation convenience).

Then, the multi-scale framework is introduced into feature extraction process. The design enables us to describe the characteristics of a shape from the global to the details. The length of curve segment between two contour points denotes the scale size. Different scales can capture different information: the scale with longer curve segment captures global shape information and inner texture information, while the shorter captures the finer details information of shape. The number of scale is determined as follows:

$$k = logN - 1 \tag{1}$$

where N is the number of the sample points on the contour. In our experiment, we set $N = 256$, so we have seven different scales. At scale $s(s = 1, 2, \ldots, k)$,

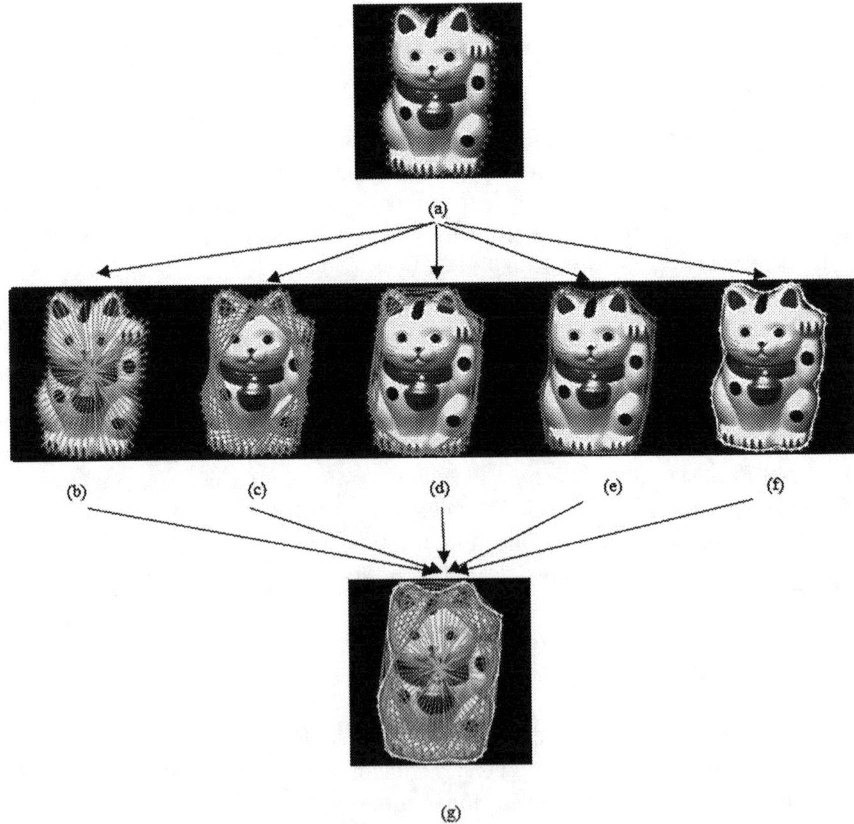

Fig. 2. (a) The downsampled contour points of a shape. In order to clearly observe the picture, only 64 points are shown here; (b)–(f) examples of different scales with $s = 1, \ldots, 5$; (g) the effect of superposition of (b)–(f).

for each contour sample point $p_i (i = 1, 2, \ldots, N)$, we get a straight line segment S_{ij} starting from p_i and ending at point p_j. The location of end point p_j, is determined as follows:

$$j = i + \frac{N}{2^s} \tag{2}$$

The smaller s is, the longer the curve segment between p_i and p_j is. And the straight line falls in a more central position of shape. Figure 2 also shows us that, the straight lines fall within the shape with the smaller s, while the straight lines fall around the contour with the bigger s. Thus, at different scales, different information about shape can be captured in the multi-scale framework, realizing to characterize the shape from center to outline and from coarse to fine.

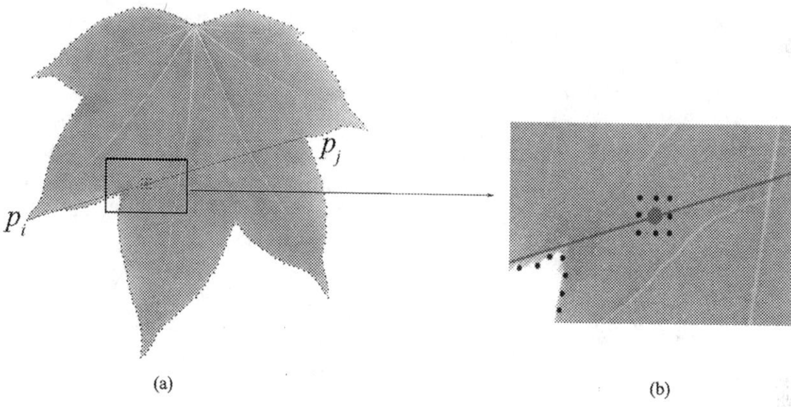

Fig. 3. (a) A straight line segment S_{ij} formed by a connection between point p_i and point p_j on the downsampled contour. (b) An example point on the straight line segment and its neighborhood using to calculate LBP value.

At each scale, two sample points p_i and p_j are connected to get a straight line segment S_{ij} passing through the shape, see Fig. 3(a) as an example. We attempt to extract five different types of features to describe the shape:

Firstly, to capture the interior information inside shape, we extract the texture features around points on the straight line segment S_{ij}. More specifically, each point on the line segment S_{ij} and its eight neighborhoods are encoded with the rotation-invariant Local Binary Pattern (LBP) [16–18] (see Fig. 3(b)). Figure 4 gives a demonstration about the specific practice of rotation-invariant LBP. After encoding with LBP, we get a binary code '10100101'. Then, constantly rotate the bits of the binary code, and get a series of binary codes. These binary codes are turned into decimal numbers, and the mean value of the eight numbers is calculated as the LBP value of the central pixel point. Different from conventional use of LBP, we apply LBP on straight line segment and its surrounding points to obtain the local information around the line. With multi-scale framework, our method can describe interior texture information inside shape from the center to the outline. After calculating the LBP value of all

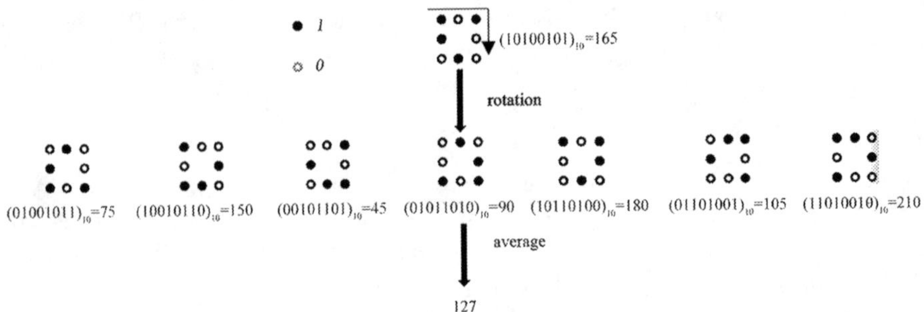

Fig. 4. An example of rotation-invariant LBP.

points on all straight line segments, the distribution of LBP can be modelled as a histogram [26] with eight bins. Then, this histogram, which is denoted as f_1, is used to represent the interior texture feature of the shape.

Secondly, we extract deviation features using the geometric properties of the distribution of these sample points on the contour. We define two point sets P_l and P_r, which consist of the sample points located on the left side and the right side of S_{ij}, respectively. With these definitions, the deviation features f_2 and f_3 can be calculated as follows:

$$f_2 = max\left(\frac{1}{N_l}\sum_{p_e \epsilon P_l} D\left(p_e, S_{ij}\right), \frac{1}{N_r}\sum_{p_e \epsilon P_r} D\left(p_e, S_{ij}\right)\right) \tag{3}$$

$$f_3 = min\left(\frac{1}{N_l}\sum_{p_e \epsilon P_l} D\left(p_e, S_{ij}\right), \frac{1}{N_r}\sum_{p_e \epsilon P_r} D\left(p_e, S_{ij}\right)\right) \tag{4}$$

where N_l, N_r denote the numbers of point set P_l and P_r, respectively. $D(p_e, S_{ij})$ defines the vertical distance from contour point p_e to the straight line segment S_{ij}, which can be calculated as follows:

$$D\left(p_e, S_{ij}\right) = \frac{\left|\left(x_e - x_i\right)\left(y_j - y_i\right) - \left(y_e - y_i\right)\left(x_j - x_i\right)\right|}{\sqrt{\left(x_i - x_j\right)^2 + \left(y_i - y_j\right)^2}} \tag{5}$$

where (x_i, y_i), (x_j, y_j) are the coordinates of the start point p_i and the end point p_j of straight line segment S_{ij}, respectively, p_e is a sample point on the contour and (x_e, y_e) is its coordinate.

Thirdly, the difference between the point number in P_l and P_r is used to describe the imbalance feature of the shape cut by S_{ij}.

$$f_4 = \left|N_l - N_r\right| \tag{6}$$

Finally, the bending degree of the curve between start point p_i and end point p_j can be calculated as follows:

$$f_5 = \frac{C_{ij}}{\left|S_{ij}\right|} \tag{7}$$

where C_{ij} is the length of curve segment between start point and end point in contour-clockwise direction and $|S_{ij}|$ is the Euclidean distance between the two points. Then we use the five features as a whole to represent the shape characteristics.

With multi-scale framework, we can obtain a representation as follows: $\{f_1^s(i), f_2^s(i), f_3^s(i), f_4^s(i), f_5^s(i), i = 1, 2, \ldots, N; s = 1, 2, \ldots, logN - 1\}$ to describe a shape using both the inner texture and contour information.

2.2 Invariance of the Descriptor

Through feature extraction process in 2.1, the shape can be represented by the descriptor $\{f_g^s(i)|i = 1, 2, \ldots, N; g = 1, 2, \ldots, 5; s = 1, 2, \ldots, logN - 1\}$. A good shape descriptor should be invariant to translation, mirroring, scaling and rotation [8]. In this subsection, the invariance of the proposed descriptor is discussed as follows.

Translation Invariance. Feature f_1 and f_4 are related to the number of points and are not affected by image translation. Feature f_2 and f_3 are designed based on distance from points to line without the effect of translation of coordinates of points, so they are invariant to translation. Feature f_5 also only relies on the distance between points and is unrelated to the coordinate translation of points, thus ensuring translation invariance.

Mirroring Invariance. From the definitions of the extracted features, the invariance to mirror is intrinsic of proposed method. Feature f_1 represents the distribution about LBP values of all points on straight line segments. The line stays the same when we interchange start points p_i and end point p_j. Thus, f_1 is not affected by the transformation of mirror. Feature f_2 and f_3 are designed unchanged because the maximum and minimum value retain the same as before if p_i and p_j are interchanged. Thus, they are invariant to mirror. Feature f_4 expresses the point number difference between the two sides of straight line segment and the absolute value is designed for mirror invariance. As f_5 is also independent to the direction of shape contour, ensuring the invariance of mirror.

Scaling Invariance. To obtain the scaling invariance, we locally normalised each feature $\{f_g^s(i), g = 1, 2, \ldots, 5\}$ by dividing its maximum value respectively. When the maximum value of a feature is 0 (In this case, the value of this feature is all 0, since the features we designed are all positive values), the normalization is omitted because the feature is already invariant to scale.

Rotation Invariance. To make the proposed descriptor invariant to rotation, Fourier transform is utilized to the descriptor we have got above. Theoretically, Fourier transform can remove the impact of the phase position change caused by the rotation of shape. Thus, for each feature at scale s, the magnitudes of Fourier transform coefficients can be calculated as

$$F_g^s(n) = \frac{1}{N}\left|\sum_{i=0}^{N-1} f_g^s(i)\, exp\left(\frac{-j2\pi in}{N}\right)\right| \tag{8}$$

where g is the number of the five features, s is the level of scales and n is the number of Fourier coefficients we set for the descriptor. For the robust to noise and compact, we select the lowest T Fourier coefficients, T is far less than N. Finally, the descriptor F of the shape can be defined as

$$F = \left\{F_g^s(n) \mid g = 1, ..., 5; s = 1, ..., logN - 1; n = 0, ..., T - 1\right\} \tag{9}$$

2.3 Dissimilarity Measure

Given two different sample shapes A and B, their descriptors are $F_g^{(A)s}(n)$ and $F_g^{(B)s}(n), g = 1, \ldots, 5, s = 1, \ldots, logN - 1, n = 0, \ldots, T - 1$, respectively. We measure the dissimilarity between them in each scale s. It can be calculated as follows,

$$D_s(A, B) = \sum_{g=1}^{5} w_g \left(\sum_{n=0}^{T-1}\left|F_g^{(A)s}(n) - F_g^{(B)s}(n)\right|\right) \tag{10}$$

where w_g is the weight to adjust the contribution of five features we have got. In order to complete the design of our method, we apply two commonly used global contour feature, eccentricity (E) and rectangularity (R), as the features of scale $s = 0$. So the dissimilarity of scale $s = 0$ can be calculated as

$$D_0(A, B) = |E(A) - E(B)| + |R(A) - R(B)| \tag{11}$$

So the dissimilarity of all scales can be defined as

$$D(A, B) = \sum_{s=0}^{logN-1} D_s(A, B) \tag{12}$$

3 Experiments

3.1 Performance Comparison on COIL20 Dataset

To evaluate the effectiveness of the proposed method, we conduct experiments on Columbia University Image Library (COIL-20) dataset [14]. COIL-20 contains 20 household object images. Each object is rotated 360° on the level and a photo is taken every 5°, so each object has 72 related images. There are 1440 images in all and all of them have the same resolution of 128 * 128. Some examples in the dataset are shown in Fig. 5, one sample image per object. The performance is measured using the commonly used bulls-eye test score [1–3, 11, 20, 21]. Table 1 shows the bulls-eye scores of the proposed method contrasted with the state-of-the-art methods. As we can see from Table 1, the proposed method performs best with the highest score of 79.8%, which is 6.3% higher than contour-based method Hierarchical String Cuts and 15.5%, 11.9% and 5.3% higher than Radon composite features, Shape Contexts and Structure Integral Transform these region-based methods respectively.

Fig. 5. 20 object samples from the COIL-20 dataset.

Table 1. Comparison of our approach with the state-of-the-art approaches on COIL-20 dataset. The value with * are from the published papers.

Algorithm	Bulls-eye test score (%)
Radon composite features (RCF) [5]	64.3*
Shape Contexts [4]	67.9*
Hierarchical String Cuts (HSC) [20]	73.5
Structure Integral Transform (SIT) [21]	74.5*
Proposed method	**79.8**

3.2 Performance Comparison on Flavia Dataset

To further verify the effectiveness and generality of the proposed method for shape recognition, we also conduct experiments on Flavia, Swedish, Leaf100 and ETH-80 dataset.

Fig. 6. 32 example images of Flavia dataset which has 1907 images including 32 classes, 50–77 images for each class. We select one image from each class.

Flavia dataset [24] is a widely used dataset for evaluating the performance of methods for shape recognition, which contains 1907 leaf images of 32 species and each species includes 50–77 images. These images have the same resolution of 1600 * 1200. Example images of the dataset are shown in Fig. 6. We choose 30 images from each species randomly as test images and 20 images as modeling images. The classification rate is used to evaluate the recognition ability of methods, which is calculated by the nearest-neighbor classification rule in experiments.

Table 2 summarizes the performance comparison results on Flavia dataset of the proposed approach and the state-of-the-art approaches. It can be observed that the proposed method maintained the highest classification rate (98.32%). Compared with HSC, the classification rate of the proposed method increases by 4.57%. In the dataset, there are some species have similar shape. At this time, our method can well express internal information which HSC cannot, so the performance is improved. And our method is able to express more meticulous texture information inside the shape than SIT, so achieves better performance.

Table 2. Comparison of our approach with the state-of-the-art approaches on Flavia dataset.

Algorithm	Classification rate (%)
Hierarchical String Cuts (HSC) [20]	93.75
Structure Integral Transform (SIT) [21]	80.25
Proposed method	**98.32**

3.3 Performance Comparison on Swedish Dataset

Swedish dataset [19] contains 15 species with 75 samples per species. 15 samples leaf images (one image per species) are shown in Fig. 7. The dataset is considered very challenging due to its high inter-species similarity. In our experiment, the same classification protocol and accuracy measurement as used in [6,11,19,20], 25 images of each species are selected as model images, and 50 images are used as testing images. The discriminative ability is also measured by the nearest-neighbor classification rule. The results are shown in the Table 3. It can be seen that the proposed method achieves the highest accuracy (99.33%) among the compared methods, 11.21% and 3.84% higher than the region-based methods, Shape Context and Structure Integral Transform respectively, 5.2%, 4.58% and 2.42% higher than inner distance Shape Context, Multi-scale convexity concavity and Hierarchical String Cuts based on shape contour respectively.

3.4 Performance Comparison on Leaf100 Dataset

The Leaf100 dataset contains 100 species with 12 samples each class. 100 samples leaf images (one image per species) are shown in Fig. 8. The challenge of the dataset lies in the high inter-class similarity and the large intra-class variations about contours. The same performance measurement as used in COIL-20 dataset

Fig. 7. 15 samples of Swedish dataset, one sample of each species.

Table 3. Comparison of our approach with the state-of-the-art approaches on Swedish dataset. The value with * are from the published papers.

Algorithm	Classification rate (%)
Shape Contexts (SC) [4]	88.12*
Inner-Distance Shape Contexts (IDSC) [11]	94.13*
Multi-scale convexity concavity (MCC) [1]	94.75*
Hierarchical String Cuts (HSC) [20]	96.91
Structure Integral Transform (SIT) [21]	95.49
Proposed method	**99.33**

Fig. 8. Samples of Leaf100 dataset, one sample of each species.

is applied in the dataset. The comparative results of the proposed method and the state-of-the-art methods are listed in Table 4. It is very encouraging to see that the proposed method consistently maintains the best score than the state-of-the-art methods. Compared with the state-of-the-art methods, our method performs better because of its excellent discrimination power when the contour differences between different classes are small.

Table 4. Comparison of our approach with the state-of-the-art approaches on Leaf100 dataset. The values with * are from the published papers

Algorithm	Bulls-eye scores (%)
Shape Contexts (SC) [4]	86.82*
Inner-Distance Shape Contexts (IDSC) [11]	85.64*
Multi-scale convexity concavity (MCC) [1]	77.10*
Hierarchical String Cuts (HSC) [20]	89.40*
Structure Integral Transform (SIT) [21]	77.23
Proposed method	**92.36**

Table 5. Comparison of our approach with the state-of-the-art approaches on ETH-80 dataset. The values with * are from the published papers.

Algorithm	Classification rate (%)
SC+DP [4]	86.40*
MDS+SC+DP [11]	86.80*
IDSC+DP [11]	88.11*
HSC [20]	83.84
SIT [21]	76.49
Proposed method	88.45

3.5 Performance Comparison on ETH-80 Dataset

The ETH-80 dataset [10] contains eight categories with 10 objects per category. For each object, there are 41 color images with different viewpoints. Thus, the dataset contains 3280 images in all. Figure 9 gives some example images of the dataset. The accuracy measurement is leave-one-object-out cross-validation [10]. This means we train with 79 objects and test with the one unknown object.

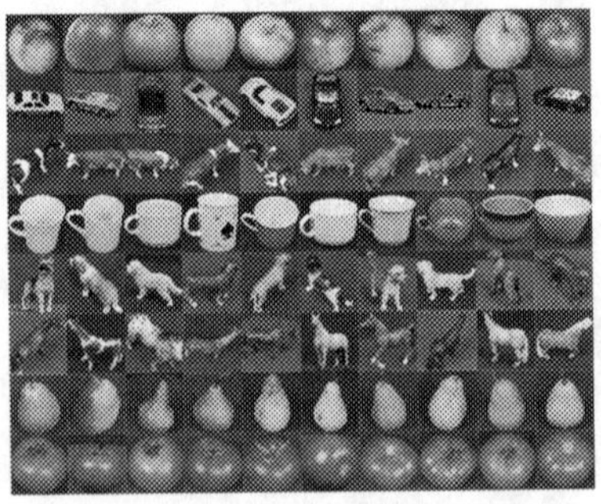

Fig. 9. Samples of ETH-80 dataset, one sample of each object.

The classification rate is averaged over all the objects. The experimental results are listed in Table 5. Our method performs better than the state-of-the-art approaches.

4 Conclusion

In this paper, we have proposed a novel hierarchical multi-scale descriptor for shape recognition. At each scale, both the contour information and the interior texture information are captured to describe the shape. Moreover, the proposed descriptor can be invariant to translation, mirroring, scaling and rotation. The dissimilarity of two shapes can be measured by comparing their shape feature using L_1 distance. The method has been evaluated on COIL-20, Flavia, Swedish, Leaf100 and ETH-80 dataset. The experimental results demonstrate the effectiveness of our method compared with the state-of-art approaches.

Acknowledgement. This work is partially supported by National Key R&D Program of China (No. 2016YFD0101903), National Natural Science Foundation of China (No. 61702386, 61672398), Major Technical Innovation Program of Hubei Province (No. 2017AAA122), Key Natural Science Foundation of Hubei Province of China (No. 2017CFA012), the Fundamental Research Funds for the Central Universities (No. 185210006).

References

1. Adamek, T., O'Connor, N.E.: A multiscale representation method for nonrigid shapes with a single closed contour. IEEE Trans. Circ. Syst. Video Technol. **14**(5), 742–753 (2004)
2. Alajlan, N., El Rube, I., Kamel, M.S., Freeman, G.: Shape retrieval using triangle-area representation and dynamic space warping. Pattern Recogn. **40**(7), 1911–1920 (2007)
3. Bai, X., Wang, B., Yao, C., Liu, W., Tu, Z.: Co-transduction for shape retrieval. IEEE Trans. Image Process. **21**(5), 2747–2757 (2012)
4. Belongie, S.J., Malik, J., Puzicha, J.: Shape matching and object recognition using shape contexts. IEEE Trans. Pattern Anal. Mach. Intell. **24**(4), 509–522 (2002)
5. Chen, Y.W., Chen, Y.Q.: Invariant description and retrieval of planar shapes using radon composite features. IEEE Trans. Sig. Process. **56**(10), 4762–4771 (2008)
6. Felzenszwalb, P.F., Schwartz, J.D.: Hierarchical matching of deformable shapes. In: IEEE Conference on Computer Vision and Pattern Recognition, CVPR 2007, pp. 1–8. IEEE (2007)
7. Hu, R.X., Jia, W., Ling, H., Huang, D.: Multiscale distance matrix for fast plant leaf recognition. IEEE Trans. Image Process. **21**(11), 4667–4672 (2012)
8. Kim, H.K., Kim, J.D.: Region-based shape descriptor invariant to rotation, scale and translation. Sig. Process. Image Commun. **16**(1), 87–93 (2000)
9. Korn, P., Sidiropoulos, N., Faloutsos, C., Siegel, E., Protopapas, Z.: Fast and effective retrieval of medical tumor shapes. IEEE Trans. Knowl. Data Eng. **10**(6), 889–904 (1998)

10. Leibe, B., Schiele, B.: Analyzing appearance and contour based methods for object categorization. In: Proceedings of the 2003 IEEE Computer Society Conference on Computer Vision and Pattern Recognition, vol. 2, p. II-409. IEEE (2003)
11. Ling, H., Jacobs, D.W.: Shape classification using the inner-distance. IEEE Trans. Pattern Anal. Mach Intell. **29**(2), 286–299 (2007)
12. Loncaric, S.: A survey of shape analysis techniques. Pattern Recogn. **31**(8), 983–1001 (1998)
13. Mouine, S., Yahiaoui, I., Verroust-Blondet, A.: A shape-based approach for leaf classification using multiscaletriangular representation. In: Proceedings of the 3rd ACM Conference on International Conference on Multimedia Retrieval, pp. 127–134. ACM (2013)
14. Nene, S.A., Nayar, S.K., Murase, H., et al.: Columbia object image library (coil-20) (1996)
15. Neumann, J., Samet, H., Soffer, A.: Integration of local and global shape analysis for logo classification. Pattern Recogn. Lett. **23**(12), 1449–1457 (2002)
16. Ojala, T., Pietikäinen, M., Harwood, D.: A comparative study of texture measures with classification based on featured distributions. Pattern Recogn. **29**(1), 51–59 (1996)
17. Ojala, T., Pietikäinen, M., Mäenpää, T.: Gray scale and rotation invariant texture classification with local binary patterns. In: Vernon, D. (ed.) ECCV 2000. LNCS, vol. 1842, pp. 404–420. Springer, Heidelberg (2000). https://doi.org/10.1007/3-540-45054-8_27
18. Ojala, T., Pietikainen, M., Maenpaa, T.: Multiresolution gray-scale and rotation invariant texture classification with local binary patterns. IEEE Trans. Pattern Anal. Mach. Intell. **24**(7), 971–987 (2002)
19. Söderkvist, O.: Computer vision classification of leaves from Swedish trees (2001)
20. Wang, B., Gao, Y.: Hierarchical string cuts: a translation, rotation, scale, and mirror invariant descriptor for fast shape retrieval. IEEE Trans. Image Process. **23**(9), 4101–4111 (2014)
21. Wang, B., Gao, Y.: Structure integral transform versus radon transform: a 2D mathematical tool for invariant shape recognition. IEEE Trans. Image Process. **25**(12), 5635–5648 (2016)
22. Wang, B., Gao, Y., Sun, C., Blumenstein, M., La Salle, J.: Can walking and measuring along chord bunches better describe leaf shapes? In: Proceedings of the IEEE Conference on Computer Vision and Pattern Recognition, pp. 6119–6128 (2017)
23. Wang, X., Feng, B., Bai, X., Liu, W., Latecki, L.J.: Bag of contour fragments for robust shape classification. Pattern Recogn. **47**(6), 2116–2125 (2014)
24. Wu, S.G., Bao, F.S., Xu, E.Y., Wang, Y.X., Chang, Y.F., Xiang, Q.L.: A leaf recognition algorithm for plant classification using probabilistic neural network. In: IEEE International Symposium on Signal Processing and Information Technology, pp. 11–16. IEEE (2007)
25. Zhang, D., Lu, G.: Review of shape representation and description techniques. Pattern Recogn. **37**(1), 1–19 (2004)
26. Zhang, H., Gao, W., Chen, X., Zhao, D.: Learning informative features for spatial histogram-based object detection. In: Proceedings of the 2005 IEEE International Joint Conference on Neural Networks, IJCNN 2005, vol. 3, pp. 1806–1811. IEEE (2005)

PReMVOS: Proposal-Generation, Refinement and Merging for Video Object Segmentation

Jonathon Luiten(✉), Paul Voigtlaender, and Bastian Leibe

Computer Vision Group, RWTH Aachen University, Aachen, Germany
{luiten,voigtlaender,leibe}@vision.rwth-aachen.de

Abstract. We address semi-supervised video object segmentation, the task of automatically generating accurate and consistent pixel masks for objects in a video sequence, given the first-frame ground truth annotations. Towards this goal, we present the PReMVOS algorithm (Proposal-generation, Refinement and Merging for Video Object Segmentation). Our method separates this problem into two steps, first generating a set of accurate object segmentation mask proposals for each video frame and then selecting and merging these proposals into accurate and temporally consistent pixel-wise object tracks over a video sequence in a way which is designed to specifically tackle the difficult challenges involved with segmenting multiple objects across a video sequence. Our approach surpasses all previous state-of-the-art results on the DAVIS 2017 video object segmentation benchmark with a $\mathcal{J}\&\mathcal{F}$ mean score of 71.6 on the `test-dev` dataset, and achieves first place in both the DAVIS 2018 Video Object Segmentation Challenge and the YouTube-VOS 1st Large-scale Video Object Segmentation Challenge.

1 Introduction

Video Object Segmentation (VOS) is the task of automatically estimating the object pixel masks in a video sequence and assigning consistent object IDs to these object masks over the video sequence. This can be seen as extension of instance segmentation from single frames to videos, and also as an extension of multi object tracking from tracking bounding boxes to tracking pixel masks. This framework motivates our work in separating the VOS problem into two sub-problems. The first being the instance segmentation task of generating accurate object segmentation mask proposals for all of the objects in each frame of the video, and the second being the multi object tracking task of selecting and merging these mask proposals to generate accurate and temporally consistent pixel-wise object tracks throughout a video sequence. Semi-supervised Video Object Segmentation focuses on the VOS task for certain objects for which the ground truth mask for the first video frame is given. The DAVIS datasets [3,26,27] present a state-of-the-art testing ground for this task. In this paper we present the PReMVOS (Proposal-generation, Refinement and Merging for Video

C. V. Jawahar et al. (Eds.): ACCV 2018, LNCS 11364, pp. 565–580, 2019.
https://doi.org/10.1007/978-3-030-20870-7_35

Object Segmentation) algorithm for tackling the semi-supervised VOS task. This method involves generating coarse object proposals using a Mask R-CNN like object detector, followed by a refinement network that produces accurate pixel masks for each proposal. We then select and link these proposals over time using a merging algorithm that takes into account an objectness score, the optical flow warping, a Re-ID feature embedding vector, and spatial constraints for each object proposal. We adapt our networks to the target video domain by fine-tuning on a large set of augmented images generated from the first-frame ground truth. An overview of our method, PReMVOS, can be seen in Fig. 1. Our method surpasses all current state-of-the-art results on all of the DAVIS benchmarks and achieves the best results in the 2018 DAVIS Video Object Segmentation Challenge [20] and the YouTube-VOS 1st Large-scale Video Object Segmentation Challenge [13].

Fig. 1. PReMVOS overview. Overlay colours represent different object proposals. (Color figure online)

2 Related Work

Current state-of-the-art methods for VOS fall into one of two paradigms. The first is *objectness* estimation with domain adaptation from first-frame finetuning. This approach, first proposed in [2], uses fully convolutional networks to estimate the *objectness* of each pixel by fine-tuning on the first-frame ground truth. This approach was expanded upon by [21] and [29,30] by using semantic segmentation guidance and iterative fine-tuning, respectively. The second paradigm, used in several state-of-the-art methods [15,17,18,25], involves propagating the mask from the previous frame using optical flow and then refining these estimates using a fully convolutional network. The methods proposed in [18] and [17] expand this idea by using a network to calculate a re-identification (ReID) embedding vector for proposed masks and using this to improve the object re-identification after an object has been occluded. [15] improves upon the mask propagation paradigm by training on a huge set of augmented images generated from the first-frame ground truth. Our method tackles the VOS task in an inherently different way than any of the previous papers in the literature. However, we adopt ideas presented in

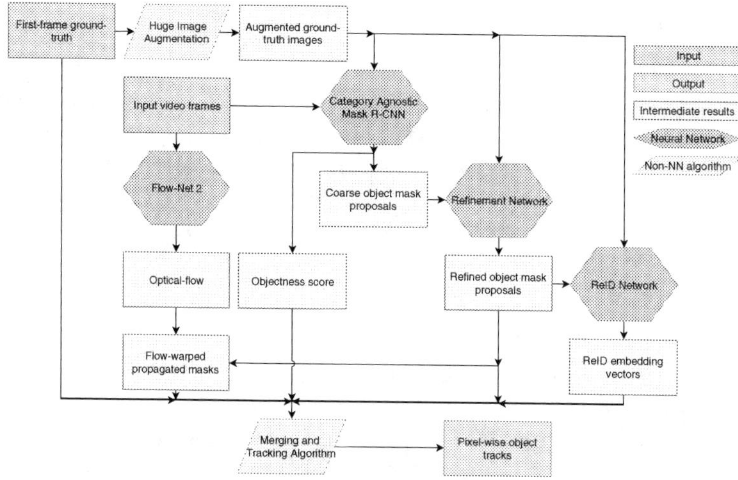

Fig. 2. Diagram showing the components of PReMVOS and their relationships.

all of the above papers such as the use of ReID embedding vectors, optical flow proposal warping and fine-tuning on a large set of images augmented from the first frame.

3 Approach

We propose PReMVOS as a novel approach for addressing the VOS task. This approach is designed to produce more accurate and temporally consistent pixel masks across a video, especially in the challenging multi-object VOS task. Instead of predicting object masks directly on the video pixels, as done in [2,21,29] and [30], a key idea of our approach is to instead detect regions of interest as coarse object proposals using an object detection network, and to then predict accurate masks only on the cropped and resized bounding boxes. We also present a new proposal merging algorithm in order to predict more temporally consistent pixel masks. The methods presented in [15,17,18,25] create temporally consistent proposals by generating their proposals directly from the previous frame's proposals warped using optical flow into the current frame. Instead, our method generates proposals independently for each frame and then selects and links these proposals using a number of cues such as optical flow based proposal warping, ReID embeddings and objectness scores, as well as taking into account the presence of other objects in the multi-object VOS scenario. This novel paradigm for solving the VOS task allows us to predict both more accurate and more temporally consistent pixel masks than all previous methods and achieves state-of-the-art results across all datasets. Figure 2 shows an overview of each of the components of the PReMVOS algorithm and how these work together to solve the VOS task.

3.1 Image Augmentation

For each video we generate a set of 2500 augmented images using the first-frame ground truth. We use the Lucid Data Dreaming method proposed in [15] but only generate single images (not image pairs). This method removes the objects, automatically fills in the background, and then randomly transforms each object and the background before randomly reassembling the objects in the scene. Fine-tuning on this set of augmented images allows us to adapt our networks directly to the target video domain.

3.2 Proposal Generation

We generate coarse object proposals using a Mask R-CNN [9] network implementation by [31] with a ResNet101 [10] backbone. We adjust this network to be category agnostic by replacing the N classes with just one class by mapping all classes to a single foreground class for detecting generic objects. We train this network starting from pre-trained ImageNet [6] weights on both the COCO [19] and Mapillary [22] datasets jointly. We then fine-tune a separate version of this network for each video for three epochs of the 2500 augmented images. This network generates coarse mask proposals, bounding boxes, and objectness scores for each image in the video sequence. We extract proposals with a score greater than 0.05 and also perform non-maximum suppression removing proposals which have an IoU of 66% or greater with a proposal with a higher score.

3.3 Proposal Refinement

The Proposal-Refinement Network is a fully convolutional network inspired by [34] and based on the DeepLabv3+ [4] architecture. This network takes as input a 385×385 image patch that has been cropped and resized from an approximate bounding box around an object of interest. A 50 pixel (in the original image) margin is first added to the bounding box in all directions. We add a fourth channel to the input image which encodes the original bounding box as a pixel mask to the input image. Starting from weights pre-trained on ImageNet [6], COCO [19], and PASCAL [7], we train this network on the Mapillary [22] dataset using random flipping, random gamma augmentations and random bounding box jitter [34] up to 5% in each dimension, to produce an accurate object segmentation, given an object's bounding box. We then fine-tune a separate version of this network for five epochs for each video on the 2500 augmented images. We then use this network to generate accurate pixel mask proposals for each of the previously generated coarse proposals, by only taking the bounding box of these proposals as input into the Refinement network and discarding the coarse mask itself.

3.4 Mask Propagation Using Optical Flow

As part of our proposal merging algorithm we use the optical flow between successive image pairs to warp a proposed mask into the next frame, to calculate the temporal consistency between two mask proposals. We calculate the Optical Flow using FlowNet 2.0 [12].

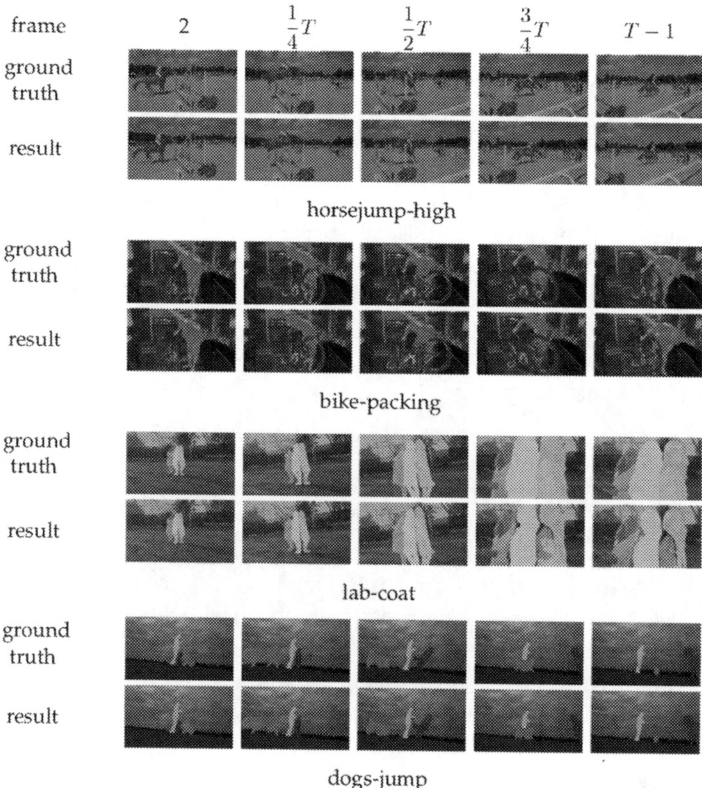

Fig. 3. Qualitative results of PReMVOS on the DAVIS 2017 `val dataset`.

3.5 ReID Embedding Vectors

We further use a triplet-loss based ReID embedding network to calculate a ReID embedding vector for each mask proposal. We use the feature embedding network proposed in [24]. This is based on a wide ResNet variant [32] pre-trained on ImageNet [6] and then trained on the COCO dataset [19] using cropped bounding boxes resized to 128×128 pixels. This uses a triplet loss to learn an embedding space in which crops of different classes are separated and crops of the same class are grouped together. It is trained using the batch-hard loss with a soft-plus margin proposed in [11]. We then fine-tune this network using the crops of each object from the generated 2500 augmented images for each of the 90 video sequences (242 objects) in the DAVIS 2017 `val`, `test-dev` and `test-challenge` datasets combined in order to have both enough positive and negative examples to train a network with a triplet-based loss. This network generates a ReID vector which differentiates all of the objects in these datasets from one other, which is used to compare the visual similarity of our generated object proposals and the first-frame ground truth object masks.

3.6 Proposal Merging

Our proposal merging algorithm works in a greedy manner. Starting from the ground truth object masks in the first-frame, it builds tracks for each frame by scoring each of the proposals on their likeliness to belong to a particular object track. We have exactly one track for each ground truth object and we make hard decisions for which proposals to add to each track each timestep in a greedy manner. The proposal with the highest track score is added to each track. This track score is calculated as an affine combination of five separate sub-scores, each with values between 0 and 1. In the following, taking the complement of a score means subtracting it from 1.

The first sub-score is the *Objectness* score. The objectness score $s_{obj,t,i,j}$ for the j-th track of the i-th proposal $c_{t,i}$ at time t is given by

$$s_{obj,t,i,j}(c_{t,i}) = MaskObj(c_{t,i}), \tag{1}$$

where $MaskObj(\cdot)$ denotes the confidence value provided by the Proposal Generation network.

The second score is a *ReID* score, calculated using the Euclidean distance between the first-frame ground truth ReID embedding vector $r(f_j)$ and the ReID embedding vector $r(c_{t,i})$ of the current mask proposal, where $r(\cdot)$ denotes applying the ReID network, $\|\cdot\|$ denotes the L2 norm, and f_j is the bounding box of the j-th ground truth object in the first frame. This distance is then normalized by dividing it by the maximum distance for all proposals in a video from the ground truth embedding vector of interest. The complement is then taken to convert from a distance into a similarity score.

$$s_{reid,t,i,j}(c_{t,i}, f_j) = 1 - \frac{\|r(c_{t,i}) - r(f_j)\|}{\max_{\tilde{t},\tilde{i}}\|r(c_{\tilde{t},\tilde{i}}) - r(f_j)\|} \tag{2}$$

The third score is a *Mask Propagation* score. This is calculated for each possible object track as the IoU between the current mask proposal and the warped proposal that was decided for in the previous time-step for this object track, warped into the current time-step using the optical flow:

$$s_{maskprop,t,i,j}(c_{t,i}, p_{t-1,j}) = IoU(c_{t,i}, warp(p_{t-1,j})), \tag{3}$$

where $p_{t-1,j}$ is is the previously selected proposal for timestep $t-1$ for object track j and $warp(\cdot)$ applies optical flow mask warping from frame $t-1$ to t.

The fourth score is an *Inverse ReID* score. This is calculated as the complement of the maximum *ReID* score for the current mask proposal and all other object tracks k except the object track of interest j:

$$s_{inv\_reid,t,i,j} = 1 - \max_{k \neq j}(s_{reid,t,i,k}). \tag{4}$$

The fifth score is an *Inverse Mask Propagation* score. This is calculated as the complement of the maximum *Mask Propagation IoU* score for the current mask proposal and all other object tracks k except the object track of interest j:

$$s_{inv\_maskprop,t,i,j} = 1 - \max_{k \neq j}(s_{maskprop,t,i,k}). \tag{5}$$

All five scores are combined together by

$$s_{comb,t,i,j} = \sum_{q \in \{objectness,reid,maskprop,inv\_reid,inv\_maskprop\}} \alpha_q s_{q,t,i,j}, \tag{6}$$

where $\sum_q \alpha_q = 1$ and all $\alpha_q \geq 0$. The greedy decisions are then made by $p_{t,j} = c_{t,k_j}$, where

$$k_j = \underset{i}{\operatorname{argmax}}\, s_{comb,t,i,j}. \tag{7}$$

In cases where the selected proposals for the different objects within one time-step overlap, we assign the overlapping pixels to the proposal with the highest combined track score. We present results with both an equal weighting for each of the five sub-score components and where the weights are tuned using random-search hyper-parameter optimisation evaluated against the DAVIS 2017 `val` set. The values of these optimised weights are shown in Table 4. We ran this optimisation for 25000 random parameter values. For the results on the 2018 DAVIS Challenge we also present results using an ensemble of the results using the top 11 sets of parameter values, using a simple pixel-wise majority vote to ensemble the results.

4 Experiments

We evaluate our algorithm on the set of DAVIS [3,26,27] datasets and benchmarks. Table 1 shows our results on the three DAVIS benchmarks. The DAVIS 2017 `test-dev` and `val` datasets contain multiple objects per video sequence, whereas the DAVIS 2016 `val` dataset contains a single object per sequence. The metrics of interest are the $\mathcal{J}$ score, calculated as the average IoU between the proposed masks and the ground truth mask, and the $\mathcal{F}$ score, calculated as an average boundary similarity measure between the boundary of the proposed masks and the ground truth masks. For more details on these metrics see [26].

On all of the datasets our method gives results better than all other state-of-the-art methods for both the $\mathcal{F}$ metric and the mean of the $\mathcal{J}$ and $\mathcal{F}$ score. We also produce either the best, or comparable to the best, results on the $\mathcal{J}$ metric for each dataset. These results show that the novel proposed VOS paradigm performs better than the current VOS paradigms in predicting both accurate and temporally consistent mask proposals.

Table 2 shows our results both with and without ensembling on the DAVIS 2017/2018 `test-challenge` dataset evaluated during the 2018 DAVIS Challenge compared to the top six other competing methods. Our method gives the best results and gets first place in the 2018 DAVIS Challenge.

Figure 3 shows qualitative results of our method on four video sequences from the 2017 `val` dataset. These results show that our method produces both accurate and temporally consistent results across the video sequences.

Table 1. Our results and other state-of-the-art results on the three DAVIS datasets: the 2017 `test-dev` set (17 T-D), the 2017 `val` set (17 Val), and the 2016 val set (16 Val). On the 17 Val and 16 Val datasets we use the naive merging component weights, whereas on the 17 T-D dataset we use the weights optimised using the 17 Val set.

			Ours	DyeNet [17]	MRF [1]	Lucid [15]	ReID [18]	OSVOS-S [21]	OnAVOS [29,30]	OSVOS [2]
17 T-D	$\mathcal{J}\&\mathcal{F}$	Mean	**71.6**	68.2	67.5	66.6	66.1	57.5	56.5	50.9
	$\mathcal{J}$	Mean	**67.5**	65.8	64.5	63.4	64.4	52.9	52.4	47.0
		Recall	**76.8**	-	-	73.9	-	60.2	-	52.1
		Decay	21.7	-	-	19.5	-	24.1	-	**19.2**
	$\mathcal{F}$	Mean	**75.7**	70.5	70.5	69.9	67.8	62.1	59.6	54.8
		Recall	**84.3**	-	-	80.1	-	70.5	-	59.7
		Decay	20.6	-	-	**19.4**	-	21.9	-	19.8
17 Val	$\mathcal{J}\&\mathcal{F}$	Mean	**77.8**	74.1	70.7	-	-	68.0	67.9	60.3
	$\mathcal{J}$	Mean	**73.9**	-	67.2	-	-	64.7	64.5	56.6
		Recall	**83.1**	-	-	-	-	74.2	-	63.8
		Decay	16.2	-	-	-	-	**15.1**	-	26.1
	$\mathcal{F}$	Mean	**81.7**	-	74.2	-	-	71.3	71.2	63.9
		Recall	**88.9**	-	-	-	-	80.7	-	73.8
		Decay	19.5	-	-	-	-	**18.5**	-	27.0
16 Val	$\mathcal{J}\&\mathcal{F}$	Mean	**86.8**	-	-	-	-	86.5	85.5	80.2
	$\mathcal{J}$	Mean	84.9	**86.2**	84.2	-	-	85.6	86.1	79.8
		Recall	96.1	-	-	-	-	**96.8**	96.1	93.6
		Decay	8.8	-	-	-	-	5.5	**5.2**	14.9
	$\mathcal{F}$	Mean	**88.6**	-	-	-	-	87.5	84.9	80.6
		Recall	94.7	-	-	-	-	**95.9**	89.7	92.6
		Decay	9.8	-	-	-	-	8.2	**5.8**	15.0
	$\mathcal{T}$	Mean	36.4	-	-	-	-	21.7	**19.0**	37.8

4.1 Proposal Refinement

We perform an ablation study to investigate the effect of the Refinement network on the accuracy of the mask proposals. We compare the coarse proposals generated from a state-of-the-art instance segmentation method, Mask R-CNN [9], to the refined proposals generated by feeding the bounding boxes of these coarse proposals into our Refinement Network. In order to evaluate these results we calculate the best proposal for each object in each frame which maximizes the IoU score with the ground-truth mask. We then evaluate using the standard DAVIS evaluation metrics using these merged proposals. This *oracle merging* algorithm allows us to evaluate the accuracy of our proposal generation separately from our merging algorithm.

Table 3 shows the quantitative IoU ($\mathcal{J}$) and boundary measure ($\mathcal{F}$) improvement for our refined proposals over the Mask R-CNN proposals. Our method

Table 2. Our results (with and without ensembling) on the DAVIS `test-challenge` dataset compared with the top five other competitors in the 2018 DAVIS Challenge.

		Ours (Ens)	Ours	DyeNet [16]	ClassAgno. VOS [35]	OnlineGen. VOS [8]	Lucid [14]	ContextBased VOS [28]
$\mathcal{J}$&$\mathcal{F}$	Mean	**74.7**	71.8	73.8	69.7	69.5	67.8	66.3
$\mathcal{J}$	Mean	71.0	67.9	**71.9**	66.9	67.5	65.1	64.1
	Recall	**79.5**	75.9	79.4	74.1	77.0	72.5	75.0
	Decay	19.0	23.2	19.8	23.1	15.0	27.7	**11.7**
$\mathcal{F}$	Mean	**78.4**	75.6	75.8	72.5	71.5	70.6	68.6
	Recall	**86.7**	82.9	83.0	80.3	82.2	79.8	80.7
	Decay	20.8	24.7	20.3	25.9	18.5	30.2	**13.5**

Table 3. Quantitative results of an ablation study on the 2017 `val` dataset showing the effect of the Refinement Network on the accuracy of generated mask proposals. Presented results are calculated using *oracle merging* (see Sect. 4.1).

	$\mathcal{J}$ mean	$\mathcal{F}$ mean	$\mathcal{J}$&$\mathcal{F}$ mean
Without refinement	71.2	77.3	74.2
With refinement	**77.1**	**85.2**	**81.2**
Boost	5.9	7.9	7.0

Fig. 4. Qualitative results showing the effect of the Refinement Network on the mask proposal accuracy. Results are calculated using *oracle merging* (Sect. 4.1).

results in a 5.9% improvement in IoU and a 7.9% improvement in boundary measure over just using the Mask R-CNN proposals.

Figure 4 also visualizes the qualitative results of the improved accuracy of the refined masks over the generated Mask R-CNN masks. In all examples the refined proposals match the ground truth masks more closely than the coarse proposals and capture the boundary contours at a much higher fidelity. This is due to the refinement network extracting deep features only over the area of interest for each object, and not over the whole image as is done in the case for Mask R-CNN. The Refinement Network is also able to recover parts of objects that were completely lost in the coarse proposals, for example in the two examples of bicycles shown. This is because the Refinement Network takes as input only the bounding box of the coarse mask proposal, not the coarse mask itself, and relies only on it's trained knowledge of what is inherently an *object* in order to generate the refined segmentation masks. Also when the bounding box does not accurately cover the whole object, as is the case with the bicycle in the second column of Fig. 4, the refinement network is still able to recover the accurate mask as it takes into account a 50 pixel margin around the coarse mask proposal bounding box.

4.2 Proposal Merging

We perform a further ablation study to investigate the effect of each of the merging algorithm sub-score components on the accuracy of the merging algorithm. Table 4 shows the results of this ablation study on the DAVIS 2017 `val` dataset.

We first present an upper bound baseline result for our merging algorithm. This is calculated by choosing the best proposal for each object in each frame which maximizes the IoU score with the ground-truth mask. This *oracle merging* method gives a 81.2 $\mathcal{J}\&\mathcal{F}$ mean score.

We then present the results of our merging algorithm where the weights for each of the five sub-score components were optimised using random-search hyper-parameter optimisation evaluated against the DAVIS 2017 `val` set. This optimisation was done by evaluating 25000 random affine combinations of the 5 component weights and selecting the set of weights that resulted in the best IoU score. This result gives another upper bound of 78.2 $\mathcal{J}\&\mathcal{F}$ mean score, as this was evaluated on the same dataset as the weight values were optimised on. Our greedy selection algorithm based on a combination of the 5 sub-component scores is able to reach a $\mathcal{J}\&\mathcal{F}$ mean score that is only 3% lower than the hypothetical maximum, showing that these carefully selected 5 sub-score components are sufficient to generate accurate and consistent object tracks, even in difficult cases such as multiple similar objects and large occlusions. These opimised weights used on the 2017 `test-dev` dataset presented in Table 1, all other dataset results in Tables 1 and 4 use equal weights for the five sub-components.

The naive combination with all 5 sub-score components has a $\mathcal{J}\&\mathcal{F}$ mean score of 77.8 which is only 0.4 below that with optimised weights. This indicates that the merging algorithm is relatively robust to the exact weights and that what is more important is the presence of all five components.

The *Objectness* sub-score separates well-defined mask proposals with accurate boundary contours from proposals with boundaries that are less likely to model a consistent object. It is also able to distinguish objects of interest given in the first frame from other objects in the scene, as this score was trained in the Mask R-CNN fine-tuning process to identify these objects and ignore the others. However, this sub-score component is unable to distinguish between different objects of interest if more than one is present in a video sequence.

Table 4. Results of an ablation study on the DAVIS `2017 val` dataset showing the effect of each of the merging algorithm sub-score components on the accuracy of the merging algorithm. The *oracle merging* result indicates an upper bound for the merging algorithm performance (Sect. 4.1). The components given as percentages indicate the optimal component weights calculated using hyper-parameter optimisation on the `2017 val` set. The components given by a checkmark (✓) have equal weights for each checked components. For each group of results with the same number of components the best result is expressed in **bold** and the worst in *italics*.

Num. Comp.	Merging sub-score components					$\mathcal{J}\&\mathcal{F}$ Mean
	Objectness	ReID	InvReID	MaskProp	InvMaskProp	
0	Oracle merging					**81.2**
5(opt.)	19%	18%	14%	22%	27%	**78.2**
5	✓	✓	✓	✓	✓	**77.8**
4	✓	✓	✓	✓	-	76.7
	✓	✓	✓	-	✓	*75.5*
	✓	✓	-	✓	✓	**76.9**
	✓	-	✓	✓	✓	76.3
	-	✓	✓	✓	✓	75.9
3	✓	✓	✓	-	-	74.2
	✓	✓	-	✓	-	75.0
	✓	✓	-	-	✓	74.2
	✓	-	✓	✓	-	73.5
	✓	-	✓	-	✓	69.6
	✓	-	-	✓	✓	71.1
	-	✓	✓	✓	-	75.8
	-	✓	✓	-	✓	*69.3*
	-	✓	-	✓	✓	**75.9**
	-	-	✓	✓	✓	74.3
2	✓	✓	-	-	-	72.7
	✓	-	✓	-	-	64.7
	✓	-	-	✓	-	69.1
	✓	-	-	-	✓	57.9
	-	✓	✓	-	-	68.7
	-	✓	-	✓	-	**74.3**
	-	✓	-	-	✓	68.8
	-	-	✓	✓	-	74.0
	-	-	✓	-	✓	*47.3*
	-	-	-	✓	✓	73.6
1	✓	-	-	-	-	*29.5*
	-	✓	-	-	-	67.4
	-	-	✓	-	-	44.3
	-	-	-	✓	-	**72.8**
	-	-	-	-	✓	34.4

The *ReID* sub-score is used to distinguish between objects that look visually different from each other. This works well to separate objects such as bikes and people from each other in the same video sequence, but does not work as well on sequences with multiple similar looking objects.

The *MaskProp* sub-score is used for temporal consistency. This can distinguish well between very similar objects if they are separated in the spatial domain of the image. However, this sub-score cannot deal with cases where objects heavily occlude each other, or completely disappear before later returning.

The *InvReID* and *InvMaskProp* sub-scores are used to force the selected mask proposals in each frame to be as distinguishable from each other as possible. Just using the other 3 components often results in failure cases where the same or very similar mask proposals are chosen for different objects. This occurs when similar looking objects overlap or when one object disappears. These two sub-components work by distinguishing proposals that are visually and temporally inconsistent with other objects in the video sequence, resulting in a signal of consistency with the object of interest. These components can separate well between the different objects of interest in a video sequence, but they are unable to separate these objects from possible background objects.

The results in Table 4 show that all five sub-scores are important for accurate proposal merging, as removing one of these components results in a loss of accuracy between 0.9, when only removing the *InvReID* sub-score, to 2.3, when removing the *MaskProp* sub-score. Without both the *InvReID* and *InvMaskProp*, the $\mathcal{J}\&\mathcal{F}$ mean score decreases by 1.9 points, showing that these sub-scores that were introduced to promote spatial separation of the chosen proposals are an integral part of the merging algorithm. Only using these two sub-components, however, results in a score decrease of 30.5 points. Removing the two main key components, the *ReID* and *MaskProp* sub-scores, results in a loss of 8.2 points, whereas only having these two components results in a loss of 3.5 points. When used by itself, the *MaskProp* sub-score is the strongest component, resulting in a loss of 5.0 points.

4.3 Runtime Evaluation

We perform a runtime evaluation of the different components of the PReMVOS algorithm. The complete PReMVOS algorithm with first-frame data augmentation and fine-tuning was designed in order to produce the most accurate results without regards for speed requirements. For further evaluation, we present in Table 5 three versions of PReMVOS. The original version, a fast-finetuned version, and a version without any fine-tuning. The fast-finetuned version is finetuned for one third of the iterations as the original method, and instead of the slow Lucid Data Dreaming [15] image augmentations, it uses simple rotations, translations, flipping and brightness augmentations. Only one set of weights are fine-tuned over the whole DAVIS val set rather than different weights for each video. A combination of the *specific* proposals from the fine-tuned proposal network and the *general* proposals from a proposal network that was not fine-tuned on the validation set first-frames are used. The not-finetuned version of PReMVOS just uses the *general* proposals without any fine-tuning. Figure 5 compares the quality and runtime of PReMVOS against other methods in the literature. Across all of the presented runtime scales, our method compares to or exceeds all other state-of-the-art results.

Table 5. Runtime analysis of the different components of the PReMVOS algorithm. Times are in seconds per frame, averaged over the DAVIS 2017 val set. Augmentation Generation is run on 48 CPU cores, and Fine-tuning is done on 8 GPUs. Otherwise, everything is run sequentially on one GPU/CPU core.

	Augm. Gen.	Fine-tuning	Prop. Gen.	Prop. Refine.	ReID	Optic. Flow	Warping	Merging	Total	Av. # Prop.	Mean $\mathcal{J}\&\mathcal{F}$
Original	23.4	12.3	0.41	1.04	0.05	0.14	0.32	0.02	37.4	17.52	77.8
Fast-finetuned	0.02	3.9	0.26	0.45	0.03	0.14	0.20	0.02	5.02	9.28	73.7
Not-finetuned	0.00	0.00	0.14	0.33	0.02	0.14	0.16	0.02	0.81	6.87	65.7

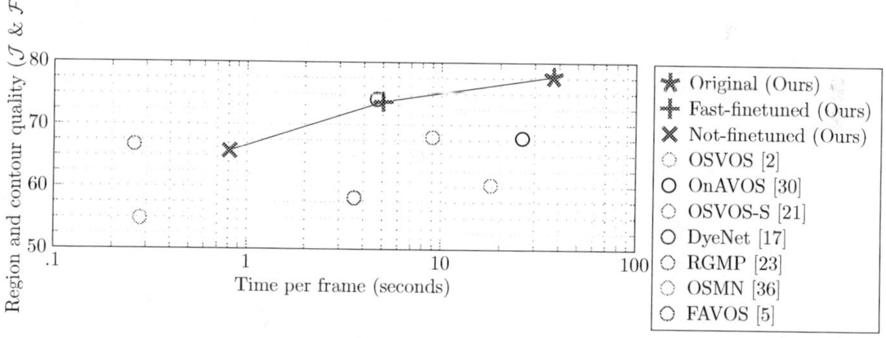

Fig. 5. Quality versus timing on the DAVIS 2017 val set. For methods that only publish runtime results on the DAVIS 2016 dataset, we take these timings as per object timings and extrapolate to the number of objects in the DAVIS 2017 val set.

4.4 Further Large-Scale Evaluation

In Table 6 we present the results of PReMVOS on the new YouTube-VOS dataset [33], the largest VOS dataset to date (508 test video compared to 30 in DAVIS), our results on the test set obtained 1st place in the 1st Large-scale Video Object Segmentation Challenge. We don't run the original PReMVOS method but the PReMVOS Fast-finetuned version (see Sect. 4.3), which can be evaluated on this larger dataset in a more reasonable amount of time. Our results are much better

Table 6. Results on the YouTube-VOS dataset, using the PReMVOS Fast-finetuned version of PReMVOS. These results obtained 1st place in the the 1st Large-scale Video Object Segmentation Challenge. '2nd', '3rd', '4th' refers to the other competitors results in this challenge with that ranking. Bold results are the best results for that metric.

	Overall	$\mathcal{J}$ seen	$\mathcal{J}$ unseen	$\mathcal{F}$ seen	$\mathcal{F}$ unseen
Ours	**72.2**	**73.7**	64.8	**77.8**	72.5
Seq2Seq [33]	70.0	66.9	**66.8**	74.1	72.3
2nd	72.0	72.5	66.3	75.2	**74.1**
3rd	69.9	73.6	62.1	75.5	68.4
4th	68.4	70.6	62.3	72.8	67.7

than [33], the only other method that has published results on this dataset. It is also better than all other methods that submitted results to the 2017 1st Large-scale Video Object Segmentation Challenge.

5 Conclusion

In this paper we have presented a new approach for solving the video object segmentation task. Our proposed approach works by dividing this task into first generating a set of accurate object segmentation mask proposals for each video frame and then selecting and merging these proposals into accurate and temporally consistent pixel-wise object tracks over a video sequence. We have developed a novel approach for each of these sub-problems and have combined these into the PReMVOS (Proposal-generation, Refinement and Merging for Video Object Segmentation) algorithm. We show that this method is particularly well suited for the difficult multi-object video object segmentation task and that it produces results better than all current state-of-the-art results for semi-supervised video object segmentation on the DAVIS benchmarks, as well as getting the best score in the 2018 DAVIS Challenge.

Acknowledgements. This project was funded, in parts, by ERC Consolidator Grant DeeViSe (ERC-2017-COG-773161).

References

1. Bao, L., Wu, B., Liu, W.: CNN in MRF: video object segmentation via inference in a CNN-based higher-order spatio-temporal MRF. arXiv preprint arXiv:1803.09453 (2018)
2. Caelles, S., Maninis, K.K., Pont-Tuset, J., Leal-Taixé, L., Cremers, D., Van Gool, L.: One-shot video object segmentation. In: CVPR (2017)
3. Caelles, S., et al.: The 2018 DAVIS challenge on video object segmentation. arXiv preprint arXiv:1803.00557 (2018)

4. Chen, L.C., Zhu, Y., Papandreou, G., Schroff, F., Adam, H.: Encoder-decoder with atrous separable convolution for semantic image segmentation. arXiv preprint arXiv:1802.02611 (2018)
5. Cheng, J., Tsai, Y.H., Hung, W.C., Wang, S., Yang, M.H.: Fast and accurate online video object segmentation via tracking parts. In: CVPR (2018)
6. Deng, J., Dong, W., Socher, R., Li, L.J., Li, K., Fei-Fei, L.: ImageNet: a large-scale hierarchical image database. In: CVPR (2009)
7. Everingham, M., Van Gool, L., Williams, C.K.I., Winn, J., Zisserman, A.: The pascal visual object classes (VOC) challenge. IJCV **88**(2), 303–338 (2010)
8. Guo, P., Zhang, L., Zhang, H., Liu, X., Ren, H., Zhang, Y.: Adaptive video object segmentation with online data generation. In: The 2018 DAVIS Challenge on Video Object Segmentation - CVPR Workshops (2018)
9. He, K., Gkioxari, G., Dollár, P., Girshick, R.: Mask R-CNN. In: ICCV (2017)
10. He, K., Zhang, X., Ren, S., Sun, J.: Deep residual learning for image recognition. In: CVPR (2016)
11. Hermans, A., Beyer, L., Leibe, B.: In defense of the triplet loss for person re-identification. arXiv preprint arXiv:1703.07737 (2017)
12. Ilg, E., Mayer, N., Saikia, T., Keuper, M., Dosovitskiy, A., Brox, T.: FlowNet 2.0: evolution of optical flow estimation with deep networks. In: CVPR (2017)
13. Luiten, J., Voigtlaender, P., Leibe, B.: PReMVOS: proposal-generation, refinement and merging for the YouTube-VOS challenge on video object segmentation 2018. In: The 1st Large-scale Video Object Segmentation Challenge - ECCV Workshops (2018)
14. Khoreva, A., Benenson, R., Ilg, E., Brox, T., Schiele, B.: Lucid data dreaming for video object segmentation. In: The 2018 DAVIS Challenge on Video Object Segmentation - CVPR Workshops (2018)
15. Khoreva, A., Benenson, R., Ilg, E., Brox, T., Schiele, B.: Lucid data dreaming for multiple object tracking. In: The 2017 DAVIS Challenge on Video Object Segmentation - CVPR Workshops (2017)
16. Li, X., Loy, C.C.: Video object segmentation with joint re-identification and attention-aware mask propagation. In: The 2018 DAVIS Challenge on Video Object Segmentation - CVPR Workshops (2018)
17. Li, X., Loy, C.C.: Video object segmentation with joint re-identification and attention-aware mask propagation. In: Ferrari, V., Hebert, M., Sminchisescu, C., Weiss, Y. (eds.) ECCV 2018. LNCS, vol. 11207, pp. 93–110. Springer, Cham (2018). https://doi.org/10.1007/978-3-030-01219-9_6
18. Li, X., et al.: Video object segmentation with re-identification. In: The 2017 DAVIS Challenge on Video Object Segmentation - CVPR Workshops (2017)
19. Lin, T.Y., et al.: Microsoft COCO: common objects in context. In: Fleet, D., Pajdla, T., Schiele, B., Tuytelaars, T. (eds.) ECCV 2014. LNCS, vol. 8693, pp. 740–755. Springer, Cham (2014). https://doi.org/10.1007/978-3-319-10602-1_48
20. Luiten, J., Voigtlaender, P., Leibe, B.: PreMVOS: proposal-generation, refinement and merging for the DAVIS challenge on video object segmentation 2018. In: The 2018 DAVIS Challenge on Video Object Segmentation - CVPR Workshops (2018)
21. Maninis, K.K., et al.: Video object segmentation without temporal information. PAMI (2017)
22. Neuhold, G., Ollmann, T., Bulo, S.R., Kontschieder, P.: The mapillary vistas dataset for semantic understanding of street scenes. In: ICCV (2017)
23. Oh, S., Lee, J., Sunkavalli, K., Kim, S.: Fast video object segmentation by reference-guided mask propagation. In: CVPR (2018)

24. Ošep, A., Voigtlaender, P., Luiten, J., Breuers, S., Leibe, B.: Large-scale object discovery and detector adaptation from unlabeled video. arXiv preprint arXiv:1712.08832 (2017)
25. Perazzi, F., Khoreva, A., Benenson, R., Schiele, B., Sorkine-Hornung, A.: Learning video object segmentation from static images. In: CVPR (2017)
26. Perazzi, F., Pont-Tuset, J., McWilliams, B., Van Gool, L., Gross, M., Sorkine-Hornung, A.: A benchmark dataset and evaluation methodology for video object segmentation. In: CVPR (2016)
27. Pont-Tuset, J., Perazzi, F., Caelles, S., Arbeláez, P., Sorkine-Hornung, A., Van Gool, L.: The 2017 DAVIS challenge on video object segmentation. arXiv preprint arXiv:1704.00675 (2017)
28. Tran, M., et al.: Context-based instance segmentation in video sequences. In: The 2018 DAVIS Challenge on Video Object Segmentation - CVPR Workshops (2018)
29. Voigtlaender, P., Leibe, B.: Online adaptation of convolutional neural networks for the 2017 DAVIS challenge on video object segmentation. In: The 2017 DAVIS Challenge on Video Object Segmentation - CVPR Workshops (2017)
30. Voigtlaender, P., Leibe, B.: Online adaptation of convolutional neural networks for video object segmentation. In: BMVC (2017)
31. Wu, Y., et al.: Tensorpack (2016). https://github.com/tensorpack/
32. Wu, Z., Shen, C., van den Hengel, A.: Wider or deeper: revisiting the ResNet model for visual recognition. arXiv preprint arXiv:1611.10080 (2016)
33. Xu, N., et al.: YouTube-VOS: sequence-to-sequence video object segmentation. arXiv preprint arXiv:1809.00461 (2018)
34. Xu, N., Price, B., Cohen, S., Yang, J., Huang, T.: Deep GrabCut for object selection. In: BMVC (2017)
35. Xu, S., Bao, L., Zhou, P.: Class-agnostic video object segmentation without semantic re-identification. In: The 2018 DAVIS Challenge on Video Object Segmentation - CVPR Workshops (2018)
36. Yang, L., Wang, Y., Xiong, X., Yang, J., Katsaggelos, A.: Efficient video object segmentation via network modulation. In: CVPR (2018)

ColorNet: Investigating the Importance of Color Spaces for Image Classification

Shreyank N. Gowda[1(✉)] and Chun Yuan[2]

[1] Computer Science Department, Tsinghua University, Beijing 10084, China
sny17@mails.tsinghua.edu.cn

[2] Graduate School at Shenzhen, Tsinghua University, Shenzhen 518055, China
yuanc@sz.tsinghua.edu.cn

Abstract. Image classification is a fundamental application in computer vision. Recently, deeper networks and highly connected networks have shown state of the art performance for image classification tasks. Most datasets these days consist of a finite number of color images. These color images are taken as input in the form of RGB images and classification is done without modifying them. We explore the importance of color spaces and show that color spaces (essentially transformations of original RGB images) can significantly affect classification accuracy. Further, we show that certain classes of images are better represented in particular color spaces and for a dataset with a highly varying number of classes such as CIFAR and Imagenet, using a model that considers multiple color spaces within the same model gives excellent levels of accuracy. Also, we show that such a model, where the input is preprocessed into multiple color spaces simultaneously, needs far fewer parameters to obtain high accuracy for classification. For example, our model with 1.75M parameters significantly outperforms DenseNet 100-12 that has 12M parameters and gives results comparable to Densenet-BC-190-40 that has 25.6M parameters for classification of four competitive image classification datasets namely: CIFAR-10, CIFAR-100, SVHN and Imagenet. Our model essentially takes an RGB image as input, simultaneously converts the image into 7 different color spaces and uses these as inputs to individual densenets. We use small and wide densenets to reduce computation overhead and number of hyperparameters required. We obtain significant improvement on current state of the art results on these datasets as well.

Keywords: Color spaces · Densenet · Fusion

1 Introduction

Image classification is one of the most fundamental applications in the field of computer vision. Most of the datasets used for image classification tend to

Supported by NSFC project Grant No. U1833101, Shenzhen Science and Technologies project under Grant No. JCYJ20160428182137473 and the Joint Research Center of Tencent and Tsinghua.

C. V. Jawahar et al. (Eds.): ACCV 2018, LNCS 11364, pp. 581–596, 2019.
https://doi.org/10.1007/978-3-030-20870-7_36

consist of color images. These color images are represented in RGB format. To a computer, these images are just numbers and do not contain any inherent meaning. Most recent models developed for classification do not perform a color space transformation to the image and instead use the RGB image directly for classification.

In this paper, we propose the use of different color spaces. The main color spaces will be discussed briefly in this section.

A color space is essentially an organization of colors. Along with physical device profiling, color spaces help us to reproduce analog and digital representations of color. Color spaces can also be thought of as an abstract mathematical model that helps us to describe colors as numbers.

RGB color space, often the most popular color space, is a system dependent color space. Commonly, it is represented using a 24-bit implementation where each channel R, G and B are given 8 bits each. This results in each channel having a range of values from 0 to 255. This color space models on the basis that all colors can be represented using different shades of red, green and blue.

Images from popular datasets such as CIFAR [2] have images present in the sRGB format. The first step is in converting the sRGB images to RGB by linearizing it by a power-law of 2.2.

Some of the other popular color spaces we shall discuss briefly are HSV, LAB, YUV, YCbCr, YPbPr, YIQ, XYZ, HED, LCH and CMYK.

HSV stands for hue, saturation and value. HSV was developed taking into consideration how humans view color. It describes color (hue) in terms of the saturation (shade) and value (brightness). H has a range from 0 to 360, S and V have range 0 to 255. The transformation from RGB to HSV can be seen in (1)–(6). R, G and B are the values of the red channel, green channel and blue channel respectively. H obtained represents the hue channel. Similarly, S represents the saturation channel and V the value channel.

$$R' = R/255, G' = G/255, B' = B/255 \tag{1}$$

$$Cmax = max(R', G', B'), Cmin = min(R', G', B') \tag{2}$$

$$\Delta = Cmax - Cmin \tag{3}$$

$$H = \begin{cases} 0^\circ & , \Delta = 0 \\ 60^\circ \left(\frac{G'-B'}{\Delta} mod 6\right) & , Cmax = R' \\ 60^\circ \left(\frac{B'-R'}{\Delta} + 2\right) & , Cmax = G' \\ 60^\circ \left(\frac{R'-G'}{\Delta} + 4\right) & , Cmax = B' \end{cases} \tag{4}$$

$$S = \begin{cases} 0 & , Cmax = 0 \\ \frac{\Delta}{Cmax} & , Cmax \neq 0 \end{cases} \tag{5}$$

$$V = Cmax \tag{6}$$

To define quantitative links between distributions of wavelengths in the EM visible spectrum (Electromagnetic) along with the physiological perceived colors in human eye sight, the CIE (Commission internationale de l' éclairage)

1931 color spaces were introduced. The mathematical relationships between these color spaces form fundamental tools to deal with color inks, color management, illuminated displays, cameras and printers.

CIE XYZ (from now on referred to as XYZ) was formed on the mathematical limit of human vision as far as color is concerned. X, Y and Z are channels extrapolated from the R, G and B channels to prevent the occurrence of negative values. Y represents luminance, Z represents a channel close to blue channel and X represents a mix of cone response curves chosen to be orthogonal to luminance and non-negative. XYZ image can be derived from RGB using (7).

$$\begin{pmatrix} X \\ Y \\ Z \end{pmatrix} = \begin{bmatrix} 0.489989 & 0.310008 & 0.2 \\ 0.176962 & 0.81240 & 0.010 \\ 0 & 0.01 & 0.99 \end{bmatrix} \begin{pmatrix} R \\ G \\ B \end{pmatrix} \tag{7}$$

LAB is another very popular color space. This color space is often used as an interchange format when dealing with different devices. This is done because it is device independent. Here, L stands for lightness, 'a' stands for color component green-red and 'b' for blue-yellow. An image in RGB can be transformed to LAB by first converting the RGB image to XYZ image.

YIQ, YUV, YPbPr, YCbCr are all color spaces that are used for television transmission. Hence, they are often called transmission primaries. YUV and YIQ are analog spaces for PAL and NTSC systems. YCbCr is used for encoding of digital color information used in video and still-image transmission and compression techniques such as JPEG and MPEG.

YUV, YCbCr, YPbPr, and YIq belong to opponent spaces. They have one channel for luminance and 2 channels for chrominace, represented in an opponency way (usually red versus green, and blue versus yellow).

The RGB color space is an additive color model, where to obtain the final image we add the individual channel values. A subtractive color model exists, called CMYK where C stands for Cyan, M stands for magenta, Y stands for yellow and K stands for key (black). The CMYK model works by masking colors on a light background. RGB to CMYK conversion can be seen in (8)–(12).

$$R' = R/255, G' = G/255, B' = B/255 \tag{8}$$

$$K = 1 - max(R', G', B') \tag{9}$$

$$C = \frac{(1 - R' - K)}{(1 - K)} \tag{10}$$

$$M = \frac{(1 - G' - K)}{(1 - K)} \tag{11}$$

$$Y = \frac{(1 - B' - K)}{(1 - K)} \tag{12}$$

LCH is another color space. It is similar to LAB. It is in the form of a sphere that has three axes: L, c and h. L stands for lightness, c stands for chroma (saturation) and h stands for hue. It is a device-independent color space and is used for retouching images in a color managed workflow that utilizes high-end editing applications. To convert from RGB to LCH, we first convert from RGB to LAB and then from LAB to LCH.

There are other color spaces that have not been explored. Only the most popular ones have been referenced. The idea behind the paper is that an image is nothing but numbers to a computer, hence, transformations of these images should be viewed as a completely new image to a computer. Essentially transforming an image into different color spaces should yield us new images in the view of the computer.

We exploit our idea by using small networks to classify images in different color spaces and combine the final layer of each network to obtain an accuracy that takes into account all the color spaces involved. To obtain a high accuracy, we need each output to be less correlated to each other. This is also something we will explain in detail in the proposed approach section.

We have proposed the following novel contributions, that have not been performed before to the best of our knowledge.

(1) We show that certain classes of images are better represented in certain color spaces.
(2) We show that combining the outputs for each color space will give us a much higher accuracy in comparison to individually using each color space.
(3) We show that a relatively small model can obtain a similar level of accuracy to recent state of the art approaches (See experimental analysis section, our model with 1.75M parameters can provide a similar accuracy to that of a densenet model with 25.6M parameters for CIFAR datasets).
(4) We also obtain new state of the art results on CIFAR-10, CIFAR-100, SVHN and imagenet, to the best of our knowledge.

2 Related Works

Image classification has been a fundamental task in the field of computer vision. This task has gained huge importance in recent times with the development of datasets such as Imagenet [10, CIFAR [2], SVHN [3], MNIST [4], CALTECH-101 [5], CALTECH-256 [6] among others.

Deep convolutional neural networks [7–9] have been developed which have drastically affected the accuracy of the image classification algorithms. These have in turn resulted in breakthroughs in many image classification tasks [10,11].

Recent research [12,13] has shown that going deeper will result in higher accuracy. In fact, current state-of-the-art approaches on the challenging Imagenet [1] dataset has been obtained by very deep networks [12–15]. Many complex computer vision tasks have also been shown to obtain great results on using deeper networks [16–20].

Clearly, depth has been giving us good results. But learning better networks is not as simple as adding more layers. A big deterrent for this is the vanishing gradient problem which hampers convergence of layers [21].

A solution to the vanishing gradient problem has been normalized initialization [14,22]. Another solution has been the introduction of intermediate normalization layers [15]. These enabled very deep networks to start converging for SGD (stochastic gradient descent) with back propagation [9].

Networks with an extremely high number of layers were giving high accuracy results on Imagenet as mentioned before. For example, [23] had 19 layers, [24,25] surpassed 100 layers. Eventually, it was seen in [26] that not going deeper, but going wider provided a higher accuracy.

The problem with deeper networks as mentioned above is the vanishing gradient problem. To solve this we could bypass signal between layers using identity connections as seen in the popular networks Resnets [24] and Highway networks [25].

Repeatedly combining multiple parallel layer sequences with a varying number of convolutional blocks was done in order to get a large nominal depth in FractalNets [27]. This was done along with maintaining multiple short paths in the network. The main similarity between [24–27] was that they all created short paths from early layers to the later layers.

Densenet [28] proposed connecting all layers to ensure information from each layer is passed on to every other layer. They also showed state-of-the-art results on popular image classification tasks.

All these recent approaches gave excellent results, however, the number of parameters has been very high. We look at the possibility of reducing the number of parameters needed for performing the same task, whilst, ensuring the accuracy of classification remains high.

Also, all these recent approaches used images from the dataset directly as it is for the task of classification. We propose transformations of these images using color space conversions as the medium to do so.

Performing image classification tasks by preprocessing input with color conversion has been explored before. In [29] for instance, YCbCr was the color space used for skin detection. Color pixel classification was done in [30] using a hybrid color space. Soccer image analysis was done using a hybrid color space in [31].

To see if color space conversion actually makes a difference, an analysis was done on skin detection [32]. They found that RGB color space was the model that gave the best results. Skin pixel classification was studied using a Bayesian model in [33] with different color spaces. In this case, the authors found LAB color space gave best results for accuracy.

Based on the works in [32,33] we can say that the authors found conflicting results. But importantly we take from these works the fact that using different color spaces gave authors different results, which means we could experiment on the same. We exploit this idea for our approach. The main modification we do, which will be explained in the proposed approach section, is that we combine the color spaces model to obtain a higher accuracy. This is due to the fact, as we shall see in the next section, that the color spaces are not completely correlated.

3 Proposed Approach

The idea was thought of while trying the effects of color space conversion on the CIFAR-10 dataset [2]. We started with a simple convolutional network. The network consisted of two convolutional layers followed by a max pooling layer. This was followed by a dropout layer, 2 more convolutional layers, one more max pooling, one more dropout layer and finished with a dense layer.

We started the classification on CIFAR-10 using the input data as it is i.e. in RGB format. We obtained an accuracy of 78.89% and time needed was 26 s. Next, we performed the classification by introducing color space conversion. We did the same with HSV, LAB, YIQ, YPbPr, YCbCr, YUV, LCH, HED, LCH and XYZ. The reason we chose the selected color spaces was due to the ease to perform the conversion using Scikit library [34]. The results of the classification can be seen in Table 1.

Table 1. Comparison of results for different color spaces on CIFAR-10 with simple CNN

Color space	Accuracy	Time
RGB	78.89	26 s
HSV	78.57	26 s
YUV	78.89	26 s
LAB	**80.43**	26 s
YIQ	78.79	26 s
XYZ	78.72	26 s
YPbPr	78.78	26 s
YCbCr	78.81	26 s
HED	78.98	26 s
LCH	78.82	26 s

From the table, we can see that the results obtained were highest for LAB color space, whilst the time of execution remained constant. However, like previous papers [32,33] showed, the accuracy levels are not too distant showing that the color space conversion results in more or less the same results while adding the time needed for the conversion.

We decided to have a closer look at the results by observing the confusion matrix for each case. The confusion matrices are shown in Fig. 1 for RGB, HSV, YUV, LAB, HED, LCH, XYZ and YPbPr.

On closer inspection, we see that each color space gives different accuracy for different classes. There are some classes that have equal classification rate in some classes, however, the majority differ in some way. For example, class 4 in CIFAR-10 is detected with 82% accuracy using YPbPr, however, the same class

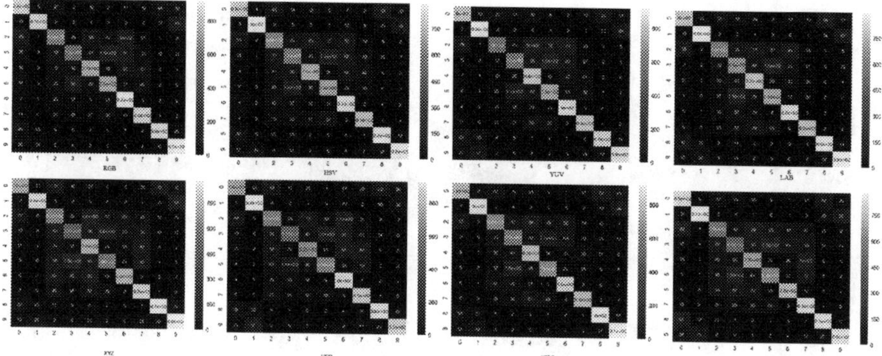

Fig. 1. Confusion matrices for various color spaces

is detected only with 72% in case of HED. Such differences can be noticed in multiple classes.

Based on these findings, we can conclude two important things. Firstly, there isn't 100% correlation between color spaces, which infers they can be used in combination to obtain better results. Secondly, certain classes of objects are being better represented by different color spaces.

We use these findings as the basis of our proposed model. We use small and wide Densenets as the base of our combination model. The proposed model is explored in the next section. Another important finding was that some color spaces are causing a loss of accuracy. We show a sample of such losses in Table 2. Here, we individually combined multiple color spaces to obtain higher classification rates using the simple CNN proposed earlier. This table was created only to show the reason we exclude certain color spaces in the next section. For this, we use RGB, HSV, XYZ, HED, LAB and YUV.

We also tried a late fusion approach. This would decrease the number of parameters in the model.

The combination being talked about above is using the output of the simple CNN with a particular color space and combining the outputs to obtain an average output of the different color spaces. The idea will be better understood in the next subsection. However, the important finding was that we can use the combination of color spaces to obtain a high accuracy of classification.

As can be seen, an early fusion approach did not significantly alter the accuracy in comparison to a model with a single color space itself. Although, the number of parameters significantly reduced in comparison to the model with late fusion, the accuracy was also lower in case of early fusion. Hence, we have chosen a late fusion model.

Table 2. Comparison of results for combination of different color spaces on CIFAR-10 with simple CNN

Color space	Accuracy	Number of color spaces used
RGB+HSV	81.42	2
RGB+YUV	81.41	2
HSV+YUV	81.97	2
RGB+LAB	81.91	2
LAB+HSV	81.95	2
YUV+LAB	82.05	2
RGB+HSV+YUV	82.33	3
RGB+HSV+LAB	82.49	3
RGB+LAB+YUV	82.62	3
LAB+HSV+YUV	82.66	3
RGB+HSV+YUV+LAB	82.96	4
RGB+HSV+YUV+LAB+HED(RHYLH)	83.61	5
RGB+HSV+YUV+LAB+HED+XYZ	82.81	6
RHYLH with Conv Layer	**84.32**	5
RHYLH with early fusion	81.63	5

3.1 Architecture of Model Used

The base of the model is using a Densenet for each color space. Essentially, the model consists of 7 Densenets, one for each color space being used, along with a final dense layer to give weighted predictions to classes.

Densenet [28] proposed the use of feed-forward connection between every layer in a network. They proposed the idea to overcome problems such as the vanishing gradient problem, but also believed that such a network could obtain remarkably high results with fewer parameters in comparison to other recent models. The Densenet model is represented as DenseNet-L-k where L stands for the depth of the model and k stands for the growth factor.

However, the model that obtained highest accuracy in both CIFAR-10 and CIFAR-100 datasets, the DenseNet-190-40 needed 25.6M parameters. We believed that this could be reduced significantly if we could find a way to pre-process the data.

We notice from our observations in the previous section, that combining the outputs from the 7 CNNs increased the accuracy of the model from 78.89% to 86.14%. Which meant a rise close to 7%. This result provoked the thought that, using a combination of smaller densenets which use far fewer parameters than the ones that obtained state of the art results could help us to reach similar levels of accuracy if not obtain better ones. Along with this, we thought of the idea that a wider densenet could possibly obtain better results than a deeper densenet based on [26].

Using these two thoughts, we decided to implement a model that consisted of small densenets for each color space. We started by using a DenseNet-BC-40-12 which used only 0.25M parameters. The BC in the name refers to the use of bottleneck layers after each block to compress the size of the model.

The color spaces that were selected based on the results obtained by individually checking if the accuracy affects the overall model are: RGB, LAB, HSV, YUV, YCbCr, HED and YIQ. The overall architecture of the model is seen in Fig. 2.

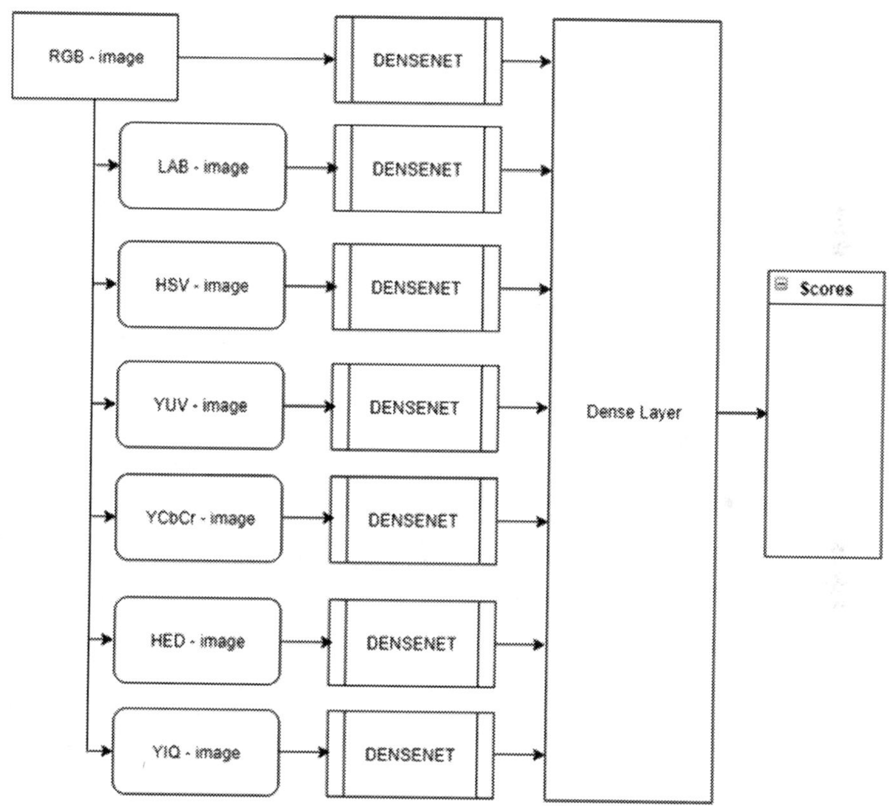

Fig. 2. Architecture of proposed model

The input RGB image is simultaneously converted into the 6 other color spaces and all 7 inputs are passed to Densenets. The output scores of each Densenet is then passed to a dense layer which helps to give weighted predictions to each color space. The output of the dense layer is used as the final classification score.

Many questions may arise for such a model, for example, the time needed for multiple color space conversions will cause an overhead. Also, the Densenets as mentioned in earlier sections has many parameters by itself, therefore, a combination of densenets will have, in this case, 7 times the number of parameters.

The first problem is something we do for the benefit of a higher accuracy which will be seen in later sections. The second, however, is solved by using smaller and wider densenets which use far fewer parameters than the models that have state of the art results on popular image classification datasets. The experimental results should help satisfy some of the questions regarding the time-accuracy trade-off.

4 Experimental Analysis

4.1 Datasets

We perform the experimental evaluation on CIFAR-10, CIFAR-100, SVHN and Imagenet.

The CIFAR-10 dataset consists of 60000 color images of size 32×32 each. There are 10 classes present. The dataset is divided into 50000 training images and 10000 test images. The CIFAR-100 dataset consists of 100 classes. We use data augmentation for these datasets and represent the results with a '+' sign. For example, C10+ refers to Cifar-10 results with augmentation. The augmentation done is horizontal flip and width/height shift.

The SVHN dataset (Street View House Numbers) contains 32×32 size images. There are 73,257 training images in the dataset and 26,032 test images in the dataset. Additionally, there are 531,131 images for extra training.

The Imagenet dataset consists 1.2 million training images and 50000 validation images. There are a total of 1000 classes. We apply single crop or 10 crop with size 224×224 at test time. We follow [25] and [28] in showing the imagenet classification score on the validation set.

4.2 Training

Since we use densenets as the base for building our model, we follow the training procedure followed in [28]. Each individual densenet is trained using stochastic gradient descent (SGD). We use a batch size of 32 for CIFAR datasets and run the model for 300 epochs. The learning rate is initially 0.1 and is reduced to 0.01 after 75 epochs and 0.001 after 150 epochs. In case of SVHN we run the model for 100 epochs and the learning rate is initially 0.1 and is reduced to 0.01 after 25 epochs and 0.001 after 50 epochs.

As with the original densenet implementation, we use a weight decay of 0.0001 and apply Nesterov momentum [35] of 0.9 without dampening. When we do not use data augmentation we add a dropout of 0.2.

There are 2 parameters that can affect the accuracy and number of parameters of our model. These are the growth factor and depth of network as was the case with original densenet [28]. With this regard, here onwards, colornet-L-k refers to a colornet that has densenets-L-k as subparts of the colornet model. L here refers to the depth of the network and k the growth factor. We use densenets with bottleneck as the densenet model part of our model.

4.3 Classification Results on CIFAR-10

Table 3 refers to the classification accuracies obtained on CIFAR-10 dataset for recent state of the art approaches. We compare the results obtained from our model with these approaches. In the table C10 refers to the accuracy of a particular model on CIFAR-10 and C10+ refers to the accuracy of the same model with data augmentation.

We compare our model with Network in Network [36], the All-CNN [37], Highway network [24], fractalnet [27], Resnet [25], Wide-Resnet [26] and Densenet [28].

Table 3. Comparison of error rates for CIFAR-10

Model name	No of parameters	C10	C10+
N-in-N [36]	-	10.41	8.81
all-CNN [37]	-	9.08	7.25
Highway network [24]	-	-	7.72
Fractalnet [27]	38.6M	10.18	5.22
Fractalnet [27] with dropout	38.6M	7.33	4.60
Resnet-101 [25]	1.7M	11.66	5.23
Resnet-1202 [25]	10.2M	-	4.91
Wide-Resnet-28 [26]	36.5M	-	4.17
Densenet-BC-100-12 [28]	0.8M	5.92	4.51
Densenet-BC-250-24 [28]	15.3M	5.19	3.62
Densenet-BC-190-40 [28]	25.6M	-	3.46
Colornet-40-12	1.75M	4.98	3.49
Colornet-40-48	19.0M	**3.14**	**1.54**

As can be seen, the Colornet-40-48 obtains an error rate of just 1.54 for CIFAR-10 with augmentation, which to the best of our knowledge obtains a new state of the art classification accuracy. Along with this a smaller Colornet model, the Colornet-40-12 with just 1.75M parameters has a better accuracy than Densenet-BC-250-24, with 15.3M parameters and is almost equal to that of Densenet-BC-190-40 which has 25.6M parameters.

4.4 Classification Results on CIFAR-100

Table 4 refers to the classification accuracies obtained on CIFAR-100 dataset for recent state of the art approaches. We compare the results obtained from our model with these approaches. In the table C100 refers to the accuracy of a particular model on CIFAR-100 and C100+ refers to the accuracy of the same model with data augmentation.

Table 4. Comparison of error rates for CIFAR-100

Model name	No of parameters	C100	C100+
N-in-N [36]	-	35.68	-
all-CNN [37]	-	-	33.71
Highway network [24]	-	-	32.29
Fractalnet [27]	38.6M	35.34	23.30
Fractalnet [27] with dropout	38.6M	28.20	23.73
Resnet-101 [25]	1.7M	37.80	24.58
Wide-Resnet-28 [26]	36.5M	-	20.50
Densenet-BC-100-12 [28]	0.8M	23.79	20.20
Densenet-BC-250-24 [28]	15.3M	19.64	17.60
Densenet-BC-190-40 [28]	25.6M	-	17.18
Colornet-40-12	1.75M	19.86	17.42
Colornet-40-48	19.0M	**15.62**	**11.68**

We compare our model with Network in Network [36], the All-CNN [37], Highway network [24], fractalnet [27], Resnet [25], Wide-Resnet [26] and Densenet [28].

As can be seen, the Colornet-40-48 obtains an error rate of 11.68 for CIFAR-10 with augmentation, which to the best of our knowledge obtains a new state of the art classification accuracy. Along with this a smaller Colornet model, the Colornet-40-12 with just 1.75M parameters has a better accuracy than Densenet-BC-250-24, with 15.3M parameters and is almost equal to that of Densenet-BC-190-40 which has 25.6M parameters.

4.5 Classification Results on Imagenet

Table 5 refers to the classification accuracies obtained on the imagenet dataset for recent state of the art approaches. Top-1 and Top-5 accuracy is compared for each approach. The error rates are represented as x/y where x represents error rate for single-crop testing and y for 10-crop testing.

We compare our model with Densenet as it is the paper that shows state of the art results for imagenet.

As can be seen, the Colornet-121, which replaces all the Densenets in the proposed model with Densenets-121 obtains a new state of the art accuracy on imagenet dataset to the best of our knowledge.

4.6 Classification Results on SVHN

Table 6 refers to the classification accuracies obtained on SVHN dataset for recent state of the art approaches. We compare the results obtained from our model with these approaches.

Table 5. Comparison of error rates for Imagenet

Model name	Top-1	Top-5
DenseNet-121	25.02/23.61	7.71/6.66
DenseNet-201	22.58/21.46	6.34/5.54
DenseNet-264	22.15/20.80	6.12/5.29
Colornet-121	**17.65/15.42**	**5.22/3.89**

We compare our model with Network in Network [36], fractalnet [27], Resnet [25], Wide-Resnet [26] and Densenet [28].

Table 6. Comparison of error rates for SVHN

Model name	No of parameters	SVHN
N-in-N [36]	-	2.35
Fractalnet [27]	38.6M	2.01
Fractalnet [27] with dropout	38.6M	1.87
Resnet-101 [25]	1.7M	1.75
Densenet-BC-100-12 [28]	0.8M	1.76
Densenet-BC-250-24 [28]	15.3M	1.74
Colornet-40-12	1.75M	1.59
Colornet-40-48	19.0M	**1.12**

As can be seen, the Colornet-40-48 obtains an error rate of 1.12 for SVHN, which to the best of our knowledge obtains new state of the art classification accuracy. Along with this a smaller Colornet model, the Colornet-40-12 with just 1.75M parameters has a better accuracy than Densenet-BC-250-24, with 15.3M parameters.

4.7 Further Analysis of Results

We further breakdown the reported results into the four error metrics namely true positives (TP), true negatives (TN), false positives (FP) and false negatives (FN) for each dataset. Table 7 highlights the same.

Table 7. Further analysis of obtained results for various datasets

Model	Dataset	TP	TN	FP	FN
Colornet-40-48	C-10	97.14	96.78	2.86	3.22
Colornet-40-48	C-10+	98.68	98.24	1.44	1.72
Colornet-40-48	C-100	84.12	84.64	15.88	15.33
Colornet-40-48	C-100+	88.65	87.99	11.35	12.01
Colornet-40-48	SVHN	98.90	98.86	1.11	1.13

5 Conclusion

We found that preprocessing images by transforming them into different color spaces yielded different results. Although, the accuracy by itself did not vary too much, on closer inspection with the aid of confusion matrices we could see that there wasn't a 100% correlation between the results. We could see that certain classes were being better represented in certain color spaces.

Using this as the idea, we dug deeper to see that the LCH, YPbPr and XYZ color spaces reduced the overall accuracy of the model and hence were discarded. We chose 7 color spaces as models that could be combined to obtain high accuracy of classification. These color spaces included RGB, YIQ, LAB, HSV, YUV, YCbCr and HED.

We used a densenet model as the base of the proposed architecture. We combined 7 densenets with the input to each being a different color space transformation of the original input image. The outputs of each densenet was sent to a dense layer to obtain weighted predictions from each densenet. Using a densenet model helped us to deal with common issues such as the vanishing gradient problem, the problem of overfitting among others.

Based on the results, we could see that state of the art results was obtained. We could compete against models with 27M parameters using a model of just 1.75M parameters.

Although the accuracy reached state of the art level, the time needed could still be optimized. For starters, the preprocessing step of converting to each color space needs a certain amount of time by itself. For small images like with the case of CIFAR or SVHN, this preprocessing can be done in real-time. However, for bigger images, like the ones in imagenet the time needed creates a cost-overhead. In addition to this, there is the computation overhead of using several densenet models. Although, we dealt with this using smaller and wider densenets.

References

1. Deng, J., Dong, W., Socher, R., Li, L.J., Li, K., Fei-Fei, L.: Imagenet: a large-scale hierarchical image database. In: IEEE Conference on Computer Vision and Pattern Recognition, CVPR 2009, pp. 248–255. IEEE, June 2009
2. Krizhevsky, A., Nair, V., Hinton, G.: The CIFAR-10 dataset (2014). http://www.cs.toronto.edu/kriz/cifar.html
3. Netzer, Y., Wang, T., Coates, A., Bissacco, A., Wu, B., Ng, A.Y.: Reading digits in natural images with unsupervised feature learning. In: NIPS Workshop on Deep Learning and Unsupervised Feature Learning, vol. 2011, no. 2, December 2011
4. LeCun, Y., Bottou, L., Bengio, Y., Haffner, P.: Gradient-based learning applied to document recognition. Proc. IEEE **86**(11), 2278–2324 (1998)
5. Fei-Fei, L., Fergus, R., Perona, P.: Learning generative visual models from few training examples: an incremental Bayesian approach tested on 101 object categories. Comput. Vis. Image Understand. **106**(1), 59–70 (2007)
6. Griffin, G., Holub, A., Perona, P.: Caltech-256 object category dataset (2007)
7. Gowda, S.N.: Human activity recognition using combinatorial deep belief networks. In: 2017 IEEE Conference on Computer Vision and Pattern Recognition Workshops (CVPRW), pp. 1589–1594. IEEE, July 2017
8. Krizhevsky, A., Sutskever, I., Hinton, G.E.: Imagenet classification with deep convolutional neural networks. In: NIPS, pp. 1097–1105 (2012)
9. LeCun, Y., et al.: Backpropagation applied to handwritten zip code recognition. Neural Comput. **1**(4), 541–551 (1989)
10. Gowda, S.N.: Face verification across age progression using facial feature extraction. In: International Conference on Signal and Information Processing (IConSIP), pp. 1–5. IEEE, 2016 October
11. Sermanet, P., Eigen, D., Zhang, X., Mathieu, M., Fergus, R., LeCun, Y.: Overfeat: Integrated recognition, localization and detection using convolutional networks. arXiv preprint arXiv:1312.6229 (2013)
12. Simonyan, K., Zisserman, A.: Very deep convolutional networks for large-scale image recognition. arXiv preprint arXiv:1409.1556 (2014)
13. Szegedy, C., et al.: Going deeper with convolutions. In: CVPR (2015)
14. He, K., Zhang, X., Ren, S., Sun, J.: Delving deep into rectifiers: surpassing human-level performance on imagenet classification. In: Proceedings of the IEEE International Conference on Computer Vision, pp. 1026–1034 (2015)
15. Ioffe, S., Szegedy, C.: Batch normalization: accelerating deep network training by reducing internal covariate shift. In: International Conference on Machine Learning, pp. 448–456, June 2015
16. Gowda, S.N.: Fiducial points detection of a face using RBF-SVM and adaboost classification. In: Chen, C.-S., Lu, J., Ma, K.-K. (eds.) ACCV 2016. LNCS, vol. 10116, pp. 590–598. Springer, Cham (2017). https://doi.org/10.1007/978-3-319-54407-6_40
17. He, K., Zhang, X., Ren, S., Sun, J.: Spatial pyramid pooling in deep convolutional networks for visual recognition. In: Fleet, D., Pajdla, T., Schiele, B., Tuytelaars, T. (eds.) ECCV 2014. LNCS, vol. 8691, pp. 346–361. Springer, Cham (2014). https://doi.org/10.1007/978-3-319-10578-9_23
18. Girshick, R.: Fast r-cnn. arXiv preprint arXiv:1504.08083 (2015)
19. Gowda, S.N.: Age estimation by LS-SVM regression on facial images. In: Bebis, G., et al. (eds.) ISVC 2016. LNCS, vol. 10073, pp. 370–379. Springer, Cham (2016). https://doi.org/10.1007/978-3-319-50832-0_36

20. Long, J., Shelhamer, E., Darrell, T.: Fully convolutional networks for semantic segmentation. In: Proceedings of the IEEE Conference on Computer Vision and Pattern Recognition, pp. 3431–3440 (2015)
21. Glorot, X., Bengio, Y.: Understanding the difficulty of training deep feedforward neural networks. In: Proceedings of the Thirteenth International Conference on Artificial Intelligence and Statistics, pp. 249–256, March 2010
22. Saxe, A.M., McClelland, J.L., Ganguli, S.: Exact solutions to the nonlinear dynamics of learning in deep linear neural networks. arXiv preprint arXiv:1312.6120 (2013)
23. Russakovsky, O., et al.: Imagenet large scale visual recognition challenge. IJCV **115**(3), 211–252 (2015)
24. Srivastava, R.K., Greff, K., Schmidhuber, J.: Training very deep networks. In Advances in Neural Information Processing Systems, pp. 2377–2385 (2015)
25. He, K., Zhang, X., Ren, S., Sun, J.: Deep residual learning for image recognition. In: Proceedings of the IEEE Conference on Computer Vision and Pattern Recognition, pp. 770–778 (2016)
26. Zagoruyko, S., Komodakis, N.: Wide residual networks. arXiv:1605.07146 (2016)
27. Larsson, G., Maire, M., Shakhnarovich, G.: Fractalnet: Ultra-deep neural networks without residuals. arXiv preprint arXiv:1605.07648 (2016)
28. Huang, G., Liu, Z., Weinberger, K.Q., van der Maaten, L.: Densely connected convolutional networks. In: Proceedings of the IEEE Conference on Computer Vision and Pattern Recognition, vol. 1, no. 2, p. 3, July 2017
29. Chai, D., Bouzerdoum, A.: A Bayesian approach to skin color classification in YCbCr color space. In: TENCON 2000 Proceedings, pp. 421–424. IEEE (2000)
30. Vandenbroucke, N., Macaire, L., Postaire, J.G.: Color pixels classification in an hybrid color space. In: Proceedings of 1998 International Conference on Image Processing, ICIP 98, vol. 1, pp. 176–180. IEEE, October 1998
31. Vandenbroucke, N., Macaire, L., Postaire, J.G.: Color image segmentation by pixel classification in an adapted hybrid color space. Application to soccer image analysis. Comput. Vis. Image Underst. **90**(2), 190–216 (2003)
32. Shin, M.C., Chang, K.I., Tsap, L.V.: Does colorspace transformation make any difference on skin detection? In: Proceedings of Sixth IEEE Workshop on Applications of Computer Vision, (WACV 2002), pp. 275–279. IEEE (2002)
33. Zarit, B.D., Super, B.J., Quek, F.K.: Comparison of five color models in skin pixel classification. In: 1999 International Workshop on Recognition, Analysis, and Tracking of Faces and Gestures in Real-Time Systems, pp. 58–63. IEEE (1999)
34. Van der Walt, S., et al.: scikit-image: image processing in Python (2014)
35. Sutskever, I., Martens, J., Dahl, G., Hinton, G.: On the importance of initialization and momentum in deep learning. In: International Conference on Machine Learning, pp. 1139–1147, February 2013
36. Lin, M., Chen, Q., Yan, S.: Network in network. arXiv:1312.4400 (2013)
37. Springenberg, J.T., Dosovitskiy, A., Brox, T., Riedmiller, M.: Striving for simplicity: The all convolutional net. arXiv preprint arXiv:1412.6806 (2014)

Pooling-Based Feature Extraction and Coarse-to-fine Patch Matching for Optical Flow Estimation

Xiaolin Tang[1(✉)], Son Lam Phung[1], Abdesselam Bouzerdoum[1,2], and Van Ha Tang[1]

[1] School of Electrical, Computer and Telecommunications Engineering, University of Wollongong, Wollongong, NSW 2522, Australia
{xt622,vht986}@uowmail.edu.au, {phung,bouzer}@uow.edu.au

[2] Division of Information and Computing Technology, College of Science and Engineering, Hamad Bin Khalifa University, PO Box 5825, Doha, Qatar

Abstract. This paper presents a pooling-based hierarchical model to extract a dense matching set for optical flow estimation. The proposed model down-samples basic image features (gradient and colour) with min and max pooling, to maintain distinctive visual features from the original resolution to the highly down-sampled layers. Subsequently, patch descriptors are extracted from the pooling results for coarse-to-fine patch matching. In the matching process, the local optimum correspondence of patches is found with a four-step search, and then refined by a velocity propagation algorithm. This paper also presents a method to detect matching outliers by checking the consistency of motion-based and colour-based segmentation. We evaluate the proposed method on two benchmarks, MPI-Sintel and Kitti-2015, using two criteria: the matching accuracy and the accuracy of the resulting optical flow estimation. The results indicate that the proposed method is more efficient, produces more matches than the existing algorithms, and improves significantly the accuracy of optical flow estimation.

Keywords: Optical flow estimation · Coarse-to-fine patch matching · Pooling-based feature extraction

1 Introduction

Optical flow estimation (OFE) aims to find velocities for all pixels in an image pair, to determine the motion of objects in a scene. It remains a challenging problem in computer vision though numerous studies [4,5,11,14,19] have been proposed to enhance OFE accuracy and efficiency. In OFE, it is difficult to track large displacement, obtain smooth flow map and crisp motion boundary, estimate optical flow under occlusion, and moreover, accelerate the estimation speed. This paper addresses these problems by using a pooling-based hierarchical model to extract a dense matching set for enhancing OFE.

C. V. Jawahar et al. (Eds.): ACCV 2018, LNCS 11364, pp. 597–612, 2019.
https://doi.org/10.1007/978-3-030-20870-7_37

Dense matching is of great importance in OFE [5,14,29]. An efficient approach to obtain good matches is using a hierarchical architecture to track objects from carse to fine [14,24]. Gaussian pyramid and convolutional neural network (CNN) [11,19,26] are two popular hierarchical architectures based on Gaussian smoothed down-sampling and by max pooling, respectively. The hierarchical model proposed in this paper combines the advantages of Gaussian pyramid and CNN model. The proposed model has a flexible architecture and maintains salient features in highly down-sampled images. It uses image gradients and colour to construct a base layer. Then, min pooling and max pooling are separately applied to the base layer to generate two branches: min-pooling-based hierarchical structure and max-pooling-based hierarchical structure. The spatial gradients and colour in salient regions are preserved by the pooling strategy to the top layer. Compared to CNN models, the adjacent layers in the proposed architecture are independent since the pooling operator is applied on the output of the previous layer directly without learning filter coefficients. This makes the proposed model more flexible. Compared to Gaussian pyramid, the proposed model down-samples the feature maps with min and max pooling, making it easier and reliable to track small objects whose motion are highly different from the background.

Based on the proposed architecture, we develop a simple and powerful descriptor for patch matching. The proposed descriptors are extracted at each scale to explore pixel-level matches from coarse to fine. As this descriptor works on the pooling layers, it is robust to small structure distortion, such as rotations and scale changes. It is also robust to variant illuminations due to z-score normalisation. After feature extraction, four-step search and velocity propagation are used to explore matches with a coarse-to-fine scheme. To enhance the searching ability, we sample four extra velocities from the nearby motion field of the neighbour to do velocity propagation. To remove the effects of matching noise in propagation, we detect outliers at level 0 by a segmentation-based method. This method is based on the observation that motion boundaries should be confirmed in the colour space. Thus, the inconsistency degree of motion-based segmentation and colour-based segmentation is a criterion to determine whether the match is an outlier or not. This noise detection method enhances correct matches and greatly reduces the outliers ratio.

The contributions of this paper are in four aspects: a pooling-based hierarchical model, a simple but powerful patch descriptor, a modified propagation strategy, and a segmentation-based noise detection method. Compared to the existing matching algorithms [14,24,29], the proposed method produces more accurate matches with fewer computation costs. The optical flow estimated by EpicFlow interpolation with the produced matches is also competitive to that of the state-of-the-art methods [11,14,23,29] in terms of the estimation accuracy and the computation costs on two of the most challenging optical flow benchmarks: *MPI-Sintel* and *Kitti-2015*. The flow accuracy is even higher than many CNN-based methods although our method does not learn any filter coefficients.

This paper is structured as follows: Sect. 2 presents the related works in OFE. Section 3 describes the proposed feature model and matching process. Section 4 presents the experiments to analyse the performance of the proposed method and compare it with other state-of-the-art methods. Section 5 gives the concluding remarks.

2 Related Work

The existing algorithms for optical flow estimation aim to improve estimation accuracy by tracking large displacement, getting crisp motion boundary, and estimating homography transformation for optical flow interpolation.

Estimating optical flow using hierarchical models has shown to cope well with large displacements [3,6,14,15,22]. Coarse-to-fine Patch Match (CPM) [14] estimates matching flow using a Gaussian pyramid from a coarse to fine scale. This method extracts denseSIFT [16,17] descriptors at each scale for patch matching and obtains a large matching set for OFE. As small objects are highly blurred at high levels of the Gaussian pyramid, it is difficult for CPM to track small objects having distinct motions. DeepMatching [24] extracts salient features layer by layer in a multi-level correlation pyramid. The final matches are extracted with a top-down correspondence extraction method which is time-consuming. K-d tree patch matching (KPM) [12] improves the optical flow accuracy of generalized patch matching (GPM) [3] by using a kd-tree assisted searching method. KPM is quite fast but contains many outliers in the matching result. CNN is also the popular hierarchical model for OFE. The published CNN models, such as FLowNet2.0 [15], PWCNet [26], and SPNet [22], estimate optical flow in real time with high accuracy. However, these models require a large dataset for training. As the network architecture is fixed, CNN models require the size of test images to be similar to or larger than that of the training images. Thus, CNN models are not as flexible as the traditional OFE method for real-world applications.

Combining segmentation with optical flow estimation enhances crisp-motion boundary indication and optical flow accuracy [10,18,25,27,30,32]. The method in [10] performs superpixel matching then pixel matching to reduce computation costs. This method conducts global search for large displacement on superpixel-level, which, however, is difficult to obtain accurate superpixel matches in homogeneous regions. The approaches proposed in [27,30,32] aim to divide the image into pieces and estimate a homography motion for each piece. These methods produce accurate optical flow and segmentation, which however, time-consuming due to pixel-level energy minimisation model for both segmentation and homography model estimation.

Estimating accurate homography transformation with a given matching set for pixel velocity interpolation yields smooth flow field. EpicFlow interpolation [23] is a popular method. It uses the edge map generated by the structured edge detector (SED) in [9] to find the k-nearest neighbours and the corresponding weight of the neighbours. This method removes matching noise and smooths seed motions using the k-nearest matches. For the pixel not in the matching set, the nearest matching seed is explored and the motion derived by this match is copied to the pixel. RicFlow is another method to perform flow interpolation with a matching set [13]. This approach segments images into superpixels with SLIC method [1] and constructs an affine model to represent the superpixel motion instead of using seed motion as in EpicFlow.

3 Proposed Method

This section presents the proposed pooling-based hierarchical model for feature extraction and coarse-to-fine path matching for enhanced optical flow estimation. Subsection 3.1 describes the pooling-based feature extraction. Subsection 3.2 presents the coarse-to-fine patch matching process. Subsection 3.3 addresses the post-processing and optical flow estimation.

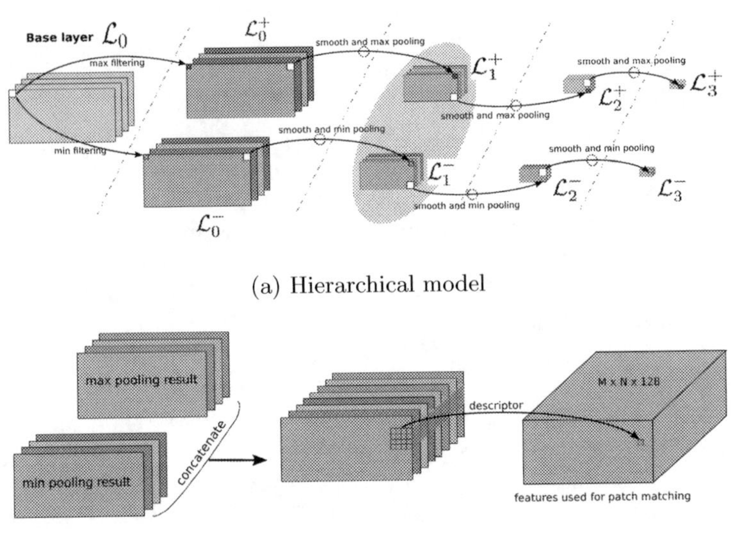

(a) Hierarchical model

(b) Feature extraction at one level

Fig. 1. Illustration of the hierarchical architecture and feature extraction.

3.1 Pooling-Based Feature Extraction

Let I be an image of size $M \times N$ pixels in the RGB colour space. Its gradients along the x and y directions of the three colour channels are denoted by three vectors $(G_{x,r}, G_{y,r})$, $(G_{x,g}, G_{y,g})$, and $(G_{x,b}, G_{y,b})$. Among these three vectors, let (G_x, G_y) be the vector with the largest magnitude. Furthermore, let Y be the luminance channel in the YCbCr colour space. We define image C as $C = (R-Y)(B-Y)$. The four features G_x, G_y, Y, and C form the base layer $\mathcal{L}_b$ of the pooling-based hierarchical model in Fig. 1(a). Applying min and max filters of size $h \times h$ pixels to each channel of $\mathcal{L}_0$ yields two layers $\mathcal{L}_0^-$ and $\mathcal{L}_0^+$, respectively. Note that the three layers $\mathcal{L}_0$, $\mathcal{L}_0^-$, and $\mathcal{L}_0^+$ have the same size $M \times N \times 4$. As shown in Fig. 1(a), $\mathcal{L}_0^-$ and $\mathcal{L}_0^+$ are the initial layers of two branches based on min pooling and max pooling. Min or max pooling down-samples the input by reducing each window of size $w \times w$ to a single value, which is the minimum or maximum of the window pixel; a stride factor of s is applied.

Let $\mathcal{L}_l^-$ and $\mathcal{L}_l^+$ be the lth layer in the min and max pooling branch, respectively. Let $\mathcal{F}_l^-$ and $\mathcal{F}_{l+}$ be a feature map (a channel) in $\mathcal{L}_l^-$ and $\mathcal{L}_l^+$, respectively. Because the pooling operation is sensitive to noise, we first apply box filtering on each channel to obtain:

$$\tilde{\mathcal{F}}_l^-(x,y) = \text{mean}\left\{\mathcal{F}_l^-(x',y') \mid |x'-x| \leq b \text{ and } |y'-y| \leq b\right\}, \tag{1}$$

$$\tilde{\mathcal{F}}_l^+(x,y) = \text{mean}\left\{\mathcal{F}_l^+(x',y') \mid |x'-x| \leq b \text{ and } |y'-y| \leq b\right\}, \tag{2}$$

where b determines the box filter size. Next, we calculate the feature maps for the $(l+1)$th layer:

$$\mathcal{F}_{l+1}^-(x,y) = \min_{(x',y') \in W(x,y)} \tilde{\mathcal{F}}_l^-(x',y'), \tag{3}$$

$$\mathcal{F}_{l+1}^+(x,y) = \max_{(x',y') \in W(x,y)} \tilde{\mathcal{F}}_l^+(x',y'). \tag{4}$$

Here, $W(x,y)$ is a window of size $w \times w$ centred on pixel $(sx + 0.5w, sy + 0.5w)$. Subsequently, applying min pooling on all feature maps of $\mathcal{L}_l^-$ we get a pooling layer $\mathcal{L}_{l+1}^-$ which has four down-sampled feature maps. Similarly, applying max pooling on all feature maps of $\mathcal{L}_l^+$ yields a pooling layer $\mathcal{L}_{l+1}^+$. In this pooling-based hierarchical model, there are eight feature maps at each level, four from $\mathcal{L}_l^-$ and four from $\mathcal{L}_l^+$. Hence, layers $\mathcal{L}_l^-$ and $\mathcal{L}_l^+$ are of size $(M/s^l) \times (N/s^l) \times 4$. The pooling process stops when the size of output layer is smaller than a predefined size.

Next, we describe how features are extracted at each level, as shown in Fig. 1(b). At the lth level, $\mathcal{F}_l^-$ and $\mathcal{F}_l^+$ are the min and max pooling results derived from the basic feature $\mathcal{F}$, where $\mathcal{F}$ can be G_x, G_y, Y, or C. The proposed descriptor is extracted from a patch consisting of $t \times t$ cells, each cell has $c \times c$ pixels. The patch is represented as a vector of size $2t^2$:

$$\mathcal{D}_{l,\mathcal{F}} = \left\{\mathcal{F}_l^-(\mathbf{p}_1), \cdots, \mathcal{F}_l^-(\mathbf{p}_{t^2})\right\} \cup \left\{\mathcal{F}_l^+(\mathbf{p}_1), \cdots, \mathcal{F}_l^+(\mathbf{p}_{t^2})\right\}, \tag{5}$$

where $\mathbf{p}_i$ is the centroid pixel of the ith cell. To reduce the effects of varying illumination, we normalise this vector as

$$\tilde{\mathcal{D}}_{l,\mathcal{F}} = \frac{\mathcal{D}_{l,\mathcal{F}} - m}{\|\mathcal{D}_{l,\mathcal{F}} - m\|_2 + \epsilon}, \tag{6}$$

where ϵ is small positive constant, and m is the mean value of vector $\mathcal{D}_{l,\mathcal{F}}$.

The overall patch descriptor is the concatenation of the four normalised vectors:

$$\tilde{\mathcal{D}}_l = \left\{\tilde{\mathcal{D}}_{l,Gx}, \tilde{\mathcal{D}}_{l,Gy}, \tilde{\mathcal{D}}_{l,Y}, \tilde{\mathcal{D}}_{l,C}\right\}. \tag{7}$$

To calculate the matching cost efficiently, this descriptor is scaled and stored as an 8-bit integer. Due to the min and max pooling, the proposed descriptor has built-in scale-invariance and is robust to small rotations. We refer to the proposed descriptor as *pooling-based salient feature transform* or PST.

3.2 Coarse-to-fine Patch Matching

The coarse-to-fine patch matching has four main steps: (1) sample seeds regularly in a grid at each level; (2) initialise the motion of seeds at level l by using the matching results of level $l+1$; (3) refine seed motions with a four-step search and the proposed propagation algorithm; (4) detect outliers with the proposed segmentation-based method.

Let g_l be the grid size at level l. We select $g_0 = 3$, $g_1 = 2$, and $g_l = 1$ if $l > 1$. Let I and I' be an image pair for patch matching. Let $\mathcal{S}_l$ be the set of seeds in scale level l. Let $\mathcal{M}_l$ be the set of matches at level l. The pseudocode of the proposed coarse-to-fine patch matching is shown in Algorithm 1. The forward (from I to I') and backward (from I' to I) patch matching are performed simultaneously.

Algorithm 1. Pseudo-code of the coarse-to-fine patch matching

Input: Feature pyramids $\mathcal{D}$ and $\mathcal{D}'$ separately derived from I and I'

Sample $\mathcal{S}_L$ and $\mathcal{S}'_L$ from the top layer $\mathcal{D}_L$ and $\mathcal{D}'_L$, respectively.
Get $\mathcal{M}_L$ and $\mathcal{M}'_L$ by exhaustively search.
for $l = L\text{-}1\text{:-}1\text{:}0$ **do**
  Sample $\mathcal{S}_l$ from $\mathcal{D}_l$, and $\mathcal{S}'_l$ from $\mathcal{D}'_l$.
  Get $\mathcal{M}_l$ and $\mathcal{M}'_l$ by motion initialisation.
  Refine matches in $\mathcal{M}_l$ and $\mathcal{M}'_l$ with the four-step search.
  if $l = 0$ **then**
    Detect matching noise in $\mathcal{M}_l$ and $\mathcal{M}'_l$.
    Set the matching cost of outliers to infinity.
  Refine matches in $\mathcal{M}_l$ and $\mathcal{M}'_l$ via velocity propagation and four-step search.
return Matching set $\mathcal{M}_0$ (forward) and $\mathcal{M}'_0$ (backward)

Matching Cost. Let $\mathbf{p}_k$ be the kth seed, and $\mathbf{v}_k$ be its velocity. The matching cost between $\mathbf{p}_k$ and $\mathbf{p}_k + \mathbf{v}_k$ is defined as the ℓ_1-norm distance between two descriptors:

$$\mathcal{C}(\mathbf{p}_k, \mathbf{v}_k) = \|\mathcal{D}(\mathbf{p}_k) - \mathcal{D}'(\mathbf{p}_k + \mathbf{v}_k)\|_1, \tag{8}$$

where $\mathcal{D}'(\mathbf{p}_k + \mathbf{v}_k)$ is the corresponding descriptor in I'. The ℓ_1-norm distance is efficient to calculate and is relatively robust to noise.

Motion Initialisation. Let $\mathbf{p}_k^{l+1}$ as the parent seed of $\mathbf{p}_k^l$. We define a set $\psi_k^{l+1} := \{\mathbf{p}_j^{l+1} \mid 3g_{l+1} > \|\mathbf{p}_j^{l+1} - \mathbf{p}_k^{l+1}\|_2\}$, and then initialise the motion of $\mathbf{p}_k^l$ as

$$\mathbf{v}_k^l = \underset{s\mathbf{v}_j^{l+1}}{\operatorname{argmin}} \left(\{\mathcal{C}(\mathbf{p}_k^l, s\mathbf{v}_j^{l+1}) \mid \mathbf{p}_j^{l+1} \in \psi_k^{l+1}\}\right), \tag{9}$$

where s is the stride in the pooling model. For seeds at the top level, their motions are initialised by exhaustive search in the corresponding image. After motion initialisation, the standard four-step search and velocity propagation are applied to refine the motions.

Velocity Propagation. In dense matching, propagation is of great significance to ensure motion smoothness and obtain a large matching set. The propagation is conducted in two directions: from $\mathbf{p}_1$ to $\mathbf{p}_K$ in even iterations, and from $\mathbf{p}_K$ to $\mathbf{p}_1$ in odd iterations, where K is the number of seeds at the current level. In each iteration, seed motion is updated by propagating the motions of verified neighbours. Suppose $\mathbf{p}_j$ is one of the 8-connected neighbours of $\mathbf{p}_k$, and $\mathbf{v}_j$ is the velocity of $\mathbf{p}_j$. For the propagation of $\mathbf{v}_j$ to $\mathbf{p}_k$, the following set Ω of five following candidates in I' are evaluated to find the best correspondence of $\mathbf{p}_k$:

$$\begin{aligned} &\mathbf{c}_1 = \mathbf{p}_j + \mathbf{v}_j, \mathbf{c}_2 = (\mathbf{p}_k + \mathbf{p}_j)/2 + \mathbf{v}_j, \mathbf{c}_3 = \mathbf{p}_k + \mathbf{v}_j, \\ &\mathbf{c}_4 = (3\mathbf{p}_k - \mathbf{p}_j)/2 + \mathbf{v}_j, \mathbf{c}_5 = 2\mathbf{p}_k - \mathbf{p}_j + \mathbf{v}_j, \end{aligned} \tag{10}$$

The motion vector of $\mathbf{p}_k$ is updated as

$$\mathbf{v}_k^* = \mathbf{c}_p - \mathbf{p}_k, \text{ if } \mathcal{C}(\mathbf{p}_k, \mathbf{v}_k) > \mathcal{C}(\mathbf{p}_k, \mathbf{c}_p - \mathbf{p}_k). \tag{11}$$

Here, $\mathbf{c}_p$ is the candidate with the smallest matching cost:

$$\mathbf{c}_p = \underset{\mathbf{c}_i \in \Omega}{\operatorname{argmin}}\ \mathcal{C}(\mathbf{p}_k, \mathbf{c}_i - \mathbf{p}_k). \tag{12}$$

Matching Noise Detection. After motion initialisation, matching noise is detected at level 0 to remove incorrect matches. Consider a seed $\mathbf{p}_k$ in I and its correspondence $\mathbf{p}_k'$ in I'. Two small windows, W centred on $\mathbf{p}_k$ and W' centred on $\mathbf{p}_k'$ are defined; the window size is $(2r+1)\times(2r+1)$. The motion dissimilarity between $\mathbf{p}_k$ and a seed in the two windows is calculated as

$$d_{k,j} = \begin{cases} \frac{|(\mathbf{v}_j - \mathbf{v}_k)^T(\mathbf{p}_j - \mathbf{p}_k)|}{\|\mathbf{p}_j - \mathbf{p}_k\|^2 + \tau_0}, \text{ if } \mathbf{p}_j \text{ in } W, \\ \frac{|(\mathbf{v}_j + \mathbf{v}_k)^T(\mathbf{p}_j - \mathbf{p}_k')|}{\|\mathbf{p}_j - \mathbf{p}_k'\|^2 + \tau_0}, \text{ if } \mathbf{p}_j \text{ in } W', \end{cases} \tag{13}$$

where τ_0 is a tolerance factor. This metric evaluates the distortion of the Euclidean distance between two seeds after separate motions. It avoids detecting matches in rotated objects as noise. According to the motion dissimilarity, seeds in W and W' are divided into two sets: L_v satisfying $d_{k,j} < 1$, and H_v for all else. Seeds in L_v have similar motions to $\mathbf{v}_k$ or $-\mathbf{v}_k$, and seeds in set H_v have distinct motions to $\mathbf{v}_k$ or $-\mathbf{v}_k$. Let m_l and m_h be the mean colour of L_v and H_v, respectively. Taking m_l and m_h as two centres, we cluster seeds in L_v into LL and LH, and seeds in H_v into HL and HH. If L_v and H_v are the accurate segmentation for seeds in the two windows, the set LH and HL should be empty, indicating segmentations based on motion and colour are consistent. The inconsistency degree is defined as

$$\mathcal{E} = \frac{|LH| + |HL|}{|L_v| + |H_v|}. \tag{14}$$

We perform colour-based segmentation on three channels (Y, Cb, and Cr) to get three inconsistency degrees, and take the minimum value as the ultimate inconsistency degree. Finally, match $(\mathbf{p}_k, \mathbf{p}_k + \mathbf{v}_k)$ is regarded as noise if $\mathcal{E}(\mathbf{p}_k) > \tau_1$. In matching-noise detection, outliers are assigned to a large matching cost to be updated in propagation.

3.3 Post-processing and Optical Flow Estimation

The coarse-to-fine patch matching finds a match for each seed at level 0. However, there are many outliers among these matches due to occlusion and miss-matching. We extract accurate matches by checking matching consistency in the forward and backward directions. For each pixel in I or I', its velocity is equal to that of the nearest seed. Match $(\mathbf{p}_k, \mathbf{p}'_k)$ is considered as an outlier if: (i) $\mathbf{p}_k$ or $\mathbf{p}'_k$ is less than τ_2 pixels from the image border; or (ii) there is a pixel $\mathbf{p}'_j$ in a $(2g_0 - 1) \times (2g_0 - 1)$ window centred on $\mathbf{p}'_k$, and the pixel velocity $\mathbf{v}'_j$ satisfies $\| \mathbf{v}_k + \mathbf{v}'_j \|_2 > \tau_2$. The first condition aims to remove image boundary effects, and the second condition ensures the matches are consistently estimated from I to I' and from I' to I. After this step, we obtain the final matching result.

From the matching result obtained from our method, we estimate dense optical flow using EpicFlow interpolation [23]. We choose EpicFlow interpolation since this method is widely used and evaluated in most state-of-the-art methods (e.g. [13,14,29]). EpicFlow estimates affine transformation locally from nearby matches to generate dense optical flow field. Therefore, the properties of matching result impact the optical flow accuracy greatly.

4 Experiments

This section describes two standard benchmarks, performance metrics, parameters of the proposed method, and the ablation study. It also presents experimental results for coarse-to-fine patch matching and optical flow estimation.

4.1 Experimental Methods

The proposed method was evaluated on two benchmarks: *MPI-Sintel* [7] and *Kitti-2015* [20,21]. *MPI-Sintel*[1] consists of video clips with multiple rapid motions and homogeneous regions. This benchmark has two passes: 'clean' and 'final'. The 'final' pass is challenging for optical flow estimation due to numerous rendering effects. The length of image sequence in each clip is up to 50, and the image size is 436 × 1024 pixels. *Kitti-2015*[2] is a collection of image pairs

[1] sintel.is.tue.mpg.de.

[2] www.cvlibs.net/datasets/kitti.

captured by drivers. There are large displacement and distortion in image pairs, especially near the image border. There are 200 image pairs in the training set and test set. The image size in *Kitti-2015* is around 372×1240 pixels.

To analyse the proposed method, we conducted experiments over different pixel sets. For *MPI-Sintel*, the average end-point error (AEE) was evaluated on three sets (s0-10, s10-40, s40+) divided by pixel velocity, or on three sets (d0-10, d10-60, d60-140) divided by the Euclidean distance between pixel and its nearest occlusion-boundary, or on two sets (occ, non) referring occlusion and non-occlusion. For *Kitti-2015*, the flow outlier (Fl) was evaluated on background regions (bg) and foreground regions (fg). For numerical analysis of the matching result, we used two more metrics: CNum is the number of correct matches per frame, ME is the ratio in percentage of the incorrect matches over the total matches.

The matching result and optical flow estimation on *MPI-Sintel* and *Kitti-2015* were evaluated. For both benchmarks, only the ground truth of training set is provided to the public. Thus, the evaluation of matching result is only performed on the training set. For optical flow, the evaluation is performed on the training set and test set.

4.2 Algorithm Parameters

For the feature extraction described in Subsect. 3.1, the min and max filter size h was set to 3. The window used in min and max pooling had a window size $w = 2$ and stride $s = 2$. The width of the top layer in the hierarchical model was 10 pixels or larger. At each level, we sampled seeds at each level from grid image. The grid size was set as $g_0 = 3$ at level 0, $g_1 = 2$ at level 1, and $g_l = 1$ at the other levels ($l > 1$). The box filter size is set as $b = 1$. The patch defined for feature extraction consists of $t \times t$ cells with $t = 4$, and each cell is of size $c \times c$ pixels with $c = 3$.

In coarse-to-fine patch matching described in Subsect. 3.2, threshold τ_0 was set to 36 and τ_2 is set to 5. We conducted experiments on the training set of *MPI-Sintel* 'final' pass and the training set of *Kitti-2015* to tune the window size r and the inconsistency cut τ_1 in noise detection. Figure 2 shows the impact of the two parameters. We set $r = 3, \tau_1 = 0.12$ for *MPI-Sintel* to get a large CNum and the lowest AEE, and set $r = 6$ and $\tau_1 = 0.28$ for *Kitti-2015* to get large CNum and the lowest flow outlier ratio (Fl-all).

4.3 Ablation Study

We evaluated the contribution of different components in the proposed method, using the training set of *MPI-Sintel* and *Kitti-2015*. The proposed method has two stages: feature extraction (F-PST) and patch matching (M-PST). Hence, we fixed one stage and changed the other, see Table 1.

Experiments 1 to 4 fixed M-PST to compare different feature maps. The hierarchical model used for feature extraction was constructed from Gx and

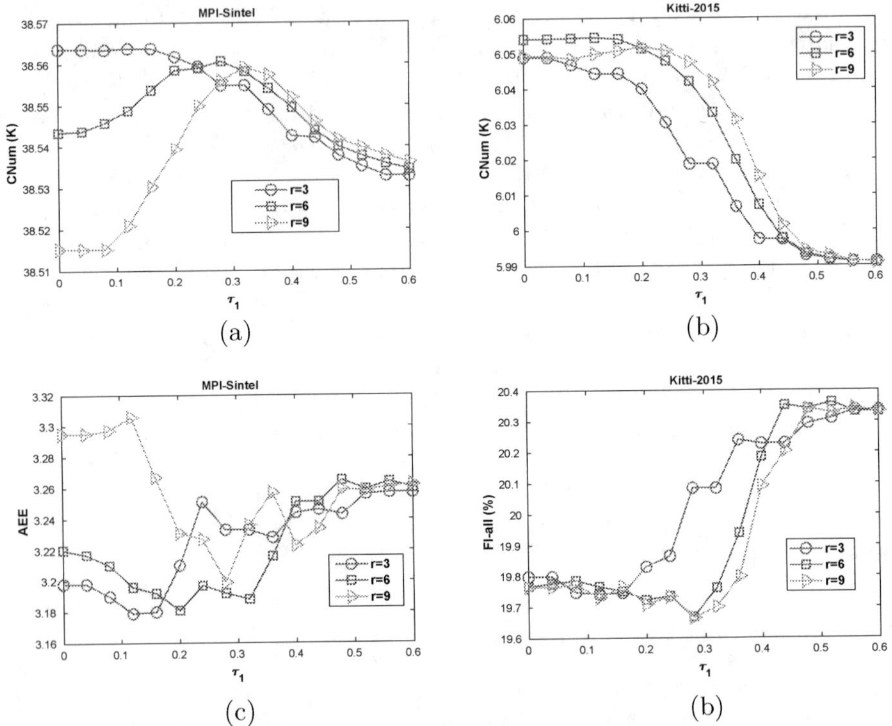

Fig. 2. Impact of r and τ_1 on *MPI-Sintel* training set of 'final' pass and *Kitti-2015* training set. (a) CNum on *MPI-Sintel*, (b) CNum on *Kitti-2015*, (c) AEE on *MPI-Sintel*, (d) Fl-all on *Kitti-2015*.

Gy in Experiment 1, and from Y and C in Experiment 2. We denote descriptors from the two models as F-PST-G and F-PST-A, respectively. DenseSIFT in Experiment 3 is the feature used in CPM. In Experiment 4, the standard proposed descriptor (F-PST) and the standard proposed matching method (M-PST) were evaluated. The experiment results show that F-PST-G yields more correct matches and lower outlier ratio than that of F-PST-A. However, the colour information enhances the number of correct matches and reduces optical flow error on two benchmarks in Experiment 4. Compared with DenseSIFT, the proposed feature yields more correct matches and more accurate optical flow under the proposed matching method.

Experiments 4 to 8 fixed the standard proposed feature (F-PST) to compare different matching methods. Here, M-PST-N denotes M-PST without matching noise detection. M-PST-E represents M-PST without using the four extra motions in propagation. CPM is the method used in [14]; SGM is the method used in [29]. The number of correct matches on two benchmarks decreased if removing the noise detection step (M-PST-N). The number of correct matches and the outlier ratio on two benchmarks increased if omitting the four extra

Table 1. Ablation study of the proposed method.

ID	Method		MPI-Sintel ('final' pass)			Kitti-2015		
	Feature	Matching	CNum(K)	ME(%)	AEE	CNum(K)	ME(%)	Fl(%)
1	F-PST-G	M-PST	39.69	**2.816**	3.374	6.12	9.597	20.467
2	F-PST-A	M-PST	37.84	3.049	3.278	5.20	13.31	21.054
3	DenseSIFT	M-PST	38.19	2.824	3.327	5.02	**8.799**	21.399
4	F-PST	M-PST	38.56	2.912	**3.176**	6.05	9.887	**19.665**
5	F-PST	M-PST-N	38.02	3.805	3.206	5.88	9.905	20.275
6	F-PST	M-PST-E	40.18	3.139	3.198	6.14	10.242	20.073
7	F-PST	CPM	**41.08**	5.001	3.536	**6.48**	14.228	21.645
8	F-PST	SGM	36.56	3.326	3.309	4.97	14.451	23.577

motion in velocity propagation (M-PST-E). M-PST outperformed SGM on the two benchmarks with the proposed descriptors (Experiment 4 vs. Experiment 8). CPM yielded more correct matches and a larger outlier ratio than that of M-PST (Experiment 4 vs. Experiment 7). Among all configurations, the combination of proposed feature (F-PST) and proposed matching method (M-PST) yields the smallest end-point error (AEE) on *MPI-Sintel*, and the smallest flow outlier ratio (Fl) on *Kitti-2015*.

4.4 Evaluation of Patch Matching

We compared the proposed method PST with two state-of-the-art methods for dense matching: DeepMatching[3] and CPM[4]. These methods use different interpolation algorithms for optical flow estimation. To remove the impact of interpolation variance, we use EpicFlow interpolation method to estimate optical flow for the compared methods. The matching results of DeepMatching and CPM were obtained using the online published code. We ran the experiments for DeepMatching, CPM and PST in a single-core 3.4 GHz CPU.

Table 2 shows the analysis of the matching results and optical flow on the training set of *MPI-Sintel* ('final' pass) and *Kitti-2015*. On *MPI-Sintel*, PST yielded the highest correct matches (CNum), the lowest outlier ratio of matches (ME), and the lowest optical flow error (AEE) over all velocity ranges (all, s0-10, s10-40, s40+). These experiment results indicate the proposed method is more robust to rendering distortion and more powerful in tracking large displacements. On *Kitti-2015*, PST generated the highest CNum over all velocity ranges although its ME scores on sets (all, s40+) were slightly higher than that of CPM. In terms of the percentage of optical flow outliers (Fl-all), PST outperformed the other two methods on sets (all, s10-40, s40+). These results confirm that PST is more reliable on tracking large displacements. In Table 2, the running

[3] Dthoth.inrialpes.fr/src/deepflow/.
[4] github.com/YinlinHu/CPM.

time includes only patch-matching computation, i.e. without EpicFlow interpolation. PST was the fastest method, requiring 1.05 s per frame on *MPI-Sintel* and 1.3 s per frame on *Kitti-2015*. For PST, the average time for feature extraction (two images) was 0.6 s on *MPI-Sintel* and 0.8 s on *Kitti-2015*; the average time for matching (forward and backward) was 0.45 s on *MPI-Sintel* and 0.5 s on *Kitti-2015*.

Figure 3 presents four examples of the matching results. To display the matching results in continuous field, the motion derived by each match is copied to the nearby pixels in a window of size $g_0 \times g_0$. As can be seen, matches generated by PST have a more compact distribution compared to those by the other methods. PST finds many matches although the objects are small, e.g. the bird in the first example and the hand in the third example. In the fourth example, CPM fails to track the foreground object for the structure distortions caused by unevenly distributed optical flow. However, DeepMatching and PST are able to extract some correct matches in this region. Moreover, PST is much faster than DeepMatching. These observations indicate that PST is powerful to track large displacements and is robust to small structure distortions.

Table 2. Analysis of the matching result and optical flow on the training set of *MPI-Sintel* and *Kitti-2015*.

Sintel 'final'	CNum (K)				ME (%)				AEE				Time (s)
	all	s0-10	s10-40	s40+	all	s0-10	s10-40	s40+	all	s0-10	s10-40	s40+	
DeepMatching [24]	5.48	4.33	0.93	0.22	6.744	2.826	14.151	34.322	3.726	0.570	3.845	25.858	48
CPM [14]	37.80	29.99	6.42	1.39	3.420	1.757	7.248	17.802	3.540	0.575	3.695	24.239	1.3
PST	**38.56**	**30.30**	**6.66**	**1.60**	**2.912**	**1.494**	**6.063**	**14.316**	**3.176**	**0.554**	**3.447**	**21.181**	**1.05**
Kitti-2015	CNum (K)				ME (%)				Fl-all (%)				Time (s)
	all	s0-10	s10-40	s40+	all	s0-10	s10-40	s40+	all	s0-10	s10-40	s40+	
DeepMatching [24]	0.91	0.38	0.39	0.14	15.662	5.873	14.134	36.709	26.943	**2.687**	12.380	65.129	59.1
CPM [14]	5.72	2.58	2.35	0.79	**10.418**	4.702	10.951	**23.951**	21.159	2.717	10.024	50.262	1.5
PST	**6.05**	**2.64**	**2.48**	**0.92**	10.575	**4.127**	**10.842**	24.511	**19.665**	2.772	**9.682**	**46.086**	**1.3**

4.5 Evaluation of Optical Flow Estimation

We compared PST and the state-of-the-art methods in terms of the optical flow accuracy on the test set of *MPI-Sintel* and *Kitti-2015*. Our comparison also indicates if a method uses CNN, CPU, or GPU.

Table 3 shows the optical flow accuracy on *MPI-Sintel* test set of 'final' pass. Among the CPU-only methods, PST is the fastest one (4.1s) and yields the lowest AEE (5.416). Compared with DCFlow, PST yields larger AEE for most cases, but a lower AEE for the case d10-60. Compared with FlowNet2 (which is a CNN method), PST generates more accurate optical flow. Compared with the other two CNN methods (PWC-Net and MRFlow), PST and DCFlow yield a larger AEE for most cases, but a lower AEE for the case s40+. This result indicates that CNN methods estimate optical flow accurately for occluded regions (occ)

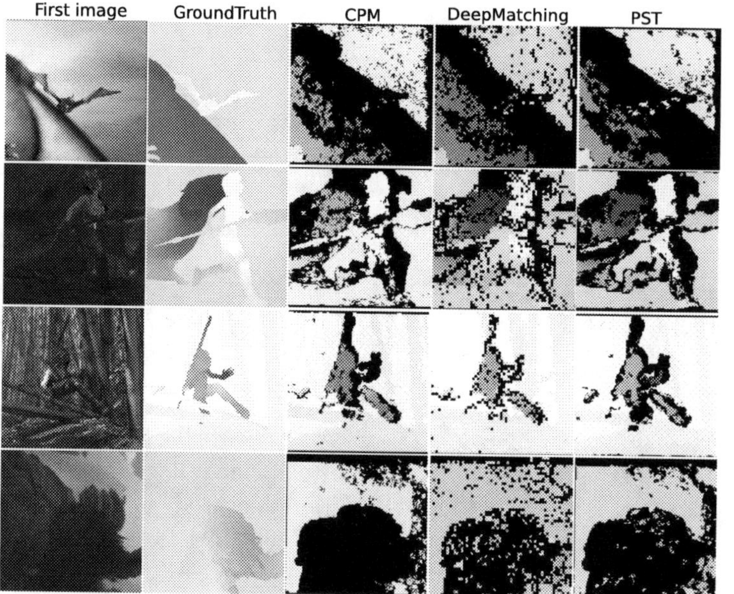

Fig. 3. Matching results of four examples in the training set of *MPI-Sintel* 'final' pass.

Table 3. Averaged end-point error (AEE) on *MPI-Sintel* test set of 'final' pass.

Method	all	noc	occ	d0-10	d10-60	d60-140	s0-10	s10-40	s40+	CPU	GPU	CNN	Time (s)
RicFlow [13]	5.620	2.765	28.907	5.146	2.366	1.679	1.088	**3.364**	33.573	✓			5
FlowFields [2]	5.810	2.621	31.799	4.851	2.232	1.682	1.157	3.739	33.890	✓			28
FullFlow [8]	5.895	2.838	30.793	4.905	2.506	1.913	1.136	3.373	35.592	✓			240
EpicFlow [23]	6.285	3.060	32.564	5.205	2.611	2.216	1.135	3.727	38.021	✓			15
CPM [14]	5.960	2.990	30.177	5.038	2.419	2.143	1.155	3.755	35.136	✓			4.3
S2F-IF [31]	5.417	2.549	28.795	4.745	2.198	1.712	1.157	3.468	31.262	✓			20–120
DCFlow [29]	**5.119**	**2.283**	**28.228**	**4.665**	2.108	**1.440**	**1.052**	3.434	**29.351**	✓	✓		8.6
PST	5.416	2.572	28.592	4.695	**2.088**	1.761	1.172	3.546	30.987	✓			**4.1**
FlowNet2 [15]	6.016	2.977	30.807	5.139	2.786	2.102	1.243	4.027	34.505		✓	✓	0.123
PWC-Net [26]	**5.042**	**2.445**	**26.221**	**4.636**	**2.087**	**1.475**	**0.799**	**2.986**	**31.070**		✓	✓	**0.03**
MRFlow [28]	5.376	2.818	26.235	5.109	2.395	1.755	0.908	3.443	32.221	✓	✓	✓	480

and low-speed regions (s0-10, s10-40). However, CNN methods do not estimate optical flow as accurately as DCFlow and PST for high-speed regions (s40+).

Table 4 shows the outlier ratio of optical flow on *Kitti-2015* test set. The evaluations are over non-occluded pixels and all pixels. PST is still the fastest CPU-only method. Using the same interpolation method, PST yields a lower percentage of flow outliers than EpicFlow and CPM for all evaluation sets. Compared with DCFlow, PST has more accurate results in foreground regions, and more errors in the background regions. In this benchmark, the background contain many occluded regions so the interpolation method affects the flow accuracy

Table 4. Flow outlier ratio in percentage on *Kitti-2015* test set.

Method	Non-occluded pixels			All pixels			CPU	GPU	CNN	Time (s)
	Fl-bg	Fl-fg	Fl-all	Fl-bg	Fl-fg	Fl-all				
CPM [14]	12.77	18.71	13.85	22.32	22.81	22.40	✓			4.2
EpicFlow [23]	15.00	24.34	16.69	25.81	28.69	26.29	✓			15
FullFlow [8]	12.97	20.58	14.35	23.09	24.79	23.37	✓			240
FlowFields+ [2]	9.69	16.82	10.98	19.51	21.26	19.80	✓			28
RicFlow [13]	9.27	**14.88**	10.29	18.73	**19.09**	18.79	✓			5
DCFlow [29]	**8.04**	19.84	**10.18**	**13.10**	23.70	**14.86**	✓	✓		8.6
PST	9.81	17.73	11.25	19.25	22.21	19.74	✓			**3.6**
PWC-Net [26]	**6.14**	**5.98**	**6.12**	**9.66**	**9.31**	**9.60**		✓	✓	**0.03**
MRFlow [28]	6.86	17.91	8.86	10.13	22.51	12.19	✓	✓	✓	480

significantly. As CNN models are efficient at modelling the relationships between adjacent structures, CNN methods (PWC-net and MRFlow) can obtain better performance than non-CNN interpolation methods for optical flow estimation on this benchmark.

5 Conclusion

This paper presents a pooling-based hierarchical model for patch matching and optical flow estimation. Features extracted from this model are robust to object size and small shape distortion. Combined with a coarse-to-fine scheme, the proposed method is powerful in tracking large displacements and small objects with distinctive motions. The proposed hierarchical model can be considered as a bridge between CNN models and hand-craft features without learning a large number of filters parameters. It is flexible in that there is no constraint on the input image size. The experiment results indicate that the proposed PST is the most efficient among several evaluated CPU-only methods, and it obtains high optical flow accuracy in *MPI-Sintel* and *Kitti-2015* benchmarks.

References

1. Achanta, R., Shaji, A., Smith, K., Lucchi, A., Fua, P., Süsstrunk, S.: SLIC superpixels compared to state-of-the-art superpixel methods. IEEE Trans. Pattern Anal. Mach. Intell. **34**(11), 2274–2281 (2012)
2. Bailer, C., Taetz, B., Stricker, D.: Flow fields: dense correspondence fields for highly accurate large displacement optical flow estimation. In: ICCV, pp. 4015–4023 (2015)
3. Barnes, C., Shechtman, E., Goldman, D.B., Finkelstein, A.: The generalized patchmatch correspondence algorithm. In: Daniilidis, K., Maragos, P., Paragios, N. (eds.) ECCV 2010. LNCS, vol. 6313, pp. 29–43. Springer, Heidelberg (2010). https://doi.org/10.1007/978-3-642-15558-1_3

4. Brox, T., Bruhn, A., Papenberg, N., Weickert, J.: High accuracy optical flow estimation based on a theory for warping. In: Pajdla, T., Matas, J. (eds.) ECCV 2004. LNCS, vol. 3024, pp. 25–36. Springer, Heidelberg (2004). https://doi.org/10.1007/978-3-540-24673-2_3
5. Brox, T., Malik, J.: Large displacement optical flow: descriptor matching in variational motion estimation. IEEE Trans. Pattern Anal. Mach. Intell. **33**, 500–513 (2011)
6. Brox, T., Malik, J., Bregler, C.: Large displacement optical flow. In: CVPR, pp. 41–48 (2009)
7. Butler, D.J., Wulff, J., Stanley, G.B., Black, M.J.: A naturalistic open source movie for optical flow evaluation. In: Fitzgibbon, A., Lazebnik, S., Perona, P., Sato, Y., Schmid, C. (eds.) ECCV 2012. LNCS, vol. 7577, pp. 611–625. Springer, Heidelberg (2012). https://doi.org/10.1007/978-3-642-33783-3_44
8. Chen, Q., Koltun, V.: Full flow: optical flow estimation by global optimization over regular grids. In: CVPR, pp. 4706–4714 (2016)
9. Dollár, P., Zitnick, C.L.: Structured forests for fast edge detection. In: ICCV, pp. 1841–1848 (2013)
10. Dong, X., Shen, J., Shao, L.: Hierarchical superpixel-to-pixel dense matching. IEEE Trans. Circ. Syst. Video Technol. **27**(12), 2518–2526 (2017)
11. Dosovitskiy, A., et al.: FlowNet: learning optical flow with convolutional networks. In: ICCV, pp. 2758–2766 (2015)
12. He, K., Sun, J.: Computing nearest-neighbor fields via propagation-assisted KD-trees. In: CVPR, pp. 111–118 (2012)
13. Hu, Y., Li, Y., Song, R.: Robust interpolation of correspondences for large displacement optical flow. In: CVPR, vol. 2017-Janua, pp. 4791–4799 (2017)
14. Hu, Y., Song, R., Li, Y.: Efficient coarse-to-fine patchmatch for large displacement optical flow. In: CVPR, pp. 5704–5712 (2016)
15. Ilg, E., Mayer, N., Saikia, T., Keuper, M., Dosovitskiy, A., Brox, T.: Flownet 2.0: evolution of optical flow estimation with deep networks. In: CVPR, pp. 1–8 (2017)
16. Liu, C., Yuen, J., Member, S., Torralba, A.: SIFT flow: dense correspondence across scenes and its applications. IEEE Trans. Pattern Anal. Mach. Intell. **33**(5), 978–994 (2011)
17. Liu, C., Yuen, J., Torralba, A., Sivic, J., Freeman, W.T.: SIFT flow: dense correspondence across different scenes. In: Forsyth, D., Torr, P., Zisserman, A. (eds.) ECCV 2008. LNCS, vol. 5304, pp. 28–42. Springer, Heidelberg (2008). https://doi.org/10.1007/978-3-540-88690-7_3
18. Lu, J., Li, Y., Yang, H., Min, D., Eng, W., Do, M.N.: PatchMatch filter: edge-aware filtering meets randomized search for visual correspondence. IEEE Trans. Pattern Anal. Mach. Intell. **39**(9), 1866–1879 (2017)
19. Mayer, N., et al.: A large dataset to train convolutional networks for disparity, optical flow, and scene flow estimation. In: CVPR, pp. 4040–4048 (2015)
20. Menze, M., Heipke, C., Geiger, A.: Joint 3D estimation of vehicles and scene flow. In: ISPRS Workshops, pp. 427–434 (2015)
21. Menze, M., Heipke, C., Geiger, A.: Object scene flow. ISPRS J. Photogrammetry Remote Sens. **140**, 60–76 (2018)
22. Ranjan, A., Black, M.J.: Optical flow estimation using a spatial pyramid network. In: CVPR, pp. 1–8 (2017)
23. Revaud, J., Weinzaepfel, P., Harchaoui, Z., Schmid, C.: Epicflow: edge-preserving interpolation of correspondences for optical flow. In: CVPR, pp. 1164–1172 (2015)
24. Revaud, J., Weinzaepfel, P., Harchaoui, Z., Schmid, C.: Deepmatching: hierarchical deformable dense matching. Int. J. Comput. Vis. **120**, 300–323 (2016)

25. Sevilla-Lara, L., Sun, D., Learned-Miller, E.G., Black, M.J.: Optical flow estimation with channel constancy. In: Fleet, D., Pajdla, T., Schiele, B., Tuytelaars, T. (eds.) ECCV 2014. LNCS, vol. 8689, pp. 423–438. Springer, Cham (2014). https://doi.org/10.1007/978-3-319-10590-1_28
26. Sun, D., Yang, X., Liu, M.Y., Kautz, J.: PWC-Net: CNNs for optical flow using pyramid, warping, and cost volume. In: CVPR, pp. 1–8 (2017)
27. Unger, M., Werlberger, M., Pock, T., Bischof, H.: Joint motion estimation and segmentation of complex scenes with label costs and occlusion modeling. In: CVPR, pp. 1878–1885 (2012)
28. Wulff, J., Sevilla-Lara, L., Black, M.J.: Optical flow in mostly rigid scenes. In: CVPR, pp. 6911–6920 (2017)
29. Xu, J., Ranftl, R., Koltun, V.: Accurate optical flow via direct cost volume processing. In: CVPR, pp. 1289–1297 (2017)
30. Yang, J., Li, H.: Dense, accurate optical flow estimation with piecewise parametric model. In: CVPR, pp. 1019–1027 (2015)
31. Yang, Y., Soatto, S.: S2F: slow-to-fast interpolator flow. In: CVPR, pp. 3767–3776 (2017)
32. Yao, J., Boben, M., Fidler, S., Urtasun, R.: Real-time coarse-to-fine topologically preserving segmentation. In: CVPR, pp. 2947–2955 (2015)

Oral Session O4: Detection, Segmentation, and Action

Unseen Object Segmentation in Videos via Transferable Representations

Yi-Wen Chen[1,2(✉)], Yi-Hsuan Tsai[3], Chu-Ya Yang[1], Yen-Yu Lin[1], and Ming-Hsuan Yang[4,5]

[1] Academia Sinica, Taipei, Taiwan
wenz116@iis.sinica.edu.tw
[2] National Taiwan University, Taipei, Taiwan
[3] NEC Laboratories America, Princeton, USA
[4] University of California, Merced, Merced, USA
[5] Google Cloud, Sunnyvale, USA

Abstract. In order to learn object segmentation models in videos, conventional methods require a large amount of pixel-wise ground truth annotations. However, collecting such supervised data is time-consuming and labor-intensive. In this paper, we exploit existing annotations in source images and transfer such visual information to segment videos with unseen object categories. Without using any annotations in the target video, we propose a method to jointly mine useful segments and learn feature representations that better adapt to the target frames. The entire process is decomposed into two tasks: (1) solving a submodular function for selecting object-like segments, and (2) learning a CNN model with a transferable module for adapting seen categories in the source domain to the unseen target video. We present an iterative update scheme between two tasks to self-learn the final solution for object segmentation. Experimental results on numerous benchmark datasets show that the proposed method performs favorably against the state-of-the-art algorithms.

1 Introduction

Nowadays, video data can be easily accessed and visual analytics has become an important task in computer vision. In this line of research, video object segmentation is one of the effective approaches to understand visual contents that facilitates various applications, such as video editing, content retrieval, and object identification. While conventional methods rely on the supervised learning strategy to effectively localize and segment objects in videos, collecting such ground truth annotations is expensive and cannot scale well to a large amount of videos.

Electronic supplementary material The online version of this chapter (https://doi.org/10.1007/978-3-030-20870-7_38) contains supplementary material, which is available to authorized users.

C. V. Jawahar et al. (Eds.): ACCV 2018, LNCS 11364, pp. 615–631, 2019.
https://doi.org/10.1007/978-3-030-20870-7_38

Recently, weakly-supervised methods for video object segmentation [31,40–42] have been developed to relax the need for annotations where only class-level labels are required. These approaches have significantly reduced the labor-intensive step of collecting pixel-wise training data on target categories. However, these categories are pre-defined and thus the trained model cannot be directly applied to unseen categories in other videos, and annotating additional categories would require more efforts, which is not scalable in practice. In this paper, we propose an algorithm to reduce efforts in both annotating pixel-level and class-level ground truths for unseen categories in videos.

To this end, we make use of existing pixel-level annotations in images from the PASCAL VOC dataset [4] with pre-defined categories, and design a framework to transfer this knowledge to unseen videos. That is, the proposed method is able to learn useful representations for segmentation from the data in the image domain and adapt these representations to segment objects in videos regardless of whether their categories are covered in the PASCAL VOC dataset. Thus, while performing video object segmentation, our algorithm does not require annotations in any forms, such as pixel-level or class-level ground truths.

We formulate the object segmentation problem for unseen categories as a joint objective of mining useful segments from videos while learning transferable knowledge from image representations. Since annotations are not provided in videos, we design an energy function to discover object-like segments in videos based on the feature representations learned from the image data. We then utilize these discovered segments to refine feature representations in a convolutional neural network (CNN) model, while a transferable module is developed to learn the relationships between multiple seen categories in images and the unseen category in videos. By jointly considering both energy functions for mining better segments while learning transferable representations, we develop an iterative optimization method to self-guide the video object segmentation process. We also note that the proposed framework is flexible as we can input either weakly-labeled or unlabeled videos.

To validate the proposed method, we conduct experiments on benchmark datasets for video object segmentation. First, we evaluate our method on the DAVIS 2016 dataset [25], where the object categories may be different from the seen categories on PASCAL VOC. Based on this setting, we compare with the state-of-the-art methods for object segmentation via transfer learning, including approaches that use the NLP-based GloVe embeddings [24] and a decoupled network [10]. In addition, we show baseline results with and without the proposed iterative self-learning strategy to demonstrate its effectiveness. Second, we adopt the weakly-supervised setting on the YouTube-Objects dataset [28] and show that the proposed method performs favorably against the state-of-the-art algorithms in terms of visual quality and accuracy.

The contributions of this work are summarized as follows. First, we propose a framework for object segmentation in unlabeled videos through a self-supervised learning method. Second, we develop a joint formulation to mine useful segments while adapting the feature representations to the target videos. Third, we design a CNN module that can transfer knowledge from multiple seen categories in images to the unseen category in videos.

2 Related Work

Video Object Segmentation. Video object segmentation aims to separate foreground objects from the background. Conventional methods utilize object proposals [15,17,26] or graphical models [21,39], while recent approaches focus on learning CNN models from image sequences with frame-by-frame pixel-level ground truth annotations to achieve the state-of-the-art performance [3,12,37]. For CNN-based methods, motion cues are usually used to effectively localize objects. Jain et al. [12] utilize a two-stream network by jointly considering appearance and motion information. The SegFlow method [3] further shows that jointly learning segmentation and optical flow in videos enhances both performance. Another line of research is to fine-tune the model based on the object mask in the first frame [1,14] and significantly improves the segmentation quality. However, in addition to annotations of the first frame in target videos [1,14], these methods require pre-training on videos with frame-by-frame pixel-level annotations [3,37] or bounding box ground truths [12] to obtain better foreground segmentation. In contrast, the proposed algorithm uses only a smaller number of existing annotations from the image dataset and transfers the feature representations to unlabeled videos for object segmentation. In addition, our method is flexible for the weakly-supervised learning setting, which cannot be achieved by the above approaches.

Object Segmentation in Weakly-supervised Videos. To reduce the need of pixel-level annotations, weakly-supervised methods have been developed to facilitate the segmentation process, where only class-level labels are required in videos. Numerous approaches are proposed to collect useful semantic segments by training segment-based classifiers [34] or ranking supervoxels [45]. However, these methods rely on the quality of generated segment proposals and may produce inaccurate results when taking low-quality segments as the input. Zhang et al. [44] propose to utilize object detectors integrated with object proposals to refine segmentations in videos. Furthermore, Tsai et al. [40] develop a co-segmentation framework by linking object tracklets from all the videos and improve the result. Recently, the SPFTN method [42] utilizes a self-paced learning scheme to fine-tune segmentation results from object proposals. Different from the above algorithms that only target on a pre-defined set of categories, our approach further extends this setting to videos without any labels for unseen object categories.

Transfer Learning for Object Recognition. Using cross-domain data for unsupervised learning has been explored in domain adaptation [6,7,23,30]. While domain adaptation methods make the assumption that the same categories are shared across different domains, transfer learning approaches focus on transferring knowledge between categories. Numerous transfer learning methods have been developed for object classification [38] and detection [9,18]. Similar efforts

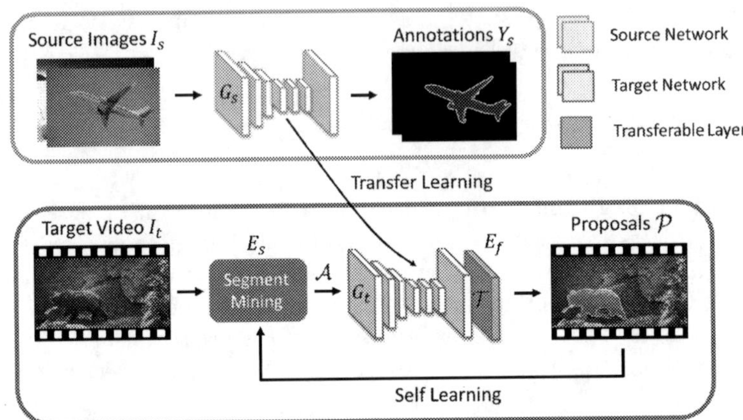

Fig. 1. Overview of the proposed algorithm. Given a set of source images $\mathcal{I}_s$ with semantic segmentation annotations Y_s, we first train a source CNN model G_s. To predict object segmentations on a target video $\mathcal{I}_t$ without knowing any annotations, we initialize the target network G_t from the parameters in G_s and perform adaptation via a transferable layer $\mathcal{T}$. We optimize the function E_s for selecting object-like segments $\mathcal{A}$ from proposals $\mathcal{P}$ and adapt feature representations in the CNN model via optimizing E_f. The entire self-learning process is performed via iteratively updating two energy functions to obtain the final segmentation results.

have been made for object segmentation. Hong et al. [10] propose a weakly-supervised semantic segmentation method by exploiting pixel-level annotations from different categories. Recently, Hu et al. [11] design a weighted transform function to transfer knowledge between the detected bounding boxes and instance segments. In this work, we share the similar motivation with [10] but remove the assumption of weak supervisions. To the best of our knowledge, this work is the first attempt for video object segmentation by transferring knowledge from annotated images to unlabeled videos between unshared categories.

3 Algorithmic Overview

3.1 Overview of the Proposed Framework

We first describe the problem context of this work. Given a number of source images $\mathcal{I}_s = \{I_s^1, ..., I_s^N\}$ with pixel-level semantic segmentation annotations $Y_s = \{y_s^1, ..., y_s^N\}$ and the target sequence $\mathcal{I}_t = \{I_t^1, ..., I_t^M\}$ without any labels, our objective is to develop a self-supervised learning algorithm that segments the object in $\mathcal{I}_t$ by transferring knowledge from $\mathcal{I}_s$ to $\mathcal{I}_t$. In this work, the object category in $\mathcal{I}_t$ is allowed to be arbitrary. It can be either covered by or different from those in $\mathcal{I}_s$.

To this end, we propose a method with two components: (1) a ranking module for mining segment proposals, and (2) a CNN model for learning transferable feature representations. Figure 1 illustrates these two components in the proposed framework. We first train a source CNN model G_s using $\mathcal{I}_s$ and Y_s as the input and the desired output, respectively. Then we initialize the target network G_t from the parameters in G_s, where this target network can generate segment proposals $\mathcal{P}$ on the target video $\mathcal{I}_t$. To find a set of object-like proposals among $\mathcal{P}$, we then develop an energy function to re-rank these proposals based on their objectness scores and mutual relationships. With the selected proposals that have higher object-like confidence, we further refine the feature representations in the target network. Since $\mathcal{I}_s$ and $\mathcal{I}_t$ may not share common object categories, we design a layer $\mathcal{T}$ that enables cross-category knowledge transfer, and append it to the target network. The entire process can be formulated as a joint optimization problem with the objective function as described below.

3.2 Objective Function

Our goal is to find high-quality segment proposals $\mathcal{P}$ from the target video $\mathcal{I}_t$ that can guide the network to learn feature representations $\mathcal{F}$ for better segmenting the given video $\mathcal{I}_t$. We carry out this task by jointly optimizing an energy function E that accounts for segment proposals $\mathcal{P}$ and features $\mathcal{F}$:

$$\max_{\mathcal{A},\theta} E(\mathcal{I}_t, \mathcal{P}, \mathcal{F}; \mathcal{A}, \theta) = \max_{\mathcal{A},\theta} E_s(\mathcal{P}, \mathcal{F}; \mathcal{A}) + E_f(\mathcal{I}_t, \mathcal{A}; \theta), \quad (1)$$

where E_s is the energy for selecting a set of high-quality segments $\mathcal{A}$ from the proposals $\mathcal{P}$ based on the features $\mathcal{F}$, while θ is the parameters of the CNN model that aims to optimize E_f and learn feature representations $\mathcal{F}$ from the selected proposals $\mathcal{A}$. Details of each energy function and the optimization process are described in the following section.

4 Transferring Visual Information for Segmentation

In this section, we describe the details of the proposed energy functions for mining segments and learning feature representations, respectively. The segment mining step is formulated as a submodular optimization problem, while the feature learning process is completed through a CNN with a transferable module. After introducing both energy functions, we present an iterative optimization scheme to jointly maximize the objective (1).

4.1 Mining Segment Proposals

Given a target video $\mathcal{I}_t$, we can generate frame-by-frame object segmentations by applying the CNN model pre-trained on the source images $\mathcal{I}_s$. However, these segments may contain many false positives that do not well cover objects. Thus, we aim to select high-quality segments and eliminate noisy ones from the generated object segmentations. The challenging part lies in that there are no ground truth annotations in the target video, and thus we cannot train a classifier to guide the selection process.

Motivated by the co-segmentation method [40], we observe that high-quality segments have higher mutual relationships. As a result, we gather all the predicted segments from the target video and construct a graph to link each segment. We then formulate segment mining as a submodular optimization problem, aiming to select a subset of object-like segments that share higher similarities.

Graph Construction on Segments. We first feed the target video $\mathcal{I}_t$ into the CNN model frame-by-frame and obtain a set of segment proposals $\mathcal{P}$, where each proposal is a connected-component in the predicted segmentation. Then we construct a graph $G = (\mathcal{V}, \mathcal{E})$ on the set $\mathcal{P}$, where each vertex $v \in \mathcal{V}$ is a segment, and each edge $e \in \mathcal{E}$ models the pairwise relationship between two segments. Our goal is to find a subset $\mathcal{A}$ within $\mathcal{P}$ that contains proposals with higher object-like confidence.

Submodular Function. We design a submodular function to find segments that meet the following criteria: (1) objects from the same category share similar features, (2) a true object has a higher response from the output of the CNN model, and (3) an object usually moves differently from the background area in the video. Therefore, we formulate the objective function for selecting object-like segments by a facility location term $\mathcal{H}$ [16] and a unary term $\mathcal{U}$. The former computes the similarity between the selected segments, while the latter estimates the probability of each selected segment being a true object. Both terms are defined based on the segment proposals $\mathcal{P}$ and the adopted feature representation $\mathcal{F}$. First, we define the facility location term as:

$$\mathcal{H}(\mathcal{P}, \mathcal{F}; \mathcal{A}) = \sum_{i \in \mathcal{A}} \sum_{j \in \mathcal{V}} W(v_i, v_j) - \sum_{i \in \mathcal{A}} \phi_i, \tag{2}$$

where W denotes the pairwise relationship between a potential facility v_i and a vertex v_j, while ϕ_i is the cost to open a facility, which is fixed to a constant α. We define W as the similarity between two segments in order to encourage the submodular function to choose a facility v_i that is similar to v_j. To estimate this similarity, we represent each segment as a feature vector and compute their inner product of the two vectors. To form the feature vector for each segment, we draw feature maps from the CNN model (**conv1** to **conv5**) and perform the global average pooling on each segment. It is the adopted feature representation $\mathcal{F}$ in this work. In addition to the facility location term, we employ a unary term to evaluate the quality of segments:

$$\mathcal{U}(\mathcal{P}, \mathcal{F}; \mathcal{A}) = \lambda_o \sum_{i \in \mathcal{A}} \Phi_o(i) + \lambda_m \sum_{i \in \mathcal{A}} \Phi_m(i), \tag{3}$$

where $\Phi_o(i)$ is the objectness score that measures the probability of segment i being a true object, and $\Phi_m(i)$ is the motion score that estimates the motion difference between segment i and the background region. λ_o and λ_m are the weights for the two terms, respectively.

The objectness score $\Phi_o(i)$ is calculated by averaging the probability map of the CNN output layer on all the pixels within the segment. For the motion score $\Phi_m(i)$, we first compute the optical flow [19] for two consecutive frames, and then we utilize the minimum barrier distance [33,43] to convert the optical flow into a saliency map, where the larger distance represents a larger motion difference with respect to the background region.

Formulation for Segment Mining. Our goal is to find a subset $\mathcal{A}$ within $\mathcal{P}$ containing segments that are similar to each other and have higher object-like confidence. Therefore, we combine the facility location term $\mathcal{H}$ and the unary term $\mathcal{U}$ as the energy E_s in (1):

$$E_s(\mathcal{P}, \mathcal{F}; \mathcal{A}) = \mathcal{H}(\mathcal{P}, \mathcal{F}; \mathcal{A}) + \mathcal{U}(\mathcal{P}, \mathcal{F}; \mathcal{A}). \tag{4}$$

We also note that the linear combination of two non-negative terms preserves the submodularity [46].

4.2 Learning Transferable Feature Representations

Given the selected set of object-like segment proposals, the ensuing task is to learn better feature representations based on these segments. To this end, we propose to use a CNN model fine-tuned on these segments via a self-learning scheme. However, since our target video may have a different set of object categories from those in the source domain, we further develop a transfer learning method where a transferable layer is augmented to the CNN model. With the proposed layer, our network is able to transfer knowledge from seen categories to the unseen category, without the need of any supervision in the target video.

Inspired by the observation that an unseen object category can be represented by a series of seen objects [29], we develop a transferable layer that approximates an unseen category as a linear combination of seen ones in terms of the output feature maps. In the following, we first present our CNN objective for learning the feature representations based on the selected segment proposals. Then we introduce the details of the proposed layer for transferring knowledge from the source domain to the target one.

Objective Function. Given the target video $\mathcal{I}_t$ and selected segment proposals $\mathcal{A}$ as described in Sect. 4.1, we use $\mathcal{A}$ as our pseudo ground truths and optimize the target network G_t with parameters θ_g to obtain better feature representations that match the target video. Specifically, we define the energy function E_f in (1) as:

$$E_f(\mathcal{I}_t, \mathcal{A}; \theta_g, \theta_{\mathcal{T}}) = -\mathcal{L}(\mathcal{T}(G_t(\mathcal{I}_t)), \mathcal{A}), \tag{5}$$

where $\theta_{\mathcal{T}}$ is the parameters of the transferable layer $\mathcal{T}$ and $\mathcal{L}$ is the cross-entropy function to measure the loss between the network prediction $\mathcal{T}(G_t(\mathcal{I}_t))$ and the pseudo ground truth $\mathcal{A}$. We also note that, we use the minus sign for the loss function $\mathcal{L}$ to match the maximization formulation in (1).

Learning Transferable Knowledge. Suppose there are C_s categories in the source domain, we aim to transfer a source network G_s pre-trained on the source images $\mathcal{I}_s$ to the target video. To achieve this, we first initialize the target network G_t using the parameters in G_s. Given the target video $\mathcal{I}_t$, we can generate frame-wise feature maps $R = G_t(\mathcal{I}_t) = \{r_c\}_{c=1}^{C_s}$ through the network with C_s channels, where r_c is the output map of source category c. Since the target category is unknown, we then approximate the desired output map, r, for the unseen category as a linear combination of these seen categories through the proposed transferable layer $\mathcal{T}$:

$$r = \mathcal{T}(R) = \sum_{c=1}^{C_s} w_c \, r_c, \tag{6}$$

where w_c is the weight of the seen category c. Specifically, the proposed transferable layer $\mathcal{T}$ can be performed via a 1×1 convolutional layer with C_s channels, in which the parameter of channel c in $\theta_{\mathcal{T}}$ corresponds to w_c.

Since w_c is not supervised by any annotations from the target video, the initialization of w_c is critical for obtaining a better combination of feature maps from the seen categories. Thus, we initialize w_c by calculating the similarity between each source category c and the target video. For each image in the source and target domains, we extract its feature maps from the **fc7** layer of the network and compute a 4096-dimensional feature vector on the predicted segment via global average pooling. By representing each image as a feature vector, we measure the similarity score between source and target images by their inner product. Finally, the initialized weight w_c^{init} for the category c can be obtained by averaging largest scores on each target frame with respect to the source images:

$$w_c^{init} = \frac{1}{|\mathcal{I}_t|} \sum_{i=1}^{|\mathcal{I}_t|} \max_j \langle \mathcal{F}_t^i, \mathcal{F}_{s,c}^j \rangle, \tag{7}$$

where $|\mathcal{I}_t|$ is the number of frames in the target video, $\mathcal{F}_t^i \in \mathbb{R}^{4096}$ is the feature vector of the ith frame of $\mathcal{I}_t$, and $\mathcal{F}_{s,c}^j \in \mathbb{R}^{4096}$ is the feature vector of the jth image of source category c.

4.3 Joint Formulation and Model Training

Based on the formulations to mine segments (4) and learn feature representations (5), we jointly solve the two objectives, i.e., E_s and E_f, in (1) by:

$$\begin{aligned}\max_{\mathcal{A},\theta} E(\mathcal{I}_t, \mathcal{P}, \mathcal{F}; \mathcal{A}, \theta) &= \max_{\mathcal{A},\theta} E_s(\mathcal{P}, \mathcal{F}; \mathcal{A}) + E_f(\mathcal{I}_t, \mathcal{A}; \theta) \\ &= \max_{\mathcal{A},\theta_g,\theta_{\mathcal{T}}} [\mathcal{H}(\mathcal{P}, \mathcal{F}; \mathcal{A}) + \mathcal{U}(\mathcal{P}, \mathcal{F}; \mathcal{A})] - \mathcal{L}(\mathcal{T}(G_t(\mathcal{I}_t)), \mathcal{A}).\end{aligned} \tag{8}$$

To optimize (8), we decompose the process into two sub-problems: (1) solving a submodular function for segment mining to generate $\mathcal{A}$, and (2) training a

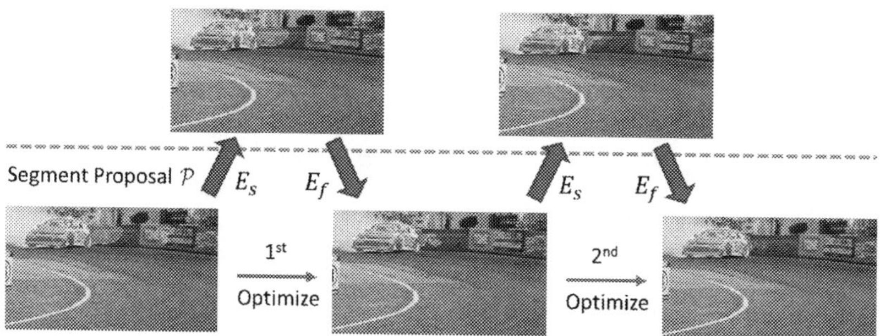

Fig. 2. Sample results of iteratively optimizing E_s and E_f. Starting from an initial set of proposals $\mathcal{P}$, we solve E_s to obtain object-like segments $\mathcal{A}$ as our pseudo ground truths to optimize E_f. By iteratively updating both energy functions, our algorithm gradually improves the quality of $\mathcal{P}$ and $\mathcal{A}$ to obtain the final segmentation results.

CNN model that optimizes θ_g and $\theta_{\mathcal{T}}$ for learning transferable representations. We adopt an iterative procedure to alternately optimize the two sub-problems. The initialization strategy and the optimization of the two sub-problems are described below.

Initialization. We first pre-train a source network G_s on the PASCAL VOC training set [4] with 20 object categories. We then initialize the target network G_t from parameters in G_s and the transferable layer $\mathcal{T}$ as described in Sect. 4.2. To obtain an initial set of segment proposals, we forward the target video $\mathcal{I}_t$ to the target model G_t with $\mathcal{T}$ and generate segments $\mathcal{P}$ with their features $\mathcal{F}$.

Fix E_f and Optimize E_s. We first fix the network parameters θ and optimize $\mathcal{A}$ in E_s of (8). We adopt a greedy algorithm similar to [40]. Starting from an empty set of $\mathcal{A}$, we add an initial element $a \in \mathcal{V}\backslash\mathcal{A}$ to $\mathcal{A}$ that gives the largest energy gain. The process is then repeated and stops when one of the following conditions is satisfied: (1) the number of selected proposals reaches a threshold, i.e., $|\mathcal{A}| > N_{\mathcal{A}}$, and (2) the ratio of the energy gain between two rounds is below a threshold, i.e., $\mathcal{D}(\mathcal{A}^i) < \beta \cdot \mathcal{D}(\mathcal{A}^{i-1})$, where $\mathcal{D}(\mathcal{A}^i)$ stands for the energy gain, i.e., difference of E_s between two rounds during the optimization process, and β is the ratio.

Fix E_s and Optimize E_f. Once obtaining $\mathcal{A}$ as the pseudo ground truths, we fix $\mathcal{A}$ and optimize the network with the transferable layer, i.e., θ_g and $\theta_{\mathcal{T}}$, in E_f of (8). We alter the problem to a task that minimizes the network loss $\mathcal{L}$ in an end-to-end fashion, jointly for θ_g and $\theta_{\mathcal{T}}$ using the SGD method.

Iterative Optimization. To obtain the final $\mathcal{A}$, θ_g and $\theta_{\mathcal{T}}$, instead of directly solving (8) for optimal solutions, we solve it via an iterative updating scheme between E_s and E_f until convergence. In practice, we measure the intersection-over-union (IoU) of selected segment proposals between two iterations. The opti-

Algorithm 1. Unseen Object Segmentation

Source Image: $\mathcal{I}_s$, Y_s
Target Video: $\mathcal{I}_t$
Initialization: pre-trained G_s on source inputs, $G_t \leftarrow G_s$, w_c^{init} via (7)
$(\mathcal{P}, \mathcal{F}) \leftarrow \mathcal{T}(G_t(\mathcal{I}_t))$
while $\mathcal{P}$ not converged **do**
  $\mathcal{A}^0 \leftarrow \emptyset$, $i \leftarrow 1$
  loop
    $a^* = \arg\max_{\{\mathcal{A}^i \in \mathcal{V}\}} E_s(\mathcal{P}, \mathcal{F}; \mathcal{A}^i)$, where $\mathcal{A}^i \leftarrow \mathcal{A}^{i-1} \cup a$, $a \in \mathcal{V} \backslash \mathcal{A}$
    if $|\mathcal{A}| > N_{\mathcal{A}}$ or $\mathcal{D}(\mathcal{A}^i) < \beta \cdot \mathcal{D}(\mathcal{A}^{i-1})$ when $i \geq 2$ **then**
      break
    end if
    $\mathcal{A}^i \leftarrow \mathcal{A}^{i-1} \cup a^*$, $i \leftarrow i + 1$
  end loop
  $\mathcal{A} \leftarrow \mathcal{A}^i$
  Optimize E_f: $(\theta_g, \theta_{\mathcal{T}}) \leftarrow \min \mathcal{L}(\mathcal{T}(G_t(\mathcal{I}_t)), \mathcal{A})$
  $(\mathcal{P}, \mathcal{F}) \leftarrow \mathcal{T}(G_t(\mathcal{I}_t))$
end while
Output: object segmentation $\mathcal{P}$ of $\mathcal{I}_t$

mization process ends when the IoU is larger than a threshold (e.g., 90%), showing that the set of $\mathcal{A}$ becomes stable. Figure 2 shows one example of gradually improved $\mathcal{P}$ and $\mathcal{A}$ via iteratively updating E_s and E_f. The overall process is summarized in Algorithm 1.

5 Experimental Results

In this section, we first present implementation details of the proposed method, and then we show experimental results on numerous benchmark datasets. In addition, ablation studies for various components in the algorithm are conducted. The source code and trained models will be made available to the public. More results are presented in the supplementary material.

5.1 Implementation Details

In the submodular function for segment mining, we set $\alpha = 1$ for the facility location term in (2), and $\lambda_o = 20$, $\lambda_m = 35$ for the unary term in (3). During the submodular optimization in (4), we use $N_{\mathcal{A}} = 0.8 \cdot |\mathcal{P}|$ and $\beta = 0.8$. All the parameters are fixed in all the experiments. For training the CNN model in (5), we employ various fully convolutional networks (FCNs) [20] including the VGG-16 [32] and ResNet-101 [8] architectures for both the source and target networks using the Caffe library. The learning rate, momentum and batch size are set as 10^{-14}, 0.99, and 1, respectively. To further refine segmentation results, we average the responses from the CNN output and a motion prior that is already computed in the motion term of (3) to account for both the appearance and temporal information.

Table 1. IoU of the selected segments with different weights of the motion term on the DAVIS dataset.

λ_m	0	5	15	25	35	45
Avg. IoU	57.2	57.4	60.5	60.6	61.0	60.3

Table 2. Results on the DAVIS 2016 dataset with categories excluded from the PASCAL VOC dataset.

Methods	bear	bswan	camel	eleph	goat	malw	rhino	Avg.
CVOS [35]	86.4	42.2	85.0	49.4	7.4	24.5	52.0	49.6
MSG [27]	85.1	52.6	75.6	68.9	73.5	4.5	90.2	64.3
FST [22]	89.8	73.2	56.2	82.4	55.4	8.7	77.6	63.3
NLC [5]	90.7	87.5	76.8	51.8	1.0	76.1	68.2	64.6
LMP [36]	69.8	50.9	78.3	78.9	75.1	38.5	76.8	66.9
TransferNet [10]	73.7	**83.4**	65.5	**76.1**	78.1	17.9	42.4	62.4
Ours (GloVe)	82.6	67.2	68.8	61.2	70.4	**64.7**	32.0	63.8
Ours (init)	80.3	75.6	70.9	70.4	83.1	40.9	57.7	68.4
Ours (opt)	88.8	80.6	68.6	71.8	82.4	43.8	67.3	71.9
Ours (final)	**89.8**	76.7	**72.0**	73.8	**83.3**	41.6	**71.0**	**72.6**
ARP [15]	**92**	88.1	**90.3**	84.2	77.6	58.3	**88.4**	82.7
FSEG [12]	91.5	89.5	76.4	**86.2**	84.1	83.3	77.6	84.1
Ours (ResNet)	91.8	**90.3**	77.5	85.7	**84.8**	**84.9**	86.0	**85.9**

5.2 DAVIS Dataset

We first conduct experiments on the DAVIS 2016 benchmark dataset [25]. Since our goal is to transfer the knowledge from seen categories in images to unseen objects in the video, we manually select all the videos with object categories that are different from the 20 categories in the PASCAL VOC dataset. In the following, we first conduct ablation studies and experiments to validate the proposed method. Second, we show that our algorithm can be applied under various settings on the entire set of the DAVIS 2016 dataset.

Impact of the Motion Term. One critical component of our framework is to mine useful segments for the further CNN model training step. In the submodular function of (3), we incorporate a motion term that accounts for object movements in the video. To validate its effectiveness, we fix the weight $\lambda_o = 20$ for the appearance and vary the weight λ_m for the motion term. In Table 1, we show the IoU of the selected segment proposals via solving (4) under various values of λ_m. The results show that the IoU is gradually improved when increasing the motion weight, which indicates that the quality of selected segments becomes better, and hence we use $\lambda_m = 35$ in all the following experiments.

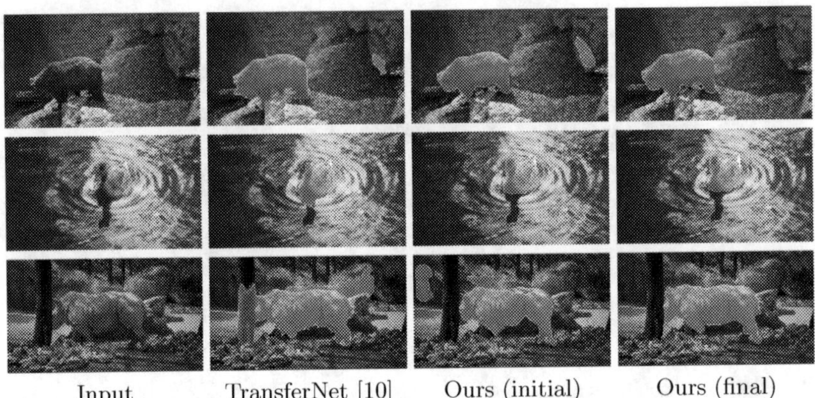

Fig. 3. Sample results on the DAVIS dataset with categories excluded from the PASCAL VOC dataset. We show that our final results are more accurate in details than the TransferNet [10] and with the noisy segments removed from the initial results.

Ablation Study. In the middle group of Table 2, we show the final segmentation results of our method using VGG-16 architecture with various baselines and settings. We first present a baseline method that uses the GloVe embeddings [24] to initialize weights, i.e., the similarity between two categories, of the transferable layer. Since the GloVe is not learned in the image domain between categories, the initialized weights may not reflect the true relationships between the seen and unseen categories, and hence the results are worse than the proposed method for initializing the transferable layer.

Furthermore, we show results at different stages, including using the model with initialization before optimizing (8), after optimization, and the final result with motion refinement. After the optimization, the IoU is improved in 5 out of 7 videos, which shows the effectiveness of the proposed self-learning scheme without using any annotations in the target video.

Overall Comparisons. In Table 2, we show the comparisons between our method and the state-of-the-art approaches. We first demonstrate the performance of our method using VGG-16 architecture. The work closest in the scope to the proposed framework is the method [10] that transfers the knowledge between two image domains with mutually exclusive categories in a weakly-supervised setting. To compare with this approach, we use the authors' public implementation and train the models with the same setting as our method. We show that our algorithm achieves better IoUs in 5 out of 7 videos and improves the overall IoU by 10.2% on average. We also note that our model with initialization already performs favorably against [10], which demonstrates that the proposed transferable layer is effective in learning knowledge from seen categories to unseen ones. Visual comparisons are presented in Fig. 3.

In addition, we present more results of video object segmentation methods in Table 2 and show that the proposed algorithm achieves better performance.

Different from existing approaches that rely on long-term trajectory [27,35] or motion saliency [5,22] to localize foreground objects, we use the proposed self-learning framework to segment unseen object categories via transfer learning. We note that the proposed method performs better than the CNN-based model [36] that utilizes synthetic videos with pixel-wise segmentation annotations.

We further employ the stronger ResNet-101 architecture and compare with state-of-the-art unsupervised video object segmentation methods. In the bottom group of Table 2, we show that our approach performs better than FSEG [12] using the same architecture and training data from PASCAL VOC, i.e., the setting of the appearance stream in FSEG [12]. In addition, compared to ARP [15] that adopts a non-learning based framework via proposal post-processing and is specifically designed for video object segmentation, our algorithm performs better and is flexible under various settings such as using weakly-supervised signals.

Results on the Entire DAVIS 2016 Dataset. In addition to performing object segmentation on unseen object categories, our method can adapt to the weakly-supervised setting by simply initializing the weights in the transferable layer as a one-hot vector, where only the known category is set to 1 and the others are 0. We evaluate this setting on the DAVIS 2016 dataset with categories shared in the PASCAL VOC dataset. Note that, we still adopt the unsupervised setting for the unseen categories. The results on the entire DAVIS 2016 dataset are shown in Table 3. In comparison with a recent weakly-supervised method [42] and the baseline model [20] (our initial result), our approach addresses the transfer learning problem and outperforms their methods by 6.5% and 6.1%, respectively.

Although the same categories are shared between the source and target domains in this setting, we can still assume that the object category is unknown in the target video. Under this fully unsupervised setting without using any pixel-wise annotations in videos during training, we show that our method improves the results of FSEG [12] and other unsupervised algorithms [5,22]. Sample results are presented in Fig. 4.

Table 3. Results on the entire DAVIS 2016 dataset.

Methods	Weak supervision			No supervision			
	SPFTN [42]	FCN [20]	Ours	FST [22]	NLC [5]	FSEG [12]	Ours
Avg. IoU	61.2	61.6	67.7	57.5	64.1	64.7	66.5

5.3 YouTube-Objects Dataset

We evaluate our method on the YouTube-Objects dataset [28] with annotations provided by [13] for 126 videos. Since this dataset contains 10 object categories that are shared with the PASCAL VOC dataset, we conduct experiments using the weakly-supervised setting. In Table 4, we compare our method with the state-of-the-art algorithms that use the class-level weak supervision. With the VGG-16 architecture, the proposed framework performs well in 6 out of 10 categories and achieves the best IoU on average. Compared to the baseline FCN model [20] used in our algorithm, there is a performance gain of 9%. In addition, while existing methods rely on training the segment classifier [34], integrating object proposals with detectors [44], co-segmentation via modeling relationships between videos [40], or self-paced fine-tuning [42], the proposed method utilizes a self-learning scheme to achieve better segmentation results. With the ResNet-101 architecture, we compare our method with DeepLab [2] and FSEG [12]. We show that the proposed method improves the performance in 6 out of 10 categories and achieves the best averaged IoU.

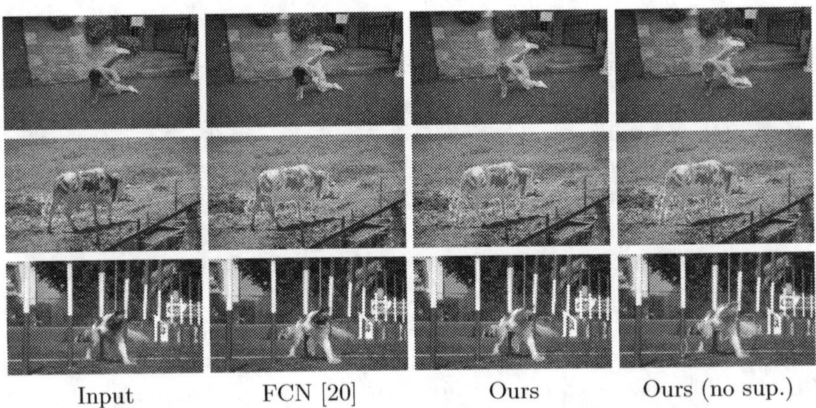

Fig. 4. Segmentation results on the DAVIS dataset with categories shared in the PASCAL VOC dataset. We show that both of our results with and without supervision have more complete object segmentations than the baseline FCN model [20] (our initial result) that uses the weak supervision.

Table 4. Results on the YouTube-Objects dataset.

Methods	aero	bird	boat	car	cat	cow	dog	horse	mbike	train	Avg.
DSA [34]	17.8	19.8	22.5	38.3	23.6	26.8	23.7	14.0	12.5	40.4	23.9
FCN [20]	68.3	65.7	55.7	76.6	52.3	50.4	55.6	52.6	35.7	55.9	56.9
DET [44]	72.4	66.6	43.0	58.9	36.4	58.2	48.7	49.6	41.4	49.3	52.4
CoSeg [40]	69.3	**76.1**	57.2	70.4	**67.7**	59.7	64.2	57.1	44.1	57.9	62.3
SPFTN [42]	**81.1**	68.8	63.4	73.8	59.7	64.5	63.4	58.2	**52.4**	45.5	63.1
Ours (VGG)	74.6	65.3	**66.9**	**79.5**	64.2	**68.3**	**67.3**	**61.7**	51.5	**59.4**	**65.9**
DeepLab [2]	80.6	67.8	66.9	73.3	55.3	61.8	63.9	45.5	54.7	56.4	62.6
FSEG [12]	83.4	60.9	**72.6**	74.5	**68.0**	69.6	69.1	**62.8**	61.9	**62.8**	68.6
Ours (ResNet)	**83.5**	**76.4**	70.0	**75.3**	65.9	**69.7**	**71.6**	54.7	**63.8**	58.7	**69.0**

6 Concluding Remarks

In this paper, we propose a self-learning framework to segment objects in unlabeled videos. By utilizing existing annotations in images, we design a model to adapt seen object categories from source images to the target video. The entire process is decomposed into two sub-problems: (1) a segment mining module to select object-like proposals, and (2) a CNN model with a transferable layer that adapts feature representations for target videos. To optimize the proposed formulation, we adopt an iterative scheme to obtain final solutions. Extensive experiments and ablation study show the effectiveness of the proposed algorithm against other state-of-the-art methods on numerous benchmark datasets.

Acknowledgments. This work is supported in part by Ministry of Science and Technology under grants MOST 105-2221-E-001-030-MY2 and MOST 107-2628-E-001-005-MY3.

References

1. Caelles, S., Maninis, K.K., Pont-Tuset, J., Leal-Taixé, L., Cremers, D., Gool, L.V.: One-shot video object segmentation. In: CVPR (2017)
2. Chen, L.C., Papandreou, G., Kokkinos, I., Murphy, K., Yuille, A.L.: Deeplab: Semantic image segmentation with deep convolutional nets, atrous convolution, and fully connected CRFs. arXiv:1606.00915 (2016)
3. Cheng, J., Tsai, Y.H., Wang, S., Yang, M.H.: Segflow: joint learning for video object segmentation and optical flow. In: ICCV (2017)
4. Everingham, M., Gool, L.J.V., Williams, C.K.I., Winn, J.M., Zisserman, A.: The Pascal visual object classes (VOC) challenge. IJCV **88**(2), 303–338 (2010)
5. Faktor, A., Irani, M.: Video segmentation by non-local consensus voting. In: BMVC (2014)
6. Ganin, Y., Lempitsky, V.: Unsupervised domain adaptation by backpropagation. In: ICML (2015)
7. Gopalan, R., Li, R., Chellappa, R.: Domain adaptation for object recognition: an unsupervised approach. In: ICCV (2011)
8. He, K., Zhang, X., Ren, S., Sun, J.: Deep residual learning for image recognition. In: CVPR (2016)
9. Hoffman, J., et al.: LSDA: large scale detection through adaptation. In: NIPS (2014)
10. Hong, S., Oh, J., Lee, H., Han, B.: Learning transferrable knowledge for semantic segmentation with deep convolutional neural network. In: CVPR (2016)
11. Hu, R., Dollár, P., He, K., Darrell, T., Girshick, R.: Learning to segment every thing. arXiv:1711.10370 (2017)
12. Jain, S., Xiong, B., Grauman, K.: FusionSeg: learning to combine motion and appearance for fully automatic segmentation of generic objects in videos. In: CVPR (2017)
13. Jain, S.D., Grauman, K.: Supervoxel-consistent foreground propagation in video. In: Fleet, D., Pajdla, T., Schiele, B., Tuytelaars, T. (eds.) ECCV 2014. LNCS, vol. 8692, pp. 656–671. Springer, Cham (2014). https://doi.org/10.1007/978-3-319-10593-2_43

14. Khoreva, A., Perazzi, F., Benenson, R., Schiele, B., Sorkine-Hornung, A.: Learning video object segmentation from static images. In: CVPR (2017)
15. Koh, Y.J., Kim, C.S.: Primary object segmentation in videos based on region augmentation and reduction. In: CVPR (2017)
16. Lazic, N., Givoni, I., Frey, B., Aarabi, P.: Floss: facility location for subspace segmentation. In: ICCV (2009)
17. Lee, Y.J., Kim, J., Grauman, K.: Key-segments for video object segmentation. In: ICCV (2011)
18. Lim, J.J., Salakhutdinov, R., Torralba, A.: Transfer learning by borrowing examples for multiclass object detection. In: NIPS (2011)
19. Liu, C.: Beyond pixels: exploring new representations and applications for motion analysis. Ph.D. thesis, MIT (2009)
20. Long, J., Shelhamer, E., Darrell, T.: Fully convolutional networks for semantic segmentation. In: CVPR (2015)
21. Märki, N., Perazzi, F., Wang, O., Sorkine-Hornung, A.: Bilateral space video segmentation. In: CVPR (2016)
22. Papazoglou, A., Ferrari, V.: Fast object segmentation in unconstrained video. In: ICCV (2013)
23. Patricia, N., Caputo, B.: Learning to learn, from transfer learning to domain adaptation: a unifying perspective. In: CVPR (2014)
24. Pennington, J., Socher, R., Manning, C.D.: Glove: Global vectors for word representation. In: EMNLP, pp. 1532–1543 (2014)
25. Perazzi, F., Pont-Tuset, J., McWilliams, B., Gool, L.V., Gross, M., Sorkine-Hornung, A.: A benchmark dataset and evaluation methodology for video object segmentation. In: CVPR (2016)
26. Perazzi, F., Wang, O., Gross, M., Sorkine-Hornung, A.: Fully connected object proposals for video segmentation. In: CVPR (2015)
27. Ochs, P., Brox, T.: Object segmentation in video: a hierarchical variational approach for turning point trajectories into dense regions. In: ICCV (2011)
28. Prest, A., Leistner, C., Civera, J., Schmid, C., Ferrari, V.: Learning object class detectors from weakly annotated video. In: CVPR (2012)
29. Rochan, M., Wang, Y.: Weakly supervised localization of novel objects using appearance transfer. In: CVPR (2015)
30. Saenko, K., Kulis, B., Fritz, M., Darrell, T.: Adapting visual category models to new domains. In: Daniilidis, K., Maragos, P., Paragios, N. (eds.) ECCV 2010. LNCS, vol. 6314, pp. 213–226. Springer, Heidelberg (2010). https://doi.org/10.1007/978-3-642-15561-1_16
31. Saleh, F.S., Aliakbarian, M.S., Salzmann, M., Petersson, L., Alvarez, J.M.: Bringing background into the foreground: making all classes equal in weakly-supervised video semantic segmentation. In: ICCV (2017)
32. Simonyan, K., Zisserman, A.: Very deep convolutional networks for large-scale image recognition. CoRR abs/1409.1556, 1187–1200 (2014)
33. Strand, R., Ciesielski, K.C., Malmberg, F., Saha, P.K.: The minimum barrier distance. CVIU **117**(4), 429–437 (2013)
34. Tang, K., Sukthankar, R., Yagnik, J., Fei-Fei, L.: Discriminative segment annotation in weakly labeled video. In: CVPR (2013)
35. Taylor, B., Karasev, V., Soatto, S.: Causal video object segmentation from persistence of occlusions. In: CVPR (2015)
36. Tokmakov, P., Alahari, K., Schmid, C.: Learning motion patterns in videos. In: CVPR (2017)

37. Tokmakov, P., Alahari, K., Schmid, C.: Learning video object segmentation with visual memory. In: ICCV (2017)
38. Tommasi, T., Orabona, F., Caputo, B.: Learning categories from few examples with multi model knowledge transfer. PAMI **36**, 928–941 (2014)
39. Tsai, Y.H., Yang, M.H., Black, M.J.: Video segmentation via object flow. In: CVPR (2016)
40. Tsai, Y.-H., Zhong, G., Yang, M.-H.: Semantic co-segmentation in videos. In: Leibe, B., Matas, J., Sebe, N., Welling, M. (eds.) ECCV 2016. LNCS, vol. 9908, pp. 760–775. Springer, Cham (2016). https://doi.org/10.1007/978-3-319-46493-0_46
41. Yan, Y., Xu, C., Cai, D., Corso, J.J.: Weakly supervised actor-action segmentation via robust multi-task ranking. In: CVPR (2017)
42. Zhang, D., Yang, L., Meng, D., Xu, D., Han, J.: SPFTN: a self-paced fine-tuning network for segmenting objects in weakly labelled videos. In: CVPR (2017)
43. Zhang, J., Sclaroff, S., Lin, Z., Shen, X., Price, B., Mech, R.: Minimum barrier salient object detection at 80 fps. In: ICCV (2015)
44. Zhang, Y., Chen, X., Li, J., Wang, C., Xia, C.: Semantic object segmentation via detection in weakly labeled video. In: CVPR (2015)
45. Zhong, G., Tsai, Y.-H., Yang, M.-H.: Weakly-supervised video scene co-parsing. In: Lai, S.-H., Lepetit, V., Nishino, K., Sato, Y. (eds.) ACCV 2016. LNCS, vol. 10111, pp. 20–36. Springer, Cham (2017). https://doi.org/10.1007/978-3-319-54181-5_2
46. Zhu, F., Jiang, Z., Shao, L.: Submodular object recognition. In: CVPR (2014)

Forget and Diversify: Regularized Refinement for Weakly Supervised Object Detection

Jeany Son[1], Daniel Kim[1,2], Solae Lee[2], Suha Kwak[2], Minsu Cho[2], and Bohyung Han[1(✉)]

[1] Computer Vision Lab., ASRI, Seoul National University, Seoul, Korea
{jeany,bhhan}@snu.ac.kr
[2] Computer Vision Lab., POSTECH, Pohang, Korea
{daniel.kim,solae,suha.kwak,mscho}@postech.ac.kr

Abstract. We study weakly supervised learning for object detectors, where training images have image-level class labels only. This problem is often addressed by multiple instance learning, where pseudo-labels of proposals are constructed from image-level weak labels and detectors are learned from the potentially noisy labels. Since existing methods train models in a discriminative manner, they typically suffer from collapsing into salient parts and also fail in localizing multiple instances within an image. To alleviate such limitations, we propose simple yet effective regularization techniques, weight reinitialization and labeling perturbations, which prevent overfitting to noisy labels by forgetting biased weights. We also introduce a graph-based mode-seeking technique that identifies multiple object instances in a principled way. The combination of the two proposed techniques reduces overfitting observed frequently in weakly supervised setting, and greatly improves object localization performance in standard benchmarks.

Keywords: Weakly supervised learning · Object detection · Regularization

1 Introduction

Object detection algorithms recently demonstrate remarkable performance thanks to advances of deep neural network technologies [5,12,13,24,27,28,30] and well-established datasets provided with bounding box annotations [11,20, 23]. Despite their great success, many object detection algorithms still suffer from a critical limitation caused by lack of training examples with proper annotations. In particular, due to substantial cost for bounding box labeling and inherent skewness of training data distributions, existing datasets for object detection are often insufficient in their quantity and diversity for majority of classes. This fact incurs overfitting to datasets and damages generalization performance of models.

C. V. Jawahar et al. (Eds.): ACCV 2018, LNCS 11364, pp. 632–648, 2019.
https://doi.org/10.1007/978-3-030-20870-7_39

Weakly supervised object detection (WSOD) has been studied as a solution to the above issues [1,2,4,21,22,39]. The primary goal of this task is to train object detectors using image-level class labels only. The limitations of the standard object detection algorithms can be alleviated by weakly supervised approaches because image-level class labels are readily available in several existing large-scale datasets for image classification, *e.g.* ImageNet [6], or easily obtainable due to their low annotation cost. However, learning object detectors based only on image-level class labels is challenging because the labels indicate presence or absence of each object class without localization information of objects.

Many recent weakly supervised object detection algorithms rely heavily on weakly supervised deep detection network (WSDDN) [2]. This approach identifies relevant bounding boxes to individual classes by applying softmax operations to score matrices across object proposals and candidate class labels. The performance of this method has been improved by adding a few refinement layers [39]. However, WSDDN and its extensions have the following critical limitations. First, as in many other weakly supervised object detection techniques, noisy annotations estimated by object detectors based on weak labels may make models converge to bad local optima in training. Second, due to characteristics of softmax functions, the method is prone to identify only a single target class and object instance in an input image. Consequently, they are not effective to handle images with multiple objects corresponding to diverse class labels.

To alleviate the limitations, we propose simple yet effective multi-round regularization techniques for handling noisy labels, and introduce a graph-based labeling method for mining multiple instances in the same class. Specifically, we integrate refinement layers into the WSDDN architecture and perform multiple rounds of training with randomly reinitialized weights of the refinement layers. This regularization technique prevents the deep neural network from overfitting by forgetting biased weights. Also, a mode-seeking algorithm is performed on a graph of object proposals to identify multiple target instances in a principled way, where the graph is constructed to diversify pseudo-labels by perturbing a threshold to connect vertices corresponding to proposals. The combination of the multi-round regularization and the graph-based labeling improves object detection accuracy substantially in the standard weakly supervised setting for object detection. Our main contributions are summarized as follows:

- We introduce simple multi-round regularization techniques for weakly supervised object detection, which are based on refinement layer reinitializations and labeling perturbations, to tackle overfitting issues caused by falling into bad local optima.
- We propose a mode-seeking technique for labeling candidate bounding boxes, where a graph structure of object proposals is constructed based on their class scores and spatial proximities. This method is helpful to identify multiple object instances of a class in a principled way.

- We demonstrate that our approach improves performance significantly with respect to the state-of-the-art methods in weakly supervised object detection on the standard benchmarks such as PASCAL VOC 2007 and 2012.

This paper has the following organization. Section 2 discusses related work and Sect. 3 presents technical background of our problem. We describe the proposed regularization and label generation techniques in Sect. 4. Experimental results with internal and external comparative study are presented in Sect. 5, and we conclude this paper in Sect. 6.

2 Related Work

This section describes existing approaches about weakly supervised object detection and regularization of deep neural networks.

2.1 Weakly Supervised Object Detection

Weakly supervised object detection algorithms typically rely only on image-level class labels in text to find all the bounding boxes corresponding to objects in target classes. There have been a large volume of research in this interesting topic [1,2,4,18,21,22,26,39,46]. Most approaches in this line of research follow the idea of Multiple Instance Learning (MIL) [8]; a set of proposals from an image constructs a bag, and its label is determined by its image-level weak labels. During training, the approaches alternate selecting the most representative proposals in positive images and learning object detectors using tentatively estimated positive and negative instances. Since a list of true positive instances per image is latent, the optimization is inherently sensitive to initializations of individual examples and prone to fall into bad local optima consequently.

Most MIL-based approaches attempt to improve initialization [7,22,36,37,45] and enhance classifiers through optimization [1,2,4,33,35,39,41]. Li *et al.* [22] collect class specific object proposals and optimize the network progressively using confident object candidates. Self-taught learning approach [17] has been proposed to obtain high-quality proposals progressively. Diba *et al.* [7] introduce cascaded networks with multiple learning stages, which incorporate class specific proposal generation and MIL in an end-to-end pipeline. Multi-fold MIL method [4] splits training data into multiple subsets and learn models to escape from local optima and avoid overfitting. Wan *et al.* [41] perform clustering of object proposals based on their scores and overlap ratios, and minimize entropy of proposal scores in the same cluster, by which it improves localization accuracy and reduces localization randomness.

WSDDN [2] is probably the most popular MIL based end-to-end deep framework, where image-level classification loss is computed by a sum of proposal scores. This framework has been investigated further and a variety of extensions have been proposed recently [4,18,33,39,41,44,45]. Kantorov *et al.* [18] integrates semantic context information to identify tight bounding boxes corresponding objects of interest. Tang *et al.* [39] diffuses labels estimated by WSDDN

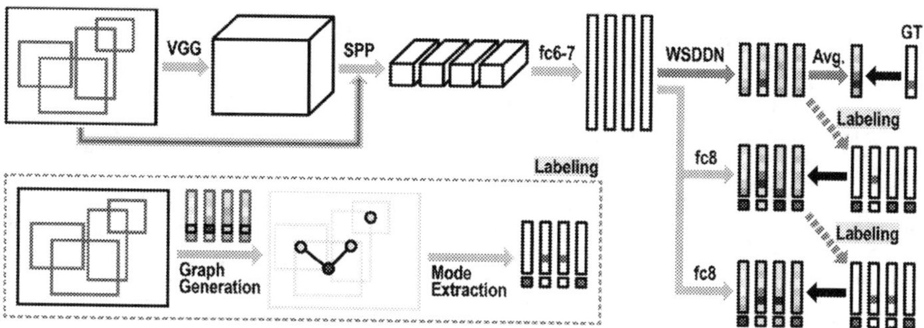

Fig. 1. The network architecture of the proposed approach. A feature of each proposal is extracted from a spatial pyramid pooling layer followed by two `fc` layers and then fed to WSDDN and multiple classifier refinements for training. Supervision for each refinement step is given by the predictions of the preceding step. Our graph-based labeling generates pseudo ground-truth labels for the proposals that are used to learn refinement layers.

to highly-overlapped bounding boxes and learns object detectors end-to-end. Saliency-guided proposal selection has been proposed in [21] to generate reliable positive examples by drawing boxes enclosing areas with heavy class-specific attention, where classification and saliency losses of the proposals are jointly optimized to localize objects. Zhang *et al.* [45] generate diverse and reliable positive examples by merging boxes with detection scores from [39]. Zhang *et al.* [44] train a detector by feeding training examples in an increasing order of difficulty. Shen *et al.* [33] present a generative adversarial learning method to train a detector, which emulates a surrogate detector similar to WSDDN, using image-level annotations only.

2.2 Regularization of Deep Neural Networks

Regularization on deep neural networks is a crucial technique to avoid overfitting that results from overparametrized nature of networks. Even simple heuristics including early stopping, weight decay, and data augmentation turn out to be effective in practice. A class of well-known techniques is regularization by noise injection, where random noises are added to input images [29], ground-truth labels [43], or network weights [19,42] during training for better generalization. In particular, dropout [38] and dropconnect [42] employ binary random noise to hidden units or connections of neural networks, and learning with stochastic depth [14,15] can be interpreted as a regularization method by noise injection into model architecture. Recently, [25] discusses theoretical aspect of regularization-by-noise techniques, and [31] proposes a confidence calibration technique based on stochastic regularization. Unlike existing methods, the proposed multi-round regularization technique is specialized to the scenario of weakly supervised object detection.

3 Preliminaries

Our approach builds on WSDDN [2] and its refinement [39]. Figure 1 illustrates the network architecture and label generation algorithm of our approach. Given an image I and its binary label vector with C classes $\mathbf{y} = [y_1, \ldots, y_C]$, WSDDN learns objectness score $s_{c,r}$ for class c of proposal r through elementwise multiplication of classification confidence, $\boldsymbol{\psi}_{\text{cls}} \in \mathbb{R}^{C\times|\mathcal{R}|}$ and localization confidence, $\boldsymbol{\psi}_{\text{loc}} \in \mathbb{R}^{C\times|\mathcal{R}|}$. The value of an element corresponding to an (r, c) pair in the resulting matrix is given by

$$\begin{aligned} s_{c,r} &= \boldsymbol{\psi}_{\text{cls}}(c;r) \cdot \boldsymbol{\psi}_{\text{loc}}(r;c) \\ &= \frac{f_{\text{cls}}(c;r)}{\sum_{i=1}^{C} \exp(f_{\text{cls}}(i;r))} \cdot \frac{f_{\text{loc}}(r;c)}{\sum_{i=1}^{|\mathcal{R}|} \exp(f_{\text{loc}}(i;c))}, \end{aligned} \tag{1}$$

where $f_{\text{cls}}(c;r)$ denotes an activation of a class c given a proposal r in the network while $f_{\text{loc}}(r;c)$ is an activation of a proposal r given a class c. Image-level class score vector, $\boldsymbol{\phi} = \{\phi_1, \ldots, \phi_C\}$, is computed by a global sum pooling over all proposals, which is given by

$$\phi_c = \sum_{r=1}^{|\mathcal{R}|} s_{c,r}, \tag{2}$$

and the score is employed to compute a multi-class cross entropy loss $\mathcal{L}_{\text{wsddn}}$ as follows:

$$\mathcal{L}_{\text{wsddn}} = -\sum_{c=1}^{C} y_c \log \phi_c + (1 - y_c) \log (1 - \phi_c). \tag{3}$$

To avoid converging discriminating parts of an object, additional refinement layers are added to WSDDN. The refinement layers are trained using pseudo ground-truth labels determined by proposal scores from preceding steps as illustrated with red dashed arrows in Fig. 1. The loss function for the kth refinement step, where $k \in \{1, 2, \ldots, K\}$, is given by

$$\mathcal{L}_{\text{refine}}^{k} = -\frac{1}{|\mathcal{R}|} \sum_{r=1}^{|\mathcal{R}|} \sum_{c=1}^{C+1} w_r^k z_{c,r}^k \log s_{c,r}^k, \tag{4}$$

where $s_{c,r}^k$ and $z_{c,r}^k$ denote the output score and the pseudo-label of a proposal r in the kth refinement for a class c, respectively, while w_r^k is the weight of the proposal, which is used to manage noisy supervision in the refinement layers and avoid unstable solution. Note that each class has a class index $c \in \{1, 2, \ldots, C+1\}$ in a fixed order and the last index $C + 1$ corresponds to background. The total loss of our overall network is obtained by combining those two losses as follows:

$$\mathcal{L} = \mathcal{L}_{\text{wsddn}} + \sum_{k=1}^{K} \mathcal{L}_{\text{refine}}^{k}. \tag{5}$$

Algorithm 1. Learning our WSOD network with multi-round regularization

```
Input: Number of training rounds T, number of refinement steps K.
for i = 1 to T do
    Initialize parameters of refinement layers randomly. (Sect. 4.1)
    Update θ_IoU for labeling perturbation. (Sect. 4.1)
    for each iteration do
        Build a proposal graph with θ_IoU in each refinement step of each image.
        Generate labels of individual labels. (Sect. 4.2)
        Train the network with K refinement steps using the loss function in Eq. (5).
    end for
end for
```

During inference, a final detection score for each proposal is computed by averaging softmax scores over all refinement classifiers.

4 Our Approach

The architecture introduced in Sect. 3 has two inherent issues. First, as the architecture is trained using pseudo-labels in refinement steps, the learning procedure is prone to fall in bad local optima. Second, due to the limitation of the labeling scheme during refinement steps, it identifies only a single object instance in an image even in the case multiple instances exist in the image.

To tackle these challenges, we propose *multi-round regularization* and *graph-based labeling* techniques in our weakly supervised object detection framework. Both components are useful to improve object detection performance. The overall learning procedure is outlined in Algorithm 1, and we discuss the details of each component in the rest of this section.

4.1 Multi-round Regularization of Refinement

Our weakly supervised object detection algorithm relies on MIL, where we obtain pseudo ground-truth labels for individual bounding boxes based on their prediction scores for training object detector. However, as expected, this strategy may incur a lot of label noises, which leads to increase of modeling bias and prediction error. To mitigate this limitation, we present multi-round regularization techniques that improve target object representation and avoid overfitting of our weakly supervised object detection network. Note that the multi-round regularization is specialized to weakly supervised learning because labels of all examples are dynamically determined in each stage depending on network parameters. We claim that multi-round regularization is useful to consider potential label noise and reduce training bias in weakly supervised setting.

Our multi-round regularization has two components, refinement layer reinitialization and label perturbation. The second component is related to graph-based label generation method. The multiple rounds of training with reinitialization and perturbation reduce the bias of the learned models affected by a fixed but potentially erroneous labels and prevent the models from being converged to bad local optima.

Reinitialization of Refinement Layers. Our refinement network is composed of a single `fc` layer in each stage, and we simply reinitialize the parameters in the refinement layers of all three stages in each round of training. Since the last `fc` layers in the classifier refinements are trained using the labels predicted by the preceding stages, these layers may be biased by noisy labels. However, if the `fc` layers are reinitialized before starting the next round, we can diversify labels and avoid overfitting problem while feature extraction parts of the network learn better representations for target classes.

Labeling Perturbation for Refinements. The pseudo ground-truth labels of individual bounding boxes are determined by a graph-based labeling algorithm, which will be discussed in Sect. 4.2. Another regularization scheme for our weakly supervised object detection is to perturb the instance labels during our training procedure. This regularization method is based on a similar motivation to the reinitialization technique discussed above, where we aim to reduce bias of learned models originated from noisy labels. Instead of random perturbation, we adjust a parameter, which directly affects label assignment for each bounding box, the graph construction in each round of training and decide the label of each proposal using the graph-based labeling algorithm with the perturbed parameters. This label perturbation strategy increases diversity in the number of detected objects, and make our models optimized towards a new objective given by a different label set in each round.

4.2 Graph-Based Label Generation

Since images often include multiple instances of a class, the label generation method should be able to handle an arbitrary number of object instances conceptually. Hence, we propose a new labeling method based on mode-seeking on a graph structure, which is illustrated inside the red dashed box of Fig. 1. Our graph-based labeling technique facilitates to identify diverse positive proposals by building a graph structure of proposals based on their overlap relations and finding multiple modes with high classification scores. This graph-based labeling allows us to obtain accurate labels by diversifying annotations and improve quality of trained models. Note that Tang *et al.* [39] regard proposals that have large overlap ($\geq$0.5 in terms of IOU) with the top-scoring bounding box as positive instances while making the remaining ones negative; selecting only positive examples from a single mode inherently limits capability to handle multiple objects in an images.

Our graph-based label generation method first constructs a neighborhood graph of proposals for each object class in each image. In the graph of class c at refinement step k, denoted by $G_c^k = (\mathcal{V}_c^k, \mathcal{E}_c^k)$, a vertex corresponds to a proposal with a sufficiently large classification score given by the preceding step, and an

Algorithm 2. Graph-based mode-seeking algorithm

Input: Graph $G = (\mathcal{V}, \mathcal{E})$ and weight vector $\mathbf{w} \in \mathbb{R}^{|V|}$
Output: A detected mode set $\mathcal{M}$
$\mathbf{h} \leftarrow [1, 2, \ldots, |V|] \in \mathbb{R}^{|V|}$ /* $\mathbf{h}$ is a cluster indicator vector */
while until $\mathbf{h}$ converges **do**
  for $u \in \mathcal{V}$ **do**
    $h(u) \leftarrow \text{argmax}_{v \in \mathcal{N}_{h(u)}} w(v)$ /* medoid-shift */
  end for
end while
$\mathcal{M} \leftarrow$ a set of unique elements of $\mathbf{h}$

edge connects two of vertices if the proposals for the vertices have sufficiently large overlap to each other. Formally, the sets of vertices and edges are defined by

$$\begin{aligned} \mathcal{V}_c^k &= \{v | s_{c,v}^{k-1} > \theta_s, \quad v \in \mathcal{R}\} \\ \mathcal{E}_c^k &= \{(u, v) | \ \text{IoU}(u, v) > \theta_{\text{IoU}}, \quad u, v \in \mathcal{R}\}, \end{aligned} \tag{6}$$

where u and v denote object proposals, $s_{c,v}^{k-1}$ is a proposal score predicted in the preceding step, θ_s is a threshold for the score, $\text{IoU}(u, v)$ is intersection-over-union measure between proposals, and θ_{IoU} is an IoU threshold.

Then we perform a mode-seeking algorithm, medoid-shift [3,32], on this graph. The algorithm is useful in practice because it finds multiple reliable modes of data distribution and requires no manual initialization and terminating conditions. Specifically, we first compute the weight of each node $u \in \mathcal{V}$ of G by

$$w_c(u) = \sum_{v \in \mathcal{V}} s_{c,v} \delta(u, v). \tag{7}$$

where $\delta(\cdot, \cdot) = 1$ if there exists an edge $(u, v) \in \mathcal{E}$, and 0 otherwise. Then, medoid-shift algorithm is applied to the graph and identifies a set of modes, where each vertex is associated with one of the modes after convergence. Since such a mode-seeking algorithm often finds spurious modes, we adopt a mode filtering technique, which maintains only salient modes based on topological persistence of a graph [9]. The proposals corresponding to the modes obtained from mode-seeking and mode filtering procedures receive positive labels. The entire procedure of the proposed method is summarized in Algorithm 2.

After finding the modes, the rest of proposals r for a class c are given a pseudo-label $z_{c,r}$ as follows:

$$z_{c,r} = \begin{cases} 1 & \text{if } \text{IoU}(m, r) > 0.5, \ m \in \mathcal{M}_c \text{ and } y_c = 1 \\ 0 & \text{otherwise} \end{cases}, \tag{8}$$

where $\mathcal{M}_c$ is a set of detected modes for class c and y_c denotes image-level binary class label for class c. In other words, proposals sufficiently overlapped with any of detected modes are labeled to be positive and the rest are given negative labels in a similar way to OICR [39]. This labeling method is employed to compute a loss in Eq. (4) for all refinement steps.

5 Experiments

This section presents performance of our regularization algorithm with graph-based labeling. We also compare the proposed approach with the state-of-the-art methods and show results from ablation study of our technique.

5.1 Implementation Details

We use VGG_M and VGG16 [34] networks pretrained on ImageNet [6] classification task to obtain image representation. To compute feature descriptors of all proposals at once, the last max-pooling layer is replaced by a spatial pyramid pooling (SPP) layer as in Fast-RCNN [12]. For training, we employ the standard stochastic gradient descent (SGD) method with batch size 2. The model is trained with 50K iterations in each round, where the learning rate of the first 40K iterations is set to 0.001 and then decreased to 0.0001 for the last 10K iterations. Initial momentum and weight decay are set to 0.9 and 0.0005, respectively. Every image is rescaled to the sizes that the length of the shorter side becomes one of {480, 576, 688, 864, 1200} while we preserve aspect ratios. Approximately 2,000 object proposals are generated for each image by applying selective search algorithm [40] in fast mode. We set the score threshold θ_s to the half of the maximum proposal scores for each class c. Our algorithm runs 4 rounds of iterative training procedure with parameter reinitialization while the number of refinement steps is set to 3, *i.e.*, $K = 3$. Our experiments run on a NVIDIA GTX Titan Xp GPU and the implementation is based on the Caffe [16] framework.

5.2 Datasets and Evaluation Metrics

We evaluate our method on PASCAL VOC 2007 [11] and 2012 [10] datasets, which consist of a total of 9,963 and 22,531 images from 20 object classes. We train our model on train+validation splits of PASCAL VOC 2007 and 2012 datasets, consisting of 5,011 and 11,540 images, respectively. Since our approach lies on weakly supervised setting, only image-level annotations for class labels are used for training. For testing, we utilize 4,952 and 10,991 test images from PASCAL VOC 2007 and 2012 datasets, respectively. All ablation studies are performed on PASCAL VOC 2007 dataset.

Our quantitative evaluation metric is the mean of Average Precisions (APs) over classes. The number of true positives is the count of object proposals that have more than 0.5 IoU overlap with ground-truths. We also measure Correct localization (CorLoc) to evaluate localization accuracy of our model on the training set. The final inference is given by averaging scores from all the refinement steps. Before evaluating and measuring AP and CorLoc scores, non-maximum suppression is applied to positive examples with 0.3 IoU threshold.

Table 1. Comparison between network refinement with and without layer reinitialization. We test VGG_M and VGG16 networks with several different numbers of refinement layers on VOC 2007 test set. We report accuracy in terms of mAP (%). RL means refinement layer in the table.

Methods (round/iterations)	(a) With layer reinitialization		(b) Without layer reinitialization	
	(R1/50k)	(R2/50k)	(–/50k)	(–/100k)
Ours-1RL-VGG_M	35.6	36.2	35.6	35.6
Ours-2RL-VGG_M	36.3	37.6	36.3	34.8
Ours-3RL-VGG_M	38.0	39.2	38.0	38.7
Ours-1RL-VGG16	36.2	40.2	36.2	37.4
Ours-2RL-VGG16	41.6	43.9	41.6	42.1
Ours-3RL-VGG16	42.6	44.6	42.6	42.2

Table 2. Comparison of two labeling methods after training for 50k iterations on VOC 2007 test set: (a) labeling example by propagating positive labels based on overlaps from the bounding box with the maximum classification score, and (b) labeling with multi-modal score distribution given by mode-seeking technique on a graph structure of proposals.

Methods	Base network	RL	mAP
(a) Maximum GT	VGG_M	1	33.5
		2	36.0
		3	36.4
	VGG16	1	35.8
		2	39.1
		3	41.8
(b) Graph-based GT (ours)	VGG_M	1	35.6
		2	36.3
		3	38.0
	VGG16	1	36.2
		2	41.6
		3	42.6

5.3 Ablation Study

Impact of Refinement Layer Reinitialization. We first validate the effectiveness of our refinement layer reinitialization scheme on PASCAL VOC 2007 test set. For the purpose, we compare mAPs of two models—with and without reinitialization of the `fc` layers for refinement—after training for the same number of iterations altogether in both cases, 50k and 100k. Both VGG_M and VGG16 networks are employed as backbone CNNs for this experiment. Table 1 summarizes the results. The performance of the models with reinitialization is

Table 3. Results with different IoU thresholds in Eq. (6) for graph construction. Note that the labels obtained from the graph are integrated into the refinement layer reinitialization. Evaluation is performed with VGG16 network on VOC 2007 test set. We report accuracy in terms of mAP (%).

Methods	θ_{IoU}	Round1	Round2	Round3	Round4	Round5
Ours-1RL	0.1	36.2	40.2	40.8	41.4	41.6
Ours-2RL		41.6	43.9	43.6	43.8	43.1
Ours-3RL		42.6	44.6	44.4	43.4	43.1
Ours-1RL	0.5	36.0	39.5	40.2	40.8	40.5
Ours-2RL		38.0	40.5	41.9	42.5	41.9
Ours-3RL		40.3	41.5	41.6	41.2	41.2
Ours-1RL	0.1 (Round 1, 2)	36.2	40.2	40.4	41.1	40.1
Ours-2RL	0.5 (Round 3, 4, 5)	41.6	43.9	44.5	44.5	43.7
Ours-3RL		42.6	44.6	45.5	45.4	44.0

improved significantly in the second round while the ones without layer reinitialization generally have marginal gains in the second half of the 100k iterations.

Impact of Graph-Based Label Generation. Table 2 illustrates results from two different methods for generation of pseudo ground-truths. The one identifies positive examples from only a single mode corresponding to the bounding box with a maximum score (maximum GT) and the other extract them from multi-modal score distribution over bounding boxes given by the mode-seeking algorithm via medoid-shift on a graph structure (graph-based GT). For this experiment, IoU threshold θ_{IoU} for graph construction is set to 0.1. After one round of training, our graph-based mode-seeking technique outperforms the naïve single GT method on both VGG_M and VGG16 networks consistently.

Impact of Labeling Perturbations. We also investigate influence of label perturbation by varying IoU threshold for edge connectivity of proposal graph. As mentioned in Sect. 4.1, definition of spatial adjacency between vertices affects pseudo ground-truth construction and final label estimation. We test with two IoU thresholds, 0.1 and 0.5. Table 3 presents the results with VGG16 network for the several tested options. The proposed labeling perturbation method works well in general, especially with more refinement steps. Also, when we use a small threshold value at the early stage of training and then increase its value later, detection accuracies are improved compared to the cases with fixed thresholds. It is probably because this strategy is effective to reject noisy examples quickly in the early stages and maintain multiple positive instances in the later ones.

Table 4. AP (%) of all compared algorithms on VOC 2007 test set. Asterisk (*) denotes the method that uses an external detector such as Fast-RCNN or SSD within its framework.

Method	aero	bike	bird	boat	bottle	bus	car	cat	chair	cow	
WSDDN-VGG16 [2]	39.4	50.1	31.5	16.3	12.6	64.5	42.8	42.6	10.1	35.7	
WSDDN+context [18]	57.1	52.0	31.5	7.6	11.5	55.0	53.1	34.1	1.7	33.1	
OICR-VGG16 [39]	58.0	62.4	31.1	19.4	13.0	65.1	62.2	28.4	24.8	44.7	
SelfTaught-VGG16 [17]	52.2	47.1	35.0	26.7	15.4	61.3	66.0	54.3	3.0	53.6	
WCCN-VGG16 [7]	49.5	60.6	38.6	29.2	16.2	70.8	56.9	42.5	10.9	44.1	
SGWSOD-VGG16 [21]	48.4	61.5	33.3	30.0	15.3	72.4	62.4	59.1	10.9	42.3	
OICR-Ens [39]	58.5	63.0	35.1	16.9	17.4	63.2	60.8	34.4	8.2	49.7	
OICR-Ens+FRCNN [39]	65.5	67.2	47.2	21.6	22.1	68.0	68.5	35.9	5.7	63.1	
GAL300-VGG16+SSD* [33]	52.0	60.5	44.6	26.1	20.6	63.1	66.2	65.3	15.0	50.1	
ZLDN-VGG16+FRCNN* [44]	55.4	68.5	50.1	16.8	20.8	62.7	66.8	56.5	2.1	57.8	
OICR-VGG16+FRCNN [39]	60.9	62.9	50.5	28.9	17.1	70.3	68.1	27.0	25.7	58.8	
Ours-3RL-VGG16	62.1	55.7	42.0	31.1	17.2	67.6	65.2	50.8	20.4	51.5	
Ours-3RL-VGG16+FRCNN	59.8	62.8	45.6	33.2	21.8	70.2	68.6	56.6	22.8	55.9	
Method	**table**	**dog**	**horse**	**mbike**	**person**	**plant**	**sheep**	**sofa**	**train**	**tv**	**Avg.**
WSDDN-VGG16 [2]	24.9	38.2	34.4	55.6	9.4	14.7	30.2	40.7	54.7	46.9	34.8
WSDDN+context [18]	49.2	42.0	47.3	56.6	15.3	12.8	24.8	48.9	44.4	47.8	36.3
OICR-VGG16 [39]	30.6	25.3	37.8	65.5	15.7	24.1	41.7	46.9	64.3	62.6	41.2
SelfTaught-VGG16 [17]	24.7	43.6	48.4	65.8	6.6	18.8	51.9	43.6	53.6	62.4	41.7
WCCN-VGG16 [7]	29.9	42.2	47.9	64.1	13.8	23.5	45.9	54.1	60.8	54.5	42.8
SGWSOD-VGG16 [21]	34.3	53.1	48.4	65.0	20.5	16.6	40.6	46.5	54.6	55.1	43.5
OICR-Ens [39]	41.0	31.3	51.9	64.8	13.6	23.1	41.6	48.4	58.9	58.7	42.0
OICR-Ens+FRCNN [39]	49.5	30.3	64.7	66.1	13.0	25.6	50.0	57.1	60.2	59.0	47.0
GAL300-VGG16+SSD* [33]	52.8	56.7	21.3	63.4	36.8	22.7	47.9	51.7	68.9	54.1	47.0
ZLDN-VGG16+FRCNN* [44]	47.5	40.1	69.7	68.2	21.6	27.2	53.4	56.1	52.5	58.2	47.6
OICR-VGG16+FRCNN [39]	41.9	20.7	42.4	65.5	7.1	24.6	51.5	61.9	62.7	56.5	45.3
Ours-3RL-VGG16	36.3	34.1	46.2	65.8	12.3	21.9	48.8	55.4	60.2	65.7	45.4
Ours-3RL-VGG16+FRCNN	47.5	40.8	59.0	65.0	9.1	22.4	49.5	64.6	57.8	57.3	**48.8**

5.4 Results on PASCAL VOC Datasets

We compare the proposed algorithm with existing state-of-the art methods for weakly supervised object detection including WSDDN [2], WSDDN+ context [18], OICR [39], SelfTaught [17], WCCN [7], SGWSOD [21], ZLDN [44], GAL300 [33]. Tables 4 and 5 present performance of all compared algorithms on PASCAL VOC 2007 dataset in terms of mean of APs and CorLoc, respectively. We also present the performances on PASCAL VOC 2012 dataset in Table 6. Best performance of each measure is marked with bold and second best is marked with underline.

To obtain the final results, we use the models trained for four rounds with refinement layer reinitialization. Our model with 3 refinement layers based on VGG16, which is denoted by Ours-3RL-VGG16 in the table, achieves significantly improved accuracy compared to OICR-VGG16 [39]. This result suggests that our training method is very effective because the two models have the exactly same network architecture. We also train a Fast-RCNN [12] (FRCNN) detector based on the labels of the proposals with the highest scores given by

Table 5. CorLoc (%) of all compared algorithms on VOC 2007 trainval set. Asterisk (*) denotes the method that uses an external detector such as Fast-RCNN or SSD within its framework.

Method	aero	bike	bird	boat	bottle	bus	car	cat	chair	cow	
WSDDN-VGG16 [2]	65.1	58.8	58.5	33.1	39.8	68.3	60.2	59.6	34.8	64.5	
WSDDN+context [18]	83.3	68.6	54.7	23.4	18.3	73.6	74.1	54.1	8.6	65.1	
OICR-VGG16 [39]	81.7	80.4	48.7	49.5	32.8	81.7	85.4	40.1	40.6	79.5	
SelfTaught-VGG16 [17]	72.7	55.3	53.0	27.8	35.2	68.6	81.9	60.7	11.6	71.6	
WCCN-VGG16 [7]	83.9	72.8	64.5	44.1	40.1	65.7	82.5	58.9	33.7	72.5	
SGWSOD-VGG16 [21]	71.0	76.5	54.9	49.7	54.1	78.0	87.4	68.8	32.4	75.2	
OICR-Ens [39]	85.4	78.0	61.6	40.4	38.2	82.2	84.2	46.5	15.2	80.1	
OICR-Ens+FRCNN [39]	85.8	82.7	62.8	45.2	43.5	84.8	87.0	46.8	15.7	82.2	
GAL300-VGG16+SSD* [33]	76.5	76.1	64.2	48.1	52.5	80.7	86.1	73.9	30.8	78.7	
ZLDN-VGG16+FRCNN* [44]	74.0	77.8	65.2	37.0	46.7	75.8	83.7	58.8	17.5	73.1	
OICR-VGG16+FRCNN [39]	86.7	81.2	64.0	50.5	30.9	83.2	85.3	38.7	45.1	80.1	
Ours-3RL-VGG16	85.4	71.4	61.6	55.9	37.0	83.2	84.2	61.3	29.7	77.4	
Ours-3RL-VGG16+FRCNN	86.3	77.6	65.5	55.9	41.6	82.7	86.7	61.6	39.7	80.8	
Method	table	dog	horse	mbike	person	plant	sheep	sofa	train	tv	Avg.
WSDDN-VGG16 [2]	30.5	43.0	56.8	82.4	25.5	41.6	61.5	55.9	65.9	63.7	53.5
WSDDN+context [18]	47.1	59.5	67.0	83.5	35.3	39.9	67.0	49.7	63.5	65.2	55.1
OICR-VGG16 [39]	35.7	33.7	60.5	88.8	21.8	57.9	76.3	59.9	75.3	81.4	60.6
SelfTaught-VGG16 [17]	29.7	54.3	64.3	88.2	22.2	53.7	72.2	52.67	68.9	75.5	56.1
WCCN-VGG16 [7]	25.6	53.7	67.4	77.4	26.8	49.1	68.1	27.9	64.5	55.7	56.7
SGWSOD-VGG16 [21]	29.5	58.0	67.3	84.5	41.5	49.0	78.1	60.3	62.8	78.9	62.9
OICR-Ens [39]	45.2	41.9	73.8	89.6	18.9	56.0	74.2	62.1	73.0	77.4	61.2
OICR-Ens+FRCNN [39]	51.0	45.6	83.7	91.2	22.2	59.7	75.3	65.1	76.8	78.1	64.3
GAL300-VGG16+SSD* [33]	62.0	71.5	46.7	86.1	60.7	47.8	82.3	74.7	83.1	79.3	**68.1**
ZLDN-VGG16+FRCNN* [44]	49.0	51.3	76.7	87.4	30.6	47.8	75.0	62.5	64.8	68.8	61.2
OICR-VGG16+FRCNN [39]	41.4	32.3	67.0	91.2	12.7	60.4	76.3	66.4	80.2	78.9	62.6
Ours-3RL-VGG16	28.1	46.3	66.0	88.0	16.6	51.3	70.1	59.7	73.8	79.2	61.3
Ours-3RL-VGG16+FRCNN	47.5	57.4	82.3	90.8	20.3	55.7	77.3	69.6	74.9	79.2	66.7

Table 6. Comparison between the proposed algorithm and the existing ones on PASCAL VOC 2012 dataset in terms of mAP (%) and CorLoc (%).

Method	mAP (%)	CorLoc (%)
WSDDN+context [18]	34.9	56.1
OICR-VGG16 [39]	37.9	62.1
SelfTaught-VGG16 [17]	38.3	58.8
WCCN-VGG16 [7]	37.9	-
SGWSOD-VGG16 [21]	39.6	62.9
SGWSOD-Ens [21]	40.6	64.2
OICR-Ens [39]	38.2	63.5
OICR-Ens+FRCNN [39]	42.5	65.6
ZLDN-VGG16+FRCNN* [44]	42.9	61.5
GAL300-VGG16+SSD* [33]	43.1	67.2
Ours-3RL-VGG16	41.2	64.1
Ours-3RL-VGG16+FRCNN	**44.1**	**68.5**

our method in individual images. Our final model (Ours-3RL-VGG16+FRCNN) shows higher mAP score than the state-of-the-art methods in both datasets. It is also noticeable that even our method without using FRCNN (Our-3RL-VGG16) outperforms even the ensemble OICR model (OICR-Ens) and the OICR-VGG16-FRCNN method. In terms of CorLoc, we achieve the second best score among the comparison methods on PASCAL VOC 2007 dataset and the top score on 2012 dataset.

Figures 2 and 3 illustrate qualitative examples and failure cases, respectively. Our method is effective in finding more accurate bounding boxes of the objects compared to OICR, but still confused with the objects that have similar appearance and background. Also, detecting highly non-rigid objects (*e.g.* `person`) is still challenging and limited to finding discriminative parts such as human faces.

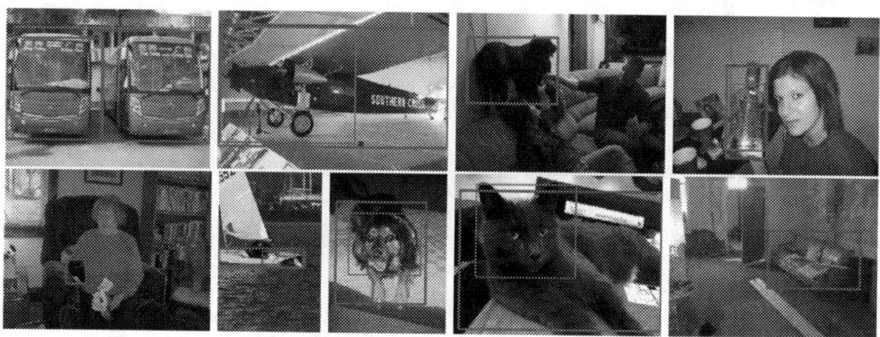

Fig. 2. Qualitative examples on PASCAL VOC 2007 test set. Red boxes indicate detection results from OICR [39] and green ones present our results. (Color figure online)

Fig. 3. Examples of failure cases. Our method is often confused with the objects with similar appearances.

6 Conclusion

We presented simple but effective regularization techniques with a graph-based labeling method for weakly supervised object detection. The proposed regularization algorithms—refinement layer reinitialization and labeling perturbation during iterative training procedure—are helpful to avoid overfitting to local optima by forgetting biased weights and diversifying pseudo-labels. A mode-seeking algorithm on a graph of object proposals contributes to identifying multiple target instances and improving detection accuracy. Our method illustrates outstanding performances on PASCAL VOC 2007 and 2012 datasets compared to existing state-of-the-art weakly supervised object detection techniques.

Acknowledgements. This research was supported in part by Naver Labs., the Institute for Information & Communications Technology Promotion (IITP) grant [2014-0-00059, 2017-0-01778] and the National Research Foundation of Korea (NRF) grant [NRF-2017R1E1A1A01077999, NRF-2018R1A5A1060031, NRF-2018R1C1B6001223] funded by the Korea government (MSIT).

References

1. Bilen, H., Pedersoli, M., Tuytelaars, T.: Weakly supervised object detection with posterior regularization. In: BMVC (2014)
2. Bilen, H., Vedaldi, A.: Weakly supervised deep detection networks. In: CVPR (2016)
3. Cho, M., Lee, K.M.: Mode-seeking on graphs via random walks. In: CVPR (2012)
4. Cinbis, R.G., Verbeek, J., Schmid, C.: Weakly supervised object localization with multi-fold multiple instance learning. TPAMI **39**, 189–203 (2017)
5. Dai, J., Li, Y., He, K., Sun, J.: R-FCN: object detection via region-based fully convolutional networks. In: NIPS, pp. 379–387 (2016)
6. Deng, J., Dong, W., Socher, R., Li, L.J., Li, K., Fei-Fei, L.: ImageNet: a large-scale hierarchical image database. In: CVPR (2009)
7. Diba, A., Sharma, V., Pazandeh, A., Pirsiavash, H., Van Gool, L.: Weakly supervised cascaded convolutional networks. In: CVPR (2017)
8. Dietterich, T.G., Lathrop, R.H., Lozano-Pérez, T.: Solving the multiple instance problem with axis-parallel rectangles. Artif. Intell. **89**(1), 31–71 (1997)
9. Edelsbrunner, H., Letscher, D., Zomorodian, A.: Topological persistence and simplification. Discrete Comput. Geom. **28**, 511–533 (2002)
10. Everingham, M., Eslami, S.A., Van Gool, L., Williams, C.K., Winn, J., Zisserman, A.: The Pascal visual object classes challenge: a retrospective. IJCV **111**(1), 98–136 (2015)
11. Everingham, M., Van Gool, L., Williams, C.K., Winn, J., Zisserman, A.: The Pascal visual object classes (VOC) challenge. IJCV **88**(2), 303–338 (2010)
12. Girshick, R.: Fast R-CNN. In: ICCV, pp. 1440–1448 (2015)
13. Girshick, R., Donahue, J., Darrell, T., Malik, J.: Region-based convolutional networks for accurate object detection and segmentation. TPAMI **38**(1), 142–158 (2016)
14. Han, B., Sim, J., Adam, H.: Branchout: regularization for online ensemble tracking with convolutional neural networks. In: CVPR (2017)
15. Huang, G., Sun, Y., Liu, Z., Sedra, D., Weinberger, K.Q.: Deep networks with stochastic depth. In: Leibe, B., Matas, J., Sebe, N., Welling, M. (eds.) ECCV 2016. LNCS, vol. 9908, pp. 646–661. Springer, Cham (2016). https://doi.org/10.1007/978-3-319-46493-0_39
16. Jia, Y., et al.: Caffe: Convolutional architecture for fast feature embedding. arXiv preprint arXiv:1408.5093 (2014)

17. Jie, Z., Wei, Y., Jin, X., Feng, J., Liu, W.: Deep self-taught learning for weakly supervised object localization. In: CVPR (2017)
18. Kantorov, V., Oquab, M., Cho, M., Laptev, I.: ContextLocNet: context-aware deep network models for weakly supervised localization. In: Leibe, B., Matas, J., Sebe, N., Welling, M. (eds.) ECCV 2016. LNCS, vol. 9909, pp. 350–365. Springer, Cham (2016). https://doi.org/10.1007/978-3-319-46454-1_22
19. Kingma, D.P., Salimans, T., Welling, M.: Variational dropout and the local reparameterization trick. In: NIPS (2015)
20. Krasin, I., et al.: Openimages: A public dataset for large-scale multi-label and multi-class image classification (2017). Dataset available from https://storage.googleapis.com/openimages/web/index.html
21. Lai, B., Gong, X.: Saliency guided end-to-end learning for weakly supervised object detection. In: IJCAI (2017)
22. Li, D., Huang, J., Li, Y., Wang, S., Yang, M.H.: Weakly supervised object localization with progressive domain adaptation. In: CVPR (2016)
23. Lin, T.-Y., et al.: Microsoft COCO: common objects in context. In: Fleet, D., Pajdla, T., Schiele, B., Tuytelaars, T. (eds.) ECCV 2014. LNCS, vol. 8693, pp. 740–755. Springer, Cham (2014). https://doi.org/10.1007/978-3-319-10602-1_48
24. Liu, W., et al.: SSD: single shot multibox detector. In: Leibe, B., Matas, J., Sebe, N., Welling, M. (eds.) ECCV 2016. LNCS, vol. 9905, pp. 21–37. Springer, Cham (2016). https://doi.org/10.1007/978-3-319-46448-0_2
25. Noh, H., You, T., Mun, J., Han, B.: Regularizing deep neural networks by noise: its interpretation and optimization. In: NIPS (2017)
26. Oquab, M., Bottou, L., Laptev, I., Sivic, J.: Is object localization for free? - weakly-supervised learning with convolutional neural networks. In: CVPR (2015)
27. Redmon, J., Farhadi, A.: Yolo9000: better, faster, stronger. In: CVPR, pp. 6517–6525 (2017)
28. Redmon, J., Divvala, S., Girshick, R., Farhadi, A.: You only look once: unified, real-time object detection. In: CVPR, June 2016
29. Reed, R., Oh, S., Marks, R.: Regularization using jittered training data. In: IJCNN (1992)
30. Ren, S., He, K., Girshick, R., Sun, J.: Faster R-CNN: towards real-time object detection with region proposal networks. In: NIPS (2015)
31. Seo, S., Seo, P.H., Han, B.: Confidence calibration in deep neural networks through stochastic inferences. In: arXiv preprint arXiv:1809.10877 (2018)
32. Sheikh, Y.A., Khan, E.A., Kanade, T.: Mode-seeking by medoidshifts. In: ICCV (2007)
33. Shen, Y., Ji, R., Zhang, S., Zuo, W., Wang, Y.: Generative adversarial learning towards fast weakly supervised detection. In: CVPR (2018)
34. Simonyan, K., Zisserman, A.: Very deep convolutional networks for large-scale image recognition. CoRR abs/1409.1556 (2014)
35. Singh, S., Gupta, A., Efros, A.A.: Unsupervised discovery of mid-level discriminative patches. In: Fitzgibbon, A., Lazebnik, S., Perona, P., Sato, Y., Schmid, C. (eds.) ECCV 2012. LNCS, pp. 73–86. Springer, Heidelberg (2012). https://doi.org/10.1007/978-3-642-33709-3_6
36. Siva, P., Russell, C., Xiang, T.: In defence of negative mining for annotating weakly labelled data. In: Fitzgibbon, A., Lazebnik, S., Perona, P., Sato, Y., Schmid, C. (eds.) ECCV 2012. LNCS, vol. 7574, pp. 594–608. Springer, Heidelberg (2012). https://doi.org/10.1007/978-3-642-33712-3_43
37. Song, H.O., Lee, Y.J., Jegelka, S., Darrell, T.: Weakly-supervised discovery of visual pattern configurations. In: NIPS (2014)

38. Srivastava, N., Hinton, G., Krizhevsky, A., Sutskever, I., Salakhutdinov, R.: Dropout: a simple way to prevent neural networks from overfitting. J. Mach. Learn. Res. **15**(1), 1929–1958 (2014)
39. Tang, P., Wang, X., Bai, X., Liu, W.: Multiple instance detection network with online instance classifier refinement. In: CVPR (2017)
40. Uijlings, J.R.R., van de Sande, K.E.A., Gevers, T., Smeulders, A.W.M.: Selective search for object recognition. IJCV **104**, 154–171 (2013)
41. Wan, F., Wei, P., Jiao, J., Han, Z., Ye, Q.: Min-entropy latent model for weakly supervised object detection. In: CVPR (2018)
42. Wan, L., Zeiler, M., Zhang, S., Le Cun, Y., Fergus, R.: Regularization of neural networks using dropconnect. In: ICML (2013)
43. Xie, L., Wang, J., Wei, Z., Wang, M., Tian, Q.: Disturblabel: regularizing CNN on the loss layer. In: CVPR (2016)
44. Zhang, X., Feng, J., Xiong, H., Tian, Q.: Zigzag learning for weakly supervised object detection. In: CVPR (2018)
45. Zhang, Y., Bai, Y., Ding, M., Li, Y., Ghanem, B.: W2f: a weakly-supervised to fully-supervised framework for object detection. In: CVPR (2018)
46. Zhou, B., Khosla, A., Lapedriza, À., Oliva, A., Torralba, A.: Learning deep features for discriminative localization. In: CVPR (2016)

Task-Adaptive Feature Reweighting for Few Shot Classification

Nan Lai[1,2], Meina Kan[1,3], Shiguang Shan[1,2,3](✉), and Xilin Chen[1,2]

[1] Key Lab of Intelligent Information Processing of Chinese Academy of Sciences (CAS), Institute of Computing Technology, CAS, Beijing, China
{lainan,kanmeina,sgshan,xlchen}@ict.ac.cn

[2] University of Chinese Academy of Sciences, Beijing, China

[3] CAS Center for Excellence in Brain Science and Intelligence Technology, Shanghai, China

Abstract. Few shot classification remains a quite challenging problem due to lacking data to train an effective classifier. Lately a few works employ the meta learning schema to learn a generalized feature encoder or distance metric, which is directly used for those unseen classes. In these approaches, the feature representation of a class remains the same even in different tasks (In meta learning, a task of few shot classification involves a set of labeled examples (support set) and a set of unlabeled examples (query set) to be classified. The goal is to get a classifier for the classes in the support set.), i.e. the feature encoder cannot adapt to different tasks. As well known, when distinguishing a class from different classes, the most discriminative feature may be different. Following this intuition, this work proposes a task-adaptive feature reweighting strategy within the framework of recently proposed prototypical network [6]. By considering the relationship between classes in a task, our method generates a feature weight for each class to highlight those features that can better distinguish it from the rest ones. As a result, each class has its own specific feature weight, and this weight is adaptively different in different tasks. The proposed method is evaluated on two few shot classification benchmarks, *mini*ImageNet and *tiered*ImageNet. The experiment results show that our method outperforms the state-of-the-art works demonstrating its effectiveness.

Keywords: Few shot classification · Feature reweighting · Meta-learning

1 Introduction

In recent years, deep learning has achieved impressive performance on image classification task [1–4]. Despite the success, it requires a large amount of data to update massive parameters. In contrast, the human visual system can learn a new visual concept quickly from few data. The ability of learning quickly from few data is very important for an artificial visual system, as in practice

C. V. Jawahar et al. (Eds.): ACCV 2018, LNCS 11364, pp. 649–662, 2019.
https://doi.org/10.1007/978-3-030-20870-7_40

labeling data manually is very expensive and training on a large scale dataset is time-consuming. Few shot classification is such a kind of technique that aims to recognize a set of new classes from few examples. The challenge of this problem is how to get an effective classifier from few data and limited class variation.

A straightforward approach is fine-tuning a pre-trained model by using those new classes in a task. However, this would cause overfitting problem, especially when the classes for pre-training have large discrepancy with the new classes [19]. Although regularization methods can be used to alleviate the overfitting problem to some extent, they cannot fully solve it. Lately, a new trend of few shot classification methods arises, i.e. quite a few works apply meta learning to few shot classification. For example, MAML [10] attempts to get a model to be easy to fine-tune by learning a good network initialization such that a small number of update steps with few data could produce good generalization performance on a new task. Matching Network [12] learns a network to get the embeddings of few labeled examples and unlabeled queries, over which a cosine similarity metric is used to predict the label of each query. Prototypical Network [6] learns a generalized distance metric space in which classification can be performed by computing distances with prototype representations of each class. On *mini*ImageNet, these approaches significantly outperform the straightforward fine-tuning methods, e.g. more than 10% improvement [12], making meta learning quite promising for few shot classification. The effectiveness of meta learning may benefit from its ability of learning to learn generalized knowledge across different tasks, which can be transferred to a new task.

Among the meta-learning approaches, prototypical network [6] is a fairly simple and elegant solution, and thus attracts much attention. In this work, we attempt to extend prototypical network [6] to further improve its performance. In this method as well as other existing approaches, the feature representation of a class remains the same even in different tasks. This means that the feature encoder cannot adapt to a specific task using the peculiar discriminant information of the task, e.g. the relationship of classes in this task. As well known, when distinguishing a class from different classes, the most discriminative feature is different, e.g. when distinguishing a dog from a cat the head plays a crucial role, while the neck matters most when distinguishing a dog from a giraffe.

Following above intuition, this work proposes a task-adaptive feature reweighting strategy within the framework of prototypical network [6]. Specifically, our method consists of three components, a feature encoder, a weight generator and a classifier, among which the generator is newly introduced module in this work. By considering the discrepancy between a class and the rest ones, the generator produces a feature weight for each class to highlight those most discriminative features to distinguish it from the rest classes. As a result, when compared with different classes, the same class is equipped with different feature weights to focus on different features for better classification. Hence, this method is more discriminative than prototypical network [6]. From the point of view of meta learning, the weight generator is a meta-learner, which learns to pick out those most discriminative features between a class and the other classes to be compared with. By training the network across different tasks as most meta learning methods do, the weight generator generalizes well to a new task. Experimental results on two commonly used few shot classification benchmarks, *mini*ImageNet and *tiered*ImageNet, show that our proposed method outperforms the state-of-the-art works demonstrating its effectiveness.

2 Related Work

Generative Approaches. In the early stage of few shot classification, most works employ generative models to solve this problem. One of the earliest work [20] develops a Bayesian probabilistic model on the features of previous classes with the premise that a prior from previous classes could be generalized to novel classes. Hierarchical Bayesian Program learning method [16] proposes to use a hierarchical Bayesian model to construct handwritten characters from strokes for digital classification. [11] proposes to compose characters from patches and construct an AND-OR graph using patches to represent each character object. Such powerful generative models perform well on classes with limited intra-class variation such as handwritten characters. However, these models cannot capture the vast variation for unconstrained classes.

Regularization and Data Augmentation Approaches. Regularization technique is a natural way to alleviate the overfitting problem, making fine-tuning a pre-trained model feasible for few shot classification. [8] proposes to group the parameters of a network into clusters and the parameters in the same cluster share the same weight and gradient, which effectively regularizes the dimensionality of parameter search space. Another straightforward method for few shot classification is data augmentation. In addition to regular augmentation techniques, e.g. random crop and rotation, color jittering and PCA jittering, modern generative networks [24,26–29] are proposed to generate realistic images. Despite significant progress, these models suffer from the problem of mode collapse and training instability.

Meta-Learning Approaches. Lately, meta learning becomes a popular way to solve few shot recognition problem. Meta learning learns at two level: (1) learns a meta-learner which extracts knowledge through a slow learning phase across all tasks and (2) then learns rapidly for a target task using the meta-learner. The strategy of training across different tasks makes the learned model (i.e. the meta-learner) well generalize to novel tasks. MAML [10] learns a good initialization of networks across all tasks. On the basis of this initialization, only few updates of parameters are enough to achieve a good performance on a new target task. Meta-SGD [9] learns a meta-learner that can not only give an initialization to a network but also give update direction and learning rate to any differentiable learner such that it can learn effectively from a few examples even in one step. Some other works [6,12,14] learn a distance metric across tasks that can be transferred to the target task. Matching Network [12] learns a network that can extract full context representation for few labeled examples and queries and then uses cosine similarity to predict the label of queries. Prototypical Network [6] builds a prototype for each class, which is computed as the average of samples in that class, and then computes the similarity between a query and each prototype via Euclidean distance. Different from [6,12], Relation Network [14] directly learns a nonlinear similarity metric to compute the similarity of two images.

Memory-Based Approaches. There are some works that use memory-based networks for few shot classification task. Memory networks are networks augmented with an external memory that can be read and written based on location and content. The external memory is used to store knowledge or past experience that is useful for few shot recognition task. In [7], the few shot classification task is formalized as a sequence classification problem. At each time step, an LSTM controller read past experience from external memory and writes current feature to external memory. And the retrieved memory is used to classify current image. Here the external memory is used to hold data samples presented at previous steps. In [5], two memory components are introduced, one called external memory used to store representations of a large set of auxiliary classes, and the other called abstraction memory used to store concise information related to target categories. Read operation is defined on the external memory to retrieve related information from auxiliary classes. Two operations are defined on the abstraction memory, one read operation to retrieve useful memory from the abstraction memory to classify current query and one write operation which updates the abstraction memory using the information of current query and the retrieved memory from external memory. To use memory networks, the key is to design how to handle the memory. And until now how to train a memory network is still a challenging problem.

3 Method

3.1 Problem

Few shot classification aims at getting an effective classifier by only using few examples for each class. A few shot classification task generally involves a support set S containing few labeled examples and a query set Q containing examples to be classified. If the support set contains N unique classes and K examples for each of these classes, the task is called N-way K-shot classification.

Recently meta learning is widely used to few shot classification task. Meta learning, also referred to as learning to learn, endeavors to learn from sparse data rapidly. It learns at two level, a gradual learning process for a meta learner which can guide a rapid learning process for a learner targeting a specific task. Meta learning approaches usually consists of two phases, meta training and meta testing. In meta-training phase, a meta learner is trained across different tasks sampled from a meta dataset. The meta dataset is usually a large labeled dataset containing C classes with many samples for each class, and has no overlap with the support set and query set of the testing task. In each training iteration, the meta learner randomly samples a N-way K-shot task from meta dataset to

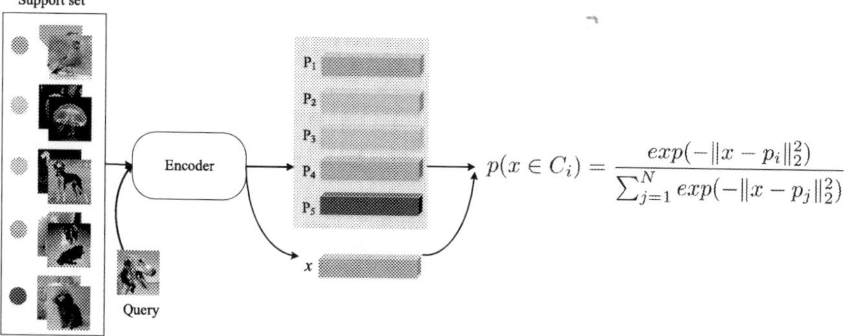

Fig. 1. Prototypical network [6]. It consists of an encoder used to extract feature and a non-parameterized classifier. The classifier computes a probability distribution over classes of query x based on its distance with the prototypes.

mimic the testing task. The selected support set together with the query set can also be called an episode. The meta learner is optimized by minimizing the classification loss on the query set in this episode. As the training process goes on, different tasks, i.e. different episodes, are sampled and used to train the meta learner. Therefore, the meta learner can learn useful and well generalized knowledge across different tasks. In the phase of meta-testing, the trained meta learner is directly used for a novel classification task.

3.2 Baseline Method: Prototypical Network [6]

Prototypical network is one of the state-of-the-art meta-learning methods for few shot classification. It is used as the baseline of our method considering its simplicity and effectiveness. Prototypical network consists of two modules, an encoder and a non-parameterized classifier, as shown in Fig. 1. The encoder E maps an input image I into a feature representation z in an embedding feature space $\mathcal{Z}$, i.e.,

$$z = E(I) \tag{1}$$

where the encoder E is usually structured as a four-layer convolutional network. In the embedding feature space, a prototype for each class p_i is computed as the mean of the few examples in the support set, formulated as follows:

$$p_i = \frac{1}{K}\sum_{k=1}^{K} z_i^k \tag{2}$$

where z_i^k is the k-th sample of i-th class in the support set. The classifier produces a softmax-like distribution over classes of a query x based on its Euclidean distances with the prototypes:

$$p(y=i|x) = \frac{exp(-d(x,p_i))}{\sum_{j=1}^{N} exp(-d(x,p_j))}, \quad i=1,2,\cdots,N. \tag{3}$$

$$d(x,p_i) = \|x-p_i\|_2^2, \quad i=1,2,\cdots,N. \tag{4}$$

where $p(y = i|x)$ is the probability of predicting query x as the i-th class. Using the standard cross-entropy loss as supervision signal, the whole network is trained across different tasks from scratch in an end-to-end manner.

In testing phase, the encoder E is directly used to a novel task to extract the feature representation of samples in support set and query set. Finally, the classification of a query sample is simply performed by finding the nearest class prototype under the Euclidean distance metric.

3.3 Our Method: Task-Adaptive Prototypical Network

In prototypical network [6], the learned feature representation is generally discriminative across many tasks, but not finely carved for a specific testing task. As well known, when distinguishing a class from different classes, the most discriminative features are different. For example, when distinguishing snow from hail, the most discriminative feature is its shape, while distinguishing snow and soil the most discriminative feature turns to color. In other words, a feature representation across the board is not optimal, and a carved one for the specific task is preferred. Following this intuition, this work proposes a task-adaptive feature reweighting strategy to extend prototypical network [6] for further improvement. Feature weighting highlights those most discriminative features that can distinguish a class from the rest classes in the same task, not from all other classes. When distinguishing one class from different classes in different tasks, those highlighted features are different. Thus our proposed network is called as Task-adaptive Prototypical Network.

Overall Framework. As Fig. 2 shows, our proposed task-adaptive Prototypical Network consists of three main components, an encoder used to extract features of examples, a feature weight generator used to produce a feature weight for each class and a non-parameterized classifier used for final classification. The feature weight generator is the newly introduced in this work and the rest two parts are the same as prototypical network [6].

In detail, for a N-way K-shot classification task, the images of the support set are fed into the encoder and the encoder outputs a feature representation for each image. Then these features are fed into the weight generator module and the module produces a feature weight for each class, which is used to re-weight the features of this class. Based on the feature weights, the distance between a query sample x and the i-th prototype p_i is computed as below:

$$d(x,p_i) = \|w_i \cdot x - w_i \cdot p_i\|_2^2 \tag{5}$$

where w_i is weight vector, p_i and x are feature vectors and $\cdot$ means dot product operation. The probability of query x belonging to the i-th class is computed as:

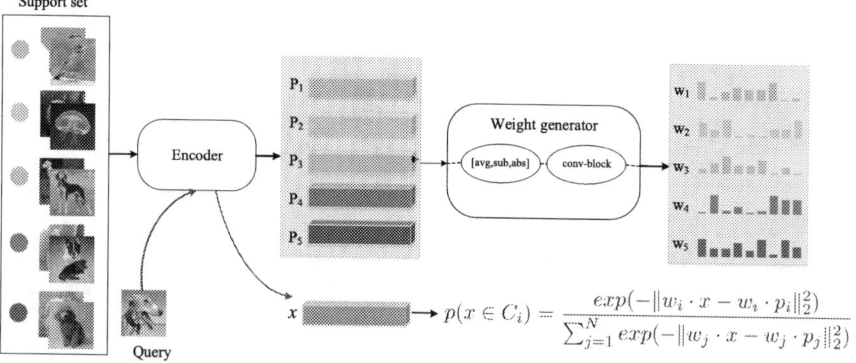

Fig. 2. Our task-adaptive prototypical network is an extension of Prototypical Network [6]. It consists of three components, an encoder used to extract feature, a newly introduced weight generator used to produce feature weight for each class and a non-parameterized classifier. The classifier computes a probability distribution over classes of query x based on its distance with the re-weighted prototypes.

$$p(y = i|x) = \frac{exp(-\|w_i \cdot x - w_i \cdot p_i)\|_2^2)}{\sum_{j=1}^{N} exp(-\|w_j \cdot x - w_j \cdot p_j)\|_2^2)} \tag{6}$$

Similar to prototypical network [6], in training phase the parameters of the encoder and weight generator can be easily optimized by using the standard cross-entropy loss as supervision signal in an end-to-end manner. In the testing phase, the encoder and weight generator is directly used to a novel task.

Weight Generator Module. It is obvious that the most discriminative feature for a class would be among those features that are different between this class and the rest ones in the same task. Therefore, the weight generator takes the feature differences between the classes as input and outputs the feature weights.

Specifically, the weight generator is structured as a small sub-network with several convolutional layers, denoted as G. As shown in Fig. 3, given a support set S of a N-class K-shot task, the weight generator computes the feature weight of one class based on the feature differences between its prototype and the rest ones, which can be formalized as:

$$w_i = G\left(\left|p_i - \frac{1}{N-1}\sum_{j \neq i} p_j\right|\right) \tag{7}$$

where w_i is the feature weight vector of the i-th class with each value between 0 and 1 and its dimension is the same as feature dimension.

The generator targets to learn how to compute discriminating power of a feature based on its inter-class variation, i.e. feature differences. Here we adopt convolutional structure to model G. The reasons are two-folded. The first one is that sharing the same kernel in the way of convolution can reduce the parameters. The second one is that the feature weight is only related to feature variations rather than the feature itself, which means that different features can use the

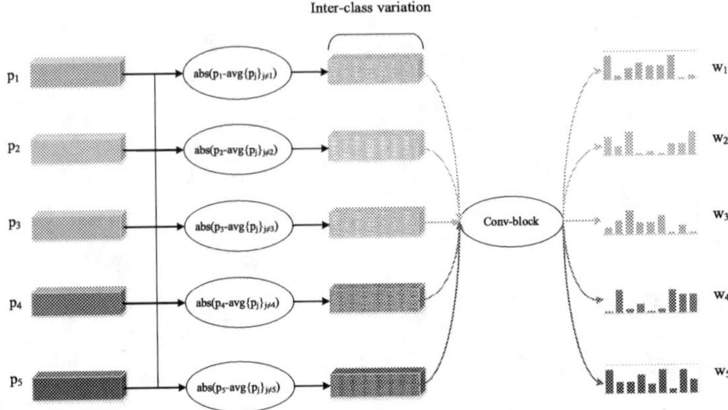

Fig. 3. The weight generator in the 5-way 1-shot classification scenario. For each class, the feature differences between its prototype and the other four prototypes are computed and averaged as inter-class variation. Then the inter-class variation together with its prototype are fed into a convolution block and the feature weight is produced. The weight generator is trained together with the encoder in an end-to-end way.

same parameters to compute their weights. Hence the generator can be naturally implemented as a convolutional structure.

This whole task-adaptive network is trained from scratch using the schema of meta learning. The standard cross-entropy loss function is taken as the supervision signal, and the back propagation and gradient descent algorithm are used to optimize the following objective in an end-to-end manner:

$$\min_{E,G} L = \sum_{I \in Q} -log(p(y = y_I|I)) \tag{8}$$

where I is an image in the query set Q of an episode and y_I is the ground truth label of image I.

4 Experiments

Our proposed method is evaluated by comparing it with the state-of-the-art ones [6,9,10,12,14] on two few shot classification benchmarks, *mini*ImageNet [12] and *tiered*ImageNet [21].

4.1 Experimental Setting

In our experiments, the encoder is composed of four convolutional blocks as prototypical network [6]. The newly introduced weight generator consists of one tiny convolutional block with kernel shared to significantly reduce the number of parameters. A detailed structure is listed in Table 1. The whole network is trained from scratch via Adam with random initialization.

Table 1. The structure of our task-adaptive prototypical network. Here, conv(n × n,c) means a convolutional layer with c channels and n is the kernel size. bn means batch normalization layer and relu is the non-linear ReLU activation layer. max-pool(n × n) is a max-pooling layer with n × n kernel size.

Encoder				Weight generator
block1	block2	block3	block4	
conv(3 × 3,64) bn relu max-pool(2 × 2)	conv(3 × 3,64) bn relu max-pool(2 × 2)	conv(3 × 3,64) bn relu max-pool(2 × 2)	conv(3 × 3,64) bn relu max-pool(2 × 2)	conv(3 × 3,2) relu conv(1 × 1,1)

For fair comparison, all methods are evaluated on the same evaluation setting, i.e. 600 episodes are randomly sampled from the test set, with each episode containing 15 query images per class in both 1-shot and 5-shot scenarios. The final classification performance is computed as the average classification accuracy over these 600 episodes.

4.2 Few-Shot Classification on *mini*ImageNet

*mini*ImageNet, firstly proposed by Matching Network [12], is a subset of ILSVRC-12 dataset [22]. This dataset contains 100 classes with 600 images in each class. We use 64 classes as training set, 16 classes as validation set and the remaining 20 classes as test set, same as the compared methods for fair comparison. All the images are resized to 84 × 84. In training process, each episode contains 30 classes and 15 queries for each class on the 1-shot scenario, and 20 classes with 15 queries for each class on the 5-shot scenario.

Table 2 shows the performance of few shot classification on the *mini*ImageNet. From Table 2, we can see that the Prototypical Network [6] performs the best in 5-shot scenario among the existing works, but only ordinarily in the 1-shot scenario. With the proposed feature re-weighting strategy, our method outperforms the Prototypical Network and other existing works in both 1-shot and 5-shot scenarios, especially on the one-shot scenario. Compared to Relation Network [14], our model with half number of parameters gets a nearly 2% higher performance on the 1-shot scenario and a nearly 4% improvement on the 5-shot scenario. The superior performance on this dataset demonstrates the effectiveness of our proposed feature re-weighting strategy. Moreover, the reweighting strategy can be easily integrated into any other framework besides prototypical network [6].

4.3 Few-Shot Classification on *tiered*ImageNet

*tiered*ImageNet is another larger dataset for few shot classification. It is proposed in [21]. Like *mini*ImageNet, it is also a subset of ILSVRC-12 [22]. This dataset contains 34 categories and 608 classes in total, with each category containing between 10 and 30 classes. These categories are split into 20 for training, 6 for

Table 2. Few-shot classification accuracies on *mini*Imagenet. All accuracy results are averaged over 600 test episodes and are reported with 95% confidence intervals. The performances of other methods are copied from their report. 'Y' in column Finetune means the method fine-tunes the model learned at meta-training stage for a test episode. The best-performing method is highlighted.

Model	Finetune	5-way	
		1-shot	5-shot
Matching network [12]	N	43.56% ± 0.84%	55.31% ± 0.73%
MAML [10]	Y	48.70% ± 1.84%	63.11% ± 0.92%
Prototypical network [6]	N	49.42% ± 0.78%	68.20% ± 0.66%
Graph network [13]	N	50.33% ± 0.36%	66.41% ± 0.63%
Meta-SGD [9]	Y	50.47% ± 1.87%	64.03% ± 0.94%
Relation network [14]	N	50.44% ± 0.82%	65.32% ± 0.70%
Ours	N	**52.10% ± 0.60%**	**69.07% ± 0.53%**

validation and 8 for testing. The classes in one category belong to the same high-level concept. Hence, the training classes are sufficiently distinct from the testing classes, making tieredImageNet a more challenging dataset.

The results are shown in Table 3. From Table 3 we can see that on this more challenging dataset, our method also achieves state-of-the-art performance on both the 1-shot and 5-shot scenarios demonstrating the effectiveness of the feature re-weighting strategy again.

4.4 Visualization of Generated Feature Weight

To better understand the weight generator, we further visualize the feature weights to see if it learned those most discriminative features between classes. Figure 4 shows the learned feature weights of two tasks, one comparing a horse to a donkey, the other comparing this horse to a zebra. Here, the visualization of one weight value is achieved by computing the gradient with respect to the input image of the feature equipped with this weight value [30]. By this way, what the feature equipped with one specific weight value looks like can be visualized. As can be seen, when comparing a horse with a donkey, the feature with the top three largest weight value focus on its head totally different from the head of the donkey. And when comparing the same horse with a zebra, the features with the top three largest weight values focus on its partial body without black and white strips which is the most different between these two classes. As expected, the most highlighted feature of the same class under different tasks is different. This result proves that the feature weight produced by the weight generator truly highlights those most discriminative features and is adaptive to different tasks.

Table 3. *tiered*Imagenet few shot classification performance. All accuracy results are averaged over 600 test episodes and are reported with 95% confidence intervals. The performances of other methods are achieved by running their released code. 'Y' in column Finetune means the method fine-tunes the model learned at meta-training stage for a test episode. For each task, the best-performing method is highlighted.

Model	Finetune	5-way	
		1-shot	5-shot
Matching network [12]	N	40.75% ± 0.80%	51.13% ± 0.71%
MAML [10]	Y	44.83% ± 1.85%	66.41% ± 0.09%
Meta-SGD [9]	Y	49.90% ± 1.92%	65.97% ± 0.09%
Graph network [13]	N	50.84% ± 0.36%	68.67% ± 0.63%
Prototypical network [6]	N	52.12% ± 0.68%	69.82% ± 0.58%
Relation network [14]	N	53.71% ± 0.94%	70.28% ± 0.77%
Ours	N	**53.85% ± 0.67%**	**72.36% ± 0.56%**

We provide more visualization results of generated weights, including success cases shown in Fig. 5 and failure cases shown in Fig. 6. These success cases further verify the effectiveness of our proposed weight generator. The failures could be roughly categorized into two kinds. The first category is caused by distraction of background with rich texture (see a, d in Fig. 6) and high-contrast global features (see b in Fig. 6). In some other cases, the features with larger weights are missing or occluded in the respective original images (see the black gradient images in c, e, f of Fig. 6).

Moreover, Fig. 7 shows some success and failure classification cases of our method and prototypical network [6]. From the figure, we can see that for those middle-level hard queries prototypical network [6] fails to classify, our method can handle them successfully.

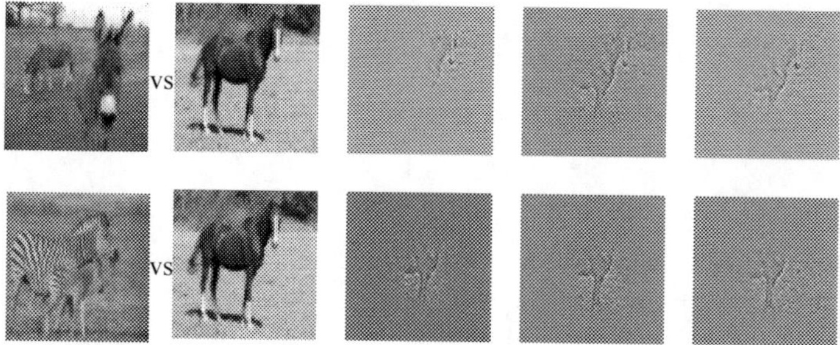

Fig. 4. Feature weight visualization for two different tasks. The first two columns are two classes to be compared in support set. The remaining three columns show the feature equipped with the top three largest weight of the horse.

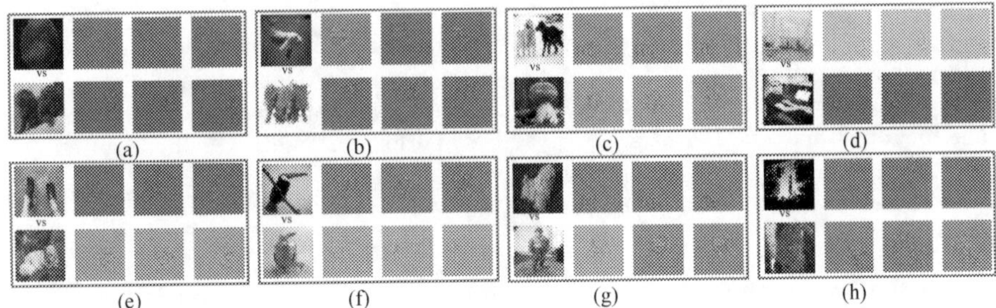

Fig. 5. Visualization of features with top-3 largest weights for each class in 2-way 1-shot setting. Eight success cases given. From these examples we can see that our reweighting mechanism truly highlights those most discriminative features.

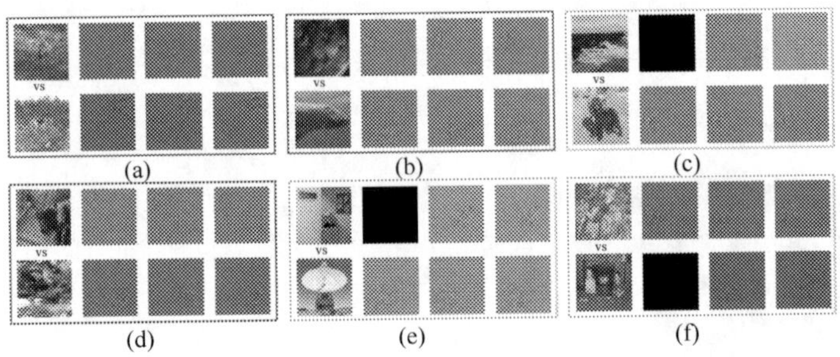

Fig. 6. Visualization of features with top-3 largest weights for each class in 2-way 1-shot setting. Six failure cases given. Failures can be categorized into two kinds: one caused by the distraction of background or high-contrast global feature, e.g. a, b, d, and the other caused by missing (occluded) feature e.g. c, e, f.

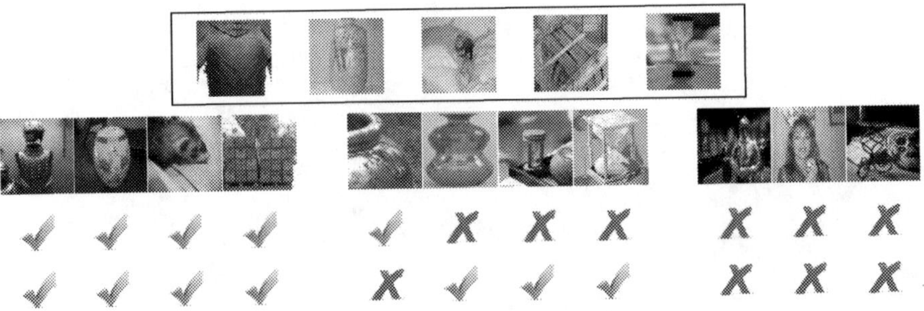

Fig. 7. An example of a 5-way 1-shot classification. The first row and the second row are respectively the support set and the query set. The third row and the fourth row respectively show the classification accuracy of prototypical network [6] and our method.

5 Conclusions

In this work, we propose a novel task-adaptive feature reweighting module to extend the recent prototypical network [6] for better classification performance. The newly introduced feature reweighting module can highlight those most discriminative features of each class to better distinguish it from the rest ones. As a result, each class has its own feature weights and these feature weights are adaptively different in different tasks. We conduct extensively experiments to evaluate the effectiveness of our method. On one hand, we qualitatively demonstrate that the feature weights produced by the weight generator can truly highlight those most discriminative features of each class and are adaptive to different tasks. On the other hand, quantitative experimental results show that our method can achieve the state-of-the-art performance on two commonly used benchmarks for few shot classification task demonstrating the effectiveness of our method.

Acknowledgements. This work was partially supported by National Key R&D Program of China under contracts No.2017YFA0700804 and Natural Science Foundation of China under contracts Nos. 61650202, 61772496, 61402443 and 61532018.

References

1. Krizhevsky A., Sutskever I., Hinton G.: ImageNet classification with deep convolutional neural networks. In: Advances in Neural Information Processing Systems (NIPS) (2012)
2. Szegedy C., et al.: Going deeper with convolutions. In: IEEE Conference on Computer Vision and Pattern Recognition (CVPR) (2015)
3. He, K., Zhang, X., Ren, S., Sun, J.: Deep residual learning for image recognition. In: IEEE Conference on Computer Vision and Pattern Recognition (CVPR) (2016)
4. Huang, G., Liu, Z., Maaten, L., Weinberger, K.: Densely connected convolutional networks. In: IEEE Conference on Computer Vision and Pattern Recognition (CVPR) (2017)
5. Xu, Z., Zhu, L., Yang, Y.: Few-shot object recognition from machine-labeled web images. In: IEEE Conference on Computer Vision and Pattern Recognition (CVPR) (2017)
6. Snell, J., Swersky, K., Zemel, R.: Prototypical networks for few-shot learning. In: Advances in Neural Information Processing Systems (NIPS) (2017)
7. Santoro, A., Bartunov, S., Botvinick, M., Wierstra, D., Lillicrap, T.: Meta-learning with memory-augmented neural networks. In: International Conference on Machine Learning (ICML) (2016)
8. Yoo, D., Fan, H., Boddeti, V., Kitani, K.: Efficient k-shot learning with regularized deep networks. In: AAAI Conference on Artificial Intelligence (AAAI) (2018)
9. Li, Z., Zhou, F., Chen, F., Li, H.: Meta-SGD: Learning to Learn Quickly for Few Shot Learning. CoRR abs/1707.09835 (2017)
10. Finn, C., Abbeel, P., Levine, S.: Model-agnostic meta-learning for fast adaptation of deep networks. In: International Conference on Machine Learning (ICML) (2017)
11. Wong, A., Yuille, A.: One shot learning via compositions of meaningful patches. In: IEEE International Conference on Computer Vision (ICCV) (2015)

12. Vinyals, O., Blundell, C., Lillicrap, T., Kavukcuoglu, K., Wierstra, D.: Matching networks for one shot learning. In: Advances in Neural Information Processing Systems (NIPS) (2016)
13. Satorras V., Estrach J.: Few-shot learning with graph neural networks. In: International Conference on Learning Representations (ICLR) (2018)
14. Sung, F., Yang, Y., Zhang, L., Xiang, T., Torr, P., Hospedales, T.: Learning to compare: relation network for few-shot learning. In: IEEE Conference on Computer Vision and Pattern Recognition (CVPR) (2018)
15. Koch, G., Zemel, R., Salakhutdinov, R.: Siamese neural networks for one-shot image recognition. In: ICML Workshop on Deep Learning (2015)
16. Lake, B., Salakhutdinov, R., Tenenbaum, J.: Human-level concept learning through probabilistic program induction. Science **350**, 1332–1338 (2015)
17. Salakhutdinov, R., Tenenbaum, J., Torralba, A.: One-shot learning with a hierarchical nonparametric Bayesian model. In: ICML Workshop on Unsupervised and Transfer Learning (2012)
18. Hariharan, B., Girshick, R.: Low-shot visual recognition by shrinking and hallucinating features. In: IEEE International Conference on Computer Vision (ICCV) (2017)
19. Yosinski, J., Clune, J., Bengio, Y., Lipson, H.: How transferable are features in deep neural networks? In: Advances in Neural Information Processing Systems (NIPS) (2014)
20. Li, F., Fergus, R., Perona, P.: One-shot learning of object categories. IEEE Trans. Pattern Anal. Mach. Intell. (TPAMI) **28**, 594–611 (2006)
21. Ren, M., et al.: Meta-learning for semi-supervised few-shot classification. In: International Conference on Learning Representations (ICLR) (2018)
22. Russakovsky, O., et al.: ImageNet large scale visual recognition challenge. Int. J. Comput. Vis. (IJCV) **115**, 211–252 (2015)
23. Guo, L., Zhang, L.: One-shot Face Recognition by Promoting Underrepresented Classes. CoRR abs/1707.05574 (2017)
24. Goodfellow, I., et al.: Generative adversarial nets. In: Advances in Neural Information Processing Systems (NIPS) (2014)
25. Rezende, D., Mohamed, S., Wierstra, D.: Stochastic backpropagation and approximate inference in deep generative models. In: International Conference on Machine Learning (ICML) (2014)
26. Mirza, M., Osindero, S.: Conditional Generative Adversarial Nets. CoRR abs/1411.1784 (2014)
27. Radford, A., Metz, L., Chintala, S.: Unsupervised Representation Learning with Deep Convolutional Generative Adversarial Networks. CoRR abs/1511.06434 (2015)
28. Mao, X., Li, Q., Xie, H., Lau, R., Wang, Z., Smolley, S.: Least squares generative adversarial networks. In: IEEE International Conference on Computer Vision (ICCV) (2017)
29. Gulrajani, I., Ahmed, F., Arjovsky, M., Dumoulin, V., Courville, A.: Improved training of wasserstein GANs. In: Advances in Neural Information Processing Systems (NIPS) (2017)
30. Simonyan, K., Vedaldi, A., Zisserman, A.: Deep Inside Convolutional Networks: Visualising Image Classification Models and Saliency Maps. CoRR abs/1312.6034 (2013)

Deep Attention-Based Classification Network for Robust Depth Prediction

Ruibo Li[1], Ke Xian[1], Chunhua Shen[2], Zhiguo Cao[1(✉)], Hao Lu[1], and Lingxiao Hang[1]

[1] Huazhong University of Science and Technology, Wuhan, China
{liruibo,kexian,zgcao}@hust.edu.cn
[2] The University of Adelaide, Adelaide, Australia

Abstract. In this paper, we present our deep attention-based classification (DABC) network for robust single image depth prediction, in the context of the Robust Vision Challenge 2018 (ROB 2018) (http://www.robustvision.net/index.php). Unlike conventional depth prediction, our goal is to design a model that can perform well in both indoor and outdoor scenes with a single parameter set. However, robust depth prediction suffers from two challenging problems: (a) How to extract more discriminative features for different scenes (compared to a single scene)? (b) How to handle the large differences of depth ranges between indoor and outdoor datasets? To address these two problems, we first formulate depth prediction as a multi-class classification task and apply a softmax classifier to classify the depth label of each pixel. We then introduce a global pooling layer and a channel-wise attention mechanism to adaptively select the discriminative channels of features and to update the original features by assigning important channels with higher weights. Further, to reduce the influence of quantization errors, we employ a soft-weighted sum inference strategy for the final prediction. Experimental results on both indoor and outdoor datasets demonstrate the effectiveness of our method. It is worth mentioning that we won the 2-nd place in single image depth prediction entry of ROB 2018, in conjunction with IEEE Conference on Computer Vision and Pattern Recognition (CVPR) 2018.

Keywords: Robust depth prediction · Attention · Classification network

1 Introduction

Single image depth prediction is a challenging task that aims to recover pixel-wise depth from monocular images, which plays an important role in many applications, such as 3D modeling, autonomous driving, and 2D-to-3D conversion. With the prosperity of deep convolutional neural networks (CNNs),

R. Li and K. Xian—Equal contribution.

C. V. Jawahar et al. (Eds.): ACCV 2018, LNCS 11364, pp. 663–678, 2019.
https://doi.org/10.1007/978-3-030-20870-7_41

many deep learning-based methods [6,17,24] have achieved state-of-the-art performance on various RGB-D datasets, such as NYUv2 [19], ScanNet [5], and KITTI [8]. However, all these methods are trained individually on each dataset, which makes models be specific to certain domains. For example, ScanNet only focuses on indoor scenes, while KITTI considers outdoor views. The large differences between indoor and outdoor patterns limit the generalization ability of the model. That is, a model achieves remarkable performance on one dataset but performs poorly on the other one, as shown in Fig. 1. In this paper, we study how to make the model robust so that it can perform well on diverse datasets.

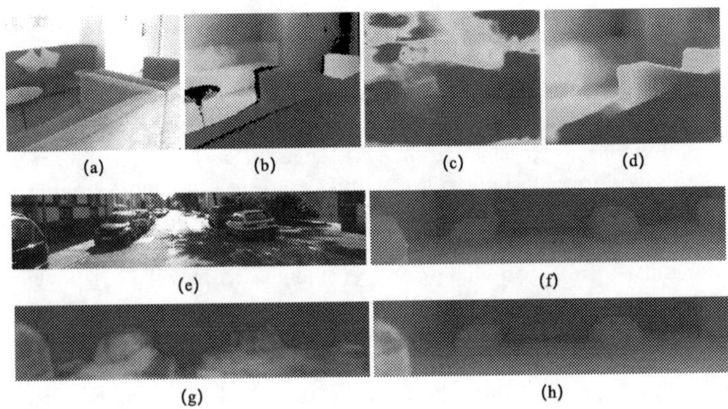

Fig. 1. Some examples on robust depth prediction. (a) and (e) are the input images from ScanNet and KITTI, respectively. (b) and (f) are corresponding ground truth depth maps. (c) is a depth map predicted by a model trained on KITTI. (g) is a depth map predicted by another model trained on ScanNet. (d) and (h) are the results predicted by our DABC model.

One challenge for robust depth prediction is how to extract discriminative features from diverse scenes. Compared with conventional depth prediction, robust depth prediction requires one single model to perform well in both indoor and outdoor scenes. Thus, the model should adapt to diverse scene layouts and tackle complex depth patterns. Another challenge is the large difference of depth ranges between indoor and outdoor. For example, the depth range of ScanNet is from 0 m to 10 m, while the depth range of KITTI is between 2.5 m and 80 m. It is worth noting that two datasets exist an overlapped depth range from 2.5 m to 10 m. In this range, different layouts belonging to indoor or outdoor scenes may correspond to the same depth value, which increases the difficulty of training models.

In this paper, we present a deep attention-based classification network (DABC) to address these problems. In order to tackle diverse scenes, our model learns a universal RGB-to-depth mapping from both the ScanNet and KITTI datasets. Our model is based on a U-shape [15,18,24] structure, where skip-connections fuse multi-scale depth cues to generate accurate and high-resolution results. To extract discriminative features, we employ a global average pooling layer and a channel-wise attention mechanism to our model. Through the global average pooling layer, the model can capture the channel-wise statistics of features that represent the global information and visual characteristics of a scene. According to the channel-wise statistics, the attention mechanism assigns important channels with higher weights and updates the original features. In addition, to tolerate the significant difference of depth ranges, we formulate depth prediction as a multi-class classification problem. By discretizing continuous depth values into several intervals, we choose a softmax layer as the predictor. In this way, each neuron in the last layer only needs to activate for a specific depth interval rather than to predict the depth value in the whole depth range, which makes the model easy to train. Further, to reduce the influence of quantization error caused by depth discretization, we employ a soft-weighted sum inference method [1] to obtain the final continuous predictions.

The contributions of this work can be summarized as follows:

- We present one of the first explorations on the task of robust depth prediction and propose a deep attention-based classification network (DABC).
- For the task of depth prediction, we are the first to employ the channel-wise attention mechanism, and verify the effectiveness of the attention module on choosing scene-specific features.
- Our method achieves state-of-the-art performance on both the ScanNet and KITTI datasets, and won the 2-nd place in the single image depth prediction entry of ROB 2018.

2 Related Work

Metric Depth Prediction. Recently, many methods have achieved impressive performance by employing CNNs to monocular depth prediction. In order to regress the depth map from a RGB image, Eigen et al. [6] proposed a multi-scale architecture which consists of two CNNs: the first one predicts the coarse depth map based on global context, the second one refines the coarse prediction using local information. Laina et al. [13] applied the residual learning [9] to the depth prediction task and presented an encoder-decoder model with a novel up-sampling module. In order to encourage spatial consistency in the predicted depth map, some researchers tried to formulate a structured regression problem by combining CNNs with Conditional Random Fields (CRFs). For instance, Liu et al. [17] proposed an end-to-end network by incorporating a CRF loss layer into a generic superpixel-wise CNN. The spatial relation of adjacent superpixels can be modeled by a CRF, and the parameters of CNN and CRF can be jointly optimized. Instead of just refining the coarse predictions, Xu et al. [26] designed a novel continuous CRF framework to merge multi-scale features derived from CNN inner layers.

Aside from regressing the exact depth values from a RGB image, Cao et al. [2] recast depth estimation as a pixel-wise classification problem to classify the depth range for each pixel. Further, Li et al. [1] proposed a soft-weighted-sum inference strategy to replace the hard-max inference used in [2] to obtain continuous depth predictions. Fu et al. [7] formulated depth estimation as an ordinal regression problem, which considered the ordering of discrete depth ranges. However, the above models are only trained on indoor and outdoor datasets individually, which greatly limits the application of these models. In contrast, we propose an attention-based classification network which is adaptive for a variety of scenes and achieves the state-of-the-art performance on the ScanNet and KITTI datasets with a single parameter set.

Relative Depth Prediction. Some recent works [4,24] focus on recovering depth ordering from unconstrained monocular images instead of predicting the metric depth value directly. The idea behind relative depth prediction is similar to robust depth prediction, because they all need models to be applicable to diverse unconstrained natural scenes. However, when using a model trained on relative depth data to predict metric depth, a transformation function that converts relative depth values to metric depth values should be provided for each dataset separately, which reduces the practicality of the model. Thus, a model that can directly estimate metric depth from unconstrained images is more practical and effective.

Attention Mechanism. Recently, attention mechanism has been successfully applied to various tasks, such as image classification [10,23], monocular depth prediction [12,27], and semantic segmentation [3,28]. Kong et al. [12] presented a pixel-wise attentional gating unit to learn spatial allocation of computation in dense labeling tasks. Xu et al. [27] proposed an attention-based CRF where a structured attention model [11] is applied to regulate the feature fusion across different scales. Unlike above methods, we focus on how to extract more discriminative features for diverse scenes with a channel-wise attention mechanism.

3 Method

In order to use a single model to estimate the depth map from an unconstrained image, we present a deep attention-based classification network (DABC) for robust depth prediction. As illustrated in Fig. 2, we reformulate robust depth prediction as a classification task and learn a universal RGB-to-depth mapping that is suitable for both indoor and outdoor scenes. In the following, we first describe the architecture of our DABC model. Then we discuss our discretization strategy and explain the technical details of learning and inference stages.

3.1 Network Architecture

As shown in Fig. 2, our deep attention-based classification model consists of three parts: feature extraction module, multi-scale feature fusion module, and prediction module. The feature extraction module is built upon ResNeXt-101 (64×4d) [25]. To make it suitable for the task of depth prediction, we first remove the last pooling layer, fully-connected layer and softmax layer. We divide ResNeXt into 4 blocks according to the size of the output feature maps. To capture global information, we attach a 1×1 convolution layer, global average pooling layer and unpooling layer to the top of the modified ResNeXt. Specifically, the 1×1 convolution layer is used to reduce the dimension of the feature maps from block4, and the global pooling layer is used to encode the global context features. The unpooling layer is used to restore the spatial resolution of the global features.

Due to max pooling and convolutional strides in ResNeXt, the size of final feature map is 1/32 of the original input image. Inspired by [16,24,28], we use a progressive refinement strategy, which aggregates high-level semantic features and low-level fine-grained features layer-by-layer, to generate high-resolution predictions. There exists a large difference between the information represented by low-level and high-level features. Thus, in each feature fusion block, we first use a feature transfer block (FTB) [28] to fine-tune the input features and adapt them for better feature fusion. The 1×1 Convolution layer in FTB is used to unify the dimension of features. Then, two groups of features are merged via an attention-based feature aggregation block (AFA) [28]. We consider that high-level features with much contextual information are more discriminative than low-level features. Thus, we leverage the attention module to enhance the discriminability of low-level features with the help of high-level features. At the beginning of each AFA block, a global pooling layer is used to capture channel-wise statistics of the two groups of features. According to the channel-wise statistics, two fully connected layers are employed to generate an attention vector that represents the importance of each channel in low-level features. Based on the attention vector, the low-level features are selectively summed to the high-level features to generate final outputs at the current scale. After the AFA, another FTB and a bilinear upsampling operation are stacked to enlarge the spatial resolution of the fused features. More specifically, the channel number of AFA connected to Block4 is 512 and the others are 256. In order to produce final score maps, we attach a prediction module to the end of the fusion module, which consists of a dropout layer, a 3×3 convolution layer and a softmax-loss layer.

3.2 Depth Discretization Strategy

To formulate depth prediction as a classification task, we discretize continuous depth values into several discrete bins in the log space. Assuming that the depth range is $[\alpha, \beta]$, the discretization strategy can be defined as

$$\begin{aligned} l &= round\left(\left(\log_{10}(d) - \log_{10}(\alpha)\right)/q\right), \\ q &= \left(\log_{10}(\beta) - \log_{10}(\alpha)\right)/K, \end{aligned} \tag{1}$$

where l is the quantized label, d is the original continuous depth value, K is the number of sub-intervals and q is the width of the quantization bin. Specifically, $[\alpha, \beta]$ are set to $[0.25, 80]$, and K is set to 150 through cross validation.

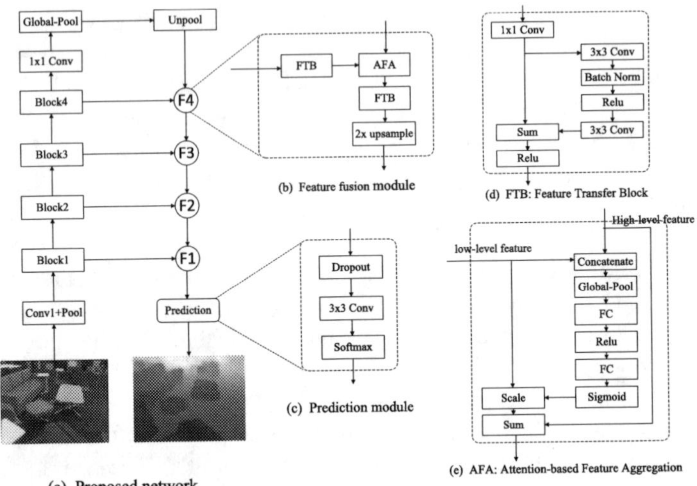

Fig. 2. Illustration of our DABC model for robust depth prediction. (a) is our proposed network. (b) shows the process of multi-scale feature fusion. (c) is a prediction module to generate score maps. (d) is a feature transfer block. (e) is an attention-based feature aggregation block to fuse multi-scale features.

3.3 Learning and Inference

At the training stage, we use the pixel-wise multinomial logistic loss function to train our DABC network:

$$L = -\frac{1}{N}\sum_{i=1}^{N}\sum_{D=1}^{K} 1\left\{y^{(i)} = D\right\} \log\left(P\left(D|c_i\right)\right), \tag{2}$$

where N is the number of valid training pixels in a mini-batch and $y^{(i)}$ is the ground truth label of pixel i. $P(D|c_i) = e^{c_{i,D}}/\sum_d^K e^{c_{i,d}}$ represents the probability of pixel i labelled with D, and $c_{i,d}$ is the output from the last 3×3 convolution layer.

At the inference stage, we use a soft-weighted sum inference strategy [1] to compute final predictions after obtaining the score maps from the softmax layer. For clarity, we use $\mathbf{p_i}$ to denote the score vector of pixel i. The depth value of pixel i can be calculated as:

$$\hat{d}_i = 10^{\mathbf{w}^T \mathbf{p_i}}, w_j = \log_{10}(\alpha) + q \cdot j, \tag{3}$$

where $\hat{d}_i$ is the predicted depth value of pixel i, $\mathbf{w}$ is a weight vector that constituted by the discretization thresholds of the original depth range in log space, and w_j is j-th element of $\mathbf{w}$.

4 Experiments

In this section, we evaluate our DABC model on two publicly available RGB-D datasets: ScanNet [5] and KITTI [21]. We first introduce the two datasets and the evaluation metrics. Then we give the details about our experimental setting. Finally, we compare our DABC model with the official baseline method and other outstanding methods that participate in this challenge.

4.1 Datasets and Metrics

Datasets. ScanNet [5] is a large-scale RGB-D dataset for indoor scene reconstruction, which contains 2.5M RGB-D images in 1513 scenes. Original RGB images are captured at a resolution of 1296×968 and depth at 640×480 pixels. Specially, the resized RGB images of the resolution 640×480 are also officially provided for the robust depth prediction task.

KITTI [21] contains street scene RGB-D videos captured by cameras and a LiDAR scanner. The resolution of RGB-D pairs is about 376×1242. In the KITTI dataset, less than 5% pixels of the raw depth map is valid, thus we fill in the missing pixels to produce dense ground truth depth maps for training via the "colorization" algorithm [14].

Evaluation Metrics. In order to measure the performance of our model, we introduce several evaluation metrics used in this robust vision challenge:

- The mean relative absolute error (absRel): $\frac{1}{Q}\sum_{i=1}^{Q}\frac{\left|d_i-\widehat{d_i}\right|}{d_i}$
- The mean relative squared error (sqRel): $\frac{1}{Q}\sum_{i=1}^{Q}\frac{\left(d_i-\widehat{d_i}\right)^2}{d_i^2}$
- The mean absolute error of the inverse depth (imae): $\frac{1}{Q}\sum_{i=1}^{Q}\left|p_i-\widehat{p_i}\right|$
- The root mean squared error of the inverse depth (irmse): $\sqrt{\frac{1}{Q}\sum_{i=1}^{Q}\left(p_i-\widehat{p_i}\right)^2}$
- Scale invariant error (SI): $\frac{1}{Q}\sum_{i=1}^{Q}\left(d_i-\widehat{d_i}+\alpha\left(d_i,\widehat{d_i}\right)\right)^2$, $\alpha\left(d_i,\widehat{d_i}\right)=\frac{1}{|S_i|}\sum\limits_{j\in S_i}\left(\widehat{d_j}-d_j\right)$
- Scale invariant logarithmic error (SILog): $\frac{1}{Q}\sum_{i=1}^{Q}\left(\log d_i-\log\widehat{d_i}+\alpha'\left(d_i,\widehat{d_i}\right)\right)^2$, $\alpha'\left(d_i,\widehat{d_i}\right)=\frac{1}{|S_i|}\sum\limits_{j\in S_i}\left(\log\widehat{d_j}-\log d_j\right)$

where d_i and $\widehat{d_i}$ denote the ground truth and estimated depth for pixel i, Q is the total number of valid pixels in the test images, p_i and $\widehat{p_i}$ represent the inverse of d_i and $\widehat{d_i}$, respectively. S_i is a set of pixels that belong to the same image with pixel i.

4.2 Experimental Setting

We implement our model using the public available `MatConvNet` [22] Library on a single Nvidia GTX 1080 GPU. The feature extraction module is initialized using ResNeXt-101 (64×4d), and the others are initialized with simple random Gaussian initialization. Data augmentation is performed on-the-fly during training. Specifically, horizontal flipping and randomly scaling are applied, and the default input resolution of our model is 256×320. We train our model using SGD with a mini-batch size of 8. The momentum and weight decay are set to 0.9 and 0.0005, respectively. We train our model with an initial learning rate of 0.001 for 30 epochs, and divide it by 10 for another 20 epochs.

During training, for ScanNet, we first downsample images to 240×320, and then pad the downsampled images to 256×320 with zeros. For KITTI, we first downsample images to 182×612. Then we randomly crop the images to the size of 182×320 by keeping the height constant, followed by padding the cropped images to 256×320 with zeros. To train our model, we use 37K officially provided training data. More specifically, the number of images from KITTI and ScanNet are 17K and 20K, respectively.

At the testing phase, we first downsample the input image to half. If the width of the image is larger than 320, we split it to two parts by keeping the height constant and the width of 320. Then, the image or image slices are padded with zeros to form the inputs of our model. After inference, we discard the invalid regions of the output depth maps and perform a bilinear interpolation to get our final predictions. Note that, for image slices, the depth values of overlapped regions are obtained by averaging the predictions of depth slices.

4.3 Experiment Results

In this section, our DABC model is compared with the official baseline method and the other three outstanding methods that participate in this challenge. Tables 1 and 2 show the results of the five models: (1) *Baseline*: an official baseline model based on GoogLeNetV1 [20]; (2) *DORN*: a deep ordinal regression network proposed by Fu et al. [7]; (3) *CSWS*: a classification model with soft-weighted-sum inference strategy trained by Li et al. [1]; (4) *APMOE*: a CNN model with pixel-wise attentional gating units proposed by Kong et al. [12]; (5) *DABC*: our proposed deep attention-based classification network. As shown in Tables 1 and 2, the errors of our DABC model are significantly lower than that of the official baseline model about by 40%–70% on both the KITTI and ScanNet. Compared with other methods, our DABC model achieves the first place on the ScanNet and the third place on the KITTI. Finally, our DABC model won the 2-nd place in single image depth prediction of ROB 2018. Some qualitative results are shown in Figs. 3 and 4, we observe our model well captures local image details and yields predictions of high visual quality in both outdoor and indoor scenes.

5 Discussion

In this section, we conduct a in-depth analysis of our DACB model. In following experiments, we use the ResNeXt-50 (32×4d) to replace the original ResNeXt-101 (64×4d) in our DABC model for fast training. Unless otherwise stated, the models are trained with the mixed ScanNet and KITTI data. In order to analyze the effectiveness of our model, we select the test images from the official validation set of these two datasets. For ScanNet, we use all images from its validation set, which contains 2537 images from 156 scenes. For KITTI, we choose one image every 5 consecutive frames from its validation set, thus creating 1370 images from 26 scenes for validation. First, we compare the DABC model against a conventional regression network. Second, we evaluate the effectiveness of the attention module in choosing discriminative features.

Table 1. Performance on the KITTI benchmark.

Method	SILog	sqRel	absRel	irmse
Baseline	33.49	24.06	29.72	35.22
CSWS [1]	14.85	3.48	11.84	16.38
APMOE [12]	14.74	3.88	11.74	15.63
DORN [7]	**13.53**	**3.06**	**10.35**	15.96
DABC	14.49	4.08	12.72	**15.53**

Table 2. Performance on the ScanNet benchmark.

Method	SI	sqRel	absRel	irmse	imae
Baseline	0.05	0.14	0.25	0.21	0.17
APMOE [12]	0.03	0.10	0.20	0.16	0.13
CSWS [1]	**0.02**	**0.06**	0.15	**0.13**	**0.10**
DORN [7]	**0.02**	**0.06**	**0.14**	**0.13**	**0.10**
DABC	**0.02**	**0.06**	**0.14**	**0.13**	**0.10**

5.1 Effect of Multi-class Classification

In order to verify the effectiveness of multi-class classification, we compare our model against a conventional regression network. In this experiment, the regression network is built upon the same basic structure as our DABC model and trained with a typical ℓ_2 loss function. Note that the attention module of the original structure is removed in the regression network, because we find this module hinders the convergence in practice. The experimental results are shown in Tables 3 and 4. Specially, all the metrics in Table 3 are multiplied by 100 for easy comparison. In particular, "Classification" refers to our DABC model, "Regression" refers to the regression model, and the symbol "*" indicates that the marked model is trained and evaluated on the same dataset.

Fig. 3. Qualitative results of our DABC model on the KITTI validation dataset: original color images (top row), ground truth depth maps (center), and predicted depth maps (bottom row). Color indicates depth (purple is far, yellow is close). (Color figure online)

From Tables 3 and 4, we observe that our DABC model is significantly better than the regression model on both the KITTI and ScanNet datasets. By comparing "Regression" against "Regression*", we find that training on the mixed data harms the accuracy of the regression model on each individual dataset. However, according to the results of "Classification" and "Classification*", we do not observe performance degradation, which suggests our DABC model can better adapt to the mixed data and avoid the mutual interference of different datasets.

Further, we draw the confusion matrices of our DABC model and the regression model on both the KITTI and ScanNet datasets. Here, each element (i, j) in the confusion matrix represents the empirical probability of each pixel known to be label i but estimated to be label j. In Fig. 5, we can observe a clear diagonal pattern in the matrices of our DABC model, which means that the accuracy of our DABC is higher than that of the regression model on the two datasets. Specially, we highlight the performance of each model on the overlapped depth ranges of two datasets, i.e. $i \in [60, 95]$. From Fig. 5(e)–(h), we find that our DABC model performs better than the regression model on this range. It indicates that our DABC model can tackle the complex depth patterns well in these easily-confusing depth ranges.

We believe that the outstanding performance of DABC model in robust depth prediction benefits from recasting depth prediction into a multi-class classification problem. When facing the complex depth patterns from indoor and outdoor

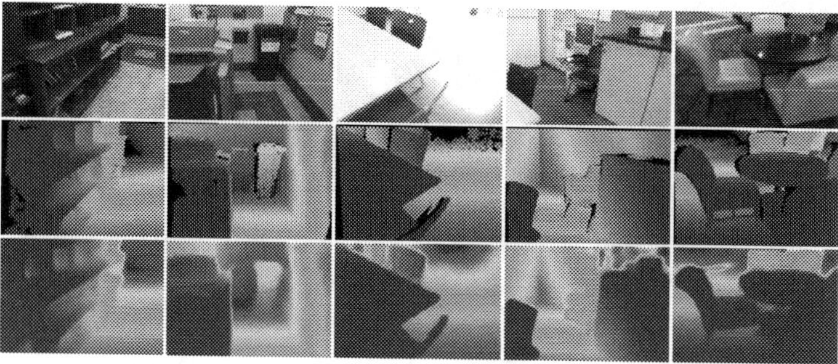

Fig. 4. Qualitative results of our DABC model on the ScanNet validation dataset: original color images (top row), ground truth depth maps (center), and predicted depth maps (bottom row). Color indicates depth (red is far, blue is close). The invalid regions in ground truth depth maps are painted black. (Color figure online)

scenes, in regression network, the last neuron should produce accurate activations for the whole depth patterns; but in the classification network, each neuron in last layer only corresponds to a specified depth interval and activates for some special depth patterns, which makes the classification network easy to train and to achieve better performance. Specially, in the overlapped depth range, the classification network shows stronger robustness. In practice, for each neuron of the last layer, if the depth value of a sample is far from the specified depth interval of this neuron, this sample is usually a easy negative example with a negligible loss contribution to the training of this neuron. Thus, the samples from outdoor scenes can hardly influence the training of the neurons that correspond to the indoor depth range, and vice versa. This is why our model can adapt to the mixed data and avoid the mutual interference of different datasets.

Table 3. Comparison between classification and regression on the ScanNet validation dataset.

Method	sqRel	absRel	irmse	imae
Regression*	5.93	17.05	18.65	11.84
Regression	6.51	17.47	18.65	11.73
Classification*	**4.33**	12.84	16.05	8.88
Classification	4.34	**12.67**	**15.93**	**8.71**

5.2 Effect of attention mechanism

In order to reveal the effectiveness of the channel-wise attention mechanism, we conduct an ablation study. Results are shown in Tables 5 and 6. Specially, each metric in Table 5 is multiplied by 100 for easy comparison. In these tables,

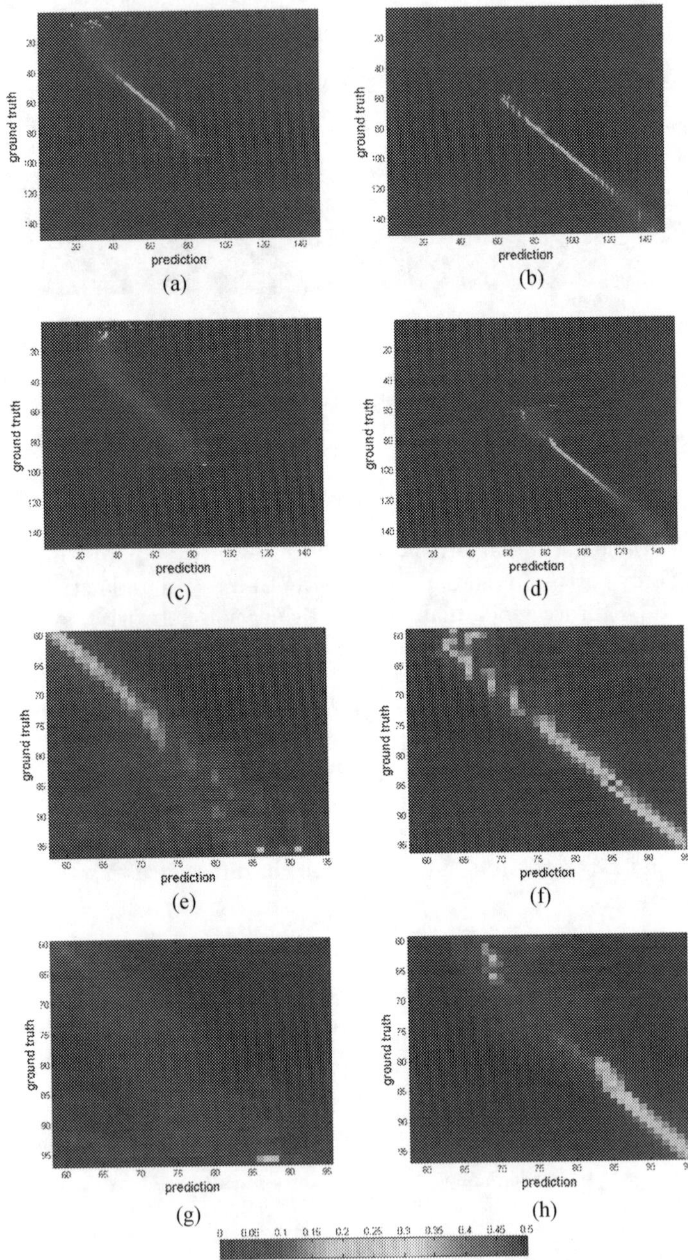

Fig. 5. Visualization of confusion matrices. (a) is the confusion matrix of our DABC model on the ScanNet. (b) is the confusion matrix of our DABC model on the KITTI. (c) is the confusion matrix of the regression network on the ScanNet. (d) is the confusion matrix of the regression network on the KITTI. (e)–(h) show the details of the above four confusion matrices in the label range of 60 to 95, respectively.

Table 4. Comparison between classification and regression on the KITTI validation dataset.

Method	SILog	sqRel	absRel	irmse
Regression*	14.55	2.26	9.33	11.45
Regression	14.49	2.28	9.44	11.63
Classification*	13.42	**1.92**	**7.86**	9.72
Classification	**13.34**	1.95	8.01	**9.58**

"DABC w/o attention" represents a DABC model that ignores the attention vectors and directly sums the multi-scale features in each fusion block. Compared with "DABC w/o attention", our DABC model makes a significant improvement on the ScanNet dataset and achieves comparable performance on the KITTI dataset.

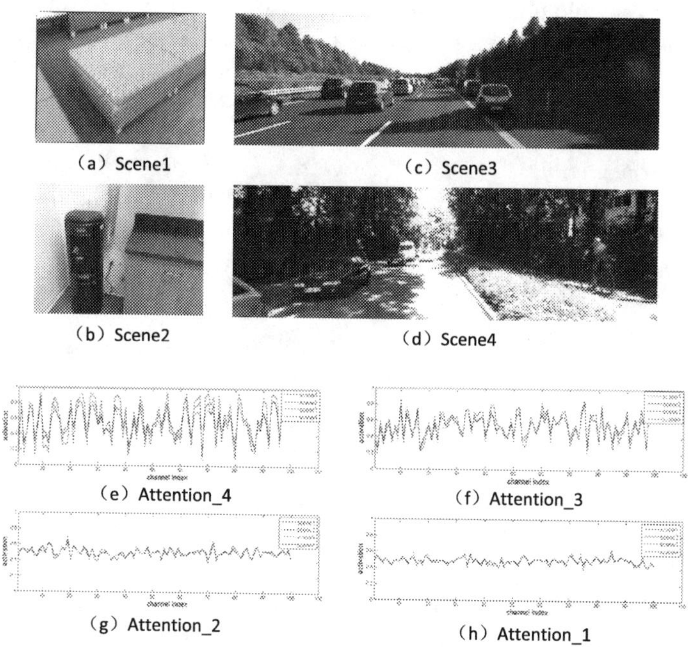

Fig. 6. Activations of different AFA modules. (a) and (b) are the color images from the ScanNet, (c) and (d) are from the KITTI. (e)–(h) are the activations of AFA modules from the high-level to the low-level in sequence.

Further, in order to visualize the activations, we choose four images from the KITTI and ScanNet datasets, and draw the activations of four AFA blocks, as shown in Fig. 6. For clarity, only one hundred activations of each block are visualized. We make three observations about the attention mechanism in robust

Table 5. Evaluation of the attention mechanism on the ScanNet validation dataset.

Method	sqRel	absRel	irmse	imae
DABC w/o attention	4.93	13.50	16.37	9.07
DABC	**4.34**	**12.67**	**15.93**	**8.71**

Table 6. Evaluation for attention mechanism on the KITTI validation dataset.

Method	SILog	sqRel	absRel	irmse
DABC w/o attention	**13.33**	2.00	**8.00**	**9.58**
DABC	13.34	**1.95**	8.01	**9.58**

depth prediction. First, we find that the activations of four scenes are more different in the high-level block than in the low-level one, which suggests that the values of each channel in the high-level features are scene-specific. Second, as per Fig. 6(e), we observe a significant difference between indoor and outdoor activations. It indicates that the attention mechanism can give different scenes with different activations based on the characteristics and the layout of the scene. Third, by comparing the activations of scene1 and scene2 in Fig. 6(e), we can also observe a non-negligible difference of activations between the two indoor scenes, which suggests that the attention mechanism still has a strong discriminating ability when processing the scenes from the same dataset.

Therefore, we consider that the channel-wise attention mechanism plays a vital role in choosing discriminative features for diverse scenes and improving the performance in robust depth prediction.

6 Conclusion

In this paper, we study the task of robust depth prediction that requires a model suitable for both indoor and outdoor scenes with a single parameter set. Unlike conventional depth prediction tasks, robust depth prediction task needs the model to extract more discriminative features for diverse scenes and to tackle the large differences in depth ranges between indoor and outdoor scenes. To this end, we proposed a deep attention-based classification network to learn a universal RGB-to-depth mapping which is suitable for both indoor and outdoor scenes, where a channel-wise attention mechanism is employed to update the features according to the importance of each channel. Experimental results on both indoor and outdoor datasets demonstrate the effectiveness of our method. Specifically, we won the 2nd place in the single image depth prediction entry of ROB 2018, in conjunction with CVPR 2018. In the future, we plan to extend our method to other dense prediction tasks.

Acknowledgement. This work was supported by the Project of the National Natural Science Foundation of China No. 61876211.

References

1. Li, B., Yuchao Dai, M.H.: Monocular depth estimation with hierarchical fusion of dilated CNNs and soft-weighted-sum inference (2018)
2. Cao, Y., Wu, Z., Shen, C.: Estimating depth from monocular images as classification using deep fully convolutional residual networks. IEEE Trans. Circ. Syst. Video Technol. **28**, 3174–3182 (2017)
3. Chen, L.C., Yang, Y., Wang, J., Xu, W., Yuille, A.L.: Attention to scale: scale-aware semantic image segmentation. In: Proceedings of the IEEE Conference on Computer Vision and Pattern Recognition, pp. 3640–3649 (2016)
4. Chen, W., Fu, Z., Yang, D., Deng, J.: Single-image depth perception in the wild. In: Advances in Neural Information Processing Systems, pp. 730–738 (2016)
5. Dai, A., Chang, A.X., Savva, M., Halber, M., Funkhouser, T., Nießner, M.: ScanNet: richly-annotated 3D reconstructions of indoor scenes. In: Proceedings of Computer Vision and Pattern Recognition (CVPR). IEEE (2017)
6. Eigen, D., Puhrsch, C., Fergus, R.: Depth map prediction from a single image using a multi-scale deep network. In: Advances in Neural Information Processing Systems, pp. 2366–2374 (2014)
7. Fu, H., Gong, M., Wang, C., Batmanghelich, K., Tao, D.: Deep ordinal regression network for monocular depth estimation. In: Proceedings of the IEEE Conference on Computer Vision and Pattern Recognition, pp. 2002–2011 (2018)
8. Geiger, A., Lenz, P., Stiller, C., Urtasun, R.: Vision meets robotics: the KITTI dataset. Int. J. Robot. Res. **32**(11), 1231–1237 (2013)
9. He, K., Zhang, X., Ren, S., Sun, J.: Deep residual learning for image recognition. In: Proceedings of the IEEE Conference on Computer Vision and Pattern Recognition, pp. 770–778 (2016)
10. Hu, J., Shen, L., Sun, G.: Squeeze-and-excitation networks. arXiv preprint arXiv:1709.01507 (2017)
11. Kim, Y., Denton, C., Hoang, L., Rush, A.M.: Structured attention networks. arXiv preprint arXiv:1702.00887 (2017)
12. Kong, S., Fowlkes, C.: Pixel-wise attentional gating for parsimonious pixel labeling. arXiv preprint arXiv:1805.01556 (2018)
13. Laina, I., Rupprecht, C., Belagiannis, V., Tombari, F., Navab, N.: Deeper depth prediction with fully convolutional residual networks. In: 2016 Fourth International Conference on 3D Vision (3DV), pp. 239–248. IEEE (2016)
14. Levin, A., Lischinski, D., Weiss, Y.: Colorization using optimization. In: ACM Transactions on Graphics (ToG), vol. 23, pp. 689–694. ACM (2004)
15. Lin, G., Milan, A., Shen, C., Reid, I.: Refinenet: multi-path refinement networks with identity mappings for high-resolution semantic segmentation. arXiv preprint arXiv:1611.06612 (2016)
16. Lin, G., Milan, A., Shen, C., Reid, I.: Refinenet: multi-path refinement networks for high-resolution semantic segmentation. In: IEEE Conference on Computer Vision and Pattern Recognition (CVPR), vol. 1, p. 3 (2017)
17. Liu, F., Shen, C., Lin, G., Reid, I.: Learning depth from single monocular images using deep convolutional neural fields. IEEE Trans. Pattern Anal. Mach. Intell. **38**(10), 2024–2039 (2016)
18. Ronneberger, O., Fischer, P., Brox, T.: U-Net: convolutional networks for biomedical image segmentation. In: Navab, N., Hornegger, J., Wells, W.M., Frangi, A.F. (eds.) MICCAI 2015. LNCS, vol. 9351, pp. 234–241. Springer, Cham (2015). https://doi.org/10.1007/978-3-319-24574-4_28

19. Silberman, N., Hoiem, D., Kohli, P., Fergus, R.: Indoor segmentation and support inference from RGBD images. In: Fitzgibbon, A., Lazebnik, S., Perona, P., Sato, Y., Schmid, C. (eds.) ECCV 2012. LNCS, vol. 7576, pp. 746–760. Springer, Heidelberg (2012). https://doi.org/10.1007/978-3-642-33715-4_54
20. Szegedy, C., et al.: Going deeper with convolutions. In: Proceedings of the IEEE Conference on Computer Vision and Pattern Recognition, pp. 1–9 (2015)
21. Uhrig, J., Schneider, N., Schneider, L., Franke, U., Brox, T., Geiger, A.: Sparsity invariant CNNs. In: International Conference on 3D Vision (3DV) (2017)
22. Vedaldi, A., Lenc, K.: Matconvnet - convolutional neural networks for matlab. In: Proceeding of the ACM International Conference on Multimedia (2015)
23. Wang, F., et al.: Residual attention network for image classification. arXiv preprint arXiv:1704.06904 (2017)
24. Xian, K., et al.: Monocular relative depth perception with web stereo data supervision. In: Proceedings of the IEEE Conference on Computer Vision and Pattern Recognition, pp. 311–320 (2018)
25. Xie, S., Girshick, R., Dollár, P., Tu, Z., He, K.: Aggregated residual transformations for deep neural networks. In: 2017 IEEE Conference on Computer Vision and Pattern Recognition (CVPR), pp. 5987–5995. IEEE (2017)
26. Xu, D., Ricci, E., Ouyang, W., Wang, X., Sebe, N.: Multi-scale continuous CRFs as sequential deep networks for monocular depth estimation. In: Proceedings of CVPR (2017)
27. Xu, D., Wang, W., Tang, H., Liu, H., Sebe, N., Ricci, E.: Structured attention guided convolutional neural fields for monocular depth estimation. In: Proceedings of the IEEE Conference on Computer Vision and Pattern Recognition, pp. 3917–3925 (2018)
28. Yu, C., Wang, J., Peng, C., Gao, C., Yu, G., Sang, N.: Learning a discriminative feature network for semantic segmentation (2018)

Predicting Video Frames Using Feature Based Locally Guided Objectives

Prateep Bhattacharjee(✉) and Sukhendu Das

Visualization and Perception Laboratory,
Department of Computer Science and Engineering,
Indian Institute of Technology Madras, Chennai, India
prateepb@cse.iitm.ac.in, sdas@iitm.ac.in

Abstract. This paper presents feature reconstruction based approach using Generative Adversarial Networks (GAN) to solve the problem of predicting future frames from natural video scenes. Recent GAN based methods often generate blurry outcomes and fail miserably in case of long-range prediction. Our proposed method incorporates an intermediate feature generating GAN to minimize the disparity between the ground truth and predicted outputs. For this, we propose two novel objective functions: (a) Locally Guided Gram Loss (LGGL) and (b) Multi-Scale Correlation Loss (MSCL) to further enhance the quality of the predicted frames. LGGL aides the feature generating GAN to maximize the similarity between the intermediate features of the ground-truth and the network output by constructing Gram matrices from locally extracted patches over several levels of the generator. MSCL incorporates a correlation based objective to effectively model the temporal relationships between the predicted and ground-truth frames at the frame generating stage. Our proposed model is end-to-end trainable and exhibits superior performance compared to the state-of-the-art on four real-world benchmark video datasets.

Keywords: Video frame prediction · GANs · Correlation loss · Guided gram loss

1 Introduction

Although video understanding has been one of the key areas of computer vision, the problem of predicting frames from natural video scenes has not been explored till recently. Compared to image reconstruction tasks, generation of multiple video frames requires understanding of non-trivial internal spatio-temporal feature representations. Past approaches in this area involve the use

Electronic supplementary material The online version of this chapter (https://doi.org/10.1007/978-3-030-20870-7_42) contains supplementary material, which is available to authorized users.

C. V. Jawahar et al. (Eds.): ACCV 2018, LNCS 11364, pp. 679–695, 2019.
https://doi.org/10.1007/978-3-030-20870-7_42

of Long Short Term Memory (LSTM) networks [9,26], recurrent neural networks [23] and action conditional deep networks [21]. Majority of the recent approaches [13,29,31] focus on predicting the semantics which is useful in decision making problems. Mathieu *et al.* [19] proposed a frame prediction model based on Generative Adversarial Networks (GAN). Contrary to the semantic based approaches, this multi-scale GAN uses the future frames (during training) as target from large amount of natural video scenes to produce crisp and clear output. This method also overcomes the issue of producing blurry output when the L2 penalty is used as the objective function, by introducing a gradient based loss (GDL). Recently, Villegas *et al.* [28] incorporates different encoding streams for motion and content by using LSTM based encoders. Another approach in synthesizing frames is to use pixel-autoregressive models [10,22]. Also, latent variable models *viz.* Variational Auto-encoders (VAE) [12] have been used for both single [33] and multi-frame predictions [1]. Although these approaches (also [15,17,30,34]) offer improvement in the quality of the produced frames over the semantic based models, they often fail to perform satisfactorily in environments differing greatly from the training set and in case of faraway predictions. Very recently, [2] used a two-stage GAN based framework and introduces two novel objective functions based on cross-correlation and a distance based divergence measure. This work captures the spatial as well as temporal information through the use of a cross-correlation based loss. Although this improves the scores over the state-of-the-art, it often fails on situations where multiple objects having very different velocity are present in the scene simultaneously. We overcome this issue by modifying the cross-correlation based objective using a multi-scale anchor based approach along with a novel GAN based architecture and a locally guided feature based objective.

Our proposed work incorporates two GAN based models: (a) feature generating GAN (F-GAN) and (b) reconstruction GAN (R-GAN). These two networks act in an encoder-decoder arrangement and are trained together end-to-end. F-GAN learns to generate intermediate feature representations, while R-GAN reconstructs the future frames from the generated feature space. The learning process of F-GAN is aided by a Locally Guided Gram Loss (LGGL) function. This minimizes the distance between the intermediate feature maps of the ground truth frames, produced by another auxiliary network and the feature maps from the F-GAN itself, by forming soft "local guidance" regions. The auxiliary network is trained simultaneously along with the two generators. The raison d'être of the feature generating network is to break the process of frame prediction from a direct coarse strategy into a finer multi-step method. The reconstruction network minimizes the L1 loss along with a multi-scale correlational objective function (MSCL), which exploits the combination of spatial features and short-ranged temporal relationships among local neighborhood patches between the predicted and the ground-truth (GT) frames (refer Fig. 1). The salient parts of our work are: (a) novel encoder-decoder type GAN based architecture in the domain of video frame prediction and (b) two novel feature based objective functions (LGGL and MSCL) for bridging the gap between the predicted and target outputs efficiently.

2 Proposed Architecture

The overall proposed system of predicting future frames mimics an encoder-decoder like arrangement via an amalgamation of two GANs [8]. Overall, these are composed of two sub-networks: (a) the Generator (G) and (b) the Discriminator (D). The generator (G) is trained to produce realistic outputs by learning the underlying true data distribution p_{data} and consequently making the job of differentiating between true and synthetic outputs by the discriminator harder. In contrast, the discriminator D learns to distinguish between the real data and the synthetic outputs produced by the generator. In short, GANs use an alternating two player min-max game-like learning strategy [8] to achieve the mixed equilibrium of generating better synthetic outputs. The objective function minimized by the GANs [8] is given by

$$\min_{G} \max_{D} v(D, G) = \mathbb{E}_{x \sim p_{data}}[log(D(x))] + \mathbb{E}_{z \sim p_z}[log(1 - D(G(z)))] \quad (1)$$

where, x is a sample from the true distribution p_{data} and vector z is sampled from a uniform (or Gaussian) noise distribution p_z. As we work deals with videos instead of arbitrary data distributions, the input to F-GAN is a sequence of video frames, while R-GAN receives a collection of 2D intermediate feature maps (refer Fig. 1). The following two sub-sections describe the working principles of the feature generation and the reconstruction stages.

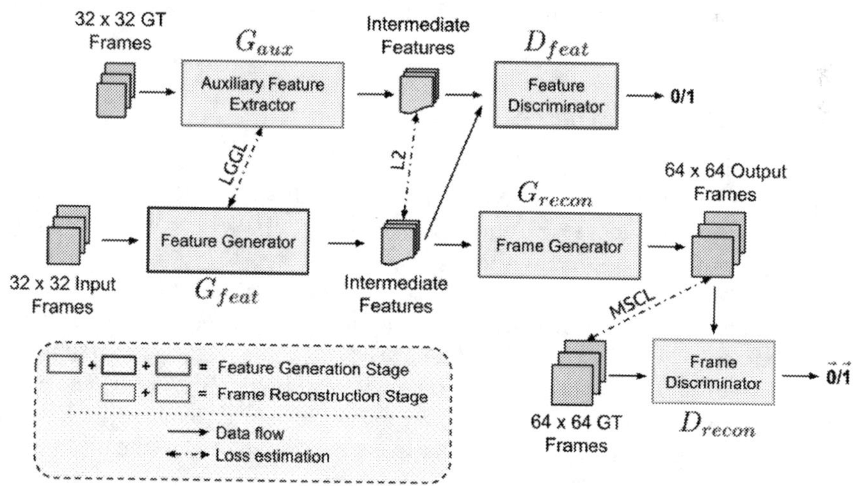

Fig. 1. The proposed GAN based network architecture for video frame prediction.

2.1 Stage-1: Feature Generation

As shown in Fig. 1, the feature generation stage comprises of a Generative Adversarial Network (G_{feat}) and an auxiliary convolutional neural network (G_{aux}).

A sequence of M frames of width W_I and height H_I (for simplicity, $W_I = H_I$) from a video are fed as input to the generator (G_{feat}). On the other hand, G_{aux} is fed with a sequence of N target or GT frames (during training). Both these component networks of the feature generation stage produce outputs of dimension $M_{int} \times W_{int} \times H_{int}$, where, M_{int} is the number of generated feature maps while W_{int} and H_{int} are the corresponding width and height (kept identical all throughout our experiments). The outputs from both these networks are fed to the feature discriminator (D_{feat}). As the motivation of using the feature generator is to bring the intermediate feature maps of the generator closer to the encoded GT data in high-dimensional feature space, the discriminator is trained to distinguish between the synthesized feature maps produced by G_{aux} and G_{feat}. The target labels chosen for features fed to D_{feat} are: '0' for the feature maps generated by G_{feat} and '1' for that from G_{aux}. Note that the auxiliary network is only used for training and is not involved in the testing phase.

Although GANs are notorious for their training instability, our proposed model of simultaneous learning of the discriminator along with the generator and the auxiliary networks is elegant and successful due to: *(a)* Although minimizing the sum squared distance (L2) is a traditional method used in optimization literature, it results in production of blurry frames. This shortcoming is evaded in our work by minimizing the L2 distance between a large number of high-dimensional feature maps instead of the pixels in the generated frames and *(b)* Projecting the input and GT frames to a high-dimensional space using a novel non-linear objective function (described in Sect. 3) increases separability for better discrimination.

2.2 Stage-2: Reconstruction

The reconstruction phase of the frame prediction framework is essentially another Generative Adversarial Network fine-tuned to produce sharp (in content) high-quality sequence of frames. This phase consists of two networks: (a) frame generator (G_{recon}) and (b) frame discriminator (D_{recon}). The intermediate feature maps of dimension $M_{int} \times W_{int} \times H_{int}$ generated by G_{feat} at stage-1 is fed as input to G_{recon}, which in turn produces an output sequence of N frames with dimension $W_O \times H_O$. The discriminator (D_{recon}) at this stage is trained to distinguish between the synthetic and true data in the RGB image space.

Exploration of different architectures for the feature generation and reconstruction stages led to an observation that using residual blocks in the reconstruction stage produces comparatively better outputs at less training time. Also, the same helps in diminishing the effect of vanishing gradients through by-passing higher level features using identity pathways.

3 Locally Guided Gram Loss (LGGL)

The joint problem of projecting the input video frame sequence in a high dimensional space shared by the features from GT frames and optimizing the discriminator to differentiate between them simultaneously is a non-trivial problem. For these situations, we use feature maps from several layers of G_{aux} and G_{feat}. By breaking the feature maps into local regions, the proposed objective function guides the neurons of G_{feat} to transform the original input data to the targeted feature space.

Let $FM_k^{feat}(X)$ and $FM_k^{aux}(Y)$ denote the feature representations of X and Y at layer k of G_{feat} and G_{aux}. Also, each of the columns of FM_k^{feat} and FM_k^{aux} are vectorized *i.e.* $FM_k \in \mathbb{R}^{W_k \times H_k \times N_k}$ where, W_k, H_k and N_k are the width, height and number of feature maps at layer k respectively. Our aim is to transform each small local (spatially) region of the feature maps from G_{feat}, at several layers by using those from G_{aux}. We divide the feature maps into R non-overlapping square regions and use the concept of Gaussian Guidance Maps (GGM). GGMs are essentially normalized ([0, 1]) image maps and specifies how much weightage is given to a specific neuron in the guiding policy. We noticed that the neurons near the border of all the R regions contribute almost equally to capture an intermediate feature; whereas, those near the center are often mutually exclusive in their role. Armed with this intuition, we assign a higher weightage for the center neurons in the GGM and lower it near the borders. This is modeled with the help of a Gaussian distribution. Note that the guidance maps have zero values for areas outside the boundaries of a particular region, thereby suppressing unwanted effects from those (*e.g. sky*) far away from the current one (*e.g. road*).

The feature maps of each of the K layers are multiplied with R Gaussian Guidance Maps to compute the Locally Guided Gram matrix (LGG) $\mathcal{G}$. This is defined as:

$$[FM_k^{feat}]_r = [GGM]_r \circ FM_k^{feat} \tag{2}$$

$$[\mathcal{G}_k^{feat}]_r = [FM_k^{feat}]_r^T [FM_k^{feat}]_r \tag{3}$$

where, $r \in R$, $\circ$ represents element-wise multiplication, $[GGM]_r$ is the normalized Gaussian Guidance Map for region r and $[\mathcal{G}_k^{feat}]_r$ is the LGG of the same. We compute the values for the feature maps of the auxiliary network simultaneously, as follows:

$$[FM_k^{aux}]_r = [GGM]_r \circ FM_k^{aux} \tag{4}$$

$$[\mathcal{G}_k^{aux}]_r = [FM_k^{aux}]_r^T [FM_k^{aux}]_r \tag{5}$$

where, all symbols follow those in Eqs. 2 and 3. Each of the LGG matrices now becomes the target for optimization for the corresponding regions in the feature space. This way, the objective function for LGGL is expressed in Sum of Squared Distance (SSD) form as:

$$\mathcal{L}_{LGGL}(X, Y) = \frac{1}{K} \sum_{k=1}^{K} \frac{1}{R^2 (N_k)^2} \sum_{r=1}^{R} \left[[\mathcal{G}_k^{feat}]_r - [\mathcal{G}_k^{aux}]_r \right]^2 \tag{6}$$

As the granularity of the extracted features vary proportionally with the depth of CNNs, $\mathcal{L}_{LGGL}$ minimizes the feature distance in a hierarchical fashion and greatly increases the stability of the feature generating stage.

4 Multi-scale Correlational Loss (MSCL)

Although the feature generating stage projects the input data into a rich space similar to that of the target, it still cannot capture the intricate temporal relationships needed to reconstruct a photo-realistic version of the target. Recently, [2] introduced an objective function based on the idea of normalized cross-correlation for minimizing the perceptual difference between local neighborhoods of the predicted output and GT frames. Although this method shows impressive results, the original objective function (termed as the Normalized Cross-Correlation Loss) performs poorly in scenes containing objects moving at very different speeds in a small region. This type of complexities often occur in real world video samples. To overcome this drawback, we modify the proposed loss (NCCL [2]) to perform correlation based matching at different scales. The intuition behind this modification is the fact that objects with less velocity will be captured by small scale windows whereas, faster objects can be tracked by the larger scale patches. Cross-correlation, a well-known similarity measuring technique [5,14,18,20,27], is mathematically defined as:

$$Corr(A, B) = \sum_{x,y} \frac{(A(x,y) - \mu_A)(B(x,y) - \mu_B)}{\sigma_A \sigma_B} \tag{7}$$

where, $A(x,y), B(x,y)$ are the sub-images with $<\mu, \sigma>$ being their <mean, standard deviation>. We define local regions, called 'anchors' at 3 different scales *viz.* 3×3, 5×5 and 7×7. Each of these anchors is defined as a 3-tuple $\langle x, y, h\rangle$ where, x, y are the top-left pixel indices and $h \in \{3, 5, 7\}$ being the scale. At each scale, we compute a correlation score between the anchors from the current time-step of the predicted frames ($\langle x, y, h\rangle_t$) and those at the previous time-step in the GT ($\langle x', y', h'\rangle_{t-1}$), where, $x' < x, y' < y$ and $h' > h$. This essentially allows the network to measure the similarity of the output generated at a certain scale with a slightly larger region around it from the target scene at the previous time-step. Using a larger neighborhood for the similarity measure enables to capture movement (small, with no eccentric motion pattern) of objects over consecutive frames.

In spite of the above assumption (slow movements), scenes may contain several objects moving at different speeds, *e.g.* crowded street scenes, where, pedestrians have predominantly lower velocity than cars running on the streets. To cope with this issue, apart from using multiple anchor scales, we also compute the similarity measure with anchors of 3 different larger dimensions of the GT frame at the previous time-step. For example, correlational similarity is computed between an anchor $\langle x, y, 5\rangle_t$ with a set of anchors $\{\langle x-2, y-2, 9\rangle_{t-1}, \langle x-3, y-3, 11\rangle_{t-1}, \langle x-4, y-4, 13\rangle_{t-1}\}$. In simpler terms, we employ difference constants $\Delta h \in \{2, 3, 4\}$, at multiple scales. Following this convention, it can be seen that the number of scales used overall for similarity computation is $n_{anchors} \times n_{\Delta h}$. To limit the overall computation time, we use 3 different anchors and 3 scale difference constants, *i.e.* $n_{anchors} = n_{\Delta h} = 3$, as stated earlier above.

Algorithm 1: Multi-Scale Correlation (MSC) score for estimating similarity between a set of reconstructed and target frame(s).

Input: Target frames (Y), Predicted frames (Y')
Output: Multi-Scale Correlation score ($Score_{MSC}$)
// W, Height (also width) of the frames
// $\mathbb{H} = \{3, 5, 7\}$, set of anchor scales
// $\Delta\mathbb{H} = \{2, 3, 4\}$, set of scale difference constants
// t, current time-step; T, number of frames predicted
Initialize: $Score_{MSC} = 0$
for $t = 1$ *to* T **do**
  foreach $\mathbf{h} \in \mathbb{H},\ \Delta\mathbf{h} \in \Delta\mathbb{H}$ **do**
    for $i = 0$ *to* W, $i \leftarrow i + \mathbf{h}$ **do**
      for $j = 0$ *to* W, $j \leftarrow j + \mathbf{h}$ **do**
        $Anchor_t^Y =< i, j, \mathbf{h} >_t$
        $Anchor_{t-1}^{Y'} =< i - \Delta\mathbf{h}, j - \Delta\mathbf{h}, \mathbf{h} + 2 \times \Delta\mathbf{h} >_{t-1}$
        $Score_{MSC} = Score_{MSC} + Corr(Anchor_t^Y, Anchor_{t-1}^{Y'})$
        // refer equation 7
      end
    end
    $Score_{MSC} \leftarrow \frac{Score_{MSC}}{\lfloor \frac{W}{\mathbf{h}} \rfloor^2}$
  end
  $Score_{MSC} \leftarrow \frac{Score_{MSC}}{|\mathbb{H}||\Delta\mathbb{H}|}$
end
$Score_{MSC} \leftarrow \frac{Score_{MSC}}{(T-1)}$

The entire process for estimating this multi-scale similarity score is given step-wise in Algorithm 1. The corresponding objective function minimized by the reconstruction stage network is $\mathcal{L}_{MSCL}(Y, Y') = -Score_{MSC}(Y, Y')$, where, Y, Y' are the reconstructed and GT frames respectively.

5 Overall Objective Function

We integrate the objective functions described in Sect. 3 and 4 with the traditional adversarial loss function [8] as well as the well-known $L1$ and $L2$ metrics for the proposed frame prediction network. The generator (G_{feat}) in the feature generation stage thus optimizes the following weighted function:

$$\mathcal{L}_{comb}^{feat} = \lambda_{adv}^{feat} \mathcal{L}_{adv}^{G_{feat}}(X) + \lambda_{LGGL} \mathcal{L}_{LGGL}(X, Y) + \lambda_{L2}^{feat} \mathcal{L}_{L2}(X_{int}, Y_{int}) \quad (8)$$

where, the optimal values for the co-efficients $\lambda_{adv}^{feat}, \lambda_{L2}^{feat}$ and λ_{LGGL} are empirically found to be $0.1, 0.45$ and 0.45. On the other hand, the combined loss function for the reconstruction phase generator (G_{recon}) is represented as:

$$\mathcal{L}_{comb}^{recon} = \lambda_{adv}^{recon} \mathcal{L}_{adv}^{G_{recon}}(X_{int}) + \lambda_{L1}^{recon} \mathcal{L}_{L1}(Y, Y') + \lambda_{MSCL} \mathcal{L}_{MSCL}(Y, Y') \quad (9)$$

In all our experiments, we also keep the weights $\lambda_{adv}^{recon}, \lambda_{L1}^{recon}$ and λ_{MSCL} as $0.15, 0.45$ and 0.45 respectively (determined empirically for best performance).

These combined objectives in Eqs. 8 and 9 when minimized simultaneously, reduce the gap in the intermediate and RGB features spaces of the target (GT) and generated frames, thereby generating better results.

6 Experiments

We evaluate our frame prediction network on four popular benchmark datasets: (a) KTH [24], (b) Weizmann [3], (c) UCF-101 [25] and (d) KITTI [7]. Among these, KTH and Weizmann contain various simple human actions in a predominantly static background. The UCF-101 dataset comprises of scenes with 101 different complex human actions. Although it contains much complex scenes than the KTH and Weizmann, it still suffers from the problem of static background which can lead the network to just learn to copy pixel values. To overcome this issue, we use Sports-1M [11], a large scale database of natural sports videos, for training. Lastly, KITTI contains street view scenes taken from a car mounted camera and generally does not suffer from the static background problem.

Quantitative studies with recent state-of-the-art and other methods have been carried out using two image quality measurement metrics: (a) Peak Signal to Noise Ratio (PSNR) [4] and (b) Structural Similarity Index Measure (SSIM) [32].

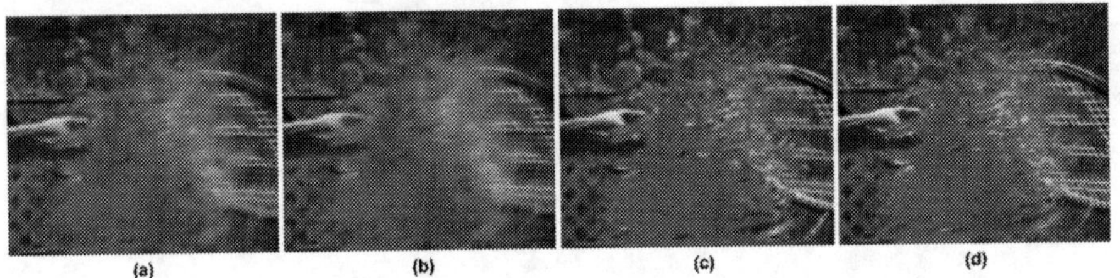

Fig. 2. Effect of layer selection in the feature generation stage. Zoomed-in patches of outputs from models optimized with LGGL taking into account: (a) early, (b) terminal and (c) optimum choice (mixed) of layers from G_{aux} and G_{feat} networks. The same patch from the ground-truth frame is shown in (d). Observe the trade-off between blurriness and sharpness in each of the cases (Best viewed in color)

6.1 Results on KTH and Weizmann

The KTH dataset comprises of 6 different human actions from 25 subjects. Videos in this dataset have rather simplistic motions which are periodic and predominantly exhibit a static background. Following [28], we use persons 1–16 for training and the rest for testing purpose. Apart from these, we also selected walking, running, one and two hands waving classes from the Weizmann database. All the experiments are done using 64×64 target frames and 32×32 dimension input frames. The network is trained using a set of 6 consecutive frames to predict up-to 10 frames in the future. For a fair comparison with [28], clips from the running and jogging classes are sampled every 3rd frame while for the rest of the classes the sample period is one in every 10 frames. As our network predicts 10 frames in the future, the sampling rate is chosen to be 10 instead of 20 (as in [28]). Additional results for deeper prediction are shown the supplementary document.

The layers conv_2, conv_4, conv_5 and conv_7 of G_{aux} and G_{feat} were found to be the optimum choice for the Locally Guided Gram Loss (LGGL) in the feature generation stage (refer sections 1 and 2 in supplementary document for architecture). Choosing only the early layers for LGGL produced features which forced G_{recon} to predict output frames having sharp edges with overall color and texture informations intact, but lacking in finer details (e.g. cloth patterns). A reverse effect was observed (sharper details but blurry edges) when features were chosen from later parts of the feature generation network (see Fig. 2).

From the quantitative results presented in Table 1, it is evident that the proposed framework is superior than its closest competitor MCNet both in terms of PSNR and SSIM quality measures. Also note that the drop in reconstruction quality is substantially less than other methods, as we go deeper into the future. This can be attributed to the additional correlational loss (MSCL) used in the reconstruction phase which captures the temporal information in locally restricted areas. MCNet uses LSTMs as well as two separate networks for capturing both the temporal and spatial information. While the complex framework of MCNet learns periodic motions, it often fails to perform in case of complex scenes with highly non-periodic motion. Also, as our method learns an intermediate feature representation that is explicitly trained to fuel the prediction quality, the output frames look much more photo-realistic (refer supplementary figures for additional illustrations).

Table 1. Comparison of performance for KTH and Weizmann datasets using PSNR/SSIM scores. Best results in bold.

Methods	Frame-1		Frame-4	
	Weizmann	KTH	Weizmann	KTH
ConvLSTM [28]	-	30.8/0.87	-	26.2/0.74
ConvLSTM + RES [28]	36.2/0.97	33.8/0.94	29.8/0.92	27.9/0.86
MCNet [28]	-	30.1/0.85	-	26.5/0.76
MCNet + RES [28]	36.8/0.97	33.9/0.94	31.9/0.94	28.3/0.88
Adv + L1 + LGGL	38.3/0.96	36.9/0.95	36.2/0.94	33.8/0.89
Adv + L1 + LGGL + MSCL (Non-res)	40.8/0.97	38.8/0.96	37.2/0.95	35.1/0.91
Adv + L1 + LGGL + MSCL	**42.5/0.98**	**40.8/0.96**	**38.1/0.96**	**36.7/0.91**

6.2 Results on UCF-101

The UCF-101 dataset contains realistic scenes of 101 types of human actions collected from YouTube. Compared to KTH and Weizmann, this database is much complex and larger in size. Following [19], we train our models using 4 consecutive frames as input and the 5th as target at the training phase. As the scenes from this dataset contains many frames having static background, we train using random 32×32 (patches) exhibiting motion, estimated using the $L2$ distance between frames in consecutive time-steps. Apart from the UCF-101 frames, Sports-1M [11] is also used for reasons similar to the experimental settings described in [19]. We sampled one in every 10 videos of the test split of UCF-101 for the evaluation phase and identified regions containing significant motion by calculating optical flow features (using [6]). The architecture is kept the same as that used for predicting frames from KTH and Weizmann dataset. Also, we again use the combination of features from convolutional layers 2, 4, 5 and 7 of the feature generation stage for calculating LGGL.

Notice the superiority of the proposed model over the recent works from the quantitative results produced in Table 2. Similar to the results obtained in case of KTH and Weizmann datasets, the trend of a slower rate of degradation (measured using PSNR and SSIM) of the output (produced) frames is also evident in the UCF-101 ablation studies. Qualitative results are shown in Fig. 4. Inclusion of residual blocks in the reconstruction stage generator plays a more involved role in UCF-101 predictions than in KTH and Weizmann datasets (Fig. 3).

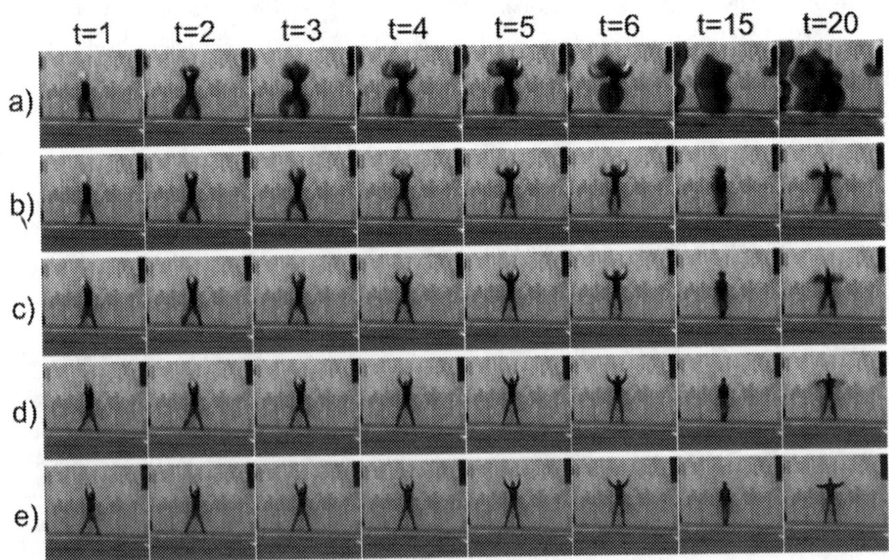

Fig. 3. Qualitative result for Weizmann dataset. The combination of models used are (a) L1 (non-adversarial), (b) LGGL + L1, (c) LGGL + L1 + MSCL (Non-residual) and (d) LGGL + L1 + MSCL. The last row represents ground-truth frames while 't' is the time-step

6.3 Results on KITTI

KITTI is a traffic scene database containing videos captured from a camera mounted on cars. In contrast to KTH, Weizmann and UCF-101, the videos from this dataset do not generally suffer from the issue of static background. Hence, we did not use any auxiliary dataset *viz.* Sports-1M for training. For all our experimental studies, videos from (a) road and (b) city have been used. The models were trained using four consecutive frames as input and the subsequent four as target. For quantitative evaluation, we selected one among every five videos from the above mentioned classes to predict 8 frames in the future. Table 2 provides the quantitative comparison of several of our models for KITTI. Interesting to note that, the bare model with only $L1$ objective and the adversarial losses fail miserably to reconstruct realistic versions of KITTI scenes. This is due to the fact that the model seems to reconstruct by averaging between every two consecutive frames producing ghost image type artifacts. This issue is almost entirely subdued by the use of LGGL (see Table 2), thereby confirming once again its role in guiding the feature generation network into building a rich intermediate feature space.

Table 2. Quantitative comparison of performance of different methods for the UCF-101 and KITTI datasets using PSNR/SSIM scores. (*) indicates that models are fine tuned on patches of size 64×64 [19]. (†) represents model trained on 2 frames as input. (-) denotes unavailability of performance results. Last 3 rows report the scores obtained using the proposed method. Best results are given in bold.

Methods	Frame-1		Frame-2	
	UCF-101	KITTI	UCF-101	KITTI
L1	28.7/0.88	-	23.8/0.83	-
GDL L1* [19]	29.9/0.90	-	26.4/0.87	-
Adv + GDL fine-tuned* [19]	32.0/0.92	-	28.9/0.89	-
Optical flow [19]	31.6/0.93	-	28.2/0.90	-
ConvLSTM [28]	27.3/0.87	-	23.3/0.78	-
ConvLSTM + RES [28]	29.8/0.90	-	25.1/0.82	-
MCNet [28]	27.9/0.87	-	23.8/0.80	-
MCNet + RES [28]	30.2/0.91	-	27.6/0.86	-
MCNet + RES UCF101 [28]	30.5/0.91	-	27.7/0.86	-
Deep Voxel Flow† [16]	35.8/0.96	-	-	-
NCCL + L1 [2]	35.4/0.94	37.1/0.91	33.9/0.92	35.4/0.90
NCCL + PCDL + L1 [2]	37.3/0.95	39.7/0.93	35.7/0.92	37.1/0.91
SNCCL + PCDL + L1 [2]	38.2/0.95	40.2/0.94	36.8/0.93	37.7/0.91
Adv + L1 + LGGL	36.2/0.94	38.3/0.92	34.4/0.91	36.8/0.90
Adv + L1 + LGGL + MSCL (Non-Res)	38.5/0.95	40.1/0.95	37.4/0.92	38.1/0.91
Adv + L1 + LGGL + MSCL (Res)	**39.1/0.96**	**41.3/0.96**	**38.2/0.94**	**39.1/0.92**

6.4 Cross-Dataset Evaluation

Apart from the ablation studies discussed above, we also tested our model for generalization using cross-dataset evaluations. For this, we chose four different combinations of datasets (listed as training → testing): (a) UCF-101 → KTH, (b) UCF-101 → Weizmann, (c) Weizmann → KTH and (d) UCF-101 → KITTI.

UCF-101 → KTH and Weizmann. Although KTH and Weizmann are simpler in nature than UCF-101 and KITTI, the scenes in these datasets are quite different in style, color and motion pattern. In spite of these inherent differences, our proposed models when trained with UCF-101 for predicting frames, performed remarkably well when tested with KTH or Weizmann videos. Figure 5 (2nd sub-figure) illustrates one example of predicting frames from KTH. The model without any of our proposed objectives (as shown in the first row of 2nd sub-figure of Fig. 5) failed miserably to reconstruct the frames. Inclusion of LGGL greatly helps to generate legible scenes whereas, combination of all the proposed objectives successfully produce near photo-realistic images. The quantitative results for UCF-101 → KTH and UCF-101 → Weizmann are shown in Table 3. As both KTH and Weizmann have a large static background, the color patterns were easy to predict (simple pixel copy). From the values in Table 3 (last two rows), it can be observed that the residual version performs significantly better than the other models. This is evident in the qualitative results also (see Fig. 5) as it produces sharp edges and maintains the overall texture and minor details (*e.g.* details of the dresses) quite successfully.

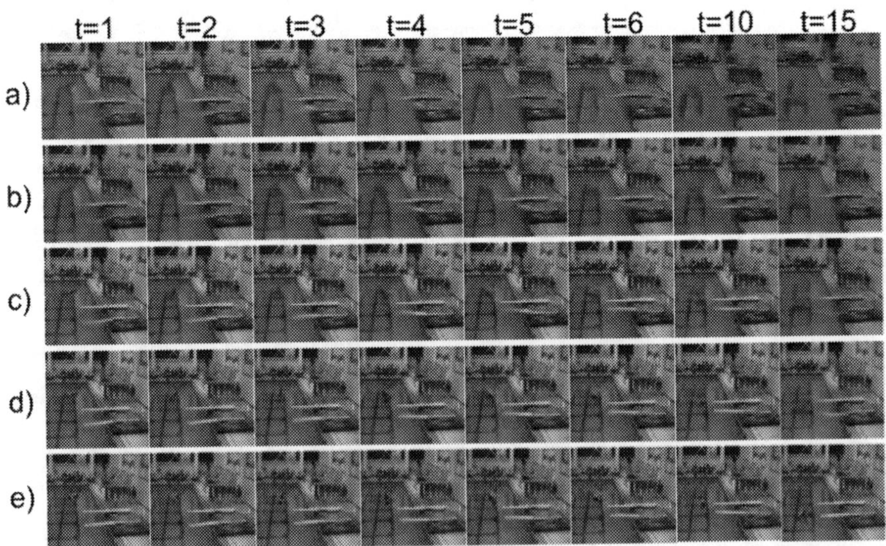

Fig. 4. Qualitative results of the proposed GAN based framework for predicting frames on a scene from the UCF-101 dataset. Different combinations of objective functions used are: (a) NCCL + PCDL [2], (b) LGGL, (c) LGGL + MSCL (Non-Res) and (d) LGGL + MSCL. The last row represents GT frames while 't' denotes the time-step (Best viewed in color)

Table 3. Comparison of cross-dataset performance using PSNR/SSIM measures for different models trained for UCF-101 and tested on KTH and Weizmann datasets. Best results in bold.

Methods	Frame-1		Frame-4		Frame-10	
	Weizmann	KTH	Weizmann	KTH	Weizmann	KTH
Adv + L1 + LGGL	36.6/0.94	33.4/0.94	32.7/0.91	28.6/0.87	26.8/0.88	24.3/0.81
Adv + L1 + LGGL + MSCL (Non-Res)	38.3/0.95	35.9/0.95	34.4/0.92	30.7/0.88	28.8/0.89	26.6/0.82
Adv + L1 + LGGL + MSCL	**40.2/0.96**	**38.2/0.95**	**36.4/0.94**	**33.9/0.90**	**31.2/0.90**	**28.9/0.84**

Weizmann → KTH. Unlike UCF-101, KTH and Weizmann are often similar in the motion patterns and therefore easier for cross-dataset evaluation. This reflects in our studies as seen in Table 4. Interesting to note that the difference in quantitative performance between the residual and non-residual versions of the models are marginal when compared to the UCF-101 → KTH and Weizmann cross-dataset studies. This is due to the simplicity of the available scenes in these particular databases. We also observed that the qualitative results were slightly inferior compared to the UCF-101 → KTH scenario. This small improvement stems from the large variation of motion patterns available in UCF-101 video samples compared to the small and simple Weizmann database.

UCF-101 → KITTI. We also tested our models trained for UCF-101 on the KITTI dataset by feeding 6 input frames to produce 8 future frames. The PSNR/SSIM values in Table 5 indicate the generalizability of our proposed models in this cross-dataset arrangement. Note that, in this particular case, the PSNR values decrease (with increasing frame number) a bit faster compared to that for other databases, while the trend of slow rate in decrease of the SSIM value remains unaltered. As PSNR is a pixel-wise difference measure, small changes in a large number of pixels result in a far worse value despite being perceptually acceptable. As SSIM uses features for measuring the similarity, it does not get affected by this undesired phenomenon. Figure 5 (1st sub-figure) shows qualitative results of this cross-dataset experimentation.

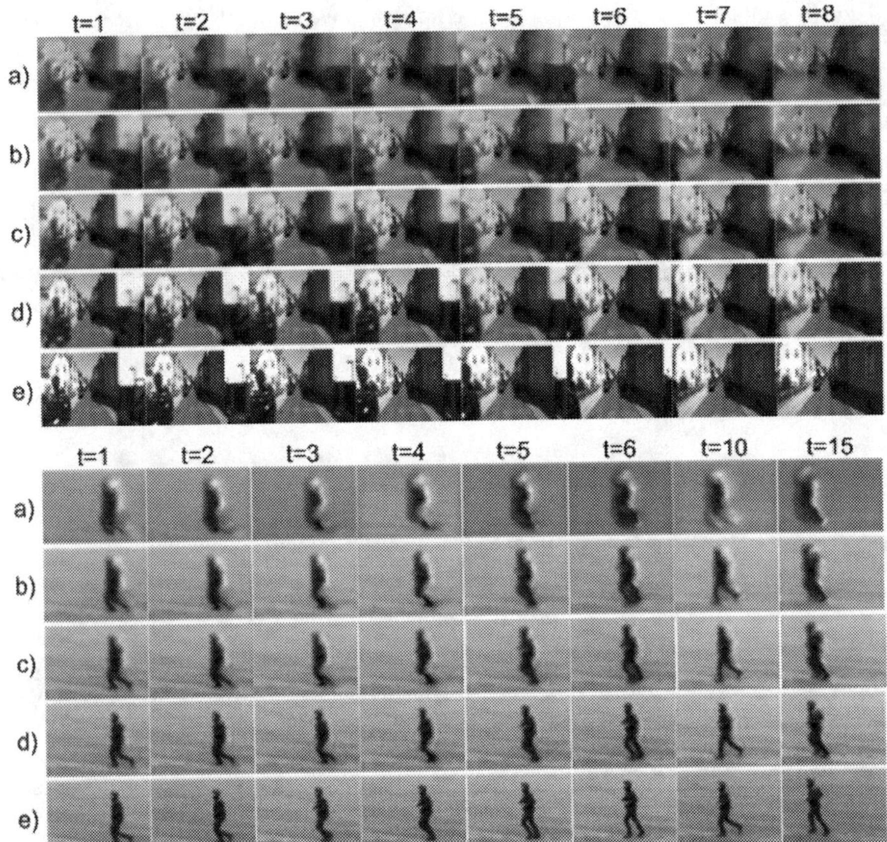

Fig. 5. Cross-dataset evaluation on KITTI and KTH using models trained for UCF-101. The combination of models used are (a) L1, (b) LGGL + L1, (c) LGGL + L1 + MSCL (Non-residual) and (d) LGGL + L1 + MSCL. The last row represents ground-truth frames while 't' is the time-step

Table 4. Comparison of cross-dataset performance using PSNR/SSIM measures for different models trained for Weizmann and tested on KTH dataset. Best results in bold.

Methods	Frame-1	Frame-4	Frame-10	Frame-20
Adv + L1 + LGGL	33.3/0.93	28.1/0.86	23.5/0.79	19.8/0.72
Adv + L1 + LGGL + MSCL (Non-res)	35.3/**0.95**	30.2/0.88	25.2/0.81	22.8/0.76
Adv + L1 + LGGL + MSCL	**36.8/0.95**	**31.4/0.89**	**26.6/0.82**	**23.1/0.77**

Table 5. Comparison of cross-dataset performance using PSNR/SSIM measures for different models trained for UCF-101 and tested on KITTI dataset. Best results in bold.

Methods	Frame-1	Frame-2	Frame-4	Frame-8
Adv + L1 + LGGL	34.5/0.90	32.8/0.86	29.5/0.81	25.8/0.75
Adv + L1 + LGGL + MSCL (Non-Res)	37.4/0.93	36.5/0.92	32.9/0.85	29.6/0.82
Adv + L1 + LGGL + MSCL	**38.6/0.94**	**37.5/0.91**	**34.2/0.86**	**31.1/0.83**

7 Conclusion

This paper proposes a 2-stage encoder-decoder type GAN for predicting photo-realistic future frames. Further, for diminishing the issues of instability and building a meaningful intricate intermediate feature space, we employed two novel region based guidance objectives: the Locally Guided Gram Loss (LGGL) and the Multi-Scale Correlation Loss (MSCL) for capturing the spatio-temporal relationships. Extensive evaluation on popular benchmark datasets and KITTI, a database previously not quite explored in the genre of frame prediction, reveal the superiority of our proposed model over the recent state-of-the-art methods.

References

1. Babaeizadeh, M., Finn, C., Erhan, D., Campbell, R.H., Levine, S.: Stochastic variational video prediction. arXiv preprint arXiv:1710.11252 (2017)
2. Bhattacharjee, P., Das, S.: Temporal coherency based criteria for predicting video frames using deep multi-stage generative adversarial networks. In: Advances in Neural Information Processing Systems, pp. 4268–4277 (2017)
3. Blank, M., Gorelick, L., Shechtman, E., Irani, M., Basri, R.: Actions as space-time shapes. In: Tenth IEEE International Conference on Computer Vision 2005, vol. 2, pp. 1395–1402 (2005)
4. Bovik, A.C.: The Essential Guide to Video Processing, 2nd edn. Academic Press, Boston (2009)
5. Briechle, K., Hanebeck, U.D.: Template matching using fast normalized cross correlation. In: Proceedings of SPIE, vol. 4387, pp. 95–102 (2001)
6. Brox, T., Bregler, C., Malik, J.: Large displacement optical flow. In: IEEE Conference on Computer Vision and Pattern Recognition, pp. 41–48 (2009)
7. Geiger, A., Lenz, P., Stiller, C., Urtasun, R.: Vision meets robotics: The KITTI dataset. Int. J. Robot. Res. **32**(11), 1231–1237 (2013)
8. Goodfellow, I., et al.: Generative adversarial nets. In: Advances in Neural Information Processing Systems, pp. 2672–2680 (2014)
9. Hochreiter, S., Schmidhuber, J.: Long short-term memory. Neural Comput. **9**(8), 1735–1780 (1997)
10. Kalchbrenner, N., et al.: Video pixel networks. In: International Conference on Machine Learning, pp. 1771–1779 (2017)

11. Karpathy, A., Toderici, G., Shetty, S., Leung, T., Sukthankar, R., Fei-Fei, L.: Large-scale video classification with convolutional neural networks. In: IEEE International Conference on Computer Vision and Pattern Recognition (2014)
12. Kingma, D.P., Welling, M.: Auto-encoding variational bayes. arXiv preprint arXiv:1312.6114 (2013)
13. Lan, T., Chen, T.-C., Savarese, S.: A hierarchical representation for future action prediction. In: Fleet, D., Pajdla, T., Schiele, B., Tuytelaars, T. (eds.) ECCV 2014. LNCS, vol. 8691, pp. 689–704. Springer, Cham (2014). https://doi.org/10.1007/978-3-319-10578-9_45
14. Lewis, J.P.: Fast normalized cross-correlation. In: Vision Interface, vol. 10, pp. 120–123 (1995)
15. Liang, X., Lee, L., Dai, W., Xing, E.P.: Dual motion GAN for future-flow embedded video prediction. arXiv preprint (2017)
16. Liu, Z., Yeh, R., Tang, X., Liu, Y., Agarwala, A.: Video frame synthesis using deep voxel flow. In: International Conference on Computer Vision (ICCV), vol. 2 (2017)
17. Lu, C., Hirsch, M., Schölkopf, B.: Flexible spatio-temporal networks for video prediction. In: Proceedings of the IEEE Conference on Computer Vision and Pattern Recognition, pp. 6523–6531 (2017)
18. Luo, J., Konofagou, E.E.: A fast normalized cross-correlation calculation method for motion estimation. IEEE Trans. Ultrason. Ferroelectr. Freq. Control **57**(6), 1347–1357 (2010)
19. Mathieu, M., Couprie, C., LeCun, Y.: Deep multi-scale video prediction beyond mean square error. In: International Conference on Learning Representations (ICLR) (2016)
20. Nakhmani, A., Tannenbaum, A.: A new distance measure based on generalized image normalized cross-correlation for robust video tracking and image recognition. Pattern Recogn. Lett. **34**(3), 315–321 (2013)
21. Oh, J., Guo, X., Lee, H., Lewis, R.L., Singh, S.: Action-conditional video prediction using deep networks in atari games. In: Advances in Neural Information Processing Systems, pp. 2863–2871 (2015)
22. van den Oord, A., Kalchbrenner, N., Kavukcuoglu, K.: Pixel recurrent neural networks. arXiv preprint arXiv:1601.06759 (2016)
23. Ranzato, M., Szlam, A., Bruna, J., Mathieu, M., Collobert, R., Chopra, S.: Video (language) modeling: a baseline for generative models of natural videos. arXiv preprint arXiv:1412.6604 (2014)
24. Schuldt, C., Laptev, I., Caputo, B.: Recognizing human actions: a local SVM approach. In: Proceedings of the 17th IEEE International Conference on Pattern Recognition 2004, vol. 3, pp. 32–36 (2004)
25. Soomro, K., Zamir, A.R., Shah, M.: UCF101: a dataset of 101 human actions classes from videos in the wild. arXiv preprint arXiv:1212.0402 (2012)
26. Srivastava, N., Mansimov, E., Salakhudinov, R.: Unsupervised learning of video representations using LSTMs. In: International Conference on Machine Learning, pp. 843–852 (2015)
27. Subramaniam, A., Chatterjee, M., Mittal, A.: Deep neural networks with inexact matching for person re-identification. In: Advances in Neural Information Processing Systems, pp. 2667–2675 (2016)
28. Villegas, R., Yang, J., Hong, S., Lin, X., Lee, H.: Decomposing motion and content for natural video sequence prediction. In: ICLR, vol. 1, no. 2 (2017)
29. Vondrick, C., Pirsiavash, H., Torralba, A.: Generating videos with scene dynamics. In: Advances In Neural Information Processing Systems, pp. 613–621 (2016)

30. Vondrick, C., Torralba, A.: Generating the future with adversarial transformers. In: IEEE Conference on Computer Vision and Pattern Recognition (CVPR) (2017)
31. Walker, J., Gupta, A., Hebert, M.: Patch to the future: unsupervised visual prediction. In: Proceedings of the IEEE Conference on Computer Vision and Pattern Recognition, pp. 3302–3309 (2014)
32. Wang, Z., Bovik, A.C., Sheikh, H.R., Simoncelli, E.P.: Image quality assessment: from error visibility to structural similarity. IEEE Trans. Image Process. (TIP) **13**(4), 600–612 (2004)
33. Xue, T., Wu, J., Bouman, K., Freeman, B.: Visual dynamics: probabilistic future frame synthesis via cross convolutional networks. In: Advances in Neural Information Processing Systems, pp. 91–99 (2016)
34. Zhou, Y., Berg, T.L.: Learning temporal transformations from time-lapse videos. In: Leibe, B., Matas, J., Sebe, N., Welling, M. (eds.) ECCV 2016. LNCS, vol. 9912, pp. 262–277. Springer, Cham (2016). https://doi.org/10.1007/978-3-319-46484-8_16

A New Temporal Deconvolutional Pyramid Network for Action Detection

Xiangli Ji, Guibo Luo, and Yuesheng Zhu(✉)

Communication and Information Security Laboratory, Shenzhen Graduate School, Peking University, Shenzhen 518055, China
{Jxiangli,luoguibo,zhuys}@pku.edu.cn

Abstract. Temporal action detection is a challenging task for detecting various action instances in untrimmed videos. Existing detection approaches are unable to localize the start and end time of action instances precisely. To address this issue, we propose a novel Temporal Deconvolutional Pyramid Network (TDPN), in which a Temporal Deconvolution Fusion (TDF) module in each pyramidal hierarchy is developed to construct strong semantic features of multiple temporal scales for detecting action instances with various durations. In the TDF module, the temporal resolution of high-level feature is expanded by a temporal deconvolution. The expanded high-level features and low-level features are fused by a fusion strategy to form strong semantic features. The fused semantic features with multiple temporal scales are used to predict action categories and boundary offsets simultaneously, which significantly improves the detection performance. Besides, a strict strategy for assigning label is proposed during training to improve the precision of temporal boundaries learned by model. We evaluate our detection approach on two public datasets, *i.e.*, THUMOS14 and MEXaction2. The experimental results have demonstrated that our TDPN model can achieve competitive performance on THUMOS14 and best performance on MEXaction2 compared with the other approaches.

Keywords: Action detection · Untrimmed videos · TDPN network

1 Introduction

Temporal action detection has numerous potential applications in video surveillance, video content analysis and intelligent home care. This task is to detect action instances in untrimmed videos, which needs to output the action categories and the precise start and end time. Since there is high variability in

Y. Zhu—This work was supported in part by the Shenzhen Municipal Development and Reform Commission (Disciplinary Development Program for Data Science and Intelligent Computing); and by Shenzhen International cooperative research projects GJHZ20170313150021171.

C. V. Jawahar et al. (Eds.): ACCV 2018, LNCS 11364, pp. 696–711, 2019.
https://doi.org/10.1007/978-3-030-20870-7_43

the duration of action from arbitrarily long video, temporal action detection is substantially challenging.

In recent years, some progress has been made in temporal action detection [3,16,22,31,33,34]. Many works regard this task as a classification problem, which contains candidate generation stage and classification stage. Earlier attempts [4,33] in temporal action detection adopt sliding windows as candidates and design hand-crafted features for classification, which is computationally expensive. Inspired by progress in image object detection [20], many approaches [22,31,34] adopt the "Proposal + Classification" framework, where a classifier is used to classify action instances generated by proposal methods [6,9]. However, there are some major drawbacks in these approaches. First, the process of proposal generation requires additional time and space costs. Second, deep convolutional features with fixed temporal resolution are used to detect action instances with various temporal scales, which limits the detection performance of these methods. Inspired by unified models [19,29] in object detection, SSAD network [16] and SS-TAD [12] network completely eliminate action proposal generation stage and predict temporal boundaries and specific action categories simultaneously. Although these approaches have a fast speed for detecting actions, the accuracy of detected temporal boundaries is still unsatisfied. For the SS-TAD [12] network, the used recurrent memory modules have a limit span of temporal attention leading to imprecise temporal boundaries. For the SSAD network [16], multiscale features are extracted by temporal convolution to detect actions, yet these features are temporally coarser, so that it cannot localize the start and end of action instances precisely. Besides, the detection performance of SSAD network is dependent heavily on feature extractor since final action classes are obtained by fusing predicted class scores and snippet-level action scores from feature extractor.

To address these issues, we propose a new Temporal Deconvolutional Pyramid Network (TDPN), which adopts Temporal Deconvolution Fusion (TDF) modules in various pyramidal hierarchies to integrate strong semantic information into feature maps with multiple temporal scales. Inspired by FPN [15] network in object detection, we introduce a top-down pathway with lateral connection into SSAD [16] network to extract temporal feature pyramid. Note that it is non-trivial to adapt the top-down architecture from object detection to temporal action detection, which needs to be designed to efficiently deal with temporal features. Different from FPN [15] network, our TDF module in top-down pathway adopts temporal deconvolution to expand temporal resolution of feature maps. To further improve detection performance, we investigate different fusion strategies for features from different pyramid hierarchies in the top-down pathway. Compared to SSAD [16] network, the fused feature sequences with same temporal resolution contains stronger semantics and more context information, which can significantly improve detection performance. The fused semantic features with multiple temporal scales are used to predict action class scores and boundary offsets simultaneously. The post-processing step of TDPN model is simple and only Non-Maximum Suppression (NMS) is used to remove repeatable detection results.

Our main contribution is the proposal of a new Temporal Deconvolutional Pyramid Network for temporal action detection that is eminent in the following aspects: (1) The TDPN model constructs strong semantic features with multiple temporal resolution by using TDF modules in various pyramidal hierarchies to detect action instances, which significantly improves detection performance. (2) Our TDPN model can learn precise temporal boundaries of action instances by using a fusion strategy for features from different pyramid hierarchies and a strict strategy for assigning label during training. (3) Our TDPN model achieves competitive performance (mAP@tIoU = 0.5 of 40.7%) on THUMOS14 dataset and outperforms other approaches on MEXaction2 dataset by increasing mAP@tIoU = 0.5 from 11.0% to 22.1%.

2 Related Work

Action Recognition. Over the past several years, great progress has been made in action recognition task. Earlier work mainly focuses on hand-crafted features, such as space-time interest points (STIP) [14] and Improved Dense Trajectory (iDT) [26]. With the remarkable performance obtained from deep neural network in image analysis, many methods adopt features extracted from deep neural networks [23,24]. Two-stream architecture [23] is proposed, which adopts two convolutional neural networks (CNNs) to extract appearance and motion features from single frame and stacked optical flow field respectively. 3D-CNN [24] learns appearance and motion features directly from frame volumes using 3D convolutional filters, which is more efficient than two-stream network. As a upgraded task, temporal action detection usually adopts action recognition models to extract spatiotemporal features. In our TDPN model, a deep two-steam network is used as feature extractor.

Object Detection. According to the used detection framework, object detection methods can be broadly divided into two categories. One is “detect by classifying object region proposals” framework, including region proposal generation stage and classification stage, such as Faster R-CNN [20] and Feature Pyramid Network (FPN) [15]. The region proposals are generated by some methods, such as SelectiveSearch [25] and RPN [20], and then classification network predicts object categories and location offsets of region proposals. The other one is unified detection framework, which skips proposal generation step and encapsulates all computation in a single network. Typical networks of this framework are YOLO [19] and SSD [29]. Object detection focuses on regions of interest in images, yet temporal action detection requires to combine temporal information to detect actions of interest in videos. Different from the FPN [15] network, our TDPN network adopts temporal deconvolution to deal with multiscale temporal features.

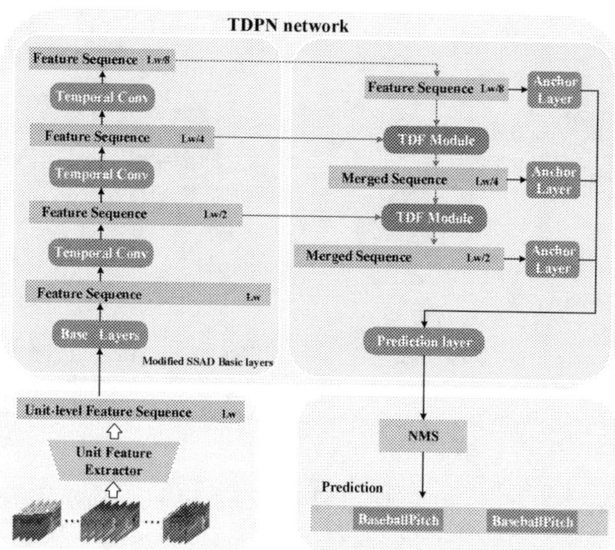

Fig. 1. Framework of our approach: the whole framework includes feature extractor, the TDPN network and the post-processing. Our TDPN network consists of modified SSAD basic layers, Temporal Deconvolution Fusion (TDF) modules, anchor layers and prediction layers. NMS is used to filter out duplicate detection results

Temporal Action Detection. Affected by the object detection methods, temporal action detection approaches are also broadly divided into "proposals by classification" framework and unified framework. For the previous framework, many methods for generating action proposals have been proposed, such as Sparse-prop [9] and TURN [6]. In the classification process, earlier works [11,17,33] mainly use hand-crafted features to classify action proposals. Recently, many approaches extract appearance and motion features using deep neural network [31,34,35] to detect action instances, which improves detection performance. Segment-CNN [35] proposes three segment-based 3D ConNets for detecting action: proposal network, classification network and localization network. Structured segment network (SSN) [34] models temporal structure of action instances via a structured temporal pyramid and a decomposed discriminative model. Based on Faster R-CNN framework, recently proposed TAL-Net [3] network improves receptive field alignment by a multi-tower network and exploits temporal context by extending receptive fields. Different from TAL-Net network, our TDPN model constructs temporal feature pyramid by using temporal convolution and deconvolution for detecting action instances directly without proposal generation process. UntrimmedNet [27] is a weakly supervised architecture, in which classification module and selection module are developed to learn action models and detect action instances respectively. Recurrent neural networks (RNNs) are also used to learn temporal information in many action detection methods [32,33]. The unified framework eliminates the proposal generation

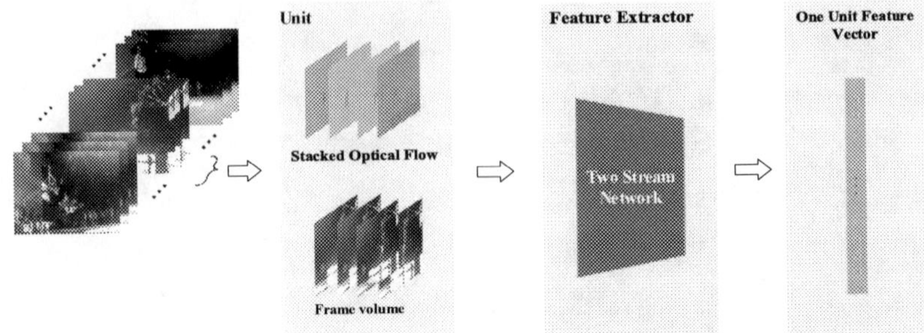

Fig. 2. Unit-level feature extraction. A untrimmed video is divided into units which consists of frame volume and stacked optical flow and unit-level feature sequences are extracted by two-steam network as the input of our TDPN model

stage and predict action categories and location offsets simultaneously, such as SSAD [16] and SS-TAD [12]. Our TDPN model also adopts the unified framework to detect action instances in untrimmed videos.

3 Approach

In this section, we introduce our Temporal Deconvolution Pyramid Network (TDPN) and the training procedure. As shown in Fig. 1, the whole architecture of system consists of feature extractor, the TDPN network and the post-processing. Initial feature pyramid is obtained by temporal convolution in modified SSAD basic layers, and a new Temporal Deconvolution Fusion (TDF) module is developed to extract strong semantic features with multiple temporal resolution. In the post-processing, NMS is used to remove repeatable results to obtain final detection results. We will describe each component and training procedure in details.

3.1 Video Unit Feature Extraction

We adopt deep two-stream network [30] to extract feature sequences as the input of TDPN model, where spatial CNN network uses ResNet [8] model and temporal CNN network adopts BN-Inception model [10]. A untrimmed video V is divided into T_v/m_u consecutive units where m_u is the number of frames in a unit and T_v is the number of frames in V. We pad the video in tail with last frame so that each unit has the same length m_u. Note that units are not overlapped with each other. As shown in Fig. 2, a frame volume with 8 frames is sampled uniformly from a unit, which is fed into the spatial network to extract features of "Flatten_673" layer. We compute the mean of these 8 feature vectors as unit-level appearance feature. Stacked optical flow field is calculated from 6 consecutive frames at the center of a unit, which is fed into the temporal network to extract motion feature of "global pool" layer. The appearance feature vector and the motion feature vector are concatenated as the feature vector of a unit.

Given a untrimmed video V, we can extract a unit-level feature sequence. Since the length of video is various, we use a sliding window with fixed length to divide the feature sequence into segments as the input of the TDPN model.

3.2 TDPN Network

We propose the TDPN model, which consists of modified SSAD basic layers, Temporal Deconvolution Fusion (TDF) modules, anchor layers and prediction layers. A key innovation is to strengthen semantics of multiscale features by using TDF modules in the top-down pathway, which improves significantly detection performance. The post-processing step of TDPN model is simple and only NMS is used to filter out duplicate detection results.

Modified SSAD Basic Layers. In the bottom-up pathway of our TDPN model, the modified SSAD basic layers is used, which consists of base layers and three temporal convolutional layers, as shown in Fig. 1.

The original base layers of SSAD [16] network contains two temporal convolutional layers for increasing the size of receptive fields and two temporal max pooling layers for shortening feature maps. Note that the max pooling layers are removed in the base layers of TDPN model since the temporal length of input features needs to remain unchanged in these layers. Then three temporal convolutional layers are stacked to extract initial feature maps with multiple temporal resolution. We denote the feature map of l-th temporal convolutional layer in the bottom-up pathway as $F_E^l \in R^{L_l \times T_l}$. The output feature maps of these convolutional layers are F_E^1, F_E^2 and F_E^3 with size $L_w/2 \times 512$, $L_w/4 \times 512$ and $L_w/8 \times 512$ respectively.

Temporal Deconvolution Fusion Module. As shown in Fig. 3, Temporal Deconvolution Fusion (TDF) module in each pyramid hierarchy of the top-down pathway is comprised of temporal deconvolutional layers, fusion sub-module, temporal convolutional layers and batch normalization layers, which is used to fuse semantically strong, temporally coarser features from top-down pathway and temporally fine features from bottom-up pathway.

The temporal deconvolution is actually the transpose of temporal convolution rather than an actual deconvolution, which is a convolutional form of sparse coding. Filters of the temporal deconvolutional layers can be parameterized by weights $W_l \in R^{T_l \times d \times T_{l-1}}$ and biases $b_l \in R^{T_l}$, where d is the duration of filters, T_l and T_{l-1} respectively indicate the number of filters in the l-th and $(l-1)$-th deconvolutional layer. The output vector E_t of the l-th deconvolutional layer at time step t is

$$E_t^l = f(\sum_{t'=1}^{d} \langle W_{t'}^l, E_{t+d-t'}^{l-1} \rangle + b^l) , \quad (1)$$

Where $f(\bullet)$ is the activation function, $E_{t+d-t'}^{l-1}$ is the activation vector of the $(l-1)$-th deconvolutional layer at the time step $(t+d-t')$.

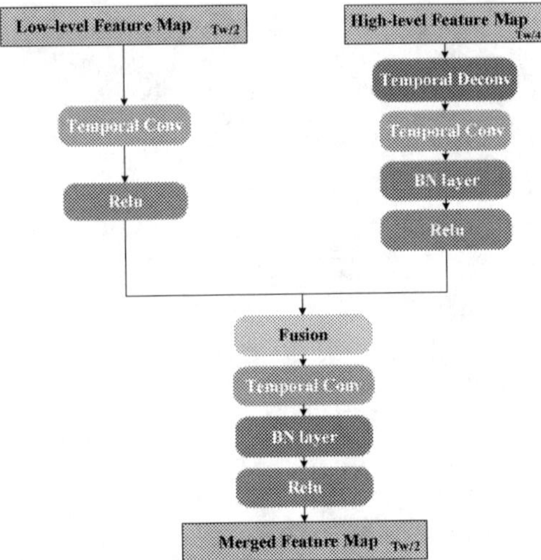

Fig. 3. TDF module. Temporal deconvolution is used to expand temporal dimension of high-level, strong semantic feature maps from top-down pathway. Low-level feature maps with high temporal resolution come from the bottom-up pathway. Fusion sub-module is adopted to fuse high-level features and low-level features

Then a temporal convolutional layer is added to further expand the temporal receptive field and a batch normalization layer is adopted to speed up training and further improve detection accuracy. With these layers, the temporal dimension of high-level feature map from top-down pathway is doubled. We adopt 1×1 convolution to match the number of channels in low-level features from bottom-up pathway. The fusion sub-module is used to fuse the high-level feature maps with expanded temporal dimension and low-level feature maps from the bottom-up pathway. To further improve detection performance, we explore different fusion methods, including element-wise sum, element-wise mean and channel concatenation.

Two TDF modules are stacked in the top-down pathway, which output feature maps F_D^1 and F_D^2 with size $L_w/2 \times 512$ and $L_w/4 \times 512$ respectively. Together with the output of the last layer $F_E^3 \in R^{L_w/8 \times 512}$ in the bottom-up pathway, the fused feature maps are used to predict action class scores and boundary offsets simultaneously.

Anchor and Prediction Layers. We use three anchor layers composed of temporal convolution to process the fused feature maps with multiple temporal scales from the top-down pathway. In each feature map of anchor layers, each temporal location is associated with K anchor instances with different scales. The scale ratios of anchors are the same as the ones used in SSAD [16] network, as shown in Table 1. When the length of video unit m_u is 16, the strides of these feature sequences are 32, 64, 128 frames respectively. The temporal scale ranges

Table 1. The anchor settings for feature sequences with different temporal resolutions in the proposed TDPN model.

Feature maps	Strides	Anchor scale ratios	Temporal scale ranges
F_D^1	32	$(1, 1.5, 2)$	32–64
F_D^2	64	$(0.5, 0.75, 1, 1.5, 2)$	32–128
F_D^3	128	$(0.5, 0.75, 1, 1.5, 2)$	64–256

of these anchor instances are 32–64, 32–128 and 64–256 frames, respectively. An important reason why the performance of our TDPN model is better than SSAD model is that the anchor instances with same temporal scales contains context information and strong semantics.

In the prediction layer, temporal convolution is adopted to predict action categories probabilities, boundaries offsets and overlap scores simultaneously. Each level of the temporal feature pyramid corresponds to a prediction layer and parameters are not shared in these layers. Similar to SSAD [16], classification scores are obtained by softmax layer and overlap scores are normalized by sigmoid function. Finally, we use NMS to remove duplicate results to obtain final detection results. The threshold in NMS is set to 0.1 by empirical validation.

3.3 Training

Label Assignment. We propose a new strategy for assigning action label to the detected action instances during training. Given a window w_i, g_i is the corresponding ground truth instances, including action categories, the starting and ending frames of action instances. Based on the time intersection-over-union (tIoU), we assign an activity label to a predicted anchor instance (1) if the highest one among the tIoUs with all ground truth instances g_i is higher than a threshold σ; (2) if it has the highest tIoU for a given ground truth instance. Note that the priority of the first case is higher than the second to avoid a predicted anchor instance being assigned multiple activity labels. When these conditions are not satisfied, it will be assigned a background label. The threshold σ is set to 0.7 by empirical validation. Our TDPN model can learn precise temporal boundaries of action instances by using this strict strategy for assigning label during training.

Optimization. Temporal action detection is a multi-task problem, including regression and classification tasks. To train the TDPN model, we need to optimize both regression and classification tasks jointly. The objective loss function is a weighted sum of the softmax loss and the smooth L_1 loss, which is given by:

$$Loss = L_{soft\max} + \lambda L_{reg} + L_2(\Theta) \ , \tag{2}$$

where $L_{soft\max}$ is a standard multi-class softmax loss function; L_{reg} is smooth L_1 loss; $L_2(\Theta)$ is the L_2 regularization loss; Θ represents the parameters of the TDPN model; λ is a loss trade-off parameter and is set to 2.

L_{reg} is defined as

$$L_{reg} = \frac{1}{N}\sum_{i=1}^{N}\sum_{z=1}^{C} l_i^z [R(\Delta\hat{c}_i^z - \Delta c_i^z) + R(\Delta\hat{w}_i^z - \Delta w_i^z)], \quad (3)$$

where Δc and Δw are location transformations of ground truth instances; $\Delta\hat{c}$ and $\Delta\hat{w}$ are the same for predicted action instances; N is the number of training samples in the mini-batch; C denotes the number of classes; R is the L_1 distance; $l_i^z = 1$ when the true class label of the i-th instance is z, otherwise, $l_i^z = 0$.

4 Experiments

In this section, the experiments are conducted to evaluate the performance of our proposed TDPN model on two detection benchmark datasets: THUMOS14 [13] and MEXaction2 [1].

4.1 Evaluation Datasets

THUMOS14 [13]**.** The whole dataset contains 1010 untrimmed videos for validation and 1574 untrimmed videos for testing. In the temporal action detection task, 200 validation set videos and 213 test set videos have temporal annotations in 20 action categories. This dataset is particularly challenging as many action instances have very short duration in pretty long videos. This dataset dose not provide the training set by itself, so the UCF-101 dataset including 13320 trimmed videos is appointed as the official training set. Following the practices, we only use its validation set for training and the test set for evaluating the TDPN network. Note that we remove two falsely annotated videos ("270", "1496") in the test set.

MEXaction2 [1]**.** This dataset contains three subsets: INA videos, YouTube clips and UCF101 Horse Riding clips. In the Mexaction2 dataset, only two action classes are annotated temporally: "BullChargeCape" and "HorseRiding". INA videos consist of 117 untrimmed videos with approximately 77 h in total, which are divided into three parts: training, parameter validation and testing. YouTube clips and UCF101 Horse Riding clips are trimmed and each clip contains one action instance, which are only used for training. Although this dataset only contains two action categories, it is particularly challenging in temporal action detection task. There are high imbalance between background and action instance of interest and high variability in point of view, image quality and action duration for "HorseRiding" in the MEXaction2 dataset.

Evaluation Metrics. We follow the convention metrics used in the THUMOS14, which use mean Average Precision (mAP) at different tIoU thresholds for evaluation and calculate Average Precision (AP) for each activity categories.

Table 2. Ablation study of TDF module in the proposed TDPN model. "SP" denotes that the network has single pathway and "TP" denotes that the network has two contrary pathway.

tIoU	0.1	0.2	0.3	0.4	0.5
SSAD [16]	50.1	47.8	43.0	35.0	24.6
re-trained SSAD (SP)	54.6	52.1	47.7	41.1	31.1
Our TDPN (TP)	58.6	56.3	51.8	44.4	35.0

On THUMOS14, the mAP with tIoU thresholds $\{0.1, 0.2, 0.3, 0.4, 0.5\}$ is used for comparing the performance of different methods and the AP at 0.5 tIoU is used for each activity category. On the MEXaction2 dataset, the mAP at 0.5 tIoU is used to compare performance of different approaches.

4.2 Implementation Details

During training, the length of sliding window is L_w and the stride size is $\frac{1}{4}L_w$. Note that the stride size is $\frac{3}{4}L_w$ during prediction. The windows of training data should contain at least one ground truth instance and the windows without ground truth instances will be held out from training. L_w is set to 32 by empirical validation. The batch size is 32 and each mini-batch is constructed from one window. To make the TDPN model converge fast, we randomly shuffle the order of training data. Similar to SSAD [16], the hard negative mining strategy is adopted to balance the proportion of positive and negative samples. Since there is no suitable pre-trained temporal deconvolutional network, the parameters of whole TDPN model are randomly initialized by the Xavier method [7]. The learning rate is initially set to 10^{-4} and then reduced by a factor of 10 after every 30 epochs. Training is terminated after a maximum of 60 epochs. We implement our system using Tensorflow [2], with training executed on a machine with 32G memory, NVIDIA Titan Xp GPU and Intel i7-6700K processor.

4.3 Ablation Study

Two Pathways vs Single Pathway. Our TDPN model contains two contrary pathways by introducing a top-down pathway into SSAD [16] network. The main strength of our TDPN model is that the features constructed by TDF modules in the top-down pathway contain more context information and stronger semantics than the ones with same temporal resolution in SSAD network. To compare fairly with SSAD network, we re-train the SSAD network using the unit-level feature sequences as our baseline model. The used strategy for label assignment is same as the one proposed in SSAD [16]. The element-wise sum is chosen as the fusion method in TDF module, which provides the best performance (See Table 3 bottom sections). Table 2 lists the detection results of our baseline model and TDPN model on THUMOS14, which shows that the mAP at 0.5

Table 3. Ablation study of methods for fusing feature sequences.

Fusion methods	mAP ($\theta = 0.5$)
Eltw-mean	37.9
Channel concatenate	38.8
Eltw-sum	40.7

Table 4. Ablation study of strategy for label assignment. "LA1" denotes the strategy for assigning label used in SSAD [16]. "LA2" denotes the strategy proposed in this paper.

tIoU	0.1	0.2	0.3	0.4	0.5
TDPN (LA1)	58.6	56.3	51.8	44.4	35.0
TDPN (LA2)	63.1	61.1	56.7	49.9	40.7

tIoU of the re-trained SSAD model increases from 24.6% to 31.1%. Compared to the SSAD model with single pathway, the mAP at 0.5 tIoU of our TDPN model increases from 31.1% to 35.0% (about 3.9% improvement). From these results, we can get two conclusions: (1) Strong semantic features with multiple temporal resolution constructed by TDF modules in the top-down pathway can significantly improve detection performance. (2) The unit-level feature sequences are effective to represent the spatiotemporal characteristics of actions.

Methods for Fusing Feature Sequences. We explore the different fusion methods in the TDF module of our TDPN model, including element-wise sum, element-wise mean and channel concatenation. During training, we use the strategy for label assignment proposed in Sect. 3.3 to train our TDPN model. The mAP at 0.5 tIoU is adopted to compare different methods on THUMOS14. As shown in Table 3, the element-wise sum method achieves best performance among these methods (the 40.7% mAP at 0.5 tIoU). Therefore, element-wise sum can effectively combine high-level feature maps with coarser temporal resolution and low-level feature maps with fine temporal resolution, which improves the performance of the TDPN detector.

Strategies for Label Assignment. Here, we evaluate that the impact of label assignment on detection performance on THUMOS14. "LA1" denotes the strategy for label assignment proposed in SSAD [16], where a predicted action instance is assigned the corresponding activity label if its highest tIoU with all ground truth instances is higher than 0.5. "LA2" denotes that the strategy for label assignment discussed in the Sect. 3.3. We use these strategies to train our TDPN model respectively. Action detection results are measured by mAP of different tIoU thresholds. As shown in Table 4, the strategy proposed in this paper achieves the best performance (about 5.7% improvement of the mAP at

Table 5. Action detection results on THUMOS14 test dataset, measured by mAP at different tIoU thresholds.

tIoU	0.1	0.2	0.3	0.4	0.5
Wang *et al.* [28]	18.2	17.0	14.0	11.7	8.3
Oneata *et al.* [18]	36.6	33.6	27.0	20.7	14.4
SLM [21]	39.7	35.7	30.0	23.2	15.2
FG [32]	48.9	44.0	36.0	26.4	17.1
PSDF [33]	51.4	42.6	33.6	26.1	18.8
S-CNN [35]	47.7	43.5	36.3	28.7	19.0
CDC [22]	-	-	40.1	29.4	23.3
SSAD [16]	50.1	47.8	43.0	35.0	24.6
TURN [6]	54.0	50.9	44.1	34.9	25.6
RC3D [31]	54.5	51.5	44.8	35.6	28.9
CBR [5]	60.1	56.7	50.1	41.3	31.0
TAL-Net [3]	59.8	57.1	53.2	48.5	**42.8**
SSAD (re-trained)	54.6	52.1	47.7	41.1	31.1
TDPN (ours)	**63.1**	**61.1**	**56.7**	**49.9**	40.7

0.5 tIoU) compared with the strategy used in SSAD [16]. Our proposed strategy increases the number of positive samples with short duration that are detected hard during training. These results demonstrate that our strict strategy for label assignment can improve the precision of temporal boundaries learned by model.

From the above comparisons, we adopt the unit-level feature sequences as the input of our TDPN model, the fused features with multiple temporal resolutions for detecting action instances and strict label assignment for training. Next, the TDPN model will be compared with other state-of-the-art approaches.

4.4 Comparison with the State of the Art

On the THUMOS14 and MEXaction2 datasets, we compare our TDPN model with existing state-of-the-art approaches, and using the matrix mentioned above reports detection performance. In our experiments, we set the unit length and window length to 16 and 32 respectively and use element-wise sum method to fuse features in the TDF module.

THUMOS14. In the last row of Table 5, our TDPN model shows about 9.6% improvement at the mAP@0.5 over our re-trained SSAD network, which indicates the importance of exploiting the feature maps with the high temporal resolution and strong semantics. Moreover, we compare the TDPN model with state-of-the-art approaches and the results during challenge [18,28]. As shown in Table 5, when the tIoU threshold is less than 0.5, our TDPN model outperforms the prior state-of-the-art approaches, including Cascaded Boundary Regression

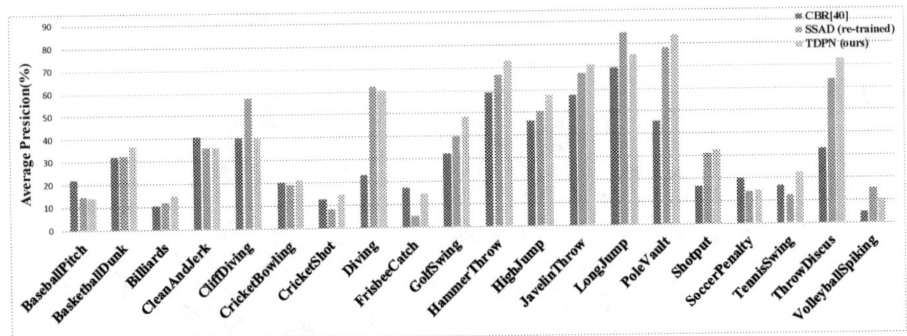

Fig. 4. Per-class AP at 0.5 tIoU threshold on THUMOS14

Table 6. Average precision on MEXaction2 dataset. The tIoU threshold is set to 0.5.

Methods	BullChargeCape	HorseRiding	mAP (%)
DTF [1]	0.3	3.1	1.7
S-CNN [35]	11.6	3.1	7.4
SSAD [16]	16.5	5.5	11.0
Our TDPN	**35.2**	**9.1**	**22.1**

(CBR) [5] and recently proposed TAL-Net [3] network. When the tIoU threshold is 0.5, our TDPN model achieves competitive performance. These results indicate that the TDPN model can detect the temporal boundaries in untrimmed video precisely. Figure 4 shows the AP at 0.5 tIoU for each action category of different methods including CBR [5], re-trained SSAD and our TDPN model. Our approach performs the best for 12 action categories compared with other methods, specially for “GolfSwing”, “HammerThrow” and “ThrowDiscus”. These results clearly demonstrates the superiority of our method. Qualitative detection results on THUMOS14 are shown in Fig. 5.

MEXaction2. We use all 38 untrimmed videos in MEXaction2 training dataset to train our TDPN model. The anchor scale ratios are the same as ones used in THUMOS14 dataset since the duration distribution of action instances on MEXaction2 is similar to the THUMOS14 dataset.

We compare TDPN model with other existing methods, including typical dense trajectory features (DTF) [1], Segment-CNN (SCNN) [35] and SSAD [16]. All methods are evaluated using standard criteria mentioned in Sect. 4.1. According to Table 6, our TDPN model outperforms other approaches for both “BullChargeCape” action and “HorseRiding” action, and the mAP at 0.5 tIoU threshold increases from 11.0% to 22.1% (about 11.1% improvement). The major challenge of this dataset is high variability in point of view, action duration for “HorseRiding” and image quality. These results indicate our TDPN model is

Fig. 5. Qualitative visualization of the actions detected by the TDPN network. Figure (a) and Figure (b) show detection results for two action classes on THUMOS14 dataset and MEXaction2 dataset respectively

capable of handing such problems. Figure 5 displays the visualization of detection results for "BullChargeCape" and "HorseRiding" respectively.

5 Conclusions

In this paper, we propose the Temporal Deconvolutional Pyramid Network (TDPN) for temporal action detection. The temporal convolutions are adopted to construct a initial feature pyramid in the bottom-up pathway. With the strong semantic features formed by Temporal Deconvolution Fusion (TDF) modules in various pyramidal hierarchies, the detection performance can be improved significantly. We explore different fusion strategies and the experiment results have showed that element-wise sum can achieve the excellent performance. To further improve detection accuracy, a strict strategy for label assignment is designed to train the model. Finally, the proposed TDPN model achieves competitive performance on THUMOS14 and outperforms other approaches on MEXaction2, which demonstrates our method is capable of localizing temporal boundaries precisely. For future work, we plan to explore end-to-end system that combines feature extractor and TDPN model to detect action instances from raw videos.

References

1. Mexaction2 (2015). http://mexculture.cnam.fr/xwiki/bin/view/Datasets/Mex+action+dataset
2. Abadi, M., Agarwal, A., et al.: TensorFlow: largescale machine learning on heterogeneous distributed systems. arXiv preprint arXiv:1603.04467 (2016)
3. Chao, Y., Vijayanarasimhan, S., Seybold, B., et al.: Rethinking the faster R-CNN architecture for temporal action localization. In: IEEE Conference on Computer Vision and Pattern Recognition. IEEE, Salt Lake City (2018)
4. Gaidon, A., Harchaoui, Z., Schmid, C.: Temporal localization of actions with actoms. IEEE Trans. Pattern Anal. Mach. Intell. **35**(11), 2782–2795 (2013)
5. Gao, J., Yang, Z., Nevatia, R.: Cascaded boundary regression for temporal action detection. In: British Machine Vision Conference. BMVA Press, London (2017)
6. Gao, J., Yang, Z., Sun, C., Chen, K., Nevatia, R.: TURN TAP: temporal unit regression network for temporal action proposals. In: IEEE International Conference on Computer Vision, pp. 3648–3656. IEEE Computer Society, Venice (2017)
7. Glorot, X., Bengio, Y.: Understanding the difficulty of training deep feedforward neural networks. In: Teh, Y.W., Titterington, M. (eds.) The Thirteenth International Conference on Artificial Intelligence and Statistics, vol. 9, pp. 249–256. PMLR, Sardinia (2010)
8. He, K., Zhang, X., Ren, S., Sun, J.: Deep residual learning for image recognition. In: IEEE Conference on Computer Vision and Pattern Recognition, pp. 770–778. IEEE, Las Vegas (2016)
9. Heilbron, F.C., Niebles, J.C., Ghanem, B.: Fast temporal activity proposals for efficient detection of human actions in untrimmed videos. In: IEEE Conference on Computer Vision and Pattern Recognition, pp. 1914–1923. IEEE, Las Vegas (2016)
10. Ioffe, S., Szegedy, C.: Batch normalization: accelerating deep network training by reducing internal covariate shift. arXiv preprint arXiv:1502.03167 (2015)
11. Jain, M., van Gemert, J.C., et al.: Action localization by tubelets from motion. In: IEEE Conference on Computer Vision and Pattern Recognition, pp. 740–747. IEEE, Columbus (2014)
12. Jain, M., Gemert, J.V., et al.: End-to-end, single-stream temporal action detection in untrimmed videos. In: British Machine Vision Conference. BMVA Press, London (2017)
13. Jiang, Y.G., Liu, J., Roshan Zamir, A., et al.: THUMOS challenge: action recognition with a large number of classes (2014). http://crcv.ucf.edu/THUMOS14/
14. Laptev, I.: On space-time interest points. Int. J. Comput. Vis. **64**(2–3), 107–123 (2005)
15. Lin, T., Dollr, P., Girshick, R., et al.: Feature pyramid networks for object detection. In: IEEE Conference on Computer Vision and Pattern Recognition, pp. 936–944. IEEE, Honolulu (2017)
16. Lin, T., Zhao, X., Shou, Z.: Single shot temporal action detection. In: Proceedings of the 2017 ACM on Multimedia Conference, pp. 988–996. ACM, New York (2017)
17. Mettes, P., van Gemert, J.C., et al.: Bag-of-fragments: selecting and encoding video fragments for event detection and recounting. In: Proceedings of the 5th ACM on International Conference on Multimedia Retrieval, pp. 427–434. ACM, New York (2015)
18. Oneata, D., Verbeek, J., Schmid, C.: The LEAR submission at Thumos 2014 (2014). https://hal.inria.fr/hal-01074442

19. Redmon, J., Divvala, S.K., Girshick, R.B., Farhadi, A.: You only look once: unified, real-time object detection. In: IEEE Conference on Computer Vision and Pattern Recognition, pp. 779–788. IEEE, Las Vegas (2016)
20. Ren, S., He, K., Girshick, R., Sun, J.: Faster R-CNN: towards real-time object detection with region proposal networks. IEEE Trans. Pattern Anal. Mach. Intell. **39**(6), 1137–1149 (2017)
21. Richard, A., Gall, J.: Temporal action detection using a statistical language model. In: IEEE Conference on Computer Vision and Pattern Recognition, pp. 3131–3140. IEEE, Las Vegas (2016)
22. Shou, Z., Chan, J., Zareian, A., Miyazawa, K., Chang, S.: CDC: convolutional-de-convolutional networks for precise temporal action localization in untrimmed videos. In: IEEE Conference on Computer Vision and Pattern Recognition (CVPR), pp. 1417–1426. IEEE, Venice (2017)
23. Simonyan, K., Zisserman, A.: Two-stream convolutional networks for action recognition in videos. In: Proceedings of the 27th International Conference on Neural Information Processing Systems, pp. 568–576. MIT Press, Cambridge (2014)
24. Tran, D., Bourdev, L., Fergus, R., et al.: Learning spatiotemporal features with 3D convolutional networks. In: 2015 IEEE International Conference on Computer Vision, pp. 4489–4497. IEEE Computer Society, Washington (2015)
25. Uijlings, J.R., Van De Sande, K.E., et al.: Selective search for object recognition. Int. J. Comput. Vis. **104**(2), 154–171 (2013). https://doi.org/10.1007/s11263-013-0620-5
26. Wang, H., Schmid, C.: Action recognition with improved trajectories. In: IEEE International Conference on Computer Vision, pp. 3551–3558. IEEE, Sydney (2013)
27. Wang, L., Xiong, Y., Lin, D., Gool, L.V.: Untrimmednets for weakly supervised action recognition and detection. In: IEEE Conference on Computer Vision and Pattern Recognition, pp. 6402–6411. IEEE, Honolulu (2017)
28. Wang, L., Qiao, Y., Tang, X.: Action recognition and detection by combining motion and appearance features (2014). http://crcv.ucf.edu/THUMOS14/
29. Liu, W., et al.: SSD: single shot multibox detector. In: Leibe, B., Matas, J., Sebe, N., Welling, M. (eds.) ECCV 2016. LNCS, vol. 9905, pp. 21–37. Springer, Cham (2016). https://doi.org/10.1007/978-3-319-46448-0_2
30. Xiong, Y., Wang, L., et al.: CUHK & ETHZ & SIAT submission to ActivityNet challenge 2016. arXiv preprint arXiv:1608.00797 (2016)
31. Xu, H., Das, A., Saenko, K.: R-C3D: region convolutional 3D network for temporal activity detection. In: IEEE International Conference on Computer Vision, pp. 5794–5803. IEEE, Venice (2017)
32. Yeung, S., Russakovsky, O., Mori, G., Fei-Fei, L.: End-to-end learning of action detection from frame glimpses in videos. In: IEEE Conference on Computer Vision and Pattern Recognition, pp. 2678–2687. IEEE, Las Vegas (2016)
33. Yuan, J., Ni, B., Yang, X., Kassim, A.A.: Temporal action localization with pyramid of score distribution features. In: IEEE Conference on Computer Vision and Pattern Recognition, pp. 3093–3102. IEEE, Las Vegas (2016)
34. Zhao, Y., Xiong, Y., Wang, L., et al.: Temporal action detection with structured segment networks. In: IEEE International Conference on Computer Vision, pp. 2933–2942. IEEE Computer Society, Venice (2017)
35. Zheng, S., Dongang, W., Fu, C.S.: Action temporal localization in untrimmed videos via multi-stage CNNs. In: IEEE Conference on Computer Vision and Pattern Recognition, pp. 1049–1058. IEEE, Las Vegas (2016)

Dynamic Temporal Pyramid Network: A Closer Look at Multi-scale Modeling for Activity Detection

Da Zhang[1](✉), Xiyang Dai[2], and Yuan-Fang Wang[1]

[1] University of California, Santa Barbara, USA
{dazhang,yfwang}@cs.ucsb.edu
[2] University of Maryland, College Park, USA
xdai@umiacs.umd.edu

Abstract. Recognizing instances at varying scales simultaneously is a fundamental challenge in visual detection problems. While spatial multi-scale modeling has been well studied in object detection, how to effectively apply a multi-scale architecture to temporal models for activity detection is still under-explored. In this paper, we identify three unique challenges that need to be specifically handled for temporal activity detection. To address all these issues, we propose Dynamic Temporal Pyramid Network (DTPN), a new activity detection framework with a multi-scale pyramidal architecture featuring three novel designs: (1) We sample frame sequence dynamically with different frame per seconds (FPS) to construct a natural pyramidal representation for arbitrary-length input videos. (2) We design a two-branch multi-scale temporal feature hierarchy to deal with the inherent temporal scale variation of activity instances. (3) We further exploit the temporal context of activities by appropriately fusing multi-scale feature maps, and demonstrate that both local and global temporal contexts are important. By combining all these components into a uniform network, we end up with a single-shot activity detector involving single-pass inferencing and end-to-end training. Extensive experiments show that the proposed DTPN achieves state-of-the-art performance on the challenging ActvityNet dataset.

Keywords: Activity detection · Multi-scale model · Pyramid network

1 Introduction

Temporal activity detection has drawn increasing interests in both academic and industry communities due to its vast potential applications in security surveillance, behavior analytics, videography and so on. Different from activity recognition, which only aims at *classifying* the categories of *manually trimmed* video clips, activity detection is *localizing* and *recognizing* activity instances from *long, untrimmed* video streams. This makes the task substantially more interesting

C. V. Jawahar et al. (Eds.): ACCV 2018, LNCS 11364, pp. 712–728, 2019.
https://doi.org/10.1007/978-3-030-20870-7_44

and challenging. With recent advances in deep learning, there has been fruitful progress in video analysis. While the performance of activity recognition has improved a lot [6,18,22,26,27,32], the detection performance still remains unsatisfactory [7,9,13,20,34].

One major obstacle that people are facing in temporal activity detection, is how to effectively model activities with various temporal length and frequency. Especially, the challenge of localizing precise temporal boundaries among activities of varying scales has been demonstrated as one major factor behind the difference in performance [9]. Luckily, the problem of scale variation is not new in computer vision researches, as it has been well studied in object detection in images [23]. In order to alleviate the problems arising from scale variation and successfully detect objects at multiple scales, extensive analysis has been conducted in recent years. Multi-scale pyramidal architecture has been widely adopted and become a general structure in many state-of-the-art object detection frameworks [14,15].

How to effectively model the temporal structure for activity detection using a multi-scale pyramidal network then? To answer this question, we first identify three unique problems that need to be specifically handled for temporal activity detection: (1) The duration of the input video is arbitrary (usually ranges from few seconds to few minutes). A naive subsampling method (resize the video) or sliding window (crop the video) will fail to fully exploit the temporal relations. (2) The temporal extent of activities varies dramatically compared to the size of objects in an image, posing a challenge to deal with large instance scale variation. (3) The spatial context of a bounding box is important to correctly classify and localize an object, and the temporal context is arguably more so than the spatial context. Thus, cross-scale analysis becomes much more crucial in temporal domain. In this work, we propose a multi-scale pyramidal deep-learning architecture with three novel elements designed to solve the above problems accordingly.

1. **How to effectively extract a feature representation for input video of arbitrary length?** A common practice in most existing works [7,9,31] is to use a high-quality video classification network for extracting a feature representation from raw frame sequence. However, when dealing with input video of arbitrary length, they only decode the video at a fixed FPS and extract features with a single resolution. To fully exploit temporal relations at multiple scales and effectively construct a feature representation, we propose to use dynamic sampling to decode the video at varying frame rates and construct a pyramidal feature representation. Thus, we are able to parse an input video of arbitrary length into a fixed-size feature pyramid without losing short-range and long-range temporal structures. Nevertheless, our extraction method is very general and can be applied to any framework and compatible with a wide range of network architectures.
2. **How to build better temporal modeling architectures for activity detection?** In dealing with the large instance scale variation, we draw inspirations from SSD [15] to build a multi-scale feature hierarchy allowing

predictions at different scales by appropriately assigning default spans. This multi-scale architecture enforces the alignment between the temporal scope of the feature and the duration of the default span. Besides, we also draw inspirations from Faster-RCNN [19] to use separate features for classification and localization since features for localization should be sensitive to pose variation while those for classification should not. We propose a new architecture to leverage the efficiency and accuracy from both frameworks while still maintaining a single shot design. In our work, we use separate temporal convolution and temporal pooling branches with matched temporal dimension at each scale, and use a late fusion scheme for final prediction.
3. **How to utilize local and global temporal contexts?** We claim both local temporal context (*i.e.*, moments immediately preceding and following an activity) and global temporal context (*i.e.*, what happens during the whole video duration) are crucial. We propose to explicitly encode local and global temporal contexts by fusing features at appropriate scales in the feature hierarchy.

Our contributions are: (1) We take a closer look at multi-scale modeling for temporal activity detection and identify three unique challenges. (2) To address all these issues in a single network, we introduce the Dynamic Temporal Pyramid Network (DTPN), which is a single shot activity detector featuring a novel multi-scale pyramidal architecture design. (3) Our DTPN achieves state-of-the-art performance on temporal activity detection task on ActivityNet benchmark [4].

2 Related Work

Here, we review relevant works in activity recognition, multi-scale pyramidal modeling, and temporal activity detection.

Activity Recognition. Activity recognition is an important research topic and has been extensively studied for a long time. In the past few years, tremendous progress has been made due to the introduction of large datasets [4,12] and the developments on deep neural networks [6,18,22,26,27]. Two-stream network [22] learned both spatial and temporal features by operating 2D ConvNet on single frames and stacked optical flows. C3D [26] used Conv3D filters to capture both spatial and temporal information directly from raw video frames. More recently, improvements on top of the C3D architecture [6,18,27] as well as advanced temporal building blocks such as non-local modules [30] were proposed to further boost the performance. However, the assumption of well-trimmed videos limits the application of these approaches in real scenarios, where the videos are usually long and untrimmed. Although they do not consider the difficult task of localizing activity instances, these methods are widely used as the backbone network for the detection task.

Multi-scale Pyramidal Modeling. Recognizing objects at vastly different scales is a fundamental challenge in computer vision. To alleviate the problems arising from scale variation, multi-scale pyramidal modeling forms the basis of

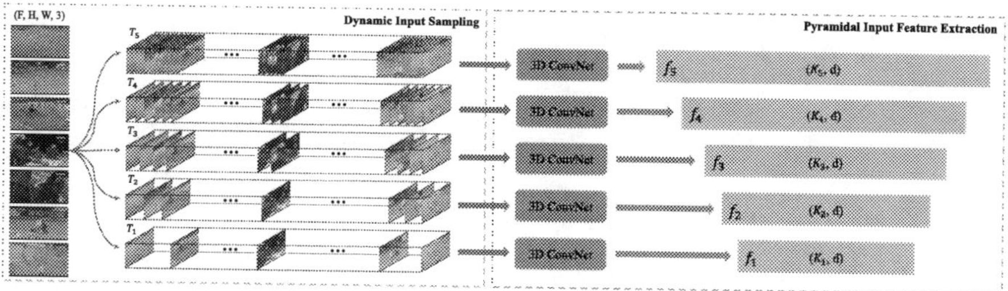

Fig. 1. An illustration of pyramidal input feature extraction with 5 sampling rates. Left: input video is sampled at different FPS to capture motion dynamics at different temporal resolutions; right: a shared 3D ConvNet is used to extract the input feature at each resolution.

a standard solution [1] and has been extensively studied in the spatial domain. For example, independent predictions at layers of different resolutions are used to capture objects of different sizes [5], training is performed over multiple scales [11], inference is performed on multiple scales of an image pyramid [8], feature pyramid is directly constructed from the input image [14].

Meanwhile, the multi-scale modeling for temporal activity detection is still under-explored: Shou *et al.* [21] used a multi-scale sliding window to generate snippets of different lengths, however, such method is often inefficient during runtime due to the nature of sliding window; Zhao *et al.* [35] used temporal pyramid pooling for modeling multi-scale structures without considering complex motion dynamics, since those features were directly pooled at different levels. In this paper, we provide a comprehensive study on temporal multi-scale modeling and propose an efficient end-to-end solution.

Temporal Activity Detection. Unlike activity recognition, the detection task focuses on learning how to localize and detect activity instances in untrimmed videos. The problem has recently received significant research attention due to its potential application in video data analysis.

Previous works on activity detection mainly use sliding windows as candidates and classify video clips inside the window with activity classifiers trained on multiple features [17]. Many recent works adopt a proposal-plus-classification framework [3,10,20,21,35] by generating segment proposals and classifying activity categories for each proposal: some of them focus on designing better proposal schemes [3,10,35], while others focus on building more accurate activity classifiers [20,21,35]. Along this line of attack, Xu *et al.* [31] proposed an end-to-end trainable activity detector based on Faster-RCNN [19]. Buch *et al.* [2] investigated the use of gated recurrent memory module in a single-stream temporal detection framework. However, all these methods rely on feature maps with a fixed temporal resolution and fail to utilize a multi-scale pyramidal architecture for handling instances with varying temporal scales.

A few very recent works [7,9,13,34] have started to model temporal scales with a multi-tower network [7] or a multi-scale feature hierarchy [13,34], and incorporated temporal contextual information [7,9]. Our method differs from all these approaches in that we identify three unique modeling problems specific to temporal activity detection and propose to solve them in one single multi-scale pyramidal network. We detail our contributions below.

3 Approach

We present a *Dynamic Temporal Pyramid Network (DTPN)*, a novel approach for temporal activity detection in long untrimmed videos. DTPN is dedicatedly designed to address the temporal modeling challenges as discussed in the introduction with a multi-scale pyramidal architecture. The overall DTPN framework is a single-shot, end-to-end activity detector featuring three novel architectural designs: pyramidal input feature extraction with dynamic sampling, multi-scale feature hierarchy with two-branch network, and local and global temporal contexts (Sects. 3.1, 3.2 and 3.3).

3.1 Pyramidal Input Feature Extraction with Dynamic Sampling

The input of our network is an untrimmed video with an arbitrary length. We denote a video ν as a series of RGB frames $\nu = \{I_i\}_{i=1}^{F}$, where $I_i \in \mathbb{R}^{H\times W\times 3}$ is the *i-th* input frame and F is the total number of frames. A common practice is to use a high-quality video classification network to extract a 1D feature representation on top of the input frame sequence [7,13,31]. This feature extraction step is beneficial for summarizing spatial-temporal patterns from raw videos into high-level semantics. The backbone classification network can be of any typical architectures, including the two-stream network [22], C3D [26], I3D [6], Res3D [27], P3D [18], etc. However, an obvious problem of the classification ConvNet in their current form is their inability in modeling long-range temporal structure. This is mainly due to their limited temporal receptive field as they are designed to operate only on a single stack of frames in a short snippet.

To tackle this issue, we propose to extract pyramidal input feature with dynamic sampling, a video-level framework to model multi-level dynamics throughout the whole video. Sparse sampling has already been proven very successful when solving the video classification problem [28], where preliminary prediction results from short snippets sparsely sampled from the video are aggregated to generate the video-level prediction. Following similar ideas, we propose a general feature extraction framework specifically for the temporal activity detection.

Formally, given an input video ν with F frames and a sampling scale index s, we divide the entire frame sequence into K_s different segments of equal duration. Suppose a classification network takes w frames as input and generates a *d-dimensional* 1D feature vector before any classification layers, we uniformly sample w frames in each segment to construct a sequence of snippets $\{T_1, T_2, \ldots, T_{K_s}\}$, where each $T_i, i \in [1, K_s]$ is a snippet of w frames which can be directly used as an input to the backbone network. Thus, we can extract features for a specific sampling scale index s as

$$f_s = \bigcup_{i=1}^{K_s} F(T_i, \mathbf{W}) \in \mathbb{R}^{K_s \times d} \tag{1}$$

where $F(T_i, \mathbf{W})$ is the function representing a ConvNet with parameter $\mathbf{W}$ which operates on snippet T_i and generates a *d-dimensional* feature vector. Thus, each single feature vector $F(T_i, \mathbf{W})$ in f_s covers a temporal span of $\frac{F}{K_s}$ frames. Suppose the input frame sequence is decoded at r FPS, then the equivalent feature-level sampling rate is given as $\frac{r \times K_s}{F}$. Instead of only extracting features at a single scale, we apply a set of different scales to construct a pyramidal input feature, which can be considered as sampling the input frame sequence with dynamic FPS. Technically, we use S different scales to sample the input video with a base scale length K_1 and an up sampling factor of 2. *i.e.* $K_s = 2^{s-1} \times K_1, s \in [1, S]$ different feature vectors will be extracted given a scale index s. This dynamic sampling procedure allows us to directly summarize both short-range and long-range temporal relations while being efficient during runtime. Finally, a pyramidal feature is constructed as

$$f_{pymd} = \bigcup_{s=1}^{S} f_s, f_s \in \mathbb{R}^{K_s \times d} \tag{2}$$

which will be used as the input to the two-branch network (Sect. 3.2).

The overall procedure is illustrated in Fig. 1. Note that our approach is different from temporal pyramid pooling [35] where higher-level features are directly pooled, and multi-scale sliding window [21] where a window size is pre-defined. Our dynamic sampling approach fixes the number of sampling windows and computes independent features by directly looking at input frames with different receptive fields. We find that both sparse and dense sampling are important for temporal detection task: sparse sampling is able to model long-range temporal relations. Dense sampling, on the other hand, provides high-resolution short-range temporal features. By using an off-the-shelf video classification network and a dynamic frame sampling strategy, we are able to construct a pyramidal input feature that naturally encodes the video at varying temporal resolutions.

Comparison with Previous Works. When extracting features from the input video, previous works [7,9,13,31,34] decode the input video with a fixed FPS (usually small for computational efficiency) and extract features using a non-overlapping sliding window, which corresponds to a fixed FPS single-scale sampling in our schema. Although advanced networks are applied to model temporal relationships, their feature extraction component fails to fully exploit the multi-scale motion context in an input video stream. More importantly, our extraction strategy is very general thus can be applied to any framework and compatible with a wide range of network architectures.

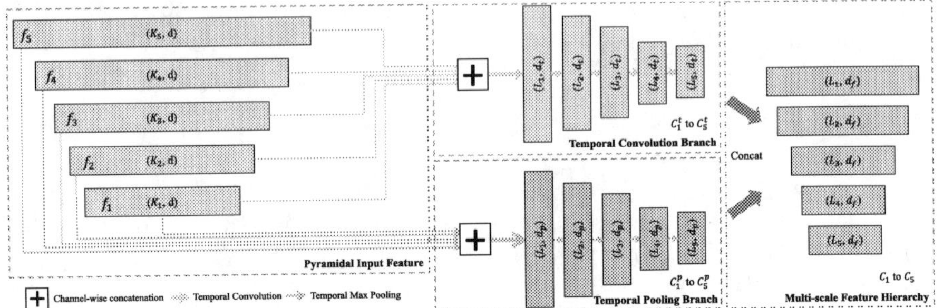

Fig. 2. An illustration of the two-branch multi-scale network with $S = N = 5$. The network combines a temporal convolution branch and a temporal pooling branch, where the features are concatenated and down sampled. Late fusion scheme is applied to build the multi-scale feature hierarchy.

3.2 Multi-scale Feature Hierarchy with Two-Branch Network

To allow the model to predict variable scale temporal spans, we follow the design of SSD to build a multi-scale feature hierarchy consisting of feature maps at several scales with a scaling step of 2. We then assign default temporal spans at each layer to get temporal predictions at multiple scales. More specifically, a multi-scale feature hierarchy is created which we denote as $\{C_i\}_{i=1}^N, C_i \in \mathbb{R}^{L_i \times d_f}$ where N is the total number of features each with a temporal dimension L_i and feature dimension d_f. For a simple and efficient design, we set $L_1 = K_1$ and $L_N = 1$, and the temporal dimension in between follows $L_i = 2L_{i+1}$.

The next question is: how do we combine the pyramidal input feature and build the multi-scale network? As illustrated in Fig. 2, we propose to use a two-branch network, *i.e.*, a temporal convolution branch and a temporal pooling branch to fuse the pyramidal input feature and aggregate these branches at the end. This design choice is inspired by the fact that pooling features contain more translation-invariant semantic information which is classification-friendly and convolutional features better model temporal dynamics which are helpful for localization [14,19].

In more detail, both branches take as input the pyramidal feature f_{pymd}. For the temporal convolution branch, a Conv1D layer with temporal kernel size $\frac{K_s}{L_1} + 1$, stride $\frac{K_s}{L_1}$ is applied to each input feature $f_s \in f_{pymd}, s \in [1, S]$ to increase the temporal receptive field and decrease the temporal dimension to L_1 (temporal stride is set to 1 for f_1 since no down sampling is needed). We use channel-wise concatenation to combine the resulting features into a single feature map $C_1^t \in \mathbb{R}^{L_1 \times d_t}$. Based on C_1^t, we stack Conv1D layers with kernel size 3 and stride 2 for progressively decreasing the temporal dimension by a factor 2 to construct C_2^t through C_N^t. For the temporal pooling branch, a non-overlapping temporal max pooling with window size $\frac{K_s}{L_1}$ is used on top of each input feature $f_s \in f_{pymd}, s \in [1, S]$ to match with the temporal dimension L_1. Similar to the temporal convolution branch, channel-wise concatenation is applied here to

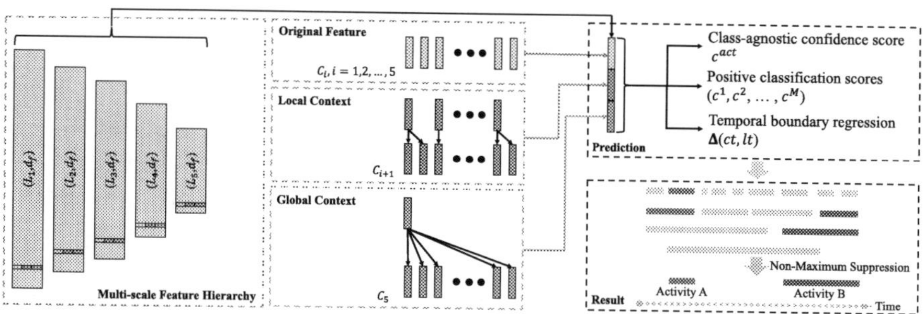

Fig. 3. An illustration of local and global contexts when setting N to 5. Every temporal feature map cell at all scales is enhanced by its local context (next scale) and global context (last scale) to produce a set of prediction parameters. Temporal NMS is applied to produce the final detection results.

construct $C_1^p \in \mathbb{R}^{L_1 \times d_p}$. Then, we use temporal max pooling with a scaling step of 2 to construct the feature hierarchy $\{C_i^p\}_{i=1}^N$. Finally, features from the two branches are aggregated together to generate the final feature hierarchy $\{C_i\}_{i=1}^N$, which will be used to further model the temporal context (Sect. 3.3).

Simplicity is central to our design and we have found that our model is robust to many design choices. We have experimented with other feature fusion blocks such as element-wise product, average pooling, etc., and more enhanced building blocks such as dilated convolution [33] and observed marginally better results. Designing better network blocks is not the focus of this paper, so we opt for the simple design described above.

Comparison with Previous Works. Previous works based on SSD framework [13,34] only use a single convolutional branch and don't apply feature fusion since only a single-scale input is applied. Our design uses two separate branches with slightly different feature designs at multiple scales. The localization branch uses temporal convolution for better localization while the classification branch uses maximum pooling to record the most prominent features for recognition. We show experimentally that our two-branch design achieves much better results compared to single-branch (Sect. 4.4).

3.3 Local and Global Temporal Contexts

Context is important in computer vision tasks [24,36]. Temporal contextual information has been shown to be critical for temporal activity detection [7,9]. There are mainly two reasons: First, it enables more precise localization of temporal boundaries. Second, it provides strong semantic cues for identifying the activity class. In order to fully utilize the temporal contextual information, we propose to use both local temporal context (*i.e.*, what happens immediately before and after an activity instance) and global temporal context (*i.e.*, what happens during the whole video duration). Both contexts help with localization and classification subtasks but with different focuses: local context focuses more on localization with immediate cues to guide temporal regression, while global context tends to look much wider at the whole video to provide classification guidance. Below, we detail our approach.

Our multi-scale feature hierarchy can easily incorporate contextual information since it naturally summarizes temporal information at different scales. To exploit the local temporal context for a specific layer C_i, we combine each temporal feature cell at C_i with a corresponding feature cell at C_{i+1}. Specifically, we first duplicate each feature cell at C_{i+1} twice to match with the temporal dimension of C_i and concatenate the feature maps together. Thus, at each feature cell location in C_i, it not only contains feature at its original location but also a local context feature at the next scale. To exploit the global temporal context, instead of looking at the feature map in the next scale, we combine the feature with the last feature map C_N which summarizes the whole video content. Similar to the local temporal context, we duplicate C_N to have the same temporal dimension with C_i. We exploit local and global contexts at all layers in our network, thus, each temporal feature cell is enhanced by its local and global temporal information. We illustrate this mechanism in Fig. 3.

Each temporal feature map can produce a fixed set of detection predictions using a set of Conv1D layers. These are indicated on top of the feature network in Fig. 3. The basic operation for predicting parameters of a potential temporal detection is a Conv1D filter that produces scores for activity presence (c^{act}) and categories (c^1 to c^M, where M is the total number of classes), and temporal offsets ($\Delta ct, \Delta lt$) relative to the default temporal location. The temporal detections at all scales are combined through temporal non-maximum suppression for generating the final detection results.

Comparison with Previous Works. Neither Zhang *et al.* [34] nor Lin *et al.* [13] exploited any context features in their network. Dai *et al.* [9] included context features in the proposal stage, but they pooled features from different scales. Chao *et al.* [7] only exploited the local temporal context. Our work considers both local and global temporal contexts and inherently extract contexts from a multi-scale temporal feature hierarchy.

4 Experiments

We evaluate the proposed framework on the ActivityNet [4] large-scale temporal activity detection benchmark. As shown in the experiments, our DTPN achieves state-of-the-art performance. We also perform a set of ablation studies to analyze the impact of different components in our network.

4.1 Experimental Settings

Dataset. ActivityNet [4] is a recently released dataset which contains 200 different types of activities and a total of 849 hours of videos collected from YouTube. ActivityNet is the largest benchmark for temporal activity detection to date in terms of both the number of activity categories and number of videos, making the task particularly challenging. There are two versions, and we use the latest version 1.3 which contains 19994 untrimmed videos in total and is divided into three disjoint subsets, training, validation, and testing by a ratio of 2:1:1. On average, each activity category has 137 untrimmed videos. Each video on average has 1.41 activities which are annotated with temporal boundaries. Since the ground-truth annotations of test videos are not public, following traditional evaluation practices on this dataset, we use the validation set for ablation studies.

Evaluation Metrics. ActivityNet dataset has its own convention of reporting performance metrics. We follow their conventions, reporting mean average precision (mAP) at different IoU thresholds 0.5, 0.75 and 0.95. The average of mAP values with IoU thresholds [0.5:0.05:0.95] is used to compare the performance between different methods.

4.2 Implementation Details

Feature Extractor. To extract the feature maps, we first train a Residual 3D ConvNet (Res3D) model [27] on the Kinetics activity classification dataset [6]. The model takes as input a stack of 8 RGB frames with spatial size 256×256, performs 3D convolutions, and extracts a feature vector with $d = 2048$ as the output of an average pooling layer. We decode each video at 30 FPS to take enough temporal information into account, and each frame is resized to 256×256. We set $K_1 = L_1 = 16$ and $S = 5$ for dynamic sampling, thus, we divide the input frame sequence into a set of $\{16, 32, 64, 128, 256\}$ segments and a snippet of window size $w = 8$ is sampled in each segment. Each snippet is then fed into our Res3D model to extract a pyramidal input feature. Note that feature extraction can be done very efficiently with a single forward pass in batches.

Temporal Anchors. In our design, we associate a set of temporal anchors with each temporal feature map cell in the multi-scale feature hierarchy $\{C_i\}_{i=1}^{5}$. As described in Sect. 3.2, the temporal dimension of C_i is given as $L_i = 2^{5-i}, i \in [1, 5]$. Regarding a feature map C_i, we set the length of each temporal anchor to be $\frac{1}{L_i}$ (as the input video length is normalized to 1), and the centers are uniformly distributed with a temporal interval of $\frac{1}{L_i}$ in between. Thus, we assign a set of $\{16, 8, 4, 2, 1\}$ temporal anchors in our network which correspond to anchors of duration between $\frac{1}{16}$ and the whole video length. This allows us to detect activity instances with varying scales.

Network Configurations. Our system is implemented in TensorFlow and its source code will be made publicly available. All evaluation experiments are performed on a work station with NVIDIA GTX 1080 Ti GPUs. For multi-scale feature hierarchy, we generate a set of features with temporal dimension $\{16, 8, 4, 2, 1\}$ through both temporal convolution branch and temporal pooling branch as described in Sect. 3.2. In temporal convolution branch, we set the number of filters to 64 for five different input features, and $d_t = 320$ for all convolutional layers after concatenation. When training the network, we randomly flip the pyramidal input feature along temporal dimension to further augment the training data. The network is trained with multi-task end-to-end loss functions involving a regression loss, a classification loss and a localization loss. The whole network is trained for 20 epochs with the learning rate set to 10^{-4} for the first 12 epochs and 10^{-5} for the last 8 epochs.

4.3 Comparison with State-of-the-Art

Table 1 shows our activity detection results on the ActivityNet v1.3 validation subset along with state-of-the-art methods [7,9,20,25,29,31] published recently. The proposed framework, using a single model instead of an ensemble, is able to achieve an average mAP of 25.72 that tops all other methods and perform well at high IoU thresholds, *i.e.*, 0.75 and 0.95. This clearly demonstrates the superiority of our method.

Table 1. Activity detection results on ActivityNet v1.3 validation subset. The performances are measured by mean average precision (mAP) for different IoU thresholds and the average mAP of IoU thresholds from 0.5:0.05:0.95.

IoU threshold	0.5	0.75	0.95	Average
Singh and Cuzzolin [25]	34.47	-	-	-
Wang and Tao [29]	45.10	4.10	0.00	16.40
Shou *et al.* [20]	45.30	26.00	0.20	23.80
Xu *et al.* [31]	26.80	-	-	12.70
Dai *et al.* [9]	36.44	21.15	**3.90**	-
Chao *et al.* [7]	38.23	18.30	1.30	20.22
DTPN (ours)	**41.44**	**25.49**	3.26	**25.72**

Note that the top half in Table 1 are top entries for challenge submission: our method is worse than [29] at IoU threshold 0.5 but their method is optimized for 0.5 overlap and its performance degrades significantly at high IoU thresholds, while our method achieves much better results (25.49 vs. 4.10 at IoU threshold 0.75); Shou *et al.* [20] builds a refinement network based on the result of [29], although they are able to improve the accuracy our method is still better when measured by the average mAP (25.72 vs. 23.80). We believe the performance gain comes from our advanced temporal modeling design for both feature extraction and feature fusion, as well as rich temporal contextual information.

4.4 Ablation Study

To understand DTPN better, we evaluate our network with different variants on ActivityNet dataset to study their effects. For all experiments, we only change a certain part of our model and use the same evaluation settings. We compare

Table 2. Results for using a single-resolution feature map as the network input.

IoU threshold	0.5	0.75	0.95	Average
Single-256	36.75	22.09	1.94	22.18
Single-128	36.93	21.93	2.86	22.32
Single-64	35.47	21.39	2.56	21.63
Single-32	35.62	21.78	2.57	21.66
Single-16	33.64	20.69	1.82	20.63
Pyramidal input	**38.89**	**23.82**	**3.25**	**24.07**

the result of different variants using the mAP at 0.5, 0.75, 0.95 and the average mAP. For a fair comparison, we don't concatenate contextual features in all experiments unless explicitly noted.

Dynamic Sampling vs. Single-Resolution Sampling. A major contribution of DTPN is using dynamic sampling to extract a pyramidal input feature as the network input. However, as a general SSD based temporal activity detector, single-resolution feature can also be applied as the input to our network. We validate the design for dynamic sampling pyramidal input by comparing with single-resolution sampling input: we keep the multi-scale feature network with 5 temporal dimensions from 16 to 1 and the two-branch architecture, but instead of taking the pyramidal feature as input we only input a separate feature map of temporal size 256, 128, 64, 32 and 16 independently. The hidden dimension for each layer is kept the same for a fair comparison. The results are reported in Table 2. Pyramidal input performs uniformly the best compared to single input, despite the network design, this clearly demonstrates the importance of multi-scale pyramidal feature extraction.

Table 3. Results for combing multiple feature maps as the network input.

256	128	64	32	16	Average mAP
✓	✓				22.52
			✓	✓	22.01
✓		✓		✓	23.11
✓	✓	✓	✓	✓	**24.07**

Multi-scale Feature Fusion. We further validate our design to combine multiple features as our network input. Instead of just using a single-resolution feature as input, we investigate the effects of combining different input features. We also keep the same hidden dimension for each layer for a fair comparison. Table 3 compares different combination schemes: we observe that only dense sampling $(256+128)$ or sparse sampling $(32+16)$ leads to inferior performance compared to sampling both densely and sparsely (256 + 64 + 16); By adding more fine-grained details (128 and 32), our pyramidal input achieves the best result.

Table 4. Results for the impact of the two-branch network architecture.

IoU threshold	0.5	0.75	0.95	Average
TConv	27.12	14.70	1.34	15.12
TPool	29.77	17.24	2.16	17.12
TConv+TPool (two-branch)	**38.89**	**23.82**	**3.25**	**24.07**

Two-Branch vs. Single-Branch. Here, we evaluate the impact of the two-branch network architecture. In our design, We propose to use a separate temporal convolution branch and temporal pooling branch and fuse the two feature hierarchies at the end. However, either branch can be used independently to predict the final detection results. Table 4 lists the performance of models with temporal convolution branch only (TConv) and temporal pooling branch only (TPool). We conclude that two-branch architecture can significantly improve the detection performance (more than 5% in comparison with single-branch).

Table 5. Results for incorporating local and global temporal contexts.

IoU threshold	0.5	0.75	0.95	Average
w/o Context	38.89	23.82	3.25	24.07
w/Local Context	40.01	24.50	3.24	24.70
w/Global Context	40.17	24.20	**3.54**	24.62
w/Local+Global Contexts	**41.44**	**25.49**	3.26	**25.72**

Local and Global Temporal Contexts. We contend that temporal contexts both locally and globally are crucial for temporal activity detection. Since local and global contextual features are extracted from different layers and combined through concatenation, we can easily separate each component and see its effect. As reported in Table 5, We compare four different models: (1) model without temporal context (w/o Context); (2) model only incorporating local context (w/Local Context); (3) model only incorporating global context (w/Global Context); (4) model incorporating both local and global contexts (w/Local+Global Contexts). We achieve higher mAP nearly at all IoU thresholds when incorporating either local or global context, and we can further boost the performance by combining both contexts at the same time.

Qualitative Results. We provide qualitative detection results on ActivityNet to demonstrate the effectiveness and robustness of our proposed DTPN. As shown in Fig. 4, different video streams contain very diversified background context and different activity instances vary a lot in temporal location and scale.

Fig. 4. Qualitative visualization of the top detected activities on ActivityNet. Each sequence consists of the ground-truth (blue) and predicted (green) activity segments and class labels. (Color figure online)

DTPN is able to predict the accurate temporal span as well as the correct activity category, and it is also robust to detect multiple instances with various length in a single video.

Table 6. Comparison of our approach and the state-of-the-art methods in the approximate computation time(s) to process each video on ActivityNet dataset.

Method	Shou *et al.* [20]	Xu *et al.* [31]	Mahasseni *et al.* [16]	DTPN (ours)
Time (s)	>930	3.2	0.35	**0.5**

Activity Detection Speed. We benchmark our network on a single GTX 1080 Ti GPU to measure the activity detection speed. One activity detection in our framework is measured as a single forward-pass of the whole network, and we follow the same strategy reported in [16] to calculate the approximate detection time for different methods. In Table 6, we compare our approach with the state-of-the art methods in the approximate computation time to process each video. Due to the single-shot end-to-end design with simple Conv3D building blocks, our DTPN is very efficient and can process a single video in 0.5 s which is significantly faster than most state-of-the-art methods [20, 31].

5 Conclusions

In this paper, we introduce DTPN, a novel network architecture specifically designed to address three key challenges arising from the scale variation problem for temporal activity detection. DTPN employs a multi-scale pyramidal structure with three novel architectural designs: (1) pyramidal input feature extraction with dynamic sampling; (2) multi-scale feature hierarchy with two-branch network; and (3) local and global temporal contexts. We achieve state-of-the-art performance on the challenging ActivityNet dataset, while maintaining an efficient single-shot, end-to-end design.

References

1. Adelson, E.H., Anderson, C.H., Bergen, J.R., Burt, P.J., Ogden, J.M.: Pyramid methods in image processing. RCA Eng. **29**(6), 33–41 (1984)
2. Buch, S., Escorcia, V., Ghanem, B., Fei-Fei, L., Niebles, J.: End-to-end, single-stream temporal action detection in untrimmed videos. In: BMVC (2017)
3. Buch, S., Escorcia, V., Shen, C., Ghanem, B., Niebles, J.C.: SST: single-stream temporal action proposals. In: 2017 IEEE Conference on Computer Vision and Pattern Recognition (CVPR), pp. 6373–6382. IEEE (2017)
4. Caba Heilbron, F., Escorcia, V., Ghanem, B., Carlos Niebles, J.: ActivityNet: a large-scale video benchmark for human activity understanding. In: Proceedings of the IEEE Conference on Computer Vision and Pattern Recognition, pp. 961–970 (2015)
5. Cai, Z., Fan, Q., Feris, R.S., Vasconcelos, N.: A unified multi-scale deep convolutional neural network for fast object detection. In: Leibe, B., Matas, J., Sebe, N., Welling, M. (eds.) ECCV 2016. LNCS, vol. 9908, pp. 354–370. Springer, Cham (2016). https://doi.org/10.1007/978-3-319-46493-0_22
6. Carreira, J., Zisserman, A.: Quo vadis, action recognition? A new model and the kinetics dataset. In: 2017 IEEE Conference on Computer Vision and Pattern Recognition (CVPR), pp. 4724–4733. IEEE (2017)
7. Chao, Y.W., Vijayanarasimhan, S., Seybold, B., Ross, D.A., Deng, J., Sukthankar, R.: Rethinking the faster R-CNN architecture for temporal action localization. In: Proceedings of the IEEE Conference on Computer Vision and Pattern Recognition, pp. 1130–1139 (2018)
8. Dai, J., et al.: Deformable convolutional networks. In: Proceedings of the IEEE International Conference on Computer Vision, pp. 764–773 (2017)
9. Dai, X., Singh, B., Zhang, G., Davis, L.S., Chen, Y.Q.: Temporal context network for activity localization in videos. In: 2017 IEEE International Conference on Computer Vision (ICCV), pp. 5727–5736. IEEE (2017)
10. Gao, J., Yang, Z., Nevatia, R.: Cascaded boundary regression for temporal action detection. In: BMVC (2017)
11. He, K., Zhang, X., Ren, S., Sun, J.: Deep residual learning for image recognition. In: Proceedings of the IEEE Conference on Computer Vision and Pattern Recognition, pp. 770–778 (2016)
12. Jiang, Y., et al.: Thumos challenge: action recognition with a large number of classes (2014)
13. Lin, T., Zhao, X., Shou, Z.: Single shot temporal action detection. In: Proceedings of the 2017 ACM on Multimedia Conference, pp. 988–996. ACM (2017)

14. Lin, T.Y., Dollár, P., Girshick, R., He, K., Hariharan, B., Belongie, S.: Feature pyramid networks for object detection. In: 2017 IEEE Conference on Computer Vision and Pattern Recognition (CVPR), pp. 936–944. IEEE (2017)
15. Liu, W., et al.: SSD: single shot multibox detector. In: Leibe, B., Matas, J., Sebe, N., Welling, M. (eds.) ECCV 2016. LNCS, vol. 9905, pp. 21–37. Springer, Cham (2016). https://doi.org/10.1007/978-3-319-46448-0_2
16. Mahasseni, B., Yang, X., Molchanov, P., Kautz, J.: Budget-aware activity detection with a recurrent policy network. In: Proceedings of the British Machine Vision Conference (BMVC) (2018)
17. Mettes, P., van Gemert, J.C., Cappallo, S., Mensink, T., Snoek, C.G.: Bag-of-fragments: selecting and encoding video fragments for event detection and recounting. In: Proceedings of the 5th ACM on International Conference on Multimedia Retrieval, pp. 427–434. ACM (2015)
18. Qiu, Z., Yao, T., Mei, T.: Learning spatio-temporal representation with pseudo-3D residual networks. In: 2017 IEEE International Conference on Computer Vision (ICCV), pp. 5534–5542. IEEE (2017)
19. Ren, S., He, K., Girshick, R., Sun, J.: Faster R-CNN: towards real-time object detection with region proposal networks. In: Advances in Neural Information Processing Systems, pp. 91–99 (2015)
20. Shou, Z., Chan, J., Zareian, A., Miyazawa, K., Chang, S.F.: CDC: convolutional-de-convolutional networks for precise temporal action localization in untrimmed videos. In: 2017 IEEE Conference on Computer Vision and Pattern Recognition (CVPR), pp. 1417–1426. IEEE (2017)
21. Shou, Z., Wang, D., Chang, S.F.: Temporal action localization in untrimmed videos via multi-stage CNNs. In: Proceedings of the IEEE Conference on Computer Vision and Pattern Recognition, pp. 1049–1058 (2016)
22. Simonyan, K., Zisserman, A.: Two-stream convolutional networks for action recognition in videos. In: Advances in Neural Information Processing Systems, pp. 568–576 (2014)
23. Singh, B., Davis, L.S.: An analysis of scale invariance in object detection-snip. In: Proceedings of the IEEE Conference on Computer Vision and Pattern Recognition, pp. 3578–3587 (2018)
24. Dai, X., Southall, B., Trinh, N., Matei, B.: Efficient fine-grained classification and part localization using one compact network. In: 2017 IEEE International Conference on Computer Vision Workshop (ICCVW), pp. 996–1004 (2017)
25. Singh, G., Cuzzolin, F.: Untrimmed video classification for activity detection: submission to activitynet challenge. arXiv preprint arXiv:1607.01979 (2016)
26. Tran, D., Bourdev, L., Fergus, R., Torresani, L., Paluri, M.: Learning spatiotemporal features with 3D convolutional networks. In: 2015 IEEE International Conference on Computer Vision (ICCV), pp. 4489–4497. IEEE (2015)
27. Tran, D., Wang, H., Torresani, L., Ray, J., LeCun, Y., Paluri, M.: A closer look at spatiotemporal convolutions for action recognition. In: Proceedings of the IEEE Conference on Computer Vision and Pattern Recognition, pp. 6450–6459 (2018)
28. Wang, L., et al.: Temporal segment networks: towards good practices for deep action recognition. In: Leibe, B., Matas, J., Sebe, N., Welling, M. (eds.) ECCV 2016. LNCS, vol. 9912, pp. 20–36. Springer, Cham (2016). https://doi.org/10.1007/978-3-319-46484-8_2
29. Wang, R., Tao, D.: Uts at activitynet 2016. AcitivityNet Large Scale Activity Recognition Challenge **2016**, 8 (2016)
30. Wang, X., Girshick, R., Gupta, A., He, K.: Non-local neural networks. In: CVPR (2018)

31. Xu, H., Das, A., Saenko, K.: R-C3D: region convolutional 3D network for temporal activity detection. In: IEEE International Conference on Computer Vision (ICCV), vol. 6, p. 8 (2017)
32. Dai, X., Signh, B., Ng, J.Y., Davis, L.S.: TAN: temporal aggregation network for dense multi-label action recognition. In: WACV (2019)
33. Yu, F., Koltun, V.: Multi-scale context aggregation by dilated convolutions. arXiv preprint arXiv:1511.07122 (2015)
34. Zhang, D., Dai, X., Wang, X., Wang, Y.F.: S3D: single shot multi-span detector via fully 3D convolutional network. In: BMVC (2018)
35. Zhao, Y., Xiong, Y., Wang, L., Wu, Z., Tang, X., Lin, D.: Temporal action detection with structured segment networks. In: 2017 IEEE International Conference on Computer Vision (ICCV), pp. 2933–2942. IEEE (2017)
36. Dai, X., Ng J.Y., Davis, L.S.: FASON: first and second order information fusion network for texture recognition. In: 2017 IEEE Conference on Computer Vision and Pattern Recognition (CVPR), pp. 7352–7360 (2017)

Global Regularizer and Temporal-Aware Cross-Entropy for Skeleton-Based Early Action Recognition

Qiuhong Ke[1(✉)], Jun Liu[2], Mohammed Bennamoun[1], Hossein Rahmani[3], Senjian An[4], Ferdous Sohel[5], and Farid Boussaid[1]

[1] The University of Western Australia, Crawley, Australia
qiuhong.ke@research.uwa.edu.au,
{mohammed.bennamoun,farid.boussaid}@uwa.edu.au
[2] Nanyang Technological University, Singapore, Singapore
jliu029@ntu.edu.sg
[3] Lancaster University, Lancashire, England
h.rahmani@lancaster.ac.uk
[4] Curtin University, Bentley, Australia
s.an@curtin.edu.au
[5] Murdoch University, Murdoch, Australia
f.sohel@murdoch.edu.au

Abstract. In this paper, we propose a new approach to recognize the class label of an action before this action is fully performed based on skeleton sequences. Compared to action recognition which uses fully observed action sequences, early action recognition with partial sequences is much more challenging mainly due to: (1) the global information of a long-term action is not available in the partial sequence, and (2) the partial sequences at different observation ratios of an action contain a number of sub-actions with diverse motion information. To address the first challenge, we introduce a global regularizer to learn a hidden feature space, where the statistical properties of the partial sequences are similar to those of the full sequences. We introduce a temporal-aware cross-entropy to address the second challenge and achieve better prediction performance. We evaluate the proposed method on three challenging skeleton datasets. Experimental results show the superiority of the proposed method for skeleton-based early action recognition.

Keywords: Early action recognition · Global regularizer · Temporal-aware cross-entropy · 3D skeleton sequences

1 Introduction

Early action recognition, which aims to infer the action class before an action is fully performed, is very important for a wide range of real-world applications, such as prevention of dangerous events in video surveillance, autonomous driving and health care systems [1]. It can also be used to enhance human-robot

C. V. Jawahar et al. (Eds.): ACCV 2018, LNCS 11364, pp. 729–745, 2019.
https://doi.org/10.1007/978-3-030-20870-7_45

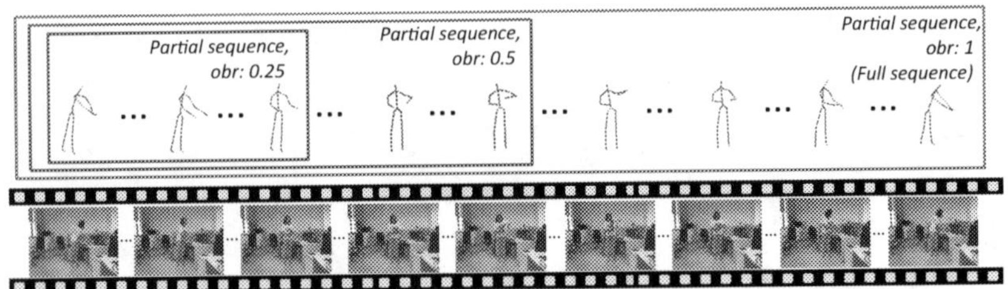

Fig. 1. A human action generally contains multiple temporal stages and sub-actions. Early action recognition aims to recognize the action class before the action sequence is fully observed, i.e., the observation ratio ('obr') is smaller than 1.

interaction, allowing robots to quickly respond to humans and improve user experience [2]. Given that human actions are performed in the 3D space, 3D skeleton sequences captured by depth cameras provide comprehensive and useful information for action analysis [3]. 3D skeleton data is also robust to clustered backgrounds and illumination variations. Besides, such data is easy to obtain due to the prevalence and affordability of 3D sensors. Moreover, the dimension of the skeleton data is quite small (75 in each frame in the skeleton sequence captured by Kinect V2). This makes skeleton data very attractive for real-time applications (such as early action recognition). In this paper, we propose a new early action recognition approach based on 3D skeleton data.

A series of advanced skeleton-based action recognition methods have been proposed in recent years and have shown promising performance [4–10]. Compared to action recognition, early action recognition is much more challenging. In action recognition, an action is recognized after the action is fully observed. In contrast, in early action recognition, the goal is to infer the action class when the action is still in progress. In other words, the observation used for early action recognition is often a partial sequence, which only contains a partial execution of the action. As a result, the long-term global information of the action, which is important for class inference, is unavailable. As shown in Fig. 1, a human action may last for a long period of time and contain multiple sub-actions, with a variety of human motions during the overall duration of the action. As a result, in order to accurately infer the action class, the long-term global information of the full action progress needs to be captured and modeled [11–13].

In this paper, we propose a global regularizer to learn a latent feature space, in which the partial sequences and the full sequences are similar. More specifically, during training, both the partial and the full sequences are fed to the network as two inputs, which are then aggregated in a hidden feature layer by using the global regularizer. The global regularizer measures the distance of the statistical properties between the partial and full sequences in the latent space. We propose to minimize the discrepancy of their statistical properties (i.e., mean and variance) rather than directly minimizing their pair-wise feature distance. This is because the estimation of the statistical properties can help reduce the effects of outliers such as actions without motions occurring at an early temporal stage. Once the network is trained, the learned network (which shares information of the full sequences) is used to process a given testing sequence to infer the action class.

Another main challenge in early action recognition is that the partial sequences of an action class often contain diverse motion information. As shown in Fig. 1, the partial sequence with a small observation ratio only contains some early sub-actions, while the partial sequence with a large observation ratio contains more information of the action. Intuitively, the partial sequence with a small observation ratio should be given a smaller weight during the training of the network as less action information is provided. To address this issue, we introduce a temporal-aware cross-entropy as the classification loss of the network. The temporal-aware cross-entropy is calculated based on the observation ratios of the partial sequences. More specifically, less penalty is given to the classification errors made by the partial sequences with smaller observation ratios. This prevents the network from over-fitting the partial sequences with small observation ratios and improves the prediction performance.

To sum up, in this paper, we address skeleton-based early action recognition. We explore two main challenges in this task, and propose a new method to handle these challenges. We summarize the main contributions of this paper as follows: (1) We propose a new network which contains a global regularizer to exploit the global information. (2) We introduce a temporal-aware cross-entropy as the classification loss for early action recognition at different observation ratios. (3) We report extensive experimental results demonstrating the superior performance of the proposed method.

2 Related Works

Skeleton-Based Action Recognition. Human action recognition and early recognition are important tasks in the area of computer vision due to their wide ranges of applications [14–22]. Due to the prevalence of affordable and highly-accurate sensing cameras, many efforts have been made on 3D skeleton-based action recognition [4–10,23–26]. Traditional methods include spatial feature learning from each frame of the sequence (*e.g.*, pairwise relative positions, rotations and translations) and temporal modelling of the features of all frames using Fourier Temporal Pyramid (FTP) [4,5]. Recently, LSTM has been developed to learn the spatial or spatial-temporal information from skeleton sequences [6,7,9]. Deep CNN has also been leveraged to process skeleton sequences as images, which hierarchically learns both the spatial and temporal information [10]. Different from the aforementioned works on action recognition by using fully-observed skeleton sequences, in this paper, we propose a new framework for the challenging skeleton-based early action recognition task.

Early Action Recognition. Compared to action recognition (which uses full sequences for action inference), early action recognition, aims to infer the action class at an early temporal stage before the action is fully observed. For RGB-based early action recognition, most of the existing works try to exploit the

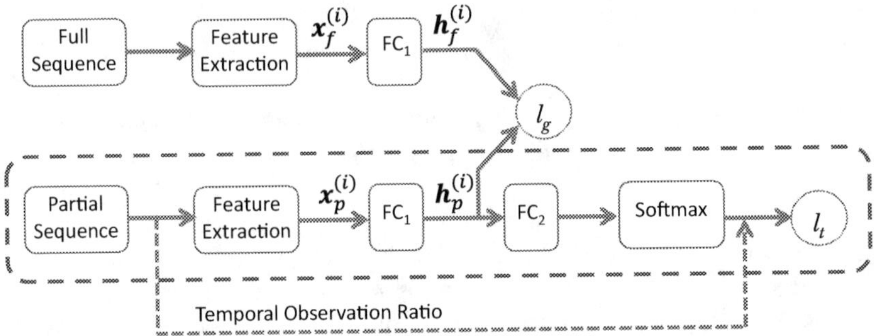

Fig. 2. The overall architecture of the proposed method. FC denotes fully connected layer. $\mathbf{x}_f^{(i)}$ and $\mathbf{x}_p^{(i)}$ denote the features of the full and partial sequences in the ith training pair, respectively. $\mathbf{h}_f^{(i)}$ and $\mathbf{h}_p^{(i)}$ denote the hidden representations of the full and partial sequences, respectively. Given a testing sequence, the sub-network shown in the red box is leveraged to process the sequence for early action recognition. The full sequence and the temporal observation ratio value are not required in the testing phase. (Color figure online)

temporal dynamics of the features of partial sequences [2,27–30]. In [30], each partial sequence is represented with spatial, temporal and structural features for early interaction recognition. Some works [31,32] focus on learning a classification model using a new loss for better early action recognition. In [31], a weighted cross-entropy is introduced for early action recognition. The new loss aims to prevent the network from over-fitting the partial sequences at an early stage. In [32], a weighted false positive classification loss is introduced and added to the standard cross-entropy as a new classification loss for action anticipation. Recently, Farha *et al.* [33] introduced two different architectures based on CNN and RNN for future action anticipation. For RGB-D early action recognition, Hu *et al.* [34] introduced a soft regression-based framework for early action recognition using RGB-D videos. Liu *et al.* [35] introduced a Scale Selection Network (SSNet) to effectively select different scales for online 3D early action recognition. In this work, we focus on early action recognition from skeleton sequences that contain a single activity.

3 Proposed Method

The overall architecture of the proposed framework is shown in Fig. 2. It contains a global regularizer, which aims to exploit the global information from partial sequences for better early action recognition. The classification loss of the network is a temporal-aware cross-entropy, which prevents the network from over-fitting the partial sequences with small observation ratios and further improves the performance. In this section, we describe the architecture in details.

3.1 Global Regularization

A human action generally contains multiple sub-actions and a high variation of human motions. The long-term global information needs to be leveraged in order to recognize the action more accurately. In early action recognition, the partial sequence does not provide the global information. This makes early action recognition very challenging. In this section, we introduce a new method to exploit the global information for early action recognition from the partial sequence. The main idea is to learn a hidden feature space, in which the partial sequences are similar to the full sequences. This similarity is enforced by minimizing a global regularizer between the full and the partial sequences in the feature space. The global regularizer is calculated based on the statistical properties of the features of the sequences. The discrepancy of the statistical properties has been shown to lead to an incompatibility between two distributions of data in domain adaptation tasks [36–39].

As shown in Fig. 2, the network has two inputs. During training, the training data is fed to the network in the form of pairs. Each pair consists of the feature of the full sequence of an action sample and the feature of a partial sequence of the same sample. Here, we denote the set of training pairs as $\{\mathbf{x}_f^{(i)}, \mathbf{x}_p^{(i)}\}_{i=1}^{n}$, where n denotes the number of training pairs in the batch. $\mathbf{x}_f^{(i)} \in \mathbb{R}^{d_1}$ and $\mathbf{x}_p^{(i)} \in \mathbb{R}^{d_1}$ are the features of the full and the partial sequences in the ith training pair, respectively. The features of the partial sequence and the corresponding full sequence in each pair are fed to the hidden layer $\texttt{FC}_1$ of the network to generate an embedding feature. We use $W \in \mathbb{R}^{d_2 \times d_1}$ and $\mathbf{b} \in \mathbb{R}^{d_2 \times 1}$ to denote the weight matrix and bias vector of the hidden layer, where d_2 is the dimension of the hidden space. The hidden representations of the full and partial sequences in the $i^{(th)}$ pair are calculated as:

$$\begin{aligned} \mathbf{h}_f^{(i)} &= g(W\mathbf{x}_f^{(i)} + \mathbf{b}) \\ \mathbf{h}_p^{(i)} &= g(W\mathbf{x}_p^{(i)} + \mathbf{b}) \end{aligned} \tag{1}$$

where g is the rectified linear unit (ReLU) activation function [40].

The global regularizer l_g between the partial and the full sequences is computed as:

$$\ell_g = \left\| \hat{\mathbf{h}}^p - \hat{\mathbf{h}}^f \right\|_2. \tag{2}$$

where $\hat{\mathbf{h}}^p$ and $\hat{\mathbf{h}}^f$ are the global representations of the partial and full sequences in the hidden space, respectively. $\hat{\mathbf{h}}^p$ and $\hat{\mathbf{h}}^f$ are calculated as:

$$\hat{\mathbf{h}}_p = \begin{bmatrix} \mathbf{m}_p \\ \mathbf{v}_p \end{bmatrix} \tag{3}$$

$$\hat{\mathbf{h}}_f = \begin{bmatrix} \mathbf{m}_f \\ \mathbf{v}_f \end{bmatrix} \tag{4}$$

where

$$\begin{aligned}
\mathbf{m}_p &= \tfrac{1}{n}\sum_{i=1}^{n}\mathbf{h}_p^{(i)} \\
\mathbf{v}_p &= \tfrac{1}{n}\sum_{i=1}^{n}\left(\mathbf{h}_p^{(i)}-\mathbf{m}_p\right)^2 \\
\mathbf{m}_f &= \tfrac{1}{n}\sum_{i=1}^{n}\mathbf{h}_f^{(i)} \\
\mathbf{v}_f &= \tfrac{1}{n}\sum_{i=1}^{n}\left(\mathbf{h}_f^{(i)}-\mathbf{m}_f\right)^2
\end{aligned} \tag{5}$$

3.2 Temporal-Aware Cross-Entropy

The network simultaneously minimizes the global regularizer and the classification loss of the partial sequences, thus the sequences do not lose their discriminative power, which is used for recognizing actions. The standard cross-entropy between the ground-truth action label and the output predictions is generally used for action recognition. Specifically, let $\mathbf{z}^{(i)} = [z_1^{(i)}, \cdots, z_m^{(i)}]^T \in \mathbb{R}^m$ denote the feature vector of the ith sample that is fed to the Softmax layer to generate the probability scores, where m denotes the number of action classes. The predicted probability of the kth class is defined as:

$$p_k^{(i)} = \frac{\exp(z_k^{(i)})}{\sum_{j=1}^{m}\exp(z_j^{(i)})} \tag{6}$$

The cross-entropy between the predicted probability and the ground-truth label is formulated as:

$$\ell_c^{(i)} = -\sum_{k=1}^{m} y_k^{(i)} \log\left(p_k^{(i)}\right) \tag{7}$$

where $y_k^{(i)}$ is the ground-truth action label corresponding to the kth class of the ith sample, i.e., assume the action class of the ith sample is $m^\star$, then $y_k^{(i)} = 1$ if $k = m^\star$, and $y_k^{(i)} = 0$ otherwise.

In contrast to action recognition, where the testing data comes with full sequences which cover the full progress of the action, the testing data in early action recognition are partial sequences with various observation ratios. Intuitively, a partial sequence with a small observation ratio should be assigned a smaller weight during the training of the network, as the partial sequence with a small observation ratio often contains less action information and more noisy information (that is irrelevant to the full action) compared to a partial sequence with a large observation ratio. Therefore, we introduce a temporal-aware cross-entropy loss function, which uses different weights that are related to the observation ratios of the partial sequences. Specifically, this loss function gives smaller penalties to the classification mistakes of the partial sequences with smaller observation ratios. This prevents the network from over-fitting. The temporal-aware cross-entropy is formulated as:

$$\ell_t^{(i)} = f(r^{(i)})\ell_c^{(i)} \tag{8}$$

where $r^{(i)} = \frac{t}{T}$ denotes the observation ratio of a partial sequence with t frames. T denotes the total number of frames of the full sequence that the partial sequence belongs to. $\ell_c^{(i)}$ is the standard cross-entropy formulated as Eq. 7 and $f(r^{(i)})$ is an increasing function. We empirically evaluated two increasing functions, including the linear form:

$$f(r^{(i)}) = r^{(i)} \tag{9}$$

and the exponential form:

$$f(r^{(i)}) = e^{r^{(i)}-1} \tag{10}$$

Both methods give smaller weights to the losses of the partial sequences with smaller observation ratios and yield better performances compared to the method without the temporal-aware cross-entropy. In the experiments, the exponential form is used to report our final prediction accuracies.

3.3 Network Training and Action Inference

The loss of the network includes the temporal-aware cross-entropy and the global regularizer:

$$\mathcal{L} = \frac{1}{n}\sum_{i=1}^{n} \ell_t^{(i)} + \lambda \ell_g \tag{11}$$

where n denotes the number of training pairs of the partial and full sequences, and λ is the weight to balance the two losses.

During training, the full sequences, which contain the fully executions of actions, are provided by each dataset. For each full sequence, we generate multiple partial sequences. We denote a full skeleton sequence as $s(1{:}J,\ 1{:}T)$, where J denotes the number of human skeletal joints in each frame, and T denotes the number of frames. We segment $s(1{:}J,\ 1{:}T)$ into k partial sequences which all start from the first frame. The ith partial sequence can be denoted as $s(1{:}J,\ 1{:}\lceil\frac{T \cdot i}{k}\rceil)$. In this case, the observation ratio of this partial sequence is $\frac{i}{k}$. Each partial sequence contains the accumulative information that starts from the first frame of the action. Consequently, the kth partial sequence is actually the full sequence containing T frames.

To feed the training data to the network, we first adapt the method in [10] to extract features from the partial and full skeleton sequences. The main idea of [10] is to transform skeleton sequences into image-based representations to extract CNN features, which hierarchically encode both the spatial and temporal information. In [10], each skeleton sequence is represented as four images to extract four features. In this paper, we aim to show the benefits of the proposed framework, rather than the feature representations of the skeleton sequences. Therefore, during training and testing, we represent each sequence as only one image and extract one feature vector for computation efficiency, rather than extracting multi-features which are computational expensive as [10]. During testing, the sub-network (shown in the red box in Fig. 2) is used to process a given partial sequence. The full sequence and the temporal observation ratio of the partial sequence are not required to predict the action.

4 Experiments

The proposed method was evaluated on three benchmark skeleton datasets, i.e., NTU Dataset [7], CMU Dataset [41] and SYSU 3D Human-Object Interaction (3DHOI) Dataset [42]. In this section, we report the experimental results and present detailed analysis.

4.1 Datasets

NTU Dataset. [7] contains more than 56000 sequences and 4 million frames. This is currently the largest skeleton-based action dataset. There are 60 action classes, including both one-person actions (e.g., eating, drinking) and two-person interactions (e.g., kicking, handshaking). These actions are performed by 40 distinct subjects and are captured by three cameras. The cameras are placed at different locations and view points, which results in 80 view points in total. The 3D coordinates of 25 joints are provided for each skeleton. This dataset is very challenging due to the large view-point, intra-class and sequence-length variations.

CMU Dataset. [41] contains 2235 sequences and about 1 million frames. This dataset has been categorized into 45 action classes (*e.g.*, walking, jumping) [8]. Each action is performed by one person. The 3D coordinates of 31 joints are provided in each skeleton. There are high sequence-number variations and intra-class diversity, which make this dataset very challenging.

SYSU 3DHOI Dataset. [42] contains 480 sequences performed by 40 subjects. There are 12 action classes, including drinking, pouring, calling with a cell phone, playing with a cell phone, wearing a backpack, packing a backpack, sitting in a chair, moving a chair, taking out a wallet, taking something out from the wallet, mopping and sweeping. Some actions are very similar at the early temporal stage since the subjects operate the same object, or the actions have the same starting sub-action, such as standing still. This makes this dataset very challenging for early action recognition.

4.2 Experimental Settings

The following methods are implemented based on the same feature for comparison:

Action Recognition Network (ARN). This network is trained using only full sequences. The network has one input and one output with a Softmax layer to generate class scores. In testing, the partial sequence is directly fed to the network for early action recognition. This baseline is used to show the importance of using partial sequences to train the early action recognition network.

Early Action Recognition Network (EARN). This baseline has the same architecture as the ARN baseline, except that the training data consists of all the available partial and full sequences. Compared to our proposed method, EARN does not include the global regularizer for early action recognition. Besides, it uses the standard cross-entropy loss for the classifier.

Early Action Recognition Network + Global Regularization (EARN + GR). In this baseline, a network with the same architecture as the proposed network is devised, except that the classification loss is the standard cross-entropy loss function. In other words, this method does not take the temporal observation ratio into account to compute the temporal cross-entropy. The loss of the network is the combination of the global regularizer and the standard cross-entropy.

Early Action Recognition Network + Global Regularization + Temporal-aware Cross-entropy (EARN + GR + TCE). This method is the proposed method, which includes the global regularizer and the temporal-aware cross-entropy for early action recognition.

Other Early Action Recognition Methods. We also compare with other state-of-the-art early action recognition methods, including the methods in [31, 32] and [34].

In our implementation, the parameter λ in Eq. 11 is set to 1 for all datasets. The number of units of the first and second fully-connected layer is set to 512 and the number of action classes, respectively. The network is trained using the stochastic gradient descent algorithm. The learning rate is set to 0.001 with a decay rate of 10^{-6}. The momentum is set to 0.9. For all datasets, we split 20% of the training data for validation to select the hyper-parameters. Each action sequence is divided into 10 partial sequences. All the partial sequences start from the first frame of the full sequence. The observation ratios of the partial sequences, in this case, are changed from 0.1 to 1, with a step of 0.1.

4.3 Results on the NTU Dataset

For the evaluation on this dataset, we follow the cross-subject testing protocol, i.e., the sequences of 20 subjects are used for training and the sequences of the other 20 subjects are used for testing. The comparisons of the proposed method to other methods are shown in Fig. 3(a) and Table 1.

EARN outperforms ARN when the observation ratio is smaller than 0.8. More specifically, when the observation ratio is 0.5, i.e., only the former 50% of the number of frames of each sequence is used for testing, the prediction accuracy of EARN is 47.13%, which is 20.63% better than ARN (26.5%). ARN outperforms EARN when the observation ratio is close to 1. The recognition accuracy (observation ratio is 1) of ARN is 66.25%. Compared to EARN (60.64%), the

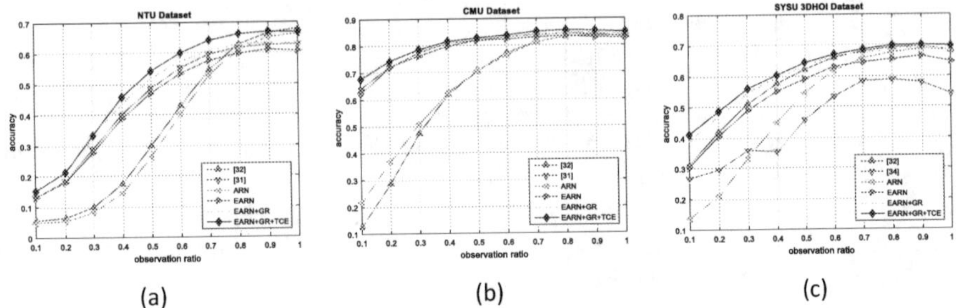

Fig. 3. Performance comparison of early action recognition on (a) NTU Dataset, (b) CMU Dataset and (c) SYSU 3DHOI Dataset. On each observation ratio r, the partial sequence that starts from the first frame to the $(rT)^{th}$ frame is used for testing. T denotes the number of frames in the full sequence. (Best viewed in color)

Table 1. Performance comparison of early action recognition on the NTU Dataset. We adapt the method in [10] to transform each skeleton into an image and extract one feature vector. The same feature is used in all methods for fair comparisons. Refer to Fig. 3(a) for more results.

Observation ratios	Methods					
	[32]	[31]	ARN	EARN	EARN+GR	EARN+GR+TCE
0.3	28.94%	9.95%	8.21%	27.87%	32.66%	**33.46%**
0.5	48.62%	29.98%	26.50%	47.13%	51.79%	**54.28%**
0.8	61.86%	62.80%	61.06%	59.88%	62.76%	**66.21%**
Average	45.15%	36.41%	34.51%	43.77%	47.27%	**49.41%**

Table 2. Performance comparison of the proposed method without and with temporal-aware cross-entropy (linear and exponential) on the NTU Dataset.

Observation ratios	EARN+GR	EARN+GR+TCE (linear)	EARN+GR+TCE (exp)
0.3	32.66%	32.63%	**33.46%**
0.5	51.79%	53.94%	**54.28%**
0.8	62.76%	65.66%	**66.21%**
Average	47.27%	48.88%	**49.41%**

improvement of ARN is 5.61%. In contrast to EARN, ARN does not use partial sequences to train the network. It clearly shows that early action recognition is different from action recognition and the partial sequences are indispensable for network training in order to predict actions at the early temporal stage.

EARN + GR is seen to significantly outperform EARN on all observation ratios. Particularly, when the observation ratio is 0.5, the prediction accuracy of the EARN + GR is 51.79%, which is 4.66% better than that of the EARN (47.13%). The improvement of the EARN + GR compared to the EARN averaged across all observation ratios is 3.5% (from 43.77% to 47.27%). EARN does not take into account the fact that the global information is not available in the partial sequences. In contrast, the proposed EARN + GR explicitly investigates the global information with a global regularizer. The global regularizer encourages the network to learn a hidden feature space, in which the partial and full sequences are similar. During testing, because the partial sequences are mapped to the hidden space which shares the global information of the full sequences, better performances are achieved. It clearly shows the benefits of the global regularizer for early action recognition.

EARN + GR + TCE further improves the performance of EARN + GR, especially at the late temporal stage. When the observation ratio is 0.5, the performance of the EARN + GR + TCE is 54.28%. Compared to the EARN + GR (51.79%), the performance of EARN + GR + TCE is 2.49% better. The improvement of EARN + GR + TCE compared to EARN + GR averaged across all observation ratios is 2.14% (from 47.27% to 49.41%). EARN + GR uses standard cross-entropy for the classification of the partial sequences. In contrast, EARN + GR + TCE takes the temporal observation ratios of the sequences into account and calculates the temporal cross-entropy as the classification loss of the partial sequences. The temporal cross-entropy prevents the network from over-fitting the sequences with small observation ratios and yields better performances.

We also compared the proposed method with state-of-the-art early action recognition methods [31,32] in Fig. 3 and Table 1. We used the same feature in [31,32] for fair comparisons. When the observation ratio is 0.5, the performance of [32] is 48.62%. EARN + GR + TCE outperforms [32] by 5.66% (from 48.62% to 54.28%). The average improvement of the proposed EARN + GR + TCE compared to [32] is 4.26%. In [32], a new loss combining the standard cross-entropy and a linearly increasing false positive loss, is introduced to prevent ambiguities in early action recognition. It does not explicitly exploit the global information for early action recognition. The EARN + GR + TCE also significantly outperforms the method in [31]. More specifically, the performance of EARN + GR + TCE (54.28%) is 24.30% better than that of the method in [31] (29.98%) on observation ratio 0.5. In [31], a weighted cross-entropy is introduced for early action recognition. The weight of the cross-entropy of each partial sequence is an exponential function in terms of the difference of the number of the frames between the partial and the full sequences. It can be seen that the performance of this method is similar to ARN (which is trained only on the full sequences). This is due to the fact that the numbers of frames of most full sequences are large, which yields zero weights for most partial sequences. In other words, the network does not take the partial sequences for training. This results in a degraded performance of early action recognition at the early temporal stage due to the under-fitting problem. The method in [31] performs better only when the number of frames of the testing sequence is similar to that of the full sequence (i.e., observation ratio is close to 1) as this method mainly focuses on full sequences for training.

Table 2 compares the performances of the proposed method with linear (Eq. 9) and exponential (Eq. 10) cross-entropy on the NTU Dataset. We refer to these two methods as EARN + GR + TCE (linear) and EARN + GR + TCE (exp). Both methods outperform EARN + GR, which uses standard cross-entropy instead of the temporal-aware cross-entropy for classification. The improvements of EARN + GR + TCE (linear) and EARN + GR + TCE (exp) compared to EARN + GR averaged across all observation ratios are 1.61% and 2.14%, respectively. EARN + GR + TCE (exp) outperforms EARN + GR + TCE (linear) on all observation ratios. EARN + GR + TCE (linear) uses the observation ratio of each partial sequence as the weight to calculate cross-entropy. This method suppresses the weight of the partial sequence with a small observation ratio to a very low value. In other words, the network does not train the partial sequences with small observation ratios, which results in low prediction accuracies during testing due to the under-fitting problem. With EARN + GR + TCE (exp), the weights of the partial sequences range from 0.37 ($\exp^{0-1}$) to 1 ($\exp^{1-1}$). In this case, the network trains the partial sequences of all observation ratios.

4.4 Results on the CMU Dataset

For this dataset, we follow the 4-fold cross-validation protocol proposed in [8] for evaluation. In particular, we use the four different splits of the data provided by [8] for training and testing. The average accuracies of the four folds are reported. The comparison results of the proposed method with the baselines and the state-of-the-art early action recognition methods [31,32] are shown in Fig. 3(b) and Table 3.

Similar to the NTU Dataset, the performance of ARN is better than EARN only when the observation ratio is close to 1. The proposed EARN + GR achieves an average accuracy of 80.55%, which outperforms EARN (78.9%) by 1.65%. EARN + GR + TCE further improves the performance of EARN + GR to 81.01%. Compared to the method in [32] and [31], the improvements of the proposed EARN + GR + TCE are by 1.67% and 18.01%, respectively. The improvements of the proposed method are smaller on this dataset compared to that on the NTU Dataset. This is due to the fact that most actions of this dataset (*e.g.*, running and jumping) are periodical and are repeated many times across the full sequences. In this case, the motions at different temporal stages are similar and the information of the partial sequences is similar to the global information of the full sequences. Therefore, the actions can be accurately recognized even without the global information, which limits the benefits of global regularizer and temporal-aware cross-entropy.

Table 3. Performance comparison of early action recognition on the CMU Dataset. The same feature is used in all methods for fair comparisons. Refer to Fig. 3(b) for more results.

Observation ratios	Methods					
	[32]	[31]	ARN	EARN	EARN+GR	EARN+GR+TCE
0.3	77.45%	47.50%	50.91%	76.22%	78.34%	**78.65%**
0.5	81.87%	70.45%	70.53%	81.95%	82.56%	**82.87%**
0.8	84.45%	83.26%	83.25%	83.53%	84.56%	**85.63%**
Average	79.34%	63.00%	65.21%	78.90%	80.55%	**81.01%**

Table 4. Performance comparison of early action recognition on the SYSU 3DHOI Dataset. The same feature is used in all methods for fair comparisons. Refer to Fig. 3(c) for more results.

Observation ratios	Methods					
	[32]	[34]	ARN	EARN	EARN+GR	EARN+GR+TCE
0.3	51.08%	35.83%	33.39%	49.01%	54.68%	**56.06%**
0.5	62.14%	45.83%	54.64%	59.01%	63.24%	**64.35%**
0.8	69.32%	58.75%	67.67%	65.44%	68.61%	**69.94%**
Average	58.51%	45.58%	50.01%	55.81%	60.40%	**61.60%**

4.5 Results on the SYSU 3DHOI Dataset

For evaluation, we followed the cross-subject setting used by [34], in which the data samples performed by half of the subjects were used for training, and the data samples from the other half were used for testing. The accuracies were averaged over 30 different combinations of training and testing subjects provided by [42]. The results are shown in Fig. 3(c) and Table 4. In this paper we only use the skeleton. We compared with [34] using their reported results based on skeleton. When the observation ratio is 0.1, the proposed EARN + GR + TCE achieves an accuracy of 41.11%. Compared to the performance of the methods in [32] and [34], the improvements are 10.1% and 15.9%, respectively.

4.6 Comparison with Pair-Wise Distance

In this paper, we enforce the similarity between the full and partial sequences based on the mean and variance. When using the pair-wise distance between each pair of the full and the partial sequences as the regularizer to enhance their similarity, the prediction accuracy averaged across all observation ratios on the NTU Dataset is 38.91%, which is 10.5% worse than the proposed method. The partial sequences at the early stage are quite different from the full sequences.

Some sequences at the beginning do not contain any motion, which introduces outliers of the samples. Using the pair-wise distance to enforce every pair of the full sequence and the partial sequence (including the outliers) to be similar makes the network difficult to converge, and results in poor performance. The proposed method minimizes the mismatch between the full and the partial sequences based on their statistical properties, which is capable of reducing the effects of the outliers and yields better performances.

4.7 Parameter Analysis

In this section, we evaluate the influence of λ in Eq. 11 on the NTU Dataset. The prediction performances of the proposed method using different λ are shown in Table 5. When $\lambda = 0$, the global regularizer is not used in the network learning. As shown in Table 5, the prediction accuracies are improved when λ is increased. It clearly shows the advantage of the global regularizer for better early action recognition. Note that when λ is assigned a large value, the performance at the early stage is slightly worse. The reason might be that the network focuses on the learning of the global pattern of the full sequences, which leads to the under-fitting problem of the partial sequences at the early stage.

Table 5. Impact of the parameter λ on early action recognition performance on the NTU Dataset.

Observation ratios	λ				
	0	0.1	0.5	1	2
0.3	27.87%	29.79%	33.80%	33.46%	33.04%
0.5	47.13%	51.92%	53.97%	54.28%	55.37%
0.8	59.88%	65.19%	65.39%	66.21%	67.49%
Average	43.77%	47.48%	49.10%	49.41%	50.08%

5 Conclusion

In this paper, we have proposed a new framework for skeleton-based early action recognition, which explicitly exploits the global information from the partial sequences using a global regularizer. The classification loss of the network is a temporal-aware cross-entropy, which prevents the network from over-fitting the partial sequences with small observation ratios. The proposed method has been tested on three benchmark datasets. Experimental results clearly show the advantages of the proposed method for early action recognition.

Acknowledgment. We greatly acknowledge NVIDIA for providing a Titan XP GPU for the experiments involved in this research. This work was partially supported by Australian Research Council grants DP150100294, DP150104251, and DE120102960.

References

1. Ryoo, M.S.: Human activity prediction: early recognition of ongoing activities from streaming videos. In: ICCV, pp. 1036–1043. IEEE (2011)
2. Lan, T., Chen, T.-C., Savarese, S.: A hierarchical representation for future action prediction. In: Fleet, D., Pajdla, T., Schiele, B., Tuytelaars, T. (eds.) ECCV 2014. LNCS, vol. 8691, pp. 689–704. Springer, Cham (2014). https://doi.org/10.1007/978-3-319-10578-9_45
3. Ma, Q., Shen, L., Chen, E., Tian, S., Wang, J., Cottrell, G.W.: WALKING WALKing walking: action recognition from action echoes. In: IJCAI, pp. 2457–2463. AAAI Press (2017)
4. Wang, J., Liu, Z., Wu, Y., Yuan, J.: Mining actionlet ensemble for action recognition with depth cameras. In: CVPR, pp. 1290–1297. IEEE (2012)
5. Vemulapalli, R., Arrate, F., Chellappa, R.: Human action recognition by representing 3D skeletons as points in a lie group. In: CVPR, pp. 588–595. IEEE (2014)
6. Du, Y., Wang, W., Wang, L.: Hierarchical recurrent neural network for skeleton based action recognition. In: CVPR, pp. 1110–1118. IEEE (2015)
7. Shahroudy, A., Liu, J., Ng, T.T., Wang, G.: NTU RGB+D: a large scale dataset for 3D human activity analysis. In: CVPR. IEEE (2016)
8. Zhu, W., et al.: Co-occurrence feature learning for skeleton based action recognition using regularized deep LSTM networks. In: AAAI, vol. 2, p. 8. AAAI Press (2016)
9. Liu, J., Shahroudy, A., Xu, D., Wang, G.: Spatio-temporal LSTM with trust gates for 3D human action recognition. In: Leibe, B., Matas, J., Sebe, N., Welling, M. (eds.) ECCV 2016. LNCS, vol. 9907, pp. 816–833. Springer, Cham (2016). https://doi.org/10.1007/978-3-319-46487-9_50
10. Ke, Q., Bennamoun, M., An, S., Boussaid, F., Sohel, F.: A new representation of skeleton sequences for 3D action recognition. In: CVPR. IEEE (2017)
11. Niebles, J.C., Chen, C.-W., Fei-Fei, L.: Modeling temporal structure of decomposable motion segments for activity classification. In: Daniilidis, K., Maragos, P., Paragios, N. (eds.) ECCV 2010. LNCS, vol. 6312, pp. 392–405. Springer, Heidelberg (2010). https://doi.org/10.1007/978-3-642-15552-9_29
12. Wang, L., Qiao, Y., Tang, X.: Latent hierarchical model of temporal structure for complex activity classification. IEEE Transa. Image Process. **23**, 810–822 (2014)
13. Donahue, J., et al.: Long-term recurrent convolutional networks for visual recognition and description. In: CVPR, pp. 2625–2634. IEEE (2015)
14. Kong, Y., Fu, Y.: Human action recognition and prediction: a survey. arXiv preprint arXiv:1806.11230 (2018)
15. Mahmud, T., Hasan, M., Roy-Chowdhury, A.K.: Joint prediction of activity labels and starting times in untrimmed videos. In: ICCV, pp. 5784–5793. IEEE (2017)
16. Bütepage, J., Black, M.J., Kragic, D., Kjellström, H.: Deep representation learning for human motion prediction and classification. In: CVPR 2017. IEEE (2017)
17. Ke, Q., Liu, J., Bennamoun, M., An, S., Sohel, F., Boussaid, F.: Chapter 5 - computer vision for human-machine interaction. In: Leo, M., Farinella, G.M., (eds.) Computer Vision for Assistive Healthcare, pp. 127–145. Academic Press (2018)
18. Tang, C., Li, W., Wang, P., Wang, L.: Online human action recognition based on incremental learning of weighted covariance descriptors. Inf. Sci. **467**, 219–237 (2018)
19. Rahmani, H., Mahmood, A., Huynh, D., Mian, A.: Histogram of oriented principal components for cross-view action recognition. PAMI **38**, 2430–2443 (2016)

20. Rahmani, H., Mian, A., Shah, M.: Learning a deep model for human action recognition from novel viewpoints. PAMI **40**(3), 667–681 (2018)
21. Rahmani, H., Bennamoun, M.: Learning action recognition model from depth and skeleton videos. In: ICCV. IEEE (2017)
22. Rahmani, H., Mian, A.: 3D action recognition from novel viewpoints. In: CVPR, pp. 1506–1515. IEEE (2016)
23. Wang, P., Li, W., Ogunbona, P., Wan, J., Escalera, S.: RGB-D-based human motion recognition with deep learning: a survey. Comput. Vis. Image Underst. **171**, 118–139 (2018)
24. Ke, Q., An, S., Bennamoun, M., Sohel, F., Boussaid, F.: Skeletonnet: mining deep part features for 3-D action recognition. IEEE Sig. Process. Lett. **24**, 731–735 (2017)
25. Ke, Q., Bennamoun, M., An, S., Sohel, F., Boussaid, F.: Learning clip representations for skeleton-based 3D action recognition. IEEE Trans. Image Process. **27**, 2842–2855 (2018)
26. Liu, J., Wang, G., Hu, P., Duan, L.Y., Kot, A.C.: Global context-aware attention LSTM networks for 3D action recognition. In: CVPR, vol. 7. IEEE (2017)
27. Ryoo, M.: Human activity prediction: early recognition of ongoing activities from streaming videos. In: ICCV, pp. 1036–1043. IEEE (2011)
28. Kong, Y., Kit, D., Fu, Y.: A discriminative model with multiple temporal scales for action prediction. In: Fleet, D., Pajdla, T., Schiele, B., Tuytelaars, T. (eds.) ECCV 2014. LNCS, vol. 8693, pp. 596–611. Springer, Cham (2014). https://doi.org/10.1007/978-3-319-10602-1_39
29. Ke, Q., Bennamoun, M., An, S., Boussaid, F., Sohel, F.: Human interaction prediction using deep temporal features. In: Hua, G., Jégou, H. (eds.) ECCV 2016. LNCS, vol. 9914, pp. 403–414. Springer, Cham (2016). https://doi.org/10.1007/978-3-319-48881-3_28
30. Ke, Q., Bennamoun, M., An, S., Sohel, F., Boussaid, F.: Leveraging structural context models and ranking score fusion forhuman interaction prediction. IEEE Trans. Multimed. **20**, 1712–1723 (2017)
31. Jain, A., Singh, A., Koppula, H.S., Soh, S., Saxena, A.: Recurrent neural networks for driver activity anticipation via sensory-fusion architecture. In: ICRA, pp. 3118–3125. IEEE (2016)
32. Aliakbarian, M.S., Saleh, F., Salzmann, M., Fernando, B., Petersson, L., Andersson, L.: Encouraging LSTMs to anticipate actions very early. In: ICCV. IEEE (2017)
33. Farha, Y.A., Richard, A., Gall, J.: When will you do what? Anticipating temporal occurrences of activities. arXiv preprint arXiv:1804.00892 (2018)
34. Hu, J.-F., Zheng, W.-S., Ma, L., Wang, G., Lai, J.: Real-time RGB-D activity prediction by soft regression. In: Leibe, B., Matas, J., Sebe, N., Welling, M. (eds.) ECCV 2016. LNCS, vol. 9905, pp. 280–296. Springer, Cham (2016). https://doi.org/10.1007/978-3-319-46448-0_17
35. Liu, J., Shahroudy, A., Wang, G., Duan, L.Y., Kot, A.C.: SSNet: scale selection network for online 3D action prediction. In: CVPR, pp. 8349–8358. IEEE (2018)
36. Herath, S., Harandi, M., Porikli, F.: Learning an invariant hilbert space for domain adaptation. arXiv preprint arXiv:1611.08350 (2016)
37. Hubert Tsai, Y.H., Yeh, Y.R., Frank Wang, Y.C.: Learning cross-domain landmarks for heterogeneous domain adaptation. In: CVPR, pp. 5081–5090. IEEE (2016)
38. Baktashmotlagh, M., Harandi, M., Salzmann, M.: Distribution-matching embedding for visual domain adaptation. J. Mach. Learn. Res. **17**, 3760–3789 (2016)

39. Pan, S.J., Tsang, I.W., Kwok, J.T., Yang, Q.: Domain adaptation via transfer component analysis. IEEE Trans. Neural Netw. **22**, 199–210 (2011)
40. Krizhevsky, A., Sutskever, I., Hinton, G.E.: Imagenet classification with deep convolutional neural networks. In: NIPS, pp. 1097–1105 (2012)
41. CMU: CMU graphics lab motion capture database (2013). http://mocap.cs.cmu.edu/
42. Hu, J.F., Zheng, W.S., Lai, J., Zhang, J.: Jointly learning heterogeneous features for RGB-D activity recognition. In: CVPR, pp. 5344–5352. IEEE (2015)

Correction to: Symmetry-Aware Face Completion with Generative Adversarial Networks

Jiawan Zhang, Rui Zhan, Di Sun, and Gang Pan

Correction to:
Chapter "Symmetry-Aware Face Completion with Generative Adversarial Networks" in: C. V. Jawahar et al. (Eds.): Computer Vision – ACCV 2018, LNCS 11364, https://doi.org/10.1007/978-3-030-20870-7_18

In the original version of this book the address of the author Di Sun was incorrect. This has now been corrected.

The updated version of this chapter can be found at
https://doi.org/10.1007/978-3-030-20870-7_18

C. V. Jawahar et al. (Eds.): ACCV 2018, LNCS 11364, p. C1, 2021.
https://doi.org/10.1007/978-3-030-20870-7_46

Author Index

Printed in the United States
by Baker & Taylor Publisher Services